# Weiss Ratings' Guide to Credit Unions

# Weiss Ratings'
# Guide to
# Credit Unions

A Quarterly Compilation of Credit Union
Ratings and Analyses

**Spring 2016**

**GREY HOUSE PUBLISHING**

Weiss Ratings
4400 Northcorp Parkway
Palm Beach Gardens, FL 33410
561-627-3300

Published by Grey House Publishing, Inc., located at 4919 Route 22, Amenia, NY 12501; telephone 518-789-8700. Grey House Publishing neither guarantees the accuracy of the data contained herein nor assumes any responsibility for errors, omissions or discrepancies. Grey House Publishing accepts no payment for listing; inclusion in the publication of any organization, agency, institution, publication, service or individual does not imply endorsement of the publisher.

4919 Route 22
PO Box 56
Amenia, NY 12501-0056

Edition No. 21, Spring 2016

ISBN: 978-1-68217-012-0
ISSN: 2162-8270

# Contents

# Terms and Conditions

This document is prepared strictly for the confidential use of our customer(s). It has been provided to you at your specific request. It is not directed to, or intended for distribution to or use by, any person or entity who is a citizen or resident of or located in any locality, state, country or other jurisdiction where such distribution, publication, availability or use would be contrary to law or regulation or which would subject Weiss Ratings or its affiliates to any registration or licensing requirement within such jurisdiction.

No part of the analysts' compensation was, is, or will be, directly or indirectly, related to the specific recommendations or views expressed in this research report.

This document is not intended for the direct or indirect solicitation of business. Weiss Ratings, LLC and its affiliates disclaims any and all liability to any person or entity for any loss or damage caused, in whole or in part, by any error (negligent or otherwise) or other circumstances involved in, resulting from or relating to the procurement, compilation, analysis, interpretation, editing, transcribing, publishing and/or dissemination or transmittal of any information contained herein.

Weiss Ratings has not taken any steps to ensure that the securities or investment vehicle referred to in this report are suitable for any particular investor. The investment or services contained or referred to in this report may not be suitable for you and it is recommended that you consult an independent investment advisor if you are in doubt about such investments or investment services. Nothing in this report constitutes investment, legal, accounting or tax advice or a representation that any investment or strategy is suitable or appropriate to your individual circumstances or otherwise constitutes a personal recommendation to you.

The ratings and other opinions contained in this document must be construed solely as statements of opinion from Weiss Ratings, LLC, and not statements of fact. Each rating or opinion must be weighed solely as a factor in your choice of an institution and should not be construed as a recommendation to buy, sell or otherwise act with respect to the particular product or company involved.

Past performance should not be taken as an indication or guarantee of future performance, and no representation or warranty, expressed or implied, is made regarding future performance. Information, opinions and estimates contained in this report reflect a judgment at its original date of publication and are subject to change without notice. Weiss Ratings offers a notification service for rating changes on companies you specify. For more information visit WeissRatings.com or call 1-877-934-7778. The price, value and income from any of the securities or financial instruments mentioned in this report can fall as well as rise.

This document and the information contained herein is copyrighted by Weiss Ratings, LLC. Any copying, displaying, selling, distributing or otherwise reproducing or delivering this information or any part of this document to any other person or entity is prohibited without the express written consent of Weiss Ratings, LLC, with the exception of a reviewer or editor who may quote brief passages in connection with a review or a news story.

## Date of Data Analyzed: September 30, 2015
Data Source: Call Report data provided by SNL Financial.

# Welcome to Weiss Ratings
## *Guide to Credit Unions*

Most people automatically assume their credit union will survive, year after year. However, prudent consumers and professionals realize that in this world of shifting risks, the solvency of financial institutions can't be taken for granted. After all, your credit union's failure could have a heavy impact on you in terms of lost time, lost money (in cases of deposits exceeding the federal insurance limit), tied-up deposits, lost credit lines, and the possibility of being shifted to another institution under not-so-friendly terms.

If you are looking for accurate, unbiased ratings and data to help you choose a credit union for yourself, your family, your company or your clients, Weiss Ratings' Guide to Credit Unions gives you precisely what you need.

# Weiss Ratings' Mission Statement

Weiss Ratings' mission is to empower consumers, professionals, and institutions with high quality advisory information for selecting or monitoring a financial services company or financial investment.

In doing so, Weiss Ratings will adhere to the highest ethical standards by maintaining our independent, unbiased outlook and approach to advising our customers.

# Why rely on Weiss Ratings?

Weiss Ratings provides fair, objective ratings to help professionals and consumers alike make educated financial decisions.

At Weiss Ratings, integrity is number one. Weiss Ratings never takes a penny from rated companies for issuing its ratings. And, we publish Weiss Safety Ratings without regard for institutions' preferences. Our analysts review and update Weiss Ratings each and every quarter, so you can be sure that the information you receive is accurate and current – providing you with advance warning of financial vulnerability early enough to do something about it.

Other rating agencies focus primarily on a company's current financial solvency and consider only mild economic adversity. Weiss Ratings also considers these issues, but in addition, our analysis covers a company's ability to deal with severe economic adversity in terms of a sharp decline in the value of its investments and a drop in the collectibility of its loans.

Our use of more rigorous standards stems from the viewpoint that a financial institution's obligations to its customers should not depend on favorable business conditions. A credit union must be able to honor its loan and deposit commitments in bad times as well as good.

Weiss's rating scale, from A to F, is easy to understand. Only a limited number of outstanding institutions receive an A (Excellent) rating, although there are many to choose from within the B (Good) category. A large group falls into the broad average range which receives C (Fair) ratings. Companies that demonstrate marked vulnerabilities receive either D (Weak) or E (Very Weak) ratings. So, there's no numbering system, star counting, or color-coding to keep track of.

# How to Use This Guide

The purpose of the *Guide to Credit Unions* is to provide consumers, businesses, financial institutions, and municipalities with a reliable source of industry ratings and analysis on a timely basis. We realize that the financial safety of a credit union is an important factor to consider when establishing a relationship. The ratings and analysis in this guide can make that evaluation easier when you are considering:

- a checking, merchant banking, or other transaction account
- an investment in a certificate of deposit or savings account
- a line of credit or commercial loan
- counterparty risk

The rating for a particular company indicates our opinion regarding that company's ability to meet its obligations – not only under current economic conditions, but also during a declining economy or in an environment of increased liquidity demands.

To use this guide most effectively, we recommend you follow the steps outlined below:

**Step 1**  To ensure you evaluate the correct company, verify the company's exact name as it was given to you. It is also helpful to ascertain the city and state of the company's main office or headquarters since no two credit unions with the same name can be headquartered in the same city. Many companies have similar names but are not related to one another, so you will want to make sure the company you look up is really the one you are interested in evaluating.

**Step 2**  Turn to Section I, the Index of Credit Unions, and locate the company you are evaluating. This section contains all federally insured credit unions. It is sorted alphabetically by the name of the company and shows the main office city and state following the name for additional verification.

  If you have trouble finding a particular institution or determining which is the right one, you may have an incorrect or incomplete institution name. There are often several institutions with the same or very similar names. So, make sure you have the exact name and proper spelling, as well as the city in which it is headquartered.

**Step 3**  Once you have located your specific company, the first column after the state shows its current Weiss Safety Rating. Turn to *About Weiss Safety Ratings* for information about what this rating means. If the rating has changed since the last edition of this guide, a downgrade will be indicated with a down triangle ▼ to the left of the company name; an upgrade will be indicated with an up triangle ▲.

**Step 4**  Following the current Weiss Safety Rating are two prior ratings for the company based on year-end data from the two previous years. Use this to discern the longer-term direction of the company's overall financial condition.

**Step 5**     The remainder of Section I, provides insight into the areas our analysts reviewed as the basis for assigning the company's rating. These areas include size, capital adequacy, asset quality, profitability, liquidity, and stability. An index within each of these categories represents a composite evaluation of that particular facet of the company's financial condition. Refer to the *Critical Ranges In Our Indexes* table for an interpretation of which index values are considered strong, good, fair, or weak. In most cases, lower-rated companies will have a low index value in one or more of the indexes shown. Bear in mind, however, that Weiss Safety Rating is the result of a complex qualitative and quantitative analysis which cannot be reproduced using only the data provided here.

**Step 6**     If the company you are evaluating is not highly rated and you want to find a credit union a higher rating, turn to the page in Section II that has your state's name at the top. This section contains Weiss Recommended Companies (rating of A+, A, A- or B+) that have a branch office in your state. If the main office telephone number provided is not a local telephone call or to determine if a branch of the credit union is near you, consult your local telephone Yellow Pages Directory under "Credit Unions Services," or "Financial Services." Here you will find a complete list of the institution's branch locations along with their telephone numbers.

**Step 7**     Once you've identified a Weiss Recommended Company in your local area, you can then refer back to Section I to analyze it.

**Step 8**     In order to use Weiss Safety ratings most effectively, we strongly recommend you consult the *Important Warnings and Cautions*. These are more than just "standard disclaimers." They are very important factors you should be aware of before using this guide. If you have any questions regarding the precise meaning of specific terms used in the guide, refer to the glossary.

**Step 9**     Make sure you stay up to date with the latest information available since the publication of this guide. For information on how to acquire follow-up reports, check ratings online or receive a more in-depth analysis of an individual company, call 1-877-934-7778 or visit www.weissratings.com.

# About Weiss Safety Ratings

The Weiss Ratings are calculated based on a complex analysis of hundreds of factors that are synthesized into five indexes: capitalization, asset quality, profitability, liquidity and stability. Each index is then used to arrive at a letter grade rating. A weak score on any one index can result in a low rating, as financial problems can be caused by any one of a number of factors, such as inadequate capital, non-performing loans and poor asset quality, operating losses, poor liquidity, or the failure of an affiliated company.

Our **Capitalization Index** gauges the institution's capital adequacy in terms of its cushion to absorb future operating losses under adverse business and economic scenarios that may impact the company's net interest margin, securities' values, and the collectability of its loans.

Our **Asset Quality Index** measures the quality of the company's past underwriting and investment practices based on the estimated liquidation value of the company's loan and securities portfolios.

Our **Profitability Index** measures the soundness of the company's operations and the contribution of profits to the company's safety. The index is a composite of five sub-factors: 1) gain or loss on operations; 2) rates of return on assets and equity; 3) management of net interest margin; 4) generation of noninterest-based revenues; and 5) overhead expense management.

Our **Liquidity Index** evaluates a company's ability to raise the necessary cash to satisfy creditors and honor depositor withdrawals.

Finally, our **Stability Index** integrates a number of sub-factors that affect consistency (or lack thereof) in maintaining financial strength over time. These include 1) risk diversification in terms of company size and loan diversification; 2) deterioration of operations as reported in critical asset, liability, income and expense items, such as an increase in loan delinquency rates or a sharp increase in loan originations; 3) years in operation; 4) former problem areas where, despite recent improvement, the company has yet to establish a record of stable performance over a suitable period of time; and 5) relationships with holding companies and affiliates.

In order to help guarantee our objectivity, we reserve the right to publish ratings expressing our opinion of a company's financial stability based exclusively on publicly available data and our own proprietary standards for safety.

Each of these indexes is measured according to the following range of values.

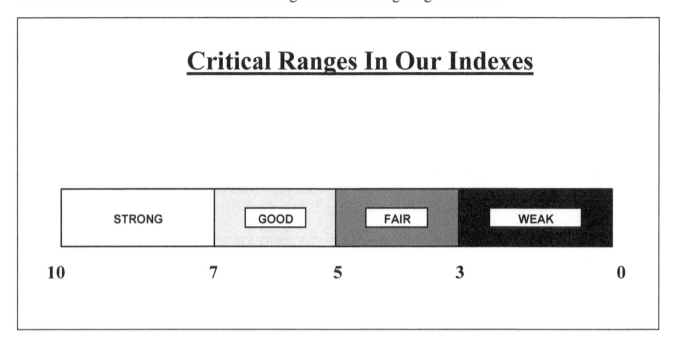

Finally, the indexes are combined to form a composite company rating which is then verified by our analysts. The resulting distribution of ratings assigned to all credit unions looks like this:

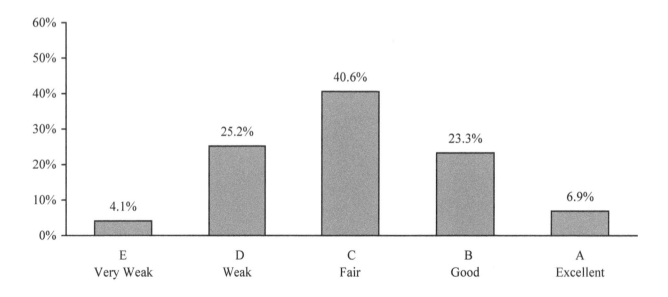

# What Our Ratings Mean

**A**     **Excellent.** The institution offers excellent financial security. It has maintained a conservative stance in its business operations and underwriting practices as evidenced by its strong equity base, high asset quality, steady earnings, and high liquidity. While the financial position of any company is subject to change, we believe that this institution has the resources necessary to deal with severe economic conditions.

**B**     **Good.** The institution offers good financial security and has the resources to deal with a variety of adverse economic conditions. It comfortably exceeds the minimum levels for all of our rating criteria, and is likely to remain healthy for the near future. Nevertheless, in the event of a severe recession or major financial crisis, we feel that this assessment should be reviewed to make sure that the company is still maintaining adequate financial strength.

**C**     **Fair.** The institution offers fair financial security, is currently stable, and will likely remain relatively healthy as long as the economic environment remains relatively stable. In the event of a severe recession or major financial crisis, however, we feel this company may encounter difficulties in maintaining its financial stability.

**D**     **Weak.** The institution currently demonstrates what, in our opinion, we consider to be significant weaknesses which could negatively impact depositors or creditors. In the event of a severe recession or major financial crisis, these weaknesses could be magnified.

**E**     **Very Weak.** The institution currently demonstrates what we consider to be significant weaknesses and has also failed some of the basic tests that we use to identify fiscal stability. Therefore, even in a favorable economic environment, it is our opinion that depositors or creditors could incur significant risks.

**F**     **Failed.** The institution has been placed under the custodianship of regulatory authorities. This implies that it will be either liquidated or taken over by another financial institution.

**+**     The **plus sign** is an indication that the institution is in the upper third of the letter grade.

**-**     The **minus sign** is an indication that the institution is in the lower third of the letter grade.

**U**     **Unrated.** The institution is unrated due to the absence of sufficient data for our ratings.

# Peer Comparison of Credit Union Safety Ratings

| Weiss Ratings | Veribanc | Bauer Financial | IDC Financial | Bankrate.com | Lace Financial |
|---|---|---|---|---|---|
| A+, A, A- | Green, Three Stars w/ Blue Ribbon recognition | 5 stars, 4 stars | 201-300 | 1, Five stars | A+, A |
| B+, B, B- | Green, Three Stars w/out Blue Ribbon recognition | 3 ½ stars | 166-200 | 2, Four stars | B+ |
| C+, C, C- | Green Two Stars, Yellow Two Stars | 3 stars | 126-165 | 3, Three stars | B, C+ |
| D+, D, D- | Green one star, Yellow one star, Green no stars | 2 stars | 76-125 | 4, Two stars | C, D |
| E+, E, E- | Yellow no stars, Red no stars | 1 star | 1-75 | 5, One star | E |

# Important Warnings and Cautions

1.  **A rating alone cannot tell the whole story.** Please read the explanatory information contained here, in the section introductions and in the appendix. It is provided in order to give you an understanding of our rating philosophy as well as to paint a more complete picture of how we arrive at our opinion of a company's strengths and weaknesses. In addition, please remember that our safety rating is not an end-all measure of an institution's safety. Rather, it should be used as a "flag" of possible troubles, suggesting a need for further research.

2.  **Safety ratings shown in this directory were current as of the publication date.** In the meantime, the rating may have been updated based on more recent data. Weiss Ratings offers online reports that may be more current. For more information call 1-877-934-7778 or visit www.weissratings.com.

3.  **When deciding to do business with a financial institution, your decision should be based on a wide variety of factors in addition to Weiss Safety Rating.** These include the institution's pricing of its deposit instruments and loans, the fees you will be charged, the degree to which it can help you meet your long-term planning needs, how these costs/benefits may change over the years, and what other choices are available to you given your current location and financial circumstances.

4.  **Weiss Safety ratings represent our opinion of a company's insolvency risk.** As such, a high rating means we feel that the company has less chance of running into financial difficulties. A high rating is not a guarantee of solvency nor is a low rating a prediction of insolvency. Weiss Safety Ratings are not deemed to be a recommendation concerning the purchase or sale of the securities of any credit union.

5.  **All firms that have the same Weiss Safety Rating should be considered to be essentially equal in safety.** This is true regardless of any differences in the underlying numbers which might appear to indicate greater strengths. Weiss Safety Rating already takes into account a number of lesser factors which, due to space limitations, cannot be included in this publication.

6.  **A good rating requires consistency.** If a company is excellent on four indicators and fair on one, the company may receive a fair rating. This requirement is necessary due to the fact that fiscal problems can arise from any *one* of several causes including poor underwriting, inadequate capital resources, or operating losses.

7.  **Our rating standards are more conservative than those used by other agencies.** We believe that no one can predict with certainty the economic environment of the near or long-term future. Rather, we assume that various scenarios – from the extremes of double-digit inflation to a severe recession – are within the range of reasonable possibilities over the next one or two decades. To achieve a top rating according to our standards, a company must be adequately prepared for the worst-case reasonable scenario, without impairing its current operations.

8.  **We are an independent rating agency and do not depend on the cooperation of the companies we rate**. Our data is derived from quarterly financial statements filed with federal regulators. Although we seek to maintain an open line of communication with the companies being rated, we do not grant them the right to influence the ratings or stop their publication. This policy stems from the fact that this guide is designed for the protection of our customers.

9. **Inaccuracies in the data issued by the federal regulators could negatively impact the quality of a company's Safety Rating.** While we attempt to find and correct as many data errors as possible, some data errors inevitably slip through. We have no method of intercepting fraudulent or falsified data and must take for granted that all information is reported honestly to the federal regulatory agencies.

10. **There are many companies with the same or similar sounding names, despite no affiliation whatsoever.** Therefore, it is important that you have the exact name, city, and state of the institution's headquarters before you begin to research the company in this guide.

11. **This publication does not include foreign credit unions, or their U.S. branches.** Therefore, our evaluation of foreign credit unions is limited to those U.S. chartered domestic credit unions owned by foreign companies. In most cases, the U.S. operations of a foreign credit union are relatively small in relation to the overall size of the company, so you may want to consult other sources as well. In any case, do not be confused by a domestic credit union with a name which is the same as – or similar to – that of a foreign company. Even if there is an affiliation between the two, we have evaluated the U.S. institution based on its own merits.

# Section I

# Index of Credit Unions

An analysis of all rated

**U.S. Credit Unions**

Institutions are listed in alphabetical order.

# Section I Contents

This section contains Weiss Safety Ratings, key rating factors, and summary financial data for all U.S. federally-insured credit unions. Companies are sorted in alphabetical order, first by company name, then by city and state.

*Left Pages*

1. **Institution Name**

The name under which the institution was chartered. If you cannot find the institution you are interested in, or if you have any doubts regarding the precise name, verify the information with the credit union itself before proceeding. Also, determine the city and state in which the institution is headquartered for confirmation. (See columns 2 and 3.)

2. **City**

The city in which the institution's headquarters or main office is located. With the adoption of intrastate and interstate branching laws, many institutions operating in your area may actually be headquartered elsewhere. So, don't be surprised if the location cited is not in your particular city.

Also use this column to confirm that you have located the correct institution. It is possible for two unrelated companies to have the same name if they are headquartered in different cities.

3. **State**

The state in which the institution's headquarters or main office is located. With the adoption of interstate branching laws, some institutions operating in your area may actually be headquartered in another state.

4. **Safety Rating**

Weiss rating assigned to the institution at the time of publication. Our ratings are designed to distinguish levels of insolvency risk and are measured on a scale from A to F based upon a wide range of factors. Please see *What Our Ratings Mean* for specific descriptions of each letter grade.

Highly rated companies are, in our opinion, less likely to experience financial difficulties than lower rated firms. See *About Weiss Safety Ratings* for more information. Also, please be sure to consider the warnings regarding the ratings' limitations and the underlying assumptions.

5. **Prior Year Safety Rating**

Weiss rating assigned to the institution based on data from December 31 of the previous year. Compare this rating to the company's current rating to identify any recent changes.

6. **Safety Rating Two Years Prior**

Weiss rating assigned to the institution based on data from December 31 two years ago. Compare this rating to the ratings in the prior columns to identify longer term trends in the company's financial condition.

**7.  Total Assets**

The total of all assets listed on the institution's balance sheet, in millions of dollars. This figure primarily consists of loans, investments (such as municipal and treasury bonds), and fixed assets (such as buildings and other real estate). Overall size is an important factor which affects the company's ability to diversify risk and avoid vulnerability to a single borrower, industry, or geographic area. Larger institutions are usually, although not always, more diversified and thus less susceptible to a downturn in a particular area. Nevertheless, do not be misled by the general public perception that "bigger is better." Larger institutions are known for their inability to quickly adapt to changes in the marketplace and typically underperform their smaller brethren. If total assets are less than $1 million then it will be noted by <1 in that field column.

**8.  One Year
Asset Growth**

The percentage change in total assets over the previous 12 months. Moderate growth is generally a positive since it can reflect the maintenance or expansion of the company's market share, leading to the generation of additional revenues. Excessive growth, however, is generally a sign of trouble as it can indicate a loosening of underwriting practices in order to attract new business.

**9.  Commercial
Loans/
Total Assets**

The percentage of the institution's asset base invested in loans to businesses. Commercial loans make up a smaller portion of the typical credit union's lending portfolio compared with consumer lending. Except maybe for the largest of credit unions.

**10.  Consumer
Loans/
Total Assets**

The percentage of the institution's asset base invested in loans to consumers, primarily credit cards. Consumer lending has grown rapidly in recent years due to the high interest rates and fees institutions are able to charge. On the down side, consumer loans usually experience higher delinquency and default rates than other loans, negatively impacting earnings down the road.

**11.  Home
Mortgage
Loans/
Total Assets**

The percentage of the institution's asset base invested in residential mortgage loans to consumers, excluding home equity loans. Only larger credit unions will offer home mortgage loans and typically are not involved in mortgages and mortgage-backed securities.

This type of loan typically experiences lower default rates. However, the length of the loan's term can be a subject for concern during periods of rising interest rates.

**12. Securities/ Total Assets**

The percentage of the institution's asset base invested in securities, including U.S. Treasury securities, mortgage-backed securities, and municipal bonds. This does not include securities the institution may be holding on behalf of individual customers. Although securities are similar to loans in that they represent obligations to pay a debt at some point in the future, they are a more liquid investment than loans and usually present less risk of default. In addition, mortgage-backed securities can present less credit risk than holding mortgage loans themselves due to the diversification of the underlying mortgages.

**13. Capitalization Index**

An index that measures the adequacy of the institution's capital resources to deal with potentially adverse business and economic situations that could arise. It is based on an evaluation of the company's degree of leverage compared to total assets as well as risk-adjusted assets. See the *Critical Ranges In Our Indexes* table for a description of the different critical levels presented in this index.

**14. Net Worth Ratio**

Net worth divided by total assets. This ratio answers the question: How much does the institution have in stockholders' equity for every dollar of assets? Thus, the Net Worth Ratio represents the amount of actual "capital cushion" the institution has to fall back on in times of trouble. We feel that this is the single most important ratio in determining financial strength because it provides the best measure of an institution's ability to withstand losses.

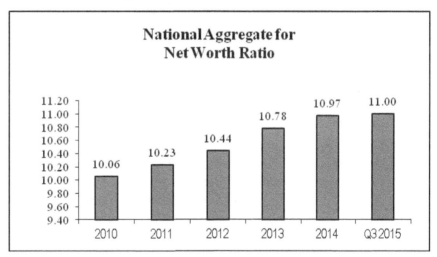

*Right Pages*

1. **Asset Quality Index**

An index that measures the quality of the institution's past underwriting and investment practices, as well as its loss reserve coverage. See the *Critical Ranges In Our Indexes* table for a description of the different critical levels presented in this index.

2. **Nonperforming Loans/ Total Loans**

The percentage of the institution's loan portfolio which is either past due on its payments by 90 days or more, or no longer accruing interest due to doubtful collectibility. This ratio is affected primarily by the quality of the institution's underwriting practices and the prosperity of the local economies where it is doing business. While only a portion of these loans will actually end up in default, a high ratio here will have several negative consequences including increased loan loss provisions, increased loan collection expenses, and decreased interest revenues.

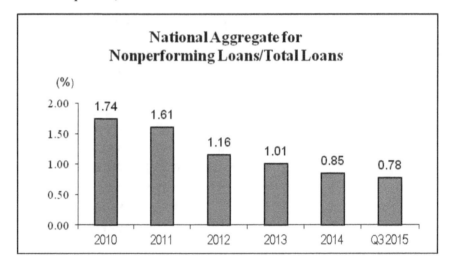

3. **Nonperforming Loans/ Capital**

The percentage of past due 90 days and nonaccruing loans to the company's core (tier 1) capital plus reserve for loan losses. This ratio answers the question: If all of the credit union's significantly past due and nonaccruing loans were to go into default, how much would that eat into capital? A large percentage of nonperforming loans signal imprudent lending practices which are a direct threat to the equity of the institution.

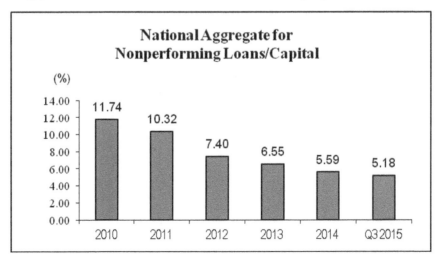

**4. Net Charge-offs/ Average Loans**

The ratio of foreclosed loans written off the institution's books since the beginning of the year (less previous write-offs that were recovered) as a percentage of average loans for the year. This ratio answers the question: What percentage of the credit union's past loans have actually become uncollectible? Past loan charge-off experience is often a very good indication of what can be expected in the future, and high loan charge-off levels are usually an indication of poor underwriting practices.

**5. Profitability Index**

An index that measures the soundness of the institution's operations and the contribution of profits to the company's financial strength. It is based on five sub-factors: 1) gain or loss on operations; 2) rates of return on assets and equity; 3) management of net interest margin; 4) generation of noninterest-based revenues; and 5) overhead expense management. See the Critical Ranges In Our Indexes table for a description of the different critical levels presented in this index.

**6. Net Income**

The year-to-date net profit or loss recorded by the institution, in millions of dollars. This figure includes the company's operating profit (income from lending, investing, and fees less interest and overhead expenses) as well as nonoperating items such as capital gains on the sale of securities, income taxes, and extraordinary items.

**7. Return on Assets**

The ratio of net income for the year (year-to-date quarterly figures are converted to a 12-month equivalent) as a percentage of average assets for the year. This ratio, known as ROA, is the most commonly used benchmark for credit union profitability since it measures the company's return on investment in a format that is easily comparable with other companies.

Historically speaking, a ratio of 1.0% or greater has been considered good performance. However, this ratio will fluctuate with the prevailing economic times. Also, larger credit unions tend to have a lower ratio.

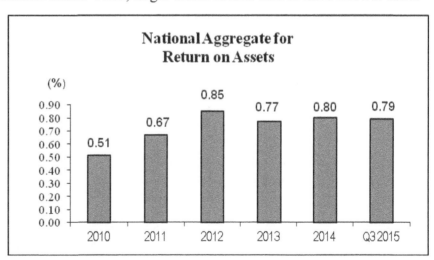

**8. Return on Equity**

The ratio of net income for the year (year-to-date quarterly figures are converted to a 12-month equivalent) as a percentage of average equity for the year. This ratio, known as ROE, is commonly used by a company's shareholders as a measure of their return on investment. It is not always a good measure of profitability, however, because inadequate equity levels at some institutions can result in unjustly high ROE's.

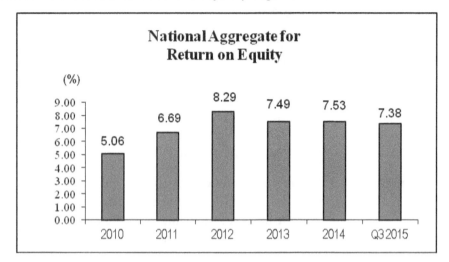

**National Aggregate for Return on Equity**

**9. Net Interest Spread**

The difference between the institution's interest income and interest expense for the year (year-to-date quarterly figures are converted to a 12-month equivalent) as a percentage of its average revenue-generating assets. Since the margin between interest earned and interest paid is generally where the company generates the majority of its income, this figure provides insight into the company's ability to effectively manage interest spreads.

A low Net Interest Spread can be the result of poor loan and deposit pricing, high levels of non-accruing loans, or poor asset/liability management.

**10. Overhead Efficiency Ratio**

Total overhead expenses as a percentage of total revenues net of interest expense. This is a common measure for evaluating an institution's ability to operate efficiently while keeping a handle on overhead expenses like salaries, rent, and other office expenses. A high ratio suggests that the company's overhead expenses are too high in relation to the amount of revenue they are generating and/or supporting. Conversely, a low ratio means good management of overhead expenses which usually results in a strong Return on Assets as well.

**11. Liquidity Index**

An index that measures the institution's ability to raise the necessary cash to satisfy creditors and honor depositor withdrawals. It is based on an evaluation of the company's short-term liquidity position, including its existing reliance on less stable deposit sources. See the Critical Ranges In Our Indexes table for a description of the different critical levels presented in this index.

**12. Liquidity Ratio**

The ratio of short-term liquid assets to deposits and short-term borrowings. This ratio answers the question: How many cents can the institution easily raise in cash to cover each dollar on deposit plus pay off its short-term debts? Due to the nature of the business, it is rare (and not expected) for an established credit union to achieve 100% on this ratio. Nevertheless, it serves as a good measure of an institution's liquidity in relation to the rest of the credit union industry.

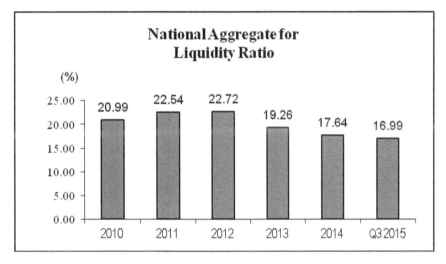

**13. Hot Money Ratio**

The percentage of the institution's deposit base that is being funded by jumbo CDs. Jumbo CDs (high-yield certificates of deposit with principal amounts of at least $100,000) are generally considered less stable (and more costly) and thus less desirable as a source of funds.

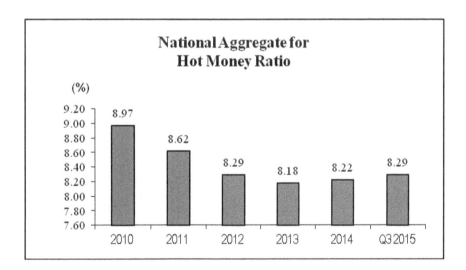

**14. Stability Index**

An index that integrates a number of factors such as 1) risk diversification in terms of company size and loan diversification; 2) deterioration of operations as reported in critical asset, liability, income and expense items, such as an increase in loan delinquency rates or a sharp increase in loan originations; 3) years in operation; 4) former problem areas where, despite recent improvement, the company has yet to establish a record of stable performance over a suitable period of time; and 5) relationships with affiliates. See the Critical Ranges In Our Indexes table for a description of the different critical levels presented in this index.

| Name | City | State | Rating | 2014 Rating | 2013 Rating | Total Assets ($Mil) | One Year Asset Growth | Asset Mix (As a % of Total Assets) | | | | Capital-ization Index | Net Worth Ratio |
|---|---|---|---|---|---|---|---|---|---|---|---|---|---|
| | | | | | | | | Comm-ercial Loans | Cons-umer Loans | Mort-gage Loans | Secur-ities | | |
| 1199 SEIU FCU | New York | NY | C- | C- | D | 61.4 | 2.98 | 0.0 | 15.6 | 21.5 | 57.8 | 6.0 | 8.0 |
| 121 FINANCIAL CU | Jacksonville | FL | B- | B | B | 499.9 | 14.14 | 11.1 | 30.3 | 24.8 | 20.0 | 9.7 | 10.8 |
| 167TH TFR FCU | Martinsburg | WV | D+ | D+ | D | 47.1 | 1.86 | 0.0 | 9.8 | 14.1 | 35.4 | 7.1 | 9.1 |
| ▲ 1ST ADVANTAGE FCU | Yorktown | VA | B | B- | B+ | 619.6 | 2.12 | 4.0 | 36.1 | 25.4 | 5.2 | 10.0 | 11.3 |
| 1ST BERGEN FCU | Hackensack | NJ | D | D | E+ | 2.3 | 3.08 | 0.0 | 8.3 | 0.0 | 0.0 | 9.1 | 10.4 |
| 1ST CHOICE CU | Atlanta | GA | C+ | C | C- | 20.5 | -3.28 | 0.0 | 49.0 | 3.5 | 26.9 | 10.0 | 13.6 |
| 1ST CLASS EXPRESS CU | Waukesha | WI | C- | C- | D | 2.5 | 2.76 | 0.0 | 61.2 | 0.0 | 0.0 | 10.0 | 12.4 |
| 1ST COMMUNITY CU | Sparta | WI | B- | B- | B | 126.9 | 5.40 | 11.9 | 20.1 | 41.6 | 0.0 | 8.7 | 10.2 |
| 1ST COMMUNITY FCU | San Angelo | TX | B- | B | B | 234.4 | 2.97 | 10.7 | 36.4 | 18.0 | 15.4 | 7.7 | 9.5 |
| 1ST COOPERATIVE FCU | Cayce | SC | C | C- | C- | 13.5 | 3.08 | 0.0 | 56.1 | 0.0 | 0.0 | 10.0 | 14.1 |
| 1ST ED CU | Chambersburg | PA | B | B | B | 125.7 | -0.97 | 0.3 | 11.7 | 7.3 | 56.6 | 10.0 | 12.8 |
| 1ST FINANCIAL FCU | Wentzville | MO | C+ | C | D | 209.2 | 5.13 | 1.1 | 67.5 | 7.9 | 5.8 | 5.9 | 7.9 |
| 1ST GATEWAY CU | Camanche | IA | B+ | B+ | B- | 121.4 | 21.03 | 4.5 | 36.3 | 39.5 | 1.1 | 8.5 | 10.0 |
| 1ST LIBERTY FCU | Great Falls | MT | D+ | D+ | C | 161.8 | 2.16 | 1.8 | 27.6 | 9.8 | 41.5 | 9.1 | 10.4 |
| 1ST MIDAMERICA CU | Bethalto | IL | B+ | B+ | B | 633.8 | 9.80 | 4.6 | 65.4 | 9.9 | 2.1 | 9.1 | 10.4 |
| 1ST MISSISSIPPI FCU | Meridian | MS | A | A | A | 56.3 | 0.50 | 0.9 | 13.6 | 12.5 | 1.8 | 10.0 | 28.9 |
| ▲ 1ST NORTHERN CALIFORNIA CU | Martinez | CA | C+ | C | C | 651.5 | 2.87 | 0.0 | 6.7 | 19.8 | 51.1 | 9.1 | 10.4 |
| 1ST RESOURCE CU | Birmingham | AL | B- | B- | B- | 31.5 | 4.98 | 0.0 | 42.2 | 39.7 | 0.0 | 9.2 | 10.5 |
| 1ST SELECT FCU | Hopkinsville | KY | E+ | D | D | 1.0 | -1.67 | 0.0 | 76.8 | 0.0 | 0.0 | 3.6 | 5.6 |
| 1ST UNITED SERVICES CU | Pleasanton | CA | B- | B- | C+ | 846.4 | 1.19 | 2.7 | 34.7 | 29.1 | 15.9 | 9.4 | 10.6 |
| 1ST UNIV CU | Waco | TX | E | E | E | 12.9 | 2.70 | 0.4 | 36.3 | 27.9 | 0.0 | 5.2 | 7.2 |
| 1ST VALLEY CU | San Bernardino | CA | C | C- | C- | 36.7 | 7.94 | 0.0 | 18.4 | 22.4 | 31.1 | 9.5 | 10.9 |
| 2 RIVERS AREA CU | Kankakee | IL | C+ | C+ | C | 15.3 | 4.67 | 0.0 | 41.1 | 0.0 | 0.0 | 10.0 | 16.9 |
| 20TH CENTURY FOX FCU | Los Angeles | CA | D+ | C- | D+ | 45.2 | -3.26 | 4.7 | 9.2 | 41.8 | 6.2 | 6.8 | 8.8 |
| 360 FCU | Windsor Locks | CT | B- | B- | C+ | 209.2 | 1.98 | 8.8 | 20.5 | 21.9 | 18.9 | 10.0 | 11.4 |
| ▲ 4FRONT CU | Traverse City | MI | B | B | B- | 415.3 | 83.87 | 3.5 | 29.4 | 22.7 | 27.8 | 10.0 | 11.5 |
| 5 STAR COMMUNITY CU | Mount Pleasant | IA | D+ | C- | C | 27.4 | 0.91 | 6.7 | 26.7 | 17.4 | 19.0 | 9.8 | 10.9 |
| 540 IBEW CU INC | Massillon | OH | C- | C- | C- | <1 | -8.27 | 0.0 | 59.0 | 0.0 | 3.2 | 10.0 | 19.2 |
| 600 ATLANTIC FCU | Boston | MA | B- | B- | B- | 25.1 | -1.88 | 0.5 | 17.5 | 21.1 | 8.7 | 10.0 | 13.2 |
| 74TH STREET DEPOT FCU | Chicago | IL | C- | C- | C | 8.4 | 0.18 | 0.0 | 40.7 | 0.0 | 0.0 | 10.0 | 23.3 |
| 77TH STREET DEPOT FCU | Chicago | IL | C | C | C+ | 18.3 | -2.72 | 0.0 | 28.5 | 0.0 | 0.0 | 10.0 | 20.1 |
| A & S FCU | Aliquippa | PA | B- | B- | B- | 24.9 | 7.55 | 0.0 | 11.8 | 15.8 | 0.0 | 10.0 | 13.3 |
| A H E PLANT NO 3 FCU | Winchester | IN | C+ | C+ | C+ | 6.9 | 5.54 | 0.0 | 22.9 | 0.0 | 0.0 | 10.0 | 17.5 |
| A M CASTLE EMPL FCU | Franklin Park | IL | D+ | D | D+ | 1.5 | -15.54 | 0.0 | 55.7 | 0.0 | 0.0 | 10.0 | 13.8 |
| A+ FCU | Austin | TX | B+ | B+ | B+ | 1188.8 | 6.71 | 3.6 | 31.5 | 17.9 | 13.1 | 7.5 | 9.3 |
| AAA FCU | South Bend | IN | C | C | C | 57.6 | -0.12 | 0.0 | 20.4 | 15.7 | 9.8 | 10.0 | 12.8 |
| AAC CU | Grand Rapids | MI | A | A | A | 114.6 | 24.77 | 3.2 | 27.5 | 24.0 | 10.6 | 10.0 | 18.6 |
| AAEC CU | Arlington Heights | IL | B | B- | B | 72.5 | 6.04 | 0.0 | 14.5 | 0.1 | 0.6 | 9.9 | 11.0 |
| AAFES FCU | Dallas | TX | C+ | C | C- | 91.6 | 0.13 | 0.0 | 23.5 | 0.8 | 19.6 | 10.0 | 13.1 |
| AB FCU | Altoona | PA | C- | C | C | 5.0 | -0.10 | 0.0 | 19.6 | 0.0 | 0.0 | 10.0 | 13.4 |
| ▼ AB&W CU INC | Alexandria | VA | C | B | B | 31.6 | 6.21 | 0.0 | 52.5 | 0.8 | 0.0 | 10.0 | 15.9 |
| ABBEVILLE COMMUNITY FCU | Abbeville | SC | C | C | C | 7.4 | 9.60 | 0.0 | 55.3 | 0.2 | 0.0 | 10.0 | 15.5 |
| ABBEY CU | Vandalia | OH | C- | C | C- | 84.2 | 2.28 | 8.5 | 45.7 | 21.8 | 8.3 | 6.3 | 8.4 |
| ABBOTT LABORATORIES EMPL CU | Gurnee | IL | B+ | B | B | 680.2 | 5.23 | 0.0 | 13.6 | 28.0 | 30.9 | 9.9 | 11.0 |
| ABCO FCU | Rancocas | NJ | C | C+ | B- | 210.9 | 2.94 | 11.5 | 21.8 | 15.4 | 7.1 | 6.0 | 8.0 |
| ABD FCU | Warren | MI | D- | D | D- | 57.6 | -2.23 | 0.0 | 19.4 | 5.6 | 14.3 | 8.5 | 10.0 |
| ABERDEEN FCU | Aberdeen | SD | A- | A- | B | 119.3 | 5.02 | 3.8 | 43.2 | 7.0 | 0.0 | 9.9 | 10.9 |
| ABERDEEN PROVING GROUND FCU | Edgewood | MD | B- | B- | B- | 1044.2 | 4.18 | 0.5 | 53.6 | 16.4 | 11.6 | 8.1 | 9.7 |
| ABILENE FCU | Abilene | TX | B | B | B | 23.6 | 5.07 | 0.0 | 59.8 | 0.0 | 0.0 | 10.0 | 18.7 |
| ABILENE TEACHERS FCU | Abilene | TX | A- | A- | A- | 406.2 | 0.12 | 0.0 | 56.5 | 1.3 | 12.2 | 10.0 | 13.6 |
| ABLE FCU | Cresaptown | MD | E+ | E+ | E+ | 8.4 | -0.21 | 0.0 | 46.4 | 1.6 | 13.2 | 5.8 | 7.8 |
| ABNB FCU | Chesapeake | VA | B+ | B+ | A- | 493.2 | 12.41 | 7.0 | 53.8 | 16.8 | 1.2 | 10.0 | 11.2 |
| ABRI CU | Romeoville | IL | C- | C- | C- | 307.7 | 1.70 | 5.5 | 15.8 | 16.8 | 34.4 | 7.0 | 9.0 |
| ABYSSINIAN BAPTIST CHURCH FCU | New York | NY | D | D | C- | <1 | -6.87 | 0.0 | 7.7 | 0.0 | 0.0 | 4.1 | 6.1 |
| AC JAACKS CU | Calumet City | IL | C | C- | C- | 4.0 | 2.78 | 0.0 | 23.8 | 0.0 | 0.0 | 10.0 | 14.0 |
| ACADEMIC EMPL CU | Columbia | MO | E | E+ | E+ | 9.9 | -0.20 | 0.0 | 51.2 | 0.0 | 0.0 | 3.6 | 5.6 |
| ACADEMIC FCU | Briarcliff Manor | NY | D- | E+ | D- | 42.0 | 0.88 | 2.9 | 18.8 | 25.7 | 36.5 | 5.3 | 7.7 |
| ACADIA FCU | Fort Kent | ME | B+ | B+ | B+ | 136.2 | 8.16 | 13.6 | 19.9 | 44.2 | 3.5 | 10.0 | 14.8 |
| ACADIAN FCU | Lafayette | LA | D- | D | D+ | 18.0 | 4.64 | 0.0 | 35.8 | 8.1 | 0.0 | 6.0 | 8.0 |
| ACADIANA MEDICAL FCU | Lafayette | LA | D+ | D+ | D+ | 10.7 | -1.81 | 0.0 | 32.7 | 0.0 | 0.0 | 10.0 | 20.9 |

| Asset Quality Index | Non-Performing Loans as a % of Total Loans | Non-Performing Loans as a % of Capital | Net Charge-Offs Avg Loans | Profitability Index | Net Income ($Mil) | Return on Assets | Return on Equity | Net Interest Spread | Overhead Efficiency Ratio | Liquidity Index | Liquidity Ratio | Hot Money Ratio | Stability Index |
|---|---|---|---|---|---|---|---|---|---|---|---|---|---|
| 3.7 | 5.07 | 21.0 | 0.37 | 3.9 | 0.2 | 0.53 | 6.45 | 3.72 | 84.7 | 4.5 | 10.4 | 0.0 | 3.8 |
| 8.2 | 0.85 | 4.9 | 0.23 | 2.1 | -0.4 | -0.10 | -0.92 | 3.60 | 99.7 | 3.7 | 10.4 | 4.8 | 6.2 |
| 7.3 | 1.96 | 6.6 | 0.13 | 1.4 | 0.0 | -0.01 | -0.09 | 2.25 | 96.4 | 6.3 | 48.6 | 1.1 | 3.4 |
| 6.2 | 1.36 | 9.2 | 0.82 | 4.5 | 2.6 | 0.57 | 5.15 | 4.55 | 75.3 | 4.0 | 13.1 | 5.0 | 7.0 |
| 0.9 | 9.00 | 39.4 | 5.08 | 3.8 | 0.0 | 0.18 | 1.90 | 5.59 | 80.3 | 7.1 | 79.5 | 0.0 | 3.2 |
| 7.2 | 0.96 | 3.4 | 0.68 | 3.7 | 0.1 | 0.31 | 2.36 | 4.92 | 97.0 | 4.4 | 16.5 | 1.5 | 6.1 |
| 1.8 | 5.13 | 27.2 | 0.12 | 9.2 | 0.0 | 1.25 | 10.29 | 7.25 | 63.1 | 3.6 | 11.8 | 0.0 | 6.5 |
| 9.1 | 0.22 | 1.7 | 0.02 | 4.5 | 0.7 | 0.68 | 6.85 | 3.28 | 82.3 | 3.4 | 11.5 | 3.0 | 6.5 |
| 6.7 | 0.39 | 4.1 | 0.57 | 4.3 | 1.0 | 0.59 | 6.40 | 3.58 | 86.1 | 2.6 | 11.5 | 13.9 | 6.0 |
| 8.4 | 0.28 | 1.4 | 0.04 | 2.3 | 0.0 | 0.19 | 1.34 | 4.22 | 95.0 | 4.7 | 31.4 | 1.3 | 7.0 |
| 9.4 | 0.93 | 2.7 | 0.11 | 3.6 | 0.4 | 0.46 | 3.74 | 1.94 | 77.8 | 4.3 | 14.8 | 4.3 | 7.3 |
| 5.1 | 1.01 | 10.0 | 0.67 | 3.9 | 0.9 | 0.58 | 7.36 | 4.49 | 77.9 | 2.5 | 2.1 | 7.9 | 4.3 |
| 6.3 | 0.22 | 9.2 | 0.36 | 8.4 | 1.0 | 1.15 | 11.69 | 5.02 | 71.7 | 3.3 | 12.1 | 5.5 | 6.4 |
| 8.2 | 0.66 | 2.3 | 0.80 | 1.1 | -0.1 | -0.05 | -0.47 | 2.68 | 96.3 | 5.3 | 29.0 | 2.9 | 5.8 |
| 6.8 | 0.52 | 4.0 | 0.43 | 4.9 | 3.0 | 0.63 | 6.09 | 3.98 | 78.8 | 2.5 | 9.9 | 13.0 | 8.3 |
| 10.0 | 0.10 | 0.3 | 0.32 | 9.8 | 0.6 | 1.32 | 4.73 | 3.54 | 73.8 | 5.7 | 45.5 | 4.1 | 9.0 |
| 10.0 | 0.13 | 0.4 | 0.07 | 3.6 | 2.5 | 0.52 | 5.05 | 1.56 | 78.9 | 4.7 | 30.3 | 10.0 | 6.7 |
| 6.8 | 0.42 | 4.9 | 0.36 | 8.2 | 0.3 | 1.20 | 11.77 | 4.64 | 65.2 | 1.7 | 12.2 | 19.7 | 6.0 |
| 6.4 | 0.00 | 0.0 | 0.00 | 0.0 | 0.0 | -2.36 | -36.36 | 6.28 | 139.6 | 3.5 | 16.0 | 0.0 | 2.7 |
| 8.6 | 0.44 | 3.3 | 0.33 | 4.3 | 3.6 | 0.56 | 5.39 | 2.98 | 80.6 | 3.2 | 17.3 | 13.0 | 6.9 |
| 4.5 | 1.16 | 11.0 | 0.18 | 3.5 | 0.0 | 0.42 | 5.77 | 6.01 | 92.7 | 4.8 | 22.0 | 0.9 | 1.7 |
| 5.1 | 1.59 | 7.6 | 0.27 | 2.2 | 0.0 | 0.09 | 0.84 | 3.14 | 95.7 | 4.0 | 10.9 | 9.3 | 4.6 |
| 8.2 | 1.42 | 3.5 | 0.50 | 2.2 | 0.0 | -0.04 | -0.27 | 4.82 | 100.7 | 5.6 | 29.3 | 0.0 | 6.5 |
| 6.5 | 0.58 | 9.0 | 0.08 | 1.4 | 0.0 | -0.11 | -1.24 | 3.05 | 101.3 | 4.8 | 22.5 | 2.1 | 3.5 |
| 8.7 | 0.63 | 4.0 | 0.23 | 3.3 | 0.4 | 0.27 | 2.59 | 3.55 | 87.5 | 4.1 | 12.5 | 4.1 | 6.6 |
| 6.6 | 1.61 | 9.2 | 0.39 | 4.9 | 2.2 | 0.75 | 6.77 | 4.26 | 83.7 | 3.5 | 8.0 | 4.5 | 5.8 |
| 5.0 | 1.54 | 11.3 | 0.18 | 1.8 | 0.0 | 0.12 | 1.17 | 3.76 | 93.5 | 3.6 | 4.7 | 0.4 | 5.0 |
| 5.5 | 6.33 | 17.4 | -0.91 | 3.0 | 0.0 | 0.34 | 1.81 | 4.89 | 92.6 | 5.6 | 41.2 | 0.0 | 6.7 |
| 9.0 | 0.09 | 0.3 | 0.14 | 3.9 | 0.1 | 0.50 | 3.91 | 2.47 | 80.0 | 3.5 | 40.0 | 17.6 | 6.6 |
| 8.9 | 2.14 | 3.6 | 1.68 | 2.2 | 0.0 | 0.19 | 0.82 | 5.76 | 79.5 | 5.5 | 32.7 | 0.0 | 5.0 |
| 7.5 | 4.80 | 6.4 | 6.00 | 2.9 | 0.1 | 0.39 | 1.97 | 5.75 | 59.0 | 4.9 | 22.5 | 9.1 | 5.6 |
| 10.0 | 0.85 | 2.0 | 0.07 | 3.4 | 0.1 | 0.40 | 3.02 | 2.42 | 87.2 | 5.2 | 25.0 | 3.2 | 6.6 |
| 10.0 | 0.97 | 1.5 | 0.94 | 4.7 | 0.0 | 0.57 | 3.26 | 2.87 | 78.1 | 6.5 | 52.3 | 0.0 | 8.1 |
| 6.1 | 2.57 | 9.7 | 0.15 | 0.6 | 0.0 | -0.08 | -0.66 | 2.74 | 105.6 | 5.3 | 50.8 | 0.0 | 4.6 |
| 8.1 | 0.44 | 3.7 | 0.45 | 6.0 | 7.5 | 0.86 | 9.24 | 3.68 | 73.4 | 3.6 | 16.1 | 8.5 | 7.2 |
| 8.4 | 1.00 | 5.6 | 0.45 | 2.3 | 0.1 | 0.15 | 1.16 | 3.05 | 93.0 | 5.2 | 44.1 | 0.4 | 5.7 |
| 9.8 | 0.61 | 1.9 | 0.36 | 9.5 | 1.1 | 1.50 | 8.30 | 4.56 | 70.0 | 2.5 | 10.4 | 17.1 | 8.8 |
| 10.0 | 0.51 | 1.0 | 0.09 | 4.9 | 0.4 | 0.78 | 7.25 | 1.97 | 59.7 | 6.0 | 39.3 | 0.0 | 5.6 |
| 9.4 | 1.36 | 3.2 | 1.00 | 3.0 | 0.3 | 0.43 | 3.52 | 2.61 | 80.8 | 4.9 | 27.3 | 1.7 | 5.3 |
| 10.0 | 0.00 | 0.0 | 0.00 | 1.8 | 0.0 | 0.05 | 0.40 | 3.06 | 99.3 | 5.2 | 32.6 | 0.0 | 7.3 |
| 5.7 | 0.59 | 8.3 | 1.83 | 1.8 | -0.1 | -0.46 | -2.80 | 5.65 | 87.9 | 6.5 | 44.6 | 0.0 | 6.2 |
| 6.7 | 0.99 | 4.1 | 0.68 | 5.1 | 0.0 | 0.64 | 4.10 | 6.04 | 83.6 | 4.5 | 28.2 | 7.7 | 4.3 |
| 4.3 | 1.28 | 10.7 | 0.83 | 2.3 | 0.1 | 0.11 | 1.37 | 3.44 | 81.2 | 3.5 | 12.4 | 5.1 | 3.5 |
| 10.0 | 0.22 | 1.0 | 0.13 | 5.6 | 4.6 | 0.88 | 8.23 | 2.44 | 67.1 | 5.0 | 33.0 | 6.8 | 8.0 |
| 4.9 | 2.57 | 19.1 | 0.70 | 3.1 | 0.3 | 0.19 | 2.49 | 3.65 | 90.3 | 4.2 | 17.0 | 1.8 | 5.0 |
| 6.2 | 2.24 | 8.1 | 3.75 | 0.1 | -0.3 | -0.74 | -7.60 | 4.09 | 95.5 | 6.7 | 56.2 | 3.1 | 3.3 |
| 6.2 | 1.08 | 8.5 | 0.20 | 7.7 | 1.0 | 1.11 | 11.87 | 3.50 | 73.1 | 4.1 | 24.4 | 4.9 | 7.1 |
| 5.3 | 0.74 | 8.3 | 0.72 | 5.0 | 6.0 | 0.77 | 9.95 | 4.14 | 75.4 | 3.0 | 9.8 | 4.0 | 5.6 |
| 6.6 | 1.44 | 4.5 | 0.91 | 7.6 | 0.2 | 1.00 | 5.43 | 4.33 | 66.9 | 3.7 | 17.9 | 6.5 | 5.7 |
| 6.3 | 0.91 | 7.1 | 0.48 | 5.0 | 2.4 | 0.78 | 5.94 | 3.23 | 74.4 | 3.1 | 13.8 | 15.7 | 8.1 |
| 4.0 | 1.52 | 10.0 | 0.00 | 1.7 | 0.0 | 0.14 | 1.86 | 3.89 | 95.7 | 5.2 | 39.9 | 0.0 | 1.0 |
| 5.2 | 0.87 | 7.5 | 1.07 | 5.1 | 1.8 | 0.48 | 4.38 | 4.80 | 76.0 | 3.0 | 9.8 | 8.7 | 6.7 |
| 8.2 | 0.51 | 2.8 | 0.33 | 1.9 | 0.3 | 0.11 | 1.20 | 3.11 | 93.3 | 4.1 | 6.2 | 2.0 | 5.2 |
| 6.8 | 0.00 | 0.0 | 31.50 | 0.0 | 0.0 | -2.06 | -32.32 | 1.63 | 60.0 | 7.3 | 69.9 | 0.0 | 2.5 |
| 9.9 | 0.11 | 0.2 | 0.00 | 2.8 | 0.0 | 0.23 | 1.68 | 3.02 | 90.7 | 5.9 | 48.6 | 0.0 | 5.8 |
| 4.1 | 0.88 | 8.5 | 1.46 | 2.6 | 0.0 | 0.16 | 2.94 | 5.42 | 87.8 | 4.9 | 20.3 | 0.0 | 1.0 |
| 4.4 | 2.50 | 16.0 | 1.40 | 0.4 | -0.1 | -0.26 | -3.72 | 4.02 | 82.0 | 3.9 | 16.4 | 10.9 | 1.1 |
| 6.9 | 0.96 | 6.6 | 0.23 | 5.0 | 0.7 | 0.72 | 4.86 | 3.73 | 75.4 | 2.8 | 12.5 | 8.1 | 8.7 |
| 4.9 | 2.57 | 17.4 | 0.09 | 1.3 | 0.0 | -0.04 | -0.55 | 3.84 | 101.7 | 4.9 | 33.7 | 5.6 | 2.5 |
| 9.8 | 0.96 | 2.0 | 0.27 | 0.8 | 0.0 | -0.09 | -0.42 | 3.25 | 98.8 | 5.7 | 34.5 | 0.0 | 6.3 |

| Name | City | State | Rating | 2014 Rating | 2013 Rating | Total Assets ($Mil) | One Year Asset Growth | Asset Mix (As a % of Total Assets) | | | | Capital-ization Index | Net Worth Ratio |
|------|------|-------|--------|-------------|-------------|---------------------|-----------------------|-------------------|---|---|---|-----------------------|-----------------|
| | | | | | | | | Comm-ercial Loans | Cons-umer Loans | Mort-gage Loans | Secur-ities | | |
| ACBA FCU (3226) | Pittsburgh | PA | C- | D+ | D | 4.5 | -2.28 | 0.0 | 47.1 | 0.0 | 0.0 | 10.0 | 21.4 |
| ▲ ACCENTRA CU | Austin | MN | C+ | C | C | 118.4 | 5.27 | 4.2 | 39.3 | 21.5 | 3.6 | 7.1 | 9.1 |
| ACCESS COMMUNITY CU | Amarillo | TX | B+ | A- | A- | 108.8 | 7.68 | 0.0 | 56.1 | 0.4 | 1.5 | 10.0 | 14.6 |
| ACCESS CU | Broadview | IL | C- | C+ | D | 50.3 | 3.75 | 1.5 | 19.4 | 14.3 | 4.8 | 10.0 | 11.9 |
| ACCESS FCU | Clinton | NY | B- | B- | B- | 152.7 | 5.25 | 8.5 | 19.1 | 9.4 | 29.1 | 6.1 | 8.1 |
| ACCESS OF LOUISIANA FCU | Sulphur | LA | C | C | C | 26.8 | 1.89 | 0.0 | 34.4 | 28.8 | 0.0 | 10.0 | 15.3 |
| ▲ ACCLAIM FCU | Greensboro | NC | C+ | C | C | 35.3 | 1.94 | 0.1 | 36.3 | 8.2 | 0.0 | 8.3 | 9.9 |
| ACE CU | Mason City | IA | C | C | C | 9.7 | -4.37 | 0.0 | 12.7 | 0.0 | 0.0 | 10.0 | 11.1 |
| ACHIEVA CU | Dunedin | FL | A- | A- | B+ | 1195.2 | 15.19 | 5.7 | 49.5 | 17.0 | 2.6 | 10.0 | 11.0 |
| ACHIEVE FINANCIAL CU | Berlin | CT | C+ | B- | B- | 118.0 | 6.03 | 0.0 | 30.5 | 27.0 | 5.9 | 5.9 | 7.9 |
| ACIPCO FCU | Birmingham | AL | A- | A- | B+ | 145.5 | 2.05 | 0.0 | 21.4 | 50.7 | 9.4 | 10.0 | 13.0 |
| ACME CONTINENTAL CU | Riverdale | IL | B | B- | C+ | 43.5 | 0.41 | 0.0 | 39.5 | 0.3 | 11.8 | 10.0 | 17.5 |
| ACME FCU | Eastlake | OH | C- | C- | D+ | 14.8 | -2.72 | 0.0 | 20.4 | 12.2 | 0.0 | 10.0 | 17.6 |
| ACMG FCU | Solvay | NY | C- | C- | C- | 56.2 | 2.78 | 0.0 | 33.7 | 12.7 | 16.4 | 5.6 | 7.6 |
| ACPE FCU | Laramie | WY | C- | C- | C- | 45.3 | 6.14 | 0.8 | 35.3 | 15.7 | 0.0 | 5.9 | 7.9 |
| ACTORS FCU | New York | NY | B+ | B+ | B+ | 212.6 | 5.40 | 10.8 | 5.9 | 28.3 | 0.0 | 7.8 | 9.6 |
| ▼ ACU CU | Abilene | TX | C- | C | C | 6.4 | -0.47 | 0.0 | 57.0 | 0.0 | 0.0 | 10.0 | 16.6 |
| ACUME CU | Moorestown | NJ | D- | D- | D- | 4.4 | 2.03 | 0.0 | 22.2 | 29.5 | 0.0 | 6.3 | 8.3 |
| ACUSHNET FCU | Acushnet | MA | C | C+ | C+ | 21.6 | 8.55 | 0.9 | 10.0 | 28.0 | 46.5 | 7.9 | 9.6 |
| ADAMS COUNTY CU | Monroe | IN | C+ | C+ | C+ | 18.2 | 2.17 | 67.3 | 1.3 | 45.2 | 0.0 | 10.0 | 18.8 |
| ADIRONDACK REGIONAL FCU | Tupper Lake | NY | C- | C- | C- | 40.9 | 3.25 | 0.7 | 26.7 | 21.0 | 13.6 | 6.0 | 8.0 |
| ADM CU | Decatur | IL | C+ | C+ | C- | 15.9 | -4.33 | 0.0 | 58.8 | 0.0 | 0.0 | 10.0 | 15.6 |
| ▼ ADVANCE FINANCIAL FCU | East Chicago | IN | D+ | C- | C | 149.0 | -3.58 | 0.0 | 57.5 | 16.7 | 10.5 | 6.0 | 8.0 |
| ADVANCED FINANCIAL FCU | New Providence | NJ | D+ | D | D | 73.9 | 2.35 | 11.0 | 7.0 | 27.8 | 29.7 | 6.4 | 8.4 |
| ADVANCIAL FCU | Dallas | TX | B | B | B | 1233.2 | 6.75 | 9.3 | 33.9 | 34.9 | 3.5 | 7.2 | 9.1 |
| ADVANTAGE CU | Newton | IA | B+ | B+ | B+ | 60.4 | 3.27 | 4.2 | 21.6 | 11.2 | 11.5 | 10.0 | 15.8 |
| ADVANTAGE CU INC | Mansfield | OH | D- | D- | D- | 36.6 | -5.33 | 2.1 | 29.1 | 23.4 | 27.9 | 6.0 | 8.1 |
| ADVANTAGE FCU | Rochester | NY | B+ | B+ | B+ | 238.6 | 7.99 | 0.0 | 47.7 | 10.8 | 11.9 | 8.8 | 10.3 |
| ADVANTAGE ONE CU | Morrison | IL | C | C | C- | 19.6 | 0.94 | 0.0 | 30.0 | 19.0 | 0.0 | 10.0 | 11.4 |
| ADVANTAGE ONE FCU | Brownstown | MI | B | B | C+ | 121.1 | 3.66 | 6.1 | 30.3 | 10.5 | 35.4 | 9.1 | 10.4 |
| ADVANTAGE PLUS FCU | Pocatello | ID | B- | C+ | C+ | 111.7 | 5.31 | 2.2 | 27.6 | 21.9 | 2.1 | 7.7 | 9.4 |
| ADVANTAGEPLUS OF INDIANA FCU | Terre Haute | IN | B- | B- | B- | 20.3 | 3.50 | 0.0 | 61.5 | 0.1 | 0.0 | 10.0 | 16.5 |
| ADVANTIS CU | Milwaukie | OR | A- | A- | A- | 1206.7 | 3.08 | 9.3 | 24.7 | 28.8 | 4.9 | 9.5 | 10.6 |
| ▲ ADVIA CU | Parchment | MI | B+ | B | A- | 1140.2 | 12.02 | 5.9 | 30.6 | 26.4 | 24.5 | 10.0 | 12.8 |
| AE GOETZE EMPL CU | Lake City | MN | D | D | D | 4.8 | 0.59 | 0.0 | 78.8 | 0.0 | 0.0 | 8.8 | 10.2 |
| AEA FCU | Yuma | AZ | F | F | F | 243.4 | 2.28 | 9.2 | 48.4 | 17.1 | 0.7 | 0.0 | 5.6 |
| AEGIS CU | Clinton | IA | B- | C+ | C+ | 12.8 | 7.24 | 0.0 | 71.7 | 0.3 | 0.0 | 10.0 | 12.1 |
| AERO FCU | Glendale | AZ | C- | C- | C- | 212.3 | 3.89 | 0.0 | 34.5 | 0.2 | 26.0 | 10.0 | 15.3 |
| ▲ AEROQUIP CU | Jackson | MI | C+ | C | C | 43.7 | 1.67 | 0.3 | 20.8 | 29.5 | 40.4 | 10.0 | 14.7 |
| AEROSPACE FCU | El Segundo | CA | C+ | C+ | C | 365.7 | 1.82 | 0.2 | 6.0 | 8.8 | 71.7 | 8.1 | 9.7 |
| AFENA FCU | Marion | IN | C | C | C+ | 54.4 | 0.72 | 0.0 | 53.7 | 10.2 | 5.0 | 8.0 | 9.7 |
| AFFILIATED TRADES CU | Collegeville | PA | C- | C- | D+ | 27.2 | -4.91 | 0.5 | 12.5 | 4.6 | 45.7 | 10.0 | 12.4 |
| AFFINITY CU | Des Moines | IA | C+ | C+ | C- | 91.5 | 15.04 | 3.8 | 51.7 | 16.7 | 0.0 | 6.8 | 8.8 |
| AFFINITY FCU | Basking Ridge | NJ | C | C+ | C+ | 2334.8 | 3.58 | 9.0 | 11.3 | 55.9 | 11.1 | 6.6 | 8.8 |
| AFFINITY FIRST FCU | Minot | ND | B+ | B | B- | 51.2 | 5.91 | 2.4 | 22.1 | 12.3 | 1.7 | 10.0 | 11.4 |
| AFFINITY ONE FCU | Jamestown | NY | D+ | C | C- | 32.1 | 1.50 | 0.0 | 18.2 | 34.4 | 21.9 | 10.0 | 14.3 |
| AFFINITY PLUS FCU | Saint Paul | MN | B- | C+ | C+ | 1727.2 | 2.72 | 0.2 | 38.8 | 24.6 | 1.4 | 6.6 | 8.6 |
| AFGM ENTERPRISES FCU | Cheektowaga | NY | C | C | C | 11.6 | 1.48 | 0.0 | 30.7 | 17.9 | 10.2 | 10.0 | 22.4 |
| AFL-CIO EMPL FCU | Landover | MD | D- | D | C- | 53.8 | -2.25 | 0.0 | 19.1 | 16.5 | 37.8 | 8.8 | 10.3 |
| AFLAC FCU | Columbus | GA | B | B | B- | 189.9 | 2.46 | 0.3 | 4.3 | 0.0 | 72.0 | 10.0 | 15.3 |
| AGASSIZ FCU | Crookston | MN | D | D | D | 13.1 | 3.41 | 21.3 | 14.6 | 26.4 | 0.0 | 6.3 | 8.3 |
| ▲ AGILITY FINANCIAL CU | Memphis | TN | C- | D | C- | 9.1 | -5.50 | 0.0 | 42.0 | 0.6 | 0.0 | 10.0 | 11.9 |
| AGRICULTURE FCU | Washington | DC | B- | B- | B- | 262.3 | 6.80 | 2.9 | 25.7 | 25.9 | 24.0 | 10.0 | 12.3 |
| AIR ACADEMY FCU | Colorado Springs | CO | C+ | C+ | C | 506.4 | 7.12 | 1.0 | 53.0 | 29.8 | 4.2 | 6.3 | 8.4 |
| AIR FORCE FCU | San Antonio | TX | C- | C- | C | 366.8 | 1.97 | 0.7 | 53.2 | 13.7 | 8.0 | 5.8 | 7.8 |
| AIR TECH CU | Milwaukee | WI | C- | C- | C- | 3.9 | 2.39 | 0.0 | 50.0 | 0.0 | 0.0 | 10.0 | 15.6 |
| AIRCO FCU | Glendale | CA | C | C | B- | 15.2 | 2.48 | 0.0 | 14.4 | 0.0 | 0.0 | 7.2 | 9.2 |
| AKRON FCU | Akron | CO | E+ | E+ | D | <1 | -0.12 | 0.0 | 52.1 | 0.0 | 0.0 | 6.1 | 8.1 |
| AKRON FIREFIGHTERS CU | Akron | OH | D- | D- | E+ | 18.6 | -2.71 | 1.5 | 34.0 | 9.7 | 4.4 | 6.4 | 8.4 |
| AKRON MUNICIPAL EMPL CU | Akron | OH | D+ | D+ | D+ | 5.6 | 1.33 | 0.0 | 30.8 | 0.0 | 47.7 | 8.7 | 10.2 |

| Asset Quality Index | Non-Performing Loans as a % of Total Loans | as a % of Capital | Net Charge-Offs / Avg Loans | Profitability Index | Net Income ($Mil) | Return on Assets | Return on Equity | Net Interest Spread | Overhead Efficiency Ratio | Liquidity Index | Liquidity Ratio | Hot Money Ratio | Stability Index |
|---|---|---|---|---|---|---|---|---|---|---|---|---|---|
| 7.6 | 1.02 | 2.3 | 3.72 | 3.8 | 0.0 | 0.47 | 2.26 | 7.72 | 68.4 | 4.4 | 19.7 | 0.0 | 3.7 |
| 5.8 | 1.09 | 10.0 | 0.22 | 3.4 | 0.4 | 0.50 | 5.90 | 3.42 | 85.4 | 3.2 | 6.9 | 3.2 | 4.9 |
| 8.4 | 0.52 | 2.5 | 0.12 | 3.5 | 0.3 | 0.34 | 2.32 | 3.35 | 88.3 | 3.0 | 29.6 | 14.5 | 8.5 |
| 8.8 | 0.96 | 3.2 | 0.45 | 1.8 | 0.0 | 0.06 | 0.49 | 3.47 | 92.5 | 4.4 | 19.5 | 1.3 | 5.1 |
| 6.2 | 1.13 | 8.8 | 0.16 | 4.4 | 0.7 | 0.64 | 8.41 | 3.14 | 83.2 | 4.0 | 20.2 | 3.8 | 5.5 |
| 9.2 | 0.69 | 3.2 | 0.00 | 2.3 | 0.0 | 0.13 | 0.85 | 3.71 | 97.8 | 4.5 | 32.2 | 4.2 | 6.8 |
| 5.4 | 2.52 | 14.7 | 0.79 | 5.2 | 0.2 | 0.67 | 7.30 | 4.78 | 80.7 | 5.3 | 39.3 | 6.1 | 4.4 |
| 10.0 | 0.11 | 0.2 | 0.00 | 2.4 | 0.0 | 0.14 | 1.24 | 1.98 | 88.8 | 7.3 | 51.0 | 0.0 | 6.0 |
| 7.0 | 0.42 | 3.9 | 0.51 | 7.4 | 9.0 | 1.05 | 9.62 | 4.35 | 72.5 | 3.3 | 11.9 | 6.6 | 7.6 |
| 3.7 | 2.47 | 24.0 | 0.46 | 3.3 | 0.2 | 0.23 | 3.06 | 4.47 | 92.3 | 3.6 | 10.7 | 3.9 | 4.5 |
| 7.8 | 0.41 | 5.7 | 0.00 | 9.1 | 2.2 | 2.05 | 17.60 | 3.81 | 45.8 | 2.4 | 13.6 | 20.7 | 8.0 |
| 9.2 | 0.84 | 2.1 | 1.46 | 4.3 | 0.2 | 0.62 | 3.66 | 4.47 | 80.0 | 4.4 | 18.5 | 2.4 | 5.9 |
| 7.7 | 2.71 | 5.5 | -0.02 | 1.9 | 0.0 | 0.23 | 1.34 | 3.29 | 92.3 | 5.9 | 47.4 | 0.0 | 6.6 |
| 5.5 | 1.39 | 12.6 | 0.63 | 3.4 | 0.1 | 0.29 | 3.88 | 4.47 | 90.5 | 4.1 | 16.2 | 2.2 | 3.0 |
| 6.5 | 0.72 | 6.6 | 0.48 | 2.8 | 0.1 | 0.18 | 2.26 | 3.13 | 91.4 | 4.2 | 34.8 | 5.0 | 3.8 |
| 6.2 | 1.69 | 9.7 | 0.16 | 7.5 | 1.7 | 1.07 | 11.54 | 2.68 | 77.0 | 5.9 | 42.4 | 4.2 | 7.1 |
| 5.1 | 3.19 | 11.1 | 0.25 | 3.6 | 0.0 | 0.29 | 1.76 | 2.70 | 78.9 | 4.3 | 12.6 | 0.0 | 7.3 |
| 9.1 | 0.20 | 1.3 | 0.00 | 1.1 | 0.0 | -0.12 | -1.45 | 3.59 | 107.6 | 5.1 | 35.0 | 0.0 | 3.1 |
| 9.9 | 0.05 | 0.2 | 0.02 | 3.1 | 0.0 | 0.19 | 2.02 | 2.27 | 93.5 | 4.7 | 22.4 | 2.6 | 5.3 |
| 4.4 | 2.08 | 6.4 | 0.00 | 6.1 | 0.1 | 0.95 | 5.21 | 2.76 | 55.0 | 5.5 | 45.3 | 4.1 | 8.1 |
| 9.0 | 0.26 | 1.6 | 0.02 | 3.8 | 0.2 | 0.49 | 6.24 | 3.87 | 89.1 | 4.3 | 21.0 | 0.7 | 2.9 |
| 8.6 | 0.39 | 1.4 | 0.51 | 5.0 | 0.1 | 0.84 | 5.63 | 4.12 | 76.3 | 4.7 | 20.3 | 0.0 | 6.1 |
| 4.5 | 1.41 | 12.9 | 1.74 | 0.5 | -0.6 | -0.52 | -6.84 | 4.03 | 77.7 | 3.1 | 14.0 | 9.3 | 3.9 |
| 2.8 | 6.21 | 34.7 | 0.27 | 3.2 | 0.2 | 0.39 | 4.72 | 4.03 | 84.3 | 4.4 | 20.6 | 8.8 | 3.2 |
| 7.1 | 0.55 | 5.0 | 0.32 | 5.2 | 7.6 | 0.83 | 9.26 | 2.98 | 72.1 | 3.0 | 14.0 | 11.4 | 6.5 |
| 7.1 | 1.40 | 5.8 | 0.55 | 9.1 | 0.6 | 1.33 | 8.77 | 4.08 | 63.6 | 4.2 | 17.9 | 2.4 | 7.6 |
| 6.8 | 0.83 | 5.7 | 0.16 | 0.2 | -0.1 | -0.44 | -5.70 | 2.79 | 102.5 | 4.2 | 17.4 | 4.6 | 2.6 |
| 8.2 | 0.33 | 2.5 | 0.48 | 5.1 | 1.2 | 0.69 | 6.86 | 3.88 | 80.3 | 2.2 | 1.8 | 13.2 | 7.6 |
| 5.7 | 3.89 | 17.2 | 0.09 | 3.0 | 0.0 | 0.21 | 1.93 | 3.53 | 89.6 | 4.8 | 30.2 | 1.2 | 5.5 |
| 8.7 | 0.54 | 3.0 | 0.45 | 5.2 | 0.8 | 0.82 | 8.23 | 3.97 | 80.6 | 4.0 | 8.5 | 1.5 | 6.1 |
| 3.7 | 2.46 | 21.2 | 0.10 | 4.3 | 0.5 | 0.61 | 6.47 | 3.80 | 90.1 | 2.9 | 9.4 | 12.2 | 5.6 |
| 5.6 | 1.70 | 8.9 | 0.84 | 7.5 | 0.1 | 0.90 | 5.60 | 5.24 | 71.4 | 3.3 | 13.5 | 0.8 | 7.4 |
| 8.6 | 0.33 | 2.5 | 0.32 | 6.7 | 8.8 | 0.99 | 9.46 | 3.22 | 66.0 | 3.3 | 10.4 | 7.0 | 8.2 |
| 6.7 | 1.35 | 7.9 | 0.66 | 6.2 | 8.8 | 1.05 | 8.78 | 3.53 | 70.6 | 3.5 | 8.5 | 4.1 | 6.6 |
| 2.6 | 2.46 | 18.1 | 0.55 | 4.8 | 0.0 | 0.66 | 6.43 | 6.19 | 83.4 | 3.5 | 16.6 | 9.8 | 2.3 |
| 0.0 | 0.59 | 111.6 | 0.48 | 9.7 | 2.4 | 1.29 | NA | 4.64 | 71.2 | 2.9 | 12.2 | 14.4 | 2.0 |
| 7.2 | 0.61 | 3.8 | -0.01 | 8.2 | 0.1 | 1.29 | 11.00 | 4.71 | 78.5 | 4.4 | 20.1 | 2.2 | 5.7 |
| 10.0 | 0.19 | 0.7 | 0.11 | 1.2 | -0.2 | -0.14 | -0.91 | 2.55 | 106.3 | 5.0 | 31.7 | 3.2 | 6.9 |
| 9.4 | 0.07 | 0.3 | 0.41 | 4.5 | 0.3 | 0.77 | 5.33 | 3.28 | 87.0 | 4.0 | 10.0 | 0.9 | 6.3 |
| 10.0 | 0.04 | 0.1 | 0.16 | 3.6 | 1.4 | 0.50 | 5.06 | 1.69 | 73.9 | 4.8 | 18.8 | 3.0 | 6.1 |
| 6.3 | 0.59 | 4.1 | 0.38 | 4.5 | 0.3 | 0.72 | 7.71 | 4.57 | 83.3 | 3.2 | 16.7 | 7.6 | 3.0 |
| 3.7 | 7.54 | 21.8 | 0.08 | 1.8 | 0.0 | 0.18 | 1.48 | 2.19 | 96.2 | 4.4 | 24.3 | 4.1 | 5.1 |
| 5.0 | 0.63 | 6.2 | 0.33 | 7.4 | 0.8 | 1.18 | 13.06 | 4.36 | 76.4 | 4.6 | 26.2 | 2.1 | 3.7 |
| 5.4 | 1.79 | 16.0 | 0.50 | 2.5 | 2.5 | 0.15 | 1.68 | 3.20 | 84.3 | 3.0 | 5.1 | 6.4 | 6.1 |
| 9.1 | 0.21 | 1.3 | 0.07 | 9.8 | 0.6 | 1.46 | 13.36 | 4.11 | 67.4 | 3.2 | 22.0 | 15.5 | 6.6 |
| 8.9 | 0.52 | 2.5 | 0.19 | 0.7 | -0.1 | -0.55 | -3.85 | 4.02 | 106.3 | 3.6 | 7.4 | 1.7 | 7.0 |
| 6.2 | 0.79 | 8.9 | 0.69 | 4.7 | 9.8 | 0.75 | 9.13 | 3.72 | 77.7 | 2.7 | 9.3 | 8.0 | 5.6 |
| 8.1 | 2.41 | 5.9 | 0.36 | 2.1 | 0.0 | 0.18 | 0.83 | 2.71 | 85.3 | 4.9 | 36.7 | 0.0 | 6.5 |
| 6.4 | 2.11 | 8.6 | 0.63 | 0.3 | -0.3 | -0.71 | -6.88 | 3.24 | 110.8 | 4.7 | 27.0 | 5.4 | 3.6 |
| 8.3 | 4.64 | 4.9 | 0.16 | 3.6 | 0.6 | 0.45 | 2.99 | 1.55 | 62.9 | 5.6 | 16.8 | 0.0 | 7.7 |
| 6.4 | 0.52 | 3.3 | 1.36 | 0.6 | -0.1 | -0.65 | -7.49 | 3.14 | 99.7 | 5.6 | 36.1 | 0.9 | 4.1 |
| 9.5 | 0.60 | 2.2 | 0.39 | 1.5 | 0.0 | 0.03 | 0.25 | 3.88 | 99.4 | 4.4 | 30.1 | 1.6 | 3.9 |
| 8.0 | 0.80 | 4.6 | 0.38 | 4.0 | 1.1 | 0.55 | 4.49 | 2.96 | 79.9 | 3.5 | 18.2 | 10.7 | 7.2 |
| 4.9 | 0.64 | 12.3 | 0.32 | 3.9 | 1.8 | 0.48 | 5.69 | 3.32 | 78.9 | 2.8 | 4.2 | 5.9 | 5.4 |
| 5.8 | 0.55 | 5.3 | 1.56 | 2.1 | 0.4 | 0.15 | 2.12 | 4.58 | 79.9 | 2.8 | 17.6 | 14.7 | 2.8 |
| 7.9 | 1.11 | 4.1 | -0.18 | 1.3 | 0.0 | -0.07 | -0.44 | 3.31 | 96.6 | 4.5 | 13.4 | 0.0 | 6.4 |
| 10.0 | 0.20 | 0.4 | 0.11 | 3.8 | 0.1 | 0.41 | 4.38 | 2.34 | 85.1 | 4.5 | 6.7 | 5.7 | 4.0 |
| 8.0 | 0.16 | 1.4 | 0.00 | 0.8 | 0.0 | -0.16 | -1.99 | 4.03 | 105.0 | 3.9 | 20.2 | 0.0 | 3.0 |
| 5.8 | 1.52 | 9.8 | 0.04 | 1.6 | 0.0 | 0.17 | 2.06 | 4.36 | 94.8 | 5.4 | 37.3 | 8.8 | 2.7 |
| 9.2 | 0.05 | 0.2 | 0.88 | 1.9 | 0.0 | 0.07 | 0.70 | 3.86 | 93.3 | 5.6 | 33.9 | 0.0 | 4.6 |

| Name | City | State | Rating | 2014 Rating | 2013 Rating | Total Assets ($Mil) | One Year Asset Growth | Asset Mix (As a % of Total Assets) | | | | Capital- ization Index | Net Worth Ratio |
|---|---|---|---|---|---|---|---|---|---|---|---|---|---|
| | | | | | | | | Comm- ercial Loans | Cons- umer Loans | Mort- gage Loans | Secur- ities | | |
| AKRON POLICE DEPT CU | Akron | OH | D | C- | C | 10.5 | -11.23 | 0.0 | 58.7 | 0.0 | 0.0 | 10.0 | 12.5 |
| AKRON SCHOOL EMPL FCU | Akron | NY | D+ | D | D+ | <1 | 3.98 | 0.0 | 57.5 | 0.0 | 27.3 | 10.0 | 19.3 |
| AL GAR FCU | Cumberland | MD | D+ | C- | C | 33.6 | -2.18 | 0.0 | 34.6 | 12.7 | 9.8 | 10.0 | 17.4 |
| ▼ ALABAMA CENTRAL CU | Birmingham | AL | C | B- | C+ | 135.1 | 3.53 | 1.3 | 47.6 | 16.8 | 6.7 | 7.1 | 9.1 |
| ALABAMA CU | Tuscaloosa | AL | A- | A- | A- | 676.3 | 4.83 | 4.4 | 14.1 | 25.3 | 40.9 | 8.7 | 10.2 |
| ALABAMA LAW ENFORCEMENT CU | Birmingham | AL | C | C | C | 8.7 | 6.93 | 0.0 | 69.2 | 0.0 | 0.0 | 10.0 | 14.2 |
| ALABAMA ONE CU | Tuscaloosa | AL | F | C- | C- | 581.9 | -4.30 | 3.5 | 14.9 | 23.0 | 35.3 | 7.7 | 9.5 |
| ALABAMA POSTAL CU | Birmingham | AL | C+ | C+ | C+ | 7.8 | 0.66 | 0.0 | 34.6 | 0.0 | 0.0 | 10.0 | 27.9 |
| ALABAMA RIVER CU | Monroeville | AL | C | C | C | 17.3 | 1.77 | 0.0 | 26.8 | 0.0 | 31.8 | 10.0 | 11.8 |
| ALABAMA RURAL ELECTRIC CU | Montgomery | AL | C | C | C | 32.9 | 1.86 | 6.4 | 35.7 | 0.0 | 0.0 | 9.8 | 10.9 |
| ▼ ALABAMA STATE EMPL CU | Montgomery | AL | C+ | B | B+ | 232.5 | 5.84 | 0.4 | 30.3 | 7.9 | 37.7 | 10.0 | 11.4 |
| ALABAMA TEACHERS CU | Gadsden | AL | A- | A | A | 257.9 | 2.76 | 13.8 | 22.3 | 38.9 | 13.6 | 10.0 | 12.8 |
| ALAMO FCU | San Antonio | TX | D- | D- | D- | 46.4 | -0.13 | 0.4 | 44.3 | 13.0 | 2.5 | 5.1 | 7.1 |
| ALASKA AIRLINES/HORIZON AIR EMPL FCU | Seatac | WA | C | C- | C- | 58.9 | 3.89 | 0.0 | 19.4 | 5.9 | 16.7 | 10.0 | 16.9 |
| ▲ ALASKA DISTRICT ENGINEERS FCU | JBER | AK | D- | E | E+ | 13.6 | 5.94 | 6.5 | 16.8 | 21.3 | 40.4 | 4.9 | 6.9 |
| ALASKA USA FCU | Anchorage | AK | B- | B- | B- | 6309.2 | 12.91 | 5.7 | 59.6 | 10.8 | 4.8 | 5.9 | 9.2 |
| ALATRUST CU | Birmingham | AL | C+ | B- | C+ | 133.7 | 1.83 | 3.9 | 19.8 | 27.1 | 21.8 | 10.0 | 12.4 |
| ALBA GOLDEN FCU | Alba | TX | B | B | B- | 11.8 | 5.24 | 0.0 | 38.4 | 0.0 | 0.0 | 10.0 | 15.4 |
| ALBANY CITY LODGE K OF P 540 FCU | Albany | NY | D | D | D | 1.7 | -13.27 | 0.0 | 27.3 | 0.0 | 0.0 | 10.0 | 15.4 |
| ALBANY FIREMENS FCU | Albany | NY | C- | C- | C+ | 13.9 | 2.74 | 0.0 | 51.7 | 2.5 | 0.0 | 10.0 | 13.0 |
| ALBION SCHOOL EMPL FCU | Albion | NY | D+ | C- | C+ | 2.1 | -8.99 | 0.0 | 42.5 | 0.0 | 0.0 | 10.0 | 19.4 |
| ▲ ALCO FCU | Wellsville | NY | C+ | C+ | C+ | 25.4 | 4.94 | 0.0 | 46.3 | 5.6 | 0.0 | 10.0 | 14.6 |
| ▲ ALCOA COMMUNITY FCU | Benton | AR | D+ | D | C- | 40.7 | 3.44 | 0.0 | 47.7 | 6.6 | 28.7 | 10.0 | 11.5 |
| ALCOA MUNICIPAL EMPL FCU | Alcoa | TN | D | D+ | D+ | 5.7 | -0.74 | 0.0 | 39.6 | 0.3 | 0.0 | 9.6 | 10.8 |
| ALCOA PITTSBURGH FCU | Pittsburgh | PA | C | C+ | C+ | 33.0 | 15.96 | 0.0 | 22.2 | 9.3 | 0.9 | 10.0 | 11.5 |
| ALCOA TENN FCU | Alcoa | TN | C+ | C | C | 196.0 | 4.96 | 1.4 | 23.9 | 36.4 | 17.7 | 9.4 | 10.6 |
| ALCON EMPL FCU | Fort Worth | TX | B- | B- | B- | 31.7 | -3.75 | 0.0 | 24.6 | 9.8 | 0.0 | 10.0 | 17.6 |
| ALCOSE CU | White Oak | PA | D+ | C- | C- | 16.5 | -2.69 | 0.3 | 27.2 | 0.8 | 0.1 | 10.0 | 13.3 |
| ALDEN CU | Chicopee | MA | C+ | C+ | C+ | 140.4 | 3.01 | 4.4 | 35.5 | 32.7 | 13.6 | 7.1 | 9.2 |
| ALDERSGATE FCU | Marion | IL | C+ | C | C- | 4.3 | 6.30 | 0.0 | 89.8 | 0.0 | 0.0 | 10.0 | 11.6 |
| ▲ ALDERSON FCI FCU | Alderson | WV | C- | C- | C- | 7.1 | 5.45 | 0.0 | 69.6 | 0.0 | 0.0 | 10.0 | 11.9 |
| ▲ ALEC FCU | Baton Rouge | LA | C | C- | D+ | 8.2 | -16.19 | 0.0 | 19.0 | 0.0 | 0.0 | 10.0 | 20.8 |
| ALEXANDRIA MUNICIPAL EMPL CU | Alexandria | LA | B- | B- | C+ | 21.3 | -0.63 | 0.0 | 27.5 | 10.7 | 0.0 | 10.0 | 12.6 |
| ALEXANDRIA SCHOOLS EMPL CU | Alexandria | MN | C | C | C+ | 4.0 | -3.40 | 0.0 | 54.7 | 0.0 | 0.0 | 10.0 | 23.0 |
| ▲ ALEXANDRIA T&P FCU | Alexandria | LA | C | C- | C- | 8.3 | 5.35 | 0.0 | 37.0 | 0.0 | 0.0 | 10.0 | 13.3 |
| ALHAMBRA CU | Phoenix | AZ | C- | C- | C- | 21.4 | 5.80 | 0.0 | 56.7 | 0.0 | 0.0 | 8.1 | 9.8 |
| ▲ ALIGN CU | Lowell | MA | C- | D+ | D+ | 563.7 | 2.54 | 4.6 | 8.7 | 41.4 | 33.1 | 10.0 | 12.2 |
| ▲ ALIQUIPPA TEACHERS FCU | Aliquippa | PA | C | C- | D+ | <1 | -22.07 | 0.0 | 36.8 | 0.0 | 0.0 | 10.0 | 25.9 |
| ALIVE CU | Jacksonville | FL | D+ | C- | C | 123.5 | -1.39 | 0.0 | 38.7 | 3.7 | 25.4 | 10.0 | 15.0 |
| ALL SAINTS CATHOLIC FCU | Fort Worth | TX | D | D | C- | <1 | -1.07 | 0.0 | 49.5 | 0.0 | 0.0 | 10.0 | 18.1 |
| ALL SAINTS FCU | Garfield Heights | OH | C- | C | C- | 23.3 | 24.13 | 0.5 | 20.0 | 15.4 | 13.9 | 10.0 | 16.8 |
| ALL SEASONS FCU | Indianapolis | IN | C+ | C+ | C+ | 9.4 | 2.51 | 0.0 | 18.3 | 0.0 | 0.0 | 10.0 | 12.6 |
| ALL SOULS FCU | New York | NY | D | D | D+ | <1 | -6.42 | 0.0 | 0.8 | 0.0 | 42.7 | 10.0 | 15.3 |
| ▲ ALLCOM CU | Worcester | MA | B- | C+ | C+ | 67.9 | 2.32 | 0.0 | 11.9 | 27.0 | 14.1 | 10.0 | 14.9 |
| ▲ ALLEGACY FCU | Winston-Salem | NC | B+ | B | B- | 1137.0 | 5.51 | 6.7 | 23.4 | 19.2 | 5.6 | 8.6 | 10.1 |
| ALLEGAN COMMUNITY FCU | Allegan | MI | C | C+ | C+ | 31.3 | 3.28 | 0.4 | 32.1 | 11.2 | 0.0 | 10.0 | 12.7 |
| ALLEGANY COUNTY TEACHERS FCU | Lavale | MD | B | B | B- | 96.2 | 1.26 | 0.7 | 39.2 | 24.8 | 11.8 | 9.9 | 11.0 |
| ALLEGANY FIRST FCU | Fillmore | NY | C- | C- | C | 13.0 | 0.18 | 0.0 | 19.9 | 5.3 | 0.0 | 9.5 | 10.7 |
| ALLEGENT COMMUNITY FCU | Pittsburgh | PA | C | C+ | C | 156.3 | -4.15 | 0.3 | 36.5 | 19.0 | 21.6 | 10.0 | 11.6 |
| ▼ ALLEGHENY CENTRAL EMPL FCU | Dunbar | PA | D+ | C- | C- | 5.6 | -4.04 | 0.0 | 46.6 | 2.9 | 0.0 | 9.4 | 10.6 |
| ALLEGHENY HEALTH SERVICES EMPL FCU | Pittsburgh | PA | D | C- | C- | 12.6 | 1.24 | 0.0 | 13.0 | 0.0 | 15.8 | 6.6 | 8.6 |
| ALLEGHENY KISKI POSTAL FCU | New Kensington | PA | D | D+ | D+ | 15.6 | -5.90 | 0.0 | 24.0 | 7.0 | 0.0 | 10.0 | 17.1 |
| ALLEGHENY LUDLUM BRACKENRIDGE FCU | Brackenridge | PA | C+ | C | C | 22.1 | 2.97 | 0.0 | 22.8 | 0.0 | 0.0 | 10.0 | 16.7 |
| ALLEGHENY METAL FCU | Leechburg | PA | B- | B- | B- | 13.6 | -1.15 | 0.0 | 33.2 | 0.0 | 0.0 | 10.0 | 14.9 |
| ALLEGHENY VALLEY FCU | Pittsburgh | PA | C- | C | C | 12.4 | -0.34 | 0.0 | 22.7 | 0.0 | 0.0 | 10.0 | 27.1 |
| ALLEGIANCE CU | Oklahoma City | OK | C+ | C+ | C | 249.6 | 0.33 | 4.6 | 43.6 | 17.7 | 5.6 | 6.0 | 8.0 |
| ALLEGIUS FCU | Burns Harbor | IN | B- | B- | C+ | 165.4 | 1.12 | 0.0 | 32.4 | 7.0 | 43.7 | 9.4 | 10.6 |
| ALLEN AME FCU | Philadelphia | PA | D- | D | D- | <1 | -11.36 | 0.0 | 30.8 | 0.0 | 0.0 | 10.0 | 18.0 |
| ALLEN HOSPITAL PERSONNEL CU | Waterloo | IA | C- | C- | C- | 5.3 | -5.52 | 0.0 | 79.6 | 0.0 | 0.0 | 10.0 | 18.9 |
| ALLENTOWN FCU | Allentown | PA | B | B | B | 55.5 | 5.46 | 0.0 | 11.1 | 40.4 | 0.0 | 10.0 | 12.5 |

| Asset Quality Index | Non-Performing Loans as a % of Total Loans | as a % of Capital | Net Charge-Offs Avg Loans | Profitability Index | Net Income ($Mil) | Return on Assets | Return on Equity | Net Interest Spread | Overhead Efficiency Ratio | Liquidity Index | Liquidity Ratio | Hot Money Ratio | Stability Index |
|---|---|---|---|---|---|---|---|---|---|---|---|---|---|
| 6.4 | 1.46 | 7.0 | 0.50 | 0.0 | -0.2 | -2.34 | -19.10 | 3.84 | 127.0 | 4.0 | 14.0 | 0.0 | 5.4 |
| 8.7 | 0.00 | 0.0 | 0.00 | 1.0 | 0.0 | 0.00 | 0.00 | 3.63 | 100.0 | 5.0 | 18.5 | 0.0 | 5.3 |
| 8.7 | 1.04 | 3.2 | 0.31 | 0.7 | -0.1 | -0.19 | -1.09 | 3.22 | 98.7 | 5.1 | 36.6 | 1.1 | 6.8 |
| 4.4 | 0.39 | 16.5 | 0.68 | 2.4 | 0.1 | 0.05 | 0.64 | 3.82 | 93.4 | 3.6 | 11.6 | 6.3 | 4.6 |
| 8.7 | 0.72 | 3.7 | 0.25 | 5.9 | 4.7 | 0.93 | 9.15 | 2.79 | 75.4 | 4.4 | 30.6 | 10.8 | 7.8 |
| 5.7 | 1.52 | 7.6 | 1.19 | 10.0 | 0.2 | 2.51 | 18.07 | 7.02 | 56.5 | 2.9 | 39.4 | 29.1 | 5.0 |
| 5.2 | 2.94 | 18.9 | 0.47 | 0.3 | -6.3 | -1.39 | -14.36 | 2.69 | 143.9 | 4.4 | 31.5 | 15.2 | 5.1 |
| 6.7 | 6.41 | 7.8 | 2.05 | 8.4 | 0.1 | 1.14 | 4.12 | 5.25 | 71.4 | 6.0 | 41.7 | 0.0 | 5.0 |
| 9.3 | 1.43 | 3.6 | 0.35 | 2.1 | 0.0 | 0.17 | 1.44 | 2.84 | 95.8 | 6.2 | 40.1 | 0.7 | 6.5 |
| 8.8 | 0.53 | 2.0 | -0.09 | 2.7 | 0.1 | 0.26 | 2.29 | 2.81 | 91.0 | 4.4 | 30.4 | 8.8 | 5.9 |
| 7.8 | 1.55 | 5.8 | 0.70 | 2.6 | 0.3 | 0.19 | 1.74 | 3.00 | 86.4 | 4.2 | 25.3 | 8.9 | 7.1 |
| 6.3 | 1.17 | 8.1 | 0.44 | 5.2 | 1.1 | 0.55 | 4.25 | 3.59 | 82.3 | 3.7 | 24.5 | 8.6 | 9.1 |
| 4.4 | 1.50 | 16.4 | 0.15 | 0.1 | -0.3 | -0.86 | -11.79 | 4.17 | 109.6 | 4.1 | 16.6 | 0.0 | 3.0 |
| 10.0 | 0.13 | 0.4 | 0.03 | 2.3 | 0.1 | 0.22 | 1.32 | 2.38 | 90.7 | 5.6 | 51.5 | 2.1 | 6.1 |
| 9.6 | 0.00 | 0.0 | 0.13 | 3.0 | 0.0 | 0.42 | 6.32 | 2.93 | 86.2 | 5.1 | 25.8 | 0.0 | 1.7 |
| 4.1 | 1.22 | 14.8 | 0.52 | 5.7 | 39.5 | 0.89 | 12.87 | 3.58 | 77.4 | 3.1 | 10.5 | 9.0 | 4.6 |
| 5.1 | 2.00 | 16.9 | 1.01 | 3.3 | 0.5 | 0.48 | 3.98 | 3.86 | 76.3 | 5.0 | 25.8 | 2.7 | 7.3 |
| 7.6 | 0.82 | 3.1 | 0.77 | 10.0 | 0.2 | 2.42 | 15.60 | 5.18 | 52.5 | 2.6 | 24.0 | 26.4 | 6.3 |
| 4.6 | 10.27 | 19.3 | 0.00 | 0.3 | 0.0 | -0.29 | -2.00 | 1.74 | 120.0 | 6.9 | 48.9 | 0.0 | 6.3 |
| 2.7 | 4.27 | 21.7 | 0.11 | 2.7 | 0.0 | 0.30 | 2.30 | 3.85 | 88.6 | 3.8 | 16.3 | 0.0 | 5.3 |
| 8.4 | 0.97 | 2.2 | 0.00 | 0.8 | 0.0 | -0.23 | -1.29 | 2.91 | 111.1 | 6.1 | 44.6 | 0.0 | 6.8 |
| 7.1 | 0.43 | 1.9 | 0.58 | 4.6 | 0.1 | 0.72 | 5.15 | 4.12 | 87.0 | 4.0 | 15.6 | 0.5 | 6.6 |
| 5.9 | 1.08 | 6.0 | 0.81 | 0.9 | 0.0 | -0.02 | -0.18 | 3.89 | 87.5 | 4.2 | 18.7 | 3.3 | 4.8 |
| 9.3 | 0.00 | 0.0 | 0.00 | 0.5 | 0.0 | -0.16 | -1.53 | 2.26 | 107.5 | 4.9 | 35.3 | 0.0 | 4.8 |
| 10.0 | 0.18 | 0.6 | 0.18 | 2.3 | 0.0 | 0.10 | 0.92 | 2.32 | 95.2 | 5.7 | 36.0 | 1.2 | 5.9 |
| 9.5 | 0.39 | 2.7 | 0.07 | 3.9 | 0.9 | 0.58 | 5.59 | 3.22 | 86.1 | 4.4 | 20.7 | 3.9 | 6.8 |
| 10.0 | 0.37 | 0.8 | 0.07 | 3.4 | 0.1 | 0.44 | 2.54 | 2.18 | 84.7 | 5.3 | 45.4 | 0.0 | 6.7 |
| 9.0 | 1.69 | 3.5 | 0.74 | 1.0 | 0.0 | -0.13 | -0.99 | 2.99 | 95.6 | 4.9 | 19.3 | 0.0 | 5.4 |
| 6.0 | 1.46 | 12.0 | 0.74 | 3.5 | 0.4 | 0.33 | 3.83 | 4.06 | 77.3 | 3.8 | 12.5 | 0.0 | 5.3 |
| 8.0 | 0.00 | 0.0 | 0.00 | 10.0 | 0.1 | 2.43 | 22.13 | 5.11 | 48.4 | 3.3 | 9.2 | 0.0 | 5.0 |
| 2.5 | 3.24 | 20.8 | 0.54 | 10.0 | 0.1 | 2.03 | 18.06 | 4.22 | 28.3 | 4.8 | 23.7 | 0.0 | 7.0 |
| 10.0 | 0.16 | 0.2 | 0.42 | 2.4 | 0.0 | 0.33 | 1.81 | 2.49 | 86.3 | 6.1 | 68.0 | 0.0 | 5.8 |
| 8.1 | 1.32 | 4.7 | -0.04 | 4.7 | 0.1 | 0.76 | 6.16 | 3.27 | 78.6 | 3.4 | 12.0 | 13.2 | 6.6 |
| 8.1 | 0.10 | 0.3 | 0.00 | 3.4 | 0.0 | 0.46 | 2.04 | 2.89 | 82.5 | 4.3 | 19.5 | 0.0 | 7.4 |
| 8.3 | 0.65 | 2.5 | 1.15 | 4.2 | 0.1 | 0.77 | 5.83 | 3.35 | 71.7 | 5.6 | 43.4 | 0.0 | 6.3 |
| 4.4 | 1.36 | 8.8 | 0.08 | 5.7 | 0.1 | 0.72 | 7.64 | 5.31 | 90.0 | 3.7 | 19.7 | 3.2 | 3.7 |
| 9.8 | 0.44 | 2.1 | 0.09 | 1.6 | 1.0 | 0.23 | 1.92 | 2.61 | 93.9 | 3.4 | 7.1 | 8.3 | 7.8 |
| 9.9 | 0.00 | 0.0 | 0.00 | 4.4 | 0.0 | 0.80 | 3.10 | 5.21 | 80.0 | 7.0 | 82.1 | 0.0 | 5.9 |
| 9.1 | 0.74 | 2.5 | 0.48 | 0.7 | -0.3 | -0.30 | -2.07 | 2.40 | 100.6 | 4.5 | 17.6 | 3.1 | 7.1 |
| 8.2 | 0.00 | 0.0 | 0.00 | 0.0 | 0.0 | -0.24 | -1.32 | 1.61 | 120.0 | 4.9 | 38.7 | 0.0 | 5.5 |
| 7.2 | 2.90 | 6.3 | 2.00 | 0.2 | -0.8 | -4.96 | -29.85 | -0.87 | -547.8 | 4.9 | 32.9 | 3.9 | 6.1 |
| 10.0 | 0.37 | 0.6 | -0.54 | 5.2 | 0.1 | 0.75 | 6.02 | 3.04 | 85.8 | 5.5 | 38.0 | 0.0 | 5.0 |
| 10.0 | 0.00 | 0.0 | 0.00 | 0.0 | 0.0 | -2.09 | -13.33 | 0.88 | 500.0 | 8.0 | 77.6 | 0.0 | 6.2 |
| 10.0 | 0.31 | 0.9 | 0.04 | 3.7 | 0.3 | 0.57 | 3.82 | 2.60 | 82.2 | 4.3 | 25.7 | 6.1 | 7.1 |
| 6.0 | 0.81 | 12.1 | 0.50 | 5.4 | 6.6 | 0.78 | 7.88 | 3.89 | 78.5 | 3.8 | 17.5 | 7.4 | 6.8 |
| 8.2 | 1.30 | 6.3 | 0.70 | 2.7 | 0.1 | 0.29 | 2.28 | 3.09 | 92.7 | 4.9 | 19.3 | 0.0 | 5.7 |
| 7.1 | 0.77 | 5.0 | 0.19 | 4.4 | 0.5 | 0.64 | 6.03 | 3.37 | 76.1 | 3.6 | 10.7 | 5.1 | 5.6 |
| 8.1 | 0.37 | 1.3 | -0.17 | 1.9 | 0.0 | 0.04 | 0.39 | 3.43 | 98.7 | 6.3 | 42.0 | 1.9 | 4.2 |
| 9.7 | 0.40 | 2.2 | 0.18 | 2.3 | 0.1 | 0.10 | 0.87 | 2.52 | 91.7 | 4.0 | 14.7 | 7.2 | 7.0 |
| 5.5 | 2.04 | 12.0 | -0.22 | 2.1 | 0.0 | -0.05 | -0.45 | 3.39 | 101.5 | 4.8 | 24.1 | 0.0 | 5.4 |
| 8.4 | 0.54 | 2.3 | 1.86 | 0.5 | 0.0 | -0.44 | -4.88 | 2.83 | 93.3 | 6.4 | 41.2 | 0.0 | 3.3 |
| 7.2 | 3.92 | 7.4 | 0.30 | 0.0 | -0.1 | -1.14 | -6.66 | 3.14 | 131.8 | 6.1 | 47.0 | 0.0 | 5.4 |
| 10.0 | 0.00 | 0.0 | 0.20 | 3.0 | 0.1 | 0.41 | 2.65 | 2.04 | 80.6 | 5.1 | 17.5 | 0.0 | 6.4 |
| 7.9 | 1.37 | 3.6 | 0.32 | 4.1 | 0.1 | 0.54 | 3.73 | 2.66 | 72.6 | 6.1 | 66.1 | 0.0 | 7.2 |
| 10.0 | 0.00 | 0.0 | 0.72 | 1.5 | 0.0 | -0.04 | -0.16 | 2.19 | 91.7 | 5.7 | 37.3 | 3.0 | 6.3 |
| 3.7 | 0.94 | 21.0 | 0.55 | 3.8 | 0.9 | 0.48 | 6.16 | 4.16 | 77.3 | 3.0 | 6.4 | 4.4 | 4.6 |
| 8.2 | 0.83 | 5.0 | 0.58 | 3.9 | 0.7 | 0.56 | 5.75 | 3.15 | 83.4 | 4.1 | 10.2 | 3.2 | 6.3 |
| 0.3 | 50.00 | 85.7 | 0.00 | 0.0 | 0.0 | -6.20 | -33.33 | 10.26 | 300.0 | 7.8 | 81.3 | 0.0 | 4.9 |
| 6.9 | 1.46 | 6.1 | 0.50 | 3.5 | 0.0 | 0.34 | 1.87 | 4.73 | 91.6 | 4.2 | 24.2 | 0.0 | 7.0 |
| 8.3 | 0.38 | 3.9 | 0.26 | 4.5 | 0.3 | 0.68 | 5.56 | 3.88 | 77.2 | 5.1 | 24.4 | 0.0 | 6.5 |

| Name | City | State | Rating | 2014 Rating | 2013 Rating | Total Assets ($Mil) | One Year Asset Growth | Commercial Loans | Consumer Loans | Mortgage Loans | Securities | Capitalization Index | Net Worth Ratio |
|------|------|-------|--------|-------------|-------------|---------------------|----------------------|------------------|----------------|----------------|------------|---------------------|-----------------|
| ALLIANCE BLACKSTONE VALLEY FCU | Pawtucket | RI | D | D+ | D+ | 35.6 | -1.22 | 1.4 | 24.0 | 20.0 | 14.1 | 6.7 | 8.7 |
| ALLIANCE CATHOLIC CU | Southfield | MI | B+ | B | B- | 410.0 | 0.75 | 9.2 | 13.0 | 22.7 | 45.7 | 9.5 | 10.6 |
| ▲ ALLIANCE CU | San Jose | CA | B | C+ | D+ | 370.2 | 5.79 | 0.5 | 39.4 | 16.9 | 18.8 | 6.7 | 8.7 |
| ALLIANCE CU | Fenton | MO | B- | C+ | C+ | 224.6 | 5.84 | 9.1 | 16.2 | 56.5 | 0.0 | 7.3 | 9.2 |
| ALLIANCE FCU | Lubbock | TX | B | B+ | A- | 224.6 | -0.63 | 6.5 | 25.8 | 21.7 | 35.8 | 10.0 | 14.6 |
| ALLIANCE NIAGARA FCU | Sanborn | NY | D- | D- | D- | 16.1 | 6.87 | 0.0 | 13.7 | 8.1 | 51.7 | 5.3 | 7.3 |
| ALLIANT CU | Dubuque | IA | B- | B | B- | 105.7 | 11.17 | 4.1 | 26.7 | 35.6 | 0.0 | 9.1 | 10.4 |
| ALLIANT CU | Chicago | IL | B+ | B+ | C+ | 8463.8 | 4.63 | 3.3 | 14.0 | 37.1 | 33.0 | 10.0 | 11.3 |
| ALLIED CU | Stockton | CA | C- | D+ | D+ | 23.3 | 2.47 | 0.0 | 8.3 | 8.7 | 0.0 | 10.0 | 12.4 |
| ALLIED FCU | Arlington | TX | C- | C- | D+ | 81.1 | 4.32 | 0.0 | 39.3 | 2.9 | 20.9 | 5.4 | 7.4 |
| ALLIED HEALTHCARE FCU | Long Beach | CA | C | C | C | 66.0 | -0.23 | 1.4 | 16.4 | 31.0 | 3.7 | 5.2 | 7.2 |
| ALLIED PLASTICS FCU | Baton Rouge | LA | C- | C- | D+ | 22.9 | 4.01 | 0.0 | 30.4 | 3.7 | 0.0 | 8.9 | 10.2 |
| ▼ ALLOY EMPL CU | Waukesha | WI | D | C- | C- | <1 | -10.00 | 0.0 | 25.6 | 0.0 | 0.0 | 10.0 | 45.7 |
| ALLOY FCU | Alloy | WV | C | C+ | C+ | 20.3 | 0.21 | 0.0 | 47.3 | 3.9 | 0.0 | 10.0 | 14.8 |
| ALLOY SCOTTDALE FCU | Scottdale | PA | D | D+ | D+ | <1 | -9.21 | 0.0 | 38.3 | 0.0 | 0.0 | 10.0 | 21.7 |
| ALLSOUTH FCU | Columbia | SC | A | A+ | A+ | 719.2 | 4.67 | 0.1 | 50.1 | 12.2 | 6.7 | 10.0 | 15.6 |
| ALLSTEEL CU | Oswego | IL | D+ | D+ | C | 22.1 | 0.97 | 0.0 | 27.7 | 22.6 | 0.0 | 10.0 | 17.8 |
| ALLUS CU | Salinas | CA | B+ | A- | A- | 36.6 | 2.88 | 0.0 | 22.0 | 0.0 | 44.9 | 10.0 | 15.3 |
| ALLVAC SAVINGS & CU | Monroe | NC | C | C | C | 7.5 | 1.87 | 0.0 | 29.9 | 0.0 | 0.0 | 10.0 | 14.9 |
| ▲ ALLWEALTH FCU | Hamilton | OH | D- | E+ | E+ | 18.7 | -2.82 | 0.0 | 23.9 | 24.9 | 0.0 | 6.1 | 8.1 |
| ALOHA PACIFIC FCU | Honolulu | HI | B- | B- | B | 743.4 | -1.01 | 8.0 | 6.8 | 27.5 | 42.9 | 10.0 | 11.0 |
| ALPENA COMMUNITY CU | Alpena | MI | C- | D+ | D+ | 21.4 | 9.15 | 1.4 | 14.7 | 29.3 | 37.8 | 6.7 | 8.7 |
| ALPENA-ALCONA AREA CU | Alpena | MI | B- | B- | B- | 303.3 | 5.13 | 0.1 | 19.7 | 19.9 | 1.1 | 7.0 | 9.0 |
| ALPHA CU | Boston | MA | D+ | D | D+ | 29.0 | 3.01 | 0.0 | 5.9 | 8.8 | 6.1 | 10.0 | 13.7 |
| ALPINE COMMUNITY CU | Alpine | TX | C | C | C | 15.2 | 2.48 | 0.0 | 40.6 | 0.0 | 0.0 | 9.3 | 10.6 |
| ALPINE CU | Orem | UT | B- | C | C+ | 168.8 | 4.06 | 0.0 | 37.8 | 15.1 | 6.4 | 10.0 | 11.5 |
| ▼ ALPS FCU | Sitka | AK | D+ | C | C+ | 64.5 | 45.26 | 11.5 | 6.3 | 15.5 | 19.0 | 6.6 | 8.6 |
| ALTA VISTA CU | Redlands | CA | C | C- | C+ | 139.6 | 4.71 | 2.8 | 19.5 | 27.2 | 5.5 | 6.3 | 8.4 |
| ALTAMAHA FCU | Jesup | GA | B | B | B | 56.2 | -0.27 | 0.0 | 43.1 | 8.4 | 10.0 | 10.0 | 13.8 |
| ALTANA FCU | Billings | MT | B | B+ | A- | 222.9 | 1.58 | 3.1 | 27.5 | 17.5 | 6.8 | 10.0 | 12.2 |
| ALTAONE FCU | Ridgecrest | CA | B | B | B | 608.4 | 4.00 | 5.9 | 42.7 | 22.9 | 1.8 | 8.1 | 9.8 |
| ALTERNATIVES FCU | Ithaca | NY | C+ | C- | C | 94.7 | 5.27 | 5.6 | 10.5 | 43.9 | 1.3 | 9.9 | 10.9 |
| ALTIER CU | Tempe | AZ | C+ | C | C | 180.6 | 3.06 | 9.9 | 40.0 | 0.9 | 3.8 | 6.0 | 8.0 |
| ALTON MUNICIPAL EMPL FCU | Alton | IL | D+ | C- | C | <1 | -2.55 | 0.0 | 83.7 | 0.0 | 0.0 | 10.0 | 27.8 |
| ALTONIZED COMMUNITY FCU | Alton | IL | C+ | C | D+ | 34.8 | -0.70 | 0.0 | 36.2 | 0.8 | 14.1 | 9.5 | 10.9 |
| ALTOONA AREA EMPL FCU | Altoona | PA | C | C | D+ | 10.3 | -1.27 | 0.0 | 29.9 | 0.0 | 0.0 | 9.6 | 10.8 |
| ALTOONA REGIONAL HEALTH SYSTEM FCU | Duncansville | PA | D+ | D+ | C | 28.7 | 3.75 | 0.0 | 23.9 | 8.3 | 3.8 | 6.9 | 8.9 |
| ALTRA FCU | Onalaska | WI | A- | A- | A- | 1114.5 | 9.26 | 10.9 | 34.7 | 37.3 | 5.1 | 10.0 | 11.2 |
| ALTURA CU | Riverside | CA | A | A | A | 1144.7 | 59.23 | 3.6 | 39.2 | 11.9 | 15.9 | 9.6 | 10.7 |
| AMARILLO COMMUNITY FCU | Amarillo | TX | B- | B- | B- | 219.0 | 2.13 | 0.0 | 51.1 | 2.9 | 10.1 | 6.7 | 8.7 |
| AMARILLO POSTAL EMPL CU | Amarillo | TX | C | B- | B- | 17.1 | 6.64 | 1.4 | 32.1 | 8.8 | 0.0 | 10.0 | 14.8 |
| ▼ AMBRAW FCU | Lawrenceville | IL | D+ | C- | C | 10.4 | 0.39 | 0.0 | 44.1 | 0.0 | 0.0 | 8.7 | 10.2 |
| AMBRIDGE AREA FCU | Baden | PA | C- | C | C+ | 11.2 | -8.72 | 0.0 | 28.0 | 0.0 | 0.0 | 10.0 | 12.5 |
| AME CHURCH FCU | Baton Rouge | LA | C- | D+ | C- | <1 | -3.06 | 0.0 | 20.0 | 0.0 | 0.0 | 10.0 | 15.8 |
| AMERICA FIRST FCU | Riverdale | UT | A- | B+ | B- | 7002.6 | 10.29 | 2.7 | 45.5 | 11.9 | 15.7 | 10.0 | 11.7 |
| AMERICAN 1 CU | Jackson | MI | A- | A- | A- | 280.1 | 4.48 | 0.0 | 57.8 | 3.1 | 0.0 | 10.0 | 16.8 |
| AMERICAN AIRLINES FCU | Fort Worth | TX | C+ | C+ | C+ | 6198.0 | 9.84 | 0.5 | 22.4 | 29.8 | 28.6 | 8.5 | 10.0 |
| AMERICAN BAPTIST ASSN CU | Pearland | TX | D+ | D+ | D+ | 1.8 | 5.18 | 0.0 | 58.1 | 0.0 | 0.0 | 9.7 | 10.8 |
| AMERICAN BROADCAST EMPL FCU | Rockville Centre | NY | C- | C- | C- | 99.9 | 0.72 | 0.8 | 23.8 | 25.4 | 3.2 | 9.2 | 10.5 |
| AMERICAN CHEMICAL SOCIETY FCU | Columbus | OH | D+ | D+ | D | 20.2 | 2.19 | 0.2 | 20.6 | 4.1 | 0.0 | 7.5 | 9.3 |
| AMERICAN EAGLE FINANCIAL CU INC | East Hartford | CT | C+ | C+ | C+ | 1398.8 | 3.94 | 0.6 | 19.9 | 33.1 | 25.6 | 9.0 | 10.3 |
| AMERICAN FCU | Mission Hills | CA | C | D+ | D+ | 16.5 | 4.22 | 8.6 | 6.6 | 49.0 | 0.0 | 10.0 | 18.2 |
| AMERICAN FIRST CU | La Habra | CA | A- | A- | B+ | 546.0 | 9.32 | 8.1 | 13.1 | 37.9 | 15.2 | 8.8 | 10.2 |
| AMERICAN HAMMERED FCU | Baltimore | MD | D | D | D | 5.1 | -2.42 | 0.0 | 22.7 | 0.0 | 0.0 | 10.0 | 14.0 |
| AMERICAN HERITAGE FCU | Philadelphia | PA | B | B | B | 1551.3 | 7.16 | 12.1 | 15.8 | 26.7 | 28.9 | 7.7 | 9.5 |
| AMERICAN LAKE CU | Lakewood | WA | C+ | B- | B- | 44.5 | -3.89 | 0.0 | 30.1 | 13.7 | 0.0 | 10.0 | 12.7 |
| AMERICAN NICKELOID EMPL CU | La Salle | IL | C | C+ | C+ | 11.3 | 11.63 | 0.0 | 22.7 | 31.2 | 12.0 | 10.0 | 15.5 |
| AMERICAN PARTNERS FCU | Reidsville | NC | B | B- | C+ | 47.4 | 0.57 | 0.7 | 55.9 | 0.0 | 1.6 | 10.0 | 11.7 |
| AMERICAN PRIDE CU | Altoona | PA | D+ | D+ | C- | 15.8 | 0.18 | 0.0 | 15.5 | 22.7 | 5.4 | 6.6 | 8.6 |
| AMERICAN SOUTHWEST CU | Sierra Vista | AZ | B- | B | B | 196.2 | 5.66 | 5.9 | 33.2 | 20.4 | 23.9 | 7.1 | 9.0 |

| Asset Quality Index | Non-Performing Loans as a % of Total Loans | Non-Performing Loans as a % of Capital | Net Charge-Offs Avg Loans | Profitability Index | Net Income ($Mil) | Return on Assets | Return on Equity | Net Interest Spread | Overhead Efficiency Ratio | Liquidity Index | Liquidity Ratio | Hot Money Ratio | Stability Index |
|---|---|---|---|---|---|---|---|---|---|---|---|---|---|
| 3.6 | 2.46 | 22.4 | 1.07 | 2.1 | 0.0 | 0.04 | 0.47 | 2.66 | 95.8 | 3.9 | 23.9 | 10.1 | 3.0 |
| 8.0 | 1.06 | 4.5 | 0.14 | 8.7 | 4.0 | 1.27 | 12.79 | 3.00 | 70.8 | 4.2 | 13.3 | 3.2 | 6.2 |
| 8.5 | 0.51 | 4.0 | 0.53 | 5.1 | 2.4 | 0.87 | 10.29 | 3.55 | 79.1 | 4.1 | 12.4 | 1.4 | 4.8 |
| 5.7 | 0.99 | 14.8 | 0.23 | 4.3 | 1.0 | 0.61 | 6.66 | 3.26 | 79.9 | 2.3 | 3.1 | 9.3 | 5.8 |
| 9.2 | 0.30 | 1.1 | 0.37 | 3.7 | 0.9 | 0.54 | 3.73 | 3.23 | 83.3 | 3.4 | 6.0 | 8.3 | 8.1 |
| 6.3 | 2.15 | 9.2 | -0.03 | 2.2 | 0.0 | 0.13 | 1.82 | 2.57 | 94.6 | 4.8 | 17.3 | 0.8 | 3.3 |
| 8.7 | 0.31 | 3.5 | 0.28 | 4.5 | 0.5 | 0.64 | 6.24 | 3.44 | 79.1 | 3.5 | 14.2 | 5.5 | 6.6 |
| 8.9 | 0.56 | 3.4 | 0.18 | 4.4 | 39.7 | 0.64 | 5.58 | 1.87 | 60.1 | 4.2 | 29.0 | 4.7 | 8.9 |
| 9.8 | 0.58 | 1.0 | 0.97 | 1.8 | 0.0 | 0.18 | 1.45 | 2.61 | 90.4 | 5.3 | 22.5 | 1.8 | 5.3 |
| 6.4 | 1.04 | 7.0 | 0.23 | 4.5 | 0.4 | 0.67 | 9.36 | 3.41 | 84.4 | 4.3 | 14.6 | 2.1 | 2.5 |
| 9.2 | 0.18 | 1.7 | 0.03 | 4.3 | 0.4 | 0.73 | 10.49 | 3.88 | 91.4 | 3.6 | 23.5 | 2.5 | 1.6 |
| 6.2 | 1.33 | 6.7 | 0.50 | 5.1 | 0.1 | 0.79 | 8.25 | 3.09 | 70.6 | 3.1 | 21.8 | 17.6 | 4.3 |
| 5.9 | 6.29 | 5.9 | 8.08 | 0.1 | 0.0 | -5.21 | -11.11 | 5.02 | 118.2 | 5.5 | 30.7 | 0.0 | 6.4 |
| 6.4 | 1.68 | 5.7 | 1.24 | 2.0 | 0.0 | 0.03 | 0.18 | 5.24 | 96.3 | 5.2 | 37.3 | 6.3 | 5.9 |
| 7.9 | 3.61 | 6.1 | 0.00 | 0.0 | 0.0 | -3.46 | -16.00 | 3.19 | 180.0 | 5.6 | 75.9 | 0.0 | 4.9 |
| 8.6 | 0.20 | 1.2 | 0.48 | 6.3 | 4.8 | 0.90 | 6.37 | 2.88 | 78.4 | 4.2 | 21.1 | 10.7 | 9.2 |
| 6.7 | 2.97 | 8.5 | 0.81 | 1.0 | 0.0 | 0.05 | 0.27 | 3.27 | 93.6 | 4.3 | 51.0 | 8.1 | 5.4 |
| 9.9 | 0.84 | 1.9 | 0.60 | 3.7 | 0.0 | 0.04 | 0.28 | 4.08 | 88.1 | 4.5 | 21.3 | 11.7 | 7.1 |
| 8.9 | 2.37 | 5.0 | 0.82 | 4.4 | 0.0 | 0.59 | 4.02 | 3.25 | 72.6 | 6.2 | 36.7 | 0.0 | 4.3 |
| 5.5 | 1.47 | 13.1 | 0.37 | 4.2 | 0.1 | 0.75 | 9.76 | 4.07 | 85.9 | 4.2 | 20.8 | 1.1 | 2.3 |
| 9.7 | 0.37 | 1.3 | 0.05 | 4.2 | 3.2 | 0.56 | 5.13 | 2.72 | 83.1 | 4.3 | 13.2 | 4.1 | 7.7 |
| 8.0 | 0.65 | 3.6 | 0.08 | 3.2 | 0.1 | 0.31 | 3.48 | 3.31 | 92.4 | 4.4 | 11.0 | 2.6 | 4.7 |
| 7.7 | 0.91 | 5.7 | 0.39 | 4.4 | 1.5 | 0.69 | 7.69 | 2.55 | 70.4 | 4.7 | 31.0 | 5.1 | 5.4 |
| 10.0 | 0.62 | 1.2 | 0.35 | 1.3 | 0.0 | 0.15 | 1.13 | 2.41 | 94.8 | 5.5 | 26.9 | 0.8 | 5.4 |
| 7.2 | 1.09 | 4.5 | 0.14 | 3.9 | 0.1 | 0.60 | 5.87 | 2.42 | 77.0 | 5.0 | 26.5 | 0.0 | 5.7 |
| 9.8 | 0.14 | 1.3 | 0.13 | 4.0 | 0.9 | 0.68 | 6.39 | 2.69 | 78.6 | 3.8 | 16.1 | 6.9 | 6.0 |
| 4.4 | 2.31 | 17.2 | 0.12 | 1.7 | 0.0 | -0.03 | -0.34 | 4.37 | 98.2 | 4.4 | 27.3 | 6.1 | 4.5 |
| 10.0 | 0.09 | 0.7 | 0.29 | 2.5 | 0.3 | 0.29 | 3.46 | 3.28 | 90.3 | 4.2 | 16.8 | 3.3 | 3.8 |
| 5.9 | 2.54 | 12.0 | 1.11 | 4.1 | 0.2 | 0.44 | 3.30 | 4.42 | 80.7 | 4.2 | 22.9 | 4.9 | 6.2 |
| 8.2 | 0.79 | 4.4 | 0.23 | 4.8 | 1.2 | 0.69 | 5.87 | 3.80 | 81.4 | 4.1 | 16.6 | 5.1 | 7.5 |
| 5.6 | 0.97 | 11.8 | 0.69 | 4.3 | 2.5 | 0.56 | 5.76 | 4.34 | 78.1 | 2.4 | 5.7 | 8.9 | 6.2 |
| 5.9 | 1.14 | 11.8 | 0.09 | 4.1 | 0.4 | 0.64 | 9.94 | 3.91 | 86.3 | 4.1 | 23.9 | 4.3 | 4.8 |
| 6.5 | 1.26 | 11.1 | 0.37 | 3.4 | 0.4 | 0.29 | 3.87 | 3.62 | 90.1 | 3.8 | 16.5 | 1.3 | 4.1 |
| 7.4 | 0.20 | 0.6 | 1.07 | 0.4 | 0.0 | -1.29 | -4.71 | 7.20 | 100.0 | 4.3 | 22.0 | 0.0 | 6.0 |
| 7.2 | 0.74 | 2.7 | 0.92 | 4.4 | 0.2 | 0.64 | 6.35 | 4.15 | 80.0 | 5.1 | 21.9 | 5.8 | 4.3 |
| 8.8 | 0.90 | 3.5 | 0.00 | 3.6 | 0.0 | 0.55 | 5.42 | 2.88 | 79.5 | 5.1 | 18.9 | 0.0 | 5.4 |
| 10.0 | 0.07 | 0.3 | 0.07 | 1.6 | 0.0 | -0.04 | -0.47 | 2.50 | 95.7 | 4.7 | 25.0 | 3.7 | 3.8 |
| 6.4 | 0.81 | 8.0 | 0.31 | 6.6 | 7.6 | 0.93 | 8.37 | 3.11 | 74.7 | 2.9 | 4.9 | 3.5 | 8.8 |
| 8.5 | 0.58 | 5.7 | 0.84 | 7.4 | 6.0 | 0.94 | 8.22 | 3.69 | 80.3 | 4.7 | 21.1 | 4.6 | 7.6 |
| 7.0 | 0.34 | 4.2 | 0.42 | 4.1 | 1.1 | 0.65 | 7.94 | 3.32 | 76.6 | 2.7 | 24.8 | 19.8 | 5.4 |
| 8.8 | 0.45 | 1.3 | 0.79 | 2.1 | 0.0 | 0.03 | 0.21 | 3.06 | 94.2 | 4.3 | 15.3 | 6.5 | 7.2 |
| 5.8 | 1.56 | 8.9 | 0.02 | 1.3 | 0.0 | -0.16 | -1.62 | 3.25 | 102.8 | 5.0 | 18.6 | 0.0 | 5.1 |
| 4.5 | 2.37 | 10.4 | 0.57 | 2.0 | 0.0 | 0.16 | 1.35 | 2.57 | 89.6 | 4.1 | 14.6 | 0.0 | 5.9 |
| 5.6 | 7.69 | 10.5 | 0.00 | 6.4 | 0.0 | 2.75 | 19.05 | 9.52 | 75.0 | 8.0 | 86.3 | 0.0 | 4.3 |
| 5.2 | 0.89 | 10.0 | 0.51 | 9.0 | 81.6 | 1.60 | 15.55 | 3.41 | 65.0 | 3.9 | 14.8 | 5.1 | 9.1 |
| 5.9 | 1.43 | 6.3 | 1.04 | 10.0 | 3.9 | 1.83 | 11.37 | 6.09 | 68.8 | 5.4 | 36.2 | 3.6 | 8.7 |
| 9.2 | 0.54 | 3.0 | 0.25 | 3.4 | 19.0 | 0.44 | 4.13 | 1.72 | 73.2 | 5.8 | 42.4 | 2.5 | 7.6 |
| 6.5 | 0.00 | 0.0 | 0.00 | 4.0 | 0.0 | 0.37 | 3.45 | 4.57 | 83.1 | 4.4 | 14.7 | 0.0 | 3.7 |
| 5.7 | 1.31 | 10.1 | 0.34 | 1.9 | 0.0 | 0.05 | 0.48 | 3.81 | 94.1 | 5.1 | 34.4 | 2.8 | 4.7 |
| 8.9 | 0.61 | 2.2 | 0.15 | 1.5 | 0.0 | -0.01 | -0.07 | 2.65 | 98.9 | 5.0 | 22.0 | 2.4 | 3.8 |
| 7.1 | 0.99 | 8.4 | 0.34 | 3.1 | 4.0 | 0.39 | 4.13 | 2.85 | 84.4 | 3.3 | 9.9 | 5.5 | 6.4 |
| 9.8 | 0.04 | 0.1 | 0.00 | 2.1 | 0.0 | 0.02 | 0.09 | 2.96 | 111.7 | 3.6 | 25.6 | 7.6 | 6.5 |
| 9.2 | 0.38 | 2.2 | -0.07 | 5.7 | 2.7 | 0.69 | 6.64 | 2.65 | 82.8 | 4.9 | 33.4 | 7.1 | 7.4 |
| 9.1 | 1.92 | 3.2 | 0.55 | 0.0 | 0.0 | -0.72 | -5.14 | 2.58 | 127.9 | 6.3 | 45.5 | 0.0 | 5.6 |
| 6.8 | 1.11 | 7.9 | 0.43 | 5.0 | 8.0 | 0.69 | 7.50 | 3.20 | 77.5 | 3.9 | 20.7 | 7.1 | 7.0 |
| 7.2 | 1.21 | 6.3 | 0.88 | 2.4 | 0.0 | 0.06 | 0.45 | 3.85 | 82.1 | 4.5 | 28.5 | 7.4 | 5.5 |
| 5.8 | 4.91 | 15.1 | 0.31 | 0.6 | -0.1 | -1.45 | -9.04 | 0.99 | 224.2 | 4.3 | 12.6 | 0.0 | 5.9 |
| 6.4 | 0.65 | 5.3 | 0.62 | 5.8 | 0.3 | 0.69 | 6.20 | 5.39 | 84.6 | 3.8 | 13.9 | 5.6 | 4.6 |
| 8.9 | 0.15 | 0.7 | 0.06 | 1.9 | 0.0 | 0.03 | 0.39 | 2.77 | 97.8 | 5.8 | 46.7 | 1.5 | 4.0 |
| 8.6 | 0.43 | 2.7 | 0.59 | 4.1 | 0.6 | 0.42 | 4.74 | 3.60 | 78.0 | 4.1 | 14.1 | 7.2 | 5.8 |

31

| Name | City | State | Rating | 2014 Rating | 2013 Rating | Total Assets ($Mil) | One Year Asset Growth | Asset Mix (As a % of Total Assets) | | | | Capital- ization Index | Net Worth Ratio |
| | | | | | | | | Comm- ercial Loans | Cons- umer Loans | Mort- gage Loans | Secur- ities | | |
|---|---|---|---|---|---|---|---|---|---|---|---|---|---|
| AMERICAN SPIRIT FCU | Newark | DE | B- | B+ | B+ | 58.8 | -10.59 | 6.5 | 15.2 | 8.8 | 46.8 | 10.0 | 16.2 |
| AMERICAN UNITED FAMILY OF CUS FCU | West Jordan | UT | B+ | B+ | B | 170.2 | 0.25 | 8.7 | 40.9 | 24.0 | 0.2 | 10.0 | 12.4 |
| AMERICAS CHRISTIAN CU | Glendora | CA | C- | C- | D+ | 303.2 | 7.94 | 54.9 | 9.8 | 52.8 | 0.0 | 8.2 | 9.8 |
| AMERICAS CU | Garland | TX | C | C | C- | 194.1 | 1.64 | 0.3 | 27.5 | 29.6 | 0.0 | 10.0 | 13.1 |
| AMERICAS FCU | Tacoma | WA | B+ | B+ | B+ | 492.6 | 13.44 | 4.9 | 60.1 | 8.6 | 9.3 | 8.3 | 9.9 |
| AMERICAS FIRST FCU | Birmingham | AL | B | B | B | 1368.8 | 3.38 | 0.0 | 27.2 | 26.7 | 20.5 | 9.7 | 10.8 |
| AMERICHOICE FCU | Mechanicsburg | PA | C- | C- | C- | 159.9 | -0.19 | 11.0 | 17.2 | 28.0 | 10.8 | 7.8 | 9.5 |
| ▲ AMERICO FCU | Erie | PA | D+ | D+ | C- | 70.0 | 0.53 | 0.0 | 22.0 | 4.9 | 4.8 | 10.0 | 11.2 |
| AMERICU CU | Rome | NY | B | B | B | 1267.3 | 0.51 | 1.1 | 33.5 | 20.6 | 1.5 | 8.0 | 9.7 |
| AMHERST FCU | Amherst | NY | C- | C- | C- | 31.0 | 7.97 | 0.0 | 21.0 | 16.1 | 33.7 | 5.7 | 7.7 |
| AMICUS FCU | Spokane | WA | C+ | C+ | C+ | 12.0 | 6.57 | 1.1 | 26.3 | 33.0 | 0.0 | 10.0 | 11.3 |
| AMNH EMPL FCU | New York | NY | C | C- | C- | <1 | 6.65 | 0.0 | 11.6 | 0.0 | 0.0 | 10.0 | 19.6 |
| AMOCO EAST TEXAS FCU | Longview | TX | E+ | E+ | E+ | 5.0 | -3.29 | 0.0 | 61.7 | 0.0 | 0.0 | 8.8 | 10.2 |
| AMOCO FCU | Texas City | TX | B- | B- | C | 741.2 | 13.60 | 0.0 | 49.9 | 8.9 | 18.8 | 6.7 | 8.9 |
| AMPLIFY FCU | Austin | TX | B+ | B+ | B | 740.7 | 4.20 | 8.0 | 38.0 | 25.8 | 7.1 | 7.3 | 9.4 |
| AMPOT FCU | Hamilton | MS | C | C | C- | 7.2 | -0.47 | 0.0 | 36.7 | 0.3 | 0.0 | 10.0 | 21.4 |
| ▼ ANCHOR SEVEN FCU | Jacksonville | FL | D- | D | C- | 1.9 | -15.02 | 0.0 | 39.4 | 0.0 | 0.0 | 7.2 | 9.2 |
| ANDALUSIA MILLS EMPL CREDIT ASSN FCU | Andalusia | AL | C | C+ | B- | 3.3 | -4.26 | 0.0 | 25.6 | 0.0 | 0.0 | 10.0 | 22.3 |
| ANDERSON COUNTY FCU | Palestine | TX | C+ | C+ | C+ | 16.9 | 1.63 | 0.0 | 18.8 | 0.0 | 0.0 | 10.0 | 16.2 |
| ANDERSON FCU | Anderson | SC | C- | C- | C- | 83.9 | -2.08 | 0.0 | 32.2 | 16.4 | 7.7 | 7.1 | 9.1 |
| ANDOVER FCU | Andover | MA | B- | B- | C+ | 26.7 | 6.59 | 0.0 | 16.1 | 0.0 | 6.9 | 10.0 | 12.1 |
| ANDREWS FCU | Suitland | MD | B | B | B | 1087.3 | 6.75 | 10.9 | 31.5 | 20.2 | 17.4 | 10.0 | 14.7 |
| ANDREWS SCHOOL FCU | Andrews | TX | C- | C- | C- | 7.9 | 2.30 | 0.0 | 29.3 | 0.0 | 0.0 | 10.0 | 19.7 |
| ▲ ANECA FCU | Shreveport | LA | C | C- | D+ | 95.8 | -6.44 | 6.8 | 20.4 | 16.6 | 16.1 | 10.0 | 19.7 |
| ▲ ANG FCU | Birmingham | AL | D- | D- | D | 18.9 | -3.69 | 0.0 | 26.9 | 7.2 | 0.0 | 5.6 | 7.6 |
| ANGELINA COUNTY TEACHERS CU | Lufkin | TX | C+ | C+ | C+ | 11.1 | 3.65 | 0.0 | 30.4 | 0.0 | 0.0 | 10.0 | 12.7 |
| ANGELINA FEDERAL EMPL CU | Lufkin | TX | B- | B- | B | 23.6 | 7.21 | 0.0 | 50.5 | 12.0 | 0.0 | 10.0 | 14.8 |
| ANHEUSER-BUSCH EMPL CU | Saint Louis | MO | B | B | B | 1532.7 | 6.19 | 7.0 | 46.6 | 26.1 | 10.1 | 8.7 | 10.2 |
| ANIMAS CU | Farmington | NM | B- | B- | B- | 125.7 | 0.69 | 7.4 | 39.5 | 13.2 | 5.8 | 7.3 | 9.2 |
| ANMED HEALTH FCU | Anderson | SC | C | C | C | 14.2 | 7.11 | 0.0 | 32.2 | 0.0 | 0.0 | 10.0 | 13.1 |
| ANN ARBOR POSTAL FCU | Milan | MI | C- | C- | C- | 1.0 | -1.74 | 0.0 | 45.9 | 0.0 | 0.0 | 10.0 | 29.5 |
| ANOKA HENNEPIN CU | Coon Rapids | MN | B+ | B+ | B- | 151.8 | 5.68 | 3.6 | 23.0 | 20.7 | 8.6 | 7.5 | 9.3 |
| ANTIOCH COMMUNITY FCU | Antioch | CA | C- | D+ | E+ | 23.2 | -2.57 | 2.3 | 10.1 | 26.2 | 0.0 | 7.3 | 9.2 |
| ANTIOCH CU | Cleveland | OH | D+ | D+ | C- | 2.7 | -11.01 | 0.0 | 9.7 | 0.5 | 14.1 | 10.0 | 36.1 |
| ANTIOCH MB FCU | Decatur | IL | D+ | C- | C | <1 | 13.43 | 0.0 | 11.2 | 0.0 | 0.0 | 10.0 | 27.0 |
| AOD FCU | Oxford | AL | B | B | B+ | 268.5 | 1.49 | 0.2 | 33.7 | 11.3 | 31.2 | 10.0 | 13.5 |
| AP FCU | Toledo | OH | D | D+ | C- | 33.3 | -4.31 | 0.0 | 29.9 | 15.2 | 5.2 | 10.0 | 13.2 |
| APC EMPL FCU | Tucson | AZ | C | C- | D | 1.3 | 5.69 | 0.0 | 57.6 | 0.0 | 0.0 | 10.0 | 19.9 |
| APCI FCU | Allentown | PA | C+ | C+ | C+ | 500.8 | 0.95 | 0.0 | 11.9 | 36.1 | 39.9 | 8.9 | 10.3 |
| APCO EMPL CU | Birmingham | AL | B | B | B | 2583.1 | 4.69 | 0.0 | 7.6 | 16.7 | 37.3 | 9.4 | 10.6 |
| APEX COMMUNITY FCU | Stowe | PA | B- | B- | B- | 35.1 | -3.53 | 0.0 | 41.1 | 27.3 | 0.0 | 10.0 | 13.2 |
| APEX FINANCIAL CU | Florissant | MO | D- | D- | D+ | 37.5 | -2.79 | 0.0 | 35.0 | 0.5 | 39.1 | 8.3 | 9.9 |
| APL FCU | Laurel | MD | C+ | C+ | C+ | 393.6 | 1.32 | 0.0 | 14.3 | 19.1 | 33.4 | 10.0 | 11.2 |
| ▼ APPALACHIAN COMMUNITY FCU | Gray | TN | C- | C | D+ | 180.3 | 2.42 | 5.3 | 25.6 | 49.1 | 2.6 | 6.0 | 8.0 |
| APPALACHIAN POWER EMPL FCU | Huntington | WV | C- | C- | C | 7.8 | -1.68 | 0.0 | 27.8 | 0.0 | 0.0 | 10.0 | 15.7 |
| APPLE FCU | Fairfax | VA | B | B | B | 2054.4 | 6.38 | 8.7 | 27.7 | 37.5 | 16.6 | 7.7 | 9.4 |
| APPLETREE CU | West Allis | WI | A | A+ | A+ | 114.6 | -4.26 | 0.0 | 15.7 | 51.8 | 0.0 | 10.0 | 23.3 |
| APPLIANCE CU | Cleveland | TN | C+ | C+ | C+ | 11.0 | 0.82 | 0.0 | 39.7 | 0.0 | 0.0 | 10.0 | 15.6 |
| APS FCU | Charleroi | PA | D- | D- | D- | 7.9 | -1.55 | 0.0 | 68.6 | 0.0 | 15.5 | 5.3 | 7.3 |
| ARABI SUGAR WORKERS FCU | New Orleans | LA | C+ | C+ | C+ | 1.4 | 5.94 | 0.0 | 85.2 | 0.0 | 0.0 | 10.0 | 40.9 |
| ARAPAHOE CU | Centennial | CO | B | B- | B | 114.2 | 8.80 | 0.0 | 26.5 | 15.0 | 0.0 | 6.9 | 8.9 |
| ARBUCKLE FCU | Ada | OK | E+ | D- | D | 10.3 | -3.12 | 5.0 | 67.5 | 0.0 | 0.0 | 4.4 | 6.4 |
| ARC FCU | Altoona | PA | C | C | C | 72.5 | 5.90 | 0.1 | 21.2 | 19.5 | 19.4 | 5.7 | 7.7 |
| ARCADE CU | Asheville | NC | D | D | C- | 7.0 | 0.16 | 0.0 | 28.2 | 0.0 | 0.0 | 10.0 | 13.5 |
| ARCADIA CU | Arcadia | WI | B+ | B+ | B+ | 66.7 | 1.58 | 1.5 | 14.7 | 58.9 | 0.0 | 10.0 | 13.1 |
| ARCH COMMUNITY CU | Saint Louis | MO | D- | D+ | D | 11.3 | -2.45 | 0.0 | 22.6 | 0.0 | 0.0 | 6.9 | 8.9 |
| ARCHER COOPERATIVE CU | Central City | NE | C+ | C | D | 56.9 | 2.42 | 64.9 | 5.8 | 55.5 | 1.8 | 9.5 | 10.6 |
| ARCHER HEIGHTS CU | Chicago | IL | C | C | C | 17.0 | 2.65 | 0.0 | 19.1 | 32.9 | 0.0 | 9.0 | 10.3 |
| AREA COMMUNITY CU | Grand Forks | ND | B | B | B | 22.0 | 2.87 | 0.1 | 28.6 | 11.1 | 0.0 | 10.0 | 14.6 |
| AREA CU | Kansas City | KS | C- | C- | C- | 7.1 | -0.27 | 0.0 | 25.9 | 0.0 | 0.0 | 10.0 | 15.4 |

| Asset Quality Index | Non-Performing Loans as a % of Total Loans | Non-Performing Loans as a % of Capital | Net Charge-Offs / Avg Loans | Profitability Index | Net Income ($Mil) | Return on Assets | Return on Equity | Net Interest Spread | Overhead Efficiency Ratio | Liquidity Index | Liquidity Ratio | Hot Money Ratio | Stability Index |
|---|---|---|---|---|---|---|---|---|---|---|---|---|---|
| 8.7 | 1.21 | 2.8 | 1.50 | 3.2 | 0.1 | 0.28 | 2.03 | 2.84 | 80.7 | 4.5 | 15.5 | 0.9 | 6.0 |
| 7.0 | 0.38 | 3.0 | 2.07 | 8.7 | 2.7 | 2.14 | 20.58 | 5.50 | 56.7 | 2.3 | 9.1 | 15.7 | 6.4 |
| 3.9 | 0.39 | 13.0 | 0.98 | 6.1 | 2.3 | 1.03 | 10.97 | 4.59 | 75.3 | 2.3 | 23.2 | 25.0 | 6.7 |
| 9.8 | 0.32 | 1.6 | 0.23 | 2.7 | 0.4 | 0.26 | 2.02 | 3.16 | 90.4 | 4.5 | 41.4 | 3.7 | 7.3 |
| 5.8 | 0.42 | 5.4 | 1.57 | 6.2 | 3.2 | 0.92 | 9.60 | 5.09 | 67.9 | 3.0 | 24.7 | 17.9 | 6.1 |
| 7.7 | 0.56 | 5.1 | 0.21 | 4.4 | 6.1 | 0.60 | 5.54 | 2.50 | 79.7 | 4.5 | 17.8 | 4.0 | 7.6 |
| 8.4 | 0.45 | 3.0 | 0.35 | 2.2 | 0.2 | 0.13 | 1.61 | 3.51 | 93.7 | 4.0 | 14.9 | 1.3 | 5.1 |
| 7.5 | 1.48 | 5.5 | 0.21 | 0.9 | 0.0 | -0.06 | -0.55 | 2.55 | 97.8 | 4.7 | 25.3 | 0.8 | 5.0 |
| 7.3 | 0.52 | 5.2 | 0.33 | 4.6 | 5.8 | 0.61 | 6.45 | 3.26 | 78.4 | 2.1 | 2.3 | 10.4 | 7.6 |
| 9.4 | 0.02 | 0.1 | 0.22 | 2.4 | 0.0 | 0.16 | 1.99 | 3.01 | 91.0 | 4.8 | 18.3 | 0.9 | 3.2 |
| 9.4 | 0.44 | 2.6 | 0.13 | 4.3 | 0.1 | 0.64 | 5.67 | 4.44 | 85.4 | 4.0 | 20.8 | 9.2 | 5.7 |
| 10.0 | 0.98 | 0.6 | -1.07 | 3.6 | 0.0 | 0.46 | 2.33 | 3.50 | 82.6 | 5.4 | 26.5 | 0.0 | 6.1 |
| 0.0 | 14.23 | 111.8 | 0.55 | 3.7 | 0.0 | 0.48 | 5.05 | 6.01 | 81.1 | 4.2 | 15.9 | 0.0 | 4.4 |
| 6.5 | 0.73 | 5.9 | 0.44 | 4.1 | 3.0 | 0.55 | 6.38 | 2.92 | 77.7 | 3.7 | 24.9 | 10.5 | 6.0 |
| 9.4 | 0.16 | 1.5 | 0.17 | 5.7 | 4.2 | 0.77 | 8.36 | 3.66 | 80.3 | 2.6 | 9.2 | 13.3 | 7.2 |
| 8.6 | 0.38 | 0.9 | -1.01 | 7.2 | 0.1 | 1.98 | 9.83 | 4.32 | 54.0 | 4.6 | 88.7 | 26.2 | 5.0 |
| 5.5 | 2.45 | 9.9 | 2.18 | 0.0 | -0.1 | -8.70 | -67.91 | 6.49 | 284.0 | 7.1 | 57.4 | 0.0 | 3.7 |
| 9.6 | 1.83 | 2.5 | 2.13 | 0.6 | 0.0 | -1.07 | -4.59 | 6.90 | 93.7 | 7.5 | 73.1 | 0.0 | 5.9 |
| 9.9 | 1.26 | 1.8 | 0.66 | 3.1 | 0.0 | 0.31 | 1.92 | 3.17 | 84.3 | 5.6 | 45.8 | 7.8 | 6.8 |
| 6.2 | 0.38 | 7.0 | 0.42 | 2.5 | 0.2 | 0.23 | 2.60 | 3.68 | 93.0 | 4.3 | 18.6 | 3.9 | 3.8 |
| 9.7 | 0.90 | 2.2 | 0.30 | 3.5 | 0.1 | 0.36 | 3.01 | 2.79 | 87.2 | 4.8 | 21.6 | 6.0 | 5.8 |
| 8.9 | 0.57 | 2.5 | 0.58 | 3.9 | 3.8 | 0.48 | 3.17 | 3.72 | 83.3 | 4.0 | 14.5 | 5.9 | 7.9 |
| 9.9 | 1.32 | 2.1 | 0.00 | 1.8 | 0.0 | 0.05 | 0.26 | 2.31 | 96.2 | 6.9 | 66.8 | 1.8 | 6.7 |
| 6.7 | 1.75 | 6.8 | 0.69 | 2.2 | 0.1 | 0.17 | 0.91 | 3.62 | 88.6 | 3.4 | 17.8 | 12.9 | 5.4 |
| 8.6 | 0.21 | 1.0 | 0.95 | 1.4 | 0.0 | 0.05 | 0.66 | 3.19 | 92.3 | 4.4 | 27.4 | 5.2 | 1.8 |
| 8.5 | 0.52 | 1.5 | 0.87 | 3.0 | 0.0 | 0.22 | 1.72 | 3.74 | 80.9 | 5.3 | 23.9 | 0.0 | 6.6 |
| 8.1 | 0.41 | 2.2 | 0.01 | 5.8 | 0.1 | 0.82 | 6.10 | 3.75 | 82.6 | 3.9 | 18.2 | 3.5 | 5.7 |
| 5.4 | 0.91 | 6.7 | 1.06 | 3.9 | 4.5 | 0.40 | 3.98 | 3.78 | 75.5 | 3.3 | 7.3 | 4.3 | 6.9 |
| 8.9 | 0.15 | 2.2 | 0.20 | 3.6 | 0.3 | 0.34 | 4.01 | 3.45 | 88.9 | 4.8 | 25.5 | 3.4 | 5.2 |
| 9.8 | 0.45 | 1.2 | 0.10 | 2.2 | 0.0 | 0.04 | 0.29 | 4.05 | 96.8 | 7.2 | 60.8 | 0.9 | 7.0 |
| 8.8 | 1.04 | 1.6 | 0.00 | 1.4 | 0.0 | -0.13 | -0.44 | 3.56 | 104.8 | 5.7 | 31.7 | 0.0 | 5.6 |
| 5.7 | 1.65 | 13.6 | 0.53 | 7.4 | 1.0 | 0.90 | 9.85 | 3.85 | 82.2 | 4.5 | 19.8 | 0.6 | 5.6 |
| 7.5 | 0.00 | 3.9 | 0.12 | 3.0 | 0.1 | 0.30 | 3.27 | 2.72 | 94.0 | 5.6 | 49.8 | 1.5 | 4.4 |
| 9.3 | 12.77 | 4.1 | 0.00 | 0.8 | 0.0 | -0.15 | -0.41 | 2.82 | 104.2 | 7.4 | 73.1 | 0.0 | 4.9 |
| 9.5 | 2.63 | 2.3 | 0.00 | 1.2 | 0.0 | 0.00 | 0.00 | 4.94 | 150.0 | 8.3 | 103.6 | 0.0 | 6.2 |
| 9.9 | 0.40 | 1.7 | 0.58 | 3.5 | 0.7 | 0.35 | 2.60 | 2.47 | 85.5 | 4.0 | 13.5 | 4.8 | 7.8 |
| 6.4 | 2.09 | 11.9 | 0.93 | 0.1 | -0.2 | -0.65 | -4.98 | 2.83 | 102.5 | 4.9 | 19.9 | 1.5 | 5.0 |
| 5.6 | 2.25 | 7.1 | -0.34 | 9.1 | 0.0 | 2.19 | 10.84 | 5.64 | 54.4 | 5.1 | 32.1 | 0.0 | 5.0 |
| 10.0 | 0.23 | 1.6 | 0.08 | 3.4 | 1.7 | 0.43 | 4.37 | 1.85 | 77.6 | 4.0 | 18.4 | 5.2 | 7.0 |
| 9.8 | 0.54 | 2.2 | 0.34 | 5.3 | 16.1 | 0.83 | 8.17 | 1.73 | 34.8 | 6.3 | 34.9 | 8.2 | 7.5 |
| 5.9 | 0.54 | 11.9 | 0.34 | 3.0 | 0.1 | 0.23 | 1.76 | 4.14 | 86.7 | 3.8 | 16.1 | 2.6 | 6.0 |
| 7.8 | 1.42 | 5.9 | 1.02 | 0.0 | -0.3 | -0.92 | -8.94 | 3.18 | 110.9 | 4.9 | 31.1 | 4.5 | 3.9 |
| 10.0 | 0.16 | 0.8 | 0.14 | 3.3 | 1.6 | 0.53 | 5.32 | 2.23 | 80.1 | 3.8 | 9.9 | 7.7 | 6.4 |
| 3.7 | 1.08 | 20.3 | 0.45 | 2.3 | 0.2 | 0.14 | 1.71 | 4.33 | 84.9 | 1.6 | 16.1 | 36.8 | 4.4 |
| 5.7 | 8.04 | 16.2 | 0.00 | 2.5 | 0.0 | 0.20 | 1.32 | 2.43 | 86.6 | 5.9 | 25.6 | 0.0 | 6.6 |
| 7.4 | 0.59 | 5.6 | 0.66 | 5.2 | 11.7 | 0.76 | 8.32 | 3.30 | 71.3 | 3.5 | 13.9 | 5.2 | 7.1 |
| 10.0 | 0.12 | 0.6 | 0.04 | 6.5 | 0.8 | 0.96 | 4.27 | 2.27 | 59.4 | 3.1 | 17.1 | 6.4 | 9.5 |
| 8.1 | 0.60 | 2.0 | 0.66 | 2.8 | 0.0 | 0.34 | 2.12 | 3.16 | 85.3 | 5.5 | 35.1 | 0.0 | 6.0 |
| 5.6 | 0.34 | 3.5 | 0.20 | 2.1 | 0.0 | 0.08 | 1.17 | 3.84 | 92.8 | 3.6 | 6.1 | 0.0 | 1.0 |
| 5.6 | 3.93 | 7.9 | 1.06 | 10.0 | 0.0 | 3.51 | 8.82 | 8.93 | 47.2 | 4.0 | 26.1 | 0.0 | 5.0 |
| 9.0 | 0.18 | 1.4 | 0.29 | 4.4 | 0.5 | 0.54 | 6.11 | 4.12 | 80.7 | 3.8 | 16.0 | 6.2 | 5.4 |
| 1.8 | 1.51 | 34.8 | 0.09 | 2.5 | 0.0 | 0.25 | 4.13 | 3.51 | 95.7 | 1.8 | 7.7 | 24.8 | 0.0 |
| 7.9 | 0.46 | 3.0 | 0.12 | 5.1 | 0.4 | 0.82 | 11.16 | 3.31 | 79.0 | 5.2 | 23.8 | 1.0 | 3.5 |
| 9.9 | 0.54 | 2.0 | 0.04 | 0.3 | 0.0 | -0.17 | -1.27 | 2.80 | 108.5 | 4.6 | 19.7 | 0.0 | 5.8 |
| 6.6 | 1.06 | 7.8 | 0.20 | 6.1 | 0.5 | 0.92 | 7.47 | 4.28 | 77.3 | 2.9 | 10.4 | 6.1 | 7.3 |
| 7.7 | 1.13 | 3.6 | 0.27 | 0.1 | -0.1 | -0.54 | -6.08 | 2.61 | 110.8 | 5.9 | 35.9 | 0.0 | 3.1 |
| 3.4 | 0.78 | 6.0 | 0.13 | 3.3 | 0.1 | 0.28 | 2.66 | 3.93 | 88.4 | 2.0 | 8.3 | 14.5 | 5.3 |
| 9.0 | 0.53 | 2.6 | 0.02 | 3.4 | 0.1 | 0.40 | 3.89 | 3.75 | 90.0 | 3.8 | 12.8 | 8.7 | 4.3 |
| 8.4 | 1.23 | 4.3 | 0.06 | 7.6 | 0.2 | 1.00 | 6.99 | 3.45 | 74.9 | 4.7 | 24.0 | 1.6 | 6.3 |
| 9.6 | 0.24 | 0.6 | 0.77 | 2.5 | 0.0 | 0.25 | 1.59 | 2.97 | 94.4 | 4.9 | 18.5 | 0.0 | 6.4 |

| Name | City | State | Rating | 2014 Rating | 2013 Rating | Total Assets ($Mil) | One Year Asset Growth | Asset Mix (As a % of Total Aseets) | | | | Capital-ization Index | Net Worth Ratio |
|------|------|-------|--------|-------------|-------------|---------------------|----------------------|------------|------------|------------|------------|---------------------|-----------------|
| | | | | | | | | Comm-ercial Loans | Cons-umer Loans | Mort-gage Loans | Secur-ities | | |
| ▲ AREA EDUCATIONAL CU | Mattoon | IL | B- | C+ | C+ | 23.9 | 0.62 | 0.0 | 24.7 | 0.0 | 0.0 | 10.0 | 22.0 |
| ARG BRADFORD FCU | Bradford | PA | C | C | C | 3.6 | -4.14 | 0.0 | 45.1 | 0.0 | 0.0 | 10.0 | 19.2 |
| ARGENT FCU | Chester | VA | C- | C- | D+ | 211.3 | 4.44 | 0.5 | 37.9 | 18.5 | 6.8 | 7.7 | 9.4 |
| ARH FCU | Middlesboro | KY | B+ | B+ | B+ | 11.5 | 0.92 | 0.0 | 30.7 | 9.1 | 0.0 | 10.0 | 23.0 |
| ▼ ARIZONA CENTRAL CU | Phoenix | AZ | C | B- | B- | 425.7 | -1.31 | 8.9 | 53.0 | 18.4 | 8.1 | 6.8 | 8.8 |
| ARIZONA FCU | Phoenix | AZ | A | A | A | 1341.4 | 6.04 | 2.0 | 26.3 | 7.4 | 38.0 | 10.0 | 14.0 |
| ARIZONA STATE CU | Phoenix | AZ | B+ | B+ | B+ | 1727.0 | 5.17 | 12.8 | 24.8 | 32.3 | 25.4 | 8.8 | 10.2 |
| ARK CITY TEACHERS CU | Arkansas City | KS | E+ | D- | D- | 4.0 | -1.91 | 0.0 | 46.2 | 0.0 | 0.0 | 6.5 | 8.5 |
| ▲ ARK VALLEY CU | Arkansas City | KS | C | C- | C | 32.8 | -1.97 | 0.0 | 39.8 | 0.0 | 0.0 | 6.6 | 8.6 |
| ARKANSAS AM&N COLLEGE FCU | Pine Bluff | AR | D | D+ | C- | 2.4 | 1.03 | 0.0 | 43.4 | 0.0 | 0.0 | 8.4 | 9.9 |
| ARKANSAS BEST FCU | Fort Smith | AR | C+ | C+ | B- | 115.4 | 2.18 | 0.0 | 48.8 | 0.0 | 3.9 | 10.0 | 13.9 |
| ARKANSAS DEMOCRAT-GAZETTE FCU | Little Rock | AR | C | C+ | C+ | 4.8 | -10.33 | 0.0 | 51.6 | 0.0 | 0.0 | 10.0 | 25.4 |
| ARKANSAS EDUCATION ASSN FCU | Little Rock | AR | C- | C- | C- | 7.2 | 3.89 | 0.0 | 58.5 | 0.0 | 0.0 | 10.0 | 13.3 |
| ▼ ARKANSAS EMPL FCU | Little Rock | AR | D | D+ | C- | 38.4 | -5.49 | 0.8 | 45.7 | 7.1 | 0.0 | 6.2 | 8.2 |
| ▼ ARKANSAS FARM BUREAU FCU | Little Rock | AR | C+ | B- | C+ | 9.7 | -3.97 | 0.0 | 41.5 | 0.0 | 0.0 | 10.0 | 17.3 |
| ARKANSAS FCU | Jacksonville | AR | B- | B- | B | 978.9 | -2.52 | 1.3 | 50.8 | 17.8 | 7.7 | 8.7 | 10.1 |
| ARKANSAS HEALTH CENTER FCU | Benton | AR | D+ | D+ | D | 7.4 | 2.95 | 0.0 | 47.5 | 0.5 | 0.0 | 9.1 | 10.4 |
| ARKANSAS KRAFT EMPL FCU | Morrilton | AR | C+ | C+ | C+ | 4.4 | 2.35 | 0.0 | 38.3 | 0.0 | 0.0 | 10.0 | 21.7 |
| ARKANSAS SUPERIOR FCU | Warren | AR | A- | A- | A- | 73.1 | 4.53 | 0.0 | 32.1 | 20.7 | 0.0 | 10.0 | 18.1 |
| ARKANSAS TEACHERS FCU | Little Rock | AR | C+ | C+ | C- | 1.4 | 5.18 | 0.0 | 67.2 | 0.0 | 0.0 | 10.0 | 19.4 |
| ▼ ARKANSAS VALLEY FCU | Las Animas | CO | D+ | C- | C- | 11.0 | 0.02 | 0.0 | 44.7 | 1.0 | 0.0 | 9.6 | 10.8 |
| ARLINGTON COMMUNITY FCU | Falls Church | VA | B+ | B+ | B | 229.8 | 7.21 | 2.7 | 34.0 | 25.1 | 1.3 | 7.8 | 9.5 |
| ARLINGTON HOTEL FCU | Hot Springs | AR | D | C- | C- | <1 | -5.80 | 0.0 | 66.8 | 0.0 | 0.0 | 10.0 | 22.8 |
| ARLINGTON MUNICIPAL FCU | Arlington | MA | D | D | C- | 9.7 | -1.77 | 0.0 | 13.5 | 0.0 | 0.0 | 10.0 | 19.7 |
| ARMSTRONG ASSOCIATES FCU | Ford City | PA | D+ | D+ | D+ | 54.3 | 1.47 | 0.0 | 28.8 | 0.0 | 0.0 | 10.0 | 13.0 |
| ▲ ARMSTRONG COUNTY FEDERAL EMPL FCU | Kittanning | PA | C | C- | C | 14.0 | 3.99 | 0.0 | 17.7 | 0.0 | 0.0 | 10.0 | 14.4 |
| ARMY AVIATION CENTER FCU | Daleville | AL | B | B | B+ | 1142.9 | 1.42 | 0.0 | 18.7 | 10.8 | 51.1 | 10.0 | 12.1 |
| ▼ ARNOLD BAKERS EMPL FCU | Greenwich | CT | C- | C- | C | 3.5 | -6.77 | 0.0 | 16.7 | 0.0 | 0.0 | 10.0 | 22.8 |
| ▼ ARRHA CU | Springfield | MA | C | C+ | C+ | 119.6 | 2.19 | 0.3 | 11.9 | 45.9 | 5.0 | 7.2 | 9.2 |
| ARROWHEAD CENTRAL CU | San Bernardino | CA | A+ | A | E- | 936.6 | 9.34 | 5.6 | 27.3 | 7.0 | 36.1 | 10.0 | 13.9 |
| ▲ ARROWPOINTE FCU | Catawba | SC | C+ | C | C | 142.2 | 0.32 | 0.0 | 23.4 | 24.2 | 12.7 | 10.0 | 11.1 |
| ARSENAL CU | Arnold | MO | B- | C+ | B- | 209.5 | 4.36 | 6.3 | 49.5 | 7.1 | 27.2 | 7.1 | 9.1 |
| ARTESIA CU | Artesia | NM | A- | A- | B+ | 93.2 | 4.58 | 1.1 | 33.3 | 10.0 | 0.0 | 10.0 | 12.4 |
| ARTESIAN CITY FCU | Albany | GA | C | C+ | B- | 16.0 | 1.34 | 0.0 | 28.8 | 4.3 | 0.0 | 10.0 | 22.1 |
| ▼ ARTMET FCU | Stoughton | MA | D+ | C | C | <1 | -10.73 | 0.0 | 39.2 | 0.0 | 4.2 | 10.0 | 16.4 |
| ASA FCU | Bloomfield | CT | D | D | D | 7.7 | 1.82 | 0.0 | 30.1 | 0.0 | 0.0 | 8.7 | 10.2 |
| ▲ ASBESTOS WORKERS LOCAL 14 FCU | Philadelphia | PA | D+ | D- | D+ | 3.3 | 1.78 | 0.0 | 30.4 | 0.0 | 0.0 | 7.5 | 9.4 |
| ASBESTOS WORKERS LOCAL 53 FCU | Kenner | LA | D | D | D | <1 | -11.97 | 0.0 | 14.1 | 0.0 | 0.0 | 10.0 | 20.4 |
| ASBURY FCU | Washington | DC | C | C | C | <1 | -2.03 | 0.0 | 3.6 | 0.0 | 0.0 | 10.0 | 18.1 |
| ASCEND FCU | Tullahoma | TN | A | A | A | 1789.3 | 5.39 | 4.4 | 23.7 | 30.3 | 29.3 | 10.0 | 17.3 |
| ▼ ASCENSION CU | Gonzales | LA | C | B- | B- | 55.2 | -0.18 | 0.0 | 27.6 | 15.1 | 0.4 | 8.0 | 9.7 |
| ASCENTIA FCU | Minot | ND | C | C+ | C+ | 11.8 | 3.74 | 3.4 | 28.5 | 22.1 | 0.0 | 10.0 | 11.3 |
| ASCENTRA CU | Bettendorf | IA | B+ | B+ | B+ | 360.4 | 7.40 | 5.0 | 28.6 | 22.7 | 4.5 | 9.2 | 10.4 |
| ASH EMPL CU | Anna | IL | C+ | C+ | C | 4.9 | 5.77 | 0.0 | 65.6 | 0.0 | 0.0 | 10.0 | 13.9 |
| ▼ ASHLAND COMMUNITY FCU | Ashland | OH | D- | D | D+ | 12.9 | 9.34 | 0.0 | 52.8 | 2.5 | 26.5 | 6.1 | 8.1 |
| ASHLAND CU | Ashland | KY | A- | A- | A- | 188.6 | 3.60 | 0.0 | 39.5 | 7.3 | 26.2 | 10.0 | 13.3 |
| ASHOKA CU | Boulder | CO | D- | E+ | E+ | 2.3 | -1.69 | 0.0 | 17.9 | 8.5 | 0.0 | 5.4 | 7.4 |
| ASI FCU | Harahan | LA | C+ | C+ | C+ | 314.0 | 1.59 | 9.3 | 28.5 | 16.7 | 9.3 | 8.9 | 10.2 |
| ASPIRE FCU | Clark | NJ | C+ | B- | B- | 178.6 | -0.45 | 11.1 | 39.6 | 6.7 | 0.6 | 9.7 | 10.8 |
| ASSEMBLIES OF GOD CU | Springfield | MO | B | B+ | B | 146.8 | 4.06 | 15.0 | 14.9 | 45.7 | 7.6 | 8.9 | 10.3 |
| ASSOCIATED CU | Norcross | GA | B | B | B | 1366.6 | 2.26 | 1.2 | 44.1 | 15.8 | 26.2 | 10.0 | 11.9 |
| ASSOCIATED CU OF TEXAS | League City | TX | A | A- | B+ | 327.9 | 7.94 | 1.1 | 37.2 | 14.1 | 13.9 | 10.0 | 11.3 |
| ASSOCIATED FCU | Elkhart | IN | D+ | D | C- | 5.0 | -7.29 | 0.0 | 19.3 | 0.0 | 0.0 | 10.0 | 26.4 |
| ASSOCIATED FEDERAL EMPL FCU | Salt Lake City | UT | C | D+ | C- | 29.7 | -5.70 | 3.2 | 16.4 | 15.7 | 16.7 | 10.0 | 15.0 |
| ▲ ASSOCIATED HEALTH CARE CU | Saint Paul | MN | C+ | C- | D+ | 98.8 | 1.38 | 0.0 | 46.8 | 7.5 | 3.4 | 8.3 | 9.9 |
| ASSOCIATED SCHOOL EMPL CU | Austintown | OH | D+ | D | D+ | 127.7 | -6.19 | 0.1 | 17.7 | 30.9 | 11.3 | 9.8 | 10.8 |
| ASSOCIATES FCU | Windsor | CT | C- | D+ | D+ | 6.7 | -0.37 | 0.0 | 22.4 | 37.4 | 0.0 | 10.0 | 16.7 |
| ASSUMPTION BEAUMONT FCU | Lumberton | TX | D- | E+ | D | <1 | -3.19 | 0.0 | 25.0 | 0.0 | 0.0 | 7.2 | 9.3 |
| ASTERA CU | Lansing | MI | D | C- | D+ | 140.9 | -3.31 | 1.8 | 39.0 | 13.7 | 14.1 | 5.8 | 7.8 |
| AT&T EMPL PITTSBURGH FCU | Pittsburgh | PA | C- | C- | C- | 9.4 | -1.67 | 0.0 | 19.1 | 0.0 | 0.0 | 10.0 | 26.3 |

| Asset Quality Index | Non-Performing Loans | | Net Charge-Offs Avg Loans | Profitability Index | Net Income ($Mil) | Return on Assets | Return on Equity | Net Interest Spread | Overhead Efficiency Ratio | Liquidity Index | Liquidity Ratio | Hot Money Ratio | Stability Index |
|---|---|---|---|---|---|---|---|---|---|---|---|---|---|
| | as a % of Total Loans | as a % of Capital | | | | | | | | | | | |
| 9.8 | 1.42 | 1.7 | 0.26 | 3.4 | 0.1 | 0.48 | 2.22 | 2.14 | 76.9 | 6.3 | 45.4 | 0.0 | 7.3 |
| 8.4 | 0.00 | 0.0 | 0.00 | 3.3 | 0.0 | 0.46 | 2.52 | 3.37 | 82.8 | 4.6 | 10.8 | 0.0 | 6.9 |
| 7.2 | 1.05 | 6.5 | 0.71 | 1.9 | 0.1 | 0.04 | 0.44 | 3.93 | 90.0 | 3.9 | 20.3 | 3.5 | 5.1 |
| 7.7 | 2.57 | 4.8 | 1.61 | 7.6 | 0.1 | 0.91 | 4.03 | 6.58 | 78.7 | 6.8 | 49.5 | 0.0 | 6.3 |
| 4.3 | 0.50 | 13.4 | 2.05 | 2.7 | 0.2 | 0.05 | 0.61 | 4.63 | 87.3 | 3.3 | 4.3 | 2.9 | 4.9 |
| 9.9 | 0.45 | 1.2 | -0.01 | 9.0 | 15.5 | 1.54 | 11.11 | 3.40 | 75.0 | 5.6 | 30.3 | 2.1 | 9.8 |
| 8.2 | 0.24 | 3.5 | 0.23 | 5.9 | 11.4 | 0.89 | 9.86 | 3.13 | 77.9 | 4.1 | 13.3 | 1.8 | 7.5 |
| 3.3 | 2.13 | 17.3 | 0.00 | 2.2 | 0.0 | 0.07 | 0.79 | 2.93 | 72.4 | 5.8 | 51.2 | 0.0 | 1.0 |
| 8.2 | 0.17 | 1.0 | 0.35 | 3.3 | 0.1 | 0.35 | 4.27 | 3.91 | 86.1 | 5.2 | 42.1 | 6.5 | 3.2 |
| 8.7 | 0.31 | 1.7 | 0.00 | 0.7 | 0.0 | -0.22 | -2.27 | 3.13 | 107.3 | 5.4 | 47.2 | 0.0 | 4.7 |
| 8.4 | 0.31 | 1.3 | 0.50 | 2.8 | 0.3 | 0.31 | 2.20 | 2.83 | 83.7 | 3.8 | 22.4 | 5.8 | 7.6 |
| 6.6 | 2.03 | 4.0 | 0.99 | 7.2 | 0.0 | 0.79 | 3.38 | 4.67 | 58.3 | 5.5 | 40.9 | 0.0 | 5.0 |
| 6.0 | 1.42 | 6.3 | 0.48 | 3.7 | 0.0 | 0.40 | 2.96 | 5.35 | 87.7 | 5.7 | 44.5 | 0.0 | 3.7 |
| 4.7 | 0.50 | 3.8 | 1.13 | 0.0 | -0.4 | -1.22 | -14.78 | 2.67 | 113.4 | 5.3 | 35.8 | 3.6 | 2.7 |
| 9.8 | 0.74 | 1.8 | -0.16 | 3.8 | 0.0 | 0.58 | 3.46 | 1.57 | 60.6 | 5.8 | 52.7 | 0.0 | 7.7 |
| 5.9 | 0.77 | 6.9 | 0.58 | 3.9 | 4.0 | 0.52 | 5.44 | 2.91 | 78.7 | 3.4 | 9.2 | 6.7 | 6.8 |
| 7.5 | 0.00 | 0.0 | 0.14 | 5.0 | 0.0 | 0.74 | 7.34 | 3.60 | 82.8 | 4.3 | 21.8 | 0.0 | 3.7 |
| 7.8 | 1.36 | 3.5 | 0.32 | 6.1 | 0.0 | 0.81 | 3.73 | 3.67 | 76.4 | 5.6 | 64.4 | 0.0 | 5.0 |
| 7.1 | 1.67 | 5.4 | 0.09 | 9.8 | 0.9 | 1.63 | 9.20 | 3.71 | 60.6 | 3.8 | 24.3 | 11.4 | 9.6 |
| 8.3 | 0.11 | 0.4 | 0.58 | 5.9 | 0.0 | 0.30 | 1.52 | 9.03 | 89.6 | 5.5 | 34.1 | 0.0 | 5.0 |
| 6.8 | 1.09 | 4.5 | -0.03 | 1.5 | 0.0 | -0.05 | -0.45 | 3.40 | 101.0 | 5.7 | 40.1 | 4.7 | 5.4 |
| 6.9 | 0.97 | 9.7 | 0.24 | 5.7 | 1.2 | 0.71 | 7.70 | 4.78 | 85.5 | 3.6 | 9.9 | 5.1 | 6.1 |
| 0.0 | 23.40 | 55.9 | -3.78 | 1.6 | 0.0 | -3.13 | -12.82 | 13.24 | 133.3 | 5.9 | 42.9 | 0.0 | 5.2 |
| 10.0 | 0.23 | 0.3 | -0.13 | 0.2 | 0.0 | -0.38 | -1.94 | 1.96 | 123.3 | 5.7 | 27.1 | 0.0 | 6.2 |
| 9.9 | 0.35 | 1.3 | 0.47 | 1.0 | 0.0 | -0.10 | -0.77 | 3.20 | 96.8 | 5.2 | 29.5 | 1.1 | 6.2 |
| 10.0 | 0.36 | 0.6 | 0.12 | 2.2 | 0.0 | 0.18 | 1.26 | 2.98 | 93.1 | 6.8 | 41.9 | 0.0 | 7.0 |
| 9.9 | 0.38 | 1.3 | 0.41 | 3.6 | 3.7 | 0.43 | 3.55 | 2.39 | 83.0 | 4.0 | 19.4 | 9.4 | 7.7 |
| 9.1 | 6.31 | 4.6 | 0.00 | 1.3 | 0.0 | 0.00 | 0.00 | 0.59 | 100.0 | 4.9 | 14.4 | 0.0 | 5.7 |
| 7.9 | 0.66 | 4.5 | 0.06 | 2.4 | 0.1 | 0.10 | 1.05 | 3.16 | 96.9 | 2.7 | 11.4 | 13.3 | 5.7 |
| 9.6 | 0.24 | 0.9 | 0.54 | 9.8 | 14.3 | 2.09 | 16.58 | 3.56 | 67.6 | 5.2 | 19.8 | 2.2 | 10.0 |
| 7.4 | 0.78 | 5.3 | 0.91 | 3.0 | 0.3 | 0.28 | 2.89 | 4.06 | 87.1 | 3.8 | 24.7 | 11.4 | 5.3 |
| 6.8 | 0.71 | 4.5 | 0.33 | 4.1 | 1.0 | 0.61 | 6.55 | 3.25 | 86.5 | 3.6 | 3.4 | 2.7 | 5.8 |
| 9.0 | 0.76 | 3.9 | 0.33 | 7.5 | 0.8 | 1.06 | 9.06 | 2.92 | 62.9 | 3.2 | 37.8 | 17.2 | 6.5 |
| 8.9 | 2.35 | 4.0 | 0.25 | 1.9 | 0.0 | 0.08 | 0.38 | 3.49 | 96.2 | 5.7 | 54.9 | 6.7 | 6.0 |
| 3.7 | 10.47 | 22.8 | 0.00 | 3.6 | 0.0 | 0.53 | 3.45 | 1.92 | 66.7 | 4.6 | 6.8 | 0.0 | 3.0 |
| 6.9 | 1.95 | 6.1 | 0.05 | 0.6 | 0.0 | -0.15 | -1.52 | 3.23 | 104.0 | 5.8 | 42.2 | 0.0 | 3.7 |
| 4.6 | 2.98 | 8.8 | -0.36 | 7.8 | 0.0 | 1.69 | 19.38 | 3.68 | 45.3 | 5.9 | 39.7 | 0.0 | 3.7 |
| 0.0 | 25.69 | 73.0 | 1.95 | 10.0 | 0.0 | 2.61 | 15.00 | 12.09 | 57.6 | 5.2 | 33.9 | 0.0 | 7.6 |
| 8.2 | 28.57 | 5.5 | 0.00 | 2.7 | 0.0 | 0.35 | 1.88 | 1.84 | 80.0 | 6.8 | 52.4 | 0.0 | 7.0 |
| 9.8 | 0.27 | 1.2 | 0.24 | 7.5 | 14.7 | 1.11 | 6.43 | 2.90 | 70.1 | 3.6 | 9.6 | 8.4 | 9.6 |
| 7.9 | 0.50 | 2.4 | 0.69 | 0.6 | -1.1 | -2.54 | -22.96 | 3.48 | 228.4 | 5.0 | 25.9 | 3.1 | 4.4 |
| 7.2 | 1.29 | 6.9 | 0.12 | 2.2 | 0.0 | 0.03 | 0.30 | 4.22 | 96.1 | 5.1 | 32.6 | 2.7 | 5.2 |
| 8.4 | 0.44 | 3.1 | 0.42 | 5.3 | 1.5 | 0.56 | 5.41 | 3.85 | 84.5 | 2.9 | 6.2 | 8.3 | 7.2 |
| 7.5 | 0.79 | 3.8 | -0.13 | 9.2 | 0.1 | 1.43 | 10.29 | 6.34 | 71.7 | 4.8 | 30.1 | 0.0 | 5.0 |
| 5.3 | 0.00 | 6.0 | 0.25 | 1.4 | 0.0 | 0.01 | 0.13 | 3.08 | 96.5 | 3.8 | 42.0 | 13.0 | 3.3 |
| 9.0 | 0.84 | 3.8 | 0.55 | 6.6 | 1.4 | 0.99 | 7.63 | 3.56 | 65.8 | 3.7 | 14.7 | 3.7 | 8.2 |
| 9.5 | 0.00 | 0.0 | 0.00 | 2.0 | 0.0 | -0.12 | -1.55 | 6.11 | 102.0 | 4.9 | 30.3 | 0.0 | 1.0 |
| 4.9 | 1.56 | 10.0 | 0.71 | 2.8 | 0.4 | 0.15 | 1.50 | 4.20 | 88.2 | 5.4 | 29.4 | 2.6 | 5.8 |
| 2.8 | 3.34 | 28.0 | 0.50 | 3.5 | 0.3 | 0.23 | 2.29 | 5.15 | 79.6 | 2.7 | 6.8 | 7.8 | 6.5 |
| 6.6 | 1.16 | 8.5 | 0.18 | 4.8 | 0.7 | 0.65 | 6.44 | 4.11 | 83.9 | 4.0 | 15.5 | 6.3 | 7.3 |
| 9.3 | 0.43 | 2.6 | 0.53 | 4.2 | 6.0 | 0.58 | 4.94 | 2.49 | 77.0 | 3.8 | 14.0 | 3.2 | 7.5 |
| 7.9 | 0.51 | 3.7 | 0.95 | 9.4 | 3.8 | 1.55 | 14.79 | 5.76 | 75.2 | 4.0 | 24.7 | 9.6 | 7.1 |
| 10.0 | 1.08 | 1.2 | 0.00 | 0.6 | 0.0 | -0.11 | -0.41 | 1.96 | 112.5 | 5.8 | 57.2 | 0.0 | 6.3 |
| 10.0 | 0.23 | 0.8 | 0.14 | 2.5 | 0.1 | 0.29 | 2.39 | 2.50 | 88.8 | 4.6 | 25.8 | 1.2 | 5.7 |
| 6.6 | 0.39 | 2.8 | 0.38 | 4.3 | 0.5 | 0.68 | 7.58 | 3.44 | 82.3 | 3.9 | 18.5 | 1.4 | 3.8 |
| 6.8 | 1.26 | 7.1 | 0.11 | 1.9 | 0.2 | 0.25 | 2.37 | 2.62 | 92.9 | 4.5 | 20.3 | 0.7 | 5.1 |
| 8.3 | 0.51 | 1.8 | -0.10 | 3.8 | 0.0 | 0.48 | 3.03 | 3.50 | 93.1 | 4.9 | 36.0 | 0.0 | 6.1 |
| 5.8 | 1.56 | 6.0 | 0.00 | 1.7 | 0.0 | 0.00 | 0.00 | 3.00 | 83.3 | 7.5 | 68.8 | 0.0 | 4.9 |
| 5.0 | 1.68 | 13.3 | 4.14 | 0.3 | -1.6 | -1.42 | -17.40 | 5.56 | 80.2 | 3.9 | 12.4 | 6.4 | 4.5 |
| 10.0 | 0.42 | 0.5 | 0.28 | 1.4 | 0.0 | 0.01 | 0.05 | 2.17 | 96.9 | 4.8 | 30.3 | 3.1 | 7.2 |

| Name | City | State | Rating | 2014 Rating | 2013 Rating | Total Assets ($Mil) | One Year Asset Growth | Asset Mix (As a % of Total Assets) | | | | Capital-ization Index | Net Worth Ratio |
|---|---|---|---|---|---|---|---|---|---|---|---|---|---|
| | | | | | | | | Comm-ercial Loans | Cons-umer Loans | Mort-gage Loans | Secur-ities | | |
| ATCHISON VILLAGE CU | Richmond | CA | C- | C | C- | 8.2 | 1.35 | 0.0 | 42.2 | 0.0 | 0.0 | 10.0 | 13.0 |
| ATD FCU | San Jose | CA | D | D | C- | 2.7 | -82.33 | 0.0 | 20.5 | 0.0 | 0.0 | 10.0 | 99.7 |
| ATHENS AREA CU | Athens | WI | C | C | C+ | 27.7 | 2.69 | 1.6 | 10.9 | 13.6 | 0.0 | 10.0 | 13.5 |
| ATHOL CU | Athol | MA | D | D | D | 88.0 | -4.07 | 0.0 | 13.3 | 39.7 | 26.2 | 7.8 | 9.5 |
| ▲ ATL FCU | Wyoming | MI | D+ | D | D | 12.6 | -1.77 | 0.0 | 39.0 | 8.5 | 28.4 | 10.0 | 11.0 |
| ATLANTA FCU | Atlanta | GA | D+ | D+ | D | 9.6 | 0.18 | 0.0 | 28.8 | 2.3 | 0.0 | 10.0 | 19.0 |
| ATLANTA POSTAL CU | Atlanta | GA | B- | B- | B- | 2039.9 | -0.86 | 8.0 | 34.1 | 16.2 | 31.6 | 10.0 | 13.2 |
| ATLANTIC CITY ELECTRIC CO EMPL FCU | Mays Landing | NJ | B- | C+ | C+ | 53.0 | 0.66 | 0.0 | 16.3 | 0.5 | 60.8 | 10.0 | 13.3 |
| ATLANTIC CITY FCU | Lander | WY | A- | A- | A- | 114.6 | 3.42 | 2.7 | 36.3 | 2.4 | 0.0 | 10.0 | 11.3 |
| ▲ ATLANTIC CITY POLICE FCU | Atlantic City | NJ | C | C- | C- | 2.3 | 1.03 | 0.0 | 13.5 | 0.0 | 0.0 | 10.0 | 13.9 |
| ATLANTIC COUNTY NJ EMPL FCU | Egg Harbor Townsh | NJ | C- | C | C | 2.7 | 1.44 | 0.0 | 13.3 | 0.0 | 0.0 | 10.0 | 21.7 |
| ▼ ATLANTIC FCU | Kenilworth | NJ | C- | C+ | C+ | 243.5 | -4.14 | 2.6 | 8.8 | 26.7 | 38.0 | 10.0 | 16.4 |
| ATLANTIC FINANCIAL FCU | Hunt Valley | MD | C+ | C | C- | 86.1 | -1.55 | 0.0 | 32.6 | 23.0 | 14.0 | 9.3 | 10.6 |
| ▲ ATLANTIC HEALTH EMPL FCU | Summit | NJ | C | C- | C- | 20.1 | 3.28 | 0.0 | 33.3 | 0.0 | 0.0 | 8.6 | 10.1 |
| ATLANTIC REGIONAL FCU | Brunswick | ME | B+ | B+ | A- | 298.9 | 6.93 | 6.4 | 10.1 | 50.2 | 19.9 | 10.0 | 13.4 |
| ATLAS CU | Hannibal | MO | C | C | C | <1 | 9.82 | 0.0 | 42.9 | 0.0 | 0.0 | 10.0 | 14.6 |
| ATOMIC CU | Piketon | OH | B- | B | B | 236.0 | 7.96 | 11.3 | 28.8 | 33.2 | 9.1 | 6.9 | 8.9 |
| ATRIUM CU INC | Middletown | OH | C+ | C+ | C+ | 7.6 | 9.10 | 0.0 | 36.6 | 12.1 | 0.0 | 10.0 | 13.6 |
| ▲ ATTICA-WYOMING CORRECTIONAL EMPL FC | Attica | NY | C | C- | C | 13.9 | 2.02 | 0.0 | 25.3 | 0.0 | 54.8 | 10.0 | 14.2 |
| ATTLEBORO ME FCU | Attleboro | MA | D+ | D+ | D+ | 16.2 | -0.83 | 0.0 | 20.4 | 6.0 | 0.0 | 10.0 | 12.7 |
| AUB EMPL CU | Athens | TN | C- | C | C | 1.6 | -1.25 | 0.0 | 54.9 | 0.0 | 0.0 | 10.0 | 23.3 |
| AUBURN COMMUNITY FCU | Auburn | NY | C- | D+ | C- | 81.7 | 6.72 | 0.0 | 10.7 | 0.2 | 46.3 | 7.6 | 9.4 |
| AUBURN UNIV FCU | Auburn | AL | C+ | B- | B | 163.5 | 3.51 | 0.3 | 16.6 | 14.2 | 42.5 | 10.0 | 11.4 |
| AUDUBON FCU | Owensboro | KY | D+ | D+ | C | 21.2 | 0.58 | 0.0 | 34.9 | 17.6 | 0.0 | 7.7 | 9.5 |
| AUGUSTA COUNTY FCU | Verona | VA | B- | B- | B- | 23.4 | 6.07 | 0.3 | 36.3 | 0.0 | 26.8 | 10.0 | 14.9 |
| AUGUSTA HEALTH CARE CU | Fishersville | VA | C+ | C | D+ | 11.5 | 2.19 | 0.0 | 43.2 | 0.0 | 49.2 | 8.8 | 10.2 |
| AUGUSTA METRO FCU | Augusta | GA | C+ | C+ | C+ | 92.6 | 13.75 | 0.0 | 71.3 | 5.8 | 1.5 | 7.0 | 9.0 |
| AUGUSTA VAH FCU | Augusta | GA | C | C+ | B- | 65.7 | 6.27 | 0.0 | 52.2 | 4.4 | 10.6 | 10.0 | 14.2 |
| AURGROUP FINANCIAL CU | Fairfield | OH | C- | C- | C- | 145.8 | 1.16 | 5.1 | 31.4 | 28.6 | 13.7 | 6.6 | 8.7 |
| AURORA CU | Milwaukee | WI | B+ | B | B- | 47.4 | 3.72 | 0.0 | 6.1 | 82.1 | 0.0 | 10.0 | 11.3 |
| AURORA FCU | Aurora | CO | A | A- | A- | 83.1 | 4.76 | 2.8 | 24.6 | 15.4 | 1.8 | 10.0 | 16.0 |
| AURORA FIREFIGHTERS CU | Aurora | IL | D+ | C- | D | 1.9 | 2.49 | 0.0 | 54.8 | 0.0 | 0.0 | 9.9 | 10.9 |
| AURORA POLICEMEN CU | Aurora | IL | B | B | B | 14.9 | 8.49 | 0.0 | 19.7 | 0.0 | 0.0 | 10.0 | 14.3 |
| AURORA POSTAL EMPL CU | Aurora | IL | C- | C- | C- | 2.0 | 4.28 | 0.0 | 59.0 | 0.0 | 0.0 | 10.0 | 20.6 |
| AURORA SCHOOLS FCU | Aurora | CO | C+ | C+ | C+ | 98.8 | -1.05 | 1.2 | 14.1 | 33.5 | 0.1 | 9.3 | 10.5 |
| AUSTIN CITY EMPL CU | Austin | MN | C | C | C | 9.3 | 5.70 | 0.0 | 32.9 | 0.0 | 8.4 | 10.0 | 12.0 |
| AUSTIN FCU | Austin | TX | D+ | D | D+ | 31.3 | 2.58 | 0.0 | 23.5 | 12.1 | 3.1 | 4.9 | 7.0 |
| AUSTIN TELCO FCU | Austin | TX | A | A | A- | 1334.6 | 3.90 | 8.6 | 14.4 | 23.0 | 44.6 | 10.0 | 11.7 |
| AUTO CLUB FCU | Cerritos | CA | D+ | D+ | D | 27.8 | -1.13 | 0.1 | 29.6 | 4.3 | 8.3 | 5.9 | 7.9 |
| AUTO-OWNERS ASSOCIATES CU | Lansing | MI | C+ | C+ | C+ | 29.2 | -0.11 | 0.0 | 24.6 | 0.0 | 37.5 | 10.0 | 12.9 |
| AUTOMATIC DATA PROCESSING FCU | Roseland | NJ | D+ | D+ | D | 64.6 | -3.31 | 0.0 | 13.6 | 16.6 | 8.4 | 8.4 | 10.0 |
| ▲ AUTOTRUCK FINANCIAL CU | Louisville | KY | B- | C+ | B | 112.1 | 4.30 | 0.6 | 22.4 | 8.5 | 5.0 | 10.0 | 11.8 |
| AVADIAN CU | Hoover | AL | B | B | B | 612.6 | 2.22 | 2.8 | 36.5 | 16.1 | 22.1 | 10.0 | 11.8 |
| AVANTI FCU | Watertown | SD | C | C- | C- | 17.0 | 12.56 | 0.0 | 22.8 | 4.2 | 2.6 | 10.0 | 11.2 |
| AVENTA CU | Colorado Springs | CO | B+ | B+ | B | 158.5 | 2.77 | 1.9 | 50.9 | 15.5 | 3.1 | 9.6 | 10.8 |
| ▲ AVENUE BAPTIST BROTHERHOOD FCU | Shreveport | LA | D+ | C- | C- | <1 | 4.28 | 0.0 | 4.5 | 0.0 | 0.0 | 10.0 | 23.7 |
| AVESTAR CU | Waterloo | WI | D+ | D | D | 21.5 | 7.46 | 1.1 | 22.5 | 43.3 | 0.0 | 6.6 | 8.7 |
| ▲ AVH FCU | Natrona Heights | PA | C | C- | C- | 5.0 | -3.48 | 0.0 | 18.5 | 0.0 | 0.0 | 10.0 | 29.1 |
| AVISTA CORP CU | Spokane | WA | A- | A- | A- | 56.4 | 3.22 | 0.0 | 18.7 | 33.4 | 34.8 | 10.0 | 15.2 |
| AVOYELLES PARISH SCHOOL BOARD EMPL | Marksville | LA | D | D | C- | 3.0 | -18.69 | 0.0 | 21.2 | 0.0 | 0.0 | 10.0 | 22.4 |
| AWAKON FCU | Onaway | MI | C+ | C+ | B- | 91.4 | 0.92 | 5.0 | 22.9 | 23.9 | 16.4 | 8.5 | 10.0 |
| AXTON FCU | Glasgow | KY | C | C- | C- | 3.0 | 4.25 | 0.0 | 44.0 | 0.0 | 0.0 | 10.0 | 27.0 |
| AZALEA CITY CU | Mobile | AL | C+ | C+ | C+ | 18.3 | -0.02 | 1.3 | 41.7 | 8.8 | 0.0 | 10.0 | 18.7 |
| B & W MISSISSIPPI EMPL FCU | West Point | MS | D+ | D+ | D+ | 7.6 | -7.50 | 0.0 | 10.1 | 16.1 | 0.0 | 10.0 | 20.4 |
| B BRAUN FCU | Allentown | PA | D | D+ | D+ | 2.6 | 5.55 | 0.0 | 20.6 | 0.0 | 0.0 | 6.1 | 8.1 |
| B E T FCU | Yonkers | NY | D- | D- | D | 7.0 | 1.06 | 0.0 | 9.6 | 0.0 | 0.0 | 5.8 | 7.8 |
| B N A FCU | Arlington | VA | D | D+ | D+ | 18.3 | -11.04 | 0.0 | 6.5 | 0.0 | 16.3 | 9.5 | 10.7 |
| ▼ B P S FCU | Beeville | TX | C | C+ | C+ | 4.2 | 2.72 | 0.0 | 16.8 | 0.0 | 0.0 | 10.0 | 38.7 |
| B&V CU | Overland Park | KS | C+ | C+ | C+ | 65.6 | 0.57 | 0.0 | 14.6 | 0.0 | 29.3 | 9.9 | 11.0 |
| B-M S FCU | New Brunswick | NJ | C | C- | C- | 102.3 | 0.91 | 0.0 | 3.3 | 8.1 | 72.2 | 10.0 | 14.9 |

| Asset Quality Index | Non-Performing Loans as a % of Total Loans | as a % of Capital | Net Charge-Offs Avg Loans | Profitability Index | Net Income ($Mil) | Return on Assets | Return on Equity | Net Interest Spread | Overhead Efficiency Ratio | Liquidity Index | Liquidity Ratio | Hot Money Ratio | Stability Index |
|---|---|---|---|---|---|---|---|---|---|---|---|---|---|
| 5.7 | 5.40 | 16.3 | 1.33 | 3.7 | -0.1 | -0.77 | -5.87 | 5.26 | 86.3 | 5.1 | 27.8 | 0.0 | 6.9 |
| 10.0 | 1.35 | 0.5 | -0.26 | 0.0 | -0.2 | -2.50 | -10.53 | 0.90 | 437.3 | 6.4 | 0.0 | 0.0 | 5.0 |
| 10.0 | 0.40 | 0.8 | 0.22 | 1.8 | 0.0 | 0.05 | 0.36 | 1.69 | 97.1 | 5.6 | 39.1 | 0.0 | 7.3 |
| 4.6 | 2.57 | 18.7 | 0.19 | 0.4 | -0.2 | -0.29 | -3.03 | 2.61 | 108.1 | 3.1 | 3.9 | 6.8 | 4.6 |
| 6.1 | 1.91 | 8.6 | 0.55 | 1.7 | 0.0 | 0.13 | 1.27 | 5.00 | 84.9 | 4.2 | 10.4 | 3.4 | 4.0 |
| 9.7 | 1.30 | 2.6 | 0.14 | 0.4 | 0.0 | -0.25 | -1.31 | 2.84 | 101.8 | 5.8 | 62.5 | 0.0 | 6.0 |
| 9.4 | 0.50 | 2.3 | 0.45 | 2.7 | 3.1 | 0.20 | 1.69 | 2.02 | 78.0 | 4.0 | 19.1 | 13.9 | 7.7 |
| 6.7 | 4.36 | 10.2 | 0.50 | 2.9 | 0.2 | 0.38 | 2.84 | 2.18 | 79.4 | 6.2 | 40.0 | 0.4 | 5.9 |
| 6.9 | 1.98 | 10.5 | 0.26 | 6.3 | 0.8 | 0.91 | 8.97 | 3.44 | 75.5 | 4.3 | 27.9 | 2.2 | 8.0 |
| 8.0 | 3.13 | 5.3 | 0.88 | 4.2 | 0.0 | 0.76 | 5.59 | 2.74 | 70.7 | 6.9 | 87.3 | 0.0 | 6.0 |
| 10.0 | 0.00 | 0.0 | 0.37 | 1.9 | 0.0 | 0.10 | 0.45 | 1.85 | 91.4 | 7.2 | 109.9 | 0.0 | 6.2 |
| 8.6 | 0.90 | 3.4 | 0.33 | 1.3 | -0.2 | -0.10 | -0.63 | 3.02 | 97.9 | 2.8 | 9.0 | 16.8 | 7.6 |
| 6.4 | 1.19 | 6.8 | 1.06 | 5.6 | 0.6 | 0.94 | 9.57 | 4.17 | 71.4 | 4.1 | 20.3 | 6.4 | 3.7 |
| 6.1 | 2.97 | 11.0 | 0.56 | 5.5 | 0.1 | 0.83 | 8.35 | 3.96 | 76.3 | 4.2 | 22.3 | 7.5 | 4.3 |
| 8.8 | 0.47 | 3.0 | 0.14 | 5.2 | 1.6 | 0.73 | 5.32 | 3.60 | 78.7 | 3.1 | 4.5 | 6.4 | 8.4 |
| 9.5 | 0.38 | 1.2 | 0.00 | 2.2 | 0.0 | -0.26 | -1.65 | 3.14 | 109.1 | 4.8 | 28.7 | 0.0 | 6.9 |
| 7.0 | 0.60 | 5.2 | 0.34 | 4.1 | 0.8 | 0.44 | 4.98 | 4.06 | 88.8 | 3.7 | 15.4 | 6.8 | 6.0 |
| 9.7 | 0.00 | 0.0 | 0.03 | 6.5 | 0.1 | 0.89 | 6.72 | 4.92 | 84.6 | 5.5 | 41.9 | 0.0 | 5.0 |
| 10.0 | 0.54 | 1.1 | 0.00 | 2.1 | 0.0 | 0.32 | 2.24 | 1.96 | 82.3 | 5.9 | 30.2 | 0.0 | 7.1 |
| 10.0 | 0.19 | 0.4 | -0.03 | 1.1 | 0.0 | 0.02 | 0.13 | 2.30 | 100.0 | 6.0 | 43.8 | 0.0 | 6.1 |
| 5.0 | 6.05 | 14.4 | 0.00 | 4.7 | 0.0 | 0.25 | 1.09 | 6.08 | 90.7 | 6.6 | 55.3 | 0.0 | 4.3 |
| 10.0 | 0.09 | 0.2 | 0.08 | 2.4 | 0.1 | 0.23 | 2.41 | 3.04 | 92.9 | 6.0 | 34.1 | 0.9 | 5.0 |
| 7.9 | 1.54 | 5.0 | 0.68 | 2.8 | 0.3 | 0.25 | 2.18 | 2.77 | 84.2 | 5.1 | 34.8 | 8.2 | 7.0 |
| 8.1 | 0.26 | 1.6 | 0.29 | 1.7 | 0.0 | 0.06 | 0.60 | 3.24 | 95.6 | 4.1 | 17.0 | 1.1 | 3.4 |
| 8.4 | 1.45 | 3.7 | 0.32 | 5.9 | 0.1 | 0.83 | 5.58 | 2.99 | 67.0 | 5.5 | 25.9 | 0.0 | 5.7 |
| 8.5 | 0.74 | 3.1 | 0.11 | 8.4 | 0.1 | 1.62 | 16.59 | 3.32 | 60.3 | 4.2 | 16.5 | 4.4 | 4.9 |
| 4.1 | 1.50 | 13.9 | 0.82 | 3.5 | 0.2 | 0.28 | 3.09 | 4.27 | 85.1 | 3.1 | 6.9 | 4.4 | 4.0 |
| 7.6 | 0.82 | 3.8 | 0.53 | 2.5 | 0.1 | 0.20 | 1.37 | 4.28 | 90.8 | 3.5 | 6.8 | 3.6 | 6.3 |
| 7.5 | 0.73 | 5.4 | 0.51 | 2.3 | 0.2 | 0.20 | 2.34 | 3.30 | 91.7 | 2.8 | 9.8 | 11.2 | 5.1 |
| 9.5 | 0.02 | 0.1 | 0.03 | 9.3 | 0.5 | 1.33 | 12.23 | 3.62 | 71.8 | 2.8 | 3.1 | 0.0 | 6.6 |
| 8.2 | 1.05 | 3.8 | 0.32 | 9.8 | 2.6 | 4.19 | 27.38 | 3.67 | 37.9 | 5.7 | 57.0 | 3.7 | 7.3 |
| 6.2 | 0.49 | 2.7 | -0.11 | 2.7 | 0.0 | 0.28 | 2.58 | 3.91 | 93.9 | 5.0 | 34.3 | 0.0 | 5.1 |
| 10.0 | 0.00 | 0.0 | 0.00 | 3.7 | 0.1 | 0.44 | 3.05 | 2.33 | 83.5 | 6.6 | 53.3 | 0.0 | 7.3 |
| 8.5 | 0.69 | 1.9 | -0.12 | 3.4 | 0.0 | 0.41 | 1.99 | 4.85 | 89.8 | 4.9 | 23.8 | 0.0 | 6.4 |
| 9.3 | 0.13 | 0.9 | 0.22 | 3.1 | 0.2 | 0.28 | 2.68 | 2.56 | 88.7 | 3.9 | 23.1 | 7.0 | 5.0 |
| 9.8 | 0.16 | 0.6 | 0.03 | 2.7 | 0.0 | 0.22 | 1.80 | 3.54 | 92.2 | 4.9 | 37.2 | 0.0 | 6.0 |
| 9.6 | 0.14 | 1.6 | 0.14 | 2.3 | 0.1 | 0.24 | 3.36 | 2.42 | 91.1 | 5.9 | 44.7 | 0.0 | 2.5 |
| 10.0 | 0.05 | 0.2 | 0.04 | 8.1 | 11.9 | 1.20 | 10.90 | 1.99 | 59.3 | 3.2 | 13.0 | 20.7 | 8.5 |
| 7.7 | 0.39 | 1.6 | 0.62 | 1.7 | 0.0 | -0.02 | -0.24 | 3.33 | 100.6 | 5.0 | 24.3 | 5.7 | 2.7 |
| 10.0 | 0.00 | 0.0 | -0.11 | 3.0 | 0.1 | 0.37 | 3.13 | 1.74 | 85.0 | 4.3 | 18.7 | 6.0 | 5.7 |
| 7.6 | 0.89 | 2.9 | 0.10 | 1.8 | 0.0 | 0.06 | 0.62 | 2.43 | 97.5 | 5.2 | 26.7 | 3.3 | 4.3 |
| 9.7 | 0.87 | 2.8 | 0.22 | 3.6 | 0.4 | 0.46 | 4.07 | 2.58 | 88.3 | 5.2 | 23.0 | 3.2 | 7.5 |
| 9.0 | 0.44 | 3.0 | 0.51 | 3.9 | 1.9 | 0.41 | 3.72 | 3.71 | 85.3 | 3.5 | 16.1 | 8.1 | 7.5 |
| 7.0 | 1.83 | 7.9 | 0.42 | 2.5 | 0.0 | 0.28 | 2.40 | 3.18 | 86.0 | 4.6 | 28.0 | 7.1 | 5.6 |
| 8.4 | 0.14 | 1.8 | 0.49 | 6.6 | 0.8 | 0.64 | 6.02 | 4.75 | 83.2 | 2.5 | 6.0 | 12.0 | 6.8 |
| 10.0 | 0.00 | 0.0 | 0.00 | 1.5 | 0.0 | 0.25 | 1.07 | 0.91 | 100.0 | 7.5 | 115.4 | 0.0 | 5.4 |
| 6.0 | 0.88 | 5.9 | -0.34 | 4.4 | 0.1 | 0.61 | 6.98 | 4.71 | 90.3 | 4.3 | 31.1 | 8.6 | 3.7 |
| 10.0 | 2.35 | 1.9 | -0.34 | 3.3 | 0.0 | 0.47 | 1.65 | 2.38 | 78.1 | 5.8 | 23.0 | 0.0 | 5.7 |
| 10.0 | 0.20 | 0.8 | 0.03 | 4.8 | 0.3 | 0.63 | 4.17 | 2.20 | 72.5 | 4.0 | 14.6 | 0.0 | 7.9 |
| 10.0 | 1.28 | 1.2 | 0.25 | 0.0 | 0.0 | -1.48 | -7.29 | 2.03 | 172.6 | 4.9 | 16.4 | 0.0 | 4.9 |
| 4.7 | 1.34 | 16.1 | 0.41 | 2.9 | 0.2 | 0.23 | 2.31 | 3.93 | 93.5 | 4.5 | 16.3 | 3.6 | 4.8 |
| 9.5 | 0.00 | 0.0 | 0.00 | 2.5 | 0.0 | 0.28 | 1.01 | 3.58 | 91.7 | 5.8 | 62.7 | 0.0 | 6.7 |
| 7.3 | 1.22 | 4.0 | 1.30 | 5.4 | 0.1 | 0.77 | 4.21 | 5.81 | 77.7 | 3.6 | 14.4 | 10.1 | 5.0 |
| 10.0 | 0.00 | 0.0 | 0.00 | 0.4 | 0.0 | -0.39 | -1.96 | 2.30 | 116.8 | 4.6 | 18.2 | 0.0 | 6.5 |
| 10.0 | 0.00 | 0.0 | 1.02 | 2.9 | 0.0 | 0.38 | 4.58 | 2.87 | 72.7 | 7.8 | 71.8 | 0.0 | 2.3 |
| 10.0 | 0.00 | 0.0 | 0.00 | 2.2 | 0.0 | 0.13 | 1.72 | 1.07 | 87.7 | 5.0 | 19.6 | 0.0 | 1.7 |
| 10.0 | 0.00 | 0.0 | 0.67 | 1.0 | 0.0 | -0.17 | -1.64 | 1.49 | 105.6 | 5.5 | 25.2 | 0.0 | 3.7 |
| 9.6 | 0.00 | 0.0 | 0.00 | 2.0 | 0.0 | 0.00 | 0.00 | 1.57 | 100.0 | 6.9 | 84.1 | 0.0 | 7.0 |
| 7.4 | 2.24 | 4.3 | 0.75 | 3.3 | 0.2 | 0.37 | 3.53 | 1.42 | 61.1 | 5.0 | 18.9 | 0.0 | 5.0 |
| 10.0 | 0.62 | 0.5 | 0.35 | 2.0 | 0.1 | 0.07 | 0.48 | 1.77 | 94.8 | 5.5 | 15.8 | 1.8 | 7.4 |

| Name | City | State | Rating | 2014 Rating | 2013 Rating | Total Assets ($Mil) | One Year Asset Growth | Commercial Loans | Consumer Loans | Mortgage Loans | Securities | Capitalization Index | Net Worth Ratio |
|---|---|---|---|---|---|---|---|---|---|---|---|---|---|
| BAB CU | Aztec | NM | C+ | C+ | C+ | 8.2 | 12.01 | 0.0 | 54.4 | 0.0 | 1.2 | 10.0 | 13.8 |
| ▼ BABBITT STEELWORKERS CU | Babbitt | MN | C- | B- | B- | 14.8 | -0.49 | 0.0 | 13.6 | 0.0 | 0.0 | 10.0 | 14.9 |
| ▼ BACHARACH EMPL FCU | New Kensington | PA | D+ | D | D | <1 | -6.11 | 0.0 | 18.6 | 0.0 | 0.0 | 10.0 | 40.0 |
| BACK MOUNTAIN FCU | Trucksville | PA | C | C | C | 10.5 | -1.33 | 0.0 | 16.3 | 0.1 | 74.4 | 10.0 | 11.9 |
| ▲ BADGER CU | Peshtigo | WI | C+ | C | C- | 14.9 | 2.78 | 0.0 | 30.1 | 35.1 | 0.0 | 10.0 | 15.0 |
| BADGER-GLOBE CU | Neenah | WI | C+ | C+ | C+ | 42.2 | 2.36 | 0.0 | 23.8 | 28.3 | 0.0 | 10.0 | 12.6 |
| ▲ BADLANDS FCU | Glendive | MT | C | C- | D+ | 27.5 | 37.61 | 0.0 | 23.0 | 0.1 | 0.0 | 7.4 | 9.2 |
| BAILEY INC EMPL CU | West Valley City | UT | E+ | E+ | D- | <1 | -14.23 | 0.0 | 77.6 | 0.0 | 0.0 | 5.6 | 7.6 |
| BAKELITE OTTAWA PLASTICS CU | Ottawa | IL | C | C+ | B- | 13.1 | 14.00 | 0.0 | 19.5 | 8.3 | 0.0 | 10.0 | 12.3 |
| ▲ BAKER FCU | Phillipsburg | NJ | D | D | D+ | 33.0 | 7.10 | 0.3 | 52.9 | 0.0 | 5.1 | 6.3 | 8.4 |
| BAKER HUGHES FCU | Houston | TX | D+ | D+ | D | 19.1 | -0.89 | 0.0 | 22.4 | 0.0 | 0.0 | 7.5 | 9.4 |
| BAKERS FCU | Omaha | NE | C | C | C | 7.2 | -4.03 | 0.0 | 40.9 | 0.0 | 10.2 | 10.0 | 14.9 |
| ▲ BAKERSFIELD CITY EMPL FCU | Bakersfield | CA | C- | D+ | D+ | 30.4 | -4.86 | 1.4 | 29.8 | 13.6 | 33.2 | 6.6 | 8.6 |
| BAKERY EMPL CU | Montebello | CA | D- | D- | D- | 6.9 | -2.29 | 0.0 | 26.1 | 0.0 | 0.0 | 6.1 | 8.1 |
| BALDWIN COUNTY FCU | Bay Minette | AL | B- | B- | B- | 20.0 | 1.66 | 0.6 | 24.3 | 11.5 | 1.0 | 10.0 | 12.7 |
| BALL STATE FCU | Muncie | IN | D+ | D+ | D+ | 90.7 | -0.09 | 0.5 | 42.2 | 19.1 | 8.8 | 5.7 | 7.7 |
| BALTIMORE COUNTY EMPL FCU | Towson | MD | C | C | C | 349.0 | 3.92 | 0.0 | 22.3 | 12.7 | 39.7 | 7.0 | 9.0 |
| BALTIMORE WASHINGTON FCU | Glen Burnie | MD | D- | D- | D- | 8.5 | -4.60 | 0.0 | 31.6 | 8.2 | 52.3 | 7.0 | 9.0 |
| BANCO DE SANTANDER FCU | Puerto Nuevo | PR | C- | C | C | 2.6 | 10.89 | 0.0 | 0.0 | 0.0 | 0.0 | 9.8 | 10.8 |
| BANGOR FCU | Bangor | ME | B- | B- | B- | 130.4 | 2.88 | 0.5 | 25.9 | 25.7 | 0.0 | 7.5 | 9.4 |
| BANK-FUND STAFF FCU | Washington | DC | B- | C+ | B | 4066.2 | 4.42 | 0.1 | 5.2 | 46.0 | 25.9 | 10.0 | 11.3 |
| BANNER FCU | Phoenix | AZ | C | C | C+ | 56.5 | 2.13 | 0.0 | 40.7 | 0.0 | 50.5 | 9.4 | 10.7 |
| BAPTIST CU | San Antonio | TX | C- | C- | C+ | 32.4 | 3.03 | 7.1 | 51.8 | 17.2 | 0.0 | 8.1 | 9.7 |
| BAPTIST HEALTH FCU | Little Rock | AR | B+ | B+ | B+ | 27.1 | 6.11 | 0.0 | 59.1 | 0.0 | 0.0 | 10.0 | 16.2 |
| BAPTIST HEALTH SOUTH FLORIDA FCU | Miami | FL | B+ | B | B- | 53.4 | 6.25 | 0.0 | 51.2 | 3.3 | 0.0 | 10.0 | 12.1 |
| ▲ BAR-CONS FCU | Columbus | IN | C- | C- | C- | 31.8 | 3.66 | 0.0 | 33.6 | 8.9 | 0.1 | 7.9 | 9.6 |
| BARABOO MUNICIPAL EMPL CU | Baraboo | WI | C- | D+ | D | 1.8 | 5.54 | 0.0 | 48.8 | 0.0 | 0.0 | 10.0 | 18.5 |
| BARAGA COUNTY FCU | Lanse | MI | D | C- | D+ | 32.4 | 1.85 | 0.0 | 24.0 | 1.1 | 48.7 | 7.0 | 9.0 |
| BARD EMPL FCU | New Providence | NJ | C | C- | D+ | 17.1 | -11.52 | 9.2 | 9.1 | 15.3 | 0.0 | 10.0 | 11.1 |
| BARDES EMPL FCU | Cincinnati | OH | D+ | C- | C | <1 | -5.53 | 0.0 | 46.1 | 0.0 | 38.4 | 9.1 | 10.6 |
| BARKSDALE FCU | Bossier City | LA | B- | B- | B- | 1208.5 | 3.30 | 1.3 | 31.0 | 12.6 | 28.0 | 8.5 | 10.0 |
| BARSTOW COMMUNITY CU | Barstow | CA | C | C | C | 7.7 | -7.39 | 0.0 | 29.6 | 0.0 | 0.0 | 10.0 | 13.3 |
| BARTON PLANT EMPL FCU | Luling | LA | B- | C+ | C+ | 18.8 | 1.81 | 0.0 | 29.4 | 10.9 | 0.0 | 10.0 | 18.6 |
| ▼ BASF CHATTANOOGA FCU | Chattanooga | TN | D+ | C- | D+ | 3.2 | 1.91 | 0.0 | 45.4 | 0.0 | 0.0 | 10.0 | 13.9 |
| BASHAS ASSOCIATES FCU | Tempe | AZ | D- | D | C | 15.9 | 3.73 | 0.0 | 33.6 | 0.0 | 0.0 | 7.8 | 9.5 |
| BATON ROUGE CITY PARISH EMPL FCU | Baton Rouge | LA | C- | C- | C | 46.1 | 1.38 | 0.0 | 27.6 | 6.6 | 0.0 | 10.0 | 16.6 |
| BATON ROUGE FIRE DEPT FCU | Baton Rouge | LA | A- | A- | A- | 44.1 | 3.44 | 0.0 | 48.2 | 25.7 | 0.0 | 10.0 | 18.4 |
| BATON ROUGE TELCO FCU | Baton Rouge | LA | B+ | B+ | B+ | 271.4 | 9.23 | 0.0 | 58.7 | 25.6 | 0.9 | 9.3 | 10.5 |
| BATTERY EMPL FCU | Attica | IN | D+ | D+ | D+ | 1.4 | 0.22 | 0.0 | 33.9 | 0.0 | 0.0 | 10.0 | 24.8 |
| ▼ BATTLE CREEK AREA COMMUNITY FCU | Springfield | MI | C- | C+ | B- | 18.7 | 3.33 | 0.0 | 14.6 | 3.4 | 72.1 | 10.0 | 17.9 |
| BAXTER CU | Vernon Hills | IL | A- | A- | B+ | 2255.2 | 13.82 | 1.9 | 33.7 | 41.4 | 0.8 | 8.6 | 10.1 |
| BAY AREA CU | Oregon | OH | B | B | B | 57.1 | 2.05 | 0.0 | 31.1 | 14.7 | 23.1 | 10.0 | 13.4 |
| BAY ATLANTIC FCU | Vineland | NJ | C | C- | D+ | 53.2 | 3.59 | 0.0 | 24.2 | 7.3 | 14.0 | 5.9 | 7.9 |
| BAY CITIES CU | Hayward | CA | C- | C- | C- | 67.2 | -0.58 | 0.0 | 31.2 | 0.0 | 0.0 | 5.8 | 7.8 |
| ▼ BAY CU | Panama City | FL | C | B | B | 81.9 | 7.53 | 0.0 | 42.8 | 15.4 | 1.6 | 8.7 | 10.2 |
| BAY FCU | Capitola | CA | B | B- | C+ | 732.7 | 2.47 | 0.3 | 26.1 | 21.3 | 18.9 | 6.6 | 8.7 |
| BAY RIDGE FCU | Brooklyn | NY | C- | C- | C+ | 201.9 | 6.03 | 58.8 | 9.4 | 27.3 | 1.5 | 7.3 | 9.2 |
| BAY RIDGE LODGE NO 632 FCU | Marlboro | NJ | C+ | C | C | <1 | -16.50 | 0.0 | 50.0 | 0.0 | 0.0 | 10.0 | 53.5 |
| ▲ BAY SHORE CU | Marinette | WI | B | B- | B- | 28.4 | 0.94 | 0.0 | 33.7 | 9.9 | 0.0 | 10.0 | 16.9 |
| BAYCEL FCU | Bay City | TX | A- | A- | A- | 50.2 | 5.67 | 0.0 | 33.0 | 12.0 | 0.5 | 10.0 | 16.7 |
| BAYER CU | Kansas City | MO | D | D | D+ | 7.6 | 3.09 | 0.0 | 33.4 | 0.0 | 1.3 | 6.6 | 8.6 |
| BAYER HERITAGE FCU | Proctor | WV | B | B | B- | 392.6 | 8.44 | 4.1 | 29.9 | 36.7 | 3.3 | 8.0 | 9.7 |
| BAYLANDS FCU | West Point | VA | D+ | D+ | D | 71.9 | 0.17 | 0.0 | 26.0 | 27.7 | 9.2 | 6.4 | 8.5 |
| ▲ BAYLOR HEALTH CARE SYSTEM CU | Dallas | TX | B+ | B- | C | 63.8 | 0.11 | 0.0 | 32.1 | 9.8 | 30.0 | 10.0 | 17.6 |
| BAYONNE CITY EMPL FCUS | Bayonne | NJ | C | C- | C- | 5.5 | 0.24 | 0.0 | 26.8 | 0.0 | 0.0 | 10.0 | 22.8 |
| ▲ BAYONNE HOSPITAL EMPL FCU | Bayonne | NJ | C- | D | D | 5.3 | -2.42 | 0.0 | 17.2 | 0.0 | 0.1 | 10.0 | 14.1 |
| ▼ BAYONNE SCHOOL EMPL FCU | Bayonne | NJ | C- | C- | C+ | 2.9 | 26.95 | 0.0 | 20.8 | 0.0 | 0.0 | 9.4 | 10.6 |
| BAYOU CITY FCU | Houston | TX | D | D+ | D+ | 24.3 | 2.24 | 0.0 | 33.2 | 0.0 | 0.0 | 6.6 | 8.6 |
| ▼ BAYOU FCU | Baton Rouge | LA | C | C+ | B- | 70.4 | 3.34 | 0.0 | 49.3 | 17.5 | 0.3 | 10.0 | 13.6 |
| BCBSNC CU | Durham | NC | B- | C+ | C | 14.3 | -6.49 | 0.0 | 24.8 | 0.0 | 57.6 | 10.0 | 12.7 |

| Asset Quality Index | Non-Performing Loans | | Net Charge-Offs/Avg Loans | Profitability Index | Net Income ($Mil) | Return on Assets | Return on Equity | Net Interest Spread | Overhead Efficiency Ratio | Liquidity Index | Liquidity Ratio | Hot Money Ratio | Stability Index |
|---|---|---|---|---|---|---|---|---|---|---|---|---|---|
| | as a % of Total Loans | as a % of Capital | | | | | | | | | | | |
| 7.1 | 0.78 | 4.0 | 0.43 | 9.3 | 0.1 | 1.45 | 10.42 | 4.15 | 65.9 | 3.9 | 21.4 | 0.0 | 5.7 |
| 10.0 | 0.62 | 0.7 | -0.80 | 1.2 | -0.1 | -0.48 | -3.16 | 2.40 | 117.1 | 5.5 | 28.3 | 0.0 | 5.4 |
| 5.8 | 4.12 | 4.6 | 0.00 | 0.0 | 0.0 | -1.31 | -3.03 | 6.01 | 260.0 | 7.5 | 88.4 | 0.0 | 5.3 |
| 7.5 | 5.70 | 8.3 | 0.22 | 3.2 | 0.0 | 0.33 | 2.80 | 1.32 | 72.6 | 5.2 | 10.4 | 0.0 | 5.4 |
| 9.6 | 0.09 | 0.4 | -0.08 | 2.7 | 0.0 | 0.18 | 1.20 | 3.91 | 95.3 | 3.3 | 21.3 | 15.8 | 6.4 |
| 6.1 | 2.47 | 11.9 | 0.01 | 2.2 | 0.0 | 0.08 | 0.65 | 3.09 | 90.4 | 4.1 | 28.1 | 2.5 | 6.0 |
| 7.9 | 1.72 | 5.2 | 0.22 | 2.8 | 0.1 | 0.23 | 2.57 | 2.20 | 87.9 | 6.9 | 49.3 | 0.0 | 4.0 |
| 5.0 | 0.00 | 0.0 | 1.64 | 0.0 | 0.0 | -2.68 | -40.00 | 8.74 | 78.0 | 4.9 | 30.7 | 0.0 | 3.5 |
| 9.8 | 1.05 | 2.7 | 0.17 | 2.3 | 0.0 | 0.14 | 1.09 | 2.61 | 96.4 | 5.6 | 28.5 | 2.9 | 5.8 |
| 2.3 | 2.49 | 22.0 | 1.53 | 3.2 | 0.1 | 0.24 | 2.91 | 5.89 | 73.1 | 3.3 | 4.0 | 0.0 | 3.4 |
| 7.9 | 1.18 | 3.1 | 0.34 | 3.2 | 0.0 | 0.24 | 2.64 | 2.71 | 92.2 | 4.5 | 11.9 | 5.6 | 3.3 |
| 9.7 | 0.08 | 0.3 | -0.04 | 2.8 | 0.0 | 0.33 | 2.24 | 3.06 | 91.8 | 4.5 | 10.8 | 0.0 | 7.4 |
| 7.1 | 0.43 | 4.0 | 0.14 | 2.6 | 0.1 | 0.26 | 3.13 | 3.29 | 89.5 | 3.8 | 14.3 | 8.9 | 3.5 |
| 8.3 | 0.44 | 1.4 | 0.91 | 1.4 | 0.0 | 0.16 | 1.94 | 3.44 | 100.0 | 5.9 | 31.9 | 0.0 | 1.0 |
| 9.9 | 0.06 | 0.3 | 0.46 | 3.2 | 0.1 | 0.43 | 3.90 | 3.89 | 83.2 | 4.9 | 18.9 | 4.2 | 5.4 |
| 3.5 | 1.66 | 21.7 | 0.43 | 2.4 | 0.2 | 0.24 | 3.16 | 3.87 | 87.4 | 3.5 | 9.2 | 5.0 | 2.8 |
| 9.4 | 0.42 | 2.3 | 0.35 | 3.0 | 0.9 | 0.33 | 3.97 | 2.50 | 83.2 | 4.5 | 22.9 | 2.7 | 4.9 |
| 9.5 | 0.25 | 1.1 | 0.40 | 0.6 | 0.0 | -0.12 | -1.37 | 2.44 | 96.4 | 4.4 | 7.9 | 0.0 | 3.7 |
| 7.0 | 0.34 | 2.4 | 1.58 | 4.0 | 0.0 | 0.05 | 0.48 | 8.36 | 83.0 | 4.7 | 22.1 | 0.0 | 3.7 |
| 7.9 | 0.58 | 4.3 | 0.14 | 3.9 | 0.5 | 0.48 | 5.13 | 3.03 | 87.0 | 2.8 | 13.8 | 12.5 | 5.6 |
| 8.8 | 0.75 | 3.7 | 0.13 | 3.9 | 18.8 | 0.62 | 5.55 | 2.00 | 67.1 | 3.9 | 22.1 | 9.4 | 8.1 |
| 9.9 | 0.02 | 0.1 | 0.13 | 2.5 | 0.1 | 0.18 | 1.71 | 2.53 | 96.1 | 4.5 | 20.0 | 0.2 | 4.8 |
| 5.8 | 0.52 | 4.2 | 0.23 | 2.1 | 0.0 | -0.10 | -1.07 | 4.86 | 100.7 | 4.5 | 31.5 | 6.8 | 4.4 |
| 7.5 | 0.94 | 3.7 | 0.13 | 4.9 | 0.1 | 0.63 | 3.93 | 3.60 | 86.1 | 4.8 | 34.8 | 2.5 | 7.4 |
| 5.8 | 1.43 | 7.9 | 0.66 | 9.9 | 0.8 | 1.96 | 17.03 | 5.66 | 72.1 | 4.2 | 14.2 | 1.3 | 6.2 |
| 9.8 | 0.07 | 0.4 | 0.11 | 2.1 | 0.0 | 0.14 | 1.48 | 2.81 | 94.4 | 4.0 | 11.7 | 1.6 | 5.0 |
| 8.0 | 0.00 | 0.0 | -0.66 | 2.8 | 0.0 | 0.39 | 2.01 | 5.18 | 90.9 | 5.9 | 44.1 | 0.0 | 5.9 |
| 9.6 | 0.14 | 0.5 | 0.60 | 0.9 | 0.0 | -0.16 | -1.72 | 2.72 | 96.7 | 5.0 | 14.9 | 2.1 | 4.2 |
| 8.5 | 0.96 | 3.6 | 0.48 | 1.9 | 0.0 | -0.02 | -0.14 | 2.83 | 90.3 | 4.8 | 19.8 | 4.9 | 4.4 |
| 6.3 | 0.00 | 0.0 | 2.53 | 1.0 | 0.0 | -1.53 | -13.84 | 4.20 | 103.5 | 5.0 | 17.5 | 0.0 | 4.7 |
| 7.3 | 1.01 | 5.4 | 0.78 | 3.7 | 3.8 | 0.42 | 4.27 | 2.98 | 80.7 | 4.2 | 17.1 | 10.7 | 6.7 |
| 9.5 | 0.18 | 0.5 | 0.00 | 2.1 | 0.0 | -0.08 | -0.65 | 5.72 | 102.5 | 6.3 | 50.1 | 1.5 | 5.3 |
| 9.9 | 0.20 | 0.5 | 0.33 | 4.1 | 0.1 | 0.67 | 3.71 | 2.87 | 73.5 | 5.1 | 46.8 | 0.0 | 6.9 |
| 2.7 | 5.93 | 21.7 | 1.51 | 3.3 | 0.0 | 0.25 | 1.80 | 4.85 | 77.1 | 6.0 | 57.9 | 10.0 | 6.6 |
| 8.7 | 0.83 | 2.8 | 0.63 | 0.0 | -0.1 | -0.66 | -6.84 | 3.69 | 105.6 | 4.8 | 24.8 | 0.0 | 3.3 |
| 9.8 | 0.57 | 1.3 | 0.00 | 1.7 | 0.0 | 0.09 | 0.56 | 2.56 | 97.2 | 5.7 | 47.1 | 0.0 | 6.9 |
| 8.2 | 0.28 | 1.3 | 0.03 | 9.2 | 0.4 | 1.31 | 7.38 | 4.08 | 69.3 | 3.6 | 14.4 | 2.5 | 8.0 |
| 6.1 | 0.64 | 5.8 | 0.43 | 4.2 | 1.0 | 0.47 | 4.54 | 2.56 | 75.5 | 1.1 | 6.3 | 22.4 | 7.5 |
| 3.7 | 15.78 | 20.8 | -0.27 | 1.5 | 0.0 | 0.00 | 0.00 | 5.94 | 138.9 | 7.2 | 63.9 | 0.0 | 5.0 |
| 10.0 | 0.19 | 0.2 | -0.09 | 1.1 | 0.0 | -0.14 | -0.75 | 2.31 | 105.1 | 4.7 | 12.7 | 2.5 | 6.3 |
| 8.2 | 0.48 | 4.2 | 0.40 | 9.6 | 21.1 | 1.26 | 12.97 | 3.63 | 73.9 | 2.4 | 5.5 | 9.8 | 7.4 |
| 9.6 | 0.52 | 2.5 | 0.11 | 3.6 | 0.2 | 0.36 | 2.79 | 3.60 | 90.9 | 3.7 | 8.7 | 2.4 | 6.6 |
| 7.0 | 0.73 | 4.5 | 0.27 | 4.0 | 0.2 | 0.47 | 6.13 | 3.80 | 93.8 | 4.6 | 24.3 | 1.8 | 3.1 |
| 8.5 | 0.48 | 2.1 | 0.51 | 2.8 | 0.1 | 0.23 | 2.95 | 3.11 | 87.8 | 4.6 | 29.0 | 2.0 | 2.7 |
| 5.9 | 0.62 | 9.1 | 0.97 | 2.5 | 0.0 | -0.06 | -0.65 | 5.58 | 86.9 | 3.5 | 16.8 | 12.5 | 4.6 |
| 6.5 | 0.90 | 6.5 | 0.35 | 6.5 | 5.4 | 0.98 | 11.92 | 3.74 | 75.6 | 4.3 | 14.7 | 2.0 | 5.9 |
| 2.5 | 1.40 | 11.8 | 0.27 | 3.1 | 0.1 | 0.08 | 0.81 | 3.31 | 72.5 | 1.6 | 17.6 | 47.6 | 7.3 |
| 8.8 | 0.00 | 0.0 | 0.00 | 6.9 | 0.0 | 1.35 | 2.96 | 8.00 | 66.7 | 7.6 | 110.0 | 0.0 | 5.0 |
| 9.5 | 0.58 | 1.8 | 0.05 | 4.0 | 0.1 | 0.63 | 3.85 | 2.98 | 83.0 | 4.6 | 29.7 | 1.1 | 7.4 |
| 8.2 | 1.13 | 3.6 | 0.29 | 9.5 | 0.6 | 1.47 | 9.01 | 3.46 | 58.1 | 3.3 | 8.7 | 10.8 | 8.0 |
| 6.8 | 1.11 | 4.9 | 0.54 | 0.3 | 0.0 | -0.30 | -3.41 | 3.16 | 101.5 | 5.5 | 31.1 | 0.0 | 3.1 |
| 5.4 | 1.30 | 12.2 | 0.68 | 4.7 | 1.6 | 0.55 | 5.64 | 3.25 | 76.7 | 2.7 | 10.2 | 9.6 | 6.8 |
| 3.5 | 2.84 | 23.0 | 0.06 | 2.7 | 0.1 | 0.19 | 2.40 | 3.62 | 97.1 | 3.6 | 12.8 | 6.5 | 3.1 |
| 8.8 | 1.46 | 3.8 | 0.35 | 5.3 | 0.5 | 0.95 | 6.00 | 3.13 | 70.5 | 4.6 | 22.7 | 0.0 | 7.3 |
| 10.0 | 0.07 | 0.1 | 0.00 | 3.1 | 0.0 | 0.41 | 1.81 | 3.26 | 84.6 | 5.8 | 39.1 | 0.0 | 5.5 |
| 9.2 | 3.21 | 4.2 | 0.00 | 1.4 | 0.0 | 0.15 | 1.08 | 2.67 | 91.9 | 5.1 | 27.3 | 0.0 | 5.1 |
| 7.1 | 0.81 | 1.6 | 0.00 | 4.6 | 0.0 | 0.83 | 7.23 | 2.51 | 56.8 | 6.2 | 26.3 | 0.0 | 3.7 |
| 5.9 | 1.58 | 11.7 | 0.61 | 2.8 | 0.0 | 0.16 | 1.86 | 3.77 | 93.2 | 4.6 | 20.1 | 4.7 | 2.3 |
| 7.8 | 0.40 | 3.8 | 0.50 | 1.7 | -0.1 | -0.10 | -0.85 | 3.59 | 94.4 | 3.3 | 12.9 | 4.3 | 7.0 |
| 9.9 | 1.34 | 2.3 | 0.95 | 6.3 | 0.1 | 1.17 | 8.93 | 4.26 | 79.6 | 5.3 | 16.6 | 3.7 | 6.4 |

| Name | City | State | Rating | 2014 Rating | 2013 Rating | Total Assets ($Mil) | One Year Asset Growth | Commercial Loans | Consumer Loans | Mortgage Loans | Securities | Capitalization Index | Net Worth Ratio |
|---|---|---|---|---|---|---|---|---|---|---|---|---|---|
| BCBST EMPL CU | Chattanooga | TN | B- | C+ | C+ | 10.0 | -0.20 | 0.0 | 27.0 | 14.8 | 0.0 | 10.0 | 19.0 |
| ▲ BCM FCU | Houston | TX | D | D- | D | 36.4 | -1.01 | 0.3 | 28.7 | 9.2 | 3.3 | 5.0 | 7.0 |
| ▼ BCS COMMUNITY CU | Wheat Ridge | CO | C+ | B- | B- | 25.6 | 4.62 | 0.0 | 34.7 | 13.0 | 0.0 | 10.0 | 17.2 |
| BEA CU | Bethalto | IL | C- | D+ | D+ | 3.7 | 3.06 | 0.0 | 80.5 | 0.0 | 0.0 | 10.0 | 14.4 |
| BEACH MUNICIPAL FCU | Virginia Beach | VA | B | B | B+ | 110.0 | -0.45 | 0.2 | 33.4 | 7.5 | 11.4 | 10.0 | 12.2 |
| BEACON COMMUNITY CU | Louisville | KY | B+ | B+ | B+ | 55.6 | 6.25 | 0.2 | 23.9 | 9.8 | 41.2 | 10.0 | 11.5 |
| BEACON CU | Wabash | IN | B | B | B | 1152.7 | 11.13 | 62.4 | 1.8 | 54.7 | 15.8 | 10.0 | 14.1 |
| ▲ BEACON CU INC | Lynchburg | VA | B- | B- | B | 158.3 | 24.45 | 2.8 | 67.8 | 3.8 | 0.0 | 6.5 | 8.6 |
| BEACON FCU | La Porte | TX | B- | C+ | C+ | 141.8 | 4.19 | 0.0 | 45.1 | 7.9 | 14.0 | 6.3 | 8.3 |
| BEACON MUTUAL FCU | Lima | OH | D | D- | D- | 12.5 | -0.95 | 0.0 | 34.8 | 0.0 | 46.7 | 6.6 | 8.6 |
| BEAR PAW CU | Havre | MT | C+ | C+ | B- | 113.4 | 10.32 | 1.0 | 25.8 | 19.2 | 0.0 | 6.3 | 8.3 |
| ▲ BEAUMONT COMMUNITY CU | Beaumont | TX | C | C+ | C+ | 26.7 | 0.78 | 0.0 | 33.1 | 0.0 | 0.0 | 10.0 | 11.6 |
| BEAUREGARD SCHOOL EMPL FCU | Deridder | LA | C+ | C+ | C+ | 21.1 | 2.53 | 0.0 | 52.6 | 0.0 | 3.1 | 10.0 | 12.7 |
| BEAVER AVENUE FCU | Pittsburgh | PA | E+ | E+ | E+ | 4.8 | -1.11 | 0.0 | 87.8 | 0.0 | 0.0 | 6.2 | 8.2 |
| BEAVER COUNTY TIMES FCU | Beaver | PA | C- | C- | D+ | <1 | -14.92 | 0.0 | 49.0 | 0.0 | 0.0 | 10.0 | 54.9 |
| BEAVER FALLS PENNSYLVANIA TEACHERS F | Wampum | PA | C | C | C | 2.5 | -4.39 | 0.0 | 64.0 | 0.0 | 0.0 | 10.0 | 17.1 |
| BEAVER VALLEY FCU | Beaver Falls | PA | C | C | C+ | 69.3 | 1.38 | 0.6 | 15.8 | 12.9 | 0.0 | 10.0 | 17.2 |
| BECCO BUFFALO FCU | Tonawanda | NY | C- | C- | C | 1.7 | 10.67 | 0.0 | 19.5 | 0.0 | 25.0 | 10.0 | 12.0 |
| BECKSTRAND & ASSOCIATES CU | Salt Lake City | UT | C+ | C+ | B- | <1 | -17.00 | 2.8 | 0.0 | 0.0 | 0.0 | 10.0 | 52.8 |
| BEDCO HOSPITAL FCU | Everett | PA | C- | C- | C | 2.2 | 6.20 | 0.0 | 66.3 | 0.0 | 0.0 | 10.0 | 14.4 |
| BEDFORD VA FCU | Bedford | MA | C | C | C | 3.2 | -3.49 | 0.0 | 42.9 | 0.0 | 0.0 | 10.0 | 24.3 |
| BEE FCU | Salisbury | MD | C | C- | C | 7.4 | -0.84 | 0.0 | 24.8 | 0.0 | 0.0 | 10.0 | 21.1 |
| BEECH ISLAND CU | Beech Island | SC | D | D | C- | 6.2 | -2.35 | 0.0 | 39.1 | 0.0 | 0.0 | 10.0 | 13.7 |
| BEEHIVE FCU | Rexburg | ID | A | A | A- | 201.6 | 6.04 | 0.2 | 33.8 | 27.9 | 7.2 | 10.0 | 11.6 |
| BEKA FCU | Rome | GA | D | D | D+ | 7.7 | 0.63 | 0.0 | 56.5 | 0.0 | 0.0 | 10.0 | 12.3 |
| BELCO COMMUNITY CU | Harrisburg | PA | C+ | B- | B- | 432.9 | 5.77 | 7.9 | 33.8 | 8.4 | 12.0 | 7.6 | 9.4 |
| ▲ BELEN RAILWAY EMPL CU | Belen | NM | B | C+ | C+ | 27.8 | 19.84 | 2.8 | 25.8 | 24.4 | 0.0 | 10.0 | 12.2 |
| BELL CU | Hutchinson | KS | C- | C | C+ | 11.6 | -1.26 | 1.2 | 45.4 | 1.6 | 2.2 | 10.0 | 13.1 |
| BELLCO CU | Greenwood Village | CO | A | A | A | 3415.4 | 18.06 | 8.8 | 33.0 | 25.9 | 3.1 | 8.6 | 10.0 |
| ▲ BELLCO FCU | Wyomissing | PA | E+ | E+ | E+ | 106.6 | -1.72 | 3.0 | 24.8 | 6.0 | 19.3 | 8.1 | 9.7 |
| ▲ BELLE RIVER COMMUNITY CU | Casco | MI | C- | D+ | D | 20.3 | -4.81 | 0.0 | 10.9 | 14.9 | 0.0 | 6.8 | 8.8 |
| ▲ BELLWETHER COMMUNITY CU | Manchester | NH | C | C | C | 417.0 | 4.95 | 2.3 | 34.1 | 27.2 | 15.8 | 10.0 | 11.1 |
| BELMONT MUNICIPAL FCU | Belmont | MA | C+ | C+ | C+ | 3.5 | -2.60 | 0.0 | 32.3 | 0.0 | 0.0 | 10.0 | 15.0 |
| BELTON FCU | Belton | TX | D | D+ | D+ | 4.3 | -0.14 | 0.0 | 28.1 | 0.0 | 9.4 | 10.0 | 11.8 |
| BELVOIR FCU | Woodbridge | VA | C+ | B- | B- | 321.0 | 1.14 | 3.5 | 41.8 | 22.2 | 12.6 | 6.3 | 8.4 |
| BEN E KEITH EMPL FCU | Fort Worth | TX | C+ | C+ | B- | 9.0 | 6.41 | 0.0 | 49.4 | 0.0 | 0.0 | 10.0 | 14.3 |
| ▼ BENCHMARK FCU | West Chester | PA | C | B- | B | 227.2 | -2.43 | 0.0 | 13.0 | 29.8 | 36.6 | 10.0 | 13.7 |
| BENT RIVER COMMUNITY CU | Davenport | IA | D | D+ | C | 22.8 | -0.16 | 8.0 | 24.2 | 27.6 | 15.2 | 9.9 | 10.9 |
| BENTON COUNTY SCHOOLS CU | Corvallis | OR | C- | C- | D+ | 46.0 | 8.50 | 0.0 | 10.1 | 32.9 | 3.6 | 5.9 | 7.9 |
| BEREA CU | Berea | KY | D+ | D+ | D+ | 1.3 | 1.91 | 0.0 | 57.3 | 0.0 | 0.0 | 10.0 | 12.0 |
| ▲ BEREA FCU | Brooklyn | NY | C+ | C | C+ | <1 | -23.73 | 0.0 | 15.6 | 0.0 | 15.6 | 10.0 | 12.6 |
| BEREAN CU | Chicago | IL | C- | C | C+ | <1 | 8.51 | 0.0 | 10.8 | 0.0 | 0.0 | 10.0 | 20.6 |
| BERGEN DIVISION FCU | Toms River | NJ | C+ | C+ | C+ | 8.7 | 6.91 | 0.0 | 54.7 | 0.0 | 0.0 | 10.0 | 17.9 |
| BERGEN FCU | Wanaque | NJ | D | D | C- | 2.8 | 2.76 | 0.0 | 9.4 | 0.0 | 69.5 | 10.0 | 16.7 |
| BERKELEY COMMUNITY FCU | Moncks Corner | SC | C | C- | C | 10.6 | 8.36 | 0.0 | 48.7 | 1.2 | 0.0 | 10.0 | 16.3 |
| BERKELEY COUNTY PUBLIC SCHOOLS FCU | Martinsburg | WV | E+ | E+ | E+ | 4.8 | 6.33 | 0.0 | 44.3 | 0.0 | 0.0 | 4.0 | 6.0 |
| BERRIEN TEACHERS FCU | Nashville | GA | C | C- | D+ | 1.3 | 0.24 | 0.0 | 49.3 | 0.0 | 0.0 | 10.0 | 14.1 |
| ▲ BERYLCO EMPL CU | Hamburg | PA | C- | D+ | C- | 2.7 | -14.51 | 0.0 | 13.0 | 0.0 | 0.0 | 10.0 | 37.6 |
| BESSEMER SYSTEM FCU | Greenville | PA | C | B- | B- | 39.3 | 0.68 | 0.0 | 24.4 | 9.2 | 0.3 | 10.0 | 14.1 |
| BESSER CU | Alpena | MI | B- | C+ | B- | 67.2 | 1.05 | 0.6 | 17.1 | 18.4 | 28.4 | 8.7 | 10.2 |
| BEST FINANCIAL CU | Muskegon | MI | A | A | A | 77.7 | -0.88 | 0.0 | 26.5 | 14.4 | 3.0 | 10.0 | 21.5 |
| BEST REWARD CU | Brook Park | OH | C- | C- | C | 151.9 | 22.56 | 0.6 | 11.6 | 3.1 | 47.6 | 10.0 | 12.5 |
| BETHANY BAPTIST CHRISTIAN FCU | Chester | PA | D+ | D | D | <1 | -2.60 | 0.0 | 0.0 | 0.0 | 0.0 | 10.0 | 20.0 |
| BETHEL AME CHURCH CU | Chicago | IL | D+ | D+ | C- | <1 | -4.23 | 0.0 | 0.0 | 0.0 | 0.0 | 10.0 | 14.7 |
| BETHEL BAPTIST CHURCH EAST CU | Detroit | MI | C- | C | C | <1 | 2.30 | 0.0 | 16.9 | 0.0 | 0.0 | 10.0 | 12.7 |
| ▼ BETHEX FCU | Bronx | NY | F | D+ | C+ | 12.2 | -25.97 | 20.4 | 16.9 | 26.6 | 26.6 | 3.6 | 5.6 |
| ▲ BETHLEHEM 1ST FCU | Bethlehem | PA | C- | D+ | D | 47.3 | -0.40 | 0.6 | 10.9 | 7.2 | 54.3 | 10.0 | 11.0 |
| BETHPAGE FCU | Bethpage | NY | B | B | B | 6186.9 | 7.67 | 12.2 | 6.8 | 39.7 | 34.4 | 6.4 | 8.4 |
| BEULAH FCU | Brooklyn | NY | C | C+ | B- | <1 | 4.05 | 0.0 | 9.4 | 0.0 | 0.0 | 6.3 | 8.3 |
| BEVERLY BUS GARAGE FCU | Evergreen Park | IL | C | C | C+ | 3.8 | 3.02 | 0.0 | 82.0 | 0.0 | 0.0 | 10.0 | 40.0 |

| Asset Quality Index | Non-Performing Loans as a % of Total Loans | Non-Performing Loans as a % of Capital | Net Charge-Offs Avg Loans | Profitability Index | Net Income ($Mil) | Return on Assets | Return on Equity | Net Interest Spread | Overhead Efficiency Ratio | Liquidity Index | Liquidity Ratio | Hot Money Ratio | Stability Index |
|---|---|---|---|---|---|---|---|---|---|---|---|---|---|
| 10.0 | 0.45 | 1.0 | 0.55 | 4.5 | 0.1 | 0.66 | 3.63 | 3.61 | 82.6 | 5.6 | 46.6 | 0.0 | 7.1 |
| 6.8 | 0.53 | 4.7 | 0.50 | 3.0 | 0.1 | 0.47 | 6.96 | 2.94 | 85.0 | 5.5 | 57.1 | 0.0 | 1.5 |
| 9.2 | 0.95 | 2.7 | 1.72 | 2.2 | -0.1 | -0.37 | -2.09 | 5.07 | 93.8 | 5.1 | 36.4 | 9.3 | 7.0 |
| 4.0 | 3.33 | 16.4 | 0.00 | 7.8 | 0.1 | 2.26 | 16.37 | 3.82 | 52.4 | 3.7 | 12.2 | 0.0 | 3.7 |
| 8.0 | 1.09 | 5.1 | 0.41 | 3.5 | 0.2 | 0.29 | 2.57 | 3.82 | 85.8 | 4.6 | 15.3 | 2.9 | 6.7 |
| 10.0 | 0.29 | 1.0 | 0.30 | 4.4 | 0.2 | 0.43 | 3.69 | 3.46 | 90.0 | 4.4 | 14.2 | 7.8 | 6.1 |
| 5.8 | 0.85 | 5.5 | 0.09 | 4.2 | 4.6 | 0.58 | 4.01 | 2.76 | 79.2 | 2.3 | 12.4 | 17.2 | 9.1 |
| 5.6 | 0.74 | 6.7 | 0.71 | 5.2 | 0.7 | 0.65 | 7.23 | 5.98 | 82.9 | 2.1 | 14.9 | 25.8 | 5.1 |
| 8.5 | 0.30 | 2.2 | 0.43 | 3.5 | 0.3 | 0.31 | 3.81 | 3.70 | 88.9 | 3.8 | 9.5 | 5.0 | 5.1 |
| 7.1 | 2.46 | 11.4 | 0.03 | 2.0 | 0.0 | 0.25 | 2.96 | 3.15 | 88.1 | 4.4 | 12.6 | 1.0 | 3.1 |
| 9.8 | 0.17 | 1.0 | 0.27 | 2.9 | 0.2 | 0.22 | 2.45 | 3.19 | 91.6 | 5.5 | 37.3 | 6.4 | 5.1 |
| 8.8 | 1.49 | 5.0 | 0.57 | 2.1 | 0.0 | 0.06 | 0.52 | 1.75 | 92.7 | 4.1 | 59.9 | 17.4 | 6.0 |
| 5.4 | 1.72 | 8.6 | 0.14 | 4.3 | 0.1 | 0.53 | 4.26 | 2.05 | 69.1 | 4.0 | 14.2 | 0.0 | 6.8 |
| 0.7 | 3.53 | 47.3 | 1.53 | 3.8 | 0.0 | 0.08 | 1.01 | 5.37 | 62.1 | 3.1 | 5.8 | 0.0 | 3.6 |
| 8.6 | 1.30 | 1.2 | 0.97 | 1.6 | 0.0 | 0.00 | 0.00 | 3.97 | 87.5 | 5.1 | 28.1 | 0.0 | 6.5 |
| 7.6 | 1.15 | 4.4 | 0.00 | 4.1 | 0.0 | 0.21 | 1.26 | 4.17 | 94.6 | 4.1 | 26.7 | 0.0 | 8.0 |
| 10.0 | 0.44 | 1.0 | 0.17 | 2.0 | 0.0 | 0.06 | 0.40 | 4.04 | 97.9 | 7.5 | 70.5 | 1.4 | 6.5 |
| 9.4 | 0.00 | 0.0 | 0.00 | 2.2 | 0.0 | 0.25 | 2.00 | 2.69 | 87.0 | 6.8 | 37.5 | 0.0 | 5.2 |
| 10.0 | 0.00 | 0.0 | 0.00 | 3.3 | 0.0 | 0.42 | 0.88 | 3.51 | 50.0 | 9.3 | 169.1 | 0.0 | 7.8 |
| 4.4 | 3.46 | 14.5 | 0.09 | 3.3 | 0.0 | 0.32 | 2.16 | 8.51 | 92.2 | 6.0 | 44.6 | 0.0 | 5.8 |
| 9.9 | 0.15 | 0.3 | 1.32 | 2.5 | 0.0 | 0.16 | 0.69 | 5.22 | 79.6 | 5.9 | 48.9 | 0.0 | 6.8 |
| 8.4 | 3.03 | 3.5 | 1.76 | 4.1 | 0.0 | 0.66 | 3.21 | 3.04 | 72.2 | 5.1 | 35.5 | 0.0 | 5.3 |
| 8.8 | 0.21 | 0.7 | 0.32 | 0.0 | -0.1 | -1.49 | -10.45 | 3.87 | 135.8 | 5.9 | 48.6 | 0.0 | 6.3 |
| 8.8 | 0.37 | 3.4 | 0.21 | 5.9 | 1.1 | 0.74 | 6.50 | 3.08 | 79.6 | 3.4 | 17.2 | 5.7 | 7.9 |
| 3.1 | 2.59 | 14.7 | 1.87 | 1.1 | 0.0 | -0.36 | -2.83 | 5.15 | 74.4 | 3.6 | 26.3 | 12.0 | 5.1 |
| 6.3 | 1.12 | 9.0 | 0.69 | 3.8 | 1.2 | 0.37 | 4.20 | 4.21 | 81.4 | 3.3 | 4.3 | 4.9 | 5.5 |
| 7.4 | 1.38 | 6.1 | 0.08 | 6.1 | 0.2 | 0.93 | 7.44 | 3.94 | 73.5 | 4.0 | 24.4 | 10.2 | 6.4 |
| 7.3 | 1.21 | 5.7 | 0.06 | 1.0 | 0.0 | -0.23 | -1.74 | 3.30 | 104.0 | 3.3 | 16.3 | 9.8 | 6.5 |
| 7.4 | 0.68 | 4.8 | 0.41 | 9.2 | 33.0 | 1.44 | 13.45 | 4.29 | 61.4 | 4.3 | 29.8 | 14.5 | 8.5 |
| 7.8 | 0.97 | 5.6 | 0.50 | 0.4 | -0.2 | -0.19 | -2.00 | 3.34 | 94.0 | 3.8 | 8.3 | 2.7 | 5.6 |
| 9.1 | 0.70 | 2.2 | 0.00 | 3.0 | 0.1 | 0.32 | 3.84 | 1.97 | 85.7 | 5.3 | 43.1 | 3.5 | 4.1 |
| 9.8 | 0.16 | 1.1 | 0.33 | 2.3 | 0.8 | 0.25 | 2.29 | 3.01 | 86.0 | 2.5 | 3.7 | 11.9 | 7.2 |
| 10.0 | 0.10 | 0.4 | -0.14 | 6.9 | 0.0 | 1.02 | 7.16 | 5.09 | 71.6 | 6.2 | 53.6 | 0.0 | 5.7 |
| 9.8 | 0.91 | 2.4 | 0.29 | 0.0 | 0.0 | -0.59 | -4.98 | 2.82 | 115.5 | 5.9 | 45.1 | 0.0 | 5.3 |
| 6.7 | 1.02 | 9.0 | 0.36 | 3.4 | 0.8 | 0.33 | 3.98 | 3.52 | 86.9 | 3.3 | 6.8 | 5.4 | 4.8 |
| 8.6 | 0.45 | 1.6 | 0.09 | 5.9 | 0.1 | 0.91 | 6.23 | 3.76 | 74.5 | 5.5 | 44.7 | 0.0 | 5.0 |
| 9.1 | 0.34 | 2.8 | 0.27 | 1.8 | -0.1 | -0.08 | -0.59 | 2.68 | 101.3 | 3.7 | 19.2 | 7.2 | 7.6 |
| 7.5 | 0.38 | 2.1 | 0.75 | 1.1 | 0.0 | -0.06 | -0.59 | 3.47 | 96.9 | 3.8 | 17.0 | 2.9 | 5.5 |
| 10.0 | 0.00 | 0.0 | 0.04 | 2.8 | 0.1 | 0.31 | 3.86 | 2.49 | 88.6 | 4.9 | 30.7 | 1.5 | 3.5 |
| 2.7 | 3.78 | 22.2 | 0.90 | 2.4 | 0.0 | 0.11 | 0.87 | 7.30 | 96.0 | 6.2 | 46.5 | 0.0 | 5.1 |
| 10.0 | 0.00 | 0.0 | 0.00 | 7.3 | 0.0 | 1.63 | 16.67 | 3.70 | 66.7 | 8.1 | 77.3 | 0.0 | 5.7 |
| 9.4 | 0.00 | 0.0 | 12.12 | 1.5 | 0.0 | 0.00 | 0.00 | 1.78 | 100.0 | 7.2 | 58.0 | 0.0 | 5.4 |
| 6.2 | 1.71 | 4.8 | 2.81 | 7.9 | 0.1 | 1.07 | 5.80 | 5.64 | 48.7 | 5.1 | 55.3 | 0.0 | 5.0 |
| 10.0 | 0.00 | 0.0 | 0.00 | 0.2 | 0.0 | -0.20 | -1.16 | 2.37 | 102.3 | 5.7 | 32.1 | 0.0 | 5.6 |
| 5.8 | 2.00 | 7.8 | 0.17 | 3.1 | 0.0 | 0.28 | 1.63 | 5.87 | 91.7 | 6.1 | 52.1 | 3.2 | 6.7 |
| 7.8 | 0.42 | 3.1 | 0.06 | 3.4 | 0.0 | 0.54 | 9.56 | 3.08 | 87.0 | 5.4 | 28.4 | 0.0 | 1.0 |
| 8.3 | 0.94 | 3.2 | 0.00 | 3.6 | 0.0 | 0.53 | 3.83 | 4.24 | 86.1 | 5.7 | 55.6 | 0.0 | 6.0 |
| 10.0 | 0.00 | 0.0 | 0.00 | 1.4 | 0.0 | 0.05 | 0.13 | 1.73 | 97.0 | 5.7 | 36.8 | 0.0 | 6.1 |
| 10.0 | 0.28 | 0.7 | 0.47 | 1.6 | 0.0 | -0.05 | -0.34 | 2.24 | 92.3 | 4.4 | 23.7 | 7.9 | 7.0 |
| 7.7 | 0.62 | 3.3 | 0.04 | 4.4 | 0.3 | 0.67 | 6.70 | 3.06 | 81.1 | 5.5 | 27.5 | 0.0 | 4.7 |
| 9.8 | 0.39 | 1.5 | 0.24 | 7.8 | 0.6 | 1.02 | 4.92 | 3.54 | 80.2 | 4.7 | 23.2 | 1.6 | 8.3 |
| 8.1 | 1.78 | 4.4 | 0.59 | 0.9 | -0.2 | -0.17 | -1.12 | 2.51 | 101.1 | 6.3 | 42.6 | 0.8 | 6.1 |
| 3.1 | 45.45 | 27.8 | 0.00 | 0.9 | 0.0 | 0.00 | 0.00 | 2.84 | 100.0 | 8.2 | 110.0 | 0.0 | 6.5 |
| 10.0 | 0.00 | 0.0 | 0.00 | 1.2 | 0.0 | 0.00 | 0.00 | 0.00 | 100.0 | 5.8 | 12.1 | 0.0 | 6.5 |
| 8.0 | 3.68 | 6.3 | 0.00 | 2.5 | 0.0 | 0.22 | 1.73 | 2.26 | 88.9 | 6.9 | 69.1 | 0.0 | 5.4 |
| 0.3 | 13.54 | 120.0 | 13.22 | 0.0 | -0.9 | -7.98 | -319.62 | 4.58 | 117.0 | 4.6 | 22.3 | 4.1 | 2.9 |
| 7.8 | 0.28 | 3.8 | 1.11 | 2.1 | 0.1 | 0.16 | 1.50 | 2.80 | 86.0 | 4.8 | 15.7 | 1.7 | 4.5 |
| 7.0 | 0.96 | 8.0 | 0.20 | 4.3 | 28.6 | 0.63 | 7.50 | 2.17 | 73.5 | 2.7 | 16.2 | 15.3 | 7.1 |
| 10.0 | 0.00 | 0.0 | 50.79 | 2.7 | 0.0 | 0.00 | 0.00 | 2.47 | 100.0 | 8.1 | 93.9 | 0.0 | 4.8 |
| 4.5 | 4.90 | 9.6 | 2.41 | 7.9 | 0.0 | 1.18 | 2.89 | 12.79 | 56.1 | 3.2 | 23.6 | 0.0 | 4.3 |

| Name | City | State | Rating | 2014 Rating | 2013 Rating | Total Assets ($Mil) | One Year Asset Growth | Asset Mix (As a % of Total Assets) | | | | Capital-ization Index | Net Worth Ratio |
|---|---|---|---|---|---|---|---|---|---|---|---|---|---|
| | | | | | | | | Comm-ercial Loans | Cons-umer Loans | Mort-gage Loans | Secur-ities | | |
| BEVERLY HILLS CITY EMPL FCU | Beverly Hills | CA | B- | B- | B- | 20.3 | 0.57 | 0.0 | 22.8 | 3.2 | 11.8 | 10.0 | 11.8 |
| BEVERLY MUNICIPAL FCU | Beverly | MA | C- | C- | D+ | 10.8 | 2.04 | 0.0 | 27.7 | 15.4 | 0.0 | 10.0 | 18.1 |
| BFG FCU | Akron | OH | D | D | D | 150.2 | -3.29 | 0.3 | 36.6 | 12.2 | 27.1 | 10.0 | 11.2 |
| BHCU | Ridley Park | PA | B+ | B+ | A | 126.8 | 0.47 | 0.6 | 12.8 | 25.5 | 44.2 | 10.0 | 17.0 |
| BI-COUNTY PTC FCU | Warren | MI | D+ | D+ | D+ | 8.4 | 0.08 | 0.0 | 39.6 | 4.1 | 28.4 | 9.1 | 10.4 |
| ▲ BIG BETHEL AME CHURCH FCU | Atlanta | GA | D | E+ | D | <1 | -9.00 | 0.0 | 8.1 | 0.0 | 0.0 | 7.3 | 9.2 |
| BIG ISLAND FCU | Hilo | HI | C+ | C+ | C | 86.1 | 6.26 | 1.0 | 25.6 | 14.7 | 6.1 | 6.9 | 8.9 |
| BIG SKY FCU | Billings | MT | C- | D+ | C- | 7.8 | -4.84 | 0.0 | 28.8 | 0.0 | 0.0 | 9.5 | 10.7 |
| BIG SPRING EDUCATION EMPL FCU | Big Spring | TX | B | B | B | 45.0 | 0.91 | 0.0 | 32.2 | 0.1 | 0.0 | 10.0 | 13.0 |
| BILLERICA MUNICIPAL EMPL CU | Billerica | MA | D+ | D+ | C | 13.9 | 3.05 | 0.0 | 13.6 | 6.4 | 0.0 | 10.0 | 22.1 |
| BILLINGS FCU | Billings | MT | A | A | A | 126.2 | 11.59 | 2.2 | 34.3 | 28.6 | 0.0 | 10.0 | 11.9 |
| BILOXI TEACHERS FCU | Biloxi | MS | D+ | D | D- | 9.4 | -1.08 | 0.0 | 26.2 | 0.0 | 0.0 | 8.9 | 10.3 |
| BINSY FCU | Memphis | TN | D+ | D | D | 1.6 | 5.89 | 0.0 | 59.3 | 0.0 | 0.0 | 10.0 | 17.8 |
| BIP FCU | Lenoir | NC | D+ | D+ | D+ | 4.3 | -3.03 | 0.0 | 48.0 | 5.7 | 0.0 | 10.0 | 13.5 |
| ▲ BIRMINGHAM-BLOOMFIELD CU | Birmingham | MI | C+ | C | C | 58.7 | 1.75 | 2.4 | 14.3 | 20.0 | 0.3 | 6.0 | 8.0 |
| BISON FCU | Shawnee | OK | C | C | C- | 35.4 | 1.93 | 0.3 | 14.7 | 0.0 | 31.5 | 7.0 | 9.0 |
| BITTERROOT COMMUNITY FCU | Darby | MT | D+ | D+ | D+ | 8.7 | 12.87 | 0.0 | 30.2 | 0.0 | 0.0 | 7.2 | 9.1 |
| BIVINS FCU | Masterson | TX | D+ | D+ | D+ | 7.7 | -5.27 | 0.0 | 47.7 | 0.0 | 0.0 | 10.0 | 12.8 |
| BLACK HILLS FCU | Rapid City | SD | A- | A- | B+ | 1052.3 | 4.67 | 7.7 | 15.4 | 30.2 | 15.1 | 10.0 | 11.5 |
| BLACKHAWK AREA CU | Savanna | IL | D+ | D | C- | 33.2 | -0.26 | 0.0 | 23.9 | 33.0 | 0.0 | 6.8 | 8.8 |
| ▲ BLACKHAWK COMMUNITY CU | Janesville | WI | B | C+ | C- | 416.0 | 4.93 | 7.4 | 25.8 | 32.8 | 14.6 | 6.6 | 8.6 |
| BLACKHAWK FCU | Beaver Falls | PA | C+ | C+ | C+ | 14.9 | -1.87 | 0.0 | 20.3 | 0.2 | 3.8 | 10.0 | 11.4 |
| ▲ BLACKSTONE RIVER FCU | Woonsocket | RI | C+ | C- | C- | 49.7 | 6.66 | 0.0 | 21.7 | 4.9 | 3.5 | 6.2 | 8.2 |
| ▲ BLAIR COUNTY FCU | Altoona | PA | C+ | C+ | C+ | 50.3 | 4.69 | 0.0 | 16.6 | 5.6 | 5.4 | 10.0 | 17.7 |
| BLAW-KNOX CU | Mattoon | IL | C | C- | C+ | 10.0 | 5.43 | 0.0 | 46.1 | 0.0 | 0.0 | 10.0 | 15.4 |
| ▼ BLOOMFIELD FIRE & POLICE FCU | Bloomfield | NJ | D+ | C- | C- | 6.6 | -4.01 | 0.0 | 57.0 | 0.0 | 0.0 | 10.0 | 15.1 |
| BLOOMINGTON MUNICIPAL CU | Bloomington | IL | B- | B- | B- | 23.7 | 3.28 | 0.0 | 34.6 | 0.0 | 0.0 | 10.0 | 11.8 |
| BLOOMINGTON POSTAL EMPL CU | Bloomington | IL | B- | B- | B- | 21.0 | 0.56 | 0.0 | 36.1 | 0.0 | 0.0 | 10.0 | 14.7 |
| BLUCURRENT CU | Springfield | MO | B | B- | C+ | 155.0 | 4.73 | 11.7 | 38.2 | 25.1 | 0.0 | 7.2 | 9.1 |
| ▲ BLUE CHIP FCU | Harrisburg | PA | B | B- | B- | 28.9 | -2.05 | 0.0 | 35.1 | 8.5 | 2.3 | 10.0 | 13.3 |
| BLUE CROSS & BLUE SHIELD OF MAINE FCU | South Portland | ME | D+ | C- | C | 6.3 | -2.71 | 0.0 | 16.3 | 0.0 | 0.0 | 10.0 | 19.9 |
| BLUE CROSS BLUE SHIELD KANSAS CITY CU | Kansas City | MO | C- | C- | D+ | 5.5 | -1.55 | 0.0 | 29.0 | 0.0 | 0.0 | 10.0 | 13.1 |
| BLUE CROSS TEXAS FCU | Richardson | TX | B+ | B+ | B+ | 36.6 | -3.22 | 0.0 | 31.5 | 9.5 | 13.7 | 10.0 | 15.6 |
| BLUE EAGLE CU | Roanoke | VA | A- | A- | A- | 136.0 | 5.56 | 0.1 | 31.3 | 18.8 | 0.0 | 10.0 | 13.0 |
| BLUE FLAME CU | Mobile | AL | C- | C | C | 7.7 | 1.90 | 1.4 | 37.3 | 10.6 | 0.0 | 10.0 | 15.0 |
| BLUE FLAME CU | Charlotte | NC | B- | C+ | B- | 33.1 | -5.49 | 0.0 | 44.5 | 8.0 | 0.0 | 10.0 | 17.3 |
| BLUE MOUNTAIN CU | College Place | WA | B | B | B | 29.6 | 0.82 | 3.4 | 25.7 | 32.8 | 0.0 | 10.0 | 12.2 |
| BLUE WATER FCU | Port Huron | MI | B- | B- | B | 13.5 | 4.03 | 0.0 | 23.7 | 6.1 | 5.6 | 10.0 | 18.5 |
| ▼ BLUEGRASS COMMUNITY FCU | Ashland | KY | D- | D | D- | 8.5 | -4.85 | 1.4 | 57.5 | 0.0 | 0.0 | 5.1 | 7.1 |
| BLUESCOPE EMPL CU | Kansas City | MO | D | D | D+ | 1.6 | -8.26 | 0.0 | 93.7 | 0.0 | 0.0 | 9.1 | 10.4 |
| BLUESTEM COMMUNITY CU | El Dorado | KS | D+ | C- | C- | 11.2 | 5.86 | 0.0 | 29.2 | 0.0 | 5.2 | 7.1 | 9.1 |
| BLUFFTON MOTOR WORKS/FRANKLIN ELEC | Bluffton | IN | C | C- | D+ | 1.6 | -3.17 | 0.0 | 17.0 | 0.0 | 0.0 | 10.0 | 15.5 |
| BMH FCU | Cleveland | TN | D+ | D | D+ | 3.0 | -2.32 | 0.0 | 37.5 | 0.0 | 0.0 | 10.0 | 22.2 |
| BMI FCU | Dublin | OH | C+ | B- | C+ | 413.1 | 5.05 | 1.2 | 16.0 | 39.2 | 24.1 | 7.5 | 9.3 |
| BOARD OF WATER SUPPLY FCU | Honolulu | HI | D | D+ | C- | 15.6 | -8.70 | 0.0 | 16.7 | 12.0 | 33.6 | 10.0 | 19.5 |
| BOEING EMPL CU | Tukwila | WA | A | A | A- | 13878.3 | 9.15 | 3.9 | 21.3 | 27.4 | 25.3 | 9.6 | 10.7 |
| ▼ BOISE FIRE DEPT CU | Boise | ID | C- | C | C- | 8.3 | -4.08 | 0.0 | 74.7 | 0.0 | 0.0 | 10.0 | 12.6 |
| BOISE SOUTHERN EMPL FCU | Deridder | LA | B+ | A- | A- | 36.8 | 2.83 | 0.0 | 35.2 | 0.0 | 47.8 | 10.0 | 15.4 |
| ▲ BOND COMMUNITY FCU | Atlanta | GA | C- | D+ | C- | 39.7 | -2.17 | 3.9 | 10.3 | 28.8 | 0.0 | 7.0 | 9.0 |
| BOOTSTRAP FCU | New York | NY | D- | D- | D+ | <1 | -11.10 | 0.0 | 7.8 | 0.0 | 0.0 | 6.3 | 8.3 |
| BOPTI FCU | San Pedro | CA | A- | A- | A- | 66.6 | 5.48 | 0.0 | 24.3 | 5.3 | 29.2 | 10.0 | 15.7 |
| BORDER FCU | Del Rio | TX | A | A | A | 137.7 | 5.13 | 0.0 | 32.3 | 26.8 | 10.9 | 10.0 | 13.1 |
| BORGER FCU | Borger | TX | C+ | C+ | C+ | 17.4 | -4.87 | 0.0 | 44.2 | 0.0 | 0.0 | 10.0 | 11.8 |
| BORINQUEN COMMUNITY FCU | Aguadilla | PR | D- | D | D+ | 18.1 | 0.89 | 0.0 | 28.3 | 18.3 | 8.9 | 9.7 | 10.8 |
| ▲ BORINQUEN SUR FCU | Penuelas | PR | D+ | D | C- | 10.1 | -0.03 | 0.0 | 31.7 | 19.2 | 0.0 | 7.7 | 9.5 |
| BOSSIER FCU | Bossier City | LA | C | C+ | B- | 163.1 | 4.17 | 0.0 | 35.2 | 2.4 | 13.0 | 9.3 | 10.6 |
| BOSTON CUSTOMS FCU | Boston | MA | C- | C- | D- | 2.6 | -11.37 | 0.0 | 37.9 | 0.0 | 0.0 | 10.0 | 12.6 |
| BOSTON FIREFIGHTERS CU | Dorchester | MA | A- | A- | B+ | 226.2 | 11.08 | 1.8 | 17.1 | 43.0 | 9.8 | 10.0 | 11.6 |
| BOTHWELL HOSPITAL EMPL CU | Sedalia | MO | D- | D- | D- | 1.9 | -7.77 | 0.0 | 77.7 | 0.0 | 0.0 | 6.8 | 8.8 |
| BOULDER DAM CU | Boulder City | NV | A- | B+ | B- | 537.5 | 8.25 | 5.7 | 2.7 | 30.8 | 52.7 | 8.6 | 10.1 |

| Asset Quality Index | Non-Performing Loans as a % of Total Loans | as a % of Capital | Net Charge-Offs Avg Loans | Profitability Index | Net Income ($Mil) | Return on Assets | Return on Equity | Net Interest Spread | Overhead Efficiency Ratio | Liquidity Index | Liquidity Ratio | Hot Money Ratio | Stability Index |
|---|---|---|---|---|---|---|---|---|---|---|---|---|---|
| 8.8 | 1.57 | 4.2 | 0.76 | 4.6 | 0.1 | 0.71 | 5.95 | 3.31 | 80.8 | 4.3 | 24.2 | 6.7 | 5.7 |
| 8.3 | 2.15 | 5.4 | 0.82 | 1.7 | 0.0 | 0.00 | 0.00 | 3.57 | 93.3 | 4.5 | 19.0 | 1.4 | 6.3 |
| 8.7 | 0.44 | 3.6 | 0.33 | 0.7 | -0.1 | -0.07 | -0.80 | 3.00 | 99.7 | 4.3 | 25.5 | 2.0 | 4.3 |
| 9.4 | 0.38 | 1.3 | 0.41 | 4.3 | 0.5 | 0.55 | 3.08 | 3.06 | 80.1 | 4.0 | 9.0 | 4.8 | 7.0 |
| 7.2 | 1.78 | 8.4 | 1.29 | 3.7 | 0.0 | 0.36 | 3.55 | 4.56 | 92.0 | 4.6 | 17.1 | 0.0 | 3.7 |
| 6.6 | 1.69 | 3.1 | 0.00 | 4.9 | 0.0 | 0.90 | 9.52 | 2.44 | 60.0 | 6.1 | 36.9 | 0.0 | 3.0 |
| 8.9 | 0.10 | 0.6 | 0.57 | 4.5 | 0.4 | 0.66 | 7.53 | 3.57 | 88.0 | 4.6 | 15.1 | 1.0 | 3.8 |
| 9.8 | 0.24 | 0.8 | 0.00 | 2.0 | 0.0 | 0.20 | 1.94 | 2.83 | 94.1 | 4.7 | 18.7 | 0.9 | 5.0 |
| 8.2 | 1.80 | 5.2 | 0.41 | 6.7 | 0.4 | 1.12 | 8.88 | 3.12 | 68.1 | 5.4 | 49.5 | 7.4 | 6.2 |
| 10.0 | 0.00 | 0.0 | -0.10 | 1.1 | 0.0 | -0.01 | -0.04 | 1.92 | 101.1 | 4.9 | 20.2 | 3.4 | 7.1 |
| 8.0 | 0.49 | 3.4 | 0.45 | 7.7 | 0.9 | 1.02 | 8.61 | 4.44 | 77.9 | 1.8 | 11.1 | 22.1 | 8.0 |
| 8.3 | 0.57 | 1.6 | -0.29 | 2.0 | 0.0 | 0.34 | 3.35 | 2.55 | 88.7 | 7.1 | 57.1 | 0.0 | 3.8 |
| 5.8 | 1.38 | 5.0 | 0.12 | 2.4 | 0.0 | 0.34 | 1.86 | 5.25 | 90.8 | 4.2 | 34.7 | 7.5 | 5.0 |
| 4.7 | 4.09 | 18.5 | 0.27 | 2.5 | 0.0 | 0.12 | 0.93 | 6.84 | 98.6 | 5.6 | 32.7 | 0.0 | 5.0 |
| 10.0 | 0.04 | 0.2 | 0.00 | 3.4 | 0.2 | 0.33 | 4.26 | 2.75 | 96.7 | 4.4 | 20.8 | 1.8 | 3.5 |
| 7.8 | 0.76 | 2.6 | 0.17 | 3.4 | 0.1 | 0.45 | 4.87 | 2.98 | 87.7 | 4.9 | 39.4 | 13.0 | 4.3 |
| 6.2 | 2.36 | 9.4 | 0.51 | 5.8 | 0.1 | 0.72 | 8.18 | 4.56 | 84.4 | 5.1 | 22.0 | 6.1 | 3.0 |
| 4.5 | 2.11 | 8.7 | 1.75 | 1.4 | 0.0 | -0.57 | -4.43 | 3.19 | 63.1 | 2.5 | 6.8 | 20.5 | 5.6 |
| 9.4 | 0.37 | 2.1 | 0.10 | 5.8 | 6.6 | 0.86 | 7.52 | 3.20 | 75.2 | 4.1 | 27.0 | 13.4 | 8.6 |
| 3.5 | 2.51 | 27.0 | 0.70 | 2.7 | 0.1 | 0.21 | 2.70 | 4.02 | 91.1 | 4.2 | 23.1 | 2.3 | 3.7 |
| 6.2 | 0.83 | 8.7 | 0.33 | 7.1 | 3.7 | 1.20 | 15.70 | 3.40 | 73.8 | 3.4 | 7.9 | 3.3 | 4.8 |
| 7.2 | 3.31 | 8.5 | 0.55 | 3.0 | 0.0 | 0.30 | 2.62 | 2.89 | 81.6 | 6.1 | 30.9 | 2.0 | 5.7 |
| 10.0 | 0.07 | 0.4 | 0.13 | 3.4 | 0.2 | 0.47 | 5.91 | 2.83 | 81.8 | 5.4 | 32.6 | 1.7 | 3.4 |
| 8.0 | 0.23 | 0.3 | 0.32 | 2.6 | 0.1 | 0.24 | 1.39 | 2.11 | 86.7 | 5.8 | 22.9 | 0.0 | 6.8 |
| 5.8 | 1.71 | 5.7 | 1.81 | 4.1 | 0.0 | 0.47 | 3.08 | 4.79 | 68.5 | 5.0 | 19.9 | 0.0 | 6.2 |
| 6.5 | 1.43 | 5.0 | 1.06 | 2.0 | 0.0 | -0.26 | -1.76 | 4.47 | 77.1 | 4.5 | 22.1 | 0.0 | 5.2 |
| 9.8 | 0.24 | 0.8 | -0.06 | 5.0 | 0.2 | 0.81 | 7.21 | 2.19 | 72.0 | 4.9 | 32.5 | 2.2 | 6.1 |
| 9.0 | 1.44 | 3.5 | 0.14 | 2.9 | 0.0 | 0.24 | 1.66 | 2.25 | 77.8 | 4.8 | 13.8 | 0.0 | 6.4 |
| 8.8 | 0.34 | 3.0 | 0.32 | 5.6 | 1.0 | 0.90 | 11.04 | 4.66 | 79.9 | 3.4 | 15.3 | 2.8 | 5.4 |
| 7.1 | 1.94 | 7.5 | 0.34 | 7.3 | 0.4 | 1.67 | 13.47 | 4.66 | 68.1 | 4.9 | 20.4 | 0.8 | 4.9 |
| 10.0 | 0.07 | 0.2 | 0.00 | 1.1 | 0.0 | -0.13 | -0.64 | 2.49 | 103.4 | 4.6 | 19.3 | 0.0 | 7.1 |
| 8.9 | 1.04 | 2.5 | 0.28 | 3.3 | 0.0 | 0.47 | 3.77 | 3.55 | 103.0 | 5.8 | 37.1 | 0.0 | 4.6 |
| 9.5 | 0.46 | 1.2 | 0.75 | 5.7 | 0.3 | 0.87 | 5.83 | 2.59 | 66.6 | 4.3 | 18.5 | 1.9 | 7.3 |
| 9.6 | 0.31 | 2.7 | 0.18 | 6.2 | 0.9 | 0.90 | 7.78 | 3.98 | 81.9 | 3.7 | 19.4 | 4.9 | 8.6 |
| 9.6 | 0.18 | 0.7 | 0.26 | 1.2 | 0.0 | -0.22 | -1.51 | 3.62 | 95.2 | 4.8 | 14.5 | 0.0 | 6.5 |
| 9.6 | 0.11 | 0.4 | 0.64 | 3.2 | 0.1 | 0.31 | 1.87 | 4.28 | 82.0 | 5.2 | 29.6 | 0.9 | 5.8 |
| 8.4 | 0.59 | 3.1 | 0.41 | 4.5 | 0.1 | 0.49 | 4.02 | 3.23 | 84.4 | 3.8 | 16.7 | 5.5 | 5.4 |
| 10.0 | 0.20 | 0.7 | -0.07 | 3.2 | 0.0 | 0.34 | 1.89 | 3.05 | 88.6 | 4.3 | 32.6 | 1.1 | 7.1 |
| 2.7 | 4.54 | 32.4 | 3.51 | 3.6 | 0.0 | 0.23 | 2.88 | 9.56 | 52.5 | 5.5 | 32.7 | 1.3 | 1.0 |
| 5.6 | 0.88 | 7.0 | -0.19 | 1.6 | 0.0 | 0.17 | 1.63 | 4.58 | 104.1 | 3.0 | 6.0 | 0.0 | 4.6 |
| 9.0 | 0.13 | 0.6 | 0.28 | 1.6 | 0.0 | -0.01 | -0.13 | 3.14 | 98.8 | 6.0 | 39.6 | 0.0 | 4.0 |
| 10.0 | 2.18 | 2.1 | 0.47 | 2.4 | 0.0 | 0.32 | 2.14 | 2.71 | 87.1 | 5.7 | 42.3 | 0.0 | 6.8 |
| 4.8 | 11.35 | 19.9 | 0.00 | 0.9 | 0.0 | -0.09 | -0.40 | 5.55 | 94.0 | 7.6 | 79.5 | 0.0 | 5.0 |
| 6.8 | 0.44 | 8.9 | 0.17 | 3.5 | 1.4 | 0.45 | 4.83 | 2.92 | 85.3 | 3.7 | 11.8 | 3.9 | 5.2 |
| 10.0 | 0.17 | 0.3 | 0.50 | 0.2 | -0.1 | -0.59 | -3.07 | 2.21 | 126.4 | 6.1 | 35.3 | 0.0 | 6.2 |
| 9.7 | 0.35 | 2.2 | 0.24 | 9.5 | 147.0 | 1.44 | 14.21 | 2.91 | 57.1 | 3.6 | 8.2 | 4.4 | 8.6 |
| 4.3 | 3.49 | 18.3 | 0.00 | 6.0 | 0.0 | 0.69 | 5.56 | 3.50 | 73.2 | 4.4 | 29.6 | 0.0 | 3.7 |
| 9.4 | 0.26 | 0.7 | 0.02 | 4.7 | 0.2 | 0.57 | 3.75 | 2.32 | 78.2 | 4.6 | 17.1 | 0.0 | 7.9 |
| 3.3 | 5.94 | 28.1 | 0.81 | 2.1 | 0.0 | -0.03 | -0.30 | 3.63 | 97.9 | 6.2 | 54.4 | 0.0 | 3.9 |
| 10.0 | 0.00 | 0.0 | 0.00 | 0.0 | 0.0 | -0.96 | -11.11 | 0.73 | 233.3 | 7.5 | 69.1 | 0.0 | 2.9 |
| 9.4 | 1.45 | 3.0 | 0.80 | 8.5 | 0.7 | 1.36 | 8.58 | 2.80 | 51.8 | 4.9 | 16.1 | 0.0 | 6.8 |
| 7.4 | 1.19 | 7.5 | 0.33 | 7.7 | 1.0 | 0.93 | 7.16 | 5.53 | 86.9 | 3.6 | 21.7 | 14.3 | 9.6 |
| 9.5 | 0.01 | 0.1 | 0.11 | 3.2 | 0.1 | 0.35 | 3.17 | 3.62 | 90.4 | 3.9 | 18.0 | 3.6 | 5.5 |
| 7.2 | 0.78 | 3.2 | 2.09 | 0.0 | -0.2 | -1.56 | -13.49 | 5.05 | 109.3 | 6.7 | 43.9 | 0.0 | 4.3 |
| 4.1 | 2.50 | 15.8 | 0.68 | 2.4 | 0.0 | 0.08 | 0.84 | 6.30 | 92.5 | 6.4 | 41.1 | 0.0 | 3.9 |
| 6.5 | 1.76 | 8.4 | 1.03 | 2.9 | 0.4 | 0.37 | 3.48 | 3.25 | 84.2 | 4.4 | 19.8 | 5.2 | 5.8 |
| 9.8 | 0.00 | 0.0 | -0.60 | 2.2 | 0.0 | 0.24 | 2.01 | 3.03 | 98.0 | 5.6 | 28.0 | 0.0 | 4.6 |
| 9.9 | 0.37 | 2.1 | 0.01 | 5.4 | 1.3 | 0.82 | 6.91 | 3.13 | 75.2 | 3.4 | 23.0 | 12.7 | 8.3 |
| 7.7 | 0.19 | 1.7 | -0.18 | 3.0 | 0.0 | 0.33 | 3.97 | 6.32 | 98.8 | 4.2 | 15.2 | 0.0 | 1.7 |
| 6.8 | 2.38 | 9.4 | 0.02 | 7.0 | 4.0 | 1.01 | 10.16 | 2.41 | 72.9 | 5.5 | 25.7 | 0.0 | 6.7 |

| Name | City | State | Rating | 2014 Rating | 2013 Rating | Total Assets ($Mil) | One Year Asset Growth | Asset Mix (As a % of Total Assets) | | | | Capital-ization Index | Net Worth Ratio |
|------|------|-------|--------|-------------|-------------|---------------------|----------------------|------------------|------------------|------------------|------------------|----------------------|-----------------|
| | | | | | | | | Comm-ercial Loans | Cons-umer Loans | Mort-gage Loans | Secur-ities | | |
| ▲ BOULEVARD FCU | Amherst | NY | C+ | C- | C | 33.6 | 9.29 | 0.0 | 27.7 | 8.3 | 0.0 | 10.0 | 12.9 |
| BOURNS EMPL FCU | Riverside | CA | A- | A- | B+ | 36.7 | 0.14 | 2.9 | 12.1 | 40.3 | 10.7 | 10.0 | 16.0 |
| BOWATER EMPL CU | Calhoun | TN | C | C+ | C | 145.1 | 3.01 | 0.0 | 33.3 | 12.3 | 13.4 | 8.0 | 9.7 |
| BOX BUTTE PUBLIC EMPL FCU | Alliance | NE | C | C | C | 4.5 | 2.07 | 0.0 | 41.0 | 0.0 | 0.0 | 10.0 | 16.6 |
| BOX ELDER COUNTY FCU | Brigham City | UT | A | A | A | 103.9 | 7.37 | 0.0 | 40.5 | 6.7 | 16.6 | 10.0 | 21.9 |
| BOYDS FCU | Boyds | MD | C- | D+ | D+ | 2.1 | 1.95 | 0.0 | 12.0 | 7.8 | 76.6 | 9.6 | 10.8 |
| BOYS TOWN FCU | Boys Town | NE | E+ | E+ | D- | 3.2 | -3.55 | 0.0 | 38.8 | 0.0 | 0.0 | 5.3 | 7.3 |
| BP FCU | Houston | TX | B- | B- | C+ | 133.2 | 3.55 | 0.0 | 21.9 | 24.6 | 28.1 | 5.7 | 7.7 |
| BRADFORD AREA FCU | Bradford | PA | C- | D+ | D+ | 7.5 | 1.84 | 0.0 | 39.2 | 0.0 | 0.0 | 10.0 | 19.9 |
| BRADFORD AREA SCHOOL EMPL FCU | Bradford | PA | D+ | D | D+ | <1 | 4.05 | 0.0 | 74.6 | 0.0 | 0.0 | 10.0 | 19.9 |
| BRADKEN CU | Atchison | KS | C- | C- | C- | 8.4 | -0.95 | 0.0 | 40.6 | 0.0 | 0.0 | 10.0 | 15.7 |
| BRADLEY INITIATIVE CU | Cleveland | TN | C | C- | D+ | 2.4 | 15.67 | 0.0 | 46.6 | 5.1 | 0.0 | 10.0 | 11.9 |
| BRAGG MUTUAL FCU | Fayetteville | NC | D | D+ | D+ | 48.8 | 2.27 | 0.0 | 24.4 | 0.1 | 27.1 | 10.0 | 12.1 |
| BRAINERD BN CU | Brainerd | MN | C+ | C+ | C+ | 67.3 | 3.76 | 2.7 | 12.9 | 37.5 | 0.0 | 10.0 | 11.6 |
| BRANCH 6000 NALC CU | Amityville | NY | E+ | E+ | D- | 9.2 | 9.08 | 0.0 | 28.2 | 4.6 | 20.7 | 4.9 | 7.2 |
| BRANTWOOD CU | Brantwood | WI | D+ | D | D | 4.8 | 8.40 | 0.0 | 47.8 | 0.0 | 0.0 | 10.0 | 14.3 |
| BRASSIES CU | Anniston | AL | C- | C- | D | 5.6 | -12.06 | 0.0 | 23.3 | 12.9 | 0.0 | 10.0 | 14.5 |
| ▲ BRAZOS COMMUNITY CU | Alvin | TX | C- | D | C- | 14.2 | 11.72 | 0.0 | 67.8 | 2.4 | 0.0 | 10.0 | 24.2 |
| ▲ BRAZOS VALLEY SCHOOLS CU | Katy | TX | C+ | C+ | C | 657.0 | 4.99 | 0.0 | 17.8 | 10.7 | 53.3 | 6.5 | 8.5 |
| BRAZOSPORT TEACHERS FCU | Clute | TX | B+ | B+ | B+ | 41.0 | 5.02 | 0.0 | 30.4 | 0.0 | 16.3 | 10.0 | 14.3 |
| BRECO FCU | Baton Rouge | LA | C- | C- | B- | 47.2 | 3.61 | 0.0 | 45.9 | 2.8 | 7.6 | 10.0 | 11.0 |
| ▲ BRENTWOOD BAPTIST CHURCH FCU | Houston | TX | D- | E+ | E+ | 1.1 | 6.37 | 0.0 | 66.0 | 0.0 | 0.0 | 6.0 | 8.0 |
| BREWER FCU | Brewer | ME | C+ | C+ | C+ | 50.0 | 5.01 | 2.3 | 37.9 | 16.1 | 0.0 | 9.1 | 10.4 |
| BREWERY CU | Milwaukee | WI | B | B | B | 38.9 | 1.51 | 6.9 | 47.7 | 24.4 | 0.0 | 10.0 | 19.5 |
| BREWSTER FCU | Brewster | OH | B | B | B | 20.3 | 6.76 | 0.0 | 41.1 | 2.5 | 0.0 | 10.0 | 14.0 |
| BREWTON MILL FCU | Brewton | AL | D+ | D | D+ | 19.5 | -0.55 | 0.0 | 46.6 | 1.9 | 0.0 | 7.8 | 9.5 |
| BRIDGE CU | Columbus | OH | B | B | B- | 52.2 | 3.61 | 4.3 | 47.0 | 15.6 | 7.3 | 10.0 | 13.0 |
| BRIDGEPORT CITY EMPL FCU | Bridgeport | CT | C | C- | C+ | 29.8 | 2.71 | 0.0 | 24.1 | 9.0 | 0.0 | 10.0 | 24.3 |
| BRIDGEPORT FAIRFIELD TEACHERS FCU | Bridgeport | CT | C | C- | C- | 5.9 | 0.19 | 0.0 | 45.7 | 0.0 | 0.0 | 10.0 | 26.0 |
| BRIDGEPORT HOSPITAL FCU | Bridgeport | CT | D+ | D | D | 20.4 | 1.09 | 0.0 | 12.2 | 6.7 | 47.4 | 6.6 | 8.6 |
| BRIDGEPORT POLICE FCU | Bridgeport | CT | B- | B- | B- | 16.4 | 10.82 | 0.0 | 38.7 | 0.0 | 0.0 | 10.0 | 13.0 |
| BRIDGEPORT POST OFFICE FCU | Bridgeport | CT | D+ | D+ | C- | 4.2 | 0.14 | 0.0 | 23.6 | 0.0 | 9.1 | 10.0 | 30.2 |
| BRIDGETON ONIZED FCU | Vineland | NJ | D | E+ | D- | 34.7 | 8.04 | 0.0 | 47.1 | 0.2 | 7.2 | 5.5 | 7.5 |
| ▼ BRIDGEWATER CU | Bridgewater | MA | C | C+ | B- | 332.4 | 0.43 | 6.2 | 24.3 | 41.6 | 17.2 | 9.8 | 10.9 |
| ▲ BRIDGEWAY FCU | Poughkeepsie | NY | C | C- | D+ | 79.1 | 4.29 | 0.7 | 41.1 | 22.6 | 0.9 | 5.9 | 7.9 |
| BRIGHT HOPE FCU | Philadelphia | PA | D+ | D | D | <1 | -13.82 | 0.0 | 10.8 | 36.1 | 0.0 | 10.0 | 15.3 |
| ▲ BRIGHTSTAR CU | Sunrise | FL | B | C+ | B- | 426.7 | -1.69 | 0.1 | 34.8 | 10.3 | 26.1 | 8.4 | 9.9 |
| BRIGHTVIEW FCU | Ridgeland | MS | D | D | D+ | 28.8 | 1.64 | 0.7 | 21.9 | 2.3 | 6.5 | 10.0 | 13.1 |
| BRISTOL VIRGINIA SCHOOL SYSTEM FCU | Bristol | VA | C | C | C | <1 | -8.39 | 0.0 | 31.7 | 0.0 | 0.0 | 10.0 | 26.3 |
| BROCKPORT FCU | Brockport | NY | E+ | D- | D- | 8.8 | 0.05 | 0.0 | 32.1 | 32.8 | 6.4 | 6.4 | 8.4 |
| BROKAW CU | Weston | WI | D+ | C- | C- | 47.9 | 1.77 | 3.2 | 25.2 | 25.0 | 9.9 | 6.3 | 8.3 |
| ▲ BRONCO FCU | Franklin | VA | C- | D | D | 180.6 | -1.09 | 5.8 | 25.7 | 31.1 | 3.8 | 5.0 | 7.1 |
| BROOKLAND FCU | West Columbia | SC | E+ | D- | E+ | 3.5 | -0.89 | 0.0 | 71.9 | 0.0 | 0.0 | 4.6 | 6.6 |
| ▲ BROOKLINE MUNICIPAL CU | Brookline | MA | C+ | C | C | 37.9 | -4.54 | 0.0 | 6.0 | 28.7 | 9.7 | 10.0 | 11.8 |
| BROOKLYN COOPERATIVE FCU | Brooklyn | NY | D- | D- | D | 19.6 | 5.98 | 10.7 | 21.1 | 42.1 | 0.0 | 6.5 | 8.5 |
| ▼ BROOKS COMMUNITY FCU | Brooks | MN | D | D+ | C- | 2.7 | -4.17 | 0.0 | 19.6 | 4.1 | 0.0 | 9.6 | 10.7 |
| ▼ BROSNAN YARD FCU | Macon | GA | D+ | C- | C- | 2.6 | 3.94 | 0.0 | 70.3 | 0.0 | 0.0 | 10.0 | 16.3 |
| BROTHERHOOD CU | Lynn | MA | D+ | C- | C- | 106.6 | -2.98 | 0.0 | 2.8 | 30.9 | 23.0 | 10.0 | 27.7 |
| ▼ BROWARD HEALTHCARE FCU | Fort Lauderdale | FL | C+ | B- | B- | 64.6 | 4.08 | 0.0 | 24.1 | 0.6 | 36.6 | 9.3 | 10.5 |
| BROWN COUNTY EMPL CU | Green Bay | WI | C- | C | C+ | 18.6 | -3.41 | 0.0 | 9.8 | 33.7 | 0.0 | 10.0 | 19.0 |
| BROWN-FORMAN EMPL CU | Louisville | KY | B- | B- | C+ | 12.3 | 3.93 | 0.0 | 39.4 | 5.2 | 0.0 | 10.0 | 11.3 |
| BROWNFIELD FCU | Brownfield | TX | C | C | B- | 12.6 | 8.71 | 0.8 | 36.5 | 0.0 | 0.0 | 10.0 | 30.2 |
| BROWNSVILLE CITY EMPL FCU | Brownsville | TX | C- | C | C+ | 6.7 | 2.72 | 0.0 | 55.6 | 0.0 | 0.0 | 10.0 | 22.5 |
| BRUNOT ISLAND FCU | Burgettstown | PA | C- | D+ | C- | 4.7 | -1.77 | 0.0 | 23.6 | 0.0 | 0.0 | 10.0 | 23.2 |
| BRUNSWICK COUNTY TEACHERS FCU | Lawrenceville | VA | D | D | D+ | <1 | -8.64 | 0.0 | 45.8 | 0.0 | 0.0 | 10.0 | 26.4 |
| BS AND CP HOSPITALS EMPL FCU | Bronx | NY | B- | B- | B- | 1.1 | 1.23 | 0.0 | 60.1 | 0.0 | 0.0 | 10.0 | 30.7 |
| BSE CU | Middleburg Heights | OH | D- | D- | D- | 17.5 | 0.08 | 0.0 | 27.8 | 0.0 | 36.5 | 5.6 | 7.7 |
| BUCKEYE COMMUNITY FCU | Perry | FL | B- | B- | B- | 73.1 | 3.29 | 3.5 | 29.3 | 10.9 | 7.5 | 10.0 | 13.1 |
| BUCKEYE STATE CU INC | Akron | OH | D- | D- | C- | 86.0 | 5.07 | 11.4 | 42.3 | 2.4 | 17.7 | 6.0 | 8.0 |
| ▼ BUCKS COUNTY EMPL CU | Doylestown | PA | C+ | B- | B | 34.0 | 5.36 | 0.0 | 10.1 | 0.0 | 0.0 | 7.6 | 9.4 |

| Asset Quality Index | Non-Performing Loans as a % of Total Loans | Non-Performing Loans as a % of Capital | Net Charge-Offs / Avg Loans | Profitability Index | Net Income ($Mil) | Return on Assets | Return on Equity | Net Interest Spread | Overhead Efficiency Ratio | Liquidity Index | Liquidity Ratio | Hot Money Ratio | Stability Index |
|---|---|---|---|---|---|---|---|---|---|---|---|---|---|
| 7.2 | 3.07 | 10.3 | 0.82 | 2.9 | 0.1 | 0.40 | 3.24 | 3.43 | 87.0 | 4.5 | 23.7 | 1.5 | 5.0 |
| 10.0 | 0.00 | 0.0 | -0.01 | 10.0 | 0.5 | 1.83 | 12.03 | 3.36 | 86.7 | 4.4 | 27.0 | 9.9 | 5.9 |
| 6.8 | 1.18 | 8.7 | 0.24 | 2.7 | 0.2 | 0.17 | 1.75 | 3.32 | 95.9 | 4.0 | 24.7 | 5.8 | 6.2 |
| 9.6 | 0.11 | 0.4 | 0.21 | 4.3 | 0.0 | 0.63 | 3.97 | 4.42 | 83.3 | 4.7 | 15.4 | 0.0 | 7.5 |
| 9.5 | 0.43 | 1.1 | 0.15 | 9.5 | 1.4 | 1.83 | 8.46 | 3.12 | 59.8 | 3.7 | 22.6 | 9.0 | 10.0 |
| 8.8 | 1.83 | 3.5 | 0.00 | 2.3 | 0.0 | 0.19 | 1.79 | 1.53 | 88.0 | 5.4 | 47.9 | 0.0 | 5.1 |
| 8.3 | 0.57 | 2.8 | 0.67 | 2.5 | 0.0 | 0.17 | 2.31 | 5.01 | 91.8 | 6.2 | 30.8 | 0.0 | 1.7 |
| 9.9 | 0.17 | 1.1 | 0.04 | 4.2 | 0.6 | 0.60 | 8.18 | 2.79 | 80.1 | 4.6 | 19.8 | 2.0 | 4.5 |
| 5.3 | 5.84 | 13.2 | 0.46 | 6.3 | 0.1 | 1.46 | 7.32 | 4.52 | 82.5 | 6.4 | 45.1 | 0.0 | 4.3 |
| 1.9 | 7.53 | 29.1 | -0.21 | 4.8 | 0.0 | 0.87 | 4.40 | 3.83 | 76.9 | 3.5 | 18.9 | 0.0 | 7.0 |
| 6.4 | 3.58 | 8.8 | 1.01 | 3.6 | 0.0 | 0.21 | 1.33 | 5.46 | 79.5 | 5.9 | 33.8 | 0.0 | 6.4 |
| 5.5 | 1.48 | 5.2 | 0.80 | 9.5 | 0.0 | 1.83 | 14.55 | 9.30 | 71.1 | 6.4 | 52.2 | 0.0 | 5.0 |
| 8.1 | 1.47 | 4.6 | 3.40 | 0.5 | -0.2 | -0.47 | -3.93 | 4.06 | 90.7 | 6.9 | 40.8 | 0.2 | 5.1 |
| 7.5 | 0.10 | 5.8 | 0.00 | 2.9 | 0.1 | 0.26 | 2.20 | 2.69 | 90.8 | 3.8 | 35.4 | 8.0 | 6.4 |
| 5.7 | 2.73 | 12.4 | 0.14 | 0.9 | 0.0 | -0.16 | -2.27 | 4.13 | 108.7 | 6.1 | 34.6 | 0.0 | 1.7 |
| 0.6 | 7.67 | 39.5 | 1.58 | 6.8 | 0.0 | 0.88 | 5.92 | 3.93 | 67.4 | 4.0 | 49.3 | 0.0 | 7.5 |
| 6.9 | 3.42 | 10.2 | 1.78 | 3.0 | 0.0 | -0.05 | -0.33 | 3.68 | 100.6 | 4.7 | 23.2 | 0.0 | 5.3 |
| 8.1 | 0.41 | 1.3 | 0.50 | 2.9 | 0.1 | 0.52 | 2.04 | 4.43 | 82.7 | 3.3 | 7.6 | 2.9 | 5.2 |
| 9.8 | 0.54 | 1.9 | 0.42 | 3.4 | 2.1 | 0.43 | 5.13 | 2.34 | 82.3 | 4.8 | 19.1 | 10.8 | 5.5 |
| 9.8 | 0.27 | 0.8 | 0.07 | 6.7 | 0.3 | 1.06 | 7.47 | 2.77 | 74.2 | 5.0 | 26.6 | 8.9 | 7.4 |
| 5.8 | 0.86 | 6.0 | 1.22 | 1.1 | -0.1 | -0.26 | -2.34 | 4.81 | 90.4 | 4.2 | 20.2 | 7.0 | 4.7 |
| 2.9 | 2.32 | 17.7 | 0.00 | 8.5 | 0.0 | 1.91 | 25.64 | 5.90 | 66.7 | 5.3 | 33.8 | 0.0 | 1.7 |
| 4.4 | 1.73 | 13.6 | 0.35 | 4.3 | 0.2 | 0.47 | 4.57 | 4.73 | 87.4 | 3.2 | 16.6 | 9.9 | 5.0 |
| 4.9 | 2.71 | 10.7 | 1.01 | 9.8 | 0.6 | 1.88 | 10.15 | 5.68 | 75.8 | 1.9 | 19.1 | 23.5 | 7.3 |
| 9.3 | 0.15 | 0.6 | 0.80 | 7.8 | 0.2 | 1.04 | 7.49 | 4.25 | 76.5 | 4.8 | 29.1 | 2.7 | 6.3 |
| 2.8 | 1.83 | 18.4 | 0.36 | 3.5 | 0.1 | 0.40 | 4.24 | 3.69 | 90.8 | 3.4 | 22.7 | 8.7 | 3.9 |
| 7.0 | 0.65 | 3.8 | 0.53 | 3.8 | 0.1 | 0.36 | 2.81 | 4.35 | 86.2 | 3.0 | 19.3 | 12.1 | 7.5 |
| 10.0 | 0.10 | 0.2 | -0.06 | 2.1 | 0.1 | 0.39 | 1.63 | 3.25 | 92.3 | 4.6 | 15.4 | 0.6 | 5.6 |
| 8.2 | 1.92 | 3.3 | 0.41 | 3.9 | 0.0 | 0.49 | 1.93 | 6.56 | 78.7 | 6.8 | 73.6 | 0.0 | 6.0 |
| 9.7 | 0.42 | 1.1 | 0.08 | 1.2 | 0.0 | -0.03 | -0.38 | 3.03 | 101.3 | 6.1 | 25.9 | 0.0 | 3.7 |
| 9.7 | 0.67 | 2.0 | 0.43 | 5.2 | 0.1 | 0.61 | 4.68 | 3.51 | 83.3 | 4.6 | 44.1 | 9.3 | 6.2 |
| 8.6 | 5.86 | 5.1 | -0.13 | 1.1 | 0.0 | -0.06 | -0.21 | 2.76 | 101.3 | 5.5 | 25.1 | 0.0 | 5.6 |
| 2.8 | 1.93 | 17.7 | 1.27 | 7.1 | 0.4 | 1.40 | 18.94 | 5.96 | 76.4 | 3.5 | 10.7 | 2.4 | 2.8 |
| 6.8 | 1.47 | 10.1 | -0.01 | 2.6 | 0.7 | 0.26 | 2.41 | 2.59 | 94.9 | 3.2 | 7.6 | 7.4 | 6.6 |
| 6.3 | 0.70 | 7.2 | 0.69 | 4.3 | 0.3 | 0.57 | 8.09 | 5.52 | 80.5 | 4.0 | 16.6 | 1.5 | 2.8 |
| 6.6 | 2.17 | 8.2 | 0.00 | 3.3 | 0.0 | 0.61 | 4.44 | 8.54 | 88.9 | 5.7 | 37.0 | 0.0 | 4.9 |
| 6.9 | 0.93 | 6.2 | 2.18 | 6.9 | 4.6 | 1.41 | 15.53 | 4.04 | 78.0 | 3.9 | 10.8 | 8.6 | 5.5 |
| 9.8 | 0.84 | 1.8 | 0.50 | 0.3 | -0.1 | -0.32 | -2.41 | 2.79 | 107.8 | 6.2 | 66.7 | 5.8 | 4.9 |
| 9.3 | 3.61 | 3.7 | -1.61 | 3.0 | 0.0 | 0.00 | 0.00 | 6.35 | 100.0 | 7.7 | 97.9 | 0.0 | 6.8 |
| 4.0 | 2.24 | 18.6 | 1.81 | 2.1 | 0.0 | -0.39 | -4.60 | 5.12 | 83.3 | 3.0 | 8.9 | 6.8 | 1.0 |
| 6.4 | 0.74 | 4.7 | 0.75 | 1.3 | -0.1 | -0.23 | -2.84 | 3.10 | 99.0 | 4.4 | 24.0 | 3.1 | 3.6 |
| 3.1 | 2.13 | 30.8 | 0.46 | 2.7 | 0.4 | 0.31 | 4.42 | 4.05 | 90.0 | 3.7 | 16.8 | 9.2 | 3.4 |
| 0.0 | 7.05 | 53.8 | 0.30 | 5.2 | 0.0 | 1.06 | 15.11 | 6.69 | 90.0 | 4.6 | 27.4 | 0.0 | 2.6 |
| 9.7 | 0.01 | 0.0 | -0.01 | 2.6 | 0.1 | 0.26 | 2.24 | 2.27 | 88.9 | 4.5 | 28.5 | 6.7 | 6.0 |
| 1.7 | 4.01 | 40.0 | 0.04 | 5.9 | 0.1 | 0.86 | 13.42 | 5.35 | 86.7 | 4.3 | 13.4 | 0.0 | 2.8 |
| 4.9 | 5.26 | 16.8 | 0.00 | 0.1 | 0.0 | -0.71 | -6.80 | 3.15 | 114.7 | 6.4 | 32.9 | 0.0 | 6.3 |
| 4.3 | 1.54 | 6.4 | 0.36 | 2.8 | 0.0 | -1.40 | -8.04 | 6.76 | 93.1 | 4.7 | 32.4 | 0.0 | 6.9 |
| 10.0 | 0.06 | 0.3 | 0.02 | 1.0 | 0.0 | 0.02 | 0.06 | 2.07 | 99.0 | 3.4 | 15.0 | 13.8 | 7.9 |
| 8.9 | 0.66 | 2.0 | 0.06 | 2.1 | 0.0 | 0.01 | 0.08 | 2.85 | 88.2 | 4.7 | 10.9 | 2.2 | 5.7 |
| 8.8 | 0.67 | 2.3 | 1.75 | 1.2 | 0.0 | -0.13 | -0.68 | 2.25 | 96.2 | 5.2 | 46.7 | 0.0 | 6.8 |
| 9.3 | 0.54 | 2.7 | 0.20 | 4.2 | 0.1 | 0.50 | 4.39 | 4.32 | 84.7 | 4.4 | 23.3 | 1.9 | 6.1 |
| 9.7 | 0.12 | 0.2 | 0.05 | 2.0 | 0.0 | 0.06 | 0.18 | 3.91 | 97.9 | 5.7 | 52.4 | 0.0 | 6.7 |
| 8.5 | 0.26 | 0.7 | 0.68 | 1.3 | 0.0 | -0.08 | -0.35 | 4.19 | 95.9 | 5.1 | 38.7 | 0.0 | 6.7 |
| 6.9 | 8.70 | 9.4 | 0.23 | 1.8 | 0.0 | 0.20 | 0.87 | 2.18 | 86.5 | 7.2 | 61.1 | 0.0 | 6.3 |
| 1.3 | 16.97 | 30.1 | 3.24 | 0.1 | 0.0 | -1.55 | -5.80 | 13.23 | 89.7 | 7.1 | 69.3 | 0.0 | 4.8 |
| 8.6 | 0.00 | 0.0 | 0.00 | 10.0 | 0.0 | 4.68 | 16.88 | 11.93 | 37.1 | 6.5 | 56.5 | 0.0 | 6.3 |
| 8.4 | 0.39 | 1.8 | 0.75 | 1.2 | 0.0 | 0.01 | 0.10 | 3.27 | 96.1 | 4.9 | 18.7 | 0.0 | 2.1 |
| 7.5 | 0.33 | 3.8 | 0.42 | 3.7 | 0.2 | 0.34 | 2.72 | 4.90 | 92.1 | 4.5 | 21.5 | 3.3 | 6.4 |
| 6.5 | 0.23 | 4.7 | 0.39 | 0.2 | -0.4 | -0.63 | -7.68 | 2.97 | 110.3 | 3.9 | 18.5 | 0.7 | 2.8 |
| 10.0 | 0.35 | 0.4 | -0.23 | 3.1 | 0.1 | 0.28 | 2.95 | 0.79 | 63.2 | 5.2 | 17.2 | 0.0 | 4.5 |

| Name | City | State | Rating | 2014 Rating | 2013 Rating | Total Assets ($Mil) | One Year Asset Growth | Asset Mix (As a % of Total Assets) | | | | Capital-ization Index | Net Worth Ratio |
|---|---|---|---|---|---|---|---|---|---|---|---|---|---|
| | | | | | | | | Comm-ercial Loans | Cons-umer Loans | Mort-gage Loans | Secur-ities | | |
| ▲ BUFFALO COMMUNITY FCU | Buffalo | NY | C- | C- | C | 73.4 | 1.09 | 0.0 | 20.0 | 14.8 | 0.0 | 10.0 | 11.1 |
| BUFFALO CONRAIL FCU | Cheektowaga | NY | C | C+ | B- | 39.4 | 1.66 | 0.0 | 14.3 | 3.2 | 27.9 | 10.0 | 20.7 |
| BUFFALO COOPERATIVE FCU | Buffalo | NY | E+ | E+ | E+ | 6.2 | -7.88 | 0.0 | 29.3 | 19.7 | 0.0 | 5.3 | 7.3 |
| BUFFALO METROPOLITAN FCU | Buffalo | NY | B | B | B | 92.1 | 4.37 | 0.0 | 41.7 | 18.2 | 0.0 | 10.0 | 11.5 |
| BUFFALO POLICE FCU | Buffalo | NY | C | C | B- | 9.2 | 3.45 | 0.0 | 48.0 | 0.0 | 0.0 | 10.0 | 14.8 |
| BUFFALO SERVICE CU | Buffalo | NY | C | D+ | C | 50.6 | 7.05 | 0.0 | 17.5 | 3.4 | 27.4 | 8.4 | 9.9 |
| BUILDING TRADES FCU | Maple Grove | MN | B | B | B+ | 123.4 | 1.85 | 0.6 | 20.1 | 23.1 | 22.2 | 10.0 | 12.2 |
| ▼ BULAB EMPL FCU | Memphis | TN | C- | C | C | 4.2 | 4.03 | 0.0 | 79.5 | 0.0 | 0.0 | 10.0 | 17.6 |
| BULL DOG FCU | Hagerstown | MD | D | D+ | D | 127.1 | -0.95 | 5.7 | 34.3 | 2.1 | 47.1 | 7.0 | 9.0 |
| BULLS EYE CU | Wisconsin Rapids | WI | C+ | C+ | C- | 136.9 | 2.14 | 0.9 | 30.8 | 25.0 | 4.7 | 8.0 | 9.7 |
| BURBANK CITY FCU | Burbank | CA | B- | C | C+ | 274.3 | 5.34 | 4.5 | 22.2 | 34.0 | 7.3 | 6.4 | 8.4 |
| BURLINGTON MUNICIPAL EMPL CU | Burlington | IA | D+ | D | D | 4.7 | 2.47 | 0.0 | 60.0 | 0.0 | 0.0 | 8.4 | 9.9 |
| BURLINGTON MUNICIPAL EMPL FCU | Burlington | MA | D | D | D | 8.8 | 6.62 | 0.8 | 33.0 | 0.0 | 7.8 | 7.1 | 9.6 |
| BURLINGTON NORTHERN SANTA FE RAILWA | Cicero | IL | D | D+ | C- | 7.1 | 2.16 | 0.0 | 21.0 | 0.0 | 0.0 | 10.0 | 19.2 |
| BURLINGTON NORTHTOWN COMMUNITY CU | North Kansas City | MO | B- | B- | B- | 11.7 | 4.78 | 0.0 | 34.5 | 0.0 | 0.0 | 10.0 | 17.5 |
| BURNS & MCDONNELL CU | Kansas City | MO | D | D | D- | 18.1 | 13.08 | 0.0 | 38.2 | 1.6 | 0.0 | 5.1 | 7.1 |
| BUSINESS & INDUSTRIAL FCU | Columbus | IN | D+ | D+ | D+ | 32.9 | -1.83 | 0.1 | 37.4 | 0.0 | 0.0 | 10.0 | 15.4 |
| BUTLER ARMCO EMPL CU | Butler | PA | A | A | A | 299.9 | 4.22 | 0.0 | 23.9 | 27.3 | 0.0 | 10.0 | 15.3 |
| ▼ BUTLER COUNTY TEACHERS FCU | Butler | PA | C- | C | C- | 27.1 | 3.34 | 0.0 | 15.0 | 7.2 | 2.0 | 6.1 | 8.1 |
| BUTLER HERITAGE FCU | Middletown | OH | D+ | D+ | C- | 11.5 | -1.62 | 0.0 | 19.6 | 26.3 | 0.0 | 9.8 | 10.9 |
| BUTTE COMMUNITY FCU | Butte | MT | D+ | D+ | C | 19.3 | 13.18 | 0.0 | 41.1 | 0.0 | 0.0 | 7.7 | 9.5 |
| ▲ BVA FCU | Belle Vernon | PA | D+ | D | C- | 28.2 | -3.93 | 0.0 | 10.2 | 22.1 | 23.1 | 7.6 | 9.4 |
| BVMSN FCU | Walnutport | PA | C- | C | C | 2.3 | 6.79 | 0.0 | 15.7 | 0.05 | 26.4 | 10.0 | 14.5 |
| ▲ BYKOTA FCU | Brooklyn | NY | D+ | D- | D | 1.4 | 1.05 | 0.0 | 0.0 | 0.0 | 0.0 | 9.2 | 10.5 |
| C & N W PROVISO CU | Northlake | IL | D- | D | D | 3.0 | 6.16 | 0.0 | 43.6 | 0.0 | 0.0 | 7.3 | 9.2 |
| ▼ C & R CU | Clay Center | KS | D+ | D+ | D- | 3.9 | 15.88 | 0.0 | 72.5 | 0.0 | 0.0 | 8.7 | 10.1 |
| C B S EMPL FCU | Studio City | CA | C | C | C | 17.1 | 2.50 | 0.0 | 19.3 | 1.8 | 2.9 | 10.0 | 14.4 |
| C C M H FCU | Parkersburg | WV | D+ | D+ | D+ | 4.2 | 0.05 | 0.0 | 78.9 | 0.0 | 0.0 | 10.0 | 12.3 |
| ▲ C C S E FCU | Salamanca | NY | B | B- | B | 32.8 | 3.98 | 0.0 | 23.8 | 4.8 | 7.5 | 10.0 | 11.0 |
| C O FCU | Charleston | SC | B- | C+ | C+ | 2.1 | 15.99 | 0.0 | 39.2 | 0.0 | 0.0 | 10.0 | 16.6 |
| ▼ C T A C AND M FCU | Oak Park | IL | C | C+ | C | 2.0 | 4.13 | 0.0 | 47.5 | 0.0 | 0.0 | 10.0 | 16.2 |
| C T A F C FCU | Chicago | IL | C- | D+ | C- | <1 | 1.04 | 0.0 | 35.7 | 0.0 | 0.0 | 10.0 | 16.0 |
| C&H SUGAR EMPL FCU | Crockett | CA | D | D | C- | 10.2 | -1.73 | 0.0 | 22.4 | 0.0 | 0.0 | 10.0 | 22.6 |
| C&O UNITED CU | Edgewood | KY | D | D+ | C- | 15.4 | 1.58 | 0.0 | 22.9 | 3.0 | 0.0 | 10.0 | 11.0 |
| C-B-W SCHOOLS FCU | Sidman | PA | B | B | B | 105.8 | -1.27 | 0.0 | 7.4 | 11.4 | 41.7 | 10.0 | 29.0 |
| C-E FCU | Houston | TX | D- | D- | E+ | 17.2 | 5.49 | 0.0 | 53.7 | 0.0 | 11.4 | 5.3 | 7.3 |
| C-F LA CU | Donaldsonville | LA | C | C | C | 9.0 | 2.49 | 0.0 | 36.0 | 0.0 | 0.0 | 10.0 | 11.9 |
| C-PLANT FCU | Paducah | KY | A- | B+ | B+ | 201.4 | 9.36 | 7.5 | 38.8 | 19.9 | 0.0 | 9.1 | 10.4 |
| C-T WACO FCU | Waco | TX | D | C- | C- | 6.5 | -3.00 | 0.0 | 59.5 | 0.0 | 0.0 | 10.0 | 12.1 |
| ▼ CAANO EMPL FCU | Kenner | LA | D | D+ | D+ | 2.7 | -7.47 | 0.0 | 46.4 | 0.0 | 7.5 | 10.0 | 12.7 |
| CABLE FCU | Marion | IN | D+ | D+ | D+ | 1.3 | -0.24 | 0.0 | 82.8 | 0.0 | 0.0 | 10.0 | 17.9 |
| CABOT & NOI EMPL CU | Pampa | TX | C- | C- | C | 31.2 | 1.21 | 0.0 | 56.0 | 10.0 | 0.0 | 7.3 | 9.2 |
| ▲ CABOT BOSTON CU | Boston | MA | D+ | D | D+ | 7.4 | 7.87 | 0.0 | 33.4 | 0.0 | 12.8 | 10.0 | 16.1 |
| CABOT EMPL CU | Franklin | LA | C | C | C+ | 2.0 | -11.69 | 0.0 | 47.3 | 0.0 | 0.0 | 10.0 | 18.3 |
| CABOT EMPL CU | Ville Platte | LA | D | D | C- | <1 | -5.22 | 0.0 | 34.4 | 0.0 | 0.0 | 10.0 | 14.6 |
| CABRILLO CU | San Diego | CA | B+ | A- | A | 226.7 | 4.82 | 0.8 | 36.7 | 13.4 | 0.0 | 10.0 | 11.3 |
| CABWAY TELCO FCU | Huntington | WV | C | C | C | 4.8 | -8.71 | 0.0 | 43.8 | 0.0 | 0.0 | 10.0 | 22.2 |
| CACL FCU | Pottsville | PA | B | B | B | 82.6 | 26.14 | 0.0 | 17.7 | 27.7 | 12.3 | 9.2 | 10.5 |
| CADDO PARISH TEACHERS FCU | Shreveport | LA | B | B | B | 11.9 | 10.44 | 0.0 | 45.5 | 0.0 | 0.0 | 10.0 | 24.2 |
| CADETS FCU | Buffalo | NY | C | C | C | 11.3 | 3.06 | 0.0 | 11.4 | 15.7 | 3.4 | 10.0 | 13.2 |
| CADMUS CU INC | Richmond | VA | D | D+ | D+ | 2.1 | -0.87 | 0.0 | 46.7 | 0.0 | 0.0 | 10.0 | 25.9 |
| CAHP CU | Sacramento | CA | B+ | B+ | B | 143.7 | 9.03 | 0.1 | 70.3 | 0.0 | 3.6 | 7.3 | 9.2 |
| CAL POLY FCU | Pomona | CA | E+ | E+ | E+ | 13.0 | 8.22 | 0.0 | 36.6 | 0.0 | 0.0 | 4.2 | 6.2 |
| CAL STATE LA FCU | Los Angeles | CA | B- | C+ | C | 42.7 | 3.33 | 0.9 | 22.1 | 31.7 | 0.0 | 8.9 | 10.3 |
| ▲ CAL-COM FCU | Port Lavaca | TX | C+ | C | C+ | 135.6 | 3.72 | 0.0 | 66.6 | 0.0 | 0.0 | 7.4 | 9.2 |
| ▲ CAL-ED FCU | Coal Center | PA | C | C- | D+ | 25.9 | -3.93 | 0.0 | 10.4 | 0.0 | 0.0 | 10.0 | 12.5 |
| CALCASIEU PARISH EMPL FCU | Lake Charles | LA | C+ | C+ | B- | 13.7 | 1.51 | 0.0 | 42.1 | 0.0 | 14.5 | 10.0 | 14.7 |
| ▲ CALCASIEU TEACHERS & EMPL CU | Lake Charles | LA | C | C- | C- | 37.8 | 0.84 | 0.5 | 17.3 | 3.2 | 0.0 | 10.0 | 13.0 |
| CALCITE CU | Rogers City | MI | B+ | B+ | B+ | 61.4 | 4.27 | 0.1 | 23.7 | 19.4 | 28.6 | 10.0 | 12.1 |
| ▲ CALCOE FCU | Yakima | WA | C- | C- | D | 26.7 | 3.72 | 0.2 | 49.3 | 12.3 | 7.3 | 7.9 | 9.6 |

| Asset Quality Index | Non-Performing Loans as a % of Total Loans | as a % of Capital | Net Charge-Offs Avg Loans | Profitability Index | Net Income ($Mil) | Return on Assets | Return on Equity | Net Interest Spread | Overhead Efficiency Ratio | Liquidity Index | Liquidity Ratio | Hot Money Ratio | Stability Index |
|---|---|---|---|---|---|---|---|---|---|---|---|---|---|
| 9.6 | 0.67 | 2.7 | 0.20 | 1.7 | 0.0 | 0.04 | 0.38 | 2.90 | 96.9 | 4.6 | 20.3 | 0.2 | 5.6 |
| 9.3 | 1.97 | 4.0 | 0.14 | 2.0 | 0.0 | 0.15 | 0.72 | 2.40 | 88.2 | 6.3 | 37.9 | 0.0 | 7.0 |
| 3.7 | 3.15 | 29.6 | -0.53 | 4.5 | 0.0 | 0.70 | 14.61 | 3.52 | 89.8 | 5.0 | 28.4 | 0.0 | 1.0 |
| 5.8 | 1.31 | 10.9 | 0.60 | 6.0 | 0.6 | 0.89 | 9.08 | 5.26 | 79.9 | 3.5 | 10.2 | 2.2 | 5.2 |
| 8.5 | 0.78 | 2.5 | 0.84 | 2.9 | 0.0 | -0.03 | -0.20 | 4.17 | 89.0 | 6.4 | 55.2 | 0.0 | 6.6 |
| 10.0 | 0.09 | 0.3 | 0.05 | 3.2 | 0.2 | 0.48 | 4.06 | 4.37 | 88.6 | 6.6 | 37.2 | 1.0 | 6.1 |
| 10.0 | 0.13 | 1.1 | 0.14 | 3.6 | 0.4 | 0.45 | 3.64 | 3.25 | 89.1 | 4.0 | 14.6 | 5.2 | 7.8 |
| 7.0 | 0.92 | 4.2 | 0.00 | 2.7 | 0.0 | 0.16 | 0.91 | 3.89 | 92.9 | 4.2 | 15.6 | 0.0 | 7.4 |
| 7.8 | 0.53 | 3.9 | 1.73 | 0.4 | -0.2 | -0.24 | -2.57 | 2.92 | 90.6 | 5.0 | 41.2 | 0.0 | 5.1 |
| 6.2 | 1.63 | 10.8 | 0.22 | 3.8 | 0.6 | 0.59 | 6.24 | 3.29 | 84.0 | 4.0 | 18.5 | 1.0 | 6.1 |
| 6.6 | 0.70 | 9.1 | 0.20 | 4.6 | 1.3 | 0.66 | 7.91 | 3.63 | 83.5 | 3.9 | 26.5 | 13.0 | 4.6 |
| 4.1 | 2.55 | 14.9 | 0.62 | 3.9 | 0.0 | 0.43 | 4.30 | 3.35 | 72.7 | 4.3 | 19.2 | 0.0 | 2.3 |
| 7.3 | 0.80 | 3.6 | 0.26 | 1.6 | 0.0 | 0.00 | 0.00 | 4.84 | 99.5 | 6.6 | 50.9 | 2.5 | 3.3 |
| 9.5 | 0.60 | 0.6 | 3.36 | 0.0 | -0.1 | -1.01 | -5.18 | 2.57 | 111.9 | 6.8 | 62.9 | 0.0 | 5.0 |
| 9.6 | 0.71 | 2.1 | 0.84 | 4.7 | 0.1 | 0.60 | 3.50 | 4.56 | 83.1 | 5.2 | 35.4 | 0.0 | 7.8 |
| 7.2 | 1.05 | 7.3 | 0.00 | 5.2 | 0.1 | 0.77 | 11.96 | 2.50 | 65.2 | 4.3 | 7.7 | 1.2 | 2.1 |
| 9.8 | 0.50 | 1.4 | 0.12 | 0.6 | 0.0 | -0.17 | -1.10 | 2.25 | 104.6 | 5.1 | 27.1 | 1.7 | 6.8 |
| 9.6 | 0.61 | 2.6 | 0.10 | 6.1 | 2.1 | 0.94 | 6.42 | 3.49 | 68.1 | 5.8 | 35.3 | 1.8 | 9.3 |
| 9.4 | 0.39 | 1.2 | 0.02 | 2.0 | 0.0 | 0.00 | 0.00 | 0.93 | 93.3 | 4.9 | 16.2 | 0.0 | 3.3 |
| 7.2 | 1.98 | 8.3 | -0.08 | 1.8 | 0.0 | 0.14 | 1.29 | 3.08 | 96.3 | 4.7 | 23.0 | 0.9 | 4.7 |
| 4.4 | 1.65 | 14.5 | 0.41 | 3.8 | 0.1 | 0.35 | 3.69 | 4.12 | 85.9 | 3.3 | 16.2 | 5.6 | 3.0 |
| 4.0 | 3.41 | 18.8 | 0.35 | 3.1 | 0.1 | 0.50 | 5.68 | 3.38 | 80.6 | 4.4 | 25.6 | 4.5 | 2.9 |
| 8.3 | 1.93 | 5.3 | 0.00 | 2.4 | 0.0 | 0.12 | 0.80 | 1.37 | 95.5 | 5.9 | 42.5 | 0.0 | 7.2 |
| 3.7 | 15.66 | 16.2 | -1.75 | 4.7 | 0.0 | 1.03 | 10.11 | 3.03 | 60.7 | 6.0 | 31.4 | 0.0 | 3.0 |
| 1.7 | 8.38 | 36.5 | -0.81 | 4.2 | 0.0 | 0.51 | 5.41 | 6.01 | 91.4 | 6.6 | 52.4 | 0.0 | 5.5 |
| 3.2 | 2.49 | 17.9 | 2.39 | 4.3 | 0.0 | 0.32 | 3.02 | 6.65 | 87.0 | 4.6 | 20.5 | 0.0 | 2.3 |
| 10.0 | 0.65 | 1.4 | 0.00 | 2.1 | 0.0 | 0.09 | 0.65 | 2.39 | 97.2 | 6.4 | 55.8 | 5.4 | 6.3 |
| 4.7 | 1.56 | 9.5 | 0.83 | 2.2 | 0.0 | -0.06 | -0.51 | 4.14 | 101.0 | 3.9 | 16.7 | 0.0 | 5.9 |
| 8.3 | 0.65 | 3.0 | -0.01 | 5.6 | 0.2 | 0.95 | 9.05 | 4.11 | 84.9 | 5.2 | 22.9 | 1.2 | 5.1 |
| 9.3 | 0.56 | 1.6 | 0.26 | 9.7 | 0.0 | 2.54 | 15.35 | 7.65 | 65.8 | 6.4 | 57.2 | 0.0 | 6.3 |
| 7.0 | 2.70 | 7.2 | 0.74 | 3.8 | 0.0 | 0.00 | 0.00 | 11.85 | 100.0 | 7.0 | 62.4 | 0.0 | 7.2 |
| 3.7 | 6.67 | 20.2 | 0.78 | 6.7 | 0.0 | 1.22 | 8.00 | 5.30 | 74.3 | 6.1 | 56.3 | 0.0 | 6.2 |
| 10.0 | 0.00 | 0.0 | 1.34 | 0.0 | -0.1 | -1.39 | -6.13 | 3.03 | 132.2 | 5.0 | 25.9 | 0.0 | 5.7 |
| 9.4 | 0.58 | 1.8 | 0.30 | 1.1 | 0.0 | -0.02 | -0.16 | 3.17 | 98.3 | 5.5 | 27.4 | 1.8 | 4.7 |
| 10.0 | 0.16 | 0.1 | 0.01 | 4.1 | 0.5 | 0.58 | 2.09 | 1.76 | 66.8 | 5.4 | 39.0 | 2.9 | 8.5 |
| 5.7 | 0.44 | 5.4 | 0.22 | 4.0 | 0.1 | 0.61 | 8.66 | 4.42 | 88.3 | 3.9 | 8.2 | 3.6 | 1.7 |
| 9.6 | 0.00 | 0.0 | 0.00 | 2.6 | 0.0 | 0.28 | 2.38 | 1.96 | 85.4 | 5.2 | 53.1 | 0.0 | 6.4 |
| 5.8 | 1.34 | 11.5 | 0.37 | 9.5 | 1.9 | 1.29 | 12.76 | 3.08 | 62.8 | 2.3 | 23.1 | 19.3 | 7.8 |
| 2.7 | 3.83 | 22.2 | 0.47 | 1.3 | 0.0 | -0.50 | -4.16 | 6.00 | 102.2 | 4.6 | 32.1 | 3.7 | 5.4 |
| 2.7 | 7.20 | 26.3 | 0.00 | 1.1 | 0.0 | -0.14 | -1.16 | 5.12 | 89.1 | 5.5 | 39.2 | 0.0 | 5.1 |
| 5.0 | 1.44 | 6.2 | 1.49 | 1.0 | 0.0 | -1.05 | -5.85 | 5.09 | 98.0 | 4.2 | 21.0 | 0.0 | 6.3 |
| 5.6 | 1.13 | 7.8 | 0.44 | 3.6 | 0.1 | 0.39 | 4.35 | 4.08 | 89.7 | 3.9 | 20.0 | 0.0 | 3.4 |
| 9.6 | 0.10 | 0.2 | 0.69 | 0.9 | 0.0 | -0.08 | -0.45 | 3.84 | 102.5 | 5.7 | 36.4 | 2.4 | 6.0 |
| 8.3 | 0.00 | 0.0 | 0.67 | 5.1 | 0.0 | 0.46 | 2.64 | 2.44 | 69.8 | 4.5 | 22.5 | 0.0 | 4.3 |
| 4.1 | 6.51 | 17.2 | 0.00 | 0.1 | 0.0 | -0.45 | -3.10 | 2.76 | 105.9 | 6.0 | 65.9 | 0.0 | 6.3 |
| 9.3 | 0.11 | 2.3 | 0.60 | 4.4 | 0.6 | 0.38 | 3.36 | 3.77 | 84.2 | 4.3 | 21.8 | 2.7 | 6.8 |
| 5.9 | 4.13 | 8.6 | 1.41 | 5.8 | 0.0 | 0.85 | 4.07 | 4.88 | 61.2 | 6.2 | 66.7 | 0.0 | 4.3 |
| 6.6 | 0.75 | 6.2 | 0.27 | 6.2 | 0.5 | 0.90 | 8.15 | 3.58 | 69.9 | 2.7 | 28.0 | 27.4 | 5.6 |
| 6.9 | 1.90 | 4.0 | 0.37 | 9.6 | 0.2 | 2.06 | 8.28 | 5.47 | 69.1 | 5.5 | 30.1 | 0.0 | 6.3 |
| 3.7 | 2.91 | 15.2 | 0.62 | 4.3 | 0.0 | 0.38 | 2.87 | 4.58 | 74.1 | 4.0 | 24.0 | 6.4 | 7.3 |
| 8.0 | 1.69 | 3.7 | 0.56 | 0.0 | 0.0 | -1.22 | -4.67 | 8.58 | 108.6 | 5.9 | 44.6 | 0.0 | 6.5 |
| 8.1 | 0.21 | 1.7 | 0.25 | 8.5 | 1.2 | 1.15 | 12.78 | 6.22 | 79.1 | 3.1 | 13.7 | 13.8 | 6.0 |
| 9.7 | 0.14 | 1.1 | 0.04 | 1.8 | 0.0 | 0.10 | 1.50 | 3.41 | 97.6 | 5.2 | 30.7 | 0.0 | 1.6 |
| 7.4 | 0.74 | 5.0 | 0.15 | 7.9 | 0.4 | 1.25 | 12.61 | 4.87 | 72.6 | 3.5 | 6.1 | 3.4 | 4.2 |
| 5.1 | 1.02 | 10.2 | 0.83 | 4.3 | 0.7 | 0.70 | 9.18 | 3.01 | 70.5 | 3.1 | 28.2 | 13.5 | 4.8 |
| 3.5 | 9.31 | 27.2 | 0.52 | 2.9 | 0.1 | 0.42 | 3.44 | 3.02 | 85.7 | 4.8 | 37.2 | 5.4 | 5.4 |
| 8.1 | 1.01 | 3.4 | 0.40 | 3.2 | 0.0 | 0.29 | 1.95 | 3.29 | 73.8 | 4.3 | 18.0 | 0.0 | 6.7 |
| 10.0 | 0.13 | 0.4 | 0.08 | 2.2 | 0.1 | 0.20 | 1.56 | 2.98 | 90.6 | 7.1 | 62.3 | 0.0 | 6.4 |
| 9.5 | 0.24 | 1.4 | 0.24 | 5.7 | 0.4 | 0.85 | 7.08 | 3.54 | 77.1 | 4.5 | 17.0 | 2.5 | 6.6 |
| 4.5 | 1.43 | 12.5 | 1.12 | 3.3 | 0.1 | 0.42 | 4.33 | 6.50 | 79.8 | 3.7 | 20.1 | 13.2 | 3.7 |

| Name | City | State | Rating | 2014 Rating | 2013 Rating | Total Assets ($Mil) | One Year Asset Growth | Asset Mix (As a % of Total Assets) Commercial Loans | Consumer Loans | Mortgage Loans | Securities | Capitalization Index | Net Worth Ratio |
|------|------|-------|--------|-------------|-------------|---------------------|-----------------------|--------------------|----------------|----------------|-----------|----------------------|-----------------|
| ▲ CALCOM FCU | Torrance | CA | B- | C+ | B- | 63.1 | 0.02 | 0.0 | 32.8 | 22.1 | 15.4 | 10.0 | 12.8 |
| ▲ CALHOUN-LIBERTY EMPL CU | Blountstown | FL | C+ | C | C- | 31.5 | 3.65 | 0.0 | 25.1 | 21.4 | 0.0 | 10.0 | 13.7 |
| ▲ CALIFORNIA ADVENTIST FCU | Glendale | CA | B- | C+ | C | 46.3 | 4.65 | 1.1 | 12.1 | 16.9 | 37.5 | 10.0 | 12.4 |
| CALIFORNIA AGRIBUSINESS CU | Buena Park | CA | D+ | D+ | D | 28.4 | 7.39 | 1.2 | 37.6 | 13.8 | 32.7 | 6.1 | 8.1 |
| CALIFORNIA BEAR CU | Los Angeles | CA | C+ | C | D | 107.0 | 3.25 | 0.0 | 26.8 | 10.3 | 12.7 | 5.3 | 7.3 |
| CALIFORNIA COAST CU | San Diego | CA | A- | A- | A- | 1947.6 | 6.46 | 13.9 | 32.8 | 33.2 | 19.5 | 10.0 | 11.6 |
| ▲ CALIFORNIA COMMUNITY CU | Sacramento | CA | C+ | C- | C+ | 58.7 | 1.01 | 0.8 | 20.4 | 12.8 | 0.0 | 10.0 | 12.3 |
| CALIFORNIA CU | Glendale | CA | B+ | B+ | B- | 1477.5 | 10.62 | 8.9 | 12.3 | 33.8 | 19.8 | 8.9 | 10.3 |
| CALIFORNIA LITHUANIAN CU | Santa Monica | CA | A- | A- | A- | 107.6 | 8.71 | 39.6 | 0.1 | 62.1 | 0.6 | 10.0 | 13.1 |
| CALIFORNIA STATE & FEDERAL EMPL #20 CU | Eureka | CA | B | B+ | B+ | 125.6 | 1.40 | 1.1 | 4.2 | 12.6 | 45.7 | 10.0 | 13.8 |
| CALL FCU | Richmond | VA | C+ | C+ | C+ | 364.5 | 2.93 | 0.0 | 34.0 | 26.2 | 18.0 | 10.0 | 11.4 |
| CALTECH EMPL FCU | La Canada Flintridg | CA | B+ | B+ | B+ | 1379.6 | 5.13 | 4.0 | 3.8 | 16.9 | 69.8 | 8.4 | 10.0 |
| CALVARY BAPTIST OF PACOIMA FCU | San Fernando | CA | C- | C- | D+ | <1 | -10.34 | 0.0 | 20.8 | 0.0 | 0.0 | 10.0 | 11.5 |
| CAMBRIDGE FIREFIGHTERS FCU | Cambridge | MA | B- | C+ | C | 10.1 | -0.89 | 0.0 | 32.2 | 21.5 | 0.0 | 10.0 | 20.4 |
| CAMBRIDGE MUNICIPAL EMPL FCU | Cambridge | MA | D | D+ | D+ | 9.1 | 3.50 | 0.0 | 17.9 | 0.0 | 0.0 | 10.0 | 21.6 |
| CAMBRIDGE TEACHERS FCU | Cambridge | MA | D+ | D+ | D+ | 30.9 | -1.24 | 0.0 | 13.1 | 2.1 | 37.2 | 7.8 | 9.6 |
| CAMC FCU | Charleston | WV | A- | A- | A- | 61.7 | 3.91 | 0.0 | 15.2 | 20.8 | 0.0 | 10.0 | 22.9 |
| CAMDEN FIREMENS CU | Moorestown | NJ | D | D | D- | <1 | 2.30 | 0.0 | 25.7 | 0.0 | 0.0 | 7.4 | 9.2 |
| CAMDEN POLICE FCU | Camden | NJ | E+ | E+ | E+ | <1 | 2.46 | 0.0 | 26.6 | 0.0 | 0.0 | 5.3 | 7.3 |
| CAMINO FCU | Montebello | CA | C | C | C+ | 139.9 | 8.15 | 0.2 | 15.0 | 32.4 | 11.4 | 8.7 | 10.1 |
| CAMP SHELBY FCU | Hattiesburg | MS | B- | B | B+ | 17.3 | -1.51 | 0.0 | 35.7 | 0.0 | 0.0 | 10.0 | 17.9 |
| CAMPBELL EMPL FCU | Cherry Hill | NJ | D+ | D+ | D+ | 143.5 | -2.03 | 3.0 | 17.2 | 5.1 | 59.3 | 9.7 | 10.8 |
| CAMPCO FCU | Gillette | WY | B | B | B | 94.9 | 13.41 | 0.0 | 45.2 | 9.3 | 0.0 | 7.4 | 9.2 |
| CAMPUS CU | Wichita | KS | C+ | C+ | C+ | 30.9 | -8.58 | 0.0 | 61.5 | 8.0 | 0.0 | 10.0 | 11.9 |
| CAMPUS FCU | Baton Rouge | LA | C | C | C | 539.2 | 3.60 | 9.5 | 29.2 | 31.6 | 20.3 | 7.5 | 9.3 |
| CAMPUS USA CU | Jonesville | FL | A- | B+ | B+ | 1363.5 | 12.31 | 5.9 | 43.5 | 27.3 | 12.6 | 10.0 | 12.6 |
| ▲ CANAAN CU | Urbana | IL | B- | C+ | C+ | <1 | 10.36 | 0.0 | 39.7 | 0.0 | 0.0 | 8.8 | 10.2 |
| CANALS & TRAILS CU | Lockport | IL | C- | D+ | D | 21.1 | 5.08 | 0.0 | 24.4 | 8.8 | 0.0 | 6.9 | 8.9 |
| CANANDAIGUA FCU | Canandaigua | NY | C | C- | C- | 22.6 | 4.12 | 0.0 | 22.2 | 18.9 | 35.6 | 10.0 | 12.3 |
| CANDO CU | Walbridge | OH | E+ | E+ | E+ | 8.8 | -1.85 | 0.0 | 42.8 | 0.0 | 0.0 | 5.8 | 7.8 |
| CANNON FCU | Clovis | NM | C- | C | B | 62.2 | -0.66 | 0.0 | 27.8 | 2.6 | 5.1 | 7.0 | 9.0 |
| CANOGA POSTAL FCU | Canoga Park | CA | C+ | C+ | C+ | <1 | 2.73 | 0.0 | 41.0 | 0.0 | 0.0 | 10.0 | 28.1 |
| ▼ CANTON POLICE & FIREMENS CU | Canton | OH | D- | D+ | C | 8.1 | 3.69 | 0.0 | 42.6 | 0.0 | 17.2 | 6.6 | 8.6 |
| CANTON SCHOOL EMPL FCU | Canton | OH | B- | B- | B- | 205.1 | 4.92 | 0.8 | 51.4 | 7.5 | 3.3 | 7.4 | 9.3 |
| ▼ CANYON STATE CU | Phoenix | AZ | C+ | B+ | B+ | 164.3 | 18.83 | 0.0 | 29.2 | 29.2 | 23.2 | 9.2 | 10.4 |
| CAPE REGIONAL CU | Cape Girardeau | MO | D- | D- | D- | 14.3 | 0.37 | 0.0 | 45.1 | 0.0 | 0.0 | 5.1 | 7.1 |
| CAPITAL AREA FCU | Augusta | ME | B+ | B+ | B | 28.3 | 5.46 | 1.0 | 36.8 | 38.4 | 0.0 | 10.0 | 14.4 |
| ▲ CAPITAL AREA REALTORS FCU | Rockville | MD | C- | D+ | D | 9.2 | 7.13 | 5.0 | 28.6 | 26.2 | 0.0 | 8.6 | 10.1 |
| CAPITAL AREA TAIWANESE FCU | Rockville | MD | D | D+ | D+ | 9.7 | 4.71 | 6.7 | 0.1 | 46.1 | 6.3 | 6.0 | 8.0 |
| CAPITAL COMMUNICATIONS FCU | Albany | NY | A | A | A- | 1226.5 | 11.57 | 6.5 | 22.0 | 51.5 | 5.3 | 10.0 | 11.1 |
| CAPITAL CU | Bismarck | ND | A- | A- | B | 396.6 | 7.04 | 21.5 | 22.3 | 21.2 | 5.4 | 9.5 | 10.7 |
| ▲ CAPITAL CU | Green Bay | WI | B+ | B+ | B+ | 1129.9 | 4.11 | 5.7 | 23.4 | 42.0 | 4.0 | 10.0 | 12.1 |
| CAPITAL EDUCATORS FCU | Meridian | ID | B | B | B | 478.0 | 21.99 | 2.5 | 50.2 | 24.6 | 1.1 | 6.0 | 8.1 |
| ▲ CAPITOL CU | Austin | TX | D+ | D | C- | 120.8 | 1.88 | 0.0 | 35.3 | 6.2 | 20.5 | 4.3 | 6.3 |
| CAPITOL VIEW CU | Des Moines | IA | B | B | B | 31.9 | 1.50 | 2.3 | 32.8 | 5.9 | 0.0 | 10.0 | 15.2 |
| CAPROCK FCU | Lamesa | TX | B- | B- | B | 28.4 | 1.45 | 0.0 | 59.2 | 10.5 | 1.8 | 10.0 | 13.6 |
| CAPROCK SANTA FE CU | Slaton | TX | A- | B+ | B+ | 41.7 | 3.10 | 0.0 | 42.4 | 0.0 | 0.0 | 10.0 | 27.5 |
| CAPSTONE FCU | Aliso Viejo | CA | C- | C | C | 38.7 | 7.38 | 0.0 | 16.4 | 11.9 | 18.8 | 6.9 | 8.9 |
| CARBONDALE HIGHWAY CU | Carbondale | IL | C- | C- | C- | 4.7 | 2.62 | 0.0 | 59.8 | 0.0 | 0.0 | 10.0 | 15.4 |
| CARCO FCU | Denton | MD | C | C- | D+ | 5.0 | 5.57 | 1.1 | 23.6 | 0.0 | 0.0 | 10.0 | 11.5 |
| ▲ CARDINAL CU INC | Mentor | OH | C+ | C | C+ | 186.9 | 6.93 | 3.8 | 37.5 | 23.1 | 3.6 | 10.0 | 11.3 |
| ▼ CARDOZO LODGE FCU | Bensalem | PA | D+ | D+ | D+ | <1 | -14.89 | 0.0 | 19.7 | 0.0 | 0.0 | 10.0 | 27.8 |
| CAREY POVERELLO FCU | Carey | OH | C | C | B- | 19.8 | 0.82 | 0.0 | 13.5 | 7.0 | 57.1 | 10.0 | 14.4 |
| CARIBE FCU | San Juan | PR | B+ | A- | A- | 316.0 | 8.86 | 5.5 | 50.4 | 12.7 | 9.5 | 10.0 | 13.3 |
| CARLE EMPL FCU | Urbana | IL | D- | D- | D+ | 14.6 | 5.94 | 0.0 | 41.6 | 0.0 | 0.0 | 5.8 | 7.8 |
| CARMEL BROTHERHOOD FCU | Cincinnati | OH | C- | D | D | <1 | 11.98 | 0.0 | 28.4 | 0.0 | 0.0 | 10.0 | 12.2 |
| CARNEGIE MELLON UNIV FCU | Pittsburgh | PA | D- | D- | D- | 11.1 | 3.82 | 0.0 | 25.3 | 0.0 | 48.2 | 6.0 | 8.0 |
| CAROLINA COLLEGIATE FCU | Columbia | SC | B | B | B | 85.6 | 0.79 | 4.3 | 34.0 | 7.9 | 7.7 | 10.0 | 13.2 |
| CAROLINA COOPERATIVE FCU | Charlotte | NC | D | D+ | D+ | 38.5 | -4.11 | 1.4 | 41.9 | 13.0 | 19.1 | 7.8 | 9.5 |
| CAROLINA FCU | Cherryville | NC | B- | B- | C+ | 42.1 | 2.48 | 0.2 | 55.7 | 0.2 | 7.6 | 10.0 | 11.6 |

| Asset Quality Index | Non-Performing Loans as a % of Total Loans | as a % of Capital | Net Charge-Offs Avg Loans | Profitability Index | Net Income ($Mil) | Return on Assets | Return on Equity | Net Interest Spread | Overhead Efficiency Ratio | Liquidity Index | Liquidity Ratio | Hot Money Ratio | Stability Index |
|---|---|---|---|---|---|---|---|---|---|---|---|---|---|
| 8.7 | 1.13 | 5.7 | 0.50 | 4.1 | 0.3 | 0.59 | 5.14 | 4.12 | 79.0 | 3.5 | 16.7 | 5.9 | 5.0 |
| 6.4 | 0.83 | 8.9 | 1.14 | 2.7 | 0.1 | 0.30 | 2.22 | 3.70 | 88.0 | 4.8 | 23.4 | 2.6 | 6.8 |
| 9.4 | 1.12 | 2.8 | 0.32 | 3.4 | 0.2 | 0.49 | 3.96 | 2.40 | 72.8 | 3.8 | 6.5 | 12.4 | 5.7 |
| 8.8 | 0.04 | 0.3 | 0.51 | 1.4 | 0.0 | 0.03 | 0.41 | 3.47 | 94.5 | 3.7 | 13.4 | 8.8 | 2.7 |
| 6.1 | 2.21 | 12.4 | 0.46 | 3.2 | 0.2 | 0.30 | 4.12 | 3.95 | 87.6 | 6.4 | 42.5 | 4.4 | 3.9 |
| 7.8 | 0.43 | 3.9 | 0.18 | 6.6 | 14.0 | 0.98 | 8.38 | 2.88 | 73.5 | 3.2 | 16.4 | 7.6 | 8.0 |
| 8.9 | 0.30 | 0.8 | 0.56 | 3.0 | 0.2 | 0.40 | 3.25 | 4.35 | 87.4 | 7.1 | 55.9 | 2.4 | 5.1 |
| 6.4 | 1.01 | 9.6 | 0.14 | 5.5 | 6.9 | 0.65 | 7.75 | 3.31 | 84.3 | 3.1 | 11.0 | 10.1 | 7.1 |
| 8.9 | 0.00 | 2.1 | -0.01 | 9.3 | 1.1 | 1.41 | 10.56 | 2.39 | 35.5 | 3.8 | 45.1 | 17.7 | 9.8 |
| 10.0 | 0.00 | 0.0 | 0.05 | 3.9 | 0.4 | 0.46 | 3.35 | 1.85 | 57.9 | 7.2 | 40.0 | 0.0 | 8.4 |
| 8.7 | 0.44 | 2.8 | 0.48 | 2.4 | 0.3 | 0.10 | 0.86 | 3.27 | 85.3 | 4.2 | 16.3 | 0.8 | 7.1 |
| 10.0 | 0.13 | 0.3 | 0.06 | 4.9 | 8.1 | 0.79 | 7.39 | 1.64 | 53.9 | 5.2 | 25.3 | 0.0 | 7.8 |
| 4.7 | 11.11 | 20.0 | -3.33 | 6.2 | 0.0 | 0.95 | 8.33 | 6.67 | 100.0 | 8.0 | 82.6 | 0.0 | 4.3 |
| 9.9 | 0.17 | 0.5 | 0.23 | 4.6 | 0.1 | 0.75 | 3.74 | 3.30 | 74.8 | 4.7 | 33.2 | 0.0 | 7.8 |
| 10.0 | 0.04 | 0.1 | 0.00 | 0.3 | 0.0 | -0.46 | -2.08 | 2.74 | 120.1 | 6.3 | 40.6 | 0.0 | 6.8 |
| 8.4 | 0.82 | 2.2 | 0.10 | 1.4 | 0.0 | 0.02 | 0.22 | 2.22 | 98.5 | 4.0 | 16.1 | 15.7 | 4.1 |
| 10.0 | 0.12 | 0.2 | 0.13 | 5.0 | 0.3 | 0.65 | 2.89 | 2.31 | 79.0 | 5.0 | 34.7 | 4.0 | 8.2 |
| 9.2 | 0.00 | 0.0 | 0.00 | 2.6 | 0.0 | 0.33 | 3.60 | 9.65 | 88.9 | 4.3 | 49.9 | 41.4 | 2.3 |
| 3.8 | 6.15 | 15.8 | 7.50 | 0.3 | 0.0 | -0.72 | -9.39 | 6.19 | 120.7 | 7.0 | 47.2 | 0.0 | 3.3 |
| 10.0 | 0.07 | 0.5 | 0.29 | 2.3 | 0.1 | 0.12 | 1.27 | 3.99 | 93.7 | 4.8 | 20.4 | 3.1 | 5.5 |
| 7.6 | 1.99 | 5.6 | 1.60 | 3.7 | 0.0 | 0.22 | 1.31 | 4.35 | 82.9 | 6.6 | 48.1 | 0.0 | 6.9 |
| 9.4 | 1.26 | 3.3 | 0.61 | 1.6 | 0.1 | 0.07 | 0.68 | 2.05 | 87.8 | 5.3 | 16.4 | 0.0 | 5.5 |
| 6.2 | 0.48 | 3.7 | 0.23 | 8.2 | 0.9 | 1.31 | 14.48 | 4.31 | 72.9 | 3.2 | 16.1 | 9.1 | 4.7 |
| 5.1 | 1.40 | 10.2 | 1.89 | 5.3 | 0.2 | 0.85 | 7.71 | 4.55 | 63.4 | 3.7 | 20.8 | 5.0 | 5.1 |
| 8.0 | 0.50 | 4.3 | 0.23 | 3.0 | 1.6 | 0.39 | 4.19 | 2.99 | 87.6 | 3.2 | 11.0 | 5.3 | 6.5 |
| 8.0 | 0.55 | 3.8 | 0.35 | 5.6 | 9.2 | 0.93 | 7.60 | 3.10 | 71.5 | 2.2 | 13.8 | 17.5 | 8.5 |
| 8.6 | 1.35 | 3.8 | 0.00 | 9.6 | 0.0 | 2.61 | 27.45 | 11.37 | 61.1 | 7.4 | 70.2 | 0.0 | 5.7 |
| 8.5 | 0.22 | 1.1 | 0.85 | 5.4 | 0.1 | 0.89 | 10.30 | 3.11 | 75.3 | 4.2 | 9.0 | 1.7 | 4.0 |
| 5.5 | 3.07 | 15.4 | 0.33 | 2.1 | 0.0 | 0.15 | 1.25 | 2.94 | 95.2 | 5.0 | 16.6 | 1.0 | 5.6 |
| 4.4 | 1.71 | 12.3 | 1.82 | 2.3 | 0.0 | 0.15 | 1.96 | 7.45 | 92.5 | 4.7 | 35.1 | 1.6 | 1.0 |
| 8.3 | 0.76 | 2.8 | 0.59 | 0.4 | -0.2 | -0.34 | -3.80 | 2.74 | 107.5 | 5.0 | 31.1 | 7.7 | 3.7 |
| 9.8 | 0.00 | 0.0 | 0.00 | 4.1 | 0.0 | 0.43 | 1.46 | 5.84 | 94.3 | 6.5 | 63.1 | 0.0 | 7.4 |
| 8.2 | 0.24 | 1.6 | 0.31 | 0.8 | -0.1 | -0.86 | -9.58 | 4.26 | 111.6 | 4.3 | 15.4 | 0.0 | 3.5 |
| 5.6 | 1.15 | 7.4 | 1.67 | 3.7 | 0.6 | 0.40 | 4.33 | 5.71 | 79.4 | 2.7 | 19.0 | 13.3 | 6.1 |
| 9.8 | 0.07 | 0.7 | 0.13 | 3.3 | 0.4 | 0.38 | 3.37 | 3.53 | 93.2 | 3.7 | 14.0 | 2.5 | 5.7 |
| 8.2 | 0.06 | 0.5 | 0.03 | 2.2 | 0.0 | 0.14 | 2.00 | 3.26 | 97.1 | 5.5 | 42.1 | 0.0 | 3.0 |
| 6.8 | 1.00 | 5.6 | 0.56 | 10.0 | 0.4 | 2.01 | 14.95 | 5.32 | 63.5 | 3.0 | 12.2 | 2.6 | 8.4 |
| 9.7 | 0.00 | 0.0 | 0.00 | 4.3 | 0.1 | 0.64 | 6.62 | 3.60 | 81.1 | 3.3 | 5.4 | 0.0 | 3.7 |
| 10.0 | 0.00 | 0.0 | 0.00 | 3.8 | 0.0 | 0.61 | 7.55 | 1.94 | 62.3 | 1.8 | 18.5 | 40.1 | 2.3 |
| 7.0 | 1.00 | 7.9 | 0.28 | 7.7 | 8.9 | 1.00 | 8.97 | 3.85 | 75.6 | 2.5 | 3.7 | 7.9 | 8.5 |
| 8.1 | 0.41 | 3.0 | 0.19 | 9.1 | 3.5 | 1.18 | 11.41 | 3.82 | 70.2 | 2.9 | 6.0 | 5.1 | 7.0 |
| 6.7 | 0.74 | 7.5 | 0.31 | 5.0 | 5.3 | 0.63 | 5.08 | 3.50 | 76.6 | 3.7 | 15.0 | 4.9 | 8.9 |
| 7.1 | 0.36 | 5.3 | 0.25 | 5.7 | 2.8 | 0.83 | 11.18 | 3.03 | 77.6 | 1.9 | 5.5 | 15.5 | 4.8 |
| 8.6 | 0.41 | 3.6 | 0.59 | 1.8 | 0.3 | 0.29 | 4.63 | 2.91 | 86.0 | 4.8 | 23.6 | 0.5 | 2.1 |
| 7.7 | 0.56 | 5.8 | 0.58 | 5.9 | 0.2 | 1.01 | 6.88 | 3.33 | 72.8 | 4.2 | 25.7 | 3.7 | 7.3 |
| 5.4 | 1.19 | 9.6 | 0.90 | 4.3 | 0.1 | 0.43 | 3.21 | 5.53 | 83.0 | 1.8 | 10.6 | 25.9 | 6.3 |
| 8.0 | 2.43 | 3.9 | 1.24 | 10.0 | 0.8 | 2.44 | 9.05 | 5.33 | 42.8 | 4.5 | 49.0 | 20.6 | 8.0 |
| 10.0 | 0.26 | 0.9 | 0.40 | 2.4 | 0.1 | 0.19 | 2.11 | 2.26 | 91.8 | 4.5 | 25.1 | 2.5 | 3.2 |
| 6.6 | 0.99 | 4.6 | 0.04 | 1.9 | 0.0 | 0.03 | 0.18 | 4.12 | 99.1 | 4.9 | 29.8 | 0.0 | 7.1 |
| 6.9 | 2.81 | 7.6 | 0.00 | 6.9 | 0.0 | 1.19 | 10.63 | 2.59 | 50.6 | 5.2 | 19.7 | 0.0 | 4.3 |
| 7.5 | 0.50 | 3.1 | 1.11 | 3.1 | 0.5 | 0.34 | 3.11 | 4.01 | 77.5 | 3.5 | 14.4 | 4.0 | 6.7 |
| 3.7 | 31.82 | 21.9 | 0.00 | 3.6 | 0.0 | 0.58 | 2.19 | 1.85 | 66.7 | 6.5 | 106.2 | 0.0 | 3.0 |
| 10.0 | 0.18 | 0.3 | 0.17 | 0.7 | -0.1 | -0.30 | -2.12 | 2.17 | 114.5 | 6.0 | 32.6 | 0.0 | 6.3 |
| 7.0 | 0.64 | 3.9 | 0.49 | 4.3 | 1.1 | 0.50 | 3.71 | 3.34 | 73.2 | 3.4 | 23.0 | 12.8 | 8.0 |
| 6.7 | 1.15 | 6.2 | 0.11 | 1.7 | 0.0 | 0.20 | 2.59 | 2.12 | 96.1 | 4.8 | 28.4 | 0.0 | 1.7 |
| 3.7 | 8.80 | 29.7 | 2.04 | 6.9 | 0.0 | 2.21 | 17.20 | 5.66 | 55.6 | 5.8 | 27.7 | 0.0 | 5.9 |
| 7.3 | 1.54 | 5.1 | 0.09 | 2.4 | 0.0 | 0.35 | 4.43 | 2.55 | 85.4 | 5.6 | 17.3 | 0.0 | 2.3 |
| 7.5 | 1.08 | 4.8 | 0.71 | 4.9 | 0.5 | 0.73 | 5.75 | 4.05 | 82.7 | 4.6 | 20.7 | 2.0 | 5.7 |
| 3.2 | 2.75 | 29.5 | 3.25 | 0.6 | -0.3 | -0.92 | -9.44 | 5.82 | 75.3 | 3.6 | 16.8 | 10.1 | 4.4 |
| 4.4 | 2.86 | 17.5 | 1.64 | 3.9 | 0.1 | 0.22 | 1.87 | 4.85 | 70.1 | 2.8 | 25.2 | 23.0 | 6.0 |

| Name | City | State | Rating | 2014 Rating | 2013 Rating | Total Assets ($Mil) | One Year Asset Growth | Commercial Loans | Consumer Loans | Mortgage Loans | Securities | Capitalization Index | Net Worth Ratio |
|------|------|-------|--------|-------------|-------------|---------------------|----------------------|------------------|----------------|----------------|------------|---------------------|-----------------|
| CAROLINA FOOTHILLS FCU | Spartanburg | SC | B- | B- | C+ | 95.9 | 3.54 | 4.8 | 34.7 | 13.3 | 0.4 | 7.8 | 9.6 |
| CAROLINA POSTAL CU | Charlotte | NC | C+ | C+ | C+ | 84.1 | -0.30 | 0.0 | 20.9 | 37.6 | 21.0 | 10.0 | 13.1 |
| CAROLINA TRUST FCU | Myrtle Beach | SC | B+ | B | B- | 199.1 | 5.59 | 1.5 | 34.5 | 10.7 | 12.4 | 7.7 | 9.5 |
| CAROLINAS TELCO FCU | Charlotte | NC | B | B | B | 389.2 | -0.52 | 0.0 | 19.8 | 17.5 | 48.1 | 10.0 | 16.5 |
| CARPENTERS FCU | Saint Paul | MN | C | C | D | 21.5 | 44.97 | 0.0 | 22.9 | 9.6 | 0.9 | 5.6 | 7.6 |
| CARROLL COUNTY SCHOOL EMPL FCU | Hillsville | VA | C | C | C | <1 | -2.08 | 0.0 | 8.0 | 0.0 | 0.0 | 10.0 | 15.9 |
| CARTER FCU | Springhill | LA | C+ | C+ | C+ | 256.4 | 6.65 | 12.7 | 36.0 | 35.1 | 2.1 | 6.1 | 8.1 |
| CARUS EMPL CU | Spring Valley | IL | C- | C- | C | <1 | -11.92 | 0.0 | 75.2 | 0.0 | 0.0 | 10.0 | 22.6 |
| CARVILLE EMPL FCU | Carville | LA | C | C | C | 10.0 | 57.85 | 0.0 | 45.1 | 20.3 | 0.0 | 10.0 | 13.5 |
| CASCADE CENTRAL CU | Hood River | OR | B+ | B+ | B+ | 57.0 | 5.54 | 4.8 | 12.1 | 27.8 | 15.2 | 10.0 | 11.9 |
| CASCADE COMMUNITY FCU | Roseburg | OR | B | B | B | 178.3 | 6.77 | 1.4 | 22.0 | 16.7 | 0.0 | 10.0 | 12.9 |
| CASCADE FCU | Kent | WA | B+ | B+ | C+ | 269.8 | 4.07 | 0.0 | 5.9 | 16.5 | 32.0 | 10.0 | 11.9 |
| CASCO FCU | Gorham | ME | C+ | C+ | C+ | 52.1 | 5.69 | 5.9 | 20.0 | 45.9 | 0.0 | 7.7 | 9.5 |
| CASE CU | Lansing | MI | B- | B- | C | 243.0 | -0.11 | 10.9 | 50.6 | 24.0 | 10.0 | 8.0 | 9.6 |
| CASE FCU | Tyler | TX | C- | D+ | D+ | 4.7 | 0.64 | 0.0 | 35.4 | 0.0 | 0.0 | 10.0 | 14.0 |
| CASEBINE COMMUNITY CU | Burlington | IA | B- | B- | B | 33.0 | 5.13 | 5.1 | 28.5 | 6.5 | 12.8 | 10.0 | 16.2 |
| CASTPARTS EMPL FCU | Portland | OR | B+ | B+ | B+ | 48.4 | 3.89 | 0.0 | 38.1 | 5.0 | 1.2 | 10.0 | 14.6 |
| ▲ CATHOLIC & COMMUNITY CU | Belleville | IL | B- | C+ | C+ | 118.1 | 3.66 | 1.3 | 49.4 | 2.0 | 32.0 | 7.8 | 9.5 |
| ▲ CATHOLIC CU | Avon Lake | OH | C | D+ | D | 10.4 | 9.65 | 2.3 | 18.3 | 0.0 | 9.1 | 8.4 | 9.9 |
| ▲ CATHOLIC CU | Superior | WI | D+ | D | C- | <1 | -1.43 | 0.0 | 46.1 | 0.0 | 0.0 | 10.0 | 26.8 |
| ▲ CATHOLIC FAMILY CU | Kansas City | MO | D | D- | D | 11.9 | -1.98 | 0.0 | 22.2 | 0.0 | 1.7 | 7.6 | 9.4 |
| CATHOLIC FAMILY FCU | Wichita | KS | C- | D | D- | 28.0 | -0.53 | 1.6 | 52.2 | 19.5 | 3.8 | 6.9 | 9.0 |
| CATHOLIC FCU | Saginaw | MI | C+ | B- | B- | 327.7 | 0.59 | 0.4 | 20.6 | 35.3 | 27.4 | 10.0 | 11.2 |
| ▲ CATHOLIC UNITED FINANCIAL CU | Saint Paul | MN | E+ | D- | D- | 16.7 | -7.16 | 0.6 | 40.7 | 0.0 | 0.9 | 10.0 | 13.1 |
| ▲ CATHOLIC VANTAGE FINANCIAL FCU | Livonia | MI | C+ | C | C- | 83.7 | 2.81 | 4.3 | 24.1 | 19.2 | 29.1 | 6.2 | 8.3 |
| ▲ CATHOLICS UNITED CU | South Hutchinson | KS | C- | C- | D+ | <1 | 8.74 | 0.0 | 57.3 | 0.0 | 0.0 | 10.0 | 16.1 |
| CATTARAUGUS COUNTY EMPL FCU | Little Valley | NY | C- | D+ | C- | 10.3 | 4.35 | 0.0 | 32.2 | 7.3 | 28.4 | 7.6 | 9.4 |
| ▲ CBC FCU | Oxnard | CA | C+ | C | B- | 443.8 | 9.47 | 7.2 | 14.2 | 34.1 | 30.5 | 7.6 | 9.4 |
| CBC FCU | Philadelphia | PA | D- | D- | D- | <1 | -8.56 | 0.0 | 1.8 | 0.0 | 0.0 | 8.4 | 10.5 |
| CBI FCU | Plainfield | IL | D+ | D+ | D+ | 19.4 | 0.68 | 0.0 | 18.9 | 19.2 | 5.2 | 6.3 | 8.3 |
| CCAC FCU | Pittsburgh | PA | C- | C- | C- | 4.5 | -4.53 | 0.0 | 39.5 | 0.0 | 0.0 | 10.0 | 11.6 |
| CCC VAN WERT CU | Van Wert | OH | D+ | D | C- | <1 | 0.91 | 0.0 | 55.0 | 0.0 | 0.0 | 10.0 | 35.8 |
| ▲ CDC FCU | Atlanta | GA | C+ | C | C | 272.7 | 3.65 | 0.1 | 16.2 | 5.3 | 53.6 | 5.8 | 7.8 |
| ▲ CDSC LOUISIANA FCU | Coushatta | LA | C+ | C- | C | 17.9 | 0.96 | 0.0 | 22.5 | 28.6 | 0.0 | 10.0 | 17.6 |
| CECIL COUNTY SCHOOL EMPL FCU | Elkton | MD | D+ | D | D+ | 25.3 | 4.78 | 0.3 | 39.4 | 0.0 | 11.5 | 6.6 | 8.6 |
| CEDAR FALLS COMMUNITY CU | Cedar Falls | IA | A | A- | A- | 98.3 | 4.01 | 4.6 | 35.4 | 24.0 | 0.0 | 10.0 | 14.8 |
| CEDAR POINT FCU | Lexington Park | MD | C+ | C+ | C+ | 426.1 | 1.89 | 8.1 | 14.2 | 22.6 | 35.9 | 8.0 | 9.6 |
| CEDARS-SINAI FCU | Los Angeles | CA | B- | B- | B | 24.7 | 7.16 | 0.0 | 13.9 | 0.0 | 3.9 | 10.0 | 13.5 |
| CELCO FCU | Narrows | VA | B- | B- | C | 101.2 | 0.50 | 0.0 | 14.3 | 17.5 | 12.4 | 10.0 | 20.0 |
| CEMC EMPL CU | Clarksville | TN | D | D | D+ | 2.6 | -7.45 | 0.0 | 55.9 | 0.0 | 0.0 | 10.0 | 22.3 |
| ▼ CEN TEX MANUFACTURING CU | Brownwood | TX | D | D+ | C- | 8.7 | -2.42 | 0.0 | 53.9 | 0.0 | 0.0 | 10.0 | 11.6 |
| CENLA FCU | Alexandria | LA | B+ | B+ | B | 108.7 | 2.94 | 0.0 | 32.6 | 10.1 | 33.5 | 10.0 | 13.4 |
| CENSUS FCU | Washington | DC | D+ | D+ | D+ | 58.7 | -5.65 | 0.0 | 7.2 | 9.9 | 69.3 | 10.0 | 16.6 |
| CENT CU | Mason City | IA | B | B | B+ | 38.7 | -0.93 | 1.0 | 26.2 | 33.7 | 0.0 | 10.0 | 16.8 |
| CENTERVILLE CLINICS EMPL FCU | Fredericktown | PA | D | D+ | C | <1 | -1.89 | 0.0 | 20.9 | 0.0 | 0.0 | 10.0 | 26.2 |
| CENTEX CITIZENS CU | Mexia | TX | A- | A- | A- | 61.9 | 3.01 | 2.5 | 36.0 | 19.2 | 1.1 | 10.0 | 20.8 |
| CENTRA CU | Columbus | IN | A- | A- | B+ | 1272.0 | 4.44 | 9.0 | 26.7 | 26.4 | 19.5 | 10.0 | 11.7 |
| ▲ CENTRAL CITY CU | Marshfield | WI | B- | C+ | C | 220.7 | 4.54 | 11.7 | 21.8 | 38.7 | 8.3 | 8.3 | 9.9 |
| ▲ CENTRAL COAST FCU | Seaside | CA | C | C | C | 123.8 | 4.11 | 1.0 | 8.9 | 25.6 | 29.3 | 6.6 | 8.7 |
| CENTRAL COMMUNICATIONS CU | Independence | MO | D+ | D+ | D+ | 47.9 | 0.83 | 1.5 | 23.0 | 7.3 | 50.6 | 7.7 | 9.5 |
| CENTRAL CU INC | Columbus | OH | D | D+ | C- | 2.7 | -0.55 | 0.0 | 48.0 | 0.0 | 0.0 | 10.0 | 11.4 |
| CENTRAL CU OF FLORIDA | Pensacola | FL | B+ | A- | A- | 136.8 | 2.96 | 0.0 | 38.2 | 14.9 | 6.4 | 10.0 | 12.1 |
| ▲ CENTRAL CU OF ILLINOIS | Bellwood | IL | C+ | C | C- | 85.1 | 2.24 | 0.0 | 41.5 | 26.7 | 0.0 | 6.6 | 8.6 |
| CENTRAL CU OF MARYLAND | Baltimore | MD | C | C- | C | 20.7 | -1.71 | 0.0 | 38.6 | 0.0 | 14.7 | 10.0 | 12.7 |
| CENTRAL ELECTRIC CU | Jefferson City | MO | E+ | E+ | E+ | 1.8 | 0.60 | 0.0 | 60.0 | 0.0 | 0.0 | 5.6 | 7.6 |
| CENTRAL FLORIDA EDUCATORS FCU | Lake Mary | FL | B- | B+ | B+ | 1604.0 | 7.76 | 0.9 | 21.1 | 19.8 | 46.4 | 10.0 | 11.3 |
| ▲ CENTRAL FLORIDA POSTAL CU | Orlando | FL | D+ | D- | D- | 68.7 | 0.92 | 2.6 | 68.9 | 13.0 | 0.0 | 6.0 | 8.0 |
| CENTRAL HANNA EMPL CU | Keewatin | MN | D+ | D+ | C- | 3.8 | -4.64 | 0.0 | 41.6 | 0.0 | 0.0 | 10.0 | 23.7 |
| CENTRAL HUDSON EMPL FCU | Poughkeepsie | NY | B | B | B | 46.5 | -1.05 | 0.0 | 6.5 | 7.6 | 20.6 | 10.0 | 21.3 |
| ▲ CENTRAL ILLINOIS CU | Champaign | IL | C- | C- | C- | 15.8 | 7.64 | 0.0 | 44.8 | 0.0 | 0.0 | 7.4 | 9.3 |

| Asset Quality Index | Non-Performing Loans as a % of Total Loans | as a % of Capital | Net Charge-Offs Avg Loans | Profitability Index | Net Income ($Mil) | Return on Assets | Return on Equity | Net Interest Spread | Overhead Efficiency Ratio | Liquidity Index | Liquidity Ratio | Hot Money Ratio | Stability Index |
|---|---|---|---|---|---|---|---|---|---|---|---|---|---|
| 6.8 | 0.69 | 5.0 | 0.52 | 4.5 | 0.4 | 0.60 | 6.48 | 4.45 | 84.7 | 4.3 | 24.3 | 3.5 | 4.3 |
| 7.7 | 0.61 | 7.1 | 0.21 | 2.6 | 0.1 | 0.16 | 1.24 | 4.22 | 93.3 | 4.3 | 17.1 | 3.5 | 6.1 |
| 8.9 | 0.27 | 2.2 | 0.64 | 6.1 | 1.4 | 0.96 | 10.39 | 3.41 | 78.7 | 4.9 | 20.9 | 2.9 | 6.4 |
| 9.6 | 0.82 | 2.3 | 0.26 | 4.3 | 1.8 | 0.62 | 4.00 | 2.86 | 83.2 | 4.3 | 6.4 | 2.6 | 7.7 |
| 9.9 | 0.21 | 1.0 | -0.06 | 9.3 | 0.3 | 1.99 | 25.92 | 2.66 | 69.3 | 5.0 | 42.3 | 0.5 | 3.1 |
| 10.0 | 1.23 | 0.6 | 0.00 | 2.1 | 0.0 | 0.00 | 0.00 | 4.07 | 100.0 | 8.0 | 69.0 | 0.0 | 6.4 |
| 5.0 | 1.10 | 14.1 | 0.39 | 3.6 | 0.7 | 0.36 | 5.55 | 3.59 | 84.7 | 1.4 | 10.4 | 22.3 | 4.4 |
| 2.6 | 8.93 | 25.4 | 0.00 | 5.6 | 0.0 | 1.07 | 5.10 | 4.66 | 77.4 | 4.2 | 20.3 | 0.0 | 6.7 |
| 7.1 | 1.06 | 5.1 | 0.96 | 2.1 | 0.0 | -0.09 | -0.70 | 4.59 | 86.3 | 4.0 | 25.2 | 0.0 | 6.0 |
| 8.8 | 0.18 | 0.8 | 0.01 | 6.7 | 0.4 | 1.07 | 8.80 | 3.23 | 63.8 | 5.9 | 35.3 | 2.5 | 6.6 |
| 9.9 | 0.02 | 0.1 | 0.03 | 4.7 | 1.0 | 0.72 | 5.64 | 2.47 | 76.9 | 4.2 | 18.8 | 3.5 | 8.4 |
| 8.8 | 1.79 | 3.7 | 0.21 | 5.4 | 1.6 | 0.82 | 6.99 | 1.68 | 61.8 | 4.5 | 26.2 | 8.4 | 7.8 |
| 5.5 | 1.52 | 11.7 | 0.33 | 3.8 | 0.1 | 0.37 | 3.79 | 4.25 | 91.4 | 3.1 | 5.7 | 5.2 | 4.3 |
| 5.1 | 1.35 | 9.3 | 0.90 | 4.9 | 1.4 | 0.74 | 7.90 | 4.67 | 73.6 | 3.3 | 5.8 | 3.6 | 6.5 |
| 9.0 | 1.51 | 4.2 | 0.00 | 2.1 | 0.0 | 0.34 | 2.44 | 2.64 | 91.1 | 6.3 | 69.3 | 0.0 | 6.6 |
| 9.6 | 0.70 | 2.0 | 0.28 | 3.3 | 0.1 | 0.34 | 2.09 | 4.47 | 91.1 | 4.7 | 29.9 | 0.0 | 6.9 |
| 9.5 | 0.60 | 2.4 | 0.20 | 5.6 | 0.2 | 0.68 | 4.66 | 3.34 | 84.4 | 3.8 | 7.5 | 4.1 | 7.1 |
| 8.0 | 0.54 | 3.2 | 0.55 | 4.6 | 0.7 | 0.76 | 7.86 | 2.65 | 73.7 | 3.7 | 6.8 | 3.3 | 5.8 |
| 9.1 | 0.37 | 1.4 | 0.00 | 3.9 | 0.1 | 0.62 | 6.24 | 3.02 | 90.4 | 5.5 | 25.9 | 0.0 | 3.8 |
| 8.2 | 0.00 | 0.0 | 0.00 | 1.1 | 0.0 | 0.00 | 0.00 | 3.61 | 105.0 | 4.2 | 27.8 | 0.0 | 6.5 |
| 6.4 | 2.97 | 8.9 | 0.00 | 1.2 | 0.0 | 0.06 | 0.60 | 2.34 | 98.3 | 5.8 | 52.5 | 0.0 | 3.6 |
| 3.7 | 1.73 | 16.1 | 0.43 | 6.9 | 0.3 | 1.15 | 13.74 | 4.77 | 69.2 | 3.2 | 8.7 | 4.1 | 3.6 |
| 8.1 | 0.38 | 3.6 | 0.28 | 2.8 | 0.6 | 0.22 | 2.00 | 3.02 | 88.3 | 3.8 | 12.3 | 2.6 | 7.0 |
| 9.8 | 0.28 | 1.1 | 0.13 | 0.9 | 0.0 | -0.12 | -0.92 | 2.38 | 102.1 | 5.4 | 43.9 | 0.8 | 4.3 |
| 8.9 | 0.54 | 3.2 | 0.25 | 3.5 | 0.3 | 0.49 | 6.10 | 3.09 | 80.8 | 4.1 | 11.2 | 0.8 | 3.3 |
| 2.3 | 7.94 | 27.8 | 0.00 | 10.0 | 0.0 | 2.75 | 17.78 | 7.11 | 50.0 | 5.7 | 43.7 | 0.0 | 9.1 |
| 9.9 | 0.00 | 0.0 | 0.00 | 2.8 | 0.0 | 0.37 | 3.94 | 3.07 | 87.6 | 5.0 | 22.9 | 0.0 | 4.6 |
| 9.3 | 0.29 | 2.1 | 0.27 | 3.4 | 1.8 | 0.57 | 5.93 | 3.36 | 81.0 | 3.5 | 22.4 | 10.5 | 6.0 |
| 1.7 | 100.00 | 45.0 | 0.00 | 0.9 | 0.0 | 0.00 | 0.00 | 3.42 | 100.0 | 8.5 | 102.0 | 0.0 | 3.7 |
| 9.4 | 0.29 | 1.4 | 0.07 | 2.7 | 0.1 | 0.35 | 4.22 | 2.68 | 85.7 | 5.0 | 23.6 | 2.1 | 3.7 |
| 8.6 | 1.35 | 5.5 | 0.12 | 2.1 | 0.0 | -0.06 | -0.51 | 4.15 | 97.7 | 5.2 | 35.9 | 2.6 | 5.5 |
| 8.6 | 0.00 | 0.0 | 0.00 | 1.1 | 0.0 | 0.00 | 0.00 | 7.70 | 100.0 | 6.1 | 46.4 | 0.0 | 5.0 |
| 8.9 | 0.95 | 3.6 | 0.51 | 3.8 | 1.5 | 0.73 | 9.69 | 2.38 | 74.1 | 5.2 | 17.2 | 1.7 | 4.1 |
| 2.7 | 9.40 | 32.0 | 0.49 | 9.5 | 0.2 | 1.58 | 9.20 | 3.43 | 51.7 | 3.9 | 12.1 | 0.0 | 8.1 |
| 5.3 | 2.62 | 13.4 | 0.94 | 1.8 | 0.0 | -0.17 | -1.94 | 3.84 | 92.9 | 3.6 | 14.2 | 13.7 | 3.2 |
| 9.2 | 0.52 | 2.4 | 0.01 | 9.8 | 1.2 | 1.66 | 12.26 | 3.23 | 59.0 | 3.3 | 17.8 | 9.4 | 7.9 |
| 8.3 | 0.67 | 3.1 | 0.43 | 3.3 | 1.0 | 0.31 | 3.31 | 2.71 | 87.8 | 4.7 | 22.8 | 5.6 | 5.9 |
| 10.0 | 0.71 | 0.7 | 0.33 | 4.6 | 0.1 | 0.69 | 4.95 | 2.65 | 71.3 | 6.0 | 29.0 | 1.5 | 6.5 |
| 9.3 | 1.45 | 3.4 | 0.15 | 3.9 | 0.4 | 0.52 | 2.95 | 2.99 | 82.6 | 4.8 | 22.9 | 0.0 | 8.1 |
| 6.0 | 2.90 | 8.2 | 2.00 | 0.2 | 0.0 | -1.29 | -5.54 | 5.39 | 108.5 | 5.6 | 33.9 | 0.0 | 5.0 |
| 1.8 | 6.65 | 34.8 | 0.95 | 2.0 | 0.0 | -0.06 | -0.53 | 5.27 | 77.4 | 2.8 | 22.7 | 15.8 | 5.2 |
| 6.7 | 1.80 | 9.2 | 0.36 | 5.1 | 0.6 | 0.71 | 5.90 | 3.54 | 74.8 | 4.1 | 13.5 | 4.8 | 7.9 |
| 8.4 | 2.50 | 3.1 | -0.34 | 1.3 | 0.0 | 0.07 | 0.42 | 2.05 | 97.0 | 5.2 | 27.7 | 4.2 | 5.8 |
| 7.1 | 0.03 | 0.6 | 0.11 | 5.9 | 0.3 | 0.95 | 5.83 | 3.60 | 74.4 | 4.1 | 18.1 | 1.4 | 7.6 |
| 10.0 | 0.00 | 0.0 | 6.20 | 0.0 | 0.0 | -1.58 | -6.87 | 4.21 | 133.3 | 7.3 | 60.5 | 0.0 | 6.6 |
| 8.5 | 1.37 | 4.3 | 0.49 | 6.6 | 0.4 | 0.76 | 3.83 | 5.55 | 83.4 | 5.4 | 40.2 | 9.4 | 7.5 |
| 9.3 | 0.28 | 1.7 | 0.24 | 6.1 | 8.9 | 0.94 | 8.14 | 2.18 | 67.2 | 4.2 | 27.2 | 10.3 | 8.4 |
| 6.8 | 0.71 | 4.9 | 0.20 | 4.2 | 1.0 | 0.62 | 6.38 | 3.58 | 83.0 | 3.8 | 15.6 | 3.2 | 6.7 |
| 9.3 | 0.81 | 3.2 | 0.10 | 2.9 | 0.3 | 0.35 | 4.07 | 2.94 | 100.9 | 4.9 | 19.1 | 5.2 | 5.0 |
| 8.0 | 0.32 | 2.0 | 0.22 | 1.7 | 0.1 | 0.15 | 1.78 | 3.12 | 95.5 | 4.3 | 3.9 | 2.2 | 3.3 |
| 6.0 | 2.61 | 11.1 | 0.30 | 0.0 | 0.0 | -1.16 | -9.58 | 4.24 | 118.8 | 5.5 | 51.7 | 0.0 | 5.7 |
| 8.8 | 0.56 | 3.6 | 0.71 | 4.3 | 0.5 | 0.47 | 3.91 | 4.37 | 80.3 | 4.4 | 28.3 | 8.0 | 7.6 |
| 7.3 | 0.41 | 3.1 | 0.59 | 3.4 | 0.3 | 0.43 | 5.08 | 4.17 | 86.2 | 3.7 | 14.3 | 0.6 | 3.8 |
| 9.7 | 0.67 | 2.2 | 0.49 | 1.9 | 0.1 | 0.39 | 3.13 | 3.34 | 91.3 | 4.5 | 32.6 | 2.2 | 4.8 |
| 4.9 | 0.90 | 9.3 | 0.00 | 1.6 | 0.0 | 0.15 | 1.92 | 4.06 | 93.9 | 4.0 | 13.1 | 0.0 | 1.0 |
| 7.0 | 1.59 | 7.1 | 2.64 | 2.6 | 0.9 | 0.08 | 0.68 | 3.22 | 73.5 | 4.3 | 10.6 | 2.2 | 7.7 |
| 1.7 | 2.05 | 21.3 | 0.98 | 5.1 | 0.5 | 0.89 | 11.60 | 5.09 | 77.4 | 2.5 | 8.4 | 8.3 | 3.2 |
| 4.9 | 5.63 | 12.8 | 0.18 | 0.5 | 0.0 | -0.43 | -1.92 | 3.82 | 113.0 | 4.6 | 29.0 | 0.0 | 6.1 |
| 9.7 | 2.65 | 2.5 | 0.05 | 3.7 | 0.2 | 0.45 | 2.17 | 2.22 | 78.7 | 5.5 | 23.1 | 0.6 | 7.1 |
| 8.8 | 0.24 | 1.2 | 0.07 | 2.1 | 0.0 | 0.11 | 1.19 | 2.54 | 96.1 | 5.7 | 44.0 | 0.0 | 4.0 |

| Name | City | State | Rating | 2014 Rating | 2013 Rating | Total Assets ($Mil) | One Year Asset Growth | Asset Mix (As a % of Total Assets) Commercial Loans | Consumer Loans | Mortgage Loans | Securities | Capitalization Index | Net Worth Ratio |
|------|------|-------|--------|-------------|-------------|---------------------|----------------------|-----------------|----------------|----------------|------------|---------------------|-----------------|
| ▲ CENTRAL JERSEY FCU | Woodbridge | NJ | E+ | E+ | D- | 68.9 | 2.36 | 3.4 | 17.3 | 13.4 | 21.0 | 4.6 | 6.6 |
| CENTRAL KANSAS CU | Hutchinson | KS | D- | D- | D- | 35.4 | 0.69 | 0.5 | 46.4 | 10.9 | 1.4 | 5.0 | 7.0 |
| CENTRAL KEYSTONE FCU | Sunbury | PA | B | B | B | 38.7 | -0.76 | 0.0 | 17.2 | 19.0 | 27.9 | 10.0 | 17.7 |
| CENTRAL MACOMB COMMUNITY CU | Clinton Township | MI | B+ | B+ | B+ | 179.5 | 4.13 | 3.3 | 30.7 | 30.2 | 20.9 | 8.9 | 10.3 |
| ▲ CENTRAL MAINE FCU | Lewiston | ME | C | C- | C | 87.5 | 0.43 | 0.6 | 11.5 | 18.8 | 0.0 | 10.0 | 12.5 |
| CENTRAL MINNESOTA CU | Melrose | MN | B | B | B | 894.6 | 5.01 | 56.8 | 9.8 | 40.2 | 1.9 | 10.0 | 14.9 |
| CENTRAL MISSOURI COMMUNITY CU | Warrensburg | MO | C- | C | C- | 94.7 | -7.07 | 0.0 | 31.1 | 20.8 | 10.6 | 5.8 | 7.8 |
| CENTRAL NEBRASKA FCU | Grand Island | NE | C- | C- | C- | 8.0 | -1.99 | 0.0 | 46.7 | 0.0 | 0.0 | 9.7 | 10.8 |
| ▼ CENTRAL OKLAHOMA FCU | Davenport | OK | C+ | B- | B- | 33.5 | -5.02 | 5.2 | 17.1 | 34.7 | 0.0 | 10.0 | 15.7 |
| CENTRAL ONE FCU | Shrewsbury | MA | B | B | B | 413.8 | 5.35 | 8.7 | 18.7 | 43.0 | 1.4 | 7.7 | 9.5 |
| CENTRAL SOYA FCU | Decatur | IN | C+ | C | C | 24.1 | -0.94 | 0.2 | 16.9 | 0.0 | 0.0 | 10.0 | 18.5 |
| CENTRAL STATE CU | Stockton | CA | C- | C | C- | 158.0 | 6.50 | 8.7 | 44.5 | 14.8 | 16.8 | 6.8 | 8.8 |
| CENTRAL SUNBELT FCU | Laurel | MS | A- | A- | A- | 199.5 | 2.38 | 0.1 | 28.5 | 6.2 | 39.5 | 10.0 | 14.1 |
| CENTRAL SUSQUEHANNA COMMUNITY FCU | Danville | PA | C | C- | C- | 24.4 | -3.23 | 0.0 | 16.7 | 0.0 | 56.9 | 10.0 | 15.3 |
| CENTRAL TEXAS TEACHERS CU | Corsicana | TX | D+ | C | C- | 13.0 | -2.63 | 0.0 | 26.6 | 0.0 | 0.0 | 10.0 | 12.1 |
| CENTRAL VALLEY FCU | Arnold | PA | D | C- | C | 2.0 | -2.58 | 0.0 | 61.4 | 0.0 | 0.0 | 9.6 | 10.8 |
| CENTRAL VERMONT MEDICAL CENTER INC | Berlin | VT | B | B | B | 11.9 | 4.27 | 0.0 | 45.4 | 0.0 | 0.0 | 10.0 | 18.0 |
| CENTRAL VIRGINIA FCU | Lynchburg | VA | C+ | B- | B | 115.5 | 4.71 | 0.2 | 23.5 | 15.0 | 0.0 | 6.6 | 8.6 |
| CENTRAL WILLAMETTE CU | Albany | OR | B | B | B | 238.8 | 4.04 | 6.0 | 40.4 | 12.3 | 7.0 | 7.0 | 9.0 |
| CENTRAL WISCONSIN CU | Plover | WI | C+ | C- | C+ | 33.0 | 0.71 | 0.3 | 15.4 | 47.9 | 0.0 | 10.0 | 11.4 |
| CENTRALALLIANCE CU | Neenah | WI | B- | C+ | B | 73.3 | 2.76 | 14.0 | 7.0 | 30.5 | 29.7 | 10.0 | 20.2 |
| CENTRIC FCU | West Monroe | LA | B- | B- | C+ | 135.5 | 21.34 | 8.0 | 38.7 | 27.0 | 2.5 | 6.3 | 8.4 |
| ▲ CENTRIS FCU | Omaha | NE | B | B- | B- | 572.9 | 8.89 | 4.6 | 41.6 | 33.1 | 0.4 | 7.8 | 9.5 |
| CENTURY CU | Saint Louis | MO | A | A | A | 87.4 | -0.16 | 0.6 | 27.0 | 21.4 | 0.1 | 10.0 | 17.2 |
| CENTURY EMPL SAVINGS FUND CU | Hickory | NC | C- | C- | D+ | 9.0 | -0.60 | 0.0 | 32.8 | 13.1 | 0.0 | 10.0 | 31.7 |
| CENTURY FCU | Cleveland | OH | C+ | C+ | B- | 351.5 | 0.48 | 0.4 | 16.5 | 38.9 | 27.0 | 7.5 | 9.3 |
| CENTURY HERITAGE FCU | Pittsburgh | PA | C- | C- | C- | 117.8 | -4.20 | 3.2 | 31.5 | 28.6 | 20.6 | 10.0 | 12.2 |
| CERROBRASS CU | Sauget | IL | D | D | C- | <1 | -1.62 | 0.0 | 0.0 | 0.0 | 83.2 | 10.0 | 16.8 |
| CES CU | Mount Vernon | OH | B- | C+ | C- | 124.8 | 2.07 | 0.0 | 25.4 | 17.5 | 0.0 | 6.4 | 8.4 |
| CF INDUSTRIES INC EMPL FCU | Deerfield | IL | D+ | D+ | D+ | 1.8 | -2.27 | 0.0 | 21.7 | 0.0 | 0.0 | 10.0 | 16.2 |
| CFCU COMMUNITY CU | Ithaca | NY | A | A | A | 954.9 | 6.60 | 7.9 | 18.2 | 42.6 | 11.9 | 10.0 | 13.0 |
| CGR CU | Macon | GA | A | A | A- | 80.7 | 10.04 | 0.1 | 31.4 | 5.2 | 20.3 | 10.0 | 15.5 |
| CHA-TEL FCU | Charleston | WV | D+ | D- | D | 10.6 | -0.52 | 0.0 | 53.9 | 0.0 | 25.0 | 6.9 | 8.9 |
| CHABOT FCU | Dublin | CA | B | B | B | 69.4 | -1.07 | 0.0 | 2.3 | 20.4 | 18.0 | 10.0 | 13.8 |
| CHACO CU INC | Hamilton | OH | C- | C- | C- | 175.1 | 0.30 | 5.1 | 44.8 | 30.6 | 5.9 | 6.3 | 8.3 |
| ▼ CHADRON FCU | Chadron | NE | C | C- | C | 9.9 | 5.01 | 0.0 | 44.2 | 10.2 | 0.0 | 10.0 | 11.8 |
| CHADWICK FCU | Norwood | MA | E- | E- | E- | 22.2 | 0.73 | 0.0 | 19.9 | 22.3 | 0.0 | 4.3 | 6.3 |
| ▲ CHAFFEY FCU | Upland | CA | B | B- | C- | 114.9 | 6.02 | 6.6 | 15.9 | 24.2 | 28.5 | 6.8 | 8.8 |
| CHAMPAIGN COUNTY SCHOOL EMPL CU | Champaign | IL | D | D | D | 12.7 | 11.11 | 0.0 | 33.2 | 0.0 | 0.0 | 6.0 | 8.0 |
| CHAMPAIGN MUNICIPAL EMPL CU | Champaign | IL | D | D | D+ | 4.4 | -4.89 | 0.0 | 80.8 | 0.0 | 0.0 | 10.0 | 11.2 |
| CHAMPAIGN POSTAL CU | Champaign | IL | D+ | C- | C | 2.5 | -4.73 | 0.0 | 40.0 | 0.0 | 0.0 | 10.0 | 18.1 |
| CHAMPION COMMUNITY CU | Courtland | AL | C | C | B- | 54.6 | -3.91 | 0.6 | 21.1 | 23.6 | 0.0 | 10.0 | 11.4 |
| ▲ CHAMPION CU | Canton | NC | B+ | B | B | 208.9 | 11.08 | 2.6 | 28.8 | 46.4 | 0.0 | 10.0 | 12.3 |
| CHAMPION CU | Toledo | OH | C- | D+ | D+ | 47.0 | -0.34 | 0.0 | 21.4 | 15.2 | 9.4 | 10.0 | 13.3 |
| CHAMPION FCU | Cambridge | OH | C- | C- | C- | 5.1 | 9.99 | 0.0 | 34.2 | 0.0 | 0.0 | 10.0 | 13.9 |
| CHANGING SEASONS FCU | Hampden | ME | C- | C | C- | 21.8 | -1.15 | 0.0 | 26.6 | 38.2 | 0.0 | 9.3 | 10.5 |
| CHARLESTON COUNTY TEACHERS FCU | Charleston | SC | D+ | D | D- | 1.6 | 0.44 | 0.0 | 53.0 | 0.0 | 0.0 | 8.2 | 9.8 |
| ▲ CHARLESTON FCU | Charleston | WV | D+ | D | D | 9.1 | -2.98 | 0.0 | 48.7 | 0.0 | 0.0 | 8.3 | 9.9 |
| CHARLESTON POSTAL FCU | Charleston | WV | D+ | D | D- | 4.0 | -0.97 | 0.0 | 80.5 | 0.0 | 0.0 | 7.5 | 9.3 |
| CHARLOTTE FIRE DEPT CU | Charlotte | NC | C | C- | D+ | 45.9 | -1.46 | 0.5 | 30.2 | 2.0 | 48.4 | 10.0 | 12.5 |
| CHARLOTTE METRO FCU | Charlotte | NC | A | A | A- | 343.9 | 4.73 | 7.5 | 31.1 | 38.3 | 0.0 | 10.0 | 11.0 |
| CHARLOTTESVILLE POSTAL FCU | Charlottesville | VA | E+ | E+ | E+ | 6.2 | -0.94 | 0.0 | 33.0 | 29.9 | 0.0 | 6.0 | 8.0 |
| CHARTER OAK FCU | Waterford | CT | B | B | B+ | 914.0 | 10.68 | 11.6 | 16.0 | 57.2 | 9.3 | 8.1 | 9.8 |
| CHARTWAY FCU | Virginia Beach | VA | C+ | C+ | C | 2050.0 | 7.24 | 1.2 | 51.0 | 14.0 | 8.7 | 5.8 | 7.8 |
| ▲ CHATHAM EBEN COOPERATIVE FCU | Chatham | MI | D+ | D | D | 7.4 | 4.35 | 0.0 | 42.1 | 0.0 | 0.0 | 8.0 | 9.6 |
| CHATTAHOOCHEE FCU | Valley | AL | C | C- | C+ | 14.5 | 3.37 | 0.0 | 47.6 | 2.1 | 0.0 | 10.0 | 12.7 |
| CHATTANOOGA AREA SCHOOLS FCU | Chattanooga | TN | B- | B- | B+ | 146.0 | 0.34 | 0.0 | 20.2 | 10.0 | 40.2 | 10.0 | 15.8 |
| CHATTANOOGA FEDERAL EMPL CU | Chattanooga | TN | B | B | B | 48.0 | -2.57 | 0.0 | 18.8 | 19.3 | 0.0 | 10.0 | 16.1 |
| ▲ CHATTANOOGA FIRST FCU | Chattanooga | TN | C- | D+ | C | 22.1 | -4.60 | 0.0 | 23.9 | 30.6 | 9.0 | 10.0 | 22.0 |
| CHAVES COUNTY SCHOOL EMPL CU | Roswell | NM | B | B | B | 23.2 | 3.80 | 0.0 | 31.8 | 0.0 | 14.8 | 10.0 | 18.1 |

| Asset Quality Index | Non-Performing Loans as a % of Total Loans | Non-Performing Loans as a % of Capital | Net Charge-Offs Avg Loans | Profitability Index | Net Income ($Mil) | Return on Assets | Return on Equity | Net Interest Spread | Overhead Efficiency Ratio | Liquidity Index | Liquidity Ratio | Hot Money Ratio | Stability Index |
|---|---|---|---|---|---|---|---|---|---|---|---|---|---|
| 1.7 | 5.75 | 48.6 | 0.59 | 2.2 | 0.1 | 0.17 | 2.75 | 3.64 | 107.2 | 4.5 | 19.9 | 0.3 | 1.8 |
| 4.9 | 0.86 | 9.0 | -0.11 | 1.9 | 0.1 | 0.17 | 2.47 | 3.40 | 94.2 | 4.2 | 20.6 | 0.0 | 1.7 |
| 8.5 | 1.15 | 3.4 | 0.09 | 4.3 | 0.2 | 0.62 | 3.57 | 2.63 | 76.4 | 4.0 | 11.9 | 4.8 | 7.5 |
| 7.8 | 0.75 | 5.1 | 0.53 | 5.2 | 1.0 | 0.71 | 7.00 | 3.38 | 82.2 | 2.9 | 10.5 | 9.7 | 6.9 |
| 10.0 | 0.45 | 1.4 | 0.12 | 2.0 | 0.1 | 0.19 | 1.58 | 2.08 | 91.1 | 4.7 | 35.8 | 5.5 | 6.2 |
| 4.4 | 1.16 | 7.8 | 0.02 | 7.7 | 6.9 | 1.05 | 7.06 | 3.90 | 75.0 | 2.8 | 15.1 | 10.5 | 10.0 |
| 6.3 | 0.86 | 6.7 | 0.41 | 2.5 | 0.2 | 0.32 | 4.26 | 3.45 | 91.9 | 3.5 | 13.5 | 7.5 | 2.4 |
| 6.2 | 0.76 | 3.5 | 0.06 | 3.0 | 0.0 | 0.00 | 0.00 | 5.03 | 99.7 | 6.2 | 48.0 | 0.0 | 5.0 |
| 3.7 | 4.81 | 20.6 | 0.60 | 2.8 | 0.0 | 0.02 | 0.10 | 4.60 | 84.1 | 3.0 | 35.9 | 33.0 | 5.8 |
| 6.9 | 0.78 | 8.2 | 0.08 | 5.5 | 2.7 | 0.87 | 9.50 | 3.03 | 75.5 | 2.5 | 4.6 | 7.7 | 6.0 |
| 9.4 | 1.54 | 2.0 | 0.09 | 2.7 | 0.1 | 0.26 | 1.45 | 1.78 | 86.7 | 6.0 | 42.4 | 0.0 | 6.9 |
| 8.7 | 0.22 | 2.5 | 0.67 | 2.5 | 0.2 | 0.18 | 2.10 | 3.74 | 91.6 | 4.4 | 16.5 | 0.0 | 5.1 |
| 8.5 | 0.90 | 3.4 | 0.96 | 6.5 | 1.5 | 1.00 | 7.19 | 3.69 | 75.1 | 5.2 | 25.9 | 5.0 | 8.1 |
| 10.0 | 0.55 | 1.0 | -0.04 | 1.8 | 0.0 | 0.02 | 0.11 | 2.24 | 100.9 | 5.0 | 20.4 | 1.2 | 6.7 |
| 9.0 | 1.61 | 4.2 | 3.27 | 0.4 | -0.1 | -1.15 | -9.17 | 3.21 | 96.4 | 5.4 | 44.3 | 3.6 | 5.7 |
| 5.1 | 1.48 | 7.9 | 0.00 | 0.4 | 0.0 | -1.28 | -11.64 | 4.42 | 128.6 | 4.0 | 15.7 | 0.0 | 5.6 |
| 6.2 | 2.16 | 6.0 | 0.76 | 10.0 | 0.2 | 1.97 | 11.46 | 5.25 | 55.9 | 5.5 | 49.3 | 1.2 | 8.6 |
| 8.9 | 0.36 | 1.9 | 0.45 | 3.2 | 0.2 | 0.27 | 3.17 | 3.48 | 88.1 | 5.2 | 26.9 | 1.2 | 4.9 |
| 8.4 | 0.30 | 2.4 | 0.38 | 5.0 | 1.3 | 0.72 | 8.14 | 3.74 | 80.7 | 3.6 | 11.6 | 2.9 | 5.3 |
| 8.8 | 0.00 | 0.0 | 0.02 | 3.2 | 0.1 | 0.48 | 4.29 | 3.32 | 85.8 | 3.8 | 17.9 | 1.4 | 6.1 |
| 7.9 | 0.04 | 4.9 | 0.02 | 3.7 | 0.3 | 0.54 | 2.75 | 3.19 | 82.3 | 5.5 | 29.6 | 2.8 | 7.2 |
| 5.9 | 1.01 | 9.5 | 0.58 | 5.3 | 0.7 | 0.74 | 8.63 | 4.91 | 84.0 | 2.4 | 14.5 | 21.0 | 5.3 |
| 6.0 | 0.91 | 9.0 | 0.48 | 5.3 | 3.5 | 0.82 | 9.72 | 3.92 | 80.5 | 2.5 | 4.7 | 6.9 | 6.3 |
| 9.5 | 0.71 | 2.5 | 0.34 | 9.3 | 0.8 | 1.26 | 7.56 | 3.11 | 63.5 | 3.7 | 20.8 | 5.4 | 8.5 |
| 9.9 | 0.48 | 0.7 | 0.06 | 2.1 | 0.0 | 0.22 | 0.70 | 3.36 | 97.9 | 4.6 | 35.7 | 2.0 | 6.3 |
| 8.1 | 0.72 | 5.5 | 0.31 | 3.2 | 1.1 | 0.40 | 4.33 | 2.54 | 77.9 | 3.8 | 21.3 | 3.8 | 5.7 |
| 8.1 | 0.64 | 3.5 | 0.06 | 1.4 | 0.0 | 0.04 | 0.33 | 2.79 | 96.3 | 3.6 | 15.6 | 3.9 | 6.8 |
| 8.4 | 4.55 | 3.6 | 0.00 | 0.0 | 0.0 | -4.29 | -22.67 | 2.04 | 325.0 | 6.5 | 104.9 | 0.0 | 6.1 |
| 9.4 | 0.37 | 2.5 | 0.24 | 3.9 | 0.5 | 0.55 | 6.85 | 2.86 | 85.9 | 4.9 | 30.1 | 0.8 | 4.5 |
| 7.9 | 3.81 | 5.2 | 0.00 | 1.1 | 0.0 | -0.08 | -0.46 | 2.54 | 106.9 | 5.4 | 27.4 | 0.0 | 6.6 |
| 8.8 | 0.77 | 4.1 | 0.22 | 5.8 | 5.7 | 0.81 | 6.17 | 3.40 | 70.7 | 4.1 | 24.8 | 12.9 | 9.4 |
| 8.7 | 0.72 | 4.0 | 0.43 | 9.3 | 0.8 | 1.34 | 8.68 | 3.39 | 76.4 | 4.8 | 38.0 | 13.9 | 7.9 |
| 6.8 | 0.42 | 2.7 | 0.02 | 4.3 | 0.1 | 0.69 | 8.00 | 3.82 | 81.4 | 4.9 | 16.2 | 0.0 | 3.6 |
| 9.4 | 1.84 | 3.6 | 0.00 | 3.5 | 0.2 | 0.33 | 2.55 | 1.98 | 80.3 | 4.3 | 24.1 | 7.6 | 7.0 |
| 6.5 | 0.78 | 9.0 | 0.13 | 2.4 | 0.3 | 0.21 | 2.62 | 3.41 | 93.5 | 2.7 | 8.3 | 9.2 | 4.5 |
| 8.3 | 0.69 | 4.0 | 0.11 | 5.5 | 0.1 | 0.85 | 7.42 | 4.66 | 82.4 | 4.0 | 27.6 | 5.4 | 4.3 |
| 7.3 | 0.40 | 3.3 | 0.41 | 1.8 | 0.0 | 0.08 | 1.33 | 2.82 | 90.3 | 4.0 | 8.3 | 1.1 | 0.7 |
| 9.1 | 0.03 | 0.2 | 0.00 | 5.0 | 0.7 | 0.80 | 9.29 | 2.85 | 78.3 | 4.3 | 20.6 | 7.4 | 5.3 |
| 8.0 | 0.42 | 1.7 | 0.97 | 1.6 | 0.0 | -0.02 | -0.26 | 2.67 | 98.0 | 6.0 | 56.0 | 0.0 | 2.7 |
| 7.8 | 0.06 | 0.4 | -0.04 | 0.7 | 0.0 | -0.20 | -1.89 | 4.05 | 105.0 | 3.3 | 13.4 | 0.0 | 5.6 |
| 9.5 | 0.72 | 1.9 | 0.00 | 1.1 | 0.0 | 0.00 | 0.00 | 2.65 | 97.7 | 5.6 | 46.0 | 0.0 | 5.2 |
| 7.8 | 1.04 | 5.1 | 0.16 | 2.0 | 0.0 | 0.09 | 0.77 | 3.05 | 96.6 | 4.2 | 24.9 | 12.8 | 5.8 |
| 6.0 | 0.86 | 11.1 | 0.49 | 5.1 | 1.1 | 0.74 | 5.87 | 4.86 | 79.7 | 3.1 | 17.4 | 14.1 | 7.5 |
| 6.8 | 3.12 | 11.4 | 0.07 | 1.7 | 0.1 | 0.20 | 1.62 | 3.27 | 94.3 | 4.4 | 21.2 | 1.0 | 5.6 |
| 5.1 | 6.26 | 16.3 | 0.34 | 1.9 | 0.0 | 0.08 | 0.56 | 3.38 | 93.5 | 6.9 | 55.4 | 0.0 | 7.1 |
| 6.9 | 0.53 | 3.7 | 0.30 | 2.5 | 0.0 | 0.08 | 0.76 | 3.36 | 94.8 | 3.6 | 25.0 | 3.8 | 4.9 |
| 3.6 | 2.89 | 15.6 | 0.14 | 5.5 | 0.0 | 0.67 | 6.88 | 11.92 | 82.5 | 6.3 | 45.6 | 0.0 | 3.0 |
| 5.2 | 1.50 | 7.5 | 0.55 | 5.6 | 0.1 | 0.96 | 10.34 | 3.34 | 62.5 | 4.6 | 30.1 | 0.0 | 3.0 |
| 6.4 | 0.72 | 5.1 | 2.14 | 4.1 | 0.0 | 0.20 | 2.18 | 7.23 | 70.3 | 4.2 | 18.3 | 0.0 | 2.3 |
| 8.4 | 1.00 | 3.3 | 0.04 | 2.0 | 0.0 | 0.12 | 0.98 | 3.06 | 99.8 | 2.7 | 11.9 | 23.7 | 5.0 |
| 9.0 | 0.38 | 2.7 | 0.46 | 9.5 | 3.2 | 1.27 | 11.91 | 3.65 | 76.6 | 3.4 | 12.9 | 8.2 | 7.7 |
| 7.3 | 0.38 | 2.9 | 0.69 | 0.1 | 0.0 | -0.70 | -8.62 | 3.99 | 99.5 | 4.0 | 11.5 | 0.0 | 3.2 |
| 8.2 | 0.42 | 3.7 | 0.16 | 4.3 | 4.4 | 0.67 | 6.70 | 2.94 | 82.8 | 2.9 | 3.2 | 6.5 | 6.9 |
| 5.7 | 0.66 | 6.8 | 0.40 | 3.8 | 9.0 | 0.59 | 7.49 | 2.96 | 75.3 | 2.6 | 13.3 | 16.2 | 5.0 |
| 7.5 | 0.35 | 1.7 | 0.30 | 4.5 | 0.0 | 0.65 | 6.91 | 4.08 | 85.8 | 4.1 | 17.7 | 10.5 | 3.0 |
| 7.5 | 0.33 | 1.4 | 0.67 | 3.2 | 0.1 | 0.42 | 3.38 | 4.22 | 88.5 | 4.2 | 28.2 | 6.2 | 4.7 |
| 9.9 | 0.12 | 0.3 | 0.05 | 3.5 | 0.6 | 0.55 | 3.52 | 1.61 | 65.5 | 4.0 | 18.0 | 8.4 | 8.3 |
| 7.8 | 1.33 | 6.5 | 0.42 | 3.9 | 0.2 | 0.53 | 3.32 | 2.69 | 79.8 | 5.1 | 67.8 | 10.5 | 6.7 |
| 8.7 | 0.98 | 3.3 | 0.52 | 2.6 | 0.1 | 0.41 | 1.94 | 3.43 | 84.2 | 3.3 | 35.6 | 14.9 | 6.4 |
| 10.0 | 0.03 | 0.1 | -0.12 | 3.5 | 0.1 | 0.37 | 2.08 | 2.35 | 86.8 | 5.5 | 24.1 | 0.0 | 7.8 |

| Name | City | State | Rating | 2014 Rating | 2013 Rating | Total Assets ($Mil) | One Year Asset Growth | Asset Mix (As a % of Total Assets) Commercial Loans | Consumer Loans | Mortgage Loans | Securities | Capitalization Index | Net Worth Ratio |
|---|---|---|---|---|---|---|---|---|---|---|---|---|---|
| ▼ CHEEKTOWAGA COMMUNITY FCU | Cheektowaga | NY | C- | C- | C- | 11.5 | 2.02 | 0.0 | 22.8 | 16.7 | 8.4 | 10.0 | 13.0 |
| CHELSEA EMPL FCU | Chelsea | MA | C- | C- | C | 12.5 | 1.85 | 0.0 | 40.6 | 0.0 | 0.0 | 8.7 | 10.2 |
| CHEM FAMILY CU | Anniston | AL | C+ | C+ | C+ | 6.1 | 0.52 | 0.1 | 4.5 | 7.6 | 46.8 | 10.0 | 18.1 |
| CHEMCEL FCU | Bishop | TX | B | B+ | B+ | 104.1 | 4.27 | 0.0 | 38.6 | 5.7 | 11.7 | 9.5 | 10.7 |
| ▼ CHEMCO CU | McIntosh | AL | D+ | C- | C+ | 5.6 | 0.66 | 0.0 | 27.9 | 1.2 | 0.0 | 10.0 | 13.5 |
| CHEMCO FCU | Louisville | KY | D- | D- | D+ | 19.2 | 1.88 | 0.0 | 31.8 | 11.1 | 0.0 | 6.7 | 8.7 |
| CHEN-DEL-O FCU | Franklin | NY | D | D | D+ | 25.0 | 2.95 | 0.0 | 25.3 | 0.0 | 52.7 | 8.1 | 9.7 |
| CHENEY FCU | Cheney | WA | B- | B | B | 84.5 | 0.79 | 0.0 | 12.3 | 22.0 | 10.5 | 10.0 | 11.3 |
| CHEROKEE COUNTY FCU | Rusk | TX | B+ | B+ | B+ | 30.0 | -0.35 | 0.0 | 63.9 | 1.8 | 0.0 | 10.0 | 23.4 |
| CHEROKEE COUNTY TEACHERS FCU | Rusk | TX | C+ | C+ | B- | 13.7 | 1.09 | 0.0 | 52.5 | 0.0 | 6.0 | 10.0 | 16.4 |
| CHEROKEE STRIP CU | Ponca City | OK | D | D+ | D | 77.0 | -7.73 | 0.0 | 69.0 | 10.3 | 0.0 | 1.7 | 4.5 |
| CHERRY EMPL FCU | Santa Ana | CA | D+ | D | C- | 3.7 | -5.40 | 0.0 | 22.9 | 0.0 | 0.0 | 10.0 | 25.8 |
| CHESHIRE COUNTY FCU | Keene | NH | D+ | C- | C | 17.0 | 7.02 | 0.0 | 28.2 | 4.6 | 0.0 | 7.2 | 9.1 |
| CHESHIRE HEALTH FCU | Keene | NH | E+ | E+ | E+ | 4.4 | 7.42 | 0.0 | 33.6 | 0.0 | 0.0 | 4.8 | 6.8 |
| CHESSIE FCU | Cumberland | MD | C | C | C | 248.3 | 1.80 | 1.1 | 28.3 | 29.8 | 3.4 | 6.4 | 8.4 |
| CHESTER UPLAND SCHOOL EMPL FCU | Chester | PA | E+ | D- | D | <1 | -3.91 | 0.0 | 46.5 | 0.0 | 0.0 | 6.9 | 8.9 |
| CHESTERFIELD FCU | Chesterfield | VA | C- | C- | D+ | 83.3 | 4.37 | 0.0 | 43.2 | 7.4 | 26.0 | 5.4 | 7.5 |
| CHESTNUT RUN FCU | Wilmington | DE | D+ | C- | C- | 68.6 | 1.43 | 0.0 | 15.0 | 5.9 | 23.2 | 9.1 | 10.5 |
| CHESWICK ATOMIC DIVISION FCU | Cheswick | PA | D+ | C | C | 5.9 | -4.78 | 0.0 | 22.4 | 0.0 | 0.0 | 10.0 | 24.6 |
| CHEVRON FCU | Oakland | CA | A- | A- | A- | 2696.2 | 9.56 | 1.9 | 6.9 | 69.7 | 7.6 | 9.3 | 10.5 |
| CHEVRON VALLEY CU | Bakersfield | CA | B- | B- | C+ | 125.4 | 2.09 | 0.0 | 41.9 | 6.6 | 24.6 | 10.0 | 11.2 |
| CHEYENNE-LARAMIE COUNTY EMPL FCU | Cheyenne | WY | C- | C- | C | 20.9 | 2.19 | 0.0 | 26.2 | 2.6 | 0.0 | 10.0 | 11.6 |
| CHHE FCU | Huntington | WV | C | C- | C- | 16.9 | -0.58 | 0.0 | 30.5 | 0.0 | 0.0 | 8.9 | 10.3 |
| CHICAGO AREA OFFICE FCU | Chicago | IL | C+ | C | C | 11.7 | -3.14 | 0.0 | 20.1 | 0.0 | 0.0 | 10.0 | 17.0 |
| CHICAGO AVENUE GARAGE FCU | Chicago | IL | D+ | D | D+ | 7.0 | -0.85 | 0.0 | 22.5 | 0.0 | 0.0 | 10.0 | 35.8 |
| CHICAGO CENTRAL & COMMERCE CU | Waterloo | IA | C | C | C | 6.8 | -10.61 | 0.0 | 23.1 | 0.0 | 0.0 | 10.0 | 20.6 |
| CHICAGO FAUCET FCU | Des Plaines | IL | C- | C- | C | <1 | 7.09 | 0.0 | 69.5 | 0.0 | 0.0 | 10.0 | 48.9 |
| CHICAGO FIRE OFFICERS ASSN CU | Chicago | IL | C+ | C+ | C+ | 9.6 | 5.15 | 0.0 | 41.9 | 0.0 | 0.0 | 10.0 | 15.2 |
| CHICAGO FIREFIGHTERS CU | Chicago | IL | B- | B- | B- | 52.6 | 7.13 | 0.0 | 39.6 | 0.0 | 0.0 | 9.7 | 10.8 |
| CHICAGO FIREMANS ASSN CU | Chicago | IL | C+ | C | C | 17.3 | 4.52 | 0.0 | 51.0 | 0.0 | 0.0 | 10.0 | 13.3 |
| CHICAGO MUNICIPAL EMPL CU | Chicago | IL | D+ | C- | C | 37.6 | 1.34 | 0.0 | 22.4 | 23.6 | 0.0 | 10.0 | 13.6 |
| ▲ CHICAGO PATROLMENS FCU | Chicago | IL | C | D | C | 371.1 | -0.17 | 3.2 | 25.3 | 25.6 | 27.6 | 6.6 | 8.6 |
| CHICAGO POST OFFICE EMPL CU | Chicago | IL | B- | B | B- | 17.8 | -1.28 | 0.0 | 56.1 | 0.0 | 0.0 | 10.0 | 26.2 |
| ▼ CHICOPEE MUNICIPAL EMPL CU | Chicopee | MA | C- | C | C | 47.2 | 0.10 | 0.0 | 8.5 | 0.0 | 15.0 | 9.8 | 10.9 |
| CHIEF FINANCIAL FCU | Rochester Hills | MI | A- | A- | B+ | 148.7 | 11.32 | 1.0 | 58.8 | 9.6 | 0.0 | 10.0 | 11.8 |
| CHILDRENS MEDICAL CENTER FCU | Cincinnati | OH | B+ | B+ | B+ | 35.1 | 4.43 | 0.0 | 38.7 | 21.7 | 0.0 | 10.0 | 13.6 |
| ▲ CHIPHONE FCU | Elkhart | IN | C- | D+ | D+ | 83.7 | -1.39 | 0.0 | 17.9 | 24.0 | 24.1 | 10.0 | 14.8 |
| CHIPPEWA COUNTY CU | Sault Sainte Marie | MI | C+ | B- | B- | 28.7 | 4.15 | 0.3 | 27.2 | 26.8 | 2.6 | 10.0 | 11.4 |
| CHIROPRACTIC FCU | Farmington | MI | C+ | C+ | C+ | 26.1 | 4.39 | 4.0 | 30.0 | 8.7 | 0.0 | 10.0 | 14.6 |
| CHIVAHO FCU | Chillicothe | OH | C+ | C+ | C+ | 25.1 | -4.57 | 0.0 | 19.7 | 16.6 | 2.0 | 10.0 | 18.2 |
| CHOCOLATE BAYOU COMMUNITY FCU | Alvin | TX | C | C- | C | 104.6 | 1.25 | 0.0 | 31.6 | 8.5 | 17.7 | 6.6 | 8.7 |
| CHOCTAW FCU | Choctaw | MS | C- | D | D | 2.0 | -0.55 | 0.0 | 83.3 | 0.0 | 0.0 | 10.0 | 22.1 |
| CHOICE ONE COMMUNITY FCU | Wilkes-Barre | PA | C | C | C- | 88.0 | 2.23 | 1.4 | 29.0 | 25.1 | 0.0 | 6.6 | 8.6 |
| CHOPTANK ELECTRIC COOP EMPL FCU | Denton | MD | B- | B- | B- | 2.8 | 5.29 | 0.0 | 27.4 | 0.0 | 16.5 | 10.0 | 18.9 |
| CHRIST THE KING PARISH FCU | Kansas City | KS | D+ | D | D+ | 1.7 | 0.78 | 0.0 | 35.4 | 0.0 | 0.0 | 10.0 | 12.1 |
| CHRISTIAN COMMUNITY CU | San Dimas | CA | A- | B+ | B- | 616.2 | 8.90 | 47.4 | 5.5 | 71.8 | 0.0 | 10.0 | 11.6 |
| CHRISTIAN FINANCIAL CU | Roseville | MI | B+ | B | B | 333.6 | 3.18 | 13.3 | 30.5 | 32.9 | 19.2 | 8.3 | 9.9 |
| CHRISTIANSTED FCU | Christiansted | VI | B | B | B | 21.6 | -3.05 | 0.0 | 18.3 | 0.0 | 0.0 | 10.0 | 19.2 |
| CHRISTO REY FCU | Ney | OH | D+ | D+ | D+ | 1.9 | -4.33 | 0.0 | 33.0 | 0.0 | 0.0 | 10.0 | 12.0 |
| ▲ CHRISTOPHER CU | Chesaning | MI | D | D | D | 2.2 | -6.81 | 0.0 | 10.9 | 0.0 | 20.2 | 8.7 | 10.1 |
| CHROME FCU | Washington | PA | A | A | A | 131.7 | 4.89 | 1.0 | 41.0 | 23.9 | 2.7 | 10.0 | 14.2 |
| CHULA VISTA CITY EMPL FCU | Chula Vista | CA | D | D | C- | 3.8 | 36.67 | 0.0 | 26.8 | 0.0 | 0.0 | 4.9 | 6.9 |
| CHURCH OF THE MASTER FCU | New York | NY | C | C- | C- | <1 | 11.06 | 0.0 | 12.9 | 0.0 | 0.0 | 10.0 | 15.6 |
| CHURCHILL COUNTY FCU | Fallon | NV | B+ | B+ | B+ | 44.2 | 0.35 | 0.0 | 29.8 | 0.0 | 14.0 | 10.0 | 17.1 |
| CINCINNATI EMPL CU | Harrison | OH | B- | C+ | C+ | 26.6 | 0.82 | 0.0 | 24.8 | 3.0 | 42.8 | 10.0 | 11.4 |
| CINCINNATI HEALTHCARE ASSOCIATES FCU | Cincinnati | OH | D | D | D+ | 19.3 | -1.10 | 0.0 | 34.2 | 0.0 | 0.0 | 7.1 | 9.1 |
| CINCINNATI INTERAGENCY FCU | Cincinnati | OH | C | C- | B- | 27.2 | 3.34 | 0.0 | 41.0 | 0.4 | 0.0 | 10.0 | 12.2 |
| CINCINNATI OHIO POLICE FCU | Cincinnati | OH | C+ | B- | B- | 105.8 | 0.74 | 3.3 | 24.3 | 11.7 | 12.3 | 10.0 | 11.7 |
| CINCO FAMILY FINANCIAL CENTER CU | Cincinnati | OH | D+ | D | D | 114.9 | -2.93 | 7.9 | 14.7 | 18.4 | 14.4 | 5.6 | 7.7 |
| CINFED FCU | Cincinnati | OH | B+ | B+ | B- | 360.3 | 8.47 | 13.1 | 18.7 | 47.0 | 10.5 | 9.4 | 10.6 |

| Asset Quality Index | Non-Performing Loans as a % of Total Loans | as a % of Capital | Net Charge-Offs Avg Loans | Profitability Index | Net Income ($Mil) | Return on Assets | Return on Equity | Net Interest Spread | Overhead Efficiency Ratio | Liquidity Index | Liquidity Ratio | Hot Money Ratio | Stability Index |
|---|---|---|---|---|---|---|---|---|---|---|---|---|---|
| 3.6 | 5.56 | 28.9 | 0.75 | 2.8 | 0.0 | 0.17 | 1.32 | 4.07 | 80.5 | 4.5 | 21.2 | 0.0 | 6.2 |
| 9.5 | 0.28 | 1.6 | 0.10 | 2.0 | 0.0 | 0.14 | 1.37 | 3.23 | 95.7 | 4.0 | 12.9 | 0.0 | 5.1 |
| 10.0 | 0.00 | 0.0 | 0.00 | 5.2 | 0.0 | 0.92 | 5.42 | 1.96 | 51.7 | 5.1 | 23.9 | 0.0 | 5.0 |
| 9.3 | 0.44 | 2.4 | 0.51 | 4.5 | 0.5 | 0.61 | 5.78 | 2.93 | 78.5 | 4.4 | 28.4 | 7.5 | 6.4 |
| 6.6 | 2.97 | 7.9 | 2.96 | 0.4 | -0.1 | -1.73 | -12.14 | 4.41 | 87.6 | 7.3 | 69.0 | 0.0 | 6.1 |
| 1.7 | 4.62 | 35.4 | 0.25 | 0.3 | -0.1 | -0.48 | -5.50 | 3.00 | 112.1 | 4.7 | 19.5 | 1.0 | 2.8 |
| 6.7 | 1.31 | 5.6 | 0.64 | 0.4 | -0.1 | -0.33 | -3.39 | 2.42 | 99.8 | 4.5 | 26.3 | 0.0 | 3.5 |
| 9.3 | 0.24 | 0.8 | 0.22 | 3.4 | 0.2 | 0.34 | 3.10 | 1.98 | 84.2 | 4.1 | 13.3 | 5.3 | 5.9 |
| 8.1 | 0.50 | 2.2 | 1.61 | 7.5 | 0.2 | 0.88 | 3.88 | 4.91 | 67.9 | 4.3 | 33.5 | 6.4 | 7.0 |
| 4.6 | 3.08 | 11.8 | 1.03 | 4.9 | 0.1 | 0.43 | 2.63 | 4.94 | 68.1 | 5.6 | 35.6 | 0.0 | 7.0 |
| 2.7 | 3.93 | 32.8 | 4.46 | 1.6 | -4.5 | -7.16 | -106.28 | 4.61 | 56.2 | 3.6 | 14.2 | 5.4 | 0.7 |
| 10.0 | 0.47 | 0.4 | 0.00 | 1.2 | 0.0 | 0.04 | 0.14 | 2.77 | 98.6 | 6.6 | 56.8 | 0.0 | 4.8 |
| 6.0 | 1.45 | 10.0 | 1.17 | 1.8 | 0.0 | -0.15 | -1.53 | 3.54 | 92.4 | 5.5 | 53.0 | 0.0 | 4.5 |
| 6.2 | 1.02 | 5.0 | 0.00 | 2.0 | 0.0 | 0.06 | 0.90 | 2.80 | 97.7 | 5.6 | 24.3 | 0.0 | 1.0 |
| 6.5 | 1.18 | 9.4 | 0.46 | 2.5 | 0.2 | 0.11 | 1.35 | 3.51 | 91.1 | 4.0 | 21.4 | 4.5 | 4.7 |
| 0.7 | 7.86 | 35.5 | 0.00 | 0.5 | 0.0 | -2.47 | -25.10 | 4.65 | 157.1 | 5.1 | 48.2 | 0.0 | 5.0 |
| 6.7 | 0.96 | 7.5 | 0.44 | 2.9 | 0.1 | 0.22 | 2.93 | 3.74 | 90.3 | 4.2 | 12.5 | 1.7 | 2.5 |
| 10.0 | 0.14 | 0.4 | 0.18 | 1.4 | 0.0 | -0.06 | -0.60 | 2.71 | 100.1 | 5.0 | 23.4 | 5.2 | 4.7 |
| 10.0 | 0.45 | 0.6 | 0.00 | 0.8 | 0.0 | -0.24 | -1.00 | 1.84 | 107.5 | 5.0 | 23.0 | 0.0 | 7.1 |
| 9.5 | 0.23 | 2.0 | 0.04 | 6.5 | 16.5 | 0.83 | 7.76 | 2.96 | 65.4 | 3.2 | 16.3 | 10.8 | 8.5 |
| 8.3 | 0.56 | 3.2 | 1.25 | 3.1 | 0.3 | 0.35 | 3.24 | 4.29 | 87.2 | 4.9 | 19.4 | 1.9 | 6.3 |
| 9.0 | 1.23 | 4.6 | 0.26 | 1.3 | 0.0 | -0.10 | -0.82 | 3.68 | 99.4 | 7.2 | 58.2 | 1.9 | 6.0 |
| 7.4 | 1.97 | 6.8 | 0.28 | 3.8 | 0.1 | 0.53 | 5.38 | 3.57 | 87.6 | 5.6 | 31.7 | 1.7 | 3.8 |
| 9.7 | 1.81 | 2.3 | 1.83 | 3.3 | 0.0 | 0.38 | 2.30 | 3.60 | 90.0 | 5.5 | 34.5 | 1.2 | 5.7 |
| 6.7 | 16.02 | 9.3 | 1.49 | 1.8 | 0.0 | 0.21 | 0.59 | 5.07 | 94.2 | 5.0 | 31.4 | 0.0 | 5.0 |
| 9.9 | 0.94 | 1.6 | 0.06 | 3.3 | 0.0 | 0.37 | 1.92 | 3.97 | 90.4 | 5.5 | 38.3 | 0.0 | 6.5 |
| 7.7 | 0.00 | 0.0 | 3.35 | 1.5 | 0.0 | 0.00 | 0.00 | 3.35 | 100.0 | 6.5 | 72.7 | 0.0 | 7.1 |
| 9.7 | 0.36 | 1.0 | 0.06 | 3.5 | 0.0 | 0.16 | 1.01 | 4.47 | 96.3 | 4.5 | 16.7 | 0.0 | 7.6 |
| 9.3 | 0.18 | 0.8 | 0.37 | 4.5 | 0.3 | 0.65 | 6.02 | 3.75 | 76.6 | 5.6 | 27.4 | 0.4 | 5.5 |
| 6.7 | 1.12 | 4.5 | -0.03 | 4.7 | 0.1 | 0.76 | 5.79 | 3.90 | 78.1 | 4.3 | 25.1 | 0.0 | 6.5 |
| 7.2 | 1.87 | 6.4 | 1.46 | 1.1 | -0.1 | -0.42 | -3.16 | 5.05 | 102.3 | 4.7 | 12.6 | 3.0 | 5.3 |
| 5.1 | 1.95 | 19.0 | 0.84 | 3.2 | 1.1 | 0.40 | 4.78 | 3.57 | 78.4 | 3.8 | 12.6 | 6.3 | 3.5 |
| 7.3 | 1.62 | 3.4 | 3.10 | 4.9 | 0.1 | 0.42 | 1.66 | 8.31 | 80.5 | 5.6 | 53.2 | 4.9 | 6.8 |
| 8.5 | 2.16 | 3.9 | 0.45 | 2.1 | 0.0 | 0.06 | 0.60 | 2.14 | 96.2 | 4.8 | 25.1 | 5.9 | 5.5 |
| 5.8 | 0.61 | 4.4 | 0.69 | 7.2 | 1.0 | 0.92 | 7.55 | 4.39 | 75.9 | 1.0 | 2.9 | 24.9 | 7.4 |
| 9.8 | 0.25 | 1.1 | 0.01 | 4.7 | 0.2 | 0.75 | 5.43 | 2.18 | 73.3 | 4.8 | 24.6 | 0.0 | 7.7 |
| 9.0 | 0.82 | 3.1 | 0.64 | 1.4 | 0.1 | 0.15 | 1.02 | 3.29 | 96.9 | 4.4 | 24.7 | 1.3 | 5.8 |
| 6.0 | 2.81 | 15.0 | 0.20 | 2.4 | 0.0 | 0.03 | 0.25 | 4.12 | 93.7 | 4.2 | 25.5 | 1.6 | 5.7 |
| 6.7 | 1.54 | 7.6 | 0.04 | 3.0 | 0.1 | 0.34 | 2.30 | 3.39 | 88.4 | 3.8 | 14.6 | 4.2 | 6.5 |
| 8.6 | 1.98 | 5.9 | 0.22 | 2.4 | 0.0 | 0.14 | 0.77 | 2.71 | 91.9 | 4.5 | 21.2 | 0.0 | 6.4 |
| 8.5 | 0.70 | 5.7 | 0.07 | 2.8 | 0.3 | 0.38 | 4.98 | 2.94 | 91.9 | 4.6 | 30.8 | 3.5 | 4.7 |
| 6.3 | 1.71 | 6.1 | 1.62 | 7.0 | 0.0 | 2.84 | 13.62 | 9.68 | 69.7 | 3.9 | 15.5 | 0.0 | 4.3 |
| 5.6 | 1.33 | 11.4 | 0.37 | 3.6 | 0.3 | 0.47 | 5.60 | 3.45 | 86.4 | 4.1 | 16.5 | 0.8 | 3.6 |
| 10.0 | 0.92 | 1.3 | -0.39 | 8.9 | 0.1 | 5.29 | 27.63 | 2.97 | 18.7 | 5.3 | 21.5 | 0.0 | 5.7 |
| 7.4 | 1.64 | 5.7 | 0.00 | 1.4 | 0.0 | 0.16 | 1.31 | 2.61 | 93.6 | 7.0 | 62.2 | 0.0 | 5.6 |
| 6.2 | 0.71 | 5.1 | 0.18 | 5.1 | 2.8 | 0.62 | 5.28 | 3.80 | 84.0 | 3.5 | 22.7 | 13.9 | 9.0 |
| 5.7 | 1.34 | 10.9 | 0.61 | 8.7 | 3.0 | 1.19 | 12.64 | 3.91 | 76.2 | 3.5 | 11.9 | 5.7 | 6.7 |
| 8.9 | 0.84 | 1.7 | 1.97 | 7.3 | 0.2 | 1.05 | 5.73 | 4.26 | 59.3 | 5.4 | 49.9 | 9.4 | 6.3 |
| 6.3 | 4.47 | 12.0 | 0.00 | 2.5 | 0.0 | 0.21 | 1.79 | 1.62 | 80.0 | 5.2 | 15.1 | 0.0 | 6.3 |
| 9.8 | 0.90 | 1.3 | 0.00 | 0.6 | 0.0 | -0.18 | -1.78 | 2.11 | 107.9 | 5.4 | 23.5 | 0.0 | 4.6 |
| 8.8 | 0.62 | 3.4 | 0.36 | 5.5 | 0.5 | 0.52 | 3.69 | 4.06 | 83.8 | 2.2 | 14.5 | 15.7 | 9.2 |
| 10.0 | 0.10 | 0.4 | 1.82 | 0.4 | 0.0 | -0.83 | -9.18 | 3.65 | 100.0 | 6.7 | 36.2 | 0.0 | 2.7 |
| 10.0 | 0.00 | 0.0 | -1.10 | 3.0 | 0.0 | 0.41 | 2.36 | 1.22 | 100.0 | 7.2 | 95.4 | 0.0 | 5.5 |
| 9.8 | 0.44 | 0.9 | 0.06 | 8.0 | 0.4 | 1.26 | 7.58 | 2.14 | 42.7 | 4.6 | 23.9 | 0.0 | 7.7 |
| 8.4 | 1.65 | 7.0 | 0.07 | 4.0 | 0.1 | 0.60 | 5.43 | 2.36 | 73.4 | 3.3 | 11.4 | 10.6 | 5.8 |
| 6.0 | 1.79 | 7.5 | 2.13 | 1.1 | 0.0 | -0.07 | -0.84 | 4.41 | 82.7 | 5.7 | 33.8 | 1.4 | 2.7 |
| 9.5 | 0.69 | 2.8 | 0.22 | 4.1 | 0.2 | 0.78 | 6.47 | 3.32 | 88.6 | 4.8 | 35.2 | 0.5 | 5.5 |
| 9.7 | 0.25 | 1.1 | 0.31 | 2.5 | 0.1 | 0.17 | 1.49 | 2.50 | 88.5 | 3.8 | 27.7 | 11.6 | 7.1 |
| 7.6 | 0.82 | 6.5 | 0.05 | 1.6 | 0.1 | 0.08 | 1.09 | 3.08 | 96.5 | 3.8 | 23.4 | 7.0 | 3.7 |
| 5.6 | 1.56 | 12.7 | 0.36 | 4.9 | 1.8 | 0.66 | 6.07 | 3.63 | 80.2 | 4.0 | 20.1 | 5.5 | 7.1 |

| Name | City | State | Rating | 2014 Rating | 2013 Rating | Total Assets ($Mil) | One Year Asset Growth | Commercial Loans | Consumer Loans | Mortgage Loans | Securities | Capitalization Index | Net Worth Ratio |
|---|---|---|---|---|---|---|---|---|---|---|---|---|---|
| | | | | | | | | Asset Mix (As a % of Total Assets) | | | | | |
| CIT-CO FCU | Sheridan | WY | D+ | D | C- | 12.5 | -8.15 | 2.0 | 74.9 | 0.0 | 0.0 | 6.6 | 8.6 |
| CITADEL FCU | Exton | PA | B+ | B+ | B+ | 2311.4 | 11.27 | 4.3 | 37.4 | 45.3 | 4.1 | 8.5 | 10.0 |
| CITIES CU | Vadnais Heights | MN | C- | C- | D+ | 27.1 | 2.87 | 0.0 | 31.9 | 4.2 | 1.6 | 6.7 | 8.7 |
| CITIZENS CHOICE FCU | Natchez | MS | D | D+ | D+ | 1.1 | 1.52 | 0.0 | 45.9 | 0.0 | 0.0 | 10.0 | 33.0 |
| CITIZENS COMMUNITY CU | Fort Dodge | IA | A | A | A- | 184.5 | 0.91 | 0.0 | 69.4 | 2.6 | 0.0 | 10.0 | 13.6 |
| CITIZENS COMMUNITY CU | Devils Lake | ND | B+ | A- | A- | 178.3 | 5.46 | 56.3 | 10.7 | 39.3 | 0.0 | 10.0 | 11.3 |
| CITIZENS EQUITY FIRST CU | Peoria | IL | A- | B+ | B+ | 5174.8 | 5.12 | 7.4 | 23.1 | 43.1 | 19.7 | 10.0 | 11.5 |
| CITIZENS FCU | Big Spring | TX | C+ | C | C- | 124.8 | 2.08 | 0.0 | 24.1 | 0.0 | 58.8 | 9.6 | 10.7 |
| CITY & COUNTY CU | Saint Paul | MN | A- | A- | A- | 449.7 | 7.09 | 6.6 | 42.1 | 14.9 | 20.5 | 10.0 | 11.3 |
| CITY & COUNTY EMPL CU | Fargo | ND | C- | D+ | D+ | 12.7 | -3.13 | 0.0 | 32.2 | 0.0 | 0.0 | 7.3 | 9.2 |
| CITY & POLICE FCU | Jacksonville | FL | C | C | C- | 65.0 | 5.36 | 0.9 | 26.0 | 12.5 | 34.2 | 7.2 | 9.3 |
| CITY AND COUNTY EMPL FCU | Albert Lea | MN | B- | B- | B- | 16.0 | 0.04 | 0.0 | 24.4 | 0.0 | 0.0 | 10.0 | 13.3 |
| ▲ CITY CENTER CU | Provo | UT | D+ | D- | E+ | 7.9 | 20.57 | 2.5 | 28.5 | 37.7 | 0.0 | 7.1 | 9.1 |
| ▼ CITY CO FCU | Pittsburgh | PA | D+ | D+ | D | 20.2 | -1.30 | 0.0 | 34.3 | 6.8 | 0.0 | 10.0 | 11.1 |
| CITY CU | Tuscaloosa | AL | C+ | C+ | C+ | 17.2 | 1.14 | 0.0 | 36.8 | 9.1 | 0.0 | 10.0 | 22.0 |
| CITY CU | Independence | MO | C+ | C+ | C | 31.4 | 2.74 | 0.7 | 41.4 | 2.1 | 0.0 | 9.2 | 10.5 |
| CITY CU | Dallas | TX | A- | A- | A- | 325.8 | 15.28 | 0.0 | 45.9 | 13.0 | 12.6 | 10.0 | 11.5 |
| CITY EMPL CU | Knoxville | TN | A- | A- | A- | 70.7 | 3.59 | 3.9 | 21.8 | 11.5 | 0.0 | 10.0 | 20.1 |
| ▲ CITY FCU | Amarillo | TX | D+ | D | D+ | 30.6 | 12.57 | 0.0 | 34.6 | 0.0 | 0.0 | 7.4 | 9.3 |
| CITY OF BIRMINGHAM GENERAL EMPL CU | Birmingham | AL | C+ | C+ | C+ | 7.8 | 8.00 | 0.0 | 62.6 | 5.6 | 0.0 | 10.0 | 14.2 |
| CITY OF BOSTON CU | Boston | MA | B | B | B- | 339.3 | 5.92 | 0.0 | 24.0 | 41.6 | 12.2 | 10.0 | 13.4 |
| ▲ CITY OF CLARKSBURG FCU | Clarksburg | WV | C | C- | C | 9.2 | 6.17 | 0.0 | 85.1 | 0.0 | 0.0 | 10.0 | 14.2 |
| CITY OF DEER PARK FCU | Deer Park | TX | C- | C+ | C+ | 5.9 | -6.44 | 0.0 | 34.0 | 0.9 | 0.0 | 10.0 | 16.3 |
| CITY OF FAIRBANKS FCU | Fairbanks | AK | D+ | D+ | D+ | 2.3 | 0.17 | 0.0 | 36.5 | 0.0 | 0.0 | 10.0 | 15.9 |
| CITY OF FAIRMONT FCU | Fairmont | WV | D | D | D | 1.2 | 5.80 | 0.0 | 58.2 | 0.0 | 0.0 | 8.3 | 9.8 |
| CITY OF FIRSTS COMMUNITY FCU | Kokomo | IN | C | C | D | 26.0 | -0.11 | 0.0 | 22.9 | 2.1 | 0.0 | 7.6 | 9.4 |
| ▲ CITY OF MCKEESPORT EMPL FCU | McKeesport | PA | D+ | D+ | D+ | 1.1 | 0.27 | 0.0 | 23.1 | 0.0 | 0.0 | 10.0 | 25.0 |
| CITY OF RALEIGH EMPL CU | Raleigh | NC | C+ | C+ | C | 21.9 | -4.52 | 0.0 | 32.7 | 0.1 | 20.3 | 10.0 | 13.6 |
| CITY OF SCHENECTADY EMPL FCU | Schenectady | NY | E+ | E+ | D- | 4.4 | 4.01 | 0.0 | 46.1 | 0.0 | 46.9 | 6.3 | 8.3 |
| CITY OF UKIAH EMPL CU | Ukiah | CA | D+ | D | C- | 4.1 | 2.61 | 0.0 | 18.7 | 0.0 | 0.0 | 9.3 | 10.5 |
| CITY PUBLIC SERVICE/IBEW FCU | San Antonio | TX | C+ | C | C | 40.7 | 1.32 | 0.0 | 21.2 | 6.3 | 27.5 | 10.0 | 11.7 |
| CITY TRUST FCU | Fort Wayne | IN | D+ | D+ | D+ | 8.9 | 0.17 | 0.7 | 20.3 | 6.6 | 0.0 | 10.0 | 13.0 |
| CITY-COUNTY EMPL CU | Clearwater | FL | C+ | C | C | 18.4 | 6.96 | 0.0 | 57.1 | 0.0 | 0.0 | 10.0 | 14.0 |
| CIVIL SERVICE EMPL ASSN CU | Cleveland | OH | D+ | D+ | C- | 6.1 | -1.23 | 0.0 | 45.5 | 2.4 | 0.0 | 10.0 | 19.0 |
| CLACKAMAS COMMUNITY FCU | Milwaukie | OR | B+ | B+ | C | 280.5 | 6.21 | 5.8 | 36.3 | 19.0 | 13.1 | 8.6 | 10.0 |
| ▲ CLAIRTON WORKS FCU | Elizabeth | PA | C- | C- | D+ | 13.3 | -2.40 | 0.0 | 17.6 | 0.0 | 9.6 | 10.0 | 11.1 |
| ▲ CLARENCE COMMUNITY & SCHOOLS FCU | Clarence | NY | D+ | D | D+ | 19.1 | -2.78 | 0.0 | 24.7 | 13.3 | 27.6 | 7.7 | 9.5 |
| ▼ CLARET FCU | Bayamon | PR | D+ | C- | C+ | <1 | -98.95 | 0.0 | 0.0 | 0.0 | 0.0 | 0.0 | .0 |
| CLARION FCU | Clarion | PA | B+ | B+ | B+ | 70.8 | 7.09 | 9.8 | 33.3 | 35.9 | 11.7 | 10.0 | 12.5 |
| ▲ CLARITY CU | Nampa | ID | D+ | D+ | C | 64.4 | 9.93 | 0.0 | 63.0 | 1.1 | 0.0 | 6.3 | 8.3 |
| CLARK COUNTY CU | Las Vegas | NV | A- | A- | A- | 569.9 | 7.47 | 10.2 | 29.9 | 24.6 | 11.7 | 10.0 | 12.4 |
| CLARKE EDUCATORS FCU | Grove Hill | AL | C+ | C+ | C+ | 3.8 | 3.47 | 0.0 | 45.2 | 0.0 | 0.0 | 10.0 | 22.6 |
| CLARKSBURG AREA POSTAL EMPL FCU | Clarksburg | WV | C+ | C+ | C+ | 13.4 | 7.79 | 0.0 | 25.7 | 25.2 | 0.2 | 9.3 | 10.6 |
| CLARKSTON BRANDON COMMUNITY CU | Clarkston | MI | C+ | C+ | C+ | 68.8 | 14.22 | 0.3 | 21.1 | 13.5 | 29.4 | 6.6 | 8.6 |
| CLASS ACT FCU | Louisville | KY | C+ | C+ | C | 182.2 | 5.45 | 0.0 | 33.3 | 10.4 | 0.0 | 9.0 | 10.3 |
| CLASSIC FCU | Amelia | OH | C+ | C+ | C | 38.9 | 7.70 | 0.4 | 37.0 | 5.1 | 0.0 | 7.8 | 9.5 |
| CLAY ELECTRIC EMPL CU | Keystone Heights | FL | D | D+ | D+ | 8.0 | -2.70 | 0.0 | 13.2 | 14.0 | 0.0 | 10.0 | 17.5 |
| ▲ CLEARCHOICE FCU | Wyomissing | PA | E+ | E- | E | 16.1 | 0.16 | 0.0 | 42.6 | 20.6 | 5.4 | 4.6 | 6.7 |
| CLEARFIELD STONE WORKERS FCU | Clearfield | PA | D | D | D+ | 2.0 | -5.50 | 0.0 | 58.1 | 0.0 | 0.0 | 10.0 | 14.1 |
| ▲ CLEARPATH FCU | Glendale | CA | B- | C | B- | 94.2 | 4.48 | 13.6 | 37.2 | 12.8 | 9.8 | 10.0 | 11.5 |
| CLEARVIEW FCU | Moon Township | PA | B- | B- | C+ | 961.5 | 5.60 | 4.8 | 34.5 | 11.3 | 20.8 | 8.6 | 10.6 |
| CLEARWATER CU | Lewiston | ID | E | E+ | E+ | 22.4 | -1.46 | 0.0 | 20.2 | 0.0 | 0.0 | 4.0 | 6.0 |
| CLEVELAND CHURCH OF CHRIST FCU | Cleveland | OH | D+ | D+ | D+ | <1 | 3.43 | 3.3 | 41.2 | 0.0 | 0.0 | 10.0 | 26.5 |
| ▲ CLEVELAND HEIGHTS TEACHERS CU INC | Cleveland Heights | OH | C | C- | C- | 7.3 | -4.83 | 0.0 | 18.7 | 7.4 | 47.7 | 10.0 | 21.2 |
| CLEVELAND POLICE CU INC | Cleveland | OH | C- | C- | D+ | 32.6 | 0.94 | 0.4 | 16.3 | 26.5 | 24.5 | 7.5 | 9.4 |
| ▼ CLEVELAND SELFRELIANCE FCU | Parma | OH | C+ | B | B | 90.3 | 1.32 | 7.6 | 0.8 | 30.6 | 12.4 | 10.0 | 16.5 |
| CLEVELAND-BRADLEY COUNTY TEACHERS | Cleveland | TN | B | B- | B- | 45.5 | 2.15 | 0.0 | 14.3 | 21.3 | 33.2 | 10.0 | 12.5 |
| CLIFFORD-JACOBS EMPL CU | Champaign | IL | C | C- | D+ | 2.0 | -2.78 | 0.0 | 20.7 | 0.0 | 0.0 | 10.0 | 22.6 |
| ▼ CLIFTON NJ POSTAL EMPL FCU | Clifton | NJ | C- | C+ | B- | 3.0 | -8.56 | 0.0 | 21.4 | 0.0 | 76.5 | 10.0 | 35.5 |
| CLIFTY CREEK EMPL FCU | Madison | IN | C+ | C+ | C+ | 12.4 | -2.34 | 0.0 | 56.6 | 0.0 | 1.6 | 10.0 | 17.6 |

| Asset Quality Index | Non-Performing Loans | | Net Charge-Offs Avg Loans | Profitability Index | Net Income ($Mil) | Return on Assets | Return on Equity | Net Interest Spread | Overhead Efficiency Ratio | Liquidity Index | Liquidity Ratio | Hot Money Ratio | Stability Index |
|---|---|---|---|---|---|---|---|---|---|---|---|---|---|
| | as a % of Total Loans | as a % of Capital | | | | | | | | | | | |
| 6.5 | 0.54 | 5.0 | 0.02 | 5.4 | 0.1 | 0.85 | 10.85 | 4.33 | 83.3 | 3.1 | 12.7 | 8.3 | 3.5 |
| 8.6 | 0.37 | 3.3 | 0.32 | 5.8 | 15.5 | 0.92 | 9.18 | 3.25 | 72.2 | 1.4 | 2.4 | 16.4 | 7.7 |
| 6.5 | 0.71 | 5.2 | 0.32 | 3.3 | 0.1 | 0.28 | 3.35 | 3.94 | 92.1 | 4.0 | 7.8 | 1.4 | 4.0 |
| 8.4 | 0.90 | 1.4 | 3.02 | 0.0 | 0.0 | -2.53 | -7.39 | 13.24 | 108.6 | 6.5 | 51.9 | 0.0 | 5.1 |
| 6.4 | 0.83 | 4.5 | 1.07 | 9.0 | 1.7 | 1.22 | 9.39 | 5.13 | 68.9 | 4.0 | 19.8 | 5.3 | 8.4 |
| 3.9 | 0.74 | 10.6 | 0.02 | 7.1 | 1.3 | 0.98 | 8.58 | 4.33 | 73.7 | 1.1 | 4.5 | 22.3 | 9.0 |
| 8.4 | 0.47 | 3.5 | 0.27 | 6.8 | 46.6 | 1.19 | 12.11 | 3.04 | 60.7 | 3.0 | 13.9 | 10.3 | 7.9 |
| 7.9 | 2.73 | 7.7 | 1.32 | 3.8 | 0.5 | 0.57 | 5.43 | 3.53 | 73.2 | 4.8 | 16.4 | 10.4 | 6.2 |
| 7.2 | 0.91 | 6.0 | 0.33 | 5.4 | 2.9 | 0.87 | 8.04 | 3.25 | 76.7 | 3.9 | 11.1 | 1.5 | 7.0 |
| 7.0 | 0.57 | 2.9 | 0.07 | 4.5 | 0.1 | 0.64 | 7.07 | 3.52 | 78.6 | 5.6 | 30.1 | 0.0 | 3.7 |
| 7.4 | 0.53 | 2.6 | 0.33 | 2.9 | 0.2 | 0.34 | 3.69 | 3.46 | 91.6 | 4.7 | 15.6 | 3.7 | 3.3 |
| 10.0 | 0.00 | 0.0 | 0.25 | 4.2 | 0.1 | 0.50 | 3.95 | 2.18 | 82.0 | 4.6 | 11.1 | 0.0 | 6.8 |
| 5.7 | 0.45 | 6.9 | 0.50 | 9.7 | 0.1 | 2.01 | 26.11 | 5.78 | 65.2 | 2.5 | 22.3 | 18.6 | 3.0 |
| 6.9 | 2.47 | 9.7 | 0.41 | 1.0 | 0.0 | -0.18 | -1.61 | 3.55 | 90.0 | 4.7 | 27.4 | 0.0 | 4.9 |
| 8.8 | 0.72 | 1.6 | 1.38 | 2.1 | 0.0 | 0.00 | 0.00 | 3.91 | 91.8 | 5.4 | 38.5 | 1.6 | 6.6 |
| 6.3 | 0.92 | 5.2 | 0.73 | 6.0 | 0.2 | 0.93 | 9.18 | 4.58 | 79.2 | 4.1 | 15.2 | 4.3 | 5.0 |
| 5.9 | 1.02 | 6.7 | 1.01 | 7.0 | 3.7 | 1.58 | 14.42 | 4.77 | 68.3 | 3.9 | 18.2 | 5.2 | 7.4 |
| 9.5 | 0.33 | 3.1 | 0.29 | 7.4 | 0.6 | 1.15 | 5.76 | 2.88 | 69.8 | 4.9 | 46.3 | 2.6 | 8.0 |
| 9.6 | 0.24 | 1.3 | 0.23 | 2.8 | 0.1 | 0.44 | 4.49 | 2.89 | 85.5 | 3.5 | 21.3 | 10.8 | 3.5 |
| 5.4 | 1.63 | 7.4 | 4.83 | 10.0 | 0.1 | 1.89 | 13.56 | 7.50 | 70.6 | 4.6 | 17.2 | 0.0 | 5.0 |
| 6.6 | 1.83 | 9.5 | 0.42 | 5.0 | 1.9 | 0.76 | 5.64 | 4.03 | 75.8 | 3.2 | 26.0 | 12.1 | 7.4 |
| 2.4 | 3.37 | 18.9 | 0.05 | 10.0 | 0.2 | 2.45 | 17.90 | 4.47 | 39.9 | 3.7 | 13.8 | 0.0 | 7.5 |
| 8.8 | 0.13 | 0.3 | 2.14 | 1.8 | 0.0 | -0.49 | -3.14 | 3.10 | 98.5 | 5.0 | 38.9 | 0.0 | 5.8 |
| 6.9 | 6.98 | 16.8 | 1.00 | 0.8 | 0.0 | -0.28 | -1.81 | 5.04 | 96.6 | 6.9 | 54.6 | 0.0 | 5.1 |
| 6.5 | 0.00 | 0.0 | 3.35 | 3.3 | 0.0 | 0.22 | 2.20 | 4.29 | 80.0 | 4.3 | 8.7 | 0.0 | 3.0 |
| 8.0 | 0.80 | 2.9 | 0.73 | 2.5 | 0.0 | 0.21 | 2.30 | 2.72 | 91.2 | 5.7 | 34.9 | 0.9 | 3.6 |
| 7.0 | 7.66 | 6.9 | 0.50 | 1.0 | 0.0 | -0.12 | -0.47 | 8.02 | 106.3 | 8.4 | 102.4 | 0.0 | 6.5 |
| 8.9 | 1.35 | 3.4 | 1.13 | 2.7 | 0.0 | 0.19 | 1.45 | 2.48 | 75.8 | 4.6 | 15.8 | 7.8 | 5.9 |
| 4.7 | 1.74 | 9.2 | 0.26 | 1.0 | 0.0 | -0.38 | -4.65 | 4.04 | 104.9 | 4.4 | 9.9 | 0.0 | 3.3 |
| 6.5 | 1.98 | 3.9 | 0.00 | 1.2 | 0.0 | 0.00 | 0.00 | 2.08 | 101.7 | 5.2 | 40.5 | 0.0 | 6.3 |
| 9.3 | 0.98 | 3.1 | 0.53 | 2.4 | 0.1 | 0.17 | 1.45 | 2.90 | 87.8 | 5.0 | 27.7 | 0.0 | 5.5 |
| 9.5 | 1.20 | 2.8 | -0.10 | 0.4 | 0.0 | -0.25 | -1.95 | 2.32 | 108.9 | 6.0 | 78.9 | 0.0 | 6.0 |
| 8.5 | 0.02 | 0.1 | -0.05 | 4.6 | 0.1 | 0.72 | 5.14 | 4.02 | 84.6 | 4.0 | 12.7 | 0.0 | 6.9 |
| 4.3 | 5.98 | 14.7 | 2.71 | 0.4 | -0.1 | -2.86 | -14.58 | 6.09 | 126.9 | 6.1 | 49.5 | 0.0 | 5.6 |
| 7.9 | 0.75 | 5.4 | 0.39 | 5.4 | 1.6 | 0.77 | 7.58 | 4.36 | 76.2 | 4.5 | 17.4 | 1.7 | 6.9 |
| 9.7 | 0.90 | 2.1 | 0.45 | 1.6 | 0.0 | -0.01 | -0.09 | 2.53 | 96.3 | 5.6 | 23.6 | 0.0 | 4.5 |
| 7.0 | 0.67 | 3.8 | 0.74 | 1.5 | 0.0 | 0.00 | 0.00 | 3.12 | 100.0 | 4.1 | 12.7 | 2.2 | 4.7 |
| 6.2 | NA | NA | 0.00 | 1.0 | 0.0 | -6.38 | -40.40 | 5.56 | 211.1 | 6.5 | 100.0 | 101.0 | 5.2 |
| 9.0 | 0.15 | 0.9 | 0.01 | 6.1 | 0.5 | 0.89 | 7.17 | 2.80 | 67.8 | 3.3 | 9.1 | 4.3 | 7.5 |
| 4.1 | 1.17 | 10.9 | 1.01 | 4.5 | 0.3 | 0.64 | 7.96 | 5.66 | 77.5 | 3.4 | 9.3 | 2.5 | 2.9 |
| 5.9 | 2.14 | 10.2 | 0.11 | 10.0 | 9.6 | 2.28 | 19.39 | 4.66 | 61.5 | 5.7 | 31.6 | 2.9 | 8.9 |
| 8.8 | 0.00 | 0.0 | -0.08 | 5.5 | 0.0 | 0.87 | 3.82 | 8.10 | 82.0 | 7.0 | 63.9 | 0.0 | 5.0 |
| 8.1 | 0.91 | 4.6 | 0.22 | 3.8 | 0.1 | 0.49 | 4.60 | 3.46 | 87.0 | 4.1 | 14.3 | 0.9 | 5.8 |
| 9.8 | 0.31 | 1.3 | 0.02 | 3.7 | 0.2 | 0.50 | 5.59 | 2.96 | 85.6 | 4.5 | 11.7 | 1.1 | 3.4 |
| 9.3 | 0.53 | 2.7 | 0.14 | 3.2 | -0.1 | -0.06 | -0.58 | 3.86 | 97.6 | 5.9 | 37.9 | 3.1 | 6.2 |
| 6.4 | 1.12 | 7.3 | 0.22 | 4.4 | 0.2 | 0.58 | 6.15 | 4.30 | 87.0 | 3.7 | 13.0 | 3.4 | 4.2 |
| 10.0 | 0.00 | 0.0 | 0.10 | 0.3 | 0.0 | -0.51 | -3.02 | 2.18 | 122.2 | 4.9 | 28.7 | 0.0 | 6.6 |
| 6.5 | 0.36 | 4.0 | 0.41 | 3.7 | 0.1 | 0.74 | 11.92 | 4.97 | 90.7 | 3.0 | 7.0 | 8.1 | 1.5 |
| 0.7 | 11.40 | 42.6 | 0.66 | 1.9 | 0.0 | 0.06 | 0.49 | 5.54 | 88.5 | 6.3 | 47.6 | 0.0 | 4.6 |
| 9.2 | 0.17 | 0.9 | 0.23 | 3.6 | 0.4 | 0.53 | 4.60 | 3.79 | 88.9 | 3.7 | 21.1 | 4.3 | 5.1 |
| 9.4 | 0.43 | 2.7 | 0.29 | 3.6 | 3.1 | 0.43 | 4.33 | 3.60 | 85.1 | 3.7 | 16.5 | 4.9 | 6.4 |
| 8.9 | 0.22 | 1.1 | 0.59 | 0.0 | -0.1 | -0.51 | -8.33 | 2.35 | 106.3 | 5.3 | 31.5 | 0.5 | 1.7 |
| 7.7 | 1.06 | 1.6 | 6.96 | 0.8 | 0.0 | -4.49 | -15.82 | 8.12 | 112.5 | 7.2 | 70.3 | 0.0 | 5.9 |
| 9.1 | 0.94 | 1.1 | 1.20 | 3.7 | 0.0 | 0.48 | 2.37 | 4.04 | 70.7 | 5.9 | 39.9 | 0.0 | 5.9 |
| 3.4 | 5.35 | 28.2 | 0.27 | 4.1 | 0.1 | 0.57 | 6.30 | 3.83 | 88.5 | 4.3 | 18.3 | 2.8 | 4.5 |
| 6.5 | 4.83 | 10.0 | 0.65 | 2.5 | 0.1 | 0.15 | 0.90 | 3.33 | 82.7 | 5.6 | 57.6 | 24.2 | 7.3 |
| 9.5 | 0.37 | 1.2 | 0.11 | 4.1 | 0.2 | 0.58 | 4.59 | 2.69 | 82.7 | 5.0 | 31.7 | 7.9 | 6.5 |
| 9.3 | 1.18 | 1.4 | -2.52 | 4.9 | 0.0 | 0.85 | 3.87 | 4.21 | 55.6 | 7.7 | 93.5 | 0.0 | 6.0 |
| 9.6 | 0.89 | 0.6 | -1.79 | 1.5 | 0.0 | -0.47 | -1.41 | 2.50 | 120.8 | 4.7 | 1.9 | 0.0 | 6.5 |
| 7.3 | 0.39 | 1.5 | 0.12 | 4.6 | 0.1 | 0.76 | 4.40 | 2.96 | 71.8 | 3.6 | 16.0 | 3.2 | 7.5 |

| Name | City | State | Rating | 2014 Rating | 2013 Rating | Total Assets ($Mil) | One Year Asset Growth | Asset Mix (As a % of Total Assets) | | | | Capital-ization Index | Net Worth Ratio |
|------|------|-------|--------|-------------|-------------|---------------------|-----------------------|------------------------|---|---|---|----------------------|-----------------|
| | | | | | | | | Comm-ercial Loans | Cons-umer Loans | Mort-gage Loans | Secur-ities | | |
| CLINCHFIELD FCU | Erwin | TN | B+ | B+ | B+ | 78.6 | 2.75 | 0.6 | 21.9 | 38.1 | 3.1 | 10.0 | 12.5 |
| CLINTON FCU | Clinton | SC | B- | B- | B- | 6.6 | 4.79 | 0.0 | 43.7 | 3.2 | 0.0 | 10.0 | 25.6 |
| CLOVERBELT CU | Wausau | WI | B+ | B | B | 201.7 | 4.90 | 2.8 | 20.0 | 45.0 | 0.0 | 10.0 | 12.9 |
| CMC-FCPI EMPL FCU | Scranton | PA | D- | D- | D- | 6.8 | 4.71 | 0.0 | 52.4 | 0.0 | 20.2 | 8.6 | 10.1 |
| CME FCU | Columbus | OH | B- | B- | C | 254.9 | 11.62 | 3.7 | 32.8 | 34.7 | 8.4 | 6.6 | 8.6 |
| CN/IC EMPL CU | Memphis | TN | C- | C- | D+ | 7.7 | -1.73 | 0.0 | 36.2 | 0.0 | 0.0 | 10.0 | 19.6 |
| CO-LIB CU | Saint Louis | MO | C- | C- | C | 1.0 | 2.78 | 0.0 | 42.4 | 0.0 | 0.0 | 10.0 | 12.0 |
| CO-NE FCU | Julesburg | CO | C- | C | C | 4.2 | 15.27 | 0.0 | 30.3 | 22.1 | 0.0 | 10.0 | 12.9 |
| CO-OP CU | Black River Falls | WI | A- | A- | A- | 286.3 | 7.17 | 11.0 | 12.3 | 64.2 | 2.1 | 10.0 | 12.4 |
| CO-OP CU OF MONTEVIDEO | Montevideo | MN | A- | A | A | 151.1 | 3.65 | 44.6 | 15.3 | 26.4 | 8.1 | 10.0 | 14.3 |
| CO-OP TOLEDO CU INC | Maumee | OH | D+ | D+ | C- | 9.5 | 9.47 | 0.0 | 67.8 | 0.0 | 2.1 | 10.0 | 12.8 |
| CO-OPERATIVE CU | Coffeyville | KS | D | D | D+ | 20.8 | 0.07 | 0.0 | 52.0 | 11.1 | 0.0 | 10.0 | 14.2 |
| CO-OPERATIVE FCU | Woodridge | NY | D | D | D | 7.4 | -10.99 | 0.0 | 12.7 | 0.0 | 5.8 | 10.0 | 12.1 |
| COAST CENTRAL CU | Eureka | CA | B+ | B | B | 1135.3 | 8.56 | 9.5 | 13.4 | 28.4 | 40.5 | 10.0 | 11.4 |
| COAST GUARD EMPL CU | New Orleans | LA | C | C- | C- | 5.4 | -5.60 | 0.0 | 25.3 | 0.0 | 0.0 | 10.0 | 22.5 |
| COAST LINE CU | South Portland | ME | A- | B+ | B+ | 49.8 | 1.87 | 0.0 | 18.9 | 40.9 | 0.0 | 10.0 | 16.4 |
| COAST-TEL FCU | Salinas | CA | E | E | E- | 15.6 | 6.38 | 0.0 | 43.6 | 0.0 | 0.0 | 4.9 | 6.9 |
| COAST360 FCU | Maite | GU | B | B | B+ | 337.7 | 3.48 | 10.1 | 37.6 | 30.6 | 10.4 | 10.0 | 14.4 |
| COASTAL BEND POST OFFICE FCU | Victoria | TX | B- | B- | B- | 15.9 | 2.60 | 0.0 | 34.5 | 0.0 | 51.6 | 10.0 | 15.3 |
| COASTAL COMMUNITY & TEACHERS CU | Corpus Christi | TX | C | C+ | B+ | 281.6 | 1.01 | 0.1 | 45.5 | 10.3 | 24.9 | 8.8 | 10.4 |
| COASTAL COMMUNITY FCU | Galveston | TX | C | C+ | C+ | 58.6 | 5.57 | 0.0 | 39.1 | 30.4 | 5.9 | 7.8 | 9.5 |
| COASTAL CU | Biloxi | MS | C- | C | C+ | 8.7 | 3.52 | 0.0 | 60.2 | 3.3 | 0.0 | 10.0 | 18.0 |
| COASTAL FCU | Raleigh | NC | B+ | A- | B+ | 2555.3 | 11.68 | 8.0 | 38.2 | 29.6 | 3.0 | 8.9 | 10.2 |
| COASTAL TEACHERS FCU | Port Lavaca | TX | E+ | D- | E+ | 4.9 | 7.98 | 0.0 | 51.1 | 0.0 | 0.0 | 6.4 | 8.4 |
| COASTHILLS CU | Lompoc | CA | B+ | B+ | B | 879.2 | 14.92 | 11.0 | 39.0 | 42.1 | 1.7 | 6.8 | 8.8 |
| COASTLAND FCU | Metairie | LA | C | C- | D+ | 111.8 | -1.06 | 0.0 | 18.9 | 30.3 | 9.7 | 10.0 | 11.7 |
| COASTLINE FCU | Jacksonville | FL | C | C- | D+ | 125.0 | -0.90 | 1.0 | 42.3 | 20.5 | 9.3 | 6.7 | 8.7 |
| COBBLESTONE COUNTRY FCU | Albion | NY | E+ | D- | D- | 8.4 | 3.33 | 0.0 | 51.8 | 0.0 | 0.0 | 5.9 | 7.9 |
| COBURN CU | Beaumont | TX | C | C | C | 7.1 | -2.58 | 0.0 | 36.4 | 0.0 | 0.0 | 10.0 | 13.6 |
| COCA-COLA FCU | Atlanta | GA | C+ | C+ | B- | 163.5 | -0.28 | 0.0 | 25.1 | 35.8 | 20.3 | 7.5 | 9.4 |
| COCHISE CU | Willcox | AZ | B | B | B | 28.1 | -0.09 | 0.0 | 53.5 | 0.0 | 0.0 | 10.0 | 15.4 |
| COCHRAN COUNTY SCHOOLS FCU | Morton | TX | C | C | C | 4.8 | 2.91 | 0.0 | 51.3 | 0.0 | 0.0 | 10.0 | 13.7 |
| COCONINO FCU | Flagstaff | AZ | C+ | C+ | C+ | 65.6 | 8.74 | 0.0 | 39.5 | 0.0 | 5.8 | 7.0 | 9.0 |
| CODE CU | Dayton | OH | B- | B | B | 110.7 | -1.03 | 11.0 | 34.1 | 11.7 | 0.9 | 10.0 | 12.2 |
| COFFEE COUNTY TEACHERS FCU | Douglas | GA | C+ | C+ | C | 3.6 | -1.76 | 0.0 | 19.9 | 0.0 | 0.0 | 10.0 | 13.2 |
| COGIC CU | Lafayette | LA | E+ | E+ | D | <1 | -12.50 | 0.0 | 35.5 | 0.0 | 0.0 | 6.5 | 8.9 |
| COLFAX POWER PLANT EMPL FCU | Springdale | PA | D+ | D+ | D+ | 7.8 | 0.18 | 0.0 | 56.6 | 0.0 | 0.0 | 10.0 | 12.0 |
| COLFAX SCHOOL EMPL CU | Raton | NM | C- | C- | C | <1 | -15.24 | 0.0 | 96.7 | 0.0 | 0.0 | 10.0 | 17.3 |
| COLGATE EMPL FCU | Piscataway | NJ | E+ | E+ | E+ | 7.0 | -5.10 | 0.0 | 59.4 | 7.4 | 0.0 | 5.0 | 7.0 |
| COLLEGE & UNIV CU | Chicago | IL | D+ | D+ | D- | 1.3 | 3.59 | 0.0 | 16.6 | 0.0 | 0.0 | 8.2 | 9.9 |
| COLLEGEDALE CU | Collegedale | TN | C- | C | C- | 40.3 | 5.75 | 9.6 | 8.1 | 25.6 | 0.0 | 7.1 | 9.1 |
| COLLEGEVILLE COMMUNITY CU | Collegeville | MN | C- | C- | C- | 11.8 | -0.25 | 1.6 | 40.0 | 2.3 | 0.1 | 8.2 | 9.8 |
| COLLINS COMMUNITY CU | Cedar Rapids | IA | B | B+ | B+ | 873.1 | 7.45 | 11.6 | 21.6 | 39.9 | 15.0 | 8.5 | 10.1 |
| COLORADO CU | Littleton | CO | B+ | B+ | B | 138.8 | 15.17 | 6.2 | 22.6 | 17.7 | 1.7 | 7.9 | 9.6 |
| COLORAMO FCU | Grand Junction | CO | B+ | B+ | B | 82.8 | 5.60 | 0.1 | 23.8 | 7.9 | 13.6 | 10.0 | 12.9 |
| COLQUITT COUNTY TEACHERS FCU | Moultrie | GA | C+ | C+ | C+ | 6.9 | 3.76 | 0.0 | 54.3 | 0.0 | 0.0 | 10.0 | 19.1 |
| COLTON FCU | Colton | CA | D | D | C- | 6.4 | -0.53 | 0.0 | 19.6 | 0.0 | 0.0 | 10.0 | 13.5 |
| COLUMBIA COMMUNITY CU | Vancouver | WA | A | A | A- | 1103.0 | 10.43 | 13.1 | 32.5 | 31.5 | 16.9 | 10.0 | 11.8 |
| ▼ COLUMBIA CU | Columbia | MO | D- | D | E+ | 21.3 | 4.26 | 2.3 | 44.6 | 7.2 | 0.0 | 5.0 | 7.0 |
| COLUMBIA GREENE FCU | Hudson | NY | C- | C- | D+ | 26.9 | 0.65 | 0.0 | 14.2 | 25.6 | 19.2 | 5.8 | 7.8 |
| COLUMBIA POST OFFICE CU | Columbia | SC | B | B | B | 33.4 | 2.01 | 0.0 | 17.7 | 0.0 | 13.9 | 10.0 | 12.8 |
| COLUMBIANA COUNTY SCHOOL EMPL CU | Lisbon | OH | C+ | B- | B- | 9.7 | -0.32 | 0.0 | 27.6 | 0.0 | 36.8 | 10.0 | 14.4 |
| ▼ COLUMBINE FCU | Centennial | CO | C | C+ | C+ | 55.0 | 8.43 | 3.3 | 20.5 | 15.3 | 17.7 | 6.8 | 9.0 |
| COLUMBUS CLUB FCU | San Fernando | CA | D+ | D+ | C- | 7.3 | -2.05 | 0.0 | 5.8 | 0.0 | 0.0 | 10.0 | 14.2 |
| COLUMBUS METRO FCU | Columbus | OH | B- | B | B | 234.5 | 0.19 | 0.1 | 69.9 | 7.6 | 0.0 | 8.5 | 10.0 |
| COLUMBUS MUNICIPAL CU | Columbus | MS | C- | C- | C+ | 11.1 | 5.90 | 0.0 | 30.4 | 0.0 | 0.0 | 10.0 | 17.1 |
| COLUMBUS UNITED FCU | Columbus | NE | C | B- | C+ | 57.1 | 4.46 | 5.4 | 35.5 | 16.0 | 4.0 | 9.3 | 10.5 |
| COMANCHE COUNTY FCU | Lawton | OK | B- | B- | B | 23.0 | 4.50 | 0.0 | 29.3 | 4.5 | 2.9 | 10.0 | 15.1 |
| COMBINED EMPL CU | Warner Robins | GA | C | C | C- | 12.2 | 3.41 | 0.6 | 68.0 | 0.0 | 0.0 | 10.0 | 12.4 |
| ▼ COMBINED FCU | Hot Springs | AR | D | D+ | D+ | 6.9 | -0.56 | 0.0 | 33.0 | 0.0 | 0.0 | 10.0 | 15.2 |

| Asset Quality Index | Non-Performing Loans as a % of Total Loans | Non-Performing Loans as a % of Capital | Net Charge- Offs Avg Loans | Profitability Index | Net Income ($Mil) | Return on Assets | Return on Equity | Net Interest Spread | Overhead Efficiency Ratio | Liquidity Index | Liquidity Ratio | Hot Money Ratio | Stability Index |
|---|---|---|---|---|---|---|---|---|---|---|---|---|---|
| 7.8 | 0.90 | 4.6 | 0.24 | 4.7 | 0.4 | 0.74 | 6.06 | 3.21 | 77.7 | 3.0 | 21.4 | 12.6 | 6.6 |
| 9.6 | 0.12 | 0.2 | -0.12 | 5.0 | 0.0 | 0.50 | 1.90 | 5.98 | 90.3 | 5.9 | 60.2 | 10.5 | 5.0 |
| 9.7 | 0.10 | 0.5 | 0.01 | 5.3 | 1.3 | 0.88 | 6.93 | 2.95 | 73.4 | 2.4 | 8.3 | 14.5 | 8.1 |
| 0.0 | 9.61 | 50.2 | 0.86 | 2.7 | 0.0 | 0.18 | 1.80 | 6.03 | 95.3 | 5.2 | 23.1 | 0.0 | 3.7 |
| 7.0 | 1.10 | 9.6 | 0.34 | 4.0 | 1.0 | 0.54 | 5.88 | 3.81 | 83.1 | 2.4 | 13.9 | 15.2 | 5.6 |
| 9.2 | 1.77 | 3.7 | -0.25 | 3.2 | 0.0 | 0.46 | 2.41 | 3.99 | 82.5 | 4.6 | 29.4 | 0.0 | 5.9 |
| 6.9 | 2.93 | 10.4 | 0.00 | 2.7 | 0.0 | 0.26 | 2.15 | 2.95 | 50.0 | 6.9 | 61.9 | 0.0 | 5.5 |
| 3.7 | 4.26 | 20.9 | -0.05 | 7.3 | 0.0 | 0.84 | 6.52 | 5.62 | 82.4 | 4.7 | 20.2 | 0.0 | 6.9 |
| 6.6 | 1.02 | 7.7 | 0.04 | 5.8 | 1.8 | 0.87 | 7.06 | 3.33 | 74.4 | 2.3 | 8.8 | 8.6 | 8.7 |
| 5.4 | 1.79 | 8.5 | 0.34 | 9.5 | 1.5 | 1.32 | 9.63 | 3.66 | 64.0 | 3.7 | 17.5 | 1.0 | 9.6 |
| 5.5 | 3.52 | 17.8 | 0.75 | 3.5 | 0.0 | 0.40 | 3.14 | 5.47 | 74.4 | 3.7 | 11.1 | 0.0 | 3.0 |
| 6.5 | 1.44 | 7.5 | 0.34 | 0.0 | -0.2 | -1.08 | -7.57 | 3.10 | 130.6 | 4.8 | 30.8 | 1.8 | 5.8 |
| 7.9 | 3.27 | 5.8 | 0.00 | 0.4 | 0.0 | -0.24 | -2.07 | 1.65 | 111.9 | 5.8 | 37.4 | 0.0 | 4.0 |
| 9.4 | 0.50 | 2.3 | 0.13 | 5.3 | 7.1 | 0.86 | 7.81 | 2.32 | 68.6 | 4.5 | 20.6 | 10.1 | 8.1 |
| 9.6 | 2.58 | 3.0 | 3.20 | 2.2 | 0.0 | 0.19 | 0.88 | 2.60 | 79.3 | 5.3 | 38.6 | 0.0 | 5.5 |
| 10.0 | 0.25 | 1.0 | 0.11 | 5.9 | 0.3 | 0.90 | 5.64 | 2.73 | 71.8 | 3.4 | 21.2 | 5.8 | 8.3 |
| 3.3 | 0.06 | 29.7 | 0.15 | 4.6 | 0.1 | 0.75 | 11.13 | 3.45 | 86.6 | 5.1 | 28.1 | 0.9 | 1.0 |
| 6.6 | 1.28 | 6.4 | 0.31 | 4.3 | 1.6 | 0.63 | 4.45 | 4.50 | 84.3 | 3.8 | 11.1 | 5.8 | 7.6 |
| 7.1 | 2.91 | 7.2 | 0.07 | 5.5 | 0.1 | 0.81 | 5.40 | 2.66 | 63.7 | 4.1 | 15.6 | 14.0 | 5.0 |
| 4.7 | 1.84 | 14.9 | 2.10 | 1.5 | -0.2 | -0.09 | -0.94 | 3.24 | 73.8 | 3.8 | 7.4 | 3.3 | 4.7 |
| 3.7 | 2.14 | 18.9 | 0.72 | 6.3 | 0.4 | 0.82 | 8.94 | 4.66 | 74.9 | 2.4 | 14.8 | 22.8 | 4.6 |
| 5.6 | 0.58 | 6.0 | 0.83 | 4.8 | 0.0 | 0.36 | 1.97 | 6.27 | 83.0 | 3.2 | 24.2 | 16.4 | 3.7 |
| 7.3 | 0.45 | 4.7 | 0.36 | 5.0 | 13.6 | 0.72 | 7.23 | 3.28 | 75.3 | 4.0 | 19.2 | 4.5 | 7.0 |
| 4.8 | 1.01 | 7.3 | 0.04 | 1.8 | 0.0 | 0.00 | 0.00 | 3.95 | 90.6 | 4.8 | 33.4 | 0.0 | 1.0 |
| 8.1 | 0.40 | 3.9 | 0.34 | 6.5 | 6.2 | 0.98 | 11.12 | 3.73 | 73.8 | 1.5 | 5.1 | 17.7 | 7.0 |
| 9.7 | 0.07 | 1.4 | 0.22 | 2.2 | 0.1 | 0.13 | 1.13 | 2.99 | 95.3 | 5.1 | 26.6 | 4.5 | 6.8 |
| 6.4 | 0.67 | 8.0 | 0.20 | 3.0 | 0.3 | 0.30 | 3.53 | 3.06 | 91.8 | 3.0 | 8.1 | 9.4 | 4.7 |
| 4.0 | 1.33 | 12.1 | 0.52 | 3.9 | 0.0 | 0.42 | 5.35 | 4.65 | 92.7 | 4.7 | 21.1 | 0.0 | 1.7 |
| 6.7 | 1.42 | 5.4 | 1.27 | 7.5 | 0.1 | 1.22 | 9.15 | 2.65 | 42.0 | 4.6 | 18.2 | 0.0 | 4.3 |
| 8.1 | 0.97 | 6.6 | 0.32 | 3.0 | 0.4 | 0.30 | 3.43 | 3.23 | 87.4 | 4.2 | 15.9 | 0.2 | 5.5 |
| 7.6 | 0.71 | 3.1 | 0.31 | 6.1 | 0.2 | 0.86 | 5.88 | 3.96 | 77.2 | 3.7 | 19.7 | 3.8 | 8.2 |
| 6.5 | 0.46 | 2.0 | 0.23 | 8.9 | 0.1 | 1.84 | 14.41 | 5.82 | 71.5 | 4.7 | 34.7 | 0.0 | 5.0 |
| 7.6 | 0.42 | 2.2 | 0.48 | 4.3 | 0.3 | 0.62 | 6.92 | 3.45 | 78.0 | 4.3 | 17.3 | 2.8 | 4.7 |
| 8.0 | 1.28 | 6.2 | 0.30 | 3.2 | 0.3 | 0.33 | 2.71 | 3.04 | 90.1 | 3.8 | 21.4 | 6.0 | 7.5 |
| 9.6 | 1.28 | 2.3 | 1.14 | 4.0 | 0.0 | 0.07 | 0.56 | 3.95 | 97.8 | 6.8 | 45.9 | 0.0 | 5.6 |
| 1.7 | 12.24 | 38.7 | 0.00 | 0.4 | 0.0 | -2.37 | -21.51 | 6.14 | 145.5 | 6.6 | 68.3 | 0.0 | 5.1 |
| 3.9 | 3.87 | 18.2 | -0.09 | 4.1 | 0.0 | 0.62 | 5.21 | 3.39 | 75.7 | 5.1 | 26.8 | 0.0 | 3.0 |
| 8.0 | 0.00 | 0.0 | 0.43 | 1.0 | 0.0 | -0.42 | -2.52 | 5.08 | 108.3 | 3.4 | 11.4 | 0.0 | 7.0 |
| 0.0 | 14.39 | 124.3 | 0.00 | 1.7 | 0.0 | 0.15 | 2.19 | 5.55 | 97.0 | 3.8 | 7.8 | 0.0 | 2.7 |
| 6.5 | 5.07 | 8.2 | 1.14 | 1.7 | 0.0 | 0.00 | 0.00 | 2.69 | 100.0 | 6.7 | 48.9 | 0.0 | 4.2 |
| 6.2 | 0.69 | 6.2 | 0.57 | 2.1 | 0.0 | 0.03 | 0.37 | 3.66 | 94.5 | 4.7 | 40.2 | 15.8 | 3.9 |
| 4.4 | 2.13 | 16.3 | 0.00 | 3.6 | 0.0 | 0.19 | 1.98 | 4.26 | 95.0 | 3.3 | 18.6 | 4.7 | 5.1 |
| 8.2 | 0.42 | 3.5 | 0.29 | 5.0 | 4.3 | 0.67 | 7.02 | 3.17 | 79.4 | 3.0 | 9.9 | 10.4 | 7.3 |
| 9.5 | 0.35 | 2.9 | 0.07 | 6.5 | 1.0 | 1.02 | 10.51 | 4.33 | 82.6 | 4.3 | 23.1 | 4.2 | 6.1 |
| 10.0 | 0.29 | 1.0 | 0.31 | 4.6 | 0.4 | 0.68 | 5.32 | 2.88 | 83.0 | 5.1 | 29.4 | 2.3 | 6.4 |
| 6.8 | 0.80 | 2.5 | 0.37 | 6.8 | 0.0 | 0.67 | 3.47 | 5.32 | 81.4 | 5.0 | 42.4 | 0.0 | 5.0 |
| 10.0 | 0.00 | 0.0 | 0.37 | 0.3 | 0.0 | -0.12 | -0.93 | 2.24 | 103.9 | 5.3 | 35.0 | 0.0 | 5.4 |
| 7.4 | 0.78 | 5.3 | 0.35 | 8.2 | 8.5 | 1.06 | 8.94 | 3.70 | 75.0 | 3.8 | 8.6 | 3.0 | 8.8 |
| 9.6 | 0.07 | 0.6 | 0.61 | 2.3 | 0.0 | -0.08 | -1.16 | 5.18 | 93.3 | 4.7 | 23.6 | 0.0 | 1.7 |
| 7.1 | 0.02 | 3.9 | -0.05 | 3.1 | 0.0 | 0.13 | 1.72 | 3.45 | 97.1 | 4.7 | 21.3 | 1.2 | 3.6 |
| 8.9 | 1.55 | 2.8 | 0.39 | 4.7 | 0.2 | 0.73 | 5.72 | 2.30 | 56.4 | 5.0 | 18.7 | 0.0 | 5.8 |
| 10.0 | 0.26 | 0.5 | 0.25 | 5.4 | 0.1 | 0.74 | 5.26 | 3.33 | 74.8 | 5.4 | 12.4 | 0.0 | 5.0 |
| 7.1 | 0.49 | 3.3 | 0.23 | 3.0 | 0.1 | 0.20 | 2.21 | 3.72 | 94.7 | 3.9 | 23.1 | 6.2 | 4.1 |
| 9.3 | 4.63 | 2.5 | 0.00 | 0.5 | 0.0 | -0.40 | -2.80 | 1.96 | 121.2 | 5.1 | 22.5 | 0.0 | 5.7 |
| 5.7 | 0.63 | 6.1 | 0.41 | 3.5 | 0.5 | 0.30 | 3.07 | 2.36 | 82.4 | 2.5 | 19.5 | 20.6 | 6.1 |
| 9.6 | 0.88 | 2.0 | 0.50 | 1.3 | 0.0 | 0.01 | 0.07 | 3.39 | 96.7 | 5.6 | 54.1 | 1.1 | 5.5 |
| 7.1 | 0.69 | 3.7 | 0.55 | 2.8 | 0.1 | 0.19 | 1.84 | 3.76 | 85.5 | 4.1 | 21.4 | 4.2 | 5.1 |
| 9.9 | 0.35 | 1.7 | 0.18 | 3.7 | 0.1 | 0.43 | 2.92 | 2.52 | 86.4 | 4.7 | 24.5 | 3.9 | 7.1 |
| 2.7 | 3.39 | 21.9 | 0.44 | 7.2 | 0.1 | 0.98 | 8.15 | 9.11 | 83.3 | 2.8 | 24.3 | 22.7 | 6.3 |
| 6.0 | 3.22 | 8.8 | 1.25 | 0.0 | -0.1 | -1.25 | -8.02 | 9.31 | 99.2 | 6.5 | 43.3 | 0.0 | 5.3 |

| Name | City | State | Rating | 2014 Rating | 2013 Rating | Total Assets ($Mil) | One Year Asset Growth | Asset Mix (As a % of Total Assets) | | | | Capitalization Index | Net Worth Ratio |
|------|------|-------|--------|-------------|-------------|---------------------|-----------------------|-----------------|--------------|----------------|-----------|----------------------|------------------|
| | | | | | | | | Commercial Loans | Consumer Loans | Mortgage Loans | Securities | | |
| COMM-SCOPE CU | Catawba | NC | B- | C | D | 29.6 | 4.76 | 1.0 | 14.0 | 22.1 | 39.2 | 10.0 | 12.8 |
| COMMODORE PERRY FCU | Oak Harbor | OH | D | D | D | 35.1 | 1.09 | 4.1 | 39.8 | 19.1 | 2.4 | 6.1 | 8.1 |
| COMMONWEALTH CENTRAL CU | San Jose | CA | B+ | B+ | B+ | 445.9 | 7.37 | 8.7 | 22.9 | 28.5 | 6.9 | 7.7 | 9.5 |
| COMMONWEALTH CU | Bourbonnais | IL | C | C | C | 74.9 | 6.75 | 0.6 | 51.1 | 25.7 | 0.0 | 8.9 | 10.3 |
| COMMONWEALTH CU | Frankfort | KY | A | A | A | 1019.8 | 4.28 | 1.4 | 32.5 | 24.5 | 20.9 | 10.0 | 19.5 |
| COMMONWEALTH ONE FCU | Alexandria | VA | C+ | C+ | C | 315.4 | 0.02 | 5.3 | 27.6 | 27.2 | 17.9 | 8.0 | 9.7 |
| COMMONWEALTH UTILITIES EMPL CU | Marion | MA | C | C+ | B- | 41.7 | -3.07 | 0.0 | 13.0 | 8.6 | 7.6 | 10.0 | 14.3 |
| COMMUNICATION FCU | Oklahoma City | OK | A- | A- | A- | 1011.4 | 7.71 | 0.0 | 53.5 | 7.9 | 19.6 | 10.0 | 14.4 |
| ▼ COMMUNITIES OF ABILENE FCU | Abilene | TX | C+ | B- | C+ | 130.7 | 4.98 | 0.0 | 21.7 | 17.0 | 27.8 | 6.4 | 8.5 |
| COMMUNITY & TEACHERS FCU | East Providence | RI | D+ | C- | C- | 23.9 | 9.22 | 4.3 | 8.8 | 45.3 | 0.0 | 6.8 | 8.8 |
| COMMUNITY 1ST CU | Ottumwa | IA | B | B | B | 553.4 | 8.84 | 12.6 | 26.7 | 46.8 | 0.0 | 6.8 | 8.8 |
| COMMUNITY 1ST CU | Dupont | WA | C- | C+ | C+ | 109.1 | -2.18 | 0.1 | 49.4 | 8.6 | 1.8 | 10.0 | 15.9 |
| COMMUNITY 1ST FCU | Miles City | MT | C | C | C- | 27.8 | 4.28 | 13.4 | 15.8 | 33.9 | 0.9 | 6.7 | 8.7 |
| COMMUNITY ALLIANCE CU | Novi | MI | C+ | C+ | C+ | 104.0 | 10.69 | 2.0 | 67.6 | 15.9 | 1.5 | 6.6 | 8.6 |
| COMMUNITY CHOICE CU | Commerce City | CO | B- | B- | B | 56.0 | 44.43 | 0.0 | 32.3 | 11.9 | 0.0 | 10.0 | 12.4 |
| ▲ COMMUNITY CHOICE CU | Johnston | IA | B | B- | B- | 433.7 | -3.04 | 6.3 | 53.8 | 13.5 | 2.8 | 8.0 | 9.7 |
| COMMUNITY CHOICE CU | Farmington Hills | MI | B+ | A- | A- | 703.1 | 33.66 | 9.3 | 32.5 | 27.1 | 11.4 | 8.6 | 10.1 |
| COMMUNITY CU | Lewiston | ME | B- | B- | B- | 46.5 | 4.48 | 3.9 | 20.5 | 33.2 | 0.0 | 10.0 | 11.9 |
| COMMUNITY CU | New Rockford | ND | B | B | B- | 163.6 | 0.02 | 16.5 | 0.4 | 8.8 | 65.0 | 10.0 | 13.2 |
| COMMUNITY CU OF FLORIDA | Rockledge | FL | A- | A- | A- | 520.1 | 11.63 | 10.7 | 37.8 | 34.9 | 3.1 | 9.9 | 10.9 |
| COMMUNITY CU OF LYNN | Lynn | MA | B | B | B | 134.5 | 1.33 | 11.7 | 41.2 | 31.2 | 4.1 | 10.0 | 13.1 |
| COMMUNITY CU OF NEW MILFORD INC | New Milford | CT | E+ | E+ | E | 10.4 | 3.83 | 0.0 | 26.5 | 0.0 | 0.0 | 5.1 | 7.1 |
| COMMUNITY CU OF SOUTHERN HUMBOLDT | Garberville | CA | B | B | B | 83.8 | 17.89 | 5.1 | 9.5 | 49.6 | 3.5 | 8.0 | 9.7 |
| COMMUNITY FCU | Chicago | IL | C- | C- | D+ | <1 | 81.02 | 0.0 | 24.6 | 0.0 | 5.2 | 10.0 | 17.3 |
| COMMUNITY FINANCIAL CU | Broomfield | CO | A- | A | A | 229.2 | 50.53 | 31.4 | 17.9 | 24.4 | 6.9 | 10.0 | 11.7 |
| COMMUNITY FINANCIAL CU | Plymouth | MI | A | A | A- | 665.4 | 15.45 | 7.8 | 32.1 | 40.7 | 0.0 | 10.0 | 12.9 |
| ▲ COMMUNITY FINANCIAL CU | Springfield | MO | C- | C- | C | 61.6 | 3.92 | 0.0 | 41.8 | 11.1 | 17.0 | 7.4 | 9.3 |
| COMMUNITY FINANCIAL SERVICES FCU | Roselle | NJ | D | D | D+ | 39.2 | -4.77 | 10.8 | 9.4 | 11.1 | 31.5 | 10.0 | 17.6 |
| COMMUNITY FIRST CU | Santa Rosa | CA | B | B | B | 186.6 | 9.44 | 8.5 | 38.6 | 23.8 | 6.8 | 6.9 | 8.9 |
| ▼ COMMUNITY FIRST CU | Hannibal | MO | D- | D | D | 7.1 | 5.82 | 0.0 | 54.2 | 9.5 | 0.0 | 8.4 | 10.0 |
| COMMUNITY FIRST CU | Ashtabula | OH | C- | C- | C+ | 73.2 | 1.62 | 3.4 | 16.9 | 9.1 | 43.8 | 10.0 | 14.6 |
| COMMUNITY FIRST CU | Appleton | WI | A | A | A | 2208.6 | 7.60 | 14.3 | 13.5 | 63.3 | 0.0 | 10.0 | 12.8 |
| COMMUNITY FIRST CU OF FLORIDA | Jacksonville | FL | A | A | B+ | 1307.6 | 4.37 | 2.9 | 28.9 | 28.5 | 26.8 | 10.0 | 12.5 |
| COMMUNITY FIRST FCU | Lakeview | MI | D+ | D- | D- | 37.0 | 25.33 | 0.0 | 28.9 | 52.4 | 0.0 | 4.4 | 6.4 |
| COMMUNITY FIRST GUAM FCU | Hagatna | GU | B- | B | B+ | 111.8 | 1.05 | 24.4 | 26.0 | 36.5 | 4.5 | 9.6 | 10.7 |
| COMMUNITY FOCUS FCU | Brownstown | MI | C- | C+ | C+ | 50.5 | 3.11 | 0.0 | 13.4 | 13.0 | 28.7 | 10.0 | 15.9 |
| COMMUNITY HEALTHCARE CU INC | Manchester | CT | E+ | E+ | E+ | 8.7 | 5.78 | 0.0 | 73.3 | 0.0 | 0.0 | 6.2 | 8.2 |
| ▲ COMMUNITY HEALTHCARE FCU | Everett | WA | D- | E+ | D- | 11.7 | 0.64 | 0.0 | 41.4 | 0.0 | 0.0 | 5.2 | 7.2 |
| COMMUNITY LINK FCU | Huntington | IN | C+ | C+ | C+ | 18.8 | 0.12 | 6.8 | 20.1 | 34.1 | 31.1 | 10.0 | 11.9 |
| COMMUNITY ONE CU OF OHIO | North Canton | OH | C- | C- | C- | 69.2 | 6.31 | 0.4 | 29.7 | 9.6 | 33.8 | 6.3 | 8.3 |
| ▲ COMMUNITY PLUS FCU | Rantoul | IL | E+ | E | E+ | 19.0 | -3.57 | 0.0 | 35.6 | 15.3 | 0.0 | 6.1 | 8.1 |
| ▼ COMMUNITY POWERED FCU | Bear | DE | D+ | C | C+ | 122.0 | 3.88 | 0.0 | 15.2 | 11.7 | 53.6 | 10.0 | 11.7 |
| COMMUNITY PROMISE FCU | Kalamazoo | MI | C | C | B- | <1 | -4.06 | 0.0 | 54.5 | 0.0 | 0.0 | 10.0 | 21.9 |
| COMMUNITY REGIONAL CU | Kingston | PA | D | D | D- | 19.5 | 0.01 | 0.0 | 15.0 | 13.6 | 0.0 | 8.4 | 9.9 |
| COMMUNITY RESOURCE CU | Baytown | TX | B | B- | B- | 370.7 | 8.54 | 4.1 | 51.7 | 20.9 | 5.1 | 8.0 | 9.7 |
| COMMUNITY RESOURCE FCU | Latham | NY | B+ | B+ | B+ | 74.8 | 1.53 | 0.0 | 33.4 | 25.0 | 7.2 | 10.0 | 12.2 |
| COMMUNITY SERVICE CU | Huntsville | TX | B- | B- | B- | 89.9 | 6.77 | 1.0 | 47.0 | 3.1 | 6.1 | 8.2 | 9.8 |
| COMMUNITY SOUTH CU | Chipley | FL | B+ | B- | B- | 103.7 | 6.62 | 3.6 | 40.8 | 23.9 | 18.0 | 10.0 | 13.5 |
| COMMUNITY SPIRIT CU | Lawrenceburg | IN | C | C | C | 13.9 | 2.07 | 0.3 | 40.0 | 4.1 | 32.6 | 10.0 | 16.5 |
| COMMUNITY STAR CU | Elyria | OH | C+ | C | C- | 63.0 | 17.61 | 1.5 | 31.4 | 13.5 | 0.0 | 7.5 | 9.4 |
| COMMUNITY TRUST CU | Gurnee | IL | C | C | C- | 196.9 | 5.54 | 0.2 | 16.8 | 32.3 | 10.2 | 6.2 | 8.3 |
| COMMUNITY TRUST FCU | Apopka | FL | E+ | E+ | E+ | 6.5 | -9.29 | 9.0 | 24.6 | 40.3 | 0.0 | 0.0 | -3.8 |
| COMMUNITY UNITED CU | Strongsville | OH | C+ | B- | C+ | 11.3 | -0.06 | 0.0 | 48.4 | 4.4 | 15.9 | 10.0 | 16.3 |
| ▲ COMMUNITY UNITED FCU | Waycross | GA | C+ | C- | C- | 20.8 | 2.91 | 0.4 | 14.7 | 51.5 | 0.0 | 9.4 | 10.6 |
| COMMUNITY WEST CU | Kentwood | MI | B+ | B | B | 162.2 | 29.34 | 0.2 | 52.0 | 22.8 | 1.7 | 10.0 | 11.3 |
| COMMUNITYAMERICA CU | Lenexa | KS | A- | A- | A- | 2127.9 | 7.47 | 1.8 | 23.4 | 27.1 | 22.7 | 10.0 | 12.8 |
| COMMUNITYWIDE FCU | South Bend | IN | B- | C+ | C+ | 391.6 | 11.66 | 0.2 | 73.2 | 6.9 | 1.2 | 10.0 | 14.6 |
| ▲ COMMUNITYWORKS FCU | Greenville | SC | C | D | U | 1.6 | 67.89 | 0.0 | 47.7 | 0.0 | 0.0 | 10.0 | 24.1 |
| COMPASS FCU | Oswego | NY | A- | A- | A- | 38.2 | 4.59 | 0.0 | 25.3 | 26.3 | 6.1 | 10.0 | 17.3 |
| COMPASS FINANCIAL FCU | Medley | FL | B | B- | B- | 25.1 | 10.80 | 0.0 | 67.5 | 2.2 | 0.1 | 10.0 | 15.9 |

| Asset Quality Index | Non-Performing Loans | | Net Charge-Offs | Profitability Index | Net Income ($Mil) | Return on Assets | Return on Equity | Net Interest Spread | Overhead Efficiency Ratio | Liquidity Index | Liquidity Ratio | Hot Money Ratio | Stability Index |
|---|---|---|---|---|---|---|---|---|---|---|---|---|---|
| | as a % of Total Loans | as a % of Capital | Avg Loans | | | | | | | | | | |
| 5.9 | 2.96 | 9.8 | 0.24 | 4.1 | 0.2 | 0.69 | 5.59 | 4.07 | 80.5 | 4.4 | 28.6 | 14.8 | 6.2 |
| 3.0 | 2.51 | 24.1 | 0.99 | 2.9 | 0.1 | 0.22 | 2.72 | 5.83 | 86.9 | 3.1 | 3.7 | 3.1 | 2.3 |
| 8.0 | 0.63 | 4.1 | 0.12 | 5.6 | 2.0 | 0.59 | 6.20 | 4.03 | 86.7 | 4.7 | 24.6 | 3.4 | 6.5 |
| 7.0 | 0.35 | 2.7 | 0.14 | 2.9 | 0.2 | 0.26 | 2.68 | 3.20 | 90.8 | 3.1 | 16.2 | 13.9 | 4.6 |
| 8.9 | 0.71 | 2.5 | 0.74 | 6.2 | 7.0 | 0.92 | 4.81 | 4.01 | 74.6 | 3.8 | 11.6 | 4.4 | 9.1 |
| 7.6 | 0.63 | 4.4 | 0.65 | 3.4 | 1.0 | 0.40 | 4.30 | 3.36 | 83.2 | 3.5 | 8.7 | 6.5 | 5.5 |
| 7.4 | 2.20 | 6.2 | 1.74 | 2.3 | 0.1 | 0.33 | 2.32 | 2.24 | 78.8 | 4.7 | 32.8 | 4.9 | 5.1 |
| 6.8 | 0.93 | 5.0 | 0.93 | 4.5 | 4.6 | 0.61 | 4.20 | 3.29 | 63.3 | 2.7 | 18.7 | 19.4 | 8.1 |
| 7.2 | 1.03 | 7.0 | 1.42 | 2.1 | 0.1 | 0.11 | 1.30 | 4.28 | 77.6 | 3.7 | 9.3 | 5.8 | 4.6 |
| 3.7 | 1.78 | 21.0 | 0.42 | 2.3 | 0.0 | 0.22 | 2.76 | 3.99 | 96.5 | 4.4 | 29.7 | 7.3 | 3.4 |
| 6.7 | 0.58 | 6.1 | 0.27 | 6.4 | 3.1 | 0.79 | 8.91 | 3.75 | 76.2 | 1.3 | 6.6 | 23.2 | 6.3 |
| 7.8 | 0.67 | 2.9 | 0.31 | 1.7 | -0.1 | -0.07 | -0.47 | 3.53 | 97.9 | 4.2 | 23.1 | 9.5 | 7.4 |
| 6.8 | 0.47 | 3.6 | 0.22 | 4.6 | 0.1 | 0.61 | 7.31 | 3.78 | 82.3 | 4.1 | 25.7 | 0.0 | 4.3 |
| 4.1 | 1.06 | 14.7 | 0.76 | 3.9 | 0.2 | 0.26 | 2.95 | 5.87 | 82.6 | 1.0 | 2.9 | 20.7 | 5.4 |
| 7.3 | 2.38 | 7.5 | 0.52 | 3.2 | -0.1 | -0.29 | -2.01 | 3.60 | 105.8 | 5.2 | 43.6 | 8.2 | 5.9 |
| 6.6 | 0.15 | 4.1 | -0.02 | 5.5 | 2.6 | 0.80 | 8.61 | 3.78 | 81.1 | 3.0 | 7.4 | 5.5 | 5.8 |
| 6.8 | 0.67 | 5.5 | 0.40 | 4.6 | 2.0 | 0.42 | 4.12 | 4.02 | 87.8 | 3.4 | 5.1 | 1.2 | 6.1 |
| 5.6 | 1.62 | 12.2 | 0.36 | 3.8 | 0.1 | 0.36 | 3.04 | 4.57 | 90.0 | 4.5 | 29.9 | 5.5 | 5.7 |
| 7.7 | 6.11 | 7.6 | -0.01 | 4.7 | 0.9 | 0.70 | 5.44 | 1.46 | 48.2 | 3.6 | 10.2 | 17.3 | 8.4 |
| 6.4 | 0.77 | 6.2 | 0.61 | 6.7 | 3.6 | 0.93 | 9.22 | 4.23 | 63.3 | 3.3 | 12.9 | 6.5 | 8.0 |
| 6.5 | 1.04 | 6.9 | 0.29 | 3.9 | 0.4 | 0.35 | 2.67 | 4.60 | 92.5 | 2.6 | 17.4 | 14.8 | 7.8 |
| 7.2 | 0.60 | 3.1 | 0.14 | 2.2 | 0.0 | 0.18 | 2.55 | 3.61 | 94.7 | 5.3 | 29.0 | 0.0 | 1.7 |
| 6.0 | 0.40 | 7.7 | 0.28 | 7.5 | 0.6 | 1.01 | 10.08 | 4.60 | 75.2 | 4.1 | 10.8 | 4.3 | 5.4 |
| 10.0 | 0.00 | 0.0 | 0.00 | 1.0 | 0.0 | -1.13 | -6.06 | 10.81 | 166.7 | 8.1 | 90.2 | 0.0 | 6.0 |
| 9.5 | 0.16 | 1.0 | 0.04 | 4.6 | 0.9 | 0.55 | 4.69 | 3.34 | 85.5 | 3.6 | 10.3 | 4.2 | 7.7 |
| 6.4 | 1.04 | 8.3 | 0.20 | 9.6 | 6.1 | 1.29 | 9.90 | 3.95 | 71.6 | 2.3 | 1.8 | 6.4 | 9.6 |
| 7.7 | 0.49 | 3.0 | 1.09 | 2.1 | 0.1 | 0.18 | 1.94 | 3.06 | 88.0 | 4.0 | 10.7 | 2.2 | 3.9 |
| 7.4 | 1.84 | 5.2 | 0.20 | 0.4 | -0.1 | -0.34 | -2.01 | 3.25 | 107.4 | 4.1 | 9.7 | 2.9 | 6.1 |
| 6.1 | 1.05 | 10.7 | 0.40 | 6.2 | 1.2 | 0.91 | 10.34 | 4.12 | 78.0 | 4.1 | 18.3 | 5.2 | 6.2 |
| 3.5 | 2.47 | 16.7 | -0.33 | 1.5 | 0.0 | -0.12 | -1.13 | 3.69 | 87.0 | 4.6 | 30.4 | 0.0 | 4.9 |
| 9.4 | 0.37 | 0.9 | 0.29 | 1.9 | 0.1 | 0.24 | 1.64 | 2.57 | 90.8 | 4.5 | 19.2 | 2.1 | 6.0 |
| 8.2 | 0.38 | 3.3 | 0.10 | 9.5 | 29.8 | 1.84 | 15.10 | 3.17 | 51.3 | 3.1 | 12.1 | 9.0 | 10.0 |
| 8.7 | 0.64 | 3.3 | 0.54 | 9.3 | 11.8 | 1.22 | 9.89 | 3.14 | 67.6 | 3.7 | 12.2 | 6.3 | 8.5 |
| 5.8 | 0.59 | 8.9 | 0.17 | 9.8 | 0.5 | 1.96 | 31.70 | 5.18 | 68.3 | 1.9 | 3.2 | 11.1 | 2.6 |
| 5.2 | 1.37 | 13.7 | 0.24 | 3.9 | 0.3 | 0.36 | 4.42 | 5.28 | 87.9 | 2.3 | 17.6 | 26.3 | 6.0 |
| 9.9 | 1.19 | 2.2 | 0.20 | 1.5 | 0.0 | -0.03 | -0.20 | 2.73 | 99.3 | 4.9 | 20.9 | 1.5 | 6.1 |
| 3.7 | 0.81 | 7.7 | 0.80 | 4.2 | 0.0 | 0.47 | 5.89 | 5.53 | 84.7 | 3.5 | 14.9 | 0.0 | 1.7 |
| 3.7 | 1.62 | 21.6 | 0.41 | 4.8 | 0.1 | 0.76 | 11.12 | 5.10 | 89.3 | 4.1 | 8.7 | 0.0 | 1.7 |
| 6.0 | 2.16 | 10.6 | 0.54 | 5.5 | 0.1 | 0.72 | 6.24 | 3.93 | 73.8 | 3.5 | 9.2 | 5.8 | 5.0 |
| 4.6 | 1.82 | 11.5 | 1.79 | 3.8 | 0.2 | 0.41 | 5.60 | 4.16 | 75.7 | 4.2 | 26.8 | 8.0 | 2.7 |
| 6.8 | 0.58 | 5.1 | 0.22 | 0.8 | 0.0 | -0.25 | -3.58 | 3.20 | 103.4 | 4.6 | 39.6 | 4.9 | 3.4 |
| 9.3 | 1.34 | 3.9 | 0.61 | 0.7 | -0.2 | -0.22 | -1.95 | 2.53 | 94.8 | 4.2 | 9.9 | 9.2 | 6.9 |
| 6.5 | 4.11 | 8.7 | -1.12 | 6.7 | 0.0 | 12.27 | 50.86 | 12.32 | 68.4 | 3.7 | 33.7 | 31.8 | 4.3 |
| 1.7 | 7.08 | 36.5 | 0.26 | 1.6 | 0.0 | 0.09 | 0.90 | 2.85 | 91.7 | 5.4 | 46.5 | 1.3 | 3.8 |
| 7.0 | 0.53 | 4.5 | 0.43 | 5.8 | 2.7 | 0.99 | 11.14 | 4.56 | 79.5 | 3.3 | 11.0 | 5.9 | 5.8 |
| 5.2 | 2.02 | 12.8 | 1.14 | 6.6 | 0.4 | 0.63 | 5.30 | 5.28 | 68.3 | 1.9 | 14.3 | 16.5 | 6.7 |
| 7.2 | 0.11 | 0.7 | 0.49 | 5.0 | 0.5 | 0.73 | 7.57 | 4.57 | 81.6 | 3.6 | 20.0 | 7.2 | 4.7 |
| 6.1 | 1.42 | 9.5 | 1.03 | 9.0 | 1.2 | 1.57 | 12.63 | 5.78 | 68.5 | 2.3 | 1.5 | 13.9 | 8.1 |
| 4.7 | 2.72 | 8.7 | 0.97 | 2.5 | 0.0 | 0.12 | 0.70 | 3.90 | 83.9 | 4.2 | 11.3 | 0.0 | 5.8 |
| 7.0 | 0.71 | 4.6 | 0.25 | 4.8 | 0.3 | 0.70 | 7.77 | 4.05 | 88.1 | 3.6 | 20.6 | 7.1 | 3.8 |
| 7.8 | 0.77 | 5.2 | 0.21 | 3.2 | 0.6 | 0.38 | 4.72 | 3.11 | 88.2 | 4.6 | 21.8 | 5.7 | 4.9 |
| 3.3 | 2.68 | NA | 14.75 | 1.1 | -0.8 | -14.42 | -273.83 | 5.05 | 87.2 | 3.9 | 8.9 | 2.3 | 2.1 |
| 7.5 | 1.17 | 4.5 | 0.59 | 1.5 | 0.0 | -0.31 | -1.95 | 4.15 | 97.2 | 3.9 | 16.5 | 1.3 | 6.6 |
| 6.2 | 1.55 | 10.3 | 0.44 | 7.2 | 0.2 | 1.14 | 11.32 | 4.29 | 70.2 | 4.2 | 37.5 | 11.0 | 5.0 |
| 5.7 | 1.27 | 9.3 | 0.23 | 4.4 | 0.6 | 0.53 | 4.57 | 3.85 | 79.0 | 2.5 | 8.4 | 7.5 | 7.1 |
| 8.4 | 0.82 | 4.0 | 0.47 | 5.5 | 12.6 | 0.81 | 6.28 | 2.63 | 83.2 | 3.8 | 11.4 | 4.9 | 8.7 |
| 3.5 | 3.29 | 19.7 | 2.26 | 10.0 | 5.2 | 1.85 | 12.64 | 5.24 | 33.7 | 1.2 | 2.4 | 23.2 | 8.9 |
| 5.1 | 6.93 | 15.7 | 5.71 | 10.0 | 0.1 | 9.44 | 65.50 | 12.79 | 49.4 | 4.7 | 69.0 | 65.1 | 2.2 |
| 9.1 | 0.35 | 1.4 | 0.22 | 10.0 | 0.5 | 1.87 | 11.26 | 5.30 | 65.4 | 4.0 | 21.0 | 8.3 | 8.0 |
| 5.9 | 1.06 | 6.7 | 1.61 | 7.0 | 0.1 | 0.73 | 4.69 | 6.99 | 76.3 | 2.6 | 25.7 | 26.5 | 7.2 |

| Name | City | State | Rating | 2014 Rating | 2013 Rating | Total Assets ($Mil) | One Year Asset Growth | Asset Mix (As a % of Total Assets) | | | | Capital- ization Index | Net Worth Ratio |
|---|---|---|---|---|---|---|---|---|---|---|---|---|---|
| | | | | | | | | Comm- ercial Loans | Cons- umer Loans | Mort- gage Loans | Secur- ities | | |
| COMPLEX COMMUNITY FCU | Odessa | TX | B+ | A- | A- | 450.2 | 5.81 | 0.0 | 35.0 | 16.0 | 21.3 | 8.7 | 10.1 |
| COMPTON MUNICIPAL EMPL FCU | Compton | CA | E+ | D | C- | <1 | -23.89 | 0.0 | 53.7 | 0.0 | 0.0 | 2.2 | 4.7 |
| COMTRUST FCU | Chattanooga | TN | C+ | C+ | C+ | 351.2 | 0.63 | 1.2 | 14.9 | 13.4 | 44.3 | 10.0 | 11.3 |
| COMUNIDAD LATINA FCU | Santa Ana | CA | C | C- | C | 3.9 | 0.83 | 0.0 | 53.9 | 0.0 | 0.0 | 10.0 | 13.9 |
| CONCHO EDUCATORS FCU | San Angelo | TX | C | C | C+ | 74.2 | 4.64 | 0.6 | 17.0 | 5.9 | 43.3 | 7.1 | 9.2 |
| CONCHO VALLEY CU | San Angelo | TX | C- | C- | C- | 16.3 | 4.98 | 0.0 | 23.5 | 23.0 | 0.0 | 9.5 | 10.6 |
| CONCORA WABASH FCU | Wabash | IN | C- | C- | C- | 1.0 | -6.31 | 0.0 | 81.1 | 0.0 | 0.0 | 10.0 | 19.2 |
| CONCORD FCU | Brooklyn | NY | C+ | C+ | C+ | 8.8 | 2.33 | 0.0 | 3.3 | 0.0 | 9.7 | 10.0 | 18.3 |
| CONCORDIA PARISH SCHOOL EMPL FCU | Ferriday | LA | E+ | E+ | E+ | 3.8 | -1.17 | 0.0 | 49.5 | 0.0 | 0.0 | 6.8 | 8.8 |
| ▼ CONE CU | Neenah | WI | C+ | B- | B- | 30.5 | 2.15 | 5.8 | 11.5 | 32.1 | 0.0 | 9.6 | 10.8 |
| CONGRESSIONAL FCU | Oakton | VA | B- | B- | C+ | 803.8 | 2.71 | 0.0 | 19.9 | 29.7 | 33.4 | 7.6 | 9.4 |
| ▼ CONNECT CU | Fort Lauderdale | FL | B- | B | B | 70.2 | 2.68 | 0.0 | 25.7 | 6.0 | 42.3 | 10.0 | 11.4 |
| CONNECTED CU | Augusta | ME | B- | B- | B | 34.3 | 5.42 | 0.7 | 26.8 | 29.7 | 0.0 | 10.0 | 11.6 |
| CONNECTICUT COMMUNITY CU INC | Pawcatuck | CT | D- | D- | D- | 20.5 | 2.81 | 0.0 | 39.5 | 0.0 | 0.0 | 4.8 | 6.8 |
| CONNECTICUT FCU | North Haven | CT | D | D | D+ | 7.5 | 6.60 | 0.0 | 7.5 | 0.0 | 3.8 | 8.4 | 9.9 |
| ▲ CONNECTICUT LABOR DEPT FCU | Wethersfield | CT | C- | D+ | C+ | 13.5 | 4.31 | 0.0 | 24.2 | 11.3 | 0.0 | 10.0 | 14.0 |
| CONNECTICUT POSTAL FCU | New Britain | CT | C+ | C+ | B- | 14.1 | -1.89 | 0.0 | 25.8 | 11.6 | 0.0 | 10.0 | 16.2 |
| CONNECTICUT STATE EMPL CU INC | Hartford | CT | C | C | C | 1694.9 | 0.93 | 0.0 | 2.7 | 15.4 | 47.7 | 6.3 | 8.3 |
| CONNECTICUT TRANSIT FCU | Hartford | CT | E+ | E+ | E+ | 1.1 | 4.61 | 0.0 | 87.6 | 0.0 | 0.0 | 4.0 | 6.0 |
| ▼ CONNECTION CU | Silverdale | WA | C- | C | D+ | 27.3 | 1.79 | 0.0 | 48.4 | 17.3 | 0.9 | 10.0 | 13.7 |
| ▲ CONNECTIONS CU | Pocatello | ID | D | D- | D | 143.9 | 6.50 | 3.6 | 27.0 | 26.1 | 3.0 | 6.2 | 8.2 |
| CONNECTS FCU | Richmond | VA | C- | C- | C- | 76.8 | 1.66 | 0.0 | 29.1 | 0.0 | 15.4 | 5.9 | 7.9 |
| CONNEX CU INC | North Haven | CT | B | B- | B+ | 445.5 | 6.41 | 0.9 | 33.0 | 16.9 | 24.6 | 10.0 | 12.0 |
| ▲ CONNEXUS CU | Wausau | WI | B- | B- | B | 1136.6 | 74.86 | 0.9 | 42.3 | 24.8 | 0.5 | 7.3 | 9.2 |
| CONSERVATION EMPL CU | Jefferson City | MO | B | B | B- | 101.5 | 5.03 | 1.8 | 25.1 | 32.4 | 15.9 | 8.3 | 9.9 |
| CONSOL EMPL CU | Canonsburg | PA | C- | C | B- | 16.3 | -3.24 | 0.0 | 19.9 | 0.0 | 23.0 | 10.0 | 14.2 |
| CONSOLIDATED CONTROLS CORP FCU | Bethel | CT | C- | C | C | 1.1 | -8.61 | 0.0 | 73.9 | 0.0 | 0.0 | 10.0 | 18.4 |
| CONSOLIDATED FCU | Portland | OR | B+ | B+ | B+ | 192.1 | 4.56 | 12.8 | 21.8 | 31.2 | 0.8 | 10.0 | 14.7 |
| CONSOLIDATED HUB-CO FCU | Aberdeen | SD | E+ | E+ | E+ | 5.5 | -8.77 | 0.6 | 47.7 | 0.0 | 0.0 | 5.9 | 7.9 |
| CONSTELLATION FCU | Reston | VA | B- | B | B- | 209.9 | 0.93 | 1.9 | 5.8 | 34.5 | 15.9 | 10.0 | 14.2 |
| ▲ CONSTRUCTION FCU | Bingham Farms | MI | C+ | C | C | 22.3 | 6.12 | 2.4 | 7.2 | 32.2 | 11.3 | 10.0 | 13.9 |
| CONSTRUCTION INDUSTRIES CU | Lincoln | NE | C- | C- | C- | 1.6 | -0.37 | 0.0 | 69.5 | 0.0 | 0.0 | 10.0 | 16.3 |
| CONSUMER CU | Greeneville | TN | B- | B | A- | 367.1 | 5.10 | 10.5 | 20.3 | 52.5 | 11.7 | 9.9 | 11.1 |
| CONSUMER HEALTHCARE FCU | Moon Township | PA | C | C | C | 21.4 | -8.80 | 0.0 | 9.7 | 5.3 | 0.0 | 10.0 | 14.1 |
| CONSUMERS COOPERATIVE CU | Gurnee | IL | B | B | B | 678.3 | 12.34 | 10.2 | 38.1 | 20.5 | 14.3 | 6.8 | 8.8 |
| CONSUMERS COOPERATIVE FCU | Alliance | NE | B | B | B | 24.5 | 4.94 | 0.0 | 57.2 | 2.8 | 0.0 | 10.0 | 17.7 |
| CONSUMERS CU | Denison | IA | C+ | C+ | C | 6.1 | 5.56 | 0.0 | 51.2 | 0.0 | 0.0 | 10.0 | 13.6 |
| CONSUMERS CU | Kalamazoo | MI | A- | A- | A- | 647.2 | 17.67 | 5.2 | 41.9 | 34.3 | 0.0 | 8.0 | 9.7 |
| ▲ CONSUMERS FCU | Brooklyn | NY | C | C | C | 56.3 | 24.51 | 10.9 | 4.1 | 64.2 | 0.0 | 10.0 | 13.1 |
| ▲ CONSUMERS FCU | Gregory | SD | D+ | D+ | D- | 10.5 | 1.59 | 19.2 | 29.9 | 14.5 | 0.0 | 6.6 | 8.6 |
| CONSUMERS PROFESSIONAL CU | Lansing | MI | B | B | C+ | 71.1 | -1.12 | 5.5 | 19.5 | 36.6 | 0.7 | 10.0 | 15.4 |
| ▲ CONSUMERS UNION EMPL FCU | Yonkers | NY | C | C- | C | 4.4 | -5.91 | 0.0 | 15.9 | 0.0 | 0.0 | 10.0 | 13.7 |
| CONTAINER MUTUAL CU | Fernandina Beach | FL | C | C- | C- | 8.3 | 1.94 | 0.0 | 36.0 | 8.2 | 0.0 | 10.0 | 31.7 |
| CONTINENTAL EMPL FCU | Alexandria | LA | D | D | D | 1.2 | -10.32 | 0.0 | 43.6 | 0.0 | 0.0 | 10.0 | 31.5 |
| COOPERATIVE CENTER FCU | Berkeley | CA | D | D+ | C- | 111.3 | 1.19 | 1.3 | 20.1 | 18.3 | 15.6 | 4.7 | 6.7 |
| COOPERATIVE EMPL CU | Anadarko | OK | C- | C- | C- | 6.9 | 2.50 | 0.0 | 57.6 | 0.0 | 4.4 | 10.0 | 13.4 |
| COOPERATIVE EXTENSION SERVICE FCU | Little Rock | AR | C | C | C | 5.1 | 3.94 | 0.0 | 59.8 | 0.0 | 0.0 | 10.0 | 24.6 |
| COOPERATIVE TEACHERS CU | Tyler | TX | A- | A- | A- | 107.4 | 44.33 | 0.0 | 17.7 | 32.6 | 31.5 | 10.0 | 11.1 |
| COOPERS CAVE FCU | Glens Falls | NY | D | D- | D | 13.0 | 1.33 | 0.0 | 17.4 | 0.0 | 17.7 | 7.1 | 9.0 |
| COORS CU | Golden | CO | A | A | A | 210.2 | 16.46 | 3.9 | 41.0 | 26.9 | 11.4 | 10.0 | 11.4 |
| COOSA PINES FCU | Childersburg | AL | B+ | B+ | A- | 230.3 | 2.55 | 0.9 | 22.4 | 24.5 | 32.9 | 10.0 | 12.6 |
| COOSA VALLEY FCU | Rome | GA | B | B- | C+ | 172.1 | 4.41 | 7.6 | 35.4 | 22.1 | 8.5 | 7.4 | 9.3 |
| ▼ COPOCO COMMUNITY CU | Bay City | MI | D | C- | C- | 99.5 | -3.39 | 1.2 | 36.5 | 25.2 | 16.3 | 7.8 | 9.6 |
| COPPER & GLASS FCU | Glassport | PA | C- | C- | D+ | 8.3 | 1.82 | 0.0 | 46.1 | 0.0 | 0.0 | 10.0 | 14.1 |
| COPPER BASIN FCU | Copperhill | TN | D | D- | D | 27.5 | 0.87 | 0.3 | 26.4 | 32.2 | 0.0 | 5.8 | 7.8 |
| ▼ CORAL COMMUNITY FCU | Fort Lauderdale | FL | C | C+ | C | 28.0 | 5.70 | 0.0 | 35.2 | 1.0 | 40.8 | 9.1 | 10.4 |
| CORCO FCU | Delaware | OH | D- | D- | E+ | <1 | -4.06 | 0.0 | 43.7 | 0.0 | 0.0 | 5.8 | 7.8 |
| CORE CU | Statesboro | GA | C+ | C+ | C | 65.7 | 8.86 | 5.9 | 31.0 | 34.3 | 0.0 | 7.3 | 9.2 |
| CORE FCU | East Syracuse | NY | B+ | A- | A- | 98.8 | 7.76 | 9.9 | 7.4 | 5.1 | 8.3 | 10.0 | 11.1 |
| ▲ COREPLUS FCU | Norwich | CT | C- | D+ | C- | 191.2 | 1.86 | 2.8 | 28.7 | 21.9 | 16.9 | 5.5 | 7.6 |

| Asset Quality Index | Non-Performing Loans as a % of Total Loans | as a % of Capital | Net Charge-Offs Avg Loans | Profitability Index | Net Income ($Mil) | Return on Assets | Return on Equity | Net Interest Spread | Overhead Efficiency Ratio | Liquidity Index | Liquidity Ratio | Hot Money Ratio | Stability Index |
|---|---|---|---|---|---|---|---|---|---|---|---|---|---|
| 8.0 | 0.72 | 4.5 | 0.78 | 5.3 | 1.8 | 0.53 | 5.42 | 3.28 | 77.9 | 3.6 | 15.2 | 13.5 | 7.2 |
| 0.0 | 15.92 | 65.9 | 7.88 | 1.0 | -0.1 | -8.74 | -94.36 | 10.86 | 197.8 | 6.7 | 54.8 | 0.0 | 5.8 |
| 9.9 | 0.61 | 2.0 | 0.09 | 2.7 | 0.6 | 0.23 | 2.03 | 2.10 | 89.4 | 5.6 | 26.4 | 4.8 | 7.2 |
| 8.7 | 0.14 | 0.5 | 0.42 | 6.2 | 0.1 | 1.96 | 15.16 | 5.54 | 77.0 | 2.8 | 58.2 | 57.8 | 5.0 |
| 7.5 | 1.75 | 6.5 | 0.04 | 2.8 | 0.2 | 0.29 | 3.15 | 2.55 | 90.8 | 4.1 | 18.3 | 17.1 | 4.4 |
| 9.8 | 0.18 | 0.9 | 0.15 | 2.6 | 0.0 | 0.28 | 2.64 | 3.03 | 90.9 | 4.3 | 45.5 | 11.3 | 5.1 |
| 8.2 | 0.00 | 0.0 | -0.17 | 1.4 | 0.0 | -0.25 | -1.33 | 4.75 | 106.3 | 4.2 | 18.9 | 0.0 | 6.3 |
| 10.0 | 0.00 | 0.0 | -0.23 | 2.8 | 0.0 | 0.21 | 1.17 | 2.05 | 87.6 | 5.9 | 14.7 | 0.0 | 7.4 |
| 0.7 | 5.37 | 38.6 | 0.47 | 3.5 | 0.0 | 0.41 | 4.78 | 7.35 | 85.4 | 5.4 | 35.6 | 0.0 | 3.4 |
| 7.0 | 0.64 | 6.0 | 0.41 | 2.8 | 0.0 | 0.17 | 1.55 | 2.34 | 86.7 | 3.9 | 10.8 | 0.0 | 5.9 |
| 7.1 | 1.15 | 7.2 | 0.32 | 3.6 | 2.6 | 0.43 | 4.77 | 3.10 | 86.6 | 4.5 | 36.3 | 5.5 | 6.3 |
| 8.0 | 1.15 | 4.6 | 0.20 | 1.4 | -0.4 | -0.74 | -6.14 | 3.55 | 80.1 | 4.4 | 11.1 | 2.0 | 6.1 |
| 9.7 | 0.34 | 1.8 | 0.03 | 3.9 | 0.2 | 0.58 | 5.02 | 3.32 | 86.4 | 4.2 | 24.1 | 1.3 | 6.5 |
| 6.5 | 1.05 | 7.0 | 0.31 | 0.0 | -0.1 | -0.72 | -10.28 | 2.75 | 115.4 | 5.3 | 28.4 | 0.8 | 2.5 |
| 9.5 | 1.62 | 1.5 | 0.58 | 0.6 | 0.0 | -0.23 | -2.32 | 2.90 | 105.2 | 5.8 | 18.2 | 0.0 | 3.7 |
| 10.0 | 0.55 | 1.4 | -0.14 | 1.4 | 0.0 | 0.08 | 0.57 | 3.71 | 87.8 | 6.1 | 40.3 | 0.0 | 5.1 |
| 10.0 | 0.45 | 1.1 | 0.05 | 3.3 | 0.1 | 0.44 | 2.76 | 2.01 | 77.1 | 6.1 | 40.7 | 2.5 | 6.5 |
| 10.0 | 0.10 | 0.2 | 0.21 | 2.5 | 2.9 | 0.23 | 2.88 | 1.07 | 66.4 | 7.5 | 49.3 | 2.0 | 5.8 |
| 1.2 | 3.29 | 34.8 | 1.54 | 0.0 | 0.0 | -2.49 | -41.18 | 9.68 | 96.0 | 3.1 | 3.5 | 0.0 | 3.1 |
| 5.4 | 0.87 | 7.7 | 1.48 | 1.4 | 0.0 | -0.11 | -0.78 | 7.08 | 75.2 | 3.8 | 10.8 | 1.9 | 6.1 |
| 5.7 | 1.35 | 11.2 | 0.46 | 2.9 | 0.2 | 0.20 | 2.39 | 3.58 | 86.3 | 4.0 | 16.3 | 5.5 | 4.5 |
| 7.6 | 0.91 | 4.0 | 0.67 | 2.1 | 0.1 | 0.08 | 1.07 | 2.87 | 92.8 | 4.7 | 18.7 | 4.5 | 2.2 |
| 7.4 | 1.00 | 7.5 | 0.20 | 4.0 | 2.0 | 0.60 | 5.03 | 2.88 | 86.0 | 3.1 | 9.3 | 9.9 | 7.1 |
| 5.9 | 1.17 | 9.8 | 0.30 | 6.3 | 5.8 | 0.72 | 6.87 | 3.36 | 74.2 | 1.9 | 7.0 | 13.7 | 7.5 |
| 7.9 | 0.55 | 4.1 | 0.16 | 4.1 | 0.4 | 0.47 | 4.93 | 2.99 | 83.6 | 3.9 | 11.8 | 4.8 | 6.5 |
| 9.9 | 1.38 | 1.9 | -0.07 | 1.4 | 0.0 | 0.06 | 0.40 | 2.97 | 96.7 | 6.3 | 34.0 | 0.0 | 5.1 |
| 8.5 | 0.00 | 0.0 | 0.00 | 2.1 | 0.0 | 0.00 | 0.00 | 5.33 | 97.3 | 4.0 | 9.3 | 0.0 | 6.6 |
| 9.5 | 0.17 | 1.0 | 0.09 | 5.1 | 1.1 | 0.80 | 5.44 | 3.25 | 83.2 | 3.8 | 26.2 | 4.7 | 8.2 |
| 4.4 | 1.25 | 9.7 | -0.04 | 3.4 | 0.0 | 0.52 | 6.89 | 4.48 | 91.7 | 4.7 | 22.8 | 0.0 | 1.0 |
| 10.0 | 0.24 | 1.1 | 0.08 | 3.0 | 0.5 | 0.33 | 2.33 | 2.70 | 87.3 | 4.0 | 27.2 | 9.7 | 8.3 |
| 10.0 | 0.00 | 0.0 | 0.03 | 2.7 | 0.1 | 0.36 | 2.63 | 2.93 | 88.3 | 4.4 | 29.2 | 14.6 | 6.6 |
| 5.6 | 2.46 | 10.4 | 0.11 | 1.9 | 0.0 | -0.08 | -0.50 | 5.01 | 100.0 | 5.6 | 35.1 | 0.0 | 6.8 |
| 9.6 | 0.05 | 0.7 | 0.00 | 4.0 | 1.3 | 0.47 | 4.30 | 2.22 | 83.6 | 2.7 | 7.8 | 13.5 | 7.8 |
| 7.8 | 3.22 | 6.0 | 0.50 | 2.3 | 0.0 | 0.26 | 1.91 | 1.88 | 84.0 | 6.0 | 32.8 | 0.0 | 5.9 |
| 8.3 | 0.34 | 3.1 | 0.37 | 4.6 | 2.3 | 0.46 | 5.44 | 3.68 | 87.2 | 3.2 | 11.0 | 7.7 | 5.9 |
| 7.3 | 1.24 | 4.7 | 0.36 | 10.0 | 0.4 | 2.31 | 13.62 | 4.76 | 47.6 | 2.9 | 38.8 | 32.0 | 6.3 |
| 8.4 | 0.17 | 0.7 | 0.00 | 5.6 | 0.0 | 0.72 | 5.40 | 5.52 | 88.8 | 6.1 | 48.7 | 4.4 | 5.0 |
| 8.3 | 0.30 | 3.3 | 0.44 | 9.7 | 5.8 | 1.27 | 12.99 | 3.76 | 76.3 | 1.7 | 5.9 | 16.1 | 7.5 |
| 3.5 | 0.00 | 26.8 | 0.11 | 4.7 | 0.3 | 0.78 | 5.23 | 3.93 | 82.3 | 2.1 | 27.3 | 25.4 | 6.0 |
| 6.6 | 0.35 | 2.6 | 0.10 | 3.9 | 0.1 | 0.64 | 8.29 | 3.22 | 84.4 | 3.4 | 24.8 | 14.3 | 3.0 |
| 9.0 | 0.61 | 2.7 | 0.12 | 5.3 | 0.5 | 0.88 | 5.85 | 3.73 | 75.6 | 2.4 | 17.1 | 23.7 | 6.8 |
| 9.0 | 2.71 | 3.1 | 2.57 | 6.7 | 0.1 | 1.42 | 11.23 | 2.02 | 52.3 | 7.2 | 53.7 | 0.0 | 4.3 |
| 8.9 | 2.71 | 4.2 | -0.10 | 4.6 | 0.1 | 0.78 | 2.43 | 3.24 | 75.8 | 5.1 | 33.9 | 0.0 | 4.3 |
| 3.3 | 6.64 | 22.9 | 4.47 | 0.0 | -0.1 | -6.35 | -19.87 | 6.02 | 136.0 | 4.7 | 23.8 | 0.0 | 5.3 |
| 6.1 | 1.00 | 10.7 | 1.76 | 0.6 | -0.3 | -0.39 | -8.98 | 3.15 | 98.7 | 4.6 | 25.7 | 1.4 | 2.1 |
| 7.6 | 0.41 | 2.4 | 0.00 | 3.7 | 0.0 | 0.33 | 2.47 | 4.88 | 93.6 | 3.8 | 17.3 | 1.7 | 6.9 |
| 8.4 | 0.64 | 1.6 | 0.58 | 2.9 | 0.0 | 0.19 | 0.74 | 4.47 | 90.4 | 5.7 | 50.0 | 0.0 | 7.1 |
| 9.6 | 0.55 | 2.6 | 0.40 | 6.5 | 0.8 | 1.03 | 8.60 | 3.29 | 65.4 | 4.9 | 20.6 | 0.0 | 8.4 |
| 7.3 | 0.52 | 2.2 | 1.31 | 1.7 | 0.0 | 0.23 | 2.56 | 3.31 | 96.5 | 5.7 | 33.1 | 0.0 | 3.2 |
| 7.4 | 1.02 | 8.1 | 0.31 | 8.4 | 1.9 | 1.22 | 10.86 | 4.08 | 72.3 | 3.2 | 7.4 | 2.9 | 7.8 |
| 9.8 | 0.48 | 2.3 | 0.37 | 4.4 | 1.1 | 0.64 | 5.13 | 3.12 | 76.3 | 4.0 | 16.4 | 5.5 | 7.3 |
| 7.3 | 0.38 | 4.7 | 0.44 | 5.7 | 1.1 | 0.86 | 9.64 | 4.79 | 79.9 | 3.8 | 13.6 | 2.5 | 5.8 |
| 3.6 | 2.15 | 20.7 | 1.77 | 1.0 | -0.2 | -0.25 | -3.07 | 4.25 | 86.6 | 3.5 | 6.1 | 3.8 | 4.2 |
| 5.0 | 2.84 | 12.0 | 1.03 | 7.1 | 0.1 | 1.07 | 7.78 | 5.46 | 76.2 | 4.8 | 21.6 | 0.0 | 4.3 |
| 0.3 | 3.85 | 50.3 | 0.25 | 3.6 | 0.1 | 0.41 | 5.56 | 4.63 | 90.2 | 4.4 | 26.0 | 5.7 | 3.1 |
| 8.6 | 0.46 | 1.9 | 0.12 | 1.7 | 0.0 | -0.10 | -0.94 | 3.48 | 91.4 | 4.5 | 9.0 | 2.5 | 5.4 |
| 8.1 | 0.00 | 0.0 | 5.45 | 0.3 | 0.0 | -2.46 | -29.33 | 4.90 | 106.7 | 6.7 | 54.6 | 0.0 | 4.1 |
| 5.0 | 0.80 | 9.6 | 0.34 | 5.9 | 0.3 | 0.58 | 6.81 | 5.20 | 87.7 | 3.5 | 20.4 | 10.4 | 4.7 |
| 7.9 | 0.77 | 4.6 | 0.04 | 5.3 | 0.6 | 0.81 | 7.63 | 3.90 | 75.5 | 6.4 | 40.1 | 0.9 | 7.1 |
| 7.5 | 0.51 | 4.7 | 0.60 | 2.1 | 0.4 | 0.29 | 4.05 | 3.01 | 86.2 | 3.3 | 11.9 | 6.4 | 3.7 |

| Name | City | State | Rating | 2014 Rating | 2013 Rating | Total Assets ($Mil) | One Year Asset Growth | Commercial Loans | Consumer Loans | Mortgage Loans | Securities | Capitalization Index | Net Worth Ratio |
|---|---|---|---|---|---|---|---|---|---|---|---|---|---|
| ▲ CORNER POST FCU | Wilkes-Barre | PA | D+ | D- | D- | 63.9 | -3.22 | 0.0 | 16.9 | 3.8 | 50.1 | 7.0 | 9.0 |
| CORNER STONE CU | Lancaster | TX | D | D+ | D+ | 21.1 | 4.87 | 0.5 | 60.2 | 3.7 | 2.3 | 6.6 | 8.6 |
| CORNERSTONE BAPTIST CHURCH FCU | Brooklyn | NY | D+ | D+ | D | <1 | 3.33 | 0.0 | 0.8 | 0.0 | 0.0 | 10.0 | 21.8 |
| CORNERSTONE COMMUNITY CU | Des Moines | IA | C | C+ | C+ | 20.8 | 9.56 | 10.0 | 29.2 | 25.0 | 3.5 | 9.4 | 10.6 |
| CORNERSTONE COMMUNITY FCU | Lockport | NY | C | C+ | B- | 367.4 | 2.89 | 0.2 | 25.0 | 8.0 | 20.3 | 5.7 | 7.7 |
| CORNERSTONE COMMUNITY FINANCIAL CU | Auburn Hills | MI | A- | A- | A- | 253.0 | 16.44 | 6.3 | 47.1 | 23.0 | 4.0 | 10.0 | 12.2 |
| CORNERSTONE CU | Caldwell | ID | E- | E- | E- | 15.8 | -14.13 | 0.0 | 47.0 | 3.4 | 0.0 | 1.2 | 4.3 |
| ▲ CORNERSTONE CU | Freeport | IL | B- | C | D+ | 101.4 | 0.96 | 1.3 | 54.4 | 8.3 | 12.9 | 10.0 | 11.7 |
| CORNERSTONE FCU | Carlisle | PA | C+ | C+ | C+ | 100.3 | 2.02 | 11.4 | 18.4 | 28.9 | 12.0 | 9.1 | 10.4 |
| CORNERSTONE FINANCIAL CU | Nashville | TN | B- | B- | B- | 283.7 | 6.23 | 1.4 | 43.5 | 19.7 | 9.7 | 8.8 | 10.2 |
| ▲ CORNING CABLE SYSTEMS CU | Hickory | NC | C- | D+ | D+ | 33.8 | -6.18 | 0.0 | 19.7 | 18.5 | 14.2 | 9.0 | 10.3 |
| CORNING FCU | Corning | NY | B- | B- | B- | 1136.3 | 4.64 | 8.7 | 27.2 | 24.0 | 16.2 | 7.6 | 9.4 |
| CORNING GLASS WORKS HARRODSBURG F | Harrodsburg | KY | C- | C- | C | 5.7 | 1.63 | 0.0 | 20.9 | 0.0 | 0.0 | 10.0 | 16.9 |
| CORPORATE AMERICA FAMILY CU | Elgin | IL | A- | B+ | A | 595.4 | 4.46 | 0.0 | 26.7 | 27.1 | 31.7 | 10.0 | 15.9 |
| CORPUS CHRISTI CITY EMPL CU | Corpus Christi | TX | C | C | C | 51.6 | 2.81 | 1.5 | 47.4 | 6.2 | 0.0 | 6.7 | 8.7 |
| CORPUS CHRISTI POSTAL EMPL CU | Corpus Christi | TX | B- | B- | B- | 14.8 | 3.11 | 0.0 | 41.3 | 0.0 | 0.0 | 10.0 | 14.9 |
| ▼ CORPUS CHRISTI SP CU | Corpus Christi | TX | D | D+ | D+ | 3.7 | -6.49 | 0.0 | 70.8 | 0.0 | 0.0 | 10.0 | 25.3 |
| ▲ CORRECTIONAL WORKERS FCU | El Reno | OK | D+ | D | D+ | 11.1 | -7.93 | 0.0 | 20.1 | 20.9 | 0.0 | 9.4 | 10.6 |
| CORRECTIONS FCU | Soledad | CA | D+ | D- | E | 12.9 | 1.17 | 0.0 | 63.8 | 0.0 | 0.0 | 7.2 | 9.1 |
| CORRY AREA SCHOOLS FCU | Corry | PA | D | D+ | D | 4.8 | 4.51 | 0.0 | 41.1 | 11.9 | 0.0 | 6.6 | 8.6 |
| CORRY FCU | Corry | PA | B- | B- | C+ | 42.6 | 4.00 | 0.0 | 26.3 | 17.2 | 3.0 | 9.9 | 11.0 |
| ▲ CORRY JAMESTOWN CU | Corry | PA | B- | C+ | C+ | 15.9 | 6.27 | 0.0 | 25.1 | 10.3 | 0.0 | 10.0 | 13.2 |
| CORY METHODIST CHURCH CU | Cleveland | OH | D | D | D | 1.7 | -5.86 | 0.0 | 16.3 | 17.7 | 0.0 | 10.0 | 24.9 |
| ▼ COSDEN FCU | Big Spring | TX | D+ | C | C+ | 37.4 | 0.34 | 0.0 | 19.2 | 0.1 | 0.0 | 10.0 | 13.5 |
| ▼ COSHOCTON FCU | Coshocton | OH | C- | C- | C- | 2.0 | 10.56 | 0.0 | 42.0 | 2.5 | 0.0 | 10.0 | 12.5 |
| COSMOPOLITAN FCU | Chicago | IL | D+ | D+ | C | <1 | -42.11 | 0.0 | 60.0 | 0.0 | 0.0 | 10.0 | 12.7 |
| ▲ COTEAU VALLEY FCU | Sisseton | SD | C- | D+ | C- | 9.1 | -0.59 | 0.0 | 28.9 | 13.4 | 0.0 | 10.0 | 11.2 |
| COTTONWOOD COMMUNITY FCU | Cottonwood | ID | B | B | B | 84.4 | 6.68 | 31.8 | 8.5 | 39.4 | 0.0 | 10.0 | 16.5 |
| COULEE DAM FCU | Coulee Dam | WA | B | B | C+ | 124.8 | 6.52 | 6.0 | 40.5 | 10.3 | 25.2 | 5.7 | 7.7 |
| COUNCILL FCU | Normal | AL | C | C | C- | 3.5 | 1.85 | 0.0 | 38.3 | 0.0 | 0.0 | 10.0 | 14.0 |
| COUNTRY FCU | Macclenny | FL | C- | C- | D- | 60.6 | 15.71 | 4.4 | 32.8 | 25.8 | 0.0 | 5.7 | 7.7 |
| ▲ COUNTRY HERITAGE CU | Buchanan | MI | B+ | B | B | 37.0 | 0.45 | 20.1 | 1.8 | 61.5 | 20.5 | 10.0 | 15.5 |
| COUNTRYSIDE FCU | East Syracuse | NY | B+ | A- | A- | 135.1 | 6.74 | 11.8 | 8.9 | 56.0 | 0.9 | 10.0 | 12.8 |
| ▲ COUNTY CU | Saint Louis | MO | C | C- | C- | 18.7 | 1.05 | 0.0 | 24.0 | 10.3 | 0.0 | 10.0 | 17.7 |
| COUNTY CU | Kenosha | WI | C | C- | D+ | 13.6 | 1.93 | 0.0 | 20.8 | 19.6 | 0.0 | 10.0 | 12.1 |
| COUNTY EDUCATORS FCU | Roselle Park | NJ | C- | C+ | B | 93.1 | -0.86 | 0.0 | 11.8 | 0.0 | 0.0 | 9.2 | 10.4 |
| ▲ COUNTY FCU | Caribou | ME | B+ | B | B | 204.3 | 2.96 | 4.8 | 32.5 | 24.3 | 8.2 | 9.7 | 10.8 |
| COUNTY SCHOOLS FCU | Ventura | CA | D+ | D+ | D+ | 52.4 | 0.34 | 2.3 | 26.6 | 21.1 | 0.5 | 5.4 | 7.4 |
| COUNTY-CITY CU | Jefferson | WI | D | D | D | 24.3 | -1.05 | 6.2 | 21.3 | 30.4 | 0.0 | 5.9 | 7.9 |
| COUNTYWIDE FCU | Beavercreek | OH | C- | C- | C- | 13.2 | -1.81 | 0.0 | 15.8 | 9.8 | 0.0 | 8.1 | 9.7 |
| COVANTAGE CU | Antigo | WI | A | A- | A- | 1224.3 | 9.18 | 18.7 | 18.9 | 45.5 | 12.5 | 10.0 | 11.3 |
| COVE FCU | Edgewood | KY | B+ | B+ | B+ | 52.4 | 14.60 | 0.0 | 54.3 | 13.6 | 0.0 | 10.0 | 15.3 |
| COVENANT SAVINGS FCU | Killeen | TX | E+ | E+ | E+ | 2.6 | -6.54 | 0.0 | 74.3 | 0.0 | 0.0 | 4.8 | 6.8 |
| COVENTRY CU | Coventry | RI | C+ | C+ | C+ | 241.0 | 3.86 | 0.3 | 2.9 | 30.5 | 4.3 | 7.0 | 9.0 |
| COVENTRY TEACHERS FCU | Coventry | RI | D | D | C- | 3.0 | -2.17 | 0.0 | 36.8 | 0.0 | 0.0 | 10.0 | 22.2 |
| COVINGTON SCHOOLS FCU | Andalusia | AL | B | B | B | 17.9 | 1.97 | 0.0 | 25.9 | 9.1 | 0.0 | 10.0 | 31.4 |
| COWBOY COUNTRY FCU | Premont | TX | C+ | C+ | C+ | 14.8 | 10.34 | 0.0 | 46.0 | 0.0 | 0.0 | 10.0 | 11.1 |
| COWETA CITIES & COUNTY EMPL FCU | Newnan | GA | B- | B- | B- | 18.0 | 5.48 | 0.0 | 33.2 | 0.0 | 0.0 | 10.0 | 15.7 |
| COXSACKIE CORRECTIONAL EMPL FCU | Coxsackie | NY | C+ | C+ | C+ | 3.4 | 5.37 | 0.0 | 41.0 | 0.0 | 0.0 | 10.0 | 27.5 |
| ▲ CP FCU | Jackson | MI | B+ | B | B | 389.9 | 1.97 | 3.3 | 31.0 | 28.5 | 10.0 | 10.0 | 11.6 |
| CPM FCU | North Charleston | SC | A- | B+ | B- | 274.4 | 5.64 | 0.1 | 20.2 | 15.5 | 15.5 | 10.0 | 11.6 |
| CPORT CU | Portland | ME | B- | B- | B- | 170.2 | 7.24 | 6.8 | 15.5 | 46.5 | 1.9 | 7.7 | 9.4 |
| CRAFTMASTER FCU | Towanda | PA | C | C | C | 9.5 | 3.69 | 0.0 | 44.2 | 0.0 | 0.0 | 10.0 | 17.8 |
| CRAIG CU | Selma | AL | D | D+ | C- | 12.4 | 8.21 | 0.0 | 46.1 | 2.4 | 0.0 | 10.0 | 18.2 |
| CRANE FCU | Odon | IN | A- | A- | A- | 477.8 | 14.74 | 7.1 | 20.2 | 33.9 | 23.2 | 10.0 | 13.6 |
| CRANSTON MUNICIPAL EMPL CU | Cranston | RI | C | C | C+ | 55.6 | -0.07 | 0.0 | 9.6 | 3.3 | 38.9 | 10.0 | 20.9 |
| CRAYOLA LLC EMPL FCU | Easton | PA | C | C | C | 7.4 | 4.29 | 0.0 | 9.7 | 29.2 | 15.2 | 10.0 | 17.9 |
| CRCH EMPL FCU | Roanoke | VA | C | C- | D- | 4.8 | 1.71 | 0.0 | 62.9 | 0.0 | 0.0 | 10.0 | 13.5 |
| CREIGHTON FCU | Omaha | NE | C | C | C | 49.2 | 4.29 | 1.7 | 10.6 | 48.0 | 9.4 | 7.8 | 9.5 |
| ▲ CRESCENT CU | Brockton | MA | B | B- | B- | 432.8 | 1.76 | 5.0 | 24.7 | 41.1 | 5.4 | 10.0 | 12.9 |

| Asset Quality Index | Non-Performing Loans as a % of Total Loans | Non-Performing Loans as a % of Capital | Net Charge-Offs / Avg Loans | Profitability Index | Net Income ($Mil) | Return on Assets | Return on Equity | Net Interest Spread | Overhead Efficiency Ratio | Liquidity Index | Liquidity Ratio | Hot Money Ratio | Stability Index |
|---|---|---|---|---|---|---|---|---|---|---|---|---|---|
| 7.7 | 1.37 | 3.7 | 0.60 | 1.3 | 0.0 | 0.06 | 0.67 | 2.12 | 89.7 | 4.8 | 10.9 | 0.6 | 3.3 |
| 5.1 | 1.22 | 8.6 | 0.44 | 1.3 | -0.1 | -0.49 | -5.43 | 5.91 | 96.7 | 3.7 | 12.2 | 3.7 | 3.7 |
| 9.1 | 100.00 | 3.3 | 0.00 | 1.2 | 0.0 | 0.00 | 0.00 | 0.00 | 0.0 | 9.3 | 127.8 | 0.0 | 6.7 |
| 6.8 | 0.21 | 3.7 | 0.73 | 3.3 | 0.1 | 0.33 | 3.08 | 3.12 | 86.5 | 1.7 | 5.0 | 32.8 | 6.1 |
| 5.7 | 1.49 | 11.8 | 0.85 | 1.6 | -0.2 | -0.07 | -0.85 | 3.47 | 87.1 | 4.0 | 13.1 | 1.6 | 4.6 |
| 5.2 | 1.00 | 8.0 | 0.64 | 9.4 | 2.9 | 1.55 | 12.86 | 4.03 | 61.1 | 2.7 | 7.8 | 7.5 | 7.5 |
| 4.1 | 0.96 | 12.9 | 0.36 | 1.2 | 0.0 | 0.07 | 1.77 | 3.94 | 98.7 | 4.6 | 14.4 | 0.0 | 0.0 |
| 5.5 | 0.87 | 5.9 | 0.85 | 3.9 | 0.5 | 0.64 | 5.88 | 4.21 | 86.2 | 3.3 | 8.4 | 5.9 | 6.1 |
| 6.4 | 1.16 | 7.9 | 0.07 | 3.3 | 0.3 | 0.42 | 4.34 | 3.08 | 86.8 | 3.6 | 13.4 | 3.7 | 6.4 |
| 8.7 | 0.40 | 3.0 | 0.15 | 4.1 | 1.1 | 0.51 | 5.57 | 3.56 | 87.2 | 3.7 | 18.1 | 3.5 | 5.6 |
| 9.7 | 0.02 | 1.3 | 0.22 | 2.1 | 0.1 | 0.25 | 2.55 | 2.85 | 91.3 | 4.8 | 20.3 | 3.4 | 4.7 |
| 9.4 | 0.30 | 2.5 | 0.12 | 4.1 | 4.9 | 0.58 | 6.36 | 2.88 | 82.7 | 3.7 | 9.2 | 6.0 | 7.3 |
| 6.1 | 12.17 | 15.3 | -0.11 | 2.7 | 0.0 | 0.31 | 1.81 | 2.91 | 84.6 | 5.8 | 28.6 | 0.0 | 6.1 |
| 8.4 | 1.19 | 4.2 | 0.54 | 4.7 | 2.4 | 0.53 | 3.39 | 3.91 | 82.9 | 3.8 | 12.8 | 3.4 | 8.2 |
| 5.7 | 0.79 | 5.1 | 0.51 | 3.4 | 0.1 | 0.28 | 3.20 | 3.91 | 86.5 | 4.2 | 29.8 | 8.5 | 3.7 |
| 9.7 | 0.32 | 1.1 | 0.00 | 5.0 | 0.1 | 0.68 | 5.14 | 5.49 | 86.3 | 6.7 | 44.8 | 0.0 | 7.7 |
| 5.0 | 4.03 | 12.2 | 1.32 | 0.4 | -0.1 | -2.58 | -9.89 | 6.07 | 109.8 | 3.0 | 23.8 | 18.6 | 6.4 |
| 9.0 | 0.59 | 2.6 | -0.03 | 1.5 | 0.0 | 0.06 | 0.57 | 2.30 | 96.3 | 5.5 | 34.5 | 0.0 | 4.8 |
| 5.9 | 0.25 | 3.8 | 0.14 | 4.9 | 0.1 | 0.85 | 9.69 | 6.38 | 93.9 | 4.2 | 18.7 | 1.5 | 3.1 |
| 0.3 | 9.76 | 71.9 | -0.04 | 0.0 | -0.3 | -7.91 | -59.39 | 3.67 | -75.7 | 5.1 | 30.0 | 0.0 | 5.2 |
| 6.1 | 1.21 | 6.3 | 0.72 | 5.3 | 0.2 | 0.47 | 4.25 | 3.70 | 78.1 | 3.1 | 14.0 | 13.2 | 5.9 |
| 9.3 | 0.25 | 0.9 | 0.52 | 5.6 | 0.1 | 0.88 | 6.94 | 3.76 | 83.0 | 4.2 | 10.5 | 1.6 | 6.6 |
| 7.8 | 0.63 | 0.8 | 8.44 | 0.0 | -0.1 | -5.99 | -21.67 | 4.12 | 180.9 | 6.6 | 50.9 | 0.0 | 5.4 |
| 7.7 | 3.10 | 5.2 | 2.63 | 0.6 | -0.1 | -0.33 | -2.44 | 2.45 | 109.0 | 5.2 | 39.3 | 5.4 | 5.1 |
| 3.7 | 5.47 | 20.6 | 0.47 | 7.4 | 0.0 | 1.72 | 13.56 | 5.26 | 76.1 | 6.2 | 41.7 | 0.0 | 5.3 |
| 8.7 | 0.00 | 0.0 | 0.00 | 7.5 | 0.0 | 4.65 | 57.14 | 7.62 | 57.1 | 6.5 | 52.1 | 0.0 | 4.3 |
| 3.7 | 1.79 | 20.2 | -0.23 | 6.7 | 0.1 | 1.51 | 13.63 | 3.12 | 60.2 | 5.3 | 43.2 | 0.0 | 5.7 |
| 4.4 | 2.17 | 14.4 | 0.11 | 10.0 | 1.2 | 1.99 | 11.95 | 4.13 | 51.4 | 3.6 | 28.4 | 8.0 | 8.7 |
| 9.2 | 0.11 | 1.1 | 0.45 | 4.6 | 0.6 | 0.62 | 8.08 | 4.13 | 84.3 | 4.6 | 23.0 | 2.4 | 5.2 |
| 7.1 | 3.07 | 9.3 | 0.00 | 5.5 | 0.0 | 0.89 | 6.51 | 4.01 | 76.3 | 6.3 | 51.6 | 0.0 | 4.3 |
| 4.7 | 0.60 | 5.7 | 0.53 | 6.1 | 0.4 | 0.87 | 11.48 | 4.84 | 77.4 | 1.6 | 8.0 | 24.6 | 3.0 |
| 9.2 | 0.19 | 0.8 | -0.02 | 8.4 | 0.4 | 1.52 | 10.24 | 3.49 | 52.7 | 2.1 | 13.3 | 23.3 | 7.0 |
| 7.2 | 0.69 | 4.8 | 0.12 | 3.1 | 0.1 | 0.05 | 0.43 | 2.88 | 92.7 | 2.2 | 14.4 | 16.2 | 8.9 |
| 8.9 | 0.70 | 5.2 | 0.34 | 2.4 | 0.0 | 0.25 | 1.38 | 3.54 | 89.6 | 5.3 | 38.5 | 0.0 | 6.6 |
| 10.0 | 0.06 | 0.2 | 0.08 | 2.5 | 0.0 | 0.25 | 2.03 | 2.65 | 89.7 | 5.0 | 31.8 | 0.0 | 6.5 |
| 9.5 | 0.69 | 1.6 | 0.11 | 1.8 | 0.0 | -0.02 | -0.25 | 2.45 | 102.2 | 5.3 | 20.5 | 1.0 | 4.0 |
| 7.1 | 0.67 | 5.0 | 0.09 | 5.5 | 1.3 | 0.89 | 8.34 | 3.00 | 73.1 | 3.5 | 20.3 | 6.2 | 7.1 |
| 4.8 | 0.55 | 9.8 | 4.21 | 2.3 | 0.1 | 0.31 | 4.21 | 4.85 | 74.4 | 3.3 | 12.9 | 8.5 | 3.0 |
| 9.0 | 0.23 | 1.9 | 0.00 | 1.2 | 0.0 | -0.18 | -2.29 | 3.89 | 103.9 | 3.8 | 14.4 | 0.5 | 3.1 |
| 9.5 | 0.51 | 1.5 | 0.07 | 2.9 | 0.0 | 0.37 | 3.91 | 2.55 | 87.0 | 5.4 | 30.8 | 0.0 | 4.3 |
| 7.8 | 0.45 | 3.7 | 0.13 | 8.5 | 12.1 | 1.37 | 12.14 | 3.30 | 63.9 | 3.2 | 11.0 | 7.1 | 8.7 |
| 8.5 | 0.33 | 2.0 | 0.30 | 7.2 | 0.3 | 0.81 | 5.14 | 4.64 | 83.3 | 3.1 | 18.0 | 4.5 | 7.6 |
| 3.0 | 1.08 | 18.7 | 0.00 | 0.9 | 0.0 | -0.24 | -3.81 | 4.42 | 96.7 | 3.5 | 10.8 | 0.0 | 1.4 |
| 5.0 | 1.49 | 16.8 | 0.35 | 3.2 | 0.8 | 0.43 | 4.83 | 2.97 | 84.7 | 3.5 | 8.1 | 6.0 | 5.1 |
| 9.9 | 0.27 | 0.5 | 0.95 | 0.0 | 0.0 | -0.94 | -4.17 | 2.01 | 151.2 | 5.2 | 38.8 | 0.0 | 6.1 |
| 9.7 | 0.52 | 0.7 | 0.21 | 4.5 | 0.1 | 0.64 | 2.04 | 2.88 | 65.7 | 6.4 | 47.4 | 0.0 | 6.9 |
| 5.8 | 1.20 | 6.3 | 0.54 | 6.9 | 0.1 | 1.03 | 9.36 | 3.52 | 74.4 | 2.4 | 16.6 | 20.4 | 5.0 |
| 9.5 | 0.52 | 1.5 | -0.03 | 3.4 | 0.1 | 0.44 | 2.76 | 3.24 | 85.1 | 5.9 | 56.3 | 1.9 | 7.3 |
| 9.4 | 1.13 | 1.9 | 0.42 | 6.9 | 0.0 | 1.15 | 4.15 | 5.60 | 57.8 | 7.1 | 73.1 | 0.0 | 5.7 |
| 6.6 | 0.71 | 6.4 | 0.84 | 5.1 | 2.3 | 0.77 | 7.32 | 4.00 | 81.7 | 4.0 | 17.0 | 3.5 | 6.4 |
| 9.9 | 0.39 | 1.9 | 0.80 | 8.1 | 3.6 | 1.76 | 16.90 | 3.38 | 77.0 | 5.2 | 30.6 | 6.1 | 6.3 |
| 8.7 | 0.35 | 2.7 | 0.15 | 4.3 | 0.7 | 0.58 | 6.12 | 3.95 | 85.3 | 4.1 | 20.1 | 4.6 | 5.9 |
| 7.5 | 2.70 | 8.2 | 0.44 | 4.8 | 0.1 | 0.70 | 4.01 | 3.26 | 67.6 | 4.8 | 36.7 | 3.9 | 4.3 |
| 0.3 | 14.93 | 43.2 | 2.17 | 2.2 | 0.0 | 0.08 | 0.41 | 7.07 | 77.9 | 5.7 | 29.7 | 0.0 | 5.8 |
| 7.5 | 1.09 | 5.4 | 0.27 | 4.9 | 2.3 | 0.69 | 5.03 | 3.25 | 76.9 | 4.0 | 22.1 | 7.0 | 8.5 |
| 10.0 | 0.00 | 0.1 | 0.76 | 1.6 | 0.2 | 0.35 | 1.54 | 2.12 | 81.7 | 5.3 | 30.7 | 10.4 | 7.3 |
| 10.0 | 0.03 | 0.1 | 0.00 | 2.6 | 0.0 | 0.16 | 0.91 | 2.95 | 93.2 | 6.3 | 49.5 | 0.0 | 7.4 |
| 6.3 | 1.70 | 7.6 | 0.79 | 7.6 | 0.0 | 1.06 | 8.02 | 6.44 | 74.9 | 4.2 | 15.7 | 2.5 | 4.3 |
| 5.7 | 1.75 | 11.7 | 0.21 | 3.2 | 0.2 | 0.41 | 4.28 | 3.35 | 89.1 | 3.8 | 19.1 | 7.4 | 4.4 |
| 9.4 | 0.28 | 1.9 | 0.05 | 4.3 | 2.1 | 0.66 | 5.16 | 2.73 | 82.0 | 2.5 | 8.4 | 9.7 | 8.1 |

| Name | City | State | Rating | 2014 Rating | 2013 Rating | Total Assets ($Mil) | One Year Asset Growth | Asset Mix (As a % of Total Assets) | | | | Capital- ization Index | Net Worth Ratio |
|---|---|---|---|---|---|---|---|---|---|---|---|---|---|
| | | | | | | | | Comm- ercial Loans | Cons- umer Loans | Mort- gage Loans | Secur- ities | | |
| CRIERS FCU | Monroe Township | NJ | C | C | C | 1.7 | -9.75 | 0.0 | 1.3 | 0.0 | 0.0 | 10.0 | 21.5 |
| CRMC EMPL CU | Douglas | GA | C+ | C+ | C+ | 2.6 | 5.75 | 0.0 | 31.9 | 0.0 | 0.0 | 10.0 | 16.3 |
| CROSS ROADS CU | Kansas City | MO | C | C | D+ | 4.4 | -1.21 | 0.0 | 40.8 | 0.0 | 0.0 | 10.0 | 16.6 |
| ▲ CROSS VALLEY FCU | Wilkes-Barre | PA | D+ | D- | D | 150.9 | -2.61 | 4.8 | 24.1 | 5.5 | 30.0 | 4.4 | 6.5 |
| CROSSROADS COMMUNITY FCU | Cheektowaga | NY | C- | C | C | 62.3 | 2.49 | 0.0 | 16.9 | 15.7 | 12.9 | 10.0 | 12.8 |
| CROSSROADS CU | Goessel | KS | C | C- | C- | 9.3 | 5.07 | 9.0 | 27.7 | 14.6 | 0.0 | 10.0 | 13.8 |
| CROSSROADS FINANCIAL FCU | Portland | IN | C | C- | C- | 46.8 | 5.69 | 0.0 | 32.3 | 12.7 | 2.4 | 5.9 | 7.9 |
| ▼ CROUSE FCU | Syracuse | NY | D+ | C- | C- | 15.1 | 4.73 | 0.0 | 44.6 | 0.0 | 0.0 | 9.9 | 10.9 |
| CROUSE HINDS EMPL FCU | Syracuse | NY | D- | E+ | E+ | 6.2 | -1.29 | 0.0 | 22.5 | 0.5 | 0.0 | 6.0 | 8.0 |
| CROW WING POWER CU | Brainerd | MN | C | C | C | 75.7 | 3.56 | 0.0 | 7.7 | 46.0 | 0.0 | 5.4 | 7.4 |
| CSC EMPL FCU | Falls Church | VA | D | D+ | C- | 77.4 | -8.68 | 0.6 | 12.0 | 16.0 | 20.9 | 10.0 | 12.9 |
| ▲ CSD CU | Kansas City | MO | C+ | C | C+ | 36.8 | 1.61 | 0.0 | 20.8 | 15.6 | 0.0 | 10.0 | 13.5 |
| CSE FCU | Lake Charles | LA | B- | B | B- | 288.1 | 2.29 | 4.3 | 24.7 | 31.5 | 11.1 | 10.0 | 12.9 |
| ▲ CSP EMPL FCU | Enfield | CT | D+ | D+ | C- | 8.3 | -1.14 | 0.0 | 26.8 | 0.0 | 0.0 | 10.0 | 15.9 |
| CSX CHICAGO TERMINAL CU | Calumet City | IL | C- | C- | D+ | 5.8 | -8.82 | 0.0 | 18.7 | 0.0 | 0.0 | 10.0 | 22.3 |
| CT1 MEDIA CU | Hartford | CT | D | D | D+ | 1.6 | 1.76 | 0.0 | 68.6 | 0.0 | 0.0 | 10.0 | 17.1 |
| ▼ CTA SOUTH FCU | Chicago | IL | C- | C+ | C+ | 1.1 | -6.01 | 0.0 | 73.1 | 0.0 | 0.0 | 10.0 | 35.1 |
| CTECU | Bellaire | TX | D | D | C- | 45.6 | -11.98 | 0.3 | 8.2 | 9.8 | 0.0 | 10.0 | 11.3 |
| ▼ CTK CU | Milwaukee | WI | D- | D | D+ | <1 | 7.69 | 0.0 | 36.3 | 0.0 | 0.0 | 5.1 | 7.1 |
| CU 1 | Anchorage | AK | A | A | A- | 924.8 | 4.19 | 0.3 | 41.7 | 24.6 | 3.1 | 10.0 | 11.9 |
| CU 1 | Rantoul | IL | C+ | C | C | 754.4 | 0.25 | 0.7 | 21.6 | 23.0 | 25.5 | 6.5 | 8.6 |
| CU ADVANTAGE | Southfield | MI | B- | B | B- | 25.8 | -3.89 | 0.0 | 20.3 | 12.1 | 56.4 | 10.0 | 12.1 |
| CU COMMUNITY CU | Springfield | MO | A | A | A | 98.4 | 3.93 | 11.5 | 23.0 | 20.8 | 11.2 | 10.0 | 14.8 |
| CU FOR ROBERTSON COUNTY | Springfield | TN | B | B | B | 44.3 | 3.94 | 0.1 | 43.7 | 18.6 | 3.2 | 10.0 | 12.2 |
| CU HAWAII FCU | Hilo | HI | B- | B | B | 252.1 | 1.79 | 4.6 | 13.2 | 19.7 | 25.5 | 10.0 | 12.1 |
| CU OF AMERICA | Wichita | KS | A- | A- | A- | 636.6 | 9.54 | 3.8 | 53.9 | 19.5 | 5.4 | 10.0 | 12.6 |
| ▲ CU OF ATLANTA | Atlanta | GA | C+ | D+ | D- | 68.9 | -0.76 | 0.3 | 31.7 | 1.7 | 25.8 | 8.6 | 10.3 |
| CU OF COLORADO A FCU | Denver | CO | C+ | B- | B | 1269.1 | 7.29 | 0.4 | 28.3 | 21.6 | 23.9 | 9.7 | 10.8 |
| CU OF DENVER | Lakewood | CO | A | A- | B+ | 630.3 | 5.95 | 2.0 | 32.5 | 16.4 | 32.1 | 10.0 | 11.7 |
| CU OF DODGE CITY | Dodge City | KS | C | C | C | 66.0 | -1.45 | 1.3 | 74.5 | 3.4 | 0.5 | 6.9 | 8.9 |
| ▲ CU OF EMPORIA | Emporia | KS | B- | C+ | C+ | 20.8 | 5.73 | 0.0 | 29.7 | 14.4 | 0.0 | 10.0 | 12.3 |
| CU OF GEORGIA | Woodstock | GA | B+ | B+ | B- | 245.0 | 6.69 | 0.2 | 33.3 | 11.6 | 20.0 | 8.1 | 9.7 |
| CU OF LEAVENWORTH COUNTY | Lansing | KS | D- | D | D+ | 7.3 | 5.40 | 0.0 | 32.3 | 2.2 | 0.0 | 8.6 | 10.1 |
| CU OF NEW JERSEY | Ewing | NJ | C | C | C | 327.7 | -0.12 | 7.6 | 26.1 | 36.6 | 1.3 | 5.9 | 7.9 |
| CU OF OHIO | Hilliard | OH | C- | C | C | 131.5 | 0.76 | 0.0 | 25.8 | 14.2 | 3.8 | 9.8 | 10.9 |
| CU OF SOUTHERN CALIFORNIA | Anaheim | CA | A- | A- | A | 989.9 | 26.19 | 9.2 | 9.9 | 29.4 | 35.0 | 10.0 | 12.6 |
| CU OF TEXAS | Dallas | TX | B+ | B | C+ | 1252.1 | 11.65 | 23.1 | 31.7 | 12.7 | 4.6 | 6.4 | 8.4 |
| CU OF THE BERKSHIRES | Pittsfield | MA | C | C | C | 20.9 | -4.60 | 0.0 | 20.5 | 1.1 | 7.0 | 10.0 | 14.0 |
| CU OF THE ROCKIES | Golden | CO | B- | B- | B- | 91.2 | 0.53 | 1.8 | 27.5 | 13.4 | 24.8 | 8.7 | 10.1 |
| CU OF VERMONT | Rutland | VT | B+ | B+ | B+ | 37.2 | 2.86 | 0.0 | 25.5 | 33.6 | 0.0 | 10.0 | 11.9 |
| CU ONE | Ferndale | MI | B | B | B | 1028.3 | 19.11 | 1.1 | 61.1 | 15.1 | 2.0 | 6.8 | 8.8 |
| CU ONE | North Jackson | OH | C+ | B- | B- | 11.4 | 5.63 | 0.0 | 32.8 | 0.0 | 0.9 | 10.0 | 16.5 |
| ▲ CU ONE OF THE OKLAHOMA | Oklahoma City | OK | D | D | D+ | 39.2 | -2.58 | 0.4 | 62.4 | 0.1 | 7.6 | 10.0 | 11.1 |
| CU PLUS | Bay City | MI | C | D+ | D- | 38.4 | -2.33 | 0.4 | 12.3 | 35.1 | 37.1 | 10.0 | 11.0 |
| CU SOUTH | Gulfport | MS | D+ | C- | C- | 8.9 | 10.06 | 0.0 | 66.0 | 5.4 | 0.0 | 10.0 | 13.2 |
| CU WEST | Glendale | AZ | A- | A- | A- | 571.5 | 4.50 | 3.6 | 41.4 | 8.4 | 6.6 | 9.9 | 10.9 |
| ▼ CUBA CU | Cuba | NM | C+ | B- | B- | 13.5 | 10.37 | 0.4 | 17.3 | 26.4 | 0.0 | 10.0 | 15.2 |
| CULVER CITY EMPL FCU | Culver City | CA | E | E+ | D- | 22.4 | -5.21 | 0.0 | 28.8 | 3.3 | 21.8 | 5.1 | 7.1 |
| CUMBERLAND COUNTY FCU | Falmouth | ME | B+ | B+ | B+ | 196.9 | 6.69 | 0.0 | 25.1 | 22.7 | 24.7 | 9.6 | 10.8 |
| CUMBERLAND MUNICIPAL EMPL FCU | Cumberland | RI | C- | C- | D+ | 8.2 | 5.35 | 0.0 | 27.6 | 0.0 | 0.0 | 10.0 | 17.3 |
| CUP FCU | Provo | UT | D+ | C- | C- | 6.1 | -5.39 | 1.5 | 36.6 | 20.0 | 0.0 | 10.0 | 16.1 |
| CURTIS FCU | Sandy Hook | CT | C- | C- | D+ | <1 | -8.15 | 0.0 | 8.6 | 0.0 | 0.0 | 10.0 | 20.4 |
| CUSA FCU | Covington | LA | B- | B- | B- | 30.3 | 6.85 | 0.3 | 36.3 | 30.9 | 22.0 | 9.6 | 10.8 |
| CUTTING EDGE FCU | Milwaukie | OR | C | C+ | C | 40.6 | 2.19 | 1.3 | 31.1 | 19.9 | 41.3 | 9.8 | 10.8 |
| CVPH EMPL FCU | Plattsburgh | NY | C- | C- | C | 8.2 | 5.29 | 0.0 | 61.1 | 0.0 | 0.0 | 9.1 | 10.4 |
| CWV TEL FCU | Clarksburg | WV | C- | C- | C | 25.3 | 1.16 | 0.0 | 28.6 | 7.2 | 0.0 | 10.0 | 15.6 |
| CY-FAIR FCU | Houston | TX | B- | B- | C+ | 208.7 | 7.03 | 0.2 | 49.0 | 18.7 | 9.9 | 5.9 | 8.0 |
| CYPRUS FCU | West Jordan | UT | A- | A- | B+ | 713.2 | 6.06 | 10.5 | 48.7 | 19.6 | 3.6 | 10.0 | 11.2 |
| DACOTAH FCU | Rapid City | SD | D | D- | D | 10.1 | -0.17 | 0.0 | 36.0 | 9.4 | 0.0 | 7.3 | 9.2 |
| DADE COUNTY FCU | Doral | FL | B+ | B+ | B | 627.2 | 6.73 | 4.4 | 38.8 | 7.2 | 30.2 | 10.0 | 12.3 |

| Asset Quality Index | Non-Performing Loans as a % of Total Loans | Non-Performing Loans as a % of Capital | Net Charge-Offs Avg Loans | Profitability Index | Net Income ($Mil) | Return on Assets | Return on Equity | Net Interest Spread | Overhead Efficiency Ratio | Liquidity Index | Liquidity Ratio | Hot Money Ratio | Stability Index |
|---|---|---|---|---|---|---|---|---|---|---|---|---|---|
| 9.3 | 0.00 | 0.0 | 0.00 | 4.0 | 0.0 | 0.62 | 2.98 | 1.13 | 42.9 | 5.8 | 35.9 | 0.0 | 6.9 |
| 8.1 | 1.97 | 4.1 | 0.32 | 4.8 | 0.0 | 0.59 | 3.53 | 2.82 | 69.4 | 5.6 | 40.1 | 0.0 | 4.3 |
| 9.3 | 0.43 | 2.2 | -0.60 | 3.4 | 0.0 | 0.41 | 2.58 | 3.90 | 107.8 | 6.2 | 55.4 | 0.0 | 5.7 |
| 4.8 | 2.28 | 16.3 | 1.94 | 2.1 | 0.4 | 0.36 | 5.98 | 3.88 | 83.0 | 5.1 | 20.6 | 0.0 | 1.6 |
| 9.6 | 0.85 | 2.6 | 0.22 | 1.8 | 0.0 | 0.01 | 0.08 | 2.37 | 97.0 | 6.2 | 44.6 | 1.4 | 6.8 |
| 7.9 | 0.91 | 3.4 | 0.37 | 6.9 | 0.1 | 1.52 | 11.55 | 3.20 | 73.5 | 4.6 | 39.4 | 0.0 | 4.3 |
| 8.6 | 0.25 | 1.8 | 0.02 | 4.9 | 0.3 | 0.74 | 9.67 | 3.89 | 83.2 | 4.3 | 15.5 | 0.3 | 3.4 |
| 8.1 | 0.45 | 1.9 | 0.65 | 1.4 | 0.0 | -0.12 | -1.05 | 3.67 | 92.6 | 4.7 | 24.7 | 0.0 | 5.5 |
| 9.4 | 0.27 | 1.4 | 0.00 | 2.3 | 0.0 | 0.32 | 4.09 | 2.35 | 85.3 | 5.3 | 23.6 | 0.0 | 1.7 |
| 8.8 | 0.25 | 2.0 | 0.06 | 4.4 | 0.4 | 0.62 | 8.57 | 2.20 | 74.3 | 3.6 | 24.2 | 7.2 | 3.2 |
| 10.0 | 0.23 | 0.5 | 0.40 | 0.2 | -0.3 | -0.47 | -3.89 | 2.03 | 112.7 | 5.0 | 23.5 | 2.2 | 4.9 |
| 10.0 | 0.21 | 0.8 | 0.18 | 2.8 | 0.1 | 0.44 | 3.24 | 2.80 | 92.9 | 3.9 | 12.5 | 5.1 | 5.8 |
| 8.4 | 0.69 | 3.7 | 0.16 | 3.0 | 0.5 | 0.25 | 1.96 | 3.34 | 91.8 | 3.6 | 15.4 | 5.3 | 7.4 |
| 10.0 | 0.18 | 0.3 | 0.00 | 0.9 | 0.0 | 0.00 | 0.00 | 2.80 | 102.4 | 4.9 | 14.1 | 0.0 | 6.4 |
| 9.4 | 1.38 | 1.1 | 0.00 | 2.0 | 0.0 | 0.20 | 0.93 | 2.71 | 86.9 | 6.0 | 61.5 | 0.0 | 5.2 |
| 2.1 | 5.52 | 21.4 | -0.26 | 2.7 | 0.0 | 0.17 | 1.01 | 3.87 | 93.6 | 5.7 | 36.4 | 0.0 | 6.0 |
| 6.7 | 1.70 | 3.1 | 2.83 | 1.6 | 0.0 | -1.02 | -2.99 | 12.75 | 72.9 | 5.4 | 37.8 | 0.0 | 5.6 |
| 10.0 | 0.04 | 0.1 | -0.08 | 0.5 | -0.1 | -0.32 | -3.01 | 1.68 | 120.7 | 4.7 | 35.4 | 9.9 | 4.5 |
| 0.3 | 17.39 | 66.7 | 0.00 | 3.5 | 0.0 | 0.74 | 10.26 | 9.20 | 88.6 | 6.9 | 47.3 | 0.0 | 3.2 |
| 6.8 | 1.31 | 8.3 | 0.76 | 5.9 | 4.5 | 0.65 | 5.47 | 4.70 | 76.2 | 4.0 | 18.3 | 7.0 | 8.9 |
| 5.6 | 1.62 | 16.6 | 0.39 | 3.8 | 3.1 | 0.53 | 6.49 | 3.59 | 86.3 | 5.4 | 28.7 | 3.7 | 5.1 |
| 9.5 | 0.85 | 2.5 | 0.55 | 2.9 | 0.1 | 0.22 | 1.94 | 2.85 | 90.5 | 4.3 | 5.4 | 3.0 | 4.4 |
| 8.8 | 0.97 | 3.4 | 0.37 | 9.3 | 1.0 | 1.37 | 9.70 | 4.06 | 63.2 | 5.4 | 33.6 | 4.6 | 8.4 |
| 7.8 | 0.93 | 5.5 | 0.57 | 6.2 | 0.3 | 0.80 | 6.62 | 5.80 | 84.7 | 3.8 | 26.1 | 8.5 | 6.0 |
| 8.3 | 0.78 | 3.6 | 0.35 | 3.4 | 0.7 | 0.39 | 3.27 | 2.82 | 87.6 | 5.0 | 22.9 | 5.0 | 7.0 |
| 6.0 | 0.85 | 6.5 | 0.42 | 8.8 | 5.2 | 1.12 | 8.96 | 3.66 | 70.2 | 2.4 | 5.9 | 10.7 | 9.4 |
| 6.2 | 2.49 | 8.2 | 1.35 | 7.6 | 1.2 | 2.32 | 26.49 | 4.59 | 84.4 | 5.1 | 27.2 | 11.8 | 4.4 |
| 9.9 | 0.29 | 1.6 | 0.29 | 3.6 | 4.8 | 0.52 | 4.63 | 3.26 | 84.2 | 5.2 | 28.8 | 6.5 | 7.7 |
| 8.6 | 0.98 | 4.7 | 0.40 | 7.1 | 5.0 | 1.08 | 9.36 | 3.21 | 65.7 | 3.8 | 16.9 | 7.7 | 8.5 |
| 4.9 | 0.52 | 6.3 | 0.46 | 3.9 | 0.2 | 0.30 | 3.55 | 4.57 | 88.5 | 2.4 | 11.2 | 14.9 | 3.7 |
| 9.4 | 0.78 | 3.1 | 0.07 | 5.0 | 0.1 | 0.90 | 7.54 | 2.88 | 70.8 | 4.2 | 15.5 | 2.6 | 7.1 |
| 9.0 | 0.33 | 4.0 | 0.17 | 9.8 | 2.5 | 1.35 | 14.48 | 3.74 | 76.1 | 4.7 | 14.0 | 0.8 | 5.7 |
| 9.1 | 0.00 | 0.0 | 0.05 | 0.0 | -0.1 | -1.18 | -11.01 | 3.42 | 135.0 | 5.2 | 23.4 | 0.0 | 5.0 |
| 4.7 | 1.65 | 17.9 | 0.92 | 3.5 | 0.9 | 0.38 | 4.82 | 4.35 | 79.8 | 2.7 | 5.6 | 4.7 | 4.3 |
| 10.0 | 0.36 | 1.5 | 0.16 | 1.7 | -0.1 | -0.05 | -0.50 | 3.14 | 101.1 | 4.3 | 28.3 | 6.5 | 6.2 |
| 7.9 | 1.37 | 5.5 | 0.26 | 7.0 | 6.0 | 0.82 | 7.35 | 3.55 | 77.9 | 4.7 | 18.0 | 7.6 | 9.3 |
| 7.7 | 0.51 | 4.9 | 0.28 | 8.3 | 11.5 | 1.28 | 15.38 | 3.86 | 74.5 | 3.5 | 13.0 | 8.3 | 5.7 |
| 10.0 | 0.77 | 1.6 | 0.00 | 1.7 | 0.0 | 0.04 | 0.27 | 2.51 | 106.7 | 5.6 | 26.0 | 1.1 | 5.9 |
| 9.0 | 0.08 | 0.5 | 0.55 | 3.4 | 0.3 | 0.45 | 4.53 | 3.22 | 84.4 | 4.4 | 19.8 | 6.1 | 4.2 |
| 9.9 | 0.02 | 0.1 | 0.18 | 5.9 | 0.3 | 0.89 | 7.74 | 3.25 | 68.9 | 3.5 | 22.5 | 5.4 | 6.8 |
| 4.8 | 1.19 | 10.9 | 0.50 | 5.6 | 4.0 | 0.58 | 6.26 | 3.70 | 79.5 | 3.2 | 8.2 | 3.5 | 6.6 |
| 9.5 | 1.55 | 3.0 | 1.01 | 2.6 | 0.0 | 0.05 | 0.28 | 4.33 | 97.5 | 6.5 | 42.3 | 0.0 | 6.8 |
| 7.3 | 0.62 | 4.0 | 0.17 | 0.3 | -0.1 | -0.30 | -2.79 | 3.44 | 103.3 | 4.7 | 20.7 | 0.8 | 5.2 |
| 3.7 | 3.34 | 21.4 | 0.94 | 3.1 | 0.1 | 0.16 | 1.49 | 3.90 | 89.4 | 4.1 | 14.8 | 3.7 | 4.8 |
| 5.8 | 1.94 | 10.9 | 1.08 | 0.5 | -0.1 | -0.94 | -6.68 | 6.89 | 99.8 | 4.3 | 26.7 | 0.0 | 5.0 |
| 9.2 | 0.21 | 1.5 | 0.34 | 4.2 | 1.0 | 0.25 | 2.39 | 4.04 | 92.3 | 3.2 | 6.9 | 4.8 | 7.6 |
| 3.7 | 9.36 | 32.6 | 0.02 | 5.8 | 0.1 | 0.74 | 4.74 | 4.17 | 81.5 | 6.0 | 49.4 | 1.1 | 7.9 |
| 6.4 | 1.33 | 6.1 | 1.15 | 0.7 | -0.1 | -0.33 | -4.66 | 2.55 | 91.5 | 4.8 | 23.8 | 0.0 | 1.3 |
| 6.5 | 1.64 | 9.5 | 0.38 | 5.6 | 1.3 | 0.87 | 8.11 | 3.15 | 72.7 | 3.5 | 17.8 | 9.6 | 7.6 |
| 7.9 | 3.06 | 5.1 | 0.06 | 2.5 | 0.0 | 0.23 | 1.33 | 2.50 | 90.5 | 3.4 | 46.8 | 23.0 | 6.2 |
| 9.2 | 0.32 | 1.4 | 0.12 | 0.7 | 0.0 | -0.26 | -1.64 | 3.24 | 105.6 | 3.6 | 12.8 | 6.1 | 6.9 |
| 9.6 | 5.56 | 3.2 | 0.00 | 1.4 | 0.0 | 0.00 | 0.00 | 1.35 | 133.3 | 7.4 | 65.1 | 0.0 | 5.2 |
| 6.6 | 0.77 | 5.2 | 0.26 | 6.6 | 0.2 | 0.98 | 9.52 | 3.63 | 67.8 | 3.3 | 3.4 | 4.8 | 6.3 |
| 4.1 | 0.23 | 19.7 | 0.63 | 3.1 | 0.1 | 0.26 | 2.45 | 4.02 | 85.5 | 4.3 | 17.2 | 2.5 | 5.4 |
| 8.2 | 0.02 | 0.1 | 0.07 | 3.1 | 0.0 | 0.27 | 2.55 | 4.01 | 90.0 | 5.5 | 32.5 | 0.0 | 5.1 |
| 10.0 | 0.86 | 2.0 | 0.15 | 1.8 | 0.0 | 0.17 | 1.16 | 2.47 | 94.1 | 5.1 | 22.4 | 0.0 | 6.7 |
| 7.0 | 0.41 | 3.7 | 0.53 | 4.5 | 1.0 | 0.63 | 8.06 | 4.12 | 81.7 | 3.9 | 9.7 | 1.8 | 4.3 |
| 5.6 | 0.27 | 4.4 | 0.40 | 8.1 | 6.1 | 1.15 | 10.98 | 3.45 | 73.0 | 3.3 | 12.7 | 6.8 | 8.0 |
| 6.2 | 0.22 | 8.1 | 0.30 | 4.5 | 0.1 | 0.83 | 9.14 | 6.76 | 90.2 | 4.5 | 24.7 | 9.8 | 2.3 |
| 8.6 | 0.72 | 3.6 | 0.51 | 4.3 | 2.8 | 0.61 | 5.27 | 4.26 | 84.8 | 4.2 | 11.2 | 3.1 | 8.4 |

| Name | City | State | Rating | 2014 Rating | 2013 Rating | Total Assets ($Mil) | One Year Asset Growth | Asset Mix (As a % of Total Assets) | | | | Capital-ization Index | Net Worth Ratio |
|---|---|---|---|---|---|---|---|---|---|---|---|---|---|
| | | | | | | | | Comm-ercial Loans | Cons-umer Loans | Mort-gage Loans | Secur-ities | | |
| DAIJO FCU | Los Angeles | CA | C | D+ | C- | 2.1 | -10.32 | 0.0 | 31.3 | 0.0 | 0.0 | 10.0 | 13.6 |
| DAIRYLAND POWER CU | La Crosse | WI | C+ | C- | C- | 12.7 | 0.63 | 0.0 | 27.0 | 22.2 | 0.0 | 10.0 | 17.9 |
| DAIRYPAK EMPL CU | Olmsted Falls | OH | C+ | C | C+ | <1 | -9.75 | 0.0 | 51.0 | 0.0 | 0.0 | 10.0 | 36.4 |
| DAKOTA PLAINS CU | Edgeley | ND | C+ | C+ | C+ | 68.3 | 7.61 | 40.4 | 24.4 | 32.7 | 0.0 | 6.3 | 8.3 |
| DAKOTA PLAINS FCU | Lemmon | SD | C | C+ | C | 52.7 | 5.14 | 25.7 | 27.4 | 14.4 | 0.0 | 6.5 | 8.5 |
| DAKOTA STAR FCU | Rapid City | SD | C | C | C | 22.0 | 12.67 | 7.2 | 35.1 | 0.0 | 0.0 | 7.8 | 9.5 |
| DAKOTA TELCO FCU | Fargo | ND | C | C | C- | 21.0 | -1.91 | 0.0 | 3.2 | 0.0 | 0.0 | 10.0 | 11.8 |
| DAKOTA WEST CU | Watford City | ND | B+ | B+ | B- | 253.0 | 3.86 | 55.6 | 4.0 | 38.4 | 16.2 | 7.5 | 9.4 |
| ▲ DAKOTALAND FCU | Huron | SD | B+ | B | B | 276.0 | 5.43 | 22.7 | 22.2 | 33.3 | 4.6 | 8.4 | 9.9 |
| DALE EMPL CU | Columbus | NE | B+ | B+ | B+ | 25.6 | 1.30 | 0.0 | 10.4 | 8.6 | 0.0 | 10.0 | 20.0 |
| DALLAS FCU | Dallas | TX | D | D | C- | 51.5 | 3.00 | 1.8 | 54.5 | 8.2 | 0.0 | 6.3 | 8.3 |
| ▲ DALLAS UP EMPL CU | Dallas | TX | B- | C+ | B- | 18.0 | 2.20 | 0.0 | 39.4 | 0.0 | 20.7 | 10.0 | 25.1 |
| DANBURY CYANAMID EMPL CU | Danbury | CT | D | D | D | 6.3 | -10.07 | 0.0 | 12.7 | 0.0 | 0.0 | 10.0 | 26.2 |
| DANE COUNTY CU | Madison | WI | B- | B- | C+ | 151.6 | 8.49 | 0.6 | 28.7 | 24.1 | 3.1 | 7.7 | 9.4 |
| DANIELS-SHERIDAN FCU | Scobey | MT | B | B | B | 55.6 | 1.49 | 30.9 | 12.1 | 9.1 | 1.7 | 10.0 | 15.4 |
| DANNEMORA FCU | Plattsburgh | NY | A- | A- | A- | 152.0 | 7.48 | 0.2 | 22.2 | 20.7 | 28.5 | 10.0 | 13.2 |
| DANVERS MUNICIPAL FCU | Danvers | MA | C- | C- | C | 7.2 | 2.10 | 0.0 | 40.2 | 0.0 | 0.0 | 10.0 | 37.6 |
| ▲ DANVILLE BELL CU | Danville | IL | C+ | D+ | C- | 13.2 | 6.36 | 0.0 | 43.9 | 4.7 | 0.0 | 10.0 | 12.8 |
| DANVILLE CITY EMPL FCU | Danville | VA | D+ | D+ | D+ | 24.3 | 0.75 | 0.0 | 15.2 | 10.8 | 0.0 | 10.0 | 22.1 |
| DATCU CU | Denton | TX | A | A | A | 801.2 | 7.65 | 0.5 | 61.4 | 13.5 | 0.6 | 10.0 | 14.7 |
| DAVENPORT POLICE DEPT CU | Davenport | IA | C | C | C | 3.9 | 3.89 | 0.0 | 16.3 | 15.9 | 44.4 | 10.0 | 14.2 |
| DAVIESS COUNTY TEACHERS FCU | Owensboro | KY | C | C+ | C+ | 38.9 | 1.61 | 0.0 | 29.3 | 29.3 | 0.0 | 8.9 | 10.3 |
| DAVISON EMPL FCU | Sulphur | LA | D | D | D | 2.9 | -0.07 | 0.0 | 61.2 | 0.0 | 0.0 | 10.0 | 27.8 |
| DAWSON CO-OP CU | Dawson | MN | B | B | B | 137.1 | 4.87 | 59.4 | 8.9 | 25.6 | 0.7 | 10.0 | 14.4 |
| DAY AIR CU | Kettering | OH | A | A | A- | 302.9 | 4.81 | 8.5 | 53.8 | 22.1 | 6.3 | 10.0 | 12.4 |
| DAY-MET CU INC | Dayton | OH | C- | C- | D+ | 83.3 | 2.79 | 7.3 | 24.7 | 29.9 | 14.0 | 9.8 | 10.8 |
| DAYTON FIREFIGHTERS FCU | Dayton | OH | C+ | C+ | C+ | 52.1 | 2.15 | 4.6 | 32.9 | 15.3 | 15.2 | 8.6 | 10.1 |
| DC FCU | Washington | DC | B- | C+ | C+ | 53.6 | 3.54 | 0.0 | 45.4 | 8.2 | 13.8 | 9.6 | 10.7 |
| DCH CU | Tuscaloosa | AL | C+ | C+ | C+ | 29.6 | -0.96 | 0.0 | 27.0 | 7.4 | 37.5 | 10.0 | 13.0 |
| ▲ DE SOTO MO-PAC CU | De Soto | MO | C | C | C | 12.4 | 10.06 | 0.0 | 54.4 | 0.7 | 0.0 | 9.3 | 10.6 |
| DEARBORN COUNTY HOSPITAL FCU | Lawrenceburg | IN | C- | C- | D+ | 15.0 | -2.91 | 0.0 | 24.8 | 0.0 | 0.0 | 9.0 | 10.4 |
| ▲ DECA CU | Cincinnati | OH | C- | D+ | D+ | 4.8 | 2.10 | 0.0 | 42.3 | 0.0 | 0.0 | 10.0 | 21.4 |
| ▲ DECATUR EARTHMOVER CU | Forsyth | IL | C- | C- | C | 264.6 | 0.28 | 0.0 | 31.1 | 17.6 | 23.6 | 10.0 | 11.1 |
| DECATUR MEDICAL DENTAL CU | Decatur | IL | C- | C- | C- | 13.0 | 4.92 | 0.0 | 45.7 | 0.0 | 28.7 | 8.7 | 10.1 |
| DECATUR POLICEMEN CU | Decatur | IL | C- | C- | C- | 4.1 | -5.63 | 0.0 | 60.6 | 0.0 | 0.0 | 10.0 | 13.9 |
| DECATUR POSTAL CU | Decatur | IL | C | C | C+ | 9.3 | -7.00 | 0.0 | 18.9 | 0.0 | 0.0 | 10.0 | 12.1 |
| DECATUR STANOLIND CU | Decatur | IL | D | D | C- | 3.5 | -15.58 | 0.0 | 17.8 | 0.0 | 0.1 | 10.0 | 21.2 |
| DEDHAM TOWN EMPL FCU | Dedham | MA | D+ | D+ | D+ | 8.1 | -0.25 | 0.0 | 48.5 | 0.0 | 0.0 | 10.0 | 12.8 |
| ▼ DEEPWATER INDUSTRIES FCU | Deepwater | NJ | D | C- | C- | 84.6 | 3.59 | 0.0 | 15.7 | 16.0 | 10.7 | 6.8 | 8.9 |
| ▲ DEER LODGE COUNTY SCHOOL EMPL FCU | Anaconda | MT | D+ | D+ | D+ | 4.6 | 4.96 | 0.0 | 29.4 | 0.0 | 0.0 | 7.5 | 9.3 |
| DEER RIVER COOPERATIVE CU | Deer River | MN | C- | D+ | D | 15.5 | -0.10 | 0.0 | 15.0 | 28.9 | 0.0 | 9.0 | 10.4 |
| DEER VALLEY CU | Phoenix | AZ | C+ | C+ | C+ | 206.7 | 2.01 | 0.0 | 32.0 | 22.8 | 25.0 | 6.9 | 8.9 |
| DEERE EMPL CU | Moline | IL | B+ | B+ | B+ | 715.5 | 6.79 | 0.0 | 29.7 | 50.2 | 0.0 | 6.5 | 8.5 |
| DEFENSE CONTRACTS SOUTH FCU | Dallas | TX | C | C | C+ | 43.5 | 1.16 | 0.2 | 23.4 | 0.0 | 0.0 | 10.0 | 12.9 |
| DEFENSE LOGISTICS FCU | Picatinny Arsenal | NJ | E+ | E+ | E+ | <1 | -4.54 | 0.0 | 63.3 | 0.0 | 22.2 | 4.3 | 6.3 |
| DEKALB COUNTY CU | Dekalb | IL | D- | D- | D- | 6.0 | -1.18 | 0.0 | 29.6 | 0.0 | 0.0 | 6.9 | 8.9 |
| DEL MET FCU | Muncie | IN | C- | C- | C- | 9.5 | -0.94 | 0.0 | 25.2 | 0.0 | 0.0 | 10.0 | 15.8 |
| DEL NORTE CU | Santa Fe | NM | B+ | A- | A- | 505.0 | 6.37 | 0.0 | 55.8 | 13.3 | 5.3 | 10.0 | 11.6 |
| DEL RIO SP CU | Del Rio | TX | D | D | C- | 5.7 | 2.53 | 0.0 | 10.7 | 0.0 | 0.0 | 10.0 | 27.9 |
| ▲ DEL-ONE FCU | Dover | DE | B | B- | B- | 356.9 | 9.55 | 2.2 | 41.2 | 26.0 | 7.6 | 8.2 | 9.8 |
| DELANCEY STREET FCU | San Francisco | CA | D+ | D+ | C- | <1 | -7.10 | 0.0 | 0.0 | 0.0 | 83.5 | 10.0 | 38.2 |
| DELAWARE ALLIANCE FCU | New Castle | DE | C+ | C | C | 20.7 | 0.25 | 0.0 | 24.2 | 7.4 | 0.0 | 10.0 | 14.5 |
| DELAWARE RIVER & BAY AUTHORITY EMPL | New Castle | DE | C | C- | D+ | 6.8 | -0.29 | 0.0 | 0.0 | 0.0 | 11.8 | 10.0 | 11.1 |
| DELAWARE RIVER EMPL FCU | Swedesboro | NJ | D | D | D | <1 | -6.90 | 0.0 | 38.8 | 0.0 | 0.0 | 10.0 | 17.2 |
| DELAWARE STATE POLICE FCU | Georgetown | DE | C+ | C | D+ | 120.2 | -0.21 | 0.4 | 18.6 | 16.3 | 43.4 | 8.6 | 10.0 |
| DELCO POSTAL CU | Upper Darby | PA | E+ | D- | D- | 14.2 | 1.50 | 0.0 | 16.2 | 26.6 | 0.0 | 6.2 | 8.2 |
| DELMAR OCF FCU | Feura Bush | NY | D | D | C- | 1.2 | -4.21 | 0.0 | 25.5 | 0.0 | 0.0 | 10.0 | 13.9 |
| DELMARVA POWER SOUTHERN DIVISION FC | Salisbury | MD | B- | B- | B- | 16.5 | -1.30 | 0.0 | 16.8 | 2.3 | 0.6 | 10.0 | 18.8 |
| DELTA COMMUNITY CU | Atlanta | GA | A- | A- | A- | 4829.7 | 4.35 | 2.6 | 35.9 | 32.0 | 20.1 | 10.0 | 11.5 |
| DELTA COUNTY CU | Escanaba | MI | B | B | B | 122.1 | 3.52 | 0.7 | 22.7 | 22.0 | 31.0 | 9.2 | 10.4 |

| Asset Quality Index | Non-Performing Loans as a % of Total Loans | as a % of Capital | Net Charge-Offs Avg Loans | Profitability Index | Net Income ($Mil) | Return on Assets | Return on Equity | Net Interest Spread | Overhead Efficiency Ratio | Liquidity Index | Liquidity Ratio | Hot Money Ratio | Stability Index |
|---|---|---|---|---|---|---|---|---|---|---|---|---|---|
| 9.6 | 0.00 | 0.0 | -4.06 | 4.5 | 0.0 | 1.04 | 7.84 | 3.36 | 97.5 | 7.2 | 66.3 | 0.0 | 4.3 |
| 9.6 | 0.09 | 0.3 | 0.00 | 3.3 | 0.1 | 0.47 | 2.73 | 3.00 | 86.1 | 4.4 | 34.0 | 1.3 | 6.8 |
| 8.7 | 0.00 | 0.0 | -1.23 | 8.1 | 0.0 | 2.01 | 5.71 | 10.34 | 65.0 | 7.2 | 85.0 | 0.0 | 5.7 |
| 5.6 | 0.61 | 6.0 | 0.01 | 6.4 | 0.5 | 0.91 | 11.01 | 4.18 | 74.2 | 1.5 | 12.9 | 21.5 | 4.6 |
| 7.9 | 0.16 | 1.4 | 0.08 | 3.9 | 0.2 | 0.46 | 5.47 | 4.23 | 89.8 | 3.1 | 9.0 | 5.8 | 4.3 |
| 8.2 | 0.20 | 1.7 | -0.05 | 7.2 | 0.2 | 1.00 | 10.60 | 4.37 | 80.6 | 3.1 | 12.1 | 2.0 | 4.3 |
| 10.0 | 0.00 | 0.0 | 0.00 | 2.7 | 0.1 | 0.34 | 2.95 | 1.00 | 64.0 | 6.2 | 40.6 | 0.0 | 6.4 |
| 3.5 | 2.26 | 14.7 | 0.09 | 9.1 | 2.5 | 1.26 | 14.86 | 3.87 | 60.8 | 4.0 | 15.5 | 5.5 | 7.5 |
| 7.3 | 0.76 | 5.7 | 0.14 | 5.6 | 1.6 | 0.80 | 8.51 | 3.57 | 78.1 | 3.2 | 11.7 | 7.1 | 7.0 |
| 10.0 | 0.58 | 1.0 | -0.12 | 5.1 | 0.1 | 0.55 | 2.80 | 2.29 | 77.1 | 4.1 | 14.4 | 7.6 | 7.9 |
| 4.0 | 1.30 | 10.4 | 1.09 | 0.7 | -0.1 | -0.37 | -4.42 | 4.05 | 86.9 | 4.1 | 31.4 | 0.2 | 2.4 |
| 9.2 | 1.08 | 1.8 | 0.54 | 5.0 | 0.1 | 0.85 | 3.43 | 3.76 | 86.5 | 5.8 | 35.4 | 0.0 | 6.4 |
| 9.1 | 2.92 | 1.8 | -0.41 | 0.0 | -0.1 | -1.33 | -5.15 | 2.67 | 136.5 | 5.3 | 29.5 | 0.0 | 4.8 |
| 6.9 | 1.12 | 9.0 | 0.29 | 4.4 | 0.6 | 0.56 | 5.90 | 3.96 | 85.3 | 3.3 | 11.6 | 6.8 | 6.2 |
| 8.6 | 0.50 | 1.7 | 0.12 | 4.4 | 0.3 | 0.58 | 3.92 | 3.27 | 86.7 | 5.1 | 40.0 | 3.1 | 7.8 |
| 8.6 | 0.58 | 3.9 | 0.06 | 5.4 | 0.9 | 0.82 | 6.33 | 3.46 | 79.4 | 4.5 | 14.0 | 1.2 | 8.7 |
| 9.9 | 0.60 | 0.7 | 0.09 | 1.4 | 0.0 | -0.04 | -0.10 | 2.04 | 100.9 | 5.7 | 91.2 | 0.0 | 7.2 |
| 9.2 | 0.43 | 2.1 | 0.35 | 3.8 | 0.1 | 0.66 | 5.09 | 5.08 | 86.3 | 4.5 | 11.8 | 0.0 | 6.6 |
| 10.0 | 0.41 | 0.5 | 0.15 | 1.2 | 0.0 | 0.02 | 0.10 | 2.19 | 96.5 | 5.6 | 34.5 | 3.4 | 5.8 |
| 7.7 | 0.38 | 2.9 | 0.20 | 9.4 | 7.8 | 1.33 | 9.16 | 3.35 | 65.8 | 2.8 | 8.1 | 5.8 | 10.0 |
| 9.7 | 0.00 | 0.0 | 0.00 | 2.4 | 0.0 | 0.20 | 1.45 | 2.51 | 90.7 | 3.7 | 36.8 | 10.9 | 7.1 |
| 8.9 | 0.15 | 0.9 | 0.10 | 2.5 | 0.1 | 0.19 | 1.88 | 3.07 | 92.7 | 4.5 | 19.1 | 1.1 | 5.4 |
| 8.2 | 1.14 | 2.6 | 0.00 | 0.0 | 0.0 | -1.34 | -4.77 | 5.61 | 134.1 | 6.2 | 48.6 | 0.0 | 6.6 |
| 4.2 | 1.29 | 6.4 | 0.03 | 9.8 | 1.9 | 1.89 | 13.74 | 3.63 | 42.1 | 3.5 | 17.7 | 5.4 | 10.0 |
| 6.5 | 0.77 | 4.9 | 0.32 | 8.9 | 3.1 | 1.36 | 11.40 | 3.34 | 66.0 | 2.9 | 9.5 | 5.2 | 8.8 |
| 6.6 | 0.85 | 5.1 | 0.20 | 1.6 | 0.0 | -0.05 | -0.48 | 3.23 | 95.8 | 3.9 | 20.8 | 5.3 | 5.0 |
| 7.4 | 0.40 | 2.8 | 0.30 | 3.9 | 0.2 | 0.54 | 5.46 | 3.05 | 75.4 | 3.1 | 20.4 | 13.8 | 5.0 |
| 4.5 | 1.47 | 10.5 | 1.72 | 4.4 | 0.2 | 0.60 | 7.94 | 5.93 | 77.1 | 3.8 | 16.3 | 12.2 | 4.0 |
| 5.9 | 5.45 | 15.6 | 1.38 | 3.5 | 0.1 | 0.50 | 3.95 | 3.38 | 83.1 | 4.2 | 37.3 | 19.7 | 5.2 |
| 4.8 | 0.77 | 5.5 | 0.31 | 7.5 | 0.1 | 1.16 | 10.91 | 3.72 | 64.9 | 4.0 | 16.2 | 0.0 | 5.9 |
| 8.7 | 1.43 | 4.1 | 0.20 | 2.6 | 0.0 | 0.27 | 2.69 | 2.36 | 88.5 | 4.9 | 16.1 | 0.0 | 4.8 |
| 8.5 | 0.57 | 1.4 | 0.00 | 1.4 | 0.0 | 0.14 | 0.66 | 3.14 | 95.8 | 5.7 | 55.0 | 0.0 | 6.2 |
| 8.3 | 0.77 | 4.0 | 0.64 | 1.6 | 0.0 | 0.02 | 0.20 | 3.27 | 89.0 | 4.7 | 23.4 | 6.3 | 5.7 |
| 8.4 | 0.23 | 1.2 | -0.08 | 2.4 | 0.0 | 0.27 | 2.65 | 2.74 | 86.5 | 4.6 | 11.7 | 0.0 | 4.1 |
| 8.0 | 0.00 | 0.0 | 0.00 | 2.8 | 0.0 | 0.29 | 2.15 | 1.59 | 81.3 | 4.3 | 15.4 | 0.0 | 6.3 |
| 9.5 | 0.84 | 1.4 | 0.62 | 3.5 | 0.0 | 0.43 | 3.73 | 1.94 | 77.4 | 5.1 | 35.4 | 0.0 | 4.0 |
| 10.0 | 0.30 | 0.3 | 0.00 | 0.0 | -0.1 | -1.87 | -9.33 | 1.14 | 254.3 | 5.8 | 53.1 | 5.4 | 6.1 |
| 6.2 | 1.67 | 6.2 | 0.30 | 3.3 | 0.0 | 0.32 | 2.58 | 4.23 | 90.5 | 3.7 | 25.9 | 12.9 | 5.3 |
| 6.1 | 1.73 | 9.0 | 1.26 | 0.5 | -0.3 | -0.44 | -5.17 | 3.20 | 90.5 | 5.2 | 28.0 | 2.4 | 3.3 |
| 9.8 | 0.00 | 0.0 | 0.00 | 3.4 | 0.0 | 0.49 | 5.42 | 2.95 | 81.4 | 4.9 | 13.0 | 0.0 | 3.0 |
| 7.2 | 0.42 | 2.4 | -0.03 | 2.6 | 0.0 | 0.35 | 3.45 | 3.30 | 88.5 | 5.2 | 37.1 | 0.0 | 5.4 |
| 9.1 | 0.50 | 3.3 | 0.08 | 3.8 | 0.7 | 0.47 | 5.45 | 3.18 | 84.8 | 3.8 | 11.1 | 2.5 | 4.8 |
| 9.7 | 0.19 | 1.9 | 0.18 | 6.9 | 5.8 | 1.09 | 13.43 | 2.58 | 70.0 | 2.0 | 9.8 | 14.8 | 6.8 |
| 8.3 | 2.92 | 6.7 | 0.96 | 1.8 | 0.0 | 0.01 | 0.07 | 1.42 | 80.8 | 5.7 | 35.0 | 0.0 | 6.2 |
| 8.2 | 0.00 | 0.0 | 0.00 | 0.3 | 0.0 | -0.28 | -4.30 | 4.19 | 103.5 | 3.9 | 20.4 | 0.0 | 2.5 |
| 7.7 | 0.79 | 3.9 | 0.34 | 1.1 | 0.0 | -0.11 | -1.25 | 2.82 | 103.1 | 5.2 | 23.5 | 0.0 | 3.3 |
| 9.3 | 1.25 | 2.2 | 0.00 | 2.2 | 0.0 | 0.15 | 0.98 | 2.05 | 90.7 | 4.9 | 14.3 | 0.0 | 7.1 |
| 7.3 | 0.78 | 5.1 | 0.49 | 4.9 | 2.3 | 0.61 | 5.25 | 3.52 | 72.3 | 3.8 | 18.3 | 7.5 | 7.8 |
| 10.0 | 0.00 | 0.0 | -0.35 | 0.2 | 0.0 | -0.49 | -1.75 | 2.16 | 128.1 | 6.0 | 58.3 | 8.7 | 6.7 |
| 5.3 | 1.60 | 13.0 | 0.73 | 5.6 | 2.2 | 0.86 | 9.38 | 4.05 | 77.2 | 2.7 | 11.3 | 10.0 | 5.9 |
| 10.0 | 0.00 | 0.0 | 0.00 | 1.3 | 0.0 | 0.00 | 0.00 | 0.94 | 100.0 | 6.2 | 24.3 | 0.0 | 6.5 |
| 7.9 | 2.29 | 5.6 | -0.39 | 2.9 | 0.1 | 0.31 | 2.15 | 3.34 | 93.2 | 4.9 | 13.9 | 0.0 | 6.5 |
| 10.0 | 2.90 | 1.9 | -0.49 | 4.8 | 0.0 | 0.77 | 7.11 | 1.42 | 40.9 | 5.4 | 27.9 | 0.0 | 4.3 |
| 6.8 | 9.13 | 19.3 | 0.00 | 0.0 | 0.0 | -2.79 | -15.07 | 1.65 | 257.1 | 6.7 | 74.1 | 0.0 | 5.7 |
| 3.7 | 4.58 | 24.7 | 0.32 | 3.8 | 0.5 | 0.53 | 5.55 | 3.56 | 80.8 | 4.1 | 14.8 | 6.6 | 5.5 |
| 3.7 | 1.56 | 21.4 | 0.46 | 2.0 | 0.0 | -0.08 | -1.03 | 5.49 | 99.6 | 5.6 | 34.6 | 0.1 | 1.7 |
| 9.7 | 1.12 | 2.3 | -1.69 | 0.0 | 0.0 | -1.95 | -13.64 | 2.52 | 195.0 | 6.5 | 43.0 | 0.0 | 6.8 |
| 7.7 | 5.33 | 6.3 | 0.18 | 4.7 | 0.1 | 0.71 | 3.79 | 2.20 | 63.0 | 5.9 | 35.4 | 0.0 | 7.1 |
| 8.3 | 0.55 | 3.7 | 0.46 | 6.4 | 36.1 | 1.00 | 8.97 | 3.11 | 68.9 | 3.4 | 6.8 | 3.5 | 8.3 |
| 7.2 | 1.01 | 5.5 | 0.70 | 4.6 | 0.6 | 0.67 | 6.41 | 3.35 | 76.4 | 3.6 | 14.4 | 10.5 | 6.9 |

| Name | City | State | Rating | 2014 Rating | 2013 Rating | Total Assets ($Mil) | One Year Asset Growth | Asset Mix (As a % of Total Aseets) | | | | Capital-ization Index | Net Worth Ratio |
|------|------|-------|--------|-------------|-------------|---------------------|----------------------|-----------|---|---|---|---|---|
| | | | | | | | | Comm-ercial Loans | Cons-umer Loans | Mort-gage Loans | Secur-ities | | |
| ▼ DELTA COUNTY FCU | Delta | CO | C+ | B- | B- | 47.0 | 9.79 | 0.2 | 7.9 | 21.5 | 0.0 | 7.5 | 9.3 |
| DELTA CU | Greenville | MS | C- | C- | C | 5.2 | 0.70 | 0.0 | 46.9 | 0.0 | 0.0 | 10.0 | 24.1 |
| DELTA REFINING CO EMPL FCU | Memphis | TN | C | C | C | 4.5 | -4.55 | 0.0 | 29.4 | 0.0 | 0.0 | 10.0 | 18.0 |
| DELTA SCHOOLS FCU | Antioch | CA | C+ | B- | C+ | 34.0 | 1.67 | 0.5 | 18.4 | 8.6 | 1.5 | 8.0 | 9.7 |
| DELUXE FCU | Burbank | CA | E+ | D- | D- | 9.1 | 16.61 | 0.0 | 31.9 | 11.6 | 0.0 | 5.4 | 7.4 |
| DEMING SCHOOLS EMPL CU | Deming | NM | C | C | C+ | 4.6 | -2.17 | 0.0 | 46.9 | 0.0 | 0.0 | 10.0 | 18.1 |
| DEMOCRACY FCU | Alexandria | VA | D+ | D+ | C | 153.8 | -1.60 | 4.1 | 25.4 | 23.1 | 24.2 | 9.0 | 10.4 |
| ▼ DEMOCRAT P&L FCU | Little Rock | AR | C- | C | C | 2.0 | -9.10 | 0.0 | 37.9 | 0.0 | 0.0 | 10.0 | 16.9 |
| DEMOPOLIS FCU | Demopolis | AL | E+ | E+ | E+ | <1 | -0.68 | 0.0 | 72.7 | 0.0 | 0.0 | 5.3 | 7.3 |
| DENALI ALASKAN FCU | Anchorage | AK | B- | B- | B- | 578.0 | 1.13 | 6.9 | 68.3 | 10.6 | 1.5 | 7.0 | 9.0 |
| ▼ DENNISON FCU | Coopersville | MI | D+ | D+ | C- | <1 | 29.75 | 0.0 | 35.8 | 0.0 | 0.0 | 10.0 | 11.2 |
| DENOCOS FCU | Crescent City | CA | D | D | D+ | 6.4 | 1.06 | 0.0 | 18.7 | 0.0 | 0.0 | 8.5 | 10.0 |
| DENVER COMMUNITY CU | Denver | CO | A | A | A | 278.1 | 4.19 | 5.0 | 22.3 | 20.2 | 18.7 | 10.0 | 14.1 |
| DENVER FIRE DEPT FCU | Denver | CO | C+ | C | C- | 142.9 | 7.11 | 4.1 | 8.4 | 22.1 | 50.9 | 9.8 | 10.9 |
| DEPT OF COMMERCE FCU | Washington | DC | B- | B | B | 339.2 | 1.46 | 0.1 | 14.8 | 29.7 | 45.0 | 7.2 | 9.1 |
| DEPT OF CORRECTIONS CU | Baton Rouge | LA | A- | A- | A- | 74.4 | 2.64 | 0.0 | 41.1 | 15.1 | 0.7 | 10.0 | 17.0 |
| ▲ DEPT OF LABOR FCU | Washington | DC | B | B | B- | 86.3 | 24.19 | 0.0 | 23.4 | 19.7 | 38.4 | 10.0 | 11.9 |
| DEPT OF PUBLIC SAFETY FCU | Oklahoma City | OK | C | C- | C- | 27.6 | -0.92 | 0.0 | 28.5 | 0.0 | 0.8 | 10.0 | 20.2 |
| DEPT OF THE INTERIOR FCU | Washington | DC | B- | B | B | 164.8 | 8.36 | 5.5 | 26.5 | 37.5 | 17.2 | 9.8 | 10.8 |
| ▲ DERRY AREA FCU | Derry | PA | D+ | D+ | D+ | 8.6 | 3.39 | 0.0 | 46.9 | 0.0 | 0.0 | 10.0 | 14.0 |
| DERTOWN SCHOOL FCU | Latrobe | PA | C | C | C | 8.2 | 2.38 | 0.0 | 37.0 | 28.8 | 27.4 | 10.0 | 34.6 |
| DES MOINES COUNTY POSTAL CU | Burlington | IA | C- | C- | C- | 2.4 | -13.09 | 0.0 | 57.9 | 0.0 | 0.0 | 10.0 | 20.0 |
| DES MOINES FIRE DEPT CU | Des Moines | IA | C- | C- | C- | 5.1 | -5.77 | 0.0 | 57.5 | 0.0 | 0.0 | 10.0 | 16.3 |
| DES MOINES METRO CU | Des Moines | IA | C+ | C+ | C+ | 50.0 | 3.88 | 3.6 | 19.0 | 15.7 | 0.0 | 10.0 | 12.1 |
| DES MOINES POLICE OFFICERS CU | Des Moines | IA | B+ | B+ | B+ | 51.0 | 14.73 | 1.1 | 33.7 | 15.6 | 2.0 | 10.0 | 14.3 |
| DES MOINES WATER WORKS CU | Des Moines | IA | D | D | D+ | 1.6 | -3.33 | 0.0 | 59.6 | 0.0 | 0.0 | 10.0 | 11.4 |
| DESCO FCU | Portsmouth | OH | B- | B- | B | 271.5 | 1.98 | 15.3 | 11.6 | 41.0 | 17.6 | 9.5 | 10.6 |
| DESERET FIRST FCU | Salt Lake City | UT | C+ | C+ | C | 494.4 | 8.40 | 4.1 | 32.0 | 25.9 | 13.1 | 4.9 | 7.0 |
| ▼ DESERT COMMUNITIES FCU | Needles | CA | E+ | D- | D- | 23.3 | 5.88 | 0.0 | 18.0 | 4.8 | 6.8 | 5.7 | 7.7 |
| ▲ DESERT MEDICAL FCU | Scottsdale | AZ | D+ | D- | C- | 10.2 | 2.42 | 0.0 | 55.4 | 0.0 | 0.0 | 6.8 | 8.8 |
| ▼ DESERT SAGE FCU | Nampa | ID | D+ | C- | C | 1.4 | -2.24 | 0.0 | 49.5 | 0.0 | 0.0 | 10.0 | 14.2 |
| DESERT SCHOOLS FCU | Phoenix | AZ | A | A | A- | 3741.4 | 5.75 | 4.0 | 16.4 | 14.8 | 44.6 | 9.9 | 10.9 |
| ▲ DESERT VALLEYS FCU | Ridgecrest | CA | D | D | D- | 27.1 | 6.43 | 1.2 | 45.4 | 0.0 | 0.0 | 4.1 | 6.1 |
| DESERTVIEW FCU | Huntington | UT | B- | B- | B- | 32.5 | -2.29 | 1.9 | 26.7 | 11.9 | 40.8 | 10.0 | 11.8 |
| DESTINATIONS CU | Baltimore | MD | D+ | C- | D+ | 60.0 | 4.51 | 0.0 | 35.5 | 9.2 | 11.1 | 10.0 | 13.1 |
| DETOUR DRUMMOND COMMUNITY CU | Drummond Island | MI | C+ | C+ | C- | 32.8 | -1.61 | 2.2 | 11.2 | 38.0 | 37.6 | 10.0 | 11.0 |
| ▼ DEVILS SLIDE FCU | Morgan | UT | C+ | C+ | C | 10.4 | 0.96 | 0.0 | 47.0 | 0.0 | 0.0 | 10.0 | 13.6 |
| DEXSTA FCU | Wilmington | DE | B- | C+ | C+ | 240.6 | 3.12 | 0.0 | 40.7 | 3.5 | 29.8 | 6.8 | 8.8 |
| DEXTER CU | Central Falls | RI | D- | D- | D- | 98.6 | -12.80 | 8.7 | 24.0 | 32.0 | 10.9 | 4.5 | 6.7 |
| DEXTER PUBLIC SCHOOLS CU | Dexter | MO | D | D | D | 4.5 | -2.56 | 0.0 | 35.2 | 0.0 | 0.0 | 8.3 | 9.9 |
| DFCU FINANCIAL CU | Dearborn | MI | A | A- | A- | 3903.7 | 6.59 | 0.2 | 5.1 | 16.2 | 64.8 | 10.0 | 12.0 |
| DIABLO VALLEY FCU | Concord | CA | C- | C | D+ | 35.0 | 9.99 | 6.6 | 23.1 | 31.7 | 3.3 | 6.0 | 8.0 |
| DIAL CU | Montgomery | IL | C- | C | C | 9.5 | -0.67 | 0.0 | 26.8 | 0.0 | 17.8 | 10.0 | 13.3 |
| DIAMOND CU | Pottstown | PA | A- | A- | A- | 476.1 | 7.47 | 1.7 | 53.5 | 20.9 | 0.6 | 10.0 | 11.0 |
| DIAMOND LAKES FCU | Malvern | AR | C- | C | C+ | 69.5 | 3.66 | 0.1 | 37.7 | 8.9 | 0.4 | 8.9 | 10.2 |
| DIAMOND VALLEY FCU | Evansville | IN | D+ | D | D | 132.5 | -0.88 | 0.0 | 26.3 | 15.3 | 0.0 | 7.6 | 9.4 |
| ▲ DIEBOLD FCU | North Canton | OH | C- | C- | C- | 16.8 | -0.58 | 2.4 | 49.2 | 11.8 | 0.0 | 7.1 | 9.1 |
| DIGITAL FCU | Marlborough | MA | A- | A- | B+ | 6519.5 | 13.14 | 10.3 | 35.9 | 34.3 | 6.1 | 7.3 | 9.2 |
| DILL FCU | Roxboro | NC | D | D | C- | 1.1 | -4.30 | 0.0 | 25.2 | 0.0 | 0.0 | 10.0 | 44.3 |
| DILLARDS FCU | Little Rock | AR | D- | D- | D- | 27.4 | -0.72 | 0.5 | 39.5 | 12.5 | 4.2 | 7.4 | 9.3 |
| DILLON CU | Hutchinson | KS | C+ | C+ | C+ | 36.8 | -2.00 | 0.0 | 35.9 | 28.0 | 0.0 | 10.0 | 15.7 |
| DILLONVALE FCU | Dillonvale | OH | D | D | D | 1.2 | -2.53 | 0.0 | 53.9 | 0.0 | 0.0 | 10.0 | 28.1 |
| DIRECT FCU | Needham | MA | A | A | A- | 439.2 | 6.44 | 0.0 | 10.6 | 37.8 | 0.6 | 10.0 | 16.2 |
| DIRECTIONS CU | Sylvania | OH | C+ | C+ | C+ | 621.1 | 4.54 | 8.7 | 22.6 | 33.2 | 14.5 | 7.1 | 9.1 |
| DIRECTORS CHOICE CU | Albany | NY | C+ | C+ | C+ | 6.9 | 2.81 | 38.3 | 13.5 | 2.4 | 0.0 | 10.0 | 16.7 |
| DISCOVERY FCU | Wyomissing | PA | C+ | C+ | C+ | 126.5 | -1.75 | 10.2 | 15.1 | 0.5 | 38.3 | 9.9 | 10.9 |
| DISTINGUISHED SERVICE CU | Youngstown | OH | D | D | C- | 1.2 | -12.80 | 0.0 | 50.0 | 0.0 | 0.0 | 10.0 | 34.5 |
| ▼ DISTRICT #6 FCU | Hornell | NY | D | C- | C- | 17.6 | 1.12 | 0.0 | 22.3 | 0.0 | 50.2 | 7.9 | 9.6 |
| DISTRICT 05 DOTD FCU | Monroe | LA | C- | C- | C- | 7.9 | 0.89 | 0.0 | 31.0 | 9.7 | 0.0 | 10.0 | 19.0 |
| DISTRICT 08 FCU | Alexandria | LA | E+ | E+ | E+ | 8.0 | 1.53 | 0.0 | 20.8 | 12.8 | 0.0 | 5.4 | 7.4 |

| Asset Quality Index | Non-Performing Loans as a % of Total Loans | as a % of Capital | Net Charge-Offs Avg Loans | Profitability Index | Net Income ($Mil) | Return on Assets | Return on Equity | Net Interest Spread | Overhead Efficiency Ratio | Liquidity Index | Liquidity Ratio | Hot Money Ratio | Stability Index |
|---|---|---|---|---|---|---|---|---|---|---|---|---|---|
| 7.4 | 0.85 | 6.1 | 0.01 | 4.0 | 0.2 | 0.45 | 4.81 | 3.19 | 85.8 | 5.0 | 26.5 | 5.7 | 5.3 |
| 4.9 | 5.05 | 10.2 | -0.25 | 3.5 | 0.0 | 0.23 | 0.96 | 3.98 | 96.1 | 4.7 | 40.7 | 0.0 | 6.6 |
| 9.9 | 0.74 | 1.3 | -0.63 | 4.0 | 0.0 | 0.61 | 3.65 | 2.07 | 78.3 | 5.5 | 44.7 | 0.0 | 7.2 |
| 10.0 | 0.11 | 0.4 | 0.23 | 2.9 | 0.1 | 0.21 | 2.21 | 3.10 | 98.2 | 5.5 | 32.4 | 1.7 | 4.2 |
| 7.3 | 1.15 | 6.1 | 2.75 | 0.0 | -0.1 | -1.07 | -13.30 | 3.49 | 101.2 | 3.6 | 23.5 | 17.4 | 3.0 |
| 5.8 | 2.91 | 7.7 | -0.59 | 5.3 | 0.0 | 0.76 | 4.25 | 4.09 | 77.7 | 4.8 | 41.5 | 0.0 | 4.3 |
| 6.9 | 1.71 | 8.8 | 1.27 | 1.4 | -0.1 | -0.06 | -0.56 | 3.98 | 87.6 | 4.1 | 16.6 | 9.9 | 5.5 |
| 8.0 | 1.19 | 3.1 | 0.89 | 1.9 | -0.1 | -0.32 | -1.95 | 3.17 | 95.1 | 4.9 | 38.1 | 7.5 | 6.3 |
| 2.5 | 1.60 | 13.9 | 2.92 | 3.7 | 0.0 | -1.62 | -20.69 | 13.24 | 84.1 | 4.9 | 25.0 | 0.0 | 1.0 |
| 4.7 | 0.91 | 10.3 | 0.65 | 6.7 | 5.0 | 1.13 | 13.55 | 5.33 | 80.5 | 2.8 | 6.5 | 4.6 | 5.6 |
| 1.7 | 13.98 | 40.6 | 0.00 | 3.2 | 0.0 | 0.32 | 2.30 | 4.81 | 72.7 | 7.4 | 72.7 | 0.0 | 6.2 |
| 5.7 | 4.20 | 8.5 | 3.50 | 1.9 | 0.0 | 0.00 | 0.00 | 2.16 | 85.1 | 5.5 | 44.8 | 0.0 | 4.7 |
| 9.9 | 0.16 | 0.8 | 0.43 | 5.5 | 1.4 | 0.66 | 4.69 | 3.43 | 81.5 | 4.8 | 40.2 | 10.9 | 8.1 |
| 10.0 | 0.00 | 0.0 | 0.09 | 2.9 | 0.6 | 0.54 | 4.93 | 1.81 | 75.1 | 4.2 | 19.9 | 6.2 | 6.7 |
| 9.8 | 0.51 | 2.4 | 0.50 | 4.1 | 1.4 | 0.53 | 5.50 | 2.89 | 76.8 | 4.1 | 81.4 | 16.7 | 5.9 |
| 7.8 | 1.16 | 4.2 | 0.68 | 6.3 | 0.4 | 0.74 | 4.45 | 5.68 | 83.7 | 5.3 | 45.3 | 5.2 | 7.1 |
| 6.4 | 2.84 | 10.8 | 0.76 | 5.7 | 0.5 | 0.84 | 7.36 | 4.56 | 76.3 | 4.1 | 19.2 | 3.3 | 5.3 |
| 9.9 | 0.97 | 1.5 | 0.11 | 2.2 | 0.1 | 0.24 | 1.20 | 2.25 | 90.3 | 5.1 | 41.6 | 7.0 | 6.9 |
| 7.5 | 0.70 | 6.1 | 0.47 | 2.7 | 0.2 | 0.16 | 1.47 | 3.33 | 87.3 | 3.2 | 21.7 | 6.3 | 6.4 |
| 6.0 | 2.16 | 8.6 | 0.41 | 2.9 | 0.0 | 0.12 | 0.89 | 3.58 | 88.4 | 4.9 | 35.4 | 0.0 | 7.0 |
| 9.6 | 0.00 | 0.0 | 0.00 | 4.3 | 0.0 | 0.70 | 2.03 | 2.39 | 70.6 | 3.6 | 14.9 | 1.9 | 7.4 |
| 8.7 | 0.57 | 1.6 | 0.41 | 2.3 | 0.0 | 0.31 | 1.68 | 3.07 | 89.5 | 4.0 | 25.7 | 0.0 | 6.8 |
| 8.6 | 0.38 | 1.4 | 0.00 | 1.6 | 0.0 | 0.03 | 0.16 | 2.80 | 97.9 | 5.2 | 44.0 | 0.0 | 6.7 |
| 6.9 | 0.52 | 7.8 | 0.21 | 2.8 | 0.1 | 0.25 | 2.11 | 2.72 | 91.7 | 5.3 | 34.2 | 2.0 | 5.9 |
| 9.6 | 0.31 | 1.4 | 0.04 | 6.5 | 0.4 | 1.02 | 7.11 | 3.09 | 70.2 | 3.4 | 12.5 | 6.5 | 8.0 |
| 2.7 | 4.46 | 26.1 | 0.00 | 1.9 | 0.0 | 0.00 | 0.00 | 4.23 | 92.1 | 4.9 | 27.4 | 0.0 | 5.5 |
| 6.2 | 0.86 | 8.3 | 0.18 | 3.7 | 0.9 | 0.43 | 4.56 | 3.40 | 87.1 | 4.0 | 22.5 | 8.3 | 6.6 |
| 6.8 | 0.85 | 7.9 | 0.50 | 5.7 | 2.8 | 0.76 | 11.12 | 3.71 | 78.1 | 4.0 | 14.5 | 5.3 | 3.8 |
| 6.1 | 3.84 | 12.9 | 0.72 | 0.5 | -0.1 | -0.35 | -4.36 | 3.19 | 109.5 | 4.5 | 11.2 | 4.8 | 2.6 |
| 8.5 | 0.00 | 0.0 | 0.07 | 4.6 | 0.1 | 0.82 | 9.73 | 3.79 | 81.1 | 4.5 | 33.2 | 0.0 | 3.1 |
| 2.5 | 7.87 | 34.7 | 1.17 | 4.5 | 0.0 | 0.47 | 3.38 | 7.47 | 93.8 | 5.0 | 29.0 | 0.0 | 6.8 |
| 9.3 | 0.43 | 2.8 | 0.19 | 8.8 | 32.6 | 1.17 | 11.12 | 2.75 | 79.0 | 5.4 | 27.0 | 2.4 | 8.1 |
| 6.5 | 0.43 | 3.6 | 0.66 | 3.3 | 0.0 | 0.15 | 2.43 | 5.03 | 90.0 | 4.2 | 13.2 | 6.2 | 2.2 |
| 5.6 | 3.84 | 14.4 | 0.36 | 4.1 | 0.1 | 0.52 | 4.67 | 3.41 | 81.8 | 3.9 | 25.2 | 4.5 | 6.2 |
| 7.4 | 0.69 | 5.5 | 0.98 | 0.5 | -0.2 | -0.42 | -3.27 | 3.60 | 97.5 | 3.4 | 8.4 | 9.0 | 5.9 |
| 3.7 | 4.86 | 23.0 | 0.13 | 2.3 | 0.0 | 0.05 | 0.44 | 3.14 | 87.7 | 4.1 | 18.9 | 9.3 | 6.2 |
| 7.8 | 0.00 | 0.0 | 0.04 | 6.7 | 0.1 | 0.87 | 6.36 | 3.58 | 69.8 | 2.9 | 26.7 | 30.6 | 4.3 |
| 7.9 | 0.83 | 4.8 | 0.58 | 3.6 | 0.9 | 0.48 | 5.72 | 3.45 | 82.8 | 4.8 | 20.9 | 2.9 | 4.6 |
| 3.7 | 1.63 | 18.0 | 0.91 | 0.0 | -1.4 | -1.83 | -29.03 | 4.09 | 119.5 | 2.4 | 5.6 | 15.2 | 0.9 |
| 8.2 | 0.28 | 1.3 | 0.06 | 2.5 | 0.0 | 0.26 | 2.75 | 1.60 | 80.4 | 5.1 | 51.4 | 0.0 | 5.0 |
| 10.0 | 0.39 | 0.9 | 0.18 | 8.1 | 40.9 | 1.40 | 11.96 | 2.23 | 53.4 | 4.5 | 7.3 | 3.5 | 8.3 |
| 6.6 | 0.12 | 5.8 | 0.14 | 3.5 | 0.1 | 0.38 | 4.70 | 4.05 | 92.1 | 4.9 | 29.3 | 2.0 | 3.8 |
| 7.8 | 2.40 | 5.1 | 1.79 | 1.4 | 0.0 | -0.21 | -1.60 | 3.72 | 102.8 | 6.3 | 50.6 | 0.0 | 6.6 |
| 6.5 | 0.52 | 4.6 | 0.61 | 5.2 | 1.8 | 0.51 | 4.64 | 4.14 | 82.4 | 2.2 | 6.6 | 12.4 | 7.4 |
| 6.2 | 0.85 | 5.0 | 0.30 | 2.5 | 0.1 | 0.26 | 2.61 | 2.98 | 91.0 | 4.3 | 21.0 | 4.5 | 4.7 |
| 8.4 | 0.55 | 3.1 | 0.43 | 2.0 | 0.4 | 0.36 | 3.98 | 3.09 | 88.4 | 4.2 | 20.8 | 3.6 | 5.0 |
| 7.7 | 0.16 | 1.4 | 0.18 | 4.4 | 0.1 | 0.49 | 5.67 | 4.86 | 92.8 | 3.0 | 17.5 | 6.2 | 3.7 |
| 7.3 | 0.57 | 5.2 | 0.33 | 9.1 | 58.5 | 1.24 | 13.80 | 2.84 | 57.7 | 3.5 | 17.3 | 4.4 | 7.9 |
| 9.8 | 0.00 | 0.0 | 3.21 | 0.0 | 0.0 | -2.41 | -5.33 | 4.52 | 173.9 | 7.5 | 72.8 | 0.0 | 6.3 |
| 9.0 | 0.10 | 0.7 | 0.43 | 0.2 | 0.0 | -0.20 | -2.19 | 2.57 | 104.1 | 4.8 | 25.0 | 1.3 | 3.0 |
| 9.5 | 0.28 | 1.3 | 0.37 | 3.1 | 0.1 | 0.46 | 3.05 | 3.24 | 81.6 | 3.6 | 24.1 | 5.0 | 7.0 |
| 6.7 | 2.24 | 4.6 | 0.00 | 0.4 | 0.0 | -0.33 | -1.18 | 3.62 | 109.7 | 5.2 | 37.3 | 0.0 | 5.1 |
| 9.1 | 0.50 | 2.6 | 0.33 | 6.9 | 2.8 | 0.87 | 5.26 | 3.16 | 78.5 | 3.1 | 12.7 | 6.3 | 8.5 |
| 7.5 | 0.53 | 4.9 | 0.28 | 3.9 | 2.7 | 0.59 | 6.63 | 3.41 | 83.5 | 3.7 | 13.0 | 3.6 | 5.9 |
| 5.4 | 0.97 | 4.5 | 0.34 | 8.9 | 0.1 | 1.57 | 9.76 | 3.11 | 71.5 | 1.9 | 17.6 | 21.1 | 5.0 |
| 7.9 | 1.57 | 6.8 | 0.16 | 3.2 | 0.3 | 0.32 | 2.99 | 2.80 | 85.2 | 4.0 | 21.8 | 4.1 | 6.5 |
| 8.8 | 0.00 | 0.0 | 0.90 | 0.0 | 0.0 | -1.52 | -4.59 | 4.17 | 131.7 | 5.8 | 59.8 | 0.0 | 5.6 |
| 5.9 | 3.02 | 13.5 | 0.77 | 0.9 | 0.0 | -0.26 | -2.75 | 2.31 | 101.6 | 4.4 | 10.3 | 1.3 | 4.1 |
| 7.7 | 1.40 | 3.8 | 0.47 | 2.3 | 0.0 | 0.02 | 0.09 | 4.12 | 90.0 | 5.7 | 55.2 | 6.3 | 5.8 |
| 6.0 | 1.75 | 9.3 | -0.04 | 2.8 | 0.0 | 0.38 | 5.29 | 4.14 | 96.2 | 6.3 | 36.9 | 0.0 | 1.0 |

| Name | City | State | Rating | 2014 Rating | 2013 Rating | Total Assets ($Mil) | One Year Asset Growth | Commercial Loans | Consumer Loans | Mortgage Loans | Securities | Capitalization Index | Net Worth Ratio |
|------|------|-------|--------|-------------|-------------|---------------------|----------------------|------------------|----------------|----------------|-----------|---------------------|-----------------|
| DISTRICT 123 FCU | Oak Lawn | IL | C+ | C+ | C+ | 3.3 | -2.43 | 0.0 | 9.6 | 0.0 | 0.0 | 10.0 | 18.5 |
| DISTRICT 58 FCU | Chase | LA | C- | C- | C | 5.1 | -0.17 | 0.0 | 55.4 | 0.0 | 0.0 | 10.0 | 13.7 |
| DISTRICT 62 HIGHWAY FCU | Hammond | LA | C+ | C+ | B- | 4.7 | 6.24 | 0.0 | 46.8 | 3.1 | 0.0 | 10.0 | 17.4 |
| DISTRICT 7 HIGHWAY CU | Joplin | MO | B- | B- | C+ | 17.1 | 4.33 | 0.0 | 14.2 | 16.0 | 0.0 | 10.0 | 11.5 |
| DISTRICT 8 HIGHWAY EMPL CU | Springfield | MO | B- | B- | B- | 16.7 | 2.03 | 0.0 | 26.0 | 5.3 | 0.0 | 10.0 | 14.6 |
| DISTRICT OF COLUMBIA FIRE DEPT FCU | Washington | DC | C- | C- | C- | 6.9 | 3.20 | 0.0 | 43.8 | 0.0 | 0.0 | 10.0 | 16.8 |
| ▲ DISTRICT OF COLUMBIA TEACHERS FCU | Washington | DC | B- | C+ | C- | 44.6 | 2.93 | 0.0 | 16.0 | 12.6 | 41.6 | 10.0 | 12.1 |
| DISTRICT ONE HIGHWAY CU | Saint Joseph | MO | C+ | B- | B- | 25.3 | 4.10 | 0.0 | 19.9 | 0.0 | 0.0 | 10.0 | 13.6 |
| DIVERSIFIED CU | Minneapolis | MN | C+ | C | C- | 31.2 | -0.94 | 0.0 | 20.0 | 1.3 | 0.0 | 9.6 | 10.7 |
| DIVERSIFIED GENERAL FCU | Logansport | IN | C- | D+ | D+ | 8.0 | 8.12 | 0.0 | 52.4 | 0.0 | 0.0 | 8.8 | 10.2 |
| DIVERSIFIED MEMBERS CU | Detroit | MI | B- | B- | B+ | 425.2 | -4.38 | 7.0 | 8.1 | 10.8 | 64.9 | 10.0 | 18.7 |
| ▲ DIVISION #6 HIGHWAY CU | Chesterfield | MO | C- | D+ | D+ | 14.1 | 0.24 | 0.0 | 25.8 | 17.3 | 0.0 | 10.0 | 16.2 |
| ▼ DIVISION 10 HIGHWAY EMPL CU | Sikeston | MO | C | C+ | B- | 12.1 | 1.11 | 0.0 | 28.3 | 0.0 | 0.0 | 10.0 | 21.5 |
| ▼ DIVISION 694 MOTOR COACH EMPL FCU | San Antonio | TX | D+ | C- | C- | 2.9 | 4.67 | 0.0 | 45.5 | 0.0 | 0.0 | 10.0 | 15.6 |
| ▼ DIVISION 726 FCU | Staten Island | NY | C- | C- | C- | 10.0 | 5.14 | 1.4 | 69.6 | 0.0 | 0.0 | 10.0 | 14.6 |
| DIVISION 819 TRANSIT EMPL CU | Irvington | NJ | C- | C- | D- | 20.0 | -4.65 | 0.0 | 23.0 | 0.0 | 59.8 | 8.3 | 9.9 |
| DIXIE CRAFT EMPL CU | Goodwater | AL | C- | D+ | D+ | 2.5 | -15.93 | 0.0 | 34.4 | 2.7 | 0.0 | 10.0 | 14.4 |
| ▲ DIXIE LINE CU | Nashville | TN | C | C- | D+ | 8.9 | 15.87 | 0.0 | 72.0 | 0.0 | 0.0 | 10.0 | 18.7 |
| DIXIES FCU | Darlington | SC | B | B | B | 40.4 | -5.60 | 2.4 | 39.3 | 22.5 | 1.2 | 10.0 | 19.2 |
| DOCHES CU | Nacogdoches | TX | B- | B- | B- | 40.6 | -0.91 | 0.1 | 33.6 | 5.6 | 0.0 | 10.0 | 13.4 |
| DOCO CU | Albany | GA | B | B- | C+ | 216.8 | 3.94 | 7.7 | 41.9 | 16.4 | 7.2 | 10.0 | 12.2 |
| ▼ DOE RUN FCU | Brandenburg | KY | D+ | D+ | D+ | 9.1 | 2.22 | 0.0 | 53.7 | 9.8 | 0.0 | 9.3 | 10.5 |
| DOMINION CU | Richmond | VA | B- | B- | B | 269.3 | 3.46 | 0.0 | 25.3 | 14.6 | 52.7 | 10.0 | 11.3 |
| DOMINO FCU | Texarkana | TX | B | B | B | 57.1 | -0.39 | 0.0 | 35.3 | 25.9 | 0.0 | 10.0 | 14.0 |
| DOR WIC FCU | Salisbury | MD | C+ | C+ | C+ | 8.4 | 4.60 | 0.0 | 33.0 | 0.0 | 60.4 | 10.0 | 20.1 |
| DORT FCU | Flint | MI | A | A | A | 643.3 | 7.33 | 3.7 | 31.8 | 25.6 | 17.4 | 10.0 | 18.3 |
| ▲ DOUGLAS COUNTY CU | Superior | WI | C- | D+ | D+ | 3.6 | 9.28 | 0.0 | 39.3 | 0.4 | 0.0 | 10.0 | 14.7 |
| DOVER FCU | Dover | DE | B | B | B- | 421.8 | 3.91 | 4.3 | 41.5 | 9.2 | 20.5 | 9.1 | 10.4 |
| DOVER-PHILA FCU | Dover | OH | A | A | A | 399.7 | 7.82 | 0.4 | 19.9 | 20.6 | 19.1 | 10.0 | 14.5 |
| DOW BUCKS COUNTY FCU | Bristol | PA | B- | B- | B- | 15.2 | 1.13 | 0.5 | 23.0 | 26.1 | 0.0 | 10.0 | 15.7 |
| DOW CHEMICAL EMPL CU | Midland | MI | C | C+ | B | 1446.6 | 1.73 | 0.0 | 17.9 | 26.2 | 42.0 | 10.0 | 11.7 |
| ▲ DOW GREAT WESTERN CU | Antioch | CA | C+ | C | C | 40.8 | 5.04 | 0.0 | 11.7 | 33.4 | 0.0 | 9.2 | 10.5 |
| DOW JONES EMPL FCU | Princeton | NJ | C- | C- | C | 13.0 | -2.53 | 0.0 | 14.6 | 22.9 | 0.0 | 10.0 | 12.1 |
| DOW NORTHEAST EMPL FCU | Philadelphia | PA | D | D | D | 21.5 | -4.78 | 0.9 | 19.5 | 8.3 | 0.0 | 10.0 | 17.3 |
| DOWAGIAC AREA FCU | Dowagiac | MI | D | D | D- | 17.0 | -0.50 | 0.0 | 21.7 | 25.3 | 0.0 | 6.3 | 8.3 |
| DOWELL FCU | Tulsa | OK | B- | C+ | C+ | 34.0 | -0.30 | 0.0 | 56.2 | 2.5 | 0.0 | 10.0 | 11.1 |
| DOWN EAST CU | Baileyville | ME | C | C | C+ | 149.0 | 17.63 | 0.8 | 45.7 | 18.0 | 0.0 | 5.5 | 7.5 |
| DOWNEY FCU | Downey | CA | B- | B- | B- | 193.3 | 4.08 | 1.0 | 12.7 | 20.6 | 24.1 | 10.0 | 11.9 |
| DOWNRIVER COMMUNITY FCU | Ecorse | MI | C+ | C+ | D+ | 143.3 | 2.04 | 5.7 | 13.5 | 26.0 | 23.7 | 6.5 | 8.5 |
| DOY FCU | Youngstown | OH | B+ | B+ | B+ | 44.8 | -0.95 | 0.0 | 3.1 | 40.7 | 8.9 | 10.0 | 15.1 |
| DPUC CU | Chicago | IL | D+ | D | C- | 4.1 | -0.58 | 0.0 | 19.7 | 0.0 | 0.0 | 10.0 | 12.6 |
| ▲ DRESSER ALEXANDRIA FCU | Pineville | LA | C- | D+ | D+ | 6.0 | -4.34 | 0.0 | 33.8 | 0.0 | 0.0 | 10.0 | 21.2 |
| ▲ DU PONT EMPL CU | Fort Madison | IA | C | C- | C- | 3.3 | 3.73 | 0.0 | 64.1 | 0.0 | 24.5 | 10.0 | 18.2 |
| DUBOIS-PIKE FCU | Jasper | IN | C | C | C- | 26.9 | 5.85 | 0.3 | 16.3 | 27.4 | 1.3 | 6.2 | 8.2 |
| DUBUQUE POSTAL EMPL CU | Dubuque | IA | C- | C- | C- | 4.4 | -1.48 | 0.0 | 19.7 | 0.0 | 11.4 | 10.0 | 11.1 |
| DUCOTE FCU | Jacksonville | FL | D | D+ | C- | 3.1 | 1.51 | 0.0 | 17.9 | 0.0 | 0.0 | 10.0 | 29.1 |
| DUGOOD FCU | Beaumont | TX | B+ | A- | A- | 253.6 | 4.07 | 4.1 | 23.6 | 33.2 | 5.9 | 10.0 | 12.3 |
| DUGWAY FCU | Dugway | UT | C- | C | C- | 3.4 | -9.16 | 0.0 | 54.2 | 0.0 | 0.0 | 10.0 | 22.8 |
| DUKE UNIV FCU | Durham | NC | B- | B- | B- | 120.5 | 6.10 | 0.0 | 26.6 | 9.2 | 16.6 | 6.1 | 8.1 |
| DULUTH FIRE DEPT CU | Duluth | MN | C | C | C | 4.9 | 3.74 | 0.0 | 39.4 | 0.0 | 0.0 | 10.0 | 19.1 |
| DULUTH POLICE DEPT EMPL CU | Duluth | MN | C | C | C- | 9.9 | -0.40 | 0.0 | 23.1 | 0.0 | 0.0 | 9.6 | 10.7 |
| DULUTH TEACHERS CU | Duluth | MN | B- | B- | B- | 96.9 | 6.65 | 2.6 | 18.8 | 31.3 | 3.0 | 7.0 | 9.0 |
| DUNLOP EMPL FCU | Buffalo | NY | C- | C- | C- | 14.6 | -4.02 | 0.0 | 20.7 | 9.7 | 0.0 | 10.0 | 12.6 |
| DUPACO COMMUNITY CU | Dubuque | IA | A | A | A | 1291.8 | 3.92 | 18.9 | 23.7 | 22.7 | 28.8 | 10.0 | 14.8 |
| DUPAGE COUNTY EMPL CU | Wheaton | IL | D+ | D+ | C- | 15.5 | 9.57 | 0.0 | 38.1 | 0.0 | 0.0 | 7.1 | 9.1 |
| DUPAGE CU | Naperville | IL | B- | B- | C- | 300.6 | 4.31 | 0.0 | 40.0 | 5.0 | 4.6 | 5.6 | 7.6 |
| DUPONT COMMUNITY CU | Waynesboro | VA | B+ | B+ | B+ | 988.3 | 5.47 | 8.5 | 17.0 | 46.4 | 11.6 | 8.9 | 10.3 |
| DUQ LITE EMPL FCU | Beaver Falls | PA | E+ | E+ | E+ | 1.6 | -1.65 | 0.0 | 66.4 | 0.0 | 0.0 | 5.6 | 7.6 |
| DUTCH POINT CU | Wethersfield | CT | B- | B- | B | 242.3 | 6.36 | 0.2 | 21.1 | 17.3 | 28.1 | 9.7 | 11.0 |
| ▲ DUTRAC COMMUNITY CU | Dubuque | IA | B | B | B | 619.5 | 2.91 | 9.9 | 25.5 | 31.9 | 28.4 | 10.0 | 12.0 |

| Asset Quality Index | Non-Performing Loans as a % of Total Loans | as a % of Capital | Net Charge-Offs Avg Loans | Profitability Index | Net Income ($Mil) | Return on Assets | Return on Equity | Net Interest Spread | Overhead Efficiency Ratio | Liquidity Index | Liquidity Ratio | Hot Money Ratio | Stability Index |
|---|---|---|---|---|---|---|---|---|---|---|---|---|---|
| 10.0 | 0.93 | 0.5 | 0.36 | 3.4 | 0.0 | 0.39 | 2.21 | 1.94 | 78.3 | 5.5 | 28.2 | 0.0 | 7.4 |
| 3.1 | 3.26 | 18.3 | 0.17 | 8.1 | 0.1 | 2.03 | 15.63 | 5.19 | 45.9 | 4.3 | 24.5 | 0.0 | 7.0 |
| 8.2 | 1.00 | 3.2 | 0.38 | 8.1 | 0.1 | 1.30 | 7.46 | 3.81 | 61.0 | 5.4 | 36.5 | 0.0 | 5.0 |
| 10.0 | 0.07 | 0.2 | 0.00 | 4.2 | 0.1 | 0.56 | 4.92 | 2.23 | 70.8 | 4.8 | 15.8 | 0.0 | 6.0 |
| 9.6 | 0.09 | 0.2 | 0.33 | 5.4 | 0.1 | 1.02 | 7.06 | 3.05 | 55.8 | 5.7 | 30.3 | 0.0 | 5.6 |
| 6.8 | 3.20 | 7.8 | 0.83 | 3.9 | 0.0 | 0.49 | 2.93 | 11.12 | 78.4 | 7.1 | 62.4 | 0.0 | 5.8 |
| 3.7 | 6.55 | 21.3 | -0.37 | 6.5 | 0.4 | 1.10 | 9.43 | 3.80 | 98.4 | 4.6 | 16.3 | 0.0 | 5.7 |
| 9.6 | 1.19 | 2.3 | 0.00 | 3.5 | 0.1 | 0.44 | 3.23 | 1.81 | 65.7 | 4.9 | 17.4 | 0.0 | 6.8 |
| 4.0 | 2.09 | 12.2 | 1.37 | 6.4 | 0.2 | 0.90 | 8.83 | 4.61 | 65.7 | 4.0 | 18.2 | 0.4 | 4.9 |
| 7.6 | 0.47 | 2.7 | 0.27 | 8.1 | 0.1 | 1.34 | 13.58 | 4.25 | 82.8 | 4.4 | 12.0 | 0.0 | 4.3 |
| 10.0 | 0.94 | 1.1 | 0.78 | 3.0 | 1.1 | 0.33 | 1.86 | 2.50 | 82.2 | 4.8 | 12.5 | 0.0 | 7.1 |
| 9.9 | 0.28 | 0.9 | 0.15 | 1.5 | 0.0 | 0.03 | 0.18 | 2.38 | 99.6 | 4.8 | 22.5 | 1.0 | 6.5 |
| 9.9 | 0.12 | 0.2 | 0.66 | 1.9 | 0.0 | 0.19 | 0.88 | 2.67 | 86.4 | 5.2 | 22.8 | 0.0 | 6.6 |
| 6.4 | 1.84 | 5.1 | 0.63 | 0.5 | 0.0 | -1.41 | -8.33 | 7.57 | 120.9 | 6.5 | 58.7 | 0.0 | 5.8 |
| 5.6 | 1.52 | 6.9 | 0.70 | 4.2 | 0.0 | 0.36 | 2.49 | 5.68 | 80.9 | 4.5 | 24.1 | 0.0 | 3.7 |
| 7.7 | 2.04 | 4.4 | 1.85 | 3.5 | 0.0 | 0.06 | 0.61 | 3.60 | 69.9 | 6.0 | 27.2 | 0.0 | 4.3 |
| 7.0 | 2.89 | 7.4 | 2.98 | 1.6 | 0.0 | 0.26 | 1.86 | 3.24 | 74.7 | 5.5 | 61.9 | 0.0 | 5.7 |
| 7.0 | 0.65 | 2.6 | -0.15 | 8.6 | 0.1 | 1.42 | 7.20 | 5.27 | 72.6 | 2.5 | 25.3 | 27.1 | 4.3 |
| 7.3 | 1.05 | 6.1 | 0.57 | 4.5 | 0.2 | 0.48 | 2.57 | 5.78 | 84.4 | 4.2 | 35.3 | 9.4 | 6.8 |
| 8.3 | 0.89 | 3.4 | 0.15 | 4.5 | 0.2 | 0.71 | 5.54 | 3.46 | 84.6 | 4.1 | 30.7 | 7.8 | 6.2 |
| 4.3 | 1.57 | 18.4 | 0.93 | 7.6 | 1.7 | 1.04 | 8.70 | 5.26 | 75.2 | 3.9 | 21.5 | 9.4 | 7.8 |
| 4.4 | 1.10 | 11.0 | 2.01 | 3.2 | 0.0 | -0.36 | -3.21 | 6.79 | 80.4 | 4.8 | 31.8 | 1.3 | 3.0 |
| 9.9 | 0.46 | 1.7 | 0.32 | 3.9 | 1.2 | 0.60 | 5.34 | 2.24 | 74.5 | 4.0 | 4.5 | 3.8 | 7.3 |
| 6.5 | 1.15 | 8.5 | 0.23 | 5.0 | 0.3 | 0.73 | 5.30 | 4.19 | 82.2 | 3.5 | 31.4 | 10.5 | 6.9 |
| 9.5 | 1.00 | 3.3 | 0.28 | 6.2 | 0.1 | 1.01 | 5.01 | 2.51 | 61.0 | 4.5 | 7.1 | 0.0 | 5.0 |
| 7.7 | 1.22 | 4.7 | 0.42 | 9.6 | 7.4 | 1.54 | 8.60 | 4.18 | 69.7 | 4.2 | 15.8 | 3.9 | 9.5 |
| 9.5 | 0.00 | 0.0 | 0.08 | 1.4 | 0.0 | 0.08 | 0.51 | 3.71 | 99.0 | 4.3 | 21.9 | 0.0 | 6.3 |
| 7.0 | 1.27 | 8.2 | 0.69 | 4.2 | 1.6 | 0.52 | 5.02 | 3.78 | 74.4 | 4.2 | 25.8 | 5.4 | 6.3 |
| 8.8 | 1.42 | 4.4 | 0.06 | 6.8 | 3.3 | 1.11 | 8.05 | 2.56 | 63.2 | 5.2 | 33.8 | 2.2 | 9.1 |
| 8.0 | 1.78 | 6.2 | 0.00 | 4.7 | 0.1 | 0.68 | 4.40 | 2.53 | 69.9 | 4.0 | 4.6 | 0.0 | 7.9 |
| 10.0 | 0.16 | 0.7 | 0.06 | 2.4 | 2.9 | 0.26 | 2.27 | 1.40 | 84.8 | 4.1 | 19.0 | 3.3 | 7.8 |
| 10.0 | 0.01 | 0.1 | 0.05 | 3.3 | 0.2 | 0.57 | 5.43 | 3.08 | 86.6 | 4.0 | 18.5 | 4.3 | 5.0 |
| 8.2 | 0.78 | 2.7 | 0.36 | 1.3 | 0.0 | -0.11 | -0.94 | 2.44 | 101.2 | 4.8 | 30.0 | 5.1 | 5.0 |
| 9.4 | 1.88 | 3.9 | 0.61 | 0.0 | -0.1 | -0.74 | -4.32 | 2.97 | 113.0 | 4.8 | 59.5 | 9.3 | 5.5 |
| 5.7 | 2.05 | 15.0 | 0.13 | 2.5 | 0.0 | 0.18 | 2.19 | 2.76 | 90.3 | 4.6 | 30.4 | 0.0 | 2.3 |
| 8.6 | 0.21 | 1.1 | 0.18 | 4.3 | 0.2 | 0.60 | 5.58 | 2.64 | 80.2 | 3.0 | 30.1 | 16.5 | 5.6 |
| 2.7 | 1.88 | 21.9 | 0.34 | 5.7 | 1.0 | 0.95 | 12.20 | 4.26 | 77.2 | 1.6 | 7.5 | 22.3 | 4.6 |
| 9.1 | 0.72 | 2.5 | 0.19 | 3.4 | 0.6 | 0.41 | 3.52 | 2.39 | 82.7 | 3.9 | 24.6 | 9.6 | 7.1 |
| 8.7 | 0.84 | 4.5 | 0.32 | 3.6 | 0.5 | 0.41 | 5.06 | 3.08 | 85.9 | 5.0 | 27.5 | 3.1 | 4.3 |
| 7.1 | 0.89 | 7.4 | 0.04 | 7.1 | 0.4 | 1.05 | 7.14 | 2.19 | 51.0 | 4.7 | 32.7 | 0.0 | 7.0 |
| 8.3 | 3.11 | 4.8 | 0.00 | 0.9 | 0.0 | 0.03 | 0.26 | 3.46 | 100.0 | 6.6 | 57.0 | 0.0 | 6.0 |
| 7.5 | 2.39 | 5.3 | 0.44 | 1.7 | 0.0 | 0.04 | 0.21 | 4.37 | 94.8 | 5.8 | 37.5 | 0.0 | 6.3 |
| 8.8 | 0.00 | 0.0 | -0.06 | 4.1 | 0.0 | 0.66 | 3.57 | 2.97 | 75.4 | 4.7 | 25.0 | 0.0 | 7.2 |
| 8.3 | 0.37 | 2.6 | 0.05 | 3.4 | 0.1 | 0.31 | 3.76 | 2.78 | 88.1 | 3.6 | 16.1 | 8.3 | 4.5 |
| 8.2 | 0.00 | 0.0 | 0.00 | 3.8 | 0.0 | 0.57 | 5.30 | 1.91 | 68.4 | 5.3 | 18.4 | 0.0 | 3.7 |
| 7.8 | 6.81 | 5.0 | 9.45 | 0.0 | -0.1 | -3.37 | -9.82 | 5.59 | 126.9 | 7.8 | 84.1 | 0.0 | 5.1 |
| 9.6 | 0.26 | 1.3 | 0.22 | 5.3 | 1.5 | 0.78 | 6.45 | 3.28 | 80.5 | 4.2 | 26.3 | 8.1 | 8.1 |
| 6.1 | 2.70 | 7.6 | 0.73 | 3.3 | 0.0 | 0.27 | 1.23 | 7.83 | 94.5 | 5.2 | 57.0 | 13.7 | 6.4 |
| 8.9 | 0.27 | 1.9 | 0.64 | 4.1 | 0.5 | 0.51 | 6.40 | 4.11 | 86.1 | 6.4 | 40.1 | 2.5 | 4.5 |
| 9.7 | 0.00 | 0.0 | 0.00 | 2.9 | 0.0 | 0.33 | 1.73 | 2.51 | 86.8 | 4.7 | 45.4 | 6.9 | 7.4 |
| 8.7 | 0.00 | 0.0 | -0.04 | 3.4 | 0.0 | 0.37 | 3.43 | 1.75 | 77.1 | 5.0 | 11.5 | 0.0 | 5.8 |
| 8.2 | 0.30 | 2.3 | 0.06 | 5.7 | 0.7 | 0.91 | 10.32 | 3.20 | 75.7 | 3.8 | 20.3 | 1.8 | 4.7 |
| 8.5 | 0.35 | 1.0 | 0.66 | 1.4 | 0.0 | -0.07 | -0.58 | 2.46 | 87.0 | 6.2 | 51.1 | 0.0 | 5.4 |
| 7.1 | 1.01 | 4.7 | 0.39 | 9.8 | 16.6 | 1.72 | 11.63 | 3.62 | 59.1 | 3.4 | 5.4 | 7.5 | 10.0 |
| 9.9 | 0.02 | 0.1 | 0.14 | 1.8 | 0.0 | 0.10 | 1.14 | 1.99 | 96.0 | 5.1 | 26.1 | 0.0 | 4.1 |
| 7.0 | 0.60 | 7.3 | 0.36 | 6.4 | 2.2 | 0.95 | 13.53 | 4.40 | 84.0 | 4.8 | 19.4 | 0.7 | 4.9 |
| 8.8 | 0.36 | 3.4 | 0.23 | 5.0 | 5.8 | 0.79 | 8.42 | 3.04 | 77.4 | 3.4 | 8.5 | 4.8 | 7.2 |
| 1.4 | 3.99 | 33.6 | 0.63 | 1.1 | 0.0 | -0.08 | -1.14 | 3.08 | 100.0 | 4.9 | 31.2 | 0.0 | 1.0 |
| 9.0 | 0.77 | 3.3 | 0.36 | 4.0 | 0.9 | 0.52 | 4.66 | 3.05 | 82.3 | 4.6 | 16.9 | 3.5 | 6.9 |
| 7.1 | 0.92 | 6.1 | 0.19 | 4.0 | 2.5 | 0.54 | 4.73 | 2.53 | 81.8 | 3.4 | 23.3 | 9.5 | 8.5 |

| Name | City | State | Rating | 2014 Rating | 2013 Rating | Total Assets ($Mil) | One Year Asset Growth | Comm-ercial Loans | Cons-umer Loans | Mort-gage Loans | Secur-ities | Capital-ization Index | Net Worth Ratio |
|---|---|---|---|---|---|---|---|---|---|---|---|---|---|
| DVA FCU | Washington | DC | D+ | D | C- | 106.3 | 1.05 | 0.0 | 24.5 | 16.3 | 33.2 | 9.7 | 10.8 |
| DYNAMIC FCU | Celina | OH | A- | A- | A- | 31.6 | 14.55 | 0.6 | 35.1 | 2.6 | 22.3 | 10.0 | 16.4 |
| E E SOUTH TEXAS CU | Corpus Christi | TX | C- | C- | C- | 7.6 | -1.70 | 0.0 | 8.2 | 0.0 | 0.0 | 10.0 | 16.7 |
| E M O T FCU | Abilene | TX | B- | B- | B- | 10.7 | -3.06 | 0.0 | 24.0 | 0.0 | 0.0 | 10.0 | 24.5 |
| E-CENTRAL CU | Pasadena | CA | A | A | A | 160.8 | 0.26 | 6.1 | 17.4 | 35.2 | 10.5 | 10.0 | 17.3 |
| EAGLE CAN EMPL FCU | Wellsburg | WV | C- | C- | C | <1 | 5.50 | 0.0 | 23.1 | 0.0 | 0.0 | 10.0 | 17.3 |
| ▲ EAGLE COMMUNITY CU | Lake Forest | CA | C+ | C- | C | 220.1 | 0.54 | 4.4 | 27.3 | 18.5 | 30.9 | 6.1 | 8.3 |
| EAGLE CU | Lodi | CA | D- | D- | C- | 19.8 | -2.16 | 0.8 | 14.4 | 7.5 | 0.0 | 5.9 | 7.9 |
| EAGLE FCU | Atchison | KS | E+ | E+ | E+ | 1.8 | 14.81 | 0.0 | 45.7 | 0.0 | 0.0 | 5.2 | 7.2 |
| EAGLE LOUISIANA FCU | Baton Rouge | LA | C+ | C+ | C | 104.3 | -0.31 | 0.4 | 73.2 | 8.9 | 0.0 | 10.0 | 11.6 |
| ▼ EAGLE ONE FCU | Claymont | DE | B- | B | B | 62.3 | 1.51 | 2.4 | 35.6 | 17.2 | 9.8 | 9.5 | 10.7 |
| EARTHMOVER CU | Oswego | IL | A | A- | B | 232.2 | 3.57 | 1.3 | 30.0 | 6.3 | 16.9 | 10.0 | 16.7 |
| EAST ALABAMA COMMUNITY FCU | Opelika | AL | B- | B- | B- | 13.3 | 7.05 | 0.0 | 52.1 | 0.2 | 0.0 | 10.0 | 17.6 |
| ▲ EAST ALLEN FCU | New Haven | IN | C- | D+ | D+ | 12.9 | 1.89 | 0.0 | 15.1 | 5.8 | 60.4 | 7.2 | 9.1 |
| ▼ EAST BATON ROUGE TEACHERS FCU | Baton Rouge | LA | D | D+ | D | 3.2 | 1.60 | 0.0 | 64.4 | 1.2 | 0.0 | 10.0 | 18.5 |
| ▲ EAST CENTRAL MISSISSIPPI CU | Newton | MS | C | D+ | C- | 4.8 | 2.74 | 0.0 | 26.1 | 2.5 | 0.0 | 10.0 | 12.4 |
| EAST CHICAGO FIREMENS CU | East Chicago | IN | D+ | D+ | D+ | <1 | -4.86 | 0.0 | 9.2 | 0.0 | 0.0 | 10.0 | 16.8 |
| EAST COUNTY SCHOOLS FCU | El Cajon | CA | C+ | C+ | C+ | 98.6 | 4.07 | 9.9 | 11.5 | 30.5 | 33.3 | 6.7 | 8.7 |
| EAST END BAPTIST TABERNACLE FCU | Bridgeport | CT | D+ | D+ | D+ | <1 | -14.67 | 0.0 | 16.6 | 0.0 | 0.0 | 10.0 | 15.9 |
| EAST END FOOD COOPERATIVE FCU | Pittsburgh | PA | E+ | E+ | D- | <1 | 13.49 | 0.0 | 27.8 | 0.0 | 0.0 | 7.1 | 9.1 |
| EAST FELICIANA TEACHERS FCU | Clinton | LA | D- | D- | D | <1 | -9.80 | 0.0 | 73.9 | 0.0 | 0.0 | 10.0 | 13.0 |
| EAST HARTFORD FCU | East Hartford | CT | D | D | D+ | 9.9 | 1.71 | 0.0 | 39.3 | 0.0 | 0.0 | 10.0 | 11.8 |
| EAST HAVEN MUNICIPAL EMPL CU | East Haven | CT | D+ | C- | C- | 2.5 | 7.70 | 0.0 | 25.1 | 0.0 | 0.0 | 10.0 | 13.9 |
| EAST IDAHO CU | Idaho Falls | ID | C | C- | C | 257.7 | 3.18 | 0.0 | 39.8 | 11.6 | 21.5 | 8.4 | 9.9 |
| EAST OHIO GAS CLEVELAND OPERATING FC | Cleveland | OH | C- | D+ | C- | 1.6 | -7.37 | 0.0 | 45.6 | 0.0 | 0.0 | 10.0 | 23.4 |
| EAST OHIO GAS YOUNGSTOWN DIV EMPL F | Youngstown | OH | C | C | C | 3.7 | 0.00 | 0.0 | 45.5 | 0.0 | 14.8 | 10.0 | 20.8 |
| EAST ORANGE FIREMENS FCU | East Orange | NJ | C- | C- | C- | 7.8 | 1.20 | 0.0 | 56.2 | 0.0 | 0.0 | 10.0 | 21.3 |
| ▲ EAST ORANGE VETERANS HOSPITAL FCU | East Orange | NJ | C+ | C | C- | 13.9 | 1.27 | 0.0 | 34.9 | 0.0 | 0.0 | 10.0 | 11.3 |
| EAST RIVER FCU | Madison | SD | B- | B- | B- | 30.6 | 2.24 | 0.0 | 43.8 | 4.8 | 11.4 | 7.4 | 9.3 |
| EAST TEXAS PROFESSIONAL CU | Longview | TX | A+ | A+ | A+ | 549.8 | 2.86 | 1.3 | 31.7 | 12.6 | 18.7 | 10.0 | 17.9 |
| ▲ EAST TRAVERSE CATHOLIC FCU | Traverse City | MI | C- | D+ | D | 50.8 | 4.70 | 2.0 | 19.2 | 29.5 | 22.5 | 6.4 | 8.4 |
| EASTERN INDIANA FCU | New Castle | IN | D+ | C- | D+ | 23.7 | 4.92 | 0.0 | 22.1 | 5.5 | 0.0 | 6.4 | 8.4 |
| ▲ EASTERN KENTUCKY FCU | Prestonsburg | KY | C- | D | D+ | 3.9 | 3.80 | 0.0 | 68.3 | 0.0 | 0.0 | 10.0 | 23.1 |
| EASTERN MAINE MEDICAL CENTER FCU | Bangor | ME | C | C- | C- | 47.0 | 3.30 | 0.0 | 17.5 | 16.3 | 16.3 | 8.5 | 10.0 |
| EASTERN PANHANDLE FCU | Martinsburg | WV | D- | E+ | E- | 14.6 | 10.43 | 0.0 | 38.1 | 6.1 | 0.0 | 5.2 | 7.2 |
| EASTERN UTAH COMMUNITY FCU | Price | UT | B- | B | B | 115.4 | 11.10 | 7.2 | 28.4 | 19.1 | 1.6 | 6.9 | 8.9 |
| EASTEX CU | Evadale | TX | B | B | B | 67.5 | 2.54 | 0.0 | 45.8 | 0.6 | 1.5 | 10.0 | 11.4 |
| EASTMAN CU | Kingsport | TN | A | A | A | 3225.0 | 7.52 | 6.6 | 21.3 | 50.1 | 3.9 | 10.0 | 13.3 |
| EASTMILL FCU | East Millinocket | ME | B- | B- | B- | 60.3 | 1.76 | 0.5 | 11.1 | 6.4 | 8.2 | 10.0 | 18.9 |
| EASTPOINTE COMMUNITY CU | Eastpointe | MI | D- | D | D | 9.3 | 7.59 | 0.0 | 37.1 | 0.0 | 35.5 | 6.9 | 8.9 |
| EATON EMPL CU | Shenandoah | IA | C | C | C- | 2.8 | 11.12 | 0.0 | 69.0 | 0.0 | 0.0 | 10.0 | 21.4 |
| EATON EMPL CU | Spencer | IA | D- | D- | D | 3.0 | 9.18 | 0.0 | 54.2 | 0.0 | 0.0 | 7.3 | 9.2 |
| EATON EMPL CU | Eden Prairie | MN | C- | D+ | D+ | 2.9 | 2.27 | 1.3 | 66.6 | 0.0 | 0.0 | 9.3 | 10.5 |
| ▼ EATON EMPL FCU | Denver | CO | C- | C | C | <1 | 8.98 | 0.0 | 36.8 | 0.0 | 0.0 | 10.0 | 18.9 |
| EATON FAMILY CU INC | Euclid | OH | C+ | C+ | C+ | 57.5 | -0.04 | 4.4 | 28.6 | 23.9 | 20.7 | 9.4 | 10.7 |
| EBSCO FCU | Birmingham | AL | D | D+ | D+ | 12.2 | -2.55 | 0.0 | 27.3 | 19.9 | 0.0 | 6.7 | 8.7 |
| ECAI FCU | Philadelphia | PA | D- | D- | D | <1 | 3.41 | 0.0 | 9.9 | 0.0 | 0.0 | 10.0 | 11.0 |
| ECCO CU | Milton | FL | B- | B- | B- | 22.8 | 1.82 | 8.4 | 10.7 | 35.6 | 0.0 | 10.0 | 16.0 |
| ECO CU | Birmingham | AL | C | C- | C- | 129.1 | 3.87 | 0.4 | 27.1 | 13.5 | 43.5 | 8.8 | 10.6 |
| ▲ ECOLAB CU | Saint Paul | MN | C- | C- | C+ | 10.9 | 4.89 | 0.0 | 43.9 | 0.0 | 6.9 | 8.6 | 10.1 |
| ECU CU | Largo | FL | D+ | D+ | D+ | 36.1 | 2.00 | 0.0 | 25.1 | 7.5 | 55.0 | 10.0 | 14.6 |
| ECUSTA CU | Brevard | NC | D+ | D+ | D+ | 55.8 | 4.63 | 0.0 | 16.5 | 14.7 | 50.3 | 10.0 | 11.6 |
| ED-MED FCU | Ogdensburg | NY | C- | C- | C- | 23.5 | 4.25 | 0.0 | 26.4 | 0.0 | 47.1 | 6.9 | 8.9 |
| EDDY FCU | Carlsbad | NM | C | B- | B+ | 56.8 | -4.93 | 0.0 | 37.6 | 0.0 | 0.0 | 10.0 | 12.2 |
| EDDY PAPER EMPL CU | White Pigeon | MI | C- | C- | C- | <1 | 12.88 | 0.0 | 57.6 | 0.0 | 0.0 | 10.0 | 14.2 |
| EDDYVILLE COOPERATIVE CU | Eddyville | NE | C | C | C | 1.4 | 7.81 | 0.0 | 17.9 | 5.0 | 0.0 | 10.0 | 21.5 |
| EDGE FCU | Liverpool | NY | C+ | B- | B- | 42.4 | 5.77 | 1.4 | 15.0 | 9.0 | 2.4 | 10.0 | 11.3 |
| EDGE MOOR DUPONT EMPL FCU | Wilmington | DE | D | D | D | 2.2 | -5.91 | 0.0 | 63.6 | 0.0 | 0.0 | 10.0 | 19.0 |
| EDINBURG TEACHERS CU | Edinburg | TX | A- | A | A | 85.8 | 5.74 | 0.0 | 19.7 | 0.1 | 58.3 | 10.0 | 23.9 |
| ▼ EDISON CU | Kansas City | MO | D- | D | C | 28.5 | -0.70 | 0.0 | 15.2 | 12.3 | 9.0 | 8.9 | 10.3 |

| Asset Quality Index | Non-Performing Loans as a % of Total Loans | as a % of Capital | Net Charge-Offs Avg Loans | Profitability Index | Net Income ($Mil) | Return on Assets | Return on Equity | Net Interest Spread | Overhead Efficiency Ratio | Liquidity Index | Liquidity Ratio | Hot Money Ratio | Stability Index |
|---|---|---|---|---|---|---|---|---|---|---|---|---|---|
| 6.3 | 3.08 | 12.4 | 0.68 | 1.5 | 0.1 | 0.12 | 1.12 | 3.17 | 92.1 | 4.4 | 28.7 | 7.0 | 5.2 |
| 9.8 | 0.74 | 2.4 | 0.03 | 9.8 | 0.5 | 1.97 | 12.20 | 3.69 | 63.6 | 5.2 | 36.6 | 0.4 | 8.0 |
| 10.0 | 1.44 | 0.9 | 0.30 | 1.3 | 0.0 | -0.09 | -0.53 | 1.14 | 113.8 | 6.8 | 68.6 | 0.0 | 7.0 |
| 9.9 | 0.82 | 1.0 | 0.26 | 4.2 | 0.1 | 0.55 | 2.32 | 2.07 | 66.5 | 4.8 | 28.4 | 0.0 | 7.0 |
| 7.8 | 1.24 | 4.5 | 0.41 | 7.3 | 1.1 | 0.92 | 5.40 | 3.73 | 81.5 | 4.7 | 39.9 | 12.3 | 8.5 |
| 7.4 | 3.66 | 4.6 | 0.00 | 2.9 | 0.0 | 0.39 | 2.20 | 4.11 | 88.9 | 6.6 | 49.6 | 0.0 | 5.9 |
| 9.4 | 0.52 | 3.2 | 0.37 | 4.2 | 1.1 | 0.69 | 8.89 | 3.45 | 85.0 | 4.5 | 21.1 | 5.4 | 4.5 |
| 8.2 | 0.14 | 0.4 | 0.46 | 0.0 | -0.1 | -0.83 | -10.13 | 3.80 | 145.5 | 5.0 | 26.4 | 0.0 | 3.3 |
| 3.3 | 2.29 | 15.9 | 0.00 | 1.6 | 0.0 | -0.08 | -1.04 | 5.43 | 92.9 | 5.6 | 48.9 | 0.0 | 1.0 |
| 7.2 | 0.51 | 3.6 | 0.44 | 2.7 | 0.2 | 0.20 | 1.74 | 4.54 | 91.2 | 2.2 | 7.8 | 12.7 | 6.7 |
| 5.5 | 2.57 | 13.4 | 1.18 | 3.8 | 0.1 | 0.11 | 0.99 | 5.33 | 89.1 | 3.8 | 15.5 | 10.7 | 5.4 |
| 7.8 | 1.21 | 5.5 | 0.50 | 8.2 | 2.1 | 1.19 | 7.30 | 3.51 | 68.8 | 4.0 | 19.7 | 7.5 | 8.2 |
| 8.6 | 0.40 | 1.2 | 0.10 | 5.7 | 0.1 | 0.85 | 4.93 | 4.74 | 88.7 | 5.2 | 26.1 | 0.0 | 5.7 |
| 9.2 | 0.37 | 0.9 | 0.84 | 2.2 | 0.0 | 0.13 | 1.48 | 2.00 | 92.9 | 5.6 | 29.6 | 0.0 | 4.3 |
| 5.2 | 3.07 | 8.9 | 3.84 | 0.0 | -0.1 | -4.33 | -21.18 | 10.14 | 93.7 | 5.5 | 37.2 | 3.5 | 5.1 |
| 9.8 | 0.06 | 0.2 | 0.33 | 4.4 | 0.0 | 0.90 | 7.49 | 4.78 | 89.6 | 5.8 | 34.7 | 0.0 | 4.3 |
| 10.0 | 0.86 | 0.6 | 0.00 | 0.7 | 0.0 | -0.14 | -0.83 | 2.82 | 100.0 | 5.2 | 21.5 | 0.0 | 5.2 |
| 8.1 | 0.49 | 2.7 | 0.05 | 2.9 | 0.2 | 0.23 | 2.58 | 2.48 | 89.3 | 4.2 | 21.3 | 6.2 | 4.2 |
| 1.6 | 37.93 | 45.8 | 0.00 | 1.8 | 0.0 | 0.00 | 0.00 | 3.21 | 100.0 | 8.1 | 99.2 | 0.0 | 5.8 |
| 3.5 | 8.59 | 23.7 | -0.88 | 2.4 | 0.0 | 0.23 | 2.56 | 3.30 | 90.9 | 5.3 | 11.2 | 0.0 | 1.7 |
| 0.2 | 12.20 | 39.7 | -3.70 | 0.5 | 0.0 | -5.20 | -39.64 | 10.30 | 131.8 | 5.3 | 39.2 | 0.0 | 4.7 |
| 9.9 | 0.00 | 0.0 | 0.44 | 0.0 | -0.1 | -1.18 | -9.48 | 3.32 | 130.0 | 4.5 | 18.4 | 0.0 | 5.7 |
| 8.5 | 1.45 | 2.6 | 2.51 | 0.5 | 0.0 | -0.39 | -2.71 | 3.12 | 93.8 | 6.0 | 31.4 | 0.0 | 6.4 |
| 9.3 | 0.36 | 2.6 | 0.54 | 2.9 | 0.6 | 0.32 | 3.28 | 3.18 | 86.8 | 4.5 | 22.6 | 5.8 | 5.5 |
| 8.7 | 0.85 | 1.6 | 0.00 | 1.6 | 0.0 | 0.16 | 0.73 | 3.71 | 91.4 | 5.3 | 20.9 | 0.0 | 4.7 |
| 8.0 | 0.59 | 1.3 | 0.00 | 6.0 | 0.0 | 0.99 | 4.83 | 2.81 | 60.0 | 5.7 | 43.3 | 0.0 | 5.0 |
| 4.6 | 4.62 | 10.9 | -0.16 | 7.7 | 0.1 | 1.22 | 5.70 | 4.51 | 70.6 | 4.6 | 34.2 | 0.0 | 4.3 |
| 8.6 | 1.42 | 4.6 | 0.38 | 3.5 | 0.1 | 0.50 | 4.61 | 4.43 | 76.1 | 6.1 | 36.8 | 0.0 | 5.5 |
| 8.7 | 0.24 | 1.7 | 0.19 | 7.8 | 0.3 | 1.13 | 12.38 | 3.87 | 75.6 | 3.6 | 7.7 | 4.0 | 4.5 |
| 9.6 | 0.47 | 1.6 | 0.16 | 9.7 | 11.4 | 2.77 | 16.17 | 3.26 | 51.5 | 4.0 | 22.6 | 7.0 | 10.0 |
| 7.2 | 0.20 | 1.5 | 0.05 | 2.6 | 0.1 | 0.36 | 4.19 | 3.85 | 91.3 | 3.7 | 8.9 | 5.8 | 3.4 |
| 7.8 | 1.27 | 5.6 | 0.22 | 3.0 | 0.0 | 0.23 | 2.70 | 2.51 | 93.9 | 5.5 | 32.1 | 1.3 | 3.6 |
| 5.7 | 2.49 | 6.7 | 0.06 | 6.0 | 0.0 | 1.51 | 6.64 | 4.57 | 108.3 | 4.5 | 25.1 | 0.0 | 3.7 |
| 10.0 | 0.14 | 0.8 | -0.02 | 2.8 | 0.1 | 0.30 | 3.09 | 3.08 | 90.9 | 5.6 | 38.1 | 2.3 | 5.1 |
| 5.7 | 1.07 | 10.9 | 0.19 | 4.0 | 0.1 | 0.64 | 9.16 | 3.63 | 87.0 | 4.6 | 24.5 | 0.0 | 1.8 |
| 6.9 | 0.85 | 7.3 | 0.31 | 3.9 | 0.4 | 0.45 | 4.92 | 3.32 | 85.9 | 3.6 | 16.1 | 6.1 | 5.6 |
| 7.7 | 0.20 | 1.4 | 0.20 | 6.3 | 0.5 | 0.99 | 9.15 | 3.71 | 79.5 | 3.4 | 13.6 | 5.8 | 5.8 |
| 9.6 | 0.16 | 1.2 | 0.19 | 9.7 | 38.0 | 1.60 | 12.44 | 3.74 | 55.2 | 2.9 | 22.1 | 18.4 | 9.8 |
| 10.0 | 0.07 | 0.1 | 0.17 | 3.2 | 0.2 | 0.37 | 1.96 | 2.10 | 84.2 | 5.4 | 47.1 | 2.3 | 7.3 |
| 7.1 | 1.31 | 6.0 | 0.21 | 2.1 | 0.0 | 0.06 | 0.64 | 4.12 | 98.6 | 5.7 | 28.8 | 0.0 | 1.7 |
| 5.9 | 1.41 | 4.4 | 1.22 | 10.0 | 0.1 | 3.69 | 17.92 | 7.82 | 43.6 | 3.0 | 32.3 | 28.2 | 5.0 |
| 0.0 | 10.24 | 61.7 | -0.13 | 4.4 | 0.0 | 0.65 | 6.91 | 5.56 | 78.7 | 5.5 | 32.0 | 0.0 | 5.7 |
| 5.7 | 1.08 | 6.9 | 0.06 | 7.4 | 0.0 | 1.26 | 12.16 | 6.14 | 79.5 | 4.4 | 26.4 | 7.7 | 3.7 |
| 3.7 | 12.20 | 22.7 | 0.00 | 3.9 | 0.0 | 0.30 | 1.59 | 3.13 | 90.0 | 6.7 | 77.0 | 0.0 | 7.9 |
| 4.4 | 2.58 | 14.7 | 1.50 | 4.2 | 0.1 | 0.31 | 2.97 | 4.73 | 76.2 | 3.0 | 10.0 | 11.1 | 5.0 |
| 9.8 | 0.00 | 0.0 | 1.01 | 0.7 | 0.0 | -0.32 | -3.68 | 2.61 | 93.9 | 6.6 | 53.3 | 0.0 | 4.5 |
| 0.2 | 30.67 | 149.0 | 0.00 | 5.6 | 0.0 | 0.78 | 7.41 | 2.08 | 58.3 | 5.5 | 39.2 | 0.0 | 5.2 |
| 9.7 | 0.00 | 0.0 | 0.34 | 5.0 | 0.1 | 0.83 | 5.17 | 2.74 | 64.3 | 4.8 | 17.0 | 0.0 | 7.6 |
| 7.8 | 1.44 | 6.8 | 0.69 | 2.9 | 0.4 | 0.39 | 4.31 | 3.15 | 84.2 | 4.4 | 10.6 | 1.5 | 4.8 |
| 8.0 | 0.02 | 2.0 | 0.59 | 2.0 | 0.0 | 0.19 | 1.82 | 3.65 | 93.2 | 5.9 | 44.5 | 1.2 | 3.2 |
| 7.4 | 2.81 | 6.9 | 0.44 | 0.5 | -0.1 | -0.26 | -1.79 | 3.03 | 107.4 | 5.9 | 31.9 | 0.0 | 5.8 |
| 9.0 | 0.20 | 0.6 | 0.39 | 1.2 | 0.0 | 0.08 | 0.66 | 2.87 | 94.1 | 5.1 | 15.5 | 0.6 | 5.6 |
| 6.9 | 1.02 | 4.2 | 0.11 | 5.2 | 0.1 | 0.83 | 9.50 | 2.10 | 61.2 | 3.6 | 21.1 | 12.4 | 3.7 |
| 8.7 | 0.47 | 1.6 | 2.86 | 2.5 | 0.0 | -0.01 | -0.08 | 4.67 | 75.5 | 7.0 | 60.5 | 1.6 | 6.6 |
| 5.1 | 3.19 | 12.5 | 1.66 | 4.8 | 0.0 | 0.78 | 5.39 | 7.90 | 84.0 | 6.4 | 47.2 | 0.0 | 3.7 |
| 7.8 | 1.34 | 4.0 | 0.00 | 4.8 | 0.0 | 0.53 | 2.64 | 7.58 | 88.1 | 5.7 | 40.8 | 2.3 | 4.3 |
| 9.3 | 0.94 | 3.1 | 0.41 | 2.3 | 0.0 | 0.12 | 1.06 | 3.34 | 93.1 | 5.5 | 27.5 | 0.0 | 5.8 |
| 4.9 | 2.78 | 9.3 | 0.00 | 1.0 | 0.0 | 0.06 | 0.33 | 4.29 | 100.0 | 3.7 | 15.2 | 8.9 | 4.7 |
| 9.8 | 2.24 | 2.2 | 1.78 | 4.9 | 0.4 | 0.67 | 2.79 | 3.65 | 76.7 | 5.8 | 21.6 | 1.2 | 6.9 |
| 9.3 | 0.43 | 1.9 | 0.18 | 0.2 | -0.1 | -0.61 | -5.89 | 2.67 | 113.4 | 4.4 | 16.6 | 1.0 | 4.5 |

| Name | City | State | Rating | 2014 Rating | 2013 Rating | Total Assets ($Mil) | One Year Asset Growth | Asset Mix (As a % of Total Assets) | | | | Capital-ization Index | Net Worth Ratio |
|---|---|---|---|---|---|---|---|---|---|---|---|---|---|
| | | | | | | | | Comm-ercial Loans | Cons-umer Loans | Mort-gage Loans | Secur-ities | | |
| EDISON CU | Springfield | OH | C- | C- | C- | 4.6 | -2.26 | 0.0 | 54.2 | 0.0 | 10.3 | 10.0 | 14.5 |
| ▲ EDISON FINANCIAL CU INC | Austintown | OH | C | D | D | 37.4 | -6.19 | 0.0 | 53.9 | 9.5 | 24.3 | 10.0 | 14.0 |
| EDISTO FCU | Orangeburg | SC | C+ | C+ | C+ | 24.9 | 0.02 | 0.0 | 23.2 | 13.5 | 0.0 | 10.0 | 12.9 |
| EDUCATION ASSNS FCU | Washington | DC | E+ | E+ | E+ | 2.7 | -0.75 | 0.0 | 80.5 | 0.0 | 0.0 | 6.1 | 8.1 |
| EDUCATION CU | Amarillo | TX | A | A | A | 236.3 | 7.27 | 0.0 | 47.5 | 19.6 | 3.7 | 10.0 | 12.9 |
| EDUCATION FIRST CU | Ogden | UT | C | C | C- | 28.0 | -1.45 | 2.7 | 40.3 | 23.2 | 0.0 | 7.5 | 9.3 |
| EDUCATION FIRST CU INC | Westerville | OH | D | D- | D+ | 87.9 | -0.11 | 0.2 | 29.5 | 23.6 | 0.0 | 8.3 | 9.9 |
| EDUCATION FIRST FCU | Beaumont | TX | A- | B+ | B- | 338.2 | 5.28 | 1.6 | 32.6 | 14.0 | 19.9 | 10.0 | 11.7 |
| EDUCATION PERSONNEL FCU | Danville | IL | B- | B | B | 46.4 | 2.04 | 0.4 | 14.2 | 10.1 | 1.1 | 10.0 | 12.6 |
| EDUCATION PLUS CU | Monroe | MI | A- | A- | A | 99.8 | 6.94 | 0.5 | 25.2 | 5.4 | 35.5 | 10.0 | 14.6 |
| ▲ EDUCATIONAL & GOVERNMENTAL EMPL FC | Hartsdale | NY | C- | D+ | D+ | 50.0 | 5.06 | 0.0 | 22.4 | 3.9 | 15.7 | 10.0 | 11.2 |
| EDUCATIONAL COMMUNITY ALLIANCE CU | Toledo | OH | D+ | C- | D+ | 43.0 | 1.72 | 0.0 | 25.5 | 4.5 | 27.1 | 9.4 | 10.6 |
| EDUCATIONAL COMMUNITY CU | Kalamazoo | MI | C+ | B- | B- | 419.2 | 3.40 | 3.7 | 22.2 | 48.7 | 11.6 | 7.8 | 9.5 |
| ▲ EDUCATIONAL COMMUNITY CU | Springfield | MO | C- | D+ | D | 56.8 | 1.93 | 0.0 | 26.3 | 11.4 | 22.8 | 6.4 | 8.4 |
| EDUCATIONAL CU | Topeka | KS | B | B | B- | 198.4 | 4.61 | 1.1 | 48.5 | 13.7 | 22.2 | 7.1 | 9.1 |
| EDUCATIONAL EMPL CU | Fresno | CA | A | A | A | 2451.6 | 9.49 | 0.2 | 25.8 | 12.1 | 46.3 | 10.0 | 12.6 |
| ▲ EDUCATIONAL SYSTEMS FCU | Greenbelt | MD | B+ | B- | C+ | 788.6 | 8.06 | 0.0 | 35.0 | 20.1 | 24.4 | 9.0 | 10.3 |
| EDUCATORS CU | Waco | TX | A | A | A | 375.6 | 4.32 | 0.0 | 21.7 | 8.8 | 40.4 | 10.0 | 15.6 |
| EDUCATORS CU | Racine | WI | A- | B+ | B+ | 1563.3 | 3.83 | 0.9 | 17.2 | 44.5 | 7.4 | 10.0 | 11.5 |
| ▼ EDWARDS FCU | Edwards AFB | CA | C+ | B- | B- | 173.3 | 3.58 | 8.5 | 18.0 | 18.6 | 40.9 | 5.9 | 7.9 |
| EECU | Fort Worth | TX | A | A | A- | 1777.2 | 8.98 | 8.3 | 54.5 | 12.4 | 5.6 | 10.0 | 11.7 |
| ▲ EFCU FINANCIAL FCU | Baton Rouge | LA | C+ | C | C | 320.7 | 5.75 | 2.7 | 55.4 | 19.6 | 7.2 | 8.6 | 10.1 |
| ▲ EFFINGHAM HIGHWAY CU | Effingham | IL | D+ | D | D | 4.8 | 3.29 | 0.0 | 64.1 | 0.0 | 0.0 | 9.2 | 10.5 |
| EGLIN FCU | Fort Walton Beach | FL | B- | B- | B | 1639.2 | 3.99 | 0.0 | 18.8 | 17.2 | 34.4 | 10.0 | 11.2 |
| ▲ EIGHT FCU | Rossford | OH | C | C- | C | 11.1 | 4.17 | 0.0 | 39.2 | 0.0 | 28.5 | 10.0 | 16.9 |
| ▲ EL CAJON FCU | El Cajon | CA | C- | D+ | D+ | 16.5 | 35.22 | 0.0 | 24.2 | 6.1 | 0.0 | 7.3 | 9.2 |
| EL MONTE COMMUNITY CU | El Monte | CA | D+ | D+ | D+ | 24.3 | 4.37 | 0.0 | 20.1 | 10.8 | 3.0 | 7.1 | 9.1 |
| EL PASO AREA TEACHERS FCU | El Paso | TX | B | B+ | A- | 587.4 | 17.24 | 0.7 | 49.3 | 3.2 | 21.9 | 10.0 | 12.0 |
| EL RENO RIL CU | El Reno | OK | C | C- | D+ | 44.6 | -0.23 | 1.0 | 14.8 | 7.3 | 14.3 | 6.1 | 8.1 |
| ELCA FCU | Chicago | IL | D | U | U | <1 | NA | 0.0 | 0.0 | 0.0 | 0.0 | 10.0 | 95.6 |
| ELCO FCU | Elberton | GA | C | C- | C- | 2.9 | 1.34 | 0.0 | 59.0 | 0.0 | 0.0 | 10.0 | 17.4 |
| ▼ ELECTCHESTER FCU | Flushing | NY | D | D+ | C | <1 | -9.16 | 0.0 | 55.4 | 0.0 | 0.0 | 10.0 | 32.5 |
| ELECTEL COOPERATIVE FCU | Raleigh | NC | B | B- | B- | 41.8 | -0.38 | 0.0 | 60.3 | 0.0 | 0.0 | 10.0 | 11.4 |
| ▲ ELECTRIC COOPERATIVES FCU | Little Rock | AR | D+ | D+ | C | 11.8 | -1.93 | 0.0 | 59.8 | 0.0 | 0.0 | 7.7 | 9.5 |
| ELECTRIC ENERGY INC EMPL CU | Metropolis | IL | D+ | D+ | C- | 2.0 | -6.12 | 0.0 | 55.0 | 0.0 | 0.0 | 10.0 | 18.8 |
| ELECTRIC MACHINERY EMPL CU | Minneapolis | MN | D+ | D+ | D+ | 9.0 | 2.80 | 0.0 | 45.8 | 5.4 | 13.0 | 10.0 | 21.1 |
| ELECTRIC SERVICE CU | Nashville | TN | C+ | C+ | C+ | 62.6 | 4.03 | 0.1 | 41.5 | 5.0 | 10.0 | 10.0 | 13.6 |
| ELECTRIC UTILITIES CU | Big Spring | TX | C- | C | D+ | 6.5 | 0.39 | 0.0 | 33.4 | 0.0 | 0.0 | 10.0 | 12.7 |
| ▲ ELECTRICAL FCU | Arvada | CO | C | C- | C- | 33.9 | 6.54 | 2.0 | 32.1 | 16.0 | 18.1 | 6.6 | 8.6 |
| ELECTRICAL INSPECTORS FCU | Bensalem | PA | D | D | C- | <1 | 21.82 | 0.0 | 22.4 | 0.0 | 0.0 | 10.0 | 13.4 |
| ELECTRICAL WORKERS CU | Collinsville | IL | D- | D- | D | 2.6 | -2.08 | 2.2 | 32.9 | 0.0 | 0.0 | 6.2 | 8.2 |
| ELECTRICAL WORKERS LOCAL 130 FCU | Metairie | LA | D | D- | D- | 5.3 | -4.61 | 0.0 | 29.4 | 7.4 | 0.1 | 8.8 | 10.3 |
| ELECTRICAL WORKERS LOCAL 58 CU | Detroit | MI | C | C- | C- | 11.8 | -10.73 | 0.0 | 35.1 | 0.0 | 37.1 | 10.0 | 12.9 |
| ELECTRICAL WORKERS NO 22 FCU | Omaha | NE | D+ | D | D+ | 9.9 | -0.93 | 0.0 | 31.9 | 0.0 | 9.1 | 7.8 | 9.6 |
| ELECTRICAL WORKERS NO 558 FCU | Sheffield | AL | B- | B- | B- | 22.3 | 4.72 | 0.0 | 45.3 | 3.0 | 0.0 | 10.0 | 20.4 |
| ELECTRICIANS LOCAL 349 CU | Miami | FL | D | D | C- | 4.3 | 3.68 | 0.0 | 25.5 | 0.9 | 0.0 | 10.0 | 19.1 |
| ▲ ELECTRO SAVINGS CU | Saint Louis | MO | B | B- | B- | 146.1 | -0.45 | 1.5 | 61.9 | 2.2 | 6.8 | 9.4 | 10.6 |
| ELECTROGAS CU | Alton | IL | D | D | C- | 1.1 | -12.23 | 0.0 | 38.4 | 0.0 | 50.1 | 10.0 | 33.8 |
| ELECTRUS FCU | Brooklyn Center | MN | C | C | C | 54.1 | 4.41 | 1.4 | 22.5 | 4.8 | 19.8 | 10.0 | 18.2 |
| ▲ ELEKTRA FCU | New York | NY | B- | C+ | C+ | 36.6 | 6.71 | 0.0 | 8.6 | 0.0 | 4.1 | 10.0 | 15.5 |
| ELEMENT FCU | Charleston | WV | B- | B- | B- | 30.5 | 9.26 | 0.0 | 80.9 | 0.0 | 0.0 | 10.0 | 11.3 |
| ELEMENTS FINANCIAL FCU | Indianapolis | IN | A- | A- | B+ | 1115.5 | 4.74 | 1.2 | 25.5 | 35.1 | 10.4 | 8.6 | 10.1 |
| ELEVATIONS CU | Boulder | CO | B+ | B+ | B+ | 1563.6 | 10.40 | 3.7 | 13.3 | 38.3 | 21.3 | 7.8 | 9.5 |
| ELEVATOR CU | Olive Branch | MS | B- | B- | B- | 13.2 | 6.20 | 0.0 | 23.2 | 0.0 | 0.0 | 10.0 | 15.5 |
| ELGA CU | Burton | MI | B+ | B- | C+ | 414.3 | 9.09 | 5.9 | 44.8 | 30.6 | 2.3 | 10.0 | 12.5 |
| ▲ ELGIN MENTAL HEALTH CENTER CU | Elgin | IL | D+ | D+ | C- | 6.1 | -13.07 | 0.0 | 28.5 | 0.0 | 7.5 | 10.0 | 12.2 |
| ELITE COMMUNITY CU | Bourbonnais | IL | C | C | C | 13.6 | 1.41 | 0.0 | 56.4 | 4.3 | 1.4 | 10.0 | 14.2 |
| ▲ ELIZABETH (NJ) FIREMENS FCU | Elizabeth | NJ | D- | E+ | E+ | 8.8 | 4.44 | 0.0 | 18.8 | 0.6 | 0.0 | 5.9 | 7.9 |
| ▼ ELIZABETH POLICE DEPT EMPL FCU | Elizabeth | NJ | D+ | C- | C | 2.9 | -10.92 | 0.0 | 29.2 | 0.0 | 0.0 | 10.0 | 34.3 |
| ELIZABETH POSTAL EMPL CU | Elizabeth | NJ | C | C- | D | <1 | 1.55 | 0.0 | 32.6 | 0.0 | 0.0 | 10.0 | 25.2 |

| Asset Quality Index | Non-Performing Loans as a % of Total Loans | as a % of Capital | Net Charge-Offs Avg Loans | Profitability Index | Net Income ($Mil) | Return on Assets | Return on Equity | Net Interest Spread | Overhead Efficiency Ratio | Liquidity Index | Liquidity Ratio | Hot Money Ratio | Stability Index |
|---|---|---|---|---|---|---|---|---|---|---|---|---|---|
| 7.4 | 0.36 | 1.4 | 0.38 | 3.8 | 0.0 | 0.53 | 3.83 | 4.15 | 85.9 | 3.5 | 39.9 | 15.9 | 3.7 |
| 5.8 | 1.64 | 7.3 | 0.14 | 2.8 | 0.2 | 0.52 | 3.73 | 3.60 | 87.5 | 3.8 | 12.6 | 1.9 | 5.1 |
| 5.8 | 5.22 | 15.0 | 0.71 | 4.8 | 0.2 | 0.78 | 6.17 | 4.07 | 89.5 | 4.3 | 28.4 | 18.0 | 6.1 |
| 3.3 | 1.81 | 16.7 | 0.00 | 3.8 | 0.0 | 0.71 | 8.85 | 5.49 | 86.1 | 4.1 | 13.4 | 0.0 | 1.0 |
| 6.1 | 1.13 | 6.1 | 1.24 | 6.4 | 0.9 | 0.52 | 4.03 | 5.70 | 75.3 | 2.6 | 15.2 | 14.4 | 9.0 |
| 6.6 | 0.75 | 5.8 | 0.02 | 4.4 | 0.1 | 0.57 | 6.30 | 3.75 | 84.0 | 3.4 | 26.0 | 14.7 | 4.3 |
| 5.4 | 1.26 | 11.2 | 0.67 | 1.1 | 0.0 | 0.03 | 0.41 | 4.30 | 93.4 | 3.7 | 16.1 | 3.7 | 3.3 |
| 6.9 | 1.35 | 7.7 | 0.78 | 5.1 | 1.7 | 0.69 | 6.77 | 3.70 | 81.8 | 3.9 | 21.9 | 6.6 | 6.5 |
| 10.0 | 0.76 | 1.7 | 0.41 | 3.2 | 0.1 | 0.33 | 2.74 | 2.07 | 82.9 | 4.7 | 11.5 | 0.0 | 6.2 |
| 7.5 | 1.12 | 5.2 | 0.59 | 7.8 | 0.9 | 1.19 | 8.28 | 3.22 | 62.1 | 4.1 | 14.8 | 5.2 | 7.1 |
| 9.8 | 0.93 | 2.2 | 0.54 | 2.0 | 0.1 | 0.30 | 2.73 | 2.89 | 89.1 | 5.5 | 28.6 | 1.5 | 4.5 |
| 7.9 | 0.40 | 1.8 | 0.58 | 1.1 | -0.1 | -0.15 | -1.37 | 4.04 | 95.2 | 4.7 | 19.7 | 2.3 | 4.3 |
| 8.9 | 0.29 | 2.2 | 0.26 | 3.5 | 1.1 | 0.36 | 3.80 | 3.60 | 89.6 | 3.6 | 8.6 | 1.0 | 6.1 |
| 7.1 | 0.60 | 3.8 | 0.46 | 2.0 | 0.1 | 0.17 | 2.03 | 3.01 | 91.1 | 4.6 | 10.1 | 2.7 | 3.8 |
| 7.3 | 0.46 | 4.1 | 0.29 | 5.9 | 1.4 | 0.94 | 10.49 | 3.49 | 75.6 | 3.4 | 14.4 | 4.3 | 6.1 |
| 10.0 | 0.47 | 1.7 | 0.45 | 8.2 | 19.8 | 1.11 | 9.04 | 2.94 | 69.7 | 4.3 | 15.5 | 11.7 | 8.9 |
| 7.5 | 0.88 | 5.2 | 0.65 | 5.4 | 3.6 | 0.61 | 6.21 | 3.19 | 80.7 | 4.1 | 25.2 | 3.4 | 6.9 |
| 10.0 | 0.49 | 1.1 | 0.10 | 6.0 | 2.4 | 0.87 | 5.62 | 2.54 | 65.2 | 5.5 | 30.5 | 9.5 | 9.5 |
| 6.9 | 1.10 | 7.3 | 0.58 | 5.8 | 10.7 | 0.92 | 8.13 | 3.31 | 72.7 | 3.3 | 9.8 | 5.0 | 7.6 |
| 8.9 | 0.52 | 3.3 | 0.73 | 3.0 | 0.3 | 0.23 | 2.92 | 3.12 | 92.8 | 4.6 | 18.4 | 2.0 | 4.6 |
| 7.7 | 0.33 | 2.5 | 0.42 | 9.1 | 17.4 | 1.34 | 11.96 | 3.07 | 61.4 | 3.8 | 20.4 | 10.9 | 9.1 |
| 8.3 | 0.25 | 2.2 | 0.13 | 3.9 | 1.4 | 0.61 | 6.30 | 3.09 | 85.9 | 2.8 | 7.0 | 8.4 | 5.7 |
| 7.2 | 0.70 | 4.0 | 0.00 | 1.5 | 0.0 | 0.09 | 0.80 | 3.09 | 98.3 | 4.0 | 29.4 | 0.0 | 5.8 |
| 9.9 | 0.30 | 1.2 | 0.33 | 3.2 | 4.7 | 0.38 | 3.71 | 2.34 | 82.5 | 6.5 | 47.0 | 4.2 | 7.0 |
| 9.5 | 0.72 | 2.1 | 0.12 | 2.2 | 0.0 | 0.24 | 1.44 | 2.85 | 92.5 | 4.9 | 29.0 | 3.9 | 6.5 |
| 10.0 | 0.00 | 0.0 | -0.11 | 5.0 | 0.1 | 0.92 | 10.85 | 3.11 | 81.2 | 5.0 | 26.2 | 2.1 | 2.9 |
| 7.9 | 0.70 | 3.0 | 0.28 | 3.4 | 0.1 | 0.50 | 5.62 | 3.22 | 90.3 | 4.5 | 28.8 | 9.1 | 3.6 |
| 7.4 | 0.68 | 3.6 | 0.95 | 4.1 | 1.8 | 0.46 | 3.88 | 3.73 | 77.7 | 3.4 | 19.9 | 15.0 | 7.4 |
| 9.7 | 0.51 | 1.5 | 0.21 | 3.7 | 0.2 | 0.56 | 7.17 | 2.00 | 77.7 | 5.3 | 63.5 | 13.5 | 3.5 |
| 10.0 | NA | 0.0 | NA | 0.0 | 0.5 | NA | NA | NA | 3.8 | 4.4 | 0.0 | 101.0 | 0.0 |
| 5.5 | 1.70 | 6.3 | 0.77 | 8.8 | 0.0 | 1.28 | 7.42 | 5.34 | 60.4 | 5.4 | 47.9 | 0.0 | 5.0 |
| 0.7 | 22.60 | 41.3 | 14.44 | 1.2 | 0.0 | -2.65 | -7.75 | 8.83 | 145.0 | 6.5 | 61.9 | 0.0 | 4.7 |
| 8.0 | 0.29 | 2.2 | 0.27 | 6.1 | 0.3 | 0.93 | 8.50 | 4.61 | 81.1 | 4.4 | 27.2 | 2.3 | 5.6 |
| 5.0 | 0.38 | 3.9 | 1.02 | 1.9 | 0.0 | -0.06 | -0.71 | 4.38 | 88.7 | 4.1 | 24.6 | 1.9 | 3.8 |
| 5.4 | 1.70 | 5.4 | 0.65 | 2.8 | 0.0 | 0.31 | 1.79 | 6.31 | 95.9 | 4.6 | 12.2 | 0.0 | 6.5 |
| 7.6 | 1.25 | 3.3 | 0.68 | 1.7 | 0.0 | 0.22 | 1.06 | 3.53 | 87.6 | 4.4 | 36.0 | 1.7 | 5.3 |
| 8.0 | 0.93 | 4.8 | 0.83 | 2.3 | 0.0 | 0.02 | 0.11 | 5.45 | 90.8 | 4.1 | 21.2 | 10.4 | 6.4 |
| 7.1 | 4.16 | 12.5 | 0.00 | 2.9 | 0.0 | 0.29 | 2.47 | 2.98 | 80.0 | 4.0 | 14.5 | 6.4 | 6.2 |
| 6.3 | 0.90 | 5.4 | 0.53 | 5.0 | 0.2 | 0.83 | 9.85 | 3.49 | 76.6 | 4.1 | 20.0 | 2.2 | 3.8 |
| 9.8 | 0.00 | 0.0 | 0.00 | 0.0 | 0.0 | -4.76 | -22.22 | 0.00 | 0.0 | 6.0 | 75.9 | 0.0 | 6.0 |
| 8.6 | 0.00 | 0.0 | 0.32 | 0.0 | 0.0 | -0.78 | -9.13 | 3.09 | 147.1 | 6.9 | 52.9 | 0.0 | 3.8 |
| 6.1 | 1.57 | 9.6 | 0.14 | 1.1 | 0.0 | 0.03 | 0.25 | 3.94 | 98.2 | 5.1 | 31.8 | 0.0 | 3.7 |
| 9.8 | 0.02 | 0.1 | -0.18 | 2.5 | 0.0 | 0.28 | 2.31 | 2.36 | 92.4 | 4.4 | 14.8 | 0.0 | 6.3 |
| 7.9 | 0.68 | 2.6 | 0.03 | 1.9 | 0.0 | 0.14 | 1.57 | 3.08 | 95.8 | 4.7 | 21.9 | 0.0 | 4.7 |
| 8.4 | 0.29 | 0.9 | 0.17 | 4.1 | 0.1 | 0.56 | 2.76 | 2.86 | 72.1 | 4.5 | 51.5 | 5.1 | 7.5 |
| 10.0 | 0.00 | 0.0 | 0.35 | 0.0 | 0.0 | -0.86 | -4.37 | 2.67 | 132.6 | 6.3 | 49.9 | 0.0 | 6.5 |
| 5.5 | 1.17 | 8.1 | 0.82 | 4.7 | 0.8 | 0.68 | 6.93 | 4.64 | 79.5 | 3.5 | 9.9 | 4.6 | 6.0 |
| 10.0 | 0.00 | 0.0 | 0.00 | 0.0 | 0.0 | -1.61 | -4.86 | 1.64 | 200.0 | 5.4 | 30.6 | 0.0 | 6.2 |
| 10.0 | 0.01 | 0.0 | 0.02 | 1.9 | 0.0 | 0.10 | 0.53 | 2.21 | 95.9 | 5.3 | 36.4 | 1.5 | 6.3 |
| 10.0 | 3.11 | 1.7 | 0.82 | 3.8 | 0.2 | 0.62 | 4.00 | 2.32 | 72.6 | 5.1 | 14.8 | 0.0 | 5.9 |
| 4.7 | 1.21 | 10.4 | 1.32 | 5.2 | 0.1 | 0.63 | 5.66 | 5.96 | 75.7 | 2.0 | 11.8 | 19.5 | 5.7 |
| 9.0 | 0.35 | 2.9 | 0.08 | 6.5 | 7.7 | 0.90 | 9.30 | 3.00 | 83.1 | 2.9 | 13.5 | 8.1 | 8.1 |
| 9.9 | 0.26 | 1.9 | 0.10 | 6.9 | 13.0 | 1.15 | 11.74 | 3.29 | 79.2 | 3.8 | 16.5 | 2.5 | 7.1 |
| 10.0 | 0.66 | 1.0 | 0.38 | 4.2 | 0.1 | 0.69 | 4.51 | 2.88 | 71.5 | 5.4 | 27.9 | 0.0 | 7.8 |
| 5.4 | 1.28 | 9.9 | 0.54 | 10.0 | 8.8 | 2.89 | 25.10 | 5.14 | 60.5 | 3.1 | 7.1 | 1.8 | 8.5 |
| 10.0 | 0.89 | 2.1 | 0.15 | 1.2 | 0.0 | 0.16 | 1.46 | 3.25 | 95.4 | 6.0 | 42.7 | 0.0 | 4.0 |
| 7.6 | 0.22 | 1.1 | 0.73 | 2.6 | 0.0 | 0.11 | 0.76 | 4.03 | 94.4 | 3.8 | 12.7 | 1.8 | 6.9 |
| 6.4 | 3.38 | 9.6 | -0.25 | 3.0 | 0.0 | 0.44 | 5.73 | 3.06 | 88.6 | 5.0 | 17.2 | 5.8 | 1.7 |
| 8.1 | 5.95 | 4.8 | 0.46 | 0.8 | -0.1 | -2.25 | -6.63 | 3.74 | 124.7 | 6.2 | 88.4 | 0.0 | 5.3 |
| 10.0 | 0.00 | 0.0 | -1.02 | 4.5 | 0.0 | 0.87 | 3.42 | 5.61 | 82.8 | 6.7 | 81.6 | 0.0 | 5.3 |

| Name | City | State | Rating | 2014 Rating | 2013 Rating | Total Assets ($Mil) | One Year Asset Growth | Commercial Loans | Consumer Loans | Mortgage Loans | Securities | Capitalization Index | Net Worth Ratio |
|---|---|---|---|---|---|---|---|---|---|---|---|---|---|
| ELKO FCU | Elko | NV | B | B | B- | 141.9 | 4.49 | 7.5 | 11.9 | 13.5 | 16.5 | 8.2 | 9.8 |
| ELLIOTT COMMUNITY FCU | Jeannette | PA | C+ | C | C- | 32.3 | 4.32 | 0.0 | 26.5 | 9.0 | 0.0 | 10.0 | 11.9 |
| ELLIS COUNTY TEACHERS & EMPL FCU | Waxahachie | TX | C+ | C+ | C+ | 13.6 | 3.41 | 0.0 | 40.6 | 0.0 | 0.0 | 10.0 | 12.0 |
| ELLIS CU | Ellis | KS | C | C | C- | 5.9 | -6.04 | 5.7 | 32.4 | 0.3 | 0.0 | 10.0 | 14.7 |
| ▼ ELLISVILLE STATE SCHOOL EMPL CU | Ellisville | MS | C- | C | C+ | 2.5 | 5.45 | 0.0 | 13.4 | 0.0 | 0.0 | 10.0 | 23.9 |
| ELLWOOD CITY SCHOOL EMPL FCU | Ellwood City | PA | C | D+ | D | 2.3 | -4.29 | 0.0 | 38.3 | 0.0 | 0.0 | 10.0 | 16.4 |
| ELM RIVER CU | Kindred | ND | B | B | B | 22.3 | 2.13 | 44.9 | 10.3 | 46.8 | 0.0 | 10.0 | 14.6 |
| ELY AREA CU | Ely | MN | B- | B- | B- | 23.2 | 5.70 | 0.0 | 13.4 | 11.5 | 0.0 | 10.0 | 11.7 |
| ▼ EM FCU | Mesa | AZ | D+ | C- | C- | 7.5 | -2.53 | 0.0 | 37.5 | 0.0 | 0.0 | 10.0 | 20.2 |
| ▲ EMBARK FCU | Great Falls | MT | B- | C+ | B | 93.5 | 2.91 | 0.1 | 34.2 | 12.0 | 25.2 | 10.0 | 11.7 |
| EMBARRASS VERMILLION FCU | Aurora | MN | B- | B- | B- | 29.3 | 7.58 | 0.2 | 27.2 | 43.6 | 0.0 | 10.0 | 11.9 |
| EMC CU | Des Moines | IA | D | D | D | 7.7 | -0.72 | 9.0 | 20.2 | 10.4 | 0.0 | 7.0 | 9.0 |
| EME CU | Easton | PA | D+ | D | D+ | 1.7 | -2.41 | 0.0 | 23.6 | 0.0 | 0.0 | 10.0 | 13.5 |
| EMERALD COAST FCU | Port Saint Joe | FL | D | D+ | D+ | 40.7 | 1.55 | 1.9 | 24.5 | 23.0 | 0.0 | 6.3 | 8.3 |
| EMERALD CREDIT ASSN FCU | Greenwood | SC | D | D | D- | 6.3 | 5.40 | 0.0 | 57.1 | 0.0 | 0.0 | 6.3 | 8.3 |
| EMERALD CU INC | Garfield Heights | OH | D | D+ | D+ | 44.2 | -5.15 | 1.9 | 31.0 | 23.4 | 22.1 | 7.4 | 9.3 |
| EMERGENCY RESPONDERS CU | Winston-Salem | NC | C+ | C+ | C+ | 18.1 | 2.48 | 0.0 | 44.5 | 1.3 | 0.7 | 10.0 | 12.6 |
| EMERY FCU | Cincinnati | OH | B- | C+ | A- | 152.9 | -1.79 | 5.8 | 22.2 | 26.6 | 11.1 | 8.3 | 9.9 |
| EMORY ALLIANCE CU | Decatur | GA | C+ | C | C | 136.6 | 3.20 | 3.7 | 21.6 | 9.9 | 27.8 | 5.6 | 7.7 |
| EMPIRE BRANCH 36 NATIONAL ASSN LE CAR | New York | NY | D+ | C- | C- | 5.2 | -2.47 | 0.0 | 33.3 | 0.0 | 0.0 | 10.0 | 13.3 |
| EMPIRT 207 FCU | New York | NY | C- | C- | C- | 4.1 | 0.24 | 0.0 | 57.9 | 0.0 | 0.0 | 10.0 | 29.0 |
| EMPL CU | Estherville | IA | A- | A- | A- | 85.0 | 1.52 | 4.0 | 34.9 | 11.1 | 0.0 | 10.0 | 19.1 |
| EMPL CU | Nashville | TN | C+ | C+ | C+ | 30.1 | -3.90 | 2.9 | 12.3 | 14.4 | 0.0 | 10.0 | 18.1 |
| EMPL CU | Dallas | TX | C- | C- | C- | 64.8 | 2.24 | 0.3 | 43.2 | 3.5 | 0.0 | 8.6 | 10.1 |
| EMPL FIRST CU | Saint Paul | MN | B | B- | C+ | 19.7 | -2.16 | 0.0 | 38.1 | 4.6 | 0.0 | 10.0 | 23.3 |
| EMPL FIRST CU | Logan | UT | C | C+ | B- | 1.8 | -7.94 | 0.0 | 21.7 | 0.0 | 0.6 | 10.0 | 25.9 |
| EMPL UNITED FCU | Paris | TX | B- | C+ | C+ | 10.4 | -0.39 | 0.0 | 29.0 | 0.0 | 0.0 | 10.0 | 27.5 |
| EMPLOYEE RESOURCES CU | Lawrenceburg | TN | C- | C | B- | 76.5 | 22.82 | 0.0 | 65.9 | 9.3 | 0.0 | 6.5 | 8.5 |
| ▼ EMPLOYEES FCU | Tulsa | OK | D- | D | C- | 21.3 | -0.15 | 1.3 | 26.3 | 12.5 | 16.5 | 6.7 | 8.7 |
| EMPLOYMENT SECURITY CU | Jefferson City | MO | C+ | C+ | B- | 65.4 | 3.89 | 0.0 | 19.3 | 7.6 | 47.4 | 10.0 | 12.0 |
| EMPLOYMENT SECURITY CU | Nashville | TN | C | C | C | 13.2 | 0.14 | 0.0 | 21.0 | 9.7 | 2.3 | 10.0 | 24.1 |
| ▲ EMPLOYMENT SECURITY EMPL CU | Topeka | KS | C- | D+ | D+ | 1.6 | 1.23 | 0.0 | 63.8 | 0.0 | 0.0 | 10.0 | 22.6 |
| EMPORIA STATE FCU | Emporia | KS | B- | B- | B- | 71.4 | 4.11 | 3.8 | 16.2 | 48.5 | 2.6 | 7.7 | 9.5 |
| EMPOWER CU | West Allis | WI | C | C | D+ | 101.6 | -5.59 | 1.5 | 6.6 | 49.4 | 8.5 | 10.0 | 16.9 |
| EMPOWER FCU | Syracuse | NY | B+ | B+ | B+ | 1353.4 | 6.93 | 5.9 | 32.2 | 17.0 | 6.6 | 8.7 | 10.1 |
| EMPOWERMENT COMMUNITY DEVEL FCU | Houston | TX | D- | D- | D+ | 1.5 | 7.63 | 0.0 | 35.2 | 0.0 | 0.0 | 6.5 | 8.6 |
| ENCENTUS FCU | Tulsa | OK | D+ | C- | C+ | 26.4 | -7.77 | 0.0 | 32.6 | 9.9 | 0.0 | 10.0 | 12.5 |
| ENCHANTED MOUNTAINS FCU | Allegany | NY | D+ | D+ | C- | 12.0 | 2.43 | 0.0 | 17.1 | 19.2 | 1.1 | 7.4 | 9.2 |
| ENCOMPASS FCU | Tipton | IN | A- | A- | B+ | 162.7 | 0.45 | 0.6 | 36.9 | 29.8 | 0.0 | 10.0 | 11.5 |
| ENCOMPASS NIAGARA CU | Niagara Falls | NY | C- | D+ | D+ | 17.6 | 0.10 | 0.0 | 52.0 | 11.8 | 4.8 | 9.6 | 10.8 |
| ENCORE FCU | Des Plaines | IL | C | B- | B- | 34.7 | -2.37 | 0.0 | 12.7 | 0.0 | 54.9 | 10.0 | 16.0 |
| ▲ ENERGIZE CU | Oklahoma City | OK | C- | D+ | C- | 24.6 | -5.99 | 0.0 | 60.2 | 0.0 | 0.0 | 10.0 | 11.1 |
| ENERGY CAPITAL CU | Houston | TX | C+ | C+ | C | 221.6 | 4.05 | 0.0 | 30.4 | 11.8 | 18.2 | 6.5 | 8.5 |
| ENERGY CU | West Roxbury | MA | D+ | D+ | D+ | 80.9 | -3.55 | 0.0 | 10.2 | 25.9 | 39.7 | 10.0 | 18.5 |
| ▼ ENERGY FCU | Rockville | MD | D+ | C | C | 97.4 | -1.11 | 0.0 | 46.7 | 12.3 | 20.6 | 5.9 | 7.9 |
| ENERGY ONE FCU | Tulsa | OK | D+ | D+ | C- | 248.8 | -3.67 | 8.2 | 13.8 | 27.6 | 2.7 | 4.8 | 6.8 |
| ENERGY PEOPLE FCU | Tabernacle | NJ | C+ | B- | B- | 15.7 | 5.93 | 0.0 | 42.6 | 27.5 | 0.0 | 10.0 | 19.3 |
| ENERGY PLUS CU | Indianapolis | IN | B- | B- | B- | 30.4 | 3.99 | 0.0 | 50.1 | 4.1 | 0.0 | 10.0 | 14.6 |
| ▲ ENERGY SERVICES FCU | Saint Cloud | MN | C | D+ | D+ | 9.8 | 6.84 | 0.0 | 32.6 | 2.6 | 0.0 | 10.0 | 16.9 |
| ENFIELD COMMUNITY FCU | Enfield | CT | D+ | D | D | 25.7 | 5.45 | 0.0 | 29.9 | 2.2 | 16.2 | 5.6 | 7.6 |
| ENGINEERS FCU | Little Rock | AR | D | D | D | 3.9 | -10.52 | 0.0 | 34.8 | 0.0 | 0.0 | 7.2 | 9.1 |
| ENLIGHTEN FCU | Jackson | TN | D+ | D+ | C- | 12.7 | 10.92 | 0.0 | 35.0 | 1.6 | 32.8 | 10.0 | 11.4 |
| ENRICHMENT FCU | Oak Ridge | TN | C | C | C | 415.2 | 5.78 | 4.3 | 18.5 | 32.7 | 19.2 | 8.9 | 10.3 |
| ENT FCU | Colorado Springs | CO | A | A | A | 4210.5 | 3.70 | 3.8 | 24.0 | 41.8 | 16.3 | 10.0 | 12.9 |
| ENTERPRISE CU | Enterprise | KS | E+ | E+ | E+ | 1.3 | 3.40 | 0.0 | 73.3 | 0.0 | 0.0 | 5.7 | 7.7 |
| ENTERPRISE CU | Brookfield | WI | D | D | D- | 27.4 | -5.78 | 0.0 | 23.3 | 1.8 | 11.0 | 5.6 | 8.0 |
| ▼ ENTERTAINMENT INDUSTRIES FCU | Elizabeth | NJ | E- | E | E- | 15.1 | 13.32 | 9.9 | 14.8 | 38.9 | 1.0 | 6.9 | 8.9 |
| ENTRUST FINANCIAL CU | Richmond | VA | C | C | C- | 75.5 | 5.31 | 1.9 | 34.6 | 15.4 | 11.2 | 6.1 | 8.1 |
| ENVISION CU | Tallahassee | FL | B- | B- | B- | 301.4 | 6.60 | 7.4 | 31.9 | 17.3 | 16.0 | 6.9 | 8.9 |
| ENVISTA CU | Topeka | KS | B+ | B | B+ | 291.0 | 11.79 | 2.5 | 52.4 | 20.8 | 6.8 | 8.5 | 10.0 |

| Asset Quality Index | Non-Performing Loans as a % of Total Loans | as a % of Capital | Net Charge-Offs Avg Loans | Profitability Index | Net Income ($Mil) | Return on Assets | Return on Equity | Net Interest Spread | Overhead Efficiency Ratio | Liquidity Index | Liquidity Ratio | Hot Money Ratio | Stability Index |
|---|---|---|---|---|---|---|---|---|---|---|---|---|---|
| 9.6 | 0.26 | 1.3 | 0.02 | 4.9 | 0.8 | 0.79 | 8.38 | 4.18 | 75.3 | 6.7 | 46.2 | 4.8 | 6.9 |
| 8.7 | 0.18 | 5.7 | 0.04 | 3.2 | 0.1 | 0.32 | 2.66 | 3.88 | 89.7 | 6.1 | 36.7 | 4.3 | 6.2 |
| 6.5 | 1.84 | 7.3 | 0.63 | 3.3 | 0.0 | 0.38 | 3.06 | 2.91 | 81.6 | 5.1 | 27.1 | 0.0 | 6.3 |
| 9.1 | 0.00 | 0.0 | 0.18 | 5.4 | 0.0 | 0.93 | 6.88 | 2.76 | 62.7 | 4.3 | 29.2 | 0.0 | 4.3 |
| 10.0 | 1.13 | 0.7 | 0.93 | 1.5 | 0.0 | -0.11 | -0.45 | 4.10 | 96.4 | 7.7 | 76.6 | 0.0 | 6.5 |
| 9.3 | 0.00 | 0.0 | 0.00 | 4.5 | 0.0 | 0.84 | 5.32 | 2.77 | 57.5 | 6.3 | 36.0 | 0.0 | 4.3 |
| 8.1 | 0.00 | 0.0 | 0.00 | 9.8 | 0.3 | 1.57 | 11.16 | 4.33 | 62.2 | 2.7 | 11.4 | 7.3 | 6.3 |
| 10.0 | 0.00 | 0.0 | 0.05 | 4.9 | 0.1 | 0.79 | 6.49 | 3.23 | 78.5 | 4.9 | 20.9 | 0.0 | 6.7 |
| 9.7 | 1.30 | 2.4 | 0.23 | 0.9 | 0.0 | -0.19 | -0.96 | 2.75 | 101.3 | 4.7 | 23.7 | 0.0 | 6.5 |
| 9.0 | 0.65 | 3.8 | 0.29 | 3.4 | 0.4 | 0.50 | 4.41 | 3.22 | 85.9 | 4.0 | 19.9 | 2.9 | 5.5 |
| 5.6 | 2.41 | 15.9 | 0.05 | 6.0 | 0.2 | 0.75 | 6.27 | 5.21 | 87.6 | 4.0 | 25.3 | 0.4 | 6.3 |
| 9.7 | 0.00 | 0.0 | 0.00 | 1.9 | 0.0 | 0.12 | 1.35 | 2.05 | 95.0 | 5.6 | 32.5 | 0.0 | 4.2 |
| 10.0 | 0.51 | 0.9 | 0.00 | 0.9 | 0.0 | 0.08 | 0.60 | 3.36 | 93.1 | 7.3 | 84.7 | 0.0 | 5.8 |
| 4.9 | 1.21 | 12.4 | 0.47 | 0.7 | -0.1 | -0.37 | -4.68 | 3.90 | 109.9 | 4.9 | 31.4 | 4.2 | 3.4 |
| 8.3 | 0.00 | 0.0 | 0.03 | 4.2 | 0.0 | 0.53 | 6.27 | 5.36 | 89.3 | 5.1 | 32.5 | 3.5 | 3.0 |
| 6.2 | 1.05 | 6.8 | 0.76 | 0.3 | -0.2 | -0.64 | -6.89 | 3.78 | 98.7 | 4.5 | 19.0 | 2.0 | 3.3 |
| 6.4 | 1.48 | 9.2 | 0.58 | 4.3 | 0.1 | 0.57 | 4.59 | 3.52 | 82.8 | 3.8 | 14.5 | 0.5 | 6.4 |
| 8.6 | 0.52 | 3.2 | 0.29 | 4.0 | 0.7 | 0.63 | 6.69 | 3.18 | 80.8 | 3.6 | 28.2 | 10.4 | 4.9 |
| 9.2 | 0.32 | 2.3 | 0.27 | 3.3 | 0.4 | 0.43 | 5.78 | 3.33 | 87.1 | 4.8 | 23.8 | 0.8 | 3.5 |
| 4.3 | 5.05 | 18.6 | 0.00 | 1.4 | -0.1 | -1.52 | -11.13 | 8.68 | 91.2 | 5.3 | 31.3 | 0.0 | 6.4 |
| 6.1 | 2.15 | 4.2 | 0.00 | 4.6 | 0.0 | 0.71 | 2.50 | 6.95 | 68.7 | 5.1 | 58.1 | 0.0 | 4.3 |
| 7.0 | 2.12 | 7.1 | 0.42 | 10.0 | 1.3 | 2.01 | 10.97 | 3.33 | 40.1 | 4.9 | 43.1 | 0.5 | 8.2 |
| 10.0 | 0.35 | 0.6 | 0.17 | 2.2 | 0.0 | 0.12 | 0.69 | 2.93 | 93.8 | 5.1 | 23.9 | 1.9 | 7.3 |
| 9.0 | 0.21 | 1.1 | 0.38 | 2.4 | 0.1 | 0.22 | 2.26 | 3.42 | 92.0 | 4.9 | 28.7 | 0.0 | 4.2 |
| 9.3 | 1.55 | 3.3 | 0.35 | 9.3 | 0.7 | 4.82 | 19.81 | 7.97 | 40.0 | 3.8 | 31.6 | 16.6 | 6.3 |
| 10.0 | 1.77 | 1.7 | 0.00 | 2.6 | 0.0 | 0.14 | 0.57 | 3.40 | 97.8 | 4.7 | 2.6 | 0.0 | 6.7 |
| 9.9 | 1.04 | 1.3 | 0.23 | 4.7 | 0.1 | 0.69 | 2.54 | 6.37 | 81.1 | 7.2 | 56.5 | 0.0 | 7.1 |
| 1.8 | 2.60 | 26.9 | 0.93 | 5.5 | 0.4 | 0.66 | 7.68 | 5.23 | 72.3 | 2.4 | 16.3 | 22.0 | 4.3 |
| 4.4 | 3.29 | 15.9 | 0.51 | 0.8 | -0.1 | -0.30 | -3.37 | 4.16 | 102.8 | 5.0 | 19.4 | 2.9 | 3.4 |
| 10.0 | 0.46 | 1.1 | 0.09 | 2.6 | 0.1 | 0.20 | 1.60 | 2.38 | 89.9 | 6.0 | 34.0 | 0.7 | 6.4 |
| 9.9 | 1.47 | 2.3 | -0.03 | 2.3 | 0.0 | 0.24 | 1.01 | 3.27 | 92.9 | 6.2 | 43.0 | 0.0 | 6.4 |
| 8.5 | 0.46 | 1.3 | 0.00 | 2.0 | 0.0 | 0.24 | 1.09 | 4.19 | 85.7 | 4.5 | 35.9 | 0.0 | 5.8 |
| 6.9 | 0.92 | 6.8 | 0.03 | 6.3 | 0.6 | 1.03 | 11.26 | 3.21 | 70.2 | 3.0 | 15.7 | 13.0 | 5.3 |
| 8.7 | 0.62 | 2.4 | 0.19 | 2.3 | 0.1 | 0.15 | 0.94 | 2.64 | 94.7 | 3.6 | 17.2 | 7.6 | 6.7 |
| 7.0 | 0.89 | 7.8 | 0.43 | 6.4 | 10.2 | 1.01 | 10.23 | 4.39 | 76.3 | 3.1 | 6.6 | 5.6 | 7.6 |
| 5.8 | 1.65 | 10.3 | 0.00 | 0.5 | 0.0 | -0.44 | -8.03 | 4.47 | 118.5 | 7.2 | 64.7 | 0.0 | 3.9 |
| 8.7 | 0.82 | 5.9 | 0.34 | 1.0 | 0.0 | -0.07 | -0.56 | 2.83 | 97.1 | 5.4 | 43.5 | 4.3 | 5.3 |
| 7.0 | 1.07 | 4.6 | 0.63 | 1.3 | 0.0 | 0.03 | 0.36 | 3.13 | 93.7 | 4.6 | 14.6 | 0.0 | 3.8 |
| 5.9 | 2.22 | 13.6 | 1.10 | 7.0 | 1.2 | 0.96 | 8.68 | 4.37 | 65.6 | 2.2 | 19.1 | 18.3 | 7.6 |
| 3.3 | 2.06 | 12.3 | 1.06 | 3.6 | 0.1 | 0.40 | 3.80 | 4.74 | 74.4 | 4.5 | 30.4 | 3.9 | 5.3 |
| 10.0 | 0.00 | 0.0 | 0.34 | 2.2 | 0.0 | 0.05 | 0.29 | 1.54 | 95.1 | 6.0 | 28.9 | 0.0 | 7.1 |
| 7.7 | 0.51 | 2.9 | -0.11 | 2.3 | 0.1 | 0.26 | 2.47 | 2.64 | 89.7 | 3.5 | 25.9 | 6.5 | 4.9 |
| 8.6 | 0.26 | 2.6 | 0.40 | 3.4 | 0.6 | 0.39 | 4.67 | 3.09 | 81.1 | 3.9 | 10.7 | 1.6 | 4.8 |
| 7.7 | 2.62 | 6.0 | 0.12 | 1.1 | 0.0 | 0.04 | 0.19 | 3.01 | 96.5 | 4.1 | 11.7 | 5.0 | 6.2 |
| 7.2 | 0.25 | 2.0 | 0.39 | 1.2 | -0.4 | -0.50 | -6.24 | 3.78 | 102.7 | 4.3 | 24.6 | 0.0 | 2.4 |
| 5.5 | 2.22 | 17.1 | 0.04 | 1.8 | 0.3 | 0.17 | 2.62 | 2.60 | 94.5 | 3.9 | 24.7 | 7.2 | 3.2 |
| 9.5 | 0.00 | 0.0 | 0.00 | 2.5 | 0.0 | 0.14 | 0.71 | 3.57 | 86.0 | 3.4 | 19.3 | 4.0 | 7.2 |
| 7.3 | 0.78 | 4.0 | 0.42 | 3.6 | 0.1 | 0.31 | 2.12 | 4.23 | 88.3 | 3.5 | 18.8 | 3.1 | 7.1 |
| 9.6 | 0.11 | 0.3 | 0.06 | 3.0 | 0.0 | 0.48 | 2.83 | 3.17 | 82.8 | 4.5 | 15.8 | 0.0 | 6.4 |
| 5.6 | 1.82 | 14.9 | 0.40 | 3.6 | 0.1 | 0.34 | 4.51 | 3.74 | 87.5 | 4.3 | 14.9 | 1.1 | 3.4 |
| 8.7 | 1.08 | 4.1 | 0.00 | 1.3 | 0.0 | -0.16 | -1.85 | 1.73 | 107.7 | 5.4 | 34.5 | 0.0 | 4.2 |
| 9.9 | 0.23 | 0.7 | 0.29 | 1.0 | 0.0 | -0.04 | -0.37 | 2.67 | 97.4 | 5.6 | 26.7 | 0.0 | 5.5 |
| 9.5 | 0.05 | 1.1 | 0.08 | 3.1 | 1.0 | 0.33 | 3.27 | 2.78 | 89.1 | 4.6 | 18.0 | 4.6 | 6.7 |
| 9.8 | 0.24 | 1.5 | 0.12 | 7.6 | 35.9 | 1.15 | 9.35 | 2.51 | 62.1 | 3.5 | 19.3 | 5.4 | 9.5 |
| 0.7 | 7.81 | 46.2 | -1.40 | 2.0 | 0.0 | 0.00 | 0.00 | 6.30 | 100.0 | 4.7 | 27.8 | 0.0 | 5.3 |
| 6.8 | 0.45 | 3.8 | 0.20 | 2.2 | 0.0 | 0.12 | 1.98 | 3.36 | 103.8 | 4.7 | 19.4 | 0.0 | 1.3 |
| 1.7 | 2.26 | 38.1 | 0.22 | 1.0 | 0.0 | -0.37 | -5.22 | 5.00 | 104.7 | 4.7 | 23.6 | 0.0 | 0.3 |
| 6.0 | 1.37 | 9.0 | 0.36 | 3.4 | 0.2 | 0.34 | 4.28 | 3.50 | 89.3 | 4.6 | 15.6 | 0.8 | 3.0 |
| 6.8 | 0.87 | 5.9 | 0.83 | 7.5 | 4.6 | 2.07 | 23.32 | 4.27 | 76.0 | 5.4 | 28.2 | 0.6 | 4.7 |
| 7.1 | 0.54 | 5.3 | 0.25 | 6.2 | 2.1 | 1.04 | 10.23 | 3.38 | 75.8 | 2.8 | 4.2 | 6.8 | 6.4 |

| Name | City | State | 2015 Rating | 2014 Rating | 2013 Rating | Total Assets ($Mil) | One Year Asset Growth | Asset Mix (As a % of Total Assets) | | | | Capital- ization Index | Net Worth Ratio |
|------|------|-------|-------------|-------------|-------------|---------------------|------------------------|---------------|---------------|---------------|---------------|-------------------------|------------------|
| | | | | | | | | Comm- ercial Loans | Cons- umer Loans | Mort- gage Loans | Secur- ities | | |
| EP FCU | Washington | DC | C | C- | D+ | 65.7 | 0.05 | 0.1 | 21.3 | 17.6 | 43.5 | 5.7 | 8.1 |
| EPA CU | Ridgeland | MS | B- | B- | B- | 20.1 | 5.30 | 5.7 | 32.7 | 0.0 | 0.0 | 10.0 | 11.8 |
| ▼ EPB EMPL CU | Chattanooga | TN | D+ | C- | C- | 28.2 | -4.28 | 0.0 | 18.9 | 7.0 | 15.4 | 10.0 | 12.5 |
| EPIPHANY FCU | Brooklyn | NY | D | D | C- | <1 | -9.23 | 0.0 | 15.8 | 0.0 | 0.0 | 10.0 | 20.9 |
| EPISCOPAL COMMUNITY FCU | Los Angeles | CA | E+ | E+ | E+ | 4.8 | -4.17 | 0.0 | 41.4 | 0.0 | 0.2 | 5.4 | 7.4 |
| EQT FCU | Pittsburgh | PA | C- | C | C+ | 40.8 | -6.48 | 0.0 | 3.9 | 0.0 | 0.0 | 9.5 | 10.7 |
| EQUISHARE CU | Wichita | KS | C- | C- | C- | 28.8 | -0.28 | 0.0 | 63.7 | 7.5 | 0.0 | 10.0 | 11.0 |
| ▲ EQUITABLE FCU | Akron | OH | C- | D+ | C- | 7.7 | 6.67 | 0.0 | 45.0 | 0.0 | 30.2 | 10.0 | 18.3 |
| ERIE CITY EMPL FCU | Erie | PA | D+ | C- | C- | 9.0 | -2.90 | 0.0 | 34.0 | 0.0 | 0.0 | 10.0 | 16.8 |
| ERIE COMMUNITY CU | Erie | PA | C+ | C+ | C+ | 105.4 | 3.47 | 0.0 | 40.9 | 0.8 | 9.6 | 6.5 | 8.6 |
| ▲ ERIE COMMUNITY FCU | Sandusky | OH | D+ | D | D+ | 24.0 | 3.25 | 10.1 | 20.3 | 21.7 | 26.3 | 7.9 | 9.7 |
| ERIE COUNTY EMPL CU | Buffalo | NY | C+ | B- | B- | 24.3 | 2.26 | 0.0 | 20.6 | 13.3 | 27.2 | 10.0 | 12.5 |
| ERIE FCU | Erie | PA | B | B | A- | 433.2 | 10.37 | 5.6 | 18.6 | 18.9 | 39.8 | 10.0 | 11.0 |
| ERIE FIREFIGHTERS FCU | Erie | PA | D- | D- | D | 8.0 | 0.70 | 0.0 | 25.6 | 1.6 | 0.0 | 6.9 | 8.9 |
| ERIE LACKAWANNA RAILROAD CO EMPL FC | Hoboken | NJ | C+ | C+ | C | 6.5 | 6.00 | 0.0 | 57.8 | 0.0 | 0.0 | 10.0 | 27.0 |
| ▲ ERIE METRO FCU | Blasdell | NY | C | C- | C | 30.1 | 3.41 | 0.0 | 21.8 | 16.4 | 2.5 | 9.6 | 10.7 |
| ERIE POLICE FCU | Erie | PA | C+ | C+ | C | 2.4 | -7.71 | 0.0 | 50.0 | 0.0 | 0.0 | 10.0 | 20.8 |
| ERIE SHORES COMMUNITY FCU | Westlake | OH | D- | D | D+ | 19.2 | -4.95 | 3.0 | 18.8 | 7.0 | 37.5 | 4.8 | 6.8 |
| ERIE TIMES FCU | Erie | PA | D | D | D | 6.7 | -1.41 | 0.0 | 22.5 | 0.0 | 0.0 | 10.0 | 18.0 |
| ERIE TPE FCU | Erie | PA | D+ | D+ | D | 2.3 | -4.75 | 0.0 | 64.7 | 13.4 | 0.0 | 10.0 | 32.2 |
| ▼ ERRL FCU | Wyndmoor | PA | E+ | D | D+ | 1.4 | -3.44 | 0.0 | 40.4 | 0.0 | 0.0 | 7.5 | 9.4 |
| ESA CU | Boise | ID | D- | D- | D | 6.2 | 2.30 | 0.0 | 23.4 | 11.4 | 0.0 | 6.7 | 8.8 |
| ESCONDIDO FCU | Escondido | CA | C+ | B- | C+ | 39.0 | 1.66 | 0.3 | 26.0 | 4.8 | 0.0 | 8.4 | 9.9 |
| ▼ ESCU FCU | Holland | OH | C- | C | C | 4.8 | -5.53 | 0.0 | 48.8 | 2.2 | 0.0 | 10.0 | 17.4 |
| ESL FCU | Rochester | NY | A+ | A+ | A+ | 5542.4 | 11.97 | 4.2 | 15.7 | 7.1 | 41.1 | 10.0 | 14.9 |
| ▼ ESPEECO FCU | Bakersfield | CA | D | C- | D | 8.6 | 5.35 | 0.0 | 38.0 | 14.0 | 4.5 | 10.0 | 18.7 |
| ESQUIRE-GOODFELLOWSHIP FCU | Brooklyn | NY | D+ | D | D | <1 | 5.80 | 0.0 | 29.2 | 0.0 | 0.0 | 10.0 | 30.6 |
| ESSENTIAL FCU | Plaquemine | LA | B+ | B+ | B- | 281.7 | 13.39 | 3.6 | 28.4 | 19.6 | 0.0 | 7.1 | 9.0 |
| ESSEX COUNTY NJ EMPL FCU | Newark | NJ | D+ | D+ | D+ | 6.8 | 0.38 | 0.0 | 35.8 | 0.0 | 0.0 | 10.0 | 11.6 |
| ESSEX COUNTY TEACHERS FCU | Bloomfield | NJ | D | D- | D- | 13.5 | 3.67 | 2.0 | 38.6 | 9.4 | 0.0 | 6.0 | 8.0 |
| ESTACADO FCU | Hobbs | NM | C- | C | C+ | 58.0 | 2.22 | 0.0 | 28.4 | 0.0 | 17.8 | 9.9 | 10.9 |
| ETHICON CU | Cornelia | GA | B- | B- | B- | 12.1 | 7.70 | 0.0 | 28.2 | 7.6 | 0.0 | 10.0 | 20.0 |
| ETHICON SUTURE CU | Chicago | IL | C- | C- | D | 1.1 | 1.27 | 0.0 | 60.4 | 0.0 | 0.0 | 9.0 | 10.3 |
| ETMA FCU | Louisville | TN | C+ | C+ | C+ | 15.6 | -2.34 | 0.0 | 33.5 | 17.5 | 0.0 | 10.0 | 15.2 |
| ETS CU | Eldora | IA | C+ | C+ | C | 2.5 | 2.78 | 0.0 | 30.6 | 0.0 | 0.0 | 10.0 | 15.0 |
| EVANGELICAL CHRISTIAN CU | Brea | CA | D- | D- | D- | 908.1 | -11.18 | 64.3 | 7.8 | 61.2 | 6.4 | 5.0 | 7.0 |
| ▲ EVANSTON FIREMENS CU | Evanston | IL | C+ | C | C+ | 1.7 | -9.77 | 0.0 | 37.0 | 0.0 | 0.0 | 10.0 | 18.0 |
| EVANSVILLE FCU | Evansville | IN | B+ | B+ | B+ | 64.1 | 5.27 | 1.1 | 27.2 | 30.3 | 2.4 | 10.0 | 11.8 |
| EVANSVILLE FIREFIGHTERS FCU | Evansville | IN | C+ | C+ | C+ | 19.8 | -1.21 | 0.5 | 29.5 | 9.0 | 0.0 | 10.0 | 11.7 |
| EVANSVILLE TEACHERS FCU | Evansville | IN | B+ | B+ | B+ | 1157.9 | 12.24 | 3.2 | 38.5 | 29.7 | 3.9 | 7.6 | 9.5 |
| EVER $ GREEN FCU | Rochester | NY | C+ | C+ | C+ | 30.2 | 5.79 | 0.5 | 18.8 | 4.2 | 13.5 | 8.1 | 9.7 |
| EVERENCE FCU | Lancaster | PA | C+ | C+ | C+ | 153.9 | 4.99 | 12.9 | 12.6 | 37.3 | 0.0 | 5.5 | 7.5 |
| EVERETT CU | Everett | MA | C | C | C | 45.9 | 0.35 | 0.0 | 6.5 | 45.3 | 20.7 | 10.0 | 13.5 |
| EVERGLADES FCU | Clewiston | FL | B | B | C+ | 32.7 | 11.03 | 0.0 | 39.4 | 18.3 | 0.0 | 10.0 | 12.4 |
| EVERGREEN CU | Portland | ME | C+ | C+ | C+ | 233.5 | 3.32 | 10.0 | 9.8 | 32.6 | 5.7 | 6.7 | 8.7 |
| EVERGREEN CU | Neenah | WI | B | B | B | 33.5 | 10.33 | 0.0 | 31.2 | 26.2 | 0.0 | 10.0 | 11.7 |
| EVERGREEN PARK SCHOOLS FCU | Evergreen Park | IL | C | C | C+ | 12.1 | 3.20 | 0.0 | 19.2 | 0.0 | 0.0 | 10.0 | 12.0 |
| EVERGREENDIRECT CU | Olympia | WA | B | B- | B- | 50.8 | 7.01 | 0.2 | 46.1 | 4.3 | 20.5 | 10.0 | 12.4 |
| EVERMAN PARKWAY CU | Fort Worth | TX | D | D+ | D+ | 4.8 | -3.41 | 0.0 | 56.2 | 0.0 | 0.0 | 10.0 | 30.9 |
| EVERYONES FCU | Tucumcari | NM | B | B | B | 26.9 | 3.92 | 9.4 | 33.7 | 4.9 | 0.0 | 10.0 | 15.1 |
| ▲ EVOLVE FCU | El Paso | TX | B- | C | C+ | 333.8 | 1.70 | 0.0 | 55.1 | 17.4 | 12.4 | 10.0 | 11.1 |
| ▲ EVONIK EMPL FCU | Theodore | AL | D+ | D+ | D+ | 7.1 | 1.62 | 0.0 | 43.4 | 0.0 | 0.0 | 7.7 | 9.5 |
| ▼ EW #401 CU | Reno | NV | D | D+ | D | 9.8 | 17.14 | 0.0 | 13.1 | 10.8 | 10.2 | 7.5 | 9.4 |
| EWA FCU | Ewa Beach | HI | C | C- | C | 12.8 | 0.87 | 0.0 | 23.8 | 0.0 | 0.0 | 10.0 | 23.0 |
| EWEB EMPL FCU | Eugene | OR | C- | D+ | D+ | 23.5 | 10.28 | 1.6 | 18.3 | 23.3 | 0.0 | 6.0 | 8.1 |
| ▲ EXCEL FCU | Norcross | GA | C | C- | C- | 96.1 | 2.16 | 16.8 | 29.3 | 27.7 | 1.6 | 9.1 | 10.4 |
| ▼ EXPRESS CU | Seattle | WA | C- | C | C | 11.7 | 6.97 | 0.0 | 73.5 | 7.3 | 0.0 | 8.8 | 10.2 |
| EXPRESS-NEWS FCU | San Antonio | TX | D+ | C- | C- | 7.3 | 7.23 | 1.6 | 27.7 | 19.3 | 0.0 | 10.0 | 11.5 |
| EXTRA CU | Warren | MI | B- | B- | C+ | 197.3 | 3.73 | 0.1 | 22.9 | 18.0 | 35.9 | 6.8 | 8.8 |
| F C FCU | Cherry Hill | NJ | D | D+ | C- | <1 | -8.86 | 0.0 | 2.8 | 7.3 | 0.0 | 10.0 | 30.9 |

| Asset Quality Index | Non-Performing Loans as a % of Total Loans | as a % of Capital | Net Charge-Offs Avg Loans | Profitability Index | Net Income ($Mil) | Return on Assets | Return on Equity | Net Interest Spread | Overhead Efficiency Ratio | Liquidity Index | Liquidity Ratio | Hot Money Ratio | Stability Index |
|---|---|---|---|---|---|---|---|---|---|---|---|---|---|
| 10.0 | 0.14 | 0.9 | -0.33 | 2.9 | 0.2 | 0.30 | 3.97 | 3.11 | 95.0 | 4.0 | 9.1 | 6.7 | 2.9 |
| 9.3 | 0.60 | 1.8 | 0.04 | 3.3 | 0.1 | 0.45 | 3.67 | 2.43 | 82.9 | 5.6 | 32.0 | 0.0 | 6.2 |
| 6.5 | 3.61 | 9.7 | 2.30 | 0.0 | -0.3 | -1.16 | -9.85 | 2.83 | 111.1 | 5.0 | 27.8 | 1.7 | 5.5 |
| 8.2 | 7.14 | 5.1 | 0.00 | 0.0 | 0.0 | -4.44 | -19.05 | 2.67 | 300.0 | 8.0 | 90.7 | 0.0 | 4.7 |
| 2.2 | 3.37 | 25.8 | 0.33 | 0.6 | 0.0 | -0.59 | -11.88 | 4.54 | 102.2 | 5.1 | 20.1 | 0.0 | 0.6 |
| 10.0 | 0.25 | 0.1 | 0.30 | 2.1 | 0.0 | 0.11 | 1.04 | 0.89 | 87.6 | 5.5 | 29.3 | 0.0 | 3.3 |
| 2.0 | 1.87 | 26.9 | 1.29 | 4.9 | 0.1 | 0.34 | 3.50 | 5.83 | 82.3 | 4.3 | 23.8 | 1.8 | 4.8 |
| 8.3 | 0.21 | 0.7 | 0.43 | 2.5 | 0.0 | 0.41 | 2.10 | 4.18 | 88.9 | 4.1 | 17.3 | 0.0 | 5.0 |
| 7.6 | 1.23 | 3.1 | 0.54 | 1.1 | 0.0 | -0.06 | -0.36 | 2.94 | 82.6 | 4.4 | 12.8 | 0.0 | 6.0 |
| 6.3 | 1.04 | 9.0 | 0.56 | 3.6 | 0.3 | 0.36 | 4.35 | 3.56 | 79.0 | 3.6 | 9.1 | 2.6 | 5.0 |
| 6.3 | 1.71 | 8.1 | 0.49 | 1.6 | 0.0 | 0.06 | 0.64 | 3.28 | 94.2 | 4.2 | 21.3 | 4.0 | 4.3 |
| 9.5 | 0.24 | 0.7 | 0.74 | 2.6 | 0.0 | 0.18 | 1.42 | 2.78 | 87.0 | 4.7 | 10.3 | 0.6 | 6.4 |
| 9.0 | 0.86 | 3.4 | 0.42 | 4.4 | 1.7 | 0.52 | 4.77 | 2.78 | 80.9 | 3.6 | 25.8 | 11.8 | 6.2 |
| 8.1 | 1.48 | 4.7 | 0.54 | 1.6 | 0.0 | 0.23 | 2.68 | 2.62 | 85.7 | 5.0 | 24.1 | 0.0 | 3.0 |
| 8.5 | 0.41 | 0.9 | 0.74 | 9.4 | 0.2 | 3.24 | 12.26 | 6.72 | 42.6 | 2.7 | 23.6 | 17.3 | 5.0 |
| 8.3 | 0.29 | 1.9 | 0.06 | 2.9 | 0.1 | 0.30 | 2.87 | 3.55 | 90.3 | 4.6 | 16.5 | 0.0 | 5.2 |
| 8.6 | 0.00 | 0.0 | 0.43 | 4.4 | 0.0 | 0.44 | 2.14 | 3.92 | 81.7 | 4.8 | 13.8 | 0.0 | 4.3 |
| 5.3 | 1.62 | 6.9 | 5.00 | 0.0 | -1.0 | -6.55 | -67.21 | 3.73 | 115.1 | 4.8 | 17.2 | 2.4 | 3.0 |
| 8.2 | 1.66 | 2.8 | 0.79 | 0.0 | 0.0 | -0.85 | -4.83 | 2.87 | 121.0 | 6.0 | 41.6 | 2.7 | 5.7 |
| 3.1 | 5.51 | 14.1 | 0.21 | 4.1 | 0.0 | 0.55 | 1.79 | 5.59 | 88.0 | 4.3 | 22.4 | 0.0 | 3.0 |
| 3.7 | 5.36 | 20.5 | 3.01 | 0.0 | 0.0 | -1.56 | -15.32 | 2.92 | 103.6 | 5.4 | 29.6 | 0.0 | 3.1 |
| 8.9 | 0.49 | 1.9 | -0.06 | 1.8 | 0.0 | 0.13 | 1.49 | 3.47 | 96.5 | 4.9 | 18.5 | 0.0 | 1.7 |
| 9.9 | 0.23 | 0.9 | 0.30 | 3.2 | 0.1 | 0.28 | 2.90 | 2.63 | 84.6 | 5.6 | 40.5 | 6.5 | 4.9 |
| 7.0 | 1.39 | 4.1 | 0.27 | 2.6 | 0.0 | 0.19 | 1.12 | 3.49 | 87.0 | 5.8 | 52.5 | 0.0 | 6.5 |
| 9.8 | 0.66 | 2.1 | 0.46 | 9.4 | 62.1 | 1.59 | 10.45 | 3.10 | 53.0 | 4.8 | 28.6 | 8.7 | 10.0 |
| 7.4 | 2.16 | 5.9 | -0.06 | 0.1 | -0.1 | -0.93 | -5.20 | 3.36 | 99.1 | 6.3 | 50.1 | 0.0 | 6.1 |
| 9.9 | 0.00 | 0.0 | 0.00 | 1.1 | 0.0 | 0.00 | 0.00 | 5.67 | 100.0 | 8.0 | 97.7 | 0.0 | 6.5 |
| 6.3 | 0.74 | 6.6 | 0.59 | 5.7 | 0.6 | 0.31 | 3.32 | 5.40 | 87.5 | 2.4 | 10.4 | 14.1 | 5.8 |
| 8.8 | 1.58 | 4.6 | 1.78 | 0.6 | 0.0 | -0.39 | -3.17 | 6.36 | 107.1 | 6.7 | 47.0 | 0.0 | 5.4 |
| 6.0 | 1.12 | 7.8 | 0.53 | 3.6 | 0.1 | 0.48 | 6.40 | 4.58 | 86.9 | 4.1 | 16.5 | 9.1 | 3.0 |
| 6.3 | 2.19 | 7.2 | 0.95 | 2.4 | 0.0 | 0.03 | 0.27 | 3.81 | 91.5 | 5.0 | 31.5 | 7.8 | 4.9 |
| 8.0 | 1.76 | 3.9 | 0.19 | 5.1 | 0.1 | 0.55 | 2.71 | 4.91 | 88.1 | 6.0 | 48.2 | 0.0 | 7.1 |
| 8.5 | 0.00 | 0.0 | 0.61 | 2.7 | 0.0 | 0.12 | 1.16 | 6.07 | 88.2 | 6.1 | 41.7 | 0.0 | 4.5 |
| 9.2 | 0.82 | 3.3 | 0.00 | 3.5 | 0.1 | 0.42 | 2.84 | 3.61 | 89.1 | 4.8 | 24.5 | 0.0 | 7.2 |
| 8.0 | 1.97 | 4.2 | -0.43 | 9.3 | 0.0 | 1.36 | 9.29 | 3.28 | 43.5 | 6.5 | 37.0 | 0.0 | 5.7 |
| 0.0 | 5.10 | 55.8 | 1.16 | 0.4 | -11.0 | -1.53 | -20.18 | 3.67 | 115.6 | 2.6 | 25.3 | 34.9 | 3.8 |
| 10.0 | 0.00 | 0.0 | 0.00 | 6.6 | 0.0 | 1.31 | 7.61 | 4.15 | 66.0 | 5.4 | 21.8 | 0.0 | 5.0 |
| 7.3 | 0.94 | 5.6 | 0.38 | 9.1 | 0.6 | 1.29 | 11.39 | 3.77 | 72.6 | 3.5 | 15.2 | 5.9 | 6.5 |
| 8.7 | 0.58 | 2.2 | 0.28 | 2.8 | 0.0 | 0.17 | 1.44 | 3.15 | 91.4 | 4.7 | 26.6 | 6.9 | 5.4 |
| 6.5 | 0.50 | 7.5 | 0.27 | 7.6 | 8.8 | 1.05 | 11.22 | 3.40 | 78.9 | 2.6 | 13.8 | 17.3 | 7.3 |
| 9.0 | 0.52 | 2.5 | -0.01 | 3.9 | 0.1 | 0.54 | 5.63 | 3.24 | 82.9 | 4.2 | 8.8 | 4.6 | 5.7 |
| 6.4 | 1.25 | 10.2 | 0.22 | 3.3 | 0.3 | 0.24 | 3.29 | 3.68 | 90.8 | 4.0 | 27.7 | 2.5 | 5.0 |
| 7.7 | 2.06 | 9.0 | 0.08 | 2.0 | 0.1 | 0.15 | 1.10 | 3.06 | 95.5 | 3.6 | 10.6 | 7.3 | 6.2 |
| 7.8 | 0.81 | 4.0 | 0.15 | 6.0 | 0.2 | 0.82 | 6.82 | 4.47 | 79.7 | 4.1 | 25.7 | 9.0 | 5.8 |
| 6.2 | 1.49 | 10.4 | 0.41 | 3.5 | 0.8 | 0.44 | 5.12 | 3.09 | 82.1 | 4.4 | 17.5 | 1.3 | 5.3 |
| 9.0 | 0.55 | 3.4 | 0.27 | 6.4 | 0.2 | 1.01 | 8.55 | 3.87 | 79.5 | 3.1 | 12.6 | 7.0 | 6.4 |
| 9.7 | 1.60 | 2.6 | 0.30 | 2.1 | 0.0 | 0.16 | 1.38 | 1.42 | 67.2 | 5.6 | 43.2 | 0.0 | 5.3 |
| 8.2 | 0.36 | 1.8 | 0.45 | 4.5 | 0.2 | 0.51 | 4.08 | 4.84 | 83.8 | 4.0 | 11.9 | 1.2 | 5.8 |
| 5.5 | 3.73 | 6.8 | 1.80 | 0.0 | 0.0 | -1.02 | -3.31 | 4.18 | 98.7 | 4.2 | 19.4 | 0.0 | 5.7 |
| 9.0 | 0.02 | 0.5 | 0.05 | 6.3 | 0.2 | 0.88 | 5.96 | 4.61 | 85.4 | 4.1 | 21.7 | 11.0 | 6.8 |
| 7.5 | 0.55 | 4.5 | 0.96 | 4.2 | 1.9 | 0.77 | 7.44 | 3.39 | 69.1 | 2.0 | 9.0 | 25.0 | 6.1 |
| 9.7 | 0.00 | 0.0 | 0.05 | 2.5 | 0.0 | 0.43 | 4.64 | 2.98 | 84.5 | 4.6 | 20.7 | 0.0 | 4.2 |
| 8.1 | 0.31 | 0.9 | 0.00 | 1.0 | -0.1 | -0.68 | -6.41 | 2.62 | 123.2 | 4.7 | 28.6 | 13.7 | 4.5 |
| 10.0 | 1.08 | 1.3 | 0.00 | 2.4 | 0.0 | 0.34 | 1.46 | 2.71 | 96.5 | 5.0 | 22.2 | 0.0 | 6.6 |
| 9.9 | 0.00 | 0.0 | 0.00 | 3.7 | 0.1 | 0.58 | 7.17 | 2.94 | 83.4 | 4.9 | 25.0 | 2.5 | 3.7 |
| 6.9 | 0.91 | 5.0 | 0.13 | 2.8 | 0.2 | 0.33 | 2.89 | 3.08 | 94.7 | 4.4 | 33.5 | 4.1 | 5.3 |
| 5.6 | 0.48 | 3.7 | 0.50 | 2.7 | 0.0 | -0.02 | -0.23 | 6.43 | 96.4 | 2.4 | 13.0 | 12.2 | 4.4 |
| 9.5 | 0.35 | 2.3 | 0.00 | 1.0 | 0.0 | -0.25 | -2.22 | 4.13 | 102.3 | 4.8 | 29.3 | 0.0 | 6.2 |
| 7.5 | 1.04 | 5.8 | 0.82 | 4.2 | 0.7 | 0.45 | 5.31 | 4.27 | 82.4 | 4.4 | 11.0 | 1.6 | 4.8 |
| 10.0 | 0.00 | 0.0 | 0.00 | 0.0 | 0.0 | -1.23 | -3.99 | 4.12 | 211.1 | 8.7 | 130.9 | 0.0 | 6.2 |

| Name | City | State | Rating | 2014 Rating | 2013 Rating | Total Assets ($Mil) | One Year Asset Growth | Asset Mix (As a % of Total Assets) | | | | Capital-ization Index | Net Worth Ratio |
|---|---|---|---|---|---|---|---|---|---|---|---|---|---|
| | | | | | | | | Comm-ercial Loans | Cons-umer Loans | Mort-gage Loans | Secur-ities | | |
| F C I FCU | Littleton | CO | D | D+ | C- | 5.0 | -4.00 | 0.0 | 33.3 | 0.0 | 0.0 | 10.0 | 23.1 |
| F C S FCU | Floydada | TX | B+ | B+ | B+ | 11.6 | 3.92 | 0.0 | 34.9 | 0.0 | 0.0 | 10.0 | 30.6 |
| F&A FCU | Monterey Park | CA | A | A | B+ | 1447.2 | 7.57 | 0.0 | 6.7 | 4.7 | 75.7 | 10.0 | 14.7 |
| ▼ FAA CU | Oklahoma City | OK | B- | B | C+ | 573.3 | 2.13 | 0.2 | 36.7 | 16.1 | 34.9 | 6.8 | 8.9 |
| FAA FCU | Memphis | TN | C+ | C+ | C | 106.2 | 0.75 | 0.0 | 23.8 | 5.4 | 6.0 | 9.5 | 10.7 |
| FAB CHURCH FCU | Savannah | GA | C | C- | D+ | <1 | -8.75 | 0.0 | 30.6 | 3.7 | 0.0 | 10.0 | 19.9 |
| FAIRFAX CITY FCU | Fairfax | VA | D+ | D+ | C- | 2.4 | 2.02 | 0.0 | 52.1 | 0.0 | 10.5 | 8.9 | 10.3 |
| FAIRFAX COUNTY FCU | Fairfax | VA | A- | A- | B | 321.8 | 10.31 | 1.4 | 6.7 | 17.0 | 19.5 | 9.0 | 10.4 |
| FAIRFIELD COUNTY FCU | Fairfield | CT | D | D | D | 29.6 | 3.25 | 0.0 | 13.9 | 31.8 | 0.0 | 5.6 | 7.6 |
| ▲ FAIRFIELD FCU | Pine Bluff | AR | C- | D | D+ | 83.2 | 1.46 | 0.0 | 31.4 | 21.6 | 0.0 | 10.0 | 20.1 |
| FAIRLEIGH DICKINSON UNIV FCU | Madison | NJ | C- | D+ | D+ | 12.5 | -4.87 | 0.0 | 28.8 | 7.3 | 0.0 | 9.2 | 10.5 |
| FAIRLESS CU | Morrisville | PA | B- | B- | B- | 45.6 | 1.34 | 0.0 | 10.5 | 5.1 | 1.1 | 10.0 | 14.5 |
| FAIRMONT FCU | Fairmont | WV | B | B | B | 310.9 | 5.06 | 3.4 | 29.3 | 39.4 | 5.2 | 7.3 | 9.2 |
| ▲ FAIRMONT SCHOOL EMPL FCU | Fairmont | MN | C- | D | D+ | 2.1 | 2.22 | 0.0 | 53.9 | 0.0 | 0.0 | 10.0 | 13.5 |
| FAIRMONT VILLAGE CU | East Saint Louis | IL | D+ | C- | D+ | 2.1 | -5.61 | 0.0 | 47.4 | 0.0 | 0.0 | 10.0 | 18.4 |
| ▲ FAIRPORT FCU | Fairport | NY | C | C- | C | 35.8 | -0.23 | 0.0 | 27.2 | 0.0 | 0.0 | 6.3 | 8.3 |
| FAIRVIEW EMPL FCU | Costa Mesa | CA | C | C+ | C | 14.1 | 2.83 | 0.0 | 13.5 | 19.4 | 0.0 | 10.0 | 11.9 |
| FAIRWINDS CU | Orlando | FL | B | B- | C+ | 1899.4 | 7.76 | 6.5 | 21.7 | 33.5 | 31.3 | 7.9 | 9.6 |
| ▼ FAITH BASED FCU | Oceanside | CA | C- | C | C- | <1 | -9.96 | 0.0 | 11.2 | 0.0 | 0.0 | 9.8 | 10.9 |
| FAITH COMMUNITY UNITED CU | Cleveland | OH | B- | B- | C+ | 12.9 | -0.81 | 5.3 | 49.1 | 6.3 | 14.3 | 10.0 | 18.5 |
| FAITH COOPERATIVE FCU | Dallas | TX | C- | D | E+ | <1 | 0.23 | 0.0 | 48.3 | 0.0 | 0.0 | 10.0 | 12.9 |
| FAITH TABERNACLE BAPTIST FCU | Stamford | CT | E+ | E+ | D | <1 | -15.43 | 0.0 | 3.1 | 0.0 | 0.0 | 6.2 | 8.2 |
| FALL RIVER MUNICIPAL CU | Fall River | MA | C | C | D+ | 198.8 | -0.95 | 3.3 | 4.8 | 46.0 | 32.8 | 10.0 | 12.7 |
| FALLON COUNTY FCU | Baker | MT | B- | C+ | C- | 11.0 | 3.25 | 0.0 | 27.8 | 20.0 | 0.0 | 10.0 | 11.9 |
| FALLS CATHOLIC CU | Cuyahoga Falls | OH | B | B | B- | 42.6 | 7.65 | 6.0 | 29.7 | 10.2 | 8.1 | 10.0 | 14.2 |
| FAMILIES & SCHOOLS TOGETHER FCU | Hanford | CA | B+ | B | B- | 135.6 | 11.14 | 12.2 | 32.7 | 25.5 | 8.4 | 7.8 | 9.5 |
| FAMILIES FIRST FCU | Casper | WY | C- | D+ | C- | 6.1 | 5.17 | 0.0 | 43.2 | 22.0 | 0.0 | 10.0 | 14.4 |
| FAMILY 1ST FCU | New Castle | PA | C | C | C | 11.0 | -1.96 | 0.0 | 65.9 | 0.0 | 0.0 | 10.0 | 13.3 |
| ▲ FAMILY 1ST OF TEXAS FCU | Fort Worth | TX | C | D+ | D+ | 14.6 | 0.66 | 0.0 | 60.9 | 2.7 | 0.0 | 10.0 | 13.5 |
| FAMILY ADVANTAGE FCU | Spring Hill | TN | C+ | C | D+ | 46.4 | 17.01 | 0.0 | 44.9 | 11.9 | 0.5 | 6.2 | 8.2 |
| ▲ FAMILY COMMUNITY CU | Charles City | IA | C+ | C- | C- | 17.3 | 4.40 | 0.0 | 28.0 | 0.0 | 0.0 | 10.0 | 12.3 |
| FAMILY CU | Davenport | IA | A- | A- | B | 141.3 | 2.29 | 1.6 | 25.5 | 21.5 | 28.7 | 10.0 | 12.5 |
| FAMILY FCU | Wilmington | CA | D+ | D+ | D+ | 7.8 | 5.49 | 0.0 | 26.6 | 38.3 | 0.0 | 9.9 | 10.9 |
| FAMILY FINANCIAL CU | Norton Shores | MI | B | B- | B- | 97.0 | 4.94 | 0.1 | 34.9 | 11.7 | 29.2 | 10.0 | 13.9 |
| ▼ FAMILY FIRST CU | Saginaw | MI | D | C | C+ | 80.6 | 6.83 | 1.7 | 29.7 | 23.5 | 27.2 | 8.1 | 9.8 |
| FAMILY FIRST FCU | Great Falls | MT | E+ | E+ | E+ | 12.7 | -5.49 | 0.0 | 21.6 | 4.4 | 0.0 | 5.6 | 7.6 |
| FAMILY FIRST OF NY FCU | Rochester | NY | B+ | B | B+ | 164.5 | 9.59 | 6.1 | 24.3 | 23.1 | 0.0 | 9.9 | 10.9 |
| FAMILY FOCUS FCU | Omaha | NE | B+ | A- | A- | 31.5 | 4.73 | 0.0 | 46.0 | 20.1 | 3.6 | 10.0 | 12.9 |
| FAMILY HORIZONS CU | Indianapolis | IN | C | C | C | 85.8 | -2.17 | 0.0 | 60.2 | 17.4 | 8.3 | 9.7 | 10.8 |
| FAMILY SAVINGS CU | Gadsden | AL | B+ | B- | B- | 343.7 | 5.69 | 0.2 | 44.8 | 21.5 | 9.0 | 10.0 | 11.3 |
| FAMILY SECURITY CU | Decatur | AL | A | A | A | 547.6 | 4.57 | 0.6 | 36.2 | 5.4 | 19.9 | 10.0 | 13.9 |
| ▲ FAMILY TRUST FCU | Rock Hill | SC | B+ | B | B | 374.8 | 6.60 | 1.1 | 31.4 | 35.4 | 1.5 | 7.5 | 9.3 |
| ▼ FANNIE B PECK OF BETHEL AME CHURCH C | Detroit | MI | C- | C | C | <1 | -2.48 | 0.0 | 0.0 | 0.0 | 0.0 | 10.0 | 19.7 |
| FANNIN COUNTY TEACHERS FCU | Bonham | TX | C+ | C | C | 8.1 | 5.83 | 0.0 | 56.7 | 0.0 | 0.0 | 10.0 | 21.5 |
| FANNIN FCU | Bonham | TX | B- | C+ | C+ | 30.3 | 13.57 | 0.0 | 46.9 | 0.0 | 0.0 | 8.7 | 10.1 |
| FAR ROCKAWAY POSTAL FCU | Far Rockaway | NY | C- | C- | C+ | <1 | -10.14 | 0.0 | 46.2 | 0.0 | 0.0 | 10.0 | 19.4 |
| FARGO FEDERAL EMPL FCU | Fargo | ND | C | C- | C | 4.8 | 4.44 | 0.0 | 27.6 | 0.0 | 0.0 | 10.0 | 11.0 |
| FARGO PUBLIC SCHOOLS FCU | Fargo | ND | B- | B- | B | 32.9 | 4.11 | 0.0 | 21.3 | 21.3 | 0.0 | 10.0 | 14.1 |
| FARGO VA FCU | Fargo | ND | C | C | C | 9.3 | 5.16 | 0.0 | 40.4 | 0.0 | 0.0 | 10.0 | 12.1 |
| FARM BUREAU FAMILY CU | Lansing | MI | D+ | D+ | D | 17.7 | 7.30 | 0.0 | 29.7 | 0.0 | 0.0 | 6.8 | 8.8 |
| FARM CREDIT EMPL FCU | Saint Paul | MN | C- | C- | D+ | 13.4 | 0.98 | 0.0 | 46.8 | 11.3 | 0.0 | 7.3 | 9.2 |
| ▼ FARMERS BRANCH CITY EMPL FCU | Farmers Branch | TX | C- | C | C | 5.3 | 1.62 | 0.0 | 29.3 | 0.0 | 0.0 | 10.0 | 19.4 |
| FARMERS CU | Hays | KS | D | D | D | 13.9 | -1.01 | 14.9 | 10.2 | 9.4 | 5.8 | 10.0 | 11.5 |
| FARMERS FCU | Jacksonville | FL | C+ | C+ | C- | 13.2 | -0.29 | 0.4 | 15.4 | 16.9 | 0.0 | 10.0 | 14.1 |
| FARMERS INSURANCE GROUP FCU | Los Angeles | CA | A- | B | B | 686.6 | 3.82 | 50.6 | 24.2 | 28.7 | 3.5 | 10.0 | 13.5 |
| FARMWAY CU | Beloit | KS | B+ | B+ | B+ | 85.7 | -3.41 | 47.3 | 16.4 | 30.6 | 0.0 | 10.0 | 22.5 |
| FASNY FCU | Albany | NY | C | C- | C | 12.2 | -3.47 | 7.0 | 19.7 | 7.5 | 0.0 | 9.5 | 10.6 |
| FASSON EMPL FCU | Painesville | OH | C | C+ | C+ | 12.6 | -0.02 | 0.0 | 16.2 | 0.0 | 21.5 | 10.0 | 17.1 |
| FAYETTE COUNTY SCHOOL EMPL CU | Uniontown | PA | B- | B- | B- | 16.2 | 2.82 | 0.0 | 40.8 | 0.4 | 1.6 | 10.0 | 15.7 |
| FAYETTE FCU | Mount Hope | WV | C- | C- | C+ | 10.5 | -5.52 | 0.0 | 8.9 | 0.0 | 0.0 | 10.0 | 16.0 |

| Asset Quality Index | Non-Performing Loans as a % of Total Loans | as a % of Capital | Net Charge-Offs Avg Loans | Profitability Index | Net Income ($Mil) | Return on Assets | Return on Equity | Net Interest Spread | Overhead Efficiency Ratio | Liquidity Index | Liquidity Ratio | Hot Money Ratio | Stability Index |
|---|---|---|---|---|---|---|---|---|---|---|---|---|---|
| 9.5 | 0.15 | 0.3 | 2.12 | 0.0 | -0.1 | -2.73 | -11.64 | 3.87 | 160.2 | 6.2 | 48.4 | 0.0 | 6.0 |
| 9.7 | 0.62 | 0.8 | 0.26 | 8.7 | 0.1 | 1.26 | 4.13 | 2.88 | 47.6 | 4.8 | 26.5 | 0.0 | 7.0 |
| 10.0 | 0.24 | 0.3 | 0.12 | 7.3 | 11.6 | 1.09 | 7.44 | 1.90 | 49.0 | 3.9 | 5.4 | 12.1 | 9.3 |
| 8.5 | 0.56 | 3.7 | 0.35 | 3.8 | 1.7 | 0.40 | 4.58 | 2.72 | 83.4 | 3.4 | 12.9 | 10.1 | 6.0 |
| 9.7 | 0.67 | 2.5 | 0.17 | 3.6 | 0.4 | 0.47 | 4.51 | 2.58 | 83.2 | 4.8 | 42.4 | 4.9 | 6.4 |
| 4.6 | 9.71 | 17.5 | 5.33 | 4.9 | 0.0 | 0.47 | 2.52 | 10.56 | 77.8 | 7.6 | 77.0 | 0.0 | 3.7 |
| 6.3 | 0.87 | 4.3 | 0.00 | 2.1 | 0.0 | 0.00 | 0.00 | 5.50 | 100.0 | 6.2 | 39.4 | 0.0 | 4.8 |
| 10.0 | 0.26 | 1.8 | -0.01 | 6.3 | 2.3 | 0.99 | 10.46 | 3.26 | 72.4 | 3.2 | 22.8 | 9.3 | 6.5 |
| 6.3 | 0.91 | 8.8 | 0.23 | 2.6 | 0.1 | 0.20 | 2.73 | 3.97 | 97.2 | 3.9 | 9.1 | 0.0 | 2.8 |
| 6.3 | 2.91 | 9.1 | 0.32 | 1.9 | 0.2 | 0.29 | 1.44 | 3.52 | 92.3 | 4.0 | 21.1 | 0.7 | 6.0 |
| 6.1 | 1.69 | 10.1 | 0.00 | 2.1 | 0.0 | 0.03 | 0.31 | 3.61 | 98.3 | 3.9 | 21.0 | 2.7 | 4.9 |
| 9.2 | 1.37 | 4.3 | -0.05 | 3.1 | 0.1 | 0.32 | 2.24 | 2.70 | 89.6 | 4.9 | 35.4 | 2.3 | 6.6 |
| 8.3 | 0.36 | 4.3 | 0.04 | 4.3 | 1.4 | 0.61 | 7.50 | 3.24 | 85.1 | 4.2 | 18.2 | 2.0 | 5.9 |
| 4.6 | 1.76 | 7.5 | 0.00 | 4.5 | 0.0 | 0.83 | 6.19 | 4.26 | 71.7 | 5.9 | 44.0 | 0.0 | 3.7 |
| 5.4 | 4.30 | 11.1 | 0.70 | 2.3 | 0.0 | 0.06 | 0.35 | 6.52 | 97.6 | 5.9 | 48.8 | 0.0 | 6.7 |
| 10.0 | 0.00 | 0.0 | 0.03 | 3.0 | 0.1 | 0.32 | 3.98 | 2.77 | 87.4 | 4.8 | 30.6 | 1.2 | 3.9 |
| 10.0 | 0.21 | 0.7 | 0.07 | 1.8 | 0.0 | 0.02 | 0.16 | 3.04 | 100.0 | 5.6 | 31.7 | 0.0 | 6.0 |
| 6.0 | 0.94 | 12.0 | 0.31 | 5.4 | 11.4 | 0.83 | 8.71 | 3.00 | 81.6 | 3.6 | 4.6 | 4.2 | 6.8 |
| 8.7 | 0.00 | 0.0 | 0.00 | 1.7 | 0.0 | -0.93 | -8.33 | 7.04 | 113.0 | 6.4 | 80.3 | 0.0 | 5.9 |
| 6.9 | 1.11 | 4.9 | 3.72 | 8.6 | 0.1 | 1.27 | 6.93 | 8.31 | 68.4 | 4.2 | 28.8 | 0.0 | 5.7 |
| 3.5 | 6.82 | 17.2 | -17.83 | 6.3 | 0.0 | 0.99 | 7.02 | 7.59 | 89.7 | 6.8 | 57.8 | 0.0 | 5.6 |
| 0.3 | 13.70 | 55.6 | 0.00 | 0.0 | 0.0 | -1.93 | -28.57 | 2.29 | 233.3 | 6.8 | 60.5 | 0.0 | 4.3 |
| 7.8 | 0.84 | 5.3 | 0.26 | 2.4 | 0.2 | 0.14 | 1.15 | 2.80 | 94.0 | 3.3 | 6.5 | 9.4 | 7.0 |
| 5.4 | 2.11 | 15.6 | 0.89 | 9.5 | 0.1 | 1.64 | 14.13 | 5.86 | 57.1 | 3.7 | 41.0 | 21.5 | 7.1 |
| 7.5 | 1.24 | 4.9 | 0.85 | 6.5 | 0.3 | 0.93 | 6.48 | 4.29 | 61.7 | 3.6 | 28.3 | 8.1 | 6.3 |
| 9.0 | 0.49 | 3.0 | 0.27 | 7.5 | 1.2 | 1.22 | 12.88 | 3.99 | 68.0 | 5.0 | 22.8 | 1.6 | 6.4 |
| 7.0 | 0.81 | 4.5 | -0.35 | 4.4 | 0.0 | 0.60 | 4.15 | 4.58 | 97.7 | 4.0 | 13.4 | 0.0 | 3.7 |
| 5.3 | 1.94 | 10.5 | 0.00 | 3.4 | 0.0 | 0.39 | 3.04 | 3.36 | 91.5 | 3.3 | 17.3 | 7.7 | 6.0 |
| 7.1 | 0.70 | 4.2 | 0.36 | 2.1 | 0.0 | 0.27 | 1.97 | 5.58 | 96.9 | 3.8 | 26.0 | 9.9 | 5.2 |
| 6.8 | 0.47 | 3.5 | 0.50 | 9.2 | 0.5 | 1.43 | 17.71 | 5.04 | 68.2 | 5.2 | 28.6 | 0.6 | 3.6 |
| 9.9 | 0.00 | 0.0 | -0.07 | 3.0 | 0.1 | 0.49 | 4.02 | 3.12 | 86.2 | 5.6 | 39.5 | 0.0 | 5.8 |
| 6.5 | 1.77 | 10.1 | 0.50 | 6.3 | 1.0 | 0.93 | 7.72 | 3.72 | 75.9 | 3.9 | 14.9 | 5.7 | 8.1 |
| 7.1 | 0.58 | 3.2 | 0.26 | 2.3 | 0.0 | 0.05 | 0.47 | 7.76 | 97.5 | 4.6 | 15.0 | 0.0 | 5.1 |
| 8.5 | 0.90 | 3.9 | 0.20 | 4.2 | 0.5 | 0.65 | 4.73 | 3.17 | 83.9 | 3.6 | 9.2 | 6.5 | 6.5 |
| 5.4 | 2.02 | 13.3 | 0.85 | 1.0 | -0.1 | -0.09 | -1.03 | 3.18 | 92.1 | 2.8 | 12.2 | 17.9 | 4.2 |
| 6.0 | 0.77 | 7.4 | 0.35 | 0.9 | 0.0 | -0.36 | -4.64 | 3.57 | 104.1 | 5.7 | 34.7 | 1.7 | 2.0 |
| 8.6 | 0.65 | 4.6 | 0.10 | 6.1 | 1.2 | 0.96 | 9.09 | 3.96 | 78.7 | 2.6 | 9.3 | 10.3 | 7.9 |
| 7.2 | 0.60 | 3.5 | 0.19 | 8.4 | 0.2 | 1.05 | 8.21 | 4.52 | 78.3 | 3.1 | 12.1 | 7.6 | 7.0 |
| 6.9 | 0.35 | 2.3 | 0.12 | 2.9 | 0.2 | 0.29 | 2.61 | 2.88 | 88.4 | 3.5 | 8.2 | 2.4 | 4.9 |
| 6.1 | 1.06 | 9.0 | 0.69 | 5.6 | 2.0 | 0.77 | 6.83 | 4.74 | 81.9 | 3.8 | 13.5 | 6.9 | 7.3 |
| 9.0 | 0.49 | 2.4 | 0.39 | 7.9 | 4.9 | 1.19 | 8.94 | 2.65 | 73.2 | 4.5 | 22.1 | 8.8 | 9.4 |
| 7.1 | 0.78 | 7.2 | 0.30 | 7.3 | 3.2 | 1.15 | 14.10 | 3.79 | 75.7 | 3.4 | 14.2 | 8.3 | 6.0 |
| 10.0 | NA | 0.0 | NA | 0.4 | 0.0 | -5.16 | -22.72 | -5.84 | -33.3 | 9.3 | 123.0 | 0.0 | 7.1 |
| 6.9 | 0.39 | 1.3 | 0.05 | 8.7 | 0.1 | 1.27 | 5.85 | 4.48 | 68.6 | 4.5 | 31.7 | 0.0 | 5.0 |
| 6.8 | 0.22 | 1.5 | 0.51 | 5.8 | 0.2 | 0.79 | 7.83 | 4.68 | 79.8 | 4.9 | 26.0 | 2.9 | 5.1 |
| 5.9 | 3.88 | 8.5 | 10.77 | 0.2 | 0.0 | -5.83 | -27.30 | 7.47 | 110.0 | 7.1 | 67.7 | 0.0 | 6.9 |
| 9.8 | 0.00 | 0.0 | 0.00 | 5.7 | 0.0 | 1.07 | 9.71 | 2.99 | 58.7 | 5.2 | 24.4 | 3.2 | 5.0 |
| 9.9 | 0.12 | 0.5 | 0.15 | 3.7 | 0.1 | 0.46 | 3.32 | 2.96 | 86.6 | 4.6 | 19.5 | 3.2 | 7.5 |
| 9.4 | 0.27 | 1.3 | 0.00 | 4.7 | 0.1 | 0.68 | 5.62 | 3.65 | 85.4 | 4.9 | 31.8 | 0.0 | 4.3 |
| 6.9 | 0.76 | 3.8 | 0.56 | 3.2 | 0.1 | 0.38 | 4.36 | 2.96 | 85.6 | 5.0 | 15.1 | 0.0 | 3.0 |
| 8.5 | 0.00 | 0.0 | 0.00 | 4.6 | 0.1 | 0.66 | 7.37 | 3.29 | 78.9 | 4.1 | 22.0 | 2.1 | 4.3 |
| 9.7 | 0.00 | 0.0 | 0.00 | 0.9 | 0.0 | -0.18 | -0.90 | 3.42 | 106.1 | 5.9 | 51.7 | 12.5 | 7.0 |
| 9.1 | 0.27 | 1.3 | -0.30 | 0.4 | 0.0 | -0.21 | -1.83 | 2.57 | 108.4 | 5.8 | 46.2 | 0.0 | 4.8 |
| 9.0 | 1.08 | 2.8 | 0.29 | 2.3 | 0.0 | 0.09 | 0.64 | 3.34 | 91.8 | 5.6 | 28.8 | 0.0 | 6.3 |
| 6.1 | 0.47 | 2.8 | 0.47 | 6.8 | 5.0 | 0.99 | 7.42 | 4.99 | 77.3 | 2.9 | 11.8 | 7.5 | 8.9 |
| 6.5 | 1.27 | 4.3 | 0.27 | 4.5 | 0.4 | 0.65 | 2.99 | 3.49 | 83.4 | 3.8 | 17.1 | 2.5 | 7.8 |
| 7.1 | 0.45 | 2.1 | 0.45 | 3.6 | 0.1 | 0.49 | 4.77 | 3.01 | 77.4 | 4.6 | 35.9 | 4.9 | 4.2 |
| 10.0 | 0.29 | 0.3 | -0.45 | 2.4 | 0.0 | 0.19 | 1.12 | 1.84 | 84.6 | 5.7 | 27.8 | 0.0 | 6.8 |
| 9.5 | 0.98 | 2.8 | 0.42 | 4.2 | 0.1 | 0.67 | 4.33 | 3.10 | 73.7 | 4.9 | 23.2 | 0.0 | 7.3 |
| 9.8 | 0.07 | 0.1 | 0.23 | 1.5 | 0.0 | 0.05 | 0.32 | 1.57 | 91.0 | 7.2 | 52.4 | 0.0 | 5.8 |

| Name | City | State | Rating | 2014 Rating | 2013 Rating | Total Assets ($Mil) | One Year Asset Growth | Commercial Loans | Consumer Loans | Mortgage Loans | Securities | Capitalization Index | Net Worth Ratio |
|------|------|-------|--------|-------------|-------------|---------------------|----------------------|------------------|----------------|----------------|-----------|---------------------|-----------------|
| FAYETTE FEDERAL EMPL FCU | Uniontown | PA | D+ | D+ | C- | 12.2 | 1.07 | 0.0 | 28.5 | 1.0 | 0.0 | 10.0 | 11.9 |
| FAYETTEVILLE POSTAL CU | Fayetteville | NC | D- | D | D | 7.5 | 1.02 | 2.0 | 53.7 | 0.0 | 0.0 | 7.9 | 9.6 |
| FCAMEC FCU | Tallahassee | FL | D | D | D | 1.6 | 3.82 | 0.0 | 35.0 | 0.0 | 0.0 | 1.6 | 4.5 |
| FCI ASHLAND FCU | Ashland | KY | C- | C- | C- | 4.9 | -2.86 | 0.0 | 64.5 | 0.0 | 0.0 | 10.0 | 22.0 |
| FCI FCU | Texarkana | TX | D+ | D+ | D+ | 7.7 | -3.90 | 0.0 | 68.3 | 0.0 | 0.0 | 10.0 | 15.6 |
| FD COMMUNITY FCU | Waterbury | CT | C+ | C+ | C+ | 65.9 | 3.67 | 1.5 | 26.5 | 18.0 | 0.9 | 8.5 | 10.0 |
| FEDCHOICE FCU | Lanham | MD | B | B | B- | 350.5 | 1.40 | 11.7 | 22.3 | 10.1 | 37.9 | 10.0 | 11.4 |
| FEDCO CU | Jefferson City | MO | D- | D- | D | 5.6 | 8.30 | 0.0 | 14.6 | 0.0 | 0.0 | 5.2 | 7.2 |
| FEDCOM CU | Grand Rapids | MI | B | B+ | B+ | 59.3 | 11.83 | 4.3 | 38.3 | 10.5 | 12.0 | 10.0 | 11.0 |
| FEDERAL EMPL CU | Birmingham | AL | C+ | C | C+ | 15.0 | 2.80 | 0.0 | 32.2 | 8.0 | 0.0 | 10.0 | 20.8 |
| FEDERAL EMPL CU | Monroe | LA | B | B | B | 17.2 | 3.53 | 0.0 | 50.6 | 1.0 | 0.0 | 10.0 | 29.8 |
| FEDERAL EMPL CU | Texarkana | TX | D+ | D+ | C | 4.4 | -5.54 | 0.0 | 28.5 | 0.0 | 0.0 | 10.0 | 15.9 |
| FEDERAL EMPL NEWARK FCU | Newark | NJ | C- | D+ | D+ | 13.5 | -2.17 | 0.0 | 15.3 | 0.0 | 0.0 | 10.0 | 20.4 |
| FEDERAL EMPL OF CHIPPEWA COUNTY CU | Sault Sainte Marie | MI | D+ | D | D | 10.5 | 5.44 | 0.0 | 55.1 | 1.4 | 0.0 | 6.1 | 8.2 |
| ▼ FEDERAL EMPL WEST FCU | Los Angeles | CA | D+ | C- | D+ | 12.3 | -1.24 | 0.0 | 18.9 | 0.0 | 2.0 | 6.8 | 8.8 |
| FEDERAL LIFE EMPL CU | Riverwoods | IL | C- | C- | C- | <1 | -11.20 | 0.0 | 3.6 | 0.0 | 0.0 | 10.0 | 13.3 |
| FEDERATED EMPL CU | Owatonna | MN | C+ | C+ | B- | 40.9 | -0.63 | 0.0 | 30.7 | 5.6 | 4.3 | 10.0 | 14.4 |
| FEDEX EMPL CREDIT ASSN FCU | Memphis | TN | A- | A- | B+ | 408.7 | 2.31 | 0.0 | 24.2 | 15.7 | 31.2 | 10.0 | 16.3 |
| FEDFINANCIAL FCU | Rockville | MD | C- | C- | C | 73.4 | 0.56 | 0.0 | 16.1 | 1.6 | 0.0 | 6.1 | 8.1 |
| FEDMONT FCU | Montgomery | AL | B- | B- | C+ | 12.5 | 3.67 | 0.0 | 36.8 | 0.6 | 5.2 | 10.0 | 14.4 |
| FEDONE FCU | Laguna Niguel | CA | D+ | D+ | C | 20.3 | 0.93 | 0.0 | 25.3 | 0.0 | 0.0 | 10.0 | 11.2 |
| ▲ FEDSTAR CU | College Station | TX | B- | C | C- | 26.5 | 5.60 | 0.0 | 34.4 | 6.0 | 0.0 | 9.1 | 10.4 |
| FEDSTAR FCU | Roanoke | VA | D+ | C- | D+ | 12.1 | 9.25 | 0.0 | 60.5 | 0.2 | 0.0 | 7.5 | 9.3 |
| FEDTRUST FCU | Memphis | TN | D- | D- | D+ | 39.9 | 1.63 | 3.0 | 25.0 | 40.5 | 0.0 | 5.4 | 7.4 |
| FELICIANA FCU | Zachary | LA | C- | C- | C+ | 26.1 | 4.18 | 1.2 | 34.6 | 21.9 | 12.6 | 10.0 | 18.5 |
| ▲ FELLOWSHIP BAPTIST CHURCH CU | Chicago | IL | C | C | D+ | <1 | 13.74 | 0.0 | 24.8 | 0.0 | 0.0 | 10.0 | 12.1 |
| FELLOWSHIP CU | Lamar | CO | C+ | C+ | C+ | 11.4 | 1.97 | 8.0 | 19.7 | 54.9 | 0.0 | 10.0 | 14.8 |
| FELLOWSHIP CU | Windcrest | TX | C+ | C+ | C+ | 18.9 | -3.08 | 2.0 | 36.3 | 21.6 | 0.0 | 10.0 | 23.8 |
| FERGUS FCU | Lewistown | MT | B+ | B+ | B+ | 60.1 | 5.22 | 10.6 | 29.8 | 13.5 | 0.0 | 10.0 | 11.4 |
| FERGUSON FCU | Monticello | MS | B+ | B | B | 57.5 | 0.94 | 0.0 | 30.1 | 16.4 | 28.4 | 10.0 | 16.1 |
| FERKO MARYLAND FCU | Frederick | MD | C- | C- | D+ | 30.4 | 1.95 | 0.0 | 25.8 | 0.0 | 0.0 | 8.7 | 10.2 |
| FIAFE FCU | Baltimore | MD | C+ | C+ | C+ | 9.0 | -0.54 | 0.0 | 16.6 | 0.0 | 0.0 | 10.0 | 24.9 |
| FIBRE FCU | Longview | WA | B | B | B | 920.5 | 18.56 | 13.3 | 27.0 | 27.2 | 25.1 | 10.0 | 13.0 |
| ▼ FIDELIS FCU | New York | NY | D+ | C | C | <1 | 12.46 | 0.0 | 24.2 | 0.0 | 0.0 | 10.0 | 29.8 |
| FIELDALE CU | Cornelia | GA | C | C | C | 9.1 | 4.82 | 0.0 | 8.1 | 4.5 | 0.0 | 10.0 | 14.3 |
| FIELDSTONE CU | Bradley | IL | B | B | B- | 42.4 | 4.96 | 0.0 | 27.6 | 21.0 | 0.0 | 10.0 | 11.4 |
| ▲ FILER CU | Manistee | MI | B+ | B | B+ | 120.4 | 5.31 | 0.2 | 15.2 | 27.0 | 49.8 | 10.0 | 12.5 |
| FINANCIAL 1ST FCU | Williamsport | PA | D | C- | C | 4.5 | 1.45 | 0.0 | 55.5 | 0.0 | 0.0 | 9.5 | 10.7 |
| FINANCIAL ADVANTAGE FCU | Homestead | PA | C- | D+ | D+ | 9.9 | -0.56 | 0.0 | 15.0 | 0.0 | 0.0 | 10.0 | 11.4 |
| FINANCIAL ASSURANCE FCU | Jersey City | NJ | E- | E | D- | 14.8 | -7.97 | 0.0 | 39.3 | 2.2 | 7.2 | 4.2 | 6.3 |
| FINANCIAL BENEFITS CU | Alameda | CA | D+ | D+ | D | 18.8 | -1.30 | 0.0 | 4.1 | 0.0 | 0.0 | 6.5 | 8.6 |
| FINANCIAL BUILDERS FCU | Kokomo | IN | A- | A- | B+ | 76.4 | 4.66 | 0.0 | 42.5 | 19.0 | 7.5 | 10.0 | 13.4 |
| FINANCIAL CENTER CU | Stockton | CA | A | A+ | A+ | 415.2 | 9.04 | 0.0 | 32.8 | 3.0 | 48.4 | 10.0 | 22.0 |
| FINANCIAL CENTER FIRST CU | Indianapolis | IN | B- | B- | B- | 495.9 | -1.21 | 9.2 | 24.8 | 39.0 | 2.8 | 10.0 | 12.3 |
| FINANCIAL EDUCATORS FCU | Daytona Beach | FL | C+ | C- | D- | 17.3 | 8.34 | 1.8 | 32.0 | 10.3 | 27.2 | 8.7 | 10.2 |
| FINANCIAL FCU | Miami | FL | C- | C- | D+ | 53.1 | 0.10 | 0.0 | 21.7 | 2.2 | 0.0 | 10.0 | 15.6 |
| FINANCIAL HEALTH FCU | Indianapolis | IN | D+ | D | D | 28.2 | 2.53 | 0.0 | 58.2 | 0.4 | 6.4 | 9.8 | 10.9 |
| FINANCIAL HORIZONS CU | Hawthorne | NV | B+ | B+ | B+ | 155.9 | 5.48 | 6.0 | 29.1 | 20.3 | 20.3 | 9.3 | 10.7 |
| FINANCIAL ONE CU | Columbia Heights | MN | B- | C+ | C- | 82.0 | 16.85 | 13.3 | 33.3 | 11.4 | 0.0 | 6.5 | 8.5 |
| FINANCIAL PARTNERS CU | Downey | CA | B- | B | B | 1058.6 | 17.56 | 12.7 | 22.3 | 41.0 | 8.4 | 8.1 | 9.7 |
| FINANCIAL PARTNERS CU | Springfield | IL | D | D | D | 8.4 | -2.82 | 0.0 | 43.9 | 0.0 | 0.0 | 7.9 | 9.8 |
| ▼ FINANCIAL PARTNERS FCU | Woodburn | IN | C- | C | C | 26.6 | -1.87 | 0.1 | 41.0 | 11.8 | 14.8 | 8.0 | 9.7 |
| FINANCIAL PLUS CU | West Des Moines | IA | B- | B- | B | 164.6 | 1.47 | 7.8 | 23.3 | 13.5 | 17.6 | 9.4 | 10.6 |
| FINANCIAL PLUS CU | Ottawa | IL | A- | A | A | 271.6 | 15.78 | 0.7 | 33.7 | 18.0 | 14.1 | 10.0 | 12.9 |
| FINANCIAL PLUS CU | Flint | MI | A- | A- | A- | 438.2 | 2.16 | 8.0 | 40.2 | 11.6 | 20.3 | 10.0 | 14.9 |
| FINANCIAL RESOURCES FCU | Bridgewater | NJ | C+ | C+ | C | 409.5 | 4.07 | 12.1 | 8.5 | 42.6 | 26.7 | 7.7 | 9.5 |
| FINANCIAL SECURITY CU | Carlsbad | NM | B | B | B+ | 40.1 | 4.41 | 0.0 | 63.5 | 0.0 | 0.0 | 10.0 | 12.4 |
| FINANCIAL TRUST FCU | Cheektowaga | NY | B- | B- | B | 66.2 | 2.52 | 0.9 | 23.5 | 21.4 | 0.0 | 10.0 | 12.7 |
| FINANCIALEDGE COMMUNITY CU | Bay City | MI | C | C+ | C+ | 84.3 | 3.32 | 3.7 | 19.6 | 36.8 | 14.7 | 8.7 | 10.2 |
| FINANS FCU | Hammond | IN | D- | D | D | 11.1 | -1.48 | 0.0 | 31.0 | 5.0 | 0.0 | 8.4 | 9.9 |

| Asset Quality Index | Non-Performing Loans as a % of Total Loans | as a % of Capital | Net Charge-Offs Avg Loans | Profitability Index | Net Income ($Mil) | Return on Assets | Return on Equity | Net Interest Spread | Overhead Efficiency Ratio | Liquidity Index | Liquidity Ratio | Hot Money Ratio | Stability Index |
|---|---|---|---|---|---|---|---|---|---|---|---|---|---|
| 10.0 | 0.11 | 0.3 | 0.50 | 1.0 | 0.0 | -0.08 | -0.64 | 2.61 | 94.7 | 5.4 | 35.3 | 1.3 | 5.9 |
| 1.4 | 4.25 | 29.9 | 2.31 | 1.4 | 0.0 | -0.32 | -3.30 | 6.28 | 82.4 | 5.0 | 30.9 | 5.2 | 1.0 |
| 3.5 | 1.79 | 17.6 | 2.59 | 2.1 | -0.1 | -5.96 | -86.06 | 6.84 | 154.2 | 5.7 | 35.2 | 0.0 | 1.0 |
| 5.8 | 2.61 | 7.4 | 0.30 | 1.9 | 0.0 | 0.08 | 0.37 | 3.14 | 88.1 | 4.4 | 34.2 | 0.0 | 6.4 |
| 5.5 | 0.92 | 4.7 | 0.04 | 0.5 | -0.1 | -0.95 | -6.00 | 4.85 | 119.5 | 4.2 | 14.9 | 0.0 | 5.9 |
| 6.1 | 1.12 | 7.9 | 0.28 | 4.2 | 0.3 | 0.52 | 5.48 | 3.77 | 85.4 | 4.0 | 17.1 | 1.9 | 4.7 |
| 8.1 | 0.83 | 3.3 | 0.25 | 5.0 | 2.0 | 0.77 | 6.51 | 3.38 | 81.7 | 5.2 | 51.5 | 3.6 | 7.6 |
| 10.0 | 0.00 | 0.0 | 0.00 | 2.1 | 0.0 | 0.15 | 2.02 | 0.41 | 64.3 | 6.6 | 88.7 | 0.0 | 1.7 |
| 6.4 | 0.71 | 4.7 | 0.08 | 4.3 | 0.2 | 0.43 | 3.88 | 4.09 | 91.6 | 3.2 | 12.3 | 4.9 | 5.5 |
| 7.5 | 3.67 | 7.9 | 0.78 | 3.7 | 0.1 | 0.57 | 2.73 | 3.92 | 83.5 | 5.2 | 26.8 | 0.0 | 6.4 |
| 8.0 | 0.68 | 1.4 | 0.53 | 10.0 | 0.3 | 1.99 | 6.88 | 4.92 | 60.6 | 4.2 | 37.3 | 10.7 | 7.0 |
| 9.9 | 0.00 | 0.0 | 0.00 | 0.8 | 0.0 | -0.21 | -1.32 | 2.81 | 105.0 | 6.1 | 47.5 | 0.0 | 5.1 |
| 10.0 | 0.63 | 1.4 | 0.34 | 1.4 | 0.0 | 0.10 | 0.49 | 3.34 | 94.8 | 5.1 | 34.2 | 0.0 | 6.3 |
| 7.7 | 0.04 | 0.3 | 0.00 | 3.7 | 0.0 | 0.46 | 5.58 | 3.97 | 86.5 | 4.4 | 20.0 | 0.0 | 3.7 |
| 8.7 | 1.11 | 3.5 | 0.44 | 0.8 | 0.0 | -0.35 | -4.13 | 2.82 | 101.3 | 5.9 | 45.2 | 5.6 | 3.2 |
| 10.0 | 0.00 | 0.0 | -8.08 | 2.0 | 0.0 | 0.17 | 1.31 | 0.89 | 100.0 | 7.0 | 33.7 | 0.0 | 4.2 |
| 9.9 | 0.06 | 0.2 | -0.01 | 2.9 | 0.1 | 0.38 | 2.70 | 2.23 | 80.6 | 4.4 | 24.9 | 0.7 | 7.0 |
| 9.7 | 0.75 | 2.6 | 0.58 | 5.5 | 2.5 | 0.81 | 5.02 | 3.44 | 79.2 | 5.6 | 28.0 | 2.5 | 8.3 |
| 8.1 | 0.86 | 2.7 | -0.11 | 2.0 | 0.0 | 0.07 | 0.88 | 2.68 | 95.0 | 4.6 | 19.6 | 2.7 | 2.5 |
| 7.7 | 1.86 | 5.1 | 0.00 | 6.1 | 0.1 | 0.71 | 4.97 | 4.44 | 84.2 | 6.5 | 68.2 | 0.0 | 5.7 |
| 9.8 | 0.76 | 1.9 | 0.81 | 1.1 | 0.0 | -0.01 | -0.12 | 2.66 | 96.9 | 5.0 | 18.2 | 0.0 | 4.7 |
| 9.1 | 0.29 | 1.3 | 0.13 | 4.6 | 0.2 | 0.78 | 7.61 | 2.67 | 74.5 | 3.9 | 14.7 | 7.2 | 5.0 |
| 5.9 | 0.61 | 4.6 | 0.88 | 3.3 | 0.0 | 0.24 | 2.50 | 6.36 | 82.2 | 4.3 | 17.6 | 0.0 | 4.3 |
| 1.7 | 4.33 | 45.6 | 0.62 | 0.9 | -0.1 | -0.31 | -4.10 | 3.86 | 95.6 | 4.0 | 26.8 | 6.2 | 3.2 |
| 8.6 | 0.37 | 2.2 | 0.70 | 1.4 | 0.0 | -0.11 | -0.58 | 5.64 | 96.1 | 4.1 | 24.8 | 7.8 | 6.2 |
| 6.1 | 3.17 | 6.5 | 0.00 | 10.0 | 0.0 | 2.12 | 19.75 | 11.24 | 44.4 | 8.0 | 83.0 | 0.0 | 5.0 |
| 5.5 | 1.47 | 11.1 | 0.37 | 6.2 | 0.1 | 0.94 | 6.57 | 7.23 | 86.9 | 3.1 | 6.5 | 0.0 | 5.0 |
| 9.6 | 0.51 | 1.3 | 0.12 | 2.7 | 0.0 | 0.19 | 0.83 | 3.16 | 90.6 | 4.2 | 26.2 | 0.0 | 7.3 |
| 8.5 | 0.35 | 1.9 | 0.07 | 5.1 | 0.3 | 0.66 | 6.22 | 4.12 | 80.6 | 4.4 | 22.2 | 7.0 | 6.8 |
| 9.1 | 0.81 | 3.3 | 0.46 | 7.5 | 0.6 | 1.39 | 8.85 | 2.92 | 50.8 | 4.7 | 21.6 | 0.0 | 7.5 |
| 6.4 | 4.20 | 10.6 | 0.23 | 0.8 | -0.1 | -0.26 | -2.60 | 2.15 | 124.5 | 7.6 | 65.2 | 0.0 | 4.4 |
| 8.8 | 3.52 | 3.0 | 0.66 | 5.6 | 0.1 | 0.85 | 3.50 | 2.01 | 56.8 | 5.0 | 27.7 | 0.0 | 5.0 |
| 9.3 | 0.33 | 2.3 | 0.25 | 3.5 | 2.7 | 0.42 | 3.06 | 3.16 | 86.6 | 3.7 | 11.7 | 5.4 | 7.8 |
| 9.5 | 3.53 | 3.2 | 3.76 | 0.5 | 0.0 | -2.00 | -7.17 | 3.33 | 183.3 | 7.1 | 65.2 | 0.0 | 6.0 |
| 10.0 | 0.74 | 0.8 | 0.59 | 1.9 | 0.0 | 0.06 | 0.41 | 0.74 | 60.4 | 6.3 | 98.3 | 0.0 | 6.7 |
| 7.1 | 1.57 | 8.0 | 0.25 | 4.8 | 0.2 | 0.62 | 5.53 | 3.49 | 83.5 | 4.4 | 29.3 | 2.2 | 6.1 |
| 8.7 | 0.69 | 3.1 | 0.20 | 5.0 | 0.7 | 0.82 | 7.00 | 2.41 | 73.7 | 4.0 | 5.0 | 3.0 | 7.4 |
| 5.5 | 1.97 | 9.8 | 0.17 | 1.5 | 0.0 | -0.51 | -4.81 | 5.88 | 100.5 | 5.2 | 27.1 | 0.0 | 4.8 |
| 10.0 | 0.15 | 0.3 | 0.09 | 1.5 | 0.0 | -0.01 | -0.12 | 2.90 | 100.9 | 5.3 | 28.5 | 0.0 | 5.4 |
| 5.1 | 1.23 | 10.4 | 1.14 | 0.3 | -0.2 | -1.83 | -28.04 | 6.09 | 96.7 | 4.5 | 20.5 | 0.0 | 0.0 |
| 8.0 | 0.00 | 0.0 | -0.05 | 1.8 | 0.0 | -0.14 | -1.56 | 5.39 | 104.9 | 4.7 | 23.7 | 3.9 | 3.8 |
| 9.3 | 0.26 | 2.9 | 0.06 | 9.7 | 0.8 | 1.45 | 11.40 | 4.57 | 79.1 | 3.2 | 11.4 | 5.3 | 6.6 |
| 9.8 | 0.52 | 1.0 | 0.81 | 7.0 | 4.5 | 1.48 | 6.68 | 4.01 | 65.6 | 5.0 | 23.1 | 1.4 | 6.7 |
| 7.4 | 0.75 | 5.3 | 0.40 | 3.3 | 1.3 | 0.33 | 2.76 | 3.72 | 85.8 | 3.1 | 12.2 | 8.7 | 7.4 |
| 7.3 | 0.14 | 3.3 | 0.04 | 9.7 | 0.2 | 1.94 | 19.25 | 4.85 | 68.9 | 4.8 | 18.7 | 1.6 | 5.0 |
| 9.9 | 0.85 | 1.8 | 0.66 | 1.2 | 0.0 | -0.06 | -0.37 | 2.35 | 98.3 | 5.0 | 31.8 | 0.0 | 5.6 |
| 4.3 | 2.18 | 12.4 | 1.28 | 8.3 | 0.3 | 1.38 | 12.91 | 7.06 | 74.5 | 4.7 | 27.9 | 4.6 | 5.3 |
| 9.4 | 0.41 | 2.5 | 0.15 | 5.2 | 0.9 | 0.75 | 7.40 | 3.30 | 78.4 | 4.0 | 18.3 | 9.8 | 7.1 |
| 5.1 | 0.80 | 8.0 | 0.87 | 8.5 | 0.7 | 1.18 | 13.55 | 5.42 | 72.2 | 1.9 | 3.4 | 12.5 | 4.2 |
| 9.1 | 0.20 | 1.5 | 0.15 | 3.9 | 3.3 | 0.44 | 4.52 | 3.29 | 84.7 | 3.0 | 12.1 | 11.3 | 6.4 |
| 8.8 | 0.19 | 0.9 | 0.54 | 3.2 | 0.0 | 0.40 | 4.29 | 4.36 | 89.0 | 4.2 | 15.8 | 3.4 | 3.0 |
| 6.1 | 1.06 | 6.8 | 0.82 | 2.3 | 0.0 | 0.07 | 0.68 | 3.34 | 84.1 | 3.9 | 15.6 | 1.1 | 4.7 |
| 6.9 | 1.19 | 8.9 | 0.39 | 4.4 | 0.7 | 0.53 | 5.12 | 3.51 | 83.1 | 6.3 | 38.6 | 3.0 | 6.4 |
| 8.8 | 0.66 | 3.3 | 0.20 | 5.7 | 1.7 | 0.87 | 6.70 | 3.37 | 76.7 | 4.7 | 22.6 | 3.3 | 8.0 |
| 7.9 | 0.59 | 3.2 | 0.76 | 5.8 | 2.3 | 0.71 | 4.86 | 3.81 | 79.9 | 3.6 | 9.3 | 2.7 | 8.3 |
| 6.1 | 1.66 | 12.4 | 0.22 | 2.8 | 0.6 | 0.20 | 2.13 | 2.96 | 91.5 | 3.7 | 12.6 | 2.0 | 6.2 |
| 5.2 | 1.11 | 6.6 | 0.27 | 8.5 | 0.4 | 1.16 | 9.89 | 5.30 | 76.2 | 2.7 | 9.3 | 15.8 | 7.1 |
| 8.1 | 0.80 | 4.0 | 0.18 | 3.9 | 0.2 | 0.47 | 3.82 | 3.14 | 83.0 | 3.9 | 19.0 | 2.6 | 6.8 |
| 5.2 | 2.01 | 14.0 | 0.26 | 3.0 | 0.1 | 0.21 | 2.08 | 4.34 | 92.0 | 4.2 | 18.9 | 5.1 | 5.2 |
| 3.7 | 7.78 | 27.8 | 2.72 | 0.0 | -0.1 | -1.04 | -10.48 | 3.12 | 96.2 | 4.5 | 18.2 | 5.1 | 4.0 |

| Name | City | State | Rating | 2014 Rating | 2013 Rating | Total Assets ($Mil) | One Year Asset Growth | Asset Mix (As a % of Total Assets) | | | | Capital-ization Index | Net Worth Ratio |
|------|------|-------|--------|-------------|-------------|---------------------|-----------------------|-----------------|----------|----------|-----------|----------------------|------------------|
| | | | | | | | | Comm-ercial Loans | Cons-umer Loans | Mort-gage Loans | Secur-ities | | |
| FINEST FCU | New York | NY | D | U | U | 4.2 | NA | 0.0 | 24.3 | 0.0 | 6.0 | 10.0 | 41.8 |
| FINEX CU | East Hartford | CT | C- | C- | D+ | 78.7 | 2.18 | 0.0 | 23.9 | 19.4 | 0.0 | 7.1 | 9.0 |
| FINGER LAKES FCU | Geneva | NY | B- | B- | B- | 105.0 | 2.62 | 0.1 | 31.4 | 24.1 | 7.4 | 6.4 | 8.4 |
| FINGER LAKES HEALTH CARE FCU | Elmira | NY | C | C+ | B- | 23.5 | 2.25 | 0.0 | 34.3 | 7.8 | 0.0 | 10.0 | 14.0 |
| FIRE DEPT CU | Superior | WI | D | D | D+ | 1.3 | -7.46 | 0.0 | 49.6 | 0.0 | 0.0 | 10.0 | 17.9 |
| FIRE FIGHTERS CU | Tulsa | OK | B | B | B | 36.9 | 4.85 | 0.0 | 48.3 | 0.0 | 0.0 | 10.0 | 15.6 |
| FIRE POLICE CITY COUNTY FCU | Fort Wayne | IN | C+ | C+ | B | 108.7 | 1.96 | 0.2 | 29.6 | 36.6 | 0.0 | 9.3 | 10.6 |
| FIREFIGHTERS COMMUNITY CU | Cleveland | OH | D+ | C- | C+ | 230.9 | 16.44 | 0.2 | 39.8 | 22.2 | 2.9 | 8.8 | 10.2 |
| FIREFIGHTERS CU | Indianapolis | IN | C | C- | C | 62.7 | 9.52 | 0.5 | 31.1 | 4.5 | 39.3 | 10.0 | 14.5 |
| FIREFIGHTERS CU | Salt Lake City | UT | B- | B- | B- | 34.9 | 2.44 | 0.2 | 40.0 | 14.6 | 2.9 | 10.0 | 12.4 |
| FIREFIGHTERS CU | La Crosse | WI | B | B- | B- | 71.9 | 11.02 | 13.4 | 13.7 | 50.0 | 0.0 | 10.0 | 13.8 |
| FIREFIGHTERS FIRST CU | Los Angeles | CA | B+ | B+ | B+ | 1051.7 | 12.90 | 13.6 | 16.2 | 56.8 | 1.9 | 8.5 | 10.0 |
| ▲ FIRELANDS FCU | Bellevue | OH | B | B | B | 239.5 | 3.17 | 2.2 | 48.2 | 13.2 | 6.3 | 9.5 | 10.6 |
| FIREMANS CU | Birmingham | AL | B- | B- | B- | 4.8 | 2.98 | 0.0 | 61.9 | 0.0 | 0.0 | 10.0 | 28.0 |
| FIRESTONE FCU | Akron | OH | C+ | C+ | C+ | 200.2 | -2.27 | 0.0 | 2.8 | 11.8 | 57.9 | 10.0 | 17.3 |
| FIRESTONE LAKE CHARLES FCU | Sulphur | LA | D+ | D+ | C- | 10.4 | 12.71 | 0.0 | 25.5 | 0.0 | 0.0 | 9.4 | 10.6 |
| FIRST ABILENE FCU | Abilene | TX | B- | B- | B | 66.9 | -1.60 | 0.0 | 56.7 | 1.5 | 0.0 | 8.3 | 9.9 |
| FIRST AFRICAN BAPTIST CHURCH FCU | Sharon Hill | PA | E+ | D- | D | <1 | -1.12 | 0.0 | 6.8 | 0.0 | 0.0 | 4.8 | 6.8 |
| FIRST ALLIANCE CU | Rochester | MN | B- | B+ | A- | 153.2 | 7.58 | 6.1 | 28.8 | 21.2 | 8.2 | 9.7 | 10.9 |
| FIRST AMERICAN CU | Casa Grande | AZ | C+ | C+ | C+ | 111.4 | 4.19 | 5.1 | 58.2 | 5.5 | 10.2 | 5.3 | 7.3 |
| FIRST AREA CU | Saginaw | MI | B- | B- | B- | 28.6 | -0.14 | 4.4 | 32.9 | 14.8 | 18.7 | 10.0 | 11.7 |
| FIRST AREA FCU | Lewistown | PA | D | D+ | C- | 16.8 | 9.36 | 0.0 | 21.3 | 2.3 | 53.2 | 8.3 | 9.9 |
| FIRST ATLANTIC FCU | Eatontown | NJ | C- | C- | C | 209.4 | -1.21 | 3.4 | 17.8 | 32.8 | 5.6 | 6.8 | 8.8 |
| FIRST BAPTIST CHURCH (STRATFORD) FCU | Stratford | CT | D | D+ | D | <1 | 48.34 | 0.0 | 12.2 | 0.0 | 0.0 | 3.7 | 6.0 |
| FIRST BAPTIST CHURCH CRANFORD NEW JE | Cranford | NJ | D | D | D | <1 | -15.53 | 0.0 | 3.5 | 0.0 | 0.0 | 10.0 | 49.4 |
| FIRST BAPTIST CHURCH FCU | East Elmhurst | NY | D | D+ | C- | <1 | -19.84 | 0.0 | 5.6 | 0.0 | 0.0 | 10.0 | 21.5 |
| FIRST BAPTIST CHURCH OF DARBY FCU | Darby | PA | C- | C- | C | <1 | 14.75 | 0.0 | 15.7 | 0.0 | 0.0 | 10.0 | 22.9 |
| FIRST BAPTIST CHURCH OF VIENNA (VA) FC | Vienna | VA | C | C- | D- | 1.4 | -3.29 | 0.0 | 0.9 | 0.9 | 0.0 | 8.2 | 9.9 |
| FIRST BASIN CU | Odessa | TX | B+ | B | B | 205.9 | 1.58 | 10.4 | 25.6 | 37.5 | 9.7 | 7.6 | 9.4 |
| ▼ FIRST BRISTOL FCU | Bristol | CT | D+ | C | C | 84.0 | -0.62 | 0.0 | 14.4 | 24.3 | 8.9 | 10.0 | 11.6 |
| FIRST CALIFORNIA FCU | Fresno | CA | D | D+ | D+ | 80.4 | 2.63 | 0.0 | 35.3 | 5.0 | 79.0 | 8.6 | 10.1 |
| FIRST CAPITAL FCU | York | PA | B | B | B | 163.4 | 5.19 | 8.9 | 22.4 | 31.2 | 4.4 | 7.9 | 9.6 |
| FIRST CAROLINA PEOPLES CU | Goldsboro | NC | D+ | C- | C- | 27.8 | 6.93 | 0.5 | 11.7 | 57.5 | 0.0 | 7.6 | 9.4 |
| FIRST CASTLE FCU | Covington | LA | C | C | C | 69.6 | 9.13 | 0.0 | 67.2 | 12.9 | 1.0 | 6.2 | 8.3 |
| FIRST CENTRAL CU | Waco | TX | B+ | B+ | B+ | 64.7 | 5.76 | 0.0 | 43.3 | 16.4 | 1.6 | 10.0 | 13.2 |
| FIRST CENTURY FCU | Sioux Falls | SD | D+ | D | D | 19.1 | -0.75 | 25.2 | 12.2 | 18.8 | 0.0 | 8.5 | 10.0 |
| ▼ FIRST CHEYENNE FCU | Cheyenne | WY | D+ | C- | C- | 27.8 | -1.08 | 0.0 | 44.0 | 15.8 | 0.0 | 7.0 | 9.0 |
| FIRST CHOICE AMERICA COMMUNITY FCU | Weirton | WV | C+ | C+ | C+ | 412.4 | 1.56 | 6.5 | 5.1 | 19.5 | 10.6 | 10.0 | 14.3 |
| FIRST CHOICE COMMUNITY CU | Niles | OH | B | B | B- | 26.9 | 3.93 | 0.2 | 14.2 | 13.2 | 53.9 | 10.0 | 12.9 |
| FIRST CHOICE COMMUNITY CU | Knoxville | TN | C+ | B- | C+ | 36.7 | 1.36 | 0.0 | 28.5 | 14.9 | 0.0 | 10.0 | 16.1 |
| FIRST CHOICE CU | West Palm Beach | FL | C+ | C | C- | 99.7 | 4.00 | 0.0 | 17.9 | 13.8 | 44.0 | 7.2 | 9.4 |
| FIRST CHOICE CU | Marshfield | WI | B | B | B | 30.4 | 4.13 | 0.0 | 21.6 | 21.0 | 8.2 | 10.0 | 15.6 |
| ▲ FIRST CHOICE CU INC | Coldwater | OH | C+ | C+ | C+ | 15.4 | 6.60 | 0.0 | 19.0 | 13.7 | 24.7 | 10.0 | 11.6 |
| FIRST CHOICE FCU | New Castle | PA | D+ | D+ | C | 40.7 | 4.71 | 0.0 | 44.0 | 0.0 | 12.7 | 6.4 | 8.4 |
| FIRST CHOICE FINANCIAL FCU | Gloversville | NY | B+ | B+ | B+ | 89.0 | 5.49 | 0.0 | 22.6 | 20.2 | 25.4 | 10.0 | 12.0 |
| FIRST CITIZENS FCU | Fairhaven | MA | B- | B | B | 664.0 | 7.62 | 6.4 | 47.6 | 36.0 | 5.4 | 8.8 | 10.2 |
| FIRST CITY CU | Los Angeles | CA | B- | B- | B | 558.5 | 5.67 | 0.0 | 37.4 | 7.4 | 27.1 | 10.0 | 11.7 |
| FIRST CLASS AMERICAN CU | Fort Worth | TX | C | C | C | 47.2 | 1.24 | 0.0 | 32.9 | 6.0 | 0.0 | 7.1 | 9.1 |
| FIRST CLASS CU | West Des Moines | IA | C- | C | C | 68.7 | 4.93 | 3.4 | 32.1 | 8.2 | 28.0 | 7.2 | 9.2 |
| FIRST CLASS FCU | Allentown | PA | B+ | B+ | B+ | 28.2 | -1.68 | 0.0 | 11.9 | 54.9 | 0.0 | 10.0 | 16.6 |
| ▲ FIRST COAST COMMUNITY CU | Palatka | FL | C+ | C+ | C+ | 105.4 | 4.53 | 0.0 | 20.5 | 7.0 | 3.1 | 10.0 | 11.8 |
| FIRST COAST FCU | Jacksonville | FL | D+ | D+ | D+ | 7.9 | 0.46 | 0.0 | 64.8 | 0.2 | 0.0 | 10.0 | 14.9 |
| FIRST COMMERCE CU | Tallahassee | FL | A- | A- | B+ | 477.2 | 11.20 | 9.7 | 33.9 | 28.9 | 0.1 | 10.0 | 12.1 |
| FIRST COMMONWEALTH FCU | Bethlehem | PA | B+ | B- | C+ | 584.9 | 4.65 | 3.3 | 19.0 | 30.5 | 24.1 | 9.3 | 10.6 |
| FIRST COMMUNITY CU | Chesterfield | MO | C+ | C+ | C+ | 2084.8 | 5.85 | 1.5 | 29.5 | 18.6 | 28.1 | 6.7 | 8.7 |
| FIRST COMMUNITY CU | Jamestown | ND | A | A | A | 540.1 | 3.52 | 58.2 | 18.8 | 39.8 | 5.3 | 10.0 | 12.7 |
| FIRST COMMUNITY CU | Coquille | OR | B | B | B- | 878.4 | 8.02 | 10.3 | 17.7 | 25.3 | 17.4 | 9.2 | 10.5 |
| FIRST COMMUNITY CU | Houston | TX | B | B | B | 1136.8 | 8.51 | 8.5 | 54.5 | 20.7 | 15.0 | 6.2 | 8.2 |
| FIRST COMMUNITY CU OF BELOIT | Beloit | WI | A | A | A- | 114.8 | 13.91 | 0.5 | 68.1 | 7.3 | 0.0 | 10.0 | 13.2 |
| FIRST CONNECTICUT CU INC | Wallingford | CT | D- | D- | D- | 41.3 | 2.77 | 0.0 | 82.8 | 0.0 | 0.0 | 4.7 | 6.7 |

| Asset Quality Index | Non-Performing Loans as a % of Total Loans | as a % of Capital | Net Charge-Offs Avg Loans | Profitability Index | Net Income ($Mil) | Return on Assets | Return on Equity | Net Interest Spread | Overhead Efficiency Ratio | Liquidity Index | Liquidity Ratio | Hot Money Ratio | Stability Index |
|---|---|---|---|---|---|---|---|---|---|---|---|---|---|
| 10.0 | 0.00 | 0.0 | NA | 0.0 | 1.7 | NA | NA | NA | 13.3 | 6.7 | 226.5 | 90.3 | 0.0 |
| 4.3 | 1.84 | 15.2 | 0.47 | 2.4 | 0.0 | 0.05 | 0.56 | 3.59 | 95.6 | 3.6 | 9.2 | 1.7 | 3.7 |
| 8.0 | 0.74 | 5.9 | 0.35 | 3.8 | 0.3 | 0.34 | 4.06 | 3.90 | 85.7 | 4.0 | 11.8 | 0.6 | 5.5 |
| 9.9 | 0.40 | 1.3 | 0.09 | 1.9 | 0.0 | 0.02 | 0.16 | 2.36 | 98.7 | 5.2 | 28.8 | 0.0 | 7.0 |
| 4.0 | 4.28 | 13.1 | 1.85 | 0.0 | 0.0 | -1.76 | -9.86 | 3.57 | 136.7 | 5.4 | 47.4 | 0.0 | 5.2 |
| 8.5 | 0.63 | 2.2 | 0.22 | 4.4 | 0.1 | 0.50 | 3.19 | 4.62 | 87.1 | 5.2 | 39.2 | 6.5 | 7.0 |
| 8.0 | 0.52 | 4.2 | 0.36 | 3.5 | 0.3 | 0.40 | 3.94 | 3.86 | 86.0 | 3.4 | 16.9 | 4.5 | 6.3 |
| 5.4 | 2.18 | 16.4 | 0.52 | 1.8 | 0.1 | 0.03 | 0.32 | 3.99 | 93.9 | 3.3 | 12.8 | 4.4 | 5.3 |
| 8.9 | 0.96 | 2.9 | 0.28 | 6.7 | 3.6 | 7.78 | 56.91 | 2.95 | 28.7 | 5.3 | 27.4 | 1.5 | 4.9 |
| 8.6 | 0.76 | 4.5 | 0.07 | 3.8 | 0.1 | 0.56 | 4.51 | 3.03 | 82.9 | 3.9 | 14.3 | 1.9 | 6.5 |
| 5.3 | 1.47 | 9.8 | 0.10 | 8.0 | 0.6 | 1.23 | 8.90 | 3.77 | 74.5 | 1.9 | 12.5 | 18.4 | 7.3 |
| 8.0 | 0.40 | 3.3 | 0.06 | 5.1 | 5.8 | 0.77 | 7.53 | 3.26 | 78.0 | 2.1 | 10.5 | 18.1 | 6.7 |
| 5.7 | 1.16 | 7.7 | 1.08 | 4.7 | 1.2 | 0.67 | 6.95 | 4.47 | 74.6 | 3.2 | 13.5 | 7.8 | 6.1 |
| 7.0 | 1.08 | 2.3 | 0.40 | 10.0 | 0.1 | 2.84 | 10.51 | 7.41 | 40.5 | 5.5 | 32.9 | 0.0 | 5.7 |
| 9.1 | 2.45 | 2.8 | 0.14 | 2.7 | 0.4 | 0.29 | 1.70 | 1.22 | 68.4 | 5.3 | 30.8 | 1.9 | 7.1 |
| 7.8 | 1.25 | 3.8 | 1.00 | 1.9 | 0.0 | 0.19 | 1.83 | 2.70 | 79.0 | 5.4 | 34.7 | 0.0 | 4.0 |
| 7.3 | 0.34 | 2.7 | 0.13 | 4.8 | 0.4 | 0.70 | 7.40 | 3.59 | 83.6 | 4.5 | 25.0 | 4.8 | 5.3 |
| 4.6 | 16.67 | 14.3 | 0.00 | 0.0 | 0.0 | -1.50 | -19.05 | 0.00 | 300.0 | 8.7 | 96.3 | 0.0 | 3.9 |
| 8.2 | 0.69 | 4.1 | 0.11 | 3.8 | 0.5 | 0.45 | 4.09 | 3.42 | 89.6 | 3.9 | 15.9 | 1.5 | 6.9 |
| 5.1 | 0.79 | 7.7 | 1.30 | 4.8 | 0.6 | 0.71 | 9.82 | 4.31 | 78.6 | 2.5 | 18.9 | 30.0 | 4.1 |
| 6.8 | 0.54 | 6.4 | 0.05 | 4.0 | 0.1 | 0.46 | 4.02 | 3.72 | 86.7 | 4.5 | 17.4 | 0.9 | 5.9 |
| 7.6 | 0.09 | 2.7 | 0.21 | 0.8 | 0.0 | -0.07 | -0.72 | 3.11 | 100.0 | 4.7 | 19.3 | 0.0 | 4.8 |
| 7.0 | 0.75 | 8.9 | 0.16 | 2.6 | 0.5 | 0.30 | 3.45 | 2.94 | 90.3 | 3.6 | 19.8 | 4.3 | 5.3 |
| 7.8 | 0.00 | 0.0 | 0.00 | 1.4 | 0.0 | -0.77 | -10.67 | 7.84 | 116.7 | 8.0 | 89.2 | 0.0 | 1.0 |
| 6.5 | 0.00 | 0.0 | 0.00 | 0.0 | 0.0 | -8.70 | -16.67 | 5.80 | 800.0 | 8.7 | 147.7 | 0.0 | 6.2 |
| 10.0 | 0.00 | 0.0 | -5.13 | 0.0 | 0.0 | -1.89 | -9.66 | 0.93 | 350.0 | 6.8 | 48.3 | 0.0 | 5.0 |
| 9.0 | 0.00 | 0.0 | 0.00 | 1.5 | 0.0 | 0.00 | 0.00 | 0.00 | 0.0 | 8.6 | 109.4 | 0.0 | 6.2 |
| 9.6 | 0.00 | 0.0 | 0.00 | 5.1 | 0.0 | 0.55 | 5.76 | 3.31 | 70.0 | 7.1 | 46.0 | 0.0 | 4.3 |
| 8.7 | 0.27 | 3.2 | 0.41 | 6.5 | 1.6 | 1.00 | 11.30 | 3.93 | 76.8 | 4.4 | 20.3 | 6.1 | 6.6 |
| 7.9 | 1.47 | 6.1 | 0.28 | 0.8 | -0.1 | -0.15 | -1.34 | 3.41 | 98.1 | 4.7 | 23.4 | 4.5 | 5.8 |
| 7.9 | 0.82 | 4.0 | 0.34 | 0.5 | -0.2 | -0.27 | -2.71 | 2.68 | 102.3 | 4.2 | 23.4 | 9.5 | 4.2 |
| 8.9 | 0.53 | 3.6 | 0.20 | 4.4 | 0.6 | 0.51 | 5.54 | 3.50 | 84.1 | 4.1 | 11.7 | 1.8 | 6.5 |
| 1.7 | 5.30 | 42.7 | 0.68 | 1.3 | -0.1 | -0.22 | -2.29 | 4.15 | 90.4 | 3.5 | 24.3 | 15.1 | 4.8 |
| 3.5 | 0.88 | 15.1 | 0.59 | 5.0 | 0.3 | 0.51 | 5.98 | 4.61 | 81.3 | 1.4 | 12.0 | 32.8 | 4.4 |
| 5.9 | 2.36 | 13.3 | 0.52 | 9.3 | 0.6 | 1.22 | 9.56 | 5.71 | 83.9 | 4.1 | 20.6 | 6.5 | 7.7 |
| 3.9 | 0.09 | 10.9 | -0.05 | 4.8 | 0.2 | 1.03 | 10.75 | 4.28 | 77.9 | 3.8 | 19.8 | 6.0 | 3.6 |
| 6.5 | 0.73 | 8.9 | 0.68 | 1.5 | 0.0 | -0.12 | -1.27 | 4.46 | 94.3 | 3.5 | 26.5 | 10.7 | 3.5 |
| 9.9 | 0.36 | 1.1 | 0.00 | 2.8 | 1.0 | 0.31 | 2.23 | 1.89 | 86.9 | 4.8 | 32.5 | 4.8 | 8.1 |
| 8.0 | 2.09 | 5.0 | 0.43 | 5.1 | 0.2 | 0.76 | 5.95 | 2.84 | 72.5 | 3.6 | 29.2 | 24.4 | 6.5 |
| 10.0 | 0.31 | 1.1 | 0.14 | 2.5 | 0.1 | 0.16 | 1.02 | 3.15 | 94.4 | 4.7 | 31.9 | 5.3 | 7.0 |
| 6.8 | 0.55 | 3.8 | 0.73 | 4.6 | 0.5 | 0.73 | 8.28 | 2.50 | 81.7 | 2.3 | 28.0 | 89.0 | 4.1 |
| 9.2 | 1.09 | 3.3 | 0.01 | 3.7 | 0.1 | 0.39 | 2.53 | 3.31 | 89.0 | 4.7 | 30.6 | 1.6 | 7.3 |
| 10.0 | 0.05 | 0.4 | 0.14 | 2.9 | 0.0 | 0.32 | 2.97 | 2.44 | 87.0 | 5.3 | 31.8 | 0.0 | 5.7 |
| 8.8 | 0.20 | 1.3 | 0.04 | 1.1 | -0.1 | -0.17 | -1.97 | 2.60 | 103.5 | 4.4 | 18.4 | 1.5 | 3.3 |
| 8.6 | 0.73 | 2.9 | 0.37 | 6.0 | 0.5 | 0.81 | 6.93 | 3.42 | 76.9 | 4.9 | 18.2 | 0.9 | 6.5 |
| 6.8 | 0.50 | 4.7 | 0.27 | 3.9 | 2.4 | 0.50 | 4.75 | 2.85 | 85.3 | 1.7 | 5.3 | 17.3 | 7.2 |
| 9.9 | 0.16 | 0.6 | 0.54 | 3.6 | 1.8 | 0.44 | 3.74 | 2.92 | 82.0 | 5.0 | 23.3 | 6.1 | 7.6 |
| 6.9 | 0.51 | 4.5 | 0.16 | 4.1 | 0.2 | 0.46 | 5.20 | 4.06 | 90.2 | 3.9 | 14.2 | 4.7 | 4.3 |
| 5.7 | 1.23 | 8.8 | 0.77 | 2.5 | 0.0 | 0.07 | 0.81 | 3.79 | 89.6 | 4.6 | 14.8 | 1.5 | 3.9 |
| 10.0 | 0.32 | 1.3 | 0.10 | 4.2 | 0.1 | 0.55 | 3.40 | 4.80 | 81.6 | 5.6 | 32.2 | 0.0 | 7.7 |
| 7.3 | 1.31 | 4.7 | 0.75 | 3.3 | 0.3 | 0.37 | 3.24 | 3.64 | 89.9 | 5.2 | 25.9 | 3.1 | 6.5 |
| 7.0 | 0.74 | 4.4 | 0.02 | 2.3 | 0.0 | 0.23 | 1.59 | 4.51 | 94.1 | 4.8 | 33.9 | 0.0 | 5.8 |
| 7.8 | 0.31 | 3.2 | 0.48 | 6.4 | 3.0 | 0.83 | 7.01 | 3.91 | 77.8 | 3.4 | 21.0 | 13.0 | 7.8 |
| 7.9 | 0.86 | 4.9 | 0.61 | 5.6 | 3.9 | 0.88 | 8.67 | 3.61 | 73.0 | 4.2 | 15.7 | 1.6 | 6.9 |
| 7.6 | 0.58 | 5.7 | 0.42 | 3.3 | 6.9 | 0.46 | 5.20 | 2.39 | 80.1 | 4.6 | 16.4 | 4.7 | 6.1 |
| 5.9 | 0.41 | 3.0 | 0.11 | 9.6 | 5.8 | 1.46 | 11.82 | 4.14 | 66.1 | 1.9 | 7.2 | 15.8 | 10.0 |
| 7.7 | 0.88 | 4.9 | 0.21 | 4.9 | 4.2 | 0.65 | 6.51 | 3.05 | 80.8 | 4.7 | 22.1 | 4.5 | 7.2 |
| 7.1 | 0.35 | 3.2 | 0.42 | 4.2 | 4.4 | 0.53 | 6.54 | 3.20 | 79.6 | 3.0 | 7.4 | 5.8 | 6.0 |
| 7.1 | 0.50 | 3.4 | 0.12 | 9.0 | 1.0 | 1.21 | 9.01 | 3.46 | 74.6 | 1.8 | 6.7 | 13.8 | 9.6 |
| 4.1 | 0.70 | 9.5 | 0.09 | 1.3 | 0.0 | 0.00 | 0.00 | 3.36 | 97.2 | 2.6 | 0.6 | 1.8 | 1.0 |

| Name | City | State | Rating | 2014 Rating | 2013 Rating | Total Assets ($Mil) | One Year Asset Growth | Asset Mix (As a % of Total Assets) | | | | Capital-ization Index | Net Worth Ratio |
|------|------|-------|--------|-------------|-------------|---------------------|-----------------------|------------------|-------------|-------------|-------------|------|------|
| | | | | | | | | Comm-ercial Loans | Cons-umer Loans | Mort-gage Loans | Secur-ities | | |
| FIRST COUNTY FCU | Muncie | IN | D- | D- | D | 15.7 | 2.12 | 0.0 | 37.4 | 0.8 | 3.5 | 5.7 | 7.7 |
| FIRST CU | Chandler | AZ | B- | B- | C+ | 417.7 | 2.45 | 1.0 | 47.1 | 8.9 | 13.0 | 7.0 | 9.0 |
| ▼ FIRST CU | Oak Creek | WI | D- | D+ | D+ | 13.0 | -8.15 | 0.9 | 54.8 | 3.3 | 0.0 | 9.1 | 10.4 |
| FIRST CU OF GAINESVILLE | Gainesville | FL | D | D | D- | 46.5 | 4.64 | 0.0 | 55.3 | 15.0 | 0.7 | 5.5 | 7.5 |
| FIRST CU OF SCRANTON | Scranton | PA | E+ | D- | E+ | 17.9 | -0.95 | 0.0 | 13.2 | 0.0 | 0.0 | 4.6 | 6.6 |
| FIRST EAGLE FCU | Owings Mills | MD | C | C | C | 91.5 | 9.29 | 0.0 | 38.3 | 8.5 | 35.5 | 6.5 | 8.5 |
| FIRST EDUCATION FCU | Cheyenne | WY | C- | D+ | D+ | 51.8 | 4.50 | 0.0 | 19.3 | 9.0 | 2.0 | 5.4 | 7.4 |
| FIRST ENTERTAINMENT CU | Hollywood | CA | B+ | B+ | B+ | 1221.1 | 9.12 | 6.0 | 12.8 | 30.0 | 32.5 | 7.7 | 9.5 |
| FIRST FAMILY FCU | Henryetta | OK | B- | B- | B- | 62.7 | 12.63 | 0.0 | 85.1 | 0.0 | 0.0 | 8.6 | 10.0 |
| FIRST FCU | Hiawatha | IA | B+ | B | C+ | 108.5 | -0.64 | 6.1 | 17.9 | 47.7 | 11.3 | 8.4 | 9.9 |
| FIRST FINANCIAL CU | West Covina | CA | B- | B- | C+ | 437.7 | 2.72 | 2.1 | 33.5 | 30.6 | 5.1 | 6.7 | 8.7 |
| FIRST FINANCIAL CU | Chicago | IL | C+ | B- | B- | 69.4 | 0.62 | 0.0 | 39.5 | 19.3 | 3.3 | 9.9 | 11.0 |
| FIRST FINANCIAL CU | Jefferson City | MO | C- | C- | C- | 70.7 | 3.42 | 1.8 | 11.6 | 9.3 | 36.3 | 10.0 | 11.3 |
| FIRST FINANCIAL CU | Albuquerque | NM | C- | C | C- | 474.7 | 11.66 | 5.4 | 47.1 | 13.8 | 18.2 | 6.4 | 8.4 |
| FIRST FINANCIAL FCU | Wall | NJ | C- | C- | D+ | 179.1 | 1.18 | 12.4 | 19.9 | 16.1 | 13.7 | 5.7 | 7.9 |
| FIRST FINANCIAL OF MARYLAND FCU | Lutherville | MD | A | A | A+ | 952.4 | 1.66 | 0.3 | 11.6 | 11.3 | 48.7 | 10.0 | 21.2 |
| FIRST FLIGHT FCU | Cary | NC | B | B | B+ | 179.4 | 6.56 | 1.1 | 49.4 | 17.1 | 0.0 | 10.0 | 12.6 |
| FIRST FLORIDA CU | Jacksonville | FL | B+ | A- | B+ | 734.2 | 3.91 | 1.3 | 27.1 | 13.5 | 43.1 | 10.0 | 16.2 |
| FIRST FRONTIER FCU | Lynbrook | NY | D | D- | E+ | <1 | -2.85 | 0.0 | 61.9 | 0.0 | 0.0 | 10.0 | 11.2 |
| FIRST GENERAL CU | Muskegon | MI | C- | C | B- | 64.7 | -0.98 | 0.0 | 50.5 | 4.7 | 9.6 | 10.0 | 17.3 |
| ▼ FIRST HAWAIIAN HOMES FCU | Hoolehua | HI | F | C+ | B- | 3.2 | -3.01 | 0.0 | 42.0 | 0.0 | 0.0 | 10.0 | 20.4 |
| ▲ FIRST HERITAGE FCU | Painted Post | NY | B | B- | B- | 411.7 | 3.68 | 4.7 | 27.9 | 16.1 | 32.5 | 10.0 | 11.1 |
| FIRST ILLINOIS CU | Danville | IL | D | D+ | C- | 45.7 | 3.47 | 0.0 | 34.6 | 17.8 | 0.0 | 5.5 | 7.5 |
| FIRST IMPERIAL CU | El Centro | CA | B | B- | B- | 83.7 | 8.14 | 1.6 | 58.9 | 8.3 | 6.2 | 9.4 | 10.6 |
| FIRST JERSEY CU | Wayne | NJ | D+ | D+ | C- | 182.8 | 18.22 | 10.2 | 20.8 | 6.6 | 18.9 | 6.0 | 8.1 |
| ▲ FIRST KINGSPORT CU | Kingsport | TN | C | C+ | B- | 44.2 | 48.49 | 0.4 | 30.3 | 27.0 | 0.0 | 10.0 | 11.1 |
| FIRST LEGACY COMMUNITY CU | Charlotte | NC | C+ | C- | D+ | 36.1 | 3.51 | 5.9 | 23.8 | 38.8 | 0.0 | 10.0 | 16.4 |
| FIRST LINCOLN FCU | Lincoln | NE | C | C | C | 17.5 | 2.41 | 0.0 | 40.6 | 10.7 | 0.0 | 10.0 | 14.5 |
| ▼ FIRST MIAMI UNIV STUDENT FCU | Oxford | OH | E+ | D | D | <1 | -20.80 | 0.0 | 71.0 | 0.0 | 0.0 | 5.3 | 7.3 |
| FIRST MISSOURI CU | Saint Louis | MO | B+ | B+ | B | 57.7 | 3.37 | 5.0 | 45.5 | 15.9 | 6.2 | 10.0 | 12.2 |
| FIRST NEBRASKA EDUCATORS & EMPL GRO | Omaha | NE | A- | A- | A- | 113.3 | 17.45 | 0.0 | 25.7 | 27.5 | 24.7 | 10.0 | 16.8 |
| FIRST NESHOBA FCU | Philadelphia | MS | D | D | C- | 14.8 | 0.34 | 0.0 | 17.1 | 0.0 | 0.0 | 10.0 | 16.0 |
| FIRST NEW YORK FCU | Albany | NY | C | C | C | 283.2 | 5.20 | 5.2 | 15.1 | 26.9 | 21.3 | 7.9 | 9.6 |
| ▲ FIRST NORTHERN CU | Chicago | IL | D+ | D | D | 310.7 | 2.14 | 0.0 | 22.6 | 13.3 | 32.0 | 5.5 | 7.5 |
| FIRST NRV FCU | Radford | VA | D+ | D+ | D+ | 15.5 | 0.00 | 0.0 | 17.2 | 2.7 | 0.0 | 6.5 | 8.5 |
| FIRST OHIO COMMUNITY FCU | North Canton | OH | D | D+ | D+ | 35.2 | 1.30 | 0.0 | 45.2 | 5.3 | 0.0 | 6.7 | 8.7 |
| FIRST OKLAHOMA FCU | Tulsa | OK | C | C | C | 33.8 | 13.33 | 0.0 | 48.4 | 13.3 | 2.2 | 6.9 | 8.9 |
| FIRST PACE CU | West Saint Paul | MN | C | C | C | 8.8 | 7.98 | 0.0 | 41.0 | 0.0 | 25.8 | 10.0 | 19.7 |
| FIRST PENNSYLVANIA TOWNSHIP EMPL FCU | King of Prussia | PA | D- | D- | D+ | 1.6 | 3.47 | 0.0 | 52.3 | 0.0 | 0.0 | 8.0 | 9.7 |
| FIRST PEOPLES COMMUNITY FCU | Cumberland | MD | A- | A- | A- | 355.8 | 7.00 | 17.0 | 17.8 | 50.0 | 2.8 | 10.0 | 12.0 |
| ▲ FIRST PIONEERS FCU | Lafayette | LA | B | B- | C+ | 25.3 | 2.03 | 0.0 | 39.9 | 18.6 | 11.7 | 10.0 | 13.0 |
| FIRST POINT FCU | Hamilton | NJ | C | C | C- | 23.0 | -1.31 | 0.0 | 10.8 | 0.0 | 7.8 | 10.0 | 11.1 |
| FIRST PRIORITY CU | East Boston | MA | B- | C | C | 107.2 | -0.83 | 12.2 | 2.7 | 49.7 | 9.3 | 10.0 | 17.3 |
| ▲ FIRST PRIORITY CU | Abilene | TX | E+ | E | E- | 14.9 | -2.73 | 0.0 | 25.5 | 6.2 | 0.0 | 6.1 | 8.1 |
| FIRST PRIORITY FCU | Barboursville | WV | B | B | B- | 54.4 | -2.30 | 1.0 | 23.8 | 21.2 | 0.0 | 10.0 | 11.6 |
| FIRST RELIANCE FCU | Athens | GA | C | C- | C- | 12.4 | 3.19 | 0.0 | 31.9 | 9.7 | 0.0 | 9.8 | 10.9 |
| FIRST SECURITY CU | Lincolnwood | IL | D- | D | D | 7.1 | -0.79 | 0.0 | 78.9 | 0.0 | 0.0 | 6.5 | 8.5 |
| ▲ FIRST SERVICE CU | Houston | TX | D+ | D- | E+ | 572.8 | 13.15 | 0.1 | 57.3 | 8.0 | 13.0 | 8.5 | 10.1 |
| FIRST SERVICE FCU | Groveport | OH | C | C | C | 137.8 | 3.25 | 8.0 | 32.3 | 17.1 | 4.5 | 7.7 | 9.5 |
| FIRST SOURCE FCU | New Hartford | NY | B+ | B+ | B+ | 415.6 | 6.38 | 2.1 | 31.7 | 41.4 | 2.9 | 8.0 | 9.6 |
| FIRST SOUTH FINANCIAL CU | Bartlett | TN | A+ | A+ | A+ | 497.0 | 3.83 | 1.9 | 25.7 | 24.4 | 17.7 | 10.0 | 26.9 |
| ▼ FIRST STATE REFINERY FCU | New Castle | DE | D+ | C | C | 6.8 | -1.92 | 0.0 | 10.2 | 0.0 | 0.0 | 10.0 | 23.7 |
| ▲ FIRST TECHNOLOGY FCU | Mountain View | CA | B+ | B- | B- | 8335.6 | 17.29 | 4.0 | 18.5 | 40.3 | 22.9 | 7.7 | 9.5 |
| ▲ FIRST TRUST CU | Michigan City | IN | B- | B- | C | 98.4 | 2.30 | 1.1 | 15.6 | 15.8 | 0.0 | 8.6 | 10.1 |
| FIRST TULSA FCU | Tulsa | OK | C+ | C+ | C+ | 11.6 | 3.81 | 0.5 | 55.4 | 16.8 | 0.0 | 10.0 | 14.9 |
| ▲ FIRST UNITED CU | Grandville | MI | C+ | C- | C | 27.9 | -3.76 | 0.2 | 41.0 | 21.1 | 1.8 | 8.6 | 10.0 |
| FIRST UNITED CU | Tyler | TX | D+ | C- | C- | 3.0 | -8.49 | 3.7 | 79.6 | 0.0 | 0.0 | 10.0 | 27.1 |
| ▼ FIRST UNITY FCU | McComb | MS | E+ | D+ | U | <1 | 504.32 | 0.0 | 53.0 | 0.0 | 0.0 | 5.0 | 7.0 |
| FIRST US COMMUNITY CU | Sacramento | CA | B+ | A- | B+ | 332.7 | 25.10 | 3.4 | 13.3 | 33.7 | 20.7 | 8.8 | 10.2 |
| FIRSTENERGY CHOICE FCU | Greensburg | PA | C+ | C+ | B- | 55.5 | -1.08 | 0.0 | 13.6 | 0.1 | 54.4 | 10.0 | 15.3 |

| Asset Quality Index | Non-Performing Loans as a % of Total Loans | as a % of Capital | Net Charge-Offs Avg Loans | Profitability Index | Net Income ($Mil) | Return on Assets | Return on Equity | Net Interest Spread | Overhead Efficiency Ratio | Liquidity Index | Liquidity Ratio | Hot Money Ratio | Stability Index |
|---|---|---|---|---|---|---|---|---|---|---|---|---|---|
| 9.3 | 0.19 | 1.1 | 0.65 | 0.4 | 0.0 | -0.38 | -4.81 | 3.42 | 100.9 | 4.0 | 13.5 | 5.4 | 2.1 |
| 6.2 | 0.35 | 6.9 | 0.85 | 3.8 | 1.2 | 0.37 | 4.49 | 4.17 | 87.4 | 4.5 | 16.4 | 1.0 | 4.6 |
| 5.2 | 1.31 | 7.4 | 0.22 | 0.1 | -0.1 | -0.74 | -7.32 | 2.89 | 117.3 | 4.3 | 23.4 | 2.2 | 4.2 |
| 2.3 | 2.56 | 23.2 | 0.95 | 4.1 | 0.2 | 0.43 | 5.86 | 7.01 | 82.3 | 3.3 | 7.5 | 6.6 | 2.7 |
| 9.7 | 0.37 | 1.6 | 0.02 | 0.1 | -0.1 | -0.63 | -9.42 | 3.42 | 118.1 | 6.3 | 30.5 | 0.0 | 0.7 |
| 9.7 | 0.13 | 0.8 | 0.31 | 2.8 | 0.2 | 0.31 | 3.65 | 2.89 | 87.3 | 4.1 | 15.3 | 5.4 | 3.6 |
| 8.1 | 0.37 | 1.8 | 0.20 | 2.9 | 0.1 | 0.36 | 4.96 | 2.85 | 89.5 | 5.1 | 14.6 | 3.5 | 3.0 |
| 9.0 | 0.55 | 3.3 | 0.23 | 5.2 | 6.5 | 0.74 | 7.59 | 2.73 | 75.2 | 4.2 | 12.6 | 5.1 | 7.5 |
| 4.5 | 0.76 | 7.1 | 0.98 | 6.9 | 0.4 | 0.82 | 8.68 | 5.35 | 73.3 | 1.7 | 12.0 | 21.8 | 5.5 |
| 6.3 | 1.66 | 9.8 | 0.47 | 6.1 | 0.6 | 0.77 | 8.09 | 3.04 | 79.2 | 2.1 | 7.8 | 15.0 | 6.9 |
| 7.2 | 0.82 | 8.6 | 0.47 | 4.2 | 1.4 | 0.42 | 4.96 | 5.01 | 88.3 | 3.1 | 3.1 | 1.7 | 4.9 |
| 5.9 | 1.64 | 9.7 | 1.55 | 3.2 | 0.1 | 0.26 | 2.40 | 5.32 | 77.5 | 3.7 | 11.6 | 8.2 | 5.0 |
| 9.0 | 0.77 | 3.2 | 0.18 | 1.9 | 0.1 | 0.11 | 0.97 | 2.77 | 93.4 | 4.5 | 13.2 | 4.2 | 5.2 |
| 2.7 | 1.50 | 20.9 | 1.02 | 2.1 | 0.1 | 0.03 | 0.30 | 3.87 | 88.7 | 3.7 | 10.2 | 6.5 | 3.8 |
| 5.6 | 1.17 | 13.6 | 0.46 | 2.2 | 0.1 | 0.04 | 0.49 | 4.38 | 93.9 | 3.4 | 5.5 | 3.2 | 3.9 |
| 10.0 | 0.11 | 0.2 | 0.20 | 5.2 | 4.4 | 0.61 | 3.04 | 2.41 | 71.2 | 6.3 | 33.3 | 2.5 | 8.1 |
| 5.7 | 0.68 | 5.5 | 0.47 | 4.2 | 0.8 | 0.59 | 4.57 | 3.94 | 88.8 | 3.3 | 16.4 | 10.7 | 7.4 |
| 9.9 | 0.66 | 1.9 | 0.38 | 4.9 | 2.1 | 0.38 | 2.20 | 2.46 | 82.5 | 4.0 | 9.1 | 5.8 | 9.6 |
| 0.3 | 11.64 | 26.5 | 0.00 | 3.1 | 0.0 | 0.00 | 0.00 | 1.59 | 100.0 | 6.6 | 59.8 | 0.0 | 6.9 |
| 5.5 | 2.03 | 7.0 | 1.27 | 1.4 | 0.0 | 0.05 | 0.31 | 4.65 | 86.8 | 3.5 | 17.1 | 8.0 | 5.3 |
| 9.2 | 0.00 | 0.0 | 0.00 | 2.5 | 0.0 | 0.20 | 1.02 | 5.58 | 96.3 | 5.6 | 48.9 | 0.0 | 8.1 |
| 9.8 | 0.10 | 0.5 | 0.16 | 4.3 | 2.0 | 0.66 | 6.06 | 2.71 | 74.2 | 3.7 | 12.2 | 8.0 | 7.2 |
| 7.1 | 0.23 | 2.9 | 0.18 | 1.7 | 0.0 | -0.10 | -1.32 | 3.78 | 100.1 | 5.2 | 27.8 | 0.5 | 3.0 |
| 4.7 | 1.19 | 8.3 | 0.78 | 6.8 | 0.6 | 1.00 | 9.97 | 5.41 | 78.0 | 2.6 | 16.7 | 22.8 | 5.9 |
| 5.7 | 2.29 | 13.3 | 1.27 | 1.2 | -0.2 | -0.15 | -1.60 | 4.21 | 88.7 | 4.7 | 33.2 | 16.2 | 4.6 |
| 6.4 | 1.46 | 9.8 | 0.50 | 2.1 | 0.0 | 0.01 | 0.05 | 4.41 | 99.4 | 3.5 | 25.2 | 14.2 | 5.1 |
| 2.7 | 8.48 | 30.3 | 2.03 | 7.4 | 0.3 | 1.18 | 7.32 | 5.98 | 84.1 | 4.7 | 28.9 | 5.0 | 5.4 |
| 6.8 | 2.01 | 8.4 | 0.17 | 3.5 | 0.1 | 0.43 | 2.98 | 3.91 | 88.0 | 3.8 | 21.0 | 4.5 | 7.1 |
| 0.0 | 9.65 | 187.5 | 3.34 | 6.1 | 0.0 | 6.24 | 700.00 | 8.58 | 52.2 | 5.2 | 27.0 | 0.0 | 2.3 |
| 7.5 | 0.76 | 4.7 | 0.42 | 6.1 | 0.4 | 0.92 | 7.63 | 4.60 | 80.0 | 3.4 | 6.6 | 1.6 | 5.8 |
| 9.9 | 0.22 | 1.1 | 0.05 | 5.7 | 0.7 | 0.83 | 4.99 | 4.43 | 84.1 | 3.9 | 8.1 | 1.5 | 8.4 |
| 9.9 | 0.25 | 0.4 | 0.56 | 0.1 | -0.1 | -0.48 | -3.02 | 3.01 | 112.4 | 6.9 | 52.4 | 0.0 | 5.6 |
| 9.9 | 0.12 | 0.8 | 0.08 | 3.1 | 0.7 | 0.31 | 3.27 | 3.25 | 91.7 | 4.2 | 14.3 | 0.9 | 6.3 |
| 9.0 | 0.48 | 2.9 | 0.54 | 1.7 | 0.3 | 0.13 | 1.73 | 2.71 | 90.6 | 4.5 | 17.8 | 1.5 | 4.0 |
| 8.8 | 0.71 | 2.2 | 0.17 | 2.3 | 0.0 | 0.18 | 2.14 | 3.30 | 94.7 | 6.1 | 30.1 | 0.0 | 3.6 |
| 6.1 | 0.65 | 4.1 | 0.26 | 0.6 | -0.1 | -0.19 | -2.12 | 2.76 | 101.7 | 4.4 | 27.8 | 2.6 | 3.4 |
| 5.6 | 0.84 | 6.0 | 0.58 | 6.3 | 0.2 | 0.99 | 11.10 | 4.71 | 76.4 | 2.0 | 11.0 | 23.6 | 4.3 |
| 9.5 | 0.73 | 2.3 | 0.21 | 4.7 | 0.0 | 0.59 | 2.95 | 3.84 | 82.0 | 3.8 | 18.7 | 5.1 | 4.3 |
| 4.1 | 2.48 | 13.1 | -0.15 | 1.5 | 0.0 | 0.18 | 1.79 | 3.37 | 92.0 | 6.1 | 49.2 | 0.0 | 3.7 |
| 5.2 | 1.69 | 14.7 | 0.22 | 5.2 | 2.0 | 0.74 | 6.28 | 3.29 | 73.5 | 2.9 | 9.3 | 7.7 | 7.6 |
| 9.2 | 0.45 | 2.1 | 0.93 | 4.9 | 0.1 | 0.73 | 5.83 | 4.28 | 80.7 | 4.0 | 13.6 | 2.2 | 6.1 |
| 9.2 | 1.03 | 2.9 | 0.85 | 2.5 | 0.0 | 0.14 | 1.25 | 2.27 | 93.6 | 4.2 | 17.2 | 6.4 | 4.8 |
| 9.2 | 0.60 | 2.2 | 0.02 | 3.7 | 0.4 | 0.48 | 2.83 | 4.44 | 87.2 | 4.6 | 24.4 | 6.2 | 7.7 |
| 7.4 | 0.61 | 2.7 | 0.71 | 2.5 | 0.0 | 0.11 | 1.44 | 2.24 | 95.5 | 4.5 | 28.2 | 4.3 | 2.3 |
| 8.5 | 0.80 | 3.2 | 0.73 | 4.5 | 0.2 | 0.54 | 4.89 | 3.63 | 88.3 | 4.2 | 16.1 | 3.2 | 6.1 |
| 6.2 | 2.27 | 9.1 | 0.22 | 3.4 | 0.0 | 0.31 | 2.81 | 4.52 | 91.9 | 5.9 | 41.8 | 2.0 | 5.1 |
| 2.5 | 3.04 | 21.1 | 1.84 | 4.7 | 0.1 | 0.89 | 10.58 | 5.43 | 63.2 | 4.3 | 26.5 | 0.0 | 1.7 |
| 6.3 | 0.65 | 5.3 | 0.92 | 8.2 | 7.3 | 1.74 | 17.93 | 4.31 | 60.3 | 2.0 | 7.8 | 19.4 | 6.6 |
| 9.0 | 0.38 | 2.9 | 0.10 | 2.6 | 0.2 | 0.23 | 2.48 | 3.09 | 90.4 | 4.3 | 17.5 | 2.8 | 5.9 |
| 8.3 | 0.44 | 4.2 | 0.29 | 6.1 | 2.8 | 0.91 | 9.84 | 4.02 | 74.5 | 3.0 | 6.8 | 2.7 | 7.1 |
| 9.9 | 0.24 | 0.5 | 0.69 | 9.3 | 5.9 | 1.61 | 6.07 | 2.05 | 61.2 | 4.2 | 34.7 | 5.9 | 9.3 |
| 10.0 | 0.00 | 0.0 | 1.93 | 0.9 | 0.0 | -0.31 | -1.33 | 2.14 | 107.8 | 5.3 | 25.5 | 0.0 | 6.0 |
| 9.4 | 0.31 | 2.3 | 0.15 | 9.1 | 73.0 | 1.24 | 11.97 | 2.71 | 63.1 | 3.3 | 10.6 | 5.3 | 8.4 |
| 6.6 | 1.78 | 5.8 | 0.47 | 4.1 | 0.4 | 0.57 | 5.78 | 2.87 | 85.9 | 4.8 | 27.7 | 1.0 | 4.6 |
| 5.4 | 1.33 | 7.0 | 0.28 | 7.5 | 0.1 | 1.12 | 7.89 | 4.64 | 78.6 | 3.6 | 23.0 | 7.1 | 7.5 |
| 5.7 | 1.19 | 8.1 | 1.29 | 5.4 | 0.2 | 0.80 | 8.29 | 5.61 | 76.2 | 2.7 | 22.5 | 12.8 | 3.8 |
| 7.6 | 1.02 | 3.1 | 0.00 | 0.5 | 0.0 | -0.43 | -1.63 | 3.62 | 113.5 | 4.0 | 19.7 | 0.0 | 6.2 |
| 8.5 | 0.00 | 0.0 | 0.00 | 0.0 | 0.0 | -10.22 | -127.41 | 10.17 | 227.3 | 6.3 | 66.0 | 0.0 | 0.0 |
| 8.8 | 1.01 | 6.3 | 0.20 | 4.6 | 1.3 | 0.54 | 5.28 | 3.16 | 81.0 | 3.7 | 14.7 | 8.0 | 6.0 |
| 10.0 | 0.28 | 0.5 | 0.10 | 2.1 | 0.0 | 0.08 | 0.56 | 1.91 | 95.9 | 5.2 | 32.9 | 1.3 | 7.2 |

| Name | City | State | Rating | 2014 Rating | 2013 Rating | Total Assets ($Mil) | One Year Asset Growth | Asset Mix (As a % of Total Aseets) | | | | Capital- ization Index | Net Worth Ratio |
|------|------|-------|--------|-------------|-------------|---------------------|-----------------------|----------------------|---|---|---|------------------------|-----------------|
| | | | | | | | | Comm- ercial Loans | Cons- umer Loans | Mort- gage Loans | Secur- ities | | |
| FIRSTENERGY FAMILY CU INC | Akron | OH | C+ | C+ | C+ | 40.8 | 0.65 | 0.0 | 32.7 | 0.0 | 17.2 | 10.0 | 13.1 |
| FIRSTLIGHT FCU | El Paso | TX | B- | B- | B- | 887.6 | 3.80 | 8.9 | 53.2 | 24.8 | 5.0 | 6.7 | 8.7 |
| FIRSTMARK CU | San Antonio | TX | B | B | B | 980.6 | 12.40 | 4.7 | 37.1 | 34.3 | 18.1 | 6.7 | 8.7 |
| FISCAL CU | Glendale | CA | D+ | D | D+ | 139.3 | 0.61 | 7.7 | 18.6 | 13.0 | 33.7 | 7.1 | 9.1 |
| FISHER SCIENTIFIC EMPL FCU | Pittsburgh | PA | C- | C- | C- | 2.6 | -1.13 | 0.0 | 46.2 | 0.0 | 0.0 | 10.0 | 12.1 |
| FITZSIMONS FCU | Aurora | CO | C | B- | B- | 172.6 | 3.66 | 8.8 | 16.3 | 26.1 | 21.9 | 10.0 | 11.8 |
| FIVE COUNTY CU | Bath | ME | C+ | C+ | C+ | 226.0 | 5.27 | 5.1 | 17.4 | 43.6 | 0.0 | 5.7 | 7.7 |
| FIVE STAR CU | Dothan | AL | B+ | B+ | B+ | 323.9 | 9.22 | 15.6 | 30.8 | 26.3 | 12.2 | 8.7 | 10.1 |
| FIVEPOINT CU | Nederland | TX | A- | A- | A- | 499.2 | 5.98 | 8.7 | 40.1 | 23.8 | 13.3 | 10.0 | 12.0 |
| FLAG CU | Tallahassee | FL | C | C | C | 35.5 | -1.75 | 1.8 | 47.6 | 8.2 | 0.0 | 9.3 | 10.5 |
| FLAGSHIP COMMUNITY FCU | Port Huron | MI | D- | E+ | E | 18.0 | 15.97 | 14.1 | 29.4 | 38.3 | 0.0 | 4.8 | 6.8 |
| FLASHER COMMUNITY CU | Flasher | ND | D+ | D- | D | 11.6 | 19.60 | 19.6 | 6.0 | 41.8 | 0.0 | 5.0 | 7.0 |
| FLEUR DE LIS FCU | Metairie | LA | C- | D+ | D- | 15.3 | -2.14 | 0.0 | 29.4 | 0.0 | 21.2 | 9.1 | 10.4 |
| FLINT AREA SCHOOL EMPL CU | Flint | MI | B- | B- | B- | 377.9 | 3.14 | 0.0 | 11.8 | 5.1 | 64.5 | 10.0 | 15.2 |
| ▲ FLINT FCU | Reynolds | GA | C | C- | C- | 2.7 | -1.05 | 0.0 | 26.2 | 4.5 | 0.0 | 10.0 | 23.8 |
| FLINT RIVER EMPL FCU | Oglethorpe | GA | C | C | D+ | 1.9 | -2.95 | 0.0 | 35.3 | 0.0 | 0.0 | 10.0 | 24.8 |
| FLOODWOOD AREA CU | Floodwood | MN | C | C | C | 18.4 | 6.74 | 2.2 | 15.6 | 29.8 | 33.6 | 10.0 | 16.0 |
| FLORENCE DUPONT EMPL FCU | Florence | SC | C- | C+ | B | 41.2 | 3.94 | 1.2 | 66.8 | 5.9 | 0.0 | 5.6 | 7.6 |
| ▲ FLORENCE FCU | Florence | AL | C | C- | C | 51.7 | -1.23 | 0.0 | 6.4 | 20.9 | 24.5 | 10.0 | 11.0 |
| FLORIDA A&M UNIV FCU | Tallahassee | FL | E+ | E+ | D- | 20.0 | 2.25 | 0.8 | 33.7 | 16.5 | 0.0 | 4.8 | 6.8 |
| FLORIDA BAPTIST CU | Jacksonville | FL | D- | D | D | 23.7 | -0.16 | 11.1 | 9.2 | 5.6 | 57.9 | 6.9 | 8.9 |
| ▼ FLORIDA CENTRAL CU | Tampa | FL | C+ | B- | B- | 402.7 | 4.15 | 1.6 | 49.0 | 13.2 | 10.0 | 8.7 | 10.2 |
| FLORIDA CU | Gainesville | FL | B | B | B+ | 705.5 | 10.86 | 9.6 | 51.6 | 21.1 | 0.0 | 9.3 | 10.6 |
| FLORIDA CUSTOMS FCU | Tampa | FL | C | C | C | 9.5 | 2.85 | 0.0 | 36.9 | 0.0 | 0.0 | 10.0 | 17.2 |
| FLORIDA DEPT OF TRANSPORTATION CU | Tallahassee | FL | C | C+ | B- | 47.9 | 0.68 | 1.0 | 21.1 | 7.7 | 38.2 | 10.0 | 18.2 |
| FLORIDA HOSPITAL CU | Altamonte Springs | FL | B- | C+ | C+ | 47.7 | 11.00 | 0.0 | 28.6 | 9.3 | 6.7 | 8.6 | 10.0 |
| FLORIDA RURAL ELECTRIC CU | Tallahassee | FL | B- | B- | B- | 20.3 | 0.54 | 0.0 | 43.9 | 1.8 | 18.3 | 10.0 | 21.8 |
| FLORIDA STATE EMPL FCU | Pensacola | FL | D- | E+ | E- | 27.3 | -6.94 | 0.0 | 40.1 | 3.5 | 0.0 | 5.2 | 7.2 |
| FLORIDA STATE UNIV CU | Tallahassee | FL | B+ | B+ | B+ | 168.5 | 9.34 | 9.7 | 55.5 | 13.6 | 0.0 | 8.3 | 9.9 |
| FLORIDA WEST COAST CU | Brandon | FL | B- | B- | C+ | 86.6 | 3.37 | 0.0 | 30.5 | 0.0 | 43.3 | 8.4 | 9.9 |
| FLORIST FCU | Roswell | NM | C- | C- | C- | 7.9 | 5.16 | 8.9 | 39.7 | 14.6 | 0.0 | 10.0 | 14.4 |
| FLOWERS EMPL CREDIT LEAGUE CU | Thomasville | GA | B | B | B | 25.4 | 2.94 | 0.0 | 56.0 | 0.0 | 0.0 | 10.0 | 26.9 |
| FLUKE EMPL FCU | Everett | WA | C- | C- | C- | 2.8 | 1.22 | 0.0 | 48.4 | 0.0 | 0.0 | 10.0 | 18.8 |
| FM FINANCIAL CU | Flint | MI | C+ | B- | B- | 32.9 | 2.66 | 0.0 | 24.6 | 3.0 | 0.0 | 10.0 | 14.6 |
| FME FCU | Saint Clair Shores | MI | C+ | C+ | C+ | 70.4 | 0.66 | 0.7 | 14.6 | 26.6 | 12.7 | 10.0 | 12.9 |
| FO ME BO CO FCU | Wabash | IN | C- | C- | C- | 3.4 | 3.05 | 0.0 | 50.9 | 0.0 | 0.0 | 10.0 | 15.2 |
| FOCAL POINT FCU | Syracuse | NY | C+ | B- | C | 46.7 | -2.75 | 0.0 | 20.2 | 13.1 | 14.0 | 10.0 | 14.1 |
| ▲ FOCUS CU | Chattahoochee | FL | C+ | C- | C- | 133.2 | 2.68 | 7.7 | 22.1 | 22.7 | 27.9 | 7.6 | 9.5 |
| FOCUS CU | Wauwatosa | WI | D | D | D | 41.6 | 1.61 | 0.1 | 65.8 | 2.9 | 0.0 | 5.0 | 7.0 |
| FOCUS FCU | Toledo | OH | D- | D- | D- | 8.4 | -10.62 | 0.0 | 44.9 | 1.3 | 4.8 | 8.0 | 9.7 |
| ▼ FOCUS FCU | Oklahoma City | OK | C | C+ | C- | 103.4 | 1.72 | 0.0 | 54.9 | 19.8 | 5.1 | 5.4 | 7.4 |
| FOCUS FIRST FCU | Rochester | NY | D | D | C- | 16.7 | 1.89 | 0.0 | 47.1 | 0.0 | 0.0 | 10.0 | 45.7 |
| FOGCE FCU | Eutaw | AL | C+ | C | D | 1.4 | 6.46 | 0.0 | 20.2 | 0.0 | 0.0 | 10.0 | 19.6 |
| FOND DU LAC CU | Fond du Lac | WI | C+ | C | C | 56.7 | 6.80 | 0.0 | 40.9 | 23.8 | 0.0 | 7.4 | 9.3 |
| ▼ FONTANA FCU | Fontana | CA | C | B- | B- | 13.3 | 1.64 | 0.0 | 27.4 | 0.0 | 0.0 | 10.0 | 12.3 |
| FOOD INDUSTRIES CU | Springfield | OR | C+ | C | C- | 23.9 | -1.46 | 2.3 | 17.0 | 29.8 | 0.0 | 10.0 | 21.1 |
| FOOTHILL FCU | Arcadia | CA | A | A | A | 339.1 | 9.40 | 4.2 | 17.7 | 21.9 | 37.6 | 10.0 | 12.4 |
| ▲ FOOTHILLS CU | Lakewood | CO | B | B- | B- | 87.5 | 26.03 | 9.3 | 21.2 | 37.8 | 0.0 | 8.8 | 10.2 |
| FOOTHILLS FCU | Loudon | TN | B- | B | B | 42.9 | 4.44 | 2.8 | 27.5 | 13.2 | 0.0 | 10.0 | 11.7 |
| FOREST AREA FCU | Fife Lake | MI | B+ | A- | B+ | 97.9 | 0.62 | 0.7 | 13.4 | 27.5 | 14.2 | 10.0 | 14.5 |
| FORMICA-EVENDALE FCU | Evendale | OH | C- | C- | C- | 1.9 | -0.47 | 0.0 | 52.3 | 0.0 | 0.0 | 10.0 | 25.4 |
| ▲ FORREST COUNTY TEACHERS FCU | Hattiesburg | MS | C- | D | D | <1 | 3.73 | 0.0 | 48.8 | 0.0 | 0.0 | 10.0 | 21.2 |
| FORREST-PETAL EDUCATIONAL FCU | Hattiesburg | MS | E+ | E+ | E+ | 1.2 | -2.94 | 0.0 | 31.9 | 0.0 | 0.0 | 6.1 | 8.2 |
| ▼ FORT BAYARD FCU | Silver City | NM | D+ | C- | C | 4.8 | 5.43 | 0.0 | 56.6 | 0.0 | 0.0 | 10.0 | 20.8 |
| FORT BILLINGS FCU | Gibbstown | NJ | D | D | D+ | 61.6 | 1.42 | 0.0 | 10.8 | 8.1 | 57.0 | 9.0 | 10.4 |
| FORT BRAGG FCU | Fayetteville | NC | C+ | C+ | C | 377.6 | -1.48 | 0.3 | 26.7 | 14.8 | 19.0 | 9.0 | 10.3 |
| FORT CAMPBELL FCU | Clarksville | TN | A- | A- | B+ | 481.1 | 2.73 | 1.1 | 47.5 | 18.3 | 13.9 | 10.0 | 14.3 |
| FORT COMMUNITY CU | Fort Atkinson | WI | A- | B+ | B+ | 215.3 | 5.82 | 6.4 | 24.6 | 25.4 | 23.9 | 10.0 | 13.2 |
| ▼ FORT DIX FCU | Fort Dix | NJ | D+ | C- | C- | 9.2 | 2.11 | 0.0 | 23.1 | 0.0 | 0.0 | 10.0 | 14.0 |
| ▲ FORT DODGE FAMILY CU | Fort Dodge | IA | B+ | B- | B- | 26.2 | 7.11 | 0.0 | 34.3 | 0.0 | 15.3 | 10.0 | 11.9 |

| Asset Quality Index | Non-Performing Loans as a % of Total Loans | as a % of Capital | Net Charge-Offs Avg Loans | Profitability Index | Net Income ($Mil) | Return on Assets | Return on Equity | Net Interest Spread | Overhead Efficiency Ratio | Liquidity Index | Liquidity Ratio | Hot Money Ratio | Stability Index |
|---|---|---|---|---|---|---|---|---|---|---|---|---|---|
| 9.9 | 0.13 | 0.6 | 0.01 | 2.2 | 0.0 | 0.09 | 0.70 | 2.39 | 95.7 | 4.7 | 28.0 | 0.0 | 6.9 |
| 4.8 | 0.91 | 9.6 | 0.77 | 3.9 | 2.6 | 0.39 | 4.51 | 3.62 | 80.5 | 2.7 | 6.0 | 9.9 | 5.7 |
| 6.5 | 0.59 | 6.9 | 0.48 | 4.7 | 5.0 | 0.70 | 8.96 | 3.50 | 78.9 | 1.9 | 9.1 | 19.0 | 5.0 |
| 9.9 | 0.20 | 0.9 | 0.26 | 1.6 | 0.1 | 0.05 | 0.50 | 3.17 | 96.5 | 4.9 | 22.7 | 6.5 | 5.0 |
| 8.3 | 0.19 | 0.9 | 0.24 | 1.9 | 0.0 | 0.00 | 0.00 | 5.83 | 102.0 | 6.1 | 43.3 | 0.0 | 5.9 |
| 9.6 | 0.39 | 1.7 | 0.39 | 2.0 | 0.0 | 0.00 | 0.03 | 3.04 | 94.7 | 3.9 | 18.4 | 4.7 | 6.9 |
| 6.2 | 1.24 | 11.4 | 0.40 | 3.2 | 0.4 | 0.24 | 3.14 | 4.39 | 90.5 | 2.8 | 22.0 | 17.1 | 4.6 |
| 5.5 | 0.87 | 10.6 | 0.84 | 9.3 | 3.0 | 1.21 | 13.26 | 5.24 | 69.6 | 2.9 | 13.3 | 17.0 | 7.9 |
| 8.0 | 0.48 | 3.3 | 0.50 | 6.7 | 3.5 | 0.95 | 8.16 | 4.71 | 78.9 | 2.2 | 7.6 | 18.6 | 7.8 |
| 4.6 | 1.25 | 7.6 | 0.42 | 3.4 | 0.1 | 0.32 | 3.28 | 4.78 | 93.2 | 5.1 | 33.1 | 4.1 | 4.2 |
| 5.5 | 0.68 | 7.6 | 0.12 | 4.5 | 0.1 | 0.77 | 11.04 | 4.39 | 83.5 | 3.5 | 6.8 | 0.0 | 1.7 |
| 4.3 | 1.28 | 11.2 | 0.00 | 6.3 | 0.1 | 0.86 | 12.11 | 4.15 | 74.5 | 6.2 | 47.5 | 0.0 | 3.0 |
| 5.0 | 2.65 | 15.4 | -0.53 | 2.5 | 0.0 | 0.23 | 2.26 | 3.57 | 99.3 | 5.1 | 33.2 | 6.6 | 5.3 |
| 10.0 | 0.90 | 1.3 | 0.16 | 4.0 | 1.7 | 0.60 | 4.23 | 2.08 | 73.8 | 5.2 | 16.9 | 1.9 | 7.8 |
| 9.1 | 2.19 | 3.3 | 0.00 | 2.4 | 0.0 | 0.35 | 1.49 | 3.15 | 87.5 | 6.4 | 82.3 | 0.0 | 6.8 |
| 9.6 | 0.86 | 1.5 | 0.00 | 3.6 | 0.0 | 0.42 | 1.67 | 4.16 | 89.3 | 6.6 | 89.3 | 0.0 | 7.1 |
| 5.4 | 5.76 | 18.1 | 0.43 | 2.7 | 0.0 | 0.26 | 1.59 | 2.92 | 91.1 | 4.9 | 23.9 | 1.4 | 7.4 |
| 0.0 | 15.18 | 124.7 | 6.88 | 3.7 | -2.4 | -7.80 | -79.95 | 5.66 | 40.9 | 3.3 | 18.3 | 14.3 | 8.6 |
| 8.8 | 0.09 | 3.7 | 0.06 | 2.2 | 0.1 | 0.26 | 2.45 | 1.92 | 92.7 | 4.3 | 24.7 | 7.6 | 5.2 |
| 3.4 | 3.48 | 23.8 | 1.53 | 1.0 | 0.0 | -0.06 | -0.86 | 5.73 | 98.3 | 5.3 | 29.0 | 4.3 | 0.0 |
| 9.7 | 0.03 | 0.1 | -0.32 | 0.3 | -0.1 | -0.44 | -4.60 | 2.13 | 118.2 | 4.6 | 17.0 | 5.0 | 3.2 |
| 5.4 | 1.34 | 12.8 | 0.75 | 2.9 | 0.4 | 0.14 | 1.49 | 4.23 | 79.7 | 4.2 | 13.9 | 2.8 | 5.7 |
| 5.2 | 0.53 | 6.4 | 0.84 | 9.7 | 6.5 | 1.26 | 12.18 | 5.25 | 72.9 | 2.5 | 17.6 | 18.5 | 8.1 |
| 8.0 | 1.83 | 4.0 | 0.74 | 3.1 | 0.0 | 0.27 | 1.56 | 3.86 | 87.2 | 4.6 | 37.3 | 12.9 | 7.0 |
| 9.1 | 2.13 | 4.0 | 0.79 | 1.7 | 0.0 | 0.03 | 0.18 | 3.26 | 97.1 | 4.3 | 9.6 | 5.5 | 6.4 |
| 9.5 | 0.36 | 1.4 | 0.70 | 5.4 | 0.3 | 0.93 | 9.02 | 3.44 | 78.3 | 5.8 | 27.4 | 0.2 | 4.3 |
| 9.1 | 0.22 | 0.9 | 0.00 | 3.2 | 0.0 | 0.29 | 1.33 | 4.22 | 93.4 | 4.2 | 19.7 | 7.3 | 6.9 |
| 3.6 | 3.22 | 20.3 | 2.65 | 0.0 | -0.3 | -1.17 | -15.74 | 4.23 | 108.4 | 4.8 | 34.2 | 11.9 | 2.7 |
| 4.9 | 0.89 | 9.0 | 0.76 | 6.8 | 1.0 | 0.79 | 8.15 | 5.00 | 75.5 | 3.9 | 11.6 | 1.2 | 6.8 |
| 9.9 | 0.05 | 0.2 | 0.15 | 4.1 | 0.4 | 0.55 | 5.61 | 2.86 | 85.0 | 4.7 | 22.5 | 5.0 | 4.5 |
| 7.4 | 0.77 | 3.1 | 0.06 | 3.7 | 0.0 | 0.45 | 3.19 | 3.68 | 85.4 | 3.8 | 17.2 | 5.9 | 3.7 |
| 7.3 | 1.39 | 3.2 | 1.49 | 7.7 | 0.2 | 0.94 | 3.38 | 6.31 | 71.5 | 5.3 | 57.1 | 4.7 | 6.3 |
| 8.7 | 0.66 | 1.7 | 0.47 | 1.5 | 0.0 | -0.14 | -0.75 | 4.54 | 97.3 | 6.1 | 54.2 | 0.0 | 6.7 |
| 7.9 | 2.40 | 5.1 | 0.98 | 2.4 | 0.0 | 0.12 | 0.84 | 3.30 | 95.2 | 5.6 | 31.2 | 1.8 | 6.1 |
| 8.9 | 0.83 | 3.0 | 0.23 | 2.6 | 0.1 | 0.22 | 1.75 | 2.85 | 92.6 | 4.4 | 24.8 | 3.0 | 5.7 |
| 8.6 | 0.00 | 0.0 | 0.00 | 3.3 | 0.0 | 0.43 | 2.88 | 2.99 | 83.6 | 4.9 | 20.3 | 0.0 | 7.1 |
| 8.0 | 1.87 | 6.4 | 0.26 | 1.1 | -0.2 | -0.61 | -4.54 | 4.30 | 112.8 | 5.0 | 21.6 | 0.7 | 5.9 |
| 5.7 | 0.92 | 13.7 | 0.58 | 3.6 | 0.5 | 0.46 | 5.92 | 3.48 | 82.5 | 4.1 | 13.0 | 7.8 | 5.0 |
| 4.2 | 1.05 | 11.2 | 0.32 | 3.7 | 0.1 | 0.36 | 5.25 | 4.12 | 91.8 | 4.1 | 16.4 | 1.8 | 2.1 |
| 8.5 | 0.73 | 4.2 | -0.17 | 0.5 | 0.0 | -0.53 | -5.70 | 4.52 | 108.8 | 4.1 | 21.2 | 0.0 | 2.9 |
| 5.5 | 0.66 | 9.3 | 0.46 | 2.2 | 0.0 | 0.03 | 0.40 | 3.61 | 88.5 | 3.3 | 8.9 | 4.8 | 4.3 |
| 8.8 | 1.08 | 1.3 | 0.28 | 0.0 | -0.2 | -1.92 | -4.15 | 2.16 | 175.5 | 3.3 | 30.5 | 16.7 | 5.6 |
| 10.0 | 0.31 | 0.4 | 0.82 | 7.3 | 0.0 | 1.25 | 6.35 | 4.05 | 73.6 | 6.0 | 23.2 | 0.0 | 5.7 |
| 6.4 | 0.83 | 6.1 | 0.22 | 4.1 | 0.3 | 0.61 | 6.61 | 3.71 | 83.0 | 3.8 | 14.3 | 2.6 | 4.7 |
| 8.0 | 0.38 | 1.1 | 4.93 | 1.7 | -0.4 | -3.83 | -28.26 | 3.56 | 121.6 | 4.1 | 27.9 | 12.3 | 6.4 |
| 10.0 | 0.00 | 0.0 | 0.12 | 3.3 | 0.1 | 0.48 | 2.23 | 3.26 | 84.0 | 4.3 | 25.2 | 8.6 | 6.5 |
| 9.7 | 0.37 | 1.5 | 0.13 | 9.2 | 3.4 | 1.37 | 11.21 | 2.87 | 66.1 | 4.1 | 14.2 | 6.0 | 8.4 |
| 7.4 | 0.35 | 2.7 | 0.12 | 5.0 | 0.5 | 0.69 | 6.88 | 3.70 | 81.0 | 3.6 | 26.0 | 8.2 | 5.0 |
| 8.4 | 1.21 | 5.6 | 0.09 | 3.3 | 0.1 | 0.26 | 2.22 | 3.58 | 89.6 | 3.6 | 12.9 | 14.5 | 5.8 |
| 7.6 | 1.82 | 7.7 | 0.87 | 4.3 | 0.1 | 0.18 | 1.24 | 3.48 | 85.2 | 3.5 | 17.3 | 10.9 | 7.1 |
| 8.6 | 0.49 | 1.0 | 1.48 | 1.3 | 0.0 | -1.47 | -5.65 | 5.34 | 96.7 | 5.4 | 47.8 | 10.8 | 7.0 |
| 5.6 | 2.38 | 5.5 | -3.28 | 6.0 | 0.0 | 1.63 | 7.69 | 13.18 | 108.3 | 6.2 | 54.8 | 0.0 | 4.3 |
| 8.9 | 0.26 | 1.0 | 0.00 | 1.2 | 0.0 | -0.22 | -2.75 | 6.68 | 96.9 | 7.4 | 70.8 | 0.0 | 3.0 |
| 4.3 | 3.91 | 11.3 | 1.57 | 1.8 | -0.1 | -2.01 | -9.44 | 6.32 | 102.5 | 4.9 | 35.4 | 0.0 | 6.2 |
| 9.0 | 0.51 | 1.6 | 0.05 | 0.6 | -0.1 | -0.23 | -2.16 | 2.49 | 108.2 | 4.4 | 18.1 | 5.6 | 4.6 |
| 8.0 | 0.73 | 4.7 | 0.38 | 3.7 | 1.3 | 0.46 | 4.59 | 2.71 | 84.1 | 4.5 | 26.2 | 8.5 | 5.7 |
| 6.2 | 0.70 | 5.3 | 0.80 | 5.7 | 2.8 | 0.80 | 5.61 | 3.66 | 74.4 | 2.5 | 11.7 | 13.9 | 8.2 |
| 6.5 | 1.52 | 7.6 | 0.43 | 6.6 | 1.7 | 1.09 | 8.24 | 3.12 | 68.7 | 4.2 | 13.3 | 3.2 | 8.0 |
| 6.7 | 5.44 | 12.5 | 0.36 | 0.4 | -0.1 | -1.25 | -8.54 | 3.45 | 92.9 | 5.4 | 34.2 | 0.0 | 5.7 |
| 7.0 | 2.03 | 7.8 | 0.15 | 8.4 | 0.2 | 1.24 | 10.65 | 3.84 | 67.9 | 5.8 | 35.5 | 4.3 | 6.3 |

| Name | City | State | Rating | 2014 Rating | 2013 Rating | Total Assets ($Mil) | One Year Asset Growth | Commercial Loans | Consumer Loans | Mortgage Loans | Securities | Capitalization Index | Net Worth Ratio |
|---|---|---|---|---|---|---|---|---|---|---|---|---|---|
| ▲ FORT FINANCIAL FCU | Fort Wayne | IN | B- | C+ | C+ | 209.1 | 8.29 | 0.0 | 56.8 | 15.0 | 0.0 | 6.8 | 8.8 |
| FORT GORDON AND COMMUNITY CU | Fort Gordon | GA | D+ | D+ | D+ | 63.7 | 3.47 | 1.1 | 30.2 | 6.0 | 4.1 | 5.9 | 7.9 |
| FORT KNOX FCU | Radcliff | KY | A+ | A+ | A+ | 1272.0 | 9.37 | 4.8 | 30.0 | 22.9 | 11.9 | 10.0 | 15.2 |
| FORT LEE FCU | Prince George | VA | C+ | C+ | B- | 157.4 | 2.58 | 0.0 | 38.7 | 6.0 | 27.2 | 8.3 | 9.9 |
| FORT LIGONIER FCU | Bolivar | PA | C+ | C+ | C+ | 2.9 | 8.46 | 0.0 | 32.8 | 0.0 | 0.0 | 10.0 | 14.1 |
| FORT MCCLELLAN CU | Anniston | AL | B+ | B+ | B+ | 205.6 | 2.16 | 0.0 | 21.7 | 12.9 | 2.0 | 10.0 | 13.5 |
| ▼ FORT MCPHERSON CU | Atlanta | GA | C- | C | D+ | 21.9 | 2.86 | 1.4 | 27.2 | 5.3 | 5.9 | 8.3 | 9.9 |
| FORT MEADE CU | Fort Meade | MD | E | E | E+ | 31.7 | -7.32 | 0.0 | 15.4 | 11.2 | 15.6 | 4.8 | 6.8 |
| ▲ FORT MORGAN SCHOOLS FCU | Fort Morgan | CO | C- | C- | C- | 4.2 | -6.60 | 0.0 | 39.2 | 23.1 | 0.0 | 10.0 | 16.4 |
| FORT PECK COMMUNITY FCU | Fort Peck | MT | C+ | C+ | C+ | 11.1 | 8.03 | 0.0 | 20.4 | 24.8 | 0.0 | 10.0 | 11.2 |
| FORT ROOTS FCU | North Little Rock | AR | D+ | C- | C- | 4.7 | 9.68 | 0.0 | 49.6 | 0.0 | 0.0 | 10.0 | 13.6 |
| FORT SILL FCU | Fort Sill | OK | C | C+ | C+ | 264.0 | 3.70 | 0.0 | 35.5 | 5.1 | 18.7 | 8.4 | 9.9 |
| FORT SMITH DIXIE CUP FCU | Fort Smith | AR | B- | B- | B- | 12.8 | 2.00 | 0.0 | 27.5 | 0.8 | 0.0 | 10.0 | 24.4 |
| FORT SMITH MUNICIPAL EMPL FCU | Fort Smith | AR | D+ | D+ | D+ | 2.6 | -3.41 | 0.0 | 19.5 | 0.0 | 0.0 | 7.4 | 9.2 |
| FORT SMITH TEACHERS FCU | Fort Smith | AR | C- | C | C | 11.6 | 6.47 | 0.0 | 18.3 | 0.0 | 0.0 | 10.0 | 19.1 |
| FORT WORTH CITY CU | Fort Worth | TX | A | A | A | 162.4 | 7.12 | 0.1 | 23.4 | 14.0 | 8.7 | 10.0 | 12.7 |
| FORT WORTH COMMUNITY CU | Bedford | TX | C- | C | C+ | 824.4 | 0.16 | 0.0 | 67.7 | 6.0 | 9.1 | 7.5 | 9.3 |
| FORTRESS FCU | Marion | IN | D+ | C- | C- | 16.2 | 6.96 | 0.0 | 76.2 | 2.0 | 0.0 | 10.0 | 18.9 |
| FORUM CU | Fishers | IN | B | B+ | A- | 1095.5 | 11.10 | 8.7 | 45.6 | 21.3 | 1.8 | 10.0 | 11.4 |
| FORWARD FINANCIAL CU | Niagara | WI | C+ | C+ | B- | 68.1 | 1.60 | 4.9 | 21.7 | 45.6 | 0.0 | 10.0 | 12.1 |
| FOUNDATION CU | Springfield | MO | B | B | B | 63.9 | 1.21 | 0.6 | 6.2 | 26.7 | 14.1 | 10.0 | 13.4 |
| FOUNDERS FCU | Lancaster | SC | A- | A- | A- | 1823.3 | 7.15 | 0.6 | 39.4 | 36.0 | 10.8 | 10.0 | 15.0 |
| FOUNTAIN VALLEY CU | Fountain Valley | CA | D+ | C- | C- | 2.1 | -1.31 | 0.0 | 36.9 | 0.0 | 0.0 | 10.0 | 18.5 |
| FOUR CORNERS FCU | Kirtland | NM | B | B- | C+ | 26.3 | 1.73 | 0.0 | 46.5 | 0.0 | 0.0 | 10.0 | 15.9 |
| FOUR FLAGS AREA CU | Niles | MI | D | D+ | C- | 3.7 | 10.52 | 0.0 | 49.7 | 0.0 | 22.9 | 10.0 | 12.1 |
| FOUR POINTS FCU | Omaha | NE | B | B | C+ | 118.0 | -1.84 | 1.4 | 13.9 | 18.3 | 31.8 | 10.0 | 12.1 |
| FOUR SEASONS FCU | Opelika | AL | D+ | D+ | C | 46.8 | -0.30 | 3.8 | 32.4 | 2.8 | 0.0 | 7.6 | 9.4 |
| FOURTH WARD FCU | Amite | LA | C- | C- | D+ | <1 | 5.77 | 0.0 | 43.5 | 10.3 | 0.0 | 10.0 | 15.1 |
| FOX COMMUNITIES CU | Appleton | WI | A- | A- | A- | 1110.0 | 9.79 | 19.5 | 18.5 | 60.4 | 4.7 | 9.8 | 10.9 |
| FOX VALLEY CU | Aurora | IL | C- | D+ | C- | 19.8 | 0.67 | 0.0 | 24.6 | 17.3 | 5.5 | 10.0 | 13.9 |
| FRANKENMUTH CU | Frankenmuth | MI | B+ | B+ | A- | 388.6 | 15.66 | 5.7 | 42.6 | 16.0 | 2.1 | 10.0 | 11.1 |
| ▲ FRANKFORT COMMUNITY FCU | Frankfort | MI | C- | D | C- | 10.9 | 8.72 | 0.0 | 24.2 | 0.0 | 0.0 | 10.0 | 14.4 |
| FRANKLIN FIRST FCU | Greenfield | MA | D+ | D+ | C | 56.4 | -2.88 | 0.0 | 21.4 | 26.0 | 6.6 | 6.0 | 8.0 |
| FRANKLIN JOHNSTOWN FCU | Johnstown | PA | D+ | D+ | C | 30.1 | 1.67 | 0.0 | 31.5 | 0.5 | 6.5 | 10.0 | 12.8 |
| FRANKLIN MINT FCU | Broomall | PA | B- | B- | B- | 885.7 | 3.32 | 6.8 | 23.9 | 27.7 | 15.5 | 6.3 | 8.4 |
| ▲ FRANKLIN REGIONAL SCHOOLS FCU | Jeannette | PA | C- | C- | C- | 3.0 | 5.24 | 0.0 | 58.9 | 0.0 | 0.0 | 10.0 | 11.9 |
| FRANKLIN TRUST FCU | Hartford | CT | C | C | C | 41.3 | 1.80 | 0.0 | 25.4 | 5.0 | 0.0 | 9.4 | 10.6 |
| FRANKLIN-OIL REGION CU | Franklin | PA | B- | C+ | C+ | 36.0 | 4.10 | 0.0 | 40.6 | 2.4 | 0.0 | 10.0 | 11.3 |
| FRANKLIN-SOMERSET FCU | Skowhegan | ME | B | B | B- | 82.0 | 2.78 | 2.0 | 24.3 | 27.8 | 0.0 | 9.7 | 10.8 |
| ▲ FRATERNAL ORDER OF POLICE CU | Tulsa | OK | D | D | D- | 35.6 | 3.68 | 0.0 | 53.6 | 0.0 | 0.0 | 8.2 | 9.8 |
| FRB FCU | Washington | DC | C+ | C+ | C+ | 74.5 | 15.05 | 0.4 | 23.5 | 13.5 | 13.6 | 6.2 | 8.2 |
| FREDERIKSTED FCU | Frederiksted | VI | C- | C | C | 11.1 | -0.19 | 0.0 | 32.8 | 13.9 | 0.0 | 10.0 | 14.4 |
| FREEDOM COMMUNITY CU | Fargo | ND | E+ | D- | D+ | 24.6 | 0.85 | 0.0 | 30.8 | 11.5 | 0.0 | 6.2 | 8.2 |
| ▼ FREEDOM CU | Springfield | MA | C+ | B- | B | 522.9 | 2.20 | 5.6 | 4.6 | 44.8 | 36.5 | 10.0 | 13.3 |
| ▲ FREEDOM CU | Warminster | PA | B | B- | B- | 670.8 | 3.55 | 0.7 | 24.5 | 22.7 | 25.4 | 8.2 | 9.8 |
| FREEDOM CU | Provo | UT | B- | B- | C+ | 28.5 | 6.02 | 5.1 | 46.2 | 14.4 | 7.8 | 9.7 | 10.8 |
| FREEDOM FCU | Bel Air | MD | C- | C+ | C+ | 270.0 | 2.45 | 6.2 | 57.0 | 19.9 | 10.5 | 6.6 | 8.6 |
| FREEDOM FCU | Rocky Mount | NC | D- | D | D | 52.9 | 2.42 | 0.0 | 62.1 | 0.0 | 0.0 | 7.1 | 9.1 |
| FREEDOM FIRST CU | Dayton | OH | C+ | C+ | C | 30.6 | 5.76 | 0.0 | 39.9 | 0.0 | 0.0 | 7.6 | 9.4 |
| FREEDOM FIRST FCU | McConnell AFB | KS | D+ | D+ | D+ | 32.1 | 2.10 | 0.0 | 18.7 | 0.0 | 12.5 | 10.0 | 14.7 |
| FREEDOM FIRST FCU | Roanoke | VA | B+ | B+ | A- | 391.2 | 10.07 | 15.4 | 34.1 | 29.3 | 4.7 | 8.3 | 9.9 |
| FREEDOM UNITED FCU | Rochester | PA | B- | B | B | 56.9 | 6.63 | 0.0 | 15.9 | 1.3 | 15.8 | 10.0 | 16.5 |
| FREESTONE CU | Teague | TX | C | C | C- | 40.2 | 4.08 | 0.0 | 23.3 | 23.1 | 19.0 | 6.9 | 8.9 |
| FREMONT FCU | Fremont | OH | A | A- | A- | 170.2 | 6.12 | 8.5 | 22.4 | 26.6 | 23.4 | 10.0 | 14.5 |
| ▲ FREMONT FIRST CENTRAL FCU | Fremont | NE | C | C | C | 39.6 | 3.74 | 0.0 | 15.6 | 17.0 | 0.0 | 10.0 | 12.1 |
| FRESNO COUNTY FCU | Fresno | CA | A | A | A- | 600.8 | 8.70 | 0.3 | 52.9 | 8.5 | 14.8 | 10.0 | 11.4 |
| FRESNO FIRE DEPT CU | Fresno | CA | C- | C- | C | 34.7 | 1.49 | 0.0 | 15.6 | 3.4 | 0.0 | 10.0 | 13.4 |
| FRESNO GRANGERS FCU | Fresno | CA | B- | B | B- | 15.5 | 19.72 | 40.6 | 0.7 | 46.4 | 0.0 | 10.0 | 25.8 |
| FRESNO POLICE DEPT CU | Fresno | CA | C+ | B- | B | 47.9 | 1.11 | 0.0 | 26.3 | 15.0 | 4.5 | 10.0 | 18.7 |
| FREUDENBERG-NOK EMPL CU | Bristol | NH | C- | C- | C | 2.8 | 5.93 | 0.0 | 29.8 | 0.0 | 0.0 | 10.0 | 23.7 |

| Asset Quality Index | Non-Performing Loans as a % of Total Loans | as a % of Capital | Net Charge-Offs Avg Loans | Profitability Index | Net Income ($Mil) | Return on Assets | Return on Equity | Net Interest Spread | Overhead Efficiency Ratio | Liquidity Index | Liquidity Ratio | Hot Money Ratio | Stability Index |
|---|---|---|---|---|---|---|---|---|---|---|---|---|---|
| 5.1 | 1.13 | 11.3 | 0.54 | 4.0 | 0.6 | 0.37 | 4.65 | 4.11 | 83.0 | 3.9 | 13.1 | 2.8 | 4.5 |
| 6.7 | 1.12 | 5.6 | 0.86 | 1.4 | 0.0 | 0.02 | 0.24 | 2.82 | 87.3 | 5.2 | 19.1 | 1.3 | 2.9 |
| 9.3 | 0.56 | 2.7 | 0.41 | 9.5 | 14.5 | 1.58 | 10.63 | 3.24 | 52.6 | 2.4 | 17.5 | 20.7 | 9.0 |
| 7.7 | 0.90 | 4.6 | 0.82 | 2.8 | 0.3 | 0.23 | 2.54 | 3.35 | 85.4 | 4.7 | 19.9 | 5.8 | 5.0 |
| 10.0 | 0.00 | 0.0 | 0.00 | 4.1 | 0.0 | 0.38 | 2.68 | 1.79 | 75.0 | 4.9 | 27.2 | 0.0 | 7.6 |
| 8.5 | 1.03 | 3.9 | 0.38 | 4.8 | 1.1 | 0.73 | 5.54 | 2.61 | 65.8 | 5.5 | 37.9 | 0.0 | 8.0 |
| 9.9 | 0.12 | 0.4 | -0.13 | 2.3 | 0.0 | 0.13 | 1.36 | 4.32 | 97.1 | 5.8 | 32.2 | 0.0 | 3.9 |
| 3.7 | 6.16 | 24.2 | 0.52 | 0.3 | -0.1 | -0.22 | -3.27 | 3.28 | 104.3 | 5.6 | 24.1 | 0.0 | 0.7 |
| 9.6 | 0.75 | 2.6 | 0.00 | 1.3 | 0.0 | 0.00 | 0.00 | 2.28 | 90.3 | 4.4 | 45.1 | 0.0 | 5.8 |
| 8.6 | 0.54 | 2.5 | 0.99 | 3.9 | 0.0 | 0.32 | 2.69 | 4.05 | 80.6 | 4.7 | 25.3 | 5.0 | 6.2 |
| 6.6 | 1.69 | 6.7 | 0.44 | 0.8 | 0.0 | -0.27 | -1.88 | 4.10 | 100.6 | 5.4 | 37.1 | 0.0 | 6.5 |
| 7.9 | 0.67 | 5.0 | 0.60 | 2.8 | 0.4 | 0.22 | 2.23 | 2.67 | 89.2 | 4.9 | 26.4 | 4.0 | 5.8 |
| 8.6 | 2.20 | 2.9 | 0.16 | 3.9 | 0.1 | 0.54 | 2.23 | 2.26 | 79.8 | 4.6 | 16.8 | 0.0 | 7.0 |
| 8.8 | 0.61 | 2.4 | 0.14 | 1.8 | 0.0 | 0.05 | 0.55 | 5.54 | 98.7 | 6.9 | 54.1 | 0.0 | 3.2 |
| 10.0 | 0.00 | 0.0 | 0.34 | 1.9 | 0.0 | 0.07 | 0.36 | 2.76 | 92.8 | 5.2 | 23.9 | 0.0 | 6.9 |
| 9.9 | 0.05 | 0.2 | 0.17 | 6.6 | 1.2 | 1.04 | 8.98 | 2.93 | 73.5 | 4.4 | 16.5 | 3.6 | 8.9 |
| 7.6 | 0.32 | 2.9 | 0.47 | 2.3 | 0.8 | 0.12 | 1.35 | 3.04 | 87.1 | 3.5 | 11.8 | 8.4 | 6.0 |
| 4.7 | 3.31 | 13.6 | 1.96 | 0.4 | -0.3 | -2.02 | -10.36 | 5.07 | 80.6 | 2.3 | 13.9 | 16.3 | 5.4 |
| 6.9 | 0.51 | 4.0 | 0.23 | 4.1 | 4.2 | 0.53 | 4.59 | 3.02 | 84.7 | 3.7 | 18.0 | 8.4 | 7.6 |
| 6.8 | 1.27 | 7.2 | 0.06 | 2.7 | 0.1 | 0.21 | 1.78 | 4.21 | 91.1 | 3.9 | 29.0 | 7.0 | 5.8 |
| 10.0 | 0.00 | 0.0 | 0.00 | 3.9 | 0.3 | 0.60 | 4.48 | 1.84 | 64.3 | 5.3 | 19.1 | 0.0 | 6.6 |
| 7.4 | 1.08 | 6.2 | 0.93 | 7.2 | 15.2 | 1.14 | 7.59 | 4.83 | 70.1 | 3.1 | 12.0 | 8.5 | 7.8 |
| 8.1 | 2.73 | 6.1 | 0.00 | 0.5 | 0.0 | -0.45 | -2.37 | 3.12 | 116.3 | 5.0 | 24.1 | 0.0 | 6.7 |
| 7.3 | 1.33 | 5.4 | 0.72 | 6.3 | 0.2 | 1.15 | 7.50 | 4.19 | 83.6 | 5.1 | 98.2 | 34.8 | 6.3 |
| 7.4 | 0.43 | 2.2 | 0.63 | 0.5 | 0.0 | -0.51 | -4.13 | 3.68 | 102.3 | 3.8 | 12.3 | 0.0 | 4.8 |
| 9.9 | 0.28 | 1.0 | 0.17 | 4.1 | 0.5 | 0.57 | 4.84 | 2.17 | 76.7 | 3.8 | 27.9 | 11.4 | 7.7 |
| 4.1 | 1.35 | 15.9 | 0.31 | 1.9 | 0.0 | 0.04 | 0.43 | 5.86 | 98.7 | 4.4 | 16.3 | 7.9 | 2.9 |
| 2.8 | 9.60 | 30.3 | 0.00 | 6.9 | 0.0 | 3.92 | 28.07 | 11.99 | 41.2 | 6.7 | 55.7 | 0.0 | 7.2 |
| 6.9 | 0.58 | 6.0 | 0.06 | 6.7 | 7.9 | 0.98 | 8.89 | 2.85 | 72.7 | 2.9 | 7.8 | 4.5 | 8.7 |
| 8.6 | 1.18 | 3.4 | 0.64 | 1.9 | 0.0 | 0.28 | 2.05 | 3.70 | 93.0 | 4.6 | 22.5 | 0.7 | 5.1 |
| 5.4 | 1.51 | 12.0 | 0.65 | 10.0 | 5.2 | 1.87 | 17.18 | 4.90 | 63.4 | 2.9 | 6.6 | 6.7 | 8.4 |
| 9.0 | 0.07 | 0.2 | 0.33 | 1.6 | 0.0 | 0.22 | 1.45 | 2.63 | 92.3 | 5.1 | 31.4 | 0.0 | 5.2 |
| 6.4 | 0.92 | 6.6 | 0.43 | 2.2 | 0.1 | 0.19 | 2.40 | 3.12 | 90.0 | 3.0 | 17.6 | 13.0 | 2.8 |
| 9.0 | 0.38 | 1.3 | 0.58 | 0.3 | -0.1 | -0.48 | -3.74 | 3.33 | 106.1 | 5.8 | 37.5 | 1.4 | 5.7 |
| 7.6 | 0.55 | 5.1 | 0.37 | 3.8 | 3.5 | 0.52 | 6.68 | 3.31 | 83.8 | 3.3 | 10.4 | 7.8 | 5.5 |
| 8.5 | 0.00 | 0.0 | 0.18 | 1.8 | 0.0 | 0.09 | 0.73 | 3.77 | 97.6 | 4.4 | 19.2 | 0.0 | 7.1 |
| 3.0 | 1.15 | 29.7 | 1.01 | 3.3 | 0.1 | 0.39 | 4.95 | 5.50 | 90.1 | 4.9 | 24.2 | 4.7 | 3.5 |
| 6.1 | 1.66 | 10.1 | 0.10 | 6.6 | 0.3 | 1.06 | 9.40 | 5.26 | 85.9 | 4.3 | 31.6 | 9.6 | 5.2 |
| 5.5 | 1.56 | 10.4 | 0.28 | 6.8 | 0.7 | 1.09 | 10.46 | 3.75 | 72.5 | 3.4 | 16.3 | 6.6 | 5.6 |
| 5.5 | 0.50 | 5.1 | 0.45 | 1.4 | 0.0 | -0.15 | -1.73 | 2.77 | 92.8 | 4.1 | 17.0 | 8.2 | 3.4 |
| 6.2 | 1.56 | 7.2 | 0.66 | 3.3 | 0.2 | 0.33 | 3.70 | 2.80 | 81.1 | 5.5 | 38.1 | 1.9 | 3.8 |
| 3.7 | 5.37 | 24.7 | 0.51 | 2.6 | 0.0 | 0.20 | 1.42 | 4.74 | 83.6 | 4.0 | 23.7 | 1.1 | 5.9 |
| 6.4 | 0.33 | 2.5 | 0.24 | 1.2 | 0.0 | 0.11 | 1.39 | 3.24 | 94.8 | 4.2 | 11.2 | 0.0 | 2.1 |
| 7.7 | 1.66 | 6.7 | 0.13 | 2.7 | 1.1 | 0.27 | 1.98 | 2.74 | 88.9 | 3.0 | 24.0 | 15.8 | 8.6 |
| 8.8 | 0.80 | 4.1 | 0.59 | 5.3 | 4.5 | 0.89 | 9.37 | 3.01 | 70.4 | 4.6 | 30.5 | 14.5 | 6.7 |
| 6.2 | 0.17 | 1.3 | 0.45 | 6.5 | 0.2 | 1.05 | 10.56 | 3.71 | 71.7 | 3.1 | 12.4 | 10.0 | 5.2 |
| 5.8 | 0.85 | 7.5 | 0.54 | 2.5 | 0.2 | 0.09 | 1.02 | 3.86 | 87.1 | 3.0 | 10.1 | 5.6 | 5.2 |
| 6.2 | 0.20 | 3.0 | 0.36 | 0.6 | -0.1 | -0.32 | -3.48 | 3.83 | 98.0 | 3.4 | 15.5 | 3.4 | 3.5 |
| 8.8 | 0.20 | 1.2 | 0.07 | 4.6 | 0.2 | 0.64 | 7.00 | 3.11 | 85.2 | 4.4 | 29.6 | 0.3 | 4.9 |
| 10.0 | 0.85 | 1.5 | 0.34 | 1.1 | 0.0 | -0.10 | -0.71 | 2.21 | 97.4 | 5.9 | 34.4 | 5.4 | 6.4 |
| 6.4 | 0.53 | 5.9 | 0.79 | 7.3 | 3.1 | 1.10 | 11.17 | 4.03 | 72.5 | 3.2 | 8.6 | 7.9 | 6.4 |
| 8.3 | 1.75 | 3.2 | 0.29 | 3.2 | 0.1 | 0.30 | 1.81 | 2.46 | 88.0 | 5.0 | 20.6 | 0.8 | 6.9 |
| 7.9 | 0.82 | 4.9 | 0.12 | 3.0 | 0.1 | 0.30 | 3.43 | 3.93 | 89.6 | 4.4 | 21.2 | 6.2 | 4.4 |
| 6.9 | 1.63 | 6.9 | 0.12 | 8.8 | 1.7 | 1.35 | 9.52 | 3.76 | 73.9 | 3.0 | 15.3 | 12.4 | 8.8 |
| 10.0 | 0.36 | 1.2 | 0.13 | 1.9 | 0.0 | 0.04 | 0.31 | 3.12 | 96.9 | 5.8 | 35.0 | 0.0 | 6.1 |
| 6.8 | 0.86 | 5.5 | 0.58 | 8.1 | 4.6 | 1.05 | 9.52 | 4.17 | 74.6 | 3.8 | 18.7 | 7.0 | 8.9 |
| 10.0 | 0.92 | 1.9 | 0.30 | 1.6 | 0.0 | 0.02 | 0.14 | 2.22 | 99.8 | 6.0 | 38.3 | 1.2 | 6.3 |
| 8.6 | 0.02 | 1.6 | 0.00 | 6.3 | 0.1 | 0.82 | 3.09 | 3.89 | 66.3 | 6.8 | 56.0 | 0.0 | 7.8 |
| 9.7 | 0.95 | 2.4 | 0.24 | 2.7 | 0.1 | 0.17 | 0.90 | 2.92 | 85.8 | 6.1 | 49.2 | 3.1 | 7.0 |
| 9.8 | 0.00 | 0.0 | -0.28 | 1.5 | 0.0 | 0.00 | 0.00 | 3.01 | 102.6 | 7.5 | 81.9 | 0.0 | 7.0 |

| Name | City | State | Rating | 2014 Rating | 2013 Rating | Total Assets ($Mil) | One Year Asset Growth | Asset Mix (As a % of Total Assets) | | | | Capital- ization Index | Net Worth Ratio |
|------|------|-------|--------|-------------|-------------|--------------------|------------------------|---------------------------------------|---|---|---|----------------------|------------------|
| | | | | | | | | Comm- ercial Loans | Cons- umer Loans | Mort- gage Loans | Secur- ities | | |
| FRICK TRI-COUNTY FCU | Uniontown | PA | B | B- | C+ | 78.1 | 6.52 | 0.0 | 19.3 | 7.8 | 38.0 | 8.3 | 9.9 |
| FRIENDLY FCU | Aliquippa | PA | B | B | B | 50.2 | 4.51 | 0.0 | 23.4 | 22.0 | 32.9 | 10.0 | 17.5 |
| FRIENDS AND FAMILY CU | Massillon | OH | C- | C- | C | 71.7 | 6.10 | 0.0 | 43.2 | 31.4 | 2.5 | 6.1 | 8.1 |
| FRIENDS FCU | Norman | OK | C- | C- | C- | 8.6 | 5.62 | 0.0 | 40.3 | 0.0 | 0.0 | 10.0 | 15.1 |
| FRIENDS FIRST CU | Owensboro | KY | E+ | E+ | E+ | 5.7 | 0.23 | 0.0 | 53.4 | 0.0 | 0.0 | 4.4 | 6.4 |
| FRIO COUNTY FCU | Pearsall | TX | B- | B- | B- | 6.1 | 6.13 | 0.0 | 55.1 | 0.0 | 0.0 | 10.0 | 21.8 |
| FRIONA TEXAS FCU | Friona | TX | B- | B- | B- | 11.9 | 0.28 | 0.0 | 12.6 | 9.8 | 0.0 | 10.0 | 18.7 |
| FROID FCU | Froid | MT | D | D+ | D+ | <1 | -18.53 | 0.0 | 26.1 | 0.0 | 0.0 | 10.0 | 13.8 |
| ▲ FRONT ROYAL FCU | Front Royal | VA | B- | C | C- | 54.1 | 4.52 | 0.0 | 16.5 | 2.5 | 0.9 | 10.0 | 13.7 |
| ▼ FRONTIER COMMUNITY CU | Fort Dodge | IA | C- | C | C+ | 18.9 | -3.95 | 0.0 | 20.1 | 0.0 | 0.0 | 10.0 | 12.2 |
| FRONTIER COMMUNITY CU | Leavenworth | KS | B+ | B+ | A- | 116.8 | 4.15 | 1.8 | 22.5 | 22.6 | 11.1 | 10.0 | 13.5 |
| FRONTIER FINANCIAL CU | Reno | NV | D | D- | E | 72.2 | 6.55 | 0.0 | 33.6 | 17.8 | 1.2 | 6.3 | 8.3 |
| FRSA CU | Winter Park | FL | D+ | D | D+ | 5.1 | 14.70 | 5.2 | 84.2 | 0.0 | 0.0 | 9.0 | 10.3 |
| FT RANDALL FCU | Pickstown | SD | C | C | C | 19.4 | 9.45 | 1.1 | 43.5 | 11.7 | 0.0 | 6.7 | 8.7 |
| FULDA AREA CU | Fulda | MN | A- | A- | B | 84.2 | 11.68 | 30.9 | 20.8 | 40.7 | 2.1 | 10.0 | 11.5 |
| FULTON TEACHERS CU | Hapeville | GA | B | B | C | 91.9 | 1.20 | 2.7 | 31.5 | 12.1 | 1.1 | 10.0 | 13.4 |
| FUNERAL SERVICE CU | Springfield | IL | D+ | C- | C- | 9.2 | 2.39 | 70.1 | 20.7 | 0.0 | 0.0 | 10.0 | 16.9 |
| G H WOODWORKERS FCU | Aberdeen | WA | D+ | D+ | D+ | 2.2 | 0.32 | 0.0 | 68.5 | 0.0 | 0.0 | 10.0 | 13.9 |
| G P M FCU | San Antonio | TX | C | C- | C- | 1.7 | 8.07 | 0.0 | 35.0 | 0.0 | 0.0 | 10.0 | 18.5 |
| ▲ GABRIELS COMMUNITY CU | Lansing | MI | B- | C+ | B- | 13.9 | 5.36 | 1.2 | 33.6 | 25.0 | 0.0 | 10.0 | 11.1 |
| GAF LINDEN EMPL FCU | Parsippany | NJ | C- | D+ | C- | 5.1 | -1.97 | 0.0 | 15.8 | 4.8 | 0.0 | 9.3 | 10.5 |
| GALAXY FCU | Franklin | PA | B | B+ | B+ | 54.7 | -0.79 | 0.5 | 15.0 | 0.0 | 0.4 | 10.0 | 14.9 |
| GALE CU | Galesburg | IL | C | C | C | 26.4 | 0.12 | 0.0 | 38.9 | 7.7 | 9.3 | 10.0 | 14.9 |
| GALESBURG BURLINGTON CU | Galesburg | IL | B | B | B | 44.4 | -0.40 | 0.0 | 33.9 | 5.5 | 0.1 | 10.0 | 26.2 |
| GALLATIN STEAM PLANT CU | Gallatin | TN | C- | C | C- | 5.0 | -10.06 | 0.0 | 44.4 | 0.0 | 0.0 | 10.0 | 19.1 |
| GALLUP FCU | Omaha | NE | B- | B- | C+ | 15.9 | -0.53 | 0.0 | 28.5 | 15.4 | 0.0 | 10.0 | 13.0 |
| GALVESTON GOVERNMENT EMPL CU | La Marque | TX | E+ | E+ | E+ | 6.1 | -0.51 | 0.0 | 59.6 | 3.4 | 0.0 | 5.3 | 7.3 |
| GALVESTON SCHOOL EMPL FCU | Galveston | TX | E+ | E+ | D- | 3.6 | -6.96 | 0.0 | 51.5 | 0.0 | 0.0 | 6.9 | 8.9 |
| ▼ GAP FCU | Johnstown | PA | C+ | B | B+ | 42.3 | 2.49 | 0.0 | 27.8 | 9.7 | 3.4 | 10.0 | 12.4 |
| GARDEN CITY TEACHERS FCU | Garden City | KS | D+ | D | D | 11.4 | 0.15 | 0.0 | 28.6 | 8.9 | 0.0 | 6.6 | 8.6 |
| GARDEN ISLAND FCU | Lihue | HI | C | C- | C- | 89.9 | 1.34 | 0.2 | 15.0 | 7.9 | 28.1 | 10.0 | 14.5 |
| GARDEN SAVINGS FCU | Parsippany | NJ | B | B | B | 304.6 | 1.81 | 4.1 | 29.8 | 18.9 | 17.6 | 9.7 | 10.8 |
| GARDEN STATE FCU | Moorestown | NJ | D+ | D- | D- | 26.3 | -0.86 | 0.0 | 11.7 | 32.6 | 13.7 | 8.2 | 9.8 |
| GARDINER FCU | Gardiner | ME | B+ | B+ | B | 41.0 | 0.72 | 0.0 | 30.3 | 28.7 | 0.0 | 10.0 | 12.2 |
| ▲ GARLAND COUNTY EDUCATORS FCU | Hot Springs | AR | C- | C | C | 3.5 | 2.50 | 0.0 | 71.9 | 0.0 | 0.0 | 9.6 | 10.7 |
| GARY FIREFIGHTERS ASSN FCU | Gary | IN | C+ | C | C | 2.0 | -2.18 | 0.0 | 41.5 | 0.0 | 0.0 | 10.0 | 33.3 |
| GARY MUNICIPAL EMPL FCU | Gary | IN | C+ | B- | B- | <1 | -2.91 | 0.0 | 31.6 | 0.0 | 0.0 | 10.0 | 50.7 |
| ▼ GARY POLICE DEPT EMPL FCU | Gary | IN | C | C+ | B- | 1.7 | -2.47 | 0.0 | 0.0 | 0.0 | 0.0 | 10.0 | 46.7 |
| GAS & ELECTRIC CU | Rock Island | IL | B+ | B+ | B | 69.3 | 9.30 | 0.0 | 25.6 | 29.9 | 22.4 | 10.0 | 11.4 |
| GAS & ELECTRIC EMPL CU | Mason City | IA | B- | B- | B- | 5.5 | 4.62 | 0.0 | 47.3 | 0.0 | 0.0 | 10.0 | 28.0 |
| ▲ GASCO EASTERN DISTRICT FCU | Bellwood | PA | C | C- | C- | 1.8 | -0.99 | 0.0 | 39.7 | 0.0 | 0.0 | 10.0 | 22.3 |
| GATES CHILI FCU | Rochester | NY | D- | D | D | 21.4 | 5.02 | 0.0 | 20.2 | 10.2 | 0.0 | 5.2 | 7.2 |
| GATEWAY CU | Clarksville | TN | E- | E- | E+ | 11.5 | -4.96 | 1.7 | 40.9 | 22.4 | 0.0 | 4.0 | 6.0 |
| GATEWAY METRO FCU | Swansea | IL | C- | C- | D | 167.5 | -1.73 | 0.0 | 34.9 | 31.1 | 17.5 | 7.2 | 9.1 |
| ▼ GCA FCU | Lake Charles | LA | D+ | C- | C- | 5.4 | 1.74 | 0.0 | 16.1 | 0.0 | 0.0 | 10.0 | 22.1 |
| GCIU LOCAL 235 CU | Independence | MO | E+ | E+ | E+ | <1 | -15.15 | 0.0 | 72.6 | 0.0 | 0.0 | 7.8 | 9.5 |
| GCS CU | Granite City | IL | C+ | C+ | C+ | 306.4 | -0.99 | 0.1 | 62.0 | 17.3 | 3.3 | 10.0 | 12.1 |
| GEA EMPL FCU | Pearisburg | VA | C | C- | C- | 1.6 | -10.30 | 0.0 | 37.4 | 0.0 | 0.0 | 10.0 | 27.1 |
| GEAUGA CU INC | Burton | OH | C- | C- | C | 35.0 | 2.30 | 5.1 | 12.7 | 4.2 | 36.9 | 10.0 | 11.3 |
| GECO FCU | Harvey | LA | D- | D- | E+ | 1.2 | -11.09 | 0.0 | 28.8 | 0.0 | 0.0 | 6.6 | 8.7 |
| GECU | El Paso | TX | B | B- | B- | 2218.7 | 6.88 | 2.5 | 63.5 | 18.9 | 6.7 | 8.0 | 9.7 |
| GEICO FCU | Chevy Chase | MD | C+ | C+ | C+ | 128.4 | 6.92 | 0.0 | 10.2 | 27.1 | 15.5 | 6.4 | 8.4 |
| ▲ GEISMAR COMPLEX FCU | Geismar | LA | C | D+ | D+ | 25.0 | 3.70 | 0.0 | 23.1 | 28.1 | 0.0 | 6.1 | 8.1 |
| ▲ GEM FCU | Minot | ND | C- | D | D+ | 23.9 | -3.90 | 0.0 | 30.9 | 1.8 | 0.0 | 6.1 | 8.1 |
| ▼ GEMC FCU | Tucker | GA | B- | B+ | B+ | 105.5 | 6.68 | 6.3 | 36.8 | 13.6 | 0.0 | 9.2 | 10.5 |
| GENCO FCU | Waco | TX | B+ | A | A | 264.8 | 5.08 | 1.0 | 52.8 | 8.7 | 8.2 | 10.0 | 12.0 |
| ▲ GENERAL CU | Fort Wayne | IN | C+ | C | D+ | 80.1 | 1.54 | 1.0 | 25.2 | 26.1 | 14.2 | 7.5 | 9.3 |
| GENERAL ELECTRIC CU | Cincinnati | OH | B+ | A- | A- | 2132.8 | 7.64 | 1.2 | 62.3 | 20.1 | 3.1 | 10.0 | 11.0 |
| GENERAL ELECTRIC EMPL FCU | Milford | CT | C | C+ | B- | 195.0 | 9.07 | 0.0 | 16.2 | 8.7 | 33.6 | 6.3 | 8.4 |
| GENERAL MILLS EMPL CU | Lansing | IL | C | C | C | 13.5 | -2.37 | 0.0 | 42.4 | 0.0 | 0.0 | 10.0 | 18.3 |

| Asset Quality Index | Non-Performing Loans | | Net Charge-Offs Avg Loans | Profitability Index | Net Income ($Mil) | Return on Assets | Return on Equity | Net Interest Spread | Overhead Efficiency Ratio | Liquidity Index | Liquidity Ratio | Hot Money Ratio | Stability Index |
|---|---|---|---|---|---|---|---|---|---|---|---|---|---|
| | as a % of Total Loans | as a % of Capital | | | | | | | | | | | |
| 6.4 | 1.63 | 8.2 | 0.66 | 6.2 | 0.5 | 0.95 | 9.98 | 3.45 | 67.3 | 4.6 | 14.6 | 0.0 | 5.2 |
| 7.8 | 1.59 | 5.0 | 0.59 | 4.2 | 0.2 | 0.55 | 3.17 | 2.93 | 73.2 | 4.1 | 13.1 | 1.6 | 6.9 |
| 9.6 | 0.10 | 1.1 | 0.15 | 2.3 | 0.1 | 0.19 | 2.47 | 3.24 | 91.7 | 2.5 | 9.3 | 11.0 | 3.2 |
| 5.0 | 7.52 | 18.4 | 3.42 | 3.7 | 0.0 | 0.20 | 1.34 | 4.98 | 69.2 | 6.0 | 45.0 | 0.0 | 3.7 |
| 6.2 | 0.26 | 2.2 | 1.04 | 1.2 | 0.0 | -0.09 | -1.52 | 5.41 | 92.9 | 4.8 | 25.3 | 4.5 | 1.0 |
| 7.8 | 0.38 | 2.5 | 0.00 | 10.0 | 0.1 | 2.15 | 10.01 | 6.34 | 66.6 | 3.7 | 10.9 | 0.0 | 5.7 |
| 9.6 | 0.07 | 3.1 | 0.00 | 3.5 | 0.1 | 0.49 | 2.73 | 2.66 | 84.9 | 6.0 | 67.1 | 2.6 | 7.3 |
| 1.7 | 11.95 | 47.4 | 0.00 | 2.6 | 0.0 | 0.26 | 2.22 | 3.63 | 94.4 | 6.1 | 46.3 | 0.0 | 6.4 |
| 9.6 | 1.70 | 2.7 | 1.42 | 3.5 | 0.2 | 0.56 | 4.14 | 2.24 | 82.4 | 5.6 | 44.4 | 1.0 | 6.0 |
| 10.0 | 0.21 | 0.4 | 1.10 | 1.1 | 0.0 | -0.17 | -1.44 | 2.61 | 94.6 | 5.8 | 28.7 | 0.0 | 5.2 |
| 9.3 | 0.70 | 2.7 | 0.30 | 3.8 | 0.4 | 0.45 | 3.34 | 2.66 | 83.3 | 4.2 | 23.3 | 1.6 | 7.6 |
| 3.6 | 1.94 | 25.0 | 0.61 | 7.0 | 0.5 | 0.91 | 11.20 | 3.80 | 88.2 | 4.2 | 17.4 | 0.9 | 3.2 |
| 4.2 | 0.86 | 6.6 | 0.13 | 8.4 | 0.1 | 1.80 | 18.47 | 6.61 | 66.0 | 3.9 | 21.9 | 0.0 | 3.7 |
| 8.6 | 0.31 | 2.4 | 0.12 | 6.0 | 0.1 | 0.87 | 10.18 | 4.55 | 83.8 | 4.0 | 14.2 | 0.1 | 4.3 |
| 5.7 | 1.19 | 9.4 | 0.10 | 8.4 | 0.7 | 1.08 | 9.50 | 4.81 | 78.0 | 2.2 | 6.1 | 11.9 | 6.4 |
| 6.5 | 1.93 | 9.3 | 0.68 | 4.2 | 0.3 | 0.41 | 3.60 | 4.79 | 86.4 | 3.9 | 25.1 | 4.5 | 6.1 |
| 5.8 | 0.02 | 0.1 | 0.00 | 2.0 | 0.0 | 0.04 | 0.26 | 2.82 | 98.3 | 2.2 | 10.7 | 13.2 | 7.2 |
| 2.0 | 6.02 | 30.3 | 0.80 | 4.6 | 0.0 | 0.56 | 4.11 | 5.06 | 88.1 | 3.9 | 16.9 | 0.0 | 5.7 |
| 7.8 | 4.33 | 8.3 | 0.00 | 4.0 | 0.0 | 0.66 | 3.50 | 1.97 | 61.9 | 6.1 | 76.9 | 0.0 | 6.9 |
| 9.8 | 0.27 | 1.6 | -0.04 | 5.4 | 0.1 | 0.66 | 6.40 | 5.46 | 82.2 | 4.8 | 26.8 | 2.0 | 5.1 |
| 9.7 | 0.45 | 1.1 | 0.59 | 2.7 | 0.0 | 0.31 | 3.04 | 2.43 | 82.4 | 5.5 | 23.8 | 0.0 | 4.9 |
| 9.6 | 0.66 | 1.3 | 0.49 | 3.7 | 0.2 | 0.42 | 2.87 | 2.22 | 70.6 | 4.7 | 19.9 | 4.5 | 7.6 |
| 8.7 | 1.24 | 4.0 | 0.41 | 2.6 | 0.1 | 0.34 | 2.35 | 3.32 | 81.7 | 4.4 | 18.1 | 0.5 | 6.6 |
| 9.1 | 2.09 | 3.2 | 0.40 | 4.9 | 0.3 | 0.81 | 3.20 | 2.72 | 63.2 | 5.3 | 37.0 | 0.0 | 7.2 |
| 9.9 | 0.40 | 0.9 | 0.69 | 1.5 | 0.0 | 0.00 | 0.00 | 2.73 | 100.0 | 6.5 | 68.2 | 0.0 | 6.1 |
| 8.7 | 0.11 | 0.7 | 0.05 | 4.4 | 0.0 | 0.18 | 1.37 | 3.85 | 95.4 | 2.4 | 2.8 | 9.5 | 7.3 |
| 7.0 | 0.00 | 0.0 | 0.67 | 2.4 | 0.0 | 0.02 | 0.30 | 5.55 | 100.7 | 3.4 | 19.0 | 1.9 | 1.0 |
| 4.4 | 2.07 | 10.7 | 0.28 | 2.7 | 0.0 | -0.07 | -0.84 | 6.96 | 104.7 | 6.0 | 56.9 | 6.1 | 1.7 |
| 9.6 | 0.61 | 2.2 | 0.54 | 1.3 | -0.1 | -0.31 | -2.48 | 2.80 | 97.8 | 4.9 | 22.8 | 0.3 | 6.5 |
| 8.9 | 0.00 | 0.0 | 0.00 | 2.3 | 0.0 | 0.03 | 0.41 | 3.90 | 101.7 | 6.0 | 48.8 | 0.0 | 3.3 |
| 9.6 | 1.86 | 3.0 | 0.15 | 2.2 | 0.1 | 0.17 | 1.17 | 2.30 | 90.7 | 4.0 | 20.0 | 11.2 | 6.3 |
| 6.0 | 2.08 | 10.9 | 0.78 | 4.7 | 1.0 | 0.42 | 3.96 | 3.69 | 78.4 | 2.9 | 12.5 | 15.0 | 6.8 |
| 4.9 | 1.33 | 7.2 | 0.44 | 1.6 | 0.1 | 0.28 | 2.88 | 3.38 | 93.9 | 4.5 | 29.3 | 0.7 | 3.3 |
| 7.4 | 0.40 | 5.4 | 0.38 | 9.2 | 0.4 | 1.24 | 10.58 | 4.12 | 72.5 | 4.1 | 24.4 | 5.4 | 7.0 |
| 8.3 | 0.00 | 0.0 | 0.05 | 2.9 | 0.0 | 0.04 | 0.35 | 5.10 | 99.2 | 4.5 | 21.6 | 0.0 | 5.6 |
| 8.6 | 2.47 | 3.1 | 0.00 | 7.8 | 0.0 | 1.39 | 4.24 | 9.44 | 76.1 | 7.4 | 86.7 | 0.0 | 5.7 |
| 9.3 | 5.11 | 3.0 | 0.00 | 3.2 | 0.0 | 0.00 | 0.00 | 6.42 | 100.0 | 8.0 | 141.1 | 0.0 | 6.6 |
| 4.4 | 10.84 | 12.1 | 6.57 | 3.7 | 0.0 | -1.61 | -3.50 | 8.21 | 78.8 | 6.8 | 88.8 | 0.0 | 8.5 |
| 8.3 | 0.72 | 4.0 | 0.03 | 6.0 | 0.5 | 0.96 | 8.88 | 2.98 | 70.1 | 4.0 | 16.6 | 4.5 | 5.8 |
| 8.5 | 0.62 | 1.1 | 0.15 | 8.8 | 0.1 | 1.22 | 4.36 | 2.63 | 51.4 | 4.2 | 18.1 | 0.0 | 5.7 |
| 9.6 | 0.00 | 0.0 | 0.00 | 2.1 | 0.0 | 0.08 | 0.33 | 3.05 | 100.0 | 6.7 | 51.2 | 0.0 | 7.1 |
| 8.4 | 0.79 | 4.7 | 0.19 | 2.8 | 0.0 | 0.27 | 3.87 | 2.90 | 91.5 | 4.5 | 17.3 | 0.0 | 2.3 |
| 5.7 | 0.42 | 4.3 | 0.51 | 2.7 | 0.0 | 0.41 | 7.08 | 4.44 | 90.3 | 2.6 | 19.6 | 18.0 | 0.0 |
| 6.1 | 1.73 | 13.8 | 0.62 | 2.1 | 0.2 | 0.16 | 1.67 | 2.72 | 83.7 | 3.7 | 11.9 | 2.6 | 5.3 |
| 8.0 | 4.94 | 4.3 | 1.94 | 0.7 | 0.0 | -0.37 | -1.66 | 2.85 | 105.2 | 5.6 | 43.8 | 0.0 | 5.6 |
| 2.0 | 3.28 | 22.2 | 0.00 | 0.4 | 0.0 | -1.37 | -14.81 | 9.70 | 125.0 | 5.2 | 29.3 | 0.0 | 2.7 |
| 7.6 | 0.36 | 3.1 | 0.40 | 3.2 | 0.8 | 0.35 | 2.97 | 3.81 | 84.8 | 3.0 | 6.2 | 3.2 | 6.9 |
| 9.2 | 2.85 | 4.0 | 0.00 | 3.7 | 0.0 | 0.47 | 1.84 | 3.69 | 87.2 | 5.9 | 40.1 | 0.0 | 6.9 |
| 6.9 | 2.87 | 7.6 | -0.31 | 1.6 | 0.0 | 0.06 | 0.54 | 2.57 | 95.8 | 5.4 | 36.0 | 0.0 | 5.3 |
| 1.7 | 14.82 | 48.1 | -0.68 | 1.3 | 0.0 | -0.21 | -2.49 | 6.75 | 104.4 | 7.6 | 72.0 | 0.0 | 1.0 |
| 4.8 | 0.92 | 11.4 | 0.68 | 6.3 | 16.1 | 0.99 | 10.48 | 4.01 | 71.9 | 1.7 | 5.5 | 17.7 | 6.9 |
| 8.4 | 0.88 | 4.6 | 0.07 | 3.0 | 0.3 | 0.33 | 4.03 | 2.38 | 90.2 | 5.1 | 38.8 | 9.8 | 5.6 |
| 9.7 | 0.09 | 0.6 | 0.04 | 4.2 | 0.1 | 0.55 | 6.99 | 3.52 | 83.9 | 5.0 | 32.6 | 0.0 | 3.0 |
| 6.9 | 1.32 | 7.6 | 0.02 | 4.6 | 0.2 | 0.86 | 11.63 | 3.05 | 74.2 | 5.0 | 23.2 | 1.0 | 3.9 |
| 9.3 | 0.08 | 0.5 | 0.16 | 3.7 | 0.3 | 0.32 | 3.06 | 3.53 | 90.9 | 4.3 | 33.1 | 2.5 | 6.8 |
| 8.3 | 0.48 | 2.6 | 0.39 | 4.5 | 1.1 | 0.56 | 4.70 | 2.92 | 82.4 | 4.2 | 23.2 | 7.4 | 7.7 |
| 5.9 | 1.18 | 8.2 | 0.26 | 3.5 | 0.3 | 0.53 | 5.83 | 3.28 | 84.6 | 4.4 | 15.7 | 1.2 | 4.2 |
| 5.8 | 0.62 | 6.3 | 0.53 | 4.8 | 10.1 | 0.63 | 5.86 | 2.11 | 49.9 | 0.8 | 3.2 | 28.5 | 7.9 |
| 6.7 | 2.27 | 12.5 | 0.43 | 2.4 | 0.2 | 0.12 | 1.53 | 2.79 | 92.6 | 4.7 | 17.8 | 2.4 | 4.2 |
| 8.1 | 1.38 | 3.3 | 0.31 | 2.6 | 0.0 | 0.24 | 1.36 | 3.79 | 90.3 | 5.6 | 34.3 | 0.0 | 6.6 |

| Name | City | State | Rating | 2014 Rating | 2013 Rating | Total Assets ($Mil) | One Year Asset Growth | Asset Mix (As a % of Total Assets) Commercial Loans | Consumer Loans | Mortgage Loans | Securities | Capitalization Index | Net Worth Ratio |
|---|---|---|---|---|---|---|---|---|---|---|---|---|---|
| ▼ GENERAL PORTLAND PENINSULAR EMPL FC | Paulding | OH | D+ | D+ | D | <1 | -16.71 | 0.0 | 65.9 | 0.0 | 0.0 | 10.0 | 16.0 |
| GENERATIONS COMMUNITY FCU | San Antonio | TX | B- | B | B | 572.5 | 13.52 | 1.3 | 41.7 | 16.4 | 23.4 | 7.0 | 9.0 |
| GENERATIONS CU | Rockford | IL | C | C+ | C+ | 16.8 | 3.50 | 0.0 | 30.1 | 16.6 | 0.4 | 10.0 | 17.7 |
| GENERATIONS CU | Olympia | WA | D- | D- | D | 26.9 | 5.19 | 5.4 | 21.9 | 19.4 | 0.1 | 4.5 | 6.5 |
| GENERATIONS FAMILY FCU | Saginaw | MI | D+ | C- | C+ | 30.5 | 0.52 | 0.0 | 22.1 | 4.8 | 57.4 | 10.0 | 11.5 |
| GENERATIONS FCU | La Porte | IN | D | D | D | 9.4 | 6.85 | 0.0 | 29.8 | 0.0 | 0.0 | 7.6 | 9.4 |
| GENESEE CO-OP FCU | Rochester | NY | D+ | C- | C- | 16.0 | 13.69 | 0.0 | 22.0 | 36.7 | 1.3 | 6.3 | 8.3 |
| GENESEE VALLEY FCU | Geneseo | NY | C+ | B- | B- | 69.2 | 4.11 | 3.1 | 15.2 | 36.1 | 0.0 | 6.8 | 8.9 |
| ▼ GENESIS EMPL CU | Zanesville | OH | C | C+ | C+ | 13.0 | 3.94 | 0.0 | 50.3 | 0.0 | 0.0 | 9.9 | 10.9 |
| GENFED FINANCIAL CU | Akron | OH | B+ | B+ | A | 221.1 | 5.33 | 0.4 | 31.5 | 36.7 | 2.0 | 10.0 | 16.3 |
| GENISYS CU | Auburn Hills | MI | A | A | A | 1930.9 | 19.61 | 3.8 | 31.3 | 17.9 | 33.3 | 10.0 | 14.9 |
| GENUINE PARTS CU | Norcross | GA | C | C | C+ | 8.9 | 1.20 | 0.0 | 26.8 | 0.0 | 0.0 | 10.0 | 28.8 |
| GEORGETOWN KRAFT CU | Georgetown | SC | A- | A- | A- | 91.0 | 3.55 | 1.8 | 31.6 | 19.6 | 1.7 | 10.0 | 14.3 |
| GEORGETOWN UNIV ALUMNI & STUDENT FC | Washington | DC | D- | D- | D- | 16.4 | -4.29 | 0.0 | 5.8 | 0.0 | 31.7 | 5.4 | 7.4 |
| GEORGIA GUARD CU | Macon | GA | D | D- | D- | 4.3 | -8.78 | 0.0 | 46.2 | 1.5 | 0.0 | 8.7 | 10.1 |
| GEORGIA HERITAGE FCU | Savannah | GA | B | B- | B+ | 83.8 | 5.15 | 0.0 | 59.2 | 11.1 | 0.6 | 10.0 | 12.8 |
| ▲ GEORGIA POWER MACON FCU | Macon | GA | D | D- | D- | 3.4 | 6.22 | 0.0 | 62.5 | 0.0 | 0.0 | 7.4 | 9.3 |
| GEORGIA POWER NORTHWEST FCU | Rome | GA | D+ | D+ | C- | 48.2 | 5.47 | 0.0 | 31.9 | 1.7 | 0.0 | 7.9 | 9.6 |
| GEORGIA POWER VALDOSTA FCU | Valdosta | GA | C | C- | C | 23.3 | -3.25 | 0.0 | 41.1 | 9.9 | 3.2 | 10.0 | 11.2 |
| GEORGIA UNITED CU | Duluth | GA | B+ | B+ | B | 1061.1 | 8.57 | 5.3 | 29.0 | 13.7 | 27.5 | 10.0 | 12.4 |
| GEORGIAS OWN CU | Atlanta | GA | B | B- | B- | 1881.5 | 3.40 | 4.6 | 42.0 | 24.4 | 12.2 | 10.0 | 11.7 |
| GEOVISTA FCU | Hinesville | GA | B | B | B | 123.3 | 14.18 | 0.0 | 47.0 | 9.5 | 3.6 | 7.4 | 9.3 |
| ▲ GERBER FCU | Fremont | MI | B | C+ | C+ | 128.5 | 3.47 | 0.1 | 17.1 | 29.7 | 19.8 | 10.0 | 11.3 |
| GERMANIA CU | Brenham | TX | C- | C- | C+ | 9.9 | 1.52 | 0.0 | 50.1 | 0.0 | 0.0 | 10.0 | 13.9 |
| GESA CU | Richland | WA | B+ | B+ | B+ | 1536.4 | 11.60 | 9.7 | 54.5 | 18.9 | 3.4 | 8.0 | 9.6 |
| GESB SHEET METAL WORKERS FCU | Portage | IN | E+ | E+ | E+ | 8.8 | 2.10 | 0.0 | 35.1 | 7.9 | 0.0 | 5.8 | 7.8 |
| GFA FCU | Gardner | MA | C+ | C | C+ | 434.6 | 3.18 | 5.7 | 11.1 | 30.6 | 38.8 | 10.0 | 11.0 |
| GGW FCU | New Orleans | LA | C+ | C+ | C+ | <1 | 1.82 | 0.0 | 51.7 | 0.0 | 0.0 | 10.0 | 30.2 |
| GHA FCU | Greenwich | CT | C | C | C+ | 23.0 | 3.73 | 0.0 | 16.2 | 0.0 | 0.9 | 9.3 | 10.5 |
| GHS FCU | Binghamton | NY | B+ | B+ | A- | 146.1 | 2.01 | 0.5 | 43.0 | 20.4 | 5.6 | 8.0 | 9.6 |
| GHS FCU | Greenville | SC | C+ | C+ | C | 37.3 | 4.69 | 0.0 | 36.1 | 0.2 | 0.0 | 8.3 | 9.9 |
| GIBBONS & REED EMPL FCU | Salt Lake City | UT | C- | C- | C- | 5.3 | -1.75 | 0.0 | 35.3 | 0.0 | 0.0 | 10.0 | 15.6 |
| GIBBS ALUMINUM FCU | Henderson | KY | C | C | C+ | 5.1 | 5.48 | 0.0 | 47.8 | 0.0 | 0.0 | 10.0 | 33.4 |
| GIDEON FCU | Waukegan | IL | C- | C- | C+ | <1 | 4.76 | 0.0 | 6.1 | 0.0 | 0.0 | 8.3 | 9.9 |
| GILT EDGE EMPL FCU | Norman | OK | D | D | D+ | 2.0 | 12.25 | 0.0 | 45.0 | 0.0 | 0.0 | 8.9 | 10.3 |
| GIRARD CU INC | Girard | OH | C- | C- | D+ | 2.1 | -7.85 | 0.0 | 36.3 | 0.0 | 0.0 | 10.0 | 16.5 |
| GLACIAL LAKES EDUCATIONAL EMPL FCU | Watertown | SD | D- | D | C- | <1 | -0.41 | 0.0 | 61.8 | 0.0 | 0.0 | 7.3 | 9.2 |
| GLACIER HILLS CU | West Bend | WI | B | B- | C+ | 105.8 | 14.81 | 0.1 | 30.7 | 23.2 | 0.0 | 6.9 | 8.9 |
| ▲ GLAMORGAN EMPL FCU | Lynchburg | VA | C | C- | C- | 1.1 | 7.84 | 0.0 | 57.5 | 0.0 | 0.0 | 10.0 | 35.4 |
| ▲ GLAMOUR COMMUNITY FCU | Quebradillas | PR | D | D- | E+ | 3.0 | -2.33 | 0.0 | 63.1 | 0.0 | 0.0 | 8.0 | 9.6 |
| ▲ GLASS CAP FCU | Connellsville | PA | B- | C | D+ | 26.7 | 2.83 | 0.0 | 29.2 | 26.5 | 0.0 | 9.6 | 10.7 |
| GLASS CITY FCU | Maumee | OH | C | C | C | 188.4 | 2.26 | 7.0 | 23.9 | 19.2 | 31.8 | 8.8 | 10.2 |
| GLATCO CU | Spring Grove | PA | C | C | C | 37.9 | 0.61 | 0.0 | 12.8 | 3.4 | 0.0 | 10.0 | 13.8 |
| GLENDALE AREA SCHOOLS FCU | Glendale | CA | B | B | B | 344.6 | 2.33 | 0.7 | 6.4 | 6.1 | 57.2 | 10.0 | 12.8 |
| GLENDALE FCU | Glendale | CA | C+ | C | C- | 62.4 | 0.19 | 0.0 | 20.8 | 19.6 | 3.7 | 10.0 | 15.3 |
| GLENDIVE BN FCU | Glendive | MT | B+ | B+ | B+ | 29.5 | -8.00 | 0.0 | 13.1 | 27.4 | 0.0 | 10.0 | 12.9 |
| GLENVIEW CU | Glenview | IL | D- | D- | D- | 13.6 | -2.46 | 0.0 | 15.8 | 0.9 | 0.0 | 5.2 | 7.2 |
| GLOBAL 1 FCU | Pennsauken | NJ | C- | C- | D+ | 7.7 | -9.12 | 0.0 | 33.2 | 3.3 | 0.0 | 10.0 | 12.4 |
| GLOBAL CU | Spokane | WA | C- | C- | C | 380.9 | 4.49 | 7.4 | 39.7 | 19.0 | 11.7 | 6.5 | 8.5 |
| GLOBE INDUSTRIES EMPL CU | Dayton | OH | D | D | D | 2.0 | 6.96 | 0.0 | 32.6 | 0.0 | 0.0 | 10.0 | 14.8 |
| GLOUCESTER FIRE DEPT CU | Gloucester | MA | B- | B- | B- | <1 | -3.35 | 0.0 | 50.9 | 0.0 | 0.0 | 10.0 | 36.0 |
| GLOUCESTER MUNICIPAL CU | Gloucester | MA | C- | C- | C- | 1.9 | 6.13 | 0.0 | 0.9 | 0.0 | 0.0 | 10.0 | 20.7 |
| GLOVER FCU | Honolulu | HI | C | C | C | 4.7 | 1.32 | 0.0 | 2.5 | 0.0 | 1.6 | 10.0 | 13.3 |
| GLYNN COUNTY FEDERAL EMPL CU | Brunswick | GA | C+ | C | C | 18.8 | 1.03 | 0.0 | 30.4 | 2.0 | 0.0 | 10.0 | 19.7 |
| GNC COMMUNITY FCU | New Castle | PA | B+ | B+ | B+ | 70.8 | -1.25 | 0.0 | 28.1 | 1.3 | 43.4 | 10.0 | 15.5 |
| GO FCU | Dallas | TX | C- | C- | D+ | 122.4 | 2.72 | 0.0 | 50.4 | 24.2 | 2.5 | 5.3 | 7.3 |
| GOETZ CU | Saint Joseph | MO | B+ | B+ | B+ | 50.0 | 8.66 | 0.0 | 35.6 | 9.9 | 0.0 | 10.0 | 13.3 |
| GOGEBIC COUNTY FCU | Bessemer | MI | C | C | C- | 16.2 | 2.07 | 0.2 | 41.2 | 0.0 | 0.0 | 8.8 | 10.2 |
| GOLD COAST FCU | West Palm Beach | FL | B- | B | B | 149.7 | 6.81 | 0.0 | 41.2 | 2.0 | 0.6 | 9.3 | 10.5 |
| GOLDEN 1 CU | Sacramento | CA | A | A | A | 9508.2 | 10.82 | 1.1 | 32.7 | 20.2 | 30.6 | 10.0 | 11.7 |

| Asset Quality Index | Non-Performing Loans as a % of Total Loans | Non-Performing Loans as a % of Capital | Net Charge-Offs Avg Loans | Profitability Index | Net Income ($Mil) | Return on Assets | Return on Equity | Net Interest Spread | Overhead Efficiency Ratio | Liquidity Index | Liquidity Ratio | Hot Money Ratio | Stability Index |
|---|---|---|---|---|---|---|---|---|---|---|---|---|---|
| 8.4 | 0.49 | 1.9 | 0.00 | 0.5 | 0.0 | -0.21 | -1.33 | 3.46 | 106.3 | 4.2 | 9.1 | 0.0 | 5.5 |
| 7.1 | 0.90 | 6.7 | 0.90 | 3.7 | 1.7 | 0.40 | 4.42 | 4.24 | 82.2 | 2.3 | 10.2 | 22.0 | 5.9 |
| 9.9 | 0.44 | 1.3 | 0.35 | 1.7 | 0.0 | 0.00 | 0.00 | 3.47 | 98.5 | 3.2 | 11.7 | 12.6 | 6.5 |
| 4.6 | 0.62 | 13.7 | 0.57 | 2.2 | 0.1 | 0.33 | 5.01 | 4.09 | 90.8 | 4.6 | 24.1 | 0.9 | 1.6 |
| 8.6 | 1.33 | 4.0 | -0.02 | 0.5 | -0.1 | -0.33 | -2.95 | 3.07 | 108.4 | 4.5 | 16.0 | 1.5 | 4.7 |
| 7.1 | 1.05 | 3.9 | -0.16 | 2.2 | 0.0 | 0.23 | 2.44 | 3.33 | 94.5 | 5.4 | 26.0 | 0.0 | 4.1 |
| 9.4 | 0.12 | 1.2 | -0.10 | 2.8 | 0.0 | 0.21 | 3.42 | 4.01 | 96.8 | 4.8 | 25.7 | 0.7 | 3.3 |
| 8.5 | 0.28 | 2.1 | 0.09 | 3.4 | 0.1 | 0.24 | 2.70 | 4.04 | 94.9 | 5.1 | 31.1 | 4.0 | 5.0 |
| 5.9 | 0.88 | 4.3 | 0.44 | 2.6 | 0.0 | 0.23 | 2.08 | 3.47 | 86.9 | 5.5 | 47.4 | 0.0 | 5.7 |
| 8.4 | 0.83 | 4.1 | 0.24 | 4.3 | 0.9 | 0.54 | 3.49 | 3.48 | 85.3 | 3.7 | 17.0 | 5.7 | 8.2 |
| 8.4 | 0.75 | 3.2 | 0.68 | 9.8 | 27.1 | 1.98 | 13.55 | 3.32 | 49.4 | 3.7 | 10.0 | 5.2 | 9.4 |
| 10.0 | 0.70 | 0.7 | -0.29 | 3.8 | 0.0 | 0.59 | 2.04 | 4.03 | 84.0 | 5.2 | 22.8 | 0.0 | 7.0 |
| 8.9 | 0.35 | 2.4 | 0.51 | 6.7 | 0.7 | 0.96 | 7.64 | 4.49 | 83.5 | 4.2 | 24.4 | 10.5 | 6.9 |
| 10.0 | 0.00 | 0.0 | -0.22 | 1.1 | 0.0 | -0.09 | -1.18 | 1.60 | 99.7 | 6.7 | 42.8 | 0.7 | 2.0 |
| 5.3 | 0.73 | 5.1 | 0.06 | 2.2 | 0.0 | 0.28 | 2.76 | 6.64 | 95.5 | 5.4 | 30.3 | 2.7 | 4.8 |
| 8.0 | 0.33 | 2.0 | 0.28 | 4.3 | 0.3 | 0.54 | 4.29 | 3.90 | 85.2 | 2.7 | 17.5 | 15.1 | 5.4 |
| 2.2 | 3.02 | 19.7 | 0.00 | 5.8 | 0.0 | 0.84 | 9.18 | 5.98 | 81.3 | 5.2 | 29.2 | 0.0 | 4.7 |
| 9.8 | 0.23 | 1.0 | 0.21 | 1.5 | 0.0 | -0.06 | -0.60 | 2.71 | 95.8 | 5.1 | 37.3 | 2.0 | 4.2 |
| 6.4 | 1.15 | 6.8 | 1.33 | 3.8 | 0.1 | 0.37 | 3.36 | 4.30 | 80.8 | 2.4 | 21.9 | 28.9 | 5.0 |
| 8.5 | 0.37 | 2.0 | 0.21 | 5.9 | 7.6 | 0.98 | 8.15 | 3.16 | 76.0 | 3.9 | 11.9 | 3.8 | 8.8 |
| 8.7 | 0.37 | 2.8 | 0.53 | 3.8 | 6.8 | 0.48 | 4.54 | 3.29 | 83.3 | 3.5 | 8.8 | 4.1 | 7.5 |
| 5.1 | 1.97 | 12.0 | 1.08 | 8.8 | 1.3 | 1.41 | 15.70 | 5.42 | 75.7 | 4.4 | 16.1 | 3.6 | 5.4 |
| 7.7 | 1.31 | 6.0 | 0.24 | 4.4 | 0.7 | 0.69 | 6.38 | 3.14 | 82.5 | 4.0 | 15.7 | 3.4 | 6.6 |
| 8.1 | 0.28 | 1.3 | 0.00 | 1.7 | 0.0 | 0.01 | 0.10 | 3.04 | 102.2 | 4.0 | 32.5 | 2.7 | 6.7 |
| 6.8 | 0.35 | 3.7 | 0.60 | 6.6 | 11.7 | 1.04 | 11.17 | 3.65 | 67.3 | 2.9 | 9.8 | 7.1 | 6.8 |
| 6.8 | 1.17 | 7.2 | 0.29 | 2.5 | 0.0 | 0.43 | 5.56 | 3.23 | 85.1 | 4.2 | 16.6 | 0.0 | 1.0 |
| 9.1 | 0.50 | 2.5 | 0.20 | 3.5 | 1.6 | 0.48 | 4.41 | 2.41 | 84.3 | 3.2 | 15.0 | 13.8 | 7.0 |
| 6.9 | 3.22 | 5.4 | 0.00 | 7.8 | 0.0 | 1.21 | 4.02 | 5.95 | 77.4 | 5.6 | 69.1 | 0.0 | 5.0 |
| 6.3 | 2.39 | 5.4 | 0.00 | 3.9 | 0.1 | 0.57 | 5.53 | 2.79 | 78.8 | 4.7 | 14.8 | 1.2 | 5.1 |
| 7.8 | 0.53 | 4.6 | 0.34 | 2.5 | -0.1 | -0.05 | -0.55 | 3.64 | 92.9 | 3.1 | 9.8 | 4.1 | 6.2 |
| 9.5 | 0.32 | 1.3 | 0.03 | 3.1 | 0.1 | 0.40 | 4.07 | 3.01 | 90.3 | 5.4 | 27.9 | 1.7 | 5.0 |
| 7.2 | 2.88 | 7.3 | -0.12 | 3.4 | 0.0 | 0.46 | 2.92 | 3.47 | 82.2 | 6.0 | 47.4 | 0.0 | 6.5 |
| 8.7 | 0.12 | 0.2 | 0.51 | 5.8 | 0.0 | 0.93 | 2.79 | 3.70 | 72.0 | 6.8 | 77.7 | 0.0 | 5.0 |
| 7.2 | 12.50 | 7.4 | 35.56 | 2.6 | 0.0 | 0.00 | 0.00 | 8.89 | 100.0 | 8.9 | 103.4 | 0.0 | 5.1 |
| 5.1 | 2.22 | 7.9 | 4.23 | 0.7 | 0.0 | -0.51 | -4.38 | 5.64 | 53.7 | 6.8 | 61.4 | 0.0 | 4.0 |
| 6.3 | 4.11 | 10.2 | 0.00 | 3.3 | 0.0 | 0.42 | 2.72 | 2.20 | 74.2 | 5.2 | 38.6 | 0.0 | 7.1 |
| 8.6 | 0.00 | 0.0 | 0.00 | 0.4 | 0.0 | -0.26 | -2.93 | 2.57 | 111.1 | 4.2 | 7.4 | 0.0 | 4.0 |
| 7.1 | 1.01 | 6.8 | 0.11 | 5.5 | 0.6 | 0.79 | 9.04 | 3.33 | 82.4 | 4.3 | 18.7 | 1.0 | 6.1 |
| 8.7 | 0.00 | 0.0 | 0.23 | 4.7 | 0.0 | 0.78 | 2.15 | 6.57 | 83.3 | 6.6 | 64.3 | 0.0 | 4.3 |
| 5.8 | 0.00 | 0.0 | 0.13 | 3.2 | 0.0 | 0.34 | 3.70 | 5.99 | 91.7 | 5.6 | 40.0 | 0.0 | 3.0 |
| 7.7 | 0.45 | 2.7 | 0.32 | 4.4 | 0.1 | 0.70 | 7.14 | 3.62 | 80.3 | 4.6 | 24.1 | 0.4 | 4.8 |
| 9.3 | 0.43 | 2.2 | 0.24 | 3.0 | 0.6 | 0.38 | 3.81 | 2.96 | 89.5 | 4.3 | 13.4 | 3.7 | 6.0 |
| 10.0 | 0.66 | 1.2 | 0.16 | 2.2 | 0.1 | 0.16 | 1.15 | 2.16 | 90.1 | 6.1 | 36.2 | 1.2 | 6.8 |
| 10.0 | 0.34 | 0.4 | 0.05 | 5.0 | 2.1 | 0.80 | 6.39 | 2.12 | 54.9 | 5.7 | 42.2 | 18.0 | 7.4 |
| 10.0 | 0.36 | 1.0 | 0.27 | 2.9 | 0.2 | 0.32 | 2.10 | 3.16 | 83.7 | 3.7 | 13.9 | 9.8 | 6.7 |
| 10.0 | 0.16 | 0.6 | 0.02 | 7.2 | 0.3 | 1.08 | 8.87 | 3.36 | 66.8 | 4.7 | 23.3 | 5.6 | 6.8 |
| 10.0 | 0.06 | 0.2 | 0.18 | 2.4 | 0.0 | 0.26 | 3.75 | 2.81 | 91.9 | 4.7 | 19.6 | 0.3 | 1.5 |
| 6.5 | 3.33 | 9.4 | 0.54 | 2.3 | -0.1 | -1.89 | -14.94 | 4.50 | 147.7 | 5.3 | 24.0 | 0.0 | 5.2 |
| 6.2 | 0.21 | 6.1 | 0.42 | 2.4 | 0.6 | 0.20 | 2.32 | 3.19 | 92.1 | 3.9 | 12.6 | 4.0 | 4.7 |
| 7.2 | 3.65 | 8.4 | 1.10 | 0.0 | 0.0 | -2.25 | -13.60 | 3.57 | 178.1 | 5.9 | 35.3 | 7.4 | 5.3 |
| 8.7 | 0.00 | 0.0 | 0.00 | 6.7 | 0.0 | 0.75 | 2.04 | 4.68 | 81.3 | 5.4 | 29.1 | 0.0 | 5.0 |
| 9.1 | 0.99 | 1.5 | 0.00 | 2.0 | 0.0 | -0.07 | -0.34 | 4.87 | 101.8 | 5.6 | 24.8 | 0.0 | 6.1 |
| 10.0 | 0.00 | 0.0 | 0.00 | 3.5 | 0.0 | 0.43 | 3.26 | 1.17 | 56.3 | 7.4 | 70.7 | 0.0 | 5.7 |
| 7.6 | 2.97 | 6.9 | -0.04 | 3.6 | 0.1 | 0.53 | 2.66 | 3.08 | 84.3 | 5.7 | 39.2 | 0.0 | 6.9 |
| 8.8 | 1.42 | 3.7 | 0.47 | 3.9 | 0.2 | 0.41 | 2.75 | 2.68 | 85.7 | 5.2 | 19.3 | 0.0 | 6.8 |
| 7.4 | 0.08 | 2.9 | 0.41 | 2.3 | 0.1 | 0.12 | 1.64 | 4.06 | 90.4 | 2.7 | 3.3 | 5.1 | 3.9 |
| 8.5 | 0.92 | 3.8 | 0.30 | 7.9 | 0.5 | 1.46 | 11.57 | 4.13 | 66.2 | 6.3 | 42.7 | 0.0 | 6.4 |
| 6.7 | 1.83 | 8.2 | 0.49 | 2.9 | 0.0 | 0.19 | 1.95 | 3.67 | 88.4 | 4.6 | 24.3 | 0.0 | 5.5 |
| 9.8 | 0.10 | 0.6 | 0.38 | 3.6 | 0.4 | 0.37 | 3.54 | 1.98 | 86.5 | 5.8 | 43.2 | 1.2 | 5.9 |
| 9.5 | 0.51 | 2.5 | 0.29 | 6.1 | 54.1 | 0.78 | 6.55 | 2.80 | 73.8 | 4.0 | 16.6 | 5.6 | 9.0 |

| Name | City | State | Rating | 2014 Rating | 2013 Rating | Total Assets ($Mil) | One Year Asset Growth | Commercial Loans | Consumer Loans | Mortgage Loans | Securities | Capitalization Index | Net Worth Ratio |
|------|------|-------|--------|-------------|-------------|---------------------|----------------------|------------------|----------------|----------------|------------|---------------------|-----------------|
| GOLDEN CIRCLE CU INC | Massillon | OH | D+ | D+ | D+ | 86.6 | -2.40 | 7.4 | 26.2 | 9.0 | 13.1 | 10.0 | 16.4 |
| GOLDEN EAGLE FCU | Tulsa | OK | D | D+ | D+ | 16.8 | 1.99 | 0.0 | 45.2 | 0.0 | 0.0 | 10.0 | 14.8 |
| GOLDEN PLAINS CU | Garden City | KS | B | B+ | B | 538.8 | 17.75 | 1.8 | 76.7 | 4.3 | 0.0 | 8.8 | 10.2 |
| GOLDEN RULE COMMUNITY CU | Ripon | WI | D+ | D+ | D | 26.5 | -1.54 | 0.0 | 22.2 | 22.4 | 0.0 | 6.0 | 8.0 |
| GOLDEN TRIANGLE FCU | Groves | TX | B | B | B+ | 27.5 | 1.92 | 0.0 | 29.4 | 8.8 | 0.0 | 10.0 | 15.6 |
| GOLDEN VALLEY FCU | Manteca | CA | C | C- | C | 25.7 | 1.26 | 0.0 | 18.9 | 5.2 | 0.0 | 8.9 | 10.2 |
| GOLDENWEST FCU | Ogden | UT | A | A | A | 1116.5 | 6.66 | 15.5 | 26.3 | 28.3 | 11.0 | 10.0 | 13.4 |
| ▼ GOLDMARK FCU | Attleboro | MA | C- | C | C | 29.6 | 3.55 | 0.0 | 6.2 | 13.8 | 0.0 | 10.0 | 12.7 |
| GOLMAR FCU | Catano | PR | B- | B- | B+ | <1 | 1.66 | 0.0 | 21.2 | 0.0 | 0.0 | 10.0 | 30.2 |
| GOOD COUNSEL FCU | Brooklyn | NY | D | D+ | C+ | <1 | -8.58 | 0.0 | 1.8 | 0.0 | 0.0 | 10.0 | 11.6 |
| GOOD SAMARITAN FCU | Sioux Falls | SD | B- | B- | B- | 25.8 | -0.74 | 0.0 | 32.5 | 0.0 | 0.0 | 10.0 | 20.3 |
| GOOD SHEPHERD CU | Chicago | IL | C | C+ | C- | <1 | -11.94 | 0.0 | 5.1 | 0.0 | 0.0 | 10.0 | 17.0 |
| GOOD STREET BAPTIST CHURCH FCU | Dallas | TX | D | D | D | <1 | -9.95 | 0.0 | 31.7 | 1.4 | 0.0 | 10.0 | 14.5 |
| GOODYEAR EMPL CU | Akron | OH | C- | C- | C- | 4.1 | 3.66 | 0.0 | 39.1 | 0.0 | 3.9 | 10.0 | 23.2 |
| GOODYEAR SAN ANGELO FCU | San Angelo | TX | C | C | C | 1.6 | 13.01 | 0.0 | 83.6 | 0.0 | 0.0 | 10.0 | 13.8 |
| ▲ GORMAN-RUPP & ASSOCIATES CU | Mansfield | OH | D+ | D+ | D+ | 8.2 | -5.55 | 0.0 | 71.4 | 1.0 | 0.0 | 10.0 | 11.5 |
| GORTONS OF GLOUCESTER EMPL FCU | Gloucester | MA | C- | C- | D+ | 1.0 | -7.19 | 0.0 | 59.5 | 0.0 | 0.0 | 10.0 | 18.2 |
| GOUVERNEUR SCHOOLS FCU | Gouverneur | NY | D | D | C- | 1.1 | 5.45 | 0.0 | 8.4 | 0.0 | 0.0 | 10.0 | 13.9 |
| GOVERNMENT EMPL FCU | Austin | TX | D+ | D+ | C- | 132.8 | -0.53 | 0.0 | 14.5 | 20.5 | 12.8 | 6.6 | 8.7 |
| GOVERNMENT PRINTING OFFICE FCU | Washington | DC | C- | C- | C+ | 38.7 | 2.38 | 0.0 | 43.1 | 0.0 | 7.3 | 10.0 | 14.3 |
| GOVERNMENTAL EMPL CU | La Crosse | WI | C+ | C+ | C+ | 60.2 | 4.33 | 4.1 | 30.6 | 43.7 | 8.4 | 8.1 | 9.7 |
| GOWANDA AREA FCU | Gowanda | NY | C- | C- | C- | 17.1 | 2.33 | 0.0 | 24.4 | 8.1 | 0.0 | 7.0 | 9.0 |
| GOYA FOODS EMPL FCU | Jersey City | NJ | C+ | C+ | C+ | 9.9 | -0.36 | 0.0 | 0.0 | 0.0 | 18.4 | 10.0 | 15.5 |
| GP COMMUNITY FCU | Plattsburgh | NY | C- | C | C | 5.9 | 2.21 | 0.0 | 55.4 | 14.3 | 0.0 | 10.0 | 11.7 |
| ▲ GP LOUISIANA FCU | Zachary | LA | C+ | C+ | C+ | 35.2 | 4.76 | 0.0 | 54.3 | 1.1 | 13.5 | 8.8 | 10.2 |
| ▲ GPA CU | Garden City | GA | C+ | C | C | 13.4 | 1.83 | 0.0 | 35.8 | 0.0 | 7.9 | 10.0 | 18.3 |
| GPCE CU | Pensacola | FL | C- | C- | C- | 36.8 | -1.98 | 0.0 | 37.7 | 6.5 | 0.9 | 8.5 | 10.0 |
| GPO FCU | New Hartford | NY | A- | A- | B+ | 224.9 | 7.93 | 9.8 | 27.5 | 4.4 | 3.3 | 9.4 | 10.6 |
| GR CONSUMERS CU | Wyoming | MI | C | C+ | B- | 38.6 | 0.23 | 0.0 | 19.5 | 8.6 | 0.3 | 10.0 | 16.0 |
| GRACE CONGREGATIONAL CHURCH FCU | New York | NY | D | D+ | D | <1 | 8.26 | 0.0 | 6.8 | 0.0 | 0.0 | 10.0 | 32.9 |
| GRACO FCU | Alma | MI | D+ | D | D- | 16.1 | 2.30 | 0.0 | 34.9 | 0.0 | 0.0 | 6.0 | 8.0 |
| ▼ GRANCO FCU | Ephrata | WA | C | B- | C+ | 53.2 | -0.08 | 0.3 | 32.6 | 35.3 | 11.7 | 10.0 | 13.1 |
| GRAND CENTRAL TERMINAL EMPL FCU | New York | NY | C+ | C | D | 8.0 | 0.95 | 0.0 | 25.2 | 3.0 | 9.6 | 10.0 | 12.3 |
| ▼ GRAND COUNTY CU | Moab | UT | D+ | C | C | 23.3 | 22.94 | 0.3 | 61.5 | 1.2 | 0.0 | 7.2 | 9.1 |
| GRAND HERITAGE FCU | La Porte | IN | D | D | D | 15.3 | 2.30 | 0.0 | 21.8 | 11.2 | 0.0 | 5.7 | 7.7 |
| GRAND JUNCTION FCU | Grand Junction | CO | A- | A- | A- | 58.3 | 6.22 | 3.9 | 22.7 | 23.3 | 13.4 | 10.0 | 17.3 |
| ▲ GRAND PRAIRIE CU | Grand Prairie | TX | C- | D+ | C- | 15.7 | 7.81 | 0.0 | 31.2 | 12.2 | 0.0 | 8.6 | 10.1 |
| GRAND TRUNK BATTLE CREEK EMPL FCU | Battle Creek | MI | B | B | B | 30.9 | 1.62 | 0.0 | 36.9 | 8.7 | 0.0 | 10.0 | 15.5 |
| GRANGE MUTUAL EMPL CU | Columbus | OH | E+ | D- | D | 7.2 | -2.91 | 0.0 | 54.7 | 0.0 | 4.2 | 5.7 | 7.7 |
| GRANITE FCU | Salt Lake City | UT | B | B | C+ | 378.1 | 9.54 | 4.8 | 35.4 | 29.6 | 13.1 | 7.8 | 9.6 |
| GRANITE FURNITURE EMPL FCU | West Jordan | UT | C- | C- | D+ | <1 | -11.72 | 0.0 | 79.8 | 0.0 | 0.0 | 10.0 | 51.2 |
| ▼ GRANITE HILLS CU | Barre | VT | C+ | B- | B- | 37.4 | 3.30 | 0.0 | 11.9 | 12.2 | 30.7 | 10.0 | 13.5 |
| GRANITE STATE CU | Manchester | NH | C+ | B- | B- | 358.5 | 7.01 | 9.1 | 25.7 | 38.2 | 7.0 | 5.9 | 7.9 |
| GRANTSVILLE FCU | Grantsville | UT | E+ | E+ | E+ | 4.6 | 0.53 | 0.0 | 21.7 | 0.0 | 0.1 | 4.8 | 6.8 |
| GRAPHIC ARTS CU | Shreveport | LA | C+ | C+ | B- | 1.7 | 1.57 | 0.0 | 59.1 | 0.0 | 0.0 | 10.0 | 37.9 |
| ▲ GRATIOT COMMUNITY CU | Alma | MI | C+ | C | C | 28.5 | 2.12 | 0.0 | 31.6 | 18.1 | 22.9 | 6.9 | 9.0 |
| GRAYS HARBOR COMMUNITY HOSP FCU | Aberdeen | WA | D | D+ | D+ | 2.1 | 1.76 | 0.0 | 25.9 | 0.0 | 0.0 | 10.0 | 13.6 |
| GREAT BASIN FCU | Reno | NV | B+ | B+ | B+ | 134.8 | 3.87 | 4.9 | 38.5 | 20.9 | 4.7 | 8.8 | 10.2 |
| GREAT ERIE FCU | Orchard Park | NY | B- | B- | B- | 75.5 | 3.98 | 0.6 | 24.3 | 12.2 | 0.0 | 8.2 | 9.8 |
| GREAT FALLS REGIONAL FCU | Lewiston | ME | C | C | C+ | 24.6 | 1.14 | 0.9 | 12.5 | 18.8 | 0.0 | 10.0 | 19.2 |
| GREAT HORIZONS FCU | Munster | IN | C- | C- | C- | 3.2 | 0.53 | 0.0 | 61.3 | 0.0 | 0.0 | 10.0 | 18.9 |
| GREAT LAKES CU | North Chicago | IL | C- | C- | C- | 690.3 | 10.37 | 6.9 | 24.1 | 26.3 | 12.5 | 8.4 | 9.9 |
| GREAT LAKES CU INC | Sylvania | OH | C- | C+ | C+ | 26.2 | 0.63 | 2.9 | 38.3 | 2.2 | 34.1 | 9.9 | 11.0 |
| GREAT LAKES FIRST FCU | Escanaba | MI | C- | D+ | D+ | 64.5 | 3.70 | 0.0 | 25.4 | 20.7 | 21.7 | 9.2 | 10.5 |
| ▼ GREAT LAKES MEMBERS CU | Dearborn | MI | C | B- | C- | 9.7 | -3.15 | 5.7 | 25.0 | 20.7 | 37.0 | 10.0 | 29.5 |
| GREAT MEADOW FCU | Granville | NY | C+ | C+ | C+ | 23.6 | 5.83 | 0.0 | 53.4 | 7.5 | 23.2 | 10.0 | 16.9 |
| GREAT NECK SCHOOL EMPL FCU | Great Neck | NY | C | C- | D+ | 3.2 | 2.91 | 0.0 | 53.2 | 0.0 | 0.0 | 10.0 | 29.4 |
| GREAT NORTHWEST FCU | Aberdeen | WA | A- | A- | A- | 121.1 | 3.32 | 8.0 | 19.3 | 20.9 | 5.2 | 10.0 | 13.4 |
| GREAT PLAINS FCU | Joplin | MO | C+ | C+ | C+ | 281.5 | 0.16 | 0.2 | 15.2 | 14.1 | 44.2 | 10.0 | 17.5 |
| GREAT RIVER COMMUNITY CU | Quincy | IL | C- | C | C+ | 20.4 | 0.35 | 0.0 | 32.5 | 0.0 | 0.0 | 10.0 | 16.8 |

| Asset Quality Index | Non-Performing Loans as a % of Total Loans | Non-Performing Loans as a % of Capital | Net Charge-Offs Avg Loans | Profitability Index | Net Income ($Mil) | Return on Assets | Return on Equity | Net Interest Spread | Overhead Efficiency Ratio | Liquidity Index | Liquidity Ratio | Hot Money Ratio | Stability Index |
|---|---|---|---|---|---|---|---|---|---|---|---|---|---|
| 8.9 | 0.92 | 2.4 | 0.45 | 0.5 | -0.2 | -0.22 | -1.35 | 2.74 | 104.5 | 4.8 | 32.5 | 1.5 | 6.8 |
| 6.7 | 1.75 | 6.2 | 0.11 | 0.0 | -0.1 | -0.59 | -3.91 | 3.19 | 113.2 | 5.6 | 43.1 | 2.4 | 5.4 |
| 4.6 | 0.81 | 11.3 | 0.46 | 5.7 | 2.9 | 0.72 | 7.24 | 3.89 | 79.2 | 1.9 | 6.2 | 14.3 | 7.7 |
| 5.2 | 1.56 | 12.6 | 0.14 | 2.2 | 0.0 | 0.15 | 1.89 | 4.12 | 96.6 | 5.3 | 46.5 | 3.0 | 3.4 |
| 9.5 | 0.81 | 2.5 | 0.09 | 4.7 | 0.1 | 0.67 | 4.70 | 3.63 | 84.4 | 4.8 | 29.2 | 2.9 | 7.1 |
| 10.0 | 0.39 | 1.0 | -0.40 | 2.6 | 0.1 | 0.37 | 3.65 | 2.70 | 87.3 | 5.2 | 14.0 | 0.5 | 4.7 |
| 9.3 | 0.32 | 2.0 | 0.14 | 9.3 | 12.2 | 1.50 | 11.31 | 2.97 | 68.0 | 3.4 | 18.3 | 8.8 | 9.0 |
| 10.0 | 0.00 | 0.0 | 0.06 | 1.2 | 0.0 | -0.12 | -0.92 | 2.20 | 108.5 | 5.0 | 47.2 | 7.8 | 6.0 |
| 9.4 | 5.13 | 3.5 | 0.00 | 7.3 | 0.0 | 1.83 | 6.12 | 4.24 | 44.4 | 7.7 | 112.1 | 0.0 | 5.7 |
| 10.0 | 0.00 | 0.0 | 0.00 | 0.0 | 0.0 | -5.12 | -40.00 | 3.51 | 200.0 | 8.8 | 102.5 | 0.0 | 6.3 |
| 9.8 | 0.45 | 0.8 | 0.06 | 2.8 | 0.1 | 0.29 | 1.38 | 1.97 | 85.9 | 5.6 | 49.1 | 0.0 | 7.4 |
| 10.0 | 0.00 | 0.0 | 0.00 | 3.6 | 0.0 | 0.00 | 0.00 | 44.44 | 200.0 | 9.0 | 114.3 | 0.0 | 6.5 |
| 3.3 | 10.28 | 27.7 | 0.30 | 0.0 | 0.0 | -3.95 | -25.78 | 6.12 | 178.1 | 7.1 | 66.5 | 0.0 | 5.8 |
| 9.8 | 0.59 | 1.1 | -0.16 | 1.9 | 0.0 | 0.16 | 0.72 | 2.79 | 94.6 | 5.4 | 56.8 | 0.0 | 6.9 |
| 7.6 | 0.00 | 0.0 | 0.00 | 7.6 | 0.0 | 1.35 | 9.66 | 3.40 | 62.5 | 2.6 | 2.2 | 0.0 | 5.0 |
| 4.4 | 2.76 | 15.2 | 0.04 | 7.0 | 0.1 | 1.04 | 9.71 | 8.05 | 82.1 | 3.1 | 38.1 | 20.8 | 3.7 |
| 8.6 | 0.00 | 0.0 | 0.00 | 2.4 | 0.0 | 0.37 | 2.16 | 5.02 | 88.6 | 4.9 | 40.9 | 0.0 | 5.9 |
| 6.3 | 19.79 | 12.4 | 0.00 | 0.0 | 0.0 | -1.84 | -13.25 | 1.79 | 277.8 | 7.5 | 51.3 | 0.0 | 6.4 |
| 10.0 | 0.27 | 1.3 | 0.05 | 1.8 | 0.1 | 0.10 | 1.18 | 2.14 | 95.3 | 5.3 | 27.3 | 1.6 | 5.2 |
| 5.6 | 3.47 | 11.5 | 0.72 | 1.1 | -0.1 | -0.30 | -2.07 | 4.15 | 93.1 | 4.3 | 19.7 | 2.9 | 5.7 |
| 4.7 | 1.73 | 15.7 | 0.20 | 3.7 | 0.2 | 0.50 | 5.35 | 3.46 | 79.1 | 2.5 | 2.4 | 7.0 | 5.0 |
| 10.0 | 0.07 | 0.3 | 0.00 | 2.4 | 0.0 | 0.23 | 2.63 | 2.03 | 88.6 | 6.1 | 56.6 | 0.0 | 4.1 |
| 10.0 | 0.63 | 0.5 | 0.00 | 2.4 | 0.0 | 0.09 | 0.61 | 1.49 | 91.5 | 5.3 | 20.5 | 0.0 | 6.5 |
| 8.2 | 0.00 | 0.0 | -0.12 | 2.6 | 0.0 | 0.06 | 0.58 | 5.10 | 101.1 | 4.4 | 20.9 | 0.0 | 5.9 |
| 4.4 | 1.04 | 6.1 | 1.09 | 6.4 | 0.2 | 0.80 | 8.13 | 4.33 | 72.8 | 2.6 | 16.4 | 28.1 | 5.0 |
| 9.2 | 1.28 | 2.6 | 0.08 | 2.8 | 0.0 | 0.37 | 1.98 | 3.29 | 89.6 | 5.1 | 28.0 | 5.4 | 7.4 |
| 9.3 | 0.06 | 0.3 | 0.03 | 2.3 | 0.0 | 0.12 | 1.23 | 3.50 | 96.6 | 5.3 | 42.9 | 3.4 | 4.5 |
| 6.8 | 1.60 | 9.1 | 0.41 | 7.7 | 1.8 | 1.08 | 10.36 | 3.50 | 67.7 | 3.8 | 24.4 | 6.2 | 7.4 |
| 10.0 | 0.94 | 1.8 | 0.16 | 2.3 | 0.1 | 0.32 | 2.04 | 2.43 | 90.9 | 5.1 | 35.5 | 0.0 | 6.8 |
| 8.0 | 11.76 | 2.3 | 25.40 | 0.0 | 0.0 | -4.74 | -14.29 | 2.80 | 66.7 | 8.6 | 124.0 | 0.0 | 5.3 |
| 7.3 | 0.50 | 2.5 | 0.10 | 4.2 | 0.1 | 0.70 | 9.20 | 3.42 | 84.4 | 6.1 | 42.8 | 0.0 | 3.5 |
| 7.1 | 1.21 | 6.7 | 0.18 | 1.9 | 0.0 | -0.03 | -0.26 | 4.20 | 97.4 | 3.3 | 12.8 | 8.8 | 6.7 |
| 7.4 | 2.46 | 5.6 | 0.70 | 10.0 | 0.1 | 1.94 | 16.34 | 5.35 | 61.7 | 5.4 | 20.5 | 0.0 | 4.9 |
| 4.3 | 0.94 | 10.7 | 0.91 | 4.7 | 0.0 | 0.11 | 1.17 | 5.45 | 79.8 | 3.2 | 9.4 | 5.1 | 3.0 |
| 9.7 | 0.35 | 1.5 | 0.10 | 0.7 | 0.0 | -0.27 | -3.48 | 2.98 | 106.5 | 5.3 | 16.4 | 0.0 | 3.0 |
| 9.5 | 0.53 | 1.7 | 0.30 | 9.2 | 0.6 | 1.49 | 8.70 | 3.63 | 60.9 | 3.0 | 16.5 | 15.2 | 7.8 |
| 8.4 | 0.42 | 2.0 | 0.09 | 2.0 | 0.0 | 0.15 | 1.44 | 3.42 | 94.9 | 5.0 | 25.3 | 0.0 | 4.2 |
| 9.2 | 1.12 | 3.4 | 0.09 | 3.9 | 0.1 | 0.49 | 3.24 | 3.48 | 83.5 | 4.3 | 27.0 | 1.8 | 7.5 |
| 5.6 | 0.52 | 3.5 | 0.29 | 0.3 | 0.0 | -0.52 | -6.91 | 3.14 | 96.4 | 4.6 | 28.7 | 0.0 | 3.0 |
| 7.4 | 0.81 | 6.4 | 0.41 | 4.9 | 2.0 | 0.73 | 7.55 | 3.39 | 78.3 | 3.7 | 14.1 | 5.4 | 6.1 |
| 8.0 | 0.17 | 0.3 | 0.00 | 3.1 | 0.0 | 0.40 | 0.83 | 4.49 | 90.5 | 3.3 | 15.4 | 0.0 | 5.0 |
| 9.5 | 0.09 | 0.2 | 0.01 | 2.6 | 0.1 | 0.19 | 1.46 | 2.86 | 95.3 | 5.9 | 33.9 | 1.1 | 7.2 |
| 6.0 | 0.87 | 8.7 | 0.53 | 3.2 | 0.5 | 0.19 | 2.36 | 3.98 | 91.5 | 3.5 | 7.6 | 3.5 | 4.8 |
| 8.7 | 0.83 | 3.4 | 1.04 | 0.0 | -0.1 | -1.51 | -20.33 | 2.80 | 138.7 | 6.5 | 66.8 | 0.0 | 1.4 |
| 7.3 | 1.09 | 1.8 | -0.74 | 9.1 | 0.0 | 1.77 | 4.74 | 5.91 | 71.1 | 4.1 | 16.7 | 0.0 | 5.0 |
| 9.6 | 0.07 | 0.4 | 0.35 | 3.8 | 0.1 | 0.49 | 5.83 | 3.62 | 84.8 | 4.4 | 15.2 | 1.7 | 4.6 |
| 9.8 | 0.00 | 0.0 | 0.23 | 0.3 | 0.0 | -0.38 | -2.74 | 1.73 | 128.0 | 6.7 | 85.1 | 0.0 | 5.9 |
| 8.5 | 0.51 | 3.3 | 0.26 | 5.6 | 0.7 | 0.68 | 6.78 | 3.76 | 82.9 | 4.0 | 18.3 | 1.4 | 5.9 |
| 6.3 | 0.70 | 6.2 | 0.64 | 4.4 | 0.3 | 0.51 | 5.21 | 3.39 | 73.4 | 4.7 | 19.8 | 0.7 | 5.2 |
| 10.0 | 0.19 | 0.3 | 0.05 | 1.9 | 0.0 | 0.11 | 0.57 | 2.58 | 98.9 | 4.8 | 34.8 | 3.6 | 6.9 |
| 4.7 | 4.71 | 19.8 | 0.05 | 3.2 | 0.0 | 0.21 | 1.09 | 4.57 | 91.8 | 3.3 | 4.0 | 0.0 | 3.0 |
| 6.4 | 1.27 | 9.2 | 0.42 | 2.3 | 1.0 | 0.21 | 2.09 | 3.49 | 90.3 | 3.6 | 11.0 | 5.5 | 6.1 |
| 7.1 | 0.90 | 3.9 | 1.45 | 0.3 | -0.2 | -1.06 | -9.88 | 4.35 | 94.5 | 4.7 | 16.8 | 2.7 | 4.9 |
| 6.7 | 1.03 | 5.2 | 0.25 | 2.1 | 0.1 | 0.17 | 1.64 | 3.49 | 92.3 | 4.5 | 25.1 | 5.4 | 5.1 |
| 9.8 | 0.42 | 0.7 | -0.07 | 2.0 | -0.1 | -1.47 | -5.02 | 3.13 | 135.4 | 4.7 | 24.7 | 0.0 | 6.6 |
| 8.4 | 0.01 | 0.1 | -0.05 | 3.9 | 0.1 | 0.51 | 2.74 | 4.15 | 97.5 | 3.5 | 5.1 | 2.1 | 6.8 |
| 7.3 | 1.06 | 1.9 | 0.50 | 4.0 | 0.0 | 0.42 | 1.57 | 6.46 | 76.6 | 6.7 | 66.2 | 0.0 | 6.1 |
| 6.9 | 1.93 | 7.9 | 0.78 | 7.3 | 1.0 | 1.11 | 8.41 | 3.77 | 72.8 | 5.4 | 33.2 | 2.6 | 8.1 |
| 10.0 | 0.62 | 1.3 | 0.43 | 2.7 | 0.6 | 0.27 | 1.58 | 2.26 | 86.0 | 4.7 | 27.2 | 10.4 | 7.7 |
| 9.5 | 0.69 | 1.4 | 0.64 | 1.1 | 0.0 | -0.18 | -1.08 | 2.95 | 100.2 | 4.8 | 27.7 | 3.0 | 6.1 |

| Name | City | State | Rating | 2014 Rating | 2013 Rating | Total Assets ($Mil) | One Year Asset Growth | Asset Mix (As a % of Total Assets) Commercial Loans | Consumer Loans | Mortgage Loans | Securities | Capitalization Index | Net Worth Ratio |
|---|---|---|---|---|---|---|---|---|---|---|---|---|---|
| GREAT RIVER FCU | Saint Cloud | MN | B- | B- | B- | 157.5 | 2.22 | 1.2 | 17.2 | 29.0 | 21.5 | 10.0 | 11.0 |
| GREATER ABBEVILLE FCU | Abbeville | SC | B | B | B | 15.3 | 12.28 | 0.0 | 72.6 | 0.0 | 0.0 | 10.0 | 16.9 |
| GREATER ABYSSINIA FCU | Cleveland | OH | D- | D- | D | <1 | -26.90 | 0.0 | 28.6 | 0.0 | 0.0 | 10.0 | 12.1 |
| ▼ GREATER ALLIANCE FCU | Paramus | NJ | D+ | C | C | 167.1 | 3.21 | 8.1 | 26.8 | 33.0 | 0.3 | 7.2 | 9.2 |
| ▼ GREATER CENTENNIAL FCU | Mount Vernon | NY | C- | C+ | C+ | <1 | -8.21 | 0.0 | 22.7 | 0.0 | 0.0 | 10.0 | 11.5 |
| GREATER CENTRAL TEXAS FCU | Killeen | TX | D | D | D | 24.0 | 0.87 | 10.1 | 13.8 | 10.2 | 34.8 | 5.3 | 7.3 |
| GREATER CHAUTAUQUA FCU | Falconer | NY | C+ | C+ | C+ | 58.0 | 2.81 | 0.4 | 34.9 | 23.1 | 6.8 | 7.5 | 9.3 |
| ▼ GREATER CHRIST BAPTIST CHURCH CU | Detroit | MI | D | D+ | C- | <1 | -9.33 | 0.0 | 27.5 | 0.0 | 1.5 | 10.0 | 26.9 |
| GREATER CINCINNATI CU | Silverton | OH | D+ | C- | C- | 91.6 | 3.15 | 0.5 | 17.1 | 29.2 | 0.0 | 4.7 | 7.6 |
| ▲ GREATER EASTERN CU | Johnson City | TN | C+ | C- | C | 50.7 | 1.97 | 3.0 | 16.1 | 30.7 | 0.0 | 10.0 | 14.6 |
| ▼ GREATER GALILEE BAPTIST CU | Milwaukee | WI | D | C- | D- | <1 | 74.16 | 0.0 | 25.2 | 0.0 | 0.0 | 4.1 | 6.5 |
| ▼ GREATER HARTFORD POLICE FCU | Hartford | CT | D | D+ | D+ | 21.4 | 7.36 | 0.0 | 45.8 | 2.0 | 19.5 | 6.7 | 8.8 |
| GREATER IOWA CU | Ames | IA | B- | C | C+ | 348.0 | -0.83 | 6.9 | 39.7 | 26.1 | 11.2 | 7.6 | 9.5 |
| ▼ GREATER KC PUBLIC SAFETY CU | Kansas City | MO | D+ | C | B- | 116.8 | 3.83 | 0.2 | 35.8 | 16.5 | 21.5 | 9.6 | 11.0 |
| GREATER KENTUCKY CU INC | Lexington | KY | B- | B- | C+ | 66.9 | 13.61 | 0.0 | 59.8 | 13.4 | 0.0 | 8.8 | 10.2 |
| GREATER KINSTON CU | Kinston | NC | D+ | D+ | D- | 11.0 | 3.19 | 0.8 | 18.5 | 52.7 | 0.0 | 7.7 | 9.5 |
| GREATER LATROBE SCHOOLS FCU | New Alexandria | PA | C | C- | C- | 2.1 | -0.84 | 0.0 | 50.7 | 0.0 | 0.0 | 10.0 | 12.9 |
| GREATER METRO FCU | Long Island City | NY | C+ | C+ | C+ | 90.4 | -2.11 | 7.4 | 6.7 | 15.6 | 29.9 | 10.0 | 14.0 |
| GREATER NEVADA CU | Carson City | NV | A- | A- | B+ | 563.6 | 11.40 | 7.1 | 24.1 | 26.4 | 9.3 | 8.7 | 10.1 |
| GREATER NEW MT MORIAH BAPTIST CHURC | Detroit | MI | C- | C | C+ | <1 | 0.33 | 0.0 | 55.0 | 0.0 | 0.0 | 10.0 | 58.3 |
| GREATER NEW ORLEANS FCU | Metairie | LA | C+ | C+ | C | 108.5 | -1.71 | 15.8 | 43.3 | 16.3 | 8.7 | 10.0 | 13.7 |
| GREATER NIAGARA FCU | Niagara Falls | NY | B- | C+ | B | 42.8 | 5.43 | 0.0 | 24.0 | 16.5 | 31.1 | 10.0 | 12.2 |
| ▲ GREATER NILES COMMUNITY FCU | Niles | MI | C- | D+ | C- | 51.6 | -3.17 | 0.0 | 10.5 | 47.4 | 0.0 | 6.5 | 8.5 |
| GREATER PIEDMONT CU | Durham | NC | E+ | E+ | D- | 15.6 | 2.13 | 0.0 | 29.7 | 12.4 | 0.0 | 5.4 | 7.4 |
| ▲ GREATER PITTSBURGH FCU | Pittsburgh | PA | C- | D | D+ | 41.9 | -1.59 | 0.0 | 17.7 | 0.0 | 0.0 | 6.9 | 8.9 |
| GREATER PITTSBURGH POLICE FCU | Pittsburgh | PA | A- | A- | A- | 63.0 | 0.70 | 0.0 | 31.5 | 0.2 | 6.7 | 10.0 | 15.8 |
| GREATER SALEM EMPL FCU | Salem | MA | D | D+ | D+ | 12.0 | -0.43 | 0.0 | 19.4 | 18.2 | 3.3 | 6.5 | 8.6 |
| GREATER SPRINGFIELD CU | Springfield | MA | A | A | A- | 145.3 | 3.52 | 0.0 | 9.2 | 33.9 | 11.3 | 10.0 | 12.6 |
| GREATER TEXAS FCU | Austin | TX | C+ | C+ | C+ | 553.5 | 3.82 | 2.7 | 31.9 | 16.2 | 14.8 | 5.7 | 7.9 |
| GREATER VALLEY CU | Fresno | CA | C | C | C | 29.7 | -2.20 | 5.3 | 16.2 | 9.5 | 0.8 | 10.0 | 14.0 |
| GREATER WATERBURY HEALTHCARE FCU | Waterbury | CT | C+ | C+ | C+ | 11.8 | -0.20 | 0.0 | 13.1 | 0.0 | 0.0 | 10.0 | 18.6 |
| GREATER WATERTOWN FCU | Watertown | CT | E+ | E+ | D- | 16.9 | 0.36 | 0.0 | 20.5 | 0.2 | 0.0 | 5.9 | 7.9 |
| GREATER WAYNE COMMUNITY FCU | Rittman | OH | D | D | D | 14.4 | 7.49 | 0.0 | 59.5 | 6.3 | 0.0 | 5.8 | 7.8 |
| GREATER WOODLAWN FCU | Blasdell | NY | B | B | B | 116.9 | 3.21 | 0.0 | 5.3 | 26.0 | 0.0 | 10.0 | 20.1 |
| GREATER WYOMING FCU | Casper | WY | C- | C | C+ | 23.7 | -3.51 | 0.8 | 38.2 | 9.4 | 0.0 | 9.0 | 10.3 |
| GREECE COMMUNITY FCU | Rochester | NY | E+ | E+ | E+ | 7.9 | 2.48 | 0.0 | 32.7 | 1.5 | 2.5 | 6.6 | 8.7 |
| GREEN COUNTRY FCU | Sand Springs | OK | C- | C- | D+ | 55.3 | 10.46 | 9.2 | 34.7 | 23.7 | 16.7 | 6.1 | 8.1 |
| ▲ GREEN MOUNTAIN CU | South Burlington | VT | D+ | D- | E+ | 34.0 | 32.38 | 3.9 | 30.6 | 44.4 | 0.0 | 5.2 | 7.2 |
| GREEN RIVER AREA FCU | Owensboro | KY | C+ | C+ | C+ | 40.3 | 2.33 | 0.0 | 16.9 | 12.9 | 0.0 | 10.0 | 19.8 |
| GREEN RIVER BASIN FCU | Green River | WY | E | E+ | D- | 11.5 | 0.12 | 0.0 | 41.3 | 0.7 | 0.0 | 4.8 | 6.9 |
| GREENBELT FCU | Greenbelt | MD | C | C- | D+ | 27.5 | 2.32 | 0.0 | 13.5 | 12.2 | 5.4 | 8.5 | 10.0 |
| GREENEVILLE CITY EMPL CU | Greeneville | TN | B- | B- | B- | 9.5 | 1.22 | 0.0 | 55.9 | 0.0 | 0.0 | 10.0 | 24.1 |
| GREENEVILLE WORKS EMPL SAVINGS ASSN | Greeneville | TN | B- | C+ | C+ | 2.1 | -0.79 | 0.0 | 49.0 | 0.0 | 0.0 | 10.0 | 34.2 |
| ▲ GREENSBORO MUNICIPAL FCU | Greensboro | NC | B- | C | C | 46.5 | 2.43 | 0.0 | 42.9 | 6.2 | 22.0 | 9.9 | 10.9 |
| GREENSBORO POSTAL CU | Greensboro | NC | D+ | D+ | C- | 23.3 | -2.95 | 0.0 | 10.3 | 20.8 | 0.0 | 10.0 | 21.8 |
| GREENSBURG TEACHERS CU | Greensburg | PA | C- | C- | C | 7.1 | -0.70 | 0.0 | 14.0 | 0.0 | 0.0 | 10.0 | 12.9 |
| GREENUP COUNTY FCU | Russell | KY | C- | C- | C | 5.3 | -3.30 | 0.0 | 40.5 | 0.0 | 42.3 | 10.0 | 11.5 |
| GREENVILLE FCU | Greenville | SC | A- | A- | A- | 193.4 | 7.40 | 5.1 | 24.7 | 27.7 | 10.9 | 9.0 | 10.3 |
| GREENVILLE HERITAGE FCU | Greenville | SC | A | A- | A- | 80.0 | 2.70 | 0.0 | 43.7 | 30.4 | 0.0 | 10.0 | 16.0 |
| GREENWICH MUNICIPAL EMPL FCU | Greenwich | CT | C- | C- | C- | 22.0 | 2.21 | 0.0 | 16.5 | 0.0 | 57.2 | 6.6 | 8.6 |
| GREENWOOD CU | Warwick | RI | B- | B | B | 426.5 | 2.96 | 9.4 | 53.7 | 16.9 | 15.8 | 7.1 | 9.0 |
| ▲ GREENWOOD MUNICIPAL FCU | Greenwood | SC | B | B | B | 36.9 | -0.97 | 0.0 | 34.3 | 1.7 | 0.0 | 10.0 | 13.9 |
| GREYLOCK FCU | Pittsfield | MA | C+ | C+ | C+ | 1073.6 | -1.64 | 6.4 | 16.3 | 42.1 | 12.3 | 8.1 | 9.7 |
| GRIFFITH INSTITUTE EMPL FCU | Springville | NY | C | C | C+ | 3.2 | 9.33 | 0.0 | 32.5 | 0.0 | 31.4 | 10.0 | 11.1 |
| GROCERS SUPPLY EMPL CU | Houston | TX | D | D+ | C | 3.4 | -3.75 | 0.0 | 10.9 | 0.0 | 0.0 | 10.0 | 15.2 |
| ▼ GROTON MUNICIPAL EMPL FCU | Groton | CT | E+ | E+ | E+ | 6.4 | 7.97 | 0.0 | 29.9 | 0.0 | 0.0 | 6.8 | 8.8 |
| GROUP SERVICE EMPL FCU | Tulsa | OK | C | C- | C- | 11.3 | -4.71 | 0.0 | 88.7 | 0.0 | 0.0 | 10.0 | 16.0 |
| ▲ GROVE CITY AREA FCU | Grove City | PA | B- | C+ | B- | 74.2 | -1.04 | 0.0 | 23.0 | 3.5 | 34.8 | 10.0 | 12.1 |
| ▼ GROW FINANCIAL FCU | Tampa | FL | B- | B | B+ | 2118.8 | 5.45 | 3.0 | 46.9 | 23.7 | 9.7 | 8.6 | 10.1 |
| GRS EMPL FCU | West Henrietta | NY | D- | D- | D- | 2.8 | -7.55 | 0.0 | 82.4 | 0.0 | 0.0 | 7.5 | 9.4 |

| Asset Quality Index | Non-Performing Loans | | Net Charge-Offs Avg Loans | Profitability Index | Net Income ($Mil) | Return on Assets | Return on Equity | Net Interest Spread | Overhead Efficiency Ratio | Liquidity Index | Liquidity Ratio | Hot Money Ratio | Stability Index |
|---|---|---|---|---|---|---|---|---|---|---|---|---|---|
| | as a % of Total Loans | as a % of Capital | | | | | | | | | | | |
| 9.6 | 0.18 | 1.1 | 0.14 | 3.3 | 0.5 | 0.39 | 3.55 | 3.02 | 87.6 | 4.3 | 22.9 | 2.1 | 6.6 |
| 4.5 | 2.64 | 13.0 | 0.89 | 10.0 | 0.3 | 2.92 | 17.82 | 9.39 | 69.2 | 3.7 | 18.3 | 6.1 | 8.6 |
| 0.3 | 28.21 | 78.6 | 0.00 | 0.0 | 0.0 | -5.64 | -39.22 | 1.90 | 500.0 | 7.1 | 68.6 | 0.0 | 4.7 |
| 1.7 | 4.82 | 45.3 | 0.80 | 5.5 | 1.1 | 0.85 | 10.81 | 4.42 | 76.8 | 3.0 | 9.4 | 7.4 | 5.9 |
| 0.3 | 60.56 | 84.3 | 0.00 | 3.7 | 0.0 | -11.29 | -72.00 | 8.25 | 83.3 | 8.3 | 91.7 | 0.0 | 6.7 |
| 8.4 | 0.31 | 1.1 | 0.89 | 2.4 | 0.0 | 0.13 | 1.83 | 3.25 | 94.3 | 5.8 | 28.8 | 0.5 | 2.2 |
| 3.7 | 1.92 | 19.4 | 0.48 | 3.0 | 0.1 | 0.17 | 1.89 | 4.19 | 89.7 | 4.0 | 19.8 | 2.9 | 4.8 |
| 9.2 | 2.90 | 3.3 | 0.00 | 0.1 | 0.0 | -0.98 | -3.66 | 2.89 | 141.7 | 6.2 | 71.4 | 0.0 | 5.9 |
| 7.2 | 0.32 | 4.0 | 0.41 | 2.6 | 0.0 | 0.04 | 0.58 | 4.62 | 95.8 | 4.3 | 18.8 | 4.4 | 2.9 |
| 10.0 | 0.46 | 1.6 | 0.09 | 3.3 | 0.2 | 0.40 | 2.75 | 3.51 | 85.6 | 4.8 | 27.1 | 8.6 | 6.7 |
| 0.3 | 13.58 | 91.7 | 0.00 | 3.1 | 0.0 | -2.56 | -26.67 | 10.26 | 144.4 | 6.6 | 50.7 | 0.0 | 5.7 |
| 3.5 | 2.96 | 17.3 | 0.54 | 3.5 | 0.1 | 0.36 | 4.11 | 4.46 | 89.1 | 4.1 | 19.2 | 7.4 | 2.3 |
| 8.0 | 0.54 | 4.8 | 0.40 | 4.7 | 1.9 | 0.73 | 7.79 | 3.64 | 77.8 | 3.2 | 4.7 | 4.0 | 5.9 |
| 8.4 | 0.87 | 5.3 | 0.31 | 1.5 | -0.1 | -0.05 | -0.47 | 3.37 | 94.3 | 3.4 | 13.9 | 12.7 | 6.4 |
| 5.2 | 0.77 | 7.0 | 0.65 | 6.3 | 0.5 | 1.05 | 10.06 | 4.01 | 70.8 | 2.4 | 14.1 | 15.6 | 4.3 |
| 6.8 | 1.13 | 7.9 | 0.79 | 2.2 | 0.0 | 0.06 | 0.64 | 6.05 | 89.5 | 2.9 | 26.0 | 33.7 | 4.3 |
| 8.1 | 0.37 | 1.7 | 0.00 | 3.4 | 0.0 | 0.41 | 3.44 | 4.68 | 89.2 | 4.7 | 20.7 | 0.0 | 6.7 |
| 7.3 | 2.51 | 6.7 | 0.28 | 2.4 | 0.1 | 0.13 | 0.96 | 2.38 | 88.7 | 4.2 | 15.5 | 12.9 | 5.9 |
| 6.9 | 0.61 | 7.4 | 0.40 | 8.8 | 5.0 | 1.22 | 12.19 | 4.12 | 79.4 | 3.9 | 16.7 | 3.1 | 7.0 |
| 4.4 | 13.30 | 13.1 | 1.39 | 4.3 | 0.0 | 0.45 | 0.76 | 9.01 | 66.7 | 7.3 | 126.5 | 0.0 | 3.7 |
| 5.8 | 0.71 | 7.0 | 0.58 | 3.3 | 0.3 | 0.37 | 2.71 | 3.99 | 84.2 | 3.1 | 14.3 | 7.5 | 6.8 |
| 9.8 | 0.38 | 1.5 | 0.12 | 3.5 | 0.2 | 0.46 | 3.82 | 3.00 | 88.6 | 4.8 | 15.0 | 0.8 | 6.4 |
| 9.9 | 0.01 | 0.1 | 0.15 | 2.0 | 0.1 | 0.13 | 1.62 | 3.07 | 96.4 | 3.9 | 27.4 | 1.9 | 3.9 |
| 0.3 | 3.52 | 53.2 | 0.87 | 2.5 | 0.0 | 0.08 | 1.02 | 6.64 | 95.6 | 5.3 | 27.9 | 1.2 | 0.0 |
| 10.0 | 0.25 | 0.7 | 0.46 | 2.3 | 0.1 | 0.37 | 4.26 | 2.44 | 81.0 | 5.1 | 26.4 | 0.4 | 3.6 |
| 9.9 | 0.24 | 0.6 | 0.30 | 4.0 | 0.2 | 0.37 | 2.37 | 2.27 | 78.0 | 4.4 | 16.5 | 2.6 | 7.4 |
| 5.1 | 2.08 | 9.8 | 0.05 | 1.8 | 0.0 | 0.07 | 0.78 | 3.40 | 98.3 | 4.9 | 18.8 | 0.0 | 3.3 |
| 10.0 | 0.11 | 0.4 | 0.02 | 8.3 | 1.3 | 1.22 | 10.10 | 2.13 | 54.0 | 3.7 | 13.1 | 7.5 | 8.7 |
| 6.7 | 0.86 | 7.1 | 0.10 | 3.9 | 2.4 | 0.57 | 7.74 | 2.68 | 82.7 | 4.3 | 16.1 | 3.4 | 5.2 |
| 7.8 | 2.23 | 5.2 | 1.15 | 2.3 | 0.0 | 0.19 | 1.35 | 2.28 | 90.6 | 4.5 | 20.8 | 8.5 | 5.8 |
| 9.5 | 3.04 | 2.5 | 1.00 | 3.3 | 0.0 | 0.44 | 2.40 | 2.38 | 81.0 | 5.2 | 20.8 | 0.0 | 6.9 |
| 6.8 | 1.01 | 5.3 | 0.32 | 1.2 | 0.0 | 0.09 | 1.21 | 3.46 | 94.9 | 4.9 | 27.1 | 2.2 | 1.8 |
| 4.5 | 1.05 | 9.9 | 0.48 | 3.5 | 0.0 | 0.30 | 3.99 | 4.76 | 87.2 | 3.5 | 13.4 | 5.9 | 1.7 |
| 10.0 | 0.61 | 1.0 | 0.30 | 4.4 | 0.5 | 0.57 | 2.87 | 2.65 | 67.8 | 6.6 | 71.1 | 8.1 | 8.1 |
| 7.0 | 0.62 | 3.4 | 0.45 | 2.6 | 0.0 | 0.11 | 1.10 | 3.78 | 95.0 | 3.6 | 10.6 | 5.7 | 4.3 |
| 6.5 | 0.99 | 6.8 | 0.12 | 2.8 | 0.0 | 0.27 | 3.36 | 4.64 | 93.6 | 4.8 | 28.7 | 0.0 | 1.7 |
| 3.9 | 1.75 | 15.8 | 0.78 | 4.6 | 0.3 | 0.66 | 8.51 | 4.73 | 84.3 | 3.0 | 5.9 | 8.8 | 2.9 |
| 5.4 | 0.57 | 6.9 | 0.50 | 8.7 | 0.4 | 1.49 | 20.37 | 5.58 | 68.8 | 2.3 | 8.5 | 10.3 | 2.4 |
| 10.0 | 0.14 | 0.2 | 0.10 | 2.8 | 0.1 | 0.27 | 1.41 | 2.78 | 89.3 | 6.8 | 49.7 | 2.0 | 7.1 |
| 6.4 | 0.52 | 4.7 | 0.67 | 0.8 | 0.0 | -0.35 | -5.01 | 4.10 | 100.8 | 5.2 | 39.1 | 5.4 | 0.7 |
| 9.1 | 0.99 | 2.7 | 0.05 | 3.1 | 0.1 | 0.42 | 4.24 | 2.41 | 83.5 | 5.7 | 26.5 | 0.0 | 4.1 |
| 8.2 | 0.46 | 1.3 | -0.04 | 8.6 | 0.1 | 1.18 | 4.91 | 3.39 | 58.4 | 4.7 | 40.5 | 0.0 | 5.7 |
| 8.4 | 1.15 | 1.9 | 0.12 | 10.0 | 0.0 | 1.99 | 5.99 | 4.89 | 71.4 | 5.5 | 64.7 | 0.0 | 5.7 |
| 6.3 | 0.67 | 4.6 | 0.36 | 5.0 | 0.3 | 0.80 | 7.51 | 4.61 | 81.5 | 3.8 | 11.9 | 7.2 | 5.1 |
| 10.0 | 0.00 | 0.0 | 0.07 | 1.0 | 0.0 | -0.05 | -0.24 | 2.23 | 100.8 | 5.6 | 30.2 | 0.0 | 6.8 |
| 10.0 | 0.56 | 0.6 | 0.00 | 1.9 | 0.0 | 0.11 | 0.87 | 1.69 | 94.3 | 5.1 | 27.6 | 0.0 | 6.2 |
| 3.4 | 6.70 | 25.8 | 1.30 | 4.4 | 0.0 | 0.54 | 4.87 | 3.22 | 77.5 | 5.0 | 13.8 | 0.0 | 6.7 |
| 8.1 | 0.89 | 5.3 | 0.33 | 8.6 | 1.8 | 1.27 | 12.51 | 4.02 | 72.1 | 4.6 | 20.3 | 3.3 | 7.2 |
| 9.2 | 0.47 | 2.9 | 0.65 | 10.0 | 1.3 | 2.10 | 13.68 | 6.09 | 67.7 | 3.9 | 18.9 | 5.0 | 8.2 |
| 9.5 | 0.00 | 0.0 | -0.06 | 2.8 | 0.1 | 0.38 | 4.58 | 2.63 | 87.2 | 4.7 | 11.8 | 0.7 | 4.5 |
| 7.8 | 0.20 | 2.1 | 0.08 | 3.9 | 1.6 | 0.50 | 5.50 | 2.23 | 81.7 | 1.7 | 6.4 | 21.3 | 5.8 |
| 9.8 | 0.12 | 0.5 | 0.36 | 4.0 | 0.1 | 0.48 | 3.80 | 3.65 | 87.1 | 4.6 | 37.8 | 5.6 | 6.6 |
| 5.4 | 2.11 | 16.4 | 0.39 | 3.5 | 3.2 | 0.39 | 4.03 | 2.80 | 84.2 | 2.5 | 6.8 | 12.3 | 6.3 |
| 8.8 | 0.00 | 0.0 | 0.86 | 5.8 | 0.0 | 0.85 | 7.60 | 2.36 | 42.6 | 5.7 | 31.4 | 0.0 | 5.0 |
| 9.6 | 4.17 | 3.1 | 6.10 | 0.0 | 0.0 | -1.25 | -8.14 | 2.40 | 102.4 | 6.7 | 58.4 | 0.0 | 5.0 |
| 5.8 | 1.18 | 6.2 | -0.05 | 1.2 | 0.0 | -0.34 | -4.00 | 4.58 | 107.9 | 5.4 | 23.1 | 0.0 | 1.0 |
| 7.2 | 0.37 | 2.0 | 0.56 | 3.0 | 0.0 | 0.35 | 2.24 | 4.63 | 84.7 | 2.9 | 3.5 | 1.1 | 6.0 |
| 7.5 | 1.86 | 8.1 | 0.14 | 3.6 | 0.3 | 0.51 | 4.37 | 2.84 | 79.8 | 4.3 | 15.1 | 1.5 | 6.3 |
| 5.7 | 0.82 | 6.8 | 1.07 | 4.0 | 6.8 | 0.44 | 4.32 | 3.93 | 77.2 | 4.0 | 20.5 | 6.2 | 6.4 |
| 2.7 | 2.53 | 22.7 | -0.31 | 4.9 | 0.0 | 0.80 | 9.25 | 5.58 | 80.7 | 3.3 | 13.0 | 7.2 | 1.7 |

| Name | City | State | Rating | 2014 Rating | 2013 Rating | Total Assets ($Mil) | One Year Asset Growth | Comm-ercial Loans | Cons-umer Loans | Mort-gage Loans | Secur-ities | Capital-ization Index | Net Worth Ratio |
|---|---|---|---|---|---|---|---|---|---|---|---|---|---|
| GSA FCU | Washington | DC | C- | C- | C- | 35.2 | -3.64 | 0.0 | 45.1 | 8.0 | 32.4 | 8.2 | 9.8 |
| GTE FCU | Tampa | FL | C+ | C | C | 1734.2 | 4.19 | 7.4 | 43.3 | 21.6 | 0.0 | 5.9 | 7.9 |
| GUADALUPE CU | Santa Fe | NM | B+ | B | C+ | 138.3 | 3.43 | 1.9 | 28.6 | 42.4 | 0.0 | 9.9 | 10.9 |
| GUADALUPE PARISH CU | Antonito | CO | B- | B- | B- | 23.2 | 7.92 | 8.8 | 5.9 | 50.0 | 0.0 | 10.0 | 30.0 |
| GUARDIAN 1ST FCU | Fort Worth | TX | E+ | E+ | E+ | 5.1 | -0.06 | 0.0 | 49.9 | 0.0 | 0.0 | 4.7 | 6.7 |
| GUARDIAN CU | Montgomery | AL | B | B+ | B+ | 321.0 | 13.71 | 0.5 | 49.9 | 13.8 | 15.8 | 10.0 | 11.1 |
| GUARDIAN CU | West Milwaukee | WI | D- | D- | D- | 247.5 | 0.79 | 4.6 | 38.0 | 18.4 | 2.6 | 4.9 | 6.9 |
| GUCO CU | Greenville | NC | C+ | C+ | C+ | 12.8 | -2.02 | 0.0 | 43.6 | 0.6 | 0.0 | 10.0 | 12.9 |
| GUERNSEY COMMUNITY FCU | Guernsey | WY | D+ | C- | C- | 1.9 | 10.17 | 0.0 | 11.1 | 22.7 | 0.0 | 10.0 | 13.3 |
| GULF COAST COMMUNITY FCU | Gulfport | MS | A- | A- | A- | 86.4 | 3.38 | 0.3 | 31.8 | 17.1 | 0.0 | 10.0 | 16.2 |
| GULF COAST EDUCATORS FCU | Pasadena | TX | A | A | A | 580.3 | 8.84 | 0.0 | 27.6 | 10.4 | 48.6 | 10.0 | 18.2 |
| GULF COAST FCU | Mobile | AL | C | C | C | 32.4 | -1.20 | 0.0 | 19.9 | 9.5 | 0.0 | 10.0 | 14.0 |
| GULF COAST FCU | Corpus Christi | TX | C+ | C+ | C+ | 182.3 | 12.12 | 0.1 | 39.2 | 43.9 | 0.0 | 8.8 | 10.2 |
| GULF CU | Groves | TX | C- | C- | D+ | 238.0 | 5.33 | 4.5 | 29.2 | 17.6 | 32.8 | 5.0 | 7.3 |
| GULF SHORE FCU | Texas City | TX | D- | D- | D | 12.9 | 2.55 | 0.0 | 46.3 | 0.0 | 0.0 | 5.7 | 7.7 |
| GULF STATES CU | Maitland | FL | B | B | B | 28.8 | 5.98 | 2.0 | 25.0 | 13.9 | 0.0 | 10.0 | 14.5 |
| GULF TRUST CU | Pascagoula | MS | C+ | C+ | B- | 24.4 | -2.30 | 0.0 | 26.1 | 18.3 | 0.0 | 10.0 | 14.2 |
| GULF WINDS FCU | Pensacola | FL | B+ | A- | A- | 551.4 | 4.03 | 0.2 | 32.2 | 21.7 | 17.0 | 10.0 | 12.4 |
| GUNDERSEN CU | La Crosse | WI | B | B+ | B+ | 39.3 | 0.99 | 0.0 | 21.5 | 35.3 | 25.3 | 10.0 | 14.1 |
| GUTHRIE FCU | Sayre | PA | B | B | B- | 65.5 | 2.97 | 0.0 | 27.4 | 41.1 | 10.9 | 9.7 | 10.8 |
| H A L E FCU | Indianapolis | IN | C+ | B- | B- | <1 | 9.10 | 0.0 | 47.9 | 0.0 | 0.0 | 10.0 | 16.4 |
| H E TELEPHONE FCU | Rochelle Park | NJ | C+ | C+ | B- | 42.6 | 4.14 | 0.0 | 15.3 | 20.1 | 4.5 | 10.0 | 13.2 |
| ▲ H M S A EMPL FCU | Honolulu | HI | B- | C | C- | 68.2 | -0.66 | 0.0 | 7.4 | 0.0 | 25.7 | 10.0 | 11.1 |
| H&H FCU | Stinnett | TX | C- | C | C- | 49.5 | 0.06 | 0.0 | 37.2 | 5.0 | 0.0 | 10.0 | 15.9 |
| HABERSHAM FCU | Clarkesville | GA | B- | B- | B- | 16.9 | 8.71 | 0.0 | 38.6 | 10.8 | 4.7 | 10.0 | 16.3 |
| ▲ HALE COUNTY TEACHERS FCU | Plainview | TX | D | E+ | E+ | 7.3 | -3.28 | 0.0 | 62.7 | 1.7 | 0.0 | 7.6 | 9.4 |
| HALIFAX COUNTY COMMUNITY FCU | South Boston | VA | C- | C- | D+ | 7.0 | -0.23 | 0.0 | 11.4 | 13.2 | 0.0 | 9.2 | 10.5 |
| HALLCO COMMUNITY CU | Gainesville | GA | C | C | C | 66.4 | 13.54 | 1.0 | 52.0 | 5.5 | 8.6 | 6.0 | 8.0 |
| HALLIBURTON EMPL FCU | Duncan | OK | B+ | B+ | B+ | 148.9 | 0.97 | 0.0 | 64.5 | 1.2 | 19.9 | 8.2 | 9.8 |
| HAMAKUA COAST COMMUNITY FCU | Pepeekeo | HI | D+ | D+ | C- | 15.1 | -3.82 | 0.0 | 28.5 | 2.4 | 7.6 | 10.0 | 16.9 |
| HAMILTON FCU | Novato | CA | D | D | C- | 22.1 | -6.29 | 0.7 | 8.2 | 34.0 | 0.0 | 10.0 | 16.1 |
| HAMILTON HORIZONS FCU | Hamilton | NJ | E+ | E+ | D- | 23.6 | -0.61 | 0.0 | 31.5 | 1.5 | 16.8 | 6.2 | 8.2 |
| ▲ HAMLET FCU | Hamlet | NC | C | C- | C | 15.4 | -0.86 | 0.0 | 31.5 | 13.7 | 0.0 | 10.0 | 11.2 |
| HAMMOND FIREFIGHTERS ASSN CU | Hammond | IN | C | C | C | 1.6 | 1.16 | 0.0 | 26.2 | 0.0 | 0.0 | 10.0 | 20.8 |
| ▲ HAMPTON ROADS CATHOLIC FCU | Virginia Beach | VA | D- | D- | D- | 5.6 | 7.69 | 1.9 | 19.8 | 10.2 | 0.0 | 5.4 | 7.4 |
| ▲ HAMPTON ROADS EDUCATORS CU INC | Hampton | VA | D | D | D | 28.5 | -2.82 | 0.0 | 42.3 | 0.0 | 0.0 | 5.7 | 7.7 |
| HAMPTON V A FCU | Hampton | VA | D | D | D+ | 6.7 | -2.99 | 0.0 | 28.6 | 1.6 | 10.4 | 10.0 | 14.2 |
| HANCOCK FCU | Findlay | OH | B- | B- | B | 73.8 | 7.76 | 11.3 | 32.4 | 33.5 | 4.8 | 10.0 | 11.2 |
| HANCOCK SCHOOL EMPL FCU | Weirton | WV | C | C- | C- | 16.6 | 2.70 | 0.0 | 10.8 | 0.0 | 0.0 | 10.0 | 13.5 |
| HANESBRANDS CU | Winston-Salem | NC | D | D | D | 50.1 | -5.06 | 0.0 | 18.5 | 18.0 | 25.6 | 10.0 | 12.1 |
| ▲ HANIN FCU | Los Angeles | CA | B- | C | D+ | 26.0 | 3.29 | 1.3 | 69.2 | 7.4 | 0.0 | 8.7 | 10.2 |
| HANNA EMPL CU | Pleasant Prairie | WI | C | C- | C- | <1 | 4.94 | 0.0 | 64.7 | 0.0 | 0.0 | 10.0 | 54.7 |
| HANSCOM FCU | Hanscom AFB | MA | B- | B- | B | 1099.6 | 2.31 | 1.2 | 27.3 | 19.5 | 9.1 | 8.5 | 10.0 |
| HAPO COMMUNITY CU | Richland | WA | B | B | B | 1342.0 | 8.77 | 0.9 | 59.8 | 19.3 | 0.0 | 6.4 | 8.4 |
| HAPPY VALLEY CU | Elizabethton | TN | B | B | B | 29.9 | 2.82 | 0.0 | 40.3 | 9.6 | 0.0 | 10.0 | 17.0 |
| HAR-CO CU | Bel Air | MD | C+ | C+ | C | 184.0 | 1.12 | 0.7 | 19.4 | 26.9 | 18.0 | 7.8 | 9.5 |
| HARBOR AREA POSTAL EMPL FCU | Lomita | CA | D | D | D+ | 20.1 | -1.14 | 0.0 | 11.6 | 20.7 | 55.6 | 10.0 | 12.1 |
| HARBOR BEACH COMMUNITY FCU | Harbor Beach | MI | D | D+ | D+ | 4.2 | -0.12 | 0.0 | 25.5 | 0.0 | 0.0 | 10.0 | 11.7 |
| ▲ HARBOR CU | Green Bay | WI | C | C- | D+ | 107.0 | 7.19 | 3.0 | 19.0 | 34.1 | 0.0 | 7.8 | 9.5 |
| HARBOR FCU | Carson | CA | B | B+ | B+ | 110.2 | 2.23 | 0.0 | 10.7 | 17.2 | 15.5 | 10.0 | 14.7 |
| HARBORLIGHT CU | Whitehall | MI | D+ | D+ | D+ | 94.6 | 0.92 | 0.0 | 20.2 | 27.2 | 10.1 | 9.6 | 10.8 |
| ▲ HARBORSTONE CU | Lakewood | WA | B- | B- | C+ | 1130.2 | 5.04 | 10.0 | 31.5 | 22.6 | 25.9 | 10.0 | 11.3 |
| HARDIN COUNTY HOSPITAL EMPL CU | Savannah | TN | C- | C- | D+ | 1.3 | -4.24 | 0.0 | 34.4 | 0.0 | 0.0 | 9.5 | 10.7 |
| HARRIS COUNTY FCU | Houston | TX | A | A | A- | 145.9 | 3.23 | 0.0 | 35.3 | 9.9 | 17.6 | 10.0 | 13.6 |
| ▲ HARRIS EMPL CU | Cordele | GA | C- | C- | D+ | 1.5 | -10.64 | 0.0 | 19.2 | 11.4 | 0.0 | 10.0 | 14.8 |
| HARRISON COUNTY FCU | Nutter Fort | WV | C- | D+ | D+ | 14.1 | 1.92 | 0.0 | 27.6 | 0.0 | 0.0 | 10.0 | 16.1 |
| ▼ HARRISON COUNTY POE FCU | Gulfport | MS | C- | C | C | 5.9 | 3.39 | 0.0 | 61.1 | 0.0 | 0.0 | 10.0 | 22.0 |
| ▼ HARRISON DISTRICT NO TWO FCU | Colorado Springs | CO | D | D+ | C- | 12.3 | 3.94 | 0.0 | 19.8 | 14.9 | 52.9 | 10.0 | 14.4 |
| ▲ HARRISON POLICE & FIREMENS FCU | Harrison | NJ | D | D- | E+ | 20.1 | -3.15 | 0.5 | 13.0 | 0.0 | 0.0 | 7.1 | 9.1 |
| ▲ HARRISON TEACHERS FCU | Harrison | NY | D- | D | D+ | 2.2 | -1.79 | 0.0 | 0.0 | 0.0 | 0.0 | 9.5 | 10.7 |

| Asset Quality Index | Non-Performing Loans as a % of Total Loans | as a % of Capital | Net Charge-Offs Avg Loans | Profitability Index | Net Income ($Mil) | Return on Assets | Return on Equity | Net Interest Spread | Overhead Efficiency Ratio | Liquidity Index | Liquidity Ratio | Hot Money Ratio | Stability Index |
|---|---|---|---|---|---|---|---|---|---|---|---|---|---|
| 6.7 | 0.39 | 2.1 | 0.31 | 2.4 | 0.0 | 0.13 | 1.36 | 2.97 | 91.0 | 4.2 | 15.1 | 0.0 | 4.0 |
| 4.5 | 1.52 | 18.8 | 1.00 | 3.5 | 4.9 | 0.38 | 5.19 | 3.53 | 84.2 | 3.0 | 8.2 | 5.0 | 4.8 |
| 6.3 | 0.85 | 7.7 | 0.48 | 8.7 | 1.3 | 1.26 | 12.88 | 5.73 | 78.2 | 2.9 | 17.8 | 14.3 | 7.2 |
| 9.7 | 0.08 | 0.2 | 0.07 | 4.9 | 0.1 | 0.77 | 2.57 | 3.43 | 75.5 | 2.8 | 23.6 | 18.1 | 7.9 |
| 4.4 | 1.33 | 10.7 | 0.14 | 1.1 | 0.0 | -0.20 | -3.14 | 6.03 | 102.0 | 4.5 | 8.1 | 0.0 | 1.0 |
| 4.7 | 1.61 | 10.3 | 1.23 | 5.0 | 1.6 | 0.70 | 6.52 | 5.09 | 74.9 | 2.5 | 19.7 | 17.0 | 7.1 |
| 0.3 | 1.99 | 63.5 | 0.42 | 2.2 | 0.2 | 0.10 | 1.44 | 2.91 | 94.1 | 3.8 | 12.6 | 2.9 | 2.9 |
| 9.1 | 0.44 | 2.9 | 0.33 | 2.6 | 0.0 | 0.23 | 1.79 | 2.82 | 88.1 | 4.6 | 26.3 | 0.0 | 5.8 |
| 5.9 | 3.08 | 10.6 | -0.29 | 2.5 | 0.0 | -1.67 | -11.33 | 5.65 | 113.6 | 5.1 | 74.8 | 30.3 | 6.0 |
| 6.5 | 1.31 | 6.1 | 1.63 | 9.8 | 1.0 | 1.49 | 9.49 | 6.88 | 72.9 | 3.0 | 19.9 | 15.5 | 8.3 |
| 9.9 | 0.40 | 0.9 | 0.40 | 7.6 | 4.5 | 1.04 | 5.88 | 2.95 | 67.2 | 3.0 | 22.3 | 22.6 | 9.8 |
| 9.4 | 0.90 | 3.8 | 0.19 | 2.4 | 0.0 | 0.12 | 0.88 | 2.82 | 94.7 | 4.3 | 21.6 | 12.4 | 6.4 |
| 3.5 | 2.14 | 24.1 | 1.09 | 6.2 | 1.1 | 0.83 | 8.78 | 4.43 | 61.8 | 1.1 | 9.2 | 33.0 | 6.9 |
| 7.4 | 0.39 | 5.5 | 0.44 | 2.9 | 0.5 | 0.29 | 5.12 | 3.18 | 90.7 | 4.1 | 10.4 | 4.1 | 2.3 |
| 5.5 | 1.10 | 7.2 | 0.06 | 2.7 | 0.0 | 0.22 | 2.84 | 3.19 | 93.8 | 4.6 | 23.6 | 1.7 | 2.3 |
| 9.7 | 0.49 | 1.7 | 0.16 | 4.6 | 0.1 | 0.67 | 4.60 | 4.28 | 84.5 | 5.3 | 34.0 | 2.4 | 6.8 |
| 6.7 | 1.47 | 9.4 | 0.20 | 2.8 | 0.1 | 0.34 | 2.44 | 3.13 | 91.2 | 3.0 | 29.5 | 18.1 | 5.8 |
| 8.8 | 0.35 | 2.0 | 0.44 | 4.9 | 2.6 | 0.64 | 5.51 | 3.09 | 83.1 | 4.3 | 20.6 | 6.6 | 8.4 |
| 10.0 | 0.11 | 0.5 | 0.07 | 3.7 | 0.1 | 0.42 | 3.05 | 2.70 | 86.0 | 3.9 | 9.6 | 0.3 | 7.2 |
| 6.5 | 0.83 | 5.7 | 0.24 | 5.7 | 0.4 | 0.76 | 7.28 | 4.01 | 82.5 | 3.5 | 13.6 | 6.2 | 5.7 |
| 8.6 | 0.54 | 1.6 | 3.07 | 3.7 | 0.0 | -0.55 | -3.23 | 6.48 | 96.3 | 7.6 | 109.9 | 0.0 | 8.5 |
| 5.9 | 2.07 | 12.7 | 0.68 | 2.3 | 0.1 | 0.15 | 1.14 | 3.34 | 80.6 | 4.8 | 33.4 | 8.8 | 6.2 |
| 10.0 | 0.94 | 1.5 | 0.21 | 3.9 | 0.3 | 0.64 | 6.00 | 1.44 | 54.7 | 5.6 | 21.5 | 0.0 | 5.1 |
| 9.5 | 0.65 | 2.0 | 0.25 | 1.6 | 0.0 | 0.00 | 0.00 | 2.40 | 94.0 | 4.9 | 54.0 | 2.9 | 7.0 |
| 9.6 | 0.02 | 0.6 | 0.06 | 3.4 | 0.0 | 0.22 | 1.27 | 5.23 | 98.3 | 5.0 | 29.3 | 1.3 | 6.7 |
| 6.7 | 0.22 | 1.7 | 0.00 | 3.8 | 0.0 | 0.61 | 6.81 | 4.02 | 83.3 | 3.5 | 24.9 | 3.6 | 2.3 |
| 6.6 | 3.47 | 8.5 | 1.24 | 3.8 | 0.0 | 0.56 | 5.39 | 2.95 | 81.4 | 6.4 | 59.2 | 0.0 | 3.7 |
| 4.6 | 1.10 | 9.9 | 0.25 | 7.2 | 0.5 | 1.15 | 14.43 | 4.27 | 76.9 | 4.5 | 24.1 | 0.0 | 3.8 |
| 6.6 | 0.79 | 6.7 | 0.32 | 4.8 | 0.8 | 0.66 | 7.05 | 2.51 | 77.4 | 3.0 | 5.3 | 7.6 | 6.0 |
| 9.6 | 0.92 | 2.6 | -0.13 | 1.2 | 0.0 | -0.05 | -0.31 | 3.26 | 100.3 | 4.7 | 17.6 | 1.8 | 5.8 |
| 9.8 | 0.70 | 1.9 | 0.48 | 0.0 | -0.1 | -0.49 | -3.33 | 2.56 | 120.9 | 4.7 | 48.2 | 7.6 | 5.1 |
| 3.7 | 2.44 | 21.5 | 0.96 | 2.0 | 0.0 | 0.12 | 1.46 | 5.49 | 96.7 | 3.4 | 3.0 | 0.0 | 1.0 |
| 8.9 | 0.17 | 2.7 | 0.28 | 2.4 | 0.0 | 0.08 | 0.78 | 4.60 | 97.5 | 5.7 | 36.0 | 4.3 | 4.6 |
| 9.4 | 2.17 | 2.5 | -1.02 | 3.7 | 0.0 | 0.51 | 2.48 | 4.38 | 84.2 | 6.3 | 37.2 | 0.0 | 7.2 |
| 9.9 | 0.15 | 0.7 | 0.00 | 2.4 | 0.0 | 0.17 | 2.28 | 3.23 | 94.9 | 5.4 | 25.0 | 0.0 | 1.7 |
| 5.4 | 0.87 | 8.3 | 1.69 | 2.3 | 0.0 | 0.06 | 1.17 | 5.24 | 82.9 | 4.7 | 17.6 | 0.0 | 1.0 |
| 9.0 | 2.02 | 4.4 | 0.25 | 0.0 | -0.1 | -1.01 | -7.16 | 4.49 | 116.5 | 7.0 | 54.4 | 0.0 | 5.0 |
| 7.1 | 0.48 | 4.9 | 0.11 | 3.0 | 0.1 | 0.23 | 1.98 | 3.33 | 94.8 | 2.8 | 5.0 | 5.4 | 6.2 |
| 10.0 | 0.10 | 0.1 | 0.00 | 2.5 | 0.0 | 0.28 | 2.11 | 2.01 | 85.8 | 5.1 | 9.6 | 0.0 | 6.7 |
| 3.7 | 5.69 | 23.7 | 1.15 | 0.3 | -0.2 | -0.52 | -4.32 | 3.06 | 101.6 | 4.9 | 21.3 | 4.7 | 4.8 |
| 7.7 | 0.19 | 1.4 | 0.02 | 7.0 | 0.2 | 1.07 | 12.82 | 7.95 | 86.3 | 2.4 | 24.4 | 38.8 | 5.3 |
| 8.4 | 0.00 | 0.0 | 0.00 | 7.8 | 0.0 | 1.57 | 2.93 | 8.82 | 66.7 | 6.8 | 84.4 | 0.0 | 5.0 |
| 9.1 | 0.35 | 2.7 | 0.18 | 4.5 | 5.4 | 0.66 | 6.96 | 2.64 | 75.9 | 3.5 | 9.5 | 4.6 | 7.2 |
| 7.6 | 0.18 | 2.9 | 0.40 | 5.4 | 7.7 | 0.80 | 10.19 | 3.80 | 74.7 | 1.8 | 10.0 | 21.3 | 6.1 |
| 8.8 | 0.89 | 2.7 | 0.22 | 5.0 | 0.2 | 0.69 | 4.13 | 3.60 | 84.2 | 3.7 | 7.1 | 6.9 | 6.2 |
| 9.1 | 0.73 | 4.6 | 0.09 | 3.2 | 0.5 | 0.31 | 3.44 | 3.62 | 91.8 | 4.7 | 19.1 | 2.9 | 5.5 |
| 10.0 | 0.18 | 0.6 | 0.25 | 0.1 | -0.1 | -0.51 | -4.16 | 2.49 | 113.3 | 3.7 | 13.3 | 10.9 | 5.3 |
| 9.2 | 1.45 | 3.3 | 0.25 | 0.5 | 0.0 | -0.29 | -2.64 | 2.34 | 116.7 | 4.6 | 17.6 | 4.9 | 5.0 |
| 7.0 | 0.69 | 4.7 | 0.53 | 2.7 | 0.3 | 0.35 | 3.74 | 2.84 | 90.7 | 4.2 | 21.2 | 0.4 | 5.3 |
| 10.0 | 0.21 | 0.4 | 0.51 | 4.1 | 0.5 | 0.62 | 4.24 | 2.40 | 84.6 | 5.7 | 45.8 | 2.6 | 7.5 |
| 8.0 | 0.72 | 3.5 | 0.17 | 1.7 | 0.1 | 0.12 | 1.10 | 3.17 | 94.6 | 4.1 | 21.3 | 3.6 | 4.9 |
| 7.8 | 0.74 | 4.3 | 0.55 | 4.2 | 5.5 | 0.65 | 5.70 | 3.24 | 75.1 | 3.6 | 9.0 | 5.1 | 7.8 |
| 6.9 | 1.31 | 4.0 | 0.78 | 1.8 | 0.0 | -0.74 | -6.67 | 3.26 | 124.0 | 7.1 | 70.0 | 0.0 | 4.7 |
| 8.5 | 1.24 | 4.5 | 0.68 | 9.1 | 1.4 | 1.29 | 10.10 | 3.89 | 62.1 | 4.3 | 19.8 | 9.9 | 8.1 |
| 7.9 | 0.00 | 5.7 | -1.87 | 1.3 | 0.0 | -0.09 | -0.62 | 2.95 | 102.9 | 6.4 | 76.9 | 0.0 | 6.0 |
| 10.0 | 1.08 | 1.8 | 0.17 | 1.5 | 0.0 | 0.02 | 0.11 | 2.26 | 99.6 | 5.6 | 26.4 | 0.0 | 6.6 |
| 6.0 | 2.16 | 6.1 | 0.40 | 4.4 | 0.0 | 0.51 | 2.27 | 5.67 | 84.1 | 4.4 | 57.4 | 17.2 | 3.7 |
| 7.6 | 2.72 | 6.8 | -0.09 | 0.1 | 0.0 | -0.46 | -3.19 | 2.91 | 114.7 | 5.6 | 36.2 | 0.0 | 5.9 |
| 4.9 | 3.14 | 10.6 | -0.13 | 3.1 | 0.1 | 0.40 | 4.63 | 2.71 | 85.1 | 4.2 | 14.6 | 6.5 | 3.0 |
| 0.3 | 18.74 | 51.3 | 0.00 | 1.4 | 0.0 | 0.00 | 0.00 | 5.69 | 97.4 | 7.4 | 65.8 | 0.0 | 4.0 |

| Name | City | State | Rating | 2014 Rating | 2013 Rating | Total Assets ($Mil) | One Year Asset Growth | Asset Mix (As a % of Total Assets) Commercial Loans | Consumer Loans | Mortgage Loans | Securities | Capitalization Index | Net Worth Ratio |
|---|---|---|---|---|---|---|---|---|---|---|---|---|---|
| HARTFORD FCU | Hartford | CT | C+ | B- | B- | 89.0 | -0.14 | 0.0 | 11.7 | 11.4 | 1.7 | 10.0 | 13.2 |
| ▲ HARTFORD FIREFIGHTERS FCU | Hartford | CT | C | C- | C- | 19.3 | 8.21 | 0.0 | 24.6 | 11.6 | 0.0 | 10.0 | 12.5 |
| HARTFORD HEALTHCARE FCU INC | Hartford | CT | C+ | C | C- | 34.0 | 4.73 | 0.0 | 31.9 | 23.6 | 1.5 | 7.8 | 9.5 |
| ▼ HARTFORD MUNICIPAL EMPL FCU | Hartford | CT | C- | C | C- | 49.8 | 15.64 | 0.0 | 62.0 | 0.0 | 0.0 | 9.4 | 10.6 |
| HARVARD COMMUNITY CU | Harvard | IL | C | C | D+ | 13.5 | 1.17 | 0.0 | 26.6 | 15.7 | 0.0 | 9.3 | 10.6 |
| ▲ HARVARD UNIV EMPL CU | Cambridge | MA | B+ | B | B | 503.3 | 8.08 | 0.2 | 12.2 | 46.9 | 10.9 | 6.6 | 8.7 |
| HARVEST FCU | Heath | OH | B- | C+ | C | 26.0 | 4.01 | 0.4 | 22.3 | 18.8 | 1.0 | 10.0 | 13.7 |
| ▼ HARVESTER FINANCIAL CU | Indianapolis | IN | C- | C | C | 51.6 | -3.46 | 0.0 | 24.3 | 19.2 | 31.2 | 7.6 | 9.4 |
| HARVESTERS FCU | Cantonment | FL | C- | C- | C- | 143.8 | 1.24 | 11.1 | 19.2 | 25.4 | 2.2 | 6.5 | 8.5 |
| HASTINGS FCU | Hastings | NE | C+ | C+ | B- | 24.7 | 7.97 | 0.0 | 36.0 | 8.8 | 0.0 | 9.4 | 10.6 |
| HATTIESBURG-LAUREL FCU | Hattiesburg | MS | E+ | E+ | D- | 7.6 | -11.00 | 0.0 | 28.7 | 0.0 | 0.0 | 7.3 | 9.2 |
| ▼ HAULPAK FCU | Peoria | IL | D+ | C- | C | 2.4 | 1.46 | 0.0 | 44.8 | 0.0 | 0.0 | 10.0 | 23.4 |
| HAVERHILL FIRE DEPT CU | Haverhill | MA | C | C | C | 17.2 | 4.54 | 0.0 | 12.2 | 14.4 | 2.4 | 10.0 | 12.6 |
| HAWAII CENTRAL FCU | Honolulu | HI | B | B | B- | 204.3 | 4.87 | 4.8 | 24.7 | 19.7 | 20.1 | 7.3 | 9.2 |
| ▼ HAWAII COMMUNITY FCU | Kailua-Kona | HI | B- | B | B- | 431.7 | 6.11 | 7.8 | 9.2 | 37.5 | 34.8 | 7.8 | 9.6 |
| HAWAII COUNTY EMPL FCU | Hilo | HI | C+ | C+ | C+ | 84.4 | 1.92 | 4.1 | 14.5 | 11.5 | 19.6 | 10.0 | 15.8 |
| HAWAII FCU | Honolulu | HI | B | B- | C+ | 79.1 | 17.81 | 0.2 | 53.8 | 6.3 | 2.3 | 8.7 | 10.1 |
| HAWAII FIRST FCU | Kamuela | HI | C- | D+ | E+ | 35.1 | 9.43 | 0.0 | 15.1 | 21.4 | 0.0 | 6.9 | 8.9 |
| ▲ HAWAII LAW ENFORCEMENT FCU | Honolulu | HI | C- | D+ | D+ | 153.3 | -0.84 | 1.1 | 21.8 | 5.0 | 36.1 | 9.0 | 10.3 |
| ▲ HAWAII NATIONAL GUARD FCU | Honolulu | HI | D+ | D | D+ | 19.9 | -0.97 | 0.0 | 26.5 | 0.0 | 0.0 | 9.2 | 10.4 |
| HAWAII PACIFIC FCU | Honolulu | HI | D+ | D+ | D | 48.4 | 2.64 | 8.4 | 16.0 | 31.5 | 28.6 | 8.1 | 10.0 |
| HAWAII SCHOOLS FCU | Honolulu | HI | C- | C- | D+ | 66.6 | -1.79 | 0.0 | 11.9 | 6.5 | 44.8 | 10.0 | 11.3 |
| HAWAII STATE FCU | Honolulu | HI | B | C+ | B- | 1385.6 | 3.45 | 2.7 | 15.8 | 15.6 | 40.2 | 10.0 | 11.4 |
| HAWAIIAN AIRLINES FCU | Honolulu | HI | D- | D- | D- | 19.8 | 2.08 | 0.0 | 22.0 | 0.0 | 9.8 | 5.9 | 7.9 |
| ▲ HAWAIIAN ELECTRIC EMPL FCU | Honolulu | HI | C- | D+ | D+ | 35.6 | -4.21 | 0.0 | 18.3 | 9.3 | 0.0 | 10.0 | 15.4 |
| HAWAIIAN TEL FCU | Honolulu | HI | A- | B+ | B+ | 553.7 | 2.13 | 11.1 | 8.1 | 34.0 | 31.2 | 10.0 | 12.0 |
| HAWAIIUSA FCU | Honolulu | HI | B+ | B+ | B+ | 1467.5 | 6.04 | 6.5 | 15.7 | 16.3 | 48.0 | 10.0 | 11.1 |
| HAXTUN COMMUNITY FCU | Haxtun | CO | C | C- | C | 5.1 | 12.94 | 0.0 | 27.5 | 45.1 | 0.0 | 10.0 | 11.8 |
| HAYNES COMMUNITY FCU | Kokomo | IN | C | C+ | B- | 24.5 | -0.95 | 3.5 | 30.5 | 33.1 | 1.0 | 10.0 | 12.3 |
| HAYWARD COMMUNITY CU | Hayward | WI | C | C+ | C | 66.0 | -1.13 | 8.6 | 5.1 | 48.0 | 25.1 | 9.4 | 10.6 |
| HAZLETON SCHOOL EMPL CU | Hazleton | PA | B | B | B | 25.5 | 6.63 | 0.0 | 7.1 | 27.6 | 28.6 | 10.0 | 13.5 |
| HB TELCO FCU | Huron | SD | D- | E+ | D- | 4.9 | -8.27 | 0.0 | 73.5 | 0.0 | 0.0 | 6.7 | 8.7 |
| HBI EMPL CU | Saint Paul | MN | C- | C- | C- | 7.2 | 8.35 | 0.0 | 22.5 | 9.1 | 0.0 | 10.0 | 13.1 |
| HEA FCU | Warner Robins | GA | D+ | D+ | D+ | 24.8 | 4.34 | 1.4 | 41.2 | 5.2 | 0.0 | 7.1 | 9.1 |
| HEALTH & EDUCATION FCU | Lexington | KY | C | C | C- | 76.7 | 5.26 | 0.0 | 23.8 | 9.8 | 14.2 | 10.0 | 12.6 |
| HEALTH ALLIANCE FCU | Somerville | MA | D+ | D+ | D+ | 3.5 | 2.86 | 0.0 | 52.6 | 0.0 | 0.0 | 8.9 | 10.3 |
| HEALTH ASSOCIATES FCU | Orange | CA | C- | C- | D+ | 46.6 | 0.09 | 5.4 | 20.0 | 15.2 | 10.8 | 5.6 | 7.7 |
| HEALTH CARE CU | Salt Lake City | UT | C | C | C | 71.8 | 0.22 | 0.5 | 11.1 | 20.3 | 60.8 | 10.0 | 13.5 |
| ▼ HEALTH CARE CU | Oshkosh | WI | C- | C- | C | 15.8 | 11.22 | 0.0 | 27.1 | 38.9 | 0.6 | 8.3 | 9.8 |
| HEALTH CARE FAMILY CU | Richmond Heights | MO | B | B+ | B+ | 54.6 | 4.66 | 0.2 | 25.6 | 10.1 | 13.0 | 10.0 | 12.3 |
| ▲ HEALTH CARE IDAHO CU | Boise | ID | B- | C- | C+ | 12.1 | 7.69 | 0.0 | 36.4 | 0.0 | 0.0 | 10.0 | 12.5 |
| HEALTH CARE OF NEW JERSEY FCU | Mount Holly | NJ | C | C | C- | 6.6 | -1.64 | 0.0 | 36.7 | 0.0 | 0.0 | 10.0 | 14.0 |
| HEALTH CARE PROFESSIONALS FCU | Richmond | IN | B | B | B | 20.8 | 3.91 | 0.0 | 34.5 | 0.0 | 10.8 | 10.0 | 15.8 |
| HEALTH CENTER CU | Augusta | GA | C- | C- | C- | 50.7 | 3.89 | 1.6 | 45.5 | 25.6 | 4.3 | 8.4 | 9.9 |
| HEALTH CU | Birmingham | AL | C+ | C+ | C+ | 20.2 | -1.91 | 0.0 | 23.1 | 11.9 | 0.0 | 10.0 | 23.5 |
| HEALTH EMPL FCU | Albany | NY | C | C+ | B | 31.2 | 1.28 | 0.0 | 20.9 | 8.2 | 0.0 | 10.0 | 14.8 |
| ▲ HEALTH FACILITIES FCU | Florence | SC | C- | C- | C- | 25.3 | 0.11 | 2.2 | 31.5 | 2.2 | 8.8 | 9.3 | 10.6 |
| ▲ HEALTH FIRST FCU | Waterville | ME | D+ | D- | D- | 16.4 | 2.27 | 0.0 | 36.8 | 0.0 | 0.0 | 6.7 | 8.7 |
| HEALTH SYSTEMS CU | Knoxville | TN | E+ | E+ | D- | 6.0 | -14.57 | 0.0 | 23.3 | 33.7 | 0.0 | 6.2 | 8.2 |
| HEALTHCARE 1ST FCU | Cumberland | MD | E+ | E+ | E+ | 8.6 | -3.29 | 0.0 | 31.7 | 0.0 | 3.5 | 5.8 | 7.8 |
| HEALTHCARE ASSOCIATES CU | Naperville | IL | A- | A- | A- | 299.2 | 10.13 | 3.3 | 28.4 | 20.5 | 33.8 | 10.0 | 14.4 |
| HEALTHCARE EMPL FCU | Princeton | NJ | C | C- | D+ | 98.8 | -0.02 | 2.1 | 19.2 | 9.2 | 3.8 | 6.2 | 8.2 |
| HEALTHCARE FINANCIAL FCU | New Haven | CT | B- | B+ | B | 33.7 | 1.55 | 0.9 | 22.9 | 0.0 | 16.8 | 10.0 | 14.9 |
| ▼ HEALTHCARE FIRST CU | Johnstown | PA | C | B- | B- | 58.3 | 2.65 | 0.1 | 23.7 | 8.5 | 25.7 | 8.9 | 10.3 |
| ▲ HEALTHCARE PLUS FCU | Aberdeen | SD | C- | D+ | D | 47.2 | 10.87 | 4.2 | 53.6 | 22.0 | 0.0 | 6.2 | 8.2 |
| HEALTHCARE SERVICES CU | Chattanooga | TN | C+ | C+ | B- | 17.3 | -0.41 | 0.0 | 48.8 | 0.0 | 0.0 | 10.0 | 14.1 |
| HEALTHCARE SYSTEMS FCU | Fairfax | VA | C | C | C | 62.8 | 3.15 | 8.1 | 33.4 | 2.2 | 29.9 | 7.0 | 9.0 |
| HEALTHNET FCU | Cordova | TN | C- | C- | C | 49.8 | 0.46 | 0.0 | 20.5 | 3.3 | 2.5 | 10.0 | 11.6 |
| HEALTHPLUS FCU | Jackson | MS | D- | D- | D | 6.7 | 1.20 | 0.0 | 51.7 | 0.0 | 0.0 | 7.4 | 9.3 |
| ▼ HEALTHSHARE CU | Greensboro | NC | C+ | B | B | 31.6 | 1.63 | 1.8 | 35.4 | 7.2 | 0.0 | 10.0 | 13.3 |

| Asset Quality Index | Non-Performing Loans as a % of Total Loans | as a % of Capital | Net Charge-Offs Avg Loans | Profitability Index | Net Income ($Mil) | Return on Assets | Return on Equity | Net Interest Spread | Overhead Efficiency Ratio | Liquidity Index | Liquidity Ratio | Hot Money Ratio | Stability Index |
|---|---|---|---|---|---|---|---|---|---|---|---|---|---|
| 8.8 | 0.24 | 1.0 | 0.83 | 2.7 | 0.2 | 0.23 | 1.84 | 3.25 | 91.7 | 4.1 | 12.3 | 1.3 | 6.5 |
| 10.0 | 0.19 | 0.6 | 0.48 | 2.2 | 0.0 | 0.21 | 1.73 | 3.61 | 89.1 | 4.8 | 19.9 | 0.0 | 5.7 |
| 5.9 | 1.41 | 11.0 | 0.08 | 5.6 | 0.2 | 0.70 | 7.63 | 5.52 | 86.1 | 3.3 | 14.9 | 2.3 | 4.2 |
| 1.9 | 3.46 | 22.1 | 1.01 | 10.0 | 0.5 | 1.45 | 13.22 | 6.87 | 74.2 | 3.4 | 32.0 | 12.6 | 5.5 |
| 6.4 | 1.99 | 7.3 | 0.52 | 4.7 | 0.1 | 0.62 | 6.22 | 4.65 | 87.2 | 4.5 | 16.3 | 0.0 | 4.3 |
| 9.4 | 0.41 | 3.5 | 0.20 | 5.3 | 2.9 | 0.78 | 9.06 | 4.00 | 77.2 | 3.3 | 8.5 | 4.6 | 6.5 |
| 5.4 | 4.81 | 16.1 | 0.45 | 3.8 | 0.1 | 0.46 | 3.40 | 3.39 | 88.7 | 4.5 | 25.1 | 2.7 | 6.2 |
| 7.0 | 0.86 | 4.5 | 0.53 | 2.2 | 0.1 | 0.12 | 1.26 | 3.08 | 92.8 | 3.7 | 20.4 | 8.3 | 3.5 |
| 7.5 | 0.50 | 5.2 | 0.75 | 1.7 | 0.0 | 0.01 | 0.18 | 2.81 | 91.5 | 5.5 | 39.4 | 2.9 | 4.2 |
| 9.7 | 0.16 | 0.7 | 0.11 | 2.9 | 0.0 | 0.21 | 2.00 | 3.94 | 94.1 | 6.3 | 47.4 | 0.7 | 5.4 |
| 7.0 | 1.33 | 4.9 | -0.19 | 0.5 | 0.0 | -0.10 | -1.15 | 3.32 | 108.9 | 4.7 | 18.8 | 0.0 | 2.2 |
| 6.2 | 6.60 | 12.3 | 0.54 | 0.4 | 0.0 | -1.03 | -4.31 | 4.80 | 130.7 | 6.7 | 51.8 | 0.0 | 5.1 |
| 9.5 | 0.64 | 2.1 | -0.11 | 1.9 | 0.0 | 0.03 | 0.25 | 3.37 | 100.0 | 5.5 | 31.4 | 0.0 | 5.6 |
| 9.2 | 0.34 | 3.3 | 0.44 | 5.3 | 1.2 | 0.77 | 9.27 | 3.92 | 74.1 | 2.5 | 8.9 | 15.6 | 6.2 |
| 6.6 | 1.34 | 9.0 | 0.06 | 3.9 | 1.5 | 0.48 | 5.07 | 2.49 | 85.5 | 4.1 | 10.3 | 2.8 | 6.7 |
| 8.3 | 3.32 | 6.9 | 0.26 | 3.1 | 0.2 | 0.39 | 2.45 | 2.44 | 83.1 | 5.1 | 25.3 | 2.8 | 7.0 |
| 4.8 | 1.35 | 8.5 | 1.16 | 8.7 | 0.7 | 1.34 | 12.68 | 5.55 | 75.3 | 3.6 | 22.0 | 9.7 | 5.0 |
| 2.4 | 2.95 | 31.6 | 0.75 | 6.5 | 0.2 | 0.84 | 10.13 | 6.06 | 98.6 | 4.3 | 12.3 | 0.3 | 4.6 |
| 10.0 | 0.28 | 1.2 | 0.08 | 2.1 | 0.4 | 0.30 | 2.86 | 2.79 | 88.5 | 4.1 | 14.4 | 5.6 | 6.3 |
| 10.0 | 0.04 | 0.1 | 0.29 | 1.6 | 0.0 | 0.05 | 0.52 | 1.76 | 95.3 | 6.3 | 42.7 | 0.0 | 4.9 |
| 8.1 | 0.32 | 1.9 | 0.15 | 1.9 | 0.1 | 0.14 | 1.50 | 3.47 | 95.7 | 4.1 | 16.2 | 3.8 | 4.1 |
| 10.0 | 0.02 | 0.4 | -0.01 | 1.7 | 0.0 | 0.06 | 0.52 | 2.37 | 98.0 | 4.3 | 15.5 | 4.2 | 5.4 |
| 9.1 | 0.83 | 3.3 | 0.20 | 4.1 | 6.9 | 0.66 | 5.85 | 2.91 | 82.3 | 4.8 | 18.0 | 3.5 | 7.3 |
| 8.5 | 0.40 | 1.9 | 0.53 | 1.0 | 0.0 | 0.02 | 0.26 | 2.64 | 100.5 | 5.5 | 23.3 | 0.0 | 2.8 |
| 10.0 | 0.21 | 0.4 | 0.36 | 1.6 | 0.0 | 0.14 | 0.95 | 1.97 | 86.0 | 4.7 | 27.5 | 2.1 | 6.6 |
| 9.7 | 0.12 | 0.5 | 0.17 | 5.7 | 4.0 | 0.96 | 8.18 | 2.68 | 68.3 | 3.9 | 16.5 | 9.9 | 8.9 |
| 10.0 | 0.40 | 1.3 | 0.41 | 5.5 | 9.6 | 0.88 | 7.93 | 2.96 | 72.9 | 5.4 | 25.2 | 2.6 | 8.2 |
| 8.4 | 0.02 | 0.2 | 0.00 | 5.1 | 0.0 | 0.80 | 6.60 | 4.36 | 77.1 | 2.1 | 16.1 | 26.8 | 4.3 |
| 6.3 | 0.93 | 9.2 | 0.41 | 2.4 | 0.0 | 0.11 | 1.10 | 3.98 | 90.5 | 3.8 | 16.6 | 1.0 | 5.0 |
| 5.5 | 0.90 | 13.4 | 0.12 | 3.0 | 0.1 | 0.23 | 2.14 | 3.70 | 93.6 | 2.6 | 14.7 | 18.1 | 5.2 |
| 9.1 | 0.23 | 0.7 | 0.04 | 5.4 | 0.2 | 0.78 | 5.80 | 2.89 | 56.9 | 6.8 | 40.2 | 0.0 | 7.5 |
| 7.7 | 0.30 | 2.3 | -0.07 | 3.2 | 0.0 | 0.46 | 5.70 | 3.64 | 83.1 | 4.0 | 10.2 | 0.0 | 1.7 |
| 9.8 | 0.00 | 0.0 | 0.22 | 2.2 | 0.0 | 0.07 | 0.56 | 3.30 | 98.6 | 5.6 | 44.1 | 1.7 | 5.9 |
| 7.4 | 0.44 | 2.4 | -0.08 | 2.2 | 0.0 | 0.12 | 1.26 | 3.42 | 96.8 | 5.3 | 30.7 | 3.1 | 4.2 |
| 10.0 | 0.44 | 1.5 | 0.15 | 2.5 | 0.2 | 0.28 | 2.42 | 2.59 | 88.4 | 5.0 | 18.9 | 0.0 | 6.4 |
| 7.1 | 0.43 | 1.9 | 0.74 | 3.7 | 0.0 | 0.50 | 4.90 | 4.38 | 77.7 | 4.6 | 35.9 | 4.8 | 3.7 |
| 9.8 | 0.17 | 0.9 | 0.23 | 3.3 | 0.1 | 0.36 | 5.07 | 2.93 | 90.6 | 5.9 | 51.1 | 1.1 | 2.2 |
| 10.0 | 0.11 | 0.3 | 0.10 | 2.0 | 0.0 | 0.08 | 0.61 | 2.14 | 97.3 | 4.5 | 15.3 | 1.9 | 6.8 |
| 7.4 | 0.81 | 6.0 | 0.00 | 2.1 | 0.0 | -0.16 | -1.58 | 3.87 | 103.5 | 4.5 | 15.9 | 0.0 | 4.4 |
| 8.7 | 0.27 | 1.6 | 0.50 | 5.3 | 0.3 | 0.82 | 6.81 | 3.52 | 77.8 | 2.6 | 19.9 | 12.8 | 6.1 |
| 9.9 | 0.25 | 0.7 | -0.36 | 6.4 | 0.2 | 2.08 | 16.91 | 2.81 | 69.2 | 5.8 | 30.2 | 0.0 | 5.7 |
| 9.4 | 0.48 | 1.5 | 1.59 | 2.8 | 0.0 | 0.18 | 1.29 | 4.20 | 83.6 | 6.1 | 40.2 | 0.0 | 6.4 |
| 9.6 | 0.96 | 2.3 | 0.75 | 4.9 | 0.1 | 0.63 | 3.99 | 3.25 | 85.5 | 4.9 | 23.4 | 2.8 | 7.0 |
| 2.4 | 1.25 | 21.3 | 0.30 | 3.3 | 0.1 | 0.35 | 3.51 | 4.00 | 91.4 | 3.0 | 8.4 | 9.5 | 4.7 |
| 8.7 | 1.28 | 2.0 | 0.58 | 4.3 | 0.1 | 0.55 | 2.39 | 3.49 | 79.8 | 4.0 | 25.2 | 12.8 | 6.8 |
| 10.0 | 0.34 | 0.7 | 1.38 | 2.0 | 0.0 | 0.08 | 0.55 | 2.72 | 79.5 | 5.9 | 49.3 | 0.0 | 5.5 |
| 7.8 | 0.68 | 4.2 | 0.92 | 2.5 | 0.0 | 0.22 | 2.14 | 4.39 | 92.3 | 5.2 | 25.4 | 2.8 | 4.5 |
| 6.7 | 0.86 | 5.4 | 0.31 | 3.7 | 0.1 | 0.60 | 6.99 | 3.93 | 83.8 | 5.2 | 38.5 | 6.7 | 3.7 |
| 6.2 | 0.14 | 9.6 | 0.26 | 1.3 | 0.0 | -0.06 | -0.81 | 3.38 | 99.5 | 4.3 | 20.0 | 0.0 | 1.0 |
| 8.5 | 0.22 | 1.3 | 0.19 | 2.9 | 0.0 | 0.32 | 4.25 | 4.44 | 91.0 | 4.6 | 18.4 | 2.9 | 1.7 |
| 8.7 | 0.61 | 2.8 | 0.40 | 5.7 | 1.7 | 0.77 | 5.38 | 3.54 | 82.1 | 4.0 | 12.4 | 1.2 | 7.9 |
| 5.5 | 1.77 | 13.1 | 0.09 | 2.9 | 0.3 | 0.37 | 4.61 | 2.90 | 88.0 | 4.2 | 19.7 | 0.0 | 4.4 |
| 9.8 | 1.05 | 2.5 | 0.45 | 1.8 | -0.1 | -0.27 | -1.85 | 3.68 | 102.6 | 5.5 | 28.8 | 0.8 | 6.5 |
| 8.1 | 0.51 | 2.4 | 0.01 | 2.4 | 0.1 | 0.12 | 1.14 | 2.56 | 96.0 | 5.0 | 51.8 | 6.5 | 5.2 |
| 4.4 | 0.86 | 8.8 | 0.48 | 5.3 | 0.3 | 0.83 | 10.84 | 4.41 | 77.1 | 1.8 | 4.3 | 13.4 | 3.5 |
| 5.9 | 2.63 | 9.1 | 1.46 | 3.6 | 0.0 | 0.10 | 0.71 | 4.80 | 83.9 | 5.4 | 38.6 | 2.8 | 6.0 |
| 6.0 | 1.13 | 6.7 | 0.51 | 4.3 | 0.3 | 0.62 | 6.81 | 4.26 | 85.8 | 3.4 | 6.7 | 5.9 | 4.0 |
| 10.0 | 0.03 | 0.1 | 0.24 | 1.3 | 0.0 | -0.07 | -0.58 | 2.05 | 100.8 | 5.5 | 34.6 | 0.2 | 5.7 |
| 4.3 | 2.58 | 13.6 | 1.36 | 0.2 | 0.0 | -0.84 | -8.72 | 8.13 | 96.4 | 5.7 | 28.9 | 0.0 | 4.1 |
| 8.6 | 1.00 | 3.6 | 0.71 | 1.3 | -0.1 | -0.22 | -1.72 | 3.19 | 95.8 | 4.7 | 19.5 | 0.4 | 6.2 |

| Name | City | State | Rating | 2014 Rating | 2013 Rating | Total Assets ($Mil) | One Year Asset Growth | Asset Mix (As a % of Total Aseets) | | | | Capital-ization Index | Net Worth Ratio |
|------|------|-------|--------|-------------|-------------|---------------------|-----------------------|------------|-----------|-----------|---------|----------------------|------------------|
| | | | | | | | | Comm-ercial Loans | Cons-umer Loans | Mort-gage Loans | Secur-ities | | |
| HEARD AME FCU | Roselle | NJ | D- | D- | D+ | <1 | -3.93 | 0.0 | 19.1 | 0.0 | 0.0 | 9.2 | 10.5 |
| HEART CENTER FCU | Roslyn | NY | C+ | C+ | C+ | 15.8 | -3.73 | 0.7 | 18.4 | 1.9 | 20.3 | 10.0 | 13.8 |
| HEART O TEXAS FCU | Waco | TX | D+ | C- | C | 54.8 | 0.31 | 2.0 | 31.7 | 10.2 | 0.0 | 6.5 | 8.5 |
| HEART OF LOUISIANA FCU | Pineville | LA | B+ | A- | A- | 96.7 | 2.76 | 2.2 | 36.7 | 16.7 | 1.0 | 10.0 | 13.1 |
| HEARTLAND AREA FCU | Omaha | NE | D+ | D+ | C- | 22.5 | -4.08 | 0.0 | 22.4 | 12.4 | 1.0 | 10.0 | 23.9 |
| HEARTLAND COMMUNITY CU | Kansas City | MO | E+ | E+ | E+ | 8.0 | -8.21 | 0.0 | 40.8 | 0.0 | 0.0 | 5.8 | 7.8 |
| HEARTLAND CU | Springfield | IL | B+ | B+ | B+ | 249.6 | 4.50 | 0.0 | 63.0 | 4.5 | 0.0 | 9.2 | 10.5 |
| HEARTLAND CU | Hutchinson | KS | B | B+ | A- | 255.3 | 8.26 | 15.6 | 33.0 | 38.1 | 8.1 | 7.1 | 9.1 |
| HEARTLAND CU | Inver Grove Heights | MN | B | B | B- | 102.5 | 5.07 | 0.0 | 34.6 | 18.4 | 7.6 | 8.5 | 10.0 |
| HEARTLAND CU | Madison | WI | B- | B- | B | 231.0 | 3.31 | 21.0 | 24.5 | 39.7 | 0.0 | 8.2 | 9.8 |
| HEARTLAND FCU | Dayton | OH | D+ | C- | D+ | 105.2 | 35.27 | 1.4 | 31.4 | 12.5 | 13.4 | 10.0 | 13.1 |
| HEB FCU | San Antonio | TX | B- | B- | B | 154.8 | 7.02 | 0.5 | 25.7 | 10.7 | 11.7 | 10.0 | 14.5 |
| ▼ HEEKIN CAN EMPL CU | Cincinnati | OH | D | D+ | C- | <1 | -3.46 | 0.0 | 53.3 | 0.0 | 0.0 | 10.0 | 40.4 |
| HEIGHTS AUTO WORKERS CU | Chicago Heights | IL | C- | C | C | 36.0 | -0.56 | 0.0 | 20.0 | 5.1 | 0.0 | 10.0 | 15.5 |
| HEIGHTS COMMUNITY FCU | Bethlehem | PA | E- | E+ | E+ | 11.2 | -11.10 | 0.0 | 21.3 | 22.3 | 0.0 | 5.4 | 7.4 |
| HEINZ - DEL MONTE FCU | Pittsburgh | PA | D+ | D | D+ | 25.0 | -8.57 | 0.0 | 22.6 | 0.0 | 28.0 | 7.5 | 9.3 |
| HELCO FCU | Hilo | HI | B | B | B | 39.3 | 2.93 | 3.0 | 20.0 | 1.7 | 6.6 | 10.0 | 18.2 |
| HELENA COMMUNITY CU | Helena | MT | B | B+ | A- | 176.4 | 15.85 | 0.5 | 37.6 | 9.9 | 11.4 | 10.0 | 11.7 |
| ▼ HEMA FCU | Silver Spring | MD | D+ | C+ | C+ | 14.9 | 3.41 | 0.0 | 35.3 | 0.0 | 49.4 | 9.6 | 10.7 |
| ▲ HEMINGFORD COMMUNITY FCU | Hemingford | NE | C- | D+ | D+ | 6.3 | -5.56 | 0.0 | 26.5 | 10.2 | 0.0 | 8.8 | 10.2 |
| HEMPFIELD AREA FCU | Greensburg | PA | C- | C- | C- | 6.2 | 1.50 | 0.0 | 23.7 | 0.0 | 0.0 | 10.0 | 11.9 |
| HENDERSON STATE UNIV FCU | Arkadelphia | AR | C | C- | D+ | 10.0 | 4.03 | 0.0 | 55.6 | 0.0 | 0.0 | 10.0 | 13.6 |
| HENRICO FCU | Henrico | VA | C+ | C+ | C+ | 207.3 | 1.48 | 0.0 | 34.7 | 9.7 | 6.2 | 6.6 | 8.6 |
| HERCULES CU | Salt Lake City | UT | B- | B- | B- | 61.6 | 2.60 | 0.1 | 14.1 | 9.6 | 12.7 | 10.0 | 11.1 |
| HEREFORD TEXAS FCU | Hereford | TX | B- | B- | B- | 45.9 | 5.01 | 8.2 | 69.8 | 0.1 | 0.0 | 10.0 | 20.0 |
| ▲ HERITAGE COMMUNITY CU | Sacramento | CA | C | C | C | 197.1 | 0.74 | 4.6 | 31.9 | 21.1 | 3.3 | 8.6 | 10.1 |
| HERITAGE CU | Lafayette | LA | C+ | C+ | C+ | 15.2 | 0.86 | 0.0 | 34.9 | 8.9 | 0.0 | 10.0 | 13.5 |
| ▲ HERITAGE CU | Madison | WI | B | B- | B- | 288.2 | 6.63 | 2.0 | 25.1 | 30.9 | 0.7 | 10.0 | 12.4 |
| HERITAGE FAMILY FCU | Rutland | VT | B+ | B+ | B+ | 388.1 | 3.94 | 11.2 | 24.5 | 35.0 | 5.4 | 8.3 | 9.8 |
| HERITAGE FCU | Newburgh | IN | B- | B | B | 514.0 | 11.00 | 0.1 | 40.7 | 20.6 | 6.5 | 8.6 | 10.1 |
| HERITAGE FCU | Butte | MT | C+ | C+ | C+ | 19.8 | 5.38 | 0.0 | 34.8 | 0.0 | 0.0 | 10.0 | 14.8 |
| ▲ HERITAGE GROVE FCU | Salem | OR | C+ | C- | C | 100.8 | 1.31 | 4.6 | 24.7 | 20.3 | 12.8 | 6.4 | 8.4 |
| HERITAGE SOUTH COMMUNITY CU | Shelbyville | TN | A | A- | A- | 165.0 | 3.20 | 11.8 | 26.9 | 22.7 | 10.6 | 10.0 | 14.3 |
| HERITAGE SOUTH CU | Sylacauga | AL | B | B | B | 101.5 | 7.73 | 1.0 | 34.4 | 32.9 | 7.0 | 10.0 | 12.0 |
| HERITAGE TRUST FCU | Summerville | SC | B | B | B- | 506.0 | 4.31 | 0.2 | 22.7 | 19.6 | 26.1 | 8.5 | 10.0 |
| HERITAGE USA FCU | Midland | TX | D+ | D+ | C- | 52.5 | -0.43 | 0.0 | 40.3 | 0.0 | 32.3 | 5.2 | 7.2 |
| ▲ HERITAGE VALLEY FCU | York | PA | C | C | C- | 73.2 | 2.27 | 0.0 | 23.4 | 10.0 | 4.7 | 10.0 | 11.0 |
| HERMANTOWN FCU | Hermantown | MN | B- | B- | B | 127.1 | 5.44 | 1.8 | 26.8 | 14.1 | 8.4 | 9.1 | 10.4 |
| HERSHEY FCU | Hummelstown | PA | C- | C- | C | 57.0 | 0.50 | 8.0 | 26.4 | 29.2 | 0.0 | 6.0 | 8.0 |
| HERSHEY ROBINSON EMPL CU | Robinson | IL | B- | B- | B- | 2.7 | -5.74 | 0.0 | 67.1 | 0.0 | 0.0 | 10.0 | 22.8 |
| HFS FCU | Hilo | HI | C+ | C+ | B- | 478.9 | 4.03 | 0.5 | 14.6 | 13.7 | 48.6 | 8.4 | 9.9 |
| HI-LAND CU | Salt Lake City | UT | A- | A- | A- | 46.2 | 5.26 | 2.4 | 14.7 | 31.4 | 25.7 | 10.0 | 17.0 |
| HIALEAH MUNICIPAL EMPL FCU | Hialeah | FL | B- | B- | B- | 10.9 | 0.42 | 0.0 | 44.1 | 0.0 | 22.3 | 10.0 | 33.8 |
| HIBBING COOPERATIVE CU | Hibbing | MN | C | C | C+ | 69.1 | -1.45 | 0.0 | 11.7 | 7.1 | 19.6 | 10.0 | 12.1 |
| HICKAM FCU | Honolulu | HI | C+ | C+ | C | 532.6 | -1.04 | 0.6 | 15.8 | 16.7 | 28.4 | 7.9 | 9.6 |
| HIDDEN RIVER CU | Pottsville | PA | D | D | C- | 112.5 | 1.92 | 0.0 | 11.3 | 11.5 | 18.7 | 9.2 | 10.4 |
| ▼ HIGH PEAKS FCU | Dillon | MT | D | D+ | D | 20.4 | 5.99 | 0.0 | 22.9 | 3.6 | 0.0 | 6.9 | 8.9 |
| ▼ HIGH PLAINS FCU | Clovis | NM | D | D+ | C+ | 37.2 | -9.15 | 0.0 | 60.1 | 0.0 | 2.7 | 7.5 | 9.4 |
| HIGH SIERRA CU | Bishop | CA | C | C+ | C+ | 13.3 | 0.82 | 0.0 | 22.2 | 0.0 | 65.3 | 10.0 | 12.2 |
| HIGH STREET BAPTIST CHURCH FCU | Roanoke | VA | D | D+ | C | 1.8 | -2.01 | 0.0 | 21.4 | 0.0 | 0.0 | 10.0 | 12.0 |
| HIGHMARK FCU | Rapid City | SD | C+ | C+ | B- | 109.2 | 4.13 | 15.0 | 32.4 | 5.0 | 0.2 | 5.8 | 7.8 |
| HIGHWAY ALLIANCE CU | Jefferson City | MO | C | C- | C- | 20.8 | 7.68 | 0.0 | 35.0 | 16.1 | 0.0 | 10.0 | 12.0 |
| HIGHWAY DISTRICT 19 EMPL CU | Atlanta | TX | D+ | D+ | D+ | 12.1 | 1.19 | 0.0 | 33.2 | 0.5 | 0.0 | 10.0 | 12.1 |
| HIGHWAY DISTRICT 2 CU | Fort Worth | TX | C | C+ | C+ | 6.2 | -2.45 | 0.0 | 36.1 | 0.0 | 0.0 | 10.0 | 19.5 |
| HIGHWAY DISTRICT 21 FCU | McAllen | TX | C | C | C | 40.6 | 1.82 | 0.0 | 43.4 | 0.0 | 0.0 | 10.0 | 15.5 |
| HIGHWAY DISTRICT 9 CU | Waco | TX | C- | C | C | 4.8 | -0.19 | 1.8 | 33.5 | 2.6 | 0.0 | 10.0 | 19.3 |
| HIGHWAY EMPL CU | Tyler | TX | C | C | C- | 1.6 | -0.86 | 0.0 | 52.7 | 0.0 | 0.0 | 10.0 | 25.0 |
| HIGHWAY FCU | Pittston | PA | C+ | C+ | C+ | 21.4 | 2.97 | 0.0 | 38.4 | 10.9 | 13.5 | 10.0 | 15.6 |
| HILCO FCU | Kerrville | TX | E+ | E+ | E+ | 8.9 | -9.10 | 0.0 | 37.2 | 0.0 | 0.0 | 5.8 | 7.8 |
| HILL DISTRICT FCU | Pittsburgh | PA | E+ | E+ | E+ | 4.3 | 3.81 | 0.0 | 34.2 | 0.0 | 0.0 | 6.4 | 8.4 |

| Asset Quality Index | Non-Performing Loans as a % of Total Loans | Non-Performing Loans as a % of Capital | Net Charge-Offs Avg Loans | Profitability Index | Net Income ($Mil) | Return on Assets | Return on Equity | Net Interest Spread | Overhead Efficiency Ratio | Liquidity Index | Liquidity Ratio | Hot Money Ratio | Stability Index |
|---|---|---|---|---|---|---|---|---|---|---|---|---|---|
| 7.1 | 0.00 | 0.0 | 0.00 | 0.2 | 0.0 | -0.59 | -6.06 | 3.42 | 116.7 | 8.0 | 87.9 | 0.0 | 4.7 |
| 8.8 | 2.25 | 4.1 | 0.18 | 2.5 | 0.0 | 0.25 | 1.85 | 2.33 | 91.9 | 5.7 | 42.1 | 3.0 | 5.8 |
| 5.6 | 0.51 | 11.1 | 0.15 | 1.4 | -0.1 | -0.16 | -1.84 | 4.30 | 102.2 | 5.2 | 34.5 | 2.5 | 3.7 |
| 5.7 | 2.20 | 12.2 | 1.32 | 3.8 | 0.1 | 0.07 | 0.54 | 4.80 | 83.4 | 4.5 | 24.3 | 0.9 | 6.7 |
| 10.0 | 0.23 | 0.3 | 0.20 | 1.2 | 0.0 | -0.02 | -0.07 | 2.48 | 100.6 | 4.4 | 20.9 | 3.3 | 6.6 |
| 4.8 | 2.10 | 11.0 | 1.13 | 2.3 | 0.0 | 0.37 | 5.02 | 4.03 | 94.3 | 5.4 | 58.4 | 0.0 | 1.0 |
| 8.5 | 0.11 | 0.8 | 0.23 | 5.3 | 1.5 | 0.82 | 8.09 | 3.31 | 76.3 | 3.8 | 18.4 | 2.9 | 6.8 |
| 6.8 | 0.85 | 7.4 | 0.27 | 4.9 | 0.9 | 0.46 | 5.05 | 3.55 | 82.4 | 2.5 | 9.0 | 14.7 | 6.8 |
| 7.6 | 0.69 | 4.2 | 0.32 | 4.9 | 0.5 | 0.68 | 7.00 | 3.29 | 81.2 | 3.5 | 10.2 | 3.5 | 6.6 |
| 8.5 | 0.29 | 2.3 | 0.19 | 4.4 | 0.9 | 0.51 | 5.68 | 3.76 | 86.7 | 3.3 | 14.4 | 6.3 | 6.1 |
| 7.5 | 2.16 | 8.1 | 0.80 | 0.9 | -0.4 | -0.46 | -3.60 | 3.22 | 101.5 | 4.4 | 22.9 | 2.5 | 5.7 |
| 10.0 | 0.19 | 0.8 | 0.11 | 3.7 | 0.5 | 0.42 | 2.90 | 3.77 | 89.8 | 4.3 | 26.7 | 10.6 | 8.4 |
| 6.4 | 4.64 | 6.0 | 0.35 | 0.2 | 0.0 | -0.83 | -2.03 | 4.27 | 118.2 | 5.4 | 43.3 | 0.0 | 6.1 |
| 9.0 | 1.69 | 2.7 | 1.68 | 1.3 | 0.0 | -0.07 | -0.44 | 4.24 | 95.1 | 6.9 | 54.5 | 3.1 | 5.3 |
| 3.5 | 3.09 | 26.5 | 1.50 | 0.8 | 0.0 | -0.02 | -0.32 | 3.85 | 103.2 | 4.5 | 20.7 | 0.0 | 0.3 |
| 8.2 | 0.79 | 2.6 | 0.26 | 1.5 | 0.0 | 0.14 | 1.55 | 2.27 | 96.0 | 5.0 | 24.2 | 0.0 | 2.3 |
| 10.0 | 0.00 | 0.0 | 0.30 | 3.8 | 0.1 | 0.40 | 2.20 | 1.96 | 79.2 | 2.8 | 16.4 | 26.6 | 6.7 |
| 9.1 | 0.15 | 1.1 | 0.18 | 3.8 | 0.6 | 0.49 | 4.14 | 3.05 | 84.6 | 3.1 | 10.0 | 9.6 | 7.1 |
| 6.2 | 2.24 | 7.3 | 1.94 | 1.5 | 0.0 | -0.14 | -1.26 | 3.65 | 87.0 | 5.5 | 23.3 | 0.0 | 5.5 |
| 9.9 | 0.00 | 0.0 | 0.00 | 2.4 | 0.0 | 0.22 | 2.31 | 2.60 | 91.5 | 5.4 | 47.7 | 0.0 | 5.0 |
| 7.7 | 2.22 | 5.2 | 0.00 | 2.9 | 0.0 | 0.30 | 2.55 | 1.80 | 79.5 | 5.1 | 31.1 | 0.0 | 5.8 |
| 3.8 | 2.27 | 11.6 | 0.43 | 9.1 | 0.1 | 1.24 | 9.45 | 4.06 | 60.3 | 2.1 | 30.5 | 25.4 | 7.4 |
| 6.8 | 0.77 | 6.0 | 0.49 | 4.0 | 0.8 | 0.49 | 6.57 | 2.77 | 83.8 | 4.0 | 21.5 | 4.3 | 4.3 |
| 10.0 | 0.06 | 1.2 | 0.17 | 3.6 | 0.2 | 0.39 | 3.99 | 3.08 | 88.2 | 5.1 | 32.6 | 2.6 | 5.1 |
| 6.3 | 1.22 | 4.5 | 0.49 | 6.5 | 0.3 | 0.99 | 5.02 | 4.96 | 77.5 | 2.6 | 16.2 | 14.3 | 7.5 |
| 9.1 | 0.46 | 2.8 | 0.24 | 2.7 | 0.4 | 0.24 | 2.47 | 3.23 | 90.5 | 3.9 | 12.9 | 1.8 | 5.8 |
| 9.0 | 0.89 | 3.3 | 0.19 | 2.5 | 0.0 | 0.02 | 0.13 | 3.34 | 96.2 | 4.6 | 25.2 | 0.0 | 6.2 |
| 9.0 | 0.38 | 2.5 | 0.18 | 4.0 | 1.1 | 0.53 | 4.31 | 3.34 | 86.2 | 3.3 | 13.8 | 5.2 | 8.0 |
| 6.6 | 0.70 | 7.3 | 0.32 | 6.1 | 2.7 | 0.94 | 11.15 | 4.33 | 78.5 | 3.4 | 7.3 | 4.2 | 5.8 |
| 8.9 | 0.44 | 3.2 | 0.39 | 4.3 | 2.1 | 0.57 | 5.47 | 3.04 | 78.7 | 3.8 | 17.9 | 7.6 | 6.5 |
| 9.6 | 0.55 | 1.8 | 0.16 | 3.1 | 0.1 | 0.37 | 2.57 | 3.05 | 89.5 | 5.7 | 45.7 | 0.8 | 6.8 |
| 7.5 | 0.76 | 7.3 | 0.10 | 4.3 | 0.6 | 0.76 | 9.23 | 3.34 | 79.7 | 4.5 | 24.2 | 4.4 | 4.2 |
| 6.3 | 1.69 | 7.9 | 0.30 | 9.8 | 2.0 | 1.62 | 11.99 | 5.06 | 69.5 | 2.5 | 14.9 | 20.3 | 8.8 |
| 7.4 | 0.61 | 5.1 | 0.49 | 4.3 | 0.4 | 0.52 | 4.76 | 4.73 | 85.2 | 4.0 | 17.3 | 8.2 | 7.7 |
| 7.9 | 0.67 | 4.6 | 0.44 | 4.9 | 2.6 | 0.68 | 6.82 | 3.73 | 85.0 | 3.8 | 14.9 | 4.3 | 7.2 |
| 7.2 | 0.64 | 6.2 | 0.28 | 1.8 | 0.0 | 0.09 | 1.32 | 3.26 | 94.1 | 4.6 | 20.8 | 4.1 | 1.9 |
| 5.9 | 1.38 | 12.0 | 0.50 | 2.7 | 0.1 | 0.23 | 2.34 | 4.45 | 92.8 | 4.4 | 19.7 | 0.3 | 4.1 |
| 6.3 | 1.13 | 7.1 | 0.50 | 4.5 | 0.6 | 0.62 | 6.04 | 3.95 | 84.4 | 3.7 | 13.4 | 2.4 | 6.2 |
| 9.6 | 0.09 | 0.8 | 0.29 | 2.0 | 0.0 | 0.06 | 0.70 | 3.29 | 92.0 | 3.8 | 16.8 | 1.5 | 3.7 |
| 8.3 | 0.00 | 0.0 | 0.00 | 8.7 | 0.0 | 1.21 | 5.34 | 5.13 | 69.2 | 6.0 | 44.4 | 0.0 | 5.7 |
| 7.8 | 1.32 | 5.3 | 0.30 | 3.3 | 1.4 | 0.38 | 3.92 | 2.85 | 87.8 | 5.0 | 18.8 | 4.2 | 6.1 |
| 10.0 | 0.15 | 0.4 | -0.24 | 8.9 | 0.4 | 1.33 | 7.67 | 2.53 | 54.2 | 3.5 | 20.1 | 17.4 | 7.2 |
| 9.8 | 0.18 | 0.2 | 0.14 | 5.5 | 0.1 | 0.79 | 2.35 | 4.23 | 76.5 | 4.6 | 29.4 | 0.0 | 7.6 |
| 7.6 | 2.60 | 6.0 | 0.51 | 2.4 | 0.1 | 0.21 | 1.90 | 1.98 | 88.4 | 6.3 | 45.3 | 0.0 | 6.5 |
| 9.7 | 0.29 | 2.0 | 0.32 | 3.3 | 1.4 | 0.35 | 3.75 | 2.43 | 82.9 | 3.7 | 17.7 | 13.7 | 6.1 |
| 10.0 | 0.20 | 0.7 | 0.01 | 0.9 | -0.1 | -0.12 | -1.20 | 2.09 | 105.5 | 4.5 | 19.1 | 2.7 | 6.7 |
| 6.4 | 1.23 | 6.8 | 0.52 | 1.2 | 0.0 | -0.13 | -1.45 | 3.33 | 98.0 | 5.3 | 28.1 | 0.0 | 4.1 |
| 7.2 | 0.17 | 1.9 | 0.43 | 0.8 | -0.1 | -0.46 | -5.27 | 2.69 | 105.9 | 4.9 | 26.0 | 0.0 | 2.6 |
| 9.0 | 1.12 | 2.7 | 0.46 | 2.3 | 0.0 | 0.21 | 1.76 | 2.49 | 87.6 | 4.8 | 20.0 | 0.0 | 5.2 |
| 10.0 | 0.00 | 0.0 | 0.00 | 0.4 | 0.0 | -0.60 | -4.78 | 2.36 | 135.0 | 7.3 | 70.4 | 1.9 | 6.3 |
| 4.5 | 1.23 | 18.6 | 0.75 | 3.0 | 0.1 | 0.12 | 1.58 | 4.08 | 86.4 | 2.5 | 9.3 | 12.3 | 4.8 |
| 9.6 | 0.57 | 2.5 | 0.20 | 2.5 | 0.1 | 0.38 | 3.20 | 2.71 | 80.5 | 4.1 | 16.9 | 4.6 | 6.4 |
| 6.3 | 2.03 | 7.5 | 0.54 | 0.4 | 0.0 | -0.25 | -2.09 | 3.12 | 105.4 | 5.5 | 48.1 | 0.0 | 5.7 |
| 9.9 | 0.00 | 0.0 | 0.29 | 1.9 | 0.0 | 0.00 | 0.00 | 3.10 | 102.3 | 4.8 | 30.5 | 0.0 | 7.1 |
| 9.4 | 0.50 | 1.7 | 0.02 | 2.5 | 0.1 | 0.32 | 2.09 | 1.77 | 80.2 | 3.1 | 49.7 | 25.2 | 6.8 |
| 8.6 | 3.48 | 6.5 | -0.08 | 3.2 | 0.0 | 0.47 | 2.46 | 2.90 | 78.8 | 4.7 | 24.5 | 0.0 | 7.0 |
| 8.1 | 0.00 | 0.0 | 0.00 | 6.2 | 0.0 | 1.00 | 4.01 | 5.65 | 83.9 | 4.4 | 41.4 | 8.3 | 5.0 |
| 6.2 | 2.59 | 9.6 | 1.01 | 5.8 | 0.1 | 0.79 | 5.11 | 4.94 | 75.6 | 4.9 | 32.2 | 7.0 | 5.0 |
| 6.1 | 1.80 | 9.4 | -0.23 | 0.2 | -0.1 | -1.42 | -18.20 | 4.26 | 131.4 | 2.3 | 18.4 | 38.5 | 3.2 |
| 0.3 | 7.37 | 79.0 | 1.15 | 4.0 | 0.0 | 0.09 | 2.37 | 5.81 | 97.5 | 6.4 | 43.5 | 0.0 | 2.3 |

| Name | City | State | Rating | 2014 Rating | 2013 Rating | Total Assets ($Mil) | One Year Asset Growth | Commercial Loans | Consumer Loans | Mortgage Loans | Securities | Capitalization Index | Net Worth Ratio |
|---|---|---|---|---|---|---|---|---|---|---|---|---|---|
| HILLCREST FCU | Tulsa | OK | D | D+ | D+ | 13.5 | -5.46 | 0.0 | 42.9 | 0.0 | 0.0 | 10.0 | 15.6 |
| HINGHAM FCU | Hingham | MA | D | D | D | 46.0 | -0.34 | 0.0 | 6.8 | 27.1 | 3.3 | 5.7 | 7.7 |
| HIWAY FCU | Saint Paul | MN | A- | A- | B+ | 994.3 | 5.22 | 2.5 | 17.3 | 36.9 | 29.7 | 9.7 | 10.8 |
| HMC (NJ) FCU | Flemington | NJ | D | D+ | C- | 6.2 | 3.14 | 0.0 | 27.7 | 0.0 | 0.0 | 10.0 | 11.8 |
| HOBART INDIANA SCHOOL EMPL FCU | Hobart | IN | D- | D- | D+ | 2.0 | 3.97 | 0.0 | 57.4 | 0.0 | 0.0 | 7.4 | 9.3 |
| HOBOKEN NEW JERSEY POLICE FCU | Hoboken | NJ | D+ | D+ | D+ | 9.3 | -1.69 | 0.0 | 18.5 | 0.0 | 0.0 | 10.0 | 20.8 |
| HOBOKEN SCHOOL EMPL FCU | Hoboken | NJ | B | B | B | 45.6 | -1.23 | 0.0 | 6.1 | 48.6 | 0.0 | 10.0 | 28.7 |
| HOCKLEY COUNTY SCHOOL EMPL CU | Levelland | TX | B- | B- | B- | 32.0 | 2.84 | 0.0 | 60.0 | 0.0 | 8.6 | 10.0 | 11.7 |
| ▲ HOLLEY CU | Paris | TN | B | B- | B- | 47.3 | 4.02 | 0.0 | 50.7 | 0.2 | 3.3 | 10.0 | 11.3 |
| ▲ HOLLYFRONTIER EMPL CU | West Bountiful | UT | C+ | C | C | 6.5 | 6.88 | 0.0 | 90.3 | 5.3 | 0.0 | 10.0 | 16.6 |
| HOLSEY TEMPLE FCU | Philadelphia | PA | D+ | D+ | D | <1 | -13.51 | 0.0 | 0.0 | 0.0 | 0.0 | 10.0 | 43.8 |
| HOLSTON METHODIST FCU | Knoxville | TN | E | E | E | 13.5 | -5.21 | 8.3 | 45.7 | 29.5 | 0.0 | 5.7 | 7.7 |
| HOLY FAMILY HOSPITAL EMPL FCU | Methuen | MA | E+ | E+ | E+ | 3.4 | 6.63 | 0.0 | 68.8 | 0.0 | 0.0 | 5.4 | 7.4 |
| HOLY FAMILY MEMORIAL CU | Manitowoc | WI | C | C | C | 14.1 | 0.03 | 0.0 | 20.5 | 36.7 | 0.0 | 9.2 | 10.5 |
| HOLY FAMILY PARMA FCU | Parma | OH | C | C | C+ | 20.9 | -0.59 | 0.0 | 7.7 | 0.0 | 57.6 | 10.0 | 14.4 |
| ▲ HOLY GHOST PARISH CU | Dubuque | IA | C- | D+ | C- | 27.0 | -2.76 | 0.0 | 0.8 | 0.0 | 0.0 | 10.0 | 11.2 |
| ▼ HOLY REDEEMER COMMUNITY OF SE WISC | Milwaukee | WI | D | D+ | C- | <1 | 3.15 | 0.0 | 9.8 | 0.0 | 0.0 | 10.0 | 19.9 |
| HOLY ROSARY CHURCH FCU | Wilkes-Barre | PA | D+ | D+ | C- | <1 | -6.18 | 0.0 | 35.1 | 0.0 | 0.0 | 10.0 | 20.4 |
| HOLY ROSARY CU | Kansas City | MO | D | D | D | 18.7 | 0.01 | 1.4 | 25.1 | 4.9 | 0.0 | 5.8 | 7.8 |
| HOLY ROSARY CU | Rochester | NH | B | B | B | 217.9 | 5.47 | 2.9 | 22.2 | 33.8 | 2.3 | 7.2 | 9.2 |
| ▲ HOLY TRINITY BAPTIST FCU | Philadelphia | PA | B- | C+ | C- | <1 | 5.26 | 0.0 | 30.0 | 0.0 | 0.0 | 10.0 | 20.0 |
| HOLYOKE COMMUNITY FCU | Holyoke | CO | D+ | D+ | D+ | 29.3 | -2.24 | 1.6 | 18.0 | 60.9 | 0.0 | 6.8 | 8.8 |
| HOLYOKE CU | Holyoke | MA | B- | B- | A- | 149.8 | 4.76 | 7.8 | 15.0 | 31.3 | 20.2 | 10.0 | 11.0 |
| HOLYOKE POSTAL CU | Holyoke | MA | C- | C- | C- | 3.5 | -2.59 | 0.0 | 10.4 | 0.0 | 28.3 | 10.0 | 21.0 |
| HOME TOWN FCU | Owatonna | MN | B- | B+ | B | 115.7 | 5.02 | 0.0 | 46.3 | 12.4 | 6.2 | 8.8 | 10.2 |
| HOMEFIELD CU | North Grafton | MA | D | D | D | 135.9 | 6.54 | 8.7 | 16.9 | 33.3 | 17.4 | 8.1 | 9.7 |
| HOMELAND CU | Chillicothe | OH | B+ | A- | A- | 362.3 | 2.16 | 0.4 | 15.1 | 10.6 | 55.8 | 10.0 | 18.1 |
| HOMELAND FCU | New Orleans | LA | D+ | D+ | D+ | 14.7 | -0.22 | 0.0 | 25.9 | 19.5 | 0.0 | 10.0 | 18.6 |
| ▼ HOMEPORT FCU | Corpus Christi | TX | D | D+ | D+ | 15.8 | -1.66 | 0.0 | 45.5 | 1.0 | 0.0 | 10.0 | 12.6 |
| HOMESTEAD FCU | Billings | MT | C | C- | D | 3.7 | 3.06 | 0.0 | 72.2 | 0.0 | 0.0 | 10.0 | 14.3 |
| ▲ HOMETOWN CU | Kulm | ND | B+ | B- | C+ | 98.7 | 13.41 | 74.4 | 5.3 | 36.2 | 0.0 | 10.0 | 12.7 |
| HOMETOWN FCU | Peru | IN | B- | B- | B- | 21.2 | 7.17 | 0.7 | 50.9 | 0.1 | 0.0 | 10.0 | 13.1 |
| HOMEWOOD FCU | Homewood | IL | D- | D- | E+ | 3.2 | -1.49 | 0.0 | 19.4 | 0.0 | 0.0 | 7.5 | 9.3 |
| HONDA FCU | Torrance | CA | A- | B+ | B | 685.7 | 4.71 | 0.1 | 35.4 | 28.8 | 18.0 | 8.3 | 9.9 |
| HONEA FCU | Fort Shafter | HI | C- | C- | C- | 25.4 | 1.65 | 0.0 | 13.9 | 3.1 | 1.1 | 8.1 | 9.8 |
| HONEYWELL PHILADELPHIA DIVISION FCU | Fort Washington | PA | D+ | D+ | D+ | 27.3 | 1.12 | 0.0 | 5.3 | 0.0 | 42.8 | 9.0 | 10.3 |
| HONOLULU FCU | Honolulu | HI | C | C | C | 242.9 | 0.86 | 1.3 | 21.1 | 15.1 | 30.6 | 10.0 | 11.4 |
| HONOLULU FIRE DEPT FCU | Honolulu | HI | C | C | C | 64.7 | 0.00 | 0.2 | 12.0 | 8.2 | 11.2 | 9.8 | 10.9 |
| HONOR CU | Saint Joseph | MI | A | A | A | 643.7 | 9.90 | 10.5 | 30.2 | 32.1 | 16.1 | 9.8 | 10.9 |
| HOOSICK FCU | Hoosick Falls | NY | C | C | C+ | 22.4 | 3.90 | 1.3 | 16.1 | 14.5 | 43.5 | 10.0 | 14.3 |
| HOOSIER HILLS CU | Bedford | IN | B | B- | B | 435.4 | 7.90 | 27.4 | 12.7 | 51.9 | 5.2 | 8.3 | 9.9 |
| ▲ HOOSIER UNITED CU | Indianapolis | IN | D | D- | D- | 20.1 | 6.36 | 0.0 | 27.0 | 0.0 | 25.3 | 6.5 | 8.5 |
| HOPE FCU | Jackson | MS | D | D- | D- | 176.0 | -1.09 | 30.4 | 4.4 | 62.9 | 9.7 | 10.0 | 11.7 |
| HOPE FCU | Bridgeport | WV | B | B- | C | 34.0 | -0.65 | 0.0 | 30.0 | 0.0 | 8.8 | 10.0 | 15.1 |
| ▲ HOPES EMPL FCU | Jamestown | NY | D+ | D | D | <1 | 0.00 | 0.0 | 61.3 | 0.0 | 0.0 | 9.6 | 10.8 |
| HOPEWELL CHEMICAL FCU | Hopewell | VA | C- | C- | C | 32.9 | 4.80 | 0.0 | 41.7 | 0.0 | 0.0 | 7.8 | 9.5 |
| HOPEWELL FCU | Heath | OH | C+ | C+ | C | 76.8 | 1.57 | 9.5 | 18.8 | 34.1 | 10.9 | 7.1 | 9.1 |
| HOPKINS COUNTY TEACHERS FCU | Madisonville | KY | C+ | C | C+ | 10.6 | -5.20 | 0.0 | 18.4 | 7.4 | 0.0 | 10.0 | 18.1 |
| HORIZON COMMUNITY CU | Green Bay | WI | C+ | C+ | C+ | 42.4 | 0.14 | 0.5 | 7.3 | 59.0 | 0.3 | 10.0 | 14.4 |
| ▲ HORIZON CU | Macon | MO | B- | C+ | C+ | 26.1 | 18.45 | 1.4 | 54.3 | 0.0 | 26.1 | 10.0 | 11.9 |
| HORIZON CU | Spokane Valley | WA | B | B+ | B+ | 709.3 | 16.78 | 0.2 | 18.8 | 19.1 | 0.8 | 10.0 | 11.4 |
| HORIZON FCU | Williamsport | PA | C- | C | C+ | 63.3 | 3.77 | 0.0 | 20.6 | 1.7 | 37.2 | 9.8 | 10.9 |
| HORIZON UTAH FCU | Farmington | UT | B | B | C+ | 125.1 | 5.42 | 4.2 | 22.9 | 18.1 | 8.2 | 9.8 | 10.9 |
| HORIZONS FCU | Binghamton | NY | B- | B | B | 100.2 | 1.37 | 0.0 | 24.8 | 23.2 | 16.6 | 10.0 | 12.1 |
| HORIZONS NORTH CU | Northglenn | CO | C- | C- | C | 72.0 | 1.43 | 16.3 | 29.1 | 12.8 | 0.9 | 6.6 | 8.6 |
| HORNELL ERIE FCU | Hornell | NY | D | D+ | D+ | 4.9 | -1.91 | 0.0 | 31.5 | 0.0 | 0.0 | 10.0 | 11.2 |
| HOTEL & TRAVEL INDUSTRY FCU | Honolulu | HI | D+ | D | D- | 32.9 | -0.64 | 1.4 | 24.8 | 10.1 | 16.7 | 7.0 | 9.0 |
| ▲ HOUSATONIC TEACHERS FCU | Stratford | CT | B- | C | C | 19.4 | -0.44 | 0.0 | 7.3 | 25.2 | 0.0 | 10.0 | 31.4 |
| HOUSTON BELT & TERMINAL FCU | Humble | TX | C | C | C- | 4.2 | 5.24 | 0.0 | 45.8 | 0.0 | 0.0 | 10.0 | 20.9 |
| HOUSTON FCU | Sugar Land | TX | B- | B- | C+ | 554.5 | 6.98 | 0.1 | 43.2 | 11.7 | 4.5 | 5.5 | 7.5 |

| Asset Quality Index | Non-Performing Loans as a % of Total Loans | as a % of Capital | Net Charge-Offs Avg Loans | Profitability Index | Net Income ($Mil) | Return on Assets | Return on Equity | Net Interest Spread | Overhead Efficiency Ratio | Liquidity Index | Liquidity Ratio | Hot Money Ratio | Stability Index |
|---|---|---|---|---|---|---|---|---|---|---|---|---|---|
| 8.8 | 0.40 | 3.8 | 0.08 | 0.3 | -0.1 | -0.45 | -2.86 | 2.94 | 115.0 | 5.0 | 44.6 | 0.0 | 5.5 |
| 5.3 | 1.28 | 12.0 | 0.05 | 2.1 | 0.1 | 0.17 | 2.24 | 3.28 | 92.6 | 3.5 | 8.8 | 2.4 | 2.8 |
| 9.6 | 0.45 | 2.8 | 0.05 | 5.9 | 6.9 | 0.93 | 8.79 | 2.79 | 77.4 | 3.9 | 25.7 | 6.9 | 8.1 |
| 10.0 | 0.00 | 0.0 | -0.07 | 0.6 | 0.0 | -0.15 | -1.27 | 2.60 | 107.0 | 4.9 | 11.6 | 0.0 | 6.2 |
| 5.2 | 0.87 | 5.0 | 0.23 | 3.6 | 0.0 | 0.67 | 7.33 | 3.97 | 74.3 | 6.3 | 45.8 | 0.0 | 2.3 |
| 6.3 | 3.94 | 12.3 | -0.17 | 2.5 | 0.0 | 0.30 | 1.47 | 3.47 | 91.1 | 2.5 | 29.9 | 17.7 | 6.3 |
| 10.0 | 0.88 | 1.7 | 0.05 | 4.5 | 0.3 | 0.72 | 2.57 | 2.90 | 73.5 | 3.5 | 24.9 | 10.9 | 7.3 |
| 5.5 | 1.40 | 7.9 | 0.67 | 5.9 | 0.3 | 1.28 | 11.19 | 4.36 | 60.0 | 1.6 | 9.1 | 38.5 | 5.7 |
| 8.0 | 0.32 | 1.7 | 0.24 | 6.1 | 0.3 | 0.97 | 8.88 | 4.02 | 74.3 | 4.9 | 29.9 | 4.1 | 6.0 |
| 8.0 | 0.16 | 0.9 | 0.09 | 8.6 | 0.1 | 1.27 | 7.57 | 4.53 | 61.1 | 2.3 | 3.4 | 5.7 | 5.0 |
| 9.9 | 0.00 | 0.0 | 0.00 | 1.2 | 0.0 | 0.00 | 0.00 | 0.00 | 0.0 | 8.9 | 166.7 | 0.0 | 4.8 |
| 5.5 | 0.15 | 5.2 | 0.22 | 1.8 | 0.0 | 0.10 | 1.31 | 4.96 | 98.0 | 3.3 | 11.5 | 4.8 | 1.0 |
| 5.1 | 0.63 | 6.2 | 0.00 | 2.1 | 0.0 | 0.08 | 1.05 | 3.85 | 93.8 | 4.1 | 14.5 | 0.0 | 1.0 |
| 9.4 | 0.12 | 0.9 | -0.01 | 3.3 | 0.0 | 0.41 | 3.96 | 3.36 | 87.3 | 3.8 | 15.3 | 0.0 | 5.4 |
| 9.7 | 1.81 | 1.8 | 0.22 | 1.8 | 0.0 | 0.05 | 0.35 | 1.67 | 95.9 | 5.0 | 27.0 | 3.9 | 6.4 |
| 10.0 | 0.39 | 0.0 | 0.00 | 2.0 | 0.0 | 0.18 | 1.69 | 0.80 | 78.6 | 5.6 | 33.8 | 0.0 | 5.4 |
| 6.5 | 19.05 | 10.4 | 8.25 | 0.0 | 0.0 | -1.93 | -10.00 | 1.51 | 220.0 | 8.2 | 108.5 | 0.0 | 6.6 |
| 5.1 | 12.39 | 18.2 | 0.00 | 0.4 | 0.0 | -0.81 | -4.04 | 10.75 | 123.1 | 7.6 | 76.0 | 0.0 | 6.6 |
| 6.8 | 0.84 | 4.3 | 1.29 | 0.8 | -0.1 | -0.39 | -4.98 | 3.70 | 98.5 | 5.3 | 37.9 | 0.0 | 4.2 |
| 7.8 | 0.66 | 5.6 | 0.36 | 5.4 | 1.3 | 0.83 | 9.24 | 3.67 | 77.4 | 2.7 | 12.5 | 12.1 | 6.1 |
| 9.9 | 0.00 | 0.0 | 0.00 | 9.3 | 0.0 | 6.35 | 33.33 | 16.67 | 0.0 | 8.0 | 93.8 | 0.0 | 6.3 |
| 8.2 | 0.16 | 1.5 | 0.11 | 1.8 | 0.0 | 0.01 | 0.16 | 3.70 | 99.5 | 3.5 | 18.0 | 5.9 | 4.0 |
| 9.4 | 0.39 | 2.2 | 0.03 | 3.7 | 0.5 | 0.45 | 4.10 | 3.14 | 89.3 | 3.9 | 17.6 | 5.2 | 7.0 |
| 10.0 | 0.25 | 0.1 | 0.00 | 1.7 | 0.0 | 0.04 | 0.18 | 1.71 | 104.9 | 5.2 | 11.0 | 0.0 | 6.0 |
| 7.5 | 0.34 | 3.3 | 0.24 | 3.8 | 0.4 | 0.48 | 4.73 | 3.37 | 86.5 | 3.7 | 12.0 | 1.0 | 6.2 |
| 5.8 | 1.47 | 14.2 | 0.21 | 0.9 | 0.1 | 0.07 | 0.72 | 3.14 | 96.1 | 3.2 | 9.7 | 12.7 | 5.7 |
| 10.0 | 0.82 | 1.4 | 0.23 | 5.2 | 2.0 | 0.74 | 4.30 | 2.13 | 68.7 | 4.0 | 14.3 | 10.7 | 8.3 |
| 9.9 | 0.06 | 0.2 | 0.10 | 0.4 | -0.1 | -0.48 | -2.57 | 4.44 | 111.6 | 5.4 | 36.8 | 0.0 | 5.8 |
| 5.3 | 2.95 | 12.5 | 1.16 | 0.0 | -0.1 | -1.10 | -8.68 | 4.85 | 105.2 | 4.6 | 24.3 | 5.8 | 5.6 |
| 3.8 | 2.25 | 13.9 | 0.51 | 10.0 | 0.1 | 2.11 | 16.04 | 7.28 | 64.0 | 0.9 | 6.3 | 28.6 | 7.1 |
| 6.2 | 0.08 | 0.6 | -0.01 | 10.0 | 1.6 | 2.24 | 18.19 | 4.27 | 42.8 | 1.4 | 8.1 | 22.2 | 8.6 |
| 5.1 | 1.84 | 9.7 | 0.68 | 10.0 | 0.3 | 2.05 | 16.56 | 5.40 | 60.8 | 3.7 | 12.7 | 1.7 | 8.0 |
| 4.8 | 4.20 | 11.0 | 0.60 | 0.8 | 0.0 | -0.38 | -3.97 | 2.29 | 118.0 | 5.5 | 18.7 | 0.0 | 3.8 |
| 9.7 | 0.22 | 1.8 | 0.20 | 5.7 | 4.0 | 0.78 | 8.02 | 3.61 | 84.1 | 3.4 | 9.5 | 9.2 | 7.6 |
| 8.2 | 0.91 | 2.9 | 0.27 | 2.2 | 0.0 | 0.10 | 1.08 | 2.10 | 89.9 | 4.7 | 34.2 | 14.1 | 4.2 |
| 7.1 | 5.30 | 7.1 | 0.34 | 1.1 | 0.0 | -0.10 | -1.04 | 2.49 | 104.9 | 6.4 | 33.5 | 0.0 | 4.6 |
| 8.2 | 0.69 | 4.1 | 0.15 | 2.5 | 0.3 | 0.16 | 1.37 | 2.57 | 95.2 | 4.7 | 23.3 | 1.6 | 6.9 |
| 10.0 | 0.25 | 0.5 | 0.12 | 2.5 | 0.1 | 0.21 | 1.93 | 2.60 | 91.9 | 4.9 | 18.3 | 2.1 | 5.4 |
| 8.5 | 0.27 | 2.3 | 0.37 | 8.4 | 5.4 | 1.15 | 10.64 | 3.59 | 73.6 | 3.2 | 10.0 | 7.1 | 9.3 |
| 6.5 | 2.24 | 7.3 | -0.05 | 2.3 | 0.1 | 0.28 | 2.00 | 3.14 | 93.1 | 4.5 | 12.7 | 3.3 | 7.1 |
| 5.1 | 1.30 | 11.9 | 0.25 | 4.6 | 2.1 | 0.66 | 6.67 | 3.83 | 80.3 | 2.8 | 12.3 | 10.8 | 6.7 |
| 9.2 | 0.72 | 2.6 | 0.11 | 1.9 | 0.0 | 0.20 | 2.36 | 2.28 | 95.9 | 5.4 | 41.4 | 0.0 | 3.2 |
| 0.3 | 8.17 | 149.6 | 0.53 | 3.6 | 0.4 | 0.27 | 10.15 | 3.91 | 86.2 | 2.0 | 20.3 | 41.0 | 5.5 |
| 9.4 | 1.79 | 3.7 | -0.02 | 4.4 | 0.2 | 0.69 | 4.76 | 2.14 | 61.5 | 5.5 | 43.3 | 0.0 | 6.9 |
| 4.5 | 0.56 | 2.7 | 3.03 | 3.0 | 0.0 | 0.46 | 4.30 | 6.44 | 94.4 | 6.1 | 43.5 | 0.0 | 5.9 |
| 7.0 | 0.90 | 4.4 | 0.34 | 2.5 | 0.1 | 0.30 | 3.10 | 3.29 | 89.0 | 4.8 | 17.9 | 2.8 | 4.2 |
| 6.8 | 0.72 | 6.2 | 0.12 | 3.3 | 0.3 | 0.43 | 5.33 | 3.28 | 90.0 | 3.7 | 9.2 | 4.4 | 3.7 |
| 10.0 | 0.42 | 0.7 | 0.08 | 3.2 | 0.0 | 0.45 | 2.67 | 2.07 | 79.4 | 5.2 | 31.3 | 0.0 | 6.6 |
| 8.3 | 0.73 | 4.1 | 0.81 | 2.1 | 0.0 | 0.10 | 0.69 | 3.37 | 93.6 | 4.4 | 28.1 | 0.9 | 7.0 |
| 8.6 | 0.25 | 1.1 | 0.30 | 3.9 | 0.1 | 0.57 | 4.70 | 4.17 | 79.7 | 4.2 | 14.1 | 5.1 | 6.4 |
| 7.7 | 0.26 | 2.7 | 0.40 | 4.4 | 2.5 | 0.48 | 4.42 | 3.81 | 83.5 | 3.0 | 12.0 | 11.6 | 7.5 |
| 7.7 | 0.90 | 3.9 | 0.29 | 1.8 | 0.0 | 0.00 | 0.04 | 2.98 | 97.1 | 4.5 | 13.7 | 1.0 | 5.9 |
| 8.7 | 0.77 | 3.6 | 0.44 | 4.4 | 0.6 | 0.66 | 6.14 | 3.25 | 80.4 | 4.1 | 17.9 | 2.7 | 6.4 |
| 7.8 | 1.09 | 5.4 | 0.55 | 3.1 | 0.2 | 0.28 | 2.35 | 3.37 | 86.3 | 3.5 | 13.5 | 5.7 | 7.4 |
| 7.3 | 0.23 | 2.5 | 0.33 | 2.2 | 0.1 | 0.12 | 1.44 | 3.62 | 92.5 | 3.6 | 8.1 | 2.3 | 3.4 |
| 5.4 | 2.77 | 10.0 | 0.41 | 1.7 | 0.0 | 0.00 | 0.00 | 3.28 | 89.6 | 4.5 | 19.4 | 0.0 | 4.6 |
| 8.4 | 0.23 | 2.1 | 0.19 | 1.7 | 0.1 | 0.23 | 2.78 | 3.07 | 93.3 | 4.8 | 11.4 | 1.0 | 3.2 |
| 10.0 | 0.27 | 0.4 | 0.10 | 3.4 | 0.1 | 0.49 | 1.61 | 2.71 | 79.6 | 4.2 | 23.4 | 3.7 | 7.5 |
| 7.2 | 0.00 | 3.1 | 0.88 | 7.5 | 0.0 | 1.29 | 6.39 | 5.47 | 71.5 | 4.9 | 33.0 | 0.0 | 5.0 |
| 7.1 | 0.87 | 7.9 | 0.41 | 5.0 | 3.2 | 0.77 | 10.60 | 2.68 | 71.9 | 4.1 | 28.0 | 6.5 | 4.8 |

| Name | City | State | Rating | 2014 Rating | 2013 Rating | Total Assets ($Mil) | One Year Asset Growth | Commercial Loans | Consumer Loans | Mortgage Loans | Securities | Capitalization Index | Net Worth Ratio |
|---|---|---|---|---|---|---|---|---|---|---|---|---|---|
| HOUSTON HIGHWAY CU | Houston | TX | D+ | D | D+ | 62.7 | 2.03 | 0.3 | 28.5 | 18.3 | 21.1 | 5.7 | 7.7 |
| HOUSTON METROPOLITAN EMPL FCU | Houston | TX | C | C+ | C+ | 47.6 | 9.72 | 0.0 | 50.6 | 6.3 | 10.4 | 8.8 | 10.2 |
| HOUSTON MUSICIANS FCU | Houston | TX | C- | C- | C | 5.0 | -1.07 | 12.0 | 10.7 | 0.0 | 0.0 | 10.0 | 13.1 |
| HOUSTON POLICE FCU | Houston | TX | A | A | A | 603.8 | 7.93 | 0.0 | 38.6 | 7.6 | 41.9 | 10.0 | 13.1 |
| HOUSTON TEXAS FIRE FIGHTERS FCU | Houston | TX | B+ | A- | A- | 248.9 | 4.95 | 0.1 | 36.7 | 8.7 | 11.5 | 10.0 | 14.6 |
| HOWARD COUNTY EDUCATION FCU | Ellicott City | MD | D | D | D+ | 20.9 | 1.76 | 0.0 | 53.1 | 4.2 | 11.8 | 7.7 | 9.5 |
| HOWARD COUNTY EMPL FCU | Big Spring | TX | C | C | C+ | 2.0 | 1.43 | 0.0 | 46.6 | 0.0 | 0.0 | 10.0 | 30.9 |
| HOWARD COUNTY SCHOOL EMPL FCU | Kokomo | IN | C- | C | C | 32.9 | 0.63 | 0.0 | 21.3 | 3.6 | 0.0 | 10.0 | 11.0 |
| HOWARD UNIV EMPL FCU | Washington | DC | D | D | D | 10.6 | -6.25 | 0.0 | 20.7 | 0.0 | 0.0 | 10.0 | 19.8 |
| HOWLAND-ENFIELD FCU | Howland | ME | E+ | E+ | E+ | 7.3 | 1.90 | 0.0 | 33.8 | 22.3 | 0.0 | 5.4 | 7.4 |
| HOYA FCU | Washington | DC | D+ | D+ | C- | 20.3 | -2.28 | 0.0 | 41.8 | 0.0 | 1.7 | 8.0 | 9.7 |
| HPC CU | Alpena | MI | B | B | B | 115.6 | 0.71 | 0.0 | 8.0 | 28.1 | 18.7 | 10.0 | 13.1 |
| HSM FCU | Hickory | NC | D+ | D+ | D+ | 4.8 | 4.62 | 0.0 | 62.8 | 0.0 | 0.0 | 10.0 | 11.8 |
| HTM AREA CU | Troy | OH | B | B | B | 22.0 | 8.79 | 1.4 | 52.6 | 3.7 | 0.0 | 10.0 | 14.6 |
| ▲ HTM CU | Haverhill | MA | C+ | B- | B- | 17.8 | 0.52 | 0.0 | 17.9 | 23.5 | 5.3 | 10.0 | 17.6 |
| ▲ HUB-CO CU | Keokuk | IA | C | C | C- | 16.4 | 5.03 | 0.0 | 23.5 | 9.1 | 16.1 | 10.0 | 11.1 |
| HUD FCU | Washington | DC | D- | D- | D- | 47.5 | -4.81 | 0.0 | 25.5 | 14.2 | 10.2 | 6.6 | 8.6 |
| HUDSON HERITAGE FCU | Middletown | NY | C | C | B- | 321.1 | 4.87 | 0.4 | 29.1 | 31.3 | 4.2 | 8.1 | 9.8 |
| HUDSON MUNICIPAL EMPL FCU | Hudson | MA | D+ | C- | C- | 6.8 | -2.09 | 0.0 | 31.4 | 3.8 | 0.0 | 10.0 | 14.3 |
| HUDSON RIVER COMMUNITY CU | Corinth | NY | A- | A- | A- | 201.1 | 10.25 | 1.1 | 30.5 | 39.6 | 5.9 | 10.0 | 13.2 |
| HUDSON RIVER FINANCIAL FCU | Mohegan Lake | NY | C- | C- | D+ | 46.5 | 3.52 | 3.0 | 11.0 | 23.9 | 39.1 | 6.6 | 8.8 |
| HUDSON VALLEY FCU | Poughkeepsie | NY | B+ | B | B | 4239.3 | 7.30 | 8.1 | 23.8 | 16.6 | 37.4 | 8.5 | 10.0 |
| HUGHES FCU | Tucson | AZ | B+ | B+ | B+ | 808.2 | 7.30 | 0.0 | 64.2 | 0.0 | 0.0 | 9.1 | 10.4 |
| HULMAN FIELD TECHNICIANS FCU | Terre Haute | IN | C- | C- | C- | 7.7 | 1.66 | 0.0 | 28.5 | 0.0 | 0.0 | 10.0 | 17.3 |
| HUNTINGTON BEACH CITY EMPL CU | Huntington Beach | CA | C+ | B | B- | 53.0 | 10.00 | 0.3 | 10.5 | 2.1 | 25.5 | 8.6 | 10.1 |
| HUNTINGTON C&O RAILWAY EMPL FCU | Huntington | WV | C+ | C | C- | 33.9 | 2.60 | 0.0 | 56.8 | 14.9 | 0.0 | 10.0 | 11.5 |
| ▲ HUNTINGTON COUNTY FCU | Huntington | IN | C- | D+ | D- | 3.4 | -0.18 | 0.0 | 62.1 | 0.0 | 0.0 | 10.0 | 11.6 |
| HUNTINGTON WEST VIRGINIA FIREMENS FC | Huntington | WV | C | C | C- | 4.1 | 2.49 | 0.0 | 57.8 | 0.0 | 0.0 | 10.0 | 16.4 |
| ▼ HUNTINGTONIZED FCU | Huntington | WV | B- | B- | B | 25.6 | 7.48 | 0.8 | 37.2 | 28.8 | 0.0 | 10.0 | 16.3 |
| HURD EMPL CU | Greeneville | TN | C+ | C+ | C | 2.9 | -0.62 | 0.0 | 70.0 | 0.0 | 0.0 | 10.0 | 42.9 |
| HURLBUT EMPL FCU | South Lee | MA | D | D+ | D+ | 1.3 | -1.56 | 0.0 | 61.5 | 0.0 | 0.0 | 10.0 | 17.4 |
| HURON AREA EDUCATION FCU | Huron | SD | D- | E+ | E | 13.5 | -2.51 | 1.3 | 18.1 | 33.2 | 0.0 | 4.7 | 6.7 |
| HURON C&NW FCU | Huron | SD | E+ | E+ | D- | 5.9 | -5.90 | 0.0 | 68.1 | 0.0 | 0.0 | 4.6 | 6.6 |
| HURRICANE CREEK FCU | Benton | AR | B- | B- | B | 26.4 | -2.09 | 0.0 | 50.1 | 0.6 | 24.9 | 10.0 | 13.6 |
| ▲ HUTCHINSON GOVERNMENT EMPL CU | Hutchinson | KS | C | D+ | C- | 19.4 | 2.49 | 0.2 | 46.8 | 14.0 | 1.3 | 10.0 | 12.1 |
| ▼ HUTCHINSON POSTAL & COMMUNITY CU | Hutchinson | KS | D+ | C- | C | 4.1 | -4.41 | 0.0 | 60.6 | 0.0 | 0.0 | 10.0 | 22.8 |
| I B E W LOCAL 56 FCU | Erie | PA | E+ | E+ | E+ | 8.2 | 1.16 | 0.0 | 27.4 | 0.0 | 0.0 | 5.4 | 7.5 |
| I C FCU | Indiana | PA | C- | C- | C | 3.0 | -3.87 | 0.0 | 48.8 | 0.0 | 0.0 | 10.0 | 13.9 |
| I C S FCU | Elma | NY | E+ | E+ | E+ | 1.6 | 6.04 | 0.0 | 58.0 | 0.0 | 0.0 | 4.8 | 6.8 |
| ▼ I F F EMPL FCU | Hazlet | NJ | D- | D | D+ | 12.4 | -3.25 | 0.0 | 13.3 | 14.3 | 36.5 | 6.5 | 8.6 |
| I H MISSISSIPPI VALLEY CU | Moline | IL | C+ | C+ | B- | 921.7 | 2.86 | 9.2 | 45.0 | 18.3 | 11.0 | 8.0 | 9.8 |
| I R E B FCU | Brooklyn | NY | C- | C- | D+ | 3.9 | -3.85 | 0.0 | 24.8 | 0.0 | 0.0 | 10.0 | 12.8 |
| I W U FCU | Bloomington | IL | C- | C- | C | 3.1 | -8.52 | 0.0 | 12.7 | 0.0 | 0.0 | 10.0 | 11.8 |
| I-C FCU | Fitchburg | MA | B- | C+ | C+ | 503.3 | -3.56 | 8.8 | 25.1 | 41.9 | 3.9 | 8.7 | 10.1 |
| IAA CU | Bloomington | IL | B+ | B+ | B+ | 205.3 | 3.09 | 0.0 | 24.1 | 37.0 | 3.6 | 9.0 | 10.3 |
| IAM COMMUNITY FCU | Daleville | AL | D | D- | D+ | 32.8 | -0.32 | 0.0 | 37.6 | 14.2 | 25.6 | 9.4 | 10.7 |
| IBERIA PARISH FCU | New Iberia | LA | D | D | D+ | <1 | -11.54 | 0.0 | 49.0 | 0.0 | 0.0 | 10.0 | 59.7 |
| ▲ IBERVILLE FCU | Plaquemine | LA | C- | D+ | C- | 5.4 | -0.26 | 0.0 | 42.1 | 0.0 | 29.5 | 10.0 | 16.1 |
| IBEW & UNITED WORKERS FCU | Portland | OR | C- | C- | C- | 69.0 | -2.29 | 1.4 | 26.8 | 8.1 | 11.5 | 6.0 | 8.0 |
| IBEW 116 FCU | Fort Worth | TX | D | D | D+ | 4.1 | 2.38 | 0.0 | 40.3 | 0.0 | 0.0 | 6.6 | 8.6 |
| IBEW 141 FCU | Wheeling | WV | D- | D | D+ | 2.2 | -5.60 | 0.0 | 20.4 | 0.0 | 0.0 | 8.7 | 10.2 |
| IBEW 175 FCU | Chattanooga | TN | C- | C- | C- | 4.6 | 5.71 | 0.0 | 65.6 | 0.0 | 0.0 | 10.0 | 12.7 |
| ▼ IBEW 26 FCU | Lanham | MD | D- | D+ | C | 26.2 | 0.87 | 0.0 | 38.3 | 0.0 | 11.0 | 5.7 | 7.7 |
| IBEW 317 FCU | Huntington | WV | D+ | D | D | 21.8 | -1.07 | 0.0 | 14.9 | 27.0 | 47.6 | 8.9 | 10.2 |
| ▲ IBEW 76 FCU | Tacoma | WA | C | C- | C- | 28.7 | -8.24 | 0.0 | 9.0 | 8.8 | 0.0 | 10.0 | 11.3 |
| IBEW 968 FCU | Parkersburg | WV | C | C | C+ | 5.2 | 7.81 | 0.0 | 19.1 | 4.2 | 16.9 | 10.0 | 13.5 |
| IBEW COMMUNITY FCU | Beaumont | TX | C- | D+ | D+ | 13.9 | -1.09 | 0.0 | 31.1 | 12.4 | 0.0 | 9.0 | 10.4 |
| IBEW LOCAL #146 CU | Decatur | IL | D+ | D+ | D+ | 3.7 | 7.02 | 0.0 | 45.6 | 0.0 | 0.0 | 7.5 | 9.3 |
| IBEW LOCAL #681 CU | Wichita Falls | TX | D+ | C- | C- | <1 | 2.74 | 0.0 | 45.1 | 0.0 | 0.0 | 10.0 | 13.5 |
| IBEW LOCAL UNION 712 FCU | Beaver | PA | D | D- | D+ | 6.7 | -1.10 | 0.0 | 30.7 | 0.0 | 1.6 | 8.8 | 10.2 |

| Asset Quality Index | Non-Performing Loans as a % of Total Loans | as a % of Capital | Net Charge- Offs Avg Loans | Profitability Index | Net Income ($Mil) | Return on Assets | Return on Equity | Net Interest Spread | Overhead Efficiency Ratio | Liquidity Index | Liquidity Ratio | Hot Money Ratio | Stability Index |
|---|---|---|---|---|---|---|---|---|---|---|---|---|---|
| 8.0 | 0.34 | 4.1 | 0.59 | 2.2 | 0.2 | 0.35 | 4.65 | 4.34 | 90.9 | 2.6 | 13.8 | 17.6 | 1.5 |
| 5.7 | 1.02 | 7.0 | 0.95 | 4.6 | 0.2 | 0.55 | 6.92 | 6.54 | 86.2 | 3.8 | 9.5 | 4.2 | 3.6 |
| 8.1 | 0.07 | 0.3 | 0.35 | 1.8 | 0.0 | 0.05 | 0.41 | 4.67 | 98.3 | 4.7 | 53.7 | 5.8 | 6.5 |
| 9.8 | 0.54 | 2.0 | 0.47 | 7.9 | 5.1 | 1.16 | 8.83 | 2.42 | 57.5 | 4.1 | 6.2 | 2.1 | 9.3 |
| 9.5 | 0.39 | 1.7 | 0.20 | 5.0 | 1.3 | 0.68 | 4.75 | 3.11 | 79.4 | 4.4 | 34.0 | 7.8 | 8.6 |
| 7.1 | 0.34 | 2.0 | 0.66 | 1.0 | 0.0 | -0.10 | -1.08 | 4.09 | 94.4 | 4.7 | 27.7 | 0.0 | 3.1 |
| 8.8 | 0.11 | 0.2 | 0.00 | 3.0 | 0.0 | 0.34 | 1.09 | 2.57 | 83.3 | 6.6 | 77.8 | 0.0 | 7.3 |
| 8.4 | 1.10 | 3.0 | 0.20 | 1.9 | 0.0 | 0.08 | 0.78 | 1.08 | 85.1 | 4.6 | 23.5 | 2.4 | 5.7 |
| 9.3 | 0.85 | 2.1 | 1.85 | 0.1 | -0.1 | -1.20 | -5.99 | 4.52 | 134.4 | 5.6 | 35.7 | 0.0 | 4.7 |
| 5.6 | 0.97 | 8.5 | 0.06 | 1.0 | 0.0 | -0.20 | -2.71 | 3.67 | 104.1 | 4.0 | 17.2 | 0.0 | 1.0 |
| 4.4 | 3.69 | 17.0 | 1.09 | 1.4 | 0.0 | -0.19 | -2.01 | 3.84 | 90.8 | 4.1 | 13.1 | 3.8 | 4.2 |
| 9.5 | 0.15 | 2.7 | 0.24 | 4.1 | 0.4 | 0.45 | 3.50 | 2.03 | 76.4 | 4.7 | 33.3 | 3.1 | 7.9 |
| 4.5 | 1.68 | 12.8 | 1.91 | 2.7 | 0.0 | 0.08 | 0.70 | 5.42 | 82.0 | 2.8 | 19.0 | 12.8 | 5.6 |
| 7.5 | 0.87 | 3.7 | 0.29 | 9.8 | 0.3 | 2.03 | 13.91 | 3.93 | 59.2 | 4.5 | 23.3 | 3.7 | 6.3 |
| 10.0 | 0.01 | 0.0 | 0.03 | 3.1 | 0.1 | 0.36 | 2.10 | 3.18 | 88.9 | 5.1 | 24.7 | 0.0 | 7.2 |
| 7.9 | 1.52 | 5.2 | 0.31 | 2.5 | 0.0 | 0.23 | 2.14 | 3.43 | 89.6 | 5.7 | 36.2 | 0.0 | 5.8 |
| 7.4 | 0.88 | 4.0 | 0.56 | 0.3 | -0.1 | -0.29 | -3.43 | 3.06 | 101.7 | 5.7 | 42.4 | 0.0 | 2.6 |
| 7.5 | 0.91 | 7.3 | 0.34 | 2.9 | 0.6 | 0.24 | 2.45 | 4.37 | 85.6 | 3.0 | 5.3 | 3.8 | 6.2 |
| 7.5 | 1.57 | 4.7 | 0.00 | 0.5 | 0.0 | -0.23 | -1.64 | 3.34 | 107.3 | 5.4 | 37.1 | 0.0 | 6.9 |
| 7.1 | 0.89 | 5.8 | 0.39 | 6.3 | 1.4 | 0.97 | 7.46 | 4.64 | 78.6 | 2.7 | 6.6 | 9.0 | 7.1 |
| 7.2 | 0.50 | 5.5 | -0.01 | 2.5 | 0.1 | 0.27 | 3.27 | 3.15 | 89.9 | 4.2 | 12.6 | 2.2 | 4.1 |
| 7.4 | 0.91 | 5.9 | 0.84 | 5.7 | 30.5 | 0.97 | 9.87 | 3.09 | 64.1 | 2.4 | 9.4 | 21.2 | 7.0 |
| 5.7 | 0.46 | 5.4 | 0.78 | 7.1 | 6.2 | 1.04 | 10.25 | 4.75 | 62.8 | 2.8 | 11.8 | 11.0 | 7.5 |
| 8.7 | 0.73 | 1.5 | -0.05 | 1.6 | 0.0 | 0.03 | 0.20 | 2.34 | 100.0 | 5.5 | 32.1 | 0.0 | 6.9 |
| 10.0 | 0.01 | 0.0 | -0.01 | 2.8 | 0.1 | 0.17 | 1.64 | 2.75 | 91.5 | 6.9 | 40.1 | 0.0 | 4.6 |
| 4.3 | 1.38 | 16.3 | 0.62 | 4.0 | 0.2 | 0.63 | 5.48 | 4.37 | 77.4 | 3.3 | 19.8 | 5.1 | 5.3 |
| 7.5 | 0.21 | 1.3 | -0.29 | 3.1 | 0.0 | 0.39 | 3.45 | 4.30 | 97.0 | 4.3 | 17.6 | 0.0 | 5.2 |
| 7.5 | 1.03 | 4.1 | 0.00 | 6.8 | 0.0 | 0.93 | 5.67 | 5.35 | 80.7 | 4.5 | 12.8 | 0.0 | 4.3 |
| 4.8 | 3.37 | 15.9 | 1.48 | 9.0 | 0.3 | 1.37 | 8.43 | 7.12 | 73.9 | 3.6 | 4.3 | 0.0 | 7.1 |
| 6.1 | 2.39 | 4.1 | 0.51 | 10.0 | 0.1 | 2.08 | 4.89 | 5.04 | 66.4 | 3.9 | 32.3 | 0.0 | 5.0 |
| 6.3 | 2.16 | 7.8 | 0.38 | 0.0 | 0.0 | -1.16 | -6.49 | 3.76 | 123.5 | 3.5 | 34.2 | 13.2 | 6.0 |
| 7.0 | 0.30 | 3.0 | 0.17 | 4.3 | 0.1 | 0.55 | 8.47 | 3.21 | 85.7 | 3.9 | 17.9 | 1.6 | 1.7 |
| 0.4 | 5.74 | 44.1 | 0.84 | 6.6 | 0.1 | 2.48 | 43.91 | 5.38 | 54.6 | 4.0 | 16.8 | 0.0 | 3.0 |
| 8.1 | 0.50 | 2.4 | 0.03 | 4.4 | 0.1 | 0.67 | 5.11 | 2.93 | 83.2 | 3.4 | 16.0 | 8.1 | 7.3 |
| 8.8 | 0.07 | 0.4 | 0.17 | 3.5 | 0.1 | 0.65 | 5.48 | 3.54 | 84.7 | 3.8 | 21.4 | 2.7 | 4.6 |
| 5.1 | 3.57 | 10.6 | 0.62 | 1.9 | 0.0 | -1.15 | -4.77 | 6.18 | 96.3 | 4.2 | 33.9 | 14.4 | 6.8 |
| 6.8 | 0.94 | 5.6 | 0.08 | 1.1 | 0.0 | -0.07 | -0.87 | 2.56 | 100.6 | 4.6 | 28.4 | 0.0 | 1.0 |
| 6.3 | 1.97 | 7.2 | 0.81 | 3.6 | 0.0 | 0.39 | 2.88 | 4.26 | 83.7 | 5.3 | 26.8 | 0.0 | 6.1 |
| 2.7 | 2.56 | 21.2 | 0.00 | 3.3 | 0.0 | 0.47 | 7.41 | 3.46 | 83.9 | 5.9 | 33.7 | 0.0 | 1.0 |
| 6.9 | 0.78 | 3.2 | 0.68 | 0.1 | -0.1 | -0.74 | -8.70 | 2.71 | 119.2 | 5.8 | 39.8 | 1.0 | 3.1 |
| 7.4 | 0.31 | 4.4 | 0.17 | 3.8 | 3.5 | 0.51 | 5.33 | 2.88 | 88.1 | 3.1 | 8.8 | 7.5 | 6.7 |
| 8.2 | 1.85 | 3.4 | 0.84 | 3.3 | 0.0 | 0.30 | 2.45 | 3.75 | 81.4 | 5.1 | 13.5 | 0.0 | 5.0 |
| 10.0 | 0.00 | 0.0 | 0.00 | 2.2 | 0.0 | 0.24 | 2.21 | 1.24 | 70.8 | 6.4 | 43.7 | 0.0 | 4.0 |
| 6.4 | 1.00 | 9.0 | 0.07 | 4.2 | 2.4 | 0.62 | 6.36 | 3.02 | 80.4 | 3.0 | 8.1 | 5.6 | 7.3 |
| 9.9 | 0.13 | 0.9 | 0.07 | 5.4 | 1.3 | 0.82 | 8.21 | 2.87 | 72.6 | 3.4 | 20.6 | 9.1 | 7.0 |
| 5.4 | 3.12 | 14.0 | 1.14 | 3.5 | 0.2 | 0.81 | 7.64 | 3.06 | 114.6 | 3.6 | 16.9 | 11.7 | 4.7 |
| 5.2 | 5.42 | 4.4 | 9.30 | 0.0 | 0.0 | -6.81 | -11.20 | 10.88 | 116.1 | 6.4 | 95.2 | 0.0 | 4.7 |
| 8.7 | 0.32 | 0.9 | 0.74 | 1.5 | 0.0 | 0.02 | 0.15 | 5.30 | 99.7 | 5.7 | 36.6 | 0.0 | 5.5 |
| 5.5 | 0.36 | 5.3 | 0.33 | 2.2 | 0.1 | 0.17 | 2.17 | 3.36 | 92.3 | 5.3 | 22.2 | 0.2 | 2.8 |
| 9.7 | 0.06 | 0.3 | 0.31 | 2.4 | 0.0 | 0.00 | 0.00 | 5.65 | 97.2 | 6.3 | 45.8 | 4.1 | 2.3 |
| 3.5 | 13.48 | 29.0 | -2.08 | 0.8 | 0.0 | 0.00 | 0.00 | 3.06 | 100.0 | 5.5 | 22.5 | 0.0 | 5.7 |
| 6.2 | 1.30 | 6.3 | -0.60 | 5.4 | 0.0 | 0.84 | 6.62 | 6.00 | 75.8 | 4.2 | 33.7 | 13.1 | 4.3 |
| 7.0 | 0.86 | 4.2 | 2.37 | 0.1 | -0.3 | -1.62 | -19.97 | 4.28 | 98.2 | 5.8 | 37.3 | 0.0 | 2.0 |
| 3.2 | 6.91 | 33.8 | 0.00 | 2.8 | 0.1 | 0.47 | 4.65 | 2.11 | 77.5 | 4.3 | 14.7 | 0.0 | 4.7 |
| 10.0 | 0.31 | 0.6 | 0.27 | 2.3 | 0.0 | 0.14 | 1.24 | 2.04 | 89.6 | 5.2 | 29.9 | 1.4 | 4.3 |
| 10.0 | 0.40 | 0.7 | 0.00 | 1.9 | 0.0 | -0.05 | -0.38 | 4.91 | 103.5 | 7.7 | 67.7 | 0.0 | 7.0 |
| 8.1 | 0.19 | 1.0 | 0.21 | 2.1 | 0.0 | -0.34 | -3.30 | 3.17 | 109.8 | 4.4 | 38.0 | 8.1 | 5.5 |
| 7.5 | 0.25 | 1.3 | -0.20 | 4.3 | 0.0 | 0.53 | 5.57 | 3.83 | 85.4 | 4.8 | 12.8 | 0.0 | 3.0 |
| 7.6 | 0.86 | 3.1 | 0.00 | 1.2 | 0.0 | 0.00 | 0.00 | 4.39 | 104.8 | 6.2 | 38.1 | 0.0 | 6.5 |
| 5.2 | 3.38 | 13.2 | -0.69 | 0.8 | 0.0 | -0.06 | -0.58 | 3.74 | 118.5 | 6.2 | 42.1 | 0.0 | 3.5 |

| Name | City | State | Rating | 2014 Rating | 2013 Rating | Total Assets ($Mil) | One Year Asset Growth | Asset Mix (As a % of Total Assets) Commercial Loans | Consumer Loans | Mortgage Loans | Securities | Capitalization Index | Net Worth Ratio |
|---|---|---|---|---|---|---|---|---|---|---|---|---|---|
| IBEW LOCAL UNION 80 FCU | Chesapeake | VA | D- | E+ | E+ | 1.4 | 18.76 | 0.0 | 22.9 | 0.0 | 0.0 | 5.5 | 7.6 |
| IBEW LU 278 FCU | Corpus Christi | TX | C- | D+ | C- | 2.7 | 1.91 | 0.0 | 48.0 | 0.0 | 0.0 | 9.6 | 10.7 |
| ▲ IBEW LU 66 FCU | Pasadena | TX | D+ | D- | D | 5.8 | 17.25 | 0.0 | 62.0 | 0.0 | 0.0 | 6.1 | 8.1 |
| IBEW-LOCAL NO 5 FCU | Pittsburgh | PA | C | C | C | 10.7 | -4.59 | 0.0 | 8.8 | 0.0 | 0.0 | 9.8 | 10.9 |
| ▲ IBEW/SJ CASCADE FCU | Salem | OR | D+ | D- | D+ | 11.5 | 9.02 | 0.0 | 38.0 | 17.8 | 0.0 | 7.7 | 9.5 |
| IBM SOUTHEAST EMPL CU | Delray Beach | FL | B+ | B+ | B | 881.3 | 1.44 | 1.5 | 22.3 | 27.6 | 21.2 | 9.3 | 10.5 |
| ICI AMERICA FCU | New Castle | DE | C- | D+ | D+ | 2.8 | 2.60 | 0.0 | 41.8 | 0.0 | 0.0 | 10.0 | 14.2 |
| ICON CU | Boise | ID | A | A | A | 248.8 | 9.15 | 2.9 | 51.2 | 14.1 | 6.6 | 10.0 | 13.3 |
| IDAHO CENTRAL CU | Chubbuck | ID | A- | A- | A- | 2267.4 | 28.52 | 6.5 | 47.3 | 32.0 | 0.0 | 6.4 | 8.4 |
| IDAHO STATE UNIV FCU | Pocatello | ID | B- | C+ | B | 153.4 | 1.92 | 0.0 | 40.6 | 23.5 | 2.9 | 7.4 | 9.3 |
| IDAHO UNITED CU | Boise | ID | D | D+ | C- | 29.3 | 5.64 | 0.0 | 61.5 | 0.0 | 0.0 | 5.3 | 7.3 |
| IDB-IIC FCU | Washington | DC | A- | B+ | B- | 507.0 | 5.56 | 2.0 | 2.6 | 61.0 | 11.5 | 10.0 | 11.6 |
| IDEAL CU | Woodbury | MN | B | B | B | 607.6 | 4.87 | 3.5 | 35.4 | 38.7 | 2.1 | 8.0 | 9.7 |
| IEC FCU | Springfield | IL | D+ | D+ | D+ | 11.3 | -9.83 | 9.5 | 44.5 | 0.0 | 0.0 | 10.0 | 14.9 |
| IH CU INC | Springfield | OH | C+ | C+ | B | 276.8 | 6.31 | 2.0 | 20.7 | 22.4 | 43.1 | 10.0 | 17.3 |
| ILA 1351 FCU | La Porte | TX | C | C | C | 13.4 | -0.57 | 0.0 | 34.0 | 0.0 | 0.0 | 10.0 | 17.9 |
| ILA 28 FCU | Pasadena | TX | B- | B- | B | 6.0 | 7.86 | 0.0 | 36.6 | 0.0 | 0.0 | 10.0 | 24.5 |
| ILA LOCAL 1235 FCU | Newark | NJ | C- | C- | C- | 7.9 | 0.56 | 0.0 | 50.2 | 0.0 | 0.0 | 10.0 | 17.2 |
| ILLIANA FINANCIAL CU | Calumet City | IL | B | B | B | 202.6 | 2.57 | 3.7 | 24.9 | 17.5 | 39.6 | 10.0 | 14.2 |
| ILLINOIS COMMUNITY CU | Sycamore | IL | B+ | B | C | 75.2 | -3.05 | 0.7 | 36.3 | 8.3 | 6.4 | 10.0 | 13.5 |
| ILLINOIS EDUCATORS CU | Springfield | IL | C | C | C | 50.1 | 3.80 | 0.0 | 65.4 | 0.0 | 9.4 | 7.8 | 9.6 |
| ILLINOIS STATE CU | Normal | IL | B- | C+ | C+ | 106.7 | 19.37 | 0.0 | 42.9 | 20.9 | 4.6 | 7.0 | 9.0 |
| ▼ ILLINOIS STATE POLICE FCU | Springfield | IL | D+ | C | C+ | 97.9 | 8.33 | 0.7 | 28.6 | 9.4 | 0.3 | 5.3 | 7.3 |
| ▲ ILLINOIS VALLEY CU | Peru | IL | C | C- | D+ | 23.7 | 2.36 | 0.0 | 36.5 | 16.8 | 1.5 | 9.9 | 11.0 |
| ILWU CU | Wilmington | CA | A | A | A | 181.7 | 13.43 | 3.9 | 28.7 | 32.4 | 11.3 | 10.0 | 12.1 |
| ILWU-FSC FCU | Oakland | CA | D | D+ | C | 25.3 | 7.60 | 0.0 | 25.9 | 0.2 | 26.2 | 9.9 | 10.9 |
| IM DETROIT DISTRICT CU | Detroit | MI | C+ | C | C- | 1.4 | 3.66 | 0.0 | 4.3 | 0.0 | 0.0 | 10.0 | 19.2 |
| IMECO FCU | South Bend | IN | D | D | C- | 8.3 | 4.91 | 0.0 | 38.5 | 16.5 | 0.0 | 10.0 | 15.6 |
| IMMACULATE CONCEPTION FALL RIVER FCU | Fall River | MA | E+ | E+ | E+ | 1.6 | -11.78 | 0.0 | 23.1 | 28.1 | 0.0 | 4.9 | 6.9 |
| IMMACULATE HEART OF MARY CU | Lafayette | LA | D+ | D | C- | <1 | -0.23 | 0.0 | 11.8 | 0.0 | 0.0 | 10.0 | 25.1 |
| IMMANUEL BAPTIST CHURCH FCU | New Haven | CT | E+ | E+ | E+ | <1 | 1.55 | 0.0 | 26.7 | 0.0 | 0.0 | 4.9 | 6.9 |
| IMPACT CU INC | Clyde | OH | C+ | B | B- | 123.9 | 4.43 | 3.9 | 30.0 | 18.1 | 3.1 | 8.4 | 9.9 |
| IMPERIAL CU | Springfield | IL | E+ | D- | D+ | <1 | -8.11 | 0.0 | 29.4 | 0.0 | 0.0 | 6.8 | 8.8 |
| INCENTA FCU | Englewood | OH | D | D- | D | 82.6 | 0.64 | 0.0 | 23.9 | 23.1 | 2.3 | 9.0 | 10.3 |
| INDEPENDENCE FCU | Independence | MO | E+ | E+ | E+ | 2.6 | 6.34 | 0.0 | 72.9 | 0.0 | 0.0 | 6.0 | 8.0 |
| INDEPENDENCE TEACHERS CU | Independence | MO | C | C | C | 14.3 | 3.17 | 0.0 | 23.3 | 0.0 | 0.0 | 8.6 | 10.1 |
| INDEPENDENT EMPLOYERS GROUP FCU | Hilo | HI | D- | D+ | D+ | 21.0 | 0.35 | 1.2 | 21.1 | 9.1 | 28.2 | 6.8 | 8.8 |
| INDEPENDENT FCU | Anderson | IN | D | D | D | 68.5 | -1.72 | 0.0 | 27.6 | 21.3 | 0.0 | 5.9 | 7.9 |
| INDIANA HEARTLAND FCU | Kokomo | IN | D+ | D+ | D+ | 10.9 | 27.22 | 0.0 | 75.0 | 0.6 | 0.0 | 8.5 | 10.0 |
| INDIANA LAKES FCU | Warsaw | IN | C+ | C+ | C+ | 18.9 | -1.42 | 4.3 | 13.3 | 31.9 | 0.0 | 10.0 | 13.2 |
| INDIANA MEMBERS CU | Indianapolis | IN | B- | B- | B- | 1530.2 | 7.39 | 7.9 | 18.4 | 29.0 | 20.7 | 10.0 | 11.0 |
| INDIANA STATE UNIV FCU | Terre Haute | IN | C- | C- | C | 81.3 | 2.08 | 3.1 | 27.5 | 25.8 | 4.2 | 8.9 | 10.3 |
| INDIANA UNITED METHODIST FCU | Kokomo | IN | D- | D | D+ | 1.2 | -2.94 | 0.0 | 66.8 | 0.0 | 0.0 | 9.5 | 10.7 |
| INDIANA UNIV CU | Bloomington | IN | A- | A- | B+ | 823.2 | 4.22 | 18.4 | 16.5 | 43.8 | 20.0 | 10.0 | 12.9 |
| INDIANAPOLIS NEWSPAPER FCU | Indianapolis | IN | D+ | D+ | D+ | 7.6 | -4.08 | 0.0 | 76.8 | 0.0 | 0.0 | 10.0 | 14.7 |
| INDIANAPOLIS POST OFFICE CU | Indianapolis | IN | C- | C- | C- | 56.0 | 1.05 | 0.0 | 15.8 | 0.0 | 19.2 | 10.0 | 20.2 |
| INDIANHEAD CU | Spooner | WI | C+ | C | C | 43.9 | -0.75 | 0.0 | 13.4 | 25.9 | 0.0 | 9.0 | 10.3 |
| ▲ INDUSTRIAL CU OF WHATCOM COUNTY | Bellingham | WA | C | C | C+ | 203.1 | 6.58 | 4.9 | 25.9 | 31.2 | 28.8 | 5.6 | 7.7 |
| INDUSTRIAL EMPL CU | Centerville | IA | C+ | C+ | C+ | 8.9 | 1.89 | 0.0 | 31.4 | 6.9 | 0.0 | 10.0 | 14.1 |
| INDUSTRIAL FCU | Lafayette | IN | B- | B | B | 170.2 | 6.77 | 0.6 | 35.0 | 15.7 | 0.0 | 9.8 | 10.9 |
| INFINITY FCU | Westbrook | ME | C | C | C- | 297.3 | 14.56 | 0.1 | 9.4 | 44.4 | 22.2 | 8.3 | 9.9 |
| INFIRMARY FCU | Mobile | AL | B | B | B+ | 17.3 | 3.28 | 0.0 | 24.7 | 5.6 | 36.4 | 10.0 | 18.0 |
| INFIRST FCU | Alexandria | VA | C+ | B- | C+ | 166.0 | 3.73 | 2.3 | 29.4 | 28.2 | 24.8 | 7.7 | 9.8 |
| INGERSOLL-RAND FCU | Athens | PA | C+ | C+ | B | 58.8 | -2.45 | 0.0 | 12.5 | 8.5 | 57.5 | 10.0 | 20.4 |
| ▲ INLAND FCU | El Cajon | CA | D+ | D | D | 10.6 | 3.88 | 0.0 | 34.2 | 30.6 | 0.0 | 6.1 | 8.1 |
| INLAND MOTOR EMPL FCU | Radford | VA | D+ | D+ | D+ | 2.1 | -7.38 | 0.0 | 42.7 | 0.0 | 0.0 | 10.0 | 18.7 |
| ▼ INLAND VALLEY FCU | Fontana | CA | C- | C | D+ | 41.4 | 10.15 | 0.3 | 21.4 | 20.6 | 3.6 | 5.5 | 7.5 |
| ▲ INNER LAKES FCU | Westfield | NY | C- | D+ | D+ | 75.6 | 4.64 | 0.1 | 19.4 | 8.7 | 20.9 | 4.9 | 6.9 |
| INNOVATIONS FCU | Panama City | FL | C+ | B | B | 165.5 | 3.21 | 6.5 | 36.3 | 28.6 | 3.5 | 7.5 | 9.3 |
| ▲ INOVA FCU | Elkhart | IN | C+ | C | C+ | 306.6 | 2.68 | 5.8 | 48.4 | 31.0 | 0.3 | 6.0 | 8.0 |

| Asset Quality Index | Non-Performing Loans as a % of Total Loans | as a % of Capital | Net Charge-Offs Avg Loans | Profitability Index | Net Income ($Mil) | Return on Assets | Return on Equity | Net Interest Spread | Overhead Efficiency Ratio | Liquidity Index | Liquidity Ratio | Hot Money Ratio | Stability Index |
|---|---|---|---|---|---|---|---|---|---|---|---|---|---|
| 6.1 | 1.89 | 5.2 | -1.08 | 6.5 | 0.0 | 2.21 | 28.99 | 5.46 | 57.1 | 7.4 | 58.4 | 0.0 | 1.6 |
| 4.5 | 1.60 | 9.1 | -0.15 | 5.6 | 0.0 | 0.81 | 7.57 | 6.60 | 84.7 | 5.6 | 37.6 | 0.0 | 3.7 |
| 7.9 | 0.08 | 0.8 | 0.03 | 7.1 | 0.1 | 1.64 | 20.23 | 5.39 | 70.1 | 3.8 | 18.6 | 0.0 | 3.0 |
| 7.1 | 4.26 | 5.6 | -0.09 | 3.5 | 0.0 | 0.29 | 2.72 | 1.56 | 79.0 | 5.4 | 16.3 | 0.0 | 4.8 |
| 6.2 | 1.29 | 8.7 | 0.45 | 1.9 | 0.0 | 0.32 | 3.36 | 3.95 | 87.1 | 4.1 | 28.8 | 1.4 | 3.5 |
| 7.7 | 0.69 | 4.7 | 0.38 | 6.3 | 6.6 | 1.00 | 10.80 | 3.68 | 76.7 | 4.4 | 19.1 | 4.5 | 6.7 |
| 7.7 | 1.66 | 4.8 | -0.64 | 5.9 | 0.0 | 1.20 | 8.33 | 3.92 | 97.5 | 5.8 | 92.2 | 0.0 | 4.3 |
| 7.8 | 0.36 | 2.4 | 0.50 | 6.8 | 1.5 | 0.80 | 6.22 | 4.31 | 78.5 | 1.6 | 4.5 | 20.0 | 8.8 |
| 8.1 | 0.16 | 1.7 | 0.09 | 9.7 | 27.7 | 1.79 | 21.66 | 2.59 | 61.5 | 1.2 | 3.0 | 19.2 | 7.0 |
| 9.4 | 0.14 | 1.3 | 0.13 | 4.4 | 0.8 | 0.69 | 7.66 | 3.64 | 85.6 | 3.8 | 12.2 | 3.5 | 5.3 |
| 4.2 | 0.53 | 10.7 | 0.69 | 1.2 | -0.1 | -0.30 | -4.04 | 5.45 | 95.5 | 5.3 | 26.7 | 0.5 | 2.7 |
| 10.0 | 0.08 | 0.5 | 0.00 | 5.6 | 3.1 | 0.83 | 7.19 | 2.06 | 60.3 | 3.7 | 28.5 | 16.0 | 9.2 |
| 7.2 | 0.62 | 6.2 | 0.20 | 5.1 | 3.7 | 0.81 | 9.12 | 3.08 | 76.7 | 3.6 | 17.6 | 8.5 | 6.7 |
| 9.1 | 0.47 | 1.8 | 0.00 | 0.4 | 0.0 | -0.39 | -2.81 | 2.43 | 114.5 | 4.0 | 18.0 | 4.4 | 6.1 |
| 9.9 | 0.38 | 1.1 | 0.35 | 3.1 | 0.9 | 0.42 | 2.39 | 2.67 | 80.5 | 3.9 | 16.2 | 5.4 | 7.7 |
| 9.6 | 0.14 | 0.3 | 0.05 | 2.6 | 0.0 | 0.28 | 1.57 | 4.14 | 93.4 | 5.4 | 38.0 | 0.0 | 7.1 |
| 9.4 | 1.78 | 3.0 | 0.17 | 8.6 | 0.1 | 1.19 | 4.92 | 3.98 | 68.0 | 4.7 | 45.3 | 4.5 | 5.7 |
| 8.8 | 0.00 | 0.0 | -0.19 | 3.6 | 0.0 | 0.73 | 4.42 | 3.77 | 90.4 | 4.2 | 16.1 | 0.0 | 5.4 |
| 8.3 | 0.69 | 4.6 | 0.78 | 4.5 | 1.1 | 0.71 | 5.09 | 3.49 | 74.4 | 3.6 | 11.4 | 9.7 | 7.7 |
| 8.2 | 0.81 | 3.3 | 0.95 | 8.5 | 1.1 | 1.94 | 15.43 | 4.89 | 90.9 | 3.3 | 11.2 | 8.7 | 6.8 |
| 5.3 | 0.87 | 6.2 | 0.84 | 3.4 | 0.1 | 0.28 | 3.02 | 4.85 | 86.5 | 3.7 | 10.7 | 1.8 | 4.7 |
| 6.5 | 1.42 | 10.7 | 0.67 | 4.7 | 0.5 | 0.56 | 6.52 | 4.65 | 81.9 | 4.0 | 15.6 | 4.8 | 5.0 |
| 5.6 | 1.05 | 11.4 | 0.73 | 1.3 | -0.1 | -0.19 | -2.56 | 2.62 | 99.7 | 4.4 | 21.0 | 3.0 | 3.0 |
| 6.7 | 1.06 | 5.3 | 0.77 | 5.3 | 0.2 | 0.89 | 8.60 | 4.72 | 71.7 | 4.0 | 25.6 | 3.2 | 4.7 |
| 8.1 | 0.78 | 4.0 | 0.24 | 9.8 | 1.9 | 1.44 | 11.83 | 5.01 | 74.9 | 3.4 | 20.4 | 9.0 | 8.7 |
| 9.7 | 0.63 | 1.5 | 0.14 | 0.5 | -0.1 | -0.29 | -2.60 | 3.47 | 113.7 | 6.6 | 55.7 | 4.0 | 4.7 |
| 8.0 | 15.25 | 3.4 | 3.98 | 5.1 | 0.0 | 0.89 | 4.65 | 1.57 | 80.0 | 8.5 | 98.6 | 0.0 | 5.0 |
| 9.8 | 0.55 | 2.0 | 0.00 | 0.0 | -0.1 | -1.03 | -6.40 | 2.19 | 143.0 | 4.3 | 28.0 | 0.0 | 6.4 |
| 1.7 | 6.05 | 41.8 | 1.98 | 1.3 | 0.0 | -1.01 | -14.69 | 8.01 | 116.1 | 6.2 | 42.1 | 0.0 | 1.0 |
| 8.0 | 10.27 | 6.7 | 0.00 | 0.3 | 0.0 | -0.31 | -1.20 | 1.46 | 125.0 | 6.7 | 66.0 | 0.0 | 6.7 |
| 0.3 | 65.71 | 230.0 | 0.00 | 8.1 | 0.0 | 3.15 | 50.00 | 11.90 | 66.7 | 7.7 | 75.4 | 0.0 | 0.9 |
| 7.3 | 0.74 | 5.4 | 0.21 | 2.7 | 0.1 | 0.14 | 1.50 | 4.26 | 93.2 | 4.5 | 20.1 | 1.6 | 5.9 |
| 0.3 | 60.00 | 75.0 | -10.26 | 7.5 | 0.0 | 4.04 | 133.33 | 10.26 | 50.0 | 8.1 | 87.1 | 0.0 | 3.1 |
| 7.7 | 0.68 | 3.4 | 0.26 | 1.2 | 0.1 | 0.09 | 0.89 | 3.05 | 94.6 | 4.2 | 13.0 | 0.7 | 4.0 |
| 0.7 | 3.41 | 35.2 | 0.29 | 4.6 | 0.0 | 0.98 | 12.31 | 6.76 | 83.7 | 5.2 | 30.2 | 0.0 | 3.0 |
| 10.0 | 0.14 | 0.3 | 0.12 | 2.2 | 0.0 | 0.13 | 1.30 | 1.66 | 89.0 | 6.5 | 39.0 | 0.0 | 5.0 |
| 6.0 | 1.64 | 12.0 | -0.39 | 0.7 | 0.0 | -0.18 | -3.65 | 3.86 | 99.8 | 5.3 | 22.4 | 0.5 | 2.3 |
| 5.5 | 1.71 | 12.8 | 0.33 | 1.8 | 0.0 | 0.05 | 0.69 | 2.89 | 97.3 | 4.3 | 19.4 | 2.6 | 2.6 |
| 1.5 | 3.38 | 31.7 | 0.78 | 10.0 | 0.2 | 2.07 | 20.52 | 4.66 | 67.5 | 2.0 | 12.1 | 15.5 | 5.7 |
| 7.9 | 1.10 | 4.3 | 0.67 | 2.6 | 0.0 | 0.15 | 1.13 | 3.01 | 90.2 | 4.6 | 14.4 | 0.0 | 6.3 |
| 9.7 | 0.08 | 0.5 | 0.05 | 4.0 | 6.5 | 0.58 | 5.27 | 2.47 | 80.0 | 5.6 | 31.0 | 5.9 | 8.0 |
| 8.3 | 0.39 | 2.4 | 0.08 | 2.1 | 0.2 | 0.24 | 2.38 | 3.02 | 92.4 | 3.8 | 12.8 | 3.0 | 5.1 |
| 5.4 | 1.59 | 9.5 | 0.00 | 0.0 | 0.0 | -3.47 | -30.56 | 4.39 | 158.1 | 4.6 | 24.2 | 0.0 | 5.3 |
| 8.7 | 0.47 | 2.3 | 0.06 | 5.8 | 5.5 | 0.90 | 6.99 | 2.98 | 73.4 | 4.4 | 20.1 | 2.5 | 9.1 |
| 5.6 | 1.73 | 8.8 | 0.25 | 2.2 | 0.0 | 0.29 | 2.05 | 4.38 | 108.9 | 3.7 | 20.9 | 0.0 | 5.0 |
| 10.0 | 0.95 | 0.9 | 1.45 | 1.2 | 0.0 | -0.07 | -0.38 | 1.69 | 93.4 | 4.9 | 15.0 | 0.0 | 6.4 |
| 7.6 | 0.94 | 4.2 | 0.22 | 3.8 | 0.2 | 0.52 | 5.21 | 3.70 | 85.9 | 6.2 | 58.3 | 1.8 | 4.7 |
| 6.5 | 1.20 | 10.9 | 0.21 | 3.6 | 0.8 | 0.51 | 8.22 | 3.55 | 92.7 | 4.0 | 11.5 | 0.8 | 3.0 |
| 9.7 | 0.40 | 1.2 | -0.10 | 4.0 | 0.0 | 0.53 | 3.88 | 2.93 | 82.3 | 5.5 | 34.4 | 0.0 | 7.3 |
| 6.0 | 1.78 | 11.1 | 0.59 | 3.6 | 0.3 | 0.24 | 2.23 | 4.81 | 89.3 | 4.4 | 21.4 | 2.3 | 7.0 |
| 7.6 | 0.73 | 5.5 | 0.14 | 2.8 | 1.4 | 0.68 | 6.46 | 2.99 | 80.4 | 2.9 | 12.3 | 14.1 | 6.1 |
| 10.0 | 0.12 | 0.2 | 0.67 | 5.8 | 0.1 | 0.96 | 5.48 | 2.85 | 86.2 | 5.7 | 31.1 | 2.4 | 6.7 |
| 6.1 | 1.23 | 9.7 | 0.43 | 2.8 | 0.3 | 0.23 | 2.61 | 3.14 | 86.9 | 2.9 | 11.6 | 11.7 | 5.2 |
| 10.0 | 1.29 | 1.7 | 0.12 | 2.8 | 0.2 | 0.32 | 1.69 | 2.61 | 87.6 | 5.4 | 32.9 | 0.5 | 6.9 |
| 8.5 | 0.20 | 1.6 | 0.33 | 3.7 | 0.0 | 0.49 | 6.21 | 3.60 | 83.3 | 3.9 | 13.6 | 0.0 | 3.0 |
| 7.0 | 2.33 | 5.2 | 0.70 | 2.6 | 0.0 | 0.13 | 0.68 | 5.03 | 107.0 | 4.4 | 4.4 | 0.0 | 5.9 |
| 8.4 | 0.69 | 3.6 | 0.41 | 3.7 | 0.1 | 0.47 | 6.17 | 3.44 | 86.9 | 4.6 | 34.3 | 13.2 | 2.9 |
| 6.4 | 1.31 | 7.6 | 0.09 | 3.5 | 0.3 | 0.47 | 6.94 | 2.66 | 83.0 | 4.9 | 27.6 | 1.7 | 2.0 |
| 5.9 | 0.78 | 10.6 | 0.94 | 2.2 | -0.2 | -0.19 | -1.94 | 5.49 | 90.1 | 3.9 | 11.8 | 2.2 | 5.6 |
| 4.4 | 0.87 | 10.6 | 0.89 | 3.9 | 1.2 | 0.50 | 6.43 | 4.14 | 78.7 | 2.3 | 9.7 | 14.4 | 4.9 |

| Name | City | State | Rating | 2014 Rating | 2013 Rating | Total Assets ($Mil) | One Year Asset Growth | Commercial Loans | Consumer Loans | Mortgage Loans | Securities | Capitalization Index | Net Worth Ratio |
|---|---|---|---|---|---|---|---|---|---|---|---|---|---|
| INSIGHT CU | Orlando | FL | B- | B+ | B+ | 542.9 | 10.59 | 8.2 | 37.1 | 15.4 | 14.6 | 8.5 | 10.1 |
| ▲ INSPIRE FCU | Bristol | PA | B- | C | C | 90.9 | 8.55 | 0.1 | 28.7 | 25.1 | 0.0 | 7.8 | 9.6 |
| INSPIRUS CU | Tukwila | WA | B- | B- | C | 1049.3 | 5.69 | 0.0 | 32.5 | 14.9 | 30.6 | 8.4 | 9.9 |
| INTEGRIS FCU | Oklahoma City | OK | C- | C- | C- | 12.7 | 1.57 | 0.0 | 30.8 | 0.0 | 0.0 | 10.0 | 12.0 |
| INTEGRITY FCU | Barberton | OH | C- | C- | C- | 38.5 | 1.22 | 0.0 | 34.2 | 10.1 | 15.5 | 9.0 | 10.3 |
| ▼ INTEGRUS CU | Dubuque | IA | D | D+ | C | 20.2 | -0.77 | 5.4 | 34.1 | 33.6 | 0.5 | 7.6 | 9.4 |
| ▲ INTER-AMERICAN FCU | Brooklyn | NY | D | D | D+ | <1 | -10.24 | 0.0 | 18.5 | 0.0 | 0.5 | 8.9 | 10.3 |
| INTERCORP CU | Amarillo | TX | C- | C- | D+ | 5.1 | -2.50 | 0.0 | 51.3 | 0.0 | 0.0 | 10.0 | 15.3 |
| INTERNAL REVENUE EMPL FCU | Greensboro | NC | C | C | C- | 22.5 | -5.33 | 0.0 | 6.9 | 11.0 | 10.8 | 10.0 | 12.8 |
| ▼ INTERNAL REVENUE FCU | New Orleans | LA | C- | C | B- | 11.9 | 1.03 | 0.0 | 25.0 | 11.4 | 0.0 | 10.0 | 17.9 |
| INTERNATIONAL UAW FCU | Detroit | MI | C | C | D | 24.2 | -7.56 | 0.0 | 10.3 | 12.7 | 0.0 | 9.1 | 10.4 |
| INTERNATIONALITES FCU | Carlsbad | NM | B | B | B- | 10.6 | 2.30 | 0.0 | 47.7 | 0.0 | 0.0 | 10.0 | 15.4 |
| INTERNET ARCHIVE FCU | New Brunswick | NJ | D- | D | E- | 2.6 | -6.98 | 0.0 | 1.5 | 0.0 | 0.0 | 10.0 | 13.5 |
| INTERRA CU | Goshen | IN | B | B | B | 759.6 | 7.66 | 30.7 | 21.1 | 39.6 | 17.0 | 10.0 | 11.7 |
| INTERSTATE UNLIMITED FCU | Jesup | GA | A- | A- | B+ | 93.9 | 19.62 | 0.1 | 52.8 | 11.9 | 16.2 | 10.0 | 12.5 |
| INTOUCH CU | Plano | TX | D+ | D+ | D+ | 750.8 | -8.26 | 1.2 | 45.4 | 25.6 | 12.3 | 7.8 | 9.6 |
| INVESTEX CU | Houston | TX | B | B- | B- | 184.1 | 3.98 | 0.0 | 41.9 | 8.5 | 33.6 | 8.0 | 9.7 |
| IOWA HEARTLAND CU | Mason City | IA | C+ | B- | B- | 22.4 | 4.30 | 0.0 | 35.5 | 16.6 | 24.2 | 10.0 | 18.7 |
| ▲ IQ CU | Vancouver | WA | B+ | B | B | 798.6 | 8.89 | 13.2 | 38.9 | 19.3 | 12.2 | 6.9 | 8.9 |
| IRCO COMMUNITY FCU | Phillipsburg | NJ | D | D | C- | 71.9 | 15.91 | 0.0 | 15.5 | 23.9 | 9.0 | 8.4 | 9.9 |
| IRON COUNTY COMMUNITY CU | Hurley | WI | C+ | C+ | C+ | 23.8 | 8.57 | 0.6 | 25.3 | 20.8 | 0.0 | 10.0 | 11.9 |
| IRON MOUNTAIN KINGSFORD COMMUNITY F | Kingsford | MI | C- | C- | C | 85.9 | 2.72 | 0.0 | 21.3 | 17.2 | 10.3 | 10.0 | 14.4 |
| IRON WORKERS FCU | Pittsburgh | PA | D- | D- | D- | 6.3 | 6.04 | 1.2 | 20.3 | 31.9 | 11.9 | 6.9 | 8.9 |
| IRONDEQUOIT FCU | Rochester | NY | E+ | E+ | E+ | 5.2 | -3.85 | 0.0 | 54.8 | 4.8 | 0.0 | 4.4 | 6.4 |
| IRS BUFFALO FCU | Buffalo | NY | E+ | E+ | E+ | 4.5 | -1.86 | 0.0 | 57.3 | 13.2 | 0.0 | 5.9 | 7.9 |
| IRSE CU | Springfield | IL | D+ | C- | C- | 8.9 | 1.85 | 0.0 | 39.8 | 0.0 | 0.0 | 10.0 | 11.1 |
| IRVIN WORKS FCU | West Mifflin | PA | B- | B- | B | 21.2 | -2.45 | 0.0 | 41.4 | 0.0 | 0.0 | 10.0 | 26.7 |
| IRVING CITY EMPL FCU | Irving | TX | C+ | C+ | B- | 54.3 | 6.52 | 0.0 | 36.9 | 3.8 | 0.0 | 10.0 | 12.8 |
| ISABELLA COMMUNITY CU | Mount Pleasant | MI | B- | B- | B- | 102.5 | 8.22 | 2.6 | 37.3 | 22.3 | 13.2 | 7.2 | 9.1 |
| ISLAND FCU | Hauppauge | NY | B- | B | B | 1060.1 | 7.03 | 0.7 | 8.2 | 22.1 | 49.7 | 7.8 | 9.6 |
| ISRAEL MEMORIAL AME FCU | Newark | NJ | D | D | C- | <1 | -7.18 | 0.0 | 15.5 | 0.0 | 0.0 | 10.0 | 29.4 |
| ISRAEL METHCOMM FCU | Chicago | IL | C- | C- | C- | 1.2 | 4.67 | 0.0 | 14.8 | 0.0 | 0.0 | 10.0 | 11.0 |
| ▲ ISSAQUENA COUNTY FCU | Mayersville | MS | C | C- | C | 1.2 | 2.43 | 0.0 | 32.7 | 0.3 | 0.0 | 10.0 | 14.0 |
| ITALO-AMERICAN FCU | Glendale | NY | B- | B- | B | 17.9 | 8.19 | 8.4 | 0.0 | 76.0 | 0.0 | 9.5 | 10.6 |
| ITRUST FCU | Memphis | TN | C+ | C+ | C+ | 18.6 | 6.14 | 0.0 | 39.1 | 0.0 | 0.0 | 10.0 | 11.8 |
| ▼ ITT ROANOKE EMPL FCU | Roanoke | VA | D- | D | D+ | 3.6 | -11.55 | 0.0 | 64.0 | 0.0 | 0.0 | 5.7 | 7.7 |
| IU 7 FCU | New Kensington | PA | C+ | C+ | C+ | 21.1 | -0.79 | 0.0 | 20.5 | 0.3 | 0.0 | 10.0 | 13.5 |
| ▲ IUPAT DC 21 FCU | Philadelphia | PA | D | D- | D- | 1.6 | -5.83 | 0.0 | 0.0 | 0.0 | 0.0 | 6.6 | 8.6 |
| J D M H FCU | Jeannette | PA | C- | C- | C- | 4.8 | -4.15 | 0.0 | 53.7 | 0.0 | 0.0 | 10.0 | 38.4 |
| ▲ JACK DANIEL EMPL CU | Lynchburg | TN | B- | C+ | C- | 27.1 | 2.66 | 0.0 | 29.6 | 27.6 | 5.2 | 7.7 | 9.4 |
| JACKSON ACCO CU | Jackson | MS | C | C | C | 2.8 | 3.22 | 0.0 | 63.7 | 0.0 | 0.0 | 10.0 | 19.1 |
| JACKSON AREA FCU | Jackson | MS | B | B | B | 64.9 | 1.66 | 0.0 | 29.7 | 0.0 | 0.0 | 10.0 | 12.5 |
| JACKSON COMMUNITY FCU | Jackson | MI | C | C | C | 23.6 | -2.27 | 0.0 | 32.2 | 22.1 | 25.1 | 10.0 | 13.8 |
| JACKSON COUNTY COOPERATIVE CU | Seymour | IN | C+ | C+ | C+ | 22.2 | -0.48 | 71.6 | 5.2 | 31.3 | 0.0 | 10.0 | 14.8 |
| JACKSON COUNTY FCU | Edna | TX | D- | D- | D- | 6.6 | 2.87 | 0.0 | 45.0 | 14.3 | 0.0 | 5.8 | 7.8 |
| JACKSON COUNTY TEACHERS CU | Marianna | FL | B+ | B+ | B | 25.4 | 1.20 | 0.0 | 45.8 | 0.0 | 0.0 | 10.0 | 24.8 |
| JACKSON COUNTY TEACHERS FCU | Edna | TX | C | C | C | 7.3 | -2.60 | 0.0 | 30.7 | 12.8 | 0.0 | 10.0 | 12.1 |
| JACKSON RIVER COMMUNITY CU | Covington | VA | C+ | C | C | 76.8 | 4.62 | 0.0 | 13.7 | 8.5 | 43.1 | 10.0 | 11.1 |
| JACKSONVILLE FIREMENS CU | Jacksonville | FL | B- | B- | B- | 31.7 | -0.99 | 1.6 | 22.4 | 22.5 | 2.4 | 10.0 | 12.2 |
| JACKSONVILLE POSTAL & PROFESSIONAL C | Jacksonville | FL | C+ | C+ | C+ | 43.7 | 1.81 | 0.0 | 16.7 | 17.2 | 5.6 | 10.0 | 18.9 |
| JACL CU | Glendale | AZ | D | D | C- | <1 | -12.37 | 0.0 | 38.4 | 0.0 | 0.0 | 10.0 | 20.9 |
| JACO FCU | Ruston | LA | C | C | C | 13.4 | -1.24 | 0.0 | 12.3 | 29.4 | 0.0 | 10.0 | 15.5 |
| JACOM CU | Los Angeles | CA | D+ | D | C- | 77.8 | -1.72 | 10.7 | 10.3 | 15.0 | 10.6 | 10.0 | 14.2 |
| JAMES WARD JR FCU | Jennings | LA | C- | C- | D+ | 2.1 | -2.86 | 2.7 | 40.1 | 11.4 | 0.0 | 10.0 | 25.9 |
| JAMESTOWN AREA COMMUNITY FCU | Jamestown | NY | D+ | C- | C | 46.7 | 4.11 | 0.0 | 27.2 | 14.9 | 0.0 | 5.5 | 7.5 |
| JAMESTOWN POST OFFICE EMPL CU | Jamestown | NY | D+ | D+ | C- | 4.7 | -0.13 | 0.0 | 27.1 | 0.0 | 0.0 | 10.0 | 13.2 |
| JAX FCU | Jacksonville | FL | B | C+ | B- | 342.9 | 5.30 | 0.4 | 40.6 | 17.1 | 9.7 | 8.5 | 10.0 |
| JAX GLIDCO EMPL FCU | Jacksonville | FL | E+ | E+ | E+ | 2.1 | -0.52 | 0.0 | 59.9 | 0.0 | 0.0 | 6.9 | 8.9 |
| ▲ JAX METRO CU | Jacksonville | FL | C+ | C | C | 39.2 | -1.26 | 2.1 | 35.2 | 9.3 | 26.3 | 10.0 | 11.6 |
| JAY BEE EMPL FCU | Bethlehem | PA | C | C | C- | 1.5 | 10.01 | 0.0 | 37.8 | 0.0 | 10.1 | 10.0 | 12.8 |

| Asset Quality Index | Non-Performing Loans as a % of Total Loans | Non-Performing Loans as a % of Capital | Net Charge-Offs Avg Loans | Profitability Index | Net Income ($Mil) | Return on Assets | Return on Equity | Net Interest Spread | Overhead Efficiency Ratio | Liquidity Index | Liquidity Ratio | Hot Money Ratio | Stability Index |
|---|---|---|---|---|---|---|---|---|---|---|---|---|---|
| 6.3 | 1.71 | 10.6 | 1.05 | 2.4 | -0.5 | -0.12 | -1.15 | 3.56 | 89.3 | 4.9 | 22.4 | 3.2 | 6.0 |
| 9.5 | 0.12 | 1.0 | 0.32 | 4.7 | 0.5 | 0.79 | 8.25 | 4.54 | 81.6 | 3.4 | 9.4 | 1.3 | 4.1 |
| 9.7 | 0.24 | 1.4 | 0.32 | 4.0 | 4.1 | 0.52 | 5.18 | 2.91 | 77.2 | 3.9 | 8.8 | 0.0 | 6.9 |
| 10.0 | 0.10 | 0.3 | 0.09 | 1.5 | 0.0 | 0.00 | 0.00 | 2.32 | 100.0 | 5.6 | 40.3 | 1.1 | 5.8 |
| 6.8 | 1.87 | 8.3 | 1.21 | 2.5 | 0.1 | 0.15 | 1.53 | 3.80 | 83.3 | 4.6 | 19.8 | 1.0 | 4.5 |
| 3.4 | 1.99 | 21.3 | 0.03 | 1.7 | 0.0 | 0.15 | 1.69 | 3.46 | 95.4 | 3.2 | 7.9 | 2.4 | 4.2 |
| 3.1 | 18.18 | 24.8 | 3.33 | 3.1 | 0.0 | 0.69 | 7.33 | 3.09 | 77.8 | 6.8 | 54.7 | 0.0 | 2.3 |
| 7.5 | 1.11 | 4.3 | 0.17 | 1.9 | 0.0 | -0.05 | -0.34 | 3.85 | 96.5 | 2.8 | 37.1 | 29.4 | 6.4 |
| 10.0 | 0.00 | 0.0 | 0.03 | 2.6 | 0.0 | 0.25 | 1.96 | 1.36 | 81.3 | 5.4 | 35.0 | 0.0 | 6.0 |
| 10.0 | 0.41 | 0.9 | 0.68 | 1.6 | 0.0 | 0.15 | 0.82 | 2.89 | 89.1 | 5.5 | 38.6 | 0.0 | 5.3 |
| 7.7 | 1.39 | 3.2 | 0.44 | 3.8 | 0.1 | 0.31 | 3.06 | 2.75 | 88.4 | 5.5 | 30.1 | 3.8 | 3.2 |
| 8.7 | 0.62 | 1.9 | 0.33 | 5.3 | 0.0 | 0.54 | 3.58 | 3.76 | 83.0 | 6.3 | 47.7 | 0.0 | 8.0 |
| 3.6 | 12.82 | NA | 0.00 | 0.1 | -0.1 | -2.66 | NA | 0.67 | 183.1 | 5.1 | 29.9 | 16.1 | 5.9 |
| 8.8 | 0.28 | 1.8 | 0.11 | 4.2 | 3.1 | 0.55 | 4.81 | 3.34 | 82.4 | 2.9 | 9.1 | 9.3 | 8.8 |
| 6.1 | 0.95 | 7.2 | 0.56 | 10.0 | 1.4 | 2.07 | 16.45 | 4.62 | 63.9 | 2.5 | 9.0 | 16.8 | 7.4 |
| 6.4 | 0.83 | 6.2 | 0.53 | 1.2 | 4.8 | 0.80 | 8.97 | 2.72 | 75.8 | 3.4 | 7.1 | 3.3 | 5.0 |
| 8.9 | 0.82 | 4.7 | 0.38 | 5.0 | 1.1 | 0.79 | 8.72 | 3.68 | 81.2 | 3.9 | 5.6 | 3.7 | 5.1 |
| 9.8 | 0.42 | 1.2 | 0.39 | 2.2 | 0.0 | 0.01 | 0.03 | 3.61 | 95.1 | 4.6 | 22.9 | 0.8 | 7.4 |
| 9.0 | 0.32 | 2.8 | 0.19 | 5.9 | 5.1 | 0.87 | 10.17 | 3.80 | 76.4 | 3.9 | 10.6 | 2.8 | 6.7 |
| 6.0 | 1.68 | 10.5 | 0.38 | 1.2 | 0.0 | -0.07 | -0.87 | 3.50 | 96.7 | 4.2 | 19.5 | 1.9 | 2.2 |
| 4.4 | 3.21 | 16.4 | 1.37 | 5.2 | 0.1 | 0.80 | 6.64 | 4.36 | 82.7 | 5.5 | 44.9 | 2.0 | 6.4 |
| 9.6 | 0.74 | 2.3 | 0.23 | 1.4 | 0.0 | 0.01 | 0.04 | 2.68 | 96.7 | 5.7 | 35.5 | 1.3 | 6.8 |
| 3.4 | 4.60 | 26.3 | 0.08 | 1.4 | 0.0 | 0.07 | 0.71 | 3.77 | 98.3 | 5.2 | 32.7 | 2.1 | 1.0 |
| 4.0 | 1.34 | 13.0 | 0.00 | 0.6 | 0.0 | -0.22 | -3.57 | 4.42 | 104.4 | 4.6 | 17.6 | 0.0 | 1.2 |
| 4.6 | 1.03 | 8.9 | 0.56 | 3.1 | 0.0 | 0.53 | 7.10 | 4.48 | 86.6 | 4.1 | 17.4 | 0.0 | 1.0 |
| 7.3 | 2.01 | 8.2 | 0.10 | 1.7 | 0.0 | 0.18 | 1.62 | 2.45 | 93.3 | 4.3 | 18.3 | 0.0 | 5.4 |
| 9.7 | 0.88 | 1.8 | 0.53 | 4.3 | 0.1 | 0.49 | 1.97 | 3.98 | 79.9 | 5.3 | 40.5 | 0.0 | 7.3 |
| 9.7 | 0.41 | 1.4 | 0.23 | 2.5 | 0.1 | 0.34 | 2.62 | 2.66 | 84.1 | 4.8 | 29.5 | 2.1 | 6.6 |
| 7.7 | 0.81 | 5.5 | 0.28 | 4.1 | 0.4 | 0.48 | 5.36 | 3.60 | 85.8 | 4.0 | 16.4 | 1.8 | 6.1 |
| 10.0 | 0.45 | 2.1 | 0.17 | 3.9 | 4.2 | 0.55 | 5.74 | 2.27 | 73.9 | 3.1 | 3.4 | 14.2 | 7.5 |
| 8.6 | 6.34 | 5.0 | 0.00 | 0.0 | 0.0 | -0.86 | -3.00 | 2.38 | 136.4 | 7.2 | 107.4 | 0.0 | 5.6 |
| 0.3 | 9.44 | 53.0 | 0.00 | 8.0 | 0.0 | 1.44 | 13.33 | 4.93 | 45.8 | 7.2 | 58.8 | 0.0 | 5.3 |
| 3.7 | 15.23 | 30.9 | 0.00 | 9.4 | 0.0 | 2.42 | 18.33 | 5.08 | 57.7 | 6.7 | 79.3 | 0.0 | 8.0 |
| 7.5 | 0.29 | 2.1 | 0.00 | 9.5 | 0.2 | 1.54 | 14.91 | 2.61 | 39.0 | 2.5 | 17.3 | 18.5 | 5.7 |
| 8.9 | 0.58 | 2.0 | 1.21 | 3.2 | 0.0 | 0.11 | 0.92 | 5.28 | 97.9 | 3.8 | 16.1 | 12.7 | 6.1 |
| 4.2 | 1.65 | 11.9 | 1.93 | 0.2 | 0.0 | -0.83 | -10.69 | 5.23 | 115.7 | 5.1 | 36.6 | 0.0 | 2.3 |
| 6.9 | 2.41 | 9.6 | 0.20 | 3.1 | 0.1 | 0.35 | 2.65 | 2.63 | 77.6 | 2.7 | 17.6 | 19.2 | 6.3 |
| 6.7 | 3.64 | 7.8 | 0.00 | 3.1 | 0.0 | 0.41 | 5.13 | 2.93 | 72.2 | 7.9 | 85.0 | 0.0 | 2.3 |
| 7.7 | 1.68 | 2.6 | 0.82 | 3.7 | 0.0 | 0.33 | 0.87 | 4.52 | 78.5 | 5.6 | 38.8 | 0.0 | 6.3 |
| 7.0 | 0.50 | 3.3 | 0.23 | 7.7 | 0.2 | 1.17 | 12.93 | 3.31 | 68.0 | 2.7 | 17.1 | 17.3 | 5.7 |
| 7.5 | 0.96 | 3.3 | -0.07 | 5.7 | 0.0 | 0.58 | 3.04 | 7.20 | 92.9 | 4.5 | 38.4 | 4.5 | 4.3 |
| 9.5 | 0.88 | 3.1 | 0.31 | 3.5 | 0.2 | 0.33 | 2.68 | 4.08 | 91.9 | 6.9 | 46.4 | 2.2 | 6.1 |
| 6.2 | 1.61 | 11.3 | 0.43 | 2.2 | 0.0 | 0.05 | 0.41 | 4.44 | 94.5 | 3.9 | 10.0 | 3.6 | 5.5 |
| 6.5 | 0.19 | 0.9 | 0.00 | 3.3 | 0.0 | 0.24 | 1.58 | 3.42 | 92.9 | 3.9 | 28.8 | 7.2 | 7.4 |
| 8.4 | 0.00 | 0.0 | -0.03 | 2.5 | 0.0 | 0.21 | 2.63 | 3.02 | 91.4 | 4.2 | 29.8 | 7.7 | 1.7 |
| 8.2 | 0.14 | 0.4 | 1.58 | 6.5 | 0.1 | 0.67 | 3.19 | 7.65 | 72.8 | 5.7 | 40.3 | 8.2 | 7.2 |
| 9.8 | 0.00 | 0.0 | 0.00 | 1.8 | 0.0 | 0.04 | 0.30 | 1.88 | 96.0 | 4.8 | 44.3 | 1.7 | 6.2 |
| 9.6 | 0.82 | 2.0 | 0.23 | 2.6 | 0.1 | 0.24 | 2.20 | 2.01 | 90.5 | 5.7 | 19.6 | 1.7 | 5.3 |
| 3.7 | 3.70 | 21.7 | 0.29 | 3.1 | 0.0 | -0.04 | -0.31 | 4.39 | 100.9 | 5.6 | 40.4 | 10.3 | 5.3 |
| 10.0 | 0.19 | 0.6 | 0.41 | 2.0 | 0.0 | 0.10 | 0.54 | 2.97 | 92.1 | 5.7 | 41.1 | 8.8 | 6.4 |
| 9.7 | 0.00 | 0.0 | 0.00 | 0.0 | 0.0 | -1.88 | -9.16 | 2.12 | 188.9 | 6.5 | 44.4 | 0.0 | 6.2 |
| 5.1 | 3.84 | 16.6 | 0.15 | 4.5 | 0.1 | 0.70 | 4.64 | 3.54 | 75.3 | 5.0 | 37.9 | 0.0 | 7.2 |
| 10.0 | 0.42 | 1.1 | -0.01 | 1.0 | 0.0 | -0.05 | -0.36 | 3.67 | 101.7 | 7.1 | 47.6 | 0.0 | 5.9 |
| 5.0 | 7.22 | 15.0 | 0.46 | 3.6 | 0.0 | 0.44 | 1.75 | 4.51 | 88.7 | 5.6 | 58.6 | 0.0 | 7.0 |
| 8.6 | 0.37 | 2.1 | -0.03 | 2.0 | 0.0 | 0.09 | 1.15 | 3.49 | 96.3 | 5.1 | 27.6 | 0.0 | 2.7 |
| 10.0 | 0.07 | 0.2 | 0.00 | 0.9 | 0.0 | -0.03 | -0.21 | 3.42 | 100.8 | 4.7 | 13.5 | 0.0 | 4.8 |
| 8.1 | 0.66 | 4.9 | 0.25 | 4.5 | 1.7 | 0.68 | 6.88 | 3.74 | 83.7 | 4.3 | 19.8 | 3.0 | 6.1 |
| 5.1 | 1.33 | 8.8 | 0.11 | 1.9 | 0.0 | 0.12 | 1.43 | 3.84 | 96.9 | 4.6 | 15.5 | 0.0 | 1.0 |
| 7.1 | 1.39 | 6.8 | 0.14 | 3.4 | 0.2 | 0.49 | 4.42 | 4.04 | 87.5 | 4.4 | 14.3 | 1.6 | 5.5 |
| 9.7 | 0.00 | 0.0 | 0.00 | 3.2 | 0.0 | 0.45 | 3.55 | 2.89 | 84.6 | 6.7 | 53.6 | 0.0 | 6.1 |

| Name | City | State | Rating | 2014 Rating | 2013 Rating | Total Assets ($Mil) | One Year Asset Growth | Asset Mix (As a % of Total Assets) | | | | Capital-ization Index | Net Worth Ratio |
|------|------|-------|--------|-------------|-------------|---------------------|----------------------|-----------------|-----------------|----------------|------------|----------------------|-----------------|
| | | | | | | | | Comm-ercial Loans | Cons-umer Loans | Mort-gage Loans | Secur-ities | | |
| JC FEDERAL EMPL CU | Jefferson City | MO | C | C | C | 2.6 | 7.29 | 0.0 | 59.2 | 0.0 | 0.0 | 10.0 | 17.7 |
| JEANNE DARC CU | Lowell | MA | C+ | C+ | C+ | 1154.6 | 8.43 | 16.5 | 9.3 | 57.1 | 16.1 | 6.2 | 8.3 |
| ▼ JEEP COUNTRY FCU | Holland | OH | C+ | B | B | 61.0 | -3.13 | 0.0 | 38.9 | 10.8 | 30.2 | 10.0 | 16.5 |
| JEFF DAVIS CU | Hazlehurst | GA | D | D | C- | 5.0 | -0.74 | 0.0 | 6.7 | 4.8 | 0.0 | 10.0 | 25.3 |
| JEFF DAVIS TEACHERS FCU | Jennings | LA | C | C+ | C+ | 2.9 | -9.27 | 0.0 | 26.4 | 0.0 | 0.0 | 10.0 | 20.9 |
| JEFF-CO SCHOOLS FCU | Mount Vernon | IL | E+ | D- | E+ | 8.6 | 8.11 | 0.0 | 45.5 | 0.0 | 0.0 | 4.5 | 6.5 |
| JEFFCO FCU | Golden | CO | B- | B- | B- | 19.6 | 3.48 | 0.0 | 14.9 | 4.4 | 0.0 | 10.0 | 14.7 |
| JEFFERSON COMMUNITY FCU | Madison | IN | D+ | D- | E+ | 11.0 | 3.42 | 0.0 | 39.7 | 11.0 | 0.0 | 6.0 | 8.0 |
| ▼ JEFFERSON COUNTY FCU | Louisville | KY | C+ | B- | B- | 120.3 | 2.53 | 1.2 | 13.5 | 18.3 | 14.6 | 10.0 | 13.4 |
| JEFFERSON COUNTY PUBLIC EMPL CU | Menan | ID | D | D | C- | <1 | -26.23 | 0.0 | 41.2 | 0.0 | 0.0 | 10.0 | 13.4 |
| JEFFERSON COUNTY TEACHERS CU | Monticello | FL | C | C | C | 9.2 | 13.28 | 0.0 | 39.5 | 0.0 | 0.0 | 10.0 | 13.3 |
| JEFFERSON CU | Hoover | AL | D+ | D+ | D+ | 65.1 | -0.64 | 1.0 | 33.2 | 12.8 | 18.1 | 7.8 | 9.5 |
| ▲ JEFFERSON FINANCIAL CU | Metairie | LA | B | B- | B- | 418.9 | 13.23 | 6.7 | 39.3 | 34.4 | 0.0 | 9.5 | 10.7 |
| JEFFERSON PARISH EMPL FCU | New Orleans | LA | B+ | B+ | B+ | 90.4 | 4.12 | 0.0 | 38.7 | 5.7 | 0.7 | 10.0 | 13.6 |
| JEMEZ VALLEY CU | Jemez Springs | NM | B | B | B | 19.9 | -0.05 | 0.5 | 14.7 | 38.0 | 0.0 | 10.0 | 14.5 |
| JERSEY CENTRAL FCU | Cranford | NJ | C+ | B- | B- | 17.1 | -4.14 | 0.0 | 66.4 | 0.0 | 0.0 | 10.0 | 22.9 |
| ▲ JERSEY CITY FIREMEN FCU | Jersey City | NJ | C+ | C | C+ | 10.3 | 4.55 | 0.0 | 32.5 | 0.0 | 0.0 | 10.0 | 44.0 |
| ▲ JERSEY CITY POLICE FCU | Jersey City | NJ | C+ | C | D+ | 10.1 | -3.20 | 0.0 | 18.8 | 0.0 | 0.0 | 10.0 | 12.3 |
| JERSEY SHORE FCU | Northfield | NJ | C- | C- | C | 126.8 | 1.92 | 8.8 | 10.3 | 20.4 | 30.1 | 5.2 | 7.2 |
| JESSOP COMMUNITY FCU | Washington | PA | D+ | D+ | D- | 33.4 | 1.05 | 0.0 | 15.5 | 2.2 | 30.0 | 7.1 | 9.0 |
| JETSTREAM FCU | Miami Lakes | FL | B+ | B+ | B- | 171.7 | 4.38 | 8.9 | 50.5 | 4.9 | 11.0 | 10.0 | 11.9 |
| JM ASSOCIATES FCU | Jacksonville | FL | A | A | A- | 102.1 | 2.49 | 0.0 | 28.3 | 5.7 | 53.5 | 10.0 | 13.9 |
| JOHN WESLEY AME ZION CHURCH FCU | Washington | DC | C+ | C+ | C- | <1 | -11.70 | 0.0 | 1.2 | 0.0 | 0.0 | 9.8 | 10.8 |
| JOHNS HOPKINS FCU | Baltimore | MD | A- | A- | A- | 377.8 | 2.67 | 0.0 | 17.3 | 24.0 | 23.2 | 10.0 | 11.5 |
| JOHNSONVILLE TVA EMPL CU | Camden | TN | B+ | B+ | B+ | 88.0 | 7.89 | 0.0 | 32.6 | 7.0 | 3.4 | 10.0 | 14.2 |
| JOHNSTOWN SCHOOL EMPL FCU | Johnstown | PA | C+ | C+ | C+ | 8.6 | 0.83 | 1.2 | 32.2 | 4.7 | 56.7 | 10.0 | 17.0 |
| JOLIET FIREFIGHTERS CU | Joliet | IL | D | D | D | 6.3 | 6.35 | 0.0 | 43.2 | 0.0 | 0.0 | 6.5 | 8.5 |
| JOLIET MUNICIPAL EMPL FCU | Joliet | IL | C- | C- | C- | 7.7 | 7.87 | 0.0 | 43.5 | 0.0 | 0.0 | 8.5 | 10.0 |
| JONES METHODIST CHURCH CU | San Francisco | CA | D | D | C- | <1 | -14.68 | 0.0 | 12.4 | 0.0 | 22.4 | 10.0 | 22.0 |
| ▲ JOPLIN METRO CU | Joplin | MO | B- | C+ | C | 26.0 | 4.28 | 0.0 | 49.2 | 0.0 | 0.0 | 8.8 | 10.2 |
| ▼ JORDAN FCU | Sandy | UT | C+ | B- | B- | 238.1 | 3.04 | 4.4 | 23.7 | 25.0 | 9.8 | 6.9 | 9.0 |
| JOSTEN EMPL CU | Owatonna | MN | C- | C- | C- | 1.2 | 3.88 | 0.0 | 85.8 | 0.0 | 0.0 | 10.0 | 31.4 |
| JOURNEY FCU | Saint Johns | MI | C | C+ | C+ | 95.2 | 0.52 | 0.3 | 25.7 | 12.7 | 14.5 | 9.4 | 10.6 |
| ▲ JOY EMPL FCU | Bluefield | VA | C | C | C | 2.3 | -4.06 | 0.0 | 67.2 | 0.0 | 0.0 | 10.0 | 14.8 |
| JPFCE FCU | Jackson | MS | C | C | C | 1.1 | 0.75 | 0.0 | 57.0 | 0.0 | 0.0 | 10.0 | 21.9 |
| JSC FCU | Houston | TX | B- | B- | B | 1875.1 | 3.20 | 0.1 | 16.9 | 7.1 | 63.0 | 9.1 | 10.4 |
| JSTC EMPL FCU | Johnstown | PA | C | C | C- | 23.4 | -0.98 | 0.0 | 27.5 | 7.8 | 0.0 | 10.0 | 15.4 |
| JUDDS FCU | Gaithersburg | MD | D+ | D+ | C- | 2.1 | 3.82 | 0.0 | 39.6 | 0.0 | 49.1 | 10.0 | 16.9 |
| JUDICIAL & JUSTICE FCU | New Orleans | LA | D+ | D+ | C- | 2.2 | 0.32 | 0.0 | 39.3 | 0.0 | 0.0 | 10.0 | 11.9 |
| ▼ JUNCTION BELL FCU | Grand Junction | CO | D- | D | C- | 20.5 | 7.71 | 2.4 | 16.8 | 12.0 | 49.8 | 9.8 | 10.8 |
| ▲ JUNIOR COLLEGE FCU | Perkinston | MS | C- | D+ | C- | 1.8 | 0.51 | 0.0 | 21.4 | 0.0 | 0.0 | 10.0 | 20.3 |
| JUSTICE FCU | Chantilly | VA | A- | B+ | B+ | 663.9 | 6.32 | 0.8 | 32.7 | 23.1 | 18.9 | 8.9 | 10.3 |
| K G C FCU | Knox | PA | D- | D | D | 5.3 | 4.17 | 0.0 | 44.6 | 0.0 | 0.0 | 6.3 | 8.4 |
| K I T FCU | Louisville | KY | D+ | D | E | 11.7 | 10.14 | 0.8 | 50.6 | 20.8 | 0.0 | 7.0 | 9.0 |
| K&E EMPL FCU | Hoboken | NJ | D+ | D+ | D+ | <1 | -1.60 | 0.0 | 15.3 | 0.0 | 0.0 | 10.0 | 28.6 |
| ▼ KAH CU | Keokuk | IA | D+ | D+ | C | 1.9 | -3.41 | 0.0 | 43.2 | 0.0 | 0.0 | 10.0 | 29.0 |
| KAHUKU FCU | Kahuku | HI | D- | D | D- | 5.4 | 8.52 | 0.0 | 87.5 | 0.0 | 0.0 | 8.7 | 10.1 |
| ▲ KAHULUI FCU | Kahului | HI | C | C- | C | 55.7 | 0.56 | 0.5 | 10.3 | 20.1 | 30.3 | 10.0 | 15.7 |
| KAIPERM FCU | Walnut Creek | CA | C+ | C+ | C+ | 70.2 | 0.78 | 2.2 | 8.4 | 17.2 | 13.9 | 10.0 | 12.8 |
| KAIPERM NORTH BAY FCU | Vallejo | CA | C | C- | C | 36.6 | 2.56 | 10.1 | 27.0 | 17.3 | 0.0 | 9.0 | 10.4 |
| KAIPERM NORTHWEST FCU | Portland | OR | B | B | B | 71.3 | 3.37 | 2.7 | 21.7 | 16.3 | 37.6 | 8.7 | 10.1 |
| KALAMAZOO BUILDING TRADES CU | Kalamazoo | MI | D | D | C- | 3.0 | -12.04 | 0.0 | 36.5 | 0.0 | 41.6 | 10.0 | 14.6 |
| ▲ KALEIDA HEALTH FCU | Buffalo | NY | D- | E+ | D- | 14.0 | 4.70 | 0.0 | 46.6 | 0.0 | 0.0 | 5.1 | 7.1 |
| KALSEE CU | Kalamazoo | MI | B- | B | B | 168.8 | 16.55 | 4.5 | 51.4 | 21.0 | 15.1 | 9.0 | 10.5 |
| KAMEHAMEHA FCU | Honolulu | HI | C- | C- | C | 36.8 | -1.55 | 0.0 | 11.7 | 11.4 | 10.8 | 10.0 | 12.8 |
| KAMIAH COMMUNITY CU | Kamiah | ID | A- | A- | A- | 66.3 | 16.89 | 1.2 | 18.4 | 50.1 | 2.7 | 10.0 | 12.4 |
| KAN COLO CU | Hoisington | KS | D | D+ | C- | <1 | 3.80 | 0.0 | 46.9 | 0.0 | 0.0 | 10.0 | 16.2 |
| ▲ KANE COUNTY TEACHERS CU | Elgin | IL | C+ | C- | D+ | 197.3 | 6.09 | 1.9 | 17.1 | 5.2 | 30.4 | 10.0 | 11.7 |
| KANKAKEE COUNTY FEDERAL EMPL FCU | Kankakee | IL | C- | C | C | 5.0 | -4.34 | 0.0 | 20.4 | 0.0 | 0.0 | 10.0 | 17.4 |
| KANKAKEE FEDERATION OF TEACHERS CU | Kankakee | IL | D+ | D+ | D+ | 8.0 | 0.81 | 0.0 | 61.8 | 0.0 | 0.0 | 10.0 | 13.9 |

| Asset Quality Index | Non-Performing Loans as a % of Total Loans | as a % of Capital | Net Charge-Offs Avg Loans | Profitability Index | Net Income ($Mil) | Return on Assets | Return on Equity | Net Interest Spread | Overhead Efficiency Ratio | Liquidity Index | Liquidity Ratio | Hot Money Ratio | Stability Index |
|---|---|---|---|---|---|---|---|---|---|---|---|---|---|
| 5.0 | 2.89 | 9.9 | 0.42 | 8.4 | 0.0 | 1.15 | 6.67 | 5.27 | 67.5 | 5.5 | 43.6 | 0.0 | 5.0 |
| 7.3 | 0.78 | 6.9 | 0.25 | 3.8 | 4.8 | 0.56 | 6.88 | 2.86 | 77.8 | 2.6 | 22.7 | 16.5 | 5.9 |
| 6.5 | 3.07 | 9.7 | 2.46 | 2.3 | -0.1 | -0.23 | -1.43 | 4.90 | 74.3 | 3.9 | 4.9 | 2.3 | 6.4 |
| 10.0 | 0.26 | 0.2 | 0.32 | 0.0 | -0.1 | -1.48 | -5.71 | 1.83 | 187.5 | 6.5 | 65.8 | 0.0 | 6.0 |
| 8.7 | 3.92 | 5.4 | 0.00 | 3.2 | 0.0 | 0.39 | 1.97 | 2.43 | 82.7 | 5.3 | 24.2 | 0.0 | 7.2 |
| 8.5 | 0.02 | 0.2 | 0.00 | 3.0 | 0.0 | 0.19 | 2.91 | 3.91 | 94.5 | 4.7 | 19.1 | 1.3 | 1.0 |
| 10.0 | 0.00 | 0.0 | -0.03 | 3.9 | 0.1 | 0.54 | 3.71 | 2.87 | 84.3 | 4.3 | 25.0 | 2.7 | 7.2 |
| 8.4 | 0.34 | 2.2 | 0.07 | 3.5 | 0.0 | 0.49 | 6.20 | 3.54 | 91.9 | 5.5 | 30.3 | 0.0 | 2.8 |
| 9.6 | 0.93 | 2.6 | 0.26 | 2.4 | 0.1 | 0.06 | 0.41 | 2.07 | 95.2 | 5.2 | 32.3 | 6.3 | 7.9 |
| 8.2 | 0.00 | 0.0 | 0.00 | 0.0 | 0.0 | -2.47 | -19.51 | 6.82 | 166.7 | 6.5 | 51.2 | 0.0 | 6.0 |
| 8.7 | 0.42 | 1.5 | -0.03 | 4.2 | 0.0 | 0.54 | 3.87 | 3.82 | 85.6 | 3.0 | 15.0 | 16.9 | 6.8 |
| 6.7 | 0.67 | 4.6 | 1.12 | 1.7 | 0.0 | 0.09 | 0.89 | 4.95 | 82.8 | 4.1 | 28.9 | 9.8 | 3.7 |
| 7.0 | 0.63 | 6.2 | 0.37 | 4.8 | 2.2 | 0.75 | 6.79 | 4.32 | 79.5 | 3.2 | 12.3 | 7.8 | 6.7 |
| 6.8 | 1.81 | 6.7 | 1.53 | 5.0 | 0.3 | 0.40 | 3.32 | 4.71 | 84.5 | 5.5 | 35.8 | 4.6 | 6.3 |
| 7.4 | 2.20 | 8.8 | 0.07 | 7.0 | 0.1 | 0.92 | 6.83 | 3.94 | 78.7 | 3.3 | 22.6 | 11.7 | 5.7 |
| 5.0 | 2.78 | 8.0 | 1.83 | 5.0 | 0.1 | 0.39 | 1.75 | 8.05 | 80.7 | 3.5 | 12.7 | 2.8 | 5.0 |
| 9.8 | 2.54 | 1.8 | 0.81 | 3.9 | 0.0 | 0.53 | 1.19 | 3.92 | 84.9 | 6.2 | 70.1 | 2.4 | 6.7 |
| 10.0 | 0.67 | 1.0 | 0.54 | 2.9 | 0.0 | 0.39 | 3.29 | 2.24 | 78.1 | 4.8 | 3.3 | 0.0 | 5.0 |
| 6.7 | 1.09 | 8.7 | 0.25 | 2.0 | 0.2 | 0.16 | 2.19 | 3.11 | 89.7 | 4.1 | 27.8 | 7.0 | 4.0 |
| 6.3 | 2.59 | 9.9 | 0.10 | 1.5 | 0.0 | 0.00 | 0.00 | 2.37 | 99.2 | 5.1 | 19.6 | 5.2 | 3.7 |
| 7.5 | 0.38 | 2.6 | 0.50 | 6.3 | 1.2 | 0.91 | 7.78 | 5.13 | 80.6 | 2.6 | 12.9 | 14.1 | 7.6 |
| 9.5 | 1.10 | 3.2 | 0.89 | 6.5 | 0.6 | 0.73 | 5.57 | 2.96 | 78.5 | 4.7 | 32.3 | 3.6 | 8.4 |
| 8.3 | 0.00 | 0.0 | 0.00 | 4.1 | 0.0 | 0.00 | 0.00 | 0.00 | 200.0 | 8.5 | 109.6 | 0.0 | 6.2 |
| 9.8 | 0.30 | 1.5 | 0.09 | 5.9 | 2.5 | 0.87 | 7.74 | 3.23 | 78.7 | 4.9 | 21.9 | 1.2 | 7.5 |
| 9.3 | 0.58 | 2.1 | 0.17 | 4.3 | 0.4 | 0.58 | 4.29 | 2.86 | 82.2 | 4.9 | 28.8 | 1.9 | 7.3 |
| 10.0 | 0.90 | 2.1 | 0.04 | 4.7 | 0.1 | 0.69 | 4.17 | 2.54 | 71.1 | 4.5 | 14.9 | 0.0 | 7.3 |
| 8.7 | 0.22 | 1.1 | -0.15 | 5.2 | 0.0 | 0.82 | 9.84 | 2.50 | 64.8 | 4.6 | 11.5 | 0.0 | 3.0 |
| 8.0 | 0.96 | 4.0 | 0.64 | 2.9 | 0.0 | 0.14 | 1.39 | 3.26 | 94.9 | 4.5 | 13.9 | 0.0 | 5.8 |
| 9.8 | 0.00 | 0.0 | 0.00 | 0.0 | 0.0 | -1.67 | -7.55 | 4.88 | 216.7 | 8.1 | 81.0 | 0.0 | 4.8 |
| 7.9 | 0.38 | 2.3 | 0.12 | 5.3 | 0.1 | 0.74 | 7.29 | 5.39 | 89.1 | 5.3 | 31.1 | 0.9 | 4.5 |
| 7.7 | 0.59 | 5.1 | 0.29 | 3.3 | 0.5 | 0.29 | 3.40 | 3.45 | 88.7 | 4.8 | 28.7 | 5.5 | 4.8 |
| 8.2 | 0.00 | 0.0 | 0.28 | 2.9 | 0.0 | 0.22 | 0.69 | 4.83 | 97.2 | 4.0 | 19.8 | 0.0 | 7.6 |
| 6.5 | 1.20 | 6.1 | 0.54 | 2.7 | 0.1 | 0.15 | 1.47 | 3.38 | 82.8 | 4.1 | 12.4 | 2.5 | 5.2 |
| 2.7 | 3.78 | 17.4 | 1.68 | 10.0 | 0.0 | 1.68 | 11.97 | 5.19 | 41.5 | 5.5 | 33.0 | 0.0 | 7.8 |
| 8.1 | 0.13 | 0.4 | -0.17 | 4.4 | 0.0 | 0.50 | 2.27 | 6.71 | 92.0 | 4.9 | 33.4 | 0.0 | 4.3 |
| 10.0 | 0.21 | 0.6 | 0.32 | 4.1 | 8.0 | 0.57 | 5.57 | 1.60 | 69.8 | 4.7 | 13.2 | 6.6 | 7.0 |
| 9.4 | 0.90 | 2.8 | 0.32 | 2.2 | 0.0 | 0.06 | 0.41 | 3.90 | 94.3 | 5.5 | 48.1 | 5.9 | 7.2 |
| 8.9 | 1.28 | 3.3 | 0.56 | 0.9 | 0.0 | -0.19 | -1.13 | 4.00 | 100.0 | 4.5 | 17.1 | 0.0 | 6.4 |
| 8.6 | 1.24 | 4.0 | 0.00 | 1.0 | 0.0 | -0.12 | -0.99 | 4.46 | 103.3 | 5.4 | 29.4 | 0.0 | 4.7 |
| 9.6 | 0.24 | 0.9 | 1.04 | 0.1 | -0.1 | -0.44 | -4.46 | 2.79 | 98.7 | 5.0 | 28.0 | 2.5 | 4.2 |
| 9.0 | 0.68 | 1.1 | 0.00 | 2.6 | 0.0 | 0.52 | 2.63 | 3.23 | 104.8 | 5.8 | 82.0 | 0.0 | 5.0 |
| 8.4 | 0.62 | 3.8 | 0.34 | 6.5 | 4.8 | 0.99 | 9.90 | 4.24 | 77.2 | 4.1 | 16.2 | 8.5 | 7.2 |
| 7.1 | 0.58 | 3.0 | 0.80 | 0.6 | 0.0 | -0.30 | -3.49 | 3.36 | 97.1 | 5.8 | 51.1 | 0.0 | 3.6 |
| 2.3 | 2.80 | 24.0 | 0.26 | 8.8 | 0.1 | 1.63 | 18.52 | 6.35 | 73.9 | 3.1 | 13.2 | 9.6 | 3.7 |
| 5.8 | 6.59 | 11.8 | 2.95 | 1.5 | 0.0 | 0.13 | 0.47 | 3.43 | 96.0 | 3.2 | 35.0 | 14.3 | 6.9 |
| 3.3 | 15.60 | 22.4 | 1.52 | 1.8 | 0.0 | -0.07 | -0.24 | 3.83 | 88.6 | 6.4 | 70.2 | 0.0 | 6.5 |
| 0.0 | 12.04 | 88.4 | 2.39 | 3.7 | 0.0 | -0.12 | -1.17 | 7.39 | 60.7 | 1.5 | 13.7 | 48.4 | 6.9 |
| 10.0 | 0.00 | 0.0 | -0.02 | 2.1 | 0.1 | 0.22 | 1.38 | 2.72 | 93.4 | 4.4 | 23.6 | 4.5 | 7.0 |
| 8.7 | 1.64 | 5.1 | 0.02 | 2.5 | 0.1 | 0.15 | 1.19 | 1.87 | 96.4 | 5.3 | 47.2 | 5.4 | 6.4 |
| 9.0 | 0.15 | 0.9 | 0.08 | 2.8 | 0.1 | 0.24 | 2.34 | 3.97 | 93.0 | 4.2 | 13.5 | 3.2 | 4.6 |
| 9.0 | 0.30 | 1.3 | 0.16 | 5.3 | 0.4 | 0.76 | 7.20 | 2.93 | 78.0 | 6.0 | 60.7 | 3.7 | 6.1 |
| 9.6 | 0.00 | 0.0 | 0.00 | 0.0 | 0.0 | -1.74 | -11.99 | 2.54 | 167.8 | 4.8 | 28.3 | 0.0 | 5.6 |
| 4.9 | 1.12 | 8.3 | 0.59 | 6.1 | 0.1 | 0.94 | 13.66 | 3.70 | 68.9 | 5.1 | 27.4 | 0.0 | 2.3 |
| 6.0 | 0.85 | 8.2 | 0.40 | 4.5 | 0.6 | 0.48 | 4.49 | 4.29 | 83.2 | 3.2 | 12.9 | 4.7 | 6.0 |
| 8.0 | 2.44 | 5.5 | 0.22 | 1.5 | 0.0 | -0.02 | -0.14 | 2.44 | 100.9 | 4.6 | 20.8 | 3.4 | 5.8 |
| 5.9 | 1.77 | 12.2 | 0.35 | 9.8 | 0.7 | 1.45 | 11.39 | 4.85 | 63.5 | 3.7 | 19.3 | 9.3 | 7.8 |
| 0.7 | 14.89 | 38.7 | -0.31 | 2.3 | 0.0 | 0.00 | 0.00 | 4.34 | 100.0 | 5.3 | 24.6 | 0.0 | 6.4 |
| 10.0 | 0.71 | 2.0 | 0.70 | 2.7 | 0.5 | 0.35 | 3.05 | 2.95 | 83.1 | 4.9 | 23.1 | 0.9 | 6.5 |
| 10.0 | 1.53 | 1.8 | -0.49 | 1.5 | 0.0 | 0.00 | 0.00 | 2.98 | 100.0 | 6.6 | 58.6 | 3.7 | 5.7 |
| 3.8 | 2.95 | 13.5 | 0.67 | 3.5 | 0.0 | 0.55 | 4.02 | 2.04 | 70.8 | 4.4 | 27.6 | 0.0 | 3.0 |

| Name | City | State | Rating | 2014 Rating | 2013 Rating | Total Assets ($Mil) | One Year Asset Growth | Comm-ercial Loans | Cons-umer Loans | Mort-gage Loans | Secur-ities | Capital-ization Index | Net Worth Ratio |
|---|---|---|---|---|---|---|---|---|---|---|---|---|---|
| | | | | | | | | Asset Mix (As a % of Total Assets) | | | | | |
| KANKAKEE TERMINAL BELT CU | Kankakee | IL | C- | C- | C- | 5.0 | 7.55 | 0.0 | 82.9 | 0.0 | 0.0 | 10.0 | 12.2 |
| KANSAS AIR GUARD CU | Topeka | KS | C | C+ | C+ | 5.0 | -3.58 | 0.0 | 71.0 | 0.0 | 0.0 | 10.0 | 15.6 |
| KANSAS BLUE CROSS-BLUE SHIELD CU | Topeka | KS | B+ | B+ | B+ | 36.4 | -1.35 | 0.0 | 31.7 | 22.2 | 4.8 | 10.0 | 15.0 |
| ▲ KANSAS CITY CU | Kansas City | MO | C+ | C+ | B- | 31.1 | 7.76 | 0.0 | 15.6 | 6.7 | 30.8 | 10.0 | 11.6 |
| KANSAS CITY KANSAS FIREMEN & POLICE C | Kansas City | KS | B- | B- | C+ | 13.1 | 7.07 | 0.0 | 53.4 | 0.0 | 0.0 | 10.0 | 18.8 |
| ▼ KANSAS CITY P&G EMPL CU | Kansas City | KS | D+ | C- | C- | 4.2 | -1.92 | 0.0 | 46.5 | 0.0 | 0.0 | 10.0 | 26.2 |
| KANSAS STATE UNIV FCU | Manhattan | KS | B- | B- | B- | 72.5 | 4.35 | 0.2 | 41.3 | 13.4 | 13.8 | 8.1 | 9.7 |
| KANSAS TEACHERS COMMUNITY CU | Pittsburg | KS | B | B | B+ | 81.6 | 1.89 | 0.1 | 34.2 | 19.1 | 14.7 | 10.0 | 11.5 |
| KASE FCU | Vandergrift | PA | C- | C- | C- | 1.4 | -8.13 | 0.0 | 44.3 | 0.0 | 0.0 | 10.0 | 14.0 |
| KASKASKIA VALLEY COMMUNITY CU | Centralia | IL | D | D- | D- | 11.5 | 2.88 | 0.0 | 67.1 | 0.0 | 0.0 | 5.8 | 7.8 |
| KATAHDIN FCU | Millinocket | ME | C+ | C+ | C+ | 68.3 | 1.30 | 1.0 | 27.5 | 37.2 | 9.2 | 10.0 | 12.6 |
| KAUAI COMMUNITY FCU | Lihue | HI | B+ | B+ | B | 413.6 | 10.15 | 0.5 | 22.5 | 18.7 | 29.2 | 8.4 | 10.0 |
| ▼ KAUAI GOVERNMENT EMPL FCU | Lihue | HI | C+ | B- | B- | 108.6 | 2.65 | 0.4 | 29.1 | 31.0 | 17.2 | 6.8 | 8.8 |
| KAUAI TEACHERS FCU | Lihue | HI | C- | D+ | D- | 29.0 | -1.30 | 0.0 | 7.8 | 10.0 | 24.7 | 6.9 | 9.4 |
| ▼ KBR CU | Tacoma | WA | C+ | B- | C | 21.6 | 0.00 | 0.0 | 21.3 | 19.3 | 0.0 | 10.0 | 14.3 |
| ▼ KBR HERITAGE FCU | Houston | TX | C+ | B | B- | 91.0 | -0.87 | 0.1 | 18.7 | 6.9 | 38.2 | 10.0 | 11.8 |
| KC AREA CU | Kansas City | MO | C | C- | D+ | 5.3 | 4.46 | 0.0 | 35.8 | 0.0 | 0.0 | 10.0 | 11.5 |
| KC FAIRFAX FCU | Kansas City | KS | C- | D+ | D+ | 9.2 | -0.09 | 0.0 | 34.8 | 3.6 | 0.0 | 10.0 | 14.5 |
| KC TERMINAL EMPL/GUADALUPE CENTER F | Kansas City | MO | D+ | D | D+ | 2.3 | 12.00 | 0.0 | 76.8 | 0.0 | 0.0 | 10.0 | 15.5 |
| KCUMB CU | Kansas City | MO | C | C- | C+ | <1 | -4.79 | 0.0 | 24.5 | 0.0 | 0.0 | 10.0 | 26.0 |
| KEARNEY FCU | Kearney | NE | C- | C- | C- | 60.8 | 56.62 | 0.2 | 71.0 | 2.5 | 1.2 | 6.0 | 8.0 |
| KEARNY MUNICIPAL EMPL FCU | Kearny | NJ | C | C- | C- | 9.5 | -2.56 | 0.0 | 12.3 | 0.0 | 84.9 | 10.0 | 15.2 |
| KEESLER FCU | Biloxi | MS | A | A | A | 2290.3 | 5.37 | 0.5 | 34.8 | 14.1 | 36.8 | 10.0 | 14.1 |
| ▲ KEKAHA FCU | Kekaha | HI | C- | D | D+ | 19.4 | 3.17 | 1.8 | 9.5 | 40.0 | 3.1 | 10.0 | 20.2 |
| ▲ KELCO FCU | Cumberland | MD | B- | C | C | 50.6 | 1.80 | 3.7 | 16.3 | 29.6 | 0.0 | 10.0 | 12.9 |
| KELLOGG COMMUNITY FCU | Battle Creek | MI | A | A- | A- | 448.5 | 4.47 | 5.7 | 14.0 | 32.6 | 19.9 | 10.0 | 13.8 |
| KELLOGG MEMPHIS EMPL FCU | Memphis | TN | D | D- | D+ | 4.8 | 10.13 | 0.0 | 46.0 | 0.0 | 0.0 | 10.0 | 24.8 |
| KELLOGG MIDWEST FCU | Omaha | NE | B- | B | B | 47.3 | -0.83 | 0.0 | 23.2 | 13.0 | 35.0 | 10.0 | 19.8 |
| KELLY COMMUNITY FCU | Tyler | TX | B+ | B+ | B | 103.1 | 9.98 | 2.4 | 28.2 | 30.9 | 10.8 | 8.5 | 10.0 |
| KEMBA CHARLESTON FCU | Dunbar | WV | C- | C+ | B- | 40.1 | 0.37 | 0.0 | 25.5 | 3.4 | 5.4 | 10.0 | 20.0 |
| KEMBA CU | West Chester | OH | A | A | A | 730.8 | 13.86 | 0.8 | 54.2 | 21.3 | 0.1 | 10.0 | 12.5 |
| KEMBA DELTA FCU | Memphis | TN | B- | B- | B- | 22.9 | -0.36 | 0.0 | 49.5 | 0.2 | 0.0 | 10.0 | 24.1 |
| KEMBA FINANCIAL CU | Gahanna | OH | A | A | A | 980.6 | 7.17 | 6.4 | 38.3 | 26.5 | 10.1 | 10.0 | 11.5 |
| KEMBA INDIANAPOLIS CU | Indianapolis | IN | C+ | C+ | B- | 66.0 | 1.17 | 0.0 | 21.0 | 13.0 | 20.4 | 10.0 | 15.3 |
| ▲ KEMBA LOUISVILLE CU | Louisville | KY | B | B- | B- | 48.7 | 2.64 | 0.0 | 22.6 | 7.9 | 4.4 | 10.0 | 19.7 |
| KEMBA PEORIA CU | Peoria | IL | D+ | C- | C- | 9.5 | 1.41 | 0.0 | 43.7 | 0.0 | 0.0 | 10.0 | 11.7 |
| ▲ KEMBA ROANOKE FCU | Salem | VA | C | C+ | C+ | 59.8 | -0.29 | 0.0 | 19.0 | 7.0 | 0.0 | 10.0 | 16.1 |
| KENMORE NY TEACHERS FCU | Buffalo | NY | C- | C | C | 36.8 | 4.32 | 0.0 | 14.1 | 27.4 | 44.4 | 6.6 | 8.6 |
| KENNAFORD FCU | Bedford | PA | C | C- | C- | 6.5 | 0.06 | 0.0 | 27.0 | 0.0 | 0.0 | 10.0 | 19.5 |
| KENNAMETAL ORWELL EMPL FCU | Orwell | OH | C+ | C+ | C+ | 1.1 | 11.17 | 0.0 | 40.7 | 0.0 | 0.0 | 10.0 | 22.1 |
| KENNEDY VETERANS ADMINISTRATION EMP | Memphis | TN | C+ | C | D+ | 21.8 | 3.96 | 0.0 | 43.4 | 0.0 | 0.0 | 10.0 | 12.3 |
| KENOSHA CITY EMPL CU | Kenosha | WI | D+ | C | C- | 9.9 | 1.09 | 0.0 | 9.7 | 4.9 | 0.0 | 10.0 | 12.2 |
| KENOSHA POLICE & FIREMENS CU | Kenosha | WI | C+ | C+ | B- | 9.7 | -2.38 | 0.0 | 19.9 | 0.0 | 3.4 | 10.0 | 33.0 |
| KENOSHA POSTAL EMPL CU | Kenosha | WI | D+ | C- | C- | 1.5 | -3.94 | 0.0 | 70.9 | 0.0 | 0.0 | 10.0 | 20.8 |
| KENOWA COMMUNITY FCU | Wyoming | MI | B- | B- | C+ | 19.3 | 7.18 | 0.0 | 29.6 | 17.3 | 0.0 | 10.0 | 13.2 |
| KENT COUNTY CU | Grand Rapids | MI | C- | C- | D+ | 41.3 | 3.62 | 0.0 | 30.1 | 2.2 | 26.1 | 8.5 | 10.0 |
| KENT COUNTY MEMORIAL HOSPITAL EMPL F | Warwick | RI | D+ | D+ | D+ | 13.8 | 7.00 | 0.0 | 45.9 | 0.5 | 0.0 | 6.6 | 8.6 |
| ▲ KENTUCKY EMPL CU | Frankfort | KY | B- | B- | B | 73.5 | 8.70 | 1.2 | 31.5 | 32.1 | 3.2 | 9.2 | 10.5 |
| KENTUCKY TELCO FCU | Louisville | KY | A | A | A | 344.9 | 4.47 | 2.0 | 41.7 | 10.9 | 10.0 | 10.0 | 11.8 |
| ▲ KERN FCU | Bakersfield | CA | B+ | B- | A- | 225.8 | 3.83 | 0.0 | 42.6 | 23.2 | 1.8 | 10.0 | 13.4 |
| KERN SCHOOLS FCU | Bakersfield | CA | A- | A- | B+ | 1322.6 | 4.50 | 1.4 | 21.9 | 28.3 | 26.2 | 9.0 | 10.4 |
| KERR COUNTY FCU | Kerrville | TX | C- | C- | C- | 60.9 | 16.91 | 0.0 | 66.5 | 0.0 | 0.0 | 5.4 | 7.4 |
| KEYPOINT CU | Santa Clara | CA | B- | B- | B- | 1024.2 | 9.80 | 9.4 | 22.7 | 42.4 | 9.6 | 6.0 | 8.0 |
| ▲ KEYS FCU | Key West | FL | E+ | F | F | 122.5 | 3.47 | 4.2 | 29.8 | 26.2 | 0.0 | 4.1 | 6.1 |
| ▼ KEYSTONE CU | Tyler | TX | D+ | C | C+ | 38.2 | -1.75 | 0.0 | 15.6 | 12.7 | 0.0 | 10.0 | 26.0 |
| KEYSTONE FCU | West Chester | PA | D | D- | D+ | 73.2 | -4.53 | 8.4 | 15.1 | 12.2 | 40.9 | 5.9 | 7.9 |
| KEYSTONE UNITED METHODIST FCU | Cranberry Township | PA | D+ | D+ | C- | 16.4 | 3.07 | 6.5 | 28.6 | 25.9 | 0.0 | 7.8 | 9.6 |
| KH NETWORK CU | Dayton | OH | B | B- | B- | 48.9 | 9.41 | 3.0 | 40.9 | 25.1 | 8.5 | 10.0 | 11.2 |
| KIEF PROTECTIVE MUTUAL BENEFIT ASSN C | Bloomfield | CT | D | D | D | 1.2 | 3.40 | 0.0 | 32.1 | 0.0 | 0.0 | 10.0 | 19.4 |
| ▼ KILGORE SHELL EMPL FCU | Kilgore | TX | C- | C | C+ | 2.4 | -14.51 | 0.0 | 42.5 | 0.0 | 0.0 | 10.0 | 14.2 |

| Asset Quality Index | Non-Performing Loans as a % of Total Loans | as a % of Capital | Net Charge-Offs Avg Loans | Profitability Index | Net Income ($Mil) | Return on Assets | Return on Equity | Net Interest Spread | Overhead Efficiency Ratio | Liquidity Index | Liquidity Ratio | Hot Money Ratio | Stability Index |
|---|---|---|---|---|---|---|---|---|---|---|---|---|---|
| 7.7 | 0.52 | 3.3 | 0.29 | 4.7 | 0.0 | 0.70 | 6.01 | 6.56 | 86.3 | 3.4 | 11.3 | 0.0 | 4.3 |
| 7.9 | 0.00 | 0.0 | 0.13 | 3.2 | 0.0 | 0.13 | 0.87 | 3.02 | 95.7 | 3.8 | 41.2 | 0.0 | 7.9 |
| 9.7 | 0.33 | 1.3 | 0.02 | 5.6 | 0.2 | 0.88 | 6.07 | 2.70 | 70.0 | 3.7 | 28.0 | 7.9 | 7.6 |
| 7.9 | 2.60 | 8.2 | 1.37 | 2.8 | 0.1 | 0.23 | 1.90 | 3.20 | 91.2 | 6.3 | 38.8 | 0.0 | 5.8 |
| 8.4 | 0.18 | 0.5 | 2.48 | 6.1 | 0.1 | 0.96 | 4.97 | 4.73 | 60.3 | 4.3 | 17.8 | 0.0 | 5.7 |
| 6.4 | 2.19 | 5.6 | 0.05 | 0.0 | -0.1 | -3.23 | -12.59 | 0.07 | 485.2 | 4.6 | 25.2 | 0.0 | 6.0 |
| 6.4 | 1.08 | 6.9 | 0.36 | 5.3 | 0.4 | 0.80 | 8.48 | 3.44 | 76.9 | 3.9 | 11.4 | 1.8 | 5.2 |
| 9.5 | 0.45 | 2.7 | 0.05 | 4.4 | 0.4 | 0.64 | 5.73 | 2.88 | 82.8 | 4.2 | 20.0 | 7.0 | 5.9 |
| 3.7 | 6.33 | 20.3 | 0.00 | 0.3 | 0.0 | -0.95 | -6.77 | 5.65 | 127.3 | 6.9 | 58.9 | 0.0 | 4.9 |
| 4.0 | 1.64 | 14.8 | 0.42 | 5.6 | 0.1 | 0.93 | 12.85 | 4.99 | 80.7 | 3.8 | 16.2 | 0.0 | 3.0 |
| 6.1 | 1.70 | 11.1 | 0.27 | 2.7 | 0.1 | 0.24 | 1.91 | 4.03 | 90.2 | 3.3 | 8.5 | 3.8 | 5.5 |
| 7.8 | 0.96 | 5.9 | 0.43 | 6.8 | 3.2 | 1.07 | 11.41 | 3.57 | 65.2 | 4.0 | 15.8 | 10.6 | 5.8 |
| 5.0 | 1.95 | 14.8 | 1.46 | 3.0 | 0.1 | 0.09 | 0.95 | 3.67 | 66.9 | 2.0 | 16.5 | 25.0 | 4.9 |
| 8.8 | 1.42 | 3.8 | 0.04 | 2.2 | 0.1 | 0.21 | 2.44 | 2.37 | 88.2 | 4.9 | 25.4 | 9.6 | 3.0 |
| 3.7 | 8.05 | 24.0 | 0.11 | 7.3 | 0.2 | 1.20 | 8.77 | 3.05 | 63.0 | 5.5 | 34.2 | 0.0 | 6.6 |
| 9.9 | 0.44 | 1.0 | 0.36 | 2.5 | 0.1 | 0.11 | 0.96 | 1.90 | 87.4 | 6.1 | 30.9 | 0.0 | 6.0 |
| 9.4 | 0.95 | 3.2 | 0.47 | 4.9 | 0.0 | 0.82 | 7.23 | 4.38 | 84.5 | 5.3 | 26.6 | 0.0 | 4.3 |
| 7.8 | 1.03 | 2.9 | 2.45 | 3.6 | 0.0 | 0.54 | 3.93 | 5.03 | 84.2 | 4.7 | 22.4 | 0.0 | 5.3 |
| 0.9 | 4.85 | 25.4 | -0.35 | 10.0 | 0.0 | 1.74 | 11.14 | 9.29 | 79.5 | 4.5 | 21.4 | 0.0 | 7.5 |
| 9.9 | 0.00 | 0.0 | 0.00 | 2.2 | 0.0 | 0.28 | 1.08 | 2.68 | 80.0 | 7.8 | 79.9 | 0.0 | 7.2 |
| 3.8 | 0.96 | 12.3 | 1.10 | 4.8 | 0.2 | 0.48 | 6.07 | 6.06 | 83.9 | 3.0 | 3.3 | 0.0 | 3.4 |
| 9.0 | 2.49 | 2.1 | -0.87 | 3.4 | 0.0 | 0.43 | 2.88 | 1.82 | 62.9 | 5.6 | 15.9 | 0.0 | 6.4 |
| 8.5 | 0.66 | 3.2 | 0.56 | 7.2 | 17.9 | 1.05 | 7.88 | 2.68 | 64.0 | 3.6 | 19.2 | 13.5 | 9.3 |
| 7.0 | 3.97 | 10.7 | -0.08 | 1.3 | 0.0 | 0.16 | 0.72 | 2.88 | 102.1 | 5.0 | 37.9 | 3.9 | 5.1 |
| 6.9 | 2.63 | 9.5 | 0.01 | 3.7 | 0.2 | 0.59 | 4.86 | 2.92 | 75.7 | 5.0 | 47.1 | 1.2 | 5.7 |
| 7.4 | 1.42 | 6.0 | 0.40 | 9.0 | 4.4 | 1.31 | 9.73 | 3.16 | 66.5 | 3.7 | 15.7 | 7.5 | 8.5 |
| 3.4 | 8.26 | 14.9 | 0.64 | 3.1 | 0.0 | 0.44 | 1.70 | 4.72 | 96.0 | 6.2 | 60.8 | 0.0 | 3.0 |
| 9.3 | 1.39 | 3.8 | -0.01 | 3.0 | 0.1 | 0.22 | 1.05 | 3.01 | 93.9 | 4.8 | 35.4 | 0.7 | 6.8 |
| 8.0 | 0.66 | 5.0 | 0.48 | 5.1 | 0.5 | 0.65 | 6.74 | 4.31 | 76.8 | 4.0 | 18.9 | 7.9 | 7.3 |
| 9.0 | 0.93 | 2.0 | 0.29 | 1.9 | 0.0 | 0.03 | 0.13 | 3.02 | 92.7 | 3.7 | 13.6 | 9.9 | 6.5 |
| 8.3 | 0.20 | 2.0 | 0.22 | 6.9 | 5.3 | 1.01 | 8.77 | 2.52 | 70.0 | 3.0 | 15.8 | 10.2 | 9.1 |
| 7.0 | 2.04 | 4.1 | 0.80 | 6.1 | 0.1 | 0.73 | 3.13 | 3.64 | 81.2 | 4.8 | 44.9 | 1.8 | 5.7 |
| 9.0 | 0.38 | 2.6 | 0.43 | 7.6 | 7.5 | 1.04 | 9.12 | 3.38 | 69.2 | 3.2 | 25.6 | 15.3 | 8.8 |
| 9.7 | 0.44 | 1.6 | 0.55 | 2.9 | 0.1 | 0.22 | 1.45 | 3.54 | 90.0 | 4.6 | 19.6 | 7.2 | 6.6 |
| 10.0 | 0.32 | 0.6 | 0.31 | 4.0 | 0.2 | 0.58 | 2.96 | 3.66 | 84.0 | 5.3 | 36.3 | 3.7 | 6.7 |
| 7.0 | 0.63 | 7.0 | -0.06 | 0.7 | 0.0 | -0.33 | -2.85 | 3.95 | 106.8 | 4.3 | 19.0 | 1.2 | 6.4 |
| 9.6 | 0.90 | 1.8 | 0.71 | 2.1 | 0.0 | 0.07 | 0.43 | 2.95 | 90.8 | 4.9 | 19.2 | 0.0 | 6.5 |
| 5.9 | 2.22 | 11.2 | -0.07 | 3.5 | 0.1 | 0.40 | 4.78 | 2.47 | 83.8 | 4.4 | 10.7 | 0.0 | 4.1 |
| 9.8 | 0.95 | 1.6 | 0.13 | 2.5 | 0.0 | 0.29 | 1.48 | 2.11 | 84.2 | 5.0 | 22.1 | 0.0 | 6.7 |
| 9.8 | 0.22 | 0.4 | -0.60 | 4.8 | 0.0 | 0.53 | 2.25 | 9.71 | 88.6 | 7.3 | 72.4 | 0.0 | 7.6 |
| 7.6 | 1.43 | 5.2 | -0.22 | 6.6 | 0.2 | 1.26 | 10.46 | 3.01 | 89.9 | 4.0 | 54.4 | 17.3 | 5.6 |
| 7.8 | 6.29 | 8.5 | 2.05 | 0.5 | -0.1 | -0.86 | -6.80 | 1.91 | 101.9 | 5.7 | 39.5 | 0.0 | 5.7 |
| 10.0 | 0.50 | 0.4 | -0.35 | 2.4 | 0.0 | 0.18 | 0.54 | 1.95 | 105.9 | 5.1 | 21.2 | 0.0 | 7.2 |
| 5.4 | 5.24 | 17.1 | 0.00 | 1.5 | 0.0 | 0.00 | 0.00 | 3.05 | 89.3 | 5.3 | 31.3 | 0.0 | 6.6 |
| 9.6 | 0.44 | 2.0 | 0.32 | 6.1 | 0.1 | 0.70 | 5.37 | 5.07 | 82.3 | 5.9 | 37.7 | 0.0 | 5.7 |
| 8.2 | 0.62 | 2.3 | 0.82 | 2.2 | 0.1 | 0.18 | 1.78 | 3.46 | 92.9 | 5.2 | 20.2 | 0.0 | 4.2 |
| 6.2 | 0.84 | 5.0 | 0.59 | 3.4 | 0.0 | 0.34 | 3.99 | 4.34 | 88.1 | 4.3 | 15.6 | 0.0 | 3.0 |
| 8.5 | 0.44 | 2.8 | 0.29 | 4.3 | 0.2 | 0.43 | 4.06 | 3.97 | 90.3 | 2.2 | 16.2 | 18.8 | 5.4 |
| 9.0 | 0.54 | 2.7 | 0.53 | 6.1 | 2.2 | 0.84 | 7.24 | 2.85 | 78.6 | 3.4 | 17.3 | 9.1 | 7.8 |
| 8.3 | 0.53 | 3.5 | 0.15 | 5.4 | 1.3 | 0.79 | 6.00 | 3.65 | 93.4 | 3.9 | 23.0 | 6.6 | 7.2 |
| 9.3 | 0.36 | 2.2 | 0.21 | 5.4 | 5.1 | 0.51 | 5.18 | 3.14 | 89.3 | 4.1 | 17.0 | 4.0 | 7.1 |
| 4.0 | 0.82 | 13.0 | 0.84 | 6.0 | 0.4 | 0.81 | 12.25 | 5.77 | 72.7 | 3.3 | 21.3 | 9.6 | 3.3 |
| 9.1 | 0.30 | 3.2 | 0.14 | 4.4 | 4.3 | 0.59 | 7.15 | 3.49 | 83.3 | 3.1 | 5.4 | 3.9 | 6.0 |
| 6.1 | 0.13 | 5.0 | 0.26 | 8.6 | 1.3 | 1.47 | 26.47 | 5.20 | 71.8 | 4.3 | 20.4 | 5.0 | 2.0 |
| 8.7 | 3.29 | 4.5 | 0.68 | 0.8 | -0.1 | -0.33 | -1.28 | 2.27 | 109.1 | 5.7 | 37.3 | 0.0 | 6.6 |
| 5.0 | 2.53 | 13.3 | 0.15 | 0.7 | -0.1 | -0.16 | -2.05 | 2.94 | 105.3 | 5.2 | 30.3 | 1.9 | 2.3 |
| 6.0 | 0.89 | 6.8 | 0.23 | 2.1 | 0.0 | 0.07 | 0.77 | 4.19 | 97.1 | 1.8 | 16.1 | 27.4 | 4.1 |
| 8.3 | 0.64 | 3.8 | 0.66 | 5.5 | 0.3 | 0.80 | 7.20 | 4.42 | 78.2 | 3.9 | 20.6 | 3.2 | 5.4 |
| 8.6 | 2.98 | 6.1 | 0.00 | 0.0 | 0.0 | -0.70 | -3.51 | 2.66 | 125.0 | 5.0 | 44.3 | 0.0 | 5.3 |
| 8.8 | 0.00 | 0.0 | 0.36 | 2.8 | 0.0 | 0.05 | 0.39 | 3.69 | 81.4 | 3.8 | 21.8 | 0.0 | 5.2 |

| Name | City | State | Rating | 2014 Rating | 2013 Rating | Total Assets ($Mil) | One Year Asset Growth | Asset Mix (As a % of Total Assets) | | | | Capital-ization Index | Net Worth Ratio |
|---|---|---|---|---|---|---|---|---|---|---|---|---|---|
| | | | | | | | | Commercial Loans | Consumer Loans | Mortgage Loans | Securities | | |
| KILOWATT COMMUNITY CU | Jefferson City | MO | E+ | E+ | D- | 6.8 | 2.95 | 0.0 | 62.2 | 0.0 | 0.0 | 5.7 | 7.7 |
| KIMBERLY CLARK CU | Memphis | TN | A | A | A | 105.6 | -0.02 | 0.0 | 50.3 | 8.3 | 20.2 | 10.0 | 22.9 |
| KINECTA FCU | Manhattan Beach | CA | B- | B- | B- | 3752.0 | 8.03 | 11.5 | 30.7 | 48.0 | 2.2 | 6.1 | 8.2 |
| KINETIC FCU | Columbus | GA | B- | B | B | 295.0 | 5.57 | 3.5 | 59.8 | 7.1 | 4.3 | 9.7 | 10.8 |
| KINGS FCU | Hanford | CA | A- | A- | A- | 90.0 | 5.75 | 0.0 | 57.4 | 3.2 | 11.9 | 10.0 | 17.5 |
| ▲ KINGS PEAK CU | Roosevelt | UT | D+ | D+ | C- | 12.9 | -15.28 | 1.3 | 41.4 | 3.2 | 0.0 | 8.3 | 9.9 |
| KINGSPORT PRESS CU | Kingsport | TN | B- | B- | B | 66.1 | 2.94 | 4.7 | 16.5 | 27.6 | 1.2 | 10.0 | 11.8 |
| ▲ KINGSTON TVA EMPL CU | Harriman | TN | C | C- | D+ | 2.1 | 2.52 | 0.0 | 64.6 | 0.0 | 0.0 | 10.0 | 25.3 |
| KINGSVILLE AREA EDUCATORS FCU | Kingsville | TX | D+ | D+ | C- | 21.0 | 8.29 | 0.0 | 26.8 | 0.0 | 0.0 | 7.3 | 9.2 |
| KINGSVILLE COMMUNITY FCU | Kingsville | TX | B- | B- | B- | 15.2 | 12.23 | 0.0 | 50.2 | 0.0 | 0.0 | 10.0 | 12.6 |
| KIRTLAND FCU | Albuquerque | NM | A- | A- | A- | 681.2 | 2.60 | 0.7 | 39.0 | 26.9 | 21.0 | 10.0 | 13.6 |
| KIT TEL FCU | Kittanning | PA | C- | C- | C- | <1 | -5.68 | 0.0 | 24.9 | 0.0 | 0.0 | 10.0 | 23.9 |
| KITSAP CU | Bremerton | WA | B+ | B | C+ | 1017.6 | 4.75 | 5.1 | 52.3 | 12.2 | 19.1 | 8.9 | 10.3 |
| KLAMATH PUBLIC EMPL FCU | Klamath Falls | OR | C- | C | B- | 34.4 | 3.41 | 0.0 | 29.7 | 3.5 | 6.1 | 8.9 | 10.3 |
| KNOLL EMPL CU | East Greenville | PA | C- | C- | C- | 7.4 | 1.81 | 0.0 | 20.6 | 21.2 | 0.0 | 10.0 | 17.4 |
| KNOX COUNTY EMPL CU | Knoxville | TN | C- | C- | C- | 8.9 | 2.29 | 0.0 | 51.7 | 0.0 | 0.0 | 10.0 | 17.7 |
| KNOX COUNTY TEACHERS FCU | Knoxville | TN | C+ | C- | D+ | 25.2 | -2.08 | 0.0 | 24.8 | 15.3 | 0.0 | 10.0 | 11.9 |
| KNOXVILLE FIREFIGHTERS FCU | Knoxville | TN | B | B+ | B+ | 26.6 | 0.17 | 0.1 | 23.5 | 22.2 | 0.0 | 10.0 | 14.2 |
| KNOXVILLE LAW ENFORCEMENT FCU | Knoxville | TN | B- | B- | C+ | 24.1 | -1.07 | 0.0 | 35.9 | 21.7 | 0.0 | 10.0 | 14.8 |
| KNOXVILLE NEWS-SENTINEL EMPL CU | Knoxville | TN | C | C | C | 7.5 | -6.40 | 0.0 | 32.9 | 27.4 | 0.0 | 10.0 | 16.7 |
| KNOXVILLE TEACHERS FCU | Knoxville | TN | B | B | B | 189.7 | 0.27 | 5.1 | 12.1 | 34.9 | 34.2 | 10.0 | 11.0 |
| KNOXVILLE TVA EMPL CU | Knoxville | TN | B+ | B+ | B+ | 1459.5 | 7.26 | 6.0 | 47.7 | 29.2 | 0.0 | 7.2 | 9.1 |
| KOHLER CU | Kohler | WI | B | B | B | 299.3 | 6.87 | 4.5 | 32.5 | 35.6 | 2.4 | 7.3 | 9.2 |
| KOKOMO HERITAGE FCU | Kokomo | IN | C- | C- | C- | 9.0 | 1.92 | 0.8 | 59.6 | 0.0 | 0.0 | 10.0 | 12.3 |
| ▲ KONE EMPL CU | Moline | IL | C- | D+ | D+ | 19.1 | -4.47 | 0.0 | 44.3 | 0.0 | 0.0 | 10.0 | 11.4 |
| KOOTENAI VALLEY FCU | Libby | MT | D | D | D+ | 4.1 | -0.39 | 0.0 | 42.5 | 0.0 | 0.0 | 8.3 | 9.9 |
| KOREAN AMERICAN CATHOLICS FCU | Flushing | NY | E- | E | E- | 26.8 | -3.18 | 0.6 | 8.9 | 19.3 | 0.0 | 3.3 | 5.3 |
| ▼ KOREAN CATHOLIC FCU | Olney | MD | D+ | D+ | C- | 1.6 | 3.20 | 0.0 | 52.4 | 0.0 | 0.0 | 10.0 | 18.4 |
| KRAFTCOR FCU | Hawesville | KY | C+ | C+ | C+ | 15.4 | 5.38 | 0.0 | 30.0 | 15.2 | 0.0 | 10.0 | 11.1 |
| ▲ KRAFTMAN FCU | Bastrop | LA | C+ | C | C | 106.0 | 0.19 | 0.0 | 11.5 | 13.2 | 51.2 | 10.0 | 15.0 |
| KRAFTSMAN FCU | Hopewell | VA | D+ | D+ | C- | 7.6 | -12.19 | 0.0 | 6.4 | 0.0 | 0.0 | 10.0 | 17.7 |
| KRATON BELPRE FCU | Belpre | OH | C | C- | C | 6.5 | 1.37 | 0.0 | 37.4 | 0.0 | 0.0 | 10.0 | 13.7 |
| KRD FCU | McCook | NE | C- | D+ | C- | 14.2 | 1.51 | 0.4 | 62.3 | 7.7 | 0.0 | 8.8 | 10.2 |
| KSW FCU | Waterville | ME | B- | C+ | C+ | 54.0 | 1.05 | 0.4 | 33.1 | 35.4 | 0.0 | 8.9 | 10.3 |
| KUAKINI MEDICAL AND DENTAL FCU | Honolulu | HI | B- | B- | B- | 44.0 | -0.64 | 0.0 | 6.0 | 4.1 | 50.9 | 10.0 | 11.9 |
| KUE FCU | Lexington | KY | B- | B- | B- | 40.6 | 3.48 | 0.0 | 15.7 | 10.0 | 15.6 | 10.0 | 12.7 |
| KUMC CU | Kansas City | KS | D+ | D+ | D+ | 26.4 | 6.07 | 0.0 | 18.4 | 2.8 | 0.0 | 7.2 | 9.2 |
| KV FCU | Augusta | ME | C+ | C+ | C+ | 59.5 | 4.41 | 0.0 | 17.7 | 31.5 | 0.0 | 9.7 | 10.8 |
| KYANG FCU | Louisville | KY | D- | E | E+ | 9.4 | -5.52 | 0.0 | 26.1 | 0.0 | 0.0 | 5.8 | 7.8 |
| KYGER CREEK CU | Cheshire | OH | C+ | C+ | B- | 17.2 | 0.77 | 0.0 | 37.4 | 20.9 | 19.9 | 10.0 | 16.6 |
| L A ELECTRICAL WORKERS CU | Pasadena | CA | D+ | C- | C+ | 45.9 | 1.72 | 0.0 | 6.5 | 0.0 | 38.6 | 10.0 | 20.6 |
| L C E FCU | Painesville | OH | D | D | D | 36.5 | 6.08 | 0.0 | 22.6 | 16.7 | 35.9 | 5.1 | 7.1 |
| L C MUNICIPAL FCU | Lake Charles | LA | D | D+ | C- | 1.3 | -6.56 | 0.0 | 33.1 | 0.0 | 0.0 | 10.0 | 15.8 |
| L G & W FCU | Memphis | TN | B | B- | C- | 93.7 | -1.37 | 0.0 | 14.7 | 16.5 | 30.8 | 10.0 | 18.6 |
| ▼ L&N EMPL CU | Birmingham | AL | C | C | C- | 9.7 | -6.46 | 0.0 | 36.0 | 33.7 | 0.0 | 10.0 | 19.9 |
| L&N FCU | Louisville | KY | A- | A- | A- | 959.9 | 7.73 | 7.3 | 8.6 | 45.9 | 22.0 | 9.3 | 10.5 |
| LA CAPITOL FCU | Baton Rouge | LA | B- | B- | B | 462.4 | 2.13 | 0.2 | 43.9 | 12.0 | 15.7 | 10.0 | 13.0 |
| LA CROSSE-BURLINGTON CU | La Crosse | WI | D+ | D | D+ | 6.6 | 0.78 | 0.0 | 35.7 | 3.5 | 0.0 | 10.0 | 14.4 |
| LA FINANCIAL FCU | Pasadena | CA | C- | C | D+ | 359.5 | 3.72 | 6.1 | 22.5 | 29.3 | 26.2 | 6.0 | 8.1 |
| LA HEALTHCARE FCU | Los Angeles | CA | D- | D- | D- | 14.9 | 5.76 | 0.0 | 31.2 | 0.0 | 1.3 | 4.7 | 6.7 |
| LA JOYA AREA FCU | La Joya | TX | B- | B | B- | 51.0 | 4.09 | 0.0 | 36.4 | 4.2 | 0.0 | 9.4 | 10.6 |
| LA LOMA FCU | Loma Linda | CA | D | D | D- | 70.4 | 6.43 | 5.3 | 17.6 | 21.5 | 28.4 | 4.1 | 6.2 |
| LA MISSION FCU | San Fernando | CA | C- | C | C | 6.9 | 10.61 | 0.0 | 11.8 | 0.0 | 0.0 | 9.0 | 10.4 |
| LA TERRE FCU | Houma | LA | D | D | C | 25.4 | 2.01 | 0.0 | 32.3 | 0.0 | 0.0 | 10.0 | 11.3 |
| LABOR CU | Neenah | WI | E+ | E+ | E+ | 1.8 | -5.01 | 0.0 | 31.5 | 40.6 | 0.0 | 6.2 | 8.2 |
| LABOR MANAGEMENT FCU | Lewisport | KY | C+ | C+ | C | 22.2 | -5.25 | 0.0 | 40.8 | 23.0 | 0.0 | 10.0 | 14.4 |
| LAFAYETTE FCU | Kensington | MD | C+ | B- | B- | 411.2 | 5.17 | 7.3 | 8.1 | 63.2 | 6.0 | 6.7 | 8.7 |
| LAFAYETTE SCHOOLS FCU | Lafayette | LA | A- | A- | A- | 188.7 | 5.12 | 0.0 | 29.9 | 28.9 | 0.0 | 10.0 | 11.6 |
| LAFCU | Lansing | MI | B | B | B | 590.6 | 2.81 | 5.0 | 37.8 | 7.6 | 19.3 | 10.0 | 11.9 |
| LAKE CHEM COMMUNITY FCU | Benton | KY | C+ | C | C- | 52.1 | 5.56 | 0.0 | 28.8 | 0.0 | 0.0 | 7.7 | 9.5 |

| Asset Quality Index | Non-Performing Loans as a % of Total Loans | Non-Performing Loans as a % of Capital | Net Charge-Offs Avg Loans | Profitability Index | Net Income ($Mil) | Return on Assets | Return on Equity | Net Interest Spread | Overhead Efficiency Ratio | Liquidity Index | Liquidity Ratio | Hot Money Ratio | Stability Index |
|---|---|---|---|---|---|---|---|---|---|---|---|---|---|
| 4.2 | 1.10 | 11.6 | 0.46 | 1.7 | 0.0 | -0.16 | -2.06 | 5.45 | 98.2 | 3.7 | 12.9 | 0.0 | 1.0 |
| 8.4 | 0.42 | 1.4 | 0.63 | 5.9 | 0.5 | 0.63 | 2.79 | 4.28 | 77.2 | 3.9 | 23.1 | 9.7 | 8.6 |
| 7.4 | 0.51 | 5.0 | 0.37 | 4.1 | 12.6 | 0.45 | 5.61 | 3.13 | 87.4 | 1.6 | 5.1 | 17.9 | 5.7 |
| 5.5 | 0.93 | 7.3 | 1.33 | 3.8 | 0.9 | 0.40 | 3.70 | 5.04 | 80.2 | 3.8 | 18.9 | 10.0 | 6.4 |
| 8.5 | 0.59 | 2.2 | 0.40 | 6.4 | 0.5 | 0.82 | 4.75 | 3.68 | 70.9 | 3.8 | 16.0 | 8.0 | 8.1 |
| 4.4 | 1.39 | 11.1 | 0.82 | 2.9 | 0.0 | 0.13 | 1.47 | 4.20 | 94.8 | 5.3 | 35.1 | 0.0 | 3.8 |
| 7.1 | 0.35 | 6.6 | 0.41 | 3.7 | 0.2 | 0.42 | 3.55 | 2.63 | 84.8 | 4.7 | 66.9 | 8.9 | 5.6 |
| 7.9 | 0.70 | 2.1 | -0.08 | 5.3 | 0.0 | 1.01 | 4.03 | 5.67 | 71.1 | 4.6 | 26.1 | 0.0 | 4.3 |
| 6.3 | 3.00 | 9.3 | 2.05 | 2.5 | 0.1 | 0.31 | 3.36 | 3.83 | 80.1 | 4.6 | 14.5 | 5.0 | 3.6 |
| 5.6 | 1.20 | 5.5 | 0.51 | 9.3 | 0.1 | 1.22 | 9.83 | 6.67 | 80.8 | 5.2 | 42.6 | 3.9 | 7.2 |
| 7.5 | 0.84 | 5.5 | 0.53 | 6.0 | 5.0 | 0.99 | 7.48 | 3.27 | 63.9 | 2.7 | 3.8 | 11.5 | 9.1 |
| 10.0 | 0.88 | 1.0 | 0.00 | 1.6 | 0.0 | 0.00 | 0.00 | 2.03 | 109.1 | 6.1 | 39.4 | 0.0 | 6.8 |
| 7.4 | 0.13 | 2.1 | 0.39 | 6.2 | 7.7 | 1.02 | 10.24 | 3.57 | 74.7 | 3.5 | 12.6 | 6.0 | 7.2 |
| 9.3 | 0.22 | 1.1 | 0.09 | 2.5 | 0.1 | 0.19 | 1.87 | 3.51 | 94.5 | 4.8 | 24.9 | 5.2 | 4.8 |
| 10.0 | 0.11 | 0.4 | 0.00 | 2.0 | 0.0 | 0.14 | 0.84 | 2.80 | 94.6 | 4.3 | 18.6 | 0.0 | 7.0 |
| 8.6 | 0.66 | 1.9 | -0.09 | 2.3 | 0.0 | 0.06 | 0.34 | 3.54 | 95.0 | 4.9 | 34.1 | 1.7 | 6.2 |
| 7.6 | 1.81 | 7.5 | 0.23 | 2.8 | 0.1 | 0.34 | 2.89 | 3.39 | 87.2 | 6.1 | 50.9 | 0.0 | 6.0 |
| 9.8 | 0.27 | 1.0 | 0.03 | 4.3 | 0.1 | 0.57 | 4.07 | 3.17 | 81.7 | 4.9 | 27.2 | 4.1 | 7.0 |
| 9.2 | 0.39 | 1.9 | 0.39 | 3.8 | 0.1 | 0.44 | 3.06 | 3.64 | 81.8 | 5.2 | 29.9 | 1.5 | 7.3 |
| 9.7 | 0.29 | 1.3 | -0.13 | 2.9 | 0.0 | 0.17 | 1.08 | 3.64 | 95.7 | 3.9 | 14.1 | 1.9 | 7.0 |
| 7.2 | 0.91 | 7.0 | 0.41 | 4.3 | 0.9 | 0.63 | 5.86 | 3.08 | 73.3 | 4.2 | 10.6 | 0.0 | 5.9 |
| 8.0 | 0.14 | 1.8 | 0.21 | 5.5 | 8.6 | 0.80 | 9.29 | 2.89 | 74.9 | 2.6 | 10.7 | 11.8 | 7.3 |
| 7.5 | 0.61 | 5.3 | 0.16 | 4.3 | 1.0 | 0.46 | 5.22 | 4.03 | 89.8 | 3.3 | 4.7 | 1.1 | 6.1 |
| 4.4 | 1.92 | 14.6 | 0.62 | 4.7 | 0.0 | 0.60 | 5.04 | 5.32 | 80.1 | 2.4 | 19.3 | 19.5 | 3.7 |
| 8.7 | 0.94 | 3.6 | 0.06 | 2.3 | 0.0 | 0.28 | 2.55 | 2.90 | 91.4 | 4.4 | 21.2 | 0.0 | 4.8 |
| 4.9 | 1.57 | 9.5 | 1.72 | 1.8 | 0.0 | -0.23 | -2.27 | 6.03 | 81.4 | 4.9 | 28.7 | 0.0 | 4.5 |
| 5.2 | 1.28 | 6.2 | 11.29 | 0.0 | -0.4 | -1.99 | -34.03 | 2.65 | 89.8 | 6.1 | 35.7 | 0.0 | 0.8 |
| 8.7 | 0.00 | 0.0 | 0.00 | 0.4 | 0.0 | -0.40 | -2.21 | 4.10 | 108.7 | 5.5 | 50.0 | 0.0 | 6.7 |
| 8.8 | 0.07 | 0.4 | 0.12 | 2.4 | 0.0 | 0.19 | 1.66 | 2.73 | 91.9 | 4.2 | 13.1 | 2.9 | 6.3 |
| 8.5 | 1.69 | 3.4 | 0.21 | 2.6 | 0.3 | 0.36 | 2.52 | 2.27 | 84.2 | 4.1 | 17.0 | 13.8 | 7.7 |
| 7.8 | 9.02 | 6.1 | 0.79 | 1.2 | 0.0 | 0.00 | 0.00 | 2.05 | 89.8 | 5.3 | 33.8 | 0.0 | 4.8 |
| 9.7 | 0.60 | 1.8 | 0.00 | 3.2 | 0.0 | 0.48 | 3.52 | 2.51 | 79.6 | 5.0 | 17.3 | 0.0 | 6.7 |
| 3.5 | 1.84 | 14.0 | 0.30 | 4.8 | 0.1 | 0.72 | 7.31 | 4.91 | 80.4 | 2.9 | 14.9 | 12.9 | 5.2 |
| 6.5 | 0.63 | 5.7 | 0.21 | 4.8 | 0.3 | 0.66 | 7.01 | 3.89 | 79.9 | 2.5 | 8.6 | 8.9 | 5.6 |
| 10.0 | 1.68 | 1.9 | 0.02 | 3.4 | 0.1 | 0.37 | 3.17 | 1.68 | 78.0 | 5.1 | 23.4 | 6.2 | 6.0 |
| 10.0 | 0.23 | 0.6 | 0.04 | 3.4 | 0.1 | 0.39 | 3.15 | 2.42 | 83.3 | 5.2 | 21.6 | 1.2 | 6.5 |
| 10.0 | 0.00 | 0.0 | 0.13 | 1.8 | 0.0 | 0.07 | 0.78 | 2.41 | 96.9 | 5.2 | 30.4 | 2.4 | 3.5 |
| 10.0 | 0.06 | 0.3 | 0.02 | 3.5 | 0.2 | 0.46 | 4.28 | 3.03 | 89.1 | 4.3 | 22.8 | 1.9 | 5.7 |
| 9.8 | 0.00 | 0.0 | -0.14 | 3.3 | 0.1 | 0.63 | 8.57 | 3.30 | 89.3 | 5.3 | 23.1 | 0.0 | 1.6 |
| 8.3 | 1.01 | 3.7 | 0.05 | 5.0 | 0.1 | 0.77 | 4.75 | 2.21 | 61.0 | 2.9 | 19.2 | 14.8 | 7.5 |
| 10.0 | 3.65 | 1.9 | 0.21 | 1.1 | 0.0 | -0.06 | -0.29 | 1.62 | 102.9 | 5.5 | 30.6 | 0.0 | 7.0 |
| 6.5 | 1.22 | 7.5 | 0.22 | 1.6 | 0.0 | 0.13 | 1.83 | 2.76 | 92.7 | 4.9 | 24.0 | 0.4 | 2.0 |
| 6.8 | 3.30 | 8.6 | 2.67 | 0.0 | 0.0 | -1.47 | -8.93 | 6.75 | 113.7 | 6.1 | 32.0 | 0.0 | 4.9 |
| 10.0 | 0.20 | 0.3 | 0.16 | 4.3 | 0.5 | 0.73 | 3.85 | 3.23 | 73.9 | 5.2 | 30.0 | 7.5 | 7.4 |
| 9.3 | 0.05 | 0.3 | 0.17 | 3.7 | 0.0 | 0.42 | 2.62 | 6.13 | 94.0 | 4.0 | 22.4 | 4.2 | 6.1 |
| 9.3 | 0.39 | 2.7 | 0.14 | 8.1 | 8.6 | 1.22 | 11.86 | 3.18 | 67.9 | 4.2 | 20.7 | 6.6 | 8.0 |
| 8.4 | 0.68 | 3.6 | 0.51 | 3.4 | 1.3 | 0.36 | 3.02 | 3.78 | 89.4 | 3.9 | 12.9 | 2.8 | 7.4 |
| 7.6 | 1.51 | 4.9 | -0.05 | 1.2 | 0.0 | 0.06 | 0.42 | 3.20 | 98.0 | 6.5 | 57.5 | 0.0 | 6.6 |
| 8.5 | 0.95 | 6.5 | 0.36 | 0.9 | -1.1 | -0.40 | -4.74 | 3.07 | 107.4 | 3.8 | 9.5 | 5.0 | 4.4 |
| 7.6 | 0.87 | 3.8 | 0.82 | 4.1 | 0.1 | 0.62 | 9.35 | 4.19 | 89.3 | 5.6 | 25.3 | 0.0 | 1.4 |
| 7.7 | 0.64 | 3.3 | 0.44 | 4.2 | 0.1 | 0.36 | 3.51 | 6.36 | 92.5 | 4.9 | 28.3 | 10.0 | 5.2 |
| 9.6 | 0.24 | 1.7 | 0.03 | 1.6 | 0.0 | 0.02 | 0.31 | 3.23 | 93.0 | 4.9 | 12.6 | 0.0 | 1.7 |
| 8.1 | 1.21 | 1.6 | 1.35 | 0.9 | -0.1 | -0.90 | -8.13 | 2.19 | 141.4 | 4.9 | 9.6 | 0.0 | 4.0 |
| 6.8 | 1.92 | 8.2 | 3.25 | 0.1 | -0.2 | -0.85 | -7.11 | 3.79 | 106.8 | 5.6 | 32.7 | 0.0 | 5.0 |
| 5.9 | 0.96 | 9.3 | 0.00 | 1.7 | 0.0 | 0.07 | 0.91 | 3.79 | 102.1 | 3.7 | 27.2 | 0.0 | 1.0 |
| 9.6 | 0.25 | 1.2 | 0.52 | 4.0 | 0.1 | 0.52 | 3.77 | 3.45 | 78.0 | 3.1 | 8.5 | 8.2 | 6.3 |
| 3.3 | 3.16 | 28.6 | 0.26 | 2.8 | 0.5 | 0.18 | 2.00 | 3.45 | 92.5 | 2.6 | 11.7 | 9.8 | 5.5 |
| 7.0 | 1.34 | 8.4 | 0.23 | 5.2 | 1.0 | 0.69 | 6.37 | 3.53 | 81.1 | 3.8 | 19.7 | 8.5 | 8.3 |
| 6.8 | 1.35 | 7.8 | 0.91 | 3.9 | 2.1 | 0.48 | 4.15 | 3.71 | 77.4 | 4.0 | 15.0 | 4.3 | 7.4 |
| 6.7 | 0.63 | 7.2 | 0.17 | 4.3 | 0.2 | 0.58 | 6.12 | 4.07 | 85.6 | 3.5 | 14.6 | 9.9 | 4.7 |

| Name | City | State | Rating | 2014 Rating | 2013 Rating | Total Assets ($Mil) | One Year Asset Growth | Asset Mix (As a % of Total Assets) | | | | Capital- ization Index | Net Worth Ratio |
|------|------|-------|--------|-------------|-------------|---------------------|-----------------------|------------|------------|------------|------------|------------------------|-----------------|
| | | | | | | | | Comm- ercial Loans | Cons- umer Loans | Mort- gage Loans | Secur- ities | | |
| LAKE COMMUNITY FCU | Hartville | OH | D | D+ | D+ | 20.9 | 8.47 | 0.0 | 52.0 | 4.4 | 0.0 | 6.5 | 8.5 |
| LAKE COUNTY EDUCATIONAL FCU | Painesville | OH | D | D | D | 19.7 | 5.17 | 0.0 | 26.3 | 10.0 | 34.6 | 5.6 | 7.6 |
| LAKE ERIE COMMUNITY FCU | Girard | PA | D- | E+ | E+ | 4.4 | -2.38 | 0.0 | 50.5 | 0.0 | 0.0 | 6.1 | 8.1 |
| ▲ LAKE HURON CU | Saginaw | MI | C+ | C- | D- | 44.1 | 1.02 | 1.7 | 39.6 | 29.6 | 7.7 | 8.1 | 9.8 |
| LAKE MICHIGAN CU | Grand Rapids | MI | A | A | A | 3920.8 | 14.07 | 6.8 | 12.9 | 54.3 | 13.1 | 10.0 | 11.7 |
| LAKE SHORE FCU | Angola | NY | C | C | C | 13.8 | 6.67 | 0.0 | 35.7 | 9.0 | 0.0 | 8.5 | 10.0 |
| LAKE SUPERIOR CU | Ontonagon | MI | D | D | D- | 5.5 | 7.56 | 0.0 | 31.9 | 0.0 | 15.4 | 7.2 | 9.1 |
| LAKE SUPERIOR REFINERY CU | Superior | WI | D+ | D+ | C- | 1.2 | -2.65 | 0.0 | 34.5 | 0.0 | 0.0 | 10.0 | 14.2 |
| ▲ LAKE TRUST CU | Brighton | MI | C+ | C | C- | 1631.3 | 2.48 | 8.7 | 22.8 | 32.5 | 8.6 | 8.8 | 10.2 |
| LAKEHURST NAVAL FCU | Lakehurst | NJ | C | C- | D+ | 27.2 | -0.28 | 0.0 | 14.6 | 12.2 | 5.9 | 7.4 | 9.2 |
| LAKELANDS FCU | Greenwood | SC | C- | D+ | C- | 10.9 | 2.97 | 0.0 | 54.6 | 0.0 | 0.0 | 10.0 | 12.4 |
| LAKES AREA FCU | Grand Rapids | MN | E- | E- | E | 24.3 | 10.20 | 2.0 | 31.4 | 22.6 | 0.0 | 5.1 | 7.1 |
| LAKES COMMUNITY CU | Lake Orion | MI | C | C+ | B- | 87.6 | -1.12 | 0.1 | 38.9 | 19.4 | 16.6 | 10.0 | 11.6 |
| ▲ LAKES FCU | Monticello | IN | D+ | D- | E+ | 18.4 | -5.07 | 0.0 | 29.8 | 13.4 | 0.0 | 6.8 | 8.8 |
| LAKESHORE COMMUNITY CU | Avon Lake | OH | D | D+ | D+ | 26.6 | -1.29 | 0.0 | 16.4 | 31.1 | 43.6 | 7.6 | 9.4 |
| LAKESHORE FCU | Muskegon | MI | C | C- | C- | 25.9 | 4.24 | 0.9 | 11.7 | 22.0 | 47.0 | 10.0 | 15.2 |
| LAKESIDE EMPL CU | New Johnsonville | TN | D+ | D+ | C- | 37.5 | 3.70 | 0.0 | 23.5 | 3.9 | 0.0 | 10.0 | 14.1 |
| LAKEVIEW FCU | Ashtabula | OH | B- | B | B | 91.8 | 3.88 | 9.3 | 7.0 | 37.9 | 29.6 | 10.0 | 12.2 |
| LAKEWOOD CU | Rib Lake | WI | B- | C+ | C+ | 11.9 | 3.87 | 0.0 | 14.0 | 23.7 | 0.0 | 10.0 | 13.9 |
| LAKEWOOD FIRE FIGHTERS CU INC | Lakewood | OH | C- | C- | C | 1.6 | -3.20 | 0.0 | 36.5 | 0.0 | 0.0 | 10.0 | 19.0 |
| LAKOTA FCU | Kyle | SD | D+ | C- | D | 4.7 | 55.41 | 0.0 | 49.4 | 0.0 | 0.0 | 7.2 | 9.1 |
| LAMAR CIVIC FCU | Lamar | CO | E+ | D | E+ | 5.5 | 7.55 | 0.0 | 42.9 | 0.0 | 0.0 | 5.2 | 7.2 |
| LAMOURE CU | Lamoure | ND | B | B- | C | 24.1 | 3.96 | 15.5 | 23.8 | 14.7 | 0.0 | 9.8 | 10.9 |
| LAMPCO FCU | Anderson | IN | D- | D- | D | 50.7 | -7.74 | 0.0 | 35.9 | 2.1 | 0.0 | 9.3 | 10.6 |
| LAN-FAIR FCU | Lancaster | OH | C | C+ | C+ | 52.9 | 0.03 | 0.0 | 5.0 | 8.5 | 38.7 | 9.6 | 10.8 |
| LANAI FCU | Lanai City | HI | C+ | C+ | C+ | 26.2 | 0.22 | 0.0 | 2.4 | 0.0 | 0.0 | 10.0 | 11.8 |
| ▲ LANCASTER PENNSYLVANIA FIREMEN FCU | Lancaster | PA | D | D | D- | <1 | -21.80 | 0.0 | 72.5 | 0.0 | 0.0 | 10.0 | 12.4 |
| LANCASTER RED ROSE CU | Lancaster | PA | C | C | C | 64.0 | 0.02 | 0.0 | 15.8 | 4.2 | 17.6 | 7.4 | 9.3 |
| ▲ LANCASTER-DEPEW FCU | Depew | NY | B- | C+ | C+ | 43.7 | 3.05 | 0.0 | 20.0 | 10.4 | 44.4 | 8.1 | 9.7 |
| LANCO FCU | Lancaster | PA | C | C | C- | 74.4 | 4.30 | 13.1 | 20.2 | 19.8 | 27.2 | 5.9 | 7.9 |
| LAND OF LINCOLN CU | Decatur | IL | B+ | B+ | A- | 217.8 | 11.13 | 4.7 | 45.7 | 9.6 | 0.7 | 9.1 | 10.4 |
| LANDINGS CU | Tempe | AZ | B- | B- | C+ | 140.1 | 3.83 | 2.7 | 36.1 | 13.5 | 15.8 | 6.8 | 8.9 |
| ▲ LANDMARK CU | Fairfield | AL | C+ | C | D+ | 44.4 | -3.37 | 1.0 | 12.6 | 48.9 | 21.8 | 10.0 | 12.0 |
| LANDMARK CU | Danville | IL | B- | B- | B- | 77.4 | 4.05 | 0.2 | 25.3 | 10.3 | 0.7 | 8.8 | 10.2 |
| LANDMARK CU | North Adams | MA | D+ | D+ | C | 25.8 | -3.67 | 0.0 | 10.2 | 18.8 | 22.9 | 10.0 | 16.1 |
| LANDMARK CU | New Berlin | WI | B | B | B | 2844.8 | 8.52 | 10.3 | 40.4 | 30.1 | 4.1 | 6.5 | 8.5 |
| LANE MEMORIAL FCU | Zachary | LA | E+ | E+ | E+ | 1.5 | -4.90 | 0.0 | 65.1 | 0.0 | 0.0 | 6.0 | 8.0 |
| LANECO FCU | Eugene | OR | D | D- | D- | 14.8 | -2.04 | 0.0 | 31.4 | 0.0 | 0.0 | 6.1 | 8.1 |
| LANGLEY FCU | Newport News | VA | B | B | B- | 2063.1 | 8.01 | 4.0 | 50.0 | 16.2 | 6.4 | 10.0 | 11.8 |
| LANGSTON BAG CO EMPL SAVINGS ASSN C | Memphis | TN | C | C- | C- | <1 | -6.12 | 0.0 | 15.2 | 0.0 | 0.0 | 10.0 | 30.4 |
| LANIER FCU | Oakwood | GA | B | B- | C | 30.6 | 10.06 | 0.0 | 40.7 | 4.8 | 0.0 | 9.0 | 10.4 |
| ▲ LANSING POSTAL COMMUNITY CU | Lansing | MI | C+ | C | C | 22.2 | 1.57 | 0.0 | 31.3 | 15.9 | 0.0 | 10.0 | 12.0 |
| ▲ LAPORTE COMMUNITY FCU | La Porte | IN | B- | B- | B- | 30.1 | 4.03 | 0.0 | 40.6 | 8.5 | 0.0 | 10.0 | 11.3 |
| LARAMIE PLAINS COMMUNITY FCU | Laramie | WY | C+ | C+ | C+ | 44.1 | 8.72 | 2.1 | 59.6 | 11.5 | 0.0 | 8.6 | 10.0 |
| LAREDO FCU | Laredo | TX | B+ | B | B- | 131.4 | 5.52 | 1.5 | 13.1 | 16.8 | 23.6 | 6.9 | 8.9 |
| LAREDO FIRE DEPT FCU | Laredo | TX | C+ | C+ | C+ | 11.0 | 0.04 | 0.0 | 80.6 | 0.0 | 0.0 | 10.0 | 12.2 |
| LAS COLINAS FCU | Irving | TX | C- | C- | C- | 67.2 | 2.94 | 0.0 | 48.6 | 5.7 | 1.0 | 6.2 | 8.2 |
| LAS VEGAS UP EMPL FCU | Las Vegas | NV | D+ | D | D+ | 4.8 | 2.69 | 0.0 | 32.7 | 0.0 | 51.5 | 10.0 | 29.4 |
| LASSEN COUNTY FCU | Susanville | CA | B- | B- | B | 64.5 | 4.86 | 3.9 | 32.6 | 4.3 | 33.1 | 10.0 | 18.1 |
| LAST FCU | Long Island City | NY | C+ | C+ | C+ | <1 | -0.60 | 0.0 | 0.0 | 0.0 | 0.0 | 10.0 | 33.1 |
| LATAH FCU | Moscow | ID | C | C | C | 83.9 | 14.48 | 6.6 | 15.8 | 20.2 | 10.6 | 6.8 | 8.9 |
| LATINO COMMUNITY CU | Durham | NC | A- | B+ | B+ | 194.4 | 32.64 | 0.4 | 24.1 | 53.9 | 0.0 | 10.0 | 11.2 |
| LATITUDE 32 FCU | Charleston | SC | C+ | C+ | C- | 50.8 | 1.17 | 0.0 | 65.5 | 1.4 | 0.0 | 8.0 | 9.6 |
| LATROBE AREA HOSPITAL FCU | Latrobe | PA | D | C- | D | 10.7 | 0.33 | 0.0 | 32.4 | 0.0 | 0.0 | 9.9 | 11.0 |
| ▲ LATROBE FCU | Latrobe | PA | B- | C | C | 10.4 | 8.50 | 0.0 | 36.1 | 0.0 | 0.0 | 10.0 | 12.6 |
| LATVIAN CLEVELAND CU | Lakewood | OH | B | B | B | 30.1 | -4.96 | 8.1 | 1.4 | 59.6 | 24.4 | 10.0 | 14.1 |
| LATVIAN CU | Minneapolis | MN | C- | C- | C- | 4.9 | -0.23 | 1.1 | 36.5 | 28.9 | 0.0 | 10.0 | 11.0 |
| LATVIAN FCU | Melville | NY | C- | C- | C- | 4.2 | -8.77 | 0.0 | 0.0 | 15.9 | 0.5 | 10.0 | 14.7 |
| LATVIAN HERITAGE FCU | Grand Rapids | MI | D | D | D+ | 5.2 | -12.28 | 0.0 | 17.0 | 38.5 | 0.0 | 2.4 | 4.8 |
| LAUDERDALE COUNTY TEACHERS CU | Florence | AL | B- | B- | C | 29.6 | 5.27 | 0.0 | 10.7 | 22.0 | 0.0 | 10.0 | 11.2 |

Arrows denote recent upgrades ▲ or downgrades ▼
122
www.weissratings.com

| Asset Quality Index | Non-Performing Loans as a % of Total Loans | Non-Performing Loans as a % of Capital | Net Charge-Offs Avg Loans | Profitability Index | Net Income ($Mil) | Return on Assets | Return on Equity | Net Interest Spread | Overhead Efficiency Ratio | Liquidity Index | Liquidity Ratio | Hot Money Ratio | Stability Index |
|---|---|---|---|---|---|---|---|---|---|---|---|---|---|
| 5.2 | 0.69 | 8.4 | 0.61 | 1.9 | 0.0 | 0.03 | 0.30 | 4.26 | 84.5 | 5.6 | 36.5 | 0.0 | 4.6 |
| 9.8 | 0.24 | 1.4 | 0.26 | 2.2 | 0.0 | 0.22 | 2.89 | 3.16 | 90.5 | 4.7 | 21.2 | 2.7 | 3.1 |
| 4.7 | 1.31 | 8.8 | 0.42 | 5.2 | 0.0 | 0.80 | 10.43 | 5.36 | 78.6 | 5.1 | 23.6 | 0.0 | 1.7 |
| 5.3 | 1.26 | 10.3 | 0.72 | 8.1 | 0.4 | 1.30 | 13.69 | 4.56 | 78.5 | 3.2 | 13.6 | 6.7 | 3.9 |
| 9.7 | 0.08 | 0.6 | 0.04 | 9.8 | 54.8 | 1.94 | 17.15 | 2.53 | 62.5 | 3.1 | 9.2 | 6.0 | 9.4 |
| 6.6 | 0.92 | 4.6 | 0.42 | 6.7 | 0.1 | 0.88 | 9.25 | 3.95 | 76.6 | 5.7 | 29.5 | 0.0 | 4.8 |
| 7.3 | 0.65 | 2.9 | 0.00 | 2.4 | 0.0 | 0.18 | 1.87 | 3.72 | 95.7 | 4.9 | 34.0 | 9.0 | 2.3 |
| 6.6 | 0.00 | 0.0 | 3.28 | 1.6 | 0.0 | 0.11 | 0.80 | 3.55 | 96.7 | 4.0 | 8.8 | 0.0 | 7.0 |
| 6.2 | 0.96 | 7.8 | 0.53 | 3.5 | 3.7 | 0.30 | 2.89 | 3.67 | 85.9 | 3.3 | 5.2 | 3.8 | 6.4 |
| 7.3 | 0.91 | 3.9 | 0.11 | 4.6 | 0.2 | 0.79 | 10.35 | 2.83 | 73.9 | 4.5 | 22.7 | 2.8 | 3.8 |
| 6.0 | 0.99 | 6.0 | 0.13 | 1.9 | 0.0 | 0.23 | 1.89 | 4.94 | 94.9 | 4.2 | 21.7 | 1.5 | 5.3 |
| 2.6 | 1.45 | 25.3 | 0.33 | 2.0 | 0.0 | 0.12 | 1.56 | 4.62 | 101.8 | 2.3 | 15.5 | 15.1 | 0.0 |
| 6.6 | 1.86 | 11.1 | 0.39 | 2.4 | 0.1 | 0.09 | 0.81 | 3.59 | 91.8 | 3.8 | 13.6 | 4.4 | 5.5 |
| 6.8 | 1.14 | 5.4 | -0.05 | 4.9 | 0.1 | 0.80 | 9.73 | 2.83 | 77.5 | 5.0 | 26.9 | 0.0 | 3.1 |
| 6.7 | 1.48 | 8.1 | 0.52 | 0.9 | 0.0 | -0.16 | -1.88 | 3.38 | 92.4 | 4.8 | 30.1 | 0.0 | 3.3 |
| 10.0 | 0.16 | 0.4 | 0.10 | 2.2 | 0.0 | 0.21 | 1.38 | 2.43 | 92.6 | 4.5 | 22.4 | 3.5 | 6.3 |
| 8.2 | 2.15 | 4.6 | 0.86 | 0.5 | -0.1 | -0.49 | -3.35 | 2.18 | 107.3 | 6.1 | 57.2 | 2.1 | 5.6 |
| 8.2 | 0.92 | 4.2 | 0.15 | 3.3 | 0.3 | 0.38 | 3.19 | 2.69 | 85.3 | 4.4 | 33.2 | 3.4 | 6.4 |
| 9.7 | 0.17 | 0.5 | 0.12 | 3.9 | 0.1 | 0.60 | 4.32 | 3.14 | 78.1 | 5.5 | 26.3 | 0.0 | 7.3 |
| 5.6 | 6.84 | 11.6 | 0.00 | 5.0 | 0.0 | 0.85 | 4.44 | 2.52 | 57.1 | 6.5 | 80.1 | 0.0 | 4.3 |
| 4.9 | 1.35 | 6.1 | 0.74 | 10.0 | 0.4 | 11.40 | 258.25 | 8.93 | 29.8 | 4.5 | 67.9 | 68.8 | 3.0 |
| 6.7 | 0.96 | 5.0 | 0.11 | 1.6 | 0.0 | -0.79 | -10.28 | 3.95 | 115.1 | 5.3 | 53.7 | 0.0 | 1.0 |
| 8.3 | 0.00 | 0.0 | 0.00 | 9.3 | 0.3 | 1.42 | 14.10 | 4.05 | 58.0 | 3.9 | 23.7 | 12.4 | 6.1 |
| 5.5 | 2.39 | 13.5 | 0.13 | 0.2 | -0.3 | -0.65 | -7.55 | 3.66 | 111.9 | 4.4 | 23.7 | 0.9 | 3.7 |
| 5.7 | 3.48 | 13.8 | -0.07 | 3.0 | 0.1 | 0.27 | 2.53 | 2.82 | 88.9 | 6.6 | 42.9 | 6.9 | 5.4 |
| 10.0 | 1.16 | 0.4 | 0.39 | 2.9 | 0.1 | 0.23 | 1.96 | 1.61 | 81.6 | 5.2 | 18.3 | 0.0 | 5.6 |
| 2.7 | 4.36 | 20.0 | 0.00 | 5.3 | 0.0 | 0.76 | 7.49 | 13.62 | 91.5 | 5.5 | 33.3 | 0.0 | 5.2 |
| 6.9 | 1.22 | 5.1 | 0.14 | 3.5 | 0.3 | 0.50 | 5.35 | 2.75 | 91.0 | 4.7 | 27.5 | 0.6 | 4.0 |
| 8.9 | 0.33 | 1.4 | 0.05 | 5.1 | 0.3 | 0.82 | 8.75 | 2.73 | 72.4 | 4.4 | 17.9 | 4.0 | 5.1 |
| 7.2 | 0.62 | 4.5 | 0.43 | 3.3 | 0.1 | 0.25 | 3.18 | 4.15 | 91.1 | 4.6 | 15.1 | 0.5 | 3.4 |
| 6.2 | 0.81 | 5.0 | 0.46 | 5.8 | 1.4 | 0.88 | 8.77 | 4.40 | 81.8 | 3.8 | 23.3 | 6.6 | 6.2 |
| 6.1 | 1.27 | 10.6 | 0.30 | 4.2 | 0.5 | 0.47 | 5.47 | 4.24 | 88.7 | 4.1 | 14.5 | 2.4 | 5.2 |
| 5.8 | 0.93 | 13.0 | 0.77 | 3.9 | 0.2 | 0.55 | 5.31 | 4.17 | 90.9 | 2.2 | 13.4 | 30.5 | 4.5 |
| 6.5 | 1.61 | 6.2 | 0.56 | 3.5 | 0.3 | 0.46 | 4.64 | 2.94 | 84.8 | 5.2 | 19.2 | 1.3 | 5.4 |
| 8.9 | 0.41 | 1.0 | 0.19 | 0.7 | 0.0 | -0.18 | -1.15 | 3.72 | 105.1 | 5.5 | 31.5 | 6.6 | 5.8 |
| 6.1 | 0.82 | 8.2 | 0.29 | 7.4 | 24.2 | 1.17 | 14.32 | 2.69 | 63.9 | 2.6 | 10.0 | 9.3 | 6.5 |
| 6.0 | 0.30 | 2.4 | 0.27 | 2.5 | 0.0 | 0.37 | 4.68 | 7.52 | 94.9 | 4.4 | 32.6 | 9.9 | 1.0 |
| 9.7 | 0.05 | 0.3 | 0.00 | 1.3 | 0.0 | 0.14 | 1.79 | 2.46 | 102.1 | 5.0 | 32.7 | 0.0 | 2.4 |
| 6.4 | 0.83 | 5.1 | 0.96 | 4.6 | 10.9 | 0.72 | 6.13 | 3.75 | 68.1 | 4.1 | 18.8 | 7.8 | 7.7 |
| 10.0 | 0.00 | 0.0 | 0.00 | 1.8 | 0.0 | 0.00 | 0.00 | 4.44 | 100.0 | 8.4 | 118.2 | 0.0 | 5.1 |
| 9.0 | 0.05 | 0.8 | 0.56 | 8.4 | 0.3 | 1.15 | 11.48 | 4.52 | 72.1 | 5.8 | 47.6 | 1.5 | 4.9 |
| 9.0 | 0.40 | 1.8 | 0.19 | 3.0 | 0.0 | 0.24 | 2.37 | 3.96 | 92.9 | 5.2 | 25.7 | 0.4 | 6.0 |
| 8.6 | 0.64 | 3.3 | 0.38 | 3.6 | 0.1 | 0.38 | 3.48 | 4.11 | 88.3 | 3.9 | 10.5 | 3.6 | 5.0 |
| 4.0 | 1.41 | 12.3 | 0.65 | 4.4 | 0.2 | 0.53 | 5.19 | 4.31 | 78.4 | 2.6 | 7.5 | 10.2 | 5.1 |
| 8.9 | 0.50 | 2.4 | 0.28 | 5.5 | 0.5 | 0.52 | 6.67 | 3.02 | 89.7 | 4.2 | 19.2 | 7.1 | 5.9 |
| 6.0 | 0.90 | 5.6 | 0.05 | 4.4 | 0.1 | 0.62 | 5.15 | 5.68 | 87.4 | 1.8 | 11.9 | 20.4 | 4.3 |
| 6.4 | 0.53 | 3.6 | 0.29 | 2.4 | 0.1 | 0.19 | 2.40 | 2.78 | 89.4 | 4.5 | 30.0 | 2.2 | 3.6 |
| 9.3 | 3.52 | 3.8 | -0.17 | 1.1 | 0.0 | -0.06 | -0.19 | 5.08 | 101.7 | 6.0 | 46.3 | 0.0 | 5.2 |
| 9.7 | 0.00 | 0.0 | 0.00 | 3.2 | 0.2 | 0.45 | 2.52 | 2.97 | 86.3 | 4.6 | 22.4 | 3.4 | 7.6 |
| 8.7 | 2.44 | 1.8 | 0.00 | 6.1 | 0.0 | 0.80 | 2.42 | 8.89 | 83.3 | 8.4 | 112.6 | 0.0 | 5.0 |
| 9.6 | 0.15 | 1.0 | 0.04 | 2.9 | 0.2 | 0.34 | 4.27 | 3.00 | 89.2 | 4.8 | 26.6 | 2.8 | 4.4 |
| 5.9 | 1.50 | 11.7 | 0.18 | 10.0 | 5.7 | 4.14 | 38.27 | 5.78 | 48.6 | 2.7 | 35.4 | 49.2 | 8.5 |
| 8.3 | 0.02 | 0.7 | 0.30 | 2.9 | 0.1 | 0.24 | 2.43 | 3.46 | 91.9 | 4.3 | 28.5 | 6.3 | 4.4 |
| 10.0 | 0.03 | 0.1 | 0.34 | 0.9 | 0.0 | -0.15 | -1.36 | 2.85 | 104.8 | 4.7 | 19.6 | 0.0 | 5.1 |
| 9.8 | 0.33 | 1.2 | 0.32 | 4.4 | 0.1 | 0.69 | 5.63 | 3.29 | 83.2 | 6.3 | 44.9 | 0.0 | 6.0 |
| 9.9 | 0.55 | 2.4 | -0.01 | 4.5 | 0.2 | 0.73 | 5.38 | 2.26 | 68.4 | 3.6 | 22.3 | 6.5 | 7.5 |
| 5.2 | 1.32 | 9.6 | 0.00 | 6.9 | 0.0 | 0.92 | 8.54 | 4.58 | 82.5 | 1.5 | 13.1 | 28.2 | 3.7 |
| 7.9 | 3.96 | 5.3 | 0.00 | 2.2 | 0.0 | 0.19 | 1.31 | 1.34 | 85.7 | 5.0 | 22.1 | 0.0 | 6.0 |
| 0.3 | 8.77 | 81.8 | 5.92 | 0.0 | -0.2 | -4.29 | -78.30 | 3.95 | 67.3 | 3.8 | 11.9 | 0.0 | 1.7 |
| 10.0 | 0.01 | 0.0 | 0.05 | 3.6 | 0.1 | 0.47 | 4.18 | 2.18 | 83.7 | 4.4 | 24.7 | 9.7 | 5.8 |

| Name | City | State | Rating | 2014 Rating | 2013 Rating | Total Assets ($Mil) | One Year Asset Growth | Comm- ercial Loans | Cons- umer Loans | Mort- gage Loans | Secur- ities | Capital- ization Index | Net Worth Ratio |
|------|------|-------|--------|-------------|-------------|---------------------|----------------------|--------------------|------------------|-----------------|-------------|-------------------------|-----------------|
| LAUHOFF EMPL CU | Danville | IL | D+ | D+ | D+ | 5.6 | 6.30 | 0.0 | 58.4 | 0.0 | 0.0 | 10.0 | 17.2 |
| LAUNCH FCU | Merritt Island | FL | B- | B | B | 676.6 | 2.67 | 0.0 | 24.1 | 13.0 | 49.2 | 10.0 | 12.2 |
| LAWILIFIE CU | Baton Rouge | LA | C- | C- | D+ | 2.8 | -4.63 | 0.0 | 29.4 | 0.0 | 0.0 | 10.0 | 18.5 |
| LAWRENCE MEMORIAL HOSPITAL EMPL FCU | New London | CT | B- | B- | B | 27.1 | -1.08 | 0.0 | 29.7 | 0.0 | 0.0 | 10.0 | 19.3 |
| LBS FINANCIAL CU | Westminster | CA | A | A | A | 1190.4 | 6.05 | 0.0 | 38.7 | 19.4 | 10.1 | 10.0 | 14.1 |
| LCO FCU | Hayward | WI | E+ | E+ | D- | 1.8 | -13.47 | 0.0 | 78.5 | 0.0 | 0.0 | 5.6 | 7.6 |
| LCRA CU | Austin | TX | D+ | D+ | C+ | 24.1 | -0.45 | 0.0 | 64.6 | 5.7 | 0.0 | 10.0 | 12.2 |
| LE ROY FCU | Le Roy | NY | D+ | D | D- | 9.9 | 10.26 | 0.0 | 26.7 | 3.9 | 0.0 | 6.1 | 8.1 |
| LEADCO COMMUNITY CU | Park Hills | MO | C- | C- | C- | 20.2 | 11.29 | 0.0 | 45.3 | 1.6 | 0.0 | 10.0 | 11.1 |
| LEADERS CU | Jackson | TN | A | A | A | 261.8 | 15.69 | 1.1 | 50.5 | 15.7 | 4.8 | 10.0 | 12.7 |
| LEAHI FCU | Honolulu | HI | E+ | E+ | E+ | 2.0 | -4.21 | 0.0 | 85.3 | 0.0 | 0.0 | 4.3 | 6.3 |
| LEATHERSTOCKING REGION FCU | Cooperstown | NY | C | C | C+ | 44.0 | 2.40 | 0.0 | 24.4 | 6.7 | 33.7 | 7.8 | 9.5 |
| LEBANON FCU | Lebanon | PA | B | B | B | 191.2 | 3.90 | 4.0 | 21.3 | 30.6 | 21.7 | 9.7 | 10.8 |
| LEE COUNTY MOSQUITO CONTROL CU | Lehigh Acres | FL | C+ | C+ | C+ | <1 | -12.64 | 0.0 | 19.7 | 0.0 | 0.0 | 10.0 | 40.5 |
| LEE FCU | Washington | DC | B- | B- | B- | 10.8 | -4.70 | 3.5 | 0.4 | 30.2 | 54.6 | 10.0 | 18.4 |
| LEECO CU | Keokuk | IA | B- | C+ | C+ | 3.7 | 10.73 | 0.0 | 52.5 | 0.0 | 0.0 | 10.0 | 18.1 |
| LEFORS FCU | Lefors | TX | D+ | D+ | C- | 4.9 | -9.22 | 0.0 | 35.2 | 12.3 | 0.0 | 10.0 | 16.7 |
| LEGACY COMMUNITY FCU | Birmingham | AL | B | B+ | A- | 409.8 | 2.24 | 2.8 | 22.3 | 18.4 | 38.3 | 10.0 | 13.5 |
| LEGACY FCU | Portland | OR | C- | D+ | C- | 45.6 | 2.71 | 0.0 | 24.0 | 5.9 | 19.1 | 9.3 | 10.6 |
| LEGAL COMMUNITY CU OF COLORADO | Littleton | CO | D- | D | C- | 4.9 | 17.27 | 0.0 | 45.7 | 28.9 | 0.0 | 5.5 | 7.5 |
| LEHIGH COUNTY EMPL FCU | Allentown | PA | C+ | C+ | C | 15.4 | 5.13 | 0.0 | 12.3 | 20.6 | 0.0 | 10.0 | 11.8 |
| LEHIGH VALLEY EDUCATORS CU | Allentown | PA | B+ | B+ | B+ | 297.5 | 2.38 | 0.0 | 13.5 | 0.8 | 60.1 | 10.0 | 16.2 |
| LEHIGH VALLEY FCU | Allentown | PA | E- | E | E+ | 15.1 | -0.29 | 0.0 | 38.8 | 18.8 | 0.0 | 3.6 | 5.6 |
| LEHRER INTERESTS CU | Garwood | TX | C | C- | C+ | 2.0 | -2.26 | 0.0 | 5.4 | 5.9 | 0.0 | 10.0 | 21.8 |
| ▲ LENCO CU | Adrian | MI | C- | D+ | C | 71.3 | 4.17 | 0.0 | 26.5 | 12.0 | 1.2 | 5.7 | 7.7 |
| ▲ LENNOX EMPL CU | Marshalltown | IA | C- | C- | C+ | 37.1 | 1.05 | 2.5 | 33.6 | 2.4 | 0.0 | 10.0 | 14.4 |
| LEO CU | Painesville | OH | B- | B- | B- | 14.4 | -6.68 | 0.0 | 27.9 | 0.0 | 56.6 | 10.0 | 16.0 |
| LEOMINSTER CU | Leominster | MA | C | C | C | 631.5 | 1.88 | 2.8 | 26.0 | 30.7 | 26.6 | 6.4 | 8.5 |
| LEOMINSTER EMPL FCU | Leominster | MA | C | C | C | 17.4 | 13.71 | 0.0 | 42.9 | 18.1 | 0.0 | 8.2 | 9.8 |
| LES FCU | Baton Rouge | LA | C+ | C | C+ | 32.2 | 4.44 | 0.0 | 44.4 | 9.0 | 0.0 | 9.2 | 10.5 |
| LESCO FCU | Latrobe | PA | C+ | C+ | C+ | 66.3 | 2.77 | 0.0 | 19.6 | 4.6 | 0.0 | 10.0 | 18.8 |
| ▲ LETCHER COUNTY TEACHERS CU | Whitesburg | KY | C- | D+ | C- | 1.1 | 2.30 | 0.0 | 33.1 | 0.0 | 0.0 | 10.0 | 18.9 |
| ▼ LETOURNEAU FCU | Longview | TX | B- | B | B | 23.3 | -2.50 | 0.0 | 9.9 | 0.7 | 0.0 | 10.0 | 21.7 |
| LEWIS CLARK CU | Lewiston | ID | B | B | C+ | 55.4 | 10.72 | 0.5 | 69.3 | 0.1 | 0.0 | 10.0 | 11.3 |
| LEWISTON MUNICIPAL FCU | Lewiston | ME | C | C | C | 21.7 | 7.64 | 0.0 | 16.2 | 31.8 | 0.0 | 8.9 | 10.3 |
| LEWISTON PORTER FCU | Youngstown | NY | C | C | C- | 10.7 | 2.61 | 0.0 | 14.8 | 26.8 | 0.0 | 9.9 | 10.9 |
| LEXINGTON AVENUE FCU | Rochester | NY | D- | D- | D+ | 17.0 | -0.62 | 0.0 | 60.1 | 0.4 | 7.0 | 6.5 | 8.5 |
| ▲ LEXINGTON MA FCU | Lexington | MA | D+ | D+ | C- | 9.8 | 1.92 | 0.0 | 34.2 | 0.0 | 0.0 | 10.0 | 11.1 |
| LEXINGTON POSTAL CU | Lexington | KY | D | D | C- | 19.5 | 2.96 | 0.0 | 22.5 | 11.9 | 2.8 | 10.0 | 14.5 |
| LEYDEN CU | Franklin Park | IL | C- | D+ | D+ | 77.1 | 6.97 | 0.0 | 11.0 | 13.7 | 16.8 | 6.6 | 8.7 |
| LGE COMMUNITY CU | Marietta | GA | A- | A- | B+ | 1025.1 | 3.55 | 2.2 | 47.4 | 26.6 | 12.6 | 10.0 | 11.7 |
| LIBERTY BAY CU | Braintree | MA | C- | C- | D+ | 659.5 | 0.60 | 1.6 | 13.6 | 29.5 | 31.1 | 10.0 | 14.5 |
| LIBERTY COUNTY TEACHERS FCU | Liberty | TX | D+ | D+ | D+ | 16.4 | 8.15 | 0.0 | 34.7 | 6.3 | 0.0 | 6.4 | 8.4 |
| LIBERTY FIRST CU | Lincoln | NE | B+ | B+ | B+ | 205.7 | 16.55 | 8.5 | 33.0 | 30.0 | 0.0 | 9.0 | 10.4 |
| LIBERTY SAVINGS FCU | Jersey City | NJ | C- | C- | C- | 80.7 | 4.13 | 0.0 | 68.5 | 5.6 | 0.0 | 10.0 | 12.0 |
| LIBERTYONE CU | Arlington | TX | B- | B- | B- | 109.8 | 5.05 | 0.0 | 43.8 | 13.8 | 9.7 | 10.0 | 11.2 |
| LIBRARY OF CONGRESS FCU | Hyattsville | MD | A- | A- | A- | 222.4 | -0.04 | 0.0 | 18.7 | 33.2 | 23.6 | 10.0 | 14.2 |
| LIFE CU | Nashville | TN | B | B | B- | 30.5 | 0.85 | 0.0 | 43.4 | 20.4 | 0.3 | 10.0 | 12.0 |
| LIFEWAY CU | Nashville | TN | B | B- | B- | 48.6 | 0.40 | 0.0 | 11.7 | 17.5 | 9.7 | 10.0 | 13.6 |
| LIGHT COMMERCE CU | Houston | TX | C | C | C | 2.6 | -2.61 | 0.0 | 57.9 | 0.0 | 0.0 | 10.0 | 20.8 |
| LIGHTHOUSE COMMUNITY CU | Vancouver | WA | D+ | C- | D- | 11.3 | 3.52 | 0.0 | 45.2 | 13.9 | 0.0 | 8.4 | 9.9 |
| LIMESTONE FCU | Manistique | MI | B- | B- | B- | 42.6 | 0.02 | 1.8 | 28.7 | 50.8 | 0.0 | 10.0 | 11.5 |
| LIMONEIRA FCU | Santa Paula | CA | D | D+ | C- | 4.7 | -5.55 | 1.4 | 28.9 | 0.0 | 0.0 | 10.0 | 11.2 |
| LINCOLN COUNTY CU | Libby | MT | A | A | A | 106.2 | 1.68 | 3.3 | 9.0 | 28.9 | 21.8 | 10.0 | 19.2 |
| LINCOLN MAINE FCU | Lincoln | ME | B | B | B | 53.5 | 6.77 | 0.0 | 30.2 | 27.7 | 0.0 | 9.8 | 10.9 |
| LINCOLN NATIONAL FCU | Greensboro | NC | D+ | D+ | C- | 17.8 | -6.35 | 0.0 | 6.0 | 10.3 | 48.2 | 10.0 | 13.5 |
| LINCOLN PARK COMMUNITY CU | Lincoln Park | MI | C- | C | B- | 50.7 | -0.65 | 0.0 | 3.9 | 2.8 | 82.6 | 10.0 | 17.5 |
| LINCOLN SDA CU | Lincoln | NE | D | D+ | C- | 12.0 | 1.91 | 1.4 | 11.5 | 7.1 | 0.0 | 10.0 | 19.5 |
| LINCOLN SUDBURY TOWN EMPL FCU | Sudbury | MA | D | D | D+ | 5.2 | -0.15 | 0.0 | 18.2 | 14.3 | 0.0 | 10.0 | 12.5 |
| LINCOLN USDA FCU | Lincoln | NE | C- | C- | C- | 5.9 | 0.44 | 0.0 | 55.7 | 0.0 | 0.0 | 10.0 | 12.0 |

| Asset Quality Index | Non-Performing Loans as a % of Total Loans | Non-Performing Loans as a % of Capital | Net Charge-Offs Avg Loans | Profitability Index | Net Income ($Mil) | Return on Assets | Return on Equity | Net Interest Spread | Overhead Efficiency Ratio | Liquidity Index | Liquidity Ratio | Hot Money Ratio | Stability Index |
|---|---|---|---|---|---|---|---|---|---|---|---|---|---|
| 6.9 | 1.12 | 3.7 | 1.59 | 0.3 | -0.1 | -1.05 | -5.98 | 4.45 | 105.0 | 4.8 | 23.0 | 0.0 | 5.1 |
| 9.9 | 0.56 | 1.7 | 0.87 | 2.9 | 1.2 | 0.23 | 1.88 | 3.01 | 83.4 | 4.7 | 8.1 | 1.8 | 7.9 |
| 9.8 | 0.00 | 0.0 | 0.00 | 1.1 | 0.0 | -0.18 | -1.02 | 3.84 | 105.7 | 5.5 | 17.9 | 0.0 | 7.0 |
| 10.0 | 0.29 | 0.6 | 0.04 | 3.1 | 0.1 | 0.35 | 1.85 | 2.35 | 89.0 | 5.2 | 44.4 | 0.6 | 7.0 |
| 9.3 | 0.26 | 1.6 | 0.17 | 6.1 | 8.1 | 0.91 | 6.83 | 3.33 | 74.1 | 3.9 | 23.5 | 12.1 | 9.3 |
| 0.0 | 13.89 | 292.4 | 1.98 | 1.7 | 0.0 | -1.30 | -50.67 | 8.77 | 83.1 | 3.5 | 11.7 | 0.0 | 2.1 |
| 8.0 | 0.06 | 0.3 | 0.23 | 0.7 | -0.1 | -0.30 | -2.39 | 2.75 | 106.5 | 3.2 | 7.7 | 4.7 | 5.6 |
| 8.9 | 0.00 | 0.0 | 0.00 | 5.6 | 0.1 | 0.88 | 11.59 | 4.08 | 83.1 | 4.4 | 20.9 | 2.5 | 3.3 |
| 4.5 | 0.49 | 12.8 | 0.28 | 3.9 | 0.1 | 0.51 | 5.20 | 3.79 | 88.0 | 4.5 | 36.7 | 4.2 | 4.8 |
| 7.0 | 0.48 | 3.3 | 0.50 | 9.5 | 2.5 | 1.35 | 10.59 | 4.10 | 73.9 | 1.6 | 7.9 | 22.8 | 9.2 |
| 0.0 | 5.18 | 51.8 | 1.39 | 3.3 | 0.0 | 0.33 | 4.69 | 7.75 | 95.8 | 3.7 | 15.3 | 0.0 | 2.6 |
| 6.4 | 0.97 | 6.6 | 0.51 | 4.0 | 0.2 | 0.54 | 5.83 | 3.09 | 85.8 | 4.5 | 18.0 | 3.0 | 3.8 |
| 7.8 | 0.89 | 4.9 | 0.59 | 4.6 | 0.9 | 0.66 | 6.25 | 3.43 | 78.0 | 3.8 | 17.2 | 5.9 | 6.9 |
| 10.0 | 0.00 | 0.0 | 0.00 | 4.4 | 0.0 | 0.71 | 1.75 | 2.12 | 60.0 | 5.8 | 58.9 | 0.0 | 7.4 |
| 7.9 | 0.00 | 0.0 | 0.00 | 3.0 | 0.0 | 0.25 | 1.35 | 1.13 | 78.2 | 6.0 | 78.1 | 0.0 | 7.7 |
| 5.7 | 3.28 | 10.5 | 0.00 | 9.8 | 0.0 | 1.61 | 9.04 | 6.93 | 60.3 | 6.1 | 43.6 | 0.0 | 5.0 |
| 6.2 | 3.49 | 11.7 | 0.77 | 0.6 | 0.0 | -0.78 | -4.79 | 4.61 | 101.3 | 5.5 | 44.9 | 0.0 | 6.0 |
| 10.0 | 0.22 | 0.9 | 0.33 | 3.6 | 1.0 | 0.34 | 2.65 | 2.48 | 86.9 | 4.7 | 20.7 | 4.3 | 7.8 |
| 8.8 | 1.18 | 3.4 | 0.24 | 1.8 | 0.0 | 0.02 | 0.22 | 2.24 | 93.9 | 5.6 | 25.1 | 0.8 | 4.7 |
| 8.6 | 0.00 | 0.0 | 0.08 | 3.1 | 0.0 | 0.18 | 2.21 | 4.93 | 97.1 | 4.3 | 23.4 | 6.9 | 1.7 |
| 8.1 | 1.57 | 4.7 | 0.00 | 3.5 | 0.1 | 0.49 | 4.25 | 3.31 | 82.4 | 7.0 | 52.6 | 0.0 | 6.5 |
| 9.6 | 1.45 | 2.5 | 0.15 | 4.4 | 1.6 | 0.72 | 4.35 | 2.11 | 68.7 | 5.0 | 36.1 | 4.4 | 7.8 |
| 6.9 | 0.34 | 4.1 | 0.73 | 0.0 | -0.2 | -1.42 | -22.71 | 3.37 | 114.6 | 4.3 | 21.7 | 0.0 | 1.3 |
| 10.0 | 0.00 | 0.0 | 0.00 | 2.1 | 0.0 | 0.19 | 0.92 | 1.62 | 81.8 | 6.4 | 67.7 | 0.0 | 7.0 |
| 8.6 | 0.53 | 3.1 | 0.15 | 2.2 | 0.2 | 0.37 | 4.84 | 2.78 | 85.6 | 4.8 | 22.4 | 2.1 | 3.0 |
| 7.8 | 1.44 | 4.8 | 0.16 | 1.7 | 0.1 | 0.17 | 1.24 | 2.89 | 92.7 | 4.2 | 16.7 | 1.7 | 6.7 |
| 9.1 | 1.83 | 3.5 | 0.00 | 4.6 | 0.1 | 0.69 | 4.49 | 3.16 | 78.7 | 4.8 | 23.4 | 3.3 | 6.6 |
| 8.4 | 0.58 | 3.8 | 0.06 | 2.8 | 1.3 | 0.27 | 2.73 | 2.57 | 89.2 | 2.7 | 1.4 | 12.0 | 6.9 |
| 5.2 | 1.97 | 13.5 | 0.33 | 4.9 | 0.1 | 0.66 | 6.59 | 4.24 | 70.3 | 4.6 | 35.1 | 8.3 | 3.7 |
| 6.1 | 1.01 | 5.6 | 0.74 | 3.4 | 0.1 | 0.40 | 3.95 | 3.93 | 87.4 | 4.5 | 38.8 | 4.2 | 5.2 |
| 10.0 | 0.26 | 0.4 | 0.11 | 3.2 | 0.2 | 0.42 | 2.24 | 2.21 | 82.3 | 5.2 | 36.0 | 6.3 | 7.1 |
| 9.9 | 0.54 | 0.9 | 0.00 | 1.8 | 0.0 | 0.13 | 0.65 | 3.84 | 96.4 | 7.0 | 81.2 | 0.0 | 7.1 |
| 10.0 | 0.75 | 0.8 | 0.58 | 3.3 | 0.1 | 0.30 | 1.43 | 2.19 | 86.1 | 5.6 | 47.2 | 3.1 | 7.6 |
| 5.8 | 0.85 | 7.1 | 0.46 | 5.7 | 0.3 | 0.74 | 7.19 | 5.01 | 81.3 | 1.8 | 6.6 | 14.9 | 4.7 |
| 9.2 | 0.05 | 0.3 | -0.07 | 4.1 | 0.1 | 0.61 | 5.97 | 2.92 | 83.8 | 3.7 | 34.6 | 15.7 | 5.5 |
| 6.7 | 0.98 | 5.1 | -0.09 | 4.3 | 0.1 | 0.69 | 6.57 | 3.10 | 76.7 | 4.6 | 14.7 | 0.6 | 6.2 |
| 1.7 | 3.26 | 28.3 | 1.39 | 1.6 | 0.0 | -0.11 | -1.37 | 6.27 | 89.1 | 2.6 | 12.2 | 14.5 | 0.3 |
| 9.4 | 0.95 | 3.4 | 0.55 | 0.9 | 0.0 | -0.11 | -0.97 | 3.45 | 103.6 | 5.4 | 25.9 | 0.0 | 4.9 |
| 10.0 | 0.17 | 0.4 | 0.22 | 0.2 | -0.1 | -0.43 | -2.86 | 3.05 | 107.6 | 6.8 | 53.8 | 0.0 | 6.2 |
| 7.6 | 1.01 | 3.4 | 0.53 | 2.0 | 0.1 | 0.10 | 1.11 | 2.92 | 93.6 | 6.5 | 35.4 | 1.7 | 2.9 |
| 8.5 | 0.11 | 0.8 | 0.27 | 6.0 | 7.3 | 0.95 | 8.33 | 2.88 | 71.8 | 3.3 | 8.1 | 3.1 | 8.2 |
| 7.5 | 1.47 | 5.8 | 0.07 | 1.6 | 1.7 | 0.36 | 2.40 | 2.37 | 87.3 | 3.6 | 11.6 | 11.5 | 7.8 |
| 5.2 | 0.77 | 7.5 | 0.42 | 5.0 | 0.1 | 0.78 | 10.90 | 4.08 | 81.7 | 5.3 | 36.4 | 0.0 | 3.0 |
| 6.9 | 1.03 | 7.3 | 0.46 | 6.5 | 1.5 | 1.05 | 9.72 | 4.81 | 80.3 | 2.6 | 12.0 | 17.6 | 6.1 |
| 1.6 | 4.93 | 25.5 | 4.75 | 6.3 | 0.3 | 0.48 | 4.08 | 9.80 | 61.4 | 4.7 | 24.9 | 0.0 | 7.1 |
| 8.1 | 0.68 | 3.8 | 0.38 | 3.7 | 0.4 | 0.52 | 4.59 | 2.72 | 75.1 | 3.4 | 16.4 | 7.9 | 7.0 |
| 9.4 | 0.54 | 3.3 | 0.33 | 6.5 | 1.7 | 1.00 | 7.20 | 2.89 | 64.9 | 3.5 | 21.2 | 9.4 | 8.2 |
| 8.4 | 0.44 | 2.6 | 0.30 | 4.5 | 0.1 | 0.39 | 3.32 | 4.70 | 93.9 | 3.1 | 11.9 | 8.3 | 5.9 |
| 6.1 | 3.16 | 10.4 | -0.05 | 6.7 | 0.4 | 1.18 | 9.06 | 3.41 | 66.6 | 5.0 | 33.9 | 1.3 | 6.7 |
| 5.3 | 1.56 | 5.3 | 0.80 | 7.4 | 0.0 | 0.86 | 4.31 | 5.58 | 77.4 | 5.4 | 34.2 | 0.0 | 5.0 |
| 2.3 | 2.41 | 23.0 | 1.40 | 3.6 | -0.1 | -0.65 | -6.37 | 6.54 | 88.7 | 4.0 | 18.3 | 0.0 | 5.4 |
| 6.7 | 0.61 | 5.3 | 0.14 | 5.9 | 0.2 | 0.73 | 6.47 | 4.44 | 85.2 | 1.5 | 13.6 | 21.9 | 5.7 |
| 9.4 | 0.21 | 0.6 | 2.18 | 0.5 | 0.0 | -0.45 | -3.93 | 3.38 | 92.7 | 5.6 | 23.1 | 0.0 | 5.0 |
| 8.9 | 0.69 | 3.8 | 0.29 | 8.7 | 0.9 | 1.18 | 6.25 | 2.53 | 56.7 | 5.2 | 29.0 | 1.0 | 10.0 |
| 6.0 | 1.32 | 8.3 | 0.17 | 5.0 | 0.2 | 0.62 | 5.70 | 3.00 | 78.3 | 3.5 | 12.6 | 3.1 | 6.0 |
| 10.0 | 0.27 | 0.4 | 0.19 | 0.6 | 0.0 | -0.26 | -1.99 | 1.35 | 117.3 | 5.6 | 32.3 | 0.0 | 5.8 |
| 10.0 | 0.37 | 0.2 | 0.07 | 1.4 | 0.0 | 0.02 | 0.12 | 1.99 | 99.3 | 5.3 | 15.2 | 0.0 | 6.2 |
| 10.0 | 0.61 | 0.6 | 0.27 | 0.0 | -0.1 | -0.69 | -3.59 | 2.30 | 136.6 | 6.0 | 38.7 | 7.4 | 6.3 |
| 3.7 | 10.90 | 30.7 | 1.96 | 0.2 | 0.0 | -0.52 | -4.26 | 2.50 | 97.8 | 4.5 | 27.3 | 8.2 | 5.7 |
| 8.4 | 0.33 | 2.0 | 0.72 | 4.2 | 0.0 | 0.58 | 4.94 | 3.63 | 84.5 | 3.7 | 28.6 | 2.9 | 6.3 |

| Name | City | State | Rating | 2014 Rating | 2013 Rating | Total Assets ($Mil) | One Year Asset Growth | Commercial Loans | Consumer Loans | Mortgage Loans | Securities | Capitalization Index | Net Worth Ratio |
|------|------|-------|--------|-------------|-------------|---------------------|----------------------|------------------|----------------|----------------|------------|---------------------|-----------------|
| | | | | | | | | asset mix | | | | | |
| LINCONE FCU | Lincoln | NE | D+ | C | C | 119.4 | 174.30 | 0.3 | 30.7 | 7.3 | 1.1 | 8.4 | 10.0 |
| LINDE EMPL FCU | New Providence | NJ | E+ | E+ | E+ | 6.3 | 10.87 | 0.0 | 31.1 | 0.0 | 51.0 | 2.1 | 4.7 |
| LINDEN NEW JERSEY POLICE & FIREMEN FC | Linden | NJ | B- | B- | B- | 10.0 | -4.78 | 0.0 | 12.2 | 0.0 | 82.3 | 10.0 | 14.6 |
| LINK FCU | Indianapolis | IN | D- | D | D | 19.0 | 2.58 | 0.9 | 58.9 | 2.8 | 0.0 | 7.4 | 9.3 |
| LINKAGE CU | Waco | TX | C | C- | C- | 13.0 | 5.04 | 0.3 | 47.1 | 0.0 | 0.0 | 10.0 | 16.1 |
| LINN AREA CU | Cedar Rapids | IA | B | B | B | 353.7 | 5.26 | 6.4 | 31.5 | 24.0 | 9.7 | 7.3 | 9.2 |
| LINN-CO FCU | Lebanon | OR | B- | B- | C+ | 87.5 | 7.63 | 0.7 | 63.7 | 2.0 | 0.0 | 9.5 | 10.7 |
| LINTON FCU | Tonawanda | NY | C- | C- | C- | 6.5 | 4.24 | 0.0 | 49.1 | 0.0 | 0.0 | 10.0 | 19.6 |
| LION FCU | El Dorado | AR | B- | B- | B- | 13.9 | 1.99 | 0.0 | 42.0 | 0.0 | 0.0 | 10.0 | 15.9 |
| LIONS SHARE FCU | Salisbury | NC | C- | C- | C- | 45.3 | 14.16 | 0.0 | 63.8 | 0.0 | 0.0 | 6.2 | 8.3 |
| LISBON COMMUNITY FCU | Lisbon | ME | C+ | B- | B- | 92.7 | 8.16 | 4.7 | 16.3 | 36.1 | 0.0 | 9.8 | 10.9 |
| LISBON FARMERS UNION CU | Lisbon | ND | D+ | C- | C | 4.6 | 2.02 | 16.2 | 8.5 | 27.2 | 0.0 | 10.0 | 66.7 |
| LISTERHILL CU | Muscle Shoals | AL | B+ | B+ | B+ | 674.5 | 4.56 | 11.6 | 27.5 | 35.5 | 13.6 | 10.0 | 11.0 |
| LITHIUM FCU | Bessemer City | NC | D+ | D+ | C- | 8.5 | 2.83 | 0.0 | 36.3 | 0.0 | 0.0 | 10.0 | 17.7 |
| LITTLE GIANT FCU | McKees Rocks | PA | D+ | D+ | C- | 9.7 | -3.23 | 0.0 | 22.0 | 0.0 | 0.0 | 10.0 | 14.1 |
| LITTLE ROCK FIRE DEPT FCU | Little Rock | AR | B | B | B- | 10.7 | 5.64 | 0.0 | 51.5 | 0.0 | 0.0 | 10.0 | 17.9 |
| LITTLEFIELD SCHOOL EMPL FCU | Littlefield | TX | C+ | C+ | C+ | 1.2 | 35.81 | 0.0 | 38.3 | 0.0 | 0.0 | 10.0 | 12.3 |
| LIVINGSTON PARISH FCU | Denham Springs | LA | C+ | C+ | C+ | 14.5 | -3.77 | 0.0 | 22.1 | 11.1 | 0.0 | 10.0 | 17.7 |
| LM FCU | Baltimore | MD | C- | C- | C- | 32.6 | 6.38 | 0.0 | 34.4 | 3.7 | 0.0 | 5.3 | 7.3 |
| ▲ LOC FCU | Farmington | MI | C | C- | C- | 173.8 | 5.81 | 3.4 | 20.8 | 17.8 | 27.8 | 5.8 | 7.8 |
| LOCAL #673 CU | Mentor | OH | D | D | D | 1.9 | 8.50 | 0.0 | 53.0 | 0.0 | 4.7 | 10.0 | 12.5 |
| LOCAL 1233 FCU | Newark | NJ | C | C+ | C+ | 9.5 | 1.14 | 0.0 | 48.2 | 0.0 | 0.0 | 10.0 | 16.1 |
| LOCAL 142 FCU | San Antonio | TX | D- | D- | D | 8.8 | 0.81 | 0.0 | 31.8 | 0.0 | 0.0 | 8.2 | 9.8 |
| LOCAL 20 IBEW FCU | Grand Prairie | TX | E+ | E+ | E+ | 7.0 | -10.92 | 1.6 | 38.6 | 0.0 | 0.0 | 5.3 | 7.4 |
| LOCAL 229 IBEW FCU | York | PA | E+ | E+ | E+ | 1.3 | -13.98 | 0.0 | 63.3 | 0.0 | 0.0 | 5.5 | 7.5 |
| LOCAL 24 EMPL FCU | Houston | TX | B- | B- | B- | 11.4 | 4.42 | 0.0 | 29.4 | 0.2 | 0.0 | 10.0 | 14.4 |
| LOCAL 265 IBEW FCU | Lincoln | NE | D+ | D | D | 4.1 | 10.80 | 0.0 | 35.3 | 4.9 | 0.0 | 7.8 | 9.5 |
| LOCAL 355 MARYLAND FCU | Baltimore | MD | C+ | C+ | C | 4.3 | 9.88 | 0.0 | 16.5 | 0.0 | 53.0 | 10.0 | 23.6 |
| LOCAL 41 IBEW FCU | Orchard Park | NY | D+ | D | D | 9.6 | -2.16 | 0.0 | 24.1 | 19.1 | 0.0 | 8.1 | 9.7 |
| ▼ LOCAL 461 FCU | Macon | GA | D | D | D+ | <1 | 0.82 | 0.0 | 43.5 | 0.0 | 0.0 | 10.0 | 19.8 |
| LOCAL 50 PLUMBERS & STEAMFITTERS FCU | Northwood | OH | D+ | D+ | D+ | 7.8 | 2.28 | 0.0 | 50.8 | 0.0 | 0.0 | 10.0 | 13.3 |
| LOCAL 520 UA FCU | Harrisburg | PA | D+ | D | C- | 8.3 | -3.61 | 0.0 | 26.9 | 0.0 | 0.0 | 10.0 | 18.1 |
| LOCAL 606 ELECTRICAL WORKERS FCU | Orlando | FL | C+ | C+ | C+ | 7.8 | -2.96 | 0.0 | 6.0 | 12.5 | 0.0 | 10.0 | 15.4 |
| LOCAL 697 FCU | Merrillville | IN | C- | D+ | D+ | 34.0 | 2.98 | 0.0 | 15.4 | 2.2 | 53.3 | 10.0 | 19.2 |
| ▼ LOCAL 804 FCU | Long Island City | NY | D | C- | C | 21.4 | -0.11 | 1.0 | 10.1 | 14.2 | 0.0 | 10.0 | 23.8 |
| ▼ LOCAL CU | Sterling Heights | MI | C- | B- | B | 90.9 | -5.09 | 1.9 | 15.8 | 17.0 | 57.3 | 10.0 | 14.9 |
| LOCAL FCU | Dallas | TX | C+ | C+ | C+ | 22.3 | -2.86 | 0.0 | 63.6 | 2.2 | 0.0 | 10.0 | 17.9 |
| LOCAL GOVERNMENT FCU | Raleigh | NC | B+ | B | B- | 1549.1 | 9.80 | 4.2 | 37.0 | 26.4 | 14.4 | 7.3 | 9.4 |
| LOCAL NO 317 IAFF CU | Charleston | WV | D+ | D | D | 7.1 | 3.49 | 0.0 | 43.2 | 0.0 | 0.0 | 6.8 | 8.8 |
| LOCAL UNION 1186 IBEW FCU | Honolulu | HI | C- | C- | D+ | 14.5 | 1.07 | 0.0 | 11.1 | 0.0 | 31.2 | 10.0 | 13.2 |
| ▲ LOCAL UNION 392 FCU | Cincinnati | OH | C- | C- | C- | 10.3 | 5.86 | 0.0 | 58.7 | 0.7 | 0.0 | 10.0 | 16.4 |
| ▼ LOCKPORT SCHOOLS FCU | Lockport | NY | C- | C | C | 11.1 | 1.65 | 0.0 | 21.0 | 13.0 | 17.2 | 9.3 | 10.5 |
| LOCO CU | Alamogordo | NM | B+ | B+ | B+ | 41.3 | 0.60 | 0.0 | 35.9 | 0.6 | 7.2 | 10.0 | 13.1 |
| LOCOGA FCU | Valdosta | GA | D | D | C- | 4.8 | -8.71 | 0.0 | 38.8 | 0.0 | 0.0 | 5.0 | 7.0 |
| LOCOMOTIVE & CONTROL EMPL FCU | Erie | PA | B- | B- | B | 18.0 | -4.84 | 0.0 | 12.9 | 17.4 | 0.0 | 10.0 | 19.3 |
| LOGAN CACHE RICH FCU | Logan | UT | B- | B- | B- | 21.6 | 2.34 | 0.0 | 33.9 | 8.5 | 0.0 | 10.0 | 13.7 |
| LOGAN COUNTY SCHOOL EMPL FCU | Logan | WV | C- | C- | C- | 1.4 | -3.17 | 0.0 | 20.1 | 0.0 | 0.0 | 10.0 | 12.2 |
| LOGAN MEDICAL FCU | Logan | UT | B | B | B | 19.1 | 5.25 | 0.0 | 31.7 | 23.9 | 1.3 | 10.0 | 15.8 |
| LOGIX FCU | Burbank | CA | A | A | A | 4180.5 | 7.56 | 11.1 | 20.3 | 52.4 | 14.2 | 10.0 | 16.6 |
| LOMTO FCU | Woodside | NY | B- | B+ | A- | 271.5 | -0.96 | 87.4 | 0.2 | 2.4 | 0.0 | 10.0 | 16.8 |
| LONE STAR CU | Dallas | TX | C+ | C | D+ | 108.2 | 6.10 | 1.2 | 40.8 | 23.8 | 5.6 | 5.5 | 7.5 |
| ▲ LONG BEACH CITY EMPL FCU | Signal Hill | CA | B | B- | B- | 300.9 | -1.63 | 0.6 | 3.9 | 23.1 | 51.1 | 9.5 | 10.7 |
| LONG BEACH FIREMENS CU | Long Beach | CA | A+ | A+ | A | 170.2 | 3.21 | 10.2 | 2.0 | 58.0 | 2.1 | 10.0 | 18.1 |
| LONG BEACH TEACHERS FCU | Long Beach | NY | D | D | C- | 3.7 | -9.29 | 0.0 | 26.2 | 0.0 | 0.0 | 10.0 | 21.8 |
| LONG ISLAND CITY POSTAL EMPL FCU | Long Island City | NY | D+ | D+ | D+ | 3.3 | -5.18 | 0.0 | 4.3 | 0.0 | 38.2 | 10.0 | 19.4 |
| ▼ LONG ISLAND COMMUNITY FCU | Port Jefferson | NY | D- | D | D- | 19.0 | -2.36 | 0.0 | 8.3 | 22.6 | 0.0 | 6.8 | 8.9 |
| LONG ISLAND REALTORS FCU | West Babylon | NY | C | C | C | 13.0 | 4.50 | 0.0 | 30.3 | 28.9 | 0.0 | 9.9 | 10.9 |
| LONG ISLAND STATE EMPL FCU | Hauppauge | NY | C- | D+ | D+ | 12.9 | 4.44 | 0.0 | 24.8 | 0.0 | 0.0 | 6.3 | 8.3 |
| LONG REACH FCU | Friendly | WV | C+ | C+ | C+ | 48.2 | 14.58 | 0.0 | 41.2 | 16.3 | 0.0 | 6.5 | 8.5 |
| LONGSHORE FCU | Hoquiam | WA | D | D | D+ | 4.4 | -2.91 | 0.0 | 51.9 | 0.9 | 0.0 | 9.2 | 10.5 |

| Asset Quality Index | Non-Performing Loans as a % of Total Loans | as a % of Capital | Net Charge-Offs Avg Loans | Profitability Index | Net Income ($Mil) | Return on Assets | Return on Equity | Net Interest Spread | Overhead Efficiency Ratio | Liquidity Index | Liquidity Ratio | Hot Money Ratio | Stability Index |
|---|---|---|---|---|---|---|---|---|---|---|---|---|---|
| 8.5 | 0.72 | 3.6 | 0.34 | 1.3 | -0.2 | -0.27 | -2.43 | 4.94 | 101.9 | 4.8 | 23.8 | 0.8 | 5.7 |
| 3.2 | 4.32 | 33.5 | 0.93 | 0.8 | 0.0 | -0.07 | -1.34 | 4.06 | 88.9 | 4.7 | 12.1 | 0.0 | 0.0 |
| 7.8 | 8.80 | 7.1 | 0.11 | 5.5 | 0.1 | 0.83 | 5.95 | 1.88 | 54.0 | 5.2 | 23.6 | 0.0 | 6.8 |
| 2.5 | 2.86 | 20.5 | 0.81 | 2.0 | 0.0 | 0.19 | 2.07 | 5.04 | 89.3 | 3.8 | 21.4 | 2.9 | 3.2 |
| 6.4 | 0.95 | 3.4 | 0.43 | 3.7 | 0.1 | 0.50 | 3.09 | 4.42 | 93.5 | 2.6 | 20.1 | 21.5 | 6.4 |
| 5.8 | 1.25 | 12.2 | 0.25 | 5.2 | 2.2 | 0.85 | 9.42 | 3.46 | 76.6 | 2.9 | 5.9 | 9.0 | 6.0 |
| 4.2 | 1.20 | 9.3 | 1.45 | 8.2 | 0.7 | 1.14 | 10.84 | 7.16 | 68.5 | 4.0 | 25.7 | 7.6 | 5.7 |
| 7.7 | 0.82 | 2.6 | 0.00 | 2.4 | 0.0 | 0.23 | 1.18 | 2.74 | 89.0 | 4.5 | 40.7 | 0.0 | 6.9 |
| 6.7 | 1.57 | 7.0 | 0.18 | 6.6 | 0.1 | 0.84 | 5.22 | 4.74 | 79.3 | 5.2 | 40.6 | 0.0 | 5.7 |
| 2.9 | 2.01 | 16.7 | 1.26 | 5.7 | 0.2 | 0.73 | 8.50 | 6.12 | 74.4 | 4.3 | 20.1 | 4.2 | 4.0 |
| 6.4 | 0.94 | 5.8 | 0.11 | 3.0 | 0.2 | 0.32 | 2.97 | 3.40 | 89.5 | 4.3 | 31.6 | 3.8 | 6.3 |
| 8.6 | 0.00 | 2.7 | 0.00 | 0.6 | 0.0 | -0.61 | -0.91 | 4.57 | 100.0 | 7.3 | 127.4 | 0.0 | 7.0 |
| 6.5 | 0.93 | 7.8 | 0.72 | 4.3 | 2.4 | 0.47 | 4.73 | 4.15 | 80.6 | 3.8 | 17.1 | 6.7 | 7.7 |
| 8.4 | 0.19 | 2.6 | 0.26 | 1.6 | 0.0 | 0.18 | 0.98 | 4.35 | 91.2 | 5.1 | 43.9 | 6.4 | 5.3 |
| 9.4 | 1.40 | 2.5 | 1.10 | 0.4 | 0.0 | -0.35 | -2.51 | 2.98 | 108.3 | 5.1 | 16.4 | 0.0 | 5.4 |
| 8.1 | 0.42 | 1.5 | 0.12 | 9.2 | 0.1 | 1.33 | 7.43 | 3.50 | 52.7 | 4.7 | 24.1 | 0.0 | 6.3 |
| 8.6 | 0.65 | 2.0 | 0.85 | 6.1 | 0.0 | 0.71 | 5.59 | 4.89 | 75.9 | 6.2 | 40.0 | 0.0 | 5.0 |
| 6.2 | 2.17 | 10.5 | 0.07 | 5.6 | 0.1 | 0.94 | 5.40 | 5.27 | 75.4 | 7.2 | 63.8 | 0.0 | 6.9 |
| 8.2 | 0.31 | 3.1 | 0.03 | 2.9 | 0.1 | 0.27 | 3.72 | 3.04 | 90.8 | 4.5 | 25.1 | 0.7 | 3.3 |
| 8.0 | 0.46 | 3.4 | 0.08 | 2.8 | 0.4 | 0.30 | 4.76 | 2.89 | 92.9 | 5.0 | 21.6 | 0.7 | 3.6 |
| 5.0 | 2.72 | 11.3 | -0.26 | 0.2 | 0.0 | -0.36 | -2.66 | 3.22 | 120.5 | 5.6 | 47.1 | 0.0 | 6.7 |
| 6.6 | 1.03 | 3.0 | 0.88 | 8.1 | 0.1 | 1.04 | 6.64 | 6.17 | 77.8 | 5.8 | 41.0 | 0.0 | 5.0 |
| 6.4 | 1.75 | 5.8 | 0.46 | 0.0 | 0.0 | -0.67 | -6.55 | 3.03 | 117.9 | 5.1 | 15.1 | 4.3 | 3.9 |
| 1.7 | 6.80 | 37.9 | 0.04 | 0.0 | -0.1 | -0.84 | -11.51 | 3.47 | 111.4 | 4.6 | 35.4 | 0.0 | 1.6 |
| 0.7 | 4.51 | 35.9 | 0.34 | 0.4 | 0.0 | -0.65 | -9.15 | 4.21 | 97.9 | 3.7 | 0.2 | 0.0 | 0.7 |
| 8.8 | 0.21 | 0.4 | 0.68 | 8.1 | 0.1 | 1.25 | 9.23 | 3.78 | 66.8 | 5.4 | 20.9 | 0.0 | 6.3 |
| 8.0 | 0.17 | 0.8 | 0.45 | 2.2 | 0.0 | 0.11 | 1.04 | 2.58 | 89.7 | 4.6 | 26.4 | 8.2 | 4.3 |
| 9.2 | 3.93 | 2.8 | 4.92 | 3.7 | 0.0 | 0.49 | 2.00 | 2.99 | 75.9 | 6.6 | 47.7 | 0.0 | 6.7 |
| 9.7 | 0.02 | 0.1 | 0.00 | 3.2 | 0.0 | 0.52 | 5.56 | 3.20 | 85.6 | 4.0 | 21.1 | 0.0 | 4.8 |
| 8.5 | 0.84 | 2.0 | -0.30 | 0.0 | 0.0 | -2.11 | -9.80 | 6.73 | 131.0 | 6.8 | 64.4 | 0.0 | 5.7 |
| 5.8 | 2.03 | 8.8 | 0.03 | 0.8 | 0.0 | -0.28 | -2.18 | 3.16 | 109.6 | 5.3 | 40.1 | 0.0 | 6.1 |
| 5.7 | 4.99 | 11.2 | -0.08 | 1.6 | 0.0 | 0.38 | 2.15 | 2.92 | 89.8 | 5.3 | 41.8 | 0.0 | 5.6 |
| 10.0 | 0.83 | 1.2 | 0.28 | 3.3 | 0.0 | 0.35 | 2.35 | 2.17 | 83.7 | 5.0 | 28.6 | 0.0 | 7.3 |
| 6.9 | 9.04 | 10.5 | 0.24 | 1.7 | 0.0 | 0.15 | 0.80 | 2.36 | 87.1 | 5.5 | 41.1 | 0.0 | 6.5 |
| 6.2 | 8.76 | 9.9 | 0.29 | 0.3 | -0.1 | -0.35 | -1.48 | 2.76 | 120.2 | 4.9 | 24.7 | 3.4 | 5.2 |
| 10.0 | 0.30 | 0.7 | 0.18 | 1.4 | -0.1 | -0.11 | -0.75 | 2.24 | 102.4 | 3.2 | 19.3 | 17.4 | 5.7 |
| 3.9 | 3.53 | 13.5 | 0.57 | 7.2 | 0.2 | 0.95 | 5.52 | 9.92 | 88.4 | 4.5 | 45.3 | 15.0 | 8.0 |
| 5.5 | 1.83 | 14.4 | 0.60 | 8.0 | 12.5 | 1.10 | 12.32 | 3.91 | 71.8 | 3.6 | 8.1 | 6.1 | 7.3 |
| 9.2 | 0.49 | 2.2 | 0.00 | 6.9 | 0.1 | 1.28 | 15.12 | 2.94 | 50.0 | 5.2 | 15.4 | 0.0 | 3.7 |
| 7.7 | 2.88 | 2.7 | 0.34 | 1.2 | 0.0 | -0.11 | -0.83 | 1.54 | 106.6 | 6.2 | 26.5 | 0.0 | 6.6 |
| 4.9 | 2.61 | 11.1 | 0.45 | 3.4 | 0.0 | 0.34 | 2.06 | 4.48 | 80.4 | 3.6 | 5.2 | 1.2 | 6.8 |
| 7.6 | 0.99 | 3.6 | 1.00 | 1.8 | 0.0 | -0.03 | -0.34 | 3.16 | 89.8 | 5.5 | 29.8 | 0.0 | 5.2 |
| 9.5 | 0.17 | 1.0 | 1.72 | 9.3 | 0.6 | 1.79 | 15.84 | 4.79 | 63.9 | 4.1 | 18.1 | 9.6 | 6.2 |
| 6.4 | 0.58 | 5.7 | 2.14 | 0.0 | -0.1 | -2.84 | -34.96 | 3.63 | 135.5 | 6.6 | 78.7 | 0.0 | 2.2 |
| 9.0 | 2.61 | 4.3 | 0.20 | 3.9 | 0.1 | 0.54 | 2.87 | 2.37 | 75.6 | 5.4 | 45.0 | 0.7 | 7.3 |
| 9.7 | 0.45 | 1.5 | 0.00 | 6.0 | 0.2 | 1.03 | 7.51 | 2.53 | 61.1 | 4.3 | 13.0 | 0.0 | 5.7 |
| 7.3 | 3.32 | 5.2 | 1.66 | 1.3 | -0.1 | -5.07 | -40.38 | 5.21 | -231.3 | 7.3 | 52.9 | 0.0 | 6.2 |
| 9.1 | 0.82 | 3.3 | 0.25 | 7.5 | 0.2 | 1.08 | 6.86 | 3.03 | 65.9 | 3.8 | 21.8 | 2.0 | 6.3 |
| 8.7 | 0.64 | 3.4 | 0.39 | 9.2 | 47.8 | 1.57 | 9.63 | 3.06 | 57.1 | 2.8 | 12.5 | 8.6 | 9.6 |
| 1.7 | 1.53 | 18.3 | 0.00 | 4.6 | 0.0 | 0.01 | 0.08 | 3.19 | 53.8 | 0.8 | 4.3 | 30.4 | 10.0 |
| 9.4 | 0.13 | 1.2 | 0.26 | 5.0 | 0.6 | 0.77 | 10.87 | 3.94 | 85.0 | 3.2 | 11.1 | 7.8 | 4.0 |
| 8.4 | 1.86 | 5.3 | 0.02 | 4.6 | 1.7 | 0.73 | 7.95 | 1.97 | 59.1 | 5.9 | 24.6 | 0.0 | 5.8 |
| 9.9 | 0.00 | 0.0 | 0.00 | 9.5 | 1.7 | 1.33 | 7.43 | 2.23 | 39.5 | 4.1 | 19.5 | 0.0 | 9.9 |
| 8.3 | 2.44 | 3.9 | 0.00 | 0.1 | 0.0 | -0.77 | -3.92 | 2.87 | 130.3 | 5.8 | 81.8 | 0.0 | 6.0 |
| 9.9 | 0.00 | 0.0 | 0.00 | 0.9 | 0.0 | -0.08 | -0.42 | 2.12 | 104.2 | 5.8 | 31.2 | 0.0 | 5.2 |
| 3.7 | 2.25 | 25.3 | 0.01 | 0.4 | -0.1 | -0.51 | -5.56 | 3.24 | 101.3 | 4.3 | 13.9 | 2.6 | 3.9 |
| 4.4 | 2.33 | 14.1 | -0.03 | 4.0 | 0.1 | 0.54 | 4.87 | 2.53 | 78.2 | 3.8 | 5.5 | 0.0 | 6.3 |
| 8.1 | 0.61 | 2.8 | 0.21 | 6.4 | 0.1 | 1.00 | 12.47 | 4.07 | 79.0 | 5.5 | 31.4 | 0.0 | 3.2 |
| 6.8 | 0.65 | 6.4 | 0.45 | 7.6 | 0.4 | 1.16 | 14.02 | 4.14 | 68.6 | 3.4 | 10.5 | 5.3 | 4.0 |
| 4.3 | 2.79 | 14.9 | 0.66 | 0.9 | 0.0 | -0.06 | -0.57 | 4.29 | 97.4 | 4.6 | 23.9 | 0.0 | 3.8 |

| Name | City | State | Rating | 2014 Rating | 2013 Rating | Total Assets ($Mil) | One Year Asset Growth | Asset Mix (As a % of Total Assets) | | | | Capital-ization Index | Net Worth Ratio |
|------|------|-------|--------|-------------|-------------|---------------------|-----------------------|-------------------|---|---|---|---------------------|----------------|
| | | | | | | | | Comm-ercial Loans | Cons-umer Loans | Mort-gage Loans | Secur-ities | | |
| LONGSHOREMENS LOCAL FOUR FCU | Vancouver | WA | B | B | B+ | 25.4 | 14.44 | 0.0 | 19.2 | 7.9 | 0.0 | 10.0 | 18.9 |
| LONGVIEW CONSOLIDATED CU | Longview | TX | B- | B | B | 9.9 | -7.28 | 0.0 | 66.7 | 0.0 | 0.0 | 10.0 | 20.6 |
| ▲ LONGVIEW FCU | White Oak | TX | C- | C- | C | 4.2 | -1.05 | 0.0 | 40.8 | 0.0 | 0.0 | 10.0 | 16.6 |
| LONZA FCU | Williamsport | PA | D+ | D+ | D+ | <1 | -7.01 | 0.0 | 55.5 | 0.0 | 0.0 | 10.0 | 16.0 |
| LOREAL USA FCU | Clark | NJ | B- | B+ | B+ | 26.2 | 0.65 | 0.0 | 23.7 | 19.4 | 16.2 | 10.0 | 20.0 |
| ▲ LORMET COMMUNITY FCU | Amherst | OH | C- | D+ | D+ | 147.0 | 1.67 | 0.0 | 46.8 | 1.0 | 23.7 | 10.0 | 11.9 |
| LOS ALAMOS SCHOOLS CU | Los Alamos | NM | C+ | C+ | C+ | 16.5 | 2.06 | 1.9 | 25.0 | 32.3 | 0.0 | 10.0 | 12.5 |
| LOS ANGELES FCU | Glendale | CA | B+ | B+ | A- | 844.4 | 5.57 | 2.2 | 16.7 | 33.0 | 35.8 | 10.0 | 11.9 |
| LOS ANGELES LEE FCU | Los Angeles | CA | D+ | D+ | C- | <1 | 2.26 | 0.0 | 25.9 | 0.0 | 0.0 | 10.0 | 22.0 |
| LOS ANGELES POLICE FCU | Van Nuys | CA | B- | B | A- | 841.6 | 6.29 | 1.8 | 21.8 | 31.9 | 22.3 | 10.0 | 12.2 |
| ▲ LOUCHEM FCU | Louisville | KY | D+ | D- | D- | 24.9 | -2.02 | 1.9 | 36.8 | 16.2 | 0.0 | 8.0 | 9.6 |
| LOUDOUN CU | Leesburg | VA | C- | C+ | B | 38.2 | 11.06 | 0.0 | 36.4 | 0.0 | 0.0 | 8.0 | 9.7 |
| LOUISE MILLS FCU | Merrimac | MA | D+ | D+ | C- | 7.9 | 0.09 | 0.0 | 27.0 | 25.7 | 0.0 | 10.0 | 14.5 |
| LOUISIANA BAPTIST FCU | Alexandria | LA | D- | D- | D- | 4.5 | -0.62 | 0.0 | 59.5 | 0.0 | 0.0 | 7.5 | 9.3 |
| LOUISIANA CATHOLIC FCU | Shreveport | LA | C- | D+ | C- | 20.6 | 2.38 | 0.0 | 27.5 | 8.1 | 0.5 | 9.3 | 10.5 |
| ▲ LOUISIANA CENTRAL CU | Harahan | LA | D- | E+ | E+ | 12.9 | 1.06 | 0.0 | 52.6 | 0.0 | 0.0 | 5.4 | 7.4 |
| LOUISIANA FCU | La Place | LA | A- | B+ | B+ | 194.0 | 7.43 | 3.6 | 46.0 | 21.0 | 11.1 | 9.5 | 10.6 |
| LOUISIANA MACHINERY EMPL FCU | Monroe | LA | C+ | C+ | C+ | 5.2 | 7.90 | 0.0 | 66.2 | 0.0 | 0.0 | 10.0 | 15.5 |
| ▲ LOUISIANA USA FCU | Baton Rouge | LA | B- | C | C | 54.9 | 3.90 | 0.0 | 34.0 | 18.9 | 22.7 | 10.0 | 11.4 |
| LOUISVILLE FCU | Louisville | KY | B- | B- | B- | 34.0 | -4.90 | 0.0 | 20.3 | 17.7 | 4.0 | 10.0 | 15.5 |
| LOUISVILLE GAS & ELECTRIC CO CU | Louisville | KY | B+ | B+ | B+ | 33.9 | 0.74 | 0.0 | 33.5 | 2.0 | 0.0 | 10.0 | 14.8 |
| LOUISVILLE METRO POLICE OFFICERS CU | Louisville | KY | D+ | D | D- | 24.2 | 3.53 | 0.0 | 66.0 | 0.0 | 0.0 | 8.9 | 10.3 |
| LOUP EMPL CU | Gonzales | LA | C+ | C+ | C+ | 10.3 | -2.48 | 0.0 | 34.9 | 0.7 | 0.0 | 10.0 | 18.0 |
| LOUVAH FCU | Louisville | KY | D | D | C- | 3.3 | -0.15 | 0.0 | 57.2 | 11.6 | 0.0 | 9.4 | 10.6 |
| LOUVIERS FCU | Newark | DE | C- | C- | C- | 216.1 | -2.74 | 0.0 | 2.1 | 10.1 | 75.9 | 8.1 | 10.2 |
| LOVE GOSPEL ASSEMBLY FCU | Bronx | NY | C- | C- | C- | <1 | 7.69 | 0.0 | 17.0 | 0.0 | 0.0 | 10.0 | 24.1 |
| LOVERS LANE CU | Saint Joseph | MO | C- | C | C+ | 5.4 | 5.37 | 0.0 | 60.8 | 0.0 | 0.0 | 10.0 | 12.2 |
| LOWELL FIREFIGHTERS CU | Lowell | MA | C+ | C+ | C+ | 17.1 | 1.02 | 0.0 | 29.2 | 5.3 | 0.0 | 10.0 | 17.4 |
| LOWELL MASSACHUSETTS MUNICIPAL EMPL | Lowell | MA | D- | D+ | D | 6.8 | 14.75 | 0.0 | 38.0 | 0.0 | 6.7 | 8.4 | 10.0 |
| LOWER COLUMBIA LONGSHOREMENS FCU | Longview | WA | C+ | C+ | B- | 66.5 | 4.11 | 0.2 | 16.9 | 32.3 | 0.8 | 8.3 | 9.9 |
| LOWER EAST SIDE PEOPLES FCU | New York | NY | C- | D+ | C- | 42.6 | 2.48 | 25.0 | 5.2 | 68.3 | 0.0 | 7.9 | 9.6 |
| LOWER VALLEY CU | Sunnyside | WA | B- | B | B+ | 98.7 | 22.92 | 1.4 | 58.5 | 7.1 | 4.9 | 8.7 | 10.2 |
| ▲ LOWLAND CU | Morristown | TN | C- | D+ | C | 85.6 | 3.30 | 0.5 | 22.7 | 10.9 | 13.8 | 7.5 | 9.6 |
| ▼ LOYOLA UNIV EMPL FCU | Maywood | IL | C+ | B- | B- | 46.5 | -1.24 | 0.0 | 11.1 | 0.0 | 22.1 | 10.0 | 11.5 |
| LPS EMPL FCU | Lincoln | NE | B | B | B | 41.1 | 0.41 | 0.0 | 19.0 | 0.8 | 9.8 | 10.0 | 13.1 |
| LU 354 IBEW FCU | Salt Lake City | UT | B- | B- | B- | 21.7 | 6.68 | 0.6 | 46.8 | 15.7 | 12.3 | 10.0 | 13.2 |
| LUBBOCK COUNTY SCHOOLS FCU | Lubbock | TX | C | C | C | 2.3 | -4.13 | 0.0 | 28.6 | 0.0 | 0.0 | 10.0 | 13.2 |
| ▼ LUBBOCK TEACHERS FCU | Lubbock | TX | C | B- | B- | 17.6 | 3.73 | 0.0 | 29.1 | 0.0 | 27.4 | 10.0 | 18.4 |
| LUBBOCK TELCO FCU | Lubbock | TX | C | C | D+ | 5.9 | -0.47 | 0.0 | 27.6 | 0.0 | 0.0 | 10.0 | 27.1 |
| LUBRIZOL EMPL CU | Deer Park | TX | B- | B- | B | 39.9 | 6.17 | 0.0 | 41.7 | 0.4 | 0.0 | 10.0 | 12.7 |
| LUFKIN FCU | Lufkin | TX | B+ | B+ | B+ | 31.2 | -1.35 | 0.4 | 33.2 | 21.1 | 0.0 | 10.0 | 21.9 |
| LUFTHANSA EMPL FCU | East Meadow | NY | B- | B- | B | 97.9 | -1.37 | 0.0 | 1.4 | 6.8 | 27.7 | 10.0 | 13.5 |
| LUSO FCU | Ludlow | MA | B- | B | B | 195.0 | 8.07 | 3.9 | 5.1 | 72.4 | 3.7 | 8.5 | 10.0 |
| LUSO-AMERICAN CU | Peabody | MA | C+ | B- | C+ | 81.9 | 4.08 | 10.7 | 8.9 | 37.9 | 27.2 | 10.0 | 14.6 |
| LUTHERAN FCU | Saint Louis | MO | D | U | U | 5.2 | NA | 0.0 | 2.1 | 0.0 | 0.0 | 10.0 | 88.0 |
| LUZERNE COUNTY FCU | Wilkes-Barre | PA | D+ | C- | C- | 15.5 | -1.06 | 0.0 | 20.2 | 4.1 | 40.7 | 9.2 | 10.5 |
| LYNCHBURG MUNICIPAL EMPL FCU | Lynchburg | VA | B | B | B | 21.5 | 2.33 | 0.0 | 28.4 | 7.5 | 0.0 | 10.0 | 17.8 |
| LYNN CO FCU | Tahoka | TX | D | D | C- | <1 | -13.33 | 0.0 | 27.5 | 0.0 | 0.0 | 10.0 | 32.5 |
| LYNN FIREMENS FCU | Lynn | MA | C- | D+ | D+ | 12.5 | 1.62 | 0.0 | 17.3 | 24.6 | 0.0 | 10.0 | 17.7 |
| ▼ LYNN MUNICIPAL EMPL CU | Lynn | MA | C+ | B- | B- | 2.4 | 4.05 | 0.0 | 45.4 | 0.0 | 0.0 | 10.0 | 22.2 |
| LYNN POLICE CU | Lynn | MA | C | C | C | 12.0 | 0.07 | 0.0 | 20.1 | 0.0 | 6.9 | 10.0 | 21.6 |
| LYNN TEACHERS CU | Lynn | MA | C- | C- | C | 4.2 | 4.06 | 0.0 | 34.3 | 0.0 | 0.0 | 10.0 | 18.2 |
| M & C MENLO PARK FCU | Iselin | NJ | E+ | E+ | E+ | 1.9 | 3.42 | 0.0 | 20.9 | 0.0 | 0.0 | 6.1 | 8.1 |
| ▼ M A FORD EMPL CU | Davenport | IA | C- | C+ | C+ | 1.6 | 5.05 | 0.0 | 44.4 | 0.0 | 0.0 | 10.0 | 13.3 |
| M C T FCU | Amsterdam | NY | D+ | D+ | D+ | 50.0 | 2.37 | 0.0 | 7.6 | 5.1 | 0.0 | 6.9 | 9.0 |
| M E C O FCU | Hondo | TX | C | C | C | 5.8 | 9.94 | 0.0 | 51.0 | 0.0 | 0.0 | 10.0 | 15.6 |
| M G & E CU | Madison | WI | C- | C- | C- | 3.2 | 1.13 | 0.0 | 73.3 | 0.0 | 0.0 | 10.0 | 13.6 |
| M G EMPL FCU | North Lewisburg | OH | C- | C | C | 3.3 | -1.29 | 0.0 | 41.0 | 0.6 | 0.0 | 10.0 | 25.0 |
| M O FCU | Huron | SD | B | B | B | 25.1 | -4.41 | 1.7 | 33.5 | 29.2 | 0.0 | 10.0 | 13.5 |
| MABC FCU | Philadelphia | PA | C | C | C | <1 | -2.27 | 0.0 | 17.8 | 0.0 | 0.0 | 10.0 | 14.0 |

| Asset Quality Index | Non-Performing Loans as a % of Total Loans | Non-Performing Loans as a % of Capital | Net Charge-Offs Avg Loans | Profitability Index | Net Income ($Mil) | Return on Assets | Return on Equity | Net Interest Spread | Overhead Efficiency Ratio | Liquidity Index | Liquidity Ratio | Hot Money Ratio | Stability Index |
|---|---|---|---|---|---|---|---|---|---|---|---|---|---|
| 9.9 | 0.91 | 1.7 | -0.02 | 4.5 | 0.1 | 0.63 | 3.15 | 3.28 | 82.0 | 5.3 | 30.2 | 4.0 | 7.4 |
| 7.8 | 0.81 | 2.8 | 0.52 | 5.3 | 0.0 | 0.48 | 2.44 | 4.93 | 84.6 | 3.0 | 33.5 | 18.0 | 5.0 |
| 6.9 | 1.83 | 5.4 | 0.00 | 2.9 | 0.0 | 0.35 | 2.15 | 3.96 | 90.9 | 4.7 | 28.4 | 0.0 | 6.6 |
| 5.2 | 2.93 | 9.7 | 1.02 | 0.9 | 0.0 | -0.75 | -4.76 | 5.43 | 103.9 | 6.4 | 51.4 | 0.0 | 6.4 |
| 7.5 | 2.96 | 7.1 | 0.90 | 3.6 | 0.1 | 0.31 | 1.54 | 4.30 | 87.1 | 6.5 | 42.9 | 2.0 | 6.6 |
| 8.7 | 0.14 | 0.7 | 0.19 | 1.5 | 0.1 | 0.07 | 0.67 | 2.14 | 93.9 | 4.4 | 15.9 | 5.8 | 6.6 |
| 7.7 | 0.31 | 1.6 | -0.08 | 2.7 | 0.0 | 0.12 | 0.97 | 3.67 | 95.8 | 3.0 | 31.3 | 25.4 | 6.6 |
| 8.9 | 0.61 | 2.7 | 0.57 | 3.5 | 2.0 | 0.32 | 2.66 | 3.16 | 85.6 | 3.9 | 11.7 | 8.3 | 7.7 |
| 10.0 | 0.00 | 0.0 | 0.00 | 1.3 | 0.0 | 0.00 | 0.00 | 1.32 | 125.0 | 7.7 | 80.7 | 0.0 | 6.2 |
| 9.9 | 0.23 | 1.1 | 0.24 | 3.3 | 1.5 | 0.25 | 2.01 | 3.59 | 91.5 | 3.7 | 18.6 | 14.3 | 8.0 |
| 6.5 | 0.81 | 5.0 | 0.27 | 2.2 | 0.0 | 0.17 | 1.79 | 3.82 | 93.0 | 4.6 | 28.4 | 3.3 | 3.7 |
| 6.7 | 1.18 | 4.7 | 0.42 | 1.7 | 0.0 | 0.04 | 0.43 | 3.43 | 90.3 | 5.0 | 19.8 | 2.5 | 4.1 |
| 10.0 | 0.00 | 0.0 | 0.23 | 0.9 | 0.0 | -0.12 | -0.81 | 3.69 | 100.9 | 3.9 | 25.1 | 0.0 | 5.8 |
| 4.5 | 0.76 | 5.4 | 0.09 | 2.6 | 0.0 | 0.21 | 2.25 | 4.46 | 94.7 | 5.1 | 28.7 | 0.0 | 2.3 |
| 5.5 | 2.46 | 11.2 | 0.15 | 4.7 | 0.1 | 0.79 | 8.06 | 3.51 | 84.8 | 5.0 | 19.1 | 3.1 | 4.3 |
| 5.8 | 0.68 | 4.7 | 0.57 | 4.1 | 0.1 | 0.84 | 12.01 | 4.79 | 87.2 | 3.7 | 11.5 | 6.7 | 1.5 |
| 6.5 | 0.57 | 3.9 | 0.43 | 8.3 | 1.8 | 1.24 | 12.09 | 4.37 | 76.2 | 3.2 | 10.8 | 7.1 | 7.0 |
| 7.5 | 0.70 | 3.4 | 0.23 | 6.6 | 0.0 | 0.98 | 6.28 | 4.67 | 72.7 | 2.6 | 26.0 | 20.6 | 4.3 |
| 7.8 | 0.66 | 3.8 | 0.21 | 3.5 | 0.2 | 0.47 | 4.16 | 3.94 | 88.9 | 3.6 | 8.8 | 5.1 | 5.9 |
| 9.6 | 0.69 | 1.9 | -0.06 | 3.8 | 0.2 | 0.56 | 3.74 | 2.60 | 78.5 | 4.4 | 19.7 | 5.6 | 7.1 |
| 10.0 | 0.08 | 0.2 | -0.01 | 4.1 | 0.1 | 0.55 | 3.85 | 2.55 | 82.4 | 4.1 | 20.1 | 5.5 | 7.6 |
| 2.7 | 2.10 | 14.1 | 2.12 | 6.4 | 0.1 | 0.70 | 6.99 | 6.17 | 58.7 | 3.5 | 17.2 | 7.7 | 5.3 |
| 9.6 | 0.00 | 0.0 | -0.36 | 3.8 | 0.0 | 0.52 | 2.91 | 3.20 | 81.5 | 4.8 | 24.7 | 0.0 | 7.0 |
| 2.3 | 3.82 | 21.9 | 1.21 | 4.2 | 0.0 | 0.70 | 6.33 | 5.99 | 96.0 | 4.6 | 20.1 | 0.0 | 5.0 |
| 9.3 | 2.00 | 3.1 | 0.15 | 2.5 | 0.4 | 0.25 | 2.71 | 1.60 | 81.9 | 4.6 | 12.2 | 4.2 | 5.3 |
| 6.4 | 0.00 | 0.0 | 0.00 | 1.0 | 0.0 | -8.56 | -58.33 | 5.56 | 300.0 | 7.8 | 79.4 | 0.0 | 7.8 |
| 2.7 | 4.07 | 22.0 | 0.78 | 7.9 | 0.1 | 1.12 | 9.42 | 6.50 | 60.9 | 5.5 | 32.9 | 0.0 | 5.8 |
| 9.2 | 1.26 | 3.3 | 0.43 | 2.9 | 0.1 | 0.35 | 2.04 | 3.16 | 87.0 | 4.4 | 29.8 | 5.4 | 7.1 |
| 7.7 | 1.16 | 4.4 | 1.31 | 0.0 | 0.0 | -0.76 | -7.07 | 3.27 | 111.4 | 5.3 | 33.6 | 0.0 | 4.2 |
| 6.2 | 1.46 | 8.1 | 0.03 | 3.6 | 0.2 | 0.44 | 4.52 | 3.25 | 89.5 | 4.0 | 26.5 | 5.5 | 5.2 |
| 2.3 | 3.38 | 29.3 | 0.14 | 4.2 | 0.0 | -0.01 | -0.19 | 5.60 | 93.8 | 4.3 | 17.5 | 0.0 | 5.1 |
| 2.7 | 0.67 | 22.8 | 1.30 | 7.9 | 0.8 | 1.13 | 11.06 | 7.91 | 69.4 | 3.5 | 39.0 | 19.0 | 6.3 |
| 7.0 | 0.98 | 4.5 | 0.90 | 2.0 | 0.1 | 0.17 | 1.84 | 3.03 | 91.0 | 4.5 | 17.0 | 4.7 | 3.5 |
| 9.8 | 2.64 | 2.6 | 0.63 | 2.5 | 0.1 | 0.17 | 1.53 | 1.93 | 90.2 | 5.1 | 12.5 | 0.0 | 5.0 |
| 8.3 | 1.22 | 3.6 | 0.05 | 4.5 | 0.2 | 0.73 | 5.67 | 2.46 | 65.1 | 5.0 | 18.1 | 0.5 | 6.9 |
| 7.1 | 0.62 | 3.6 | -0.04 | 6.6 | 0.2 | 1.01 | 7.67 | 3.55 | 77.2 | 2.8 | 11.5 | 9.8 | 5.7 |
| 6.4 | 5.62 | 13.3 | 1.13 | 4.8 | 0.0 | 0.57 | 4.54 | 5.90 | 78.4 | 7.1 | 57.0 | 0.0 | 4.3 |
| 8.4 | 3.44 | 5.4 | 0.41 | 1.8 | 0.0 | -0.01 | -0.04 | 3.14 | 71.8 | 5.6 | 26.9 | 5.3 | 6.7 |
| 9.6 | 0.00 | 1.4 | 0.00 | 2.4 | 0.0 | 0.16 | 0.59 | 4.33 | 94.4 | 7.1 | 56.7 | 0.0 | 6.7 |
| 9.7 | 0.15 | 0.5 | 0.09 | 3.5 | 0.2 | 0.51 | 3.98 | 2.88 | 85.0 | 4.6 | 22.3 | 0.0 | 6.7 |
| 9.2 | 1.05 | 3.0 | 0.46 | 8.9 | 0.4 | 1.64 | 7.79 | 3.97 | 66.2 | 4.1 | 21.6 | 0.4 | 8.0 |
| 10.0 | 0.24 | 0.2 | 0.03 | 3.1 | 0.3 | 0.40 | 3.06 | 0.67 | 51.2 | 5.8 | 19.0 | 1.0 | 6.1 |
| 7.2 | 1.02 | 8.1 | 0.03 | 4.0 | 0.8 | 0.55 | 5.41 | 2.66 | 77.4 | 0.9 | 7.9 | 37.5 | 6.8 |
| 10.0 | 0.39 | 1.6 | 0.05 | 2.8 | 0.1 | 0.20 | 1.29 | 3.19 | 93.8 | 3.6 | 12.6 | 10.1 | 7.2 |
| 10.0 | 0.00 | 0.0 | NA | 0.0 | -0.5 | NA | NA | NA | 7733.3 | 7.0 | 0.0 | 0.0 | 0.0 |
| 5.6 | 3.81 | 14.4 | 0.78 | 1.5 | 0.0 | 0.01 | 0.08 | 2.93 | 100.0 | 4.8 | 21.8 | 1.1 | 4.8 |
| 10.0 | 0.01 | 0.0 | -0.03 | 5.5 | 0.1 | 0.83 | 4.73 | 3.80 | 77.9 | 5.9 | 38.3 | 0.0 | 7.6 |
| 9.7 | 0.00 | 0.0 | 1.57 | 0.0 | 0.0 | -3.34 | -10.21 | 7.52 | 164.0 | 7.6 | 85.4 | 0.0 | 4.8 |
| 10.0 | 0.30 | 0.9 | 0.22 | 1.4 | 0.0 | 0.14 | 0.78 | 2.64 | 91.8 | 4.4 | 29.4 | 1.0 | 6.2 |
| 7.8 | 2.19 | 4.3 | 0.61 | 3.7 | 0.0 | -0.06 | -0.25 | 7.21 | 77.0 | 6.9 | 64.2 | 0.0 | 8.3 |
| 8.5 | 3.50 | 5.0 | 0.00 | 2.5 | 0.0 | 0.28 | 1.28 | 1.71 | 79.5 | 3.1 | 31.4 | 24.5 | 6.3 |
| 9.3 | 0.91 | 1.7 | 0.00 | 2.1 | 0.0 | 0.03 | 0.18 | 5.29 | 98.1 | 7.2 | 66.3 | 0.0 | 6.9 |
| 5.1 | 4.49 | 15.2 | -0.51 | 0.3 | 0.0 | -0.22 | -2.60 | 2.93 | 108.6 | 5.5 | 30.6 | 0.0 | 2.5 |
| 3.7 | 7.95 | 22.5 | 0.00 | 3.8 | 0.0 | 0.36 | 2.55 | 3.04 | 45.0 | 6.9 | 53.8 | 0.0 | 6.9 |
| 8.3 | 1.59 | 2.6 | 0.71 | 1.8 | 0.0 | 0.07 | 0.84 | 2.02 | 92.0 | 6.0 | 30.4 | 1.9 | 4.2 |
| 8.4 | 0.12 | 0.4 | 0.08 | 5.6 | 0.0 | 0.71 | 4.33 | 4.54 | 82.7 | 5.0 | 48.6 | 8.1 | 5.0 |
| 8.3 | 0.00 | 0.0 | 0.00 | 3.3 | 0.0 | 0.38 | 2.76 | 4.21 | 95.3 | 3.8 | 23.0 | 0.0 | 7.1 |
| 3.7 | 14.72 | 25.3 | 1.85 | 4.0 | 0.0 | 0.25 | 0.97 | 4.42 | 80.5 | 6.7 | 56.0 | 0.0 | 7.0 |
| 9.7 | 0.24 | 1.2 | 0.12 | 3.6 | 0.1 | 0.34 | 2.58 | 3.27 | 85.9 | 3.5 | 15.9 | 4.6 | 6.9 |
| 8.4 | 0.00 | 0.0 | 0.00 | 2.2 | 0.0 | 0.00 | 0.00 | 3.76 | 100.0 | 7.6 | 92.9 | 0.0 | 6.6 |

| Name | City | State | Rating | 2014 Rating | 2013 Rating | Total Assets ($Mil) | One Year Asset Growth | Asset Mix (As a % of Total Assets) Commercial Loans | Consumer Loans | Mortgage Loans | Securities | Capitalization Index | Net Worth Ratio |
|---|---|---|---|---|---|---|---|---|---|---|---|---|---|
| MAC FCU | Fairbanks | AK | A- | A- | A- | 98.3 | 4.68 | 0.0 | 60.7 | 2.5 | 6.1 | 10.0 | 15.6 |
| ▼ MACHINISTS-BOILERMAKERS FCU | Gladstone | OR | E+ | D | D | 4.3 | -3.23 | 0.0 | 60.1 | 0.0 | 0.0 | 6.8 | 8.8 |
| MACON FIREMENS CU | Macon | GA | B- | B- | B- | 4.7 | -0.19 | 0.0 | 60.2 | 0.0 | 0.0 | 10.0 | 25.3 |
| ▼ MACON WATER WORKS CU | Macon | GA | C | B- | B | 1.5 | 4.77 | 0.0 | 0.0 | 0.0 | 0.0 | 10.0 | 14.2 |
| ▲ MACON-BIBB EMPL CU | Macon | GA | D+ | E+ | E+ | 2.7 | -21.89 | 0.0 | 72.5 | 0.0 | 0.0 | 8.6 | 10.1 |
| MADCO CU | Edwardsville | IL | D | D+ | D+ | 1.7 | 2.93 | 0.0 | 36.3 | 0.0 | 0.0 | 9.8 | 10.9 |
| ▲ MADISON COUNTY FCU | Anderson | IN | D+ | D- | D | 67.0 | 0.67 | 4.4 | 25.6 | 21.6 | 14.5 | 5.6 | 7.6 |
| MADISON CU | Madison | WI | D+ | C- | C- | 37.8 | 5.41 | 0.0 | 25.6 | 16.5 | 39.6 | 7.8 | 9.5 |
| ▲ MADISON EDUCATION ASSOCIATES CU | Madison | FL | C | C- | C- | 4.7 | 4.67 | 0.0 | 44.9 | 0.0 | 0.0 | 10.0 | 17.2 |
| MADISON FIRE DEPT CU | Madison | WI | D+ | D+ | C- | 3.7 | 3.55 | 0.0 | 52.5 | 0.0 | 0.0 | 10.0 | 15.6 |
| MAGNIFY CU | Mulberry | FL | C+ | C | C | 71.9 | 6.61 | 10.3 | 21.5 | 32.1 | 6.8 | 10.0 | 12.6 |
| ▼ MAGNOLIA FCU | Jackson | MS | B- | B | B- | 138.1 | 7.79 | 0.0 | 41.4 | 3.3 | 13.2 | 10.0 | 14.2 |
| MAINE FAMILY FCU | Lewiston | ME | B- | B- | B- | 130.1 | 5.39 | 0.0 | 25.0 | 22.2 | 6.4 | 8.5 | 10.0 |
| MAINE HIGHLANDS FCU | Dexter | ME | C | C | C | 97.2 | 3.27 | 1.1 | 17.7 | 38.3 | 0.0 | 6.6 | 8.7 |
| MAINE MEDIA FCU | South Portland | ME | C- | D+ | D | 4.2 | -4.49 | 0.0 | 43.9 | 28.1 | 0.0 | 10.0 | 23.0 |
| MAINE SAVINGS FCU | Hampden | ME | C+ | C+ | B- | 296.4 | 3.00 | 12.2 | 15.1 | 40.7 | 3.4 | 6.1 | 8.1 |
| MAINE STATE CU | Augusta | ME | B | B | B | 361.9 | 2.23 | 2.0 | 21.0 | 28.2 | 31.0 | 10.0 | 13.5 |
| MAINSTREET FCU | Lenexa | KS | C+ | B- | B- | 382.5 | 7.79 | 0.0 | 23.0 | 13.4 | 25.0 | 7.0 | 9.0 |
| ▼ MALDEN TEACHERS FCU | Malden | MA | C- | C | C | 22.9 | 3.68 | 0.0 | 9.2 | 5.0 | 0.0 | 10.0 | 18.2 |
| MALHEUR FCU | Ontario | OR | B | B- | B- | 104.6 | 8.57 | 7.2 | 28.5 | 21.1 | 20.5 | 7.1 | 9.1 |
| MAMTA FCU | Larchmont | NY | D+ | C- | C- | 11.6 | 4.56 | 0.0 | 11.6 | 0.0 | 0.0 | 6.6 | 8.6 |
| MANATEE COMMUNITY FCU | Bradenton | FL | B+ | B+ | B | 30.1 | 9.87 | 0.0 | 52.9 | 0.2 | 3.3 | 10.0 | 22.7 |
| ▼ MANATROL DIVISION EMPL CU | Elyria | OH | D+ | C | C | <1 | -6.03 | 0.0 | 53.0 | 0.0 | 0.0 | 10.0 | 14.3 |
| MANCHESTER FCU | Manchester | MA | C- | D+ | D+ | 1.7 | 1.23 | 0.0 | 40.6 | 0.0 | 0.0 | 10.0 | 12.2 |
| ▲ MANCHESTER MUNICIPAL FCU | Manchester | CT | C | C- | C | 19.7 | 6.31 | 0.0 | 37.3 | 0.0 | 0.6 | 8.2 | 9.8 |
| MANISTEE FCU | Manistee | MI | E+ | E+ | E+ | 5.1 | 5.88 | 0.0 | 34.9 | 0.0 | 0.0 | 5.0 | 7.0 |
| MANISTIQUE FCU | Manistique | MI | C- | D+ | D+ | 23.5 | -1.08 | 0.0 | 23.4 | 21.5 | 24.2 | 8.1 | 9.7 |
| MANVILLE AREA FCU | Manville | NJ | C | C- | D+ | 29.5 | -1.26 | 0.0 | 9.3 | 50.8 | 0.0 | 7.5 | 9.4 |
| MAPLE FCU | Lafayette | LA | B+ | B+ | B+ | 27.4 | 5.22 | 0.0 | 44.5 | 0.0 | 0.0 | 10.0 | 13.2 |
| MAPLETON PUBLIC SCHOOLS FCU | Denver | CO | C+ | C+ | C+ | 2.4 | 9.77 | 0.0 | 21.7 | 0.0 | 0.0 | 10.0 | 13.8 |
| MARATHON COUNTY EMPL CU | Wausau | WI | B- | C+ | C+ | 22.9 | 3.22 | 0.0 | 34.7 | 44.7 | 0.0 | 10.0 | 15.9 |
| MARATHON REPUBLIC FCU | Texas City | TX | D+ | D | D | 7.2 | -4.69 | 0.0 | 48.9 | 0.0 | 0.0 | 10.0 | 12.5 |
| MARBLEHEAD MUNICIPAL FCU | Marblehead | MA | C | C | C | 8.9 | 0.28 | 0.0 | 36.7 | 0.0 | 0.0 | 10.0 | 18.2 |
| ▲ MARIN COUNTY FCU | San Rafael | CA | C+ | C+ | C | 61.3 | 2.93 | 0.0 | 19.1 | 0.0 | 58.1 | 7.5 | 9.3 |
| MARINE CU | La Crosse | WI | B- | B- | C+ | 578.9 | 14.28 | 4.0 | 26.7 | 41.3 | 0.3 | 9.3 | 10.5 |
| MARINE FCU | Jacksonville | NC | C- | C+ | C+ | 712.4 | -1.97 | 7.3 | 41.2 | 18.5 | 15.7 | 6.3 | 8.3 |
| MARION & POLK SCHOOLS CU | Salem | OR | B | B- | C+ | 542.3 | 8.81 | 10.2 | 24.4 | 27.4 | 14.7 | 5.7 | 7.7 |
| MARION COMMUNITY CU | Marion | OH | C | C | C | 58.7 | 3.41 | 5.3 | 48.1 | 8.7 | 21.3 | 8.9 | 10.6 |
| MARION COUNTY SCHOOL EMPL FCU | Fairmont | WV | C+ | C+ | B- | 9.3 | -6.11 | 0.0 | 22.3 | 0.0 | 0.0 | 10.0 | 17.9 |
| MARISOL FCU | Phoenix | AZ | C+ | C+ | C | 33.9 | 3.03 | 0.0 | 33.6 | 11.2 | 4.3 | 8.0 | 9.8 |
| ▲ MARKET USA FCU | Laurel | MD | B | B- | C+ | 94.5 | -0.46 | 2.6 | 28.8 | 7.8 | 16.5 | 10.0 | 20.0 |
| MAROON FINANCIAL CU | Chicago | IL | C- | C | C | 43.9 | 0.25 | 0.0 | 15.7 | 22.9 | 22.5 | 6.0 | 8.2 |
| MARQUETTE COMMUNITY FCU | Marquette | MI | C | C | C+ | 68.0 | 4.76 | 0.5 | 24.5 | 2.9 | 36.9 | 6.7 | 8.7 |
| MARRIOTT EMPL FCU | Bethesda | MD | C+ | C | C | 170.3 | -0.16 | 0.0 | 33.2 | 13.4 | 13.4 | 10.0 | 11.8 |
| MARSHALL COMMUNITY CU | Marshall | MI | A | A | A | 163.3 | 4.07 | 10.2 | 14.7 | 49.0 | 12.3 | 10.0 | 16.8 |
| MARSHALL COUNTY FCU | Moundsville | WV | C- | D+ | C- | 12.8 | 6.50 | 0.0 | 44.7 | 0.0 | 0.0 | 6.3 | 8.3 |
| MARSHALL T&P EMPL FCU | Marshall | TX | B- | B- | B- | 11.1 | 0.19 | 0.0 | 53.9 | 0.0 | 0.0 | 10.0 | 17.4 |
| MARSHFIELD MEDICAL CENTER CU | Marshfield | WI | C | C | C- | 60.0 | 2.30 | 0.0 | 14.9 | 34.6 | 27.5 | 6.0 | 8.2 |
| MARSHLAND COMMUNITY FCU | Brunswick | GA | B+ | B- | C | 127.8 | 6.33 | 2.4 | 18.1 | 14.7 | 10.3 | 10.0 | 11.0 |
| MARTIN COUNTY COOPERATIVE CU | Loogootee | IN | C+ | C+ | C+ | 11.7 | 2.07 | 2.7 | 15.4 | 59.8 | 0.0 | 10.0 | 12.7 |
| MARTIN FCU | Orlando | FL | D | D+ | C- | 112.1 | 2.98 | 4.5 | 34.9 | 22.3 | 17.9 | 4.2 | 6.2 |
| MARTIN LUTHER KING CU | Houston | TX | C | C | C+ | <1 | -14.04 | 0.0 | 27.7 | 0.0 | 0.0 | 10.0 | 43.7 |
| ▲ MARTINSBURG VA CENTER FCU | Kearneysville | WV | C | D+ | D+ | 12.7 | 4.13 | 0.0 | 25.7 | 0.9 | 0.0 | 9.8 | 10.8 |
| MARVEL CITY FCU | Bessemer | AL | C- | C | C | 7.2 | -1.51 | 0.0 | 19.4 | 9.3 | 0.0 | 10.0 | 14.4 |
| MARYKNOLL OF LOS ANGELES FCU | Los Angeles | CA | D+ | D+ | D+ | <1 | -0.95 | 0.0 | 28.0 | 0.0 | 15.2 | 9.3 | 10.5 |
| ▲ MARYLAND POSTAL FCU | Gaithersburg | MD | C- | D+ | C- | 2.9 | -2.52 | 0.0 | 57.1 | 0.0 | 38.6 | 10.0 | 13.0 |
| MARYVALE SCHOOLS FCU | Cheektowaga | NY | D+ | D+ | C- | 8.5 | -1.28 | 1.4 | 16.4 | 6.8 | 0.0 | 10.0 | 16.1 |
| MARYVILLE MUNICIPAL CU | Maryville | TN | B | B | B | 15.2 | -2.22 | 0.0 | 14.8 | 8.8 | 0.0 | 10.0 | 14.4 |
| MASON COUNTY SCHOOL EMPL CU | Ludington | MI | C+ | C+ | C+ | 5.9 | 0.52 | 0.0 | 25.0 | 0.0 | 0.0 | 10.0 | 18.2 |
| MASS BAY CU | South Boston | MA | C+ | C+ | B- | 211.0 | 3.50 | 1.8 | 14.4 | 44.1 | 20.3 | 9.9 | 10.9 |

| Asset Quality Index | Non-Performing Loans | | Net Charge-Offs | Profitability Index | Net Income ($Mil) | Return on Assets | Return on Equity | Net Interest Spread | Overhead Efficiency Ratio | Liquidity Index | Liquidity Ratio | Hot Money Ratio | Stability Index |
|---|---|---|---|---|---|---|---|---|---|---|---|---|---|
| | as a % of Total Loans | as a % of Capital | Avg Loans | | | | | | | | | | |
| 6.0 | 0.90 | 5.8 | 1.74 | 8.8 | 0.9 | 1.17 | 7.72 | 6.47 | 68.8 | 3.5 | 20.4 | 12.8 | 8.3 |
| 4.4 | 0.66 | 5.7 | 0.38 | 1.3 | -0.1 | -2.24 | -23.03 | 5.69 | 124.0 | 3.8 | 14.9 | 0.0 | 1.0 |
| 7.5 | 1.58 | 3.7 | 0.46 | 9.5 | 0.1 | 1.87 | 7.57 | 5.65 | 67.3 | 4.3 | 43.1 | 0.0 | 5.7 |
| 5.3 | 3.12 | 11.8 | 3.23 | 2.3 | 0.0 | -0.35 | -2.40 | 6.77 | 70.9 | 6.2 | 43.3 | 0.0 | 7.1 |
| 7.1 | 0.10 | 0.7 | 2.31 | 6.5 | 0.0 | 1.64 | 16.79 | 8.29 | 64.0 | 3.6 | 28.4 | 12.3 | 3.4 |
| 5.3 | 3.11 | 10.7 | 0.78 | 0.8 | 0.0 | -0.57 | -4.99 | 4.78 | 118.0 | 7.0 | 62.4 | 0.0 | 5.8 |
| 3.3 | 2.24 | 20.0 | 0.97 | 3.5 | 0.3 | 0.54 | 8.35 | 4.36 | 85.6 | 4.6 | 19.3 | 0.3 | 2.4 |
| 6.3 | 1.75 | 7.9 | 0.77 | 1.9 | 0.0 | 0.14 | 1.49 | 3.25 | 87.6 | 4.8 | 14.4 | 0.6 | 3.5 |
| 8.2 | 0.35 | 1.0 | -0.06 | 4.6 | 0.0 | 0.74 | 4.25 | 3.25 | 76.2 | 4.4 | 27.5 | 0.0 | 4.3 |
| 7.2 | 1.09 | 4.9 | -0.50 | 1.1 | 0.0 | -0.04 | -0.23 | 2.85 | 101.3 | 4.5 | 44.7 | 0.0 | 6.4 |
| 6.3 | 0.40 | 7.8 | 0.61 | 2.8 | 0.2 | 0.32 | 2.56 | 3.90 | 88.1 | 3.6 | 16.3 | 5.6 | 5.1 |
| 6.6 | 1.90 | 8.2 | 2.59 | 2.7 | 0.0 | 0.00 | -0.02 | 7.23 | 84.9 | 5.0 | 30.5 | 4.9 | 7.2 |
| 7.0 | 1.42 | 8.5 | 0.37 | 3.7 | 0.4 | 0.41 | 4.11 | 2.92 | 84.4 | 4.1 | 16.1 | 3.4 | 6.3 |
| 3.6 | 2.11 | 19.6 | 0.19 | 3.9 | 0.4 | 0.49 | 5.79 | 4.11 | 85.9 | 3.0 | 11.7 | 9.6 | 4.1 |
| 8.0 | 0.94 | 3.8 | 0.35 | 2.8 | 0.0 | 0.34 | 1.53 | 4.14 | 85.5 | 2.7 | 4.3 | 0.0 | 6.3 |
| 7.7 | 0.45 | 4.4 | 0.10 | 3.4 | 0.6 | 0.28 | 3.62 | 3.03 | 91.8 | 3.0 | 12.6 | 10.0 | 5.6 |
| 9.0 | 0.90 | 3.7 | 0.36 | 4.8 | 2.0 | 0.75 | 6.11 | 3.26 | 73.2 | 4.0 | 11.0 | 6.0 | 8.1 |
| 9.3 | 0.33 | 2.6 | 0.26 | 2.9 | 0.6 | 0.21 | 2.33 | 2.82 | 92.1 | 5.0 | 21.6 | 2.1 | 5.3 |
| 10.0 | 0.00 | 0.0 | -0.01 | 1.6 | 0.0 | -0.03 | -0.19 | 2.47 | 106.6 | 4.8 | 26.1 | 0.0 | 7.0 |
| 6.3 | 1.71 | 10.2 | 0.22 | 7.5 | 0.8 | 1.10 | 12.18 | 4.17 | 74.7 | 3.9 | 19.4 | 7.0 | 6.0 |
| 10.0 | 0.00 | 0.0 | 0.00 | 2.3 | 0.0 | 0.09 | 1.08 | 1.54 | 89.9 | 5.2 | 22.2 | 0.0 | 3.8 |
| 8.7 | 0.15 | 1.0 | 0.41 | 5.4 | 0.1 | 0.65 | 2.75 | 5.05 | 88.9 | 4.5 | 35.8 | 2.2 | 6.5 |
| 8.7 | 0.00 | 0.0 | 0.00 | 1.0 | 0.0 | -0.49 | -3.45 | 7.79 | 110.7 | 6.5 | 50.2 | 0.0 | 6.7 |
| 7.6 | 1.14 | 3.7 | 0.18 | 2.1 | 0.0 | 0.08 | 0.63 | 3.86 | 97.0 | 7.0 | 59.8 | 0.0 | 6.2 |
| 6.9 | 1.54 | 8.5 | -0.04 | 6.2 | 0.2 | 1.02 | 10.81 | 3.13 | 75.5 | 4.1 | 7.9 | 0.0 | 4.3 |
| 8.3 | 0.40 | 2.5 | 0.00 | 0.1 | 0.0 | -0.35 | -4.80 | 2.87 | 111.4 | 6.1 | 38.2 | 0.0 | 3.4 |
| 6.1 | 0.61 | 9.6 | 0.11 | 3.7 | 0.1 | 0.50 | 5.31 | 3.72 | 81.5 | 5.9 | 40.8 | 1.9 | 4.8 |
| 6.6 | 1.04 | 6.9 | 0.02 | 3.4 | 0.1 | 0.47 | 5.17 | 2.55 | 82.3 | 3.9 | 38.0 | 8.5 | 4.7 |
| 9.3 | 0.29 | 1.3 | 0.43 | 6.4 | 0.2 | 0.78 | 6.02 | 3.51 | 77.0 | 4.2 | 25.1 | 3.5 | 7.4 |
| 10.0 | 0.00 | 0.0 | 1.86 | 2.6 | 0.0 | 0.29 | 2.03 | 2.67 | 88.6 | 6.4 | 83.9 | 0.0 | 7.0 |
| 9.3 | 0.36 | 1.8 | 0.27 | 6.4 | 0.2 | 0.96 | 6.02 | 4.60 | 79.3 | 3.3 | 8.7 | 0.0 | 5.7 |
| 5.8 | 1.32 | 6.6 | -0.06 | 1.2 | 0.0 | -0.05 | -0.45 | 3.86 | 101.2 | 4.0 | 16.5 | 0.0 | 5.2 |
| 9.7 | 0.54 | 1.3 | -0.04 | 2.6 | 0.0 | 0.21 | 1.16 | 3.26 | 88.7 | 6.2 | 48.3 | 0.7 | 7.0 |
| 8.8 | 0.34 | 1.1 | 0.73 | 3.5 | 0.2 | 0.44 | 4.77 | 2.76 | 82.1 | 4.7 | 15.8 | 2.8 | 3.7 |
| 3.7 | 2.96 | 20.1 | 0.54 | 9.8 | 5.9 | 1.41 | 13.55 | 6.49 | 75.8 | 4.0 | 21.1 | 6.5 | 7.6 |
| 6.7 | 0.79 | 6.3 | 1.49 | 0.6 | -6.4 | -1.17 | -13.58 | 3.86 | 97.1 | 4.1 | 12.2 | 6.4 | 5.0 |
| 8.4 | 0.30 | 3.1 | 0.11 | 7.4 | 4.4 | 1.11 | 14.41 | 4.00 | 77.8 | 4.2 | 18.5 | 2.4 | 5.4 |
| 5.9 | 0.80 | 5.0 | 0.15 | 2.8 | 0.2 | 0.35 | 3.47 | 2.81 | 92.4 | 3.1 | 3.8 | 9.4 | 4.6 |
| 9.6 | 0.85 | 1.2 | 0.69 | 2.6 | 0.0 | 0.11 | 0.64 | 2.53 | 88.8 | 6.7 | 51.3 | 0.0 | 6.6 |
| 8.8 | 0.36 | 1.9 | 0.49 | 4.9 | 0.2 | 0.67 | 7.09 | 4.73 | 86.3 | 4.9 | 21.1 | 0.4 | 4.4 |
| 8.9 | 1.22 | 2.7 | 0.83 | 4.2 | 0.4 | 0.58 | 2.97 | 3.87 | 85.6 | 5.5 | 32.2 | 0.7 | 6.2 |
| 7.8 | 0.59 | 3.5 | 0.19 | 4.1 | 0.2 | 0.46 | 5.56 | 3.12 | 87.1 | 4.4 | 32.0 | 12.3 | 2.9 |
| 7.1 | 1.29 | 5.9 | 0.21 | 3.8 | 0.3 | 0.53 | 6.10 | 3.07 | 84.4 | 5.2 | 19.3 | 0.2 | 4.2 |
| 9.3 | 0.83 | 3.4 | 0.80 | 2.8 | 0.4 | 0.31 | 2.72 | 3.42 | 87.5 | 4.5 | 22.9 | 2.0 | 6.8 |
| 7.0 | 1.53 | 7.3 | 0.25 | 9.5 | 1.8 | 1.49 | 9.22 | 3.65 | 62.5 | 3.1 | 14.3 | 10.3 | 9.4 |
| 9.8 | 0.00 | 0.0 | -0.05 | 3.4 | 0.0 | 0.36 | 4.50 | 4.08 | 88.2 | 7.0 | 57.3 | 0.0 | 4.0 |
| 8.0 | 0.09 | 0.4 | 0.26 | 8.5 | 0.1 | 1.38 | 7.97 | 4.20 | 58.8 | 3.1 | 37.4 | 15.4 | 6.3 |
| 9.8 | 0.04 | 0.3 | 0.08 | 2.9 | 0.1 | 0.32 | 4.03 | 2.56 | 85.7 | 3.8 | 12.6 | 4.5 | 4.1 |
| 6.0 | 1.29 | 13.8 | 0.95 | 5.4 | 0.7 | 0.79 | 7.19 | 4.31 | 84.5 | 4.9 | 26.4 | 6.9 | 6.4 |
| 5.2 | 2.17 | 15.8 | 0.23 | 7.4 | 0.1 | 1.18 | 9.73 | 3.36 | 65.2 | 2.0 | 15.4 | 17.2 | 5.0 |
| 5.0 | 1.17 | 11.1 | 0.83 | 1.0 | -0.1 | -0.09 | -1.47 | 4.03 | 87.4 | 4.2 | 11.2 | 0.8 | 2.2 |
| 5.0 | 20.41 | 14.9 | 1.25 | 2.5 | 0.0 | 0.00 | 0.00 | 6.89 | 90.0 | 6.4 | 42.0 | 0.0 | 5.6 |
| 9.0 | 0.99 | 2.7 | -0.07 | 2.8 | 0.0 | 0.46 | 4.32 | 2.79 | 86.0 | 5.2 | 23.0 | 1.9 | 4.9 |
| 8.4 | 1.71 | 3.7 | 0.33 | 3.3 | 0.0 | 0.33 | 2.32 | 3.77 | 83.9 | 5.9 | 56.6 | 1.8 | 6.2 |
| 6.6 | 1.56 | 4.7 | 0.00 | 2.2 | 0.0 | 0.00 | 0.00 | 1.43 | 114.3 | 5.7 | 73.2 | 17.1 | 6.1 |
| 7.4 | 0.59 | 2.6 | 0.00 | 3.8 | 0.0 | 0.64 | 5.06 | 4.80 | 87.4 | 3.9 | 4.9 | 0.0 | 3.7 |
| 10.0 | 0.34 | 0.7 | 0.00 | 1.2 | 0.0 | 0.08 | 0.49 | 2.28 | 95.3 | 5.9 | 31.3 | 0.0 | 6.4 |
| 10.0 | 0.13 | 0.2 | 0.03 | 4.2 | 0.1 | 0.62 | 4.40 | 2.71 | 75.2 | 6.5 | 50.2 | 0.0 | 7.4 |
| 10.0 | 0.82 | 1.2 | 0.00 | 5.3 | 0.0 | 0.87 | 4.87 | 2.05 | 54.8 | 5.1 | 37.2 | 0.0 | 5.0 |
| 7.5 | 1.02 | 6.7 | 0.10 | 3.2 | 0.5 | 0.32 | 2.91 | 3.49 | 92.3 | 3.0 | 6.8 | 10.9 | 6.8 |

| Name | City | State | Rating | 2014 Rating | 2013 Rating | Total Assets ($Mil) | One Year Asset Growth | Commercial Loans | Consumer Loans | Mortgage Loans | Securities | Capitalization Index | Net Worth Ratio |
|------|------|-------|--------|-------------|-------------|--------------------|-----------------------|-----------|---------|----------|-----------|----------------------|-----------------|
| | | | | | | | | Asset Mix (As a % of Total Aseets) | | | | | |
| MASSACHUSETTS FAMILY CU | Lynn | MA | B- | B- | B | 21.2 | 2.07 | 0.0 | 20.9 | 27.8 | 0.0 | 10.0 | 16.0 |
| MASSACHUSETTS INST OF TECHNOLOGY FC | Cambridge | MA | B- | B- | B- | 444.0 | 6.11 | 0.0 | 14.1 | 33.3 | 10.8 | 5.8 | 7.9 |
| MASSMUTUAL FCU | Springfield | MA | C+ | B- | B- | 236.3 | 2.05 | 0.0 | 12.1 | 19.5 | 34.1 | 8.9 | 10.2 |
| MASTERS MATES & PILOTS FCU | Linthicum Heights | MD | D | C- | D+ | 1.5 | 12.10 | 0.0 | 61.7 | 0.0 | 0.0 | 6.4 | 8.5 |
| MATADORS COMMUNITY CU | Chatsworth | CA | B | B- | C+ | 173.2 | 11.05 | 0.9 | 27.9 | 18.0 | 0.0 | 9.8 | 10.9 |
| MATAGORDA COUNTY CU | Bay City | TX | C- | C- | C- | 24.9 | 2.74 | 0.0 | 35.2 | 3.2 | 0.0 | 10.0 | 11.4 |
| MATANUSKA VALLEY FCU | Palmer | AK | B+ | B+ | B+ | 441.5 | 5.50 | 20.1 | 13.3 | 35.5 | 32.9 | 9.6 | 10.7 |
| MATERION FCU | Elmore | OH | B- | B- | B- | 18.0 | 8.25 | 1.7 | 48.4 | 17.2 | 0.0 | 10.0 | 14.8 |
| MATERNITY BVM CU | Bourbonnais | IL | C+ | C+ | C+ | 11.3 | -1.80 | 0.0 | 32.1 | 0.0 | 0.9 | 10.0 | 11.5 |
| MATSON EMPL FCU | Oakland | CA | B+ | B+ | A- | 32.4 | -1.19 | 0.0 | 8.1 | 1.3 | 0.0 | 10.0 | 22.2 |
| MATTEL FCU | El Segundo | CA | D+ | D+ | D | 24.7 | -12.72 | 0.0 | 22.8 | 16.7 | 4.0 | 7.4 | 9.2 |
| MAUI COUNTY FCU | Wailuku | HI | A | A- | A- | 256.7 | 3.62 | 1.3 | 8.0 | 34.3 | 34.0 | 10.0 | 13.7 |
| MAUI FCU | Kahului | HI | B- | C+ | C- | 97.3 | 3.78 | 3.2 | 10.8 | 14.6 | 49.8 | 10.0 | 14.8 |
| MAUI TEACHERS FCU | Wailuku | HI | B | B- | C- | 33.9 | -2.93 | 0.0 | 6.5 | 0.0 | 30.1 | 10.0 | 11.9 |
| MAUMEE EDUCATORS FCU | Maumee | OH | C- | C- | C- | 3.0 | 2.97 | 0.0 | 30.8 | 0.0 | 23.5 | 10.0 | 12.2 |
| ▲ MAUMEE VALLEY CU | Toledo | OH | C | C- | C | 19.6 | -0.57 | 0.2 | 43.1 | 0.0 | 0.0 | 10.0 | 13.1 |
| MAWC CU | Saint Louis | MO | C- | C- | D+ | 2.6 | 4.64 | 0.0 | 45.1 | 0.0 | 0.0 | 9.3 | 10.5 |
| MAX CU | Montgomery | AL | A- | A- | A- | 1139.4 | 7.64 | 12.2 | 32.2 | 17.4 | 29.5 | 10.0 | 14.3 |
| MAYO EMPL FCU | Rochester | MN | A- | A- | A- | 755.9 | 8.67 | 0.0 | 16.2 | 15.4 | 27.0 | 8.7 | 10.2 |
| MAZUMA CU | Overland Park | KS | B+ | B | C+ | 535.7 | 6.85 | 3.0 | 25.1 | 28.4 | 20.0 | 6.8 | 8.8 |
| ▼ MBFT FCU | Thurmont | MD | C | C+ | C+ | <1 | -13.66 | 0.0 | 32.0 | 0.0 | 0.0 | 10.0 | 32.9 |
| ▼ MBHS FCU | Jackson | MS | C+ | B- | B- | 9.3 | 5.35 | 0.0 | 48.3 | 0.3 | 0.5 | 10.0 | 14.9 |
| MCALESTER AAP FCU | McAlester | OK | B- | C+ | B- | 13.5 | -2.96 | 0.0 | 13.3 | 0.0 | 0.0 | 10.0 | 22.8 |
| MCALESTER CU | McAlester | OK | D | D | C- | 2.8 | -17.56 | 0.0 | 25.4 | 0.0 | 0.0 | 10.0 | 22.5 |
| MCBRYDE FCU | Eleele | HI | A | A | A | 86.8 | 3.52 | 0.1 | 7.8 | 1.5 | 80.6 | 10.0 | 23.6 |
| MCCABE HAMILTON & RENNY FCU | Honolulu | HI | C- | D | D | 6.2 | 4.59 | 0.0 | 39.9 | 0.0 | 28.8 | 10.0 | 13.7 |
| MCCLATCHY EMPL CU | Sacramento | CA | C | C | C | 15.7 | -1.30 | 0.0 | 14.9 | 10.8 | 20.0 | 10.0 | 12.9 |
| ▼ MCCOMB FCU | McComb | MS | D+ | C- | C- | 12.4 | 2.86 | 0.0 | 37.7 | 1.4 | 0.0 | 9.7 | 10.8 |
| MCCONE COUNTY FCU | Circle | MT | B+ | B+ | B+ | 66.7 | 4.32 | 47.8 | 5.2 | 36.7 | 0.0 | 10.0 | 11.9 |
| MCCOY FCU | Orlando | FL | B | B | B | 502.7 | 4.53 | 1.0 | 30.4 | 14.0 | 37.0 | 7.4 | 9.3 |
| MCDONALD COMMUNITY FCU | McDonald | OH | D+ | D+ | D+ | 4.4 | -2.85 | 0.0 | 23.2 | 0.0 | 0.0 | 10.0 | 19.0 |
| MCDOWELL CORNERSTONE CU | Marion | NC | C+ | C+ | C+ | 26.1 | 7.48 | 0.0 | 6.4 | 38.0 | 0.0 | 10.0 | 18.5 |
| MCDOWELL COUNTY FCU | Welch | WV | C- | C- | C+ | <1 | 17.65 | 0.0 | 0.0 | 0.0 | 0.0 | 10.0 | 35.0 |
| MCGRAW HILL FCU | East Windsor | NJ | D+ | D+ | C+ | 377.2 | 7.45 | 0.1 | 29.9 | 22.7 | 17.8 | 10.0 | 11.7 |
| MCINTOSH CHEMICAL FCU | McIntosh | AL | D+ | D+ | C- | 21.5 | -1.04 | 0.0 | 23.1 | 7.6 | 0.0 | 10.0 | 16.2 |
| MCKEESPORT AREA PUBLIC SCHOOL EMPL | McKeesport | PA | C+ | C+ | C+ | 3.4 | 8.52 | 0.0 | 62.5 | 0.0 | 0.0 | 10.0 | 17.7 |
| ▼ MCKEESPORT BELL FCU | McKeesport | PA | D- | D+ | C- | 10.8 | 4.16 | 0.0 | 12.4 | 0.0 | 0.0 | 8.2 | 9.8 |
| MCKEESPORT CONGREGATIONAL FCU | McKeesport | PA | C+ | C+ | C+ | <1 | 1.03 | 0.0 | 0.0 | 0.0 | 0.0 | 10.0 | 16.6 |
| MCKENZIE VALLEY FCU | Springfield | OR | E+ | E+ | E+ | 2.8 | -0.99 | 0.0 | 64.4 | 0.0 | 0.0 | 5.5 | 7.5 |
| MCKESSON EMPL FCU | San Francisco | CA | C- | C- | D- | 27.8 | 4.47 | 3.6 | 30.4 | 25.9 | 20.3 | 6.1 | 8.1 |
| ▲ MCKESSON FCU | Stratford | CT | C- | D | D+ | 24.4 | 0.23 | 0.0 | 11.6 | 14.6 | 2.5 | 8.3 | 9.9 |
| MCLENNAN COUNTY EMPL FCU | Waco | TX | B | B | B | 18.6 | 0.84 | 0.0 | 29.6 | 0.0 | 0.0 | 10.0 | 25.5 |
| MCMILLEN MASTER CU | Gibson City | IL | C+ | C+ | C- | <1 | 3.27 | 0.0 | 87.1 | 0.0 | 0.0 | 10.0 | 25.9 |
| MCMURREY FCU | Tyler | TX | C | C | C | 23.7 | 1.48 | 0.0 | 39.0 | 18.3 | 0.0 | 10.0 | 11.8 |
| MCNAIRY COUNTY EMPL CU | Adamsville | TN | C- | C- | D+ | 1.3 | -0.97 | 0.0 | 58.9 | 0.0 | 0.0 | 10.0 | 33.4 |
| MCNEESE FCU | Lake Charles | LA | D+ | D+ | C- | 15.8 | 5.64 | 0.0 | 24.5 | 0.0 | 0.0 | 10.0 | 12.4 |
| MCPHERSON COMMUNITY FCU | Tryon | NE | E+ | E+ | E+ | <1 | -5.54 | 0.0 | 31.7 | 22.9 | 0.0 | 4.1 | 6.1 |
| ▲ MCPHERSON COOPERATIVE CU | McPherson | KS | C+ | C | C- | 33.6 | 0.43 | 0.0 | 29.4 | 16.3 | 5.2 | 7.8 | 9.5 |
| MCT CU | Port Neches | TX | B+ | B | B | 242.6 | 5.31 | 7.3 | 24.4 | 32.9 | 3.4 | 10.0 | 11.1 |
| MCU FINANCIAL CENTER CU | Racine | WI | D- | D- | D | 25.4 | 4.42 | 0.0 | 63.4 | 9.4 | 0.0 | 6.0 | 8.0 |
| MDU EMPL FCU | Glendive | MT | C | C | C | 4.5 | -1.94 | 0.0 | 44.2 | 0.0 | 0.0 | 10.0 | 13.2 |
| ▲ ME EMPL CU | Wausau | WI | C | D+ | D+ | 10.2 | 5.35 | 0.0 | 28.4 | 55.1 | 0.0 | 10.0 | 17.4 |
| ▼ MEA CU | White Heath | IL | D | C- | D+ | <1 | 8.10 | 0.0 | 46.3 | 0.0 | 0.0 | 7.7 | 9.5 |
| MEA FCU | Columbus | GA | B- | B | B | 65.2 | -2.97 | 0.2 | 33.2 | 2.5 | 4.2 | 10.0 | 15.5 |
| MEAD COATED BOARD FCU | Phenix City | AL | B | B+ | A- | 51.6 | 3.00 | 0.0 | 11.4 | 6.0 | 29.4 | 10.0 | 14.2 |
| MEAD EMPL CU | Atlanta | GA | D+ | D+ | C- | 4.4 | -9.79 | 0.0 | 44.7 | 0.0 | 0.0 | 10.0 | 34.0 |
| MEADOW GOLD EMPL CU | Salt Lake City | UT | C- | C- | C- | 4.6 | -7.10 | 0.0 | 43.8 | 0.0 | 0.0 | 10.0 | 24.0 |
| ▲ MEADOW GROVE FCU | Meadow Grove | NE | C+ | C- | C- | 4.5 | -9.10 | 4.7 | 13.3 | 45.8 | 0.0 | 10.0 | 14.4 |
| ▼ MEADOWLAND CU | Sheboygan Falls | WI | C- | C+ | B | 17.8 | 13.40 | 0.0 | 21.7 | 43.0 | 0.0 | 7.6 | 9.4 |
| ▲ MEADOWS CU | Arlington Heights | IL | C- | D | E+ | 106.6 | 0.31 | 1.6 | 24.7 | 28.9 | 4.0 | 4.4 | 6.4 |

| Asset Quality Index | Non-Performing Loans as a % of Total Loans | as a % of Capital | Net Charge-Offs Avg Loans | Profitability Index | Net Income ($Mil) | Return on Assets | Return on Equity | Net Interest Spread | Overhead Efficiency Ratio | Liquidity Index | Liquidity Ratio | Hot Money Ratio | Stability Index |
|---|---|---|---|---|---|---|---|---|---|---|---|---|---|
| 9.9 | 0.38 | 1.7 | 0.41 | 4.8 | 0.1 | 0.73 | 4.60 | 3.95 | 77.2 | 2.9 | 42.6 | 46.3 | 7.5 |
| 6.7 | 1.23 | 12.4 | 0.10 | 4.5 | 2.0 | 0.61 | 7.96 | 3.47 | 82.7 | 3.2 | 8.1 | 3.9 | 5.2 |
| 8.2 | 0.89 | 4.7 | 0.19 | 3.4 | 0.7 | 0.38 | 3.88 | 2.00 | 78.7 | 3.7 | 15.7 | 6.4 | 6.7 |
| 7.3 | 0.54 | 3.6 | -0.16 | 5.3 | 0.0 | 0.88 | 11.30 | 3.77 | 80.0 | 5.4 | 38.3 | 0.0 | 3.0 |
| 7.8 | 0.81 | 5.4 | 0.20 | 9.6 | 2.6 | 2.06 | 19.27 | 5.25 | 61.2 | 3.6 | 21.9 | 12.1 | 7.4 |
| 9.7 | 0.36 | 1.8 | 0.19 | 1.8 | 0.0 | 0.17 | 1.46 | 2.83 | 91.3 | 5.5 | 26.3 | 0.0 | 5.5 |
| 6.6 | 0.80 | 7.4 | 0.18 | 5.9 | 3.0 | 0.93 | 8.42 | 3.60 | 74.7 | 4.2 | 30.8 | 3.7 | 7.9 |
| 7.6 | 0.26 | 1.4 | 0.29 | 8.4 | 0.2 | 1.40 | 9.72 | 4.04 | 67.0 | 3.4 | 14.8 | 3.4 | 6.3 |
| 9.0 | 0.63 | 2.0 | 0.26 | 2.3 | 0.0 | 0.23 | 2.07 | 2.15 | 88.8 | 4.7 | 19.4 | 0.0 | 6.4 |
| 10.0 | 0.83 | 0.4 | 0.33 | 4.7 | 0.1 | 0.53 | 2.42 | 2.11 | 74.5 | 5.4 | 31.9 | 0.0 | 6.4 |
| 4.5 | 3.66 | 17.6 | 1.00 | 1.8 | 0.0 | -0.03 | -0.35 | 2.87 | 101.2 | 3.7 | 5.9 | 6.0 | 3.4 |
| 7.1 | 2.12 | 7.3 | 0.45 | 9.2 | 3.1 | 1.62 | 12.41 | 3.05 | 68.3 | 3.8 | 10.8 | 6.4 | 8.2 |
| 10.0 | 0.33 | 0.6 | -0.08 | 6.0 | 0.7 | 0.96 | 6.39 | 2.78 | 68.4 | 5.3 | 27.9 | 4.8 | 8.2 |
| 10.0 | 0.05 | 0.1 | 0.36 | 4.2 | 0.2 | 0.67 | 5.72 | 2.03 | 63.3 | 5.4 | 17.7 | 0.0 | 6.2 |
| 7.5 | 0.00 | 0.0 | 1.82 | 2.7 | 0.0 | 0.32 | 2.59 | 2.35 | 81.8 | 5.4 | 26.1 | 0.0 | 5.1 |
| 9.4 | 0.14 | 0.6 | 0.65 | 2.0 | 0.1 | 0.31 | 2.37 | 3.56 | 93.5 | 3.1 | 12.6 | 10.2 | 4.7 |
| 8.7 | 0.00 | 0.0 | 0.11 | 2.3 | 0.0 | -0.21 | -1.94 | 2.94 | 103.9 | 5.4 | 41.7 | 0.0 | 5.5 |
| 7.7 | 1.02 | 4.2 | 0.62 | 5.2 | 6.6 | 0.79 | 5.48 | 3.21 | 75.7 | 4.2 | 14.7 | 5.8 | 9.1 |
| 10.0 | 0.26 | 1.3 | -0.01 | 6.6 | 5.7 | 1.03 | 10.29 | 2.34 | 67.4 | 4.5 | 15.6 | 2.7 | 8.3 |
| 6.3 | 1.16 | 9.8 | 0.97 | 4.9 | 2.0 | 0.52 | 5.77 | 3.75 | 81.6 | 3.6 | 14.8 | 5.6 | 6.8 |
| 9.3 | 3.94 | 3.7 | -3.21 | 1.9 | 0.0 | -0.56 | -1.90 | 7.50 | 114.3 | 8.1 | 101.7 | 0.0 | 4.7 |
| 8.7 | 0.06 | 0.2 | 0.15 | 6.8 | 0.1 | 0.81 | 5.54 | 3.20 | 84.8 | 5.2 | 25.8 | 0.0 | 5.0 |
| 9.6 | 0.78 | 1.1 | 0.00 | 4.9 | 0.1 | 0.90 | 4.09 | 2.81 | 65.4 | 5.5 | 46.6 | 0.0 | 7.3 |
| 6.1 | 8.68 | 11.7 | 0.74 | 0.0 | 0.0 | -0.78 | -4.03 | 2.73 | 139.6 | 7.1 | 75.9 | 0.0 | 4.8 |
| 10.0 | 2.09 | 1.0 | 0.92 | 6.6 | 0.8 | 1.31 | 5.40 | 1.69 | 38.2 | 5.2 | 23.5 | 0.0 | 7.6 |
| 5.3 | 2.75 | 7.8 | -0.32 | 6.0 | 0.1 | 2.99 | 21.81 | 5.03 | 65.1 | 6.0 | 32.4 | 0.0 | 4.3 |
| 10.0 | 0.20 | 1.7 | -0.06 | 2.5 | 0.0 | 0.29 | 2.27 | 1.76 | 91.6 | 5.0 | 21.1 | 0.0 | 5.5 |
| 3.6 | 4.86 | 18.4 | 4.22 | 1.2 | -0.1 | -0.79 | -7.39 | 8.18 | 82.5 | 6.9 | 51.7 | 0.0 | 5.7 |
| 7.1 | 0.15 | 0.9 | 0.01 | 6.2 | 0.5 | 0.94 | 8.15 | 3.47 | 68.6 | 1.9 | 17.0 | 20.4 | 7.2 |
| 8.8 | 0.74 | 3.7 | 1.09 | 5.0 | 2.7 | 0.73 | 7.78 | 3.53 | 80.6 | 4.1 | 12.4 | 9.1 | 6.2 |
| 9.3 | 2.13 | 2.6 | 0.00 | 0.4 | 0.0 | -0.35 | -1.90 | 2.40 | 115.6 | 5.7 | 34.9 | 0.0 | 6.7 |
| 6.0 | 4.52 | 11.9 | 0.59 | 3.1 | 0.1 | 0.27 | 1.41 | 4.21 | 89.8 | 6.6 | 53.3 | 3.4 | 6.6 |
| 6.2 | 8.33 | 6.3 | 0.00 | 2.0 | 0.0 | 0.00 | 0.00 | 12.12 | 100.0 | 8.3 | 116.0 | 0.0 | 7.5 |
| 8.5 | 0.47 | 3.2 | 0.22 | 0.4 | -1.1 | -0.40 | -3.32 | 3.29 | 108.1 | 3.0 | 5.2 | 9.3 | 7.1 |
| 9.1 | 1.27 | 2.8 | 0.70 | 1.4 | 0.0 | 0.06 | 0.39 | 2.09 | 91.5 | 5.1 | 35.8 | 0.0 | 5.9 |
| 7.8 | 0.89 | 3.1 | -0.06 | 8.5 | 0.0 | 1.32 | 7.61 | 4.00 | 55.7 | 4.3 | 40.0 | 0.0 | 5.0 |
| 9.2 | 0.96 | 1.6 | 0.76 | 0.2 | 0.0 | -0.49 | -4.71 | 1.97 | 127.4 | 6.6 | 41.5 | 0.5 | 4.2 |
| 9.0 | 0.00 | 0.0 | 0.00 | 7.1 | 0.0 | 1.37 | 8.33 | 2.04 | 25.0 | 5.8 | 65.5 | 0.0 | 5.0 |
| 1.8 | 2.89 | 25.1 | 0.00 | 0.7 | 0.0 | -0.29 | -3.79 | 7.17 | 103.8 | 4.9 | 34.8 | 8.1 | 1.9 |
| 9.0 | 0.13 | 1.1 | 0.25 | 3.4 | 0.1 | 0.35 | 4.28 | 3.92 | 90.4 | 4.1 | 22.5 | 2.9 | 3.0 |
| 6.6 | 2.15 | 6.6 | -0.04 | 2.0 | 0.1 | 0.25 | 2.57 | 2.28 | 90.3 | 5.5 | 39.5 | 4.1 | 4.7 |
| 8.8 | 2.10 | 3.0 | 0.78 | 6.9 | 0.1 | 0.90 | 3.61 | 2.71 | 63.6 | 5.4 | 51.1 | 9.9 | 6.3 |
| 7.4 | 0.00 | 0.0 | 0.00 | 9.4 | 0.0 | 2.18 | 9.15 | 7.60 | 65.0 | 4.0 | 18.4 | 0.0 | 5.0 |
| 7.5 | 0.50 | 3.2 | 0.12 | 3.4 | 0.1 | 0.40 | 3.76 | 2.84 | 84.0 | 2.8 | 44.5 | 22.6 | 5.3 |
| 8.0 | 1.50 | 2.8 | -0.16 | 3.2 | 0.0 | 0.40 | 1.20 | 4.75 | 93.8 | 5.1 | 52.9 | 0.0 | 7.1 |
| 10.0 | 0.00 | 0.0 | 0.12 | 1.1 | 0.0 | -0.05 | -0.41 | 2.03 | 102.5 | 5.2 | 27.9 | 0.0 | 6.6 |
| 9.7 | 0.00 | 0.0 | 0.00 | 1.2 | 0.0 | -0.48 | -8.51 | 3.96 | 113.0 | 4.3 | 8.5 | 0.0 | 1.0 |
| 9.4 | 0.30 | 1.6 | 0.11 | 3.5 | 0.1 | 0.47 | 5.13 | 2.67 | 85.5 | 3.3 | 36.5 | 15.6 | 4.3 |
| 6.6 | 0.94 | 6.6 | 0.18 | 6.0 | 1.8 | 1.00 | 10.57 | 4.30 | 79.6 | 3.9 | 24.6 | 3.3 | 6.5 |
| 2.8 | 1.89 | 17.4 | 0.14 | 0.6 | -0.1 | -0.26 | -3.17 | 3.43 | 106.9 | 2.7 | 11.9 | 10.7 | 3.5 |
| 9.8 | 0.00 | 0.0 | -0.06 | 2.1 | 0.0 | 0.14 | 1.12 | 2.65 | 96.3 | 5.5 | 44.4 | 0.0 | 6.5 |
| 7.7 | 0.77 | 3.7 | 0.33 | 2.1 | 0.0 | 0.11 | 0.61 | 3.71 | 96.4 | 3.6 | 14.9 | 0.0 | 6.3 |
| 7.1 | 0.00 | 0.0 | 0.00 | 1.5 | 0.0 | -0.44 | -4.60 | 3.98 | 125.0 | 7.0 | 58.6 | 0.0 | 4.6 |
| 7.1 | 1.41 | 6.1 | 1.52 | 1.8 | -0.1 | -0.29 | -1.88 | 4.71 | 90.7 | 4.7 | 18.7 | 2.3 | 6.5 |
| 9.3 | 2.47 | 3.4 | 0.19 | 3.9 | 0.2 | 0.49 | 3.48 | 1.28 | 61.2 | 4.8 | 6.8 | 0.0 | 7.2 |
| 9.5 | 1.87 | 2.6 | -0.18 | 0.7 | 0.0 | -0.47 | -1.41 | 3.92 | 108.4 | 5.3 | 26.0 | 0.0 | 5.6 |
| 8.5 | 1.66 | 3.9 | 0.00 | 3.5 | 0.0 | 0.45 | 1.94 | 4.44 | 91.5 | 4.2 | 23.6 | 3.4 | 6.5 |
| 8.9 | 0.52 | 2.3 | 0.00 | 7.0 | 0.0 | 1.10 | 8.53 | 3.84 | 75.3 | 4.4 | 33.2 | 0.7 | 5.0 |
| 4.9 | 1.91 | 14.1 | 0.07 | 2.3 | 0.0 | 0.10 | 1.04 | 3.89 | 88.3 | 3.0 | 10.9 | 9.8 | 4.8 |
| 3.7 | 0.90 | 28.1 | 0.34 | 4.5 | 0.5 | 0.62 | 10.44 | 3.21 | 82.8 | 3.9 | 11.5 | 0.2 | 2.2 |

| Name | City | State | Rating | 2014 Rating | 2013 Rating | Total Assets ($Mil) | One Year Asset Growth | Commercial Loans | Consumer Loans | Mortgage Loans | Securities | Capitalization Index | Net Worth Ratio |
|---|---|---|---|---|---|---|---|---|---|---|---|---|---|
| MEADVILLE AREA FCU | Meadville | PA | C | C | C | 67.4 | 5.91 | 0.3 | 55.0 | 6.0 | 0.3 | 6.5 | 8.5 |
| MED PARK CU | Grand Forks | ND | C+ | C+ | C+ | 17.4 | 5.61 | 0.0 | 27.0 | 0.0 | 0.0 | 9.9 | 10.9 |
| MED5 FCU | Rapid City | SD | C | C | D+ | 54.4 | 3.89 | 3.9 | 53.5 | -0.2 | 0.0 | 6.4 | 8.4 |
| MEDFORD MUNICIPAL EMPL FCU | Medford | MA | C | C | C | 6.6 | 2.63 | 0.0 | 25.1 | 0.0 | 0.0 | 10.0 | 21.1 |
| MEDIA CITY COMMUNITY CU | Burbank | CA | B | B- | C+ | 32.2 | 0.45 | 3.2 | 21.0 | 14.9 | 20.2 | 10.0 | 12.7 |
| MEDIA MEMBERS FCU | Conshohocken | PA | B- | B- | B- | 42.8 | 0.89 | 0.0 | 14.2 | 13.7 | 15.4 | 10.0 | 23.8 |
| MEDICAL EMPL OF STATEN ISLAND FCU | Staten Island | NY | E+ | E+ | E+ | 3.1 | 1.54 | 0.0 | 48.3 | 0.0 | 0.0 | 4.9 | 6.9 |
| MEDINA COUNTY FCU | Wadsworth | OH | C | C+ | B | 68.0 | 1.15 | 2.0 | 17.0 | 12.2 | 47.2 | 10.0 | 11.5 |
| MEDISYS EMPL FCU | Jamaica | NY | C | C+ | C+ | 27.0 | 2.38 | 10.6 | 13.8 | 0.0 | 0.0 | 9.3 | 10.5 |
| MEIJER CU | Grand Rapids | MI | C- | C | C+ | 58.9 | 2.54 | 1.0 | 26.6 | 22.2 | 15.0 | 9.2 | 10.6 |
| MELROSE CU | Briarwood | NY | B+ | A- | A- | 2083.7 | 0.53 | 87.3 | 0.0 | 22.1 | 3.4 | 10.0 | 17.3 |
| ▼ MELROSE SCHOOL & MUNICIPAL EMPL FCU | Melrose | MA | C+ | C+ | C+ | 10.1 | -1.76 | 0.0 | 12.6 | 26.5 | 0.0 | 10.0 | 18.8 |
| MEM FCU | Pittsburgh | PA | C- | C- | C | 18.7 | -0.84 | 0.0 | 21.1 | 0.0 | 0.0 | 8.9 | 10.3 |
| MEMBER ONE FCU | Roanoke | VA | B+ | B+ | B+ | 748.9 | 12.58 | 0.5 | 56.1 | 10.0 | 6.9 | 8.0 | 9.7 |
| MEMBER PREFERRED FCU | Fort Worth | TX | C | C | C- | 9.5 | 30.87 | 0.0 | 94.4 | 0.0 | 0.0 | 9.9 | 11.0 |
| MEMBERFOCUS COMMUNITY CU | Dearborn | MI | D+ | D+ | C- | 97.3 | 3.47 | 0.0 | 11.1 | 10.2 | 61.2 | 9.8 | 11.1 |
| MEMBERS 1ST COMMUNITY FCU | Columbus | MS | D | D | D- | 2.6 | 0.28 | 0.0 | 22.8 | 0.0 | 0.0 | 8.0 | 9.7 |
| MEMBERS 1ST CU | Redding | CA | B- | B | B | 118.0 | 9.48 | 0.1 | 53.4 | 12.0 | 10.1 | 10.0 | 11.1 |
| MEMBERS 1ST CU | Saint Louis | MO | C | D+ | D- | 26.5 | 6.04 | 5.0 | 12.4 | 19.8 | 0.0 | 6.3 | 8.4 |
| MEMBERS 1ST CU | Brattleboro | VT | D+ | D | D- | 14.6 | 9.23 | 0.0 | 31.1 | 21.6 | 0.0 | 6.9 | 8.9 |
| MEMBERS 1ST FCU | Mechanicsburg | PA | B | B | B | 2925.4 | 5.63 | 12.6 | 34.2 | 19.3 | 12.0 | 6.7 | 8.7 |
| MEMBERS 1ST OF NJ FCU | Vineland | NJ | D | D | D | 49.8 | 4.01 | 0.0 | 29.6 | 1.8 | 19.3 | 5.9 | 7.9 |
| ▲ MEMBERS ADVANTAGE COMMUNITY CU | Barre | VT | B | B- | B- | 91.4 | 4.37 | 0.0 | 21.6 | 18.6 | 0.0 | 8.9 | 10.3 |
| MEMBERS ADVANTAGE CU | Michigan City | IN | C | C | C+ | 90.0 | 1.08 | 0.0 | 19.5 | 17.8 | 43.0 | 9.6 | 10.8 |
| MEMBERS ADVANTAGE CU | Wisconsin Rapids | WI | A- | A- | A- | 94.5 | 4.40 | 7.5 | 24.5 | 30.9 | 0.0 | 10.0 | 16.4 |
| MEMBERS ALLIANCE CU | Rockford | IL | C+ | C+ | C | 167.4 | 5.95 | 0.0 | 27.9 | 17.3 | 9.4 | 5.9 | 8.1 |
| MEMBERS CHOICE CU | Peoria | IL | B- | B- | B- | 111.5 | -1.17 | 0.0 | 35.2 | 4.7 | 2.4 | 10.0 | 14.2 |
| MEMBERS CHOICE CU | Ashland | KY | B+ | B+ | A- | 203.4 | 4.64 | 0.3 | 32.1 | 24.4 | 19.4 | 10.0 | 11.1 |
| MEMBERS CHOICE CU | Greenville | OH | B+ | B+ | B | 18.3 | 4.49 | 0.0 | 27.1 | 25.8 | 0.0 | 10.0 | 19.6 |
| ▲ MEMBERS CHOICE CU | Houston | TX | B- | C+ | C | 494.2 | 2.83 | 4.2 | 17.1 | 41.3 | 14.6 | 6.2 | 8.6 |
| MEMBERS CHOICE FCU | Bloomington | IN | D- | D- | E+ | 14.5 | 0.24 | 0.5 | 27.4 | 12.1 | 0.0 | 5.9 | 7.9 |
| MEMBERS CHOICE FCU | Denton | TX | C | C | C | 12.4 | -3.96 | 0.0 | 51.4 | 13.4 | 0.0 | 10.0 | 18.8 |
| MEMBERS CHOICE FINANCIAL CU | Danville | PA | C | C | C | 128.2 | 2.10 | 7.0 | 30.4 | 27.2 | 17.1 | 6.8 | 8.9 |
| MEMBERS CHOICE OF CENTRAL TEXAS FCU | Waco | TX | A- | A- | A- | 168.4 | 2.50 | 1.0 | 52.4 | 31.8 | 6.9 | 10.0 | 13.0 |
| MEMBERS CHOICE WV FCU | Charleston | WV | B+ | A | A | 82.9 | -3.16 | 3.6 | 20.6 | 4.9 | 4.8 | 10.0 | 17.9 |
| ▲ MEMBERS COMMUNITY CU | Muscatine | IA | C+ | C | C- | 51.7 | -0.39 | 5.7 | 22.3 | 31.8 | 1.8 | 7.3 | 9.2 |
| MEMBERS COOPERATIVE CU | Cloquet | MN | A- | A | A- | 633.3 | 58.96 | 9.7 | 34.9 | 25.6 | 4.2 | 10.0 | 11.7 |
| ▲ MEMBERS CU | Cos Cob | CT | D | E+ | D- | 26.2 | -2.00 | 0.0 | 22.2 | 0.0 | 0.0 | 5.1 | 7.1 |
| MEMBERS CU | Winston-Salem | NC | C+ | C+ | C+ | 267.6 | 5.54 | 0.0 | 34.9 | 1.5 | 36.5 | 8.4 | 10.0 |
| MEMBERS CU | Cleburne | TX | C | C | C | 73.1 | 8.40 | 1.8 | 48.5 | 0.9 | 0.0 | 6.4 | 8.4 |
| MEMBERS EXCHANGE CU | Ridgeland | MS | A | A | A | 93.4 | 8.65 | 0.0 | 42.7 | 0.0 | 0.1 | 10.0 | 16.6 |
| ▼ MEMBERS FINANCIAL FCU | Midland | TX | D- | D | D+ | 46.0 | -8.34 | 0.0 | 63.1 | 0.0 | 0.0 | 5.9 | 7.9 |
| MEMBERS FIRST COMMUNITY CU | Quincy | IL | A- | A- | A- | 49.2 | 8.76 | 0.0 | 33.2 | 27.1 | 0.0 | 10.0 | 15.5 |
| MEMBERS FIRST CU | Midland | MI | B- | B- | B- | 352.8 | 5.17 | 4.7 | 29.4 | 21.7 | 9.6 | 9.5 | 10.7 |
| MEMBERS FIRST CU | Corpus Christi | TX | A+ | A+ | A+ | 114.2 | 1.38 | 0.8 | 30.6 | 15.4 | 7.4 | 10.0 | 19.2 |
| ▲ MEMBERS FIRST CU | Brigham City | UT | B+ | B- | B- | 102.0 | 4.09 | 1.0 | 49.1 | 6.7 | 21.0 | 9.8 | 10.9 |
| MEMBERS FIRST CU | Madison | WI | B- | B- | C- | 20.8 | 2.91 | 0.0 | 44.1 | 29.9 | 0.0 | 10.0 | 11.8 |
| MEMBERS FIRST CU OF FLORIDA | Pensacola | FL | B- | B | B | 169.2 | 4.40 | 0.0 | 25.2 | 18.5 | 7.9 | 10.0 | 14.5 |
| MEMBERS FIRST CU OF NH | Manchester | NH | C+ | B- | C+ | 160.9 | 6.84 | 4.5 | 15.8 | 39.7 | 25.2 | 7.0 | 9.1 |
| ▼ MEMBERS FIRST OF MARYLAND FCU | Baltimore | MD | D- | D | D- | 31.4 | 2.53 | 0.0 | 31.5 | 21.7 | 23.8 | 8.7 | 10.2 |
| MEMBERS HERITAGE CU INC | Lexington | KY | B- | B- | C+ | 345.0 | -1.06 | 1.5 | 30.8 | 15.2 | 9.3 | 10.0 | 12.3 |
| MEMBERS PLUS CU | Medford | MA | B- | C+ | C+ | 222.1 | -1.88 | 1.6 | 6.2 | 53.6 | 20.0 | 10.0 | 15.3 |
| ▲ MEMBERS PREFERRED CU | Idaho Falls | ID | B- | C | D+ | 21.9 | 6.65 | 0.0 | 47.3 | 17.6 | 0.0 | 9.3 | 10.5 |
| MEMBERS SOURCE CU | Merrillville | IN | C+ | C+ | C | 72.5 | -0.66 | 0.0 | 18.9 | 11.4 | 60.7 | 10.0 | 11.8 |
| MEMBERS TRUST FCU | Mason | OH | B- | C+ | B- | 23.1 | 6.78 | 0.0 | 27.8 | 19.6 | 0.0 | 10.0 | 16.4 |
| MEMBERS TRUST OF THE SOUTHWEST FCU | Houston | TX | B- | B- | C | 97.5 | 11.02 | 15.2 | 20.6 | 23.3 | 11.1 | 7.8 | 9.5 |
| MEMBERS UNITED CU | Albany | GA | B- | B- | C+ | 59.7 | 12.79 | 0.0 | 48.3 | 6.6 | 3.9 | 10.0 | 13.2 |
| ▲ MEMBERS1ST COMMUNITY CU | Marshalltown | IA | C | C- | C- | 151.3 | 3.28 | 5.0 | 24.2 | 11.1 | 0.0 | 7.9 | 9.6 |
| MEMBERSFIRST CU | Decatur | GA | B | B+ | B | 146.4 | 25.25 | 9.4 | 46.9 | 14.7 | 7.1 | 9.6 | 10.8 |
| MEMBERSOURCE CU | Houston | TX | C | C | C | 196.1 | 1.11 | 0.0 | 33.3 | 7.3 | 21.7 | 5.8 | 7.8 |

| Asset Quality Index | Non-Performing Loans as a % of Total Loans | as a % of Capital | Net Charge-Offs Avg Loans | Profitability Index | Net Income ($Mil) | Return on Assets | Return on Equity | Net Interest Spread | Overhead Efficiency Ratio | Liquidity Index | Liquidity Ratio | Hot Money Ratio | Stability Index |
|---|---|---|---|---|---|---|---|---|---|---|---|---|---|
| 4.3 | 1.17 | 10.0 | 0.69 | 5.3 | 0.4 | 0.79 | 9.25 | 4.95 | 76.9 | 3.8 | 12.6 | 3.9 | 3.1 |
| 9.7 | 0.06 | 0.3 | -0.03 | 4.2 | 0.1 | 0.66 | 6.18 | 3.37 | 79.8 | 4.9 | 24.4 | 0.0 | 6.2 |
| 6.3 | 0.23 | 3.2 | 0.27 | 8.2 | 0.5 | 1.19 | 14.89 | 3.95 | 73.9 | 1.4 | 3.1 | 18.3 | 3.2 |
| 10.0 | 0.66 | 0.8 | -0.55 | 3.4 | 0.0 | 0.34 | 1.64 | 2.94 | 87.7 | 5.0 | 32.4 | 0.0 | 6.8 |
| 8.1 | 1.63 | 5.7 | 0.11 | 4.4 | 0.1 | 0.58 | 4.51 | 3.06 | 84.4 | 4.2 | 30.0 | 8.3 | 5.8 |
| 9.7 | 1.35 | 1.9 | 0.54 | 2.8 | 0.1 | 0.26 | 1.08 | 2.89 | 85.9 | 5.3 | 24.7 | 0.0 | 6.4 |
| 4.0 | 2.25 | 14.0 | 2.39 | 1.2 | 0.0 | -0.22 | -3.06 | 5.03 | 84.1 | 5.3 | 37.8 | 0.0 | 1.0 |
| 10.0 | 0.05 | 0.2 | 0.27 | 2.4 | 0.2 | 0.35 | 3.03 | 2.38 | 88.4 | 5.6 | 32.4 | 1.1 | 5.3 |
| 7.2 | 1.69 | 3.9 | 0.10 | 1.6 | 0.0 | -0.11 | -1.03 | 3.21 | 104.6 | 6.8 | 55.8 | 5.3 | 4.9 |
| 7.5 | 0.40 | 2.1 | 0.42 | 2.3 | 0.1 | 0.15 | 1.40 | 3.35 | 97.2 | 4.0 | 11.7 | 1.6 | 5.3 |
| 1.8 | 6.28 | 30.1 | 0.04 | 1.6 | -21.2 | -1.35 | -7.64 | 2.51 | 46.5 | 0.5 | 1.6 | 30.9 | 9.8 |
| 10.0 | 0.26 | 0.6 | -0.09 | 1.8 | 0.0 | 0.00 | 0.00 | 3.17 | 100.0 | 5.3 | 30.6 | 1.5 | 7.2 |
| 7.4 | 2.04 | 6.6 | 0.19 | 2.2 | 0.0 | 0.15 | 1.53 | 2.79 | 94.2 | 5.0 | 32.5 | 7.1 | 5.1 |
| 6.0 | 0.91 | 7.1 | 0.81 | 7.7 | 5.7 | 1.07 | 11.27 | 3.85 | 64.6 | 2.0 | 6.8 | 18.5 | 7.2 |
| 5.0 | 0.67 | 5.8 | 0.10 | 10.0 | 0.2 | 3.31 | 31.13 | 6.64 | 61.5 | 1.4 | 1.8 | 14.4 | 4.3 |
| 7.7 | 1.21 | 3.3 | 0.51 | 1.6 | 0.0 | -0.01 | -0.13 | 2.40 | 97.8 | 4.7 | 17.1 | 0.9 | 5.5 |
| 8.0 | 0.37 | 1.2 | 1.26 | 0.7 | 0.0 | -0.56 | -5.84 | 3.71 | 103.5 | 7.1 | 57.2 | 0.0 | 4.6 |
| 8.6 | 0.03 | 0.4 | 0.16 | 3.2 | 0.3 | 0.34 | 3.03 | 3.51 | 90.9 | 3.6 | 16.2 | 5.4 | 7.2 |
| 7.4 | 0.36 | 2.9 | 0.02 | 4.3 | 0.1 | 0.57 | 6.94 | 3.38 | 85.3 | 4.0 | 17.3 | 0.4 | 3.9 |
| 2.8 | 2.77 | 21.8 | 0.38 | 7.8 | 0.1 | 1.16 | 13.67 | 6.01 | 70.6 | 3.5 | 23.6 | 14.1 | 4.4 |
| 6.6 | 0.70 | 7.0 | 0.51 | 5.8 | 19.1 | 0.88 | 11.13 | 3.63 | 73.9 | 3.2 | 10.7 | 8.4 | 5.9 |
| 6.4 | 0.77 | 6.4 | 1.12 | 1.1 | -0.2 | -0.49 | -6.23 | 4.74 | 96.0 | 4.4 | 10.9 | 0.5 | 2.8 |
| 6.6 | 1.62 | 8.0 | 0.27 | 5.4 | 0.5 | 0.73 | 7.25 | 3.78 | 77.6 | 4.4 | 15.7 | 2.8 | 5.4 |
| 8.1 | 0.73 | 2.9 | 0.22 | 2.6 | 0.1 | 0.18 | 1.65 | 2.80 | 92.7 | 4.5 | 15.3 | 3.3 | 5.6 |
| 9.4 | 0.22 | 1.0 | 0.05 | 8.2 | 0.8 | 1.12 | 7.03 | 3.58 | 74.2 | 3.3 | 11.7 | 4.4 | 8.2 |
| 6.3 | 1.61 | 10.9 | 0.70 | 3.6 | 0.5 | 0.41 | 5.51 | 3.39 | 83.2 | 4.4 | 18.5 | 1.2 | 4.7 |
| 9.7 | 0.67 | 2.3 | 0.30 | 3.1 | 0.3 | 0.35 | 2.52 | 2.69 | 87.9 | 4.1 | 20.9 | 3.2 | 7.4 |
| 5.8 | 1.36 | 7.4 | 0.65 | 7.4 | 1.8 | 1.16 | 10.84 | 3.67 | 65.9 | 3.8 | 14.6 | 9.5 | 7.2 |
| 9.8 | 0.04 | 0.1 | -0.01 | 7.6 | 0.1 | 1.03 | 5.27 | 3.45 | 74.3 | 4.9 | 26.6 | 1.6 | 6.3 |
| 7.8 | 0.56 | 5.0 | 0.16 | 4.3 | 3.2 | 0.85 | 10.87 | 4.19 | 80.0 | 3.7 | 8.5 | 2.2 | 5.5 |
| 6.2 | 0.94 | 6.5 | 0.20 | 1.7 | 0.0 | -0.09 | -1.16 | 3.62 | 104.5 | 4.7 | 18.0 | 0.9 | 2.8 |
| 7.3 | 0.76 | 3.8 | 0.53 | 2.4 | 0.0 | 0.08 | 0.46 | 5.04 | 92.9 | 2.3 | 22.3 | 20.6 | 6.1 |
| 3.7 | 1.67 | 25.5 | 0.01 | 2.9 | 0.3 | 0.36 | 4.16 | 3.17 | 88.6 | 3.1 | 7.8 | 5.9 | 5.5 |
| 6.7 | 0.25 | 4.6 | 1.49 | 9.5 | 1.8 | 1.44 | 11.29 | 5.41 | 64.1 | 1.6 | 5.7 | 18.2 | 8.3 |
| 9.5 | 0.83 | 1.6 | 0.39 | 4.8 | 0.4 | 0.61 | 3.50 | 2.13 | 70.6 | 4.9 | 27.5 | 4.1 | 7.6 |
| 6.1 | 1.19 | 9.0 | 0.09 | 4.7 | 0.3 | 0.71 | 8.18 | 3.67 | 82.7 | 3.4 | 11.9 | 4.6 | 4.5 |
| 6.8 | 1.16 | 7.6 | 0.59 | 4.5 | 1.2 | 0.34 | 2.75 | 3.36 | 80.4 | 2.7 | 16.0 | 17.0 | 8.1 |
| 8.1 | 0.19 | 1.8 | 0.00 | 3.1 | 0.1 | 0.43 | 6.57 | 4.21 | 93.5 | 3.9 | 20.2 | 0.0 | 1.8 |
| 9.7 | 0.49 | 2.6 | 0.96 | 3.5 | 1.0 | 0.47 | 4.75 | 3.43 | 82.8 | 4.8 | 25.4 | 2.5 | 5.3 |
| 5.4 | 0.61 | 4.0 | 0.54 | 3.7 | 0.2 | 0.34 | 4.01 | 3.64 | 90.1 | 4.3 | 27.5 | 5.9 | 4.0 |
| 8.9 | 0.81 | 2.9 | 1.83 | 10.0 | 1.1 | 1.57 | 9.54 | 6.41 | 69.0 | 4.0 | 39.2 | 19.8 | 8.5 |
| 3.5 | 1.78 | 16.9 | 1.17 | 1.0 | -0.2 | -0.44 | -5.61 | 4.69 | 95.1 | 4.3 | 29.2 | 8.1 | 1.8 |
| 9.6 | 0.27 | 1.1 | 0.34 | 9.5 | 0.5 | 1.39 | 9.27 | 5.14 | 73.6 | 5.1 | 33.1 | 3.6 | 8.0 |
| 8.8 | 0.59 | 3.2 | 0.67 | 4.5 | 1.7 | 0.66 | 6.31 | 4.15 | 79.8 | 3.9 | 16.4 | 3.8 | 6.3 |
| 9.7 | 0.47 | 1.6 | 0.49 | 9.7 | 1.1 | 1.32 | 7.43 | 3.71 | 68.9 | 4.7 | 20.2 | 3.6 | 9.3 |
| 7.2 | 0.53 | 3.6 | 0.02 | 5.5 | 0.7 | 0.92 | 8.73 | 3.41 | 81.4 | 3.5 | 8.4 | 4.0 | 6.5 |
| 9.4 | 0.31 | 1.8 | 0.30 | 7.8 | 0.2 | 1.06 | 9.19 | 5.17 | 81.4 | 1.7 | 10.8 | 21.1 | 5.7 |
| 7.9 | 1.40 | 5.3 | 0.42 | 3.1 | 0.2 | 0.19 | 1.31 | 4.12 | 92.6 | 5.5 | 35.4 | 4.0 | 7.4 |
| 9.2 | 0.17 | 1.2 | 0.14 | 2.8 | 0.3 | 0.25 | 2.67 | 2.73 | 90.7 | 3.7 | 20.0 | 7.7 | 5.7 |
| 7.6 | 0.56 | 2.9 | 0.70 | 0.1 | -0.1 | -0.42 | -4.08 | 3.15 | 104.8 | 4.7 | 22.1 | 0.7 | 3.7 |
| 7.9 | 0.87 | 4.1 | 1.00 | 3.1 | 0.6 | 0.21 | 1.82 | 4.01 | 81.8 | 5.9 | 44.1 | 5.7 | 6.7 |
| 8.4 | 1.27 | 5.6 | 0.08 | 3.3 | 0.7 | 0.40 | 2.68 | 2.83 | 86.3 | 3.3 | 13.3 | 6.6 | 8.1 |
| 7.9 | 0.04 | 0.3 | 0.32 | 9.3 | 0.2 | 1.46 | 14.05 | 4.44 | 73.5 | 3.8 | 16.5 | 3.3 | 4.4 |
| 10.0 | 0.40 | 1.1 | 0.18 | 2.8 | 0.1 | 0.26 | 2.24 | 2.48 | 90.5 | 4.4 | 8.8 | 1.9 | 5.2 |
| 10.0 | 0.12 | 0.4 | 0.15 | 3.9 | 0.1 | 0.51 | 3.09 | 3.08 | 86.8 | 4.7 | 22.8 | 0.8 | 7.2 |
| 6.5 | 0.49 | 3.6 | 0.15 | 6.4 | 0.6 | 0.83 | 9.96 | 3.21 | 77.5 | 2.4 | 7.4 | 17.1 | 4.8 |
| 6.7 | 0.97 | 4.8 | 0.26 | 4.5 | 0.3 | 0.71 | 5.25 | 4.27 | 79.4 | 3.1 | 13.7 | 11.7 | 5.9 |
| 6.8 | 0.36 | 7.2 | 0.18 | 2.7 | 0.4 | 0.38 | 4.06 | 2.60 | 85.3 | 4.3 | 17.1 | 2.6 | 5.8 |
| 6.5 | 0.42 | 6.2 | 0.43 | 4.5 | 0.5 | 0.46 | 4.39 | 3.86 | 88.5 | 3.7 | 20.7 | 7.9 | 6.0 |
| 9.4 | 0.30 | 2.3 | 0.48 | 2.3 | 0.2 | 0.14 | 1.83 | 3.28 | 90.3 | 4.0 | 15.0 | 5.6 | 4.0 |

| Name | City | State | Rating | 2014 Rating | 2013 Rating | Total Assets ($Mil) | One Year Asset Growth | Asset Mix (As a % of Total Assets) | | | | Capital-ization Index | Net Worth Ratio |
|------|------|-------|--------|-------------|-------------|---------------------|----------------------|-----------------|---|---|---|-----------------------|------------------|
| | | | | | | | | Comm-ercial Loans | Cons-umer Loans | Mort-gage Loans | Secur-ities | | |
| ▼ MEMBERSOWN CU | Lincoln | NE | D+ | C | C- | 102.1 | 17.33 | 0.0 | 22.4 | 4.0 | 51.3 | 6.6 | 8.7 |
| MEMORIAL CU | Chattanooga | TN | C- | C- | D+ | 7.7 | -0.10 | 0.0 | 35.8 | 3.2 | 0.0 | 10.0 | 16.7 |
| ▼ MEMORIAL CU | Houston | TX | C | C+ | C | 72.0 | 0.21 | 0.0 | 60.2 | 4.6 | 0.0 | 7.4 | 9.3 |
| MEMORIAL EMPL FCU | Hollywood | FL | B- | B- | C | 59.4 | 10.96 | 0.0 | 27.8 | 0.6 | 37.9 | 9.4 | 10.6 |
| ▲ MEMORIAL FCU | Gulfport | MS | C+ | C | C | 8.9 | -2.16 | 0.0 | 21.0 | 0.0 | 0.0 | 10.0 | 21.8 |
| MEMORIAL HEALTH CU | Savannah | GA | C | C | C | 17.4 | 2.69 | 0.0 | 36.2 | 8.8 | 0.1 | 10.0 | 18.9 |
| MEMPHIS CITY EMPL CU | Memphis | TN | A- | A | A | 248.5 | 3.76 | 0.8 | 24.6 | 14.7 | 34.6 | 10.0 | 18.6 |
| ▲ MEMPHIS MUNICIPAL EMPL FCU | Memphis | TN | C+ | C | D+ | 12.9 | 1.05 | 0.0 | 32.6 | 0.7 | 0.0 | 10.0 | 32.3 |
| MENARD CU | Chester | IL | D | D | C- | <1 | 2.54 | 0.0 | 48.8 | 0.0 | 0.0 | 5.9 | 7.9 |
| ▲ MENDO LAKE CU | Ukiah | CA | C+ | C+ | C+ | 204.5 | 9.64 | 0.1 | 49.1 | 6.2 | 32.6 | 5.9 | 7.9 |
| MENLO SURVEY FCU | Menlo Park | CA | B- | B | C+ | 59.7 | -1.24 | 0.7 | 8.0 | 33.7 | 0.0 | 10.0 | 11.5 |
| MENOMINEE AREA CU | Menominee | MI | C | C | C | 8.7 | 8.30 | 0.0 | 39.8 | 0.0 | 0.0 | 10.0 | 17.2 |
| MENOMINEE COUNTY FCU | Powers | MI | C | C+ | C+ | 97.3 | 3.96 | 0.0 | 15.1 | 30.4 | 20.9 | 6.8 | 8.8 |
| MERCED MUNICIPAL EMPL CU | Merced | CA | D+ | D+ | C- | 2.1 | 1.70 | 0.0 | 59.7 | 0.0 | 0.0 | 9.2 | 10.5 |
| MERCED SCHOOL EMPL FCU | Merced | CA | B+ | B+ | B | 426.8 | 4.59 | 0.4 | 18.8 | 13.0 | 45.0 | 8.0 | 9.7 |
| MERCER COUNTY COMMUNITY FCU | Hermitage | PA | C- | C | C | 72.2 | 3.85 | 0.0 | 22.7 | 1.9 | 1.1 | 6.5 | 8.5 |
| ▲ MERCER COUNTY IMPROVEMENT AUTHORIT | Hamilton | NJ | C | C | C | <1 | -0.76 | 0.0 | 58.4 | 0.0 | 0.0 | 10.0 | 20.6 |
| ▲ MERCER COUNTY NJ TEACHERS FCU | Hamilton Square | NJ | D | D- | D- | 28.1 | 1.96 | 0.0 | 12.7 | 0.0 | 9.1 | 5.1 | 7.1 |
| MERCER COUNTY WEST VIRGINIA TEACHER | Bluefield | WV | D- | D- | D | 8.1 | -3.54 | 0.0 | 59.4 | 0.0 | 0.0 | 8.6 | 10.1 |
| MERCER CU | Aledo | IL | D | D+ | D | 2.8 | -2.38 | 0.0 | 67.5 | 0.0 | 0.0 | 10.0 | 11.1 |
| ▼ MERCK EMPL FCU | Rahway | NJ | B- | B | B | 1896.3 | 0.68 | 0.0 | 1.1 | 7.5 | 82.3 | 9.6 | 10.8 |
| MERCK SHARP & DOHME FCU | Chalfont | PA | B- | B- | B | 498.0 | 1.17 | 1.1 | 12.8 | 13.9 | 32.2 | 7.7 | 9.5 |
| MERCO CU | Merced | CA | B- | B- | C+ | 96.8 | 5.84 | 0.0 | 27.8 | 11.6 | 5.5 | 7.0 | 9.0 |
| MERCY CU | Springfield | MO | D+ | C- | C | 49.2 | 2.45 | 0.0 | 51.5 | 1.5 | 11.8 | 8.1 | 9.8 |
| MERCY FCU | Savannah | GA | C+ | C+ | C+ | 7.0 | 4.19 | 0.0 | 40.2 | 0.0 | 0.0 | 10.0 | 15.7 |
| MERCY HEALTH PARTNERS FCU | Toledo | OH | C | C | C+ | 21.0 | 1.97 | 0.0 | 24.0 | 12.0 | 26.3 | 10.0 | 14.1 |
| MERHO FCU | Johnstown | PA | C | C | C | 44.2 | -4.58 | 0.0 | 15.9 | 7.7 | 1.0 | 9.3 | 10.6 |
| MERIDEN POSTAL EMPL FCU | Southington | CT | D | D+ | C- | <1 | -18.97 | 0.0 | 32.4 | 0.0 | 0.0 | 10.0 | 26.5 |
| MERIDEN SCHOOLS FCU | Meriden | CT | C+ | C+ | C+ | 61.7 | 0.50 | 0.0 | 14.0 | 16.4 | 3.3 | 7.9 | 9.6 |
| MERIDIA COMMUNITY FCU | Hamburg | NY | A- | A- | A- | 59.3 | 8.00 | 0.0 | 34.4 | 10.4 | 0.0 | 10.0 | 11.7 |
| MERIDIAN CU | Ottumwa | IA | B+ | B+ | B+ | 29.3 | 0.72 | 5.2 | 20.0 | 22.4 | 36.0 | 10.0 | 13.6 |
| ▲ MERIDIAN MISSISSIPPI AIR NATIONAL GUAR | Meridian | MS | C+ | C- | D+ | 16.3 | -2.06 | 0.0 | 23.2 | 13.8 | 0.0 | 9.6 | 10.7 |
| MERIDIAN MUTUAL FCU | Meridian | MS | B- | B+ | B+ | 34.0 | 4.64 | 0.0 | 13.3 | 14.9 | 0.0 | 10.0 | 13.0 |
| MERIDIAN TRUST FCU | Cheyenne | WY | B | B+ | A- | 315.7 | 5.69 | 5.9 | 32.7 | 25.5 | 3.0 | 9.5 | 10.7 |
| MERITRUST CU | Wichita | KS | B+ | A- | B+ | 1072.2 | 13.16 | 3.0 | 64.0 | 17.5 | 1.4 | 8.6 | 10.1 |
| MERIWEST CU | San Jose | CA | B+ | B+ | B- | 1157.0 | 8.72 | 7.5 | 18.9 | 34.0 | 18.7 | 7.7 | 9.4 |
| MERRIMACK VALLEY FCU | Lawrence | MA | B- | B- | B- | 538.5 | 6.76 | 3.0 | 7.4 | 29.5 | 26.8 | 8.7 | 10.1 |
| MERRITT FCU | Wilton | CT | D+ | D+ | D+ | 13.7 | 0.43 | 0.0 | 24.6 | 32.7 | 10.4 | 10.0 | 12.7 |
| ▲ MESQUITE CU | Mesquite | TX | D- | E+ | E+ | 29.7 | -16.35 | 0.0 | 37.0 | 5.0 | 0.0 | 5.1 | 7.1 |
| ▲ MESSIAH BAPTIST CHURCH FCU | East Orange | NJ | D+ | D | D- | <1 | -7.27 | 0.0 | 13.7 | 0.0 | 8.2 | 8.2 | 10.2 |
| MESSIAH BAPTIST-JUBILEE FCU | Brockton | MA | C | C- | C | <1 | 13.77 | 0.0 | 34.0 | 0.0 | 0.0 | 10.0 | 15.0 |
| ▼ MET TRAN FCU | Houston | TX | C- | C+ | C+ | 8.7 | 2.83 | 0.0 | 30.1 | 0.0 | 0.0 | 10.0 | 18.5 |
| METCO CU | Cedar Rapids | IA | B- | B- | B- | 27.8 | 3.22 | 8.6 | 22.9 | 22.6 | 0.0 | 10.0 | 11.9 |
| METHODIST HEALTHCARE FCU | Cordova | TN | A- | A- | A- | 34.5 | 2.48 | 0.0 | 24.2 | 0.4 | 1.1 | 10.0 | 15.7 |
| METHODIST HOSPITAL EMPL FCU | Dallas | TX | C- | C- | C- | 8.8 | 1.36 | 0.0 | 33.7 | 0.0 | 0.0 | 9.7 | 10.8 |
| METHUEN FCU | Methuen | MA | D+ | C- | C | 20.8 | 3.64 | 0.0 | 31.3 | 5.5 | 0.0 | 10.0 | 14.1 |
| METREX FCU | Kenilworth | NJ | C | C- | D | 5.1 | -1.10 | 0.0 | 56.4 | 0.0 | 0.0 | 10.0 | 18.5 |
| METRO COMMUNITY FCU | Huntington | WV | C- | C- | C- | 29.4 | 8.06 | 0.0 | 32.0 | 5.6 | 0.9 | 6.4 | 8.4 |
| METRO CU | Chelsea | MA | C+ | B- | B | 1462.9 | 9.58 | 6.6 | 28.7 | 32.9 | 7.9 | 8.8 | 10.2 |
| METRO CU | Springfield | MO | B- | B | B | 52.9 | 1.78 | 0.3 | 20.1 | 3.4 | 0.0 | 10.0 | 12.1 |
| METRO EMPL CU | Lexington | KY | B- | B- | B | 24.1 | 8.54 | 0.0 | 37.1 | 6.1 | 2.7 | 10.0 | 11.5 |
| METRO FCU | Arlington Heights | IL | D | D | D | 38.5 | 3.53 | 0.1 | 19.7 | 19.0 | 20.8 | 5.4 | 7.4 |
| METRO HEALTH SERVICES FCU | Omaha | NE | A | A | A- | 267.0 | 9.57 | 0.3 | 46.2 | 15.3 | 5.7 | 10.0 | 11.8 |
| METRO MEDICAL CU | Dallas | TX | C+ | B- | B- | 66.9 | 3.11 | 0.0 | 13.1 | 9.1 | 1.8 | 10.0 | 12.1 |
| METRO NORTH FCU | Jacksonville | FL | B- | B- | B- | 15.6 | 2.51 | 0.0 | 21.8 | 22.7 | 0.0 | 10.0 | 19.7 |
| METRO NORTH FCU | Waterford | MI | D+ | D+ | D | 39.2 | 4.85 | 0.0 | 40.6 | 9.0 | 4.9 | 6.9 | 8.9 |
| METRO SHORES CU | Trenton | MI | C- | C- | C- | 64.1 | 1.75 | 0.0 | 22.2 | 3.2 | 50.2 | 6.0 | 8.0 |
| ▲ METRO WIRE FCU | Plains | PA | D+ | D- | D- | 4.5 | -5.66 | 0.0 | 10.4 | 0.0 | 75.9 | 10.0 | 12.0 |
| METROPOLITAN CHURCH FCU | Suffolk | VA | C+ | C+ | C | 7.8 | 2.26 | 0.0 | 36.7 | 0.0 | 0.0 | 10.0 | 34.1 |
| METROPOLITAN DISTRICT EMPL CU | Hartford | CT | C+ | C+ | B- | 24.4 | 5.50 | 0.0 | 18.6 | 30.8 | 6.4 | 10.0 | 14.1 |

| Asset Quality Index | Non-Performing Loans | | Net Charge-Offs Avg Loans | Profitability Index | Net Income ($Mil) | Return on Assets | Return on Equity | Net Interest Spread | Overhead Efficiency Ratio | Liquidity Index | Liquidity Ratio | Hot Money Ratio | Stability Index |
|---|---|---|---|---|---|---|---|---|---|---|---|---|---|
| | as a % of Total Loans | as a % of Capital | | | | | | | | | | | |
| 7.5 | 1.16 | 6.0 | 0.67 | 1.2 | -0.2 | -0.23 | -2.68 | 2.24 | 102.1 | 4.2 | 28.6 | 7.8 | 4.3 |
| 9.7 | 0.12 | 0.3 | -0.08 | 2.2 | 0.0 | 0.17 | 1.04 | 4.31 | 100.0 | 5.2 | 24.2 | 0.0 | 5.8 |
| 6.8 | 0.27 | 2.5 | 0.53 | 1.7 | -0.1 | -0.25 | -2.57 | 3.68 | 100.5 | 3.7 | 10.9 | 7.2 | 4.1 |
| 8.1 | 0.85 | 2.6 | 0.57 | 4.1 | 0.2 | 0.55 | 5.09 | 3.20 | 86.5 | 5.5 | 20.4 | 0.0 | 5.0 |
| 10.0 | 0.79 | 0.9 | 0.88 | 6.5 | 0.1 | 1.17 | 5.36 | 2.49 | 62.0 | 5.3 | 26.8 | 0.0 | 5.0 |
| 6.5 | 2.80 | 8.2 | 0.78 | 4.8 | 0.1 | 0.70 | 3.76 | 5.24 | 83.3 | 4.2 | 16.7 | 5.1 | 6.0 |
| 10.0 | 0.31 | 0.7 | 0.35 | 5.4 | 1.4 | 0.76 | 4.39 | 2.95 | 79.8 | 4.3 | 20.2 | 6.2 | 8.3 |
| 9.1 | 1.95 | 2.2 | 1.96 | 3.1 | 0.0 | 0.35 | 1.09 | 3.96 | 90.1 | 5.8 | 68.0 | 5.5 | 5.4 |
| 6.3 | 0.51 | 2.8 | 0.67 | 0.7 | 0.0 | -0.31 | -3.92 | 7.19 | 94.7 | 6.0 | 54.6 | 0.0 | 3.2 |
| 5.7 | 0.92 | 7.1 | 0.72 | 3.9 | 0.7 | 0.51 | 6.16 | 4.11 | 78.5 | 3.8 | 11.4 | 2.6 | 4.9 |
| 10.0 | 0.26 | 1.1 | -0.03 | 3.2 | 0.1 | 0.31 | 2.73 | 2.27 | 83.0 | 5.8 | 55.1 | 3.0 | 6.1 |
| 9.5 | 0.96 | 2.5 | 0.00 | 2.6 | 0.0 | 0.12 | 0.71 | 3.65 | 96.4 | 5.1 | 24.8 | 0.0 | 7.2 |
| 7.8 | 0.45 | 3.8 | 0.27 | 2.7 | 0.1 | 0.20 | 2.23 | 2.73 | 87.5 | 5.0 | 36.1 | 9.6 | 4.4 |
| 6.5 | 0.56 | 3.1 | 0.00 | 1.6 | 0.0 | 0.00 | 0.00 | 5.19 | 98.6 | 5.5 | 43.9 | 0.0 | 4.2 |
| 10.0 | 0.28 | 1.0 | 0.11 | 5.7 | 2.5 | 0.78 | 8.20 | 3.04 | 78.3 | 5.5 | 28.7 | 4.7 | 5.6 |
| 9.3 | 0.36 | 2.0 | 0.04 | 2.0 | 0.0 | 0.05 | 0.61 | 2.40 | 96.4 | 5.3 | 24.9 | 0.4 | 4.1 |
| 8.6 | 0.00 | 0.0 | -1.98 | 3.8 | 0.0 | 0.34 | 1.67 | 15.84 | 96.8 | 6.5 | 54.5 | 0.0 | 7.0 |
| 6.6 | 1.12 | 6.9 | 0.63 | 2.2 | 0.1 | 0.25 | 5.87 | 2.37 | 84.2 | 6.2 | 41.8 | 0.0 | 0.9 |
| 0.7 | 5.67 | 35.9 | 1.39 | 5.0 | 0.1 | 0.87 | 9.56 | 7.38 | 76.1 | 5.4 | 34.2 | 2.8 | 4.7 |
| 2.0 | 5.63 | 34.8 | -0.06 | 2.7 | 0.0 | 0.19 | 1.72 | 2.49 | 91.5 | 4.6 | 31.6 | 0.0 | 5.8 |
| 10.0 | 0.98 | 1.0 | 0.05 | 3.9 | 6.7 | 0.47 | 4.42 | 0.71 | 37.8 | 5.5 | 20.8 | 0.0 | 7.6 |
| 10.0 | 0.20 | 1.0 | 0.21 | 3.7 | 1.7 | 0.42 | 4.57 | 2.70 | 81.6 | 4.8 | 23.7 | 5.9 | 6.7 |
| 8.9 | 0.29 | 1.3 | 0.48 | 5.0 | 0.5 | 0.70 | 7.85 | 3.35 | 82.7 | 5.2 | 40.6 | 2.3 | 4.2 |
| 7.0 | 0.38 | 2.3 | 0.11 | 1.6 | 0.0 | 0.01 | 0.11 | 2.58 | 97.2 | 4.9 | 23.7 | 0.0 | 4.8 |
| 8.7 | 1.66 | 4.3 | 0.74 | 7.1 | 0.1 | 0.94 | 5.98 | 5.27 | 81.9 | 6.2 | 68.4 | 5.7 | 5.0 |
| 8.9 | 1.93 | 5.3 | 0.41 | 1.8 | 0.0 | 0.02 | 0.13 | 3.11 | 97.1 | 6.0 | 35.7 | 1.4 | 6.3 |
| 8.1 | 0.92 | 3.2 | 0.23 | 2.7 | 0.1 | 0.25 | 2.45 | 2.23 | 88.6 | 4.3 | 10.0 | 2.5 | 5.0 |
| 5.7 | 10.50 | 12.1 | 0.00 | 0.2 | 0.0 | -0.38 | -1.47 | 3.24 | 113.3 | 6.1 | 43.3 | 0.0 | 6.6 |
| 7.4 | 1.08 | 4.3 | 0.20 | 3.3 | 0.2 | 0.44 | 4.67 | 2.68 | 82.4 | 5.4 | 27.2 | 1.5 | 4.5 |
| 7.5 | 0.78 | 5.4 | 0.45 | 5.7 | 0.3 | 0.73 | 6.33 | 4.01 | 75.9 | 3.6 | 7.7 | 0.2 | 6.9 |
| 8.8 | 1.22 | 4.0 | 0.46 | 4.2 | 0.1 | 0.46 | 3.45 | 3.12 | 84.2 | 4.9 | 24.6 | 3.0 | 6.7 |
| 9.4 | 0.32 | 1.2 | 0.06 | 3.5 | 0.1 | 0.53 | 5.05 | 2.35 | 82.1 | 5.8 | 62.5 | 0.0 | 5.3 |
| 10.0 | 0.37 | 0.9 | 0.39 | 3.2 | 0.1 | 0.24 | 2.05 | 4.04 | 92.2 | 7.0 | 53.1 | 3.2 | 7.1 |
| 8.8 | 0.39 | 2.8 | 0.37 | 4.8 | 1.7 | 0.74 | 7.01 | 3.19 | 74.0 | 3.2 | 14.1 | 7.0 | 6.9 |
| 6.8 | 0.40 | 4.3 | 0.83 | 5.9 | 5.9 | 0.79 | 7.68 | 4.10 | 68.9 | 1.5 | 12.0 | 21.5 | 7.3 |
| 6.9 | 0.96 | 8.5 | 0.10 | 5.0 | 5.6 | 0.68 | 7.94 | 3.00 | 80.5 | 3.1 | 13.2 | 7.6 | 6.1 |
| 9.1 | 0.60 | 3.1 | 0.05 | 4.2 | 2.6 | 0.66 | 6.43 | 2.62 | 79.1 | 4.7 | 22.9 | 8.1 | 7.4 |
| 5.2 | 3.78 | 17.5 | 0.14 | 0.9 | 0.0 | -0.14 | -1.07 | 3.73 | 103.7 | 4.3 | 28.1 | 5.3 | 4.9 |
| 6.1 | 0.52 | 5.7 | 2.09 | 0.3 | -0.2 | -0.68 | -10.31 | 3.47 | 92.7 | 4.6 | 21.3 | 0.0 | 1.7 |
| 6.2 | 5.13 | 7.4 | 0.00 | 4.1 | 0.0 | 0.52 | 5.56 | 3.49 | 75.0 | 7.1 | 40.6 | 0.0 | 3.0 |
| 7.9 | 0.75 | 1.7 | 0.00 | 7.2 | 0.0 | 1.42 | 9.72 | 2.49 | 50.0 | 4.7 | 28.3 | 0.0 | 5.0 |
| 9.8 | 0.72 | 1.3 | 0.34 | 1.4 | 0.0 | -0.55 | -2.94 | 5.19 | 106.7 | 6.6 | 62.4 | 0.0 | 6.4 |
| 7.0 | 0.22 | 6.1 | -0.05 | 4.0 | 0.1 | 0.56 | 4.80 | 4.06 | 87.8 | 4.9 | 28.7 | 2.2 | 6.5 |
| 9.4 | 0.66 | 1.1 | 1.82 | 6.5 | 0.2 | 0.93 | 6.02 | 4.17 | 81.6 | 6.4 | 43.9 | 1.9 | 7.1 |
| 6.5 | 1.60 | 5.1 | 0.95 | 6.0 | 0.1 | 0.94 | 9.05 | 3.71 | 76.3 | 5.1 | 44.5 | 3.9 | 3.7 |
| 9.7 | 0.54 | 2.0 | 0.32 | 0.6 | -0.1 | -0.29 | -2.07 | 2.87 | 109.4 | 4.8 | 30.3 | 0.0 | 6.7 |
| 8.3 | 0.00 | 0.0 | -0.08 | 4.9 | 0.0 | 0.86 | 4.75 | 4.50 | 79.2 | 4.8 | 37.0 | 0.0 | 4.3 |
| 5.9 | 1.25 | 7.3 | 0.37 | 2.7 | 0.1 | 0.30 | 3.63 | 3.35 | 89.0 | 4.5 | 22.7 | 6.1 | 3.9 |
| 9.1 | 0.29 | 2.7 | 0.06 | 3.0 | 3.4 | 0.32 | 3.45 | 2.47 | 89.6 | 2.9 | 5.8 | 6.0 | 6.2 |
| 10.0 | 0.60 | 1.8 | 0.14 | 3.1 | 0.1 | 0.29 | 2.49 | 2.88 | 93.7 | 5.0 | 26.9 | 0.7 | 6.1 |
| 9.7 | 0.10 | 0.4 | 0.20 | 6.0 | 0.2 | 0.86 | 7.56 | 4.54 | 85.2 | 6.0 | 46.0 | 3.0 | 6.6 |
| 6.1 | 0.52 | 3.4 | 0.97 | 2.6 | 0.1 | 0.23 | 3.10 | 3.67 | 85.8 | 5.0 | 18.2 | 0.0 | 2.3 |
| 6.0 | 1.34 | 7.9 | 0.49 | 9.3 | 2.7 | 1.39 | 12.07 | 4.38 | 76.9 | 3.3 | 20.8 | 9.0 | 8.3 |
| 10.0 | 0.81 | 1.6 | 0.48 | 3.2 | 0.2 | 0.37 | 3.17 | 1.82 | 86.0 | 4.8 | 18.4 | 1.9 | 6.1 |
| 8.4 | 1.10 | 3.9 | 0.19 | 2.9 | 0.0 | 0.17 | 0.87 | 3.39 | 94.4 | 5.2 | 47.3 | 4.3 | 6.6 |
| 6.4 | 0.83 | 5.4 | 0.34 | 2.0 | 0.0 | 0.08 | 0.85 | 3.51 | 95.4 | 4.1 | 11.7 | 0.3 | 3.5 |
| 7.7 | 1.10 | 5.1 | 0.52 | 2.2 | 0.0 | 0.08 | 0.99 | 2.29 | 90.3 | 4.0 | 16.0 | 7.0 | 3.2 |
| 6.4 | 4.82 | 7.9 | 1.02 | 2.1 | 0.0 | 0.20 | 1.74 | 2.41 | 92.6 | 4.8 | 7.1 | 0.0 | 3.8 |
| 3.7 | 10.60 | 21.9 | -0.14 | 10.0 | 0.1 | 1.31 | 3.96 | 7.84 | 72.7 | 4.3 | 39.0 | 7.6 | 7.6 |
| 10.0 | 0.18 | 0.7 | 0.04 | 3.4 | 0.1 | 0.40 | 2.83 | 2.73 | 84.3 | 2.9 | 17.3 | 17.9 | 6.5 |

| Name | City | State | Rating | 2014 Rating | 2013 Rating | Total Assets ($Mil) | One Year Asset Growth | Commercial Loans | Consumer Loans | Mortgage Loans | Securities | Capitalization Index | Net Worth Ratio |
|---|---|---|---|---|---|---|---|---|---|---|---|---|---|
| METROPOLITAN FCU | Kansas City | MO | D | D | C- | 10.1 | 0.81 | 0.0 | 20.5 | 0.0 | 0.0 | 10.0 | 20.0 |
| METROPOLITAN L FCU | Oak Park | IL | C | C | C | 7.4 | 8.36 | 0.0 | 26.8 | 0.0 | 0.0 | 10.0 | 18.8 |
| METROPOLITAN SERVICE FCU | Philadelphia | PA | D+ | D | E+ | 22.4 | -2.03 | 0.4 | 30.5 | 9.9 | 16.6 | 7.4 | 9.3 |
| METROPOLITAN SERVICES CU | Saint Paul | MN | D | D | D | 8.3 | 9.20 | 0.8 | 43.3 | 17.8 | 6.8 | 6.2 | 8.7 |
| METROPOLITAN TEACHERS CU | Nashville | TN | D | D | D+ | 3.1 | -6.37 | 0.0 | 21.5 | 0.0 | 8.9 | 10.0 | 33.3 |
| ▲ METROWEST COMMUNITY FCU | Framingham | MA | C- | D+ | D+ | 91.1 | -5.02 | 0.0 | 25.5 | 3.0 | 18.6 | 10.0 | 11.1 |
| METRUM COMMUNITY CU | Centennial | CO | A- | A- | A- | 60.4 | 3.34 | 0.0 | 25.1 | 30.9 | 0.0 | 10.0 | 13.1 |
| MIAMI FCU | Miami | FL | B | B | B- | 32.3 | 3.45 | 0.9 | 23.5 | 20.1 | 0.0 | 10.0 | 14.2 |
| MIAMI FIREFIGHTERS FCU | Miami | FL | C | C | C- | 87.2 | 4.79 | 0.1 | 18.5 | 12.1 | 20.5 | 6.7 | 8.7 |
| ▲ MIAMI POSTAL SERVICE CU | Miami | FL | B | C+ | C | 121.2 | 2.37 | 0.0 | 35.8 | 0.7 | 25.1 | 10.0 | 11.5 |
| MIAMI UNIV COMMUNITY FCU | Oxford | OH | C | C | C+ | 59.9 | 4.13 | 3.1 | 16.9 | 28.5 | 30.9 | 7.9 | 9.6 |
| MICHAEL BAKER JR FCU | Moon Township | PA | C+ | C+ | C+ | 7.7 | 0.62 | 0.0 | 48.3 | 0.0 | 0.0 | 10.0 | 16.6 |
| MICHIGAN COASTAL CU | Muskegon | MI | C | C+ | C | 17.2 | 39.62 | 0.0 | 42.5 | 26.4 | 11.8 | 7.2 | 9.1 |
| ▲ MICHIGAN COLUMBUS FCU | Livonia | MI | C- | D+ | D | 43.3 | 0.34 | 0.9 | 11.1 | 23.1 | 6.5 | 7.7 | 9.4 |
| MICHIGAN COMMUNITY CU | Jackson | MI | B | B | B+ | 142.4 | 9.49 | 6.2 | 44.0 | 24.3 | 11.3 | 7.8 | 9.6 |
| MICHIGAN EDUCATIONAL CU | Plymouth | MI | B- | B- | C+ | 715.6 | 3.36 | 0.1 | 22.3 | 23.0 | 34.4 | 10.0 | 12.2 |
| MICHIGAN FIRST CU | Lathrup Village | MI | A | A | A | 758.5 | 9.40 | 5.4 | 22.0 | 17.8 | 32.8 | 10.0 | 14.7 |
| MICHIGAN LEGACY CU | Pontiac | MI | B | B+ | B | 164.1 | 2.82 | 1.1 | 21.0 | 10.5 | 46.7 | 10.0 | 11.2 |
| MICHIGAN ONE COMMUNITY CU | Ionia | MI | C | C | C+ | 94.4 | 4.23 | 0.6 | 61.9 | 6.9 | 4.2 | 6.9 | 8.9 |
| MICHIGAN SCHOOLS AND GOVERNMENT CU | Clinton Township | MI | A- | A- | A- | 1526.8 | 0.79 | 4.4 | 35.8 | 31.7 | 11.3 | 10.0 | 11.3 |
| MICHIGAN STATE UNIV FCU | East Lansing | MI | A- | A- | A- | 2941.7 | 8.94 | 6.6 | 26.4 | 30.3 | 20.9 | 10.0 | 11.2 |
| MICHIGAN TECH EMPL FCU | Houghton | MI | C- | C | C- | 65.0 | 8.01 | 0.6 | 20.9 | 17.8 | 32.6 | 5.9 | 7.9 |
| MICHOUD CU | New Orleans | LA | D | D | C- | 4.0 | -9.81 | 0.0 | 58.7 | 0.0 | 0.0 | 10.0 | 17.0 |
| MICO EMPL CU | North Mankato | MN | C | C | C | 2.1 | 5.95 | 0.0 | 48.9 | 0.0 | 0.0 | 10.0 | 14.4 |
| MID AMERICAN CU | Wichita | KS | B | B | B | 261.8 | 14.01 | 2.3 | 71.1 | 13.9 | 0.0 | 7.6 | 9.4 |
| MID CAROLINA CU | Lugoff | SC | C | C | C | 109.4 | 3.51 | 0.3 | 43.6 | 12.4 | 18.1 | 10.0 | 15.9 |
| ▲ MID DELTA CU | Indianola | MS | C | C | C+ | 1.8 | 1.90 | 0.0 | 40.2 | 0.0 | 0.0 | 10.0 | 29.6 |
| MID EAST TENNESSEE COMMUNITY CU | Decatur | TN | E+ | E+ | D- | 7.6 | -22.11 | 0.0 | 60.0 | 0.0 | 0.0 | 6.0 | 8.0 |
| MID MINNESOTA FCU | Baxter | MN | B+ | A- | B+ | 274.2 | 6.63 | 9.0 | 42.4 | 21.7 | 1.2 | 10.0 | 11.1 |
| MID MISSOURI CU | Fort Leonard Wood | MO | C | C | C | 220.0 | 5.47 | 1.9 | 35.7 | 10.0 | 23.8 | 7.4 | 9.2 |
| MID OREGON FCU | Bend | OR | B | B | B | 213.3 | 10.38 | 10.4 | 27.2 | 20.7 | 0.8 | 7.2 | 9.1 |
| ▲ MID PLAINS CU | Glasco | KS | C | C | C- | 1.4 | 6.65 | 0.0 | 75.6 | 0.0 | 0.0 | 10.0 | 11.4 |
| MID-ATLANTIC FCU | Germantown | MD | C+ | C+ | C | 291.5 | 6.53 | 8.3 | 17.9 | 25.4 | 9.0 | 6.4 | 8.4 |
| MID-CITIES CU | Compton | CA | C+ | C | C | 22.2 | -1.53 | 0.0 | 47.6 | 17.7 | 5.4 | 10.0 | 21.7 |
| MID-HUDSON VALLEY FCU | Kingston | NY | C- | C | C | 804.6 | 1.15 | 10.0 | 21.7 | 28.3 | 25.4 | 7.3 | 9.2 |
| MID-ILLINI CU | Bloomington | IL | D+ | D+ | D | 49.5 | 5.88 | 1.0 | 75.3 | 3.5 | 0.0 | 5.6 | 7.6 |
| MID-ISLAND FCU | Christiansted | VI | C- | C- | D+ | 8.8 | 1.07 | 0.0 | 39.2 | 1.7 | 0.0 | 10.0 | 11.1 |
| MID-KANSAS CU | Moundridge | KS | D+ | D+ | C | 49.5 | -6.68 | 16.8 | 9.4 | 21.5 | 21.5 | 9.3 | 10.6 |
| MID-STATE FCU | Carteret | NJ | D+ | D | C- | 14.9 | -3.29 | 10.1 | 12.1 | 13.4 | 0.0 | 10.0 | 12.9 |
| MID-TEX FCU | Brownwood | TX | D | D | D | 20.8 | 6.07 | 0.0 | 52.2 | 1.6 | 0.0 | 5.6 | 7.6 |
| MIDCOAST FCU | Bath | ME | A- | A- | A- | 146.7 | 6.57 | 2.8 | 21.7 | 31.8 | 21.9 | 10.0 | 12.3 |
| MIDDCONN FCU | Middletown | CT | E+ | E | E | 20.2 | 2.10 | 0.0 | 23.9 | 9.4 | 0.0 | 4.8 | 6.8 |
| MIDDLE TENNESSEE FCU | Cookeville | TN | D+ | C- | C+ | 28.3 | 3.99 | 0.0 | 31.8 | 17.1 | 0.0 | 6.9 | 8.9 |
| MIDDLESEX COUNTY NEW JERSEY EMPL FC | New Brunswick | NJ | C | C | C | 9.2 | 3.18 | 0.0 | 28.4 | 0.0 | 0.0 | 10.0 | 17.1 |
| ▲ MIDDLESEX-ESSEX POSTAL EMPL FCU | North Reading | MA | C- | C- | D+ | 5.2 | -2.36 | 0.0 | 43.6 | 0.0 | 0.0 | 10.0 | 27.6 |
| MIDDLETOWN AREA SCHOOLS CU | Middletown | OH | D+ | C- | C- | 7.1 | -1.88 | 0.0 | 50.5 | 0.0 | 0.0 | 10.0 | 12.3 |
| MIDFLORIDA CU | Lakeland | FL | A- | A- | B+ | 2322.2 | 12.31 | 11.4 | 37.0 | 26.5 | 11.0 | 9.3 | 10.6 |
| MIDLAND CO-OP CU | Minneapolis | MN | D+ | D+ | D+ | 10.1 | 1.42 | 0.0 | 24.0 | 0.0 | 0.0 | 8.7 | 10.2 |
| MIDLAND CU | Urbandale | IA | B- | B- | B- | 46.0 | 4.98 | 4.0 | 28.9 | 31.6 | 18.6 | 10.0 | 14.1 |
| MIDLAND MUNICIPAL EMPL CU | Midland | TX | C- | D+ | C- | 17.8 | 2.67 | 0.0 | 17.8 | 0.0 | 66.3 | 7.8 | 9.5 |
| MIDSOUTH COMMUNITY FCU | Macon | GA | B | B | B | 226.3 | 9.45 | 1.8 | 55.3 | 6.3 | 14.2 | 10.0 | 11.8 |
| MIDUSA CU | Middletown | OH | C- | C- | D+ | 205.6 | 5.46 | 7.5 | 44.3 | 22.7 | 10.4 | 8.2 | 9.9 |
| MIDVALLEY FCU | Murray | UT | D | D | C- | 5.8 | -7.38 | 0.0 | 9.5 | 29.0 | 0.0 | 10.0 | 32.8 |
| ▼ MIDWAY FCU | Winchester | VA | C | C+ | C+ | 13.1 | -5.03 | 0.0 | 14.9 | 3.1 | 25.7 | 10.0 | 15.1 |
| MIDWEST AMERICA FCU | Fort Wayne | IN | B+ | B+ | B+ | 508.8 | 2.31 | 14.4 | 39.8 | 25.2 | 9.9 | 10.0 | 13.5 |
| MIDWEST CARPENTERS & MILLWRIGHTS FC | Hobart | IN | C | C | C | 94.1 | -0.19 | 0.1 | 23.7 | 17.8 | 30.2 | 6.7 | 8.7 |
| MIDWEST COMMUNITY CU | Sioux City | IA | C- | D+ | D+ | 26.1 | 5.73 | 0.4 | 14.8 | 5.1 | 32.6 | 6.8 | 8.8 |
| MIDWEST COMMUNITY FCU | Defiance | OH | C- | C- | C+ | 140.9 | 3.76 | 7.8 | 15.4 | 18.2 | 12.9 | 8.0 | 9.7 |
| ▲ MIDWEST CU | Florissant | MO | D+ | D | C- | 11.2 | -2.73 | 0.0 | 47.8 | 0.0 | 0.0 | 10.0 | 18.0 |
| ▼ MIDWEST FAMILY FCU | Portage | IN | D+ | C- | D+ | 26.9 | 1.74 | 0.0 | 25.9 | 14.8 | 13.8 | 5.7 | 7.7 |

| Asset Quality Index | Non-Performing Loans | | Net Charge-Offs Avg Loans | Profitability Index | Net Income ($Mil) | Return on Assets | Return on Equity | Net Interest Spread | Overhead Efficiency Ratio | Liquidity Index | Liquidity Ratio | Hot Money Ratio | Stability Index |
|---|---|---|---|---|---|---|---|---|---|---|---|---|---|
| | as a % of Total Loans | as a % of Capital | | | | | | | | | | | |
| 10.0 | 0.25 | 0.6 | 0.00 | 0.0 | -0.1 | -0.99 | -4.87 | 2.00 | 140.9 | 6.5 | 41.7 | 0.0 | 6.4 |
| 10.0 | 1.35 | 2.0 | 0.61 | 3.4 | 0.0 | 0.41 | 2.13 | 3.99 | 87.9 | 5.6 | 51.6 | 0.0 | 5.3 |
| 3.3 | 6.52 | 30.7 | 1.18 | 4.0 | 0.1 | 0.48 | 5.38 | 5.67 | 91.0 | 5.8 | 26.3 | 1.5 | 3.0 |
| 8.5 | 0.28 | 2.5 | 0.28 | 4.6 | 0.0 | 0.40 | 4.62 | 4.69 | 89.3 | 4.2 | 14.0 | 0.0 | 2.3 |
| 9.7 | 4.55 | 3.0 | 1.44 | 0.0 | -0.1 | -2.61 | -7.93 | 4.67 | 158.8 | 7.8 | 97.4 | 0.0 | 4.7 |
| 9.0 | 0.65 | 2.8 | 0.40 | 1.8 | 0.1 | 0.10 | 0.93 | 2.55 | 90.1 | 3.8 | 20.3 | 10.4 | 4.6 |
| 9.9 | 0.21 | 1.0 | 0.08 | 6.4 | 0.4 | 0.96 | 7.53 | 3.15 | 74.9 | 3.8 | 28.2 | 7.4 | 6.7 |
| 8.0 | 1.16 | 6.6 | 0.86 | 3.4 | 0.1 | 0.28 | 1.95 | 3.45 | 84.7 | 5.2 | 28.6 | 0.0 | 6.6 |
| 9.3 | 0.44 | 2.3 | -0.03 | 3.1 | 0.3 | 0.43 | 5.03 | 2.64 | 88.9 | 4.4 | 16.1 | 2.7 | 3.9 |
| 7.8 | 1.66 | 7.7 | 0.91 | 4.1 | 0.6 | 0.63 | 5.61 | 3.95 | 79.7 | 4.2 | 21.4 | 15.1 | 6.3 |
| 9.5 | 0.19 | 1.0 | 0.20 | 2.8 | 0.1 | 0.23 | 2.37 | 2.78 | 93.0 | 4.2 | 20.8 | 5.6 | 4.5 |
| 8.8 | 0.05 | 0.2 | 0.08 | 3.2 | 0.0 | 0.38 | 2.33 | 3.29 | 83.4 | 5.8 | 37.0 | 0.0 | 7.0 |
| 6.2 | 0.57 | 4.9 | 0.44 | 8.9 | 0.2 | 1.64 | 17.07 | 4.82 | 82.1 | 1.6 | 3.6 | 21.9 | 3.5 |
| 5.8 | 0.76 | 8.0 | 1.53 | 2.3 | 0.1 | 0.20 | 2.20 | 2.68 | 75.7 | 4.6 | 14.7 | 2.7 | 4.1 |
| 8.6 | 0.23 | 2.1 | 0.34 | 5.0 | 0.8 | 0.75 | 7.62 | 4.10 | 77.3 | 2.0 | 8.7 | 16.4 | 6.2 |
| 10.0 | 0.29 | 1.3 | 0.13 | 3.4 | 2.2 | 0.40 | 3.22 | 2.62 | 81.9 | 4.5 | 16.1 | 3.6 | 8.1 |
| 7.4 | 1.23 | 5.6 | 1.46 | 5.4 | 3.4 | 0.60 | 4.15 | 4.77 | 79.4 | 3.7 | 7.3 | 6.3 | 8.4 |
| 8.3 | 1.52 | 5.3 | 0.50 | 4.1 | 0.6 | 0.51 | 4.53 | 3.52 | 87.6 | 4.5 | 10.0 | 1.5 | 6.6 |
| 4.9 | 0.56 | 5.4 | 0.21 | 4.4 | 0.5 | 0.74 | 8.36 | 3.24 | 82.3 | 2.8 | 6.3 | 6.0 | 3.9 |
| 7.3 | 0.59 | 5.2 | 0.62 | 5.7 | 9.7 | 0.84 | 7.74 | 3.47 | 65.3 | 3.3 | 16.5 | 9.5 | 8.0 |
| 8.1 | 0.63 | 4.1 | 0.55 | 6.7 | 19.9 | 0.91 | 8.66 | 3.52 | 69.7 | 3.0 | 11.5 | 11.3 | 8.4 |
| 8.1 | 0.25 | 2.6 | 0.14 | 2.6 | 0.1 | 0.26 | 3.29 | 3.42 | 93.6 | 3.6 | 3.6 | 2.6 | 3.8 |
| 5.9 | 1.44 | 8.7 | 0.18 | 0.0 | -0.1 | -2.69 | -15.40 | 6.44 | 138.4 | 5.0 | 21.3 | 0.0 | 4.9 |
| 8.6 | 0.00 | 0.0 | 0.00 | 1.8 | 0.0 | 0.06 | 0.43 | 1.82 | 76.5 | 6.1 | 37.6 | 0.0 | 6.8 |
| 4.9 | 0.61 | 9.5 | 0.66 | 5.0 | 1.2 | 0.61 | 6.62 | 4.44 | 76.5 | 0.9 | 4.3 | 25.9 | 5.9 |
| 8.3 | 0.83 | 3.3 | 0.62 | 2.6 | 0.2 | 0.21 | 1.41 | 3.66 | 88.1 | 3.9 | 9.3 | 3.2 | 7.4 |
| 9.1 | 0.00 | 0.0 | 0.00 | 3.9 | 0.0 | 0.62 | 2.05 | 4.67 | 92.4 | 5.6 | 33.4 | 0.0 | 5.6 |
| 0.0 | 5.88 | 55.9 | -0.21 | 7.3 | 0.1 | 2.03 | 42.53 | 10.18 | 68.4 | 2.4 | 17.2 | 29.7 | 3.0 |
| 5.9 | 0.69 | 9.0 | 0.23 | 4.5 | 0.9 | 0.42 | 3.77 | 4.06 | 90.0 | 3.3 | 7.7 | 2.4 | 6.9 |
| 6.2 | 0.83 | 8.4 | 0.71 | 2.7 | 0.5 | 0.28 | 3.00 | 3.62 | 82.8 | 3.9 | 25.3 | 13.1 | 5.5 |
| 5.3 | 1.65 | 11.7 | 0.41 | 6.5 | 1.3 | 0.84 | 9.15 | 3.79 | 78.1 | 3.7 | 11.4 | 1.8 | 5.8 |
| 2.4 | 3.63 | 24.0 | 0.00 | 10.0 | 0.0 | 1.80 | 16.78 | 4.72 | 54.8 | 4.5 | 20.1 | 0.0 | 6.9 |
| 6.2 | 1.43 | 11.7 | 0.21 | 2.7 | 0.4 | 0.20 | 2.34 | 3.83 | 95.8 | 3.9 | 14.3 | 2.9 | 5.1 |
| 7.2 | 0.77 | 3.0 | 2.92 | 4.0 | 0.1 | 0.65 | 3.09 | 8.21 | 81.8 | 4.8 | 33.0 | 6.6 | 5.0 |
| 5.2 | 2.06 | 16.8 | 0.59 | 2.1 | 0.7 | 0.11 | 1.30 | 3.26 | 88.2 | 3.4 | 7.4 | 8.4 | 5.7 |
| 4.1 | 1.30 | 13.1 | 0.63 | 3.8 | 0.2 | 0.41 | 5.43 | 5.74 | 82.5 | 3.0 | 9.6 | 7.1 | 3.0 |
| 6.2 | 3.34 | 14.0 | 1.22 | 5.4 | 0.1 | 0.80 | 7.24 | 5.98 | 80.1 | 6.5 | 41.3 | 0.0 | 4.3 |
| 4.8 | 3.14 | 13.2 | 0.07 | 1.7 | 0.1 | 0.16 | 1.61 | 2.72 | 93.9 | 4.1 | 16.1 | 3.4 | 3.9 |
| 9.1 | 0.09 | 0.3 | -0.06 | 1.1 | 0.0 | 0.00 | 0.00 | 3.09 | 100.0 | 3.5 | 16.6 | 12.7 | 4.4 |
| 5.2 | 0.78 | 6.1 | 0.08 | 5.2 | 0.1 | 0.67 | 9.11 | 4.94 | 86.2 | 4.3 | 16.5 | 0.7 | 2.3 |
| 7.6 | 1.07 | 6.2 | 0.21 | 5.8 | 0.9 | 0.82 | 7.36 | 3.89 | 80.5 | 3.6 | 11.1 | 4.2 | 8.2 |
| 8.3 | 0.89 | 5.4 | 0.20 | 1.4 | 0.0 | -0.01 | -0.20 | 2.84 | 101.0 | 4.4 | 14.8 | 1.1 | 1.0 |
| 5.8 | 1.16 | 6.8 | 0.68 | 1.8 | 0.1 | 0.22 | 2.57 | 4.30 | 88.7 | 4.4 | 21.6 | 0.6 | 3.2 |
| 8.8 | 1.67 | 2.7 | 2.71 | 2.5 | 0.0 | -0.07 | -0.42 | 4.51 | 81.6 | 5.0 | 10.4 | 0.0 | 6.1 |
| 9.8 | 0.88 | 1.4 | -0.06 | 1.4 | 0.0 | -0.10 | -0.37 | 3.93 | 102.0 | 4.4 | 9.1 | 0.0 | 7.0 |
| 6.8 | 0.64 | 3.2 | 1.88 | 0.4 | -0.1 | -1.17 | -9.28 | 4.46 | 94.0 | 4.8 | 24.9 | 0.0 | 5.4 |
| 8.0 | 0.41 | 3.6 | 0.30 | 8.0 | 20.4 | 1.23 | 12.81 | 3.20 | 71.5 | 3.7 | 13.1 | 6.3 | 7.4 |
| 9.8 | 0.00 | 0.0 | 0.00 | 1.3 | 0.0 | -0.01 | -0.13 | 2.37 | 98.3 | 5.4 | 34.8 | 0.0 | 4.9 |
| 8.5 | 0.97 | 5.5 | 0.26 | 3.2 | 0.1 | 0.36 | 2.51 | 3.20 | 89.9 | 4.0 | 20.9 | 3.6 | 7.0 |
| 6.8 | 2.01 | 5.2 | 0.03 | 2.3 | 0.0 | 0.32 | 3.42 | 1.63 | 75.9 | 4.9 | 18.5 | 0.0 | 4.4 |
| 7.0 | 0.54 | 3.0 | 1.82 | 4.9 | 1.2 | 0.73 | 6.25 | 4.17 | 64.3 | 3.0 | 9.5 | 14.0 | 6.9 |
| 6.0 | 1.64 | 12.7 | 0.52 | 2.4 | 0.3 | 0.20 | 1.96 | 3.22 | 84.6 | 2.5 | 3.1 | 12.0 | 5.8 |
| 7.8 | 5.38 | 7.3 | 0.00 | 0.0 | 0.0 | -0.87 | -2.69 | 2.73 | 126.2 | 4.3 | 20.3 | 2.6 | 5.2 |
| 8.9 | 2.66 | 4.0 | 1.46 | 0.9 | 0.0 | -0.38 | -2.61 | 2.48 | 96.3 | 5.0 | 26.7 | 0.0 | 5.9 |
| 9.1 | 0.18 | 1.1 | 0.16 | 5.1 | 2.8 | 0.74 | 5.55 | 3.00 | 79.1 | 3.4 | 15.1 | 4.8 | 8.6 |
| 5.4 | 1.43 | 8.6 | 0.54 | 2.8 | 0.2 | 0.22 | 2.57 | 2.31 | 86.4 | 3.8 | 15.3 | 7.3 | 3.6 |
| 6.6 | 0.07 | 0.3 | -0.13 | 3.0 | 0.1 | 0.33 | 3.91 | 2.58 | 89.1 | 5.5 | 24.8 | 0.0 | 4.5 |
| 8.8 | 0.73 | 3.8 | 0.17 | 2.2 | 0.2 | 0.22 | 2.34 | 3.05 | 92.8 | 3.4 | 24.3 | 12.6 | 5.9 |
| 8.6 | 0.77 | 2.2 | 0.21 | 0.6 | 0.0 | -0.15 | -0.95 | 3.61 | 104.6 | 5.5 | 39.4 | 0.0 | 5.6 |
| 7.5 | 0.69 | 4.8 | 0.73 | 1.2 | 0.0 | -0.18 | -2.28 | 3.71 | 94.6 | 4.5 | 24.6 | 2.8 | 3.0 |

139

| Name | City | State | Rating | 2014 Rating | 2013 Rating | Total Assets ($Mil) | One Year Asset Growth | Asset Mix (As a % of Total Assets) | | | | Capital-ization Index | Net Worth Ratio |
|------|------|-------|--------|-------------|-------------|---------|---------|---------|---------|---------|---------|---------|---------|
| | | | | | | | | Comm-ercial Loans | Cons-umer Loans | Mort-gage Loans | Secur-ities | | |
| MIDWEST OPERATING ENGINEERS CU | Countryside | IL | C- | C | C- | 48.3 | 1.76 | 0.0 | 20.1 | 9.8 | 0.0 | 6.5 | 8.5 |
| MIDWEST REGIONAL CU | Kansas City | KS | D+ | C- | C | 59.6 | 2.63 | 0.0 | 23.2 | 18.5 | 1.7 | 7.6 | 9.4 |
| MIDWESTERN STATE UNIV CU | Wichita Falls | TX | D | D | D+ | 7.0 | 0.33 | 0.0 | 17.9 | 6.7 | 0.0 | 10.0 | 14.8 |
| ▲ MIL-WAY FCU | Texarkana | AR | C+ | C | C+ | 112.5 | 2.46 | 0.0 | 44.6 | 10.0 | 0.0 | 9.2 | 10.4 |
| MILDRED MITCHELL-BATEMAN HOSPITAL FC | Huntington | WV | C+ | C+ | C+ | <1 | -15.56 | 0.0 | 52.6 | 0.0 | 0.0 | 10.0 | 81.6 |
| MILE HIGH FCU | Butte | MT | B- | B- | B- | 22.5 | 5.81 | 0.0 | 24.9 | 0.0 | 0.0 | 10.0 | 13.7 |
| MILES CITY FCU | Miles City | MT | C- | C- | C- | 3.2 | 10.92 | 0.0 | 33.5 | 0.0 | 0.0 | 10.0 | 17.5 |
| MILFORD MEMORIAL FCU | Milford | DE | C- | D+ | C | 3.4 | 4.46 | 0.0 | 43.4 | 0.0 | 0.0 | 10.0 | 11.6 |
| ▼ MILL CITY CU | Minnetonka | MN | B- | B | B- | 313.3 | 3.11 | 0.0 | 18.2 | 29.4 | 20.9 | 9.9 | 10.9 |
| MILL TOWN CU | Everett | WA | B | B | B | 46.8 | 1.87 | 0.0 | 18.2 | 5.8 | 0.0 | 10.0 | 24.5 |
| MILLARD COUNTY CU | Fillmore | UT | B- | B- | C+ | 30.8 | 5.79 | 4.4 | 29.7 | 13.4 | 1.8 | 10.0 | 11.6 |
| MILLBURY FCU | Millbury | MA | C- | C- | C- | 299.5 | 3.44 | 10.3 | 11.6 | 53.4 | 11.0 | 5.7 | 7.7 |
| MILLEDGEVILLE COMMUNITY CU | Milledgeville | IL | D | D | D | 4.1 | -3.11 | 0.0 | 37.8 | 0.0 | 0.0 | 9.4 | 10.6 |
| MILLER TRANSPORTERS FCU | Jackson | MS | C- | D | D+ | 3.5 | 5.62 | 0.0 | 28.5 | 0.0 | 1.0 | 10.0 | 17.1 |
| MILLS42 FCU | Lowell | MA | C+ | C+ | C+ | 17.9 | 9.69 | 0.0 | 44.3 | 24.2 | 0.0 | 9.3 | 10.6 |
| MILLSTREAM AREA CU | Findlay | OH | B- | B- | B- | 35.8 | 8.38 | 0.5 | 36.1 | 15.7 | 6.9 | 10.0 | 11.2 |
| MILLWRIGHTS/PILE DRIVERS OF PITTSBURG | Saltsburg | PA | D | D | C- | <1 | -13.48 | 0.0 | 40.8 | 0.0 | 0.0 | 10.0 | 14.1 |
| ▼ MINERVA AREA FCU | Minerva | OH | C- | C | C | 7.4 | 9.38 | 0.0 | 53.3 | 0.4 | 0.0 | 10.0 | 11.6 |
| MINGO COUNTY EDUCATION FCU | Williamson | WV | C+ | C+ | C+ | 2.0 | 12.85 | 0.0 | 93.2 | 0.0 | 0.0 | 10.0 | 17.5 |
| MINI-CASSIA EMPL CU | Burley | ID | C | C | C | <1 | 4.20 | 0.0 | 40.7 | 0.0 | 0.0 | 10.0 | 13.3 |
| MINNCO CU | Cambridge | MN | B+ | B+ | B | 232.0 | 7.64 | 3.1 | 28.1 | 11.4 | 24.9 | 8.6 | 10.1 |
| MINNEQUA WORKS CU | Pueblo | CO | B+ | B | B- | 172.4 | 4.03 | 0.0 | 22.0 | 9.3 | 15.3 | 10.0 | 11.4 |
| MINNESOTA CATHOLIC CU | Little Canada | MN | D+ | D+ | D | 27.9 | 6.77 | 5.7 | 24.2 | 14.8 | 5.8 | 6.9 | 8.9 |
| MINNESOTA ORE OPERATIONS EMPL CU | Hibbing | MN | D | D | D+ | 8.1 | -0.56 | 0.0 | 22.1 | 0.0 | 10.1 | 10.0 | 18.8 |
| MINNESOTA POWER EMPL CU | Duluth | MN | B- | B- | B+ | 91.8 | 3.55 | 5.0 | 19.4 | 19.4 | 23.0 | 10.0 | 16.8 |
| MINNESOTA VALLEY FCU | Mankato | MN | A- | A- | B | 120.0 | 12.69 | 1.4 | 23.7 | 12.0 | 17.3 | 8.0 | 9.7 |
| MINOT AREA SCHOOLS FCU | Minot | ND | D | D | D | 9.7 | -3.84 | 0.0 | 36.8 | 0.0 | 0.0 | 6.0 | 8.0 |
| MINT VALLEY FCU | Longview | WA | C- | D+ | D | 16.1 | -5.48 | 0.0 | 40.5 | 10.6 | 0.0 | 10.0 | 16.8 |
| MINUTEMAN FCU | Rapid City | SD | D+ | D+ | D+ | 13.8 | 6.62 | 0.0 | 53.8 | 0.0 | 0.0 | 8.4 | 10.0 |
| MIRAMAR FCU | San Diego | CA | D+ | D+ | C- | 171.6 | 0.35 | 4.9 | 7.4 | 37.5 | 21.6 | 10.0 | 13.2 |
| MISSION CITY FCU | Santa Clara | CA | C+ | C+ | C+ | 82.5 | 6.73 | 0.0 | 15.0 | 21.3 | 21.6 | 6.6 | 8.6 |
| MISSION FCU | San Diego | CA | A | A | A | 2798.0 | 9.16 | 4.6 | 27.0 | 30.2 | 25.4 | 10.0 | 12.2 |
| MISSISSIPPI CENTRAL FCU | Morton | MS | D+ | D+ | D+ | 3.3 | 5.09 | 0.0 | 71.9 | 0.0 | 0.0 | 10.0 | 17.1 |
| MISSISSIPPI COLLEGE EMPL CU | Clinton | MS | C | C+ | C | 2.6 | -2.01 | 0.0 | 30.0 | 0.0 | 0.0 | 10.0 | 13.0 |
| MISSISSIPPI DHS FCU | Jackson | MS | C | C | C | 7.7 | 6.12 | 0.0 | 24.3 | 0.0 | 0.0 | 10.0 | 15.9 |
| MISSISSIPPI FARM BUREAU EMPL CU | Jackson | MS | C- | C- | C | 13.8 | 2.70 | 0.0 | 21.4 | 0.0 | 0.0 | 10.0 | 13.2 |
| MISSISSIPPI FCU | Jackson | MS | A- | A- | A- | 105.9 | 5.10 | 0.0 | 26.9 | 19.8 | 5.2 | 10.0 | 12.3 |
| MISSISSIPPI HIGHWAY SAFETY PATROL FCU | Jackson | MS | D+ | D+ | C- | 11.0 | -3.27 | 0.0 | 21.8 | 0.0 | 0.0 | 10.0 | 19.4 |
| MISSISSIPPI NATIONAL GUARD FCU | Jackson | MS | D | D | D- | 16.3 | 8.64 | 0.0 | 66.1 | 0.0 | 0.0 | 6.5 | 8.6 |
| MISSISSIPPI POSTAL EMPL FCU | Jackson | MS | B | B | B- | 61.5 | 1.25 | 0.0 | 22.4 | 4.6 | 4.5 | 10.0 | 20.2 |
| ▲ MISSISSIPPI PUBLIC EMPL CU | Jackson | MS | C+ | C+ | B- | 22.3 | 6.65 | 0.0 | 25.9 | 0.0 | 1.1 | 10.0 | 16.1 |
| MISSISSIPPI TELCO FCU | Pearl | MS | B | B | B | 174.3 | 1.07 | 0.0 | 12.7 | 11.7 | 46.1 | 10.0 | 13.2 |
| MISSOULA FCU | Missoula | MT | C+ | C+ | C- | 423.0 | 6.06 | 9.0 | 18.1 | 12.7 | 53.4 | 7.8 | 9.5 |
| MISSOURI BAPTIST CU | Jefferson City | MO | E+ | E+ | E+ | 6.3 | -0.55 | 0.0 | 36.7 | 0.0 | 0.0 | 6.5 | 8.5 |
| MISSOURI CENTRAL CU | Lee's Summit | MO | C+ | C+ | C+ | 46.9 | 7.12 | 0.0 | 22.6 | 1.2 | 2.6 | 10.0 | 11.8 |
| MISSOURI CU | Columbia | MO | C+ | C+ | B- | 291.2 | 6.13 | 0.0 | 48.7 | 12.3 | 4.0 | 7.8 | 9.5 |
| MISSOURI ELECTRIC COOPERATIVES EMPL | Jefferson City | MO | B+ | B+ | B+ | 155.0 | 3.36 | 0.7 | 22.8 | 13.7 | 38.3 | 8.2 | 9.8 |
| MISSOURI VALLEY FCU | Saint Peters | MO | C- | C- | D+ | 32.4 | -1.42 | 0.0 | 62.8 | 0.2 | 0.1 | 7.9 | 9.6 |
| ▼ MM EMPL FCU | Missoula | MT | D | D+ | D+ | 1.5 | 18.07 | 0.0 | 57.9 | 0.0 | 0.0 | 5.9 | 7.9 |
| ▼ MNCPPC FCU | College Park | MD | D | D | D | 12.3 | 1.55 | 0.0 | 32.8 | 4.9 | 24.0 | 7.9 | 9.6 |
| MOBILE EDUCATORS CU | Mobile | AL | C | C | C | 77.3 | 0.26 | 0.0 | 9.5 | 3.4 | 25.7 | 8.3 | 9.8 |
| MOBILE GOVERNMENT EMPL CU | Mobile | AL | B- | B- | B- | 22.1 | 0.55 | 0.0 | 12.3 | 15.1 | 0.0 | 10.0 | 15.0 |
| MOBILE POSTAL EMPL CU | Mobile | AL | C+ | C+ | C+ | 10.8 | -3.72 | 0.0 | 49.2 | 0.0 | 0.0 | 10.0 | 13.3 |
| MOBILITY CU | Irving | TX | D+ | C- | C- | 183.7 | 3.54 | 3.7 | 36.5 | 19.7 | 29.0 | 6.2 | 8.3 |
| MOBILOIL FCU | Beaumont | TX | A | A | A | 567.1 | 7.97 | 13.0 | 44.7 | 29.8 | 5.3 | 10.0 | 11.8 |
| MOCSE FCU | Modesto | CA | C+ | C+ | C | 251.4 | 6.54 | 0.0 | 22.1 | 3.5 | 32.5 | 5.9 | 7.9 |
| ▼ MODERN EMPL FCU | Owensboro | KY | D+ | C- | D+ | 5.3 | -2.09 | 0.0 | 35.8 | 24.7 | 0.0 | 10.0 | 24.0 |
| MODESTOS FIRST FCU | Modesto | CA | C+ | C- | C | 30.4 | -0.23 | 0.0 | 17.1 | 1.0 | 3.6 | 10.0 | 13.6 |
| MOFFAT COUNTY SCHOOLS FCU | Craig | CO | C- | C- | D | 4.7 | 0.13 | 0.0 | 35.0 | 0.0 | 0.0 | 9.6 | 10.7 |
| ▼ MOHAVE COMMUNITY FCU | Kingman | AZ | D+ | D+ | D+ | 29.5 | 10.66 | 0.0 | 54.9 | 0.0 | 0.0 | 5.3 | 7.3 |

| Asset Quality Index | Non-Performing Loans as a % of Total Loans | as a % of Capital | Net Charge-Offs Avg Loans | Profitability Index | Net Income ($Mil) | Return on Assets | Return on Equity | Net Interest Spread | Overhead Efficiency Ratio | Liquidity Index | Liquidity Ratio | Hot Money Ratio | Stability Index |
|---|---|---|---|---|---|---|---|---|---|---|---|---|---|
| 8.8 | 0.56 | 1.8 | 0.03 | 2.1 | 0.0 | 0.07 | 0.81 | 2.48 | 97.5 | 4.5 | 20.6 | 3.9 | 3.9 |
| 7.6 | 0.48 | 2.5 | 0.19 | 1.3 | 0.0 | -0.02 | -0.19 | 3.03 | 98.0 | 5.4 | 37.9 | 1.6 | 3.4 |
| 9.9 | 0.12 | 0.3 | 0.11 | 0.0 | -0.1 | -1.19 | -7.37 | 2.18 | 148.8 | 4.7 | 22.9 | 0.0 | 5.9 |
| 8.5 | 0.49 | 4.2 | 0.05 | 3.8 | 0.5 | 0.56 | 5.52 | 3.43 | 84.7 | 3.7 | 25.3 | 8.6 | 6.7 |
| 8.7 | 0.00 | 0.0 | 0.00 | 5.1 | 0.0 | 0.00 | 0.00 | 6.06 | 100.0 | 8.4 | 257.1 | 0.0 | 5.0 |
| 9.7 | 0.01 | 0.0 | 0.44 | 3.0 | 0.1 | 0.35 | 2.58 | 2.90 | 84.6 | 5.4 | 35.1 | 1.4 | 6.9 |
| 9.6 | 0.00 | 0.0 | 0.10 | 1.4 | 0.0 | -0.13 | -0.72 | 3.86 | 102.3 | 5.5 | 33.1 | 0.0 | 6.6 |
| 9.9 | 0.27 | 1.0 | 0.73 | 1.4 | 0.0 | -0.12 | -1.01 | 4.76 | 95.2 | 5.7 | 27.8 | 0.0 | 5.3 |
| 9.8 | 0.03 | 0.2 | 0.00 | 3.9 | 1.1 | 0.48 | 4.31 | 2.91 | 86.3 | 3.6 | 20.1 | 10.0 | 6.7 |
| 6.1 | 3.18 | 8.2 | 0.68 | 6.0 | 0.3 | 0.91 | 3.77 | 3.94 | 70.2 | 4.8 | 33.3 | 3.3 | 6.9 |
| 9.3 | 0.15 | 1.1 | 0.10 | 3.9 | 0.1 | 0.55 | 4.97 | 3.82 | 84.6 | 5.5 | 37.2 | 0.0 | 6.1 |
| 2.8 | 1.47 | 30.5 | 0.03 | 2.3 | 0.5 | 0.21 | 2.73 | 3.05 | 94.6 | 2.9 | 4.3 | 8.9 | 4.7 |
| 4.4 | 2.97 | 11.6 | 1.81 | 1.2 | 0.0 | -0.13 | -1.21 | 3.05 | 96.0 | 5.0 | 37.0 | 0.0 | 5.3 |
| 8.0 | 2.49 | 5.1 | -0.11 | 3.0 | 0.0 | 0.47 | 2.71 | 3.54 | 89.7 | 5.3 | 34.1 | 0.0 | 5.5 |
| 9.5 | 0.18 | 1.4 | -0.01 | 3.4 | 0.1 | 0.40 | 3.80 | 4.26 | 91.6 | 2.2 | 9.1 | 15.6 | 4.5 |
| 6.2 | 0.66 | 6.9 | 0.51 | 7.2 | 0.3 | 0.92 | 8.50 | 4.99 | 87.2 | 4.0 | 14.3 | 3.2 | 5.9 |
| 4.3 | 6.03 | 10.1 | 27.51 | 0.5 | -0.1 | -11.64 | -69.70 | 15.16 | 34.5 | 7.6 | 79.2 | 0.0 | 6.3 |
| 4.3 | 3.49 | 16.7 | 1.55 | 4.4 | 0.0 | 0.31 | 2.62 | 8.76 | 86.5 | 6.0 | 40.0 | 0.0 | 3.7 |
| 5.7 | 1.04 | 5.5 | 0.00 | 9.5 | 0.0 | 1.33 | 7.91 | 6.38 | 76.7 | 2.8 | 6.4 | 0.0 | 5.0 |
| 7.9 | 0.00 | 0.0 | 0.00 | 3.1 | 0.0 | 0.23 | 1.69 | 5.09 | 85.7 | 6.1 | 43.3 | 0.0 | 7.1 |
| 7.4 | 0.43 | 5.4 | 0.27 | 6.7 | 1.9 | 1.09 | 10.90 | 3.11 | 76.3 | 4.1 | 11.8 | 2.7 | 6.5 |
| 6.7 | 2.59 | 9.8 | 0.56 | 5.6 | 1.1 | 0.89 | 8.16 | 2.70 | 73.4 | 4.6 | 25.1 | 3.6 | 6.6 |
| 5.9 | 1.15 | 8.0 | 0.07 | 2.3 | 0.0 | 0.10 | 1.33 | 3.57 | 96.2 | 4.6 | 34.9 | 2.0 | 3.3 |
| 9.9 | 0.68 | 1.0 | 0.00 | 0.5 | 0.0 | -0.21 | -1.13 | 2.00 | 110.6 | 5.3 | 35.2 | 0.0 | 6.8 |
| 9.5 | 0.03 | 0.5 | 0.03 | 3.4 | 0.3 | 0.44 | 2.66 | 3.44 | 87.9 | 4.1 | 24.0 | 3.3 | 7.4 |
| 8.1 | 0.76 | 4.6 | 0.08 | 9.2 | 1.3 | 1.55 | 16.21 | 3.15 | 65.3 | 4.0 | 10.7 | 1.9 | 7.0 |
| 9.6 | 0.00 | 0.0 | 0.00 | 2.1 | 0.0 | 0.15 | 2.09 | 2.07 | 92.7 | 4.9 | 24.2 | 0.0 | 3.5 |
| 9.0 | 0.70 | 2.3 | 0.47 | 2.0 | 0.0 | 0.28 | 1.69 | 4.51 | 93.7 | 4.0 | 35.4 | 23.7 | 4.8 |
| 4.4 | 1.01 | 8.1 | 0.22 | 4.5 | 0.1 | 0.62 | 6.46 | 3.97 | 81.6 | 1.6 | 13.1 | 28.2 | 3.7 |
| 10.0 | 0.42 | 1.6 | 0.06 | 0.4 | -0.7 | -0.54 | -4.32 | 1.95 | 127.1 | 3.6 | 23.8 | 13.0 | 6.8 |
| 10.0 | 0.07 | 0.4 | 0.11 | 3.0 | 0.2 | 0.26 | 3.02 | 2.74 | 88.9 | 3.9 | 12.9 | 9.0 | 3.9 |
| 9.8 | 0.23 | 1.3 | 0.21 | 8.2 | 23.9 | 1.17 | 9.67 | 2.69 | 70.5 | 4.3 | 26.2 | 5.8 | 8.7 |
| 4.1 | 4.59 | 15.5 | 6.99 | 2.7 | 0.0 | -1.03 | -5.69 | 11.09 | 59.6 | 4.5 | 17.7 | 0.0 | 6.7 |
| 7.6 | 2.70 | 6.1 | 2.67 | 6.4 | 0.0 | 0.75 | 6.17 | 3.71 | 56.1 | 5.1 | 26.1 | 0.0 | 5.0 |
| 10.0 | 0.72 | 1.4 | 0.63 | 5.3 | 0.0 | 0.67 | 4.19 | 5.25 | 87.6 | 6.3 | 47.3 | 6.4 | 5.0 |
| 10.0 | 0.12 | 0.2 | -0.17 | 1.8 | 0.0 | 0.08 | 0.58 | 1.76 | 96.7 | 5.7 | 39.5 | 0.0 | 6.3 |
| 9.5 | 0.67 | 2.9 | 0.40 | 6.1 | 0.7 | 0.90 | 7.42 | 3.54 | 76.9 | 3.9 | 18.5 | 8.9 | 8.4 |
| 10.0 | 0.33 | 0.5 | 0.47 | 1.3 | 0.0 | -0.02 | -0.13 | 2.48 | 96.4 | 5.5 | 37.7 | 0.0 | 6.4 |
| 1.0 | 3.70 | 32.8 | 0.16 | 8.8 | 0.2 | 1.51 | 18.00 | 4.14 | 70.3 | 3.6 | 9.9 | 0.0 | 3.6 |
| 9.3 | 1.54 | 3.3 | 0.98 | 3.8 | 0.2 | 0.45 | 2.48 | 3.32 | 79.1 | 4.6 | 25.0 | 3.5 | 7.0 |
| 9.6 | 1.75 | 3.0 | 0.38 | 2.9 | 0.0 | 0.20 | 1.23 | 4.54 | 93.5 | 6.3 | 35.2 | 0.5 | 6.7 |
| 10.0 | 0.39 | 1.0 | 0.31 | 4.0 | 0.8 | 0.57 | 4.23 | 1.87 | 71.3 | 4.4 | 13.6 | 9.7 | 8.0 |
| 7.4 | 0.76 | 5.4 | 0.35 | 3.8 | 2.5 | 0.79 | 7.81 | 3.08 | 73.4 | 4.4 | 18.8 | 3.1 | 6.0 |
| 6.6 | 0.12 | 5.4 | 0.68 | 0.9 | 0.0 | -0.41 | -4.69 | 3.74 | 91.3 | 4.3 | 10.5 | 0.0 | 2.7 |
| 9.4 | 0.69 | 2.6 | 0.31 | 2.4 | 0.1 | 0.19 | 1.55 | 3.02 | 91.2 | 4.6 | 27.1 | 1.2 | 5.8 |
| 7.8 | 0.44 | 4.0 | 0.35 | 3.7 | 1.2 | 0.56 | 6.02 | 3.43 | 82.3 | 4.4 | 20.0 | 1.5 | 5.3 |
| 9.9 | 0.02 | 0.1 | 0.00 | 6.4 | 1.2 | 1.06 | 10.97 | 2.16 | 60.4 | 3.5 | 3.7 | 4.5 | 7.2 |
| 5.1 | 0.77 | 5.8 | 0.95 | 2.9 | 0.1 | 0.26 | 2.86 | 4.08 | 83.8 | 3.4 | 8.8 | 1.0 | 3.9 |
| 8.3 | 0.00 | 0.0 | 0.00 | 3.3 | 0.0 | 0.30 | 3.33 | 4.92 | 91.4 | 5.9 | 37.4 | 0.0 | 2.3 |
| 8.1 | 0.17 | 0.7 | -0.46 | 1.0 | 0.0 | -0.03 | -0.30 | 3.78 | 86.4 | 6.0 | 32.7 | 1.8 | 4.1 |
| 9.9 | 0.81 | 1.1 | 0.13 | 2.8 | 0.1 | 0.21 | 2.14 | 2.31 | 94.3 | 6.2 | 32.4 | 0.0 | 4.6 |
| 10.0 | 0.30 | 0.6 | 0.25 | 3.3 | 0.1 | 0.41 | 2.73 | 2.12 | 78.2 | 5.6 | 24.8 | 0.0 | 6.8 |
| 5.2 | 1.34 | 8.2 | 1.35 | 7.3 | 0.1 | 1.13 | 9.10 | 5.02 | 76.9 | 3.9 | 13.8 | 0.0 | 5.0 |
| 7.3 | 0.52 | 4.9 | 0.11 | 1.1 | -0.2 | -0.16 | -1.99 | 2.38 | 104.8 | 2.3 | 9.6 | 19.7 | 3.8 |
| 7.7 | 0.40 | 3.1 | 0.57 | 9.4 | 5.2 | 1.24 | 10.87 | 4.15 | 61.9 | 2.4 | 9.3 | 14.2 | 9.4 |
| 10.0 | 0.21 | 1.0 | 0.05 | 3.2 | 0.6 | 0.34 | 4.14 | 3.34 | 90.6 | 7.0 | 51.9 | 0.0 | 4.7 |
| 9.7 | 0.00 | 0.0 | 0.27 | 0.8 | 0.0 | -0.29 | -1.24 | 3.91 | 100.6 | 4.5 | 22.5 | 0.0 | 6.5 |
| 7.8 | 0.52 | 6.2 | 0.18 | 2.5 | 0.1 | 0.30 | 2.29 | 2.34 | 99.3 | 4.4 | 18.1 | 6.8 | 4.6 |
| 9.4 | 0.00 | 0.0 | -0.06 | 4.2 | 0.0 | 0.69 | 6.43 | 2.98 | 87.5 | 5.1 | 38.0 | 0.0 | 5.0 |
| 7.3 | 0.14 | 1.3 | 0.78 | 3.4 | 0.1 | 0.34 | 4.52 | 5.50 | 87.2 | 4.2 | 21.2 | 4.0 | 2.4 |

| Name | City | State | Rating | 2014 Rating | 2013 Rating | Total Assets ($Mil) | One Year Asset Growth | Asset Mix (As a % of Total Assets) | | | | Capital- ization Index | Net Worth Ratio |
|------|------|-------|--------|-------------|-------------|---------------------|-----------------------|-----------|-----------|-----------|---------|-----------------------|-----------------|
| | | | | | | | | Comm- ercial Loans | Cons- umer Loans | Mort- gage Loans | Secur- ities | | |
| MOHAWK PROGRESSIVE FCU | Schenectady | NY | D- | D- | E+ | 8.5 | 0.59 | 0.0 | 22.5 | 7.4 | 17.7 | 7.2 | 9.1 |
| ▼ MOHAWK VALLEY FCU | Marcy | NY | B- | B | B | 31.9 | 1.87 | 0.0 | 31.5 | 9.3 | 0.0 | 10.0 | 12.6 |
| MOJAVE PLANT EMPL FCU | Mojave | CA | D+ | D+ | D+ | 2.0 | 1.56 | 0.0 | 29.2 | 0.0 | 0.0 | 9.4 | 10.6 |
| MOKELUMNE FCU | Stockton | CA | B | B | B- | 47.6 | 4.62 | 0.0 | 27.9 | 1.8 | 18.1 | 10.0 | 12.0 |
| ▼ MOLEX EMPL FCU | Lisle | IL | D | D+ | D+ | 8.0 | 8.83 | 0.0 | 52.9 | 0.0 | 0.0 | 7.0 | 9.0 |
| MOLINE MUNICIPAL CU | Moline | IL | B+ | B+ | B+ | 30.5 | 0.40 | 0.0 | 28.9 | 36.9 | 0.0 | 10.0 | 15.1 |
| ▼ MOLOKAI COMMUNITY FCU | Kaunakakai | HI | C- | C | D+ | 20.3 | 1.36 | 0.0 | 31.2 | 0.0 | 1.2 | 8.9 | 10.3 |
| MON VALLEY COMMUNITY FCU | Allenport | PA | A- | A- | A- | 151.7 | 2.82 | 3.6 | 4.1 | 22.4 | 19.5 | 10.0 | 22.3 |
| ▲ MONAD FCU | Pasco | WA | D+ | D | D | 13.6 | -4.29 | 0.8 | 20.8 | 10.5 | 0.0 | 6.9 | 8.9 |
| MONARCH FCU | Miamisburg | OH | D | D | C- | 10.1 | -3.50 | 0.0 | 36.1 | 8.8 | 35.8 | 10.0 | 19.4 |
| MONESSEN SCHOOL EMPL FCU | Monessen | PA | C- | C- | D+ | <1 | 1.10 | 0.0 | 84.5 | 0.0 | 0.0 | 10.0 | 17.4 |
| MONEY FCU | Syracuse | NY | B | B | B | 40.6 | -3.20 | 0.0 | 31.4 | 30.1 | 20.5 | 10.0 | 13.5 |
| MONEY ONE FCU | Largo | MD | B+ | B | C+ | 117.7 | 11.40 | 8.9 | 53.7 | 13.7 | 1.0 | 10.0 | 12.8 |
| MONMOUTH COUNTY POSTAL EMPL CU | Red Bank | NJ | C- | D+ | C- | 25.9 | -0.76 | 0.0 | 7.1 | 0.0 | 14.3 | 10.0 | 18.4 |
| MONMOUTH FCU | Monmouth | ME | E+ | D- | D | 19.0 | 7.66 | 0.0 | 33.4 | 12.6 | 0.0 | 5.3 | 7.3 |
| MONOFRAX EMPL FCU | Falconer | NY | D+ | C- | B- | <1 | -12.69 | 0.0 | 33.5 | 0.0 | 0.0 | 10.0 | 24.2 |
| MONROE COUNTY COMMUNITY CU | Monroe | MI | B- | B- | C+ | 173.8 | 8.54 | 12.0 | 27.0 | 24.6 | 20.7 | 6.5 | 8.6 |
| ▼ MONROE COUNTY TEACHERS FCU | Key West | FL | C- | C+ | C | 27.2 | 18.27 | 0.0 | 49.5 | 22.6 | 0.0 | 6.0 | 8.0 |
| MONROE CU | Monroe | LA | D- | D- | D | 3.4 | -4.82 | 0.0 | 57.8 | 0.0 | 0.0 | 7.2 | 9.2 |
| MONROE EDUCATION EMPL FCU | Monroeville | AL | D | D+ | D- | 5.0 | 13.51 | 0.0 | 76.1 | 0.0 | 0.0 | 10.0 | 11.3 |
| MONROE TELCO FCU | West Monroe | LA | C- | C- | D+ | 39.0 | 3.82 | 0.3 | 29.4 | 4.0 | 0.3 | 7.7 | 9.5 |
| ▼ MONROEVILLE BORO FCU | Monroeville | PA | D+ | C- | C- | <1 | 5.35 | 0.0 | 25.0 | 0.0 | 0.0 | 10.0 | 18.4 |
| ▲ MONROVIA CITY EMPL FCU | Monrovia | CA | D+ | C- | D+ | 3.5 | -1.15 | 0.0 | 26.3 | 0.0 | 0.0 | 10.0 | 12.1 |
| ▲ MONTANA EDUCATORS CU | Missoula | MT | C- | D | D | 15.7 | 0.27 | 0.0 | 26.7 | 12.8 | 0.0 | 6.9 | 8.9 |
| MONTANA FCU | Great Falls | MT | B | B | B | 212.9 | 6.43 | 0.1 | 29.9 | 9.1 | 12.3 | 8.7 | 10.2 |
| MONTANA HEALTH FCU | Billings | MT | D+ | C- | C | 24.2 | -6.72 | 1.3 | 49.1 | 3.1 | 0.0 | 7.8 | 9.6 |
| ▼ MONTAUK CU | New York | NY | F | B- | B+ | 179.5 | 7.14 | 91.3 | 0.0 | 0.1 | 0.0 | 9.3 | 10.5 |
| MONTCALM PUBLIC EMPL CU | Edmore | MI | B- | B- | B- | 12.7 | 0.56 | 0.0 | 31.5 | 0.0 | 0.0 | 10.0 | 18.6 |
| MONTCLAIR POSTAL EMPL CU | West Caldwell | NJ | C- | C- | C- | 6.8 | -0.35 | 0.0 | 30.2 | 0.0 | 9.8 | 10.0 | 19.3 |
| ▲ MONTELL FCU | Westlake | LA | C | D+ | D+ | 4.6 | -1.98 | 0.0 | 35.4 | 0.0 | 0.0 | 10.0 | 27.1 |
| MONTEREY CU | Monterey | CA | B+ | B+ | A | 220.0 | 4.40 | 0.0 | 44.5 | 3.0 | 32.1 | 10.0 | 14.0 |
| MONTGOMERY COUNTY CU | Dayton | OH | F | F | D+ | 26.4 | -4.48 | 0.0 | 29.4 | 0.0 | 36.1 | 6.6 | 8.6 |
| MONTGOMERY COUNTY EMPL FCU | Germantown | MD | B- | C+ | C+ | 108.5 | 7.03 | 4.7 | 36.4 | 18.4 | 14.4 | 6.6 | 8.6 |
| MONTGOMERY VA FCU | Montgomery | AL | C | C | C- | 6.2 | 4.67 | 0.0 | 43.0 | 0.0 | 0.0 | 10.0 | 19.5 |
| MONTOURSVILLE AREA FCU | Montoursville | PA | D+ | C- | C- | 3.3 | 3.47 | 0.0 | 38.6 | 0.0 | 0.0 | 9.8 | 10.9 |
| MOOG EMPL FCU | East Aurora | NY | A- | A- | A- | 155.7 | 1.94 | 0.0 | 5.2 | 35.9 | 0.0 | 10.0 | 19.1 |
| MOONLIGHT CU | Worthington | PA | B+ | B+ | B+ | 29.1 | 2.73 | 0.3 | 31.7 | 2.7 | 0.0 | 10.0 | 14.6 |
| MOORE COUNTY SCHOOLS FCU | Dumas | TX | D | D | D+ | 8.4 | -0.29 | 0.0 | 36.0 | 0.0 | 0.0 | 9.3 | 10.5 |
| MOORE WEST FCU | San Leandro | CA | D+ | D | D | 17.9 | -7.74 | 0.0 | 8.7 | 6.8 | 61.7 | 8.0 | 9.7 |
| MOPAC EMPL FCU | Palestine | TX | C- | C | C | 15.3 | 6.87 | 0.0 | 48.4 | 0.0 | 0.0 | 8.9 | 10.3 |
| MOREHEAD COMMUNITY FCU | Morehead | KY | C | C+ | B- | 29.6 | 1.05 | 0.0 | 22.9 | 15.9 | 0.0 | 9.9 | 11.0 |
| MORGAN CITY FCU | Morgan City | LA | D+ | D+ | D+ | 6.7 | 1.79 | 0.0 | 43.0 | 0.0 | 34.1 | 8.6 | 10.1 |
| MORGANTOWN AES FCU | Morgantown | WV | C- | C- | C+ | 42.4 | 2.63 | 0.0 | 39.3 | 12.3 | 0.0 | 7.2 | 9.1 |
| MORNING STAR BAPTIST FCU | Clairton | PA | C+ | C+ | C+ | <1 | 0.18 | 0.0 | 20.9 | 0.0 | 0.0 | 10.0 | 20.7 |
| MORNING STAR FCU | Tulsa | OK | D | D | D | <1 | 1.24 | 0.0 | 79.6 | 0.0 | 0.0 | 10.0 | 11.6 |
| ▼ MORRIS SHEPPARD TEXARKANA FCU | Texarkana | TX | D+ | C- | C- | 7.1 | 0.28 | 0.0 | 71.5 | 0.0 | 0.0 | 10.0 | 14.6 |
| ▼ MORRISON EMPL CU | Dubuque | IA | D+ | C | C+ | 1.7 | 11.71 | 0.0 | 11.9 | 0.0 | 0.0 | 10.0 | 30.3 |
| MORROW COUNTY FCU | Mount Gilead | OH | C | C | C | 5.8 | 5.51 | 0.0 | 32.6 | 0.0 | 0.0 | 10.0 | 17.7 |
| MORTON CU | South Hutchinson | KS | D | D+ | D+ | 3.8 | 2.32 | 0.0 | 41.2 | 0.0 | 0.0 | 10.0 | 13.0 |
| MORTON FCU | Taunton | MA | D | D | C- | 8.6 | -2.22 | 0.0 | 14.3 | 14.9 | 1.2 | 10.0 | 15.3 |
| MORTON LANE FCU | Buffalo | NY | B+ | B+ | B+ | 40.5 | 3.61 | 0.0 | 21.6 | 9.2 | 3.4 | 10.0 | 13.6 |
| MORTON SALT CU | Rittman | OH | D | D | D+ | 4.2 | -7.25 | 0.0 | 39.6 | 0.0 | 0.0 | 10.0 | 19.1 |
| ▲ MORTON WEEKS FCU | New Iberia | LA | D+ | D | D | 9.9 | -0.60 | 0.0 | 28.1 | 0.0 | 0.0 | 8.1 | 9.8 |
| MOSAIC FCU | Harrisonburg | VA | E- | E- | E | 13.0 | 0.50 | 1.6 | 78.5 | 0.0 | 0.0 | 5.6 | 7.6 |
| MOSES FCU | North Reading | MA | C- | C- | C- | 1.8 | 4.02 | 0.0 | 33.3 | 0.0 | 0.0 | 10.0 | 18.1 |
| MOTION FCU | Linden | NJ | E | E | D- | 74.0 | -6.19 | 8.3 | 24.1 | 41.0 | 3.3 | 4.7 | 6.7 |
| ▼ MOTOR CITY COOPERATIVE CU | Clinton Township | MI | D+ | C- | B- | 130.2 | -0.45 | 2.4 | 18.1 | 9.9 | 54.8 | 10.0 | 13.8 |
| ▼ MOTOR COACH EMPL CU | East Saint Louis | IL | D+ | C- | C- | 1.9 | -4.98 | 0.0 | 47.4 | 0.0 | 0.0 | 10.0 | 21.2 |
| MOTOROLA EMPL CU | Schaumburg | IL | B | B- | B- | 859.6 | 1.82 | 3.4 | 12.8 | 31.2 | 31.4 | 9.4 | 10.6 |
| MOUNT CARMEL BAPTIST FCU | Philadelphia | PA | C- | C- | D | <1 | 1.68 | 0.0 | 13.3 | 0.0 | 0.0 | 10.0 | 28.5 |

| Asset Quality Index | Non-Performing Loans as a % of Total Loans | as a % of Capital | Net Charge-Offs Avg Loans | Profitability Index | Net Income ($Mil) | Return on Assets | Return on Equity | Net Interest Spread | Overhead Efficiency Ratio | Liquidity Index | Liquidity Ratio | Hot Money Ratio | Stability Index |
|---|---|---|---|---|---|---|---|---|---|---|---|---|---|
| 6.8 | 0.61 | 3.6 | -0.09 | 1.8 | 0.0 | 0.05 | 0.52 | 3.91 | 98.1 | 4.6 | 19.2 | 0.0 | 4.2 |
| 3.7 | 5.60 | 22.6 | 0.29 | 5.3 | 0.2 | 0.71 | 5.74 | 3.64 | 76.8 | 4.9 | 22.2 | 0.0 | 6.8 |
| 4.7 | 5.92 | 15.4 | -0.56 | 2.4 | 0.0 | 0.13 | 1.29 | 3.00 | 113.3 | 7.3 | 73.9 | 0.0 | 5.2 |
| 9.8 | 0.52 | 1.2 | 0.34 | 5.8 | 0.3 | 0.98 | 8.31 | 3.88 | 77.9 | 5.8 | 35.0 | 0.6 | 5.9 |
| 8.4 | 0.29 | 1.7 | 0.00 | 3.0 | 0.0 | 0.31 | 3.57 | 2.41 | 79.6 | 4.7 | 23.7 | 0.0 | 2.3 |
| 9.8 | 0.18 | 0.8 | 0.11 | 7.9 | 0.3 | 1.11 | 7.70 | 3.97 | 68.9 | 4.4 | 20.8 | 2.4 | 7.7 |
| 6.6 | 1.60 | 5.2 | 1.17 | 2.3 | 0.0 | -0.26 | -2.53 | 4.40 | 88.8 | 4.7 | 12.0 | 2.2 | 4.8 |
| 7.8 | 4.22 | 6.2 | 0.08 | 5.0 | 0.9 | 0.82 | 3.80 | 2.83 | 57.8 | 7.4 | 63.4 | 1.6 | 9.1 |
| 9.1 | 0.18 | 0.7 | 0.39 | 2.2 | 0.0 | 0.30 | 3.60 | 3.13 | 93.1 | 5.6 | 30.1 | 0.0 | 3.2 |
| 8.1 | 1.48 | 3.8 | -0.80 | 0.0 | 0.0 | -0.53 | -2.77 | 3.07 | 102.2 | 4.8 | 21.7 | 0.0 | 5.3 |
| 8.2 | 0.00 | 0.0 | 0.00 | 3.6 | 0.0 | 0.48 | 2.81 | 5.86 | 90.5 | 4.2 | 17.7 | 0.0 | 7.3 |
| 8.1 | 0.96 | 5.1 | 0.31 | 4.9 | 0.2 | 0.72 | 5.52 | 3.54 | 77.8 | 3.2 | 12.8 | 9.9 | 6.8 |
| 5.7 | 0.93 | 6.2 | 0.75 | 4.9 | 0.6 | 0.65 | 5.77 | 5.20 | 82.2 | 2.0 | 7.6 | 16.5 | 6.6 |
| 8.0 | 5.18 | 5.8 | 0.87 | 1.7 | 0.0 | 0.10 | 0.54 | 1.63 | 93.7 | 5.2 | 30.5 | 0.0 | 6.7 |
| 1.7 | 5.45 | 40.0 | 1.16 | 1.4 | -0.1 | -1.01 | -12.49 | 4.40 | 88.1 | 5.3 | 49.8 | 9.5 | 0.0 |
| 4.7 | 8.51 | 11.1 | 6.01 | 2.2 | 0.0 | -0.19 | -0.87 | 8.89 | 100.0 | 7.8 | 88.2 | 0.0 | 6.8 |
| 5.9 | 1.74 | 11.0 | 0.37 | 4.3 | 0.6 | 0.45 | 5.08 | 4.35 | 82.9 | 4.9 | 25.5 | 1.8 | 5.2 |
| 4.4 | 0.87 | 10.5 | 1.31 | 3.7 | -0.2 | -0.87 | -9.60 | 4.12 | 74.8 | 2.6 | 26.8 | 20.9 | 5.7 |
| 0.0 | 19.29 | 131.0 | 0.40 | 0.0 | -0.1 | -2.20 | -21.53 | 6.64 | 113.1 | 4.9 | 26.5 | 0.0 | 4.1 |
| 0.7 | 6.40 | 46.9 | 1.38 | 10.0 | 0.1 | 2.04 | 18.72 | 8.47 | 63.3 | 4.8 | 22.8 | 0.0 | 6.2 |
| 7.2 | 0.80 | 3.9 | 0.34 | 1.7 | 0.0 | 0.02 | 0.25 | 2.44 | 94.9 | 5.3 | 49.2 | 5.2 | 3.9 |
| 10.0 | 0.00 | 0.0 | 0.00 | 0.7 | 0.0 | -0.63 | -3.35 | 5.70 | 162.5 | 8.2 | 91.9 | 0.0 | 6.5 |
| 10.0 | 0.80 | 1.8 | 0.54 | 0.9 | 0.0 | -0.11 | -0.94 | 2.08 | 136.2 | 4.3 | 11.0 | 6.6 | 5.8 |
| 8.5 | 0.28 | 1.7 | -0.06 | 3.6 | 0.1 | 0.52 | 6.17 | 3.71 | 86.2 | 4.3 | 17.5 | 4.5 | 4.0 |
| 9.2 | 0.63 | 3.2 | 0.22 | 4.5 | 1.0 | 0.60 | 6.05 | 2.79 | 79.9 | 5.4 | 32.6 | 2.4 | 6.6 |
| 8.2 | 0.15 | 1.1 | 0.11 | 1.7 | 0.0 | 0.05 | 0.58 | 3.17 | 97.6 | 3.5 | 3.1 | 0.6 | 3.9 |
| 0.0 | 9.79 | 66.4 | 0.01 | 2.9 | -1.6 | -1.21 | -10.66 | 2.65 | 45.9 | 1.1 | 22.7 | 38.7 | 9.4 |
| 7.3 | 2.94 | 5.6 | 0.03 | 6.3 | 0.1 | 0.88 | 4.96 | 3.06 | 74.2 | 4.6 | 23.6 | 3.0 | 5.7 |
| 6.5 | 5.85 | 8.7 | 1.06 | 4.3 | 0.0 | 0.65 | 3.41 | 3.95 | 67.7 | 3.7 | 26.2 | 13.4 | 3.7 |
| 7.1 | 5.21 | 7.9 | 0.46 | 4.2 | 0.0 | 0.89 | 3.33 | 3.79 | 73.5 | 6.1 | 57.1 | 0.0 | 6.9 |
| 8.4 | 0.80 | 3.8 | 0.85 | 4.5 | 1.1 | 0.66 | 4.70 | 4.02 | 79.3 | 4.1 | 14.0 | 1.3 | 7.3 |
| 6.1 | 2.40 | 8.8 | 1.87 | 0.0 | -0.2 | -0.91 | -10.57 | 3.15 | 122.4 | 6.1 | 39.1 | 0.9 | 3.4 |
| 8.0 | 0.65 | 4.6 | 0.47 | 4.4 | 0.6 | 0.67 | 7.98 | 4.48 | 83.6 | 4.4 | 14.5 | 0.7 | 5.3 |
| 7.1 | 3.23 | 8.1 | -0.33 | 6.5 | 0.0 | 0.90 | 4.59 | 7.26 | 89.0 | 6.2 | 43.1 | 0.0 | 5.0 |
| 9.8 | 0.05 | 0.3 | -0.06 | 1.1 | 0.0 | -0.32 | -2.98 | 5.62 | 107.0 | 6.1 | 42.0 | 0.0 | 4.8 |
| 10.0 | 0.44 | 1.2 | 0.18 | 5.7 | 1.0 | 0.84 | 4.53 | 2.33 | 50.3 | 4.7 | 27.1 | 0.6 | 8.9 |
| 9.9 | 0.38 | 1.8 | 0.05 | 5.6 | 0.2 | 0.88 | 6.49 | 2.93 | 68.0 | 3.8 | 23.2 | 4.5 | 6.7 |
| 4.5 | 3.94 | 16.9 | -0.17 | 0.6 | 0.0 | -0.38 | -3.58 | 2.60 | 110.1 | 4.0 | 22.1 | 8.3 | 4.1 |
| 9.9 | 0.52 | 1.1 | -2.75 | 1.1 | 0.0 | -0.04 | -0.38 | 2.19 | 133.9 | 3.8 | 12.9 | 13.1 | 2.5 |
| 4.5 | 0.96 | 5.7 | 0.66 | 2.9 | 0.0 | 0.12 | 1.19 | 5.00 | 96.9 | 5.1 | 28.8 | 2.6 | 4.4 |
| 5.4 | 2.44 | 13.0 | 1.46 | 2.4 | 0.0 | 0.11 | 1.03 | 3.35 | 77.0 | 4.7 | 51.6 | 10.2 | 5.1 |
| 7.8 | 0.42 | 2.1 | 0.11 | 2.9 | 0.0 | 0.28 | 2.78 | 4.39 | 93.7 | 4.1 | 12.5 | 0.0 | 4.5 |
| 6.8 | 0.25 | 6.0 | 0.54 | 1.8 | 0.0 | 0.02 | 0.28 | 2.86 | 95.8 | 4.3 | 19.6 | 0.0 | 3.6 |
| 6.6 | 10.17 | 10.0 | 6.84 | 8.9 | 0.0 | 1.65 | 8.19 | 2.89 | 36.4 | 7.2 | 98.9 | 0.0 | 5.0 |
| 0.0 | 9.21 | 60.3 | 0.00 | 2.8 | 0.0 | 0.27 | 2.34 | 3.96 | 91.7 | 3.5 | 10.4 | 0.0 | 6.7 |
| 5.0 | 1.67 | 9.6 | 0.28 | 1.7 | 0.0 | -0.06 | -0.38 | 3.62 | 96.2 | 3.3 | 13.5 | 0.0 | 6.8 |
| 9.8 | 5.08 | 2.5 | 0.00 | 0.9 | 0.0 | -0.16 | -0.53 | 1.34 | 114.3 | 6.4 | 52.8 | 0.0 | 6.6 |
| 8.3 | 1.97 | 4.5 | 0.30 | 5.4 | 0.0 | 0.82 | 4.73 | 3.71 | 73.7 | 4.5 | 26.9 | 0.0 | 4.3 |
| 9.7 | 0.00 | 0.0 | 0.67 | 0.5 | 0.0 | -0.49 | -3.80 | 4.21 | 105.5 | 5.8 | 42.0 | 0.0 | 6.2 |
| 10.0 | 0.00 | 0.0 | 0.42 | 0.0 | -0.1 | -1.16 | -7.71 | 2.30 | 149.7 | 6.1 | 58.9 | 0.0 | 6.1 |
| 10.0 | 0.20 | 0.7 | 0.20 | 5.6 | 0.3 | 0.83 | 6.21 | 3.15 | 75.2 | 4.3 | 11.7 | 0.0 | 7.6 |
| 7.9 | 2.10 | 5.1 | 0.00 | 0.2 | 0.0 | -0.41 | -2.13 | 3.00 | 110.0 | 4.8 | 24.2 | 0.0 | 5.3 |
| 8.4 | 0.60 | 2.2 | 0.00 | 2.5 | 0.0 | 0.27 | 2.80 | 2.65 | 89.6 | 5.6 | 35.5 | 0.0 | 4.3 |
| 1.3 | 3.13 | 30.6 | 0.78 | 2.7 | 0.0 | 0.17 | 2.33 | 7.33 | 86.0 | 2.6 | 19.8 | 23.4 | 0.3 |
| 10.0 | 0.50 | 0.9 | 0.00 | 1.0 | 0.0 | -0.22 | -1.21 | 10.78 | 107.6 | 7.7 | 79.2 | 0.0 | 6.6 |
| 1.7 | 2.65 | 35.1 | 0.50 | 1.2 | 0.0 | 0.04 | 0.65 | 4.25 | 91.5 | 3.7 | 14.4 | 1.9 | 0.6 |
| 9.9 | 0.69 | 1.6 | 0.73 | 0.9 | -0.2 | -0.20 | -1.46 | 2.53 | 94.6 | 4.4 | 14.5 | 5.1 | 6.6 |
| 6.3 | 2.39 | 5.1 | 1.62 | 1.0 | 0.0 | -0.46 | -2.27 | 6.87 | 105.6 | 4.8 | 11.3 | 0.0 | 5.6 |
| 7.3 | 0.82 | 6.6 | 0.31 | 4.5 | 4.7 | 0.72 | 6.92 | 2.79 | 70.8 | 3.8 | 6.2 | 2.1 | 7.1 |
| 7.2 | 16.53 | 8.2 | 0.00 | 3.5 | 0.0 | 0.64 | 2.21 | 2.60 | 60.0 | 8.1 | 98.0 | 0.0 | 7.0 |

| Name | City | State | Rating | 2014 Rating | 2013 Rating | Total Assets ($Mil) | One Year Asset Growth | Asset Mix (As a % of Total Assets) | | | | Capital- ization Index | Net Worth Ratio |
|------|------|-------|--------|-------------|-------------|---------------------|----------------------|-------------------------------------|---|---|---|------------------------|-----------------|
| | | | | | | | | Comm- ercial Loans | Cons- umer Loans | Mort- gage Loans | Secur- ities | | |
| MOUNT CARMEL CHURCH FCU | Houston | TX | D+ | D+ | D+ | 5.1 | 2.58 | 0.0 | 31.0 | 0.0 | 0.0 | 10.0 | 16.5 |
| MOUNT GILEAD FCU | Washington | DC | C- | C- | C+ | <1 | 7.41 | 0.0 | 34.5 | 0.0 | 0.0 | 9.0 | 12.1 |
| MOUNT LEBANON FCU | Baltimore | MD | D- | E+ | D- | <1 | -1.46 | 0.0 | 67.4 | 0.0 | 0.0 | 5.4 | 7.4 |
| MOUNT OLIVE BAPTIST CHURCH FCU | Arlington | TX | B- | B- | B- | 6.2 | 19.72 | 0.0 | 57.9 | 0.0 | 0.0 | 10.0 | 12.3 |
| MOUNT PLEASANT AREA SCHOOL EMPL FCU | Mount Pleasant | PA | C | C | C | 2.8 | 1.92 | 0.0 | 28.0 | 0.0 | 0.0 | 10.0 | 14.1 |
| MOUNT PLEASANT BAPTIST CHURCH FCU | Alexandria | VA | C+ | C- | C- | <1 | 6.04 | 0.0 | 14.6 | 0.0 | 0.0 | 10.0 | 14.6 |
| ▼ MOUNT ST MARYS HOSPITAL FCU | Lewiston | NY | D | D+ | C- | 2.2 | 1.11 | 0.0 | 39.7 | 0.0 | 0.0 | 9.0 | 10.4 |
| MOUNT VERNON BAPTIST CHURCH CU | Durham | NC | D | D | C- | <1 | -5.76 | 0.0 | 8.9 | 0.0 | 0.0 | 10.0 | 33.9 |
| MOUNT VERNON NY POSTAL EMPL FCU | Mount Vernon | NY | D | D- | D | 1.8 | -7.37 | 0.0 | 46.2 | 0.0 | 0.0 | 10.0 | 11.1 |
| ▼ MOUNT ZION INDIANAPOLIS FCU | Indianapolis | IN | D+ | C- | D+ | <1 | -3.92 | 0.0 | 64.2 | 0.0 | 0.0 | 7.1 | 9.0 |
| MOUNT ZION WOODLAWN FCU | Cincinnati | OH | D | D | D+ | <1 | -8.49 | 0.0 | 29.9 | 0.0 | 0.0 | 10.0 | 12.4 |
| MOUNTAIN AMERICA FCU | West Jordan | UT | A- | A- | B+ | 4823.7 | 19.14 | 9.4 | 48.1 | 32.5 | 1.0 | 8.0 | 9.7 |
| ▲ MOUNTAIN CU | Waynesville | NC | B+ | B | B | 172.2 | 4.18 | 0.0 | 42.8 | 11.5 | 0.3 | 10.0 | 11.0 |
| MOUNTAIN EMPIRE FCU | Marion | VA | D- | E+ | D- | 15.8 | -0.02 | 0.0 | 46.5 | 3.9 | 0.0 | 6.0 | 8.1 |
| MOUNTAIN GEM CU | Nampa | ID | D+ | D+ | D | 18.7 | 5.89 | 0.0 | 69.8 | 10.1 | 0.0 | 6.3 | 8.3 |
| MOUNTAIN HERITAGE FCU | Parkersburg | WV | C+ | C | C- | 32.0 | 0.62 | 0.0 | 42.9 | 24.0 | 0.0 | 8.0 | 9.6 |
| MOUNTAIN LAKES COMMUNITY FCU | Piney Flats | TN | D+ | D+ | D+ | 24.4 | 1.07 | 1.4 | 32.9 | 31.7 | 0.0 | 7.1 | 9.1 |
| MOUNTAIN LAUREL FCU | Saint Marys | PA | B+ | B+ | A- | 95.2 | 45.35 | 0.0 | 37.1 | 8.4 | 0.7 | 10.0 | 12.9 |
| ▲ MOUNTAIN RIVER CU | Salida | CO | D- | D- | E | 23.5 | 4.43 | 0.1 | 22.4 | 20.6 | 0.0 | 6.5 | 8.5 |
| MOUNTAIN STAR FCU | El Paso | TX | C- | C | D+ | 26.9 | 1.09 | 0.0 | 36.8 | 0.0 | 0.0 | 8.1 | 9.8 |
| MOUNTAIN STATES CU | Johnson City | TN | D | D+ | D | 15.8 | -0.17 | 0.0 | 27.7 | 25.9 | 0.0 | 7.0 | 9.0 |
| MOUNTAIN WEST FCU | Butte | MT | B- | B- | B- | 6.7 | 7.04 | 0.0 | 46.7 | 0.0 | 0.0 | 10.0 | 30.4 |
| ▲ MOUNTAINCREST CU | Arlington | WA | C | C | C- | 89.4 | 4.02 | 0.0 | 47.1 | 14.7 | 6.6 | 6.5 | 8.5 |
| MOWER COUNTY CATHOLIC PARISHES CU | Austin | MN | C- | C- | C | 4.8 | 4.10 | 0.0 | 35.8 | 0.0 | 0.0 | 10.0 | 15.9 |
| ▲ MOWER COUNTY EMPL CU | Austin | MN | C | C- | C | 5.1 | -0.14 | 0.0 | 53.6 | 0.0 | 0.0 | 10.0 | 23.4 |
| ▲ MPD COMMUNITY CU | Nashville | TN | C- | D+ | C- | 25.0 | 2.34 | 0.0 | 56.3 | 12.9 | 0.0 | 6.4 | 8.4 |
| MSA EMPL FCU | Cranberry Township | PA | C | C+ | C+ | 10.8 | -0.35 | 0.0 | 27.1 | 0.0 | 0.0 | 10.0 | 11.8 |
| MSBA EMPL FCU | Rockville Centre | NY | E+ | E+ | E+ | 5.7 | -2.08 | 0.0 | 38.0 | 0.0 | 0.0 | 4.1 | 6.1 |
| MSD FCU | Louisville | KY | C+ | C+ | B- | 4.8 | 1.49 | 0.0 | 55.0 | 0.0 | 0.0 | 10.0 | 22.5 |
| MSTC FCU | Clinton | MS | D | D | C- | 3.0 | -6.50 | 0.0 | 16.7 | 0.0 | 0.2 | 10.0 | 13.0 |
| MSU FCU | Murray | KY | D | D | D | 19.4 | -0.14 | 0.0 | 36.1 | 0.0 | 0.0 | 5.7 | 7.7 |
| MT AIRY BAPTIST CHURCH FCU | Washington | DC | C | C- | C+ | 1.3 | -10.75 | 0.0 | 23.8 | 0.0 | 0.0 | 10.0 | 17.9 |
| ▼ MT JEZREEL FCU | Silver Spring | MD | C- | C | C | <1 | 7.50 | 0.0 | 7.0 | 0.0 | 0.0 | 10.0 | 11.6 |
| MT LEBANON FCU | Pittsburgh | PA | B- | B- | B- | 10.1 | 2.08 | 0.0 | 13.9 | 0.0 | 8.9 | 10.0 | 18.6 |
| MT RAINIER FCU | Puyallup | WA | C+ | C+ | B- | 11.8 | 0.38 | 0.0 | 37.1 | 0.0 | 0.0 | 10.0 | 13.1 |
| MT TAYLOR FCU | Grants | NM | C+ | C+ | C+ | 1.9 | -1.32 | 0.0 | 28.8 | 0.0 | 0.0 | 10.0 | 18.3 |
| MT ZION CU | Zion | IL | C | D+ | D+ | <1 | -8.16 | 0.0 | 28.9 | 0.0 | 0.0 | 10.0 | 18.7 |
| MTC FCU | Greenville | SC | A | A | A | 159.4 | 6.51 | 0.0 | 38.9 | 22.5 | 2.9 | 10.0 | 15.6 |
| MTCU | Midland | TX | B+ | B+ | B | 115.9 | 7.45 | 0.0 | 34.6 | 10.4 | 14.3 | 8.4 | 9.9 |
| ▼ MUHLENBERG COMMUNITY HOSPITAL CU | Greenville | KY | C | B- | B- | <1 | -6.72 | 0.0 | 17.6 | 0.0 | 0.0 | 10.0 | 18.2 |
| MULTIPLE EMPL GROUP FCU | Thomasville | GA | D+ | C- | C | 4.6 | 0.09 | 0.0 | 10.7 | 0.5 | 0.0 | 10.0 | 26.6 |
| ▼ MUNA FCU | Meridian | MS | C | B | B | 30.6 | 2.90 | 0.1 | 22.0 | 7.4 | 0.4 | 10.0 | 11.1 |
| ▲ MUNCIE FCU | Muncie | IN | C | C | C | 13.4 | 4.21 | 0.0 | 33.9 | 0.8 | 0.0 | 10.0 | 11.0 |
| MUNCIE POST OFFICE CU | Muncie | IN | C- | C- | C- | <1 | -7.00 | 0.0 | 57.2 | 0.0 | 0.0 | 10.0 | 20.2 |
| ▲ MUNI EMPL CU | Ottumwa | IA | D+ | D | D | <1 | -8.62 | 0.0 | 64.9 | 0.0 | 0.0 | 10.0 | 13.2 |
| ▲ MUNICIPAL CU | Sioux City | IA | C | C- | C | 15.4 | 2.95 | 2.1 | 10.5 | 22.9 | 0.0 | 7.3 | 9.2 |
| MUNICIPAL CU | New York | NY | C | C | C+ | 2215.2 | 8.74 | 0.0 | 33.7 | 28.1 | 14.0 | 6.4 | 8.4 |
| MUNICIPAL CU | Beloit | WI | C- | C- | C- | 17.1 | 1.39 | 0.0 | 17.8 | 15.0 | 0.0 | 10.0 | 11.2 |
| MUNICIPAL EMPL CU | La Porte | IN | D+ | C- | C | 1.0 | -2.01 | 0.0 | 69.1 | 0.0 | 0.0 | 10.0 | 20.1 |
| MUNICIPAL EMPL CU OF BALTIMORE INC | Baltimore | MD | B | C+ | C+ | 1177.7 | -1.65 | 2.6 | 24.7 | 22.9 | 33.7 | 10.0 | 11.6 |
| MUNICIPAL EMPL CU OF OKLAHOMA CITY | Oklahoma City | OK | B- | B- | B- | 151.6 | 11.11 | 1.5 | 57.7 | 20.6 | 0.8 | 6.6 | 8.6 |
| MUNICIPAL EMPL FCU | Bogalusa | LA | C | C | C | 1.4 | 1.53 | 0.0 | 20.6 | 0.0 | 0.0 | 10.0 | 19.6 |
| MUNSEETOWN COMMUNITY FCU | Muncie | IN | D- | E+ | E+ | 9.8 | 0.30 | 0.0 | 38.8 | 0.0 | 0.0 | 6.9 | 9.0 |
| MUSICIANS FCU | Arlington | TX | D | D- | E+ | <1 | 3.23 | 0.0 | 15.3 | 0.0 | 0.0 | 7.4 | 9.3 |
| MUSICIANS INTERGUILD CU | Los Angeles | CA | D | D- | E+ | 72.5 | -5.77 | 0.0 | 7.8 | 31.3 | 11.6 | 5.2 | 7.2 |
| MUSKEGON CO-OP FCU | Muskegon | MI | B | B | B | 52.0 | 2.76 | 0.0 | 66.8 | 2.2 | 4.3 | 10.0 | 12.9 |
| MUSKEGON GOVERNMENTAL EMPL FCU | Muskegon | MI | C | C | C | 47.7 | 4.02 | 0.0 | 15.1 | 15.6 | 19.0 | 9.9 | 10.9 |
| MUSKEGON PATTERNMAKERS FCU | Muskegon Heights | MI | D+ | D+ | C- | 3.1 | -2.48 | 0.0 | 38.1 | 0.0 | 46.0 | 10.0 | 28.2 |
| MUSKEGON SAINT JOSEPH FCU | Muskegon | MI | C- | D+ | C- | 10.4 | 4.82 | 0.0 | 29.0 | 18.0 | 0.0 | 10.0 | 14.8 |
| MUSKOGEE FCU | Muskogee | OK | D | D- | D- | 66.5 | 0.40 | 0.0 | 38.2 | 7.7 | 0.0 | 4.7 | 6.7 |

| Asset Quality Index | Non-Performing Loans as a % of Total Loans | as a % of Capital | Net Charge-Offs Avg Loans | Profitability Index | Net Income ($Mil) | Return on Assets | Return on Equity | Net Interest Spread | Overhead Efficiency Ratio | Liquidity Index | Liquidity Ratio | Hot Money Ratio | Stability Index |
|---|---|---|---|---|---|---|---|---|---|---|---|---|---|
| 8.4 | 0.79 | 1.9 | -0.14 | 1.2 | 0.0 | -0.05 | -0.32 | 3.30 | 99.2 | 5.0 | 18.4 | 0.0 | 6.4 |
| 6.6 | 0.00 | 0.0 | 0.00 | 2.0 | 0.0 | 0.00 | 0.00 | 6.67 | 100.0 | 7.6 | 76.5 | 0.0 | 7.2 |
| 0.0 | 16.21 | 111.3 | 0.00 | 10.0 | 0.0 | 2.52 | 37.04 | 8.04 | 52.2 | 6.2 | 56.7 | 0.0 | 3.8 |
| 5.3 | 1.91 | 8.7 | 0.35 | 10.0 | 0.1 | 2.80 | 22.01 | 5.17 | 23.0 | 6.1 | 45.0 | 0.0 | 5.0 |
| 9.9 | 0.12 | 0.3 | 0.00 | 3.0 | 0.0 | 0.39 | 2.77 | 1.65 | 60.0 | 7.2 | 65.5 | 0.0 | 7.3 |
| 10.0 | 0.00 | 0.0 | 0.00 | 6.4 | 0.0 | 2.61 | 19.05 | 3.33 | 40.0 | 8.4 | 97.0 | 0.0 | 5.7 |
| 8.2 | 0.23 | 0.9 | 0.88 | 0.6 | 0.0 | -0.38 | -3.43 | 2.91 | 102.4 | 7.0 | 64.6 | 0.0 | 4.7 |
| 7.4 | 12.50 | 3.1 | 7.41 | 0.6 | 0.0 | 0.00 | 0.00 | 1.54 | 66.7 | 6.4 | 79.8 | 0.0 | 4.7 |
| 4.4 | 3.91 | 14.7 | 0.00 | 3.4 | 0.0 | 0.57 | 5.53 | 4.36 | 77.6 | 4.6 | 27.9 | 0.0 | 3.0 |
| 2.8 | 2.02 | 16.7 | 0.00 | 10.0 | 0.0 | 2.18 | 27.05 | 9.12 | 70.0 | 5.0 | 25.1 | 0.0 | 5.1 |
| 0.3 | 41.38 | 75.0 | -4.44 | 0.4 | 0.0 | -2.56 | -20.51 | 8.89 | 150.0 | 8.0 | 83.5 | 0.0 | 4.8 |
| 5.7 | 0.84 | 7.8 | 0.35 | 9.8 | 53.2 | 1.56 | 16.28 | 3.66 | 69.1 | 2.4 | 3.2 | 6.7 | 7.7 |
| 7.5 | 1.32 | 7.9 | 0.37 | 6.2 | 1.2 | 0.93 | 8.57 | 4.19 | 76.9 | 4.0 | 12.4 | 2.5 | 7.2 |
| 4.8 | 1.00 | 6.8 | 0.71 | 2.3 | 0.0 | 0.22 | 2.88 | 4.55 | 94.5 | 5.0 | 21.6 | 1.4 | 1.7 |
| 5.1 | 0.56 | 5.4 | 0.52 | 5.0 | 0.1 | 0.57 | 6.93 | 5.72 | 88.1 | 3.5 | 13.7 | 3.7 | 3.0 |
| 3.4 | 2.97 | 22.8 | 0.73 | 6.3 | 0.2 | 0.82 | 8.60 | 4.33 | 73.4 | 3.7 | 17.8 | 3.1 | 3.8 |
| 5.6 | 1.51 | 12.0 | 0.29 | 2.2 | 0.0 | 0.09 | 0.96 | 3.74 | 92.8 | 4.0 | 22.5 | 4.3 | 3.9 |
| 9.5 | 0.53 | 2.2 | 0.14 | 4.9 | 0.4 | 0.59 | 4.70 | 3.24 | 82.8 | 5.0 | 29.2 | 0.6 | 7.0 |
| 6.0 | 1.25 | 7.3 | 0.09 | 2.1 | 0.0 | 0.05 | 0.54 | 3.59 | 98.3 | 4.2 | 15.5 | 4.1 | 4.0 |
| 5.6 | 1.14 | 7.0 | 0.01 | 2.1 | 0.0 | 0.10 | 1.01 | 4.00 | 98.0 | 4.5 | 25.8 | 3.6 | 3.9 |
| 7.9 | 0.33 | 2.0 | 0.71 | 0.5 | -0.1 | -0.70 | -7.58 | 3.53 | 108.5 | 5.3 | 35.9 | 1.7 | 4.0 |
| 8.3 | 0.60 | 1.1 | 0.10 | 9.2 | 0.1 | 1.19 | 4.01 | 5.96 | 82.7 | 5.0 | 28.9 | 0.0 | 5.7 |
| 5.3 | 0.56 | 4.6 | 0.35 | 3.6 | 0.2 | 0.31 | 3.77 | 4.11 | 92.3 | 4.8 | 25.1 | 2.3 | 3.1 |
| 7.9 | 1.42 | 3.6 | 0.35 | 1.2 | 0.0 | -0.16 | -1.04 | 2.75 | 100.0 | 5.0 | 44.9 | 0.0 | 7.0 |
| 6.7 | 0.00 | 0.0 | 0.88 | 6.1 | 0.0 | 1.03 | 4.49 | 3.69 | 69.6 | 3.7 | 9.1 | 2.6 | 4.3 |
| 8.4 | 0.13 | 1.1 | 0.09 | 4.6 | 0.1 | 0.67 | 8.27 | 4.44 | 87.0 | 3.8 | 12.9 | 5.0 | 3.4 |
| 8.3 | 3.01 | 7.4 | 0.04 | 3.1 | 0.0 | 0.40 | 3.51 | 3.00 | 87.1 | 5.4 | 26.0 | 0.0 | 5.4 |
| 2.9 | 5.45 | 30.8 | 0.99 | 0.0 | -0.1 | -1.67 | -25.82 | 4.75 | 120.6 | 4.9 | 13.9 | 0.0 | 2.8 |
| 7.6 | 1.50 | 4.3 | 0.00 | 6.4 | 0.0 | 0.83 | 3.92 | 5.07 | 90.7 | 4.8 | 32.9 | 0.0 | 4.3 |
| 10.0 | 0.19 | 0.3 | 3.21 | 0.0 | 0.0 | -0.72 | -5.65 | 2.37 | 116.3 | 4.9 | 4.8 | 0.0 | 4.1 |
| 8.9 | 0.00 | 0.0 | 0.23 | 0.9 | 0.0 | -0.08 | -1.07 | 2.42 | 99.7 | 4.1 | 15.3 | 3.4 | 2.8 |
| 8.4 | 0.20 | 0.4 | 2.91 | 7.3 | 0.0 | 1.32 | 7.50 | 4.27 | 32.1 | 6.9 | 54.8 | 0.0 | 5.0 |
| 8.2 | 5.88 | 3.9 | 7.02 | 0.9 | 0.0 | -0.64 | -5.13 | 2.36 | 66.7 | 7.6 | 53.7 | 0.0 | 5.7 |
| 10.0 | 0.19 | 0.3 | 0.50 | 5.1 | 0.0 | 0.58 | 3.10 | 2.25 | 66.0 | 5.6 | 24.2 | 0.0 | 5.0 |
| 9.6 | 0.56 | 1.9 | 0.08 | 3.7 | 0.1 | 0.55 | 4.31 | 2.91 | 87.6 | 5.0 | 26.3 | 0.0 | 6.1 |
| 9.9 | 0.00 | 0.0 | -0.21 | 2.4 | 0.0 | 0.20 | 1.14 | 2.72 | 91.7 | 6.2 | 50.0 | 0.0 | 6.9 |
| 5.1 | 10.29 | 11.9 | -7.51 | 7.8 | 0.0 | 1.72 | 9.76 | 6.23 | 40.0 | 7.6 | 73.2 | 0.0 | 4.3 |
| 9.1 | 0.56 | 2.6 | 0.36 | 10.0 | 2.3 | 1.98 | 12.89 | 6.43 | 69.3 | 4.8 | 29.1 | 4.5 | 9.7 |
| 7.9 | 1.55 | 8.1 | 0.34 | 4.4 | 0.4 | 0.50 | 5.72 | 3.98 | 81.2 | 4.4 | 17.9 | 8.7 | 6.5 |
| 10.0 | 0.76 | 0.7 | 1.75 | 1.9 | 0.0 | -0.36 | -1.92 | 3.29 | 94.1 | 6.3 | 34.8 | 0.0 | 7.9 |
| 10.0 | 1.40 | 0.7 | 1.25 | 0.3 | 0.0 | -0.64 | -2.38 | 2.70 | 122.2 | 5.5 | 42.0 | 7.5 | 6.7 |
| 8.8 | 0.82 | 3.6 | 1.24 | 1.9 | -0.1 | -0.21 | -1.88 | 5.54 | 93.5 | 6.0 | 40.8 | 6.8 | 5.3 |
| 9.9 | 0.11 | 0.5 | 1.15 | 4.9 | 0.1 | 0.76 | 7.15 | 3.13 | 70.0 | 3.0 | 14.8 | 16.6 | 5.1 |
| 7.1 | 1.20 | 3.1 | -0.56 | 2.9 | 0.0 | 0.32 | 1.59 | 7.83 | 88.9 | 4.9 | 29.2 | 0.0 | 5.6 |
| 4.7 | 1.20 | 6.9 | 0.00 | 2.5 | 0.0 | 0.36 | 2.84 | 4.26 | 90.9 | 3.9 | 16.9 | 0.0 | 5.9 |
| 8.3 | 0.54 | 2.5 | -0.02 | 4.6 | 0.1 | 0.75 | 8.55 | 3.34 | 77.9 | 6.0 | 55.2 | 0.0 | 4.3 |
| 5.5 | 1.38 | 16.2 | 0.55 | 2.6 | 2.0 | 0.12 | 2.42 | 5.19 | 93.0 | 5.0 | 22.6 | 1.1 | 5.3 |
| 10.0 | 0.17 | 0.5 | 0.07 | 1.2 | 0.0 | -0.13 | -1.11 | 1.98 | 104.2 | 4.6 | 15.0 | 1.4 | 6.1 |
| 1.5 | 6.09 | 21.2 | 1.33 | 6.2 | 0.0 | 0.66 | 3.30 | 4.90 | 85.7 | 4.3 | 30.1 | 0.0 | 7.1 |
| 6.3 | 2.54 | 12.3 | 1.07 | 4.5 | 6.5 | 0.71 | 6.41 | 3.59 | 75.8 | 3.9 | 18.9 | 7.7 | 7.0 |
| 5.9 | 0.59 | 7.9 | 1.04 | 5.9 | 0.9 | 0.78 | 8.98 | 4.80 | 73.6 | 1.6 | 10.9 | 25.5 | 5.5 |
| 8.5 | 3.14 | 3.3 | 0.00 | 2.1 | 0.0 | 0.10 | 0.49 | 3.33 | 95.7 | 7.4 | 64.0 | 0.0 | 7.3 |
| 6.0 | 2.00 | 9.2 | -0.12 | 2.7 | 0.0 | 0.35 | 3.99 | 2.94 | 91.4 | 3.9 | 16.4 | 12.0 | 1.7 |
| 8.5 | 0.00 | 0.0 | 0.00 | 2.0 | 0.0 | 0.16 | 1.69 | 5.06 | 96.0 | 5.7 | 37.4 | 0.0 | 2.8 |
| 3.4 | 4.77 | 25.7 | 0.49 | 4.2 | 0.3 | 0.59 | 8.04 | 2.50 | 97.5 | 3.1 | 19.5 | 16.2 | 2.5 |
| 8.0 | 0.32 | 2.4 | 0.45 | 5.3 | 0.3 | 0.70 | 5.70 | 4.25 | 81.5 | 2.9 | 14.8 | 10.7 | 6.9 |
| 10.0 | 0.16 | 0.6 | 0.39 | 2.7 | 0.1 | 0.35 | 3.19 | 2.52 | 86.0 | 4.2 | 30.6 | 11.2 | 5.3 |
| 9.9 | 0.33 | 0.5 | 0.10 | 0.8 | 0.0 | -0.21 | -0.75 | 2.29 | 108.3 | 5.4 | 27.5 | 0.0 | 6.2 |
| 3.7 | 7.67 | 23.2 | 0.10 | 3.6 | 0.0 | 0.39 | 2.64 | 2.37 | 80.8 | 4.1 | 8.1 | 0.0 | 7.0 |
| 6.1 | 0.98 | 8.9 | 0.15 | 2.7 | 0.1 | 0.26 | 4.02 | 2.80 | 92.3 | 4.8 | 30.6 | 0.4 | 2.1 |

| Name | City | State | Rating | 2014 Rating | 2013 Rating | Total Assets ($Mil) | One Year Asset Growth | Commercial Loans | Consumer Loans | Mortgage Loans | Securities | Capitalization Index | Net Worth Ratio |
|------|------|-------|--------|-------------|-------------|--------|--------|-----------|---------|---------|--------|---------|--------|
| MUTUAL CU | Vicksburg | MS | C+ | B- | C+ | 187.9 | 3.50 | 0.0 | 21.5 | 16.0 | 15.1 | 8.2 | 9.8 |
| ▲ MUTUAL FIRST FCU | Omaha | NE | C- | D | D+ | 105.5 | -0.55 | 10.0 | 20.2 | 25.3 | 26.8 | 5.9 | 8.0 |
| ▲ MUTUAL SAVINGS CU | Hoover | AL | D | D | D- | 178.8 | 33.11 | 8.3 | 16.1 | 36.2 | 10.2 | 7.1 | 9.0 |
| MUTUAL SAVINGS CU | Atlanta | GA | C+ | C+ | C+ | 67.6 | -1.51 | 3.0 | 26.9 | 25.1 | 7.5 | 10.0 | 12.6 |
| ▲ MUTUAL SECURITY CU | Shelton | CT | C+ | C- | C- | 252.9 | 3.43 | 0.1 | 32.7 | 44.4 | 0.0 | 6.0 | 8.0 |
| MUW EMPL FCU | Columbus | MS | C | C- | C- | 3.5 | 5.21 | 0.0 | 47.1 | 0.0 | 15.0 | 10.0 | 18.7 |
| MWD FCU | Los Angeles | CA | C | C | C | 45.2 | 0.87 | 0.0 | 20.5 | 9.0 | 14.4 | 10.0 | 12.3 |
| ▲ MWPH GRAND LODGE OF ILLINOIS FCU | Chicago | IL | D | D | D+ | <1 | -2.62 | 0.0 | 1.9 | 0.0 | 0.0 | 10.0 | 11.3 |
| MWRD EMPL CU | Chicago | IL | C+ | B- | B | 30.0 | 5.58 | 0.0 | 17.8 | 21.9 | 20.9 | 10.0 | 15.2 |
| MY CHOICE FCU | Tulsa | OK | E+ | E+ | E+ | 1.8 | -7.99 | 0.0 | 73.5 | 0.0 | 0.0 | 5.4 | 7.5 |
| MY COMMUNITY FCU | Midland | TX | B+ | A- | A- | 320.8 | 5.76 | 1.9 | 54.4 | 12.9 | 8.6 | 9.0 | 10.5 |
| ▲ MY CU | Redwood City | CA | D | D | D- | 32.7 | -5.91 | 13.1 | 16.2 | 38.3 | 2.8 | 6.5 | 8.5 |
| MY CU | Watauga | TX | C- | C- | C | 44.2 | 3.74 | 0.0 | 34.3 | 16.7 | 0.0 | 6.6 | 8.6 |
| ▲ MY HEALTHCARE FCU | Gainesville | FL | C | D | D | 25.3 | -8.86 | 0.0 | 33.2 | 4.8 | 0.0 | 10.0 | 15.6 |
| MY PENSACOLA FCU | Pensacola | FL | A- | A- | B+ | 62.5 | -1.42 | 0.0 | 25.3 | 8.3 | 5.5 | 10.0 | 18.2 |
| MY PERSONAL CU | Wyoming | MI | B- | B- | B- | 116.0 | 2.68 | 11.1 | 19.5 | 20.1 | 36.8 | 7.5 | 9.3 |
| MY POSTAL CU | Pontiac | MI | D+ | D | C- | 15.1 | -1.87 | 0.0 | 7.3 | 5.1 | 76.4 | 10.0 | 21.2 |
| MYCOM FCU | Pittsfield | MA | C+ | C+ | C+ | 16.4 | -1.48 | 0.0 | 34.8 | 2.6 | 0.0 | 10.0 | 12.7 |
| N A E FCU | Chesapeake | VA | B+ | B+ | A- | 91.1 | 3.23 | 2.5 | 65.1 | 6.6 | 10.3 | 10.0 | 16.0 |
| N C P D FCU | Plainview | NY | A | A | A | 701.7 | 4.97 | 0.3 | 6.5 | 14.7 | 68.4 | 10.0 | 13.1 |
| N C S E CU INC | Lovingston | VA | D+ | C- | C | 1.2 | -7.35 | 0.0 | 34.4 | 0.0 | 0.0 | 10.0 | 16.9 |
| N J LATVIAN FCU | Freehold | NJ | C- | C- | C | 10.9 | 7.95 | 0.0 | 1.0 | 0.8 | 50.8 | 7.5 | 11.9 |
| N Y TEAM FCU | Hicksville | NY | C+ | C+ | C+ | 36.7 | 10.65 | 9.4 | 31.9 | 9.5 | 0.0 | 8.2 | 9.8 |
| ▼ NABISCO EMPL CU | Richmond | VA | D | C- | C+ | 5.6 | -7.04 | 0.0 | 32.6 | 0.0 | 0.0 | 10.0 | 19.8 |
| NAFT FCU | Pharr | TX | B+ | B+ | B+ | 72.6 | 6.99 | 0.0 | 48.7 | 0.0 | 0.0 | 10.0 | 12.4 |
| NAHEOLA CU | Pennington | AL | A- | B+ | B | 82.7 | 1.18 | 3.8 | 14.3 | 33.4 | 21.5 | 10.0 | 22.3 |
| NAPFE FCU | Washington | DC | D | D | D+ | 3.6 | -5.07 | 0.0 | 22.9 | 0.0 | 0.0 | 10.0 | 37.2 |
| NARC FCU | Beltsville | MD | D- | D | D- | 23.7 | -3.43 | 0.0 | 8.0 | 0.0 | 71.5 | 5.7 | 7.7 |
| NAS JRB CU | New Orleans | LA | D | D | D | 27.7 | -5.29 | 0.0 | 62.2 | 0.0 | 0.0 | 6.8 | 8.8 |
| NASA FCU | Upper Marlboro | MD | A | A | A- | 1663.9 | 15.91 | 5.1 | 39.5 | 28.3 | 7.6 | 9.5 | 10.7 |
| NASCOGA FCU | Gainesville | TX | C | C+ | C+ | 85.5 | 0.94 | 5.8 | 27.4 | 21.0 | 8.0 | 6.4 | 8.4 |
| NASHVILLE FIREMENS CU | Nashville | TN | C+ | C+ | D+ | 21.7 | 7.28 | 0.0 | 54.1 | 2.5 | 0.9 | 10.0 | 17.2 |
| NASHVILLE POST OFFICE CU | Nashville | TN | C- | C+ | C+ | 71.9 | 1.84 | 0.0 | 17.6 | 16.6 | 24.3 | 10.0 | 17.8 |
| ▼ NASHWAUK FCU | Nashwauk | MN | C- | C | C | 5.0 | 16.46 | 0.0 | 28.7 | 3.7 | 0.0 | 10.0 | 11.4 |
| NASSAU EDUCATORS FCU | Westbury | NY | B+ | B+ | B | 2318.5 | 9.36 | 7.2 | 27.3 | 26.8 | 17.8 | 8.3 | 9.9 |
| NASSAU FINANCIAL FCU | Westbury | NY | D+ | C- | D+ | 394.5 | 1.46 | 18.3 | 9.1 | 16.4 | 16.8 | 8.0 | 9.6 |
| ▼ NATCHEZ-ADAMS EDUCATORS CU | Natchez | MS | C+ | B | A- | 1.6 | -8.79 | 0.0 | 26.6 | 0.0 | 0.0 | 10.0 | 34.7 |
| NATCO CU | Richmond | IN | B | B | B | 69.9 | 4.88 | 0.3 | 51.2 | 7.4 | 16.6 | 10.0 | 12.5 |
| NATCO EMPL FCU | West Warwick | RI | C | D+ | C | <1 | 8.33 | 0.0 | 24.0 | 0.0 | 0.0 | 10.0 | 15.4 |
| NATIONAL EMPL FCU | Bluefield | WV | C- | C- | D | 11.1 | 4.77 | 0.0 | 49.1 | 0.0 | 0.0 | 9.5 | 10.7 |
| NATIONAL GEOGRAPHIC FCU | Washington | DC | D+ | C- | C- | 13.7 | -6.58 | 0.0 | 36.1 | 0.0 | 31.5 | 10.0 | 14.3 |
| NATIONAL INSTITUTES OF HEALTH FCU | Rockville | MD | C+ | C | C- | 552.9 | 0.77 | 5.2 | 14.2 | 31.2 | 28.8 | 6.8 | 9.0 |
| NATIONAL JACL CU | Salt Lake City | UT | C- | C- | C+ | 29.9 | -5.20 | 3.0 | 11.2 | 14.9 | 12.8 | 10.0 | 11.9 |
| NATIONAL OILWELL VARCO EMPL CU | Houston | TX | B+ | B+ | B+ | 17.0 | 0.57 | 0.0 | 21.2 | 0.0 | 0.0 | 10.0 | 16.6 |
| NATIONAL WESTERN LIFE FCU | Austin | TX | D+ | D | D | 2.4 | 5.97 | 0.0 | 51.4 | 0.0 | 0.0 | 9.6 | 10.7 |
| NATRIUM EMPL FCU | Proctor | WV | D- | D- | D- | 8.8 | 0.83 | 0.0 | 22.5 | 0.0 | 0.0 | 5.6 | 7.6 |
| NATURAL RESOURCES CONSERVATION SER | Fort Worth | TX | D+ | D+ | C- | 10.3 | -2.67 | 0.0 | 41.8 | 0.0 | 0.0 | 10.0 | 12.5 |
| ▼ NATURAL STATE FCU | Searcy | AR | D+ | C | C | 5.5 | -3.72 | 0.0 | 65.8 | 0.0 | 0.0 | 10.0 | 15.4 |
| NAVARRO CU | Corsicana | TX | C | C- | C | 3.2 | -7.17 | 0.0 | 46.2 | 0.0 | 0.0 | 10.0 | 28.9 |
| ▲ NAVEO CU | Somerville | MA | C | C- | C- | 115.4 | 2.13 | 9.7 | 5.2 | 38.6 | 18.0 | 5.9 | 7.9 |
| ▲ NAVFAC FCU | Honolulu | HI | D+ | D | D- | 27.5 | -7.38 | 0.0 | 19.0 | 0.0 | 16.3 | 10.0 | 11.4 |
| NAVIGANT CU | Smithfield | RI | B | B- | B- | 1532.5 | 5.33 | 11.6 | 3.2 | 56.8 | 12.1 | 10.0 | 12.0 |
| NAVIGATOR CU | Pascagoula | MS | A- | A- | A- | 304.6 | 5.16 | 0.4 | 57.8 | 13.5 | 1.3 | 10.0 | 13.1 |
| NAVY ARMY COMMUNITY CU | Corpus Christi | TX | A- | A- | A- | 2317.5 | 6.74 | 3.8 | 42.0 | 35.5 | 4.8 | 9.0 | 10.4 |
| NAVY FCU | Vienna | VA | A | A | A | 71967.7 | 15.14 | 0.5 | 34.5 | 33.1 | 20.1 | 9.7 | 10.8 |
| ▼ NBA CU | Bristol | PA | C- | C+ | C+ | 43.2 | 0.26 | 4.1 | 12.1 | 47.5 | 7.7 | 10.0 | 15.2 |
| NBC (NY) EMPL FCU | New York | NY | B | B | B | 34.3 | 6.57 | 1.0 | 6.9 | 24.3 | 39.6 | 10.0 | 12.4 |
| NCE CU | Corpus Christi | TX | C | C+ | C+ | 5.0 | 6.89 | 0.0 | 61.9 | 0.0 | 0.0 | 10.0 | 18.8 |
| ▼ NE PA COMMUNITY FCU | Stroudsburg | PA | D+ | C | C | 103.0 | 2.37 | 0.3 | 14.7 | 22.3 | 35.4 | 6.9 | 8.9 |
| NEA FCU | Bardonia | NY | C | C+ | B- | 102.1 | 0.54 | 11.0 | 9.7 | 17.0 | 19.5 | 8.7 | 10.1 |

| Asset Quality Index | Non-Performing Loans as a % of Total Loans | Non-Performing Loans as a % of Capital | Net Charge-Offs Avg Loans | Profitability Index | Net Income ($Mil) | Return on Assets | Return on Equity | Net Interest Spread | Overhead Efficiency Ratio | Liquidity Index | Liquidity Ratio | Hot Money Ratio | Stability Index |
|---|---|---|---|---|---|---|---|---|---|---|---|---|---|
| 8.0 | 1.05 | 5.6 | 0.85 | 2.3 | 0.2 | 0.15 | 1.75 | 3.47 | 86.6 | 5.7 | 29.4 | 1.3 | 5.1 |
| 6.1 | 1.28 | 10.2 | 0.28 | 2.4 | 0.3 | 0.42 | 5.47 | 3.70 | 84.2 | 4.0 | 22.1 | 3.7 | 3.8 |
| 3.1 | 1.45 | 32.2 | 0.39 | 3.7 | 0.6 | 0.59 | 8.27 | 3.73 | 90.9 | 4.0 | 18.2 | 6.7 | 3.6 |
| 8.8 | 0.65 | 3.4 | 0.35 | 3.3 | 0.2 | 0.47 | 3.77 | 3.27 | 81.2 | 2.7 | 29.5 | 17.3 | 5.3 |
| 5.1 | 1.44 | 17.5 | 0.31 | 3.8 | 1.1 | 0.56 | 7.27 | 3.69 | 82.7 | 2.7 | 9.0 | 6.2 | 4.3 |
| 8.3 | 1.05 | 2.7 | 0.24 | 7.0 | 0.0 | 1.63 | 8.41 | 6.44 | 67.6 | 5.4 | 32.5 | 0.0 | 5.0 |
| 10.0 | 0.13 | 0.4 | 0.26 | 1.7 | 0.0 | -0.03 | -0.26 | 2.68 | 100.0 | 4.6 | 30.4 | 8.6 | 5.5 |
| 9.3 | 7.14 | 2.2 | 0.00 | 0.4 | 0.0 | -0.32 | -3.03 | 1.55 | 133.3 | 8.3 | 107.0 | 0.0 | 4.4 |
| 10.0 | 0.36 | 1.1 | -0.03 | 2.4 | 0.0 | 0.16 | 1.04 | 3.63 | 95.4 | 5.1 | 15.6 | 0.0 | 7.0 |
| 1.6 | 2.94 | 33.5 | -0.09 | 1.4 | 0.0 | 0.07 | 0.99 | 5.78 | 98.7 | 4.4 | 20.9 | 0.0 | 1.0 |
| 6.9 | 0.71 | 4.8 | 0.72 | 5.0 | 1.4 | 0.57 | 5.59 | 3.57 | 76.9 | 3.4 | 13.6 | 10.0 | 6.8 |
| 10.0 | 0.06 | 0.4 | -0.04 | 0.6 | 0.0 | -0.17 | -2.01 | 3.10 | 108.3 | 3.7 | 18.5 | 3.9 | 3.0 |
| 5.8 | 1.64 | 9.8 | 0.26 | 1.6 | -0.1 | -0.19 | -2.16 | 3.67 | 101.8 | 5.2 | 45.3 | 1.6 | 4.0 |
| 9.6 | 0.88 | 3.0 | 0.60 | 3.1 | 0.1 | 0.58 | 3.99 | 4.29 | 90.3 | 4.2 | 19.9 | 3.9 | 4.8 |
| 9.8 | 0.58 | 1.5 | 0.14 | 4.8 | 0.2 | 0.32 | 1.82 | 2.73 | 89.5 | 4.9 | 29.6 | 2.9 | 8.5 |
| 7.1 | 0.95 | 5.3 | 0.03 | 3.6 | 0.4 | 0.50 | 5.56 | 3.48 | 89.4 | 3.9 | 11.6 | 4.0 | 5.2 |
| 10.0 | 0.80 | 0.5 | 0.30 | 0.6 | 0.0 | -0.14 | -0.66 | 2.03 | 106.7 | 5.7 | 31.8 | 0.9 | 5.8 |
| 9.8 | 0.65 | 2.1 | 0.26 | 3.6 | 0.1 | 0.40 | 3.19 | 3.68 | 88.1 | 4.7 | 27.2 | 2.3 | 5.6 |
| 8.3 | 0.18 | 1.2 | 0.46 | 4.3 | 0.3 | 0.41 | 2.88 | 5.27 | 85.8 | 2.3 | 10.2 | 21.6 | 6.3 |
| 9.3 | 1.62 | 3.0 | 0.17 | 8.6 | 6.3 | 1.22 | 9.67 | 1.99 | 35.7 | 5.0 | 16.2 | 0.0 | 9.7 |
| 5.9 | 4.76 | 9.2 | 3.86 | 2.3 | 0.0 | 0.00 | 0.00 | 5.78 | 61.5 | 6.9 | 49.4 | 0.0 | 5.8 |
| 8.6 | 15.36 | 4.0 | 0.00 | 2.6 | 0.0 | 0.16 | 1.66 | 0.80 | 81.4 | 5.5 | 284.1 | 25.9 | 5.7 |
| 3.5 | 2.65 | 21.3 | 0.46 | 4.1 | 0.1 | 0.40 | 6.56 | 5.52 | 88.9 | 6.2 | 49.7 | 0.0 | 3.6 |
| 8.0 | 3.20 | 4.5 | -0.63 | 0.0 | -0.1 | -2.26 | -10.84 | 2.58 | 170.2 | 5.5 | 53.8 | 0.0 | 5.3 |
| 7.9 | 0.46 | 2.4 | 0.28 | 4.9 | 0.3 | 0.63 | 5.46 | 4.03 | 84.5 | 5.7 | 35.2 | 1.4 | 6.6 |
| 8.7 | 1.00 | 3.7 | 0.35 | 6.7 | 0.7 | 1.12 | 5.23 | 3.48 | 72.1 | 3.2 | 20.5 | 11.9 | 7.4 |
| 6.8 | 11.97 | 7.4 | 4.50 | 0.0 | 0.0 | -1.37 | -3.65 | 3.47 | 109.6 | 7.6 | 120.0 | 6.4 | 4.7 |
| 10.0 | 0.19 | 0.4 | 0.00 | 0.4 | -0.1 | -0.28 | -6.14 | 1.43 | 118.5 | 6.2 | 28.7 | 0.0 | 2.1 |
| 3.1 | 2.10 | 14.6 | 2.16 | 1.5 | 0.0 | -0.08 | -0.98 | 6.19 | 81.5 | 5.0 | 28.4 | 0.9 | 2.5 |
| 7.7 | 0.68 | 5.3 | 0.57 | 8.7 | 14.0 | 1.18 | 10.98 | 4.04 | 63.7 | 2.9 | 18.4 | 13.9 | 8.1 |
| 7.8 | 0.56 | 4.1 | 0.06 | 2.8 | 0.2 | 0.29 | 3.48 | 2.67 | 90.5 | 3.5 | 21.3 | 12.2 | 4.0 |
| 8.2 | 0.47 | 1.8 | -0.06 | 4.4 | 0.1 | 0.64 | 3.70 | 4.34 | 86.4 | 4.4 | 29.2 | 7.1 | 6.5 |
| 7.8 | 1.67 | 5.8 | 0.74 | 1.5 | 0.0 | -0.08 | -0.47 | 2.57 | 96.9 | 3.4 | 33.4 | 20.2 | 6.6 |
| 7.6 | 1.47 | 5.9 | 0.00 | 2.0 | 0.0 | 0.06 | 0.48 | 3.46 | 97.7 | 5.0 | 29.5 | 0.0 | 6.6 |
| 6.8 | 0.98 | 7.5 | 0.38 | 5.4 | 14.2 | 0.82 | 8.73 | 2.75 | 67.9 | 2.6 | 6.6 | 11.6 | 7.1 |
| 5.0 | 2.87 | 16.8 | 0.33 | 1.4 | -0.1 | -0.03 | -0.26 | 2.04 | 93.7 | 3.6 | 22.0 | 6.6 | 5.7 |
| 9.9 | 2.05 | 1.6 | 0.59 | 4.4 | 0.0 | 0.46 | 1.42 | 5.62 | 86.4 | 6.6 | 82.3 | 0.0 | 7.2 |
| 6.2 | 1.33 | 6.9 | 0.75 | 4.1 | 0.2 | 0.31 | 2.52 | 6.31 | 88.2 | 4.0 | 11.3 | 0.0 | 6.0 |
| 10.0 | 0.00 | 0.0 | -6.15 | 6.0 | 0.0 | 1.28 | 8.89 | 8.21 | 50.0 | 8.2 | 90.9 | 0.0 | 5.0 |
| 4.4 | 1.23 | 5.7 | 3.14 | 2.6 | 0.0 | 0.17 | 1.59 | 7.20 | 87.1 | 6.0 | 31.5 | 0.0 | 5.5 |
| 7.7 | 2.08 | 8.3 | 0.51 | 0.4 | -0.1 | -0.66 | -4.71 | 3.88 | 107.8 | 4.5 | 23.1 | 0.3 | 5.3 |
| 7.4 | 1.15 | 7.7 | 0.02 | 3.7 | 2.2 | 0.53 | 6.54 | 2.96 | 85.9 | 4.1 | 13.0 | 5.4 | 5.6 |
| 8.5 | 0.66 | 1.8 | 0.49 | 1.2 | 0.0 | 0.00 | 0.04 | 2.55 | 99.8 | 4.5 | 18.9 | 4.8 | 4.6 |
| 10.0 | 0.84 | 1.2 | 0.06 | 9.5 | 0.2 | 1.34 | 8.23 | 1.88 | 35.7 | 6.1 | 86.1 | 0.0 | 7.0 |
| 5.4 | 1.05 | 4.8 | 1.09 | 1.7 | 0.0 | 0.00 | 0.00 | 0.83 | 53.3 | 4.8 | 53.7 | 0.0 | 5.9 |
| 8.1 | 0.87 | 2.8 | -0.17 | 2.6 | 0.0 | 0.18 | 2.42 | 2.17 | 92.7 | 5.5 | 42.6 | 0.0 | 1.7 |
| 8.5 | 1.01 | 3.9 | 0.29 | 0.7 | 0.0 | -0.17 | -1.35 | 2.52 | 103.3 | 5.1 | 61.8 | 6.2 | 5.8 |
| 8.1 | 0.14 | 0.7 | 0.16 | 0.8 | 0.0 | -0.36 | -2.34 | 4.24 | 105.8 | 4.5 | 21.7 | 0.0 | 7.5 |
| 5.7 | 4.17 | 7.6 | -0.16 | 8.6 | 0.1 | 2.78 | 9.61 | 5.22 | 53.9 | 5.2 | 23.5 | 0.0 | 4.3 |
| 9.9 | 0.09 | 0.6 | 0.00 | 3.0 | 0.3 | 0.40 | 5.00 | 3.21 | 88.4 | 4.4 | 18.8 | 8.8 | 5.2 |
| 10.0 | 0.86 | 1.7 | 0.44 | 1.4 | 0.0 | 0.09 | 0.85 | 2.31 | 92.8 | 4.5 | 14.4 | 4.4 | 3.6 |
| 7.4 | 0.75 | 5.4 | 0.10 | 4.7 | 8.5 | 0.75 | 6.50 | 2.73 | 74.6 | 2.6 | 9.6 | 11.0 | 8.3 |
| 5.6 | 0.80 | 5.8 | 1.32 | 5.1 | 1.4 | 0.64 | 4.84 | 5.34 | 72.0 | 3.0 | 25.3 | 19.6 | 7.4 |
| 6.6 | 0.74 | 8.6 | 0.88 | 9.2 | 24.4 | 1.42 | 14.75 | 3.70 | 49.5 | 2.2 | 20.2 | 30.2 | 8.0 |
| 7.5 | 0.91 | 5.8 | 1.36 | 8.6 | 618.9 | 1.21 | 11.34 | 4.48 | 56.8 | 2.7 | 3.3 | 10.9 | 9.3 |
| 8.2 | 0.84 | 3.6 | 1.11 | 0.3 | -0.5 | -1.56 | -9.88 | 3.53 | 128.5 | 3.8 | 7.5 | 1.6 | 6.8 |
| 9.4 | 0.64 | 1.9 | 0.06 | 6.0 | 0.2 | 0.87 | 7.13 | 3.23 | 74.6 | 4.1 | 12.7 | 4.7 | 6.5 |
| 8.3 | 0.00 | 0.0 | -0.08 | 4.6 | 0.0 | 0.60 | 3.17 | 4.76 | 93.7 | 4.6 | 28.3 | 6.1 | 4.3 |
| 7.2 | 0.89 | 5.4 | 1.05 | 1.3 | -0.1 | -0.11 | -1.26 | 2.84 | 87.7 | 4.9 | 29.7 | 6.1 | 5.6 |
| 3.4 | 2.67 | 23.5 | 0.47 | 1.6 | -0.1 | -0.12 | -1.13 | 4.33 | 101.9 | 3.3 | 10.1 | 11.8 | 5.2 |

| Name | City | State | Rating | 2014 Rating | 2013 Rating | Total Assets ($Mil) | One Year Asset Growth | Commercial Loans | Consumer Loans | Mortgage Loans | Securities | Capitalization Index | Net Worth Ratio |
|---|---|---|---|---|---|---|---|---|---|---|---|---|---|
| NEBO CU | Springville | UT | A- | B+ | B | 74.4 | 6.45 | 0.9 | 51.8 | 7.9 | 14.5 | 10.0 | 17.2 |
| NEBRASKA ENERGY FCU | Columbus | NE | A | A | A- | 241.5 | -2.17 | 1.6 | 16.9 | 42.4 | 5.8 | 10.0 | 13.0 |
| NEBRASKA RURAL COMMUNITY FCU | Morrill | NE | E+ | D- | E+ | 2.2 | 9.49 | 0.0 | 30.2 | 22.5 | 0.0 | 5.9 | 7.9 |
| NEBRASKA RURAL ELECTRIC ASSN CU | Lincoln | NE | C | C | C | 6.3 | 3.19 | 0.0 | 41.5 | 0.0 | 0.0 | 10.0 | 12.1 |
| ▲ NEBRASKA STATE EMPL CU | Lincoln | NE | C- | D | D- | 28.7 | 21.74 | 0.0 | 18.5 | 5.4 | 0.0 | 8.1 | 9.7 |
| NECHES FCU | Port Neches | TX | A | A | A | 441.3 | 8.62 | 4.8 | 44.6 | 20.7 | 3.2 | 10.0 | 14.0 |
| NEIGHBORHOOD COMMUNITY FCU | Omaha | NE | C+ | C+ | C | 23.7 | -0.02 | 0.0 | 20.1 | 0.4 | 0.0 | 10.0 | 14.0 |
| NEIGHBORHOOD CU | Dallas | TX | B+ | B | B | 377.5 | 10.25 | 0.0 | 41.4 | 7.2 | 8.0 | 8.1 | 9.7 |
| NEIGHBORHOOD TRUST FCU | New York | NY | C- | C- | C- | 9.2 | 2.23 | 12.0 | 9.9 | 42.9 | 0.0 | 10.0 | 13.2 |
| ▲ NEIGHBORS 1ST FCU | Waynesboro | PA | E+ | E- | E- | 10.5 | -10.91 | 0.0 | 21.9 | 1.3 | 8.6 | 5.8 | 7.8 |
| NEIGHBORS CU | Saint Louis | MO | A- | B | A- | 314.8 | 3.51 | 8.1 | 28.7 | 19.0 | 18.4 | 10.0 | 15.4 |
| NEIGHBORS FCU | Baton Rouge | LA | B- | B- | B- | 724.7 | 3.66 | 2.8 | 65.4 | 9.0 | 3.1 | 6.6 | 8.6 |
| NEIGHBORS UNITED FCU | Greenwood | SC | B | B | B | 42.6 | 4.69 | 1.1 | 26.9 | 21.6 | 8.5 | 10.0 | 13.4 |
| NEIMAN MARCUS GROUP EMPL FCU | Dallas | TX | C+ | C+ | C- | 13.3 | 6.36 | 0.0 | 56.6 | 0.0 | 0.0 | 8.8 | 10.2 |
| NEKOOSA CU | Nekoosa | WI | C+ | C+ | B- | 20.4 | 3.92 | 1.8 | 6.0 | 45.1 | 0.0 | 10.0 | 25.7 |
| NEOSHO SCHOOL EMPL CU | Neosho | MO | C | C- | C | 2.3 | 8.31 | 0.0 | 39.0 | 0.0 | 0.0 | 10.0 | 12.9 |
| NEPHI WESTERN EMPL FCU | Nephi | UT | A- | A- | A- | 30.2 | 0.58 | 0.0 | 35.2 | 31.3 | 0.0 | 10.0 | 30.5 |
| ▲ NESC FCU | Methuen | MA | C+ | C | C- | 77.1 | 2.78 | 0.4 | 25.7 | 40.6 | 5.4 | 7.7 | 9.5 |
| NESTLE (FREEHOLD) EMPL FCU | Freehold | NJ | C+ | C+ | C+ | 2.6 | 1.51 | 0.0 | 48.8 | 0.0 | 0.0 | 10.0 | 19.5 |
| NET FCU | Olyphant | PA | B- | B | B | 176.8 | 1.23 | 0.0 | 13.9 | 4.8 | 26.9 | 10.0 | 15.6 |
| NEW ALLIANCE FCU | Ambridge | PA | D | D | C- | 68.5 | -1.21 | 0.0 | 15.6 | 22.0 | 4.0 | 9.2 | 10.4 |
| NEW BEDFORD CU | New Bedford | MA | C | C | C | 115.8 | 0.96 | 0.0 | 17.1 | 26.6 | 17.4 | 7.9 | 9.6 |
| NEW BRUNSWICK POSTAL FCU | Edison | NJ | D | D+ | C+ | 10.1 | -1.44 | 0.0 | 21.2 | 26.3 | 39.0 | 10.0 | 11.5 |
| NEW CASTLE BELLCO FCU | New Castle | PA | D+ | D+ | D+ | 11.8 | -3.72 | 0.0 | 16.1 | 2.8 | 75.8 | 9.3 | 10.5 |
| NEW CASTLE COUNTY DELAWARE EMPL FC | New Castle | DE | D+ | D+ | C | 22.1 | 4.87 | 0.0 | 14.4 | 0.0 | 0.0 | 9.0 | 10.3 |
| NEW CASTLE COUNTY SCHOOL EMPL FCU | New Castle | DE | D- | D | D | 44.9 | 4.35 | 0.0 | 30.6 | 0.1 | 0.0 | 5.8 | 7.8 |
| ▲ NEW CENTURY FCU | Joliet | IL | D+ | D+ | D+ | 51.9 | -0.89 | 0.0 | 9.8 | 7.5 | 3.9 | 10.0 | 11.9 |
| ▲ NEW COMMUNITY FCU | Newark | NJ | C+ | D+ | D- | 3.4 | 8.00 | 0.0 | 2.9 | 55.0 | 0.0 | 10.0 | 11.3 |
| NEW COVENANT DOMINION FCU | Bronx | NY | D+ | D+ | C | 1.9 | 65.89 | 0.0 | 20.2 | 0.0 | 0.0 | 6.8 | 8.9 |
| ▼ NEW CU | Oconto Falls | WI | C | B | B | 79.1 | 4.04 | 0.0 | 17.3 | 43.9 | 0.0 | 10.0 | 11.4 |
| NEW CUMBERLAND FCU | New Cumberland | PA | C- | C | C+ | 142.1 | 2.42 | 0.0 | 32.5 | 6.8 | 14.4 | 5.6 | 7.6 |
| NEW DIMENSIONS FCU | Waterville | ME | C- | C- | C- | 77.7 | 12.66 | 7.5 | 31.0 | 48.6 | 0.0 | 5.9 | 7.9 |
| NEW ENGLAND FCU | Williston | VT | A- | A | A | 1085.0 | 5.39 | 10.3 | 10.9 | 48.6 | 14.6 | 10.0 | 12.4 |
| NEW ENGLAND LEE FCU | Boston | MA | C- | C- | C- | 4.5 | 18.79 | 2.2 | 0.0 | 5.7 | 0.0 | 10.0 | 32.0 |
| NEW ENGLAND TEAMSTERS FCU | Arlington | MA | D+ | C- | C- | 58.8 | 1.49 | 0.3 | 9.1 | 26.7 | 36.8 | 10.0 | 13.8 |
| NEW GENERATIONS FCU | Richmond | VA | D- | D- | D- | 62.1 | 0.06 | 0.0 | 45.5 | 15.5 | 10.4 | 6.4 | 8.4 |
| NEW HAMPSHIRE FCU | Concord | NH | B | B | B | 243.5 | 3.62 | 0.0 | 13.6 | 35.5 | 32.0 | 10.0 | 13.5 |
| NEW HAMPSHIRE POSTAL CU | Manchester | NH | B- | B- | B | 41.0 | 5.35 | 0.0 | 22.1 | 0.0 | 0.0 | 10.0 | 20.8 |
| NEW HAVEN COUNTY CU | North Haven | CT | E | E- | E- | 18.5 | -6.88 | 0.0 | 25.4 | 0.0 | 25.4 | 4.5 | 6.5 |
| NEW HAVEN FIREFIGHTERS CU | New Haven | CT | C+ | C+ | C+ | 6.6 | 0.11 | 0.0 | 33.5 | 0.0 | 0.0 | 10.0 | 20.3 |
| ▲ NEW HAVEN POLICE AND MUNICIPAL FCU | New Haven | CT | C- | D | C- | 5.5 | 1.76 | 0.0 | 42.1 | 0.0 | 0.0 | 10.0 | 25.1 |
| NEW HAVEN TEACHERS FCU | New Haven | CT | C- | C- | C- | 8.9 | -1.85 | 0.0 | 12.1 | 0.0 | 0.0 | 10.0 | 29.6 |
| NEW HORIZON CU | Danville | IL | D+ | D+ | C- | 12.3 | 0.67 | 0.0 | 47.2 | 5.9 | 0.0 | 10.0 | 12.6 |
| NEW HORIZON FCU | Barberton | OH | B- | B- | B- | 17.7 | 10.39 | 0.0 | 39.4 | 11.6 | 28.7 | 9.9 | 10.9 |
| NEW HORIZONS CU | Mobile | AL | B- | C+ | C+ | 219.3 | 6.55 | 0.0 | 32.1 | 16.2 | 34.5 | 8.8 | 10.2 |
| NEW HORIZONS CU | West Point | MS | C | C- | D+ | 9.1 | 3.09 | 0.0 | 36.1 | 0.0 | 0.0 | 10.0 | 19.6 |
| NEW HORIZONS CU | Cincinnati | OH | D+ | C- | C- | 43.1 | 6.44 | 6.2 | 27.9 | 25.5 | 16.7 | 6.3 | 8.3 |
| NEW JERSEY COMMUNITY FCU | Moorestown | NJ | E+ | E+ | E+ | 8.7 | -0.30 | 0.0 | 19.7 | 14.6 | 0.0 | 4.6 | 6.6 |
| NEW JERSEY LAW & PUBLIC SAFETY CU | Trenton | NJ | B | B | B | 45.2 | -2.31 | 0.0 | 32.8 | 0.9 | 0.1 | 10.0 | 14.2 |
| NEW KENSINGTON MUNICIPAL FCU | New Kensington | PA | C | C | C | 2.1 | 0.91 | 0.0 | 29.3 | 16.4 | 0.0 | 10.0 | 22.4 |
| NEW LIFE FCU | Philadelphia | PA | C- | D | D | <1 | -20.59 | 0.0 | 41.2 | 0.0 | 0.0 | 10.0 | 18.1 |
| NEW LONDON MUNICIPAL EMPL CU | New London | CT | C- | C- | C- | 3.0 | -8.31 | 0.0 | 48.0 | 0.0 | 37.2 | 10.0 | 23.7 |
| NEW OLIVET BAPTIST CHURCH CU | Memphis | TN | C | C- | C- | <1 | -1.49 | 0.0 | 13.4 | 0.0 | 0.0 | 10.0 | 12.6 |
| NEW ORLEANS CLERK & CHECKERS FCU | Metairie | LA | C+ | C | C | 10.2 | 1.16 | 0.0 | 19.2 | 26.4 | 0.0 | 10.0 | 15.0 |
| ▲ NEW ORLEANS FIREMENS FCU | Metairie | LA | C | C- | C | 154.3 | -1.05 | 0.3 | 57.6 | 11.9 | 8.9 | 6.2 | 8.2 |
| NEW ORLEANS POLICE DEPT EMPL CU | New Orleans | LA | B+ | B+ | B+ | 19.2 | 2.59 | 0.0 | 49.6 | 0.0 | 0.0 | 10.0 | 42.4 |
| ▼ NEW ORLEANS PUBLIC BELT RR FCU | Metairie | LA | C | C+ | C+ | <1 | -8.21 | 0.0 | 51.8 | 0.0 | 0.0 | 10.0 | 24.2 |
| NEW PILGRIM FCU | Birmingham | AL | D | D- | D- | 1.3 | -18.12 | 0.0 | 44.9 | 0.0 | 0.0 | 9.7 | 10.8 |
| ▲ NEW RISING STAR FCU | Detroit | MI | C- | D+ | C- | <1 | -9.92 | 0.0 | 19.3 | 0.0 | 0.0 | 10.0 | 12.8 |
| NEW SOUTH CU | Knoxville | TN | B+ | B+ | B+ | 42.2 | 3.39 | 0.4 | 34.7 | 13.7 | 0.0 | 10.0 | 16.9 |

| Asset Quality Index | Non-Performing Loans as a % of Total Loans | Non-Performing Loans as a % of Capital | Net Charge-Offs Avg Loans | Profitability Index | Net Income ($Mil) | Return on Assets | Return on Equity | Net Interest Spread | Overhead Efficiency Ratio | Liquidity Index | Liquidity Ratio | Hot Money Ratio | Stability Index |
|---|---|---|---|---|---|---|---|---|---|---|---|---|---|
| 6.2 | 1.03 | 6.0 | 0.15 | 10.0 | 1.0 | 1.89 | 11.21 | 4.69 | 67.1 | 3.2 | 7.3 | 6.1 | 8.6 |
| 9.9 | 0.04 | 0.2 | 0.05 | 8.0 | 2.4 | 1.32 | 10.73 | 2.21 | 47.1 | 3.8 | 17.3 | 0.0 | 8.2 |
| 1.7 | 3.77 | 43.6 | 2.26 | 4.3 | 0.0 | 0.00 | 0.00 | 5.90 | 85.6 | 3.2 | 26.3 | 15.1 | 1.0 |
| 9.8 | 0.49 | 1.7 | 0.00 | 3.4 | 0.0 | 0.30 | 2.46 | 2.21 | 86.7 | 4.9 | 20.4 | 0.0 | 2.3 |
| 8.2 | 1.15 | 4.9 | 0.04 | 2.2 | 0.0 | 0.17 | 2.07 | 2.50 | 93.3 | 5.4 | 36.6 | 1.2 | 3.0 |
| 9.2 | 0.34 | 2.0 | 0.34 | 9.2 | 4.2 | 1.29 | 9.31 | 3.77 | 71.0 | 2.9 | 18.6 | 11.0 | 9.0 |
| 10.0 | 0.61 | 1.2 | -0.29 | 2.8 | 0.0 | 0.23 | 1.66 | 2.37 | 92.6 | 4.9 | 26.8 | 0.0 | 6.0 |
| 7.4 | 0.36 | 5.8 | 0.63 | 8.5 | 4.0 | 1.45 | 14.96 | 3.84 | 71.0 | 3.4 | 17.6 | 9.9 | 6.0 |
| 3.7 | 3.75 | 21.3 | 1.21 | 3.7 | 0.0 | -0.51 | -5.38 | 5.25 | 96.5 | 5.3 | 33.1 | 0.0 | 5.6 |
| 5.8 | 2.30 | 10.6 | 0.24 | 1.6 | 0.0 | 0.14 | 1.96 | 3.10 | 103.9 | 5.2 | 20.1 | 0.7 | 1.9 |
| 7.8 | 1.46 | 6.2 | 0.44 | 7.4 | 3.2 | 1.36 | 9.08 | 3.26 | 75.4 | 3.7 | 11.6 | 4.1 | 6.8 |
| 5.7 | 0.51 | 5.6 | 0.44 | 3.9 | 2.5 | 0.46 | 5.60 | 3.22 | 82.3 | 1.5 | 6.7 | 21.8 | 5.9 |
| 6.2 | 2.34 | 11.0 | 0.60 | 3.4 | 0.1 | 0.18 | 1.33 | 4.62 | 91.3 | 5.0 | 28.8 | 7.6 | 7.1 |
| 6.3 | 0.59 | 3.1 | 1.21 | 7.2 | 0.1 | 0.79 | 7.74 | 5.36 | 70.7 | 5.2 | 34.7 | 0.0 | 4.7 |
| 9.9 | 0.00 | 0.0 | 0.00 | 2.9 | 0.1 | 0.31 | 1.20 | 3.01 | 89.9 | 4.4 | 12.7 | 2.2 | 7.6 |
| 6.6 | 1.92 | 5.5 | 0.50 | 5.2 | 0.0 | 0.73 | 5.33 | 3.50 | 67.4 | 6.1 | 42.6 | 0.0 | 4.3 |
| 9.0 | 0.43 | 1.1 | -0.08 | 10.0 | 0.5 | 2.35 | 7.91 | 4.12 | 43.4 | 3.7 | 20.9 | 0.0 | 8.0 |
| 7.8 | 0.38 | 3.3 | 0.22 | 3.4 | 0.3 | 0.45 | 4.80 | 4.31 | 88.9 | 3.4 | 12.2 | 3.9 | 4.3 |
| 7.1 | 1.16 | 2.8 | 0.00 | 6.3 | 0.0 | 1.00 | 5.06 | 4.18 | 62.7 | 5.0 | 39.1 | 0.0 | 5.0 |
| 9.9 | 1.05 | 2.4 | 0.35 | 2.9 | 0.3 | 0.19 | 1.30 | 2.46 | 89.8 | 4.8 | 17.9 | 2.0 | 7.9 |
| 6.7 | 1.77 | 6.9 | 0.79 | 0.7 | -0.1 | -0.15 | -1.48 | 3.07 | 100.4 | 4.3 | 12.4 | 4.0 | 4.1 |
| 7.0 | 1.50 | 9.1 | 0.17 | 3.0 | 0.2 | 0.25 | 2.67 | 2.86 | 94.7 | 4.6 | 32.9 | 7.0 | 5.4 |
| 9.3 | 0.61 | 2.7 | 0.39 | 0.6 | 0.0 | -0.40 | -3.44 | 4.27 | 98.9 | 4.2 | 10.2 | 2.6 | 4.2 |
| 10.0 | 0.00 | 0.0 | 0.00 | 1.9 | 0.0 | 0.07 | 0.63 | 1.81 | 96.7 | 4.6 | 7.5 | 1.0 | 4.7 |
| 9.8 | 0.41 | 0.9 | 0.08 | 1.3 | 0.0 | 0.07 | 0.71 | 2.41 | 100.3 | 5.4 | 20.8 | 0.0 | 4.0 |
| 6.7 | 1.43 | 5.9 | 0.49 | 0.0 | -0.2 | -0.68 | -8.50 | 2.83 | 111.8 | 4.8 | 13.6 | 0.0 | 2.4 |
| 7.8 | 2.42 | 5.1 | 0.07 | 0.8 | 0.0 | -0.08 | -0.71 | 2.24 | 103.1 | 4.7 | 21.0 | 4.2 | 5.4 |
| 9.5 | 0.33 | 1.8 | 0.00 | 7.1 | 0.0 | 0.87 | 7.82 | 5.21 | 90.4 | 5.9 | 54.8 | 0.0 | 5.0 |
| 7.5 | 2.93 | 6.5 | 0.00 | 5.1 | 0.0 | 0.83 | 9.80 | 9.55 | 89.8 | 8.4 | 100.4 | 0.0 | 3.7 |
| 7.4 | 0.90 | 5.2 | 0.50 | 1.8 | -0.1 | -0.11 | -0.99 | 3.33 | 92.3 | 3.6 | 19.9 | 4.6 | 6.0 |
| 9.7 | 0.22 | 1.7 | 0.58 | 2.6 | 0.2 | 0.17 | 2.26 | 3.70 | 86.6 | 4.4 | 23.7 | 7.4 | 4.4 |
| 4.8 | 1.25 | 13.8 | 0.26 | 6.2 | 0.5 | 0.98 | 12.43 | 4.88 | 77.3 | 1.3 | 7.5 | 21.2 | 3.4 |
| 8.8 | 0.49 | 2.9 | 0.18 | 4.8 | 5.5 | 0.68 | 5.61 | 2.93 | 79.3 | 3.9 | 18.1 | 8.6 | 9.0 |
| 10.0 | 1.21 | 0.9 | 0.00 | 1.8 | 0.0 | 0.10 | 0.28 | 1.64 | 91.9 | 7.4 | 88.5 | 0.0 | 6.7 |
| 9.7 | 0.86 | 2.8 | 0.08 | 0.6 | -0.4 | -0.95 | -6.54 | 3.51 | 124.2 | 3.5 | 11.5 | 15.4 | 6.8 |
| 4.5 | 1.39 | 10.3 | 0.41 | 0.0 | -0.5 | -1.02 | -11.79 | 3.90 | 110.0 | 3.8 | 22.3 | 5.4 | 3.1 |
| 10.0 | 0.01 | 0.1 | 0.04 | 3.8 | 0.9 | 0.49 | 3.67 | 2.38 | 80.5 | 4.1 | 16.8 | 3.5 | 8.2 |
| 10.0 | 0.24 | 0.4 | 0.03 | 3.4 | 0.1 | 0.41 | 1.94 | 3.25 | 84.8 | 7.1 | 54.2 | 0.0 | 7.3 |
| 6.2 | 1.28 | 9.3 | 1.03 | 3.2 | 0.1 | 0.59 | 9.91 | 3.55 | 89.2 | 5.3 | 24.9 | 2.5 | 0.2 |
| 10.0 | 0.00 | 0.0 | -0.12 | 4.3 | 0.0 | 0.57 | 2.82 | 3.71 | 84.4 | 4.6 | 15.8 | 0.0 | 7.7 |
| 9.8 | 0.62 | 1.1 | 0.00 | 1.5 | 0.0 | 0.15 | 0.58 | 3.83 | 95.2 | 5.8 | 44.4 | 0.0 | 6.1 |
| 10.0 | 0.00 | 0.0 | 0.00 | 1.8 | 0.0 | 0.08 | 0.30 | 1.44 | 94.6 | 6.4 | 103.0 | 0.0 | 7.0 |
| 8.6 | 0.64 | 2.5 | 0.07 | 0.4 | 0.0 | -0.29 | -2.33 | 3.10 | 104.8 | 4.6 | 9.4 | 0.0 | 5.6 |
| 9.9 | 0.04 | 0.2 | 0.25 | 4.6 | 0.1 | 0.65 | 5.93 | 3.89 | 84.1 | 4.6 | 21.9 | 2.8 | 5.3 |
| 7.2 | 1.41 | 9.7 | 0.28 | 4.9 | 1.4 | 0.86 | 10.20 | 3.13 | 81.7 | 3.8 | 29.0 | 6.9 | 4.8 |
| 9.5 | 0.33 | 0.8 | 0.03 | 3.4 | 0.0 | 0.50 | 2.57 | 3.63 | 87.6 | 4.4 | 19.6 | 0.0 | 6.5 |
| 5.6 | 0.91 | 6.0 | 1.28 | 0.1 | -0.4 | -1.15 | -13.23 | 3.50 | 102.8 | 3.3 | 24.7 | 15.9 | 2.9 |
| 4.4 | 2.49 | 17.4 | 1.15 | 1.9 | 0.0 | 0.23 | 3.53 | 3.79 | 95.6 | 5.1 | 33.9 | 0.0 | 1.0 |
| 9.4 | 0.52 | 2.1 | 0.88 | 4.7 | 0.2 | 0.61 | 4.42 | 4.13 | 76.6 | 4.0 | 21.9 | 2.9 | 6.4 |
| 9.6 | 0.00 | 0.0 | 0.00 | 2.3 | 0.0 | 0.13 | 0.57 | 3.36 | 96.0 | 3.7 | 30.7 | 0.0 | 7.2 |
| 1.6 | 20.50 | 40.6 | 1.49 | 10.0 | 0.0 | 4.14 | 29.44 | 10.14 | 32.0 | 7.4 | 71.6 | 0.0 | 5.3 |
| 8.8 | 0.06 | 0.1 | -0.09 | 1.6 | 0.0 | -0.04 | -0.19 | 4.20 | 102.4 | 4.9 | 16.7 | 0.0 | 5.3 |
| 7.6 | 2.29 | 5.2 | 4.47 | 4.1 | 0.0 | 0.64 | 5.23 | 6.63 | 81.8 | 7.4 | 66.2 | 0.0 | 6.7 |
| 8.0 | 1.14 | 3.9 | 0.02 | 3.5 | 0.0 | 0.48 | 3.26 | 4.40 | 86.5 | 5.2 | 27.2 | 0.0 | 6.9 |
| 4.2 | 1.78 | 16.4 | 1.18 | 3.5 | 0.5 | 0.41 | 5.28 | 5.87 | 80.0 | 3.0 | 8.6 | 9.0 | 4.3 |
| 8.6 | 1.09 | 1.3 | 0.00 | 9.2 | 0.2 | 1.52 | 3.49 | 3.92 | 53.6 | 6.7 | 87.5 | 0.0 | 7.0 |
| 7.2 | 0.00 | 0.0 | 3.13 | 3.5 | 0.0 | 0.00 | 0.00 | 8.04 | 103.2 | 5.9 | 65.2 | 0.0 | 7.0 |
| 3.1 | 2.77 | 25.8 | 1.65 | 3.2 | 0.0 | 0.59 | 5.63 | 4.24 | 70.0 | 4.9 | 42.5 | 0.0 | 2.3 |
| 7.2 | 0.00 | 0.0 | 0.00 | 1.8 | 0.0 | 0.00 | 0.00 | 11.59 | 150.0 | 8.4 | 93.7 | 0.0 | 6.2 |
| 9.7 | 0.13 | 0.4 | 0.10 | 4.4 | 0.2 | 0.64 | 3.75 | 3.47 | 83.7 | 3.7 | 15.6 | 6.4 | 7.5 |

| Name | City | State | Rating | 2014 Rating | 2013 Rating | Total Assets ($Mil) | One Year Asset Growth | Commercial Loans | Consumer Loans | Mortgage Loans | Securities | Capitalization Index | Net Worth Ratio |
|------|------|-------|--------|-------------|-------------|---------------------|----------------------|-----------|---------|----------|-----------|----------------------|-----------------|
| ▲ NEW YORK STATE EMPL FCU | New York | NY | D+ | D | D | 2.2 | 2.34 | 0.0 | 61.8 | 0.0 | 0.0 | 10.0 | 12.7 |
| NEW YORK TIMES EMPL FCU | New York | NY | C | C+ | B- | 72.3 | -3.93 | 6.5 | 12.4 | 25.4 | 17.6 | 10.0 | 17.4 |
| ▼ NEW YORK UNIV FCU | New York | NY | C- | C- | D | 16.5 | 9.87 | 10.3 | 21.7 | 26.8 | 0.0 | 7.0 | 9.0 |
| ▼ NEWARK BOARD OF EDUCATION EMPL CU | Newark | NJ | C | B- | C+ | 35.0 | -6.73 | 0.0 | 29.4 | 3.3 | 31.4 | 10.0 | 25.1 |
| ▼ NEWARK FIREMEN FCU | Newark | NJ | D+ | C- | C | 17.7 | -2.48 | 0.0 | 40.9 | 0.0 | 7.9 | 10.0 | 14.3 |
| NEWARK POLICE FCU | Newark | NJ | C+ | C+ | C | 5.7 | 0.76 | 0.0 | 52.7 | 0.0 | 0.2 | 10.0 | 23.6 |
| ▲ NEWARK POST OFFICE EMPL CU | Newark | NJ | C- | D | D | 3.1 | -9.78 | 0.0 | 0.0 | 0.0 | 0.0 | 10.0 | 31.3 |
| NEWAYGO COUNTY SERVICE EMPL CU | Fremont | MI | D | D | D | 22.3 | 0.21 | 0.0 | 25.8 | 4.2 | 0.0 | 6.0 | 8.0 |
| NEWELL FCU | Newell | PA | D- | D- | E+ | 5.5 | -2.42 | 0.0 | 26.9 | 0.0 | 0.0 | 6.6 | 8.6 |
| NEWPORT NEWS MUNICIPAL EMPL CU | Newport News | VA | D+ | C- | D | 41.6 | -0.15 | 2.7 | 20.6 | 23.0 | 40.2 | 6.7 | 8.8 |
| NEWPORT NEWS SHIPBUILDING EMPL CU | Newport News | VA | B | B+ | A- | 1409.3 | 4.05 | 7.4 | 36.7 | 28.4 | 18.2 | 10.0 | 13.2 |
| NEWRIZONS FCU | Hoquiam | WA | C | C- | D- | 11.7 | 0.60 | 1.5 | 53.1 | 3.4 | 0.0 | 10.0 | 11.4 |
| ▲ NEWSPAPER EMPL CU | Albany | NY | D+ | D+ | D+ | <1 | 2.35 | 0.0 | 37.3 | 0.0 | 24.1 | 10.0 | 38.0 |
| NEWTON TEACHERS CU | Newtonville | MA | D | D | D+ | 2.1 | -1.25 | 0.0 | 20.5 | 0.0 | 2.0 | 10.0 | 15.1 |
| ▲ NFG #2 FCU | Warren | PA | C+ | C | C- | 23.6 | 2.39 | 0.0 | 19.9 | 0.0 | 31.6 | 10.0 | 11.4 |
| NFO IRVINE FCU | Warren | PA | D+ | C- | D+ | 8.7 | -0.42 | 0.0 | 29.5 | 0.6 | 3.4 | 10.0 | 18.4 |
| NGH CU | Nashville | TN | D | D | C- | 6.9 | 0.25 | 0.0 | 44.5 | 6.5 | 19.3 | 10.0 | 12.3 |
| NGM EMPL FCU | Keene | NH | D+ | D+ | D+ | 5.3 | 1.26 | 0.0 | 49.4 | 0.0 | 15.2 | 10.0 | 11.1 |
| NGPL EMPL CU | Saint Charles | IA | C | C | C | 3.4 | 1.05 | 0.0 | 8.3 | 0.0 | 0.0 | 10.0 | 23.0 |
| NH COMMUNITY FCU | Claremont | NH | E+ | E+ | E+ | 8.9 | 3.51 | 0.0 | 22.9 | 6.8 | 0.0 | 5.0 | 7.0 |
| NIAGARA FALLS AIR FORCE FCU | Niagara Falls | NY | B- | B- | B- | 12.7 | 2.66 | 0.0 | 18.6 | 11.1 | 56.0 | 10.0 | 14.5 |
| NIAGARA FALLS MEMORIAL MEDICAL CTR F | Niagara Falls | NY | D | D | C- | 4.5 | -1.70 | 0.0 | 59.4 | 0.0 | 0.0 | 10.0 | 16.1 |
| ▲ NIAGARA FALLS TEACHERS FCU | Niagara Falls | NY | C | C- | D+ | 11.6 | 4.33 | 0.0 | 19.9 | 12.4 | 0.0 | 10.0 | 14.8 |
| ▼ NIAGARA FRONTIER FEDERAL MUNICIPAL C | Niagara Falls | NY | D | D | C- | 2.8 | -5.46 | 0.0 | 55.8 | 0.0 | 29.8 | 10.0 | 15.4 |
| NIAGARA MOHAWK POWER CORE TROY EAS | Troy | NY | D | D | D | 3.7 | 1.97 | 0.0 | 66.5 | 0.0 | 0.0 | 10.0 | 16.7 |
| NIAGARA REGIONAL FCU | North Tonawanda | NY | B- | B- | B | 26.9 | 0.58 | 0.5 | 21.8 | 34.3 | 23.8 | 10.0 | 11.5 |
| ▲ NIAGARA-WHEATFIELD FCU | Sanborn | NY | E+ | E | E+ | 17.0 | 1.49 | 0.0 | 12.4 | 14.2 | 47.7 | 5.2 | 7.2 |
| ▲ NIAGARAS CHOICE FCU | Niagara Falls | NY | C+ | C | C | 147.4 | 8.11 | 1.7 | 21.1 | 18.9 | 33.1 | 7.6 | 9.4 |
| ▼ NICE FCU | Saint Charles | IL | D | C- | C | 1.3 | 7.11 | 0.0 | 69.8 | 0.0 | 0.0 | 10.0 | 11.6 |
| NICKEL STEEL FCU | Lima | OH | C | C | C+ | 5.3 | -0.87 | 0.0 | 35.6 | 13.9 | 0.0 | 10.0 | 24.1 |
| ▲ NIKKEI CU | Gardena | CA | C- | D | D+ | 66.6 | -3.42 | 4.0 | 7.4 | 22.9 | 32.9 | 10.0 | 11.9 |
| NISHNA VALLEY CU | Atlantic | IA | C | C | C | 30.0 | 4.80 | 7.1 | 35.6 | 8.6 | 0.0 | 6.1 | 8.1 |
| ▼ NIU EMPL FCU | DeKalb | IL | E | E- | E | 14.3 | -3.96 | 0.0 | 32.8 | 0.0 | 0.0 | 5.0 | 7.0 |
| NIZARI PROGRESSIVE FCU | Sugar Land | TX | A | A | A | 112.4 | 6.81 | 4.0 | 40.5 | 29.7 | 3.6 | 10.0 | 14.2 |
| NJ GATEWAY FCU | Monmouth Junction | NJ | D+ | D+ | D | 27.1 | 2.35 | 0.0 | 8.9 | 7.2 | 36.2 | 10.0 | 11.0 |
| NJT EMPL FCU | Waldwick | NJ | C | C | C | 11.4 | 3.78 | 0.0 | 25.7 | 0.0 | 0.0 | 8.0 | 9.7 |
| NMA FCU | Virginia Beach | VA | C- | D+ | D | 61.3 | 5.68 | 0.3 | 47.9 | 2.9 | 25.7 | 6.6 | 8.8 |
| NO PORT COMMISSION EMPL CU | New Orleans | LA | D | D | D | 4.5 | -4.18 | 0.0 | 47.7 | 0.0 | 1.0 | 9.5 | 10.7 |
| NODA FCU | New Orleans | LA | C- | C | C | 35.5 | 0.10 | 0.0 | 24.2 | 11.3 | 2.1 | 10.0 | 17.9 |
| ▲ NONE SUFFER LACK FCU | Suitland | MD | C+ | D+ | C | 20.1 | 17.53 | 4.6 | 7.2 | 5.9 | 3.7 | 10.0 | 12.0 |
| NORDSTROM FCU | Seattle | WA | C | C | C | 51.8 | 8.80 | 0.0 | 37.0 | 0.0 | 23.5 | 6.4 | 8.5 |
| NORFOLK COMMUNITY FCU | Norfolk | MA | C | C | C- | 16.2 | 0.93 | 0.0 | 50.0 | 20.9 | 0.0 | 8.5 | 10.0 |
| NORFOLK FIRE DEPT FCU | Norfolk | VA | C- | C+ | C+ | 22.0 | -0.82 | 0.2 | 25.1 | 0.0 | 0.0 | 10.0 | 12.0 |
| NORFOLK MUNICIPAL FCU | Norfolk | VA | D | D+ | D+ | 25.7 | -2.18 | 0.0 | 19.8 | 5.9 | 4.0 | 10.0 | 11.6 |
| NORFOLK SCHOOLS FCU | Norfolk | VA | E+ | E+ | D | 2.9 | -2.32 | 0.0 | 52.2 | 0.0 | 0.0 | 5.3 | 7.3 |
| NORFOLK VIRGINIA POSTAL CU | Norfolk | VA | E+ | D- | D | 3.9 | -7.84 | 0.0 | 56.5 | 15.6 | 0.0 | 6.3 | 8.3 |
| NORMAL CITY EMPL FCU | Normal | IL | D | D | D- | 4.4 | 3.95 | 0.0 | 74.9 | 0.0 | 5.5 | 7.3 | 9.2 |
| ▲ NORRISTOWN BELL CU | Blue Bell | PA | B- | B | B- | 50.6 | -1.87 | 0.1 | 5.9 | 19.9 | 26.5 | 10.0 | 12.0 |
| NORSTAR FCU | Britton | SD | B+ | B+ | B+ | 35.0 | 3.58 | 19.3 | 21.7 | 23.8 | 0.0 | 10.0 | 13.5 |
| NORSTATE FCU | Madawaska | ME | B- | B- | B- | 175.6 | 0.59 | 21.0 | 16.8 | 53.5 | 4.8 | 10.0 | 12.7 |
| NORTH ADAMS ME FCU | North Adams | MA | D+ | D+ | C- | 1.8 | -7.46 | 0.0 | 46.3 | 0.0 | 0.0 | 10.0 | 26.1 |
| NORTH ALABAMA EDUCATORS CU | Huntsville | AL | C | C | D+ | 85.8 | 1.91 | 0.0 | 29.3 | 9.2 | 21.6 | 5.7 | 7.7 |
| NORTH ALABAMA PAPERMAKERS FCU | Stevenson | AL | C- | C- | D+ | 2.1 | 1.20 | 0.0 | 42.3 | 0.0 | 0.0 | 10.0 | 22.7 |
| NORTH CAROLINA COMMUNITY FCU | Goldsboro | NC | D | D+ | C | 65.2 | 3.45 | 5.2 | 10.1 | 29.5 | 14.3 | 9.5 | 10.6 |
| NORTH CAROLINA PRESS ASSN FCU | Raleigh | NC | C+ | C+ | C+ | 6.9 | 9.10 | 0.0 | 14.3 | 12.9 | 0.0 | 10.0 | 13.5 |
| NORTH CENTRAL AREA CU | Houghton Lake | MI | C | C | C | 105.1 | 3.75 | 1.2 | 31.4 | 12.3 | 30.8 | 7.9 | 9.6 |
| NORTH COAST CU | Fairview Park | OH | D | D | C- | 12.6 | -0.54 | 0.0 | 33.7 | 5.6 | 0.0 | 10.0 | 45.4 |
| NORTH COAST CU | Bellingham | WA | B- | B- | B- | 190.4 | 6.23 | 17.0 | 20.6 | 43.1 | 17.1 | 6.5 | 8.7 |
| NORTH COUNTRY FCU | South Burlington | VT | B | B | B | 476.9 | 6.28 | 8.9 | 24.7 | 32.3 | 9.2 | 7.3 | 9.2 |
| NORTH COUNTY CU | San Diego | CA | C+ | B- | B- | 60.3 | 2.79 | 2.1 | 25.4 | 28.5 | 7.8 | 7.9 | 9.7 |

| Asset Quality Index | Non-Performing Loans as a % of Total Loans | Non-Performing Loans as a % of Capital | Net Charge-Offs Avg Loans | Profitability Index | Net Income ($Mil) | Return on Assets | Return on Equity | Net Interest Spread | Overhead Efficiency Ratio | Liquidity Index | Liquidity Ratio | Hot Money Ratio | Stability Index |
|---|---|---|---|---|---|---|---|---|---|---|---|---|---|
| 5.0 | 1.56 | 7.0 | 1.52 | 3.5 | 0.0 | 0.49 | 4.06 | 14.89 | 92.7 | 5.9 | 39.0 | 0.0 | 5.0 |
| 5.1 | 5.94 | 17.3 | 0.39 | 1.9 | 0.0 | 0.07 | 0.41 | 3.07 | 92.6 | 5.2 | 43.5 | 8.9 | 5.6 |
| 3.7 | 3.87 | 28.0 | 0.69 | 9.2 | 0.2 | 1.69 | 20.14 | 5.35 | 73.5 | 4.8 | 21.2 | 0.0 | 4.0 |
| 2.4 | 11.06 | 20.9 | 0.00 | 1.1 | -0.7 | -2.36 | -9.90 | 5.16 | 60.8 | 4.3 | 8.5 | 0.0 | 5.9 |
| 4.6 | 4.17 | 12.5 | 1.15 | 0.9 | 0.0 | -0.30 | -2.12 | 3.71 | 101.2 | 4.1 | 10.6 | 3.1 | 5.5 |
| 8.1 | 0.98 | 2.0 | 0.08 | 10.0 | 0.1 | 1.59 | 6.80 | 7.18 | 66.4 | 5.9 | 40.3 | 0.0 | 5.7 |
| 6.2 | 4.78 | 7.1 | 0.17 | 6.0 | 0.1 | 5.91 | 21.18 | 11.57 | 76.4 | 7.0 | 73.3 | 0.0 | 4.3 |
| 6.2 | 1.18 | 6.2 | 0.10 | 2.7 | 0.0 | 0.25 | 3.12 | 2.74 | 94.7 | 5.7 | 55.3 | 0.0 | 2.3 |
| 7.4 | 1.18 | 4.3 | 0.43 | 3.4 | 0.0 | 0.22 | 2.57 | 3.55 | 94.6 | 5.8 | 28.7 | 0.0 | 1.7 |
| 6.9 | 0.76 | 4.0 | 0.58 | 1.0 | -0.1 | -0.45 | -5.08 | 3.62 | 97.6 | 4.8 | 14.6 | 1.0 | 3.9 |
| 8.0 | 0.78 | 5.5 | 0.58 | 3.8 | 4.7 | 0.45 | 3.66 | 3.24 | 80.7 | 3.7 | 13.6 | 4.9 | 8.3 |
| 4.8 | 1.30 | 8.5 | 1.81 | 3.9 | 0.0 | 0.28 | 2.69 | 5.92 | 69.9 | 3.6 | 16.1 | 0.0 | 5.1 |
| 8.5 | 0.30 | 0.3 | 0.00 | 1.5 | 0.0 | 0.00 | 0.00 | 8.64 | 100.0 | 6.9 | 65.8 | 0.0 | 5.9 |
| 7.0 | 8.78 | 12.2 | 0.00 | 0.0 | 0.0 | -1.05 | -6.97 | 2.99 | 134.2 | 6.8 | 52.7 | 0.0 | 5.4 |
| 9.8 | 0.79 | 2.0 | 0.02 | 2.7 | 0.1 | 0.39 | 3.30 | 2.89 | 86.1 | 4.4 | 7.0 | 2.8 | 5.7 |
| 9.5 | 1.79 | 2.9 | 0.42 | 0.4 | 0.0 | -0.38 | -2.07 | 3.88 | 108.8 | 6.1 | 36.1 | 0.0 | 5.3 |
| 0.3 | 19.33 | 74.7 | 8.96 | 2.1 | 0.0 | -0.29 | -2.29 | 6.37 | 84.4 | 5.4 | 29.4 | 3.4 | 4.8 |
| 5.0 | 2.62 | 10.6 | 0.50 | 3.6 | 0.0 | 0.29 | 2.44 | 4.64 | 72.9 | 5.5 | 24.7 | 0.0 | 5.5 |
| 10.0 | 1.36 | 0.5 | 4.05 | 2.1 | 0.0 | 0.12 | 0.51 | 1.27 | 93.1 | 5.3 | 19.4 | 0.0 | 6.7 |
| 1.7 | 3.78 | 37.7 | -0.05 | 1.0 | 0.0 | -0.41 | -5.89 | 4.56 | 108.8 | 4.1 | 17.0 | 0.0 | 1.0 |
| 9.3 | 0.89 | 2.1 | -0.03 | 2.9 | 0.0 | 0.28 | 1.98 | 2.79 | 90.5 | 5.1 | 16.2 | 0.0 | 7.0 |
| 1.9 | 7.36 | 26.2 | 6.30 | 1.3 | -0.1 | -3.48 | -19.73 | 6.56 | 99.5 | 6.3 | 47.6 | 0.0 | 6.0 |
| 9.8 | 0.72 | 1.6 | 0.25 | 2.1 | 0.0 | 0.27 | 1.87 | 2.80 | 87.9 | 5.4 | 31.3 | 0.0 | 6.5 |
| 8.6 | 0.06 | 0.2 | -0.66 | 0.3 | 0.0 | -0.42 | -2.68 | 2.80 | 134.5 | 4.9 | 19.7 | 0.0 | 5.4 |
| 2.3 | 8.19 | 31.9 | 0.31 | 0.0 | -0.1 | -2.68 | -15.63 | 4.09 | 163.0 | 4.6 | 14.3 | 0.0 | 5.2 |
| 9.4 | 0.55 | 3.2 | 0.11 | 3.4 | 0.1 | 0.30 | 2.71 | 3.54 | 91.4 | 3.5 | 19.8 | 5.4 | 6.2 |
| 5.2 | 3.14 | 11.7 | 0.45 | 2.5 | 0.1 | 0.38 | 5.57 | 2.81 | 84.2 | 6.3 | 33.0 | 0.0 | 1.7 |
| 8.4 | 1.08 | 5.6 | 0.07 | 3.4 | 0.6 | 0.51 | 5.44 | 2.92 | 85.3 | 4.2 | 9.9 | 0.6 | 5.4 |
| 0.7 | 3.41 | 42.0 | 0.00 | 3.8 | 0.0 | 0.20 | 1.74 | 8.53 | 95.1 | 4.6 | 19.6 | 0.0 | 5.8 |
| 9.7 | 0.42 | 0.9 | 0.09 | 5.1 | 0.0 | 0.93 | 3.96 | 3.84 | 77.0 | 5.1 | 55.5 | 0.0 | 5.0 |
| 7.0 | 2.82 | 8.5 | 1.04 | 1.6 | 0.1 | 0.23 | 2.02 | 2.49 | 87.1 | 4.6 | 17.2 | 4.6 | 4.8 |
| 8.8 | 0.28 | 1.6 | 0.04 | 3.4 | 0.1 | 0.36 | 4.52 | 3.77 | 92.5 | 4.6 | 19.3 | 0.0 | 4.3 |
| 4.3 | 3.06 | 19.6 | -0.02 | 2.9 | 0.0 | 0.31 | 4.64 | 2.52 | 89.8 | 5.3 | 43.1 | 0.0 | 0.7 |
| 9.6 | 0.15 | 0.8 | 0.13 | 8.8 | 1.1 | 1.28 | 9.07 | 4.69 | 68.0 | 4.0 | 17.7 | 6.2 | 9.2 |
| 7.4 | 3.47 | 9.0 | 0.41 | 1.3 | 0.0 | 0.01 | 0.09 | 2.46 | 100.4 | 5.4 | 16.9 | 0.0 | 5.0 |
| 8.8 | 0.77 | 2.0 | 2.20 | 4.2 | 0.0 | 0.47 | 4.92 | 5.43 | 40.8 | 8.1 | 81.0 | 0.0 | 4.3 |
| 4.7 | 1.34 | 8.9 | 1.13 | 3.1 | 0.1 | 0.25 | 2.82 | 4.51 | 83.9 | 3.4 | 12.9 | 14.8 | 3.2 |
| 4.9 | 1.90 | 8.0 | 1.53 | 4.3 | 0.0 | 0.43 | 4.22 | 4.19 | 66.9 | 4.4 | 17.9 | 0.0 | 3.0 |
| 8.8 | 1.28 | 4.1 | 0.16 | 1.6 | 0.0 | 0.01 | 0.06 | 2.40 | 96.9 | 4.9 | 30.0 | 0.0 | 6.7 |
| 10.0 | 0.12 | 0.2 | 0.04 | 3.1 | 0.1 | 0.56 | 4.65 | 1.22 | 78.8 | 5.6 | 11.9 | 0.0 | 5.7 |
| 9.1 | 0.48 | 2.2 | 0.24 | 2.6 | 0.1 | 0.19 | 2.18 | 3.30 | 95.4 | 5.6 | 34.2 | 1.2 | 3.1 |
| 6.3 | 0.36 | 2.7 | 0.17 | 7.7 | 0.1 | 1.02 | 10.51 | 4.50 | 73.6 | 3.8 | 26.1 | 8.2 | 5.0 |
| 9.9 | 0.19 | 0.5 | 2.61 | 1.3 | 0.0 | -0.08 | -0.66 | 2.78 | 111.6 | 5.5 | 25.1 | 0.0 | 5.0 |
| 10.0 | 0.03 | 0.1 | 0.78 | 0.0 | -0.2 | -0.95 | -8.22 | 2.53 | 116.1 | 5.2 | 23.1 | 2.1 | 4.6 |
| 4.2 | 1.91 | 13.9 | 0.20 | 1.0 | 0.0 | -0.55 | -7.44 | 5.52 | 104.9 | 5.3 | 40.2 | 0.0 | 2.4 |
| 7.5 | 0.00 | 0.0 | 0.49 | 0.4 | 0.0 | -1.26 | -15.17 | 6.53 | 119.3 | 4.3 | 17.9 | 0.0 | 2.5 |
| 4.6 | 0.98 | 7.6 | 0.38 | 5.3 | 0.0 | 0.59 | 6.53 | 3.05 | 66.3 | 4.0 | 21.1 | 0.0 | 2.3 |
| 10.0 | 0.01 | 0.0 | 0.37 | 3.6 | 0.2 | 0.48 | 3.99 | 2.81 | 80.0 | 4.4 | 14.9 | 6.7 | 6.2 |
| 8.7 | 0.00 | 0.0 | -0.04 | 6.7 | 0.2 | 0.91 | 6.88 | 3.39 | 65.0 | 4.2 | 28.0 | 5.1 | 7.8 |
| 3.0 | 1.95 | 25.8 | 0.52 | 3.7 | -0.1 | -0.04 | -0.31 | 4.10 | 80.1 | 2.0 | 5.4 | 16.3 | 8.1 |
| 6.8 | 2.22 | 4.1 | 0.00 | 0.5 | 0.0 | -0.45 | -1.74 | 4.34 | 108.0 | 5.3 | 28.3 | 0.0 | 6.0 |
| 7.4 | 0.76 | 4.2 | 0.19 | 3.3 | 0.3 | 0.42 | 5.64 | 3.14 | 87.7 | 5.0 | 23.0 | 1.5 | 2.9 |
| 9.5 | 0.00 | 0.0 | 0.00 | 2.0 | 0.0 | 0.13 | 0.56 | 4.07 | 101.9 | 6.1 | 44.2 | 0.0 | 6.4 |
| 6.2 | 2.14 | 9.6 | 0.45 | 1.1 | -0.1 | -0.11 | -1.06 | 3.27 | 98.5 | 4.2 | 23.4 | 5.4 | 5.4 |
| 9.6 | 1.58 | 3.1 | 0.16 | 7.4 | 0.1 | 1.19 | 8.82 | 1.56 | 56.0 | 6.5 | 80.7 | 0.0 | 5.7 |
| 9.2 | 0.53 | 2.8 | 0.24 | 3.1 | 0.4 | 0.47 | 4.97 | 3.21 | 86.0 | 3.9 | 6.7 | 3.3 | 6.1 |
| 9.9 | 0.74 | 1.3 | -0.09 | 0.0 | -0.1 | -1.13 | -2.42 | 3.94 | 128.0 | 6.7 | 75.6 | 0.0 | 5.8 |
| 5.7 | 0.10 | 11.0 | 0.08 | 4.3 | 0.9 | 0.63 | 7.59 | 3.49 | 85.4 | 3.4 | 15.9 | 6.1 | 5.5 |
| 6.0 | 1.18 | 10.4 | 0.48 | 5.5 | 2.5 | 0.71 | 7.88 | 3.69 | 74.7 | 2.6 | 10.8 | 13.0 | 6.7 |
| 7.5 | 0.36 | 3.3 | 0.27 | 3.0 | 0.1 | 0.22 | 2.54 | 3.28 | 88.9 | 3.5 | 19.1 | 14.9 | 4.3 |

| Name | City | State | Rating | 2014 Rating | 2013 Rating | Total Assets ($Mil) | One Year Asset Growth | Asset Mix (As a % of Total Assets) | | | | Capital-ization Index | Net Worth Ratio |
|------|------|-------|--------|-------------|-------------|---------|--------|-----------|-----------|-----------|-----------|--------|--------|
| | | | | | | | | Comm-ercial Loans | Cons-umer Loans | Mort-gage Loans | Secur-ities | | |
| NORTH DISTRICTS COMMUNITY CU | Gibsonia | PA | B- | B- | B- | 33.7 | 3.94 | 0.0 | 23.6 | 0.0 | 0.0 | 9.2 | 10.5 |
| NORTH EAST KENTUCKY CAP FCU | Olive Hill | KY | D | D | C- | <1 | -17.20 | 0.0 | 14.1 | 0.0 | 0.0 | 10.0 | 14.8 |
| NORTH EAST TEXAS CU | Lone Star | TX | B | B+ | A- | 146.8 | 8.53 | 7.6 | 18.9 | 23.4 | 21.9 | 9.6 | 10.8 |
| NORTH EAST WELCH FCU | North East | PA | C+ | C | C | 13.4 | 6.89 | 0.0 | 40.7 | 3.1 | 0.0 | 10.0 | 16.1 |
| NORTH FRANKLIN FCU | Malone | NY | B | B- | B | 50.1 | 10.80 | 0.0 | 33.6 | 10.8 | 0.0 | 10.0 | 12.8 |
| ▼ NORTH GEORGIA COMMUNITY FCU | Ringgold | GA | D+ | C- | C- | 18.2 | 28.22 | 0.0 | 54.5 | 4.9 | 0.0 | 9.3 | 10.6 |
| ▲ NORTH GEORGIA CU | Toccoa | GA | B | B- | C+ | 50.2 | 0.70 | 0.0 | 30.5 | 43.6 | 0.0 | 10.0 | 11.0 |
| NORTH IOWA COMMUNITY CU | Mason City | IA | C- | C- | C | 61.8 | -3.25 | 1.7 | 34.2 | 28.3 | 1.7 | 9.5 | 10.7 |
| NORTH ISLAND FINANCIAL CU | San Diego | CA | A- | A- | B+ | 1179.7 | 4.28 | 12.1 | 16.8 | 37.8 | 12.7 | 10.0 | 11.0 |
| NORTH JERSEY FCU | Totowa | NJ | C- | C | C- | 223.5 | 4.12 | 4.9 | 11.6 | 18.9 | 16.7 | 8.9 | 10.3 |
| NORTH LITTLE ROCK EDUCATORS FCU | North Little Rock | AR | D | D+ | C- | 1.1 | -8.33 | 0.0 | 11.7 | 0.0 | 0.0 | 10.0 | 14.4 |
| NORTH MEMORIAL FCU | Robbinsdale | MN | C | C | C | 35.4 | 0.80 | 0.0 | 33.3 | 10.4 | 3.5 | 8.5 | 10.0 |
| NORTH MISSISSIPPI HEALTH SERV EMPL FC | Tupelo | MS | C+ | C+ | B- | 13.2 | 1.53 | 0.0 | 28.9 | 0.0 | 0.0 | 10.0 | 11.7 |
| NORTH OLMSTED SCHOOL EMPL FCU | North Olmsted | OH | D+ | C- | D+ | 5.1 | 4.56 | 0.0 | 8.1 | 0.5 | 47.6 | 10.0 | 11.7 |
| ▲ NORTH PENN FCU | Colmar | PA | C- | D+ | D | 16.1 | 0.82 | 0.0 | 15.9 | 0.0 | 24.2 | 7.9 | 9.6 |
| NORTH PLATTE UNION PACIFIC EMPL CU | North Platte | NE | B | B | B | 31.2 | 11.89 | 0.0 | 41.8 | 0.0 | 9.3 | 10.0 | 16.3 |
| NORTH SANPETE FCU | Mount Pleasant | UT | C- | C- | C- | 1.1 | -1.90 | 0.0 | 67.4 | 0.0 | 0.0 | 10.0 | 20.5 |
| NORTH SHORE FCU | Silver Bay | MN | A | A | A | 144.4 | 1.57 | 8.6 | 7.1 | 63.6 | 2.7 | 10.0 | 15.1 |
| NORTH SHORE LIJ HEALTH SYSTEM FCU | Jericho | NY | C | C | C | 115.9 | 4.62 | 9.5 | 27.0 | 14.8 | 22.1 | 10.0 | 13.0 |
| NORTH SIDE COMMUNITY FCU | Chicago | IL | E+ | E+ | E- | 8.6 | -9.41 | 0.0 | 26.4 | 17.8 | 7.0 | 5.4 | 7.4 |
| NORTH STAR COMMUNITY CU | Cherokee | IA | B- | B- | B- | 82.0 | 4.55 | 1.4 | 32.2 | 17.4 | 7.1 | 8.5 | 10.0 |
| NORTH STAR COMMUNITY CU | Maddock | ND | A- | A- | A- | 165.0 | -0.80 | 47.6 | 13.3 | 26.5 | 1.5 | 10.0 | 13.4 |
| NORTH STAR CU | Cook | MN | B | B | B- | 33.0 | 6.98 | 11.0 | 18.5 | 56.9 | 0.0 | 9.1 | 10.4 |
| NORTH WESTERN EMPL CU | Council Bluffs | IA | C+ | C+ | C+ | 7.7 | -2.81 | 0.0 | 41.3 | 0.0 | 0.0 | 10.0 | 17.6 |
| NORTHAMPTON AREA SCHOOL DISTRICT EM | Northampton | PA | C | C+ | C+ | 8.4 | 5.26 | 0.0 | 30.2 | 0.0 | 0.0 | 10.0 | 15.2 |
| NORTHAMPTON VAF FCU | Leeds | MA | C- | D+ | C- | 7.5 | 3.25 | 0.0 | 26.9 | 0.0 | 0.0 | 10.0 | 12.8 |
| NORTHEAST ALABAMA POSTAL FCU | Anniston | AL | B- | B- | C+ | 12.6 | -3.06 | 0.0 | 28.4 | 36.2 | 0.0 | 10.0 | 17.8 |
| NORTHEAST ARKANSAS FCU | Blytheville | AR | B | B | B- | 106.1 | 2.56 | 0.0 | 50.7 | 21.7 | 5.6 | 7.9 | 9.6 |
| NORTHEAST COMMUNITY CU | Elizabethton | TN | A | A | A- | 106.2 | 3.83 | 0.4 | 19.7 | 61.8 | 0.0 | 10.0 | 13.6 |
| NORTHEAST COMMUNITY FCU | San Francisco | CA | C | C- | C- | 12.6 | 20.11 | 3.7 | 2.2 | 29.4 | 0.0 | 10.0 | 14.7 |
| NORTHEAST CU | Portsmouth | NH | B | B | B | 1067.9 | 6.01 | 1.1 | 63.8 | 17.2 | 0.0 | 9.1 | 10.4 |
| NORTHEAST FAMILY FCU | Manchester | CT | C+ | C+ | C+ | 73.5 | -0.10 | 0.8 | 13.3 | 20.8 | 5.7 | 7.8 | 9.5 |
| NORTHEAST MISSISSIPPI FCU | Amory | MS | C | C | C+ | 4.6 | -6.98 | 0.0 | 40.2 | 29.1 | 0.0 | 10.0 | 16.1 |
| ▲ NORTHEAST NEBRASKA FCU | Norfolk | NE | C- | D+ | C | 9.5 | -4.24 | 0.0 | 34.7 | 11.8 | 0.0 | 9.5 | 10.7 |
| NORTHEAST PANHANDLE TEACHERS FCU | Perryton | TX | C+ | C+ | C+ | 23.1 | -1.65 | 0.0 | 44.9 | 0.0 | 0.0 | 10.0 | 12.5 |
| NORTHEAST REGIONAL CU | Hannibal | MO | D+ | C- | C- | 1.3 | 12.90 | 0.0 | 71.1 | 0.0 | 0.0 | 10.0 | 13.1 |
| NORTHEAST SCHOOLS & HOSPITAL CU | Newport | VT | D+ | D | D- | 4.2 | -5.68 | 0.0 | 70.8 | 0.0 | 0.0 | 9.1 | 10.4 |
| NORTHEAST TEXAS TEACHERS FCU | Paris | TX | C+ | C | B- | 23.4 | 1.48 | 0.0 | 29.1 | 2.5 | 0.0 | 10.0 | 14.4 |
| NORTHEASTERN CT HEALTHCARE CU INC | Putnam | CT | C | C | C+ | 9.8 | -2.02 | 0.0 | 47.9 | 0.0 | 0.0 | 10.0 | 12.7 |
| ▲ NORTHEASTERN ENGINEERS FCU | Richmond Hill | NY | D+ | D- | D | 72.0 | 7.01 | 1.6 | 1.9 | 55.8 | 13.2 | 5.5 | 7.5 |
| NORTHEASTERN UNIV FCU | Boston | MA | D | E+ | E | 27.7 | -7.83 | 0.0 | 27.9 | 21.8 | 0.0 | 6.0 | 8.0 |
| NORTHERN CALIFORNIA LATVIAN CU | San Francisco | CA | D | D | D+ | 1.6 | -2.86 | 0.0 | 8.5 | 0.0 | 48.4 | 10.0 | 17.5 |
| ▲ NORTHERN CHAUTAUQUA FCU | Silver Creek | NY | D | D- | E+ | 3.9 | 4.84 | 0.0 | 41.4 | 0.0 | 33.8 | 7.4 | 9.2 |
| ▲ NORTHERN COLORADO CU | Greeley | CO | B- | C+ | B- | 46.8 | 2.10 | 14.9 | 17.0 | 36.3 | 6.4 | 10.0 | 12.9 |
| NORTHERN COMMUNITIES CU | Duluth | MN | D | D | D+ | 72.7 | 0.93 | 2.8 | 26.3 | 18.6 | 0.4 | 5.2 | 7.2 |
| ▲ NORTHERN EAGLE FCU | Nett Lake | MN | B- | D- | U | <1 | 74.83 | 0.0 | 21.9 | 0.0 | 0.0 | 10.0 | 13.4 |
| NORTHERN ENERGY FCU | Mankato | MN | C- | C- | C- | 2.2 | 32.84 | 0.0 | 85.9 | 0.0 | 0.0 | 10.0 | 13.8 |
| NORTHERN FCU | Watertown | NY | C | C | C | 211.2 | 4.14 | 1.9 | 17.2 | 35.3 | 0.0 | 5.1 | 7.1 |
| ▲ NORTHERN HILLS FCU | Sturgis | SD | C+ | C- | C- | 78.4 | -3.63 | 3.4 | 31.6 | 19.7 | 0.5 | 8.1 | 9.7 |
| NORTHERN INDIANA FCU | Merrillville | IN | D | D | D | 32.3 | 1.40 | 0.0 | 25.6 | 13.7 | 0.8 | 5.4 | 7.4 |
| NORTHERN KENTUCKY EDUCATORS FCU | Highland Heights | KY | D | D | D+ | 18.1 | 3.73 | 0.0 | 35.0 | 0.0 | 0.0 | 5.8 | 7.8 |
| NORTHERN LIGHTS CU | Saint Johnsbury | VT | D+ | C- | D+ | 20.3 | 8.48 | 0.0 | 39.4 | 2.7 | 0.0 | 7.2 | 9.1 |
| ▲ NORTHERN MONTANA HOSPITAL FCU | Havre | MT | C- | D+ | C- | <1 | 1.24 | 0.0 | 37.7 | 0.0 | 0.0 | 10.0 | 16.1 |
| NORTHERN NEW MEXICO SCHOOL EMPL FC | Santa Fe | NM | C- | D+ | D+ | 19.3 | 1.76 | 0.0 | 42.9 | 0.0 | 0.0 | 7.2 | 9.1 |
| NORTHERN PACIFIC DULUTH FCU | Duluth | MN | D | D | C- | 2.3 | -5.78 | 0.0 | 63.5 | 0.0 | 0.0 | 10.0 | 25.3 |
| NORTHERN PAPER MILLS CU | Green Bay | WI | C- | C | C+ | 23.2 | -4.62 | 0.0 | 14.8 | 50.6 | 0.0 | 10.0 | 18.5 |
| NORTHERN PIEDMONT FCU | Warrenton | VA | D- | D- | D | 18.8 | 3.92 | 0.0 | 36.0 | 6.1 | 0.0 | 0.9 | 4.1 |
| NORTHERN REDWOOD FCU | Arcata | CA | D | D- | D- | 18.5 | 5.37 | 1.0 | 39.6 | 14.9 | 0.0 | 5.5 | 7.5 |
| NORTHERN SKIES FCU | Anchorage | AK | B+ | B+ | B | 90.6 | 11.70 | 0.0 | 46.5 | 2.4 | 0.8 | 9.1 | 10.4 |
| NORTHERN STAR CU INC | Portsmouth | VA | B- | B- | C+ | 82.2 | 0.24 | 8.2 | 25.7 | 11.6 | 22.7 | 10.0 | 11.9 |

| Asset Quality Index | Non-Performing Loans as a % of Total Loans | as a % of Capital | Net Charge-Offs Avg Loans | Profitability Index | Net Income ($Mil) | Return on Assets | Return on Equity | Net Interest Spread | Overhead Efficiency Ratio | Liquidity Index | Liquidity Ratio | Hot Money Ratio | Stability Index |
|---|---|---|---|---|---|---|---|---|---|---|---|---|---|
| 6.6 | 1.56 | 7.9 | 0.17 | 3.5 | 0.1 | 0.45 | 4.33 | 3.29 | 80.2 | 5.4 | 38.8 | 1.4 | 6.2 |
| 9.0 | 0.00 | 0.0 | 9.09 | 0.0 | 0.0 | -1.30 | -8.89 | 1.77 | 200.0 | 8.1 | 96.3 | 0.0 | 6.2 |
| 8.1 | 0.36 | 4.1 | 0.24 | 4.2 | 0.5 | 0.45 | 4.19 | 3.77 | 90.5 | 4.4 | 15.8 | 5.9 | 7.2 |
| 7.8 | 1.19 | 3.8 | 0.47 | 2.3 | 0.0 | 0.12 | 0.75 | 3.24 | 87.2 | 4.5 | 28.5 | 0.0 | 6.6 |
| 9.2 | 0.43 | 2.2 | 0.65 | 4.6 | 0.3 | 0.74 | 5.70 | 3.79 | 72.4 | 5.7 | 49.9 | 4.1 | 6.6 |
| 2.9 | 1.74 | 18.6 | 0.26 | 1.6 | -0.1 | -0.45 | -4.58 | 5.43 | 107.8 | 4.7 | 20.6 | 0.0 | 3.8 |
| 7.0 | 0.79 | 9.3 | 0.79 | 6.5 | 0.3 | 0.85 | 8.02 | 5.93 | 77.8 | 3.5 | 15.2 | 9.2 | 5.2 |
| 2.8 | 1.88 | 18.4 | 0.52 | 2.1 | 0.0 | 0.06 | 0.57 | 4.02 | 89.4 | 2.7 | 14.4 | 12.0 | 5.1 |
| 7.1 | 0.90 | 5.3 | 0.13 | 6.7 | 7.8 | 0.89 | 8.25 | 3.41 | 81.4 | 4.3 | 14.1 | 2.3 | 8.6 |
| 6.2 | 2.14 | 13.8 | 0.65 | 1.9 | 0.0 | 0.02 | 0.21 | 3.62 | 91.7 | 4.6 | 27.5 | 7.4 | 5.3 |
| 7.9 | 5.52 | 4.8 | -0.81 | 0.0 | 0.0 | -1.44 | -10.26 | 3.69 | 180.0 | 8.3 | 98.9 | 0.0 | 6.1 |
| 7.1 | 0.47 | 3.2 | 0.13 | 2.8 | 0.1 | 0.36 | 3.63 | 4.07 | 90.8 | 3.4 | 16.2 | 6.5 | 4.3 |
| 10.0 | 0.00 | 0.0 | 0.47 | 2.9 | 0.0 | 0.37 | 3.05 | 2.11 | 74.0 | 6.9 | 78.9 | 0.0 | 5.7 |
| 6.6 | 7.30 | 13.7 | 0.00 | 1.3 | 0.0 | -0.08 | -0.66 | 3.21 | 102.9 | 6.9 | 43.7 | 0.0 | 5.3 |
| 7.8 | 1.48 | 3.8 | 0.33 | 2.4 | 0.0 | 0.33 | 3.49 | 2.46 | 89.2 | 5.7 | 39.1 | 0.0 | 3.9 |
| 8.0 | 1.22 | 3.7 | 0.01 | 4.8 | 0.2 | 0.73 | 4.40 | 2.49 | 75.1 | 4.6 | 19.2 | 1.3 | 7.5 |
| 7.0 | 0.58 | 2.1 | 0.00 | 3.4 | 0.0 | 0.48 | 2.42 | 3.40 | 82.6 | 4.6 | 23.0 | 0.0 | 6.6 |
| 6.8 | 0.54 | 8.1 | 0.19 | 7.6 | 1.2 | 1.09 | 7.21 | 3.53 | 70.1 | 3.6 | 16.5 | 7.1 | 9.9 |
| 5.9 | 2.53 | 12.4 | 0.43 | 2.9 | 0.1 | 0.13 | 1.04 | 3.71 | 85.1 | 4.1 | 11.2 | 1.2 | 7.7 |
| 0.3 | 8.93 | 93.7 | 2.75 | 0.1 | -0.1 | -2.08 | -57.14 | 4.23 | 105.0 | 3.6 | 15.1 | 9.9 | 1.1 |
| 6.7 | 0.75 | 5.3 | 0.65 | 4.3 | 0.4 | 0.66 | 6.77 | 2.93 | 77.5 | 3.5 | 17.0 | 9.2 | 5.1 |
| 4.0 | 1.96 | 11.6 | 0.12 | 6.5 | 1.1 | 0.92 | 7.31 | 3.98 | 74.6 | 2.8 | 8.7 | 9.6 | 8.9 |
| 7.9 | 0.27 | 2.2 | -0.03 | 8.3 | 0.3 | 1.07 | 10.30 | 4.51 | 76.7 | 2.2 | 8.8 | 13.0 | 6.3 |
| 9.6 | 0.16 | 0.4 | 0.23 | 6.2 | 0.1 | 0.97 | 5.72 | 4.25 | 74.4 | 6.5 | 65.6 | 0.0 | 5.0 |
| 8.5 | 2.05 | 6.6 | 0.25 | 4.7 | 0.0 | 0.68 | 4.48 | 2.33 | 68.1 | 4.4 | 16.9 | 0.0 | 4.3 |
| 9.9 | 0.29 | 0.7 | 0.17 | 1.6 | 0.0 | 0.06 | 0.42 | 1.52 | 94.9 | 5.0 | 28.6 | 0.0 | 5.7 |
| 8.7 | 0.18 | 3.3 | 0.00 | 6.0 | 0.1 | 0.97 | 5.67 | 3.46 | 67.5 | 4.0 | 43.0 | 14.5 | 5.7 |
| 5.9 | 0.68 | 6.1 | 0.22 | 5.6 | 0.6 | 0.77 | 8.88 | 3.51 | 76.4 | 3.8 | 10.9 | 3.1 | 6.3 |
| 6.1 | 1.83 | 12.6 | 0.13 | 9.2 | 1.0 | 1.22 | 9.16 | 3.80 | 66.9 | 3.5 | 13.5 | 5.9 | 10.0 |
| 6.4 | 4.09 | 14.5 | 0.43 | 3.0 | 0.0 | 0.39 | 2.79 | 3.66 | 83.3 | 4.7 | 61.8 | 37.7 | 5.3 |
| 6.9 | 0.41 | 3.5 | 0.39 | 4.8 | 4.8 | 0.61 | 6.11 | 2.73 | 72.3 | 2.0 | 10.1 | 14.4 | 8.1 |
| 7.0 | 0.75 | 4.4 | 0.92 | 2.9 | 0.2 | 0.26 | 2.80 | 3.16 | 86.8 | 4.2 | 14.8 | 1.3 | 4.2 |
| 4.7 | 3.54 | 18.0 | 0.31 | 9.3 | 0.0 | 1.24 | 7.81 | 5.52 | 76.6 | 3.7 | 26.1 | 0.0 | 4.3 |
| 8.2 | 0.18 | 0.9 | 0.88 | 3.3 | 0.0 | 0.37 | 3.63 | 4.46 | 88.4 | 5.6 | 34.7 | 0.0 | 5.9 |
| 9.6 | 0.01 | 0.0 | -0.04 | 2.8 | 0.1 | 0.33 | 2.76 | 1.76 | 80.7 | 5.2 | 50.1 | 0.0 | 6.2 |
| 2.8 | 3.19 | 17.9 | 0.00 | 3.8 | 0.0 | 0.10 | 0.78 | 6.18 | 94.6 | 4.1 | 26.4 | 0.0 | 5.3 |
| 4.3 | 0.56 | 3.3 | 1.57 | 7.7 | 0.0 | 1.16 | 12.12 | 7.90 | 70.3 | 5.4 | 31.5 | 0.0 | 3.7 |
| 8.4 | 1.86 | 5.0 | 0.10 | 2.3 | 0.0 | 0.04 | 0.28 | 2.94 | 98.0 | 6.3 | 52.8 | 0.0 | 6.7 |
| 8.7 | 0.36 | 1.4 | 0.38 | 2.5 | 0.0 | 0.23 | 1.84 | 2.76 | 86.4 | 4.3 | 27.9 | 0.0 | 6.3 |
| 3.5 | 3.28 | 28.4 | 0.09 | 3.7 | 0.3 | 0.56 | 7.38 | 3.08 | 81.1 | 4.9 | 21.2 | 0.0 | 2.9 |
| 4.6 | 2.72 | 16.3 | 0.45 | 2.5 | 0.0 | 0.08 | 1.06 | 3.71 | 88.0 | 4.1 | 25.1 | 0.0 | 2.3 |
| 7.5 | 12.93 | 6.1 | 0.00 | 0.0 | 0.0 | -1.35 | -7.66 | 1.14 | 253.9 | 6.2 | 44.5 | 0.0 | 6.2 |
| 4.4 | 2.78 | 17.0 | -2.71 | 7.1 | 0.0 | 1.36 | 16.22 | 2.49 | 105.8 | 4.2 | 24.1 | 0.0 | 3.0 |
| 9.5 | 0.01 | 0.9 | 0.00 | 3.5 | 0.2 | 0.49 | 3.80 | 3.29 | 85.6 | 3.8 | 18.2 | 4.0 | 6.4 |
| 6.2 | 0.48 | 5.4 | 0.75 | 1.7 | 0.1 | 0.16 | 2.26 | 3.69 | 91.1 | 3.9 | 10.4 | 1.1 | 1.5 |
| 7.7 | 1.74 | 4.6 | 2.32 | 10.0 | 0.0 | 3.08 | 23.61 | 12.75 | 86.2 | 7.3 | 63.1 | 0.0 | 3.1 |
| 7.4 | 0.66 | 4.0 | -0.17 | 2.9 | 0.0 | -0.07 | -0.43 | 4.45 | 103.5 | 3.8 | 13.9 | 0.0 | 5.8 |
| 5.2 | 0.82 | 11.7 | 0.47 | 4.1 | 0.8 | 0.48 | 6.84 | 4.94 | 85.9 | 3.3 | 7.2 | 0.0 | 4.1 |
| 7.8 | 0.39 | 3.0 | 0.10 | 4.5 | 0.4 | 0.76 | 8.00 | 3.73 | 82.9 | 3.7 | 10.2 | 3.3 | 4.2 |
| 3.6 | 3.55 | 20.1 | 1.16 | 2.4 | 0.0 | 0.13 | 1.78 | 2.98 | 83.5 | 4.9 | 31.1 | 0.0 | 2.3 |
| 8.0 | 0.48 | 2.4 | 0.34 | 2.2 | 0.0 | 0.10 | 1.33 | 2.74 | 92.7 | 5.5 | 31.6 | 0.0 | 2.9 |
| 5.5 | 0.60 | 6.8 | 0.16 | 4.3 | 0.1 | 0.48 | 5.19 | 4.77 | 89.0 | 3.6 | 11.1 | 4.3 | 3.7 |
| 3.4 | 11.38 | 26.7 | 4.54 | 5.6 | 0.0 | 0.83 | 4.89 | 5.78 | 75.0 | 7.2 | 58.9 | 0.0 | 6.4 |
| 9.3 | 0.31 | 1.6 | -0.01 | 3.4 | 0.1 | 0.43 | 4.75 | 3.94 | 93.5 | 4.5 | 10.4 | 0.0 | 3.9 |
| 7.8 | 0.51 | 1.4 | 0.50 | 0.0 | 0.0 | -1.27 | -5.05 | 5.28 | 119.1 | 4.6 | 28.7 | 0.0 | 5.6 |
| 9.4 | 0.00 | 0.0 | 0.47 | 1.4 | 0.0 | -0.09 | -0.50 | 3.26 | 102.8 | 3.9 | 25.7 | 1.7 | 7.0 |
| 4.6 | 1.22 | 14.1 | 0.63 | 7.5 | 0.2 | 1.50 | 43.74 | 4.68 | 78.6 | 5.5 | 23.4 | 0.0 | 0.3 |
| 7.2 | 0.00 | 2.7 | 0.18 | 1.4 | 0.0 | -0.18 | -2.28 | 4.65 | 100.0 | 5.2 | 33.8 | 0.0 | 3.0 |
| 5.3 | 0.42 | 4.2 | 0.49 | 10.0 | 0.9 | 1.36 | 13.37 | 5.03 | 69.5 | 1.1 | 13.6 | 42.9 | 5.9 |
| 3.7 | 1.46 | 26.2 | 0.73 | 4.1 | 0.3 | 0.46 | 3.85 | 6.06 | 84.7 | 4.6 | 14.2 | 2.0 | 4.9 |

| Name | City | State | Rating | 2014 Rating | 2013 Rating | Total Assets ($Mil) | One Year Asset Growth | Comm-ercial Loans | Cons-umer Loans | Mort-gage Loans | Secur-ities | Capital-ization Index | Net Worth Ratio |
|---|---|---|---|---|---|---|---|---|---|---|---|---|---|
| | | | | | | | | Asset Mix (As a % of Total Assets) | | | | | |
| NORTHERN STATES POWER CO EMPL FCU | Grand Forks | ND | D | D- | D | 1.4 | -3.39 | 0.0 | 35.7 | 5.0 | 0.0 | 6.5 | 8.6 |
| NORTHERN STATES POWER ST PAUL CU | Saint Paul | MN | C+ | C+ | C | 47.2 | -2.76 | 0.0 | 27.8 | 18.8 | 23.0 | 10.0 | 13.1 |
| NORTHERN TIER FCU | Minot | ND | B- | B- | C | 116.5 | 5.56 | 9.7 | 33.4 | 5.5 | 9.5 | 7.5 | 9.3 |
| NORTHERN UNITED FCU | Escanaba | MI | C | C- | C- | 19.9 | 3.94 | 0.0 | 22.8 | 18.9 | 11.2 | 10.0 | 15.3 |
| NORTHERN VALLEY FCU | Grand Forks | ND | C | C | C | 14.6 | 5.07 | 0.0 | 32.4 | 1.8 | 0.0 | 8.6 | 10.0 |
| NORTHLAND AREA FCU | Oscoda | MI | B+ | A- | B | 310.6 | 8.23 | 10.5 | 20.5 | 42.6 | 18.7 | 9.4 | 10.6 |
| NORTHLAND TEACHERS COMMUNITY CU | Gladstone | MO | C- | C- | C- | 10.2 | 3.54 | 0.0 | 18.3 | 0.0 | 0.0 | 10.0 | 12.7 |
| ▼ NORTHPARK COMMUNITY CU | Indianapolis | IN | D- | D+ | D+ | 61.4 | 1.90 | 0.4 | 61.2 | 5.1 | 0.1 | 5.0 | 7.0 |
| NORTHRIDGE COMMUNITY CU | Hoyt Lakes | MN | B | B | B | 37.7 | 3.13 | 0.7 | 31.6 | 27.7 | 16.5 | 10.0 | 13.6 |
| NORTHROP GRUMMAN FCU | Gardena | CA | B | B | B+ | 1001.2 | 4.21 | 0.7 | 16.6 | 20.4 | 45.8 | 10.0 | 11.8 |
| NORTHSIDE FCU | Atlanta | GA | D | C- | C- | 13.4 | 5.36 | 0.0 | 45.4 | 0.0 | 0.0 | 8.6 | 10.1 |
| NORTHSIDE L FCU | Broadview | IL | D | D+ | D+ | 6.7 | -14.76 | 0.0 | 55.2 | 0.0 | 0.0 | 10.0 | 21.7 |
| ▲ NORTHSTAR CU | Warrenville | IL | B | C | C | 103.4 | 4.50 | 11.1 | 43.0 | 17.0 | 2.3 | 8.2 | 9.8 |
| NORTHUMBERLAND COUNTY SCHOOLS FCU | Milton | PA | C+ | C+ | C | 18.1 | 0.37 | 0.0 | 30.4 | 32.2 | 18.6 | 10.0 | 11.3 |
| NORTHWEST ADVENTIST FCU | Portland | OR | C+ | C | C | 28.8 | -1.25 | 0.0 | 25.6 | 37.9 | 1.7 | 7.4 | 9.2 |
| ▲ NORTHWEST ARKANSAS FCU | Fayetteville | AR | D- | E+ | E | 10.9 | 14.25 | 0.0 | 59.6 | 0.0 | 0.0 | 5.2 | 7.2 |
| NORTHWEST CHRISTIAN CU | Nampa | ID | B- | B- | B | 49.9 | 14.72 | 30.0 | 11.4 | 37.2 | 0.0 | 8.9 | 10.2 |
| NORTHWEST COMMUNITY CU | Morton Grove | IL | D+ | D+ | D+ | 59.7 | -2.12 | 0.8 | 15.4 | 35.5 | 17.1 | 9.2 | 10.4 |
| NORTHWEST COMMUNITY CU | Eugene | OR | B | B | B | 976.1 | 8.30 | 8.9 | 43.6 | 21.3 | 2.4 | 7.9 | 9.6 |
| NORTHWEST CONSUMERS FCU | Traverse City | MI | C | C- | D+ | 17.8 | 3.51 | 1.0 | 41.0 | 28.2 | 0.0 | 9.9 | 10.9 |
| NORTHWEST FCU | Herndon | VA | B | B | A- | 2967.9 | 14.24 | 5.6 | 36.3 | 18.6 | 30.9 | 7.7 | 9.7 |
| NORTHWEST GEORGIA CU | Rome | GA | C | C | C- | 74.2 | 9.29 | 0.0 | 43.8 | 7.6 | 0.0 | 7.3 | 9.2 |
| NORTHWEST HILLS CU | Torrington | CT | D- | D- | D- | 31.1 | -3.43 | 0.0 | 25.9 | 12.1 | 0.0 | 5.1 | 7.1 |
| NORTHWEST LOUISIANA FCU | Shreveport | LA | C | C+ | C+ | 10.6 | 3.35 | 0.0 | 40.2 | 12.7 | 0.0 | 10.0 | 30.6 |
| NORTHWEST MISSOURI REGIONAL CU | Maryville | MO | D | D | D | 8.6 | 12.69 | 0.0 | 57.8 | 0.2 | 0.0 | 6.3 | 8.3 |
| NORTHWEST MUNICIPAL FCU | Des Plaines | IL | C | C | C | 28.2 | 5.69 | 0.0 | 28.0 | 0.0 | 0.0 | 6.6 | 8.6 |
| NORTHWEST PLUS CU | Everett | WA | B+ | B | B | 164.3 | 5.36 | 2.2 | 29.6 | 30.4 | 15.3 | 10.0 | 11.4 |
| NORTHWEST UNITED FCU | Arvada | CO | C+ | C+ | C+ | 83.3 | 3.86 | 0.0 | 12.6 | 18.6 | 2.4 | 6.9 | 8.9 |
| NORTHWESTERN ENERGY EMPL FCU | Butte | MT | D | C- | C- | 31.1 | 3.07 | 0.0 | 24.8 | 0.0 | 10.7 | 8.9 | 10.3 |
| NORTHWESTERN FCU | Bryan | OH | D+ | D+ | D | 11.3 | 0.96 | 0.0 | 31.9 | 0.0 | 0.0 | 8.1 | 9.7 |
| NORTHWESTERN MUTUAL CU | Milwaukee | WI | B | B | B+ | 148.4 | 4.75 | 0.0 | 5.7 | 31.3 | 34.6 | 10.0 | 11.7 |
| NORTHWOOD FCU | Philadelphia | PA | C+ | C+ | C | 11.7 | -9.65 | 2.9 | 1.9 | 21.0 | 42.0 | 10.0 | 12.2 |
| NORTHWOODS COMMUNITY CU | Park Falls | WI | D | C- | C | 75.0 | -3.20 | 6.8 | 29.2 | 23.8 | 5.9 | 9.9 | 10.9 |
| NORTHWOODS CU | Cloquet | MN | B+ | B | B | 78.1 | 4.28 | 0.0 | 33.6 | 25.7 | 0.0 | 10.0 | 11.8 |
| NORTON-TROY EMPL CU | Watervliet | NY | D+ | D+ | D+ | 8.3 | -6.30 | 0.0 | 10.6 | 18.3 | 0.0 | 10.0 | 11.8 |
| NORWALK HOSPITAL CU | Norwalk | CT | D+ | D | C- | 34.0 | -3.02 | 0.0 | 10.2 | 0.0 | 12.2 | 8.0 | 9.7 |
| NORWALK POSTAL EMPL FCU | Norwalk | CT | D | D+ | D+ | <1 | -10.70 | 0.0 | 57.0 | 0.0 | 0.0 | 5.6 | 7.6 |
| NORWESCO CU | Saint Francis | KS | C | C | B- | <1 | -31.08 | 0.0 | 66.7 | 0.0 | 0.0 | 10.0 | 26.5 |
| NORWICH TELOPS FCU | Norwich | NY | C- | C- | D+ | 7.4 | 7.67 | 0.0 | 54.1 | 0.0 | 0.0 | 10.0 | 11.1 |
| NORWIN TEACHERS FCU | North Huntingdon | PA | D | D | D | 22.7 | 3.66 | 0.0 | 21.4 | 0.0 | 0.0 | 6.2 | 8.3 |
| NORWOOD TOWN EMPL FCU | Norwood | MA | C+ | C+ | C | 4.8 | 2.77 | 0.0 | 55.7 | 0.0 | 0.0 | 10.0 | 22.8 |
| NOTEWORTHY FCU | Cleveland | OH | D | D+ | D | 2.3 | 2.97 | 9.4 | 8.2 | 0.0 | 0.0 | 6.4 | 8.4 |
| NOTRE DAME 2901 FCU | Baltimore | MD | C- | C- | D+ | 1.8 | -2.23 | 0.0 | 12.0 | 0.0 | 0.0 | 10.0 | 11.2 |
| NOTRE DAME COMMUNITY FCU | Fall River | MA | C | C | C | 46.6 | 0.50 | 3.7 | 4.1 | 30.4 | 42.9 | 10.0 | 12.7 |
| ▲ NOTRE DAME FCU | Notre Dame | IN | C | C- | D+ | 467.0 | 0.04 | 1.6 | 24.6 | 32.7 | 8.6 | 5.8 | 7.9 |
| ▼ NOVAMONT EMPL FCU | Kenova | WV | D+ | C- | C- | <1 | 4.00 | 0.0 | 49.6 | 0.0 | 0.0 | 10.0 | 18.6 |
| NOVARTIS FCU | East Hanover | NJ | C+ | C+ | B- | 130.9 | -1.46 | 0.0 | 5.2 | 11.1 | 16.4 | 7.1 | 9.1 |
| NOVATION CU | Oakdale | MN | B | B | B- | 111.3 | 5.62 | 0.0 | 32.2 | 30.8 | 4.0 | 6.3 | 8.4 |
| NOVO FCU | Norco | CA | C+ | C+ | C | 8.2 | -10.04 | 0.0 | 82.2 | 0.0 | 0.0 | 10.0 | 17.2 |
| NOXEN COMMUNITY FCU | Monroe Township | PA | C- | C | C- | 1.5 | -6.65 | 0.0 | 19.2 | 0.0 | 0.0 | 10.0 | 23.7 |
| ▲ NRL FCU | Alexandria | VA | C+ | C | C | 438.5 | -0.26 | 0.0 | 18.6 | 29.5 | 33.7 | 8.8 | 10.4 |
| NRS COMMUNITY DEVEL FCU | Birmingham | AL | C- | D | D- | 1.0 | 5.89 | 0.0 | 59.6 | 0.0 | 0.0 | 9.2 | 10.4 |
| NSWC FCU | Dahlgren | VA | D+ | D+ | D+ | 327.8 | 3.57 | 0.0 | 18.8 | 9.3 | 46.1 | 7.9 | 9.7 |
| NU COMMUNITY CU | Milton | PA | C- | C- | C- | 18.9 | 6.50 | 0.0 | 43.0 | 0.7 | 0.0 | 10.0 | 11.9 |
| NUCOR EMPL CU | Florence | SC | B | B | B | 32.7 | 3.68 | 0.0 | 58.4 | 1.3 | 0.0 | 10.0 | 16.3 |
| NUCOR EMPL FCU | Fort Payne | AL | C | C | C | 3.3 | 3.30 | 0.0 | 25.6 | 0.0 | 0.0 | 10.0 | 21.0 |
| NUEVA ESPERANZA COMMUNITY CU | Toledo | OH | D- | D- | E+ | 1.5 | -0.58 | 0.0 | 51.6 | 4.7 | 0.0 | 7.5 | 9.3 |
| NUL FCU | New York | NY | D+ | D+ | D+ | <1 | -0.22 | 0.0 | 7.8 | 0.0 | 0.0 | 10.0 | 15.9 |
| NUMARK CU | Joliet | IL | A- | A- | A- | 210.8 | 8.35 | 3.1 | 34.6 | 16.9 | 2.6 | 10.0 | 13.6 |
| NUMERICA CU | Spokane Valley | WA | A | A | A | 1538.3 | 11.92 | 16.9 | 35.5 | 25.5 | 7.4 | 10.0 | 11.1 |

| Asset Quality Index | Non-Performing Loans as a % of Total Loans | Non-Performing Loans as a % of Capital | Net Charge-Offs Avg Loans | Profitability Index | Net Income ($Mil) | Return on Assets | Return on Equity | Net Interest Spread | Overhead Efficiency Ratio | Liquidity Index | Liquidity Ratio | Hot Money Ratio | Stability Index |
|---|---|---|---|---|---|---|---|---|---|---|---|---|---|
| 9.6 | 0.00 | 0.0 | 0.00 | 3.7 | 0.0 | 0.54 | 6.72 | 1.78 | 66.7 | 4.6 | 34.4 | 0.0 | 3.0 |
| 7.0 | 1.55 | 7.8 | -0.03 | 2.7 | 0.1 | 0.20 | 1.69 | 3.09 | 104.8 | 4.0 | 19.3 | 3.7 | 5.2 |
| 5.7 | 0.61 | 5.4 | 0.46 | 5.3 | 0.6 | 0.74 | 8.33 | 3.41 | 70.3 | 2.6 | 16.1 | 17.9 | 5.8 |
| 8.4 | 1.33 | 4.3 | 0.03 | 2.2 | 0.0 | 0.18 | 1.19 | 4.04 | 93.8 | 5.8 | 29.9 | 1.6 | 6.6 |
| 9.5 | 0.07 | 0.4 | 0.02 | 3.0 | 0.0 | 0.32 | 3.14 | 3.18 | 90.0 | 4.5 | 28.6 | 4.8 | 5.6 |
| 8.2 | 0.76 | 5.1 | 0.22 | 6.5 | 2.1 | 0.92 | 8.81 | 3.96 | 75.5 | 3.9 | 9.7 | 3.4 | 7.3 |
| 10.0 | 0.48 | 1.2 | 0.66 | 1.6 | 0.0 | -0.09 | -0.72 | 3.73 | 92.7 | 5.3 | 37.9 | 4.3 | 6.3 |
| 1.8 | 1.92 | 24.4 | 0.68 | 1.1 | -0.2 | -0.33 | -4.76 | 4.37 | 87.1 | 2.8 | 4.5 | 3.0 | 2.8 |
| 7.3 | 0.66 | 5.3 | 0.13 | 5.4 | 0.2 | 0.76 | 5.74 | 3.90 | 83.8 | 3.9 | 11.4 | 2.7 | 7.1 |
| 9.6 | 0.62 | 2.6 | 0.30 | 4.2 | 3.7 | 0.50 | 4.57 | 2.48 | 77.9 | 4.0 | 23.5 | 11.4 | 7.8 |
| 6.2 | 1.18 | 5.3 | 1.18 | 0.7 | 0.0 | -0.37 | -3.61 | 4.58 | 94.0 | 6.4 | 51.6 | 0.0 | 4.1 |
| 3.6 | 7.65 | 18.1 | 2.35 | 0.0 | -0.2 | -3.46 | -15.57 | 6.42 | 117.9 | 6.0 | 51.9 | 0.0 | 5.0 |
| 7.1 | 0.47 | 3.3 | 0.43 | 6.1 | 0.7 | 0.93 | 9.95 | 4.86 | 73.9 | 3.0 | 16.4 | 10.7 | 6.1 |
| 5.3 | 2.38 | 15.6 | 0.30 | 6.7 | 0.1 | 0.86 | 7.85 | 3.85 | 75.0 | 4.2 | 12.5 | 0.0 | 5.0 |
| 8.4 | 0.67 | 4.8 | 0.13 | 5.0 | 0.2 | 0.77 | 8.38 | 4.00 | 81.4 | 4.9 | 32.7 | 3.1 | 4.1 |
| 3.5 | 0.66 | 6.3 | 0.30 | 5.0 | 0.1 | 0.69 | 9.55 | 4.36 | 85.9 | 4.6 | 23.3 | 5.9 | 1.7 |
| 8.9 | 0.09 | 0.5 | 0.08 | 3.9 | 0.2 | 0.48 | 4.58 | 3.27 | 87.0 | 4.2 | 16.6 | 1.6 | 5.4 |
| 6.0 | 1.93 | 9.6 | 0.35 | 1.9 | 0.1 | 0.16 | 1.53 | 2.46 | 92.8 | 3.0 | 11.6 | 13.5 | 4.7 |
| 6.2 | 0.67 | 8.0 | 0.40 | 5.4 | 5.1 | 0.72 | 7.29 | 4.31 | 80.6 | 2.6 | 8.6 | 11.7 | 7.4 |
| 3.3 | 4.11 | 26.3 | 0.47 | 9.0 | 0.2 | 1.70 | 16.43 | 4.58 | 67.5 | 3.9 | 11.3 | 2.5 | 5.4 |
| 8.5 | 0.58 | 3.8 | 0.43 | 5.2 | 17.0 | 0.80 | 8.35 | 2.62 | 74.9 | 2.7 | 19.9 | 15.0 | 5.9 |
| 6.0 | 0.91 | 6.5 | 0.54 | 3.3 | 0.2 | 0.33 | 3.62 | 3.84 | 86.7 | 5.3 | 37.9 | 0.0 | 4.2 |
| 6.2 | 1.45 | 8.6 | 0.59 | 0.7 | -0.1 | -0.32 | -4.51 | 3.57 | 96.1 | 4.3 | 17.8 | 1.3 | 2.1 |
| 7.1 | 4.04 | 7.4 | 0.43 | 2.4 | 0.0 | 0.05 | 0.16 | 4.44 | 89.6 | 4.2 | 41.6 | 12.5 | 6.3 |
| 5.9 | 0.38 | 2.9 | -0.12 | 6.2 | 0.1 | 0.98 | 11.57 | 6.08 | 83.4 | 5.0 | 20.2 | 0.0 | 2.3 |
| 9.1 | 0.02 | 0.1 | 0.68 | 3.6 | 0.1 | 0.50 | 5.94 | 2.09 | 70.4 | 4.5 | 17.5 | 0.0 | 4.3 |
| 8.9 | 0.54 | 3.7 | 0.39 | 5.5 | 1.0 | 0.84 | 7.48 | 3.80 | 76.9 | 4.2 | 15.6 | 6.0 | 7.2 |
| 8.4 | 0.72 | 3.9 | 0.16 | 3.8 | 0.3 | 0.47 | 5.32 | 2.69 | 83.0 | 3.9 | 13.7 | 4.1 | 4.1 |
| 8.1 | 0.56 | 2.3 | 0.45 | 1.0 | 0.0 | -0.09 | -0.87 | 2.74 | 102.8 | 6.2 | 45.6 | 0.0 | 3.9 |
| 7.5 | 1.04 | 3.7 | -0.07 | 1.4 | 0.0 | -0.01 | -0.12 | 2.53 | 100.4 | 4.3 | 20.2 | 5.8 | 3.5 |
| 9.5 | 0.00 | 0.0 | 0.00 | 4.5 | 0.8 | 0.67 | 5.85 | 1.96 | 67.2 | 4.3 | 16.7 | 2.4 | 8.3 |
| 3.7 | 11.95 | 24.9 | 0.22 | 6.0 | 0.1 | 0.72 | 6.26 | 2.71 | 71.2 | 3.7 | 10.5 | 12.9 | 6.4 |
| 3.0 | 5.80 | 28.8 | 0.07 | 1.2 | 0.1 | 0.08 | 0.77 | 3.22 | 89.3 | 4.4 | 22.5 | 5.3 | 5.0 |
| 7.5 | 0.78 | 4.9 | 0.49 | 5.2 | 0.3 | 0.58 | 4.85 | 5.36 | 82.2 | 3.0 | 13.6 | 9.8 | 6.5 |
| 10.0 | 0.04 | 0.1 | 0.21 | 0.7 | 0.0 | -0.17 | -1.48 | 2.00 | 109.1 | 5.7 | 61.8 | 0.0 | 5.0 |
| 3.7 | 7.36 | 25.2 | 1.02 | 1.6 | 0.0 | 0.16 | 1.68 | 2.04 | 74.8 | 4.8 | 19.1 | 2.1 | 3.2 |
| 3.7 | 1.85 | 13.0 | 0.00 | 0.0 | 0.0 | -8.43 | -91.36 | 0.00 | 0.0 | 5.7 | 34.8 | 0.0 | 3.7 |
| 4.5 | 0.00 | 0.0 | 5.93 | 7.5 | 0.0 | 2.17 | 9.52 | 5.86 | 50.0 | 6.1 | 46.7 | 0.0 | 4.3 |
| 5.5 | 2.31 | 11.1 | -0.13 | 2.7 | 0.0 | 0.19 | 1.64 | 5.02 | 95.7 | 5.9 | 47.4 | 0.0 | 5.1 |
| 7.1 | 0.65 | 3.7 | 0.47 | 0.9 | 0.0 | -0.24 | -2.90 | 2.89 | 96.5 | 4.6 | 18.2 | 0.0 | 3.9 |
| 7.1 | 2.73 | 6.6 | -0.05 | 9.4 | 0.1 | 2.12 | 9.59 | 4.52 | 61.6 | 4.3 | 27.7 | 0.0 | 5.7 |
| 6.2 | 0.00 | 0.0 | 0.00 | 6.2 | 0.0 | 0.41 | 4.84 | 7.17 | 89.7 | 2.2 | 17.3 | 26.1 | 2.3 |
| 6.2 | 11.52 | 12.8 | 0.00 | 2.3 | 0.0 | 0.15 | 1.32 | 1.18 | 84.6 | 7.1 | 72.2 | 0.0 | 5.9 |
| 5.9 | 4.18 | 16.0 | 0.37 | 2.1 | 0.0 | 0.11 | 0.94 | 2.42 | 94.9 | 3.7 | 21.7 | 12.7 | 6.1 |
| 6.3 | 0.84 | 8.3 | 0.45 | 2.8 | 1.3 | 0.38 | 5.16 | 3.41 | 84.1 | 2.8 | 8.4 | 10.8 | 4.5 |
| 5.5 | 4.59 | 14.0 | 1.27 | 1.7 | 0.0 | 0.14 | 0.77 | 1.69 | 80.0 | 4.8 | 14.7 | 0.0 | 6.8 |
| 7.8 | 2.04 | 6.2 | 0.01 | 3.5 | 0.3 | 0.33 | 3.90 | 1.92 | 84.7 | 4.6 | 20.7 | 4.1 | 5.0 |
| 8.7 | 0.36 | 3.4 | 0.09 | 5.3 | 0.6 | 0.76 | 9.54 | 3.50 | 83.6 | 3.3 | 7.5 | 0.7 | 5.0 |
| 7.0 | 1.39 | 6.5 | 0.04 | 8.1 | 0.1 | 1.21 | 8.22 | 6.64 | 79.4 | 3.2 | 17.8 | 5.2 | 5.0 |
| 5.0 | 23.26 | 16.2 | 3.00 | 4.2 | 0.0 | 0.43 | 1.88 | 2.48 | 65.4 | 6.7 | 109.2 | 0.0 | 3.7 |
| 8.7 | 0.79 | 4.1 | 0.05 | 3.4 | 1.8 | 0.53 | 5.28 | 2.80 | 86.5 | 4.2 | 23.6 | 2.7 | 5.7 |
| 4.6 | 0.14 | 8.7 | 0.22 | 10.0 | 0.0 | 2.65 | 26.40 | 7.94 | 71.2 | 5.9 | 42.9 | 0.0 | 3.5 |
| 10.0 | 0.43 | 1.4 | 0.39 | 1.3 | 0.1 | 0.03 | 0.31 | 2.39 | 94.3 | 5.0 | 15.7 | 4.3 | 5.3 |
| 2.3 | 5.86 | 29.0 | 1.09 | 3.1 | 0.0 | 0.14 | 1.21 | 4.82 | 76.0 | 4.6 | 23.5 | 0.0 | 6.3 |
| 5.5 | 2.15 | 8.2 | 0.15 | 6.1 | 0.2 | 0.95 | 6.01 | 4.70 | 79.4 | 4.8 | 25.3 | 4.6 | 7.4 |
| 10.0 | 1.28 | 1.7 | 0.00 | 2.1 | 0.0 | 0.08 | 0.38 | 2.52 | 98.1 | 6.7 | 89.8 | 0.0 | 6.4 |
| 2.6 | 3.37 | 21.1 | 0.15 | 2.6 | 0.0 | -2.33 | -22.93 | 6.40 | 121.2 | 3.9 | 4.4 | 0.0 | 1.7 |
| 9.8 | 5.71 | 2.7 | 0.00 | 0.9 | 0.0 | 0.00 | 0.00 | 1.69 | 100.0 | 8.8 | 109.3 | 0.0 | 6.8 |
| 7.5 | 0.96 | 4.2 | 0.61 | 7.9 | 1.8 | 1.12 | 8.39 | 4.43 | 76.9 | 3.1 | 12.5 | 8.6 | 8.4 |
| 7.8 | 0.36 | 3.0 | 0.53 | 8.0 | 12.1 | 1.09 | 9.84 | 3.86 | 68.1 | 2.8 | 13.4 | 13.0 | 8.6 |

| Name | City | State | Rating | 2014 Rating | 2013 Rating | Total Assets ($Mil) | One Year Asset Growth | Commercial Loans | Consumer Loans | Mortgage Loans | Securities | Capitalization Index | Net Worth Ratio |
|---|---|---|---|---|---|---|---|---|---|---|---|---|---|
| NUSENDA FCU | Albuquerque | NM | B+ | A- | A- | 1650.7 | 9.60 | 17.0 | 40.2 | 27.3 | 15.4 | 9.5 | 10.7 |
| NUTMEG STATE FINANCIAL CU | Rocky Hill | CT | B+ | B+ | B+ | 376.9 | 2.44 | 2.8 | 31.9 | 30.2 | 13.7 | 10.0 | 13.7 |
| NUVISION FCU | Huntington Beach | CA | B | B- | B- | 1364.3 | 4.32 | 10.5 | 22.9 | 37.0 | 23.5 | 10.0 | 12.3 |
| NUVISTA FCU | Montrose | CO | C- | D+ | D | 80.2 | 3.76 | 1.0 | 26.1 | 30.2 | 0.0 | 6.0 | 8.0 |
| NW IOWA CU | Le Mars | IA | B | B | B- | 42.0 | 11.17 | 0.0 | 34.2 | 13.9 | 0.0 | 9.7 | 10.8 |
| NW PREFERRED FCU | Tigard | OR | B- | C+ | C- | 123.5 | 2.70 | 18.6 | 25.1 | 27.3 | 8.5 | 6.3 | 8.3 |
| NW PRIORITY CU | Portland | OR | C+ | C+ | C+ | 232.1 | 0.13 | 0.4 | 14.5 | 15.9 | 56.0 | 10.0 | 12.0 |
| NYB & FMC FCU | Jersey City | NJ | D | D | C- | 6.1 | -1.81 | 0.0 | 28.6 | 0.0 | 0.0 | 10.0 | 14.6 |
| NYM FCU | Brooklyn | NY | B- | C+ | C+ | 15.4 | -3.08 | 3.5 | 25.3 | 0.0 | 60.9 | 10.0 | 16.8 |
| NYMEO FCU | Frederick | MD | A- | A- | A- | 252.8 | 3.43 | 8.2 | 31.8 | 26.1 | 1.2 | 10.0 | 12.2 |
| O AND R UTILITIES EMPL FCU | Monroe | NY | D+ | D | D+ | 13.2 | -3.34 | 0.0 | 18.4 | 16.5 | 0.0 | 10.0 | 14.1 |
| O BEE CU | Tumwater | WA | B- | B- | B- | 207.2 | 8.08 | 3.5 | 45.2 | 27.5 | 0.0 | 6.4 | 8.4 |
| ▲ OAHE FCU | Pierre | SD | B- | B- | B- | 20.8 | 10.37 | 0.0 | 30.4 | 3.6 | 0.0 | 10.0 | 12.5 |
| OAHU FCU | Honolulu | HI | C | C | C- | 49.1 | 0.58 | 4.0 | 15.0 | 8.2 | 12.1 | 9.6 | 10.7 |
| OAK CLIFF CHRISTIAN FCU | Dallas | TX | D+ | D+ | D | 4.1 | 5.11 | 0.0 | 75.1 | 0.0 | 0.0 | 6.9 | 8.9 |
| OAK FARMS EMPL CU | Houston | TX | C | C | C+ | 4.0 | 3.69 | 0.0 | 75.0 | 0.0 | 0.0 | 10.0 | 24.0 |
| OAK LAWN MUNICIPAL EMPL CU | Oak Lawn | IL | D | D+ | D+ | 4.2 | 5.41 | 0.0 | 27.4 | 0.0 | 0.0 | 9.5 | 10.6 |
| OAK POINT EMPL CU | Belle Chasse | LA | B- | B- | B- | 8.8 | 6.46 | 0.0 | 69.2 | 0.0 | 0.0 | 10.0 | 33.2 |
| OAK TRUST CU | Plainfield | IL | B- | B- | C+ | 45.4 | 3.38 | 0.0 | 32.2 | 7.5 | 5.3 | 10.0 | 19.7 |
| ▲ OAKDALE CU | Oakdale | WI | D+ | D | D | 62.1 | 6.00 | 2.3 | 23.0 | 41.3 | 0.0 | 5.2 | 7.2 |
| ▲ OAKLAND COUNTY CU | Waterford | MI | B+ | B | B | 297.8 | 5.81 | 0.0 | 25.9 | 18.7 | 18.1 | 7.8 | 9.5 |
| OAS STAFF FCU | Washington | DC | C | C | C | 182.8 | 8.77 | 2.2 | 5.7 | 37.3 | 25.9 | 5.6 | 7.6 |
| OCALA COMMUNITY CU | Ocala | FL | B- | B | C+ | 29.9 | 7.58 | 0.0 | 28.4 | 11.8 | 16.4 | 10.0 | 11.6 |
| OCEAN COMMUNITIES FCU | Biddeford | ME | C- | C- | C | 158.3 | 4.24 | 7.4 | 24.2 | 43.2 | 3.8 | 5.3 | 7.3 |
| OCEAN COUNTY EMPL FCU | Toms River | NJ | D+ | D | D+ | 1.8 | -1.46 | 0.0 | 27.4 | 0.0 | 0.0 | 8.6 | 10.1 |
| OCEAN CREST FCU | Signal Hill | CA | D | D | D | 35.6 | 2.04 | 0.0 | 13.2 | 14.5 | 0.0 | 6.3 | 8.3 |
| OCEAN SPRAY EMPL FCU | Lakeville | MA | D+ | D+ | D+ | 11.3 | 0.08 | 0.0 | 25.5 | 19.7 | 0.0 | 10.0 | 12.4 |
| OCEANSIDE CHRISTOPHER FCU | Oceanside | NY | B | B- | B- | 293.6 | 3.08 | 10.1 | 9.7 | 29.5 | 24.5 | 7.2 | 9.2 |
| OCNAC NO 1 FCU | Jersey City | NJ | D+ | D+ | D+ | 6.3 | -1.96 | 0.0 | 39.7 | 0.0 | 0.0 | 10.0 | 11.9 |
| ODESSA EMPL CU | Odessa | TX | B | B | B | 16.4 | 1.78 | 0.0 | 32.4 | 14.0 | 0.0 | 10.0 | 14.2 |
| ODJFS FCU | Columbus | OH | C- | C- | C- | 10.0 | 6.52 | 0.0 | 40.2 | 2.2 | 30.9 | 10.0 | 12.3 |
| OF TOALSTON FCU | Logan | WV | C+ | C+ | C+ | <1 | -7.01 | 0.0 | 85.2 | 0.0 | 0.0 | 10.0 | 19.3 |
| OHIO CATHOLIC FCU | Garfield Heights | OH | B+ | B | C | 151.7 | -0.99 | 4.6 | 10.8 | 43.7 | 1.3 | 9.7 | 10.8 |
| OHIO COUNTY PUBLIC SCHOOLS FCU | Wheeling | WV | C | C | C | 5.9 | 2.82 | 0.0 | 21.8 | 0.0 | 0.0 | 10.0 | 15.7 |
| OHIO EDUCATIONAL CU | Cleveland | OH | D+ | D+ | D | 127.3 | 1.95 | 4.2 | 32.4 | 13.0 | 8.4 | 5.4 | 7.4 |
| OHIO HEALTHCARE FCU | Dublin | OH | C- | C- | C- | 73.5 | 5.21 | 1.0 | 48.3 | 7.4 | 9.4 | 6.3 | 8.4 |
| OHIO OPERATING ENGINEERS FCU | Cleveland | OH | E+ | E+ | E+ | 5.8 | 5.70 | 0.0 | 47.2 | 0.0 | 0.0 | 5.5 | 7.5 |
| ▲ OHIO TEAMSTERS CU INC | Independence | OH | C | D+ | C- | 13.7 | -13.85 | 0.3 | 30.0 | 22.3 | 18.7 | 10.0 | 26.9 |
| OHIO UNIV CU | Athens | OH | B | B- | B- | 306.0 | 3.09 | 9.9 | 22.1 | 25.3 | 11.5 | 9.0 | 10.3 |
| ▲ OHIO VALLEY COMMUNITY CU | Clarington | OH | C- | D+ | D+ | 131.2 | -2.81 | 1.4 | 20.5 | 15.4 | 26.7 | 6.6 | 8.6 |
| OHIO VALLEY FCU | Batavia | OH | D- | D | D | 23.1 | 7.94 | 4.3 | 28.3 | 7.0 | 13.1 | 7.0 | 9.0 |
| OHIOS FIRST CLASS CU | Cleveland | OH | C- | C- | D+ | 38.3 | 0.52 | 0.0 | 54.0 | 0.0 | 9.7 | 10.0 | 16.6 |
| ▼ OIL COUNTRY FCU | Titusville | PA | C- | C+ | C+ | 18.7 | -0.52 | 0.0 | 38.1 | 7.9 | 0.0 | 10.0 | 13.7 |
| ▲ OK FCU | Bartlesville | OK | C- | D+ | D | 19.8 | -0.73 | 0.0 | 40.0 | 0.0 | 0.0 | 6.9 | 9.0 |
| ▲ OK MEMBERS FIRST FCU | Tulsa | OK | C | C- | C- | 20.5 | -0.51 | 0.0 | 48.9 | 6.1 | 0.0 | 10.0 | 14.9 |
| OKALOOSA COUNTY TEACHERS FCU | Crestview | FL | C+ | C+ | C+ | 76.0 | 8.95 | 0.0 | 27.0 | 10.5 | 7.8 | 8.3 | 9.8 |
| OKLAHOMA CENTRAL CU | Tulsa | OK | B- | B- | B- | 504.3 | 3.59 | 5.8 | 25.1 | 15.0 | 43.8 | 10.0 | 13.2 |
| ▲ OKLAHOMA EDUCATORS CU | Oklahoma City | OK | B | B- | C- | 119.5 | 6.05 | 0.0 | 54.2 | 10.8 | 21.7 | 6.6 | 8.8 |
| OKLAHOMA EMPL CU | Oklahoma City | OK | A- | A- | A- | 478.3 | 9.86 | 4.9 | 54.0 | 15.9 | 18.7 | 10.0 | 12.2 |
| OKLAHOMA FCU | Oklahoma City | OK | A | A | A- | 111.4 | 1.95 | 0.2 | 51.7 | 17.4 | 14.4 | 10.0 | 13.0 |
| OLATHE FCU | Olathe | CO | D+ | D+ | C- | <1 | -7.13 | 0.0 | 33.6 | 0.0 | 0.0 | 10.0 | 12.5 |
| OLD DOMINION UNIV CU INC | Norfolk | VA | D+ | D+ | D+ | 28.4 | 1.38 | 0.0 | 14.3 | 21.5 | 0.0 | 7.7 | 9.5 |
| OLD HICKORY CU | Old Hickory | TN | D | D | C- | 223.5 | 1.72 | 9.2 | 24.7 | 21.0 | 29.6 | 6.5 | 8.5 |
| OLD OCEAN FCU | Old Ocean | TX | C | C | C | 30.2 | 1.25 | 0.0 | 39.5 | 0.0 | 28.4 | 6.8 | 8.8 |
| OLD SOUTH FCU | Natchez | MS | D+ | D+ | C- | 19.0 | 1.31 | 0.0 | 26.9 | 0.0 | 0.0 | 10.0 | 14.1 |
| OLD SPANISH TRAIL CU | Westlake | LA | D | D | C- | 9.2 | -7.30 | 0.0 | 34.9 | 0.0 | 0.0 | 10.0 | 17.5 |
| OLD WEST FCU | John Day | OR | D- | D- | D- | 124.8 | 2.06 | 33.7 | 4.5 | 39.8 | 7.8 | 8.1 | 9.7 |
| OLEAN AREA FCU | Olean | NY | A | A | A | 250.9 | 1.11 | 9.6 | 20.4 | 32.9 | 26.3 | 10.0 | 13.4 |
| OLEAN TEACHERS AND POSTAL FCU | Olean | NY | C- | C- | C- | 16.4 | 2.65 | 0.0 | 16.1 | 20.9 | 35.9 | 7.0 | 9.0 |
| OLIVE VIEW EMPL FCU | Sylmar | CA | B+ | B+ | B+ | 38.2 | 6.38 | 0.0 | 39.0 | 0.0 | 7.2 | 10.0 | 21.9 |

| Asset Quality Index | Non-Performing Loans as a % of Total Loans | Non-Performing Loans as a % of Capital | Net Charge-Offs Avg Loans | Profitability Index | Net Income ($Mil) | Return on Assets | Return on Equity | Net Interest Spread | Overhead Efficiency Ratio | Liquidity Index | Liquidity Ratio | Hot Money Ratio | Stability Index |
|---|---|---|---|---|---|---|---|---|---|---|---|---|---|
| 7.3 | 0.64 | 4.7 | 0.41 | 5.0 | 8.2 | 0.68 | 6.72 | 3.21 | 77.3 | 3.5 | 12.5 | 4.1 | 7.7 |
| 7.8 | 0.66 | 4.1 | 0.69 | 3.7 | 1.0 | 0.34 | 2.58 | 3.77 | 81.7 | 2.9 | 6.2 | 7.4 | 8.0 |
| 8.1 | 0.44 | 4.2 | 0.33 | 4.7 | 6.4 | 0.62 | 5.60 | 3.32 | 80.0 | 2.9 | 14.8 | 13.6 | 8.1 |
| 5.6 | 1.53 | 12.7 | 0.36 | 2.2 | 0.0 | 0.06 | 0.79 | 3.62 | 97.2 | 2.5 | 24.4 | 18.2 | 3.1 |
| 8.4 | 0.45 | 2.5 | -0.10 | 5.5 | 0.3 | 0.89 | 8.41 | 2.67 | 70.5 | 4.1 | 29.3 | 2.2 | 5.8 |
| 5.4 | 0.85 | 7.2 | 0.61 | 4.2 | 0.5 | 0.50 | 6.23 | 4.59 | 80.4 | 3.8 | 17.0 | 7.2 | 4.9 |
| 10.0 | 0.53 | 1.5 | 0.16 | 2.2 | 0.3 | 0.16 | 1.34 | 2.09 | 89.6 | 4.8 | 27.2 | 3.9 | 6.7 |
| 8.1 | 2.82 | 5.3 | 0.86 | 0.0 | -0.1 | -1.82 | -12.42 | 4.74 | 128.7 | 7.2 | 58.6 | 0.0 | 5.0 |
| 9.9 | 0.25 | 0.5 | 0.03 | 5.9 | 0.1 | 1.07 | 6.67 | 3.62 | 76.2 | 5.2 | 28.7 | 0.0 | 5.7 |
| 5.2 | 2.72 | 15.8 | 1.62 | 3.7 | -0.1 | -0.07 | -0.58 | 5.14 | 77.3 | 3.7 | 22.8 | 5.8 | 7.6 |
| 8.2 | 1.22 | 4.3 | 0.41 | 0.4 | 0.0 | -0.16 | -1.14 | 3.03 | 104.9 | 4.5 | 35.6 | 1.8 | 6.0 |
| 6.2 | 0.40 | 6.6 | 0.66 | 5.5 | 1.2 | 0.80 | 9.56 | 4.54 | 75.4 | 3.2 | 14.9 | 6.3 | 5.3 |
| 9.0 | 0.41 | 1.9 | 0.08 | 4.8 | 0.1 | 0.76 | 6.07 | 3.51 | 79.1 | 5.1 | 32.9 | 0.8 | 6.5 |
| 8.3 | 1.16 | 3.6 | 0.09 | 2.5 | 0.1 | 0.26 | 2.38 | 2.52 | 88.7 | 4.8 | 23.2 | 1.5 | 5.5 |
| 5.0 | 1.17 | 9.5 | 0.44 | 9.3 | 0.1 | 1.45 | 17.29 | 4.38 | 67.6 | 4.4 | 26.3 | 0.0 | 3.0 |
| 7.4 | 1.10 | 3.6 | 0.00 | 8.4 | 0.0 | 1.35 | 5.70 | 6.97 | 80.6 | 2.8 | 14.7 | 16.8 | 5.0 |
| 8.9 | 1.30 | 3.3 | 0.00 | 1.2 | 0.0 | -0.03 | -0.30 | 2.07 | 91.8 | 6.0 | 79.8 | 0.0 | 3.7 |
| 7.8 | 1.21 | 2.4 | 0.00 | 10.0 | 0.2 | 2.70 | 8.08 | 4.12 | 21.2 | 4.6 | 47.4 | 0.0 | 5.7 |
| 9.0 | 0.42 | 1.6 | 0.33 | 2.7 | 0.0 | 0.05 | 0.25 | 4.12 | 94.4 | 2.8 | 16.2 | 12.0 | 5.2 |
| 4.4 | 0.85 | 12.7 | 0.33 | 3.6 | 0.2 | 0.48 | 6.91 | 3.77 | 84.0 | 3.8 | 11.5 | 1.9 | 3.0 |
| 7.8 | 0.52 | 4.1 | 0.55 | 8.1 | 2.6 | 1.19 | 13.48 | 3.59 | 74.8 | 3.8 | 10.0 | 3.4 | 6.0 |
| 6.3 | 1.40 | 12.0 | 0.17 | 2.9 | 0.4 | 0.31 | 3.90 | 2.77 | 85.7 | 2.9 | 35.4 | 22.4 | 5.2 |
| 9.3 | 0.85 | 3.4 | 0.13 | 3.6 | 0.1 | 0.51 | 4.51 | 3.34 | 80.8 | 4.4 | 33.8 | 9.4 | 6.2 |
| 5.5 | 1.39 | 16.3 | 0.45 | 2.2 | 0.2 | 0.14 | 1.82 | 3.65 | 91.3 | 3.3 | 10.3 | 6.1 | 4.1 |
| 7.1 | 2.65 | 7.0 | 0.52 | 0.9 | 0.0 | -0.15 | -1.50 | 6.48 | 92.3 | 6.8 | 59.8 | 0.0 | 3.2 |
| 6.3 | 2.66 | 9.5 | 0.48 | 1.4 | 0.0 | 0.04 | 0.50 | 3.52 | 95.5 | 5.3 | 24.5 | 0.0 | 2.6 |
| 9.9 | 0.17 | 0.7 | 0.68 | 0.6 | 0.0 | -0.26 | -2.08 | 3.31 | 98.2 | 5.1 | 33.3 | 2.4 | 6.0 |
| 5.4 | 1.87 | 14.7 | 0.18 | 4.7 | 1.3 | 0.62 | 7.30 | 2.77 | 71.4 | 4.4 | 16.1 | 6.4 | 6.0 |
| 5.7 | 4.23 | 12.5 | 4.67 | 2.4 | 0.0 | 0.11 | 0.90 | 7.21 | 71.6 | 6.0 | 42.3 | 0.0 | 5.5 |
| 9.3 | 0.59 | 2.2 | 0.27 | 5.2 | 0.1 | 0.62 | 4.42 | 3.72 | 81.7 | 5.2 | 33.2 | 0.7 | 8.1 |
| 9.7 | 0.65 | 2.3 | 0.68 | 2.1 | 0.0 | 0.05 | 0.43 | 3.73 | 92.2 | 5.5 | 38.2 | 0.0 | 6.1 |
| 7.2 | 0.93 | 3.7 | 0.38 | 7.2 | 0.0 | 1.04 | 5.80 | 8.71 | 87.0 | 3.6 | 15.4 | 0.0 | 5.0 |
| 9.4 | 0.24 | 2.1 | 0.41 | 6.1 | 1.1 | 0.96 | 9.21 | 3.85 | 77.0 | 3.3 | 11.0 | 4.6 | 6.4 |
| 7.6 | 3.69 | 5.7 | 0.92 | 2.8 | 0.0 | 0.27 | 1.74 | 2.93 | 83.3 | 6.9 | 63.0 | 0.0 | 6.9 |
| 6.8 | 1.02 | 8.8 | 0.55 | 1.5 | 0.0 | 0.02 | 0.31 | 3.44 | 92.1 | 4.0 | 12.6 | 3.0 | 4.2 |
| 5.6 | 0.57 | 4.6 | 0.41 | 3.7 | 0.3 | 0.48 | 5.83 | 4.25 | 86.1 | 3.8 | 16.5 | 0.7 | 3.3 |
| 6.4 | 0.31 | 2.2 | 0.21 | 4.6 | 0.0 | 0.59 | 7.84 | 3.93 | 86.2 | 4.7 | 28.5 | 0.0 | 1.7 |
| 4.7 | 6.21 | 10.5 | 3.80 | 3.1 | 0.1 | 0.49 | 1.90 | 4.14 | 90.8 | 5.9 | 42.4 | 0.0 | 5.7 |
| 7.9 | 0.64 | 4.4 | 0.58 | 4.3 | 1.5 | 0.64 | 6.34 | 3.32 | 78.7 | 3.6 | 14.1 | 7.4 | 6.1 |
| 8.7 | 0.62 | 3.0 | 0.38 | 2.1 | 0.2 | 0.19 | 2.50 | 2.48 | 87.8 | 4.8 | 28.1 | 4.0 | 4.5 |
| 4.3 | 1.86 | 14.5 | -0.07 | 1.5 | 0.0 | 0.14 | 1.49 | 3.29 | 98.8 | 3.4 | 9.4 | 5.2 | 2.4 |
| 6.7 | 1.56 | 5.6 | 0.43 | 2.0 | 0.0 | 0.13 | 0.78 | 4.41 | 94.8 | 4.1 | 12.5 | 0.0 | 6.0 |
| 6.8 | 1.84 | 6.9 | 1.86 | 1.4 | -0.1 | -0.75 | -5.45 | 4.32 | 94.7 | 4.9 | 24.2 | 2.7 | 6.8 |
| 8.8 | 0.22 | 2.5 | 0.03 | 3.5 | 0.1 | 0.56 | 6.50 | 2.60 | 82.3 | 4.4 | 36.6 | 11.1 | 4.0 |
| 7.5 | 0.60 | 2.6 | 0.12 | 2.1 | 0.0 | 0.19 | 1.31 | 3.34 | 93.2 | 4.3 | 41.2 | 4.6 | 6.5 |
| 6.2 | 1.64 | 8.3 | 1.12 | 3.6 | 0.2 | 0.39 | 4.00 | 3.62 | 83.3 | 4.7 | 32.0 | 5.5 | 4.3 |
| 9.7 | 0.38 | 1.3 | 0.36 | 3.2 | 1.6 | 0.43 | 3.28 | 2.97 | 84.7 | 4.3 | 20.3 | 3.8 | 8.4 |
| 6.8 | 0.60 | 5.5 | 0.59 | 8.3 | 1.2 | 1.32 | 16.16 | 4.16 | 64.0 | 2.8 | 7.7 | 11.3 | 5.2 |
| 7.5 | 0.51 | 3.7 | 0.31 | 5.6 | 2.7 | 0.76 | 6.56 | 3.31 | 75.8 | 2.7 | 6.9 | 12.3 | 8.8 |
| 8.5 | 0.09 | 1.1 | 0.54 | 9.8 | 1.1 | 1.38 | 11.28 | 3.67 | 65.2 | 1.6 | 13.8 | 32.2 | 8.6 |
| 4.6 | 7.89 | 19.4 | 0.88 | 1.3 | 0.0 | -0.28 | -2.30 | 5.60 | 108.3 | 7.4 | 73.9 | 0.0 | 4.4 |
| 1.7 | 9.87 | 37.5 | 1.66 | 3.1 | 0.0 | 0.19 | 2.05 | 3.68 | 75.2 | 5.9 | 41.3 | 0.0 | 4.2 |
| 5.7 | 0.52 | 10.1 | 0.56 | 1.2 | 0.0 | 0.00 | 0.02 | 2.65 | 92.8 | 4.7 | 16.3 | 2.6 | 4.2 |
| 8.2 | 0.42 | 2.1 | 0.31 | 4.2 | 0.1 | 0.49 | 5.82 | 3.98 | 89.0 | 4.2 | 15.4 | 2.0 | 3.6 |
| 7.6 | 2.09 | 5.1 | 1.28 | 1.2 | 0.0 | -0.08 | -0.63 | 3.85 | 96.3 | 7.1 | 71.4 | 0.0 | 5.3 |
| 9.7 | 0.00 | 0.0 | 1.62 | 0.3 | 0.0 | -0.31 | -1.82 | 2.84 | 111.2 | 5.5 | 70.3 | 0.0 | 6.4 |
| 0.3 | 3.37 | 58.1 | -0.03 | 2.5 | 0.1 | 0.13 | 1.33 | 4.90 | 97.0 | 5.0 | 22.3 | 2.5 | 5.4 |
| 8.5 | 0.70 | 3.2 | 0.31 | 6.3 | 1.7 | 0.88 | 6.67 | 3.04 | 68.0 | 3.8 | 18.3 | 5.3 | 9.2 |
| 7.7 | 1.40 | 6.0 | 0.02 | 2.2 | 0.0 | 0.12 | 1.36 | 2.76 | 94.9 | 5.9 | 30.0 | 1.0 | 4.5 |
| 9.8 | 0.26 | 0.5 | 0.27 | 7.9 | 0.4 | 1.31 | 6.07 | 3.43 | 65.1 | 5.5 | 38.3 | 2.3 | 6.8 |

| Name | City | State | Rating | 2014 Rating | 2013 Rating | Total Assets ($Mil) | One Year Asset Growth | Asset Mix (As a % of Total Assets) | | | | Capital- ization Index | Net Worth Ratio |
|---|---|---|---|---|---|---|---|---|---|---|---|---|---|
| | | | | | | | | Comm- ercial Loans | Cons- umer Loans | Mort- gage Loans | Secur- ities | | |
| OLYMPIA CU | Olympia | WA | D+ | D | C- | 32.7 | 1.74 | 3.1 | 25.9 | 9.9 | 31.0 | 6.5 | 8.5 |
| ▲ OMAHA DOUGLAS FCU | Omaha | NE | C | C- | C- | 30.7 | 4.00 | 0.0 | 22.8 | 8.2 | 0.8 | 10.0 | 12.0 |
| ▲ OMAHA FCU | Omaha | NE | C- | D | D | 69.9 | -0.70 | 0.5 | 23.1 | 13.0 | 0.0 | 5.7 | 7.7 |
| OMAHA FIREFIGHTERS CU | Omaha | NE | B+ | A- | A | 53.9 | 2.08 | 0.0 | 20.0 | 9.6 | 14.5 | 10.0 | 16.8 |
| OMAHA POLICE FCU | Omaha | NE | C- | C | C | 64.0 | 5.15 | 0.0 | 29.3 | 26.6 | 5.5 | 6.1 | 8.2 |
| OMAHA PUBLIC POWER DISTRICT EMPL FCU | Omaha | NE | C- | D+ | D+ | 30.1 | -2.69 | 0.0 | 28.0 | 0.0 | 46.6 | 10.0 | 22.7 |
| OMC EMPL CU | Charleston | TN | C+ | C+ | C+ | 27.8 | -2.32 | 0.0 | 23.2 | 30.0 | 17.6 | 7.6 | 9.4 |
| OMEGA FCU | Pittsburgh | PA | C+ | C | C | 85.7 | 1.29 | 0.5 | 26.6 | 10.6 | 0.0 | 7.3 | 9.2 |
| OMEGA PSI PHI FRATERNITY FCU | Lawrenceville | GA | D+ | D | D- | 1.1 | 15.91 | 0.0 | 45.5 | 15.3 | 0.0 | 6.8 | 8.9 |
| OMNI COMMUNITY CU | Battle Creek | MI | A- | A- | A- | 328.7 | 4.74 | 6.6 | 27.4 | 15.8 | 43.9 | 10.0 | 14.5 |
| ▼ ON THE GRID FINANCIAL FCU | Atlanta | GA | C | C+ | B- | 36.4 | 1.81 | 0.0 | 48.9 | 9.9 | 3.3 | 10.0 | 13.9 |
| ONE COMMUNITY FCU | Parkersburg | WV | C- | C- | C- | 72.1 | 2.96 | 0.4 | 25.0 | 27.0 | 0.1 | 6.4 | 8.4 |
| ONE CU | Springfield | VT | D+ | D+ | D+ | 135.5 | 2.15 | 3.3 | 23.8 | 29.5 | 8.9 | 9.7 | 10.8 |
| ONE DETROIT CU | Detroit | MI | C- | C+ | C+ | 30.5 | 0.10 | 0.0 | 57.1 | 14.7 | 8.7 | 10.0 | 11.8 |
| ONE NEVADA CU | Las Vegas | NV | A | A- | B- | 749.2 | 4.83 | 8.9 | 27.3 | 20.6 | 4.0 | 10.0 | 11.7 |
| ▼ ONE SOURCE FCU | El Paso | TX | D+ | C | C | 92.5 | 0.55 | 0.0 | 58.1 | 10.8 | 11.6 | 6.6 | 8.7 |
| ONE THIRTEEN CU | Colorado Springs | CO | E+ | D | D | 8.8 | 1.78 | 0.0 | 38.7 | 0.0 | 0.0 | 5.8 | 7.8 |
| ONE TWENTY CU | Roslindale | MA | C- | C | C+ | <1 | 8.99 | 0.0 | 45.1 | 0.0 | 18.0 | 10.0 | 13.4 |
| ▲ ONE VISION FCU | Clarksville | IN | C | D+ | D+ | 50.9 | -0.04 | 0.1 | 19.9 | 16.2 | 0.0 | 10.0 | 12.0 |
| ▲ ONEAL CU | Birmingham | AL | C+ | C | C | 2.7 | -1.98 | 0.0 | 55.9 | 0.0 | 0.0 | 10.0 | 22.7 |
| ONEIDA COUNTY FCU | Utica | NY | C- | C- | C | 12.8 | 4.96 | 0.0 | 30.1 | 0.0 | 0.0 | 9.1 | 10.4 |
| ONOMEA FCU | Papaikou | HI | C- | C- | C- | 15.9 | 0.02 | 0.0 | 18.7 | 9.8 | 50.4 | 10.0 | 18.3 |
| ONPOINT COMMUNITY CU | Portland | OR | A | A | A- | 3838.0 | 8.11 | 3.1 | 23.6 | 28.0 | 24.8 | 10.0 | 11.2 |
| ONTARIO MONTCLAIR SCHOOL EMPL FCU | Ontario | CA | B- | B- | C | 93.2 | 6.95 | 1.6 | 27.6 | 14.0 | 30.7 | 9.5 | 10.6 |
| ONTARIO PUBLIC EMPL FCU | Ontario | CA | D | D | D+ | 19.0 | 5.23 | 0.0 | 39.7 | 4.4 | 12.9 | 6.2 | 8.2 |
| ONTARIO SHORES FCU | Newfane | NY | B- | B- | B- | 64.1 | 6.49 | 0.0 | 9.8 | 23.6 | 37.1 | 7.7 | 9.4 |
| OPC FCU | Durkee | OR | C | C | C | 2.5 | 5.19 | 0.0 | 56.4 | 0.0 | 0.0 | 10.0 | 16.0 |
| OPERATING ENGINEERS LOCAL #148 CU | Granite City | IL | C | C | C | 17.3 | -2.54 | 0.0 | 43.3 | 0.0 | 0.0 | 10.0 | 16.5 |
| OPERATING ENGINEERS LOCAL UNION #3 F | Livermore | CA | A | A- | A- | 912.4 | 4.39 | 2.4 | 22.4 | 21.2 | 34.8 | 10.0 | 14.4 |
| OPP-MICOLAS CU | Opp | AL | D+ | D+ | C- | 13.6 | -2.05 | 0.5 | 11.0 | 16.8 | 0.0 | 10.0 | 24.0 |
| ▼ OPPORTUNITIES CU | Winooski | VT | B- | B | B- | 37.4 | -1.13 | 8.6 | 2.7 | 52.3 | 0.0 | 10.0 | 15.2 |
| OPS EMPL FCU | Bensalem | PA | C- | D+ | C | 1.2 | -2.82 | 0.0 | 7.1 | 0.0 | 0.0 | 10.0 | 14.0 |
| OPTION 1 CU | Grand Rapids | MI | B+ | B+ | B | 280.0 | 2.20 | 7.9 | 16.6 | 39.9 | 17.1 | 10.0 | 16.3 |
| ORAL FCU | Honolulu | HI | D | D | C- | 2.4 | -4.89 | 0.0 | 28.0 | 0.0 | 0.0 | 10.0 | 14.8 |
| ORANGE COUNTY TEACHERS CU | Orange | TX | C- | C- | C- | 2.1 | -4.26 | 0.0 | 21.2 | 0.0 | 0.0 | 10.0 | 20.5 |
| ORANGE COUNTYS CU | Santa Ana | CA | A- | B+ | B+ | 1299.6 | 11.54 | 9.4 | 16.6 | 38.6 | 23.8 | 7.9 | 9.6 |
| ORANGE SCHOOL EMPL CU | Pepper Pike | OH | C | C | C | 3.0 | -2.19 | 0.0 | 28.8 | 0.0 | 0.0 | 10.0 | 20.5 |
| OREGON COMMUNITY CU | Eugene | OR | B- | B- | B | 1382.6 | 8.73 | 0.6 | 65.0 | 13.5 | 0.6 | 6.3 | 8.3 |
| OREGON PIONEER FCU | Portland | OR | D | D | D- | 24.1 | -5.89 | 0.6 | 11.9 | 22.3 | 32.6 | 6.4 | 8.4 |
| OREGON STATE CU | Corvallis | OR | A- | A | A | 962.4 | 8.73 | 10.1 | 28.2 | 20.3 | 29.6 | 10.0 | 11.1 |
| OREGONIANS FCU | Milwaukie | OR | B- | B- | B- | 303.6 | 1.94 | 5.2 | 7.1 | 16.6 | 52.9 | 10.0 | 12.1 |
| ▲ OREM CITY EMPL FCU | Orem | UT | D+ | D | D+ | 3.5 | -4.67 | 0.0 | 35.9 | 0.0 | 28.4 | 10.0 | 11.8 |
| ORGANIZED LABOR CU | Modesto | CA | D | D+ | D | 21.8 | 10.95 | 0.0 | 20.8 | 2.0 | 0.0 | 5.5 | 7.5 |
| ORION FCU | Memphis | TN | B | B- | B- | 574.6 | 6.40 | 3.9 | 32.1 | 29.4 | 11.9 | 10.0 | 11.3 |
| ORLANDO FCU | Orlando | FL | B+ | B+ | B+ | 199.8 | 4.12 | 0.3 | 48.4 | 19.2 | 4.3 | 9.0 | 10.5 |
| ▲ ORLEANS PARISH CRIMINAL SHERIFFS CU | New Orleans | LA | C+ | C- | C- | 6.2 | -3.10 | 0.0 | 28.1 | 0.0 | 0.0 | 10.0 | 30.3 |
| ORLEX GOVERNMENT EMPL CU | Newport | VT | E+ | E+ | E+ | 5.9 | 3.53 | 0.0 | 69.8 | 0.0 | 0.0 | 6.3 | 8.3 |
| ORNL FCU | Oak Ridge | TN | B+ | A- | A- | 1690.9 | 7.42 | 3.7 | 37.1 | 29.7 | 7.7 | 9.9 | 11.0 |
| OSHKOSH COMMUNITY CU | Oshkosh | WI | D+ | D+ | D+ | 16.5 | 19.56 | 0.7 | 29.7 | 48.4 | 0.0 | 6.7 | 8.7 |
| OSHKOSH POSTAL EMPL CU | Oshkosh | WI | D- | D- | D | 4.7 | 0.32 | 0.0 | 54.4 | 22.1 | 0.0 | 6.9 | 8.9 |
| ▲ OSHKOSH TRUCK CU | Oshkosh | WI | C | C- | C | 15.0 | -2.61 | 0.8 | 19.5 | 19.6 | 0.0 | 10.0 | 16.1 |
| ▲ OSNOVA UKRAINIAN FCU | Parma | OH | C | D+ | D | 8.8 | 4.84 | 4.8 | 2.2 | 75.9 | 0.0 | 9.6 | 10.7 |
| OSU INSTITUTE OF TECHNOLOGY FCU | Okmulgee | OK | E+ | E+ | E+ | 5.1 | 10.71 | 0.0 | 20.4 | 0.9 | 0.0 | 5.5 | 7.5 |
| ▼ OSWEGO COUNTY FCU | Oswego | NY | C | C+ | C+ | 65.1 | 10.43 | 0.0 | 45.1 | 3.3 | 1.8 | 6.2 | 8.3 |
| OSWEGO HERITAGE FCU | Fulton | NY | D | D+ | D+ | 13.8 | 0.61 | 0.0 | 26.0 | 9.3 | 0.0 | 6.9 | 8.9 |
| OSWEGO TEACHERS EMPL FCU | Oswego | NY | B | B | B | 32.9 | 4.59 | 0.0 | 16.5 | 7.2 | 16.4 | 10.0 | 11.2 |
| OTEEN VA FCU | Asheville | NC | D | D | D | 25.2 | 1.40 | 0.0 | 13.7 | 9.1 | 0.0 | 5.8 | 7.8 |
| ▲ OTERO COUNTY TEACHERS FCU | La Junta | CO | D+ | D+ | D+ | 4.2 | -5.83 | 0.0 | 33.7 | 0.0 | 0.0 | 9.3 | 10.6 |
| OTERO FCU | Alamogordo | NM | B+ | B+ | A- | 283.8 | 3.43 | 0.0 | 34.6 | 11.2 | 31.1 | 10.0 | 13.9 |
| OTIS FCU | Jay | ME | A- | B+ | B | 141.4 | 4.14 | 0.0 | 20.5 | 19.8 | 0.4 | 10.0 | 17.1 |

| Asset Quality Index | Non-Performing Loans as a % of Total Loans | Non-Performing Loans as a % of Capital | Net Charge-Offs as a % of Avg Loans | Profitability Index | Net Income ($Mil) | Return on Assets | Return on Equity | Net Interest Spread | Overhead Efficiency Ratio | Liquidity Index | Liquidity Ratio | Hot Money Ratio | Stability Index |
|---|---|---|---|---|---|---|---|---|---|---|---|---|---|
| 4.9 | 2.71 | 15.5 | 0.06 | 2.8 | 0.1 | 0.41 | 4.81 | 2.98 | 87.6 | 4.4 | 28.5 | 5.0 | 3.0 |
| 8.3 | 2.08 | 6.0 | 0.31 | 2.0 | 0.1 | 0.20 | 1.68 | 2.79 | 91.0 | 4.6 | 18.0 | 2.4 | 5.8 |
| 6.0 | 0.75 | 6.7 | 0.11 | 5.0 | 0.5 | 0.97 | 13.12 | 3.86 | 75.2 | 2.6 | 14.0 | 12.5 | 2.7 |
| 10.0 | 0.00 | 0.0 | 0.04 | 4.5 | 0.3 | 0.70 | 4.28 | 2.35 | 72.2 | 5.4 | 21.9 | 0.0 | 8.5 |
| 9.5 | 0.03 | 0.2 | 0.18 | 2.3 | 0.1 | 0.18 | 2.15 | 3.15 | 92.3 | 4.8 | 25.2 | 1.6 | 4.1 |
| 10.0 | 0.41 | 0.5 | 0.00 | 1.6 | 0.0 | 0.07 | 0.31 | 1.29 | 94.9 | 5.1 | 18.7 | 0.0 | 7.1 |
| 9.3 | 0.28 | 1.7 | 0.01 | 3.9 | 0.2 | 0.72 | 8.02 | 2.26 | 69.5 | 4.6 | 27.1 | 1.7 | 4.2 |
| 6.8 | 0.81 | 5.5 | 0.21 | 3.5 | 0.3 | 0.43 | 4.74 | 4.32 | 85.5 | 4.9 | 24.1 | 1.3 | 4.0 |
| 5.0 | 0.96 | 6.8 | 0.00 | 8.8 | 0.0 | 1.40 | 15.94 | 8.56 | 82.8 | 5.2 | 29.9 | 0.0 | 3.0 |
| 7.9 | 1.20 | 4.6 | 0.51 | 8.8 | 3.5 | 1.39 | 9.93 | 3.53 | 70.1 | 3.5 | 9.9 | 9.9 | 8.0 |
| 8.6 | 0.23 | 1.1 | 0.41 | 1.1 | -0.1 | -0.48 | -3.46 | 3.95 | 101.9 | 4.0 | 22.5 | 3.8 | 5.7 |
| 7.6 | 0.35 | 3.0 | 0.30 | 2.2 | 0.1 | 0.11 | 1.37 | 3.14 | 96.5 | 4.1 | 28.3 | 5.8 | 4.4 |
| 5.8 | 1.24 | 14.6 | 0.34 | 1.6 | 0.0 | -0.02 | -0.15 | 3.71 | 95.3 | 4.1 | 15.2 | 1.0 | 6.1 |
| 4.4 | 2.06 | 10.7 | 3.75 | 0.3 | -0.2 | -0.78 | -6.54 | 7.13 | 95.2 | 3.4 | 10.4 | 4.2 | 5.0 |
| 8.8 | 0.55 | 2.3 | 1.14 | 9.0 | 8.0 | 1.42 | 12.84 | 4.77 | 79.7 | 7.0 | 48.2 | 1.2 | 7.9 |
| 2.4 | 2.29 | 18.2 | 1.99 | 1.1 | -0.8 | -1.17 | -12.81 | 4.91 | 80.6 | 2.9 | 25.1 | 15.2 | 4.1 |
| 6.4 | 0.47 | 2.9 | 1.27 | 0.3 | 0.0 | -0.44 | -5.39 | 4.09 | 96.0 | 5.0 | 36.6 | 4.0 | 2.0 |
| 6.0 | 5.11 | 7.7 | 1.45 | 1.8 | 0.0 | -0.35 | -1.43 | 3.24 | 112.5 | 6.4 | 55.2 | 0.0 | 7.9 |
| 9.6 | 0.57 | 1.9 | 0.16 | 2.4 | 0.1 | 0.26 | 2.22 | 2.69 | 91.4 | 4.4 | 23.6 | 2.4 | 6.2 |
| 6.9 | 1.48 | 3.5 | 0.93 | 8.9 | 0.0 | 1.29 | 5.86 | 5.46 | 72.2 | 6.0 | 38.1 | 0.0 | 5.0 |
| 7.2 | 1.65 | 5.2 | 0.48 | 2.2 | 0.0 | 0.15 | 1.42 | 3.89 | 91.3 | 7.0 | 50.0 | 1.0 | 4.9 |
| 9.8 | 1.30 | 2.4 | 0.27 | 1.8 | 0.0 | 0.06 | 0.32 | 2.97 | 93.9 | 5.3 | 16.6 | 0.0 | 6.5 |
| 9.7 | 0.28 | 1.6 | 0.12 | 8.0 | 36.4 | 1.31 | 11.74 | 2.91 | 68.3 | 4.4 | 18.9 | 4.7 | 8.1 |
| 9.9 | 0.17 | 0.8 | 0.19 | 4.5 | 0.5 | 0.67 | 6.68 | 3.03 | 80.1 | 4.1 | 26.5 | 9.1 | 4.7 |
| 6.2 | 1.51 | 8.6 | 0.13 | 1.0 | -0.1 | -0.35 | -4.11 | 4.27 | 103.1 | 5.0 | 26.2 | 1.6 | 3.6 |
| 8.1 | 0.43 | 2.4 | 0.00 | 4.4 | 0.3 | 0.67 | 7.35 | 2.76 | 77.3 | 4.5 | 16.7 | 2.2 | 5.5 |
| 8.6 | 0.00 | 0.0 | 0.00 | 4.9 | 0.0 | 0.93 | 5.93 | 3.26 | 61.7 | 6.2 | 51.6 | 0.0 | 4.3 |
| 9.5 | 0.96 | 2.9 | 0.19 | 1.8 | 0.0 | 0.07 | 0.42 | 3.11 | 95.8 | 4.7 | 31.6 | 3.5 | 6.3 |
| 9.9 | 0.46 | 1.7 | 0.08 | 8.5 | 9.3 | 1.38 | 9.71 | 3.20 | 70.2 | 3.1 | 18.5 | 15.7 | 8.6 |
| 7.3 | 5.87 | 7.7 | -0.09 | 0.8 | 0.0 | -0.04 | -0.16 | 3.27 | 100.9 | 5.4 | 49.7 | 0.0 | 6.6 |
| 5.0 | 2.98 | 17.2 | 0.13 | 3.6 | 0.0 | 0.00 | 0.03 | 3.35 | 99.8 | 4.0 | 32.8 | 4.3 | 7.7 |
| 9.7 | 1.10 | 1.2 | 0.00 | 1.8 | 0.0 | 0.22 | 1.63 | 0.82 | 75.0 | 5.8 | 63.1 | 0.0 | 5.0 |
| 8.5 | 0.76 | 3.1 | 0.23 | 5.0 | 1.4 | 0.67 | 4.23 | 3.76 | 84.9 | 3.7 | 6.5 | 1.6 | 7.7 |
| 9.9 | 0.38 | 0.8 | 0.00 | 0.0 | 0.0 | -1.91 | -12.02 | 2.04 | 221.4 | 6.2 | 47.8 | 0.0 | 5.7 |
| 9.6 | 1.88 | 2.0 | 1.86 | 1.8 | 0.0 | 0.00 | 0.00 | 3.50 | 100.0 | 7.7 | 75.6 | 0.0 | 5.7 |
| 8.6 | 0.43 | 2.8 | 0.07 | 6.3 | 9.3 | 0.99 | 10.24 | 3.06 | 76.4 | 4.2 | 15.9 | 7.6 | 7.1 |
| 6.4 | 3.62 | 8.5 | 0.71 | 6.4 | 0.0 | 0.98 | 4.86 | 3.70 | 67.1 | 4.9 | 13.6 | 0.0 | 4.3 |
| 6.7 | 0.36 | 4.4 | 0.54 | 5.2 | 8.2 | 0.82 | 9.84 | 3.29 | 72.5 | 2.8 | 8.9 | 6.5 | 6.1 |
| 8.3 | 0.15 | 0.7 | 0.01 | 3.1 | 0.1 | 0.41 | 4.94 | 3.23 | 91.2 | 4.6 | 17.1 | 0.9 | 2.3 |
| 8.2 | 0.60 | 3.3 | 0.25 | 6.1 | 6.6 | 0.94 | 8.54 | 2.98 | 73.2 | 4.0 | 15.6 | 1.9 | 8.4 |
| 9.7 | 0.58 | 1.6 | 0.18 | 4.0 | 1.4 | 0.61 | 5.13 | 2.39 | 78.8 | 5.7 | 67.9 | 2.5 | 7.0 |
| 8.8 | 0.77 | 2.6 | -0.57 | 0.8 | 0.0 | -0.04 | -0.32 | 2.40 | 130.2 | 6.3 | 73.0 | 10.8 | 4.2 |
| 9.4 | 0.11 | 0.3 | 0.26 | 2.5 | 0.0 | 0.16 | 2.07 | 2.83 | 96.2 | 5.0 | 15.1 | 0.0 | 2.3 |
| 8.9 | 0.41 | 3.0 | 0.35 | 4.2 | 2.5 | 0.59 | 5.21 | 2.73 | 84.2 | 4.0 | 13.5 | 1.7 | 7.6 |
| 5.1 | 1.23 | 10.0 | 1.69 | 3.7 | -0.4 | -0.27 | -2.46 | 5.66 | 77.8 | 4.2 | 17.2 | 2.7 | 7.2 |
| 10.0 | 2.12 | 1.9 | 0.47 | 6.4 | 0.1 | 1.68 | 5.50 | 2.85 | 44.1 | 6.3 | 59.4 | 0.0 | 5.0 |
| 1.8 | 2.23 | 21.2 | 0.08 | 3.1 | 0.0 | 0.35 | 4.18 | 5.45 | 93.6 | 4.4 | 18.5 | 0.0 | 1.0 |
| 6.2 | 0.78 | 8.7 | 0.40 | 4.6 | 6.6 | 0.53 | 4.94 | 3.11 | 80.9 | 2.8 | 8.8 | 10.1 | 7.9 |
| 6.0 | 0.49 | 4.8 | 0.31 | 5.5 | 0.1 | 0.99 | 11.00 | 4.60 | 80.6 | 2.8 | 7.5 | 4.8 | 3.0 |
| 8.5 | 0.00 | 0.0 | 0.00 | 1.5 | 0.0 | -0.09 | -0.95 | 5.54 | 97.3 | 4.2 | 17.1 | 0.0 | 3.1 |
| 10.0 | 0.76 | 1.9 | 0.02 | 1.9 | 0.0 | 0.17 | 1.05 | 3.36 | 95.7 | 5.5 | 29.5 | 0.0 | 6.6 |
| 9.4 | 0.15 | 1.1 | -0.09 | 8.3 | 0.1 | 1.32 | 12.86 | 3.52 | 64.2 | 2.0 | 20.9 | 36.8 | 4.3 |
| 4.7 | 4.70 | 16.1 | 0.29 | 1.0 | 0.0 | 0.06 | 0.70 | 2.47 | 88.1 | 5.7 | 51.7 | 2.4 | 1.0 |
| 4.0 | 1.30 | 12.7 | 0.72 | 5.4 | 0.4 | 0.74 | 9.00 | 5.83 | 79.2 | 3.3 | 8.8 | 1.6 | 3.5 |
| 9.1 | 0.33 | 1.6 | 0.07 | 1.1 | 0.0 | 0.07 | 0.77 | 3.18 | 102.2 | 4.4 | 20.0 | 5.2 | 2.9 |
| 10.0 | 0.62 | 1.9 | 0.08 | 4.8 | 0.2 | 0.66 | 6.19 | 2.76 | 68.2 | 5.4 | 23.5 | 0.0 | 5.7 |
| 9.8 | 0.36 | 1.1 | 0.38 | 1.0 | 0.0 | -0.06 | -0.74 | 2.17 | 102.7 | 5.0 | 27.9 | 5.5 | 2.9 |
| 7.4 | 1.13 | 3.9 | -0.49 | 1.9 | 0.0 | 0.03 | 0.31 | 3.79 | 100.0 | 6.2 | 58.5 | 2.7 | 5.0 |
| 9.8 | 0.24 | 1.6 | 0.25 | 4.9 | 1.6 | 0.75 | 5.47 | 3.09 | 76.8 | 4.8 | 26.8 | 5.1 | 8.3 |
| 8.2 | 1.22 | 4.2 | 0.11 | 6.0 | 1.1 | 1.04 | 6.12 | 2.69 | 69.6 | 5.0 | 42.9 | 4.8 | 8.3 |

| Name | City | State | Rating | 2014 Rating | 2013 Rating | Total Assets ($Mil) | One Year Asset Growth | Asset Mix (As a % of Total Assets) | | | | Capital-ization Index | Net Worth Ratio |
|------|------|-------|--------|-------------|-------------|---------------------|----------------------|---------------------------------|---|---|---|----------------------|------------------|
| | | | | | | | | Comm-ercial Loans | Cons-umer Loans | Mort-gage Loans | Secur-ities | | |
| OTS EMPL FCU | Honolulu | HI | C | C- | D+ | 13.8 | 9.13 | 0.0 | 78.0 | 0.0 | 0.0 | 10.0 | 13.1 |
| OTTAWA HIWAY CU | Ottawa | IL | C+ | C+ | C+ | 9.5 | 4.52 | 0.0 | 35.2 | 0.0 | 0.0 | 10.0 | 13.7 |
| OTTER TAIL CU | Fergus Falls | MN | D | D | D | 15.1 | 1.59 | 0.0 | 21.7 | 0.0 | 0.0 | 6.7 | 8.7 |
| OU FCU | Norman | OK | C- | C- | D+ | 47.9 | -2.77 | 0.0 | 27.8 | 0.0 | 19.8 | 5.8 | 7.8 |
| OUACHITA VALLEY FCU | West Monroe | LA | A | A | A | 192.8 | 9.07 | 1.9 | 44.0 | 9.6 | 8.7 | 10.0 | 12.8 |
| ▼ OUACHITA VALLEY HEALTH SYSTEM FCU | Camden | AR | D+ | C- | C+ | <1 | 12.80 | 0.0 | 45.4 | 0.0 | 0.0 | 10.0 | 30.5 |
| OUR COMMUNITY CU | Shelton | WA | A | A- | B+ | 307.8 | 6.81 | 1.6 | 28.6 | 9.6 | 49.9 | 10.0 | 11.4 |
| OUR CU | Royal Oak | MI | B- | B- | B- | 219.1 | 3.33 | 7.2 | 21.0 | 22.3 | 38.3 | 7.4 | 9.3 |
| ▲ OUR FAMILY SOCIAL CU | Omaha | NE | D- | E+ | D- | <1 | -1.61 | 0.0 | 57.2 | 0.0 | 0.0 | 7.2 | 9.1 |
| OUR LADY OF SNOWS CU | Henley | MO | D- | D- | D- | 5.0 | 2.40 | 0.0 | 33.7 | 0.0 | 0.0 | 5.6 | 7.6 |
| OUR LADY OF THE ANGELS FCU | Fall River | MA | E+ | E+ | E+ | 2.6 | -0.19 | 0.0 | 32.1 | 9.3 | 0.0 | 5.7 | 7.7 |
| OUR LADY OF VICTORY INSTITUTIONS FCU | Lackawanna | NY | D | D | C- | 4.7 | -4.42 | 0.0 | 2.3 | 8.9 | 68.8 | 10.0 | 15.2 |
| ▼ OUR MOTHER OF MERCY PARISH HOUSTON | Houston | TX | D- | D | D+ | 2.4 | -4.32 | 0.0 | 38.6 | 0.0 | 0.0 | 7.9 | 9.6 |
| OUR SUNDAY VISITOR EMPL FCU | Huntington | IN | C+ | C+ | C+ | 2.8 | 9.04 | 0.0 | 83.1 | 0.0 | 0.0 | 10.0 | 14.0 |
| OUTREACH COMMUNITY FCU | Hermitage | TN | C+ | C+ | C+ | 18.8 | 1.83 | 0.0 | 28.0 | 13.1 | 0.0 | 10.0 | 13.2 |
| ▼ OWENSBORO FCU | Owensboro | KY | D+ | C | C+ | 55.0 | -0.91 | 0.0 | 19.6 | 22.3 | 0.0 | 10.0 | 11.9 |
| OWOSSO WBC FCU | Owosso | MI | D+ | D+ | C- | 3.3 | -7.39 | 0.0 | 50.8 | 0.2 | 0.0 | 10.0 | 18.1 |
| OXFORD FCU | Mexico | ME | A- | A- | B+ | 153.3 | 7.18 | 0.1 | 26.5 | 38.2 | 0.4 | 10.0 | 14.6 |
| ▲ OZARK FCU | Poplar Bluff | MO | B- | B- | B | 47.8 | 8.47 | 0.4 | 33.0 | 25.2 | 0.0 | 9.8 | 10.9 |
| P & S CU | Salt Lake City | UT | D | D | C | 13.8 | -3.31 | 0.0 | 39.8 | 10.7 | 3.5 | 7.0 | 9.0 |
| P C FCU | Port Allegany | PA | C- | D+ | D+ | 10.3 | 9.46 | 0.0 | 48.6 | 0.0 | 0.0 | 10.0 | 12.4 |
| P S E FCU | Somerset | NJ | C+ | C+ | C | 10.8 | -2.87 | 0.0 | 39.2 | 0.0 | 0.0 | 10.0 | 11.9 |
| ▲ P&G MEHOOPANY EMPL FCU | Tunkhannock | PA | C+ | C+ | C | 103.8 | 0.59 | 2.0 | 34.6 | 19.8 | 10.7 | 6.7 | 8.7 |
| PA HEALTHCARE CU | Sewickley | PA | C- | C- | C- | 25.3 | -4.69 | 0.0 | 18.1 | 0.0 | 60.6 | 10.0 | 12.8 |
| PAAC TRANSIT DIVISION FCU | Pittsburgh | PA | C- | D+ | D+ | 28.2 | -2.37 | 0.0 | 14.6 | 0.0 | 18.7 | 10.0 | 14.1 |
| PACE FCU | Huntington | WV | D | D+ | D+ | 7.6 | -0.77 | 0.0 | 33.7 | 0.0 | 0.0 | 10.0 | 16.6 |
| PACE KENNER FCU | Kenner | LA | D+ | D+ | D+ | 2.6 | 1.04 | 0.0 | 39.4 | 11.0 | 0.0 | 10.0 | 13.4 |
| PACE RESOURCES FCU | York | PA | D+ | D | E+ | 5.3 | -0.95 | 0.0 | 28.6 | 0.0 | 0.0 | 8.6 | 10.1 |
| PACIFIC CASCADE FCU | Eugene | OR | C | C- | C | 98.4 | 2.68 | 0.0 | 48.8 | 10.1 | 6.5 | 6.0 | 8.0 |
| ▲ PACIFIC COMMUNITY CU | Fullerton | CA | C+ | C+ | B- | 188.6 | 1.33 | 0.9 | 21.5 | 10.4 | 23.1 | 10.0 | 14.3 |
| ▲ PACIFIC CREST FCU | Klamath Falls | OR | C+ | C- | C | 153.0 | 2.46 | 5.9 | 30.0 | 19.9 | 2.4 | 6.6 | 8.7 |
| PACIFIC FCU | Diamond Bar | CA | D+ | D+ | C- | 17.6 | -0.64 | 1.1 | 17.4 | 0.0 | 0.0 | 10.0 | 17.1 |
| PACIFIC HORIZON CU | Springville | UT | C+ | C+ | C | 48.7 | 7.49 | 4.3 | 51.5 | 22.7 | 0.0 | 8.9 | 10.3 |
| PACIFIC MARINE CU | Oceanside | CA | B | B+ | B+ | 722.5 | 4.47 | 1.8 | 27.1 | 30.7 | 16.1 | 10.0 | 14.3 |
| ▲ PACIFIC NORTHWEST IRONWORKERS FCU | Portland | OR | C- | D | D- | 19.5 | 25.15 | 0.0 | 73.8 | 0.0 | 0.0 | 8.6 | 10.1 |
| PACIFIC NW FCU | Portland | OR | B | B | B- | 147.3 | 7.83 | 3.7 | 28.5 | 22.7 | 10.3 | 6.2 | 8.2 |
| PACIFIC POSTAL CU | San Jose | CA | B | B+ | B | 212.3 | 3.81 | 0.1 | 12.5 | 10.6 | 37.9 | 10.0 | 13.5 |
| ▲ PACIFIC SERVICE CU | Concord | CA | B- | C+ | C+ | 1108.5 | 2.49 | 0.8 | 15.2 | 11.1 | 47.7 | 10.0 | 13.2 |
| PACIFIC SPRUCE FCU | Toledo | OR | D- | D- | D+ | 3.3 | -3.76 | 0.0 | 40.7 | 0.0 | 0.0 | 6.8 | 8.9 |
| ▼ PACIFIC TRANSPORTATION FCU | Gardena | CA | C | B- | B- | 66.2 | -1.73 | 1.0 | 16.0 | 31.2 | 18.9 | 10.0 | 18.5 |
| PACOE FCU | Johnstown | PA | D | D | D+ | 4.9 | -3.90 | 0.0 | 34.6 | 0.0 | 0.0 | 10.0 | 18.2 |
| PACOIMA DEVEL FCU | Pacoima | CA | E+ | E+ | E+ | 4.5 | 4.71 | 54.7 | 9.3 | 12.1 | 0.0 | 6.0 | 8.0 |
| ▲ PADUCAH TEACHERS FCU | Paducah | KY | D+ | D | D+ | 9.6 | 1.68 | 0.0 | 54.6 | 0.0 | 0.0 | 9.5 | 10.7 |
| PAGODA FCU | Reading | PA | D- | D- | D- | 24.0 | 3.63 | 0.0 | 27.6 | 21.2 | 0.0 | 5.6 | 7.6 |
| PAHO/WHO FCU | Washington | DC | B- | B- | B- | 202.5 | 0.32 | 0.8 | 9.4 | 38.9 | 33.7 | 10.0 | 18.4 |
| PAHRANAGAT VALLEY FCU | Alamo | NV | C+ | C+ | C | 20.1 | 5.88 | 1.8 | 19.4 | 22.6 | 0.0 | 10.0 | 11.2 |
| PAINESVILLE CU | Painesville | OH | B- | C | C | 26.1 | -0.08 | 4.1 | 38.1 | 19.0 | 4.4 | 10.0 | 11.6 |
| PAKCO EMPL FCU | Latrobe | PA | C | C | D+ | <1 | 6.54 | 0.0 | 53.7 | 0.0 | 0.0 | 10.0 | 22.3 |
| PALACE CITY FCU | Mitchell | SD | C+ | C | C | 10.4 | 8.64 | 0.0 | 38.0 | 0.0 | 0.0 | 10.0 | 12.1 |
| PALCO FCU | Muncy | PA | C | C- | C- | 72.4 | 1.01 | 0.0 | 17.7 | 8.7 | 56.4 | 10.0 | 11.9 |
| ▼ PALISADES FCU | Pearl River | NY | C | C+ | D+ | 145.1 | -10.74 | 5.4 | 20.1 | 14.0 | 11.6 | 10.0 | 13.8 |
| PALMETTO CITIZENS FCU | Columbia | SC | A- | A- | A- | 668.2 | 6.48 | 1.1 | 27.2 | 23.1 | 20.2 | 10.0 | 11.0 |
| ▲ PALMETTO FIRST FCU | Florence | SC | B | B- | B- | 36.1 | 0.72 | 0.0 | 43.5 | 9.7 | 18.7 | 10.0 | 14.3 |
| PALMETTO HEALTH CU | Columbia | SC | A- | B+ | B | 60.4 | 3.83 | 0.0 | 43.3 | 7.5 | 6.2 | 10.0 | 13.9 |
| PALMETTO TRUST FCU | Columbia | SC | D+ | D | D- | 18.2 | 0.90 | 0.0 | 39.1 | 1.2 | 7.7 | 6.5 | 8.5 |
| PAMCEL COMMUNITY FCU | Pampa | TX | D | D | C- | 14.0 | 5.52 | 0.0 | 27.7 | 0.0 | 0.0 | 10.0 | 16.2 |
| PAMPA MUNICIPAL CU | Pampa | TX | E+ | E+ | D- | 3.4 | 4.68 | 0.0 | 68.8 | 0.0 | 0.0 | 5.6 | 7.6 |
| ▲ PAMPA TEACHERS FCU | Pampa | TX | C- | D+ | D+ | 13.1 | 8.15 | 0.0 | 64.8 | 8.8 | 0.0 | 8.4 | 9.9 |
| PAN AMOCO FCU | Metairie | LA | D+ | D | D- | 8.6 | -10.27 | 0.0 | 44.7 | 0.0 | 0.0 | 10.0 | 11.9 |
| PANHANDLE COOPERATIVE FCU | Scottsbluff | NE | E+ | E+ | E+ | 3.7 | -2.16 | 0.0 | 32.6 | 0.0 | 0.0 | 4.2 | 6.2 |

| Asset Quality Index | Non-Performing Loans | | Net Charge-Offs Avg Loans | Profitability Index | Net Income ($Mil) | Return on Assets | Return on Equity | Net Interest Spread | Overhead Efficiency Ratio | Liquidity Index | Liquidity Ratio | Hot Money Ratio | Stability Index |
|---|---|---|---|---|---|---|---|---|---|---|---|---|---|
| | as a % of Total Loans | as a % of Capital | | | | | | | | | | | |
| 2.9 | 4.26 | 19.5 | 1.70 | 7.6 | 0.2 | 2.29 | 18.14 | 6.45 | 62.9 | 1.6 | 3.8 | 20.1 | 5.7 |
| 9.5 | 0.41 | 1.5 | -0.03 | 4.9 | 0.1 | 0.71 | 5.31 | 3.36 | 76.2 | 4.9 | 13.0 | 0.0 | 7.5 |
| 9.7 | 0.31 | 1.1 | 0.14 | 1.1 | 0.0 | -0.04 | -0.51 | 2.40 | 102.3 | 5.6 | 26.6 | 0.0 | 3.8 |
| 8.8 | 0.57 | 3.3 | 0.71 | 2.5 | 0.1 | 0.27 | 3.51 | 2.77 | 84.4 | 4.3 | 9.9 | 0.5 | 2.4 |
| 6.6 | 1.07 | 6.4 | 0.51 | 5.8 | 1.0 | 0.73 | 6.11 | 4.11 | 80.9 | 3.8 | 21.6 | 8.4 | 8.6 |
| 5.5 | 6.55 | 9.2 | 0.00 | 2.0 | 0.0 | -0.37 | -1.17 | 7.38 | 93.3 | 6.8 | 76.3 | 0.0 | 4.7 |
| 9.9 | 0.55 | 2.0 | 0.52 | 6.8 | 2.4 | 1.05 | 8.62 | 3.83 | 74.0 | 5.0 | 56.9 | 6.7 | 7.7 |
| 7.5 | 0.86 | 5.0 | 0.54 | 3.7 | 1.1 | 0.65 | 7.32 | 2.85 | 79.5 | 4.1 | 12.4 | 3.5 | 5.5 |
| 4.4 | 1.39 | 7.6 | 0.00 | 2.0 | 0.0 | 0.00 | 0.00 | 7.07 | 100.0 | 5.9 | 38.4 | 0.0 | 6.1 |
| 2.9 | 3.70 | 25.0 | 0.05 | 2.8 | 0.0 | 0.25 | 3.23 | 2.08 | 78.8 | 4.8 | 15.2 | 0.0 | 1.0 |
| 3.5 | 1.38 | 11.8 | 0.00 | 3.9 | 0.0 | 0.31 | 4.10 | 9.73 | 94.2 | 4.7 | 20.7 | 0.0 | 1.0 |
| 10.0 | 0.00 | 0.0 | 0.27 | 0.0 | 0.0 | -0.87 | -5.63 | 2.22 | 133.0 | 5.8 | 32.6 | 0.0 | 6.6 |
| 3.9 | 3.67 | 15.5 | 2.97 | 0.3 | 0.0 | -2.23 | -20.66 | 5.19 | 104.6 | 6.6 | 59.4 | 4.6 | 3.2 |
| 5.6 | 1.38 | 8.3 | -0.06 | 9.9 | 0.0 | 1.83 | 13.08 | 4.52 | 61.4 | 2.7 | 14.7 | 4.2 | 5.0 |
| 9.8 | 0.03 | 0.1 | 0.70 | 2.2 | 0.0 | 0.16 | 1.19 | 3.12 | 88.7 | 3.8 | 51.9 | 21.3 | 6.1 |
| 8.8 | 1.05 | 5.0 | 0.47 | 0.5 | -0.2 | -0.42 | -4.25 | 2.66 | 104.4 | 5.4 | 28.5 | 0.9 | 4.9 |
| 7.3 | 0.97 | 3.3 | -0.19 | 2.4 | 0.0 | 0.38 | 2.24 | 4.60 | 93.9 | 4.4 | 22.5 | 0.0 | 4.8 |
| 7.8 | 0.69 | 4.3 | 0.21 | 8.6 | 1.7 | 1.52 | 10.55 | 3.59 | 66.8 | 2.9 | 18.6 | 9.4 | 8.9 |
| 7.3 | 0.67 | 4.0 | 0.12 | 4.3 | 0.2 | 0.59 | 5.46 | 4.13 | 85.1 | 3.8 | 21.1 | 2.7 | 5.7 |
| 8.3 | 0.20 | 1.1 | -0.05 | 1.2 | 0.0 | -0.41 | -4.64 | 3.59 | 102.9 | 4.0 | 29.8 | 5.8 | 3.7 |
| 2.6 | 4.33 | 24.8 | -0.02 | 2.7 | 0.0 | 0.07 | 0.53 | 4.32 | 95.5 | 4.5 | 23.4 | 5.0 | 6.8 |
| 7.3 | 1.40 | 4.4 | 2.61 | 5.8 | 0.1 | 0.92 | 7.89 | 1.99 | 52.5 | 5.0 | 37.1 | 0.0 | 5.7 |
| 6.4 | 1.69 | 12.0 | 0.49 | 3.9 | 0.4 | 0.52 | 6.39 | 4.37 | 77.1 | 4.2 | 24.6 | 2.2 | 5.3 |
| 9.5 | 1.82 | 2.9 | 0.28 | 1.1 | 0.0 | -0.19 | -1.49 | 2.17 | 103.0 | 6.0 | 28.5 | 0.8 | 5.4 |
| 8.6 | 1.57 | 1.8 | 0.78 | 1.3 | 0.0 | 0.02 | 0.13 | 1.96 | 93.2 | 7.4 | 73.4 | 0.0 | 5.5 |
| 9.0 | 1.48 | 3.0 | 1.44 | 0.0 | -0.1 | -0.90 | -5.32 | 2.71 | 111.1 | 5.1 | 26.0 | 0.0 | 6.3 |
| 5.6 | 4.50 | 17.5 | 0.29 | 2.3 | 0.0 | 0.10 | 0.76 | 5.54 | 92.3 | 6.5 | 52.5 | 0.0 | 5.8 |
| 7.3 | 1.75 | 5.6 | 0.51 | 3.1 | 0.0 | 0.25 | 2.50 | 3.35 | 87.6 | 6.0 | 58.0 | 0.0 | 3.0 |
| 6.4 | 0.34 | 3.8 | 0.14 | 4.7 | 0.6 | 0.79 | 9.93 | 4.13 | 85.2 | 4.6 | 22.0 | 0.3 | 3.0 |
| 10.0 | 0.38 | 1.3 | 0.38 | 3.6 | 0.7 | 0.51 | 3.70 | 3.40 | 83.0 | 5.0 | 32.0 | 2.4 | 6.7 |
| 6.9 | 1.43 | 9.4 | 0.32 | 3.7 | 0.6 | 0.48 | 5.63 | 3.93 | 88.9 | 4.3 | 23.2 | 4.3 | 4.5 |
| 9.0 | 2.24 | 4.2 | 0.19 | 0.9 | 0.0 | -0.14 | -0.91 | 2.90 | 104.4 | 5.9 | 45.3 | 3.7 | 5.3 |
| 4.2 | 0.89 | 8.3 | 0.65 | 7.0 | 0.4 | 0.98 | 9.85 | 4.19 | 72.9 | 2.8 | 15.3 | 13.3 | 5.4 |
| 9.8 | 0.24 | 1.2 | 0.26 | 4.3 | 3.4 | 0.64 | 4.52 | 3.07 | 86.1 | 3.8 | 16.0 | 6.7 | 8.3 |
| 3.9 | 0.99 | 11.7 | 0.23 | 10.0 | 0.4 | 3.03 | 44.34 | 6.73 | 59.7 | 0.7 | 4.8 | 30.1 | 3.1 |
| 9.5 | 0.10 | 0.7 | 0.22 | 5.2 | 0.8 | 0.76 | 9.30 | 3.85 | 83.1 | 4.9 | 23.0 | 0.4 | 5.0 |
| 10.0 | 0.50 | 0.9 | 0.35 | 3.6 | 0.6 | 0.36 | 2.66 | 3.12 | 87.5 | 6.7 | 59.4 | 4.1 | 7.4 |
| 10.0 | 0.06 | 0.3 | 0.02 | 3.9 | 5.0 | 0.60 | 4.58 | 2.18 | 80.9 | 4.7 | 26.9 | 11.1 | 7.5 |
| 7.0 | 0.00 | 3.3 | 0.08 | 0.0 | 0.0 | -0.88 | -9.65 | 3.14 | 122.1 | 6.0 | 51.4 | 0.0 | 4.3 |
| 7.2 | 2.49 | 9.0 | 0.36 | 0.8 | -0.3 | -0.60 | -3.18 | 4.05 | 113.3 | 4.2 | 22.8 | 7.2 | 5.8 |
| 9.9 | 0.22 | 0.4 | 0.07 | 0.0 | 0.0 | -0.81 | -4.52 | 2.56 | 132.2 | 5.6 | 38.1 | 0.0 | 6.4 |
| 0.4 | 1.30 | 20.7 | 0.00 | 0.7 | 0.0 | -0.60 | -11.89 | 6.18 | 109.5 | 2.1 | 19.2 | 32.5 | 1.8 |
| 3.8 | 1.34 | 7.4 | 1.02 | 4.4 | 0.1 | 0.74 | 7.07 | 3.94 | 63.7 | 4.2 | 25.1 | 0.0 | 3.0 |
| 8.3 | 0.25 | 2.6 | 0.27 | 1.7 | 0.0 | 0.02 | 0.22 | 3.59 | 99.7 | 4.7 | 22.7 | 0.0 | 2.9 |
| 8.2 | 1.15 | 3.8 | 0.51 | 3.7 | 0.7 | 0.47 | 2.63 | 2.47 | 74.7 | 3.6 | 44.9 | 23.0 | 8.0 |
| 6.0 | 1.96 | 9.3 | 2.10 | 5.7 | 0.1 | 0.61 | 5.41 | 3.71 | 87.6 | 3.4 | 11.0 | 10.1 | 5.0 |
| 7.5 | 1.36 | 6.7 | 0.46 | 5.0 | 0.2 | 0.82 | 7.32 | 4.61 | 86.4 | 3.3 | 14.3 | 8.7 | 5.4 |
| 8.7 | 0.00 | 0.0 | -0.93 | 3.6 | 0.0 | 0.52 | 2.30 | 3.44 | 81.3 | 6.5 | 60.6 | 0.0 | 6.4 |
| 9.9 | 0.00 | 0.0 | 0.00 | 3.0 | 0.0 | 0.34 | 2.80 | 2.82 | 89.5 | 5.7 | 33.8 | 3.2 | 6.2 |
| 9.0 | 1.23 | 3.2 | 0.18 | 2.6 | 0.2 | 0.36 | 3.18 | 2.28 | 87.7 | 4.8 | 26.5 | 2.0 | 5.5 |
| 5.5 | 2.12 | 13.5 | 1.09 | 1.9 | 0.1 | 0.06 | 0.49 | 3.46 | 86.7 | 3.7 | 18.8 | 4.0 | 6.8 |
| 7.3 | 0.93 | 7.3 | 0.62 | 8.8 | 6.1 | 1.23 | 11.54 | 3.28 | 68.6 | 4.0 | 22.4 | 4.9 | 8.3 |
| 6.2 | 1.90 | 9.9 | 0.94 | 6.7 | 0.3 | 0.98 | 7.23 | 5.74 | 75.0 | 4.6 | 18.0 | 3.6 | 6.8 |
| 8.8 | 0.42 | 1.8 | 0.31 | 10.0 | 0.9 | 1.95 | 14.95 | 5.05 | 71.0 | 4.0 | 19.2 | 10.5 | 5.9 |
| 5.5 | 1.77 | 9.1 | -0.07 | 3.5 | 0.0 | 0.31 | 3.63 | 5.73 | 97.7 | 6.9 | 52.3 | 0.7 | 3.0 |
| 9.6 | 1.60 | 3.0 | 0.06 | 0.0 | -0.1 | -0.77 | -4.75 | 2.21 | 130.2 | 5.4 | 30.7 | 0.0 | 5.5 |
| 3.9 | 1.14 | 10.7 | 0.00 | 4.3 | 0.0 | 0.80 | 10.62 | 5.23 | 80.0 | 4.2 | 19.2 | 0.0 | 1.0 |
| 3.1 | 1.72 | 12.7 | 0.63 | 5.8 | 0.1 | 0.98 | 10.06 | 4.47 | 70.4 | 2.7 | 40.2 | 32.9 | 5.6 |
| 9.2 | 0.35 | 1.4 | 0.03 | 0.6 | 0.0 | -0.18 | -1.54 | 3.31 | 106.9 | 4.5 | 14.1 | 0.0 | 4.5 |
| 1.7 | 7.82 | 35.3 | 2.20 | 0.0 | 0.0 | -1.30 | -19.92 | 3.17 | 115.4 | 7.1 | 63.7 | 0.0 | 2.7 |

| Name | City | State | Rating | 2014 Rating | 2013 Rating | Total Assets ($Mil) | One Year Asset Growth | Comm-ercial Loans | Cons-umer Loans | Mort-gage Loans | Secur-ities | Capital-ization Index | Net Worth Ratio |
|---|---|---|---|---|---|---|---|---|---|---|---|---|---|
| | | | | | | | | Asset Mix (As a % of Total Assets) | | | | | |
| PANHANDLE EDUCATORS FCU | Panama City | FL | A | A | A | 146.9 | 7.01 | 9.7 | 19.0 | 27.8 | 9.1 | 10.0 | 13.0 |
| PANHANDLE FCU | Wellington | KS | B- | B- | B | 51.8 | 2.78 | 1.1 | 9.0 | 28.3 | 0.0 | 10.0 | 15.1 |
| PANNONIA FCU | Feasterville Trevose | PA | C | C | C- | 12.8 | 5.47 | 10.1 | 2.1 | 73.8 | 0.0 | 10.0 | 33.6 |
| PANTEX FCU | Borger | TX | B | B+ | B+ | 224.0 | -2.43 | 0.0 | 16.3 | 2.8 | 61.4 | 10.0 | 17.1 |
| PAPER CONVERTERS LOCAL 286/1034 FCU | Philadelphia | PA | C- | D+ | D+ | 1.5 | -1.89 | 0.0 | 50.8 | 0.0 | 0.0 | 10.0 | 11.1 |
| PAR-DEL EMPL FCU | Wyoming | PA | C- | C- | C- | 8.4 | 2.43 | 0.0 | 20.4 | 0.0 | 34.2 | 10.0 | 11.1 |
| PARADISE VALLEY FCU | National City | CA | B | B | C+ | 83.8 | -1.37 | 10.6 | 13.8 | 35.1 | 0.0 | 10.0 | 13.2 |
| PARAMOUNT BAPTIST CHURCH FCU | Washington | DC | B- | C+ | C+ | <1 | 8.33 | 0.0 | 52.9 | 0.0 | 0.0 | 10.0 | 31.7 |
| PARDA FCU | Auburn Hills | MI | B- | B | C+ | 166.8 | -2.61 | 2.8 | 22.4 | 16.5 | 36.6 | 10.0 | 14.3 |
| PARIS DISTRICT CU | Paris | TX | C- | D+ | C- | <1 | -3.76 | 0.0 | 49.2 | 0.0 | 0.0 | 10.0 | 17.4 |
| PARIS FCU | Paris | AR | D | D | C- | <1 | -30.16 | 1.0 | 34.9 | 5.9 | 0.0 | 10.0 | 14.2 |
| PARIS HIGHWAY CU | Paris | IL | C | C | C+ | 8.7 | 0.20 | 0.0 | 69.2 | 0.0 | 21.2 | 10.0 | 13.4 |
| PARISH FCU | Toledo | OH | C | C | C- | 15.1 | 4.73 | 0.7 | 30.7 | 15.5 | 0.0 | 9.2 | 10.5 |
| ▲ PARISH MEMBERS CU | Metamora | IL | D | D- | E+ | 3.9 | -9.56 | 0.0 | 29.1 | 0.0 | 0.0 | 7.1 | 9.1 |
| PARISHIONERS FCU | Torrance | CA | D | D | D | 39.8 | 6.42 | 0.0 | 11.5 | 13.8 | 33.4 | 5.8 | 8.7 |
| PARK CITY CU | Merrill | WI | B- | C | C | 158.0 | 3.17 | 8.7 | 16.3 | 42.7 | 11.3 | 9.0 | 10.5 |
| ▲ PARK COMMUNITY CU INC | Louisville | KY | B | B | B+ | 765.7 | 10.17 | 1.5 | 40.6 | 19.0 | 3.4 | 8.1 | 9.8 |
| PARK MANOR CHRISTIAN CHURCH CU | Chicago | IL | C- | C | C | <1 | 3.58 | 0.0 | 12.3 | 0.0 | 0.0 | 9.9 | 10.9 |
| PARK SIDE CU | Whitefish | MT | B- | B- | A- | 200.4 | 6.24 | 1.7 | 35.5 | 34.0 | 3.3 | 10.0 | 11.3 |
| PARK VIEW FCU | Harrisonburg | VA | B- | B- | B- | 139.7 | 5.77 | 19.4 | 9.2 | 39.4 | 6.9 | 6.9 | 8.9 |
| PARKER COMMUNITY CU | Janesville | WI | C- | C- | D | 96.7 | 1.93 | 0.4 | 31.4 | 35.4 | 13.5 | 6.1 | 8.2 |
| ▲ PARKS HERITAGE FCU | Glens Falls | NY | C | C- | C | 27.5 | 8.25 | 0.0 | 27.8 | 27.6 | 18.7 | 10.0 | 12.6 |
| PARKSIDE CU | Livonia | MI | A- | A- | A- | 84.4 | 5.29 | 3.5 | 21.3 | 15.0 | 19.2 | 10.0 | 14.7 |
| PARKVIEW COMMUNITY FCU | McKeesport | PA | C | C+ | B | 39.3 | 1.01 | 0.0 | 30.8 | 0.0 | 24.1 | 10.0 | 13.2 |
| PARKWAY FCU | Redford | MI | D | D | D | 23.3 | 2.30 | 3.5 | 13.4 | 27.3 | 0.0 | 10.0 | 11.5 |
| PARLIN DUPONT EMPL FCU | Sayreville | NJ | D | D+ | D+ | 4.5 | 0.07 | 0.0 | 41.4 | 0.0 | 0.2 | 7.3 | 9.2 |
| PARSONS FCU | Pasadena | CA | B+ | B+ | B+ | 217.1 | -1.95 | 0.0 | 5.4 | 18.1 | 32.8 | 10.0 | 12.1 |
| ▼ PARTHENON FCU | Nashville | TN | D+ | C | C+ | 15.0 | -0.30 | 0.0 | 18.8 | 10.8 | 0.0 | 10.0 | 14.8 |
| PARTNER COLORADO CU | Arvada | CO | B+ | B | B | 301.6 | 7.19 | 2.1 | 62.0 | 8.8 | 1.7 | 10.0 | 12.3 |
| ▼ PARTNERS 1ST FCU | Fort Wayne | IN | C- | C+ | B- | 260.7 | 0.83 | 0.5 | 28.8 | 8.3 | 9.0 | 10.0 | 11.3 |
| PARTNERS FCU | Burbank | CA | A- | A- | B+ | 1339.4 | 9.47 | 3.0 | 42.2 | 31.9 | 3.1 | 10.0 | 12.0 |
| PARTNERS FINANCIAL FCU | Glen Allen | VA | D- | D- | D- | 85.7 | -4.72 | 0.0 | 29.7 | 26.0 | 17.4 | 5.1 | 7.1 |
| PARTNERSHIP FCU | Arlington | VA | C- | C- | C | 146.2 | 0.49 | 0.0 | 31.0 | 15.6 | 16.1 | 7.1 | 9.1 |
| PARTNERSHIP FINANCIAL CU | Morton Grove | IL | C- | C- | C- | 164.1 | 11.70 | 0.0 | 11.5 | 14.1 | 1.2 | 8.5 | 10.0 |
| ▲ PASADENA FCU | Pasadena | CA | D+ | D | C | 148.3 | 0.07 | 1.5 | 17.3 | 13.4 | 28.9 | 9.6 | 10.7 |
| PASADENA MUNICIPAL FCU | Pasadena | TX | B- | C+ | C+ | 11.4 | 1.63 | 0.0 | 40.7 | 0.0 | 0.0 | 10.0 | 18.5 |
| PASADENA POSTAL CU | Pasadena | TX | D+ | D+ | D+ | 1.5 | -5.74 | 0.0 | 93.0 | 0.0 | 0.0 | 10.0 | 14.3 |
| ▲ PASADENA SERVICE FCU | Pasadena | CA | C+ | C- | C- | 102.3 | -1.64 | 5.4 | 27.5 | 22.9 | 25.5 | 6.9 | 8.9 |
| PASSAIC POLICE FCU | Passaic | NJ | C+ | C | C | 5.4 | 8.18 | 0.0 | 37.7 | 0.0 | 0.0 | 10.0 | 14.3 |
| PASSAIC POSTAL EMPL CU | Passaic | NJ | D+ | D+ | C- | <1 | 0.00 | 0.0 | 48.4 | 0.0 | 0.0 | 10.0 | 16.7 |
| PATA FCU | Pittsburgh | PA | E+ | E+ | E+ | 3.0 | 3.74 | 0.0 | 68.1 | 0.0 | 0.0 | 5.2 | 7.2 |
| PATELCO CU | Pleasanton | CA | A | A | A | 4579.2 | 10.31 | 4.8 | 19.7 | 35.5 | 22.1 | 10.0 | 12.0 |
| PATENT AND TRADEMARK OFFICE FCU | Alexandria | VA | D | D- | D- | 39.6 | 3.53 | 0.9 | 20.2 | 9.9 | 21.4 | 4.6 | 6.6 |
| PATERSON POLICE FCU | Paterson | NJ | C+ | C+ | C+ | 4.9 | 2.90 | 0.0 | 25.3 | 0.0 | 0.0 | 10.0 | 16.5 |
| PATH FCU | Jersey City | NJ | B | B | B | 11.4 | -5.23 | 0.0 | 37.1 | 0.0 | 0.0 | 10.0 | 34.8 |
| PATHWAY CU | Cleveland | TN | D- | D- | D+ | 5.0 | -1.82 | 0.0 | 39.8 | 3.5 | 0.0 | 9.1 | 10.4 |
| ▲ PATHWAYS FINANCIAL CU INC | Columbus | OH | D- | E+ | E+ | 234.5 | 9.01 | 5.0 | 30.5 | 21.8 | 9.0 | 7.5 | 9.3 |
| PATRIOT CU | Saint Louis | MO | D- | D- | D- | 9.3 | 19.66 | 0.0 | 38.0 | 0.0 | 0.0 | 5.0 | 7.0 |
| PATRIOT EQUITY CU | Jackson | TN | D | D+ | D | 23.5 | 2.40 | 0.0 | 31.5 | 15.8 | 0.0 | 10.0 | 15.3 |
| PATRIOT FCU | Chambersburg | PA | B | B | A- | 510.5 | 2.93 | 0.0 | 29.8 | 14.1 | 24.9 | 10.0 | 13.3 |
| PATTERSON FCU | Arkadelphia | AR | C- | C- | C | 17.2 | 4.78 | 0.5 | 51.7 | 4.4 | 0.0 | 8.4 | 9.9 |
| PATTERSON PUMP FCU | Toccoa | GA | C+ | C+ | C | 2.4 | 0.38 | 0.0 | 33.5 | 0.0 | 0.0 | 10.0 | 17.6 |
| ▼ PAUL QUINN FCU | Flushing | NY | D | D+ | D | <1 | -5.04 | 0.0 | 17.1 | 0.0 | 0.0 | 10.0 | 22.7 |
| PAWTUCKET CU | Pawtucket | RI | B+ | B+ | B+ | 1747.0 | 7.65 | 4.5 | 15.9 | 62.4 | 4.4 | 7.9 | 9.6 |
| PAWTUCKET MUNICIPAL EMPL FCU | Pawtucket | RI | C | C | C- | 3.9 | 0.66 | 0.0 | 60.4 | 0.0 | 16.5 | 10.0 | 15.5 |
| ▲ PBA FCU | Pine Bluff | AR | C- | D+ | D+ | 10.8 | -2.38 | 0.0 | 32.7 | 0.0 | 0.0 | 10.0 | 29.8 |
| PBC CU | West Palm Beach | FL | A | A | A- | 129.8 | 8.12 | 0.0 | 41.1 | 8.1 | 1.1 | 10.0 | 12.2 |
| PCM CU | Green Bay | WI | A | A | A | 193.6 | 15.12 | 1.3 | 12.8 | 58.0 | 4.3 | 10.0 | 14.8 |
| ▲ PEABODY MUNICIPAL FCU | Peabody | MA | C+ | C | C | 25.2 | 7.96 | 0.0 | 19.6 | 0.0 | 4.2 | 10.0 | 11.3 |
| PEACH STATE FCU | Lawrenceville | GA | B- | B- | B- | 295.7 | 12.04 | 10.4 | 25.3 | 23.4 | 13.7 | 6.2 | 8.2 |

| Asset Quality Index | Non-Performing Loans as a % of Total Loans | as a % of Capital | Net Charge-Offs Avg Loans | Profitability Index | Net Income ($Mil) | Return on Assets | Return on Equity | Net Interest Spread | Overhead Efficiency Ratio | Liquidity Index | Liquidity Ratio | Hot Money Ratio | Stability Index |
|---|---|---|---|---|---|---|---|---|---|---|---|---|---|
| 8.6 | 0.39 | 2.6 | 0.42 | 8.9 | 1.5 | 1.37 | 10.53 | 4.11 | 70.1 | 4.5 | 28.8 | 11.0 | 8.4 |
| 10.0 | 0.47 | 1.2 | -0.02 | 3.5 | 0.2 | 0.44 | 3.03 | 2.05 | 80.5 | 5.2 | 37.7 | 2.2 | 7.4 |
| 9.1 | 1.15 | 2.6 | 0.04 | 2.3 | 0.0 | 0.05 | 0.16 | 3.87 | 93.2 | 4.6 | 23.2 | 0.0 | 7.3 |
| 10.0 | 0.46 | 1.0 | 0.30 | 3.7 | 0.7 | 0.41 | 2.32 | 1.99 | 80.8 | 5.5 | 40.1 | 7.6 | 8.1 |
| 6.1 | 2.17 | 9.3 | 0.00 | 5.3 | 0.0 | 0.91 | 8.44 | 7.68 | 86.1 | 6.7 | 54.0 | 0.0 | 4.3 |
| 9.7 | 0.15 | 0.3 | 0.48 | 1.6 | 0.0 | 0.06 | 0.57 | 2.53 | 96.5 | 6.8 | 40.1 | 0.0 | 4.6 |
| 5.5 | 2.67 | 14.0 | 0.19 | 5.1 | 0.4 | 0.69 | 5.32 | 3.20 | 77.5 | 2.3 | 23.1 | 30.2 | 6.5 |
| 4.4 | 10.91 | 17.7 | 0.00 | 10.0 | 0.0 | 6.94 | 21.51 | 8.77 | 16.7 | 6.4 | 62.0 | 0.0 | 10.0 |
| 8.2 | 1.01 | 4.6 | 0.38 | 3.1 | 0.5 | 0.39 | 2.80 | 3.42 | 89.9 | 4.0 | 7.9 | 2.6 | 7.2 |
| 8.3 | 0.00 | 0.0 | 0.83 | 1.7 | 0.0 | 0.00 | 0.00 | 5.77 | 84.2 | 5.3 | 45.5 | 0.0 | 6.1 |
| 7.8 | 0.00 | 0.0 | 0.00 | 0.0 | 0.0 | -1.47 | -10.98 | 2.61 | 180.0 | 5.3 | 24.8 | 0.0 | 5.4 |
| 7.2 | 0.49 | 2.6 | 0.49 | 8.0 | 0.1 | 1.38 | 10.77 | 3.50 | 50.9 | 4.1 | 38.1 | 0.0 | 5.0 |
| 7.1 | 1.11 | 5.3 | -0.08 | 4.3 | 0.1 | 0.62 | 6.01 | 3.41 | 85.6 | 4.6 | 26.0 | 2.1 | 5.8 |
| 7.3 | 1.51 | 4.7 | 0.98 | 1.9 | 0.0 | 0.07 | 0.76 | 2.52 | 95.7 | 5.7 | 37.8 | 0.0 | 4.5 |
| 10.0 | 0.07 | 0.3 | 0.09 | 0.5 | -0.1 | -0.19 | -2.31 | 2.45 | 105.8 | 4.9 | 19.3 | 3.2 | 2.8 |
| 5.6 | 1.34 | 10.8 | 0.08 | 4.0 | 0.7 | 0.58 | 5.71 | 3.83 | 86.1 | 4.2 | 12.9 | 1.3 | 6.6 |
| 7.4 | 0.51 | 4.8 | 0.47 | 5.2 | 4.8 | 0.86 | 9.93 | 3.21 | 71.4 | 3.2 | 13.9 | 8.8 | 6.5 |
| 6.5 | 10.17 | 15.7 | 0.00 | 2.1 | 0.0 | 0.00 | 0.00 | 2.92 | 100.0 | 8.0 | 90.3 | 0.0 | 6.3 |
| 8.5 | 0.45 | 3.5 | 0.29 | 3.6 | 0.6 | 0.38 | 3.33 | 4.19 | 88.8 | 2.4 | 11.3 | 14.3 | 6.3 |
| 6.0 | 0.72 | 9.7 | 0.12 | 6.0 | 1.0 | 1.00 | 11.63 | 4.23 | 77.6 | 3.3 | 13.9 | 9.0 | 5.7 |
| 6.1 | 0.51 | 5.6 | 0.48 | 3.3 | 0.3 | 0.42 | 6.17 | 3.13 | 97.4 | 3.1 | 8.7 | 6.7 | 2.7 |
| 5.9 | 1.58 | 8.1 | 0.51 | 2.0 | 0.0 | 0.21 | 1.67 | 4.07 | 89.7 | 3.6 | 13.6 | 7.5 | 5.7 |
| 8.9 | 1.01 | 2.7 | 0.81 | 4.9 | 0.3 | 0.47 | 3.20 | 3.37 | 90.4 | 4.8 | 22.5 | 2.7 | 7.2 |
| 9.5 | 0.77 | 2.8 | 0.06 | 1.9 | 0.0 | 0.00 | 0.00 | 3.30 | 98.0 | 4.6 | 21.2 | 0.0 | 6.4 |
| 6.3 | 3.93 | 13.7 | -0.06 | 0.3 | -0.1 | -0.43 | -3.78 | 3.42 | 106.0 | 5.5 | 40.7 | 1.9 | 5.2 |
| 8.8 | 0.00 | 0.0 | 0.68 | 0.6 | 0.0 | -0.57 | -6.32 | 4.69 | 100.7 | 5.1 | 29.7 | 0.0 | 3.3 |
| 10.0 | 0.26 | 0.5 | 0.03 | 4.4 | 0.9 | 0.57 | 4.58 | 2.02 | 73.4 | 5.0 | 29.2 | 8.1 | 7.5 |
| 9.0 | 1.09 | 2.4 | 1.19 | 0.8 | 0.0 | -0.31 | -2.07 | 3.07 | 100.5 | 5.1 | 26.7 | 1.6 | 6.0 |
| 5.5 | 1.31 | 8.5 | 0.66 | 5.9 | 2.7 | 1.26 | 10.02 | 3.91 | 74.8 | 3.7 | 22.7 | 12.5 | 7.4 |
| 9.9 | 0.32 | 1.2 | 0.67 | 1.6 | 0.0 | -0.01 | -0.13 | 2.75 | 96.0 | 4.4 | 21.2 | 1.3 | 6.1 |
| 6.7 | 0.85 | 6.6 | 0.82 | 9.1 | 14.1 | 1.41 | 12.12 | 4.47 | 70.2 | 1.9 | 6.8 | 15.5 | 8.2 |
| 6.7 | 0.72 | 6.0 | 0.32 | 0.4 | -0.1 | -0.14 | -1.95 | 3.32 | 101.7 | 3.8 | 15.8 | 3.9 | 1.5 |
| 9.3 | 0.46 | 2.6 | 0.27 | 2.5 | 0.3 | 0.22 | 2.51 | 3.33 | 91.3 | 4.2 | 18.2 | 2.7 | 4.8 |
| 7.4 | 1.86 | 7.6 | 0.32 | 2.2 | 0.2 | 0.16 | 1.68 | 2.35 | 89.9 | 4.9 | 37.6 | 3.3 | 5.6 |
| 7.8 | 0.53 | 5.0 | 0.10 | 1.5 | 0.1 | 0.10 | 0.97 | 2.61 | 93.8 | 4.1 | 20.3 | 10.6 | 5.6 |
| 9.7 | 0.08 | 0.2 | 0.11 | 4.7 | 0.1 | 0.84 | 4.51 | 2.57 | 63.1 | 5.4 | 35.5 | 0.0 | 7.0 |
| 8.1 | 0.00 | 0.0 | 0.10 | 0.9 | 0.0 | -1.14 | -8.41 | 9.81 | 82.7 | 0.8 | 5.5 | 27.0 | 4.7 |
| 8.3 | 0.39 | 2.5 | 0.76 | 4.4 | 0.6 | 0.82 | 9.26 | 3.62 | 80.5 | 4.2 | 32.7 | 5.3 | 4.9 |
| 8.6 | 1.48 | 3.7 | 0.89 | 9.4 | 0.1 | 1.44 | 10.27 | 2.10 | 27.9 | 4.9 | 35.3 | 0.0 | 5.0 |
| 6.9 | 1.14 | 3.1 | 1.62 | 0.6 | 0.0 | -0.73 | -4.40 | 4.59 | 116.7 | 5.4 | 39.1 | 0.0 | 5.4 |
| 3.6 | 1.47 | 12.7 | 0.42 | 2.7 | 0.0 | 0.18 | 2.52 | 7.05 | 86.4 | 5.2 | 30.4 | 0.0 | 1.0 |
| 7.1 | 1.47 | 7.9 | 0.26 | 6.0 | 27.3 | 0.83 | 6.97 | 2.72 | 67.9 | 4.4 | 23.7 | 5.4 | 8.1 |
| 8.0 | 0.56 | 3.7 | 0.02 | 2.5 | 0.1 | 0.25 | 3.91 | 2.94 | 91.6 | 5.7 | 30.7 | 0.0 | 1.9 |
| 10.0 | 0.55 | 0.8 | -0.11 | 5.7 | 0.0 | 0.81 | 4.91 | 3.05 | 70.1 | 5.4 | 24.9 | 0.0 | 5.0 |
| 8.9 | 3.69 | 4.4 | -0.12 | 9.2 | 0.2 | 2.08 | 6.29 | 5.17 | 68.6 | 5.1 | 21.0 | 0.0 | 6.2 |
| 6.4 | 1.87 | 7.9 | 0.22 | 0.4 | 0.0 | -0.26 | -2.53 | 3.23 | 105.3 | 3.6 | 23.8 | 12.5 | 3.9 |
| 8.2 | 0.47 | 3.4 | 0.17 | 3.3 | 0.8 | 0.44 | 4.66 | 3.10 | 86.9 | 3.7 | 11.4 | 3.4 | 5.4 |
| 3.6 | 2.95 | 26.0 | 0.10 | 2.1 | 0.0 | 0.19 | 2.47 | 2.88 | 93.7 | 5.1 | 39.2 | 0.0 | 1.0 |
| 9.9 | 0.34 | 1.1 | 0.53 | 0.2 | -0.1 | -0.44 | -2.82 | 2.92 | 107.3 | 4.7 | 31.0 | 2.8 | 5.9 |
| 8.2 | 0.79 | 4.3 | 0.65 | 3.7 | 1.9 | 0.49 | 4.08 | 3.19 | 77.8 | 3.4 | 14.3 | 8.7 | 8.2 |
| 4.5 | 1.21 | 8.1 | -0.21 | 5.4 | 0.1 | 0.69 | 7.09 | 4.40 | 92.2 | 4.3 | 27.9 | 1.2 | 3.7 |
| 9.7 | 1.27 | 2.6 | 0.91 | 4.8 | 0.0 | 0.61 | 3.54 | 3.63 | 77.8 | 5.5 | 45.3 | 0.0 | 7.4 |
| 7.2 | 4.76 | 3.6 | 16.90 | 0.0 | 0.0 | -2.39 | -9.76 | 2.60 | 83.3 | 7.2 | 65.9 | 0.0 | 5.3 |
| 9.3 | 0.09 | 1.7 | 0.13 | 5.3 | 9.7 | 0.75 | 7.93 | 2.41 | 69.8 | 1.3 | 6.3 | 20.1 | 7.5 |
| 8.5 | 0.37 | 1.4 | -0.06 | 4.2 | 0.0 | 0.55 | 3.55 | 5.13 | 87.5 | 4.8 | 23.8 | 0.0 | 6.3 |
| 9.7 | 1.94 | 2.4 | 0.00 | 1.5 | 0.0 | 0.19 | 0.63 | 2.27 | 92.7 | 4.7 | 23.3 | 0.0 | 6.3 |
| 9.4 | 0.21 | 1.0 | 0.79 | 8.7 | 1.3 | 1.33 | 11.18 | 5.42 | 75.4 | 5.6 | 33.7 | 0.5 | 8.1 |
| 9.7 | 0.36 | 2.0 | 0.10 | 8.5 | 1.7 | 1.18 | 8.04 | 3.44 | 71.2 | 3.0 | 12.6 | 6.5 | 9.1 |
| 9.7 | 0.73 | 1.3 | 0.91 | 2.7 | 0.1 | 0.35 | 3.04 | 2.76 | 86.7 | 5.6 | 33.6 | 6.1 | 5.3 |
| 5.6 | 1.25 | 16.4 | 0.60 | 4.9 | 1.4 | 0.67 | 8.25 | 4.21 | 83.2 | 5.0 | 22.9 | 2.6 | 5.0 |

| Name | City | State | Rating | 2014 Rating | 2013 Rating | Total Assets ($Mil) | One Year Asset Growth | Asset Mix (As a % of Total Assets) | | | | Capital-ization Index | Net Worth Ratio |
|------|------|-------|--------|-------------|-------------|---------------------|-----------------------|------------------------------------|---|---|---|----------------------|-----------------|
| | | | | | | | | Comm-ercial Loans | Cons-umer Loans | Mort-gage Loans | Secur-ities | | |
| ▼ PEAR ORCHARD FCU | Beaumont | TX | D | D | D+ | <1 | -4.28 | 0.0 | 72.9 | 0.0 | 0.0 | 10.0 | 18.6 |
| PEARL HAWAII FCU | Waipahu | HI | C- | D+ | D | 335.1 | -1.02 | 1.6 | 21.5 | 11.3 | 45.4 | 8.1 | 9.7 |
| PEARL MUNICIPAL CU | Pearl | MS | C+ | C+ | C+ | 1.1 | -2.25 | 0.0 | 56.1 | 0.0 | 0.0 | 10.0 | 15.6 |
| PECO FCU | Mineral Wells | TX | D- | D | D | 5.4 | -1.49 | 0.0 | 32.0 | 0.0 | 0.0 | 7.5 | 9.4 |
| PEE DEE FCU | Florence | SC | A- | B+ | B- | 26.2 | 3.24 | 0.0 | 41.5 | 21.5 | 0.0 | 10.0 | 16.3 |
| PEGASUS COMMUNITY CU | Dallas | TX | D+ | C- | C- | 204.8 | -15.79 | 0.0 | 47.3 | 1.0 | 25.6 | 10.0 | 11.7 |
| PELICAN STATE CU | Baton Rouge | LA | B | B | B | 247.6 | 6.05 | 1.9 | 48.6 | 18.7 | 3.4 | 8.6 | 10.1 |
| PEN AIR FCU | Pensacola | FL | A- | A- | B+ | 1279.0 | 1.71 | 3.8 | 23.5 | 15.8 | 44.4 | 10.0 | 12.0 |
| PENINSULA COMMUNITY FCU | Shelton | WA | C | C | C | 162.6 | 7.30 | 0.0 | 41.2 | 14.4 | 3.3 | 5.5 | 7.5 |
| ▲ PENINSULA FCU | Escanaba | MI | B- | C+ | C+ | 124.4 | 4.09 | 0.0 | 25.0 | 46.0 | 0.0 | 10.0 | 12.4 |
| ▲ PENINSULA GENERAL HOSPITAL & MEDICAL | Salisbury | MD | C | C- | C+ | 3.1 | 7.50 | 0.0 | 51.3 | 0.0 | 0.0 | 10.0 | 22.3 |
| PENLANCO FCU | Lancaster | PA | C | C | C | 23.6 | 0.42 | 0.0 | 18.9 | 7.0 | 0.0 | 10.0 | 12.0 |
| PENN EAST FCU | Scranton | PA | C | B- | B- | 143.0 | 0.02 | 10.3 | 37.6 | 2.2 | 8.9 | 10.0 | 12.2 |
| PENN HILLS MUNICIPAL FCU | Pittsburgh | PA | C | C | C | 2.5 | 5.29 | 0.0 | 47.5 | 0.0 | 0.0 | 10.0 | 12.6 |
| ▲ PENN SOUTH COOPERATIVE FCU | New York | NY | D+ | D | D+ | 6.2 | 7.87 | 0.0 | 2.2 | 86.6 | 0.0 | 6.6 | 8.6 |
| PENN STATE FCU | Bellefonte | PA | C- | C- | C- | 161.5 | 3.96 | 8.4 | 16.4 | 9.6 | 30.3 | 6.2 | 8.3 |
| PENN WILCO FCU | Wilkes-Barre | PA | C | C | C | 12.5 | -4.99 | 0.0 | 4.9 | 0.0 | 61.5 | 10.0 | 12.2 |
| PENN-TRAFFORD SCHOOL EMPL FCU | Trafford | PA | D+ | D+ | C- | 4.8 | 0.76 | 0.0 | 49.0 | 0.0 | 0.0 | 9.2 | 10.5 |
| PENNFORMER COMMUNITY FCU | Canonsburg | PA | D | D | C- | 6.4 | 0.05 | 0.0 | 26.2 | 0.0 | 0.0 | 10.0 | 25.2 |
| PENNINGTON MUNICIPAL & COUNTY EMPL C | Thief River Falls | MN | C- | C- | D+ | 1.5 | -12.85 | 0.0 | 36.6 | 0.0 | 0.0 | 10.0 | 12.1 |
| PENNSTAR FCU | Hermitage | PA | B- | B | B | 40.2 | 0.23 | 0.0 | 27.0 | 9.2 | 4.1 | 10.0 | 17.0 |
| PENNSYLVANIA CENTRAL FCU | Harrisburg | PA | D+ | C- | C- | 70.3 | -0.54 | 0.0 | 59.2 | 12.2 | 3.8 | 6.9 | 8.9 |
| PENNSYLVANIA STATE EMPL CU | Harrisburg | PA | B+ | B- | B+ | 4326.6 | 4.23 | 0.3 | 49.9 | 18.3 | 6.8 | 9.7 | 10.8 |
| PENNSYLVANIA-AMERICAN WATER FCU | Bethel Park | PA | D | D | D+ | 14.3 | 1.20 | 0.0 | 38.7 | 1.0 | 0.0 | 7.0 | 9.0 |
| PENNTECH EMPL FCU | Johnsonburg | PA | C- | D+ | C- | 10.8 | -1.64 | 0.0 | 39.3 | 0.0 | 31.4 | 10.0 | 11.3 |
| PENNYPACK FCU | Philadelphia | PA | E+ | E+ | E+ | 4.6 | 0.22 | 0.0 | 30.4 | 2.1 | 0.0 | 5.4 | 7.4 |
| PENOBSCOT COUNTY FCU | Old Town | ME | B- | B | B | 54.9 | 2.89 | 3.8 | 34.1 | 23.6 | 0.0 | 8.9 | 10.3 |
| PENSACOLA L&N FCU | Pensacola | FL | C | C | C- | 8.1 | -3.51 | 0.0 | 62.8 | 0.4 | 0.0 | 10.0 | 18.1 |
| PENTAGON FCU | Alexandria | VA | B | B | B+ | 19223.1 | 3.55 | 0.2 | 21.7 | 59.5 | 3.4 | 8.6 | 10.1 |
| PEOPLE DRIVEN CU | Southfield | MI | C | C+ | C+ | 242.4 | 1.13 | 1.4 | 27.7 | 16.0 | 35.3 | 7.7 | 9.5 |
| ▼ PEOPLE FIRST FCU | Allentown | PA | C- | C+ | B- | 468.6 | 6.37 | 5.6 | 23.1 | 17.4 | 34.4 | 6.1 | 8.5 |
| ▲ PEOPLES ADVANTAGE FCU | Petersburg | VA | C | C | C- | 69.1 | 1.07 | 0.0 | 32.9 | 1.5 | 45.0 | 10.0 | 12.3 |
| PEOPLES ALLIANCE FCU | Hauppauge | NY | C+ | C+ | C+ | 242.4 | 0.88 | 9.9 | 39.4 | 16.9 | 18.5 | 7.5 | 9.4 |
| PEOPLES CHOICE CU | Coffeyville | KS | C | C | C | 7.2 | 0.07 | 0.0 | 23.7 | 0.0 | 6.8 | 10.0 | 22.1 |
| PEOPLES CHOICE CU | Medford | WI | C- | C- | C- | 29.4 | 9.92 | 9.0 | 25.4 | 36.7 | 16.6 | 6.9 | 9.0 |
| PEOPLES CHOICE FCU | Duryea | PA | E+ | E+ | E+ | 7.8 | 17.78 | 0.8 | 29.1 | 0.0 | 25.8 | 4.7 | 6.7 |
| ▲ PEOPLES COMMUNITY CU | Hopkins | MN | C- | D+ | D+ | 20.0 | 8.22 | 0.0 | 38.6 | 0.0 | 0.0 | 10.0 | 22.0 |
| PEOPLES COMMUNITY FCU | Vancouver | WA | B | B | B | 183.8 | 4.41 | 14.1 | 5.6 | 24.8 | 34.0 | 10.0 | 12.1 |
| PEOPLES CU | Springfield | CO | B | B | B | 40.6 | 0.81 | 53.8 | 7.7 | 45.9 | 0.0 | 10.0 | 17.4 |
| ▲ PEOPLES CU | Webster City | IA | B- | C | C | 30.6 | 29.04 | 1.0 | 31.1 | 9.5 | 0.0 | 10.0 | 13.3 |
| PEOPLES CU | Rayne | LA | C | C | C | 24.1 | -0.12 | 0.0 | 19.1 | 10.6 | 0.0 | 10.0 | 18.1 |
| PEOPLES CU | Middletown | RI | B- | C+ | C+ | 406.0 | 3.36 | 11.2 | 15.4 | 60.8 | 2.9 | 10.0 | 11.2 |
| ▲ PEOPLES ENERGY CU | Chicago | IL | B | B- | B | 34.9 | 0.37 | 0.0 | 21.5 | 0.0 | 0.0 | 10.0 | 13.9 |
| PEOPLES FCU | Amarillo | TX | C | C | C | 171.7 | 5.34 | 0.0 | 38.1 | 1.4 | 37.8 | 6.3 | 8.3 |
| PEOPLES FCU | Nitro | WV | C- | C- | C- | 86.5 | -2.92 | 2.6 | 39.6 | 20.0 | 2.5 | 7.8 | 9.5 |
| ▼ PEOPLES FIRST FCU | Birmingham | AL | D+ | C- | C- | 5.0 | -11.12 | 0.0 | 25.4 | 41.6 | 0.0 | 10.0 | 13.2 |
| ▲ PEOPLES INDEPENDENT CHURCH FCU | Los Angeles | CA | D- | E+ | D- | <1 | 25.33 | 0.0 | 28.7 | 0.0 | 0.0 | 5.5 | 7.5 |
| PEOPLES NATURAL GAS GENERAL OFFICE E | Pittsburgh | PA | C- | C- | C- | 2.9 | -8.72 | 0.0 | 10.1 | 0.0 | 0.0 | 10.0 | 16.9 |
| PEOPLES TRANSPORT FCU | Mount Ephraim | NJ | C | C+ | C+ | 9.0 | 10.65 | 0.0 | 64.7 | 0.0 | 0.0 | 10.0 | 12.2 |
| PEOPLES TRUST FCU | Houston | TX | B- | B | B | 500.6 | 5.70 | 10.5 | 40.7 | 20.6 | 11.1 | 6.3 | 8.3 |
| PEOPLES-NEIGHBORHOOD FCU | Washington | DC | C | C- | D+ | <1 | -15.10 | 0.0 | 4.9 | 0.0 | 0.0 | 10.0 | 16.0 |
| PEOPLESCHOICE CU | Saco | ME | C | C | C | 167.5 | 6.61 | 5.1 | 13.8 | 45.4 | 7.4 | 6.7 | 8.8 |
| PEORIA BELL CU | Peoria | IL | C- | D+ | C- | 8.5 | -0.42 | 0.0 | 48.4 | 0.0 | 0.0 | 10.0 | 31.9 |
| ▲ PEORIA CITY EMPL CU | Peoria | IL | C- | C- | C | 4.8 | 0.19 | 0.0 | 41.6 | 0.9 | 0.0 | 10.0 | 21.5 |
| ▲ PEORIA FIRE FIGHTERS CU | Peoria | IL | C+ | C | C | 4.2 | 10.45 | 0.0 | 57.1 | 0.0 | 0.0 | 10.0 | 20.8 |
| ▲ PEORIA HIWAY CU | Peoria | IL | C | C- | D+ | 3.1 | 10.22 | 0.0 | 70.9 | 0.0 | 0.0 | 9.2 | 10.5 |
| PEORIA POSTAL EMPL CU | Peoria | IL | C- | C | C | 10.6 | 0.05 | 0.0 | 48.2 | 0.0 | 7.5 | 10.0 | 22.2 |
| ▲ PEPCO FCU | Washington | DC | D+ | D- | D+ | 32.5 | -1.69 | 0.0 | 25.1 | 0.1 | 0.0 | 8.0 | 9.7 |
| PERFECT CIRCLE CU | Hagerstown | IN | C- | C | C | 50.9 | 1.16 | 0.8 | 34.5 | 18.4 | 15.5 | 9.8 | 10.8 |
| PERRY POINT FCU | Perry Point | MD | D+ | C- | C+ | 19.6 | 3.85 | 0.0 | 33.0 | 0.0 | 0.0 | 8.4 | 10.0 |

| Asset Quality Index | Non-Performing Loans as a % of Total Loans | as a % of Capital | Net Charge-Offs as a % of Avg Loans | Profitability Index | Net Income ($Mil) | Return on Assets | Return on Equity | Net Interest Spread | Overhead Efficiency Ratio | Liquidity Index | Liquidity Ratio | Hot Money Ratio | Stability Index |
|---|---|---|---|---|---|---|---|---|---|---|---|---|---|
| 0.0 | 13.42 | 55.7 | 0.36 | 5.4 | 0.0 | 1.01 | 5.73 | 5.70 | 76.5 | 4.5 | 22.2 | 0.0 | 5.4 |
| 10.0 | 0.32 | 1.7 | 0.33 | 2.3 | 0.7 | 0.28 | 3.03 | 2.56 | 82.9 | 4.2 | 10.5 | 6.1 | 5.2 |
| 6.9 | 0.00 | 0.0 | 0.43 | 10.0 | 0.0 | 2.81 | 19.41 | 6.96 | 66.2 | 5.2 | 52.0 | 15.3 | 5.7 |
| 0.3 | 19.32 | 87.4 | 0.76 | 0.3 | 0.0 | -1.00 | -10.14 | 4.82 | 96.7 | 5.9 | 56.8 | 0.0 | 3.3 |
| 9.6 | 0.19 | 0.8 | 0.55 | 10.0 | 0.4 | 1.77 | 11.33 | 6.30 | 67.7 | 5.4 | 34.1 | 1.4 | 7.1 |
| 6.4 | 0.58 | 4.1 | 1.70 | 0.8 | 0.6 | 0.39 | 3.71 | 2.69 | 63.1 | 4.0 | 17.2 | 11.1 | 6.8 |
| 4.2 | 1.62 | 14.1 | 1.52 | 6.5 | 1.7 | 0.91 | 9.20 | 6.62 | 78.6 | 3.0 | 7.7 | 3.6 | 6.1 |
| 8.6 | 0.53 | 3.2 | 0.91 | 5.1 | 6.5 | 0.68 | 5.78 | 3.01 | 72.4 | 3.8 | 29.9 | 15.1 | 8.1 |
| 8.6 | 0.32 | 4.0 | 0.38 | 2.6 | 0.1 | 0.09 | 1.22 | 3.71 | 92.3 | 3.6 | 13.0 | 3.8 | 4.2 |
| 8.9 | 0.44 | 2.8 | 0.11 | 3.4 | 0.4 | 0.39 | 3.17 | 3.58 | 86.9 | 2.9 | 9.9 | 7.8 | 7.7 |
| 2.3 | 8.03 | 17.0 | 2.84 | 9.4 | 0.1 | 2.99 | 12.67 | 10.09 | 49.0 | 6.8 | 64.2 | 0.0 | 7.8 |
| 9.7 | 0.38 | 1.0 | 0.35 | 2.5 | 0.1 | 0.30 | 2.59 | 1.21 | 59.6 | 5.1 | 27.0 | 0.1 | 5.5 |
| 9.2 | 0.32 | 2.0 | 0.12 | 2.0 | 0.1 | 0.05 | 0.44 | 3.83 | 96.5 | 4.2 | 14.0 | 2.2 | 7.8 |
| 8.6 | 0.00 | 0.0 | 0.00 | 5.7 | 0.0 | 0.96 | 7.53 | 2.68 | 57.5 | 5.4 | 30.8 | 0.0 | 5.0 |
| 3.5 | 3.10 | 25.4 | 0.03 | 10.0 | 0.1 | 1.90 | 24.79 | 3.91 | 50.0 | 3.8 | 18.3 | 0.0 | 7.5 |
| 8.1 | 0.97 | 4.5 | 0.19 | 2.1 | 0.2 | 0.13 | 1.56 | 2.73 | 93.1 | 5.0 | 23.1 | 0.7 | 5.0 |
| 8.6 | 3.60 | 4.1 | 0.00 | 2.3 | 0.0 | 0.19 | 1.67 | 1.32 | 81.9 | 6.1 | 22.9 | 0.0 | 5.7 |
| 7.0 | 0.29 | 1.5 | 0.00 | 3.4 | 0.0 | 0.31 | 2.96 | 3.71 | 88.3 | 5.9 | 44.0 | 0.0 | 5.6 |
| 10.0 | 0.00 | 0.0 | 0.00 | 0.0 | -0.1 | -1.17 | -4.56 | 2.64 | 148.7 | 5.9 | 46.0 | 0.0 | 6.0 |
| 9.1 | 0.47 | 2.0 | 0.00 | 1.9 | 0.0 | 0.00 | 0.00 | 4.57 | 100.0 | 6.1 | 38.6 | 0.0 | 6.0 |
| 8.5 | 1.79 | 4.2 | 0.10 | 3.3 | 0.1 | 0.40 | 2.39 | 2.12 | 83.6 | 4.6 | 18.0 | 1.6 | 7.5 |
| 5.1 | 0.52 | 6.5 | 0.10 | 1.5 | 0.0 | -0.05 | -0.49 | 3.17 | 101.2 | 3.3 | 7.5 | 1.7 | 3.6 |
| 6.8 | 0.63 | 4.3 | 0.86 | 6.5 | 37.4 | 1.15 | 10.97 | 4.23 | 61.7 | 4.1 | 20.2 | 5.4 | 6.6 |
| 7.0 | 1.01 | 4.5 | 0.05 | 0.7 | 0.0 | -0.13 | -1.44 | 2.89 | 106.2 | 4.8 | 19.2 | 0.9 | 3.9 |
| 9.2 | 0.71 | 2.5 | 0.00 | 1.6 | 0.0 | 0.05 | 0.44 | 2.34 | 99.4 | 5.0 | 33.7 | 0.0 | 5.9 |
| 3.4 | 5.87 | 20.9 | -0.18 | 0.8 | 0.0 | -0.49 | -6.55 | 5.43 | 114.3 | 7.2 | 57.9 | 0.0 | 2.3 |
| 5.5 | 0.75 | 9.2 | 0.26 | 4.9 | 0.2 | 0.38 | 4.16 | 5.24 | 90.8 | 2.5 | 26.9 | 21.7 | 4.6 |
| 7.3 | 0.52 | 2.0 | 0.31 | 4.9 | 0.0 | 0.62 | 3.50 | 6.29 | 82.9 | 4.3 | 27.1 | 7.4 | 4.3 |
| 9.3 | 0.26 | 2.8 | 0.30 | 5.3 | 111.8 | 0.81 | 8.20 | 1.95 | 55.8 | 0.9 | 6.7 | 27.6 | 7.8 |
| 7.6 | 1.44 | 7.6 | 0.64 | 3.0 | 0.5 | 0.28 | 3.13 | 3.54 | 92.7 | 4.3 | 20.3 | 2.5 | 4.6 |
| 7.1 | 1.29 | 7.7 | 0.62 | 2.0 | -0.1 | -0.01 | -0.19 | 3.36 | 94.1 | 4.8 | 28.7 | 5.5 | 4.6 |
| 9.6 | 0.70 | 2.9 | 0.50 | 5.3 | 0.5 | 1.04 | 11.76 | 3.36 | 78.9 | 4.3 | 13.0 | 5.5 | 4.1 |
| 7.1 | 0.81 | 6.8 | 0.83 | 3.0 | 0.4 | 0.20 | 2.95 | 3.87 | 86.1 | 3.3 | 18.6 | 8.4 | 4.5 |
| 9.5 | 2.72 | 3.4 | 0.00 | 4.2 | 0.0 | 0.61 | 2.88 | 3.52 | 81.1 | 5.3 | 21.5 | 0.0 | 6.8 |
| 6.2 | 0.72 | 5.4 | 0.05 | 2.1 | 0.0 | 0.09 | 1.02 | 3.25 | 93.5 | 1.8 | 13.0 | 26.8 | 4.5 |
| 0.3 | 7.73 | 70.4 | 0.69 | 0.5 | 0.0 | -0.51 | -6.69 | 4.25 | 108.3 | 5.5 | 30.8 | 0.0 | 1.9 |
| 8.0 | 1.17 | 3.8 | 0.73 | 2.1 | 0.0 | 0.28 | 1.26 | 5.17 | 88.7 | 3.4 | 11.9 | 6.5 | 5.7 |
| 9.8 | 0.40 | 1.1 | -0.12 | 4.1 | 0.8 | 0.59 | 4.93 | 2.77 | 80.0 | 6.3 | 32.6 | 2.4 | 7.7 |
| 5.5 | 0.43 | 2.1 | 0.19 | 9.9 | 0.6 | 2.03 | 12.20 | 4.28 | 56.2 | 1.1 | 5.6 | 21.6 | 7.9 |
| 7.2 | 0.77 | 3.9 | 0.06 | 5.7 | 0.2 | 1.02 | 7.46 | 3.59 | 76.4 | 3.1 | 12.0 | 10.8 | 6.6 |
| 8.1 | 1.75 | 4.1 | 1.32 | 1.9 | 0.0 | 0.10 | 0.58 | 2.44 | 77.4 | 4.8 | 27.0 | 0.0 | 6.6 |
| 6.8 | 0.77 | 6.0 | 0.43 | 3.3 | 1.0 | 0.35 | 3.46 | 3.61 | 84.0 | 2.6 | 9.5 | 10.1 | 6.3 |
| 10.0 | 0.18 | 0.3 | 0.02 | 3.9 | 0.2 | 0.60 | 4.37 | 2.13 | 72.3 | 4.8 | 21.1 | 0.0 | 5.9 |
| 8.1 | 1.13 | 7.1 | 0.15 | 2.6 | 0.3 | 0.22 | 2.66 | 2.63 | 92.0 | 4.7 | 13.0 | 4.3 | 5.0 |
| 5.1 | 0.66 | 12.1 | 0.27 | 2.5 | 0.1 | 0.16 | 1.78 | 3.56 | 90.5 | 2.9 | 12.0 | 10.1 | 4.2 |
| 5.8 | 2.52 | 15.1 | 0.85 | 0.8 | -0.1 | -2.14 | -15.58 | 4.55 | 133.1 | 4.8 | 25.3 | 0.0 | 6.0 |
| 10.0 | 0.00 | 0.0 | 0.00 | 6.9 | 0.0 | 1.43 | 19.05 | 9.09 | 66.7 | 7.5 | 73.6 | 0.0 | 1.9 |
| 9.9 | 4.14 | 2.4 | 0.00 | 2.0 | 0.0 | 0.13 | 0.82 | 1.44 | 78.6 | 8.2 | 86.1 | 0.0 | 5.7 |
| 5.4 | 0.96 | 4.5 | 2.42 | 6.4 | 0.0 | 0.49 | 3.92 | 9.18 | 72.1 | 4.3 | 73.2 | 25.6 | 4.3 |
| 9.1 | 0.29 | 2.6 | 0.49 | 2.5 | -0.1 | -0.04 | -0.46 | 3.46 | 88.0 | 3.7 | 7.9 | 3.2 | 5.5 |
| 10.0 | 0.00 | 0.0 | -14.81 | 2.1 | 0.0 | 0.00 | 0.00 | 2.96 | 75.0 | 6.2 | 20.4 | 0.0 | 4.7 |
| 5.8 | 1.79 | 15.4 | 0.16 | 2.9 | 0.4 | 0.31 | 3.70 | 3.19 | 89.4 | 3.3 | 13.6 | 9.1 | 5.2 |
| 8.7 | 0.63 | 0.9 | -0.07 | 1.7 | 0.0 | 0.05 | 0.15 | 2.83 | 98.3 | 4.4 | 19.2 | 0.0 | 6.5 |
| 9.2 | 1.15 | 2.3 | 1.19 | 1.4 | 0.0 | -0.03 | -0.13 | 3.92 | 88.9 | 6.0 | 53.0 | 0.0 | 5.8 |
| 8.0 | 0.00 | 0.0 | 0.00 | 7.0 | 0.0 | 1.10 | 5.30 | 3.60 | 63.0 | 5.2 | 37.5 | 0.0 | 5.0 |
| 4.5 | 1.80 | 11.6 | 0.00 | 10.0 | 0.0 | 1.53 | 14.62 | 5.65 | 66.4 | 5.1 | 34.2 | 0.0 | 4.3 |
| 7.9 | 1.78 | 3.9 | 0.39 | 1.8 | 0.0 | 0.03 | 0.11 | 3.04 | 91.5 | 4.4 | 29.7 | 2.5 | 6.7 |
| 6.9 | 1.83 | 5.3 | 0.78 | 1.6 | 0.1 | 0.22 | 2.32 | 3.10 | 87.5 | 4.1 | 27.1 | 13.7 | 3.1 |
| 6.1 | 1.28 | 8.5 | 0.38 | 2.5 | 0.1 | 0.16 | 1.51 | 3.70 | 92.3 | 3.9 | 17.5 | 3.1 | 5.0 |
| 8.9 | 0.73 | 2.9 | 0.13 | 1.6 | 0.0 | 0.17 | 1.72 | 2.96 | 102.7 | 4.5 | 19.3 | 1.9 | 3.8 |

| Name | City | State | Rating | 2014 Rating | 2013 Rating | Total Assets ($Mil) | One Year Asset Growth | Asset Mix (As a % of Total Assets) | | | | Capital- ization Index | Net Worth Ratio |
|------|------|-------|--------|-------------|-------------|--------------------|-----------------------|-----------------------------------|--|--|--|------------------------|------------------|
| | | | | | | | | Comm- ercial Loans | Cons- umer Loans | Mort- gage Loans | Secur- ities | | |
| ▲ PERSONAL CARE AMERICA FCU | Trumbull | CT | D | D- | D+ | 19.2 | -9.09 | 0.0 | 29.7 | 13.9 | 0.0 | 8.3 | 9.9 |
| PERU FCU | Peru | NY | B | B | B | 16.6 | 7.83 | 0.0 | 29.8 | 12.0 | 0.0 | 10.0 | 16.2 |
| PERU MUNICIPAL CU | Peru | IL | D+ | D | D | <1 | 20.74 | 0.0 | 77.9 | 0.0 | 0.0 | 10.0 | 12.9 |
| PETERSBURG FEDERAL REFORMATORY CU | Hopewell | VA | C+ | B- | B- | 4.0 | -2.72 | 0.0 | 57.8 | 0.0 | 0.0 | 10.0 | 23.6 |
| ▼ PFD FIREFIGHTERS CU INC | Portsmouth | VA | B- | B- | C+ | 25.3 | 3.94 | 1.3 | 51.2 | 25.8 | 0.0 | 10.0 | 13.7 |
| PG & W EMPL FCU | Wilkes-Barre | PA | D | D+ | C- | 18.2 | -3.90 | 0.3 | 8.4 | 0.0 | 0.0 | 9.8 | 10.9 |
| PHB EMPL FCU | Fairview | PA | C+ | C+ | C+ | 5.8 | 2.95 | 0.0 | 42.3 | 0.0 | 0.0 | 10.0 | 19.4 |
| PHENIX PRIDE FCU | Phenix City | AL | C- | C | C | 8.0 | 17.30 | 0.0 | 73.2 | 3.6 | 0.0 | 9.5 | 10.6 |
| PHI BETA SIGMA FCU | Washington | DC | D+ | C- | C | <1 | 7.93 | 0.0 | 53.2 | 0.0 | 0.0 | 10.0 | 16.7 |
| PHI FCU | Lafayette | LA | D- | D- | D | 9.1 | 3.39 | 0.8 | 42.9 | 0.0 | 0.0 | 5.5 | 7.5 |
| PHILADELPHIA FCU | Philadelphia | PA | A- | A- | A- | 939.5 | 3.25 | 15.0 | 18.6 | 26.0 | 11.9 | 10.0 | 13.5 |
| PHILADELPHIA GAS WORKS EMPL FCU | Philadelphia | PA | D | D | D | 17.5 | 0.62 | 0.0 | 27.5 | 0.0 | 0.0 | 5.6 | 7.6 |
| PHILADELPHIA LETTER CARRIERS FCU | Philadelphia | PA | D+ | D | D+ | 5.5 | -6.66 | 0.0 | 44.3 | 11.2 | 3.6 | 10.0 | 14.6 |
| PHILADELPHIA MINT FCU | Philadelphia | PA | D | D | D | <1 | 7.14 | 0.0 | 19.8 | 0.0 | 0.0 | 10.0 | 14.3 |
| PHILADELPHIA POST OFFICE EMPL CU | Yeadon | PA | C | D+ | C- | 2.6 | 1.79 | 0.0 | 19.7 | 0.0 | 0.0 | 10.0 | 39.7 |
| PHILCORE FCU | Guayama | PR | D | C- | C | 5.4 | 1.45 | 0.0 | 62.6 | 0.0 | 4.3 | 10.0 | 14.0 |
| PHONE-CO CU | Chicago | IL | D | D | D | 5.9 | -8.58 | 0.0 | 42.5 | 0.0 | 0.0 | 10.0 | 15.3 |
| PIAS CU | Nashville | TN | C- | C- | C | 5.5 | 0.92 | 0.0 | 30.7 | 9.3 | 0.0 | 10.0 | 19.1 |
| PICATINNY FCU | Dover | NJ | C+ | C+ | C+ | 305.9 | 3.61 | 0.5 | 11.8 | 15.8 | 35.9 | 6.6 | 8.6 |
| PICKENS FCU | Pickens | SC | B- | C+ | C- | 19.5 | 6.40 | 6.9 | 20.2 | 11.6 | 2.3 | 10.0 | 16.1 |
| PIE CU | Houston | TX | C+ | B- | B- | 14.0 | 1.88 | 0.0 | 30.7 | 5.9 | 0.0 | 10.0 | 14.0 |
| PIEDMONT ADVANTAGE CU | Winston-Salem | NC | C | C | C+ | 307.8 | 6.06 | 0.0 | 51.7 | 16.9 | 4.8 | 9.2 | 10.5 |
| PIEDMONT CU | Statesville | NC | D+ | D+ | C- | 4.9 | -2.31 | 0.0 | 65.4 | 0.0 | 0.0 | 10.0 | 13.0 |
| PIEDMONT CU | Danville | VA | D+ | C | C- | 56.7 | 5.68 | 0.5 | 54.9 | 6.4 | 6.7 | 6.0 | 8.0 |
| PIEDMONT PLUS FCU | Atlanta | GA | C+ | B- | B | 33.1 | -2.94 | 0.0 | 48.6 | 0.0 | 0.0 | 10.0 | 13.9 |
| PIKE TEACHERS CU | Troy | AL | C- | C- | C- | 8.1 | 0.93 | 0.0 | 27.9 | 0.0 | 9.2 | 10.0 | 14.3 |
| ▲ PIKES PEAK CU | Colorado Springs | CO | C+ | C | C | 74.7 | 2.98 | 1.1 | 68.5 | 12.0 | 1.1 | 8.2 | 9.8 |
| PILGRIM BAPTIST CU | Chicago | IL | C- | C- | C- | <1 | -0.24 | 0.0 | 17.0 | 0.0 | 13.4 | 10.0 | 15.8 |
| PILGRIM CUCC FCU | Houston | TX | D- | D- | D | 1.2 | -14.61 | 0.0 | 64.9 | 0.0 | 0.0 | 7.0 | 9.0 |
| PIMA FCU | Tucson | AZ | B+ | B+ | B- | 459.7 | 7.23 | 0.0 | 38.4 | 10.9 | 34.2 | 9.0 | 10.3 |
| PINAL COUNTY FCU | Casa Grande | AZ | C+ | C+ | C | 116.8 | 6.88 | 4.7 | 52.1 | 4.4 | 9.8 | 5.4 | 7.5 |
| PINE BELT FCU | Hattiesburg | MS | B- | B- | B- | 10.6 | 11.84 | 0.6 | 37.3 | 6.8 | 0.0 | 10.0 | 30.4 |
| ▼ PINE BLUFF COTTON BELT FCU | Pine Bluff | AR | C- | C+ | B- | 65.5 | 0.47 | 0.5 | 26.9 | 26.2 | 0.0 | 10.0 | 12.1 |
| ▲ PINE BLUFF POSTAL FCU | Pine Bluff | AR | C | C- | C | <1 | -5.58 | 0.0 | 63.7 | 0.0 | 0.0 | 10.0 | 24.0 |
| PINE CREEK FCU | Weston | OR | C- | D+ | C- | 4.7 | 6.55 | 0.0 | 52.4 | 0.0 | 2.2 | 10.0 | 13.4 |
| PINE FCU | Pine Bluff | AR | B+ | B+ | A- | 39.3 | 6.61 | 0.0 | 46.9 | 6.8 | 0.0 | 10.0 | 23.5 |
| ▼ PINE TREE COMMUNITY CU | Grangeville | ID | B- | B | B | 41.0 | 8.66 | 0.7 | 27.4 | 23.9 | 0.5 | 9.4 | 10.6 |
| PINELLAS FCU | Largo | FL | B+ | B+ | B+ | 109.7 | 6.73 | 0.0 | 52.1 | 0.6 | 0.0 | 10.0 | 16.2 |
| PINEY HILLS FCU | Simsboro | LA | C- | C- | C- | 3.7 | 4.38 | 0.0 | 52.2 | 2.0 | 0.0 | 10.0 | 15.4 |
| PINN MEMORIAL FCU | Philadelphia | PA | C+ | C+ | C | <1 | 22.77 | 0.0 | 8.5 | 0.0 | 0.0 | 10.0 | 12.9 |
| PINNACLE CU | Atlanta | GA | D | D- | D+ | 75.0 | -6.27 | 0.7 | 33.4 | 9.9 | 20.1 | 4.6 | 6.6 |
| PINNACLE FCU | Edison | NJ | D | D- | D | 145.2 | 5.58 | 40.9 | 9.7 | 16.0 | 1.1 | 5.4 | 7.4 |
| ▲ PIONEER COMMUNITY FCU | Palisade | NE | D | D- | D+ | 3.2 | -0.09 | 0.0 | 70.2 | 1.5 | 0.0 | 7.9 | 9.6 |
| PIONEER FCU | Mountain Home | ID | B | B | B | 374.1 | 4.82 | 1.5 | 49.4 | 12.7 | 10.0 | 7.3 | 9.4 |
| PIONEER MUTUAL FCU | Sugar Land | TX | A | A | A | 123.4 | 23.71 | 4.0 | 30.9 | 9.0 | 0.0 | 10.0 | 15.0 |
| PIONEER VALLEY FCU | Springfield | MA | B+ | B+ | B+ | 55.1 | 4.63 | 0.0 | 43.5 | 26.9 | 0.0 | 10.0 | 12.1 |
| PIONEER WEST VIRGINIA FCU | Charleston | WV | B- | C+ | B | 190.5 | 0.29 | 0.1 | 40.8 | 37.0 | 3.0 | 7.4 | 9.2 |
| PIPEFITTERS-STEAMFITTERS CU | Woodbury | MN | C+ | C | B- | 32.5 | 6.17 | 3.7 | 31.0 | 9.3 | 6.7 | 10.0 | 12.6 |
| PISCATAWAY TOWNSHIP EMPL FCU | Piscataway | NJ | C- | C- | D+ | 1.8 | -1.11 | 0.0 | 35.3 | 0.0 | 0.0 | 10.0 | 13.0 |
| PITNEY BOWES EMPL FCU | Shelton | CT | C | C | C | 65.7 | -5.42 | 3.9 | 9.9 | 11.0 | 5.9 | 10.0 | 15.7 |
| PITTSBURGH CENTRAL FCU | Sewickley | PA | E- | E+ | D- | 35.9 | -11.30 | 2.0 | 23.3 | 0.0 | 2.2 | 4.1 | 6.2 |
| PITTSBURGH CITY HALL EMPL FCU | Pittsburgh | PA | B- | B- | B- | 49.7 | 2.25 | 0.0 | 17.3 | 0.0 | 58.0 | 9.9 | 10.9 |
| PITTSBURGH FCU | Pittsburgh | PA | D | D | D+ | 7.3 | 0.81 | 0.0 | 32.2 | 0.0 | 0.0 | 7.2 | 9.2 |
| PITTSBURGH FIREFIGHTERS FCU | Pittsburgh | PA | B+ | B+ | B+ | 78.6 | -2.34 | 0.0 | 8.7 | 0.0 | 12.9 | 10.0 | 13.9 |
| PITTSFORD FCU | Mendon | NY | B | B | B | 358.0 | 1.31 | 0.0 | 5.5 | 52.3 | 9.9 | 10.0 | 11.1 |
| PITTSTON AREA SCHOOL EMPL FCU | Hughestown | PA | D | D+ | C- | 1.3 | -6.83 | 0.0 | 50.0 | 0.0 | 0.0 | 10.0 | 17.8 |
| ▲ PLAIN DEALER FCU | Cleveland | OH | D+ | D | C- | 17.3 | 0.27 | 0.0 | 20.0 | 10.5 | 42.7 | 10.0 | 17.7 |
| PLAINFIELD CU | Plainfield | NJ | C | C | C | 1.4 | -6.42 | 0.0 | 16.4 | 0.0 | 0.0 | 10.0 | 17.4 |
| ▲ PLAINFIELD POLICE & FIREMENS FCU | Plainfield | NJ | D- | E+ | E+ | 4.0 | -3.85 | 0.0 | 34.0 | 0.0 | 0.0 | 6.5 | 8.5 |
| PLAINS FCU | Plainview | TX | D+ | C- | D+ | 4.0 | -1.42 | 0.0 | 48.9 | 0.0 | 0.0 | 10.0 | 14.6 |

| Asset Quality Index | Non-Performing Loans as a % of Total Loans | as a % of Capital | Net Charge-Offs / Avg Loans | Profitability Index | Net Income ($Mil) | Return on Assets | Return on Equity | Net Interest Spread | Overhead Efficiency Ratio | Liquidity Index | Liquidity Ratio | Hot Money Ratio | Stability Index |
|---|---|---|---|---|---|---|---|---|---|---|---|---|---|
| 6.1 | 1.77 | 7.9 | 0.15 | 1.7 | 0.0 | 0.06 | 0.64 | 4.57 | 93.3 | 5.1 | 32.4 | 0.0 | 2.8 |
| 9.6 | 0.52 | 1.5 | 2.20 | 7.4 | 0.1 | 0.98 | 6.14 | 4.93 | 63.8 | 4.8 | 17.0 | 1.9 | 6.3 |
| 8.2 | 0.00 | 0.0 | 0.00 | 1.6 | 0.0 | 0.30 | 2.15 | 3.33 | 85.7 | 3.5 | 21.6 | 0.0 | 6.1 |
| 8.6 | 0.00 | 0.0 | 0.99 | 5.7 | 0.0 | 0.68 | 2.87 | 4.12 | 67.0 | 4.6 | 46.2 | 12.1 | 5.0 |
| 6.2 | 1.55 | 9.2 | 0.00 | 8.0 | 0.2 | 1.02 | 7.56 | 4.22 | 68.5 | 3.1 | 15.5 | 6.2 | 5.7 |
| 9.8 | 0.81 | 1.4 | -0.04 | 0.3 | -0.1 | -0.44 | -4.07 | 1.74 | 111.8 | 5.7 | 35.9 | 0.0 | 4.4 |
| 9.6 | 1.15 | 2.5 | 0.11 | 4.8 | 0.0 | 0.61 | 3.27 | 4.21 | 84.7 | 6.0 | 55.7 | 0.0 | 6.9 |
| 3.9 | 0.43 | 14.2 | 0.38 | 10.0 | 0.1 | 2.36 | 25.38 | 9.39 | 75.0 | 3.8 | 11.4 | 3.1 | 5.0 |
| 0.9 | 7.67 | 26.4 | 0.00 | 5.1 | 0.0 | 0.00 | 0.00 | 4.72 | 100.0 | 5.7 | 35.6 | 0.0 | 8.5 |
| 8.8 | 0.14 | 1.0 | 0.00 | 2.9 | 0.0 | 0.37 | 4.96 | 3.77 | 88.7 | 4.9 | 25.1 | 0.0 | 1.7 |
| 5.8 | 2.44 | 11.9 | 0.97 | 5.6 | 5.7 | 0.80 | 6.49 | 4.99 | 70.8 | 5.1 | 25.1 | 5.7 | 7.8 |
| 5.6 | 3.28 | 13.3 | 0.59 | 3.2 | 0.1 | 0.36 | 4.95 | 4.26 | 88.3 | 6.3 | 36.2 | 0.0 | 2.1 |
| 6.8 | 1.01 | 3.9 | 0.08 | 1.6 | 0.0 | 0.14 | 0.99 | 5.81 | 95.8 | 4.4 | 32.4 | 6.6 | 4.7 |
| 8.0 | 0.00 | 0.0 | 0.58 | 0.0 | 0.0 | -3.30 | -20.29 | 8.56 | 150.0 | 5.6 | 44.5 | 0.0 | 5.0 |
| 10.0 | 0.00 | 0.0 | -0.74 | 3.3 | 0.0 | 0.51 | 1.29 | 3.77 | 85.0 | 6.6 | 59.1 | 0.0 | 5.9 |
| 1.1 | 6.35 | 35.0 | 1.78 | 2.1 | 0.0 | -0.35 | -2.84 | 7.75 | 86.9 | 5.6 | 33.6 | 0.0 | 5.8 |
| 7.3 | 2.86 | 7.5 | 1.08 | 0.0 | -0.1 | -3.04 | -19.01 | 3.54 | 162.4 | 5.1 | 52.6 | 4.0 | 4.7 |
| 7.3 | 0.80 | 6.6 | -0.05 | 1.1 | 0.0 | -0.39 | -3.30 | 4.43 | 109.5 | 4.7 | 25.6 | 7.6 | 6.2 |
| 8.2 | 1.14 | 5.4 | 0.12 | 3.0 | 0.5 | 0.24 | 2.74 | 2.42 | 91.9 | 4.6 | 24.4 | 2.2 | 4.9 |
| 9.4 | 0.13 | 1.0 | 0.13 | 4.5 | 0.1 | 0.52 | 3.19 | 4.81 | 89.6 | 6.7 | 44.5 | 0.0 | 5.8 |
| 9.9 | 0.66 | 1.8 | 0.76 | 2.4 | 0.0 | 0.07 | 0.48 | 2.35 | 86.1 | 4.6 | 20.3 | 5.1 | 6.7 |
| 5.1 | 1.17 | 9.7 | 0.98 | 3.5 | 1.2 | 0.50 | 4.91 | 4.19 | 77.3 | 3.6 | 10.2 | 4.6 | 6.8 |
| 7.1 | 0.49 | 2.4 | 0.25 | 2.8 | 0.0 | 0.25 | 1.90 | 5.20 | 83.0 | 4.8 | 28.1 | 0.0 | 5.4 |
| 2.1 | 3.14 | 25.6 | 1.73 | 1.6 | -0.1 | -0.28 | -3.32 | 5.59 | 84.8 | 2.9 | 9.6 | 13.2 | 2.8 |
| 5.8 | 2.10 | 7.5 | 1.96 | 1.3 | 0.0 | -0.11 | -0.83 | 5.93 | 86.4 | 5.9 | 36.1 | 3.3 | 5.7 |
| 5.1 | 3.96 | 8.4 | -0.11 | 2.2 | 0.0 | 0.23 | 1.62 | 2.32 | 84.9 | 6.5 | 58.9 | 0.0 | 6.4 |
| 5.0 | 0.78 | 6.4 | 0.35 | 4.3 | 0.4 | 0.69 | 7.25 | 3.12 | 73.6 | 2.3 | 15.8 | 15.5 | 4.3 |
| 3.7 | 22.86 | 22.5 | 0.00 | 4.6 | 0.0 | 0.32 | 2.08 | 2.74 | 83.3 | 7.2 | 50.7 | 0.0 | 7.4 |
| 5.6 | 0.00 | 0.0 | 3.42 | 1.1 | 0.0 | -1.30 | -14.57 | 7.52 | 90.9 | 5.8 | 37.8 | 0.0 | 4.3 |
| 9.7 | 0.20 | 2.0 | 0.75 | 5.2 | 2.8 | 0.82 | 8.38 | 3.72 | 77.3 | 4.0 | 8.6 | 1.8 | 6.0 |
| 5.3 | 0.98 | 9.5 | 0.66 | 3.9 | 0.2 | 0.25 | 3.76 | 4.63 | 85.9 | 4.3 | 15.9 | 1.5 | 3.9 |
| 9.1 | 2.07 | 3.5 | -0.03 | 6.9 | 0.1 | 0.90 | 2.90 | 5.86 | 86.8 | 4.8 | 39.2 | 9.3 | 6.3 |
| 3.7 | 4.48 | 22.3 | 0.40 | 0.4 | -0.3 | -0.54 | -4.39 | 2.89 | 110.2 | 2.8 | 9.5 | 14.0 | 5.8 |
| 8.2 | 0.00 | 0.0 | 0.00 | 4.2 | 0.0 | 0.68 | 2.88 | 6.29 | 86.7 | 5.4 | 37.3 | 0.0 | 6.8 |
| 6.2 | 1.64 | 6.1 | 0.59 | 2.4 | 0.0 | 0.06 | 0.43 | 3.96 | 94.9 | 5.4 | 42.9 | 0.0 | 6.5 |
| 5.3 | 2.96 | 9.6 | 0.58 | 9.2 | 0.4 | 1.29 | 5.58 | 3.99 | 59.9 | 4.6 | 28.5 | 2.1 | 8.1 |
| 5.6 | 1.94 | 12.3 | 0.73 | 5.3 | 0.2 | 0.72 | 6.69 | 3.89 | 68.8 | 3.9 | 20.4 | 9.9 | 6.0 |
| 5.2 | 2.18 | 10.4 | 2.05 | 3.9 | 0.3 | 0.33 | 2.08 | 4.84 | 73.3 | 4.5 | 22.9 | 3.5 | 7.4 |
| 6.1 | 1.33 | 4.8 | 0.46 | 1.7 | 0.0 | -0.15 | -0.94 | 5.91 | 96.8 | 6.2 | 48.9 | 0.0 | 6.3 |
| 9.7 | 0.00 | 0.0 | 0.00 | 5.4 | 0.0 | 0.60 | 4.17 | 3.13 | 66.7 | 7.6 | 55.1 | 0.0 | 5.0 |
| 6.2 | 0.85 | 8.4 | 0.80 | 2.9 | 0.2 | 0.28 | 4.52 | 3.59 | 92.9 | 4.3 | 10.5 | 3.3 | 1.7 |
| 5.5 | 1.33 | 14.6 | 0.09 | 1.1 | 0.0 | 0.03 | 0.36 | 3.07 | 105.7 | 2.6 | 16.8 | 9.2 | 3.2 |
| 2.3 | 2.83 | 22.7 | 0.32 | 5.3 | 0.0 | 0.71 | 7.71 | 5.79 | 85.4 | 4.4 | 20.0 | 0.0 | 5.2 |
| 5.4 | 0.96 | 9.0 | 0.29 | 6.1 | 2.3 | 0.83 | 9.18 | 3.22 | 75.5 | 1.6 | 6.5 | 27.0 | 6.0 |
| 9.4 | 0.53 | 1.6 | 0.00 | 8.9 | 1.0 | 1.20 | 7.64 | 3.07 | 65.5 | 6.3 | 35.5 | 0.4 | 10.0 |
| 7.1 | 0.78 | 4.8 | 1.03 | 6.5 | 0.3 | 0.79 | 6.74 | 5.02 | 81.0 | 2.6 | 12.6 | 12.3 | 6.2 |
| 8.6 | 0.27 | 3.2 | 0.25 | 4.4 | 0.9 | 0.63 | 7.02 | 4.14 | 79.6 | 2.8 | 4.8 | 7.0 | 5.7 |
| 9.5 | 0.15 | 0.6 | 0.17 | 2.3 | 0.1 | 0.28 | 2.19 | 2.91 | 89.3 | 4.7 | 29.9 | 1.9 | 5.9 |
| 8.3 | 1.11 | 3.0 | 0.00 | 3.1 | 0.0 | 0.30 | 2.31 | 5.65 | 91.7 | 6.3 | 46.0 | 0.0 | 5.5 |
| 8.8 | 1.65 | 3.6 | 0.29 | 1.6 | 0.0 | -0.04 | -0.24 | 2.23 | 98.2 | 5.4 | 29.7 | 0.0 | 6.1 |
| 2.5 | 4.09 | 31.0 | 2.74 | 0.0 | -0.7 | -2.26 | -35.58 | 3.09 | 107.1 | 4.6 | 30.3 | 2.9 | 0.8 |
| 8.4 | 1.25 | 2.7 | 0.10 | 3.8 | 0.2 | 0.50 | 4.72 | 1.92 | 67.4 | 4.3 | 7.1 | 6.1 | 5.9 |
| 6.1 | 1.76 | 7.9 | 0.18 | 3.6 | 0.0 | 0.36 | 4.04 | 4.05 | 89.4 | 4.9 | 22.9 | 0.0 | 2.3 |
| 6.9 | 3.38 | 8.4 | 0.52 | 4.4 | 0.4 | 0.71 | 5.30 | 2.40 | 66.5 | 6.4 | 40.4 | 0.0 | 6.8 |
| 8.5 | 0.54 | 3.6 | 0.06 | 4.2 | 1.6 | 0.58 | 5.41 | 2.59 | 74.1 | 4.0 | 17.3 | 2.2 | 7.3 |
| 8.8 | 0.00 | 0.0 | 0.00 | 0.4 | 0.0 | -0.49 | -2.86 | 3.79 | 117.9 | 5.1 | 25.9 | 0.0 | 5.9 |
| 10.0 | 0.17 | 0.3 | 0.34 | 0.7 | 0.0 | -0.05 | -0.30 | 2.99 | 101.8 | 5.9 | 36.1 | 1.5 | 5.0 |
| 9.9 | 2.56 | 2.3 | 4.64 | 3.9 | 0.0 | 0.57 | 3.24 | 2.23 | 68.2 | 7.1 | 101.4 | 0.0 | 5.7 |
| 4.0 | 5.14 | 17.0 | 2.78 | 5.9 | 0.0 | 0.67 | 8.36 | 4.16 | 78.3 | 5.1 | 30.8 | 0.0 | 2.3 |
| 8.5 | 0.45 | 1.7 | 0.06 | 0.8 | 0.0 | -0.30 | -2.03 | 3.94 | 107.1 | 4.7 | 36.7 | 0.0 | 6.5 |

| Name | City | State | Rating | 2014 Rating | 2013 Rating | Total Assets ($Mil) | One Year Asset Growth | Asset Mix (As a % of Total Assets) | | | | Capital- ization Index | Net Worth Ratio |
|---|---|---|---|---|---|---|---|---|---|---|---|---|---|
| | | | | | | | | Comm- ercial Loans | Cons- umer Loans | Mort- gage Loans | Secur- ities | | |
| ▲ PLANITES CU | Chicago | IL | C | C- | C | 32.2 | 4.68 | 0.0 | 10.9 | 20.1 | 6.1 | 8.1 | 9.7 |
| PLANTERS FCU | Suffolk | VA | C- | C- | C- | 4.4 | 6.60 | 0.0 | 43.9 | 0.0 | 0.0 | 10.0 | 12.5 |
| ▼ PLATINUM FCU | Duluth | GA | B- | B | B- | 67.2 | 14.36 | 8.6 | 52.0 | 13.4 | 0.0 | 6.6 | 8.6 |
| PLATTSBURGH CITY SCHOOL DISTRICT FCU | Plattsburgh | NY | D+ | C- | C- | 6.7 | 5.26 | 0.0 | 46.2 | 0.0 | 0.0 | 10.0 | 17.3 |
| PLUMBERS & FITTERS LOCAL 675 FCU | Honolulu | HI | C- | C- | D+ | 2.5 | 2.41 | 0.0 | 17.8 | 0.0 | 0.0 | 10.0 | 11.5 |
| PLUMBERS LOCAL #27 FCU | McKees Rocks | PA | D- | D | D+ | 2.1 | 2.91 | 0.0 | 27.8 | 0.0 | 0.0 | 9.5 | 10.7 |
| PLUMBERS LOCAL 55 FCU | Cleveland | OH | C- | C- | C- | 3.3 | -0.73 | 0.0 | 29.5 | 0.0 | 0.0 | 10.0 | 16.5 |
| PLUS CU | Las Vegas | NV | A- | A- | B+ | 79.9 | 0.01 | 0.6 | 22.7 | 23.2 | 1.3 | 10.0 | 13.3 |
| PLUS4 CU | Houston | TX | B- | B | C | 106.7 | 2.00 | 0.0 | 52.8 | 2.1 | 0.9 | 8.2 | 9.8 |
| PLYMOUTH COUNTY TEACHERS FCU | West Wareham | MA | D | D+ | D+ | 42.6 | 1.98 | 0.0 | 14.8 | 26.8 | 0.0 | 8.7 | 10.1 |
| PMI EMPL FCU | Washington | DC | D | D+ | C- | <1 | -7.62 | 0.0 | 25.9 | 0.0 | 66.6 | 10.0 | 16.2 |
| PNG NORTHERN FCU | North Apollo | PA | D+ | D+ | C- | 3.8 | 12.90 | 0.0 | 76.7 | 0.0 | 0.0 | 9.4 | 10.6 |
| ▲ POCATELLO SIMPLOT CU | Pocatello | ID | C | D+ | C+ | 31.5 | 1.67 | 0.0 | 41.4 | 5.8 | 1.6 | 10.0 | 18.1 |
| POCONO MEDICAL CENTER FCU | East Stroudsburg | PA | D- | D- | D- | 5.8 | 0.61 | 0.0 | 31.6 | 0.0 | 18.9 | 6.9 | 8.9 |
| POINT BREEZE CU | Hunt Valley | MD | B | B | B- | 723.7 | -0.06 | 2.3 | 14.5 | 27.8 | 37.0 | 10.0 | 13.4 |
| POINT LOMA CU | San Diego | CA | C+ | C+ | C | 443.5 | 2.22 | 9.3 | 12.6 | 47.3 | 12.7 | 5.9 | 7.9 |
| POINT WEST CU | Portland | OR | C- | C- | D+ | 94.0 | -0.69 | 1.6 | 48.7 | 4.5 | 14.8 | 5.2 | 7.2 |
| POINTE COUPEE EDUCATION ASSN FCU | New Roads | LA | E+ | E+ | D- | <1 | 0.64 | 0.0 | 20.9 | 0.0 | 0.0 | 5.0 | 7.1 |
| POLAM FCU | Los Angeles | CA | B | B- | C | 53.2 | 4.67 | 7.0 | 2.1 | 50.7 | 0.4 | 10.0 | 11.1 |
| POLAM FCU | Redwood City | CA | C- | D+ | D- | 68.9 | 11.31 | 13.3 | 0.7 | 40.5 | 0.0 | 10.0 | 11.1 |
| POLICE & FIRE FCU | Philadelphia | PA | A+ | A+ | A+ | 4311.0 | 0.90 | 0.1 | 15.0 | 31.4 | 12.2 | 10.0 | 16.9 |
| POLICE CU | Green Bay | WI | C- | D+ | C- | 1.2 | -15.53 | 0.0 | 91.2 | 0.0 | 0.0 | 10.0 | 14.4 |
| ▲ POLICE CU | Sheboygan | WI | C | C- | C- | <1 | 0.00 | 0.0 | 84.7 | 0.0 | 0.0 | 10.0 | 16.8 |
| POLICE FCU | Upper Marlboro | MD | B | B | B- | 141.9 | 0.86 | 0.0 | 27.1 | 22.1 | 34.6 | 10.0 | 12.8 |
| POLICEMENS FCU | South Bend | IN | B | B | B | 55.9 | -1.78 | 0.0 | 24.5 | 15.1 | 0.0 | 10.0 | 14.3 |
| POLISH & SLAVIC FCU | Brooklyn | NY | B- | B- | C- | 1647.2 | 3.99 | 16.7 | 3.8 | 46.5 | 38.5 | 8.0 | 9.6 |
| POLISH NATIONAL CU | Chicopee | MA | C+ | B- | C+ | 468.9 | -0.29 | 0.2 | 1.8 | 44.0 | 20.3 | 10.0 | 15.1 |
| ▲ POLISH-AMERICAN FCU | Troy | MI | B | B- | C | 100.1 | -3.28 | 2.5 | 5.2 | 60.6 | 0.5 | 7.5 | 9.3 |
| ▲ POLK COUNTY CU | Des Moines | IA | C- | D | D+ | 5.0 | 13.15 | 0.0 | 78.9 | 0.0 | 0.0 | 10.0 | 15.8 |
| POLK COUNTY SCHOOLS EMPL CU | Urbandale | IA | C- | C | C+ | 10.5 | -2.00 | 0.0 | 26.7 | 0.0 | 0.0 | 9.9 | 11.0 |
| POLLOCK EMPL CU | Dallas | TX | D+ | D | D | 4.8 | 3.77 | 0.0 | 60.1 | 0.0 | 0.0 | 10.0 | 12.8 |
| POLY SCIENTIFIC EMPL FCU | Blacksburg | VA | C- | C- | C- | 8.9 | -3.95 | 0.0 | 16.4 | 14.4 | 0.0 | 10.0 | 15.0 |
| POMONA POSTAL FCU | Pomona | CA | C- | C | C+ | 4.6 | -2.98 | 0.0 | 69.7 | 0.0 | 0.0 | 10.0 | 16.9 |
| POMPANO BEACH CITY EMPL CU | Pompano Beach | FL | B | B | B | 18.5 | 6.63 | 0.0 | 69.6 | 0.0 | 0.0 | 10.0 | 22.8 |
| PONTIAC DWIGHT PRISON EMPL CU | Pontiac | IL | C | C | C+ | 6.0 | -2.10 | 0.0 | 34.3 | 0.0 | 0.0 | 10.0 | 12.4 |
| POPA FCU | Cerritos | CA | A- | B | A- | 196.6 | 5.92 | 0.6 | 24.0 | 31.0 | 10.4 | 10.0 | 13.0 |
| PORT ARTHUR COMMUNITY FCU | Port Arthur | TX | C+ | C+ | C+ | 19.0 | 5.72 | 0.0 | 52.1 | 12.1 | 0.0 | 10.0 | 12.2 |
| PORT ARTHUR TEACHERS FCU | Port Arthur | TX | C | C+ | C+ | 27.6 | 0.72 | 0.0 | 30.5 | 0.0 | 0.0 | 10.0 | 13.6 |
| PORT CHESTER TEACHERS FCU | Rye Brook | NY | D+ | C- | C- | 31.5 | 3.92 | 0.0 | 18.4 | 0.0 | 32.7 | 5.5 | 7.5 |
| PORT CITY FCU | Muskegon | MI | C- | C | C+ | 28.9 | 1.61 | 0.0 | 13.1 | 25.1 | 0.0 | 10.0 | 13.5 |
| PORT CONNEAUT FCU | Conneaut | OH | C | B- | B- | 26.2 | -0.03 | 0.5 | 24.7 | 14.7 | 31.2 | 10.0 | 11.9 |
| PORT IVORY FCU | Avenel | NJ | D | D | D | 2.3 | -11.90 | 0.0 | 40.2 | 0.0 | 0.0 | 10.0 | 11.9 |
| ▼ PORT OF HAMPTON ROADS ILA FCU | Norfolk | VA | D+ | C- | C | 6.1 | 1.45 | 0.0 | 60.9 | 0.0 | 0.0 | 10.0 | 25.3 |
| PORT OF HOUSTON CU | Houston | TX | C+ | C+ | C+ | 6.2 | 7.48 | 0.0 | 79.4 | 0.0 | 0.0 | 10.0 | 23.8 |
| PORT OF HOUSTON WAREHOUSE FCU | Houston | TX | C+ | C | C- | 4.3 | 3.86 | 0.0 | 20.2 | 0.0 | 0.0 | 10.0 | 14.7 |
| PORT TERMINAL FCU | Houston | TX | D+ | D+ | C- | 10.7 | 1.41 | 0.0 | 20.0 | 0.0 | 0.0 | 10.0 | 27.7 |
| ▲ PORT WASHINGTON FCU | Port Washington | NY | B+ | B | B- | 30.1 | -1.48 | 0.4 | 6.4 | 54.5 | 24.4 | 10.0 | 12.6 |
| PORT WASHINGTON TEACHERS FCU | Port Washington | NY | C- | C- | C+ | 11.3 | -2.41 | 0.0 | 10.9 | 0.0 | 0.0 | 10.0 | 29.7 |
| PORTALLIANCE FCU | Norfolk | VA | B- | B- | B- | 91.6 | 2.62 | 0.0 | 78.1 | 0.1 | 4.9 | 8.2 | 9.8 |
| PORTER FCU | Denver | CO | D+ | D+ | C | 22.3 | -1.63 | 0.0 | 11.3 | 5.8 | 0.0 | 10.0 | 16.0 |
| ▲ PORTLAND FCU | Portland | MI | B+ | B | C+ | 267.0 | 8.46 | 1.8 | 26.6 | 34.2 | 3.1 | 8.6 | 10.0 |
| ▲ PORTLAND LOCAL 8 FCU | Portland | OR | D | E+ | D | 32.3 | -2.00 | 0.1 | 32.4 | 21.6 | 23.2 | 5.5 | 7.5 |
| ▲ PORTSMOUTH SCHOOLS FCU | Portsmouth | VA | C- | C | C | 2.1 | -1.72 | 0.0 | 44.6 | 0.0 | 0.0 | 10.0 | 16.3 |
| PORTSMOUTH VIRGINIA CITY EMPL FCU | Portsmouth | VA | D- | D | D | 2.1 | -2.56 | 0.0 | 28.9 | 0.0 | 0.0 | 7.7 | 9.5 |
| POST COMMUNITY CU | Battle Creek | MI | B- | C+ | D | 81.3 | -5.39 | 5.4 | 17.6 | 46.2 | 3.6 | 10.0 | 11.9 |
| ▲ POST OFFICE CU | Madison | WI | C | C- | C- | 35.8 | -4.63 | 0.0 | 44.4 | 9.6 | 1.5 | 10.0 | 20.2 |
| POST OFFICE CU OF MARYLAND INC | Baltimore | MD | C | C- | C- | 32.5 | 0.49 | 0.0 | 12.8 | 0.0 | 80.8 | 10.0 | 27.2 |
| ▲ POST OFFICE EMPL CU | Metairie | LA | C+ | C | C- | 25.2 | 1.87 | 5.0 | 25.3 | 16.4 | 10.1 | 10.0 | 12.0 |
| ▼ POST OFFICE EMPL FCU | Shreveport | LA | D- | D- | D- | 42.4 | 2.89 | 0.9 | 22.2 | 19.3 | 25.7 | 5.5 | 7.8 |
| POST-GAZETTE FCU | Clinton | PA | B- | B- | B | 11.9 | -2.49 | 0.0 | 44.0 | 0.0 | 0.0 | 10.0 | 43.0 |

| Asset Quality Index | Non-Performing Loans as a % of Total Loans | Non-Performing Loans as a % of Capital | Net Charge-Offs Avg Loans | Profitability Index | Net Income ($Mil) | Return on Assets | Return on Equity | Net Interest Spread | Overhead Efficiency Ratio | Liquidity Index | Liquidity Ratio | Hot Money Ratio | Stability Index |
|---|---|---|---|---|---|---|---|---|---|---|---|---|---|
| 10.0 | 0.08 | 0.2 | 0.20 | 2.9 | 0.1 | 0.36 | 3.81 | 1.89 | 87.5 | 3.0 | 13.7 | 18.2 | 4.6 |
| 6.5 | 3.05 | 10.8 | 0.54 | 4.6 | 0.0 | 0.48 | 3.67 | 4.51 | 84.0 | 5.6 | 30.8 | 0.0 | 4.3 |
| 6.1 | 0.32 | 2.6 | 0.07 | 6.6 | 0.4 | 0.76 | 8.40 | 4.42 | 87.3 | 4.6 | 26.4 | 6.1 | 5.1 |
| 5.9 | 2.22 | 7.9 | 0.06 | 1.6 | 0.0 | -0.14 | -0.80 | 4.51 | 86.0 | 3.0 | 22.9 | 26.8 | 6.1 |
| 9.0 | 1.11 | 2.0 | 1.86 | 3.3 | 0.0 | 0.44 | 3.84 | 2.04 | 75.0 | 5.6 | 13.5 | 0.0 | 4.9 |
| 3.6 | 8.73 | 22.5 | 5.67 | 0.0 | 0.0 | -2.41 | -21.65 | 3.14 | 110.0 | 6.9 | 45.7 | 0.0 | 5.5 |
| 7.2 | 3.02 | 5.6 | -0.66 | 2.4 | 0.0 | 0.24 | 1.50 | 3.24 | 91.9 | 5.1 | 20.4 | 0.0 | 6.2 |
| 8.3 | 1.18 | 5.2 | 0.22 | 5.9 | 0.4 | 0.59 | 4.52 | 4.55 | 92.3 | 5.4 | 35.8 | 2.0 | 5.6 |
| 8.6 | 0.04 | 1.1 | 0.31 | 3.7 | 0.1 | 0.10 | 1.40 | 4.27 | 97.0 | 1.8 | 8.0 | 17.2 | 5.7 |
| 7.8 | 0.78 | 3.8 | 0.31 | 0.5 | -0.1 | -0.32 | -3.10 | 2.74 | 102.8 | 4.1 | 26.0 | 4.7 | 4.7 |
| 10.0 | 0.51 | 0.8 | 0.00 | 0.0 | 0.0 | -0.85 | -5.29 | 1.15 | 133.3 | 6.2 | 84.2 | 0.0 | 4.7 |
| 3.4 | 1.15 | 9.1 | 0.80 | 3.5 | 0.0 | 0.22 | 2.00 | 5.04 | 82.6 | 3.9 | 14.9 | 0.0 | 3.0 |
| 9.3 | 1.33 | 3.4 | 0.17 | 2.7 | 0.1 | 0.46 | 2.55 | 2.93 | 79.1 | 5.0 | 21.9 | 2.3 | 6.3 |
| 4.7 | 3.16 | 10.6 | -0.65 | 6.3 | 0.1 | 1.42 | 16.57 | 2.90 | 73.8 | 5.2 | 38.4 | 0.0 | 1.7 |
| 8.9 | 0.98 | 3.7 | 0.23 | 4.3 | 3.0 | 0.55 | 4.22 | 2.59 | 76.2 | 4.9 | 20.9 | 3.6 | 8.5 |
| 7.1 | 0.57 | 4.7 | 0.69 | 3.7 | 1.7 | 0.50 | 6.40 | 3.34 | 89.1 | 4.1 | 16.1 | 3.4 | 4.4 |
| 6.8 | 0.36 | 3.3 | 0.34 | 3.4 | 0.2 | 0.32 | 4.77 | 3.87 | 93.2 | 4.1 | 15.3 | 2.2 | 2.9 |
| 6.9 | 2.55 | 6.3 | -2.76 | 0.3 | 0.0 | -0.29 | -3.92 | 3.67 | 117.4 | 6.7 | 75.9 | 0.0 | 2.5 |
| 8.9 | 0.01 | 1.9 | 0.04 | 5.1 | 0.3 | 0.88 | 8.01 | 3.07 | 70.8 | 2.7 | 14.6 | 23.9 | 6.1 |
| 3.4 | 0.00 | 30.5 | -0.07 | 6.5 | 0.5 | 0.93 | 8.32 | 4.12 | 74.9 | 5.7 | 30.6 | 4.0 | 4.8 |
| 9.2 | 0.85 | 3.3 | 0.42 | 9.7 | 44.4 | 1.36 | 8.12 | 3.72 | 53.4 | 6.5 | 56.0 | 5.9 | 10.0 |
| 6.5 | 0.27 | 1.6 | 0.00 | 3.4 | 0.0 | 0.51 | 3.79 | 2.85 | 96.3 | 3.3 | 8.9 | 0.0 | 6.6 |
| 6.6 | 1.09 | 5.1 | 0.00 | 5.7 | 0.0 | 1.10 | 6.50 | 4.18 | 58.8 | 4.2 | 18.4 | 0.0 | 4.3 |
| 7.7 | 1.38 | 5.5 | 0.06 | 4.9 | 0.8 | 0.73 | 5.82 | 2.75 | 81.0 | 3.3 | 18.4 | 11.4 | 7.1 |
| 9.9 | 0.06 | 0.2 | 0.05 | 3.9 | 0.2 | 0.51 | 3.65 | 2.26 | 81.7 | 5.2 | 48.1 | 0.0 | 6.5 |
| 6.4 | 1.65 | 10.0 | 0.17 | 3.7 | 6.6 | 0.54 | 5.66 | 2.76 | 81.6 | 3.6 | 7.0 | 5.8 | 6.7 |
| 9.6 | 0.44 | 1.8 | -0.01 | 2.5 | 0.6 | 0.18 | 1.16 | 2.07 | 91.8 | 3.4 | 14.0 | 8.5 | 8.3 |
| 7.0 | 1.21 | 9.6 | 0.16 | 5.7 | 0.7 | 0.96 | 10.80 | 3.00 | 70.6 | 3.6 | 15.3 | 2.7 | 5.2 |
| 8.3 | 0.41 | 2.0 | -0.04 | 2.8 | 0.0 | 0.55 | 3.47 | 4.40 | 85.4 | 4.5 | 24.3 | 0.0 | 5.2 |
| 10.0 | 0.00 | 0.0 | -0.26 | 0.9 | 0.0 | -0.06 | -0.58 | 3.32 | 102.1 | 6.9 | 50.6 | 0.0 | 4.4 |
| 6.1 | 0.38 | 4.1 | 0.08 | 1.4 | 0.0 | 0.11 | 0.87 | 4.80 | 98.9 | 3.8 | 9.5 | 0.0 | 6.1 |
| 6.7 | 4.53 | 9.1 | -0.19 | 1.4 | 0.0 | -0.01 | -0.10 | 2.02 | 94.7 | 6.4 | 64.1 | 0.0 | 6.5 |
| 5.2 | 3.06 | 10.3 | 0.59 | 5.2 | 0.0 | 0.53 | 3.27 | 10.31 | 72.2 | 5.7 | 39.0 | 0.0 | 3.7 |
| 8.4 | 0.20 | 0.6 | -0.03 | 6.7 | 0.1 | 0.88 | 3.83 | 5.56 | 87.9 | 3.5 | 20.1 | 9.9 | 5.7 |
| 10.0 | 0.24 | 0.7 | 0.00 | 2.3 | 0.0 | 0.24 | 2.00 | 2.76 | 87.4 | 6.5 | 36.4 | 0.0 | 6.8 |
| 8.9 | 0.67 | 2.9 | -0.19 | 7.7 | 2.4 | 1.61 | 12.89 | 4.53 | 84.4 | 4.4 | 26.7 | 11.1 | 6.5 |
| 7.8 | 0.41 | 2.2 | 0.06 | 4.5 | 0.1 | 0.59 | 4.93 | 3.96 | 85.0 | 2.6 | 15.4 | 15.4 | 6.0 |
| 8.7 | 1.17 | 2.9 | 0.82 | 1.9 | 0.0 | 0.03 | 0.25 | 3.35 | 94.4 | 5.7 | 51.8 | 0.9 | 6.0 |
| 9.0 | 0.00 | 0.0 | 1.38 | 2.0 | 0.0 | 0.10 | 1.37 | 2.38 | 95.3 | 6.5 | 38.9 | 0.0 | 2.9 |
| 10.0 | 0.08 | 0.3 | 0.17 | 1.5 | 0.0 | -0.09 | -0.69 | 2.18 | 101.9 | 4.5 | 25.0 | 3.0 | 6.7 |
| 7.2 | 1.45 | 7.5 | 0.12 | 2.0 | 0.0 | -0.08 | -0.68 | 4.05 | 99.8 | 4.2 | 16.2 | 2.7 | 5.4 |
| 6.1 | 2.04 | 10.4 | 0.51 | 0.0 | 0.0 | -1.31 | -11.15 | 4.84 | 121.2 | 5.2 | 29.9 | 0.0 | 5.0 |
| 6.1 | 3.80 | 9.2 | -0.67 | 1.9 | 0.0 | 0.04 | 0.17 | 9.13 | 99.4 | 5.4 | 37.9 | 2.2 | 5.5 |
| 7.9 | 0.67 | 2.4 | 0.39 | 9.2 | 0.1 | 1.61 | 6.88 | 7.26 | 73.7 | 3.3 | 16.5 | 8.9 | 5.7 |
| 9.4 | 1.79 | 3.3 | -0.11 | 5.5 | 0.0 | 0.97 | 6.78 | 7.34 | 70.8 | 7.6 | 68.0 | 0.0 | 5.0 |
| 10.0 | 0.28 | 0.2 | 0.94 | 0.6 | 0.0 | -0.26 | -0.90 | 2.18 | 102.7 | 6.3 | 69.6 | 0.0 | 6.6 |
| 10.0 | 0.30 | 1.6 | 0.08 | 7.9 | 0.3 | 1.26 | 10.79 | 2.74 | 62.6 | 3.9 | 16.7 | 0.0 | 6.5 |
| 10.0 | 0.07 | 0.1 | 0.00 | 1.7 | 0.0 | 0.13 | 0.44 | 2.37 | 90.7 | 5.4 | 28.3 | 0.0 | 7.0 |
| 5.8 | 0.54 | 4.1 | 0.72 | 5.8 | 0.6 | 0.84 | 8.90 | 5.62 | 78.8 | 1.9 | 23.3 | 56.3 | 4.3 |
| 10.0 | 0.93 | 1.1 | 0.50 | 0.5 | -0.1 | -0.39 | -2.42 | 1.60 | 114.7 | 5.7 | 68.0 | 5.3 | 6.2 |
| 6.1 | 1.19 | 9.4 | 0.39 | 5.8 | 1.7 | 0.84 | 8.49 | 3.99 | 78.1 | 3.3 | 12.7 | 5.0 | 6.5 |
| 3.3 | 0.11 | 26.6 | 1.97 | 6.8 | 0.3 | 1.39 | 20.48 | 5.08 | 68.4 | 3.4 | 17.4 | 16.7 | 1.5 |
| 9.8 | 0.54 | 1.4 | 1.32 | 1.8 | 0.0 | 0.12 | 0.81 | 12.22 | 92.7 | 7.0 | 62.4 | 0.0 | 5.2 |
| 7.3 | 1.13 | 3.1 | 1.72 | 0.0 | 0.0 | -2.56 | -24.64 | 6.24 | 138.6 | 7.4 | 69.4 | 0.0 | 4.1 |
| 7.5 | 0.57 | 3.8 | 0.15 | 3.8 | 0.3 | 0.54 | 4.78 | 4.10 | 88.2 | 3.7 | 15.9 | 1.3 | 5.0 |
| 9.6 | 0.32 | 1.5 | 0.14 | 2.0 | 0.1 | 0.20 | 1.01 | 2.98 | 90.0 | 4.1 | 35.8 | 4.5 | 6.4 |
| 10.0 | 1.64 | 0.8 | 0.40 | 2.1 | 0.0 | 0.14 | 0.51 | 1.88 | 93.7 | 5.1 | 11.0 | 0.0 | 7.3 |
| 6.4 | 1.11 | 10.9 | 0.14 | 3.1 | 0.1 | 0.30 | 2.60 | 5.31 | 95.2 | 4.6 | 27.6 | 0.9 | 5.7 |
| 1.7 | 6.85 | 40.5 | 0.51 | 0.6 | -0.2 | -0.75 | -9.68 | 3.69 | 105.8 | 4.7 | 18.6 | 7.8 | 3.1 |
| 8.5 | 4.04 | 4.5 | 0.92 | 3.2 | 0.0 | 0.23 | 0.55 | 3.10 | 79.9 | 4.3 | 17.4 | 0.0 | 6.5 |

| Name | City | State | Rating | 2014 Rating | 2013 Rating | Total Assets ($Mil) | One Year Asset Growth | Asset Mix (As a % of Total Assets) | | | | Capital-ization Index | Net Worth Ratio |
|------|------|-------|--------|-------------|-------------|----------|-------------|-----------------|--------------|------------|------------|-------|-------|
| | | | | | | | | Comm-ercial Loans | Cons-umer Loans | Mort-gage Loans | Secur-ities | | |
| POSTAL & COMMUNITY CU | Saint Joseph | MO | C- | D+ | C- | 41.9 | 4.79 | 0.0 | 44.2 | 4.7 | 0.0 | 6.6 | 8.6 |
| POSTAL CU | Baton Rouge | LA | D+ | C- | C+ | 27.3 | -1.17 | 0.0 | 21.5 | 14.2 | 38.5 | 10.0 | 18.2 |
| POSTAL CU | Meridian | MS | C | C | C+ | 6.0 | -1.41 | 0.0 | 12.4 | 0.0 | 0.0 | 10.0 | 15.5 |
| ▲ POSTAL EMPL CU | Huntsville | AL | C+ | C | C- | 3.1 | -1.46 | 0.0 | 37.8 | 5.4 | 0.0 | 10.0 | 14.8 |
| POSTAL EMPL CU | Yardville | NJ | B- | B- | B- | 40.6 | -2.79 | 0.0 | 15.5 | 0.0 | 23.9 | 10.0 | 14.3 |
| POSTAL EMPL OF TROY NY FCU | Troy | NY | D | D+ | C- | 1.5 | -5.10 | 0.0 | 26.1 | 0.0 | 0.0 | 10.0 | 36.1 |
| POSTAL EMPL REGIONAL FCU | Pawtucket | RI | C- | C- | C- | 6.2 | -3.83 | 0.0 | 37.7 | 0.0 | 0.0 | 10.0 | 42.7 |
| POSTAL FAMILY CU | Cincinnati | OH | C | C+ | C+ | 60.1 | -2.09 | 7.4 | 10.6 | 25.3 | 13.6 | 10.0 | 12.9 |
| ▲ POSTAL FAMILY FCU | Fargo | ND | C | C | C+ | 21.0 | 3.81 | 0.0 | 31.2 | 0.6 | 0.0 | 10.0 | 12.3 |
| ▼ POSTAL GOVERNMENT EMPL FCU | Providence | RI | C+ | B- | B- | 44.3 | 0.64 | 0.0 | 19.6 | 21.7 | 0.0 | 10.0 | 13.8 |
| POSTCITY FINANCIAL CU | Long Beach | CA | C- | D+ | C- | 73.7 | -1.69 | 1.5 | 15.9 | 13.5 | 3.2 | 10.0 | 12.8 |
| POSTEL FAMILY CU | Wichita Falls | TX | C- | C- | C | 66.8 | -3.61 | 1.2 | 29.9 | 27.4 | 3.9 | 6.6 | 8.6 |
| POSTMARK CU | Harrisburg | PA | D+ | D+ | D+ | 28.1 | -0.46 | 0.0 | 9.0 | 14.3 | 13.7 | 10.0 | 16.1 |
| POTLATCH NO ONE FCU | Lewiston | ID | A- | A- | A- | 776.5 | 15.26 | 4.2 | 54.2 | 9.1 | 0.0 | 8.1 | 9.7 |
| POTOMAC FCU | Cumberland | MD | B- | B- | B- | 22.9 | -0.54 | 0.0 | 59.6 | 13.6 | 0.0 | 10.0 | 15.2 |
| ▲ POWELL SCHOOLS FCU | Powell | WY | D+ | D+ | D | 2.2 | 10.65 | 0.0 | 60.8 | 0.0 | 0.0 | 6.8 | 8.8 |
| POWER CO-OP EMPL CU | Humboldt | IA | B+ | B+ | B+ | 30.8 | 2.85 | 9.4 | 18.3 | 16.6 | 11.6 | 10.0 | 14.8 |
| POWER CU | Pueblo | CO | B | C+ | B- | 84.5 | 3.00 | 1.1 | 36.1 | 8.9 | 8.0 | 10.0 | 11.6 |
| POWER FINANCIAL CU | Pembroke Pines | FL | C+ | C+ | C | 533.3 | 3.87 | 4.9 | 7.8 | 54.4 | 18.3 | 10.0 | 12.0 |
| POWER ONE FCU | Fort Wayne | IN | C+ | C+ | B- | 13.8 | 9.53 | 0.4 | 40.5 | 21.5 | 0.0 | 10.0 | 11.7 |
| POWERCO FCU | Atlanta | GA | C | C | C- | 172.2 | 0.87 | 0.0 | 15.1 | 20.7 | 13.8 | 10.0 | 13.2 |
| POWERNET CU | Tampa | FL | B- | B- | C+ | 74.5 | 2.63 | 4.0 | 15.6 | 33.9 | 22.2 | 8.0 | 9.7 |
| PPG & ASSOCIATES FCU | Creighton | PA | D | D | C- | 23.0 | 4.21 | 0.0 | 12.2 | 2.2 | 29.3 | 10.0 | 13.9 |
| PPL GOLD CU | Allentown | PA | B- | B- | B- | 121.6 | -0.89 | 0.3 | 12.0 | 30.9 | 26.4 | 10.0 | 14.8 |
| PRAIRIE FCU | Minot | ND | A | A- | A- | 118.7 | 7.23 | 10.9 | 18.6 | 41.7 | 4.2 | 10.0 | 11.4 |
| PRAIRIE VIEW FCU | Prairie View | TX | D- | D- | D | 4.6 | -4.08 | 0.0 | 24.5 | 0.0 | 0.0 | 6.9 | 8.9 |
| PRAIRIELAND FCU | Normal | IL | B | B | B- | 66.7 | 6.21 | 0.0 | 61.2 | 18.2 | 0.0 | 10.0 | 12.3 |
| PRECISION FCU | Keene | NH | C | C | C | 15.6 | 0.54 | 0.0 | 13.1 | 38.7 | 0.0 | 10.0 | 13.5 |
| PREFERRED CU | Grand Rapids | MI | A- | A- | B+ | 158.6 | 3.94 | 0.4 | 41.9 | 8.7 | 48.4 | 10.0 | 12.8 |
| PREMIER AMERICA CU | Chatsworth | CA | A- | B+ | B | 2123.6 | 23.98 | 15.7 | 9.9 | 53.6 | 9.9 | 8.0 | 9.7 |
| ▼ PREMIER COMMUNITY CU | Stockton | CA | C | C+ | B- | 131.8 | 2.69 | 8.2 | 16.8 | 19.2 | 27.8 | 8.3 | 9.9 |
| PREMIER CU | Des Moines | IA | B+ | B+ | B- | 141.9 | 15.68 | 0.8 | 31.6 | 17.7 | 3.1 | 8.6 | 10.0 |
| PREMIER FCU | Greensboro | NC | B+ | A- | B+ | 169.4 | 7.95 | 2.6 | 43.2 | 3.6 | 10.4 | 10.0 | 13.7 |
| PREMIER FINANCIAL CU | New Holstein | WI | B | B | B | 78.6 | 5.96 | 11.7 | 12.0 | 50.2 | 0.0 | 10.0 | 11.5 |
| ▲ PREMIER MEMBERS CU | Boulder | CO | C+ | B- | B | 856.9 | 163.45 | 5.0 | 20.6 | 22.0 | 18.4 | 9.6 | 10.8 |
| PREMIER SOURCE CU | East Longmeadow | MA | C- | C+ | B- | 71.0 | 2.33 | 0.0 | 12.5 | 29.7 | 23.9 | 10.0 | 12.8 |
| PREMIERONE CU | San Jose | CA | B- | B- | C | 361.1 | 6.60 | 0.0 | 17.9 | 22.7 | 13.2 | 7.8 | 9.6 |
| ▼ PRESCOTT FCU | Prescott | AZ | C- | C | C | 6.5 | -0.84 | 0.0 | 63.6 | 0.0 | 0.0 | 10.0 | 15.2 |
| ▲ PRESIDENTS FCU | Cleves | OH | C- | D- | E+ | 10.6 | 6.39 | 0.0 | 46.3 | 0.0 | 0.0 | 8.3 | 9.8 |
| ▲ PRESSERS UNION LOCAL 12 ILGWU CU | Boston | MA | C | C- | B- | <1 | 18.45 | 0.0 | 27.1 | 0.0 | 0.0 | 10.0 | 11.5 |
| PRESTIGE COMMUNITY CU | Dallas | TX | B- | B- | C+ | 80.6 | 3.06 | 42.4 | 25.8 | 1.4 | 4.2 | 7.0 | 9.0 |
| PRESTO LEWISTON EMPL CU | Lewiston | UT | C | C- | C- | <1 | -0.27 | 0.0 | 63.8 | 0.0 | 0.0 | 10.0 | 23.8 |
| PRESTON FCU | Kingwood | WV | B- | B- | B- | 24.4 | 3.60 | 0.0 | 20.1 | 11.0 | 0.0 | 10.0 | 12.1 |
| PRICE CHOPPER EMPL FCU | Schenectady | NY | D- | D- | D | 22.5 | -2.01 | 0.0 | 13.6 | 4.9 | 0.0 | 8.4 | 10.0 |
| PRIME CARE CU | Norfolk | VA | B- | B- | B | 19.3 | 3.66 | 0.0 | 22.0 | 4.3 | 0.0 | 10.0 | 12.4 |
| PRIME FINANCIAL CU | Cudahy | WI | C+ | C | D+ | 110.5 | -0.51 | 1.9 | 50.1 | 30.1 | 0.0 | 5.7 | 7.7 |
| PRIMESOURCE CU | Spokane | WA | B+ | B+ | B+ | 68.0 | 9.02 | 0.0 | 41.6 | 17.8 | 0.4 | 10.0 | 13.0 |
| PRIMETRUST FINANCIAL FCU | Muncie | IN | C | D+ | C | 149.5 | 3.63 | 8.4 | 36.5 | 24.7 | 0.3 | 9.7 | 10.8 |
| PRIMEWAY FCU | Houston | TX | C+ | C+ | C- | 448.9 | 1.99 | 2.2 | 46.9 | 17.4 | 11.8 | 6.7 | 8.7 |
| PRINCE GEORGES COMMUNITY FCU | Bowie | MD | B | C+ | C+ | 148.7 | 4.42 | 6.7 | 31.2 | 21.2 | 8.8 | 8.7 | 10.1 |
| PRINCETON FCU | Princeton | NJ | D+ | D+ | D | 134.9 | 1.75 | 0.0 | 10.8 | 20.6 | 48.6 | 9.3 | 10.5 |
| ▲ PRINTING INDUSTRIES CU | Riverside | CA | E+ | E- | E- | 23.0 | -2.63 | 0.0 | 64.9 | 14.2 | 0.0 | 4.9 | 6.9 |
| PRINTING OFFICE EMPL CU | Covina | CA | D | D | D | 4.2 | -5.98 | 0.0 | 18.9 | 0.0 | 0.0 | 10.0 | 18.1 |
| PRIORITY FCU | Russellville | AR | D- | D- | E+ | 9.4 | 11.14 | 0.0 | 67.9 | 0.0 | 0.0 | 6.6 | 8.6 |
| PRIORITY FIRST FCU | Du Bois | PA | C+ | C+ | C+ | 69.7 | 2.87 | 0.0 | 42.3 | 21.9 | 0.7 | 6.8 | 8.9 |
| PRIORITY ONE CU | South Pasadena | CA | C+ | C+ | C+ | 153.1 | 2.40 | 0.0 | 19.2 | 18.6 | 39.8 | 7.0 | 9.1 |
| PRIORITYONE CU | Sunrise | FL | B- | B- | C+ | 81.7 | 6.71 | 0.0 | 27.6 | 11.9 | 7.2 | 9.0 | 10.4 |
| PROCESSORS-INDUSTRIAL COMMUNITY CU | Granite City | IL | D- | D- | D | 9.8 | 0.28 | 0.0 | 47.0 | 0.0 | 0.0 | 7.7 | 9.5 |
| PROCTOR & GAMBLE ST LOUIS EMPL CU | Saint Louis | MO | C | C | C | <1 | 1.48 | 0.0 | 60.1 | 0.0 | 0.0 | 10.0 | 15.6 |
| PROCTOR FCU | Proctor | MN | B- | B- | C+ | 34.6 | 0.63 | 0.0 | 31.5 | 12.2 | 0.0 | 10.0 | 11.3 |

| Asset Quality Index | Non-Performing Loans as a % of Total Loans | as a % of Capital | Net Charge-Offs Avg Loans | Profitability Index | Net Income ($Mil) | Return on Assets | Return on Equity | Net Interest Spread | Overhead Efficiency Ratio | Liquidity Index | Liquidity Ratio | Hot Money Ratio | Stability Index |
|---|---|---|---|---|---|---|---|---|---|---|---|---|---|
| 7.3 | 0.48 | 3.5 | 0.30 | 3.0 | 0.1 | 0.38 | 4.43 | 2.87 | 86.3 | 4.3 | 19.7 | 1.7 | 3.5 |
| 8.4 | 1.11 | 2.2 | 0.36 | 0.6 | -0.1 | -0.34 | -1.89 | 2.86 | 103.3 | 5.5 | 38.8 | 0.2 | 5.8 |
| 10.0 | 0.20 | 0.2 | 0.14 | 2.2 | 0.0 | 0.16 | 1.01 | 1.47 | 82.3 | 5.4 | 27.8 | 0.0 | 6.5 |
| 9.6 | 0.00 | 0.0 | 0.00 | 6.9 | 0.1 | 2.23 | 16.08 | 5.01 | 40.7 | 5.6 | 27.1 | 0.0 | 5.0 |
| 7.4 | 3.17 | 5.5 | 1.78 | 3.6 | 0.2 | 0.53 | 3.77 | 2.87 | 66.5 | 5.4 | 46.4 | 12.9 | 5.6 |
| 10.0 | 0.00 | 0.0 | -0.34 | 0.2 | 0.0 | -0.60 | -1.71 | 2.06 | 138.1 | 6.2 | 94.2 | 0.0 | 5.3 |
| 9.2 | 3.32 | 3.6 | 0.00 | 3.2 | 0.0 | 0.43 | 1.02 | 4.03 | 77.8 | 4.9 | 40.5 | 0.0 | 5.9 |
| 7.7 | 1.45 | 5.5 | 0.27 | 1.9 | 0.0 | 0.05 | 0.36 | 2.46 | 95.5 | 5.0 | 38.4 | 3.2 | 6.1 |
| 8.8 | 1.16 | 4.2 | 0.00 | 2.6 | 0.1 | 0.35 | 2.85 | 3.64 | 89.6 | 4.6 | 21.5 | 1.4 | 5.5 |
| 6.8 | 2.51 | 10.5 | 0.13 | 1.2 | -0.1 | -0.35 | -2.52 | 3.42 | 87.1 | 4.4 | 29.3 | 5.1 | 6.9 |
| 7.9 | 2.22 | 6.3 | 0.08 | 1.6 | 0.1 | 0.12 | 0.99 | 2.73 | 97.4 | 4.8 | 30.2 | 3.6 | 5.4 |
| 4.2 | 2.16 | 17.8 | 0.79 | 2.8 | 0.2 | 0.29 | 3.55 | 3.96 | 82.2 | 3.7 | 15.9 | 9.6 | 3.4 |
| 10.0 | 0.41 | 0.7 | 0.07 | 0.8 | 0.0 | -0.06 | -0.36 | 2.22 | 101.8 | 5.6 | 29.8 | 2.2 | 6.3 |
| 6.5 | 0.41 | 4.1 | 0.47 | 8.0 | 6.4 | 1.14 | 12.08 | 3.40 | 68.6 | 2.5 | 11.2 | 14.3 | 7.5 |
| 8.4 | 0.05 | 0.3 | 0.04 | 7.7 | 0.3 | 1.44 | 9.97 | 4.75 | 83.3 | 3.3 | 20.8 | 8.1 | 5.7 |
| 8.3 | 0.00 | 0.0 | 0.50 | 5.2 | 0.0 | 0.74 | 8.65 | 2.60 | 51.2 | 3.9 | 5.6 | 0.0 | 3.0 |
| 7.8 | 0.64 | 4.7 | -0.02 | 9.4 | 0.4 | 1.78 | 12.59 | 2.64 | 38.3 | 5.0 | 38.7 | 0.0 | 8.0 |
| 9.4 | 0.30 | 1.8 | 0.68 | 4.7 | 0.5 | 0.73 | 6.45 | 3.79 | 78.2 | 3.7 | 17.0 | 12.8 | 5.2 |
| 8.6 | 0.46 | 3.8 | 0.07 | 2.9 | 1.5 | 0.37 | 3.43 | 2.85 | 89.3 | 4.1 | 21.4 | 1.0 | 7.4 |
| 5.8 | 2.36 | 12.9 | 0.18 | 3.7 | 0.0 | 0.39 | 3.41 | 4.28 | 86.8 | 4.0 | 18.3 | 0.0 | 5.6 |
| 9.7 | 0.43 | 1.3 | 0.05 | 2.2 | 0.3 | 0.19 | 1.50 | 2.87 | 93.0 | 6.4 | 47.5 | 4.1 | 7.5 |
| 7.8 | 0.90 | 5.1 | 0.21 | 3.5 | 0.2 | 0.31 | 3.21 | 3.11 | 89.4 | 4.7 | 31.3 | 7.6 | 4.6 |
| 10.0 | 0.56 | 1.0 | 0.69 | 0.0 | -0.2 | -0.87 | -6.80 | 2.27 | 140.9 | 5.7 | 25.3 | 0.0 | 5.2 |
| 10.0 | 0.07 | 0.2 | 0.07 | 3.1 | 0.4 | 0.38 | 2.67 | 2.55 | 84.8 | 4.0 | 18.7 | 3.8 | 8.2 |
| 8.7 | 0.34 | 2.4 | 0.04 | 8.7 | 1.3 | 1.41 | 12.97 | 3.23 | 60.3 | 2.8 | 6.1 | 4.6 | 8.2 |
| 6.6 | 1.91 | 4.8 | 0.00 | 0.1 | 0.0 | -0.60 | -6.75 | 4.15 | 111.0 | 6.4 | 48.6 | 0.0 | 4.5 |
| 5.3 | 1.83 | 11.5 | 0.85 | 5.4 | 0.3 | 0.54 | 4.40 | 4.82 | 76.5 | 1.8 | 16.8 | 35.7 | 6.4 |
| 7.7 | 2.10 | 8.7 | -0.02 | 2.2 | 0.0 | 0.11 | 0.83 | 3.41 | 97.2 | 4.5 | 28.6 | 2.3 | 6.4 |
| 8.7 | 0.98 | 4.2 | 0.30 | 7.3 | 1.3 | 1.05 | 8.49 | 3.89 | 76.3 | 4.0 | 13.8 | 3.9 | 7.9 |
| 8.4 | 0.64 | 4.5 | 0.06 | 6.0 | 11.2 | 0.82 | 8.32 | 3.24 | 74.2 | 3.8 | 28.8 | 17.5 | 7.8 |
| 6.6 | 2.03 | 10.8 | 0.53 | 2.5 | 0.1 | 0.12 | 1.14 | 2.90 | 94.9 | 5.1 | 28.6 | 2.6 | 6.0 |
| 7.4 | 0.29 | 5.9 | 0.15 | 6.6 | 1.3 | 1.25 | 12.76 | 3.57 | 69.9 | 3.4 | 16.7 | 11.1 | 6.7 |
| 7.3 | 1.00 | 5.3 | 1.52 | 5.5 | 0.9 | 0.74 | 5.35 | 5.56 | 76.2 | 4.2 | 30.8 | 14.8 | 7.4 |
| 7.7 | 0.57 | 3.6 | 0.11 | 4.1 | 0.3 | 0.49 | 4.73 | 3.67 | 86.3 | 3.7 | 16.1 | 1.5 | 6.1 |
| 8.7 | 0.67 | 4.6 | 0.43 | 5.0 | 3.2 | 0.72 | 6.56 | 3.73 | 70.3 | 4.0 | 14.9 | 6.3 | 6.4 |
| 7.3 | 1.85 | 6.6 | 1.06 | 1.2 | -0.2 | -0.30 | -2.24 | 3.39 | 101.9 | 3.9 | 18.5 | 7.9 | 5.1 |
| 10.0 | 0.09 | 0.5 | 0.27 | 4.2 | 1.5 | 0.57 | 5.81 | 3.17 | 84.7 | 4.7 | 19.2 | 2.7 | 5.6 |
| 6.5 | 1.89 | 7.5 | 0.76 | 4.5 | 0.0 | 0.61 | 4.09 | 5.08 | 79.7 | 3.9 | 11.2 | 0.0 | 3.7 |
| 3.4 | 2.00 | 15.9 | 0.22 | 8.6 | 0.2 | 2.21 | 24.32 | 6.49 | 65.7 | 2.7 | 10.7 | 14.6 | 3.5 |
| 10.0 | 0.00 | 0.0 | 0.00 | 1.9 | 0.0 | 0.00 | 0.00 | 3.92 | 200.0 | 8.0 | 82.6 | 0.0 | 4.7 |
| 6.7 | 0.62 | 5.5 | 0.49 | 4.4 | 0.3 | 0.51 | 5.98 | 3.76 | 80.5 | 3.4 | 20.2 | 12.3 | 3.8 |
| 8.1 | 0.00 | 0.0 | 0.00 | 3.2 | 0.0 | 0.39 | 1.53 | 6.78 | 87.5 | 5.0 | 32.0 | 0.0 | 7.1 |
| 9.6 | 0.86 | 2.3 | 0.00 | 6.2 | 0.2 | 0.86 | 7.25 | 2.12 | 56.3 | 4.4 | 8.8 | 3.0 | 5.7 |
| 9.8 | 0.31 | 0.6 | 0.18 | 0.4 | -0.1 | -0.26 | -2.71 | 1.87 | 112.7 | 5.6 | 34.7 | 0.0 | 3.6 |
| 10.0 | 0.32 | 0.7 | 0.14 | 3.7 | 0.1 | 0.39 | 3.16 | 2.09 | 90.8 | 6.3 | 53.4 | 2.0 | 6.2 |
| 4.7 | 0.84 | 9.6 | 0.68 | 3.9 | 0.2 | 0.29 | 3.81 | 4.11 | 88.8 | 3.4 | 12.6 | 5.6 | 4.3 |
| 6.0 | 1.09 | 8.0 | 0.35 | 5.9 | 0.4 | 0.75 | 6.39 | 5.01 | 80.5 | 2.3 | 15.5 | 23.9 | 7.2 |
| 7.6 | 0.66 | 4.5 | 0.53 | 3.3 | 0.4 | 0.39 | 4.06 | 4.39 | 89.2 | 3.4 | 14.9 | 6.7 | 4.9 |
| 6.0 | 0.81 | 8.5 | 0.65 | 3.5 | 2.1 | 0.63 | 9.18 | 3.87 | 79.9 | 3.3 | 9.8 | 4.4 | 3.4 |
| 6.4 | 0.92 | 10.9 | 0.38 | 5.1 | 0.8 | 0.69 | 6.94 | 4.28 | 83.6 | 3.7 | 15.0 | 4.8 | 6.1 |
| 9.4 | 0.62 | 3.6 | 0.38 | 1.9 | 0.1 | 0.09 | 0.82 | 2.82 | 93.7 | 4.2 | 32.7 | 10.2 | 6.1 |
| 4.0 | 1.06 | 10.6 | 1.19 | 4.6 | 0.1 | 0.26 | 3.86 | 6.01 | 83.6 | 3.3 | 9.1 | 1.0 | 1.7 |
| 10.0 | 0.60 | 0.6 | 1.42 | 0.0 | -0.1 | -1.47 | -7.90 | 3.34 | 147.5 | 5.4 | 11.1 | 0.0 | 4.8 |
| 3.6 | 1.58 | 12.9 | 0.42 | 4.0 | 0.0 | 0.51 | 5.54 | 3.95 | 86.2 | 4.0 | 12.4 | 1.6 | 1.7 |
| 8.3 | 0.51 | 4.7 | 0.17 | 3.8 | 0.3 | 0.52 | 6.34 | 3.82 | 84.4 | 3.7 | 10.8 | 2.4 | 4.3 |
| 7.4 | 1.11 | 8.1 | 0.13 | 3.3 | 0.4 | 0.39 | 4.36 | 3.40 | 91.8 | 4.4 | 19.8 | 4.3 | 5.2 |
| 8.9 | 0.33 | 1.8 | 0.81 | 3.7 | 0.2 | 0.40 | 3.86 | 4.16 | 85.6 | 4.3 | 19.9 | 0.9 | 5.2 |
| 5.4 | 1.59 | 7.0 | 2.13 | 1.1 | 0.0 | -0.32 | -3.40 | 4.42 | 96.8 | 4.5 | 26.9 | 0.0 | 3.6 |
| 8.2 | 0.00 | 0.0 | 0.70 | 2.2 | 0.0 | 0.00 | 0.00 | 6.91 | 90.0 | 5.9 | 39.4 | 0.0 | 7.3 |
| 7.1 | 1.68 | 9.8 | 0.00 | 3.6 | 0.1 | 0.41 | 3.69 | 3.27 | 89.2 | 3.9 | 32.2 | 3.4 | 6.0 |

| Name | City | State | Rating | 2014 Rating | 2013 Rating | Total Assets ($Mil) | One Year Asset Growth | Comm-ercial Loans | Cons-umer Loans | Mort-gage Loans | Secur-ities | Capital-ization Index | Net Worth Ratio |
|---|---|---|---|---|---|---|---|---|---|---|---|---|---|
| PRODUCERS EMPL CU | Columbus | OH | B- | C+ | C | <1 | -3.03 | 0.0 | 37.2 | 0.0 | 0.0 | 10.0 | 15.3 |
| PROFED FCU | Fort Wayne | IN | C | C | C | 379.0 | 3.85 | 1.8 | 20.1 | 16.6 | 17.9 | 7.7 | 9.5 |
| PROFESSIONAL FIRE FIGHTERS CU | Shreveport | LA | B+ | B+ | B+ | 38.3 | 2.92 | 0.0 | 31.8 | 10.7 | 0.0 | 10.0 | 18.6 |
| PROFESSIONAL POLICE OFFICERS CU | Indianapolis | IN | B | B | B- | 40.4 | 1.37 | 0.0 | 20.3 | 0.0 | 17.8 | 10.0 | 14.3 |
| PROFINANCE FCU | Merrillville | IN | D+ | D+ | C- | 13.9 | -4.66 | 1.3 | 9.7 | 17.6 | 43.5 | 10.0 | 23.1 |
| PROGRESSIONS CU | Spokane | WA | C+ | C | C- | 54.2 | 2.21 | 0.0 | 43.6 | 16.5 | 2.8 | 7.0 | 9.0 |
| PROGRESSIVE CU | New York | NY | B+ | B+ | B+ | 676.2 | 1.17 | 87.2 | 0.0 | 12.9 | 3.2 | 10.0 | 41.0 |
| PROGRESSIVE FCU | Mobile | AL | C- | C- | D+ | 5.8 | 0.33 | 0.0 | 27.1 | 1.3 | 0.0 | 10.0 | 23.9 |
| ▲ PROJECTOR FCU | Melville | NY | D+ | D | D | <1 | -2.36 | 0.0 | 15.0 | 0.0 | 0.0 | 7.2 | 9.2 |
| PROMEDICA FCU | Toledo | OH | C+ | B- | B- | 49.3 | 0.92 | 0.1 | 35.2 | 3.9 | 40.2 | 10.0 | 12.6 |
| PROMISE CU | Houston | TX | E+ | D- | D- | 5.3 | -0.19 | 0.0 | 66.5 | 0.0 | 0.0 | 7.8 | 9.6 |
| PROPONENT FCU | Nutley | NJ | B | B | C+ | 503.4 | -5.02 | 9.3 | 10.0 | 45.6 | 23.4 | 10.0 | 11.5 |
| PROSPECTORS FCU | Diamond Bar | CA | B- | B- | C+ | 63.3 | 4.40 | 4.8 | 24.4 | 14.6 | 41.2 | 10.0 | 12.1 |
| PROSPERA CU | Appleton | WI | B- | B | B- | 186.3 | 13.29 | 18.9 | 17.8 | 54.4 | 0.0 | 6.6 | 8.6 |
| PROVIDENCE FCU | Milwaukie | OR | B- | B- | C+ | 125.3 | 0.80 | 1.4 | 26.7 | 9.7 | 43.1 | 10.0 | 12.0 |
| PROVIDENT CU | Redwood City | CA | B+ | B+ | B+ | 2115.6 | 4.98 | 10.3 | 11.5 | 39.7 | 30.8 | 10.0 | 11.6 |
| PROVIDENT FCU | Dover | DE | D | D+ | D+ | 9.9 | -3.64 | 0.0 | 50.4 | 3.2 | 1.0 | 10.0 | 17.2 |
| ▲ PROVO POLICE & FIRE DEPT CU | Provo | UT | C- | D+ | D+ | 2.9 | -0.59 | 0.0 | 55.7 | 0.0 | 0.0 | 10.0 | 11.1 |
| PRR SOUTH FORK FCU | South Fork | PA | C+ | B- | B- | 42.1 | 0.53 | 0.0 | 10.3 | 4.0 | 23.2 | 10.0 | 15.7 |
| PS LOCAL 821 FCU | Jersey City | NJ | C+ | C+ | C | 1.0 | -3.52 | 0.0 | 0.0 | 0.0 | 0.0 | 10.0 | 22.5 |
| PSE CU INC | Parma | OH | D- | D | D | 122.6 | 3.22 | 0.3 | 26.4 | 7.1 | 16.8 | 6.2 | 8.2 |
| ▼ PSE&G NUCLEAR EMPL FCU | Hancocks Bridge | NJ | D- | D | D+ | 9.3 | 3.77 | 0.0 | 38.3 | 0.0 | 0.0 | 5.8 | 7.8 |
| PSTC EMPL FCU | Upper Darby | PA | B- | B | B | 34.7 | 1.46 | 1.3 | 22.5 | 33.0 | 3.3 | 10.0 | 16.1 |
| PUBLIC EMPL CU | Waterloo | IA | C+ | C+ | B- | 25.6 | -0.54 | 0.0 | 26.1 | 0.0 | 0.0 | 10.0 | 15.0 |
| PUBLIC EMPL CU | Austin | TX | C+ | C+ | C+ | 303.7 | 4.12 | 0.0 | 43.7 | 4.2 | 27.9 | 6.0 | 8.2 |
| ▲ PUBLIC SERVICE #3 CU | Fort Wayne | IN | B | B- | B- | 50.8 | -1.55 | 0.0 | 23.2 | 14.8 | 44.5 | 10.0 | 12.2 |
| PUBLIC SERVICE CU | Lone Tree | CO | A | A- | A- | 1590.3 | 13.49 | 6.2 | 52.0 | 11.6 | 12.6 | 9.9 | 10.9 |
| PUBLIC SERVICE CU | Romulus | MI | B+ | A- | A- | 146.2 | 0.98 | 6.9 | 29.8 | 26.4 | 22.6 | 10.0 | 14.3 |
| PUBLIC SERVICE CU | Wausau | WI | C | C | C | 13.0 | 3.01 | 0.0 | 11.8 | 31.5 | 0.0 | 10.0 | 20.7 |
| PUBLIC SERVICE ED TRENTON FCU | Lawrence Township | NJ | D | D | C- | 4.1 | -3.25 | 0.0 | 9.1 | 0.0 | 0.0 | 10.0 | 30.3 |
| PUBLIC SERVICE EDWARDSPT PLE FCU | Linton | IN | D+ | D | D+ | 1.7 | 4.80 | 0.0 | 58.4 | 0.0 | 0.0 | 10.0 | 11.3 |
| PUBLIC SERVICE FCU | Middlesex | NJ | B- | B | B | 31.6 | 9.08 | 0.0 | 18.2 | 11.7 | 6.5 | 9.8 | 10.9 |
| PUBLIC SERVICE HC EMPL FCU | Toms River | NJ | C- | C- | C | 8.6 | -2.35 | 0.0 | 27.1 | 0.5 | 63.9 | 10.0 | 29.2 |
| PUBLIC SERVICE PLAZA FCU | Newark | NJ | C- | C- | C- | 20.0 | -3.38 | 0.0 | 8.0 | 0.0 | 0.7 | 10.0 | 11.6 |
| PUBLIC SERVICE SEWAREN FCU | Sewaren | NJ | D | D | C- | <1 | -25.83 | 0.0 | 17.4 | 0.0 | 0.0 | 10.0 | 19.6 |
| PUBLIX EMPL FCU | Lakeland | FL | A- | B+ | A- | 813.7 | 11.72 | 2.6 | 23.3 | 9.3 | 38.9 | 10.0 | 13.0 |
| PUD FCU | Longview | WA | C | C | C | 7.4 | -3.02 | 0.0 | 43.5 | 0.0 | 0.0 | 10.0 | 16.2 |
| PUEBLO GOVERNMENT AGENCIES FCU | Pueblo | CO | C- | C- | C- | 29.2 | 5.43 | 0.9 | 26.0 | 8.2 | 0.0 | 10.0 | 13.1 |
| PUEBLO HORIZONS FCU | Pueblo | CO | D+ | D+ | D | 28.5 | 1.89 | 0.0 | 19.4 | 14.2 | 44.1 | 10.0 | 12.8 |
| PUERTO RICO FCU | Caparra | PR | B- | B- | B | 130.8 | 3.38 | 0.0 | 29.6 | 12.1 | 24.1 | 10.0 | 16.6 |
| ▲ PUGET SOUND COOPERATIVE CU | Bellevue | WA | C | D+ | D+ | 98.2 | 13.05 | 0.4 | 8.5 | 14.7 | 0.0 | 6.1 | 8.1 |
| PUGET SOUND FCU | Seattle | WA | E | E | E+ | 16.5 | -5.06 | 3.9 | 15.8 | 37.8 | 29.5 | 5.5 | 7.5 |
| PUGET SOUND REFINERY FCU | Anacortes | WA | C- | C- | C- | 10.7 | 6.57 | 0.0 | 50.1 | 0.0 | 0.0 | 10.0 | 13.4 |
| PURDUE FCU | West Lafayette | IN | B+ | A- | A- | 954.2 | 13.59 | 14.7 | 13.2 | 43.9 | 20.1 | 6.9 | 8.9 |
| PURITY DAIRIES EMPL FCU | Nashville | TN | C- | C- | C- | 3.4 | -5.08 | 0.0 | 41.1 | 0.0 | 0.0 | 10.0 | 17.5 |
| PUTNAM SCHOOL EMPL FCU | Eleanor | WV | B- | B- | B- | 11.8 | 4.05 | 0.0 | 32.9 | 0.0 | 0.0 | 10.0 | 13.2 |
| ▲ PVHMC FCU | Pomona | CA | C+ | C- | C- | 10.3 | 4.88 | 0.0 | 51.4 | 0.0 | 0.0 | 9.3 | 10.6 |
| PWC EMPL CU | Woodbridge | VA | B+ | B+ | B+ | 52.9 | 2.88 | 0.0 | 27.9 | 0.0 | 48.6 | 10.0 | 13.3 |
| PYRAMID FCU | Tucson | AZ | C+ | C+ | C | 136.8 | 2.20 | 0.7 | 46.0 | 19.7 | 14.1 | 8.1 | 9.7 |
| ▲ QSIDE FCU | Queens Village | NY | C- | D+ | D- | 46.9 | -1.06 | 0.0 | 40.2 | 7.7 | 24.8 | 6.7 | 8.8 |
| ▲ QUAD CITIES POSTAL CU | Moline | IL | C- | D | C- | 6.7 | -2.66 | 0.0 | 32.0 | 29.2 | 0.0 | 8.9 | 10.3 |
| QUAKER OATS CU | Cedar Rapids | IA | C- | C- | C- | 8.5 | 5.84 | 0.0 | 55.7 | 0.0 | 0.0 | 10.0 | 15.6 |
| QUALSTAR CU | Redmond | WA | A | A | A- | 396.9 | 8.52 | 1.2 | 26.9 | 18.6 | 2.5 | 10.0 | 13.4 |
| ▼ QUALTRUST CU | Irving | TX | C | B- | C+ | 190.5 | 0.87 | 0.0 | 30.2 | 19.9 | 8.4 | 8.5 | 10.0 |
| ▼ QUAY SCHOOLS FCU | Tucumcari | NM | C+ | B- | B- | 6.5 | -4.62 | 0.0 | 44.7 | 0.0 | 0.0 | 10.0 | 15.8 |
| QUEEN EMPL CU | Albert Lea | MN | D+ | C- | C- | 2.0 | 3.76 | 0.0 | 37.3 | 0.0 | 0.0 | 10.0 | 27.3 |
| QUEEN OF PEACE ARLINGTON FCU | Arlington | VA | C | C | C | 2.4 | -5.08 | 0.0 | 17.0 | 0.0 | 15.4 | 10.0 | 13.1 |
| QUEENS CLUSTER FCU | Hicksville | NY | C- | C+ | C+ | <1 | 4.97 | 0.0 | 42.6 | 0.0 | 0.0 | 9.0 | 10.4 |
| ▼ QUEENS FCU | Honolulu | HI | C- | B- | C | 53.5 | 4.17 | 0.3 | 18.1 | 3.5 | 6.5 | 7.9 | 9.6 |
| QUEST CU | Topeka | KS | C+ | C+ | C+ | 263.8 | -3.28 | 0.3 | 23.2 | 9.3 | 49.0 | 8.3 | 9.9 |

| Asset Quality Index | Non-Performing Loans as a % of Total Loans | as a % of Capital | Net Charge-Offs Avg Loans | Profitability Index | Net Income ($Mil) | Return on Assets | Return on Equity | Net Interest Spread | Overhead Efficiency Ratio | Liquidity Index | Liquidity Ratio | Hot Money Ratio | Stability Index |
|---|---|---|---|---|---|---|---|---|---|---|---|---|---|
| 8.2 | 0.42 | 0.9 | 4.65 | 9.8 | 0.0 | 2.16 | 14.49 | 4.51 | 35.7 | 7.0 | 73.8 | 0.0 | 5.7 |
| 9.7 | 0.26 | 1.9 | 0.08 | 3.2 | 1.2 | 0.42 | 4.54 | 2.55 | 90.2 | 5.0 | 28.6 | 1.3 | 6.0 |
| 9.1 | 1.08 | 3.3 | 0.04 | 7.2 | 0.3 | 1.16 | 6.32 | 3.30 | 62.9 | 4.1 | 47.1 | 23.4 | 7.0 |
| 10.0 | 0.00 | 0.0 | -0.03 | 4.1 | 0.2 | 0.56 | 4.04 | 2.42 | 80.1 | 4.3 | 18.9 | 5.4 | 7.0 |
| 7.3 | 3.50 | 5.2 | 0.95 | 0.9 | 0.0 | -0.04 | -0.16 | 3.11 | 99.2 | 4.7 | 16.4 | 0.0 | 6.0 |
| 8.0 | 0.10 | 1.2 | 0.12 | 5.1 | 0.3 | 0.83 | 9.40 | 4.28 | 87.9 | 3.3 | 13.3 | 8.6 | 3.2 |
| 4.7 | 1.05 | 2.4 | 0.65 | 8.0 | 5.6 | 1.07 | 2.74 | 3.93 | 38.2 | 0.9 | 7.0 | 28.2 | 10.0 |
| 7.3 | 3.10 | 4.8 | 3.10 | 2.9 | 0.0 | 0.11 | 0.48 | 7.60 | 95.4 | 6.7 | 55.9 | 2.5 | 5.4 |
| 10.0 | 0.00 | 0.0 | 0.00 | 2.9 | 0.0 | 0.40 | 4.49 | 0.81 | 70.0 | 6.7 | 61.8 | 0.0 | 4.9 |
| 9.9 | 0.16 | 0.6 | 0.31 | 2.7 | 0.1 | 0.23 | 1.91 | 2.88 | 94.1 | 4.5 | 27.1 | 2.5 | 5.8 |
| 1.9 | 2.62 | 34.8 | 4.12 | 1.9 | 0.0 | 0.00 | 0.00 | 7.09 | 79.6 | 3.5 | 39.8 | 49.6 | 1.0 |
| 6.4 | 2.06 | 12.7 | 0.18 | 4.1 | 2.0 | 0.51 | 4.79 | 3.24 | 84.2 | 3.3 | 17.8 | 7.1 | 7.3 |
| 9.8 | 0.11 | 0.4 | 0.08 | 3.8 | 0.3 | 0.54 | 4.45 | 3.11 | 83.7 | 3.9 | 11.7 | 10.3 | 6.0 |
| 6.3 | 0.53 | 5.5 | 0.07 | 5.8 | 1.3 | 0.98 | 11.61 | 3.38 | 80.3 | 3.0 | 13.0 | 11.3 | 5.2 |
| 9.6 | 0.48 | 2.0 | 0.41 | 3.8 | 0.6 | 0.61 | 5.07 | 3.07 | 79.7 | 4.1 | 15.5 | 3.2 | 7.1 |
| 9.8 | 0.10 | 0.5 | 0.08 | 4.7 | 11.6 | 0.74 | 6.32 | 2.39 | 78.2 | 4.2 | 16.4 | 3.7 | 8.3 |
| 6.6 | 1.61 | 5.2 | 1.38 | 0.7 | 0.0 | -0.22 | -1.25 | 4.90 | 98.7 | 4.2 | 31.7 | 6.3 | 5.1 |
| 6.1 | 0.61 | 2.9 | 0.00 | 3.0 | 0.0 | 0.19 | 1.67 | 4.75 | 87.7 | 6.1 | 43.0 | 0.0 | 6.3 |
| 10.0 | 0.24 | 0.3 | 0.08 | 2.7 | 0.1 | 0.24 | 1.53 | 1.14 | 81.6 | 5.6 | 40.5 | 0.0 | 7.4 |
| 8.0 | 3.64 | 4.1 | 0.97 | 7.6 | 0.0 | 1.17 | 5.31 | 5.00 | 71.0 | 6.8 | 66.7 | 0.0 | 5.0 |
| 7.8 | 0.88 | 4.3 | 0.37 | 0.5 | -0.3 | -0.27 | -3.24 | 2.82 | 102.8 | 5.1 | 27.5 | 1.6 | 4.7 |
| 7.2 | 0.57 | 3.2 | -0.10 | 3.6 | 0.1 | 0.73 | 9.93 | 3.92 | 76.9 | 6.2 | 38.6 | 0.0 | 1.7 |
| 6.3 | 4.16 | 13.2 | 2.97 | 3.9 | 0.1 | 0.18 | 1.12 | 5.48 | 63.9 | 3.6 | 34.9 | 27.1 | 7.0 |
| 9.9 | 0.00 | 0.0 | 0.01 | 3.2 | 0.1 | 0.39 | 2.63 | 2.26 | 82.5 | 4.2 | 24.2 | 5.3 | 7.6 |
| 9.3 | 0.35 | 3.2 | 0.15 | 3.3 | 0.9 | 0.41 | 5.20 | 2.60 | 83.0 | 4.7 | 17.7 | 2.2 | 4.6 |
| 10.0 | 0.20 | 0.7 | 0.07 | 5.2 | 0.2 | 0.63 | 4.99 | 2.84 | 81.5 | 4.6 | 19.7 | 1.0 | 6.7 |
| 7.7 | 0.37 | 3.0 | 0.50 | 9.6 | 18.0 | 1.58 | 14.65 | 4.13 | 65.7 | 4.1 | 18.4 | 4.9 | 8.3 |
| 6.5 | 0.62 | 5.4 | 1.88 | 5.6 | 0.4 | 0.35 | 2.58 | 3.92 | 78.9 | 3.3 | 13.4 | 9.6 | 8.0 |
| 9.9 | 0.51 | 1.2 | 0.00 | 2.0 | 0.0 | 0.10 | 0.45 | 2.49 | 94.4 | 4.1 | 17.0 | 3.6 | 7.3 |
| 10.0 | 2.17 | 0.7 | 0.00 | 0.3 | 0.0 | -0.32 | -1.08 | 1.54 | 114.6 | 6.7 | 51.5 | 0.0 | 6.2 |
| 1.8 | 4.87 | 31.2 | 0.00 | 3.6 | 0.0 | 0.58 | 5.07 | 4.01 | 83.3 | 4.6 | 25.6 | 0.0 | 5.9 |
| 10.0 | 0.33 | 1.0 | 0.07 | 3.7 | 0.1 | 0.46 | 4.20 | 2.85 | 81.4 | 4.7 | 24.1 | 6.2 | 6.0 |
| 9.2 | 3.41 | 3.2 | 1.29 | 2.7 | 0.0 | 0.32 | 1.12 | 3.59 | 82.8 | 5.2 | 29.6 | 0.0 | 6.3 |
| 10.0 | 0.90 | 0.7 | 0.00 | 1.6 | 0.0 | 0.03 | 0.29 | 0.87 | 96.3 | 5.0 | 9.5 | 0.0 | 5.7 |
| 10.0 | 0.00 | 0.0 | 0.00 | 0.0 | 0.0 | -6.78 | -32.00 | 4.17 | 700.0 | 8.6 | 105.0 | 0.0 | 4.8 |
| 8.1 | 1.20 | 4.3 | 0.56 | 5.9 | 5.7 | 0.95 | 7.45 | 2.92 | 74.2 | 4.7 | 18.7 | 6.2 | 7.9 |
| 9.1 | 0.88 | 3.0 | 0.00 | 2.7 | 0.0 | 0.24 | 1.46 | 2.77 | 91.2 | 4.7 | 45.2 | 5.2 | 7.5 |
| 7.8 | 0.65 | 5.3 | 0.45 | 1.8 | 0.0 | 0.08 | 0.63 | 3.18 | 93.8 | 5.6 | 48.9 | 1.8 | 6.4 |
| 8.7 | 0.62 | 4.6 | 0.38 | 0.4 | -0.1 | -0.27 | -2.07 | 3.00 | 104.2 | 4.5 | 25.8 | 9.3 | 5.9 |
| 8.1 | 0.77 | 3.9 | 0.87 | 2.8 | 0.2 | 0.22 | 1.34 | 2.51 | 74.4 | 5.4 | 38.7 | 8.5 | 7.0 |
| 5.4 | 0.36 | 4.4 | 0.22 | 8.1 | 0.9 | 1.23 | 16.26 | 3.98 | 71.7 | 2.4 | 9.8 | 6.9 | 3.8 |
| 6.3 | 0.47 | 3.7 | 1.29 | 0.9 | 0.0 | -0.12 | -1.59 | 3.93 | 97.0 | 4.2 | 15.6 | 0.0 | 1.4 |
| 7.7 | 1.16 | 4.4 | -0.07 | 1.8 | 0.0 | 0.16 | 1.22 | 2.64 | 92.4 | 6.3 | 50.8 | 0.0 | 6.3 |
| 9.5 | 0.21 | 1.5 | 0.19 | 4.4 | 3.9 | 0.56 | 6.12 | 3.45 | 83.5 | 4.0 | 21.9 | 6.2 | 6.7 |
| 7.5 | 2.68 | 6.1 | 0.40 | 1.6 | 0.0 | -0.04 | -0.23 | 2.00 | 97.8 | 5.9 | 55.2 | 0.0 | 5.8 |
| 9.4 | 1.00 | 2.8 | 0.00 | 5.3 | 0.1 | 0.78 | 5.99 | 3.31 | 67.9 | 6.5 | 69.0 | 0.0 | 7.2 |
| 8.6 | 0.25 | 1.2 | 0.00 | 6.1 | 0.1 | 0.90 | 8.62 | 7.33 | 79.1 | 6.8 | 53.1 | 0.0 | 5.5 |
| 9.2 | 0.54 | 1.4 | 0.89 | 5.7 | 0.3 | 0.64 | 4.81 | 3.58 | 76.3 | 5.1 | 21.1 | 1.6 | 6.7 |
| 6.3 | 0.70 | 5.9 | 0.59 | 3.0 | 0.2 | 0.23 | 2.57 | 3.99 | 89.2 | 3.6 | 11.7 | 2.8 | 4.9 |
| 7.1 | 0.59 | 3.5 | 1.03 | 2.7 | 0.1 | 0.20 | 2.28 | 5.71 | 93.7 | 4.1 | 15.2 | 2.6 | 3.8 |
| 9.8 | 0.04 | 0.3 | -0.31 | 3.2 | 0.0 | 0.44 | 4.50 | 4.90 | 89.8 | 4.9 | 27.8 | 0.0 | 4.1 |
| 7.5 | 1.22 | 5.2 | -0.05 | 1.4 | 0.0 | -0.27 | -1.71 | 4.78 | 105.0 | 4.8 | 24.4 | 0.0 | 6.1 |
| 7.9 | 1.16 | 4.5 | 0.48 | 9.7 | 5.2 | 1.79 | 13.66 | 3.73 | 65.5 | 4.5 | 33.0 | 5.7 | 8.0 |
| 6.3 | 1.19 | 8.2 | 0.79 | 1.8 | -0.2 | -0.12 | -1.23 | 4.05 | 90.2 | 4.5 | 22.0 | 3.1 | 5.9 |
| 8.6 | 0.80 | 3.1 | 0.81 | 6.4 | 0.0 | 0.60 | 4.03 | 5.86 | 75.9 | 4.4 | 37.7 | 1.3 | 5.0 |
| 9.7 | 0.00 | 0.0 | 0.00 | 0.6 | 0.0 | -0.20 | -0.74 | 3.55 | 108.6 | 7.2 | 73.7 | 0.0 | 6.3 |
| 9.9 | 0.00 | 0.0 | 0.00 | 2.9 | 0.0 | 0.39 | 2.99 | 2.48 | 82.9 | 5.9 | 38.6 | 0.0 | 6.1 |
| 7.8 | 1.07 | 4.7 | 0.00 | 0.1 | 0.0 | -2.37 | -20.00 | 4.58 | 120.0 | 6.1 | 41.1 | 0.0 | 7.7 |
| 8.7 | 1.22 | 2.8 | 0.68 | 1.9 | 0.0 | -0.05 | -0.52 | 2.73 | 99.3 | 5.8 | 24.2 | 0.0 | 5.0 |
| 9.6 | 0.47 | 1.7 | 0.25 | 3.1 | 0.7 | 0.33 | 3.30 | 2.47 | 90.1 | 5.5 | 44.6 | 5.2 | 5.0 |

| Name | City | State | Rating | 2014 Rating | 2013 Rating | Total Assets ($Mil) | One Year Asset Growth | Commercial Loans | Consumer Loans | Mortgage Loans | Securities | Capitalization Index | Net Worth Ratio |
|---|---|---|---|---|---|---|---|---|---|---|---|---|---|
| QUEST FCU | Kenton | OH | B | B | C+ | 91.2 | 5.37 | 7.0 | 22.2 | 35.4 | 4.1 | 8.9 | 10.3 |
| QUESTA CU | Questa | NM | B- | B- | B+ | 7.4 | 3.76 | 2.1 | 11.1 | 21.5 | 0.0 | 10.0 | 25.5 |
| QUINCY CU | Quincy | MA | B+ | B+ | B+ | 466.9 | 3.31 | 0.0 | 16.2 | 33.8 | 27.3 | 10.0 | 13.1 |
| QUINCY MUNICIPAL CU | Quincy | IL | C | C | C | 3.6 | 0.86 | 0.0 | 43.8 | 0.0 | 0.0 | 10.0 | 14.3 |
| QUINCY POSTAL EMPL CU | Quincy | IL | C- | D+ | D+ | 2.3 | 3.92 | 0.0 | 33.4 | 0.0 | 0.0 | 10.0 | 12.5 |
| QUINDARO HOMES FCU | Kansas City | KS | D+ | D+ | D+ | 1.2 | -13.04 | 0.0 | 0.0 | 0.0 | 0.0 | 10.0 | 21.3 |
| QUINNIPIAC VALLEY COMMUNITY FCU | Wallingford | CT | C | C | C | 7.4 | 0.57 | 0.0 | 36.4 | 0.0 | 0.0 | 10.0 | 14.5 |
| QUORUM FCU | Purchase | NY | C | C+ | C+ | 933.3 | 10.79 | 10.5 | 7.6 | 38.3 | 8.7 | 5.8 | 7.8 |
| R T P FCU | Durham | NC | C | C | C | 104.4 | -0.44 | 8.0 | 30.6 | 9.7 | 22.1 | 7.4 | 9.3 |
| ▲ R-G FCU | Raymore | MO | D | D- | D+ | 75.0 | 2.95 | 0.0 | 24.4 | 19.0 | 9.9 | 6.3 | 8.3 |
| R-S BELLCO FCU | New Brighton | PA | D- | D- | D | 24.4 | 4.83 | 0.0 | 22.3 | 0.3 | 12.6 | 5.2 | 7.2 |
| RABUN-TALLULAH FCU | Tiger | GA | C+ | C+ | C | <1 | 4.99 | 0.0 | 38.8 | 0.0 | 0.0 | 10.0 | 25.8 |
| ▼ RACINE MUNICIPAL EMPL CU | Racine | WI | C | B- | B- | 14.7 | 8.53 | 0.0 | 24.1 | 21.1 | 0.0 | 10.0 | 13.9 |
| RADIO CAB CU | Portland | OR | C+ | C+ | C+ | 4.9 | 7.92 | 0.0 | 1.4 | 0.0 | 4.1 | 10.0 | 16.8 |
| ▼ RADIO TELEVISION & COMMUNICATIONS FC | New York | NY | D | D+ | D+ | 4.2 | -5.00 | 0.0 | 27.2 | 24.6 | 0.0 | 10.0 | 19.8 |
| ▼ RAFE FCU | Riverside | CA | C | C | C- | 23.4 | 2.94 | 0.0 | 61.6 | 2.6 | 3.6 | 10.0 | 15.4 |
| RAH FCU | Randolph | MA | C- | C | C | 15.4 | 8.68 | 0.0 | 22.0 | 27.6 | 0.0 | 10.0 | 11.9 |
| RAILROAD & INDUSTRIAL FCU | Tampa | FL | A- | A- | A- | 291.7 | 5.07 | 0.3 | 13.1 | 6.2 | 55.5 | 10.0 | 11.8 |
| RAILROAD FCU | Irondale | AL | C | C | C | 105.6 | 1.52 | 0.0 | 9.5 | 0.6 | 76.5 | 10.0 | 12.3 |
| RAILS WEST FCU | Chubbuck | ID | C- | D+ | D | 54.7 | -1.76 | 0.0 | 42.9 | 28.2 | 0.0 | 5.9 | 7.9 |
| RAILWAY CU | Mandan | ND | A- | A- | A- | 93.0 | 5.61 | 10.3 | 29.1 | 12.4 | 0.7 | 10.0 | 12.9 |
| RAILWAY EMPL CU | Muscle Shoals | AL | C+ | C+ | C+ | 17.4 | 2.06 | 0.0 | 17.6 | 22.7 | 0.0 | 10.0 | 23.8 |
| RAINBOW FCU | Lewiston | ME | A- | A- | A- | 187.4 | 3.28 | 0.0 | 15.0 | 47.7 | 5.4 | 10.0 | 14.2 |
| RALEIGH COUNTY EDUCATORS FCU | Beckley | WV | B- | B- | B- | 22.1 | 3.37 | 0.0 | 30.1 | 0.0 | 36.0 | 10.0 | 16.7 |
| ▲ RALEIGH COUNTY FCU | Beckley | WV | B | C+ | C+ | 10.3 | 11.27 | 0.0 | 59.1 | 0.0 | 0.0 | 10.0 | 11.5 |
| RANCHO FCU | Downey | CA | D | D+ | D | 88.2 | 5.80 | 0.2 | 20.3 | 32.2 | 16.8 | 5.9 | 7.9 |
| RANCOCAS FCU | Willingboro | NJ | D+ | D+ | C | 2.9 | -6.07 | 0.0 | 14.9 | 8.6 | 0.0 | 6.1 | 8.1 |
| RANDOLPH COUNTY SCHOOL EMPL FCU | Elkins | WV | D+ | C- | C- | 1.4 | -10.84 | 0.0 | 28.6 | 0.0 | 0.0 | 10.0 | 13.0 |
| RANDOLPH-BROOKS FCU | Live Oak | TX | A+ | A+ | A+ | 6665.4 | 10.21 | 4.8 | 35.5 | 29.8 | 19.4 | 10.0 | 12.4 |
| ▼ RAPIDES FCU | Alexandria | LA | C- | C | C | 6.5 | 2.33 | 0.0 | 27.4 | 0.0 | 0.0 | 10.0 | 25.4 |
| RAPIDES GENERAL HOSPITAL EMPL FCU | Alexandria | LA | C | C | C- | 11.5 | 2.80 | 0.0 | 29.2 | 1.0 | 0.0 | 10.0 | 14.1 |
| RARITAN BAY FCU | Sayreville | NJ | C- | C- | D+ | 78.4 | 0.32 | 0.0 | 29.4 | 3.3 | 42.0 | 5.5 | 7.5 |
| ▲ RAVALLI COUNTY FCU | Hamilton | MT | B | B- | C+ | 37.9 | 3.33 | 0.8 | 20.0 | 16.7 | 29.8 | 9.5 | 10.7 |
| RAVENSWOOD FCU | Ravenswood | WV | B- | B- | C+ | 32.6 | 3.07 | 0.0 | 48.8 | 5.8 | 0.0 | 10.0 | 13.3 |
| RAY FCU | Kearny | AZ | C- | C- | C+ | 8.6 | 9.16 | 0.0 | 71.5 | 11.1 | 2.9 | 10.0 | 13.0 |
| RAYTOWN-LEES SUMMIT COMMUNITY CU | Raytown | MO | D | D | D+ | 61.4 | 0.64 | 0.0 | 62.9 | 3.9 | 0.0 | 5.6 | 7.6 |
| RCT FCU | Augusta | GA | E+ | D | D | 6.7 | -3.62 | 0.0 | 50.3 | 0.0 | 0.0 | 6.4 | 8.4 |
| REACH FCU | Menlo Park | CA | C+ | C+ | C+ | 97.3 | 1.71 | 1.8 | 17.6 | 25.5 | 21.0 | 7.1 | 9.2 |
| READING BERKS SCHOOL EMPL CU | Reading | PA | C+ | C | C | 19.9 | -5.62 | 0.0 | 8.5 | 0.0 | 0.0 | 10.0 | 11.4 |
| READING FCU | Cincinnati | OH | C- | C- | D+ | 7.9 | -7.06 | 0.0 | 14.8 | 0.0 | 0.0 | 10.0 | 13.2 |
| READING MASS TOWN EMPL FCU | Reading | MA | D | D | C- | 8.0 | 6.94 | 0.0 | 28.7 | 8.0 | 0.0 | 10.0 | 15.2 |
| REAVIS-STICKNEY CU | Burbank | IL | D+ | D | D+ | 1.1 | -8.48 | 0.0 | 22.1 | 0.0 | 0.0 | 8.4 | 9.9 |
| ▼ RECTOR FCU | Philadelphia | PA | D- | D- | D- | <1 | -37.30 | 0.0 | 49.7 | 0.0 | 0.0 | 10.0 | 45.8 |
| RED CANOE CU | Longview | WA | B | B | B | 650.3 | 2.40 | 7.0 | 27.5 | 37.3 | 8.2 | 10.0 | 12.0 |
| RED CROWN FCU | Tulsa | OK | B- | B- | C+ | 164.0 | 8.18 | 3.5 | 53.9 | 16.4 | 10.9 | 6.0 | 8.0 |
| RED LAKE CO-OP FCU | Red Lake Falls | MN | D | D- | E+ | 6.6 | -0.20 | 1.0 | 26.7 | 25.9 | 0.0 | 6.7 | 8.7 |
| RED RIVER FCU | Altus | OK | C | C | C- | 75.8 | -5.17 | 0.0 | 44.0 | 6.4 | 28.8 | 10.0 | 12.0 |
| RED RIVER FCU | Texarkana | TX | A- | B+ | B+ | 710.2 | 5.03 | 11.8 | 35.1 | 19.4 | 18.4 | 9.5 | 10.7 |
| RED RIVER MILL EMPL FCU | Natchitoches | LA | C- | C | C+ | 6.8 | 11.12 | 0.0 | 71.3 | 0.3 | 3.4 | 10.0 | 20.2 |
| ▼ RED ROCKS CU | Highlands Ranch | CO | B- | B | B | 246.6 | 4.64 | 0.0 | 31.2 | 27.8 | 6.9 | 7.6 | 9.5 |
| RED WING CU | Red Wing | MN | B | B | B- | 87.1 | 9.35 | 2.0 | 20.2 | 11.1 | 22.1 | 8.5 | 10.0 |
| REDBRAND CU | Bartonville | IL | B- | B- | C | 51.4 | 0.76 | 0.0 | 36.9 | 9.0 | 19.4 | 10.0 | 11.3 |
| REDFORD MUNICIPAL EMPL CU | Redford | MI | E+ | E+ | E+ | 2.5 | -2.50 | 0.0 | 50.6 | 0.0 | 0.0 | 5.7 | 7.8 |
| ▼ REDIFORM NIAGARA FALLS NY FCU | Niagara Falls | NY | D+ | C- | D+ | 10.3 | -6.38 | 0.0 | 37.9 | 16.0 | 0.2 | 10.0 | 15.9 |
| REDLANDS CITY EMPL FCU | Redlands | CA | D+ | D+ | D | 6.9 | -9.09 | 0.0 | 79.4 | 0.0 | 1.2 | 10.0 | 22.1 |
| REDSTONE FCU | Huntsville | AL | A- | A- | A- | 3881.0 | 5.92 | 1.8 | 18.5 | 8.6 | 60.0 | 10.0 | 11.5 |
| REDWOOD CU | Santa Rosa | CA | A | A | A- | 2702.9 | 11.20 | 9.9 | 21.4 | 40.3 | 0.1 | 10.0 | 11.7 |
| REED CU | Houston | TX | D+ | C- | C- | 18.5 | -5.76 | 0.0 | 1.6 | 0.0 | 0.0 | 10.0 | 14.1 |
| REEVES COUNTY TEACHERS CU | Pecos | TX | D+ | D | D+ | 10.7 | 13.63 | 0.0 | 65.7 | 4.6 | 0.0 | 8.1 | 9.7 |
| REFUGIO COUNTY FCU | Refugio | TX | B | B | B | 10.8 | 3.14 | 0.0 | 46.5 | 0.0 | 0.0 | 10.0 | 15.2 |

| Asset Quality Index | Non-Performing Loans as a % of Total Loans | as a % of Capital | Net Charge-Offs Avg Loans | Profitability Index | Net Income ($Mil) | Return on Assets | Return on Equity | Net Interest Spread | Overhead Efficiency Ratio | Liquidity Index | Liquidity Ratio | Hot Money Ratio | Stability Index |
|---|---|---|---|---|---|---|---|---|---|---|---|---|---|
| 5.2 | 1.96 | 12.6 | 0.63 | 6.5 | 0.6 | 0.93 | 9.32 | 4.96 | 77.0 | 4.4 | 24.2 | 4.1 | 4.9 |
| 10.0 | 0.00 | 0.0 | 0.00 | 5.2 | 0.0 | 0.71 | 2.78 | 4.19 | 80.8 | 6.5 | 53.6 | 0.0 | 5.0 |
| 9.6 | 0.30 | 1.4 | 0.16 | 4.2 | 2.0 | 0.56 | 4.33 | 2.63 | 76.8 | 4.0 | 15.6 | 6.4 | 7.9 |
| 8.2 | 1.19 | 3.6 | 0.08 | 3.7 | 0.0 | 0.40 | 2.86 | 3.21 | 79.8 | 5.3 | 31.6 | 0.0 | 6.9 |
| 6.0 | 4.04 | 12.0 | 2.04 | 1.6 | 0.0 | 0.00 | 0.00 | 3.18 | 100.0 | 5.5 | 32.5 | 0.0 | 6.2 |
| 3.6 | 8.12 | 15.2 | 0.00 | 3.7 | 0.0 | 0.40 | 2.04 | 6.06 | 85.7 | 7.3 | 73.8 | 0.0 | 6.3 |
| 9.9 | 0.00 | 0.0 | 0.08 | 3.2 | 0.0 | 0.46 | 3.28 | 4.09 | 100.5 | 5.6 | 42.2 | 0.0 | 7.3 |
| 4.1 | 1.71 | 18.7 | 0.79 | 3.9 | 3.7 | 0.54 | 7.37 | 4.00 | 72.1 | 2.1 | 4.1 | 14.2 | 5.0 |
| 9.3 | 0.45 | 2.7 | 0.06 | 3.1 | 0.3 | 0.33 | 3.65 | 3.14 | 91.1 | 4.5 | 12.0 | 2.2 | 5.5 |
| 6.8 | 0.58 | 5.5 | 0.82 | 0.9 | 0.0 | -0.01 | -0.11 | 3.02 | 100.1 | 4.6 | 19.4 | 0.6 | 1.9 |
| 8.1 | 0.38 | 2.5 | 0.09 | 0.5 | -0.1 | -0.27 | -3.80 | 3.02 | 106.4 | 5.3 | 30.1 | 1.0 | 3.0 |
| 8.6 | 2.04 | 3.0 | 0.00 | 4.9 | 0.0 | 0.43 | 1.65 | 5.56 | 90.9 | 7.6 | 82.1 | 0.0 | 8.1 |
| 9.3 | 0.91 | 3.4 | 0.48 | 1.8 | 0.0 | -0.07 | -0.46 | 2.96 | 89.2 | 5.1 | 35.1 | 3.3 | 7.4 |
| 8.8 | 0.00 | 0.0 | 0.06 | 7.1 | 0.0 | 1.06 | 6.40 | 3.74 | 66.9 | 6.1 | 65.1 | 0.0 | 5.7 |
| 7.4 | 3.07 | 8.5 | 4.13 | 0.0 | -0.1 | -4.07 | -18.76 | 5.07 | 114.4 | 4.9 | 27.8 | 0.0 | 5.8 |
| 1.9 | 6.76 | 29.4 | 2.56 | 9.8 | 0.5 | 3.09 | 21.54 | 12.20 | 63.9 | 3.9 | 20.8 | 10.6 | 7.8 |
| 9.2 | 0.64 | 3.5 | 0.04 | 1.6 | 0.0 | 0.09 | 0.72 | 3.48 | 96.1 | 4.5 | 13.5 | 1.4 | 5.7 |
| 9.9 | 0.38 | 1.5 | 0.47 | 4.8 | 1.2 | 0.57 | 4.93 | 2.77 | 84.1 | 4.7 | 24.3 | 14.1 | 7.2 |
| 10.0 | 0.53 | 0.6 | 0.57 | 2.0 | 0.1 | 0.10 | 0.81 | 1.19 | 87.8 | 4.2 | 7.8 | 10.8 | 6.8 |
| 5.4 | 0.70 | 6.7 | 0.31 | 4.5 | 0.3 | 0.64 | 8.51 | 4.21 | 82.6 | 3.4 | 9.0 | 1.5 | 2.1 |
| 9.2 | 0.13 | 0.7 | 0.07 | 8.2 | 0.8 | 1.21 | 9.64 | 3.73 | 68.7 | 3.0 | 7.5 | 9.5 | 7.6 |
| 9.8 | 0.39 | 0.7 | 0.71 | 2.5 | 0.0 | 0.15 | 0.62 | 4.18 | 93.2 | 6.5 | 43.3 | 0.0 | 7.3 |
| 7.3 | 1.24 | 7.7 | 0.12 | 5.3 | 1.1 | 0.77 | 6.02 | 3.24 | 79.0 | 4.1 | 21.0 | 6.3 | 8.8 |
| 9.6 | 1.01 | 1.9 | 0.42 | 5.8 | 0.1 | 0.83 | 5.09 | 3.20 | 64.4 | 7.0 | 46.1 | 0.0 | 7.0 |
| 8.3 | 0.20 | 1.1 | 0.04 | 9.8 | 0.1 | 1.37 | 12.06 | 4.75 | 72.7 | 3.4 | 8.7 | 7.0 | 6.3 |
| 7.6 | 0.83 | 5.9 | 0.27 | 0.7 | -0.2 | -0.25 | -3.04 | 3.74 | 100.7 | 4.4 | 18.2 | 2.8 | 3.1 |
| 9.7 | 0.31 | 1.2 | -0.25 | 0.0 | 0.0 | -1.43 | -17.20 | 3.41 | 141.9 | 5.7 | 39.6 | 0.0 | 3.1 |
| 3.7 | 11.36 | 23.9 | 0.00 | 2.2 | 0.0 | 0.00 | 0.00 | 6.37 | 94.7 | 7.9 | 80.5 | 0.0 | 6.0 |
| 8.5 | 0.53 | 3.3 | 0.25 | 8.3 | 54.8 | 1.13 | 8.96 | 2.91 | 71.3 | 3.2 | 12.3 | 6.1 | 10.0 |
| 9.0 | 3.18 | 4.0 | 0.43 | 1.1 | 0.0 | -0.25 | -0.96 | 3.54 | 100.0 | 6.9 | 56.8 | 0.0 | 6.2 |
| 8.9 | 1.01 | 2.8 | 0.15 | 2.2 | 0.0 | 0.10 | 0.74 | 2.58 | 93.5 | 4.6 | 19.8 | 0.0 | 7.0 |
| 5.7 | 1.76 | 10.8 | 0.89 | 1.7 | -0.1 | -0.10 | -1.35 | 3.89 | 94.1 | 4.3 | 11.5 | 0.3 | 3.2 |
| 7.9 | 0.52 | 2.9 | -0.09 | 7.6 | 0.3 | 1.20 | 11.73 | 3.27 | 76.3 | 4.4 | 21.1 | 2.8 | 5.3 |
| 5.3 | 2.29 | 12.2 | 0.33 | 3.9 | 0.1 | 0.28 | 2.27 | 4.00 | 89.1 | 5.1 | 22.8 | 1.2 | 7.0 |
| 4.9 | 1.48 | 8.8 | 1.27 | 3.7 | 0.0 | 0.20 | 1.56 | 8.50 | 88.1 | 3.4 | 13.5 | 8.6 | 3.7 |
| 3.6 | 1.26 | 15.3 | 0.25 | 1.5 | 0.0 | 0.02 | 0.26 | 3.44 | 91.5 | 3.7 | 22.4 | 9.6 | 2.5 |
| 2.5 | 4.69 | 30.0 | 2.46 | 1.8 | -0.1 | -0.88 | -10.19 | 7.25 | 94.7 | 4.9 | 35.8 | 5.5 | 1.0 |
| 8.4 | 0.44 | 2.4 | 0.26 | 3.0 | 0.2 | 0.25 | 2.78 | 2.79 | 89.0 | 4.3 | 29.8 | 3.5 | 3.4 |
| 8.8 | 0.44 | 1.3 | 0.06 | 2.4 | 0.0 | 0.14 | 1.30 | 1.66 | 94.4 | 5.6 | 29.5 | 0.0 | 5.5 |
| 8.6 | 3.39 | 3.8 | 2.87 | 3.6 | 0.0 | 0.38 | 2.94 | 3.19 | 68.4 | 3.6 | 23.6 | 19.2 | 5.2 |
| 9.7 | 0.55 | 1.4 | 0.05 | 0.1 | 0.0 | -0.41 | -2.63 | 2.50 | 112.8 | 5.9 | 56.4 | 0.0 | 5.6 |
| 10.0 | 0.00 | 0.0 | 0.00 | 2.2 | 0.0 | 0.24 | 2.54 | 2.13 | 92.9 | 5.6 | 32.2 | 0.0 | 4.4 |
| 0.0 | 43.42 | 37.9 | 7.75 | 0.0 | 0.0 | -12.00 | -30.00 | 4.62 | 116.7 | 7.5 | 110.8 | 0.0 | 4.7 |
| 6.9 | 0.68 | 5.5 | 0.36 | 4.6 | 2.9 | 0.59 | 4.88 | 3.93 | 85.5 | 3.7 | 13.3 | 7.6 | 7.6 |
| 7.0 | 0.51 | 5.6 | 0.32 | 5.4 | 1.0 | 0.83 | 11.05 | 3.59 | 76.2 | 2.8 | 10.7 | 11.2 | 5.0 |
| 8.3 | 0.15 | 1.2 | 0.00 | 5.0 | 0.0 | 0.73 | 8.59 | 3.90 | 81.6 | 4.3 | 19.3 | 0.0 | 3.0 |
| 7.3 | 0.79 | 5.1 | 0.57 | 1.7 | 0.0 | 0.07 | 0.61 | 3.06 | 91.6 | 3.9 | 6.8 | 3.7 | 5.0 |
| 7.9 | 0.44 | 3.8 | 0.52 | 6.8 | 5.8 | 1.11 | 10.72 | 3.79 | 68.7 | 3.4 | 18.5 | 14.9 | 7.2 |
| 7.9 | 0.12 | 0.5 | 0.07 | 2.3 | 0.0 | -0.22 | -1.05 | 4.62 | 104.3 | 2.0 | 7.5 | 15.0 | 6.7 |
| 9.3 | 0.38 | 3.4 | 0.14 | 3.9 | 0.9 | 0.49 | 5.30 | 3.27 | 83.7 | 2.7 | 11.9 | 11.6 | 6.1 |
| 8.1 | 0.44 | 2.0 | 0.36 | 4.5 | 0.4 | 0.57 | 5.56 | 3.03 | 78.5 | 5.0 | 24.9 | 0.5 | 5.4 |
| 8.1 | 0.93 | 4.8 | 0.81 | 3.7 | 0.2 | 0.37 | 3.75 | 4.53 | 85.2 | 4.2 | 14.8 | 1.8 | 4.8 |
| 3.9 | 2.27 | 13.8 | 0.82 | 1.5 | 0.0 | 0.00 | 0.00 | 3.55 | 94.7 | 5.7 | 38.9 | 0.0 | 1.0 |
| 8.3 | 1.02 | 3.9 | 0.02 | 0.9 | 0.0 | -0.22 | -1.44 | 3.71 | 104.7 | 4.6 | 24.7 | 3.6 | 5.7 |
| 6.7 | 0.87 | 3.2 | 0.08 | 2.4 | 0.0 | 0.13 | 0.62 | 4.76 | 78.5 | 3.2 | 13.8 | 0.0 | 5.4 |
| 9.7 | 0.63 | 2.1 | 0.74 | 5.4 | 24.1 | 0.83 | 7.53 | 2.47 | 74.2 | 4.5 | 18.4 | 3.0 | 7.9 |
| 8.3 | 0.56 | 3.5 | 0.09 | 9.8 | 34.0 | 1.74 | 15.23 | 3.98 | 60.5 | 5.0 | 25.7 | 3.3 | 8.9 |
| 10.0 | 0.18 | 0.0 | 0.26 | 0.6 | -0.1 | -0.32 | -2.34 | 1.59 | 117.3 | 5.7 | 37.4 | 0.0 | 5.7 |
| 1.5 | 2.91 | 22.5 | 0.09 | 5.8 | 0.1 | 0.66 | 6.45 | 5.79 | 87.1 | 3.6 | 7.8 | 0.0 | 5.3 |
| 7.3 | 0.99 | 3.6 | 0.79 | 7.9 | 0.1 | 1.18 | 7.74 | 3.64 | 66.9 | 5.1 | 48.6 | 0.0 | 6.3 |

| Name | City | State | Rating | 2014 Rating | 2013 Rating | Total Assets ($Mil) | One Year Asset Growth | Commercial Loans | Consumer Loans | Mortgage Loans | Securities | Capitalization Index | Net Worth Ratio |
|---|---|---|---|---|---|---|---|---|---|---|---|---|---|
| REGIONAL FCU | Hammond | IN | C- | C | C | 126.2 | 1.42 | 0.6 | 15.7 | 13.2 | 61.9 | 9.3 | 10.5 |
| REGIONAL MEDICAL CENTER HOPKINS COU | Madisonville | KY | D+ | D+ | D+ | 10.1 | 2.64 | 0.0 | 30.7 | 0.0 | 0.0 | 7.1 | 9.1 |
| ▲ REGIONAL MEMBERS FCU | Columbus | GA | D | D- | E+ | 8.6 | 7.04 | 0.0 | 42.3 | 0.0 | 7.6 | 8.1 | 9.8 |
| REGIONAL WATER AUTHORITY EMPL CU | New Haven | CT | C- | C- | C- | 6.4 | -4.37 | 0.0 | 6.9 | 0.0 | 0.0 | 10.0 | 11.1 |
| REGISTER GUARD FCU | Springfield | OR | C+ | C+ | C | 20.4 | -3.68 | 9.4 | 20.3 | 33.7 | 0.0 | 10.0 | 15.8 |
| REID TEMPLE FCU | Glenn Dale | MD | E+ | D- | D+ | 1.5 | -1.68 | 0.0 | 23.4 | 0.0 | 0.0 | 5.1 | 7.1 |
| RELIANCE CU | Kansas City | KS | B- | B | B | 23.8 | 21.31 | 0.0 | 33.0 | 14.5 | 0.0 | 10.0 | 16.4 |
| RELIANCE FCU | King Of Prussia | PA | D+ | D- | E | 23.9 | -0.05 | 3.4 | 19.5 | 1.7 | 5.8 | 7.0 | 9.0 |
| RELIANT COMMUNITY FCU | Sodus | NY | B- | B- | B- | 388.8 | 4.74 | 5.8 | 23.5 | 24.2 | 16.4 | 7.8 | 9.5 |
| RELIANT FCU | Casper | WY | B- | C+ | B | 116.0 | 5.55 | 0.4 | 36.2 | 12.3 | 12.8 | 7.2 | 9.1 |
| REMINGTON FCU | Ilion | NY | C- | D+ | C- | 41.1 | -2.43 | 0.0 | 18.8 | 3.3 | 37.2 | 10.0 | 12.2 |
| ▼ RENAISSANCE COMMUNITY DEVEL CU | Somerset | NJ | E- | E+ | E+ | <1 | -5.80 | 0.0 | 51.9 | 0.0 | 0.0 | 3.6 | 5.6 |
| RENO CITY EMPL FCU | Reno | NV | D+ | D | D | 30.4 | 4.44 | 0.0 | 19.8 | 14.0 | 0.0 | 6.5 | 8.5 |
| RESEARCH 1166 FCU | Paulsboro | NJ | D | D+ | D+ | 17.2 | 9.88 | 0.0 | 12.0 | 3.5 | 30.1 | 7.0 | 9.0 |
| ▲ RESOURCE FCU | Jackson | TN | D+ | D+ | D+ | 32.5 | 6.23 | 0.0 | 20.0 | 8.5 | 0.8 | 7.4 | 9.3 |
| RESOURCE ONE CU | Dallas | TX | A- | A- | B | 421.2 | 7.54 | 2.3 | 39.6 | 23.0 | 0.2 | 8.3 | 9.9 |
| RESURRECTION LUTHERAN FCU | Chicago | IL | C- | C- | C+ | <1 | -1.08 | 0.0 | 36.1 | 0.0 | 0.0 | 10.0 | 24.0 |
| REVERE FIREFIGHTERS CU | Revere | MA | C | C | C- | 6.3 | 3.14 | 0.0 | 17.2 | 0.0 | 10.8 | 10.0 | 15.1 |
| REVERE MUNICIPAL EMPL FCU | Revere | MA | D+ | D+ | D+ | 10.4 | 3.53 | 0.0 | 47.8 | 0.0 | 0.0 | 10.0 | 13.6 |
| RHEEM ARKANSAS FCU | Fort Smith | AR | D+ | D+ | D+ | 5.3 | 8.19 | 0.0 | 65.4 | 0.0 | 0.0 | 10.0 | 15.8 |
| RHODE ISLAND CU | Providence | RI | C- | D+ | D+ | 255.5 | 1.65 | 0.0 | 27.5 | 15.5 | 16.5 | 9.6 | 10.8 |
| RIA FCU | Bettendorf | IA | C+ | B- | C+ | 368.4 | 6.15 | 0.2 | 53.2 | 12.9 | 17.1 | 7.4 | 9.3 |
| RICHFIELD-BLOOMINGTON CU | Bloomington | MN | B | B | C | 264.9 | 2.63 | 7.8 | 26.7 | 26.8 | 26.5 | 8.1 | 9.7 |
| RICHLAND FCU | Sidney | MT | A- | A- | A- | 86.8 | 0.70 | 33.5 | 7.4 | 13.9 | 2.2 | 10.0 | 11.0 |
| ▼ RICHLAND PARISH SCHOOLS FCU | Rayville | LA | C+ | B- | B- | <1 | 6.68 | 0.0 | 28.3 | 0.0 | 0.0 | 10.0 | 17.9 |
| RICHMOND CITY EMPL FCU | Richmond | IN | D+ | D | D+ | 5.0 | -0.78 | 0.0 | 51.7 | 0.0 | 0.0 | 10.0 | 11.7 |
| ▲ RICHMOND COUNTY HEALTH DEPT EMPL CU | Augusta | GA | D+ | D+ | D | <1 | 2.10 | 0.0 | 33.7 | 0.0 | 0.0 | 10.0 | 22.9 |
| RICHMOND HERITAGE FCU | Richmond | VA | D- | D- | D- | 6.9 | 1.07 | 0.0 | 48.5 | 0.0 | 0.0 | 5.5 | 7.5 |
| ▲ RICHMOND LIGHT EMPL FCU | Richmond | IN | D+ | D | C- | 1.1 | -1.61 | 0.0 | 31.4 | 0.0 | 0.0 | 10.0 | 19.1 |
| RICHMOND POSTAL CU INC | Richmond | VA | B- | B+ | B- | 74.4 | -3.96 | 0.0 | 22.6 | 15.3 | 30.5 | 10.0 | 15.0 |
| RICHMOND VIRGINIA FIRE POLICE CU INC | Richmond | VA | C | C+ | C+ | 20.4 | 37.05 | 0.0 | 44.5 | 0.0 | 0.0 | 10.0 | 13.1 |
| RIEGEL FCU | Milford | NJ | C- | C- | C- | 115.6 | 3.61 | 0.3 | 9.9 | 14.7 | 28.1 | 10.0 | 11.5 |
| RIEGELWOOD FCU | Riegelwood | NC | C | B- | B | 95.1 | -2.72 | 0.0 | 45.2 | 3.5 | 3.6 | 10.0 | 13.2 |
| RIG EMPL CU | Macon | GA | C | C | C | 7.8 | 4.78 | 0.0 | 41.7 | 0.0 | 0.0 | 10.0 | 28.4 |
| RIM COUNTRY FCU | Snowflake | AZ | C | C | C+ | 13.6 | 3.85 | 0.0 | 21.6 | 28.6 | 28.2 | 9.3 | 10.5 |
| RIMROCK CU | Billings | MT | C | C- | C- | 36.5 | -1.70 | 0.1 | 20.2 | 4.1 | 0.0 | 10.0 | 15.6 |
| RINCONES PRESBYTERIAN CU | Chacon | NM | C- | C- | C- | 3.3 | 2.54 | 0.0 | 56.9 | 0.0 | 0.0 | 10.0 | 11.8 |
| RIO BLANCO SCHOOLS FCU | Rangely | CO | B- | B- | B- | 5.8 | 5.13 | 0.0 | 45.2 | 0.0 | 0.0 | 10.0 | 19.5 |
| RIO GRANDE CU | Albuquerque | NM | A | A | A | 268.4 | 9.79 | 1.4 | 54.7 | 13.5 | 2.5 | 10.0 | 14.3 |
| RIO GRANDE FCU | Grand Junction | CO | B | B | B | 47.3 | 3.87 | 4.8 | 18.4 | 13.8 | 0.0 | 10.0 | 18.8 |
| RIO GRANDE VALLEY CU | Harlingen | TX | C+ | C+ | C+ | 83.4 | 4.77 | 0.0 | 36.5 | 9.9 | 28.2 | 8.3 | 9.9 |
| RIPCO CU | Rhinelander | WI | C+ | C+ | B- | 113.9 | 0.26 | 0.5 | 27.4 | 17.2 | 15.6 | 8.5 | 10.0 |
| RIVER BEND FCU | South Bend | IN | C | C- | D+ | 5.2 | 0.41 | 0.0 | 38.7 | 5.4 | 0.0 | 10.0 | 15.0 |
| RIVER CITIES COMMUNITY CU | Atchison | KS | E+ | D- | D- | 3.0 | 9.17 | 0.0 | 84.1 | 0.0 | 0.0 | 5.9 | 7.9 |
| ▲ RIVER CITIES CU | Alexandria | LA | D+ | D | C- | 8.6 | -1.20 | 0.0 | 22.7 | 2.1 | 0.0 | 10.0 | 11.5 |
| RIVER CITY FCU | San Antonio | TX | D | D- | D | 117.6 | -6.22 | 2.1 | 53.0 | 17.9 | 7.9 | 4.9 | 7.0 |
| RIVER COMMUNITY CU | Ottumwa | IA | C | C | C+ | 17.2 | -1.30 | 1.8 | 40.8 | 7.8 | 1.2 | 10.0 | 13.9 |
| ▲ RIVER REGION CU | Jefferson City | MO | B | B- | C+ | 115.5 | 12.03 | 0.9 | 62.5 | 8.4 | 0.0 | 6.6 | 8.6 |
| ▼ RIVER REGION FCU | Lutcher | LA | B- | B | B | 33.6 | 3.62 | 0.0 | 12.1 | 14.3 | 0.0 | 10.0 | 20.2 |
| RIVER TO RIVER CU | Vienna | IL | D+ | D+ | D+ | 17.0 | 3.68 | 0.0 | 34.6 | 1.9 | 0.0 | 6.0 | 8.0 |
| ▲ RIVER TOWN FCU | Fort Smith | AR | C- | D+ | D+ | 13.6 | -3.15 | 0.0 | 52.5 | 0.0 | 0.0 | 10.0 | 11.1 |
| ▼ RIVER VALLEY COMMUNITY FCU | Camden | AR | D+ | C- | C- | 40.6 | 1.51 | 0.0 | 47.2 | 8.8 | 0.0 | 10.0 | 12.4 |
| RIVER VALLEY CU | Ames | IA | B+ | B+ | B+ | 54.6 | 2.72 | 4.8 | 22.6 | 22.4 | 0.0 | 10.0 | 11.7 |
| RIVER VALLEY CU | Ada | MI | C- | C | B- | 83.7 | 12.12 | 5.1 | 27.8 | 7.3 | 11.1 | 7.6 | 9.4 |
| ▼ RIVER VALLEY CU | Miamisburg | OH | B- | B | B | 311.0 | 0.76 | 10.3 | 48.8 | 24.7 | 9.6 | 7.6 | 9.4 |
| RIVER VALLEY CU | Brattleboro | VT | C | C | C | 88.1 | 5.73 | 5.4 | 19.0 | 36.4 | 0.0 | 5.4 | 7.4 |
| RIVER WORKS CU | Lynn | MA | A | A- | B+ | 106.9 | 4.91 | 21.4 | 13.0 | 50.9 | 0.0 | 10.0 | 12.1 |
| RIVER-RAIL COMMUNITY FCU | Casper | WY | D+ | C- | D+ | 35.6 | 0.34 | 3.4 | 30.3 | 17.1 | 0.0 | 6.7 | 8.7 |
| ▲ RIVERDALE CU | Selma | AL | B | B | B | 64.6 | 0.99 | 0.0 | 60.7 | 8.0 | 0.6 | 10.0 | 12.8 |
| RIVERFALL CU | Tuscaloosa | AL | B+ | B+ | B | 117.9 | -0.69 | 0.0 | 14.3 | 14.4 | 51.3 | 10.0 | 14.1 |

| Asset Quality Index | Non-Performing Loans as a % of Total Loans | as a % of Capital | Net Charge-Offs Avg Loans | Profitability Index | Net Income ($Mil) | Return on Assets | Return on Equity | Net Interest Spread | Overhead Efficiency Ratio | Liquidity Index | Liquidity Ratio | Hot Money Ratio | Stability Index |
|---|---|---|---|---|---|---|---|---|---|---|---|---|---|
| 9.6 | 0.75 | 2.1 | 0.23 | 2.2 | 0.3 | 0.27 | 2.55 | 2.61 | 85.1 | 5.4 | 44.3 | 0.8 | 5.8 |
| 9.1 | 0.07 | 0.4 | -0.02 | 3.7 | 0.0 | 0.41 | 4.47 | 3.86 | 88.6 | 5.8 | 41.0 | 0.0 | 3.0 |
| 5.4 | 2.05 | 12.0 | 0.35 | 3.0 | 0.0 | 0.28 | 2.93 | 3.46 | 92.7 | 4.0 | 21.4 | 2.9 | 2.3 |
| 10.0 | 0.00 | 0.0 | 0.57 | 1.5 | 0.0 | 0.00 | 0.00 | 1.98 | 100.0 | 4.9 | 22.6 | 0.0 | 5.8 |
| 6.8 | 1.56 | 5.1 | 0.02 | 4.8 | 0.1 | 0.58 | 3.79 | 5.11 | 86.8 | 6.3 | 48.2 | 0.0 | 5.7 |
| 0.3 | 28.36 | 63.4 | 0.00 | 0.2 | 0.0 | -1.41 | -17.54 | 5.42 | 63.8 | 8.1 | 89.1 | 0.0 | 2.8 |
| 9.1 | 0.93 | 3.1 | 0.22 | 4.7 | 0.1 | 0.53 | 3.30 | 3.74 | 81.2 | 4.4 | 13.4 | 0.0 | 6.6 |
| 7.4 | 0.21 | 2.4 | 0.83 | 2.4 | 0.0 | 0.00 | 0.00 | 4.09 | 86.8 | 5.1 | 29.2 | 3.3 | 3.9 |
| 9.7 | 0.18 | 1.4 | 0.11 | 4.2 | 1.6 | 0.56 | 6.03 | 3.77 | 86.1 | 3.8 | 11.1 | 1.4 | 6.4 |
| 8.7 | 0.46 | 3.5 | 0.36 | 4.1 | 0.5 | 0.53 | 6.26 | 3.68 | 80.0 | 4.4 | 20.4 | 3.8 | 5.4 |
| 8.0 | 2.52 | 6.0 | 0.12 | 2.0 | 0.1 | 0.35 | 2.96 | 2.67 | 92.4 | 6.0 | 39.9 | 0.4 | 4.6 |
| 2.0 | 0.54 | NA | -0.35 | 6.0 | 0.0 | 1.77 | NA | 7.58 | 71.2 | 6.8 | 58.3 | 0.0 | 0.3 |
| 9.7 | 0.40 | 1.6 | 0.10 | 1.6 | 0.0 | 0.05 | 0.57 | 2.59 | 98.5 | 5.3 | 42.9 | 7.6 | 3.2 |
| 9.2 | 0.46 | 2.4 | 0.09 | 0.4 | 0.0 | -0.17 | -2.11 | 2.67 | 105.3 | 5.6 | 28.2 | 0.0 | 4.3 |
| 9.7 | 0.29 | 1.1 | 0.04 | 1.6 | 0.0 | 0.05 | 0.49 | 2.36 | 98.4 | 5.2 | 30.0 | 3.4 | 4.0 |
| 6.6 | 0.87 | 7.5 | 0.89 | 5.7 | 1.9 | 0.62 | 6.27 | 5.16 | 80.7 | 3.5 | 17.7 | 11.0 | 6.2 |
| 9.4 | 0.00 | 0.0 | 0.00 | 1.5 | 0.0 | 0.00 | 0.00 | 3.03 | 66.7 | 5.7 | 30.9 | 0.0 | 6.2 |
| 10.0 | 0.00 | 0.0 | 0.00 | 3.2 | 0.0 | 0.42 | 2.88 | 1.83 | 75.9 | 4.9 | 10.4 | 0.0 | 7.9 |
| 8.8 | 0.04 | 0.2 | 0.09 | 1.3 | 0.0 | 0.01 | 0.09 | 3.54 | 99.6 | 4.0 | 23.2 | 0.0 | 6.0 |
| 4.1 | 2.84 | 15.0 | 0.26 | 2.4 | 0.0 | 0.00 | 0.00 | 5.55 | 96.9 | 4.3 | 29.8 | 8.1 | 6.9 |
| 9.4 | 0.40 | 2.4 | 0.17 | 2.5 | 0.4 | 0.21 | 2.14 | 3.56 | 92.7 | 3.9 | 11.6 | 2.2 | 5.6 |
| 6.5 | 0.56 | 5.0 | 0.72 | 3.3 | 0.8 | 0.28 | 2.88 | 3.77 | 82.9 | 3.3 | 7.2 | 5.1 | 5.6 |
| 6.1 | 1.95 | 13.3 | 0.31 | 4.2 | 1.1 | 0.53 | 5.47 | 3.35 | 85.5 | 3.8 | 17.0 | 2.8 | 6.3 |
| 8.1 | 0.76 | 3.1 | 0.03 | 7.8 | 0.7 | 1.10 | 10.87 | 3.01 | 62.1 | 5.5 | 41.7 | 2.2 | 6.4 |
| 10.0 | 1.01 | 1.4 | 7.02 | 3.7 | 0.0 | -0.19 | -1.03 | 6.55 | 66.7 | 7.6 | 88.6 | 0.0 | 7.4 |
| 7.2 | 1.16 | 5.0 | -0.05 | 2.7 | 0.0 | 0.54 | 4.67 | 3.25 | 91.6 | 5.3 | 25.8 | 0.0 | 5.0 |
| 6.5 | 7.63 | 10.6 | 0.00 | 0.6 | 0.0 | -0.34 | -1.50 | 4.17 | 100.0 | 6.6 | 60.3 | 0.0 | 6.5 |
| 4.6 | 1.61 | 10.1 | 1.18 | 0.9 | 0.0 | -0.29 | -3.74 | 6.03 | 90.6 | 4.8 | 37.9 | 4.8 | 2.4 |
| 9.0 | 2.24 | 4.3 | 0.00 | 0.8 | 0.0 | 0.00 | 0.00 | 2.04 | 100.0 | 5.8 | 53.9 | 0.0 | 5.8 |
| 7.7 | 1.80 | 5.5 | 0.78 | 2.8 | 0.0 | -0.06 | -0.44 | 3.84 | 84.9 | 6.1 | 41.3 | 0.0 | 6.0 |
| 6.7 | 2.28 | 10.4 | 0.13 | 5.8 | 0.1 | 0.90 | 6.93 | 5.16 | 88.3 | 4.7 | 26.3 | 1.9 | 5.0 |
| 9.8 | 0.10 | 0.3 | 0.24 | 1.9 | 0.1 | 0.09 | 0.75 | 2.41 | 94.3 | 5.5 | 25.0 | 1.6 | 6.9 |
| 4.2 | 3.21 | 17.1 | 0.65 | 2.7 | 0.2 | 0.29 | 2.24 | 5.04 | 85.5 | 4.2 | 21.7 | 6.2 | 4.8 |
| 9.8 | 0.00 | 0.0 | 0.00 | 2.8 | 0.0 | 0.24 | 0.84 | 2.68 | 90.3 | 5.8 | 37.4 | 0.0 | 7.5 |
| 7.5 | 0.41 | 3.0 | 0.42 | 2.9 | 0.0 | 0.27 | 2.64 | 4.25 | 88.8 | 4.1 | 8.9 | 0.0 | 5.9 |
| 9.9 | 0.49 | 1.1 | 0.18 | 2.0 | 0.1 | 0.17 | 1.13 | 2.67 | 94.3 | 5.5 | 36.8 | 2.3 | 6.7 |
| 4.7 | 1.64 | 10.1 | 0.16 | 5.3 | 0.0 | 0.71 | 6.35 | 4.87 | 80.5 | 3.6 | 17.0 | 0.0 | 3.7 |
| 8.3 | 0.00 | 0.0 | 0.00 | 9.5 | 0.1 | 1.44 | 7.49 | 4.01 | 59.1 | 5.5 | 41.1 | 0.0 | 5.7 |
| 8.0 | 0.37 | 2.6 | 0.65 | 9.4 | 3.2 | 1.62 | 11.45 | 4.49 | 63.6 | 2.2 | 11.7 | 17.8 | 8.8 |
| 9.6 | 0.41 | 0.8 | 0.14 | 4.5 | 0.2 | 0.64 | 3.44 | 2.81 | 78.6 | 4.8 | 42.3 | 12.2 | 7.3 |
| 7.1 | 0.71 | 4.5 | 0.25 | 3.3 | 0.2 | 0.36 | 3.68 | 3.64 | 87.0 | 4.7 | 16.2 | 1.6 | 4.9 |
| 7.5 | 0.84 | 4.3 | 0.45 | 3.5 | 0.5 | 0.53 | 5.37 | 3.42 | 86.9 | 4.2 | 21.9 | 2.3 | 5.7 |
| 8.6 | 0.20 | 0.6 | 0.11 | 5.3 | 0.0 | 0.82 | 5.58 | 3.81 | 79.1 | 4.7 | 25.9 | 0.0 | 4.3 |
| 3.5 | 1.57 | 14.3 | 0.47 | 3.9 | 0.0 | 0.47 | 5.67 | 6.32 | 80.4 | 3.9 | 12.3 | 0.0 | 1.0 |
| 8.2 | 0.89 | 3.2 | 0.81 | 0.8 | 0.0 | 0.08 | 0.67 | 2.48 | 98.1 | 5.1 | 28.4 | 0.0 | 5.6 |
| 5.6 | 0.77 | 8.0 | 1.11 | 0.9 | -0.1 | -0.13 | -1.92 | 4.78 | 86.0 | 2.7 | 9.0 | 11.6 | 2.2 |
| 8.2 | 0.96 | 5.2 | 0.44 | 1.8 | 0.0 | -0.01 | -0.11 | 3.03 | 94.0 | 4.4 | 29.4 | 4.5 | 6.6 |
| 5.0 | 1.03 | 9.3 | 0.90 | 8.4 | 1.1 | 1.30 | 15.39 | 3.66 | 63.4 | 1.9 | 6.7 | 15.4 | 6.0 |
| 8.2 | 1.74 | 4.3 | 0.71 | 2.1 | 0.0 | -0.04 | -0.18 | 3.15 | 80.7 | 6.9 | 51.4 | 1.6 | 7.4 |
| 7.6 | 0.59 | 3.8 | 0.11 | 3.3 | 0.1 | 0.36 | 4.56 | 2.96 | 88.1 | 5.0 | 30.9 | 2.3 | 3.0 |
| 5.5 | 1.31 | 9.8 | 0.36 | 1.8 | 0.0 | -0.01 | -0.09 | 4.05 | 92.9 | 3.4 | 24.8 | 13.3 | 5.0 |
| 5.6 | 0.84 | 5.2 | 0.17 | 0.9 | -0.1 | -0.23 | -1.79 | 3.70 | 101.1 | 4.0 | 17.5 | 2.5 | 6.1 |
| 8.4 | 0.90 | 4.6 | 0.03 | 4.5 | 0.3 | 0.66 | 5.68 | 2.75 | 80.4 | 4.3 | 25.8 | 2.9 | 6.5 |
| 7.2 | 0.68 | 3.8 | 0.19 | 2.1 | 0.2 | 0.32 | 3.53 | 3.32 | 93.0 | 4.7 | 20.5 | 0.3 | 3.7 |
| 6.1 | 0.75 | 6.5 | 0.56 | 3.8 | 0.9 | 0.37 | 3.79 | 3.06 | 83.0 | 3.0 | 8.8 | 6.5 | 6.4 |
| 3.1 | 2.15 | 24.5 | 0.30 | 5.4 | 0.5 | 0.75 | 10.34 | 5.06 | 84.8 | 3.4 | 8.1 | 0.7 | 3.6 |
| 8.9 | 0.19 | 1.9 | 0.24 | 7.4 | 0.9 | 1.08 | 9.17 | 4.62 | 71.7 | 2.3 | 13.8 | 19.8 | 8.7 |
| 5.7 | 0.89 | 8.5 | 0.06 | 2.4 | 0.0 | 0.07 | 0.82 | 4.28 | 96.8 | 4.1 | 26.3 | 10.0 | 4.3 |
| 4.2 | 2.86 | 15.4 | 2.21 | 8.2 | 0.6 | 1.13 | 9.15 | 7.37 | 56.8 | 3.4 | 9.9 | 4.9 | 6.7 |
| 7.3 | 2.35 | 7.1 | 0.27 | 3.6 | 0.3 | 0.38 | 2.99 | 2.17 | 84.7 | 3.9 | 30.7 | 13.5 | 8.5 |

www.weissratings.com
177
Data as of September 30, 2015

| Name | City | State | Rating | 2014 Rating | 2013 Rating | Total Assets ($Mil) | One Year Asset Growth | Asset Mix (As a % of Total Assets) | | | | Capital-ization Index | Net Worth Ratio |
|---|---|---|---|---|---|---|---|---|---|---|---|---|---|
| | | | | | | | | Comm-ercial Loans | Cons-umer Loans | Mort-gage Loans | Secur-ities | | |
| RIVERFORK FCU | Grand Forks | ND | C | C- | C- | 23.2 | 1.11 | 0.0 | 34.6 | 1.5 | 0.0 | 8.9 | 10.2 |
| RIVERFRONT FCU | Reading | PA | D | D | C- | 170.3 | 1.35 | 0.0 | 39.8 | 3.6 | 31.9 | 7.8 | 9.5 |
| RIVERLAND FCU | New Orleans | LA | C+ | C | C+ | 195.1 | 2.36 | 0.8 | 56.3 | 8.6 | 0.0 | 6.3 | 8.3 |
| RIVERMARK COMMUNITY CU | Beaverton | OR | B+ | B | B | 694.7 | 16.15 | 3.9 | 46.2 | 23.6 | 2.5 | 7.2 | 9.2 |
| RIVERSET CU | Pittsburgh | PA | B- | C+ | C | 114.5 | -2.02 | 0.0 | 44.2 | 20.5 | 3.5 | 10.0 | 21.1 |
| RIVERSIDE BEAVER COUNTY FCU | Ellwood City | PA | D+ | D+ | D+ | 1.6 | -9.20 | 0.0 | 39.7 | 0.1 | 0.0 | 10.0 | 12.5 |
| ▲ RIVERSIDE COMMUNITY CU | Kankakee | IL | C | C- | C- | 27.8 | 5.90 | 0.0 | 18.6 | 19.3 | 2.7 | 6.7 | 8.7 |
| RIVERSIDE COMMUNITY FCU | Marion | IN | C+ | C+ | C+ | 34.3 | 0.97 | 11.8 | 53.9 | 9.7 | 0.0 | 9.4 | 10.6 |
| RIVERSIDE FCU | Buffalo | NY | D | D+ | C- | 55.3 | -7.62 | 0.0 | 28.0 | 28.7 | 4.8 | 9.0 | 10.3 |
| RIVERSIDE HEALTH SYSTEM EMPL CU | Newport News | VA | C- | C | C | 8.5 | -3.15 | 0.0 | 46.0 | 0.0 | 0.0 | 10.0 | 16.9 |
| ▲ RIVERTOWN COMMUNITY FCU | Grandville | MI | D+ | D | D+ | 62.4 | -0.30 | 0.0 | 44.5 | 11.3 | 24.7 | 10.0 | 14.9 |
| RIVERTRACE FCU | Richmond | VA | D+ | C- | C- | 24.3 | 16.00 | 0.0 | 47.4 | 14.6 | 11.6 | 8.8 | 10.4 |
| RIVERVIEW COMMUNITY FCU | Saint Clair | MI | C | C | D+ | 26.0 | 2.48 | 4.0 | 30.4 | 15.0 | 14.5 | 7.3 | 9.2 |
| RIVERVIEW CU | South Saint Paul | MN | C- | C- | C- | 5.4 | 1.40 | 0.0 | 37.8 | 10.2 | 0.0 | 10.0 | 17.5 |
| RIVERVIEW CU | Belpre | OH | C+ | C+ | C | 51.3 | -4.38 | 0.8 | 21.9 | 0.0 | 12.0 | 10.0 | 17.2 |
| RIVERWAYS FCU | Rolla | MO | C | C- | C- | 40.7 | 11.74 | 4.1 | 26.1 | 37.8 | 3.9 | 5.8 | 7.8 |
| ROANOKE VALLEY COMMUNITY FCU | Roanoke | VA | C | C | C+ | 67.3 | 2.52 | 0.0 | 22.2 | 1.1 | 12.3 | 7.5 | 9.3 |
| ROANOKE VIRGINIA FIREMEN FCU | Roanoke | VA | D | D+ | C- | 2.7 | -5.82 | 0.0 | 60.3 | 0.0 | 0.0 | 10.0 | 24.3 |
| ROBBINS & MYERS EMPL FCU | Springfield | OH | D+ | D+ | D+ | 3.3 | -2.52 | 0.0 | 56.3 | 0.0 | 0.0 | 8.4 | 9.9 |
| ROBERTS DAIRY EMPL FCU | Omaha | NE | D+ | D+ | C- | 7.6 | -1.74 | 0.0 | 31.3 | 0.0 | 0.0 | 10.0 | 24.6 |
| ROBINS FCU | Warner Robins | GA | A+ | A+ | A+ | 2066.5 | 7.17 | 4.2 | 32.9 | 16.0 | 32.0 | 10.0 | 16.2 |
| ▲ ROCHESTER & MONROE COUNTY EMPL FCU | Rochester | NY | C | C | C- | 25.4 | -1.86 | 0.0 | 22.0 | 39.5 | 12.4 | 10.0 | 11.3 |
| ROCHESTER AREA STATE EMPL FCU | Rochester | NY | D- | D | D | 13.4 | 1.81 | 0.0 | 31.6 | 1.4 | 0.0 | 8.7 | 10.1 |
| ROCHESTER POLISH FCU | Rochester | NY | C | C | C | 8.6 | 4.07 | 0.0 | 3.7 | 17.6 | 0.0 | 10.0 | 16.5 |
| ROCK COMMUNITY FCU | Rock | MI | D- | D- | D- | 6.1 | 3.76 | 0.0 | 27.5 | 1.3 | 0.0 | 6.9 | 9.0 |
| ROCK VALLEY FCU | Loves Park | IL | B- | B | B- | 88.2 | 5.80 | 2.1 | 38.3 | 32.8 | 6.0 | 9.5 | 10.7 |
| ROCKDALE FCU | Rockdale | TX | C | C | C | 75.1 | 3.96 | 0.2 | 14.8 | 10.5 | 0.0 | 10.0 | 11.5 |
| ROCKET CITY FCU | Huntsville | AL | B | B | A- | 45.9 | 3.71 | 0.9 | 31.0 | 9.5 | 1.0 | 10.0 | 15.6 |
| ROCKET FCU | McGregor | TX | D+ | D+ | D | 16.5 | 4.23 | 0.0 | 39.8 | 20.6 | 3.9 | 6.9 | 8.9 |
| ▲ ROCKFORD BELL CU | Loves Park | IL | C- | D | C- | 30.6 | 0.40 | 0.0 | 27.5 | 34.4 | 0.0 | 10.0 | 16.0 |
| ▲ ROCKFORD MUNICIPAL EMPL CU | Rockford | IL | C- | C- | D+ | 18.5 | 4.19 | 0.0 | 31.2 | 0.0 | 0.2 | 10.0 | 11.2 |
| ROCKFORD POSTAL EMPL CU | Machesney Park | IL | C | C | C+ | 17.4 | 2.85 | 0.0 | 29.8 | 0.0 | 0.0 | 10.0 | 14.0 |
| ROCKLAND EMPL FCU | Spring Valley | NY | D | D- | D- | 34.7 | 26.95 | 0.0 | 46.4 | 15.7 | 10.3 | 5.9 | 7.9 |
| ROCKLAND FCU | Rockland | MA | A- | A- | A- | 1413.8 | 7.14 | 6.4 | 53.5 | 28.6 | 1.4 | 10.0 | 11.4 |
| ROCKY MOUNTAIN CU | Helena | MT | B+ | B+ | B | 183.9 | 15.79 | 10.7 | 30.6 | 33.4 | 1.2 | 9.0 | 10.4 |
| ROCKY MOUNTAIN LAW ENFORCEMENT FCU | Denver | CO | A+ | A+ | A+ | 183.0 | 3.95 | 0.0 | 25.1 | 29.4 | 0.7 | 10.0 | 17.1 |
| ▼ ROGERS EMPL FCU | Rogers | CT | D- | D+ | C- | 4.5 | -4.72 | 0.0 | 14.0 | 0.0 | 0.0 | 8.4 | 10.0 |
| ROGUE CU | Medford | OR | A- | A- | B | 1044.8 | 14.31 | 9.8 | 42.8 | 19.6 | 11.3 | 8.0 | 9.6 |
| ROGUE RIVER COMMUNITY CU | Sparta | MI | C | C+ | C+ | 39.2 | 7.54 | 0.0 | 23.1 | 11.8 | 49.2 | 7.2 | 9.1 |
| ROLLING F CU | Turlock | CA | C- | C | C | 46.3 | 1.70 | 0.0 | 11.2 | 2.2 | 14.8 | 9.5 | 10.7 |
| ROME FCU | Rome | NY | D | D | D | 18.2 | 8.18 | 0.0 | 26.8 | 18.7 | 0.0 | 5.9 | 7.9 |
| ROME KRAFT EMPL CU | Rome | GA | D+ | C- | C- | 15.9 | -2.95 | 0.9 | 30.0 | 0.0 | 0.0 | 10.0 | 21.8 |
| ROME TEACHERS FCU | Rome | NY | C+ | C+ | C+ | 34.7 | 4.33 | 0.0 | 31.8 | 9.4 | 16.3 | 10.0 | 13.4 |
| ROMEOVILLE COMMUNITY CU | Romeoville | IL | E+ | E+ | D | 4.1 | 4.14 | 0.0 | 16.2 | 0.0 | 0.0 | 6.0 | 8.1 |
| ROMNEY FCU | Romney | WV | C- | C- | C- | 6.0 | 2.46 | 0.0 | 47.8 | 0.4 | 0.0 | 10.0 | 13.5 |
| ROPER CORP EMPL CU | Lafayette | GA | C+ | C+ | C+ | 1.7 | -1.43 | 0.0 | 30.1 | 0.0 | 0.0 | 10.0 | 15.1 |
| ROSE CITY FCU | Thomasville | GA | C- | C- | C | 29.4 | 1.34 | 0.0 | 32.8 | 8.6 | 4.2 | 6.5 | 8.5 |
| ▼ ROSLYN CATHOLIC FCU | Roslyn | PA | D | D | C- | <1 | -10.61 | 0.0 | 0.9 | 0.0 | 0.0 | 10.0 | 15.0 |
| ▲ ROSWELL COMMUNITY FCU | Roswell | NM | B+ | B- | C+ | 25.7 | -0.78 | 0.6 | 35.4 | 16.1 | 19.7 | 10.0 | 11.0 |
| ▼ ROUTE 1 CU | Paris | IL | D+ | C- | D+ | 4.8 | -0.87 | 0.0 | 46.3 | 0.0 | 2.2 | 10.0 | 11.1 |
| ROUTT SCHOOLS FCU | Steamboat Springs | CO | D- | E+ | E+ | 4.6 | -0.68 | 0.0 | 20.4 | 3.3 | 0.0 | 6.1 | 8.1 |
| ROYAL CU | Eau Claire | WI | A- | A- | B | 1648.3 | 10.13 | 38.2 | 26.7 | 43.2 | 0.5 | 10.0 | 11.5 |
| RPI EMPL FCU | Troy | NY | E+ | E+ | D- | 4.8 | 3.89 | 0.0 | 19.5 | 0.0 | 0.0 | 5.3 | 7.3 |
| RSC YO/CL OFFICES FCU | Youngstown | OH | C- | C- | C- | 6.2 | -3.76 | 0.0 | 18.5 | 0.6 | 63.6 | 10.0 | 12.5 |
| RTA BROOKLYN FCU | Cleveland | OH | E+ | E+ | E+ | 7.6 | 1.06 | 0.0 | 28.8 | 1.3 | 3.3 | 5.1 | 7.1 |
| RTA HAYDEN FCU | East Cleveland | OH | C- | C | C- | 1.7 | 0.29 | 0.0 | 44.0 | 0.0 | 0.0 | 10.0 | 25.5 |
| RTN FCU | Waltham | MA | C+ | C+ | C+ | 813.4 | 1.30 | 2.1 | 12.1 | 27.7 | 40.4 | 10.0 | 11.6 |
| RURAL COOPERATIVES CU INC | Louisville | KY | C+ | C+ | B- | 38.7 | -0.51 | 7.7 | 38.3 | 6.0 | 0.0 | 10.0 | 12.5 |
| RUSHMORE ELECTRIC FCU | Rapid City | SD | C- | C- | C+ | 20.2 | -4.39 | 0.0 | 36.1 | 0.2 | 0.0 | 10.0 | 11.4 |
| ▼ RUSSELL COUNTRY FCU | Great Falls | MT | C+ | B- | B- | 61.9 | 1.85 | 0.0 | 40.9 | 11.4 | 0.0 | 9.1 | 10.4 |

| Asset Quality Index | Non-Performing Loans as a % of Total Loans | as a % of Capital | Net Charge-Offs Avg Loans | Profitability Index | Net Income ($Mil) | Return on Assets | Return on Equity | Net Interest Spread | Overhead Efficiency Ratio | Liquidity Index | Liquidity Ratio | Hot Money Ratio | Stability Index |
|---|---|---|---|---|---|---|---|---|---|---|---|---|---|
| 6.4 | 1.16 | 6.5 | 0.05 | 5.2 | 0.1 | 0.75 | 7.54 | 3.04 | 74.2 | 5.3 | 34.6 | 3.4 | 4.3 |
| 9.3 | 0.51 | 3.0 | 0.49 | 0.3 | -0.5 | -0.39 | -4.07 | 2.70 | 102.1 | 4.5 | 20.7 | 1.5 | 4.6 |
| 5.7 | 0.40 | 4.1 | 0.50 | 3.9 | 0.7 | 0.48 | 6.03 | 3.63 | 76.1 | 3.6 | 14.8 | 4.3 | 4.3 |
| 5.9 | 0.56 | 7.0 | 0.43 | 8.4 | 6.2 | 1.26 | 13.70 | 3.92 | 71.2 | 3.5 | 9.3 | 5.0 | 6.2 |
| 9.5 | 0.45 | 1.6 | 0.41 | 3.6 | 0.4 | 0.48 | 2.41 | 3.59 | 81.1 | 3.7 | 11.5 | 2.1 | 7.5 |
| 6.1 | 2.88 | 10.1 | -0.19 | 0.7 | 0.0 | -0.58 | -4.62 | 2.72 | 120.0 | 5.4 | 46.7 | 0.0 | 4.8 |
| 9.5 | 0.26 | 1.3 | 0.19 | 2.9 | 0.1 | 0.32 | 3.70 | 3.15 | 90.4 | 4.4 | 9.7 | 0.0 | 4.1 |
| 5.5 | 0.55 | 3.8 | 0.17 | 3.8 | 0.1 | 0.42 | 4.12 | 3.45 | 87.7 | 3.2 | 14.7 | 5.1 | 5.1 |
| 4.9 | 1.98 | 15.2 | 0.87 | 0.8 | -0.1 | -0.24 | -2.49 | 3.18 | 93.1 | 3.6 | 18.4 | 7.0 | 4.0 |
| 7.7 | 1.19 | 3.2 | 0.72 | 2.8 | 0.0 | 0.38 | 2.26 | 7.70 | 88.7 | 6.9 | 62.3 | 0.0 | 5.8 |
| 7.6 | 1.13 | 4.6 | 0.69 | 1.1 | 0.0 | -0.07 | -0.48 | 3.74 | 96.8 | 3.9 | 14.2 | 1.4 | 5.1 |
| 5.9 | 1.69 | 10.8 | 0.43 | 1.8 | 0.0 | -0.06 | -0.55 | 5.22 | 82.7 | 3.8 | 9.6 | 0.0 | 3.6 |
| 7.7 | 0.54 | 3.1 | 0.38 | 4.4 | 0.1 | 0.65 | 7.48 | 4.59 | 82.4 | 4.9 | 24.8 | 2.6 | 4.1 |
| 9.6 | 0.39 | 1.5 | 0.00 | 2.3 | 0.0 | 0.15 | 0.85 | 3.97 | 95.9 | 4.5 | 32.4 | 2.3 | 6.7 |
| 9.9 | 0.61 | 1.1 | 0.31 | 2.5 | 0.1 | 0.15 | 0.86 | 2.21 | 91.5 | 4.5 | 8.1 | 3.1 | 6.2 |
| 6.6 | 0.63 | 6.5 | 0.11 | 5.6 | 0.3 | 0.86 | 11.28 | 4.62 | 82.1 | 3.4 | 11.7 | 1.6 | 3.4 |
| 7.4 | 0.88 | 4.5 | 0.33 | 3.4 | 0.2 | 0.30 | 3.31 | 3.72 | 88.4 | 5.7 | 26.3 | 0.5 | 4.1 |
| 7.5 | 1.77 | 4.5 | 0.25 | 0.5 | 0.0 | -0.19 | -0.83 | 3.99 | 106.9 | 6.0 | 48.6 | 0.0 | 5.7 |
| 6.9 | 0.53 | 3.1 | -0.12 | 3.8 | 0.0 | 0.31 | 3.28 | 4.32 | 95.1 | 4.8 | 23.5 | 0.0 | 3.0 |
| 9.8 | 0.37 | 0.5 | -0.05 | 0.4 | 0.0 | -0.33 | -1.34 | 2.40 | 112.5 | 5.1 | 32.9 | 0.0 | 6.5 |
| 9.7 | 0.41 | 1.6 | 0.41 | 9.5 | 28.4 | 1.87 | 11.89 | 2.93 | 49.0 | 4.4 | 15.6 | 5.5 | 10.0 |
| 6.9 | 1.46 | 9.8 | 0.11 | 2.6 | 0.1 | 0.23 | 2.10 | 4.59 | 95.2 | 3.9 | 20.9 | 0.5 | 5.2 |
| 8.1 | 0.97 | 3.1 | -0.12 | 0.6 | 0.0 | -0.19 | -1.87 | 2.10 | 108.6 | 6.0 | 61.1 | 0.0 | 4.8 |
| 10.0 | 0.00 | 0.0 | 0.00 | 2.6 | 0.0 | 0.26 | 1.51 | 1.79 | 84.8 | 5.5 | 37.4 | 2.1 | 7.3 |
| 6.0 | 2.42 | 8.6 | 0.00 | 2.8 | 0.0 | 0.26 | 2.96 | 4.00 | 89.9 | 6.7 | 43.2 | 0.0 | 2.3 |
| 5.5 | 1.38 | 10.0 | 0.74 | 3.9 | 0.2 | 0.31 | 2.94 | 4.56 | 87.1 | 2.8 | 7.9 | 8.9 | 5.4 |
| 10.0 | 0.37 | 0.9 | 0.19 | 1.9 | 0.1 | 0.11 | 0.94 | 2.24 | 96.2 | 5.3 | 42.7 | 3.4 | 6.4 |
| 9.6 | 0.80 | 2.8 | 0.15 | 3.4 | 0.1 | 0.37 | 2.53 | 3.47 | 88.9 | 5.4 | 40.4 | 3.8 | 7.1 |
| 7.1 | 0.71 | 5.6 | 0.00 | 3.3 | 0.1 | 0.46 | 5.19 | 3.43 | 88.3 | 3.6 | 16.4 | 3.0 | 3.0 |
| 6.5 | 2.43 | 9.9 | 0.25 | 1.5 | 0.0 | 0.16 | 1.04 | 3.28 | 91.5 | 4.0 | 22.3 | 1.4 | 6.0 |
| 9.1 | 0.79 | 2.7 | 1.04 | 1.4 | 0.0 | -0.01 | -0.06 | 3.01 | 90.1 | 5.5 | 29.5 | 0.0 | 5.2 |
| 10.0 | 0.10 | 0.2 | -0.13 | 2.2 | 0.0 | 0.24 | 1.76 | 2.79 | 90.8 | 4.8 | 25.6 | 0.0 | 5.8 |
| 1.8 | 3.62 | 33.2 | 0.73 | 7.4 | 0.5 | 2.13 | 26.48 | 7.20 | 74.3 | 4.6 | 20.9 | 1.2 | 2.6 |
| 7.5 | 0.39 | 2.9 | 0.11 | 6.2 | 9.6 | 0.93 | 8.21 | 2.36 | 63.8 | 2.1 | 7.7 | 12.3 | 9.2 |
| 8.4 | 0.32 | 2.4 | 0.21 | 6.9 | 1.4 | 1.10 | 10.45 | 4.05 | 75.2 | 3.4 | 14.0 | 8.3 | 7.1 |
| 9.9 | 0.02 | 0.1 | 0.22 | 7.5 | 1.3 | 0.97 | 5.69 | 3.84 | 75.3 | 4.0 | 34.1 | 12.6 | 9.8 |
| 7.3 | 2.82 | 4.6 | -0.37 | 0.0 | -0.1 | -1.63 | -15.85 | 2.99 | 147.8 | 4.9 | 15.8 | 0.0 | 3.6 |
| 6.3 | 1.14 | 9.6 | 0.43 | 10.0 | 13.1 | 1.76 | 18.15 | 4.86 | 61.4 | 3.2 | 9.9 | 5.9 | 7.9 |
| 6.2 | 1.48 | 7.7 | 0.74 | 3.6 | 0.1 | 0.36 | 4.02 | 2.81 | 89.1 | 4.0 | 6.5 | 4.7 | 4.2 |
| 9.0 | 0.41 | 0.6 | 0.39 | 2.1 | 0.1 | 0.31 | 2.95 | 2.28 | 88.8 | 6.4 | 39.7 | 0.0 | 4.2 |
| 5.0 | 1.51 | 11.1 | -0.20 | 3.6 | 0.1 | 0.39 | 4.93 | 4.09 | 90.7 | 4.8 | 25.4 | 3.4 | 2.3 |
| 9.5 | 1.56 | 2.9 | 0.73 | 0.7 | 0.0 | -0.32 | -1.46 | 2.05 | 115.0 | 5.5 | 61.9 | 0.0 | 6.0 |
| 9.9 | 0.42 | 1.5 | 0.46 | 3.2 | 0.1 | 0.45 | 3.38 | 2.88 | 82.6 | 4.7 | 28.4 | 0.8 | 7.0 |
| 5.5 | 3.27 | 6.7 | 0.00 | 1.4 | 0.0 | -0.20 | -2.48 | 3.86 | 95.7 | 7.2 | 48.0 | 0.0 | 1.0 |
| 8.7 | 0.10 | 0.4 | 0.32 | 1.8 | 0.0 | 0.23 | 1.67 | 3.17 | 90.6 | 5.0 | 19.1 | 0.0 | 5.6 |
| 10.0 | 0.00 | 0.0 | -0.47 | 2.7 | 0.0 | 0.08 | 0.52 | 8.50 | 98.4 | 7.4 | 64.8 | 0.0 | 7.1 |
| 6.8 | 0.77 | 4.0 | 0.57 | 1.7 | 0.0 | -0.09 | -1.01 | 4.36 | 92.8 | 5.8 | 33.0 | 0.9 | 4.0 |
| 9.8 | 0.00 | 0.0 | 0.00 | 0.0 | 0.0 | -0.85 | -5.63 | 3.29 | 150.0 | 8.8 | 108.8 | 0.0 | 6.2 |
| 9.2 | 0.00 | 0.0 | 0.09 | 9.6 | 0.3 | 1.53 | 14.75 | 4.31 | 69.4 | 2.4 | 13.6 | 17.5 | 5.7 |
| 2.7 | 5.33 | 20.9 | 0.05 | 4.3 | 0.0 | 0.03 | 0.24 | 4.91 | 80.3 | 4.9 | 44.1 | 8.7 | 6.1 |
| 8.7 | 0.28 | 1.0 | 0.19 | 2.0 | 0.0 | 0.23 | 2.85 | 2.64 | 92.1 | 5.5 | 26.7 | 0.0 | 1.7 |
| 6.7 | 0.51 | 4.4 | 0.33 | 9.5 | 16.4 | 1.36 | 12.06 | 3.58 | 70.6 | 2.4 | 5.2 | 9.5 | 8.3 |
| 8.8 | 1.31 | 3.6 | 1.06 | 1.0 | 0.0 | -0.11 | -1.52 | 2.79 | 104.4 | 6.1 | 47.3 | 0.0 | 2.0 |
| 8.2 | 3.24 | 5.5 | 0.11 | 2.0 | 0.0 | 0.17 | 1.38 | 1.54 | 86.8 | 5.2 | 20.3 | 0.0 | 6.1 |
| 3.9 | 2.62 | 16.9 | 2.35 | 0.6 | -0.1 | -1.06 | -14.40 | 3.48 | 94.7 | 5.1 | 31.2 | 0.0 | 1.9 |
| 9.6 | 0.00 | 0.0 | 2.27 | 1.3 | 0.0 | -1.11 | -4.14 | 5.32 | 101.6 | 6.4 | 50.2 | 0.0 | 6.9 |
| 9.4 | 0.67 | 3.0 | 0.26 | 2.9 | 1.5 | 0.24 | 2.41 | 2.78 | 88.4 | 3.5 | 11.7 | 13.0 | 7.0 |
| 8.9 | 0.55 | 2.2 | 0.12 | 2.3 | 0.1 | 0.19 | 1.53 | 3.46 | 94.3 | 4.2 | 22.3 | 4.8 | 5.9 |
| 9.5 | 0.00 | 0.0 | 0.04 | 1.6 | 0.0 | 0.12 | 1.10 | 2.31 | 95.1 | 3.8 | 25.0 | 8.1 | 5.2 |
| 8.2 | 0.72 | 4.2 | 0.14 | 3.4 | 0.1 | 0.29 | 2.82 | 2.99 | 90.9 | 3.9 | 23.7 | 5.0 | 4.7 |

| Name | City | State | Rating | 2014 Rating | 2013 Rating | Total Assets ($Mil) | One Year Asset Growth | Asset Mix (As a % of Total Assets) Commercial Loans | Consumer Loans | Mortgage Loans | Securities | Capitalization Index | Net Worth Ratio |
|---|---|---|---|---|---|---|---|---|---|---|---|---|---|
| RUTGERS FCU | New Brunswick | NJ | C | C- | D+ | 87.5 | 7.40 | 8.6 | 15.7 | 15.0 | 43.2 | 5.5 | 7.5 |
| RUTHERFORD POSTAL DISTRICT EMPL FCU | Lakewood | NJ | E+ | E+ | E+ | 8.1 | -0.83 | 0.0 | 4.5 | 0.0 | 0.0 | 5.3 | 7.3 |
| RYDER SYSTEM FCU | Miami | FL | C- | C | C | 42.7 | 4.71 | 0.0 | 9.4 | 25.6 | 19.0 | 10.0 | 21.1 |
| S AND J SCHOOL EMPL FCU | Wintersville | OH | E+ | E+ | E+ | 3.6 | 3.44 | 0.0 | 42.1 | 0.0 | 0.0 | 4.0 | 6.0 |
| S C H D DISTRICT 7 FCU | Orangeburg | SC | C | C- | C- | 2.8 | -2.91 | 0.0 | 48.6 | 0.0 | 0.0 | 10.0 | 17.6 |
| S C I FCU | Florence | SC | C+ | C- | D+ | 15.8 | 2.56 | 0.0 | 44.6 | 3.3 | 0.0 | 10.0 | 18.9 |
| S E A CU | Richfield | UT | C | C | C+ | 4.7 | 15.08 | 0.0 | 47.6 | 0.0 | 0.0 | 10.0 | 22.7 |
| ▼ S E C U CU | Keokuk | IA | C | C+ | C+ | 2.2 | 5.94 | 0.0 | 24.8 | 0.0 | 0.0 | 10.0 | 21.1 |
| S I EMPL FCU | Saratoga Springs | NY | C+ | C+ | B- | <1 | 4.47 | 0.0 | 27.4 | 0.0 | 0.0 | 10.0 | 26.8 |
| ▲ S I PHILADELPHIA FCU | Philadelphia | PA | C | C- | C | <1 | 0.89 | 0.0 | 12.4 | 0.0 | 0.0 | 10.0 | 33.6 |
| S M H FCU | Peru | IL | D+ | C- | D+ | <1 | -1.89 | 0.0 | 22.0 | 0.0 | 0.0 | 10.0 | 18.0 |
| S T A R COMMUNITY CU | Chico | CA | C | C+ | C+ | 42.7 | 5.04 | 5.3 | 11.0 | 5.4 | 45.8 | 6.8 | 8.8 |
| ▲ S T O F F E FCU | Solon | OH | C- | C- | C- | 5.7 | -1.30 | 0.0 | 61.2 | 0.0 | 0.0 | 10.0 | 21.1 |
| ▲ S W E FCU | Kilgore | TX | D | D- | D | 1.1 | -13.42 | 0.0 | 70.3 | 0.0 | 0.0 | 8.2 | 9.9 |
| S&S M H EMPL FCU | Wellsboro | PA | D- | D+ | D+ | 4.8 | -2.19 | 0.0 | 35.8 | 0.0 | 26.9 | 8.2 | 9.8 |
| SABATTUS REGIONAL CU | Sabattus | ME | B | B | B | 37.0 | 5.53 | 0.0 | 16.6 | 24.9 | 0.0 | 10.0 | 11.9 |
| SABINE FCU | Orange | TX | B- | B- | C+ | 169.5 | 3.13 | 0.0 | 38.6 | 18.3 | 13.6 | 10.0 | 12.2 |
| SABINE SCHOOL EMPL FCU | Many | LA | C | C | C | 4.8 | 1.12 | 0.0 | 52.0 | 0.0 | 41.8 | 10.0 | 12.8 |
| SAC FCU | Papillion | NE | B- | B- | B- | 782.2 | 6.17 | 6.6 | 67.6 | 19.4 | 0.0 | 6.5 | 8.5 |
| SACO VALLEY CU | Saco | ME | B+ | B | C+ | 102.2 | 2.76 | 1.1 | 15.5 | 48.2 | 0.0 | 8.9 | 10.2 |
| SACRAMENTO CU | Sacramento | CA | A | A | A | 396.1 | 3.44 | 5.0 | 20.7 | 9.6 | 14.5 | 10.0 | 13.5 |
| SACRED HEART FCU | Metairie | LA | D | D | C- | 1.3 | -6.74 | 0.0 | 13.3 | 0.0 | 0.0 | 10.0 | 27.0 |
| SACRED HEART OF CORPUS CHRISTI FCU | White Oak | PA | D+ | D+ | D | <1 | -17.59 | 0.0 | 55.9 | 0.0 | 0.0 | 10.0 | 16.6 |
| SACRED HEART PARISH HALLETTSVILLE FC | Hallettsville | TX | C | C | C | 41.0 | 0.66 | 0.2 | 22.9 | 4.2 | 0.0 | 6.3 | 8.3 |
| SAFE 1 CU | Bakersfield | CA | A | A | A | 404.5 | 7.91 | 0.0 | 54.4 | 11.2 | 8.5 | 10.0 | 15.8 |
| SAFE CU | Folsom | CA | B | B+ | B+ | 2295.5 | 8.57 | 5.9 | 30.1 | 27.7 | 22.6 | 7.7 | 9.4 |
| SAFE CU | Beaumont | TX | D- | D | D+ | 11.5 | 4.35 | 0.0 | 41.6 | 0.4 | 0.0 | 9.0 | 10.3 |
| SAFE FCU | Sumter | SC | B | B | B+ | 929.1 | 4.85 | 0.1 | 33.5 | 19.2 | 29.0 | 9.1 | 10.4 |
| SAFE HARBOR CU | Ludington | MI | C+ | C+ | C | 44.9 | 5.11 | 1.1 | 15.1 | 33.8 | 21.7 | 7.0 | 9.0 |
| ▲ SAFEAMERICA CU | Pleasanton | CA | B- | C | C- | 353.5 | 12.90 | 0.2 | 48.6 | 28.8 | 4.5 | 6.9 | 9.0 |
| SAFEWAY FCU | Spokane | WA | B+ | B+ | B+ | 55.5 | 4.08 | 0.0 | 26.8 | 12.6 | 0.0 | 10.0 | 21.2 |
| SAG-AFTRA FCU | Burbank | CA | C+ | C | C | 223.8 | 1.80 | 4.4 | 15.7 | 18.8 | 29.4 | 6.4 | 8.4 |
| SAGELINK CU | Durand | MI | C+ | C | C | 173.4 | 3.76 | 0.0 | 21.4 | 14.8 | 20.1 | 10.0 | 11.5 |
| SAGINAW COUNTY EMPL CU | Saginaw | MI | C- | C- | C- | 32.9 | -0.20 | 1.5 | 17.9 | 24.0 | 0.0 | 6.8 | 8.8 |
| SAGINAW MEDICAL FCU | Saginaw | MI | B- | B- | B- | 123.2 | 4.03 | 3.4 | 27.5 | 10.8 | 46.4 | 9.6 | 10.8 |
| ▲ SAIF FCU | Baton Rouge | LA | D- | E+ | D- | 9.9 | 7.46 | 0.0 | 40.8 | 0.5 | 0.0 | 5.6 | 7.6 |
| SAINT AGNES FCU | Baltimore | MD | C- | C- | C- | 51.3 | 13.69 | 0.0 | 23.1 | 10.1 | 4.6 | 7.8 | 9.5 |
| SAINT ALPHONSUS MEDICAL CU | Boise | ID | E+ | E+ | E+ | 4.6 | -2.55 | 0.0 | 54.1 | 0.0 | 0.0 | 5.2 | 7.2 |
| SAINT ANTHONY HOSPITAL FCU | Rockford | IL | D | D | D+ | 4.2 | 2.77 | 0.0 | 35.8 | 0.0 | 0.0 | 7.4 | 9.2 |
| SAINT DOMINICS FCU | Swansea | MA | B | B | B | 28.9 | -0.62 | 0.0 | 20.0 | 29.9 | 0.0 | 10.0 | 16.3 |
| SAINT EDWARD MERCY HOSPITAL FCU | Fort Smith | AR | C- | C- | C | 3.0 | 3.03 | 0.0 | 40.3 | 0.0 | 0.0 | 10.0 | 14.0 |
| SAINT ELIZABETH CU | Chicago | IL | C- | C+ | C | <1 | -12.27 | 0.0 | 0.0 | 0.0 | 0.0 | 10.0 | 22.8 |
| SAINT FRANCIS EMPL FCU | Tulsa | OK | D+ | D+ | D+ | 35.1 | -3.00 | 0.0 | 34.7 | 0.0 | 3.0 | 5.7 | 7.7 |
| SAINT GABRIELS FCU | Washington | DC | D+ | C- | C- | <1 | 12.53 | 0.0 | 19.7 | 0.0 | 0.0 | 8.9 | 10.3 |
| SAINT JOHN AME FCU | Niagara Falls | NY | D+ | D | D+ | <1 | -2.04 | 0.0 | 41.2 | 0.0 | 0.0 | 10.0 | 15.6 |
| SAINT LAWRENCE FCU | Ogdensburg | NY | B+ | B+ | A- | 122.7 | 13.18 | 0.0 | 22.4 | 33.5 | 20.1 | 9.3 | 10.6 |
| SAINT LUKES COMMUNITY FCU | Houston | TX | D | D- | D- | 1.3 | -7.27 | 0.0 | 19.1 | 0.0 | 0.0 | 7.4 | 9.2 |
| SAINT LUKES CU | Kansas City | MO | C | C+ | C+ | 23.5 | 4.09 | 0.6 | 28.0 | 0.0 | 0.0 | 9.9 | 10.9 |
| SAINT NORBERTS CU | Pittsburgh | PA | B- | B- | B | <1 | -4.16 | 0.0 | 53.6 | 0.0 | 9.2 | 10.0 | 22.7 |
| SAINT PETER PAUL FCU | Brooklyn | NY | D | D+ | C- | 1.7 | -8.52 | 0.0 | 10.6 | 0.0 | 0.0 | 10.0 | 21.5 |
| SAINT VINCENT ERIE FCU | Erie | PA | D+ | D+ | C- | 14.1 | 0.28 | 0.0 | 18.5 | 0.0 | 0.0 | 7.8 | 9.5 |
| SAINT VINCENT HOSPITAL CU | Worcester | MA | C- | C- | C- | 12.1 | 0.61 | 0.0 | 31.1 | 0.0 | 31.0 | 7.7 | 9.5 |
| ▲ SAINTS MARGARET & GREGORY FCU | South Euclid | OH | C | C- | C- | 11.5 | 3.14 | 0.0 | 69.5 | 0.0 | 9.2 | 9.6 | 10.7 |
| ▼ SAKER SHOP RITE FCU | Freehold | NJ | C- | C- | C | 7.0 | 2.78 | 0.0 | 28.1 | 0.0 | 69.0 | 10.0 | 25.2 |
| SALAL CU | Seattle | WA | C+ | C+ | C+ | 417.7 | 13.02 | 7.7 | 40.9 | 30.9 | 19.6 | 7.5 | 9.5 |
| SALEM BAPTIST FCU | Jersey City | NJ | C+ | C+ | B- | <1 | -6.02 | 0.0 | 18.6 | 0.0 | 0.0 | 10.0 | 20.5 |
| SALEM SCHOOL SYSTEM CU | Salem | IL | C- | C | C | 2.3 | 2.03 | 0.0 | 48.4 | 0.0 | 0.0 | 10.0 | 22.3 |
| ▼ SALEM VA MEDICAL CENTER FCU | Salem | VA | D | D+ | C- | 80.2 | 3.56 | 0.0 | 46.0 | 4.6 | 0.0 | 6.3 | 8.3 |
| ▲ SALINA INTERPAROCHIAL CU | Salina | KS | C+ | C | C | 16.1 | -0.44 | 0.0 | 53.7 | 0.0 | 0.0 | 10.0 | 27.6 |
| SALINA MUNICIPAL CU | Salina | KS | D | C- | C- | 2.1 | -3.20 | 0.0 | 50.0 | 0.0 | 0.0 | 10.0 | 11.4 |

| Asset Quality Index | Non-Performing Loans as a % of Total Loans | Non-Performing Loans as a % of Capital | Net Charge-Offs Avg Loans | Profitability Index | Net Income ($Mil) | Return on Assets | Return on Equity | Net Interest Spread | Overhead Efficiency Ratio | Liquidity Index | Liquidity Ratio | Hot Money Ratio | Stability Index |
|---|---|---|---|---|---|---|---|---|---|---|---|---|---|
| 7.0 | 0.27 | 3.3 | 0.58 | 4.0 | 0.4 | 0.63 | 8.50 | 2.91 | 75.2 | 4.7 | 21.1 | 1.7 | 3.1 |
| 9.2 | 2.81 | 1.9 | 0.00 | 1.7 | 0.0 | 0.00 | 0.00 | 0.87 | 100.0 | 5.3 | 29.3 | 0.0 | 1.0 |
| 9.8 | 0.14 | 2.2 | -0.07 | 1.2 | 0.0 | -0.12 | -0.56 | 3.03 | 104.0 | 5.9 | 37.8 | 3.5 | 6.9 |
| 9.5 | 0.11 | 0.9 | 0.00 | 0.5 | 0.0 | -0.41 | -6.85 | 4.19 | 107.7 | 4.5 | 27.2 | 0.0 | 1.5 |
| 6.2 | 2.39 | 6.3 | -0.10 | 7.8 | 0.0 | 1.87 | 11.18 | 5.97 | 64.9 | 5.2 | 42.1 | 5.0 | 4.3 |
| 9.8 | 0.55 | 1.5 | 0.12 | 3.6 | 0.1 | 0.56 | 2.99 | 3.64 | 83.0 | 5.2 | 32.8 | 1.0 | 6.6 |
| 4.6 | 3.22 | 8.4 | 2.95 | 5.0 | 0.0 | 0.48 | 2.03 | 4.40 | 72.5 | 6.4 | 51.3 | 0.0 | 4.3 |
| 8.0 | 3.82 | 5.5 | 0.00 | 2.3 | 0.0 | -0.13 | -0.56 | 4.70 | 104.6 | 7.5 | 74.0 | 0.0 | 7.9 |
| 9.7 | 0.00 | 0.0 | 3.53 | 2.4 | 0.0 | 0.00 | 0.00 | 5.49 | 60.0 | 8.0 | 99.8 | 0.0 | 6.7 |
| 9.6 | 7.14 | 2.6 | 0.00 | 3.5 | 0.0 | 0.58 | 1.75 | 2.75 | 60.0 | 7.2 | 130.0 | 0.0 | 5.2 |
| 10.0 | 0.54 | 0.7 | 0.00 | 0.6 | 0.0 | -0.17 | -0.88 | 3.28 | 100.0 | 7.5 | 65.0 | 0.0 | 5.5 |
| 10.0 | 0.30 | 0.9 | 0.13 | 3.0 | 0.1 | 0.24 | 2.60 | 2.55 | 91.0 | 5.7 | 32.9 | 3.5 | 4.5 |
| 8.5 | 0.27 | 0.8 | 0.12 | 1.7 | 0.0 | 0.07 | 0.33 | 2.96 | 96.5 | 5.0 | 32.2 | 0.0 | 6.8 |
| 7.0 | 0.00 | 0.0 | 0.00 | 2.0 | 0.0 | 0.11 | 1.22 | 2.38 | 95.0 | 4.2 | 21.0 | 0.0 | 3.9 |
| 4.1 | 0.64 | 2.9 | 0.41 | 0.4 | 0.0 | -0.83 | -8.37 | 3.38 | 115.8 | 5.5 | 22.4 | 0.0 | 4.7 |
| 7.5 | 1.27 | 5.2 | 0.12 | 4.4 | 0.2 | 0.62 | 5.22 | 2.97 | 86.5 | 4.6 | 23.9 | 0.7 | 6.4 |
| 8.5 | 0.71 | 3.9 | 0.38 | 3.6 | 0.6 | 0.44 | 3.69 | 3.78 | 85.5 | 3.8 | 15.3 | 6.7 | 7.2 |
| 5.2 | 2.64 | 10.8 | 0.00 | 7.4 | 0.0 | 1.06 | 8.54 | 3.62 | 63.6 | 4.9 | 51.7 | 0.0 | 4.3 |
| 4.9 | 0.98 | 9.4 | 0.85 | 4.7 | 3.6 | 0.61 | 7.30 | 3.58 | 69.7 | 1.8 | 3.1 | 13.8 | 6.0 |
| 7.6 | 0.36 | 5.0 | -0.02 | 5.5 | 0.6 | 0.78 | 8.05 | 3.29 | 79.0 | 4.1 | 38.3 | 4.5 | 6.9 |
| 9.7 | 0.54 | 1.8 | -0.08 | 7.0 | 3.3 | 1.11 | 8.39 | 2.41 | 71.9 | 5.0 | 27.5 | 2.9 | 8.0 |
| 7.0 | 16.84 | 9.3 | 0.00 | 0.0 | 0.0 | -1.97 | -7.20 | 1.54 | 228.6 | 6.7 | 115.6 | 0.0 | 4.9 |
| 0.7 | 11.95 | 41.3 | 0.00 | 4.6 | 0.0 | 0.70 | 4.88 | 4.09 | 83.3 | 4.5 | 45.1 | 0.0 | 6.9 |
| 9.6 | 0.08 | 0.4 | 0.00 | 4.2 | 0.2 | 0.63 | 7.82 | 2.33 | 74.0 | 4.6 | 31.8 | 2.6 | 4.3 |
| 8.2 | 0.47 | 2.4 | 0.25 | 8.1 | 3.2 | 1.09 | 6.88 | 3.01 | 69.3 | 2.8 | 17.7 | 18.9 | 9.3 |
| 7.1 | 1.02 | 7.8 | 0.43 | 4.1 | 9.2 | 0.56 | 5.70 | 2.93 | 83.6 | 4.1 | 14.2 | 4.9 | 6.1 |
| 5.5 | 3.18 | 12.9 | 0.76 | 0.0 | -0.1 | -1.09 | -10.13 | 3.17 | 110.9 | 6.1 | 52.2 | 1.0 | 4.1 |
| 9.8 | 0.24 | 1.6 | 0.22 | 4.7 | 5.2 | 0.75 | 7.38 | 2.39 | 79.8 | 3.8 | 21.1 | 13.7 | 7.1 |
| 9.9 | 0.19 | 1.2 | 0.03 | 4.3 | 0.2 | 0.56 | 6.31 | 3.07 | 83.5 | 3.7 | 13.9 | 7.1 | 4.5 |
| 7.0 | 0.34 | 4.1 | 0.27 | 4.4 | 1.7 | 0.66 | 8.26 | 3.78 | 79.0 | 2.6 | 7.0 | 10.2 | 4.3 |
| 7.9 | 2.07 | 4.3 | 0.41 | 4.8 | 0.3 | 0.70 | 3.27 | 2.44 | 67.4 | 4.4 | 29.3 | 4.6 | 7.6 |
| 9.4 | 0.66 | 3.1 | 0.33 | 3.4 | 0.7 | 0.40 | 5.03 | 3.27 | 96.7 | 5.9 | 27.0 | 1.1 | 4.3 |
| 9.6 | 0.41 | 1.4 | 0.25 | 3.2 | 0.6 | 0.45 | 3.97 | 2.95 | 85.2 | 4.7 | 23.7 | 1.5 | 6.8 |
| 7.1 | 0.68 | 4.8 | 0.41 | 3.1 | 0.1 | 0.26 | 3.02 | 2.97 | 90.4 | 4.7 | 39.2 | 3.3 | 3.3 |
| 9.5 | 0.73 | 2.8 | 0.15 | 3.5 | 0.4 | 0.39 | 3.66 | 2.86 | 88.4 | 4.5 | 18.1 | 2.1 | 6.6 |
| 7.0 | 0.51 | 3.1 | 0.52 | 2.3 | 0.0 | 0.09 | 1.24 | 3.70 | 97.9 | 3.7 | 26.2 | 15.4 | 2.3 |
| 10.0 | 0.14 | 0.7 | 0.01 | 2.3 | 0.1 | 0.32 | 3.43 | 2.88 | 93.6 | 4.2 | 14.5 | 3.2 | 3.9 |
| 2.5 | 0.12 | 22.3 | 1.90 | 0.4 | 0.0 | -0.43 | -5.93 | 3.34 | 103.6 | 4.4 | 12.5 | 0.0 | 2.7 |
| 6.8 | 1.33 | 5.3 | 0.63 | 1.0 | 0.0 | -0.03 | -0.34 | 2.61 | 93.6 | 4.7 | 27.6 | 0.0 | 4.0 |
| 7.7 | 1.46 | 5.4 | 0.01 | 6.0 | 0.2 | 0.90 | 5.70 | 3.36 | 71.8 | 2.3 | 20.8 | 24.3 | 8.2 |
| 9.6 | 0.44 | 1.4 | 0.19 | 2.0 | 0.0 | 0.13 | 0.96 | 4.90 | 88.8 | 6.0 | 36.7 | 0.0 | 5.8 |
| 2.2 | 10.61 | 28.6 | 0.00 | 6.8 | 0.0 | 0.66 | 3.10 | 9.30 | 77.8 | 5.9 | 42.3 | 0.0 | 5.2 |
| 9.5 | 0.21 | 1.0 | 0.13 | 2.5 | 0.1 | 0.20 | 2.74 | 2.15 | 93.2 | 4.6 | 17.7 | 3.7 | 2.7 |
| 6.7 | 7.34 | 14.0 | 3.70 | 1.2 | 0.0 | 0.00 | 0.00 | 2.74 | 55.6 | 5.5 | 11.9 | 0.0 | 5.3 |
| 5.7 | 2.80 | 9.7 | 0.00 | 1.6 | 0.0 | 0.00 | 0.00 | 6.20 | 100.0 | 6.4 | 50.6 | 0.0 | 5.5 |
| 8.7 | 0.41 | 3.1 | 0.19 | 5.1 | 0.7 | 0.78 | 7.38 | 3.39 | 78.4 | 2.7 | 9.4 | 14.1 | 6.6 |
| 8.2 | 0.71 | 1.6 | 0.89 | 2.6 | 0.0 | 0.19 | 2.26 | 0.97 | 88.9 | 6.3 | 50.9 | 0.0 | 4.4 |
| 9.0 | 0.40 | 1.3 | 0.34 | 2.4 | 0.0 | 0.10 | 0.89 | 2.55 | 95.0 | 4.8 | 27.2 | 1.5 | 5.8 |
| 8.7 | 0.00 | 0.0 | 0.00 | 8.8 | 0.0 | 3.07 | 13.19 | 5.59 | 40.0 | 5.1 | 35.7 | 0.0 | 5.7 |
| 6.2 | 20.00 | 9.5 | 3.03 | 0.0 | 0.0 | -1.32 | -6.18 | 1.04 | 288.9 | 8.2 | 113.9 | 0.0 | 4.9 |
| 6.4 | 3.58 | 10.9 | 0.66 | 2.1 | 0.0 | 0.24 | 2.61 | 3.23 | 90.4 | 4.9 | 20.4 | 0.0 | 3.7 |
| 7.0 | 1.22 | 4.8 | 0.86 | 1.8 | 0.0 | -0.03 | -0.35 | 4.04 | 93.2 | 5.7 | 32.2 | 0.0 | 3.8 |
| 5.9 | 0.50 | 3.3 | -0.11 | 3.7 | 0.0 | 0.43 | 4.15 | 3.53 | 83.1 | 3.7 | 14.2 | 0.0 | 5.2 |
| 6.8 | 7.95 | 8.4 | 6.72 | 3.6 | 0.0 | 0.19 | 0.75 | 5.29 | 68.1 | 4.8 | 24.6 | 0.0 | 6.2 |
| 8.8 | 0.30 | 2.1 | 0.75 | 7.2 | 4.8 | 1.60 | 17.19 | 4.18 | 63.2 | 3.0 | 13.2 | 7.6 | 5.5 |
| 10.0 | 0.00 | 0.0 | 0.00 | 2.7 | 0.0 | 0.00 | 0.00 | 2.05 | 66.7 | 8.2 | 98.4 | 0.0 | 6.7 |
| 4.9 | 5.99 | 13.8 | 0.00 | 2.9 | 0.0 | 0.29 | 1.30 | 3.13 | 90.6 | 4.1 | 4.5 | 0.0 | 7.7 |
| 2.5 | 2.45 | 20.1 | 1.15 | 1.1 | -0.2 | -0.32 | -4.25 | 4.69 | 88.6 | 4.4 | 28.0 | 4.1 | 3.0 |
| 6.6 | 3.03 | 5.5 | 0.73 | 4.7 | 0.1 | 0.76 | 2.82 | 3.16 | 46.4 | 5.6 | 83.5 | 4.9 | 6.0 |
| 8.4 | 0.00 | 0.0 | 0.00 | 0.7 | 0.0 | -0.12 | -1.13 | 3.46 | 107.3 | 4.6 | 26.0 | 0.0 | 5.8 |

| Name | City | State | Rating | 2014 Rating | 2013 Rating | Total Assets ($Mil) | One Year Asset Growth | Asset Mix (As a % of Total Assets) Commercial Loans | Consumer Loans | Mortgage Loans | Securities | Capitalization Index | Net Worth Ratio |
|---|---|---|---|---|---|---|---|---|---|---|---|---|---|
| SALINA RAILROAD CU | Salina | KS | E+ | E+ | E+ | <1 | -2.17 | 0.0 | 92.1 | 0.0 | 0.0 | 4.5 | 6.5 |
| SALINE COUNTY TEACHERS CU | Salina | KS | C- | C- | C- | 2.6 | 8.07 | 0.0 | 56.7 | 0.0 | 0.0 | 10.0 | 26.1 |
| SALT CREEK CU | Westchester | IL | E+ | D- | D | 8.3 | 1.88 | 2.2 | 18.9 | 0.0 | 0.0 | 4.6 | 6.6 |
| SALT EMPL FCU | Grand Saline | TX | C- | D+ | D+ | 2.0 | 3.49 | 0.0 | 36.8 | 0.0 | 0.0 | 10.0 | 33.0 |
| SAN ANGELO FCU | San Angelo | TX | D | D | D+ | 22.3 | 3.99 | 0.0 | 53.8 | 0.6 | 16.0 | 6.3 | 8.3 |
| SAN ANTONIO CITIZENS FCU | San Antonio | FL | C+ | C+ | C+ | 173.0 | 11.78 | 5.9 | 18.2 | 25.0 | 31.4 | 6.9 | 9.2 |
| SAN ANTONIO FCU | San Antonio | TX | B- | B- | B- | 2772.3 | 0.83 | 0.0 | 39.0 | 8.1 | 0.0 | 10.0 | 12.4 |
| SAN DIEGO COUNTY CU | San Diego | CA | A+ | A+ | A+ | 7094.2 | 7.61 | 5.5 | 17.2 | 45.6 | 21.0 | 10.0 | 13.7 |
| SAN DIEGO FIREFIGHTERS FCU | San Diego | CA | C | C | C | 91.5 | 4.36 | 4.4 | 13.4 | 30.2 | 36.3 | 5.8 | 7.8 |
| SAN DIEGO METROPOLITAN CU | San Diego | CA | B | B | C+ | 253.6 | 1.18 | 4.8 | 14.4 | 27.5 | 8.4 | 7.0 | 9.0 |
| SAN FERNANDO VALLEY JAPANESE CU | Northridge | CA | D | D | C- | <1 | -6.83 | 0.0 | 58.4 | 0.0 | 0.0 | 10.0 | 25.6 |
| SAN FRANCISCO FCU | San Francisco | CA | C+ | B- | B- | 974.9 | 6.78 | 8.3 | 6.9 | 33.9 | 44.4 | 9.2 | 10.5 |
| SAN FRANCISCO FIRE CU | San Francisco | CA | B | B- | B- | 1084.9 | 9.28 | 11.5 | 15.9 | 40.2 | 10.5 | 6.0 | 8.0 |
| SAN FRANCISCO LEE FCU | San Francisco | CA | B- | C+ | C+ | 11.6 | 1.23 | 11.3 | 0.2 | 31.6 | 0.0 | 10.0 | 39.3 |
| SAN FRANCISCO MUNICIPAL RAILWAY EMPL | San Francisco | CA | D- | D | C- | 5.3 | -8.56 | 0.0 | 1.9 | 8.1 | 0.0 | 9.1 | 10.4 |
| SAN GABRIEL VALLEY POSTAL CU | Covina | CA | B- | C+ | C+ | 20.0 | 3.38 | 0.0 | 43.5 | 3.3 | 0.0 | 10.0 | 13.3 |
| SAN JOAQUIN POWER EMPL CU | Fresno | CA | B- | B- | B- | 130.2 | 2.41 | 11.7 | 18.5 | 34.4 | 15.1 | 10.0 | 16.6 |
| ▲ SAN JUAN CU | Blanding | UT | D | D | C- | 16.5 | 3.17 | 0.4 | 56.3 | 1.5 | 0.0 | 6.4 | 8.4 |
| SAN JUAN MOUNTAINS CU | Montrose | CO | C+ | C+ | C- | 27.3 | 4.47 | 0.0 | 17.9 | 38.4 | 0.0 | 7.7 | 9.4 |
| SAN MATEO CITY EMPL FCU | San Mateo | CA | B | B | B- | 32.8 | 6.11 | 0.0 | 8.1 | 0.9 | 0.0 | 10.0 | 12.4 |
| SAN MATEO CU | Redwood City | CA | B+ | B+ | B | 847.2 | 7.31 | 1.0 | 32.6 | 24.1 | 27.3 | 8.1 | 9.7 |
| SAN PATRICIO COUNTY TEACHERS FCU | Sinton | TX | B | B | B | 31.0 | 5.77 | 0.0 | 67.7 | 2.6 | 0.0 | 10.0 | 13.2 |
| SAN TAN CU | Chandler | AZ | E+ | E+ | E+ | 9.4 | 2.80 | 0.0 | 66.2 | 0.0 | 0.0 | 5.1 | 7.1 |
| SANDHILLS FCU | Ulysses | KS | D+ | C- | C- | 1.1 | -20.06 | 0.0 | 51.5 | 0.0 | 0.0 | 10.0 | 15.3 |
| SANDIA AREA FCU | Albuquerque | NM | A- | A- | A- | 548.2 | 8.41 | 6.9 | 74.8 | 14.4 | 0.0 | 10.0 | 11.1 |
| SANDIA LABORATORY FCU | Albuquerque | NM | A- | A- | A- | 2170.2 | 3.77 | 7.9 | 14.3 | 29.9 | 39.5 | 10.0 | 11.0 |
| SANDUSKY OHIO EDISON EMPL FCU | Sandusky | OH | D+ | D+ | D+ | <1 | 8.42 | 0.0 | 48.5 | 0.0 | 0.0 | 10.0 | 20.4 |
| SANGAMO-OCONEE EMPL FCU | West Union | SC | D | D | C- | 3.7 | 0.81 | 0.0 | 20.1 | 0.0 | 0.0 | 10.0 | 21.5 |
| ▲ SANTA ANA FCU | Santa Ana | CA | C | D+ | C- | 62.3 | -0.46 | 0.0 | 24.8 | 11.0 | 18.5 | 6.1 | 8.1 |
| SANTA BARBARA COUNTY FCU | Santa Barbara | CA | C | C | C- | 39.6 | -0.43 | 0.0 | 9.1 | 3.0 | 10.7 | 6.4 | 8.4 |
| SANTA BARBARA TEACHERS FCU | Santa Barbara | CA | C+ | C+ | B- | 219.6 | 1.99 | 0.0 | 2.9 | 22.9 | 45.8 | 9.0 | 10.4 |
| SANTA CLARA COUNTY FCU | San Jose | CA | B | B | B- | 636.3 | 9.61 | 0.0 | 25.2 | 9.8 | 33.8 | 6.8 | 8.8 |
| ▲ SANTA CRUZ COMMUNITY CU | Santa Cruz | CA | C- | C- | C- | 105.5 | -0.56 | 13.2 | 30.1 | 17.6 | 7.8 | 6.2 | 8.2 |
| SANTA FE FCU | Amarillo | TX | B+ | A- | B | 124.7 | 5.22 | 0.0 | 37.5 | 0.1 | 39.7 | 10.0 | 13.8 |
| SANTA MARIA ASSOCIATED EMPL FCU | Santa Maria | CA | D- | D- | D- | 3.5 | 4.01 | 0.0 | 49.9 | 0.0 | 0.0 | 6.5 | 8.5 |
| SANTA ROSA COUNTY FCU | Milton | FL | B- | B- | B | 107.2 | 7.68 | 0.0 | 23.3 | 7.7 | 15.6 | 10.0 | 12.2 |
| ▲ SANTEE COOPER CU | Moncks Corner | SC | C+ | C- | C- | 48.8 | 4.07 | 0.0 | 44.9 | 3.7 | 0.0 | 7.7 | 9.5 |
| SANTO CHRISTO FCU | Fall River | MA | C- | C | C | 10.4 | 2.79 | 1.9 | 28.1 | 33.8 | 0.0 | 9.6 | 10.8 |
| SARASOTA MUNICIPAL EMPL CU | Sarasota | FL | B- | B- | C+ | 27.2 | 0.27 | 0.0 | 33.2 | 0.2 | 0.0 | 10.0 | 11.6 |
| SARATOGAS COMMUNITY FCU | Saratoga Springs | NY | E | D- | D- | 37.8 | -0.09 | 0.3 | 31.5 | 21.7 | 0.0 | 4.5 | 6.5 |
| SARCO FCU | Bethlehem | PA | C- | C- | C- | 7.2 | -2.72 | 0.0 | 29.2 | 10.5 | 0.0 | 10.0 | 21.1 |
| SARGENT FCU | Washington | DC | E+ | E+ | E+ | <1 | 12.28 | 0.0 | 48.0 | 0.0 | 0.0 | 5.2 | 7.2 |
| SAVANNAH FCU | Savannah | GA | C | C- | C- | 19.9 | -0.56 | 3.3 | 21.1 | 10.5 | 21.3 | 10.0 | 19.3 |
| ▲ SAVANNAH POSTAL CU | Savannah | GA | B- | C | C+ | 19.3 | 2.00 | 0.0 | 24.2 | 5.2 | 0.0 | 10.0 | 15.3 |
| SAVANNAH SCHOOLS FCU | Savannah | GA | C+ | C+ | C+ | 28.8 | 3.91 | 0.6 | 26.6 | 2.4 | 0.0 | 10.0 | 12.9 |
| SAVASTATE TEACHERS FCU | Savannah | GA | C | C | D+ | 3.8 | 4.38 | 0.0 | 26.3 | 0.0 | 0.0 | 10.0 | 16.9 |
| SB COMMUNITY FCU | Muskegon | MI | D | D+ | D | 12.9 | 1.30 | 0.0 | 48.1 | 20.6 | 17.5 | 6.4 | 8.4 |
| SB1 FCU | Philadelphia | PA | B- | C+ | B- | 590.2 | 1.93 | 1.0 | 13.7 | 32.5 | 30.3 | 9.9 | 10.9 |
| SC STATE FCU | Columbia | SC | A- | B+ | A- | 657.5 | 6.75 | 0.0 | 29.2 | 4.0 | 14.8 | 10.0 | 11.6 |
| SC TELCO FCU | Greenville | SC | A | A | A | 294.0 | 10.42 | 2.4 | 33.2 | 26.4 | 5.9 | 10.0 | 12.1 |
| SCE FCU | Irwindale | CA | B | B | B | 632.6 | 2.84 | 9.9 | 29.7 | 24.5 | 20.8 | 8.3 | 9.9 |
| SCENIC COMMUNITY CU | Hixson | TN | B- | B- | B | 115.3 | 2.88 | 4.2 | 17.9 | 22.7 | 0.0 | 10.0 | 12.6 |
| ▲ SCENIC FALLS FCU | Idaho Falls | ID | C- | C- | C- | 64.0 | 4.38 | 0.0 | 59.0 | 1.0 | 0.0 | 6.8 | 8.8 |
| ▲ SCF WESTCHESTER NY EMPL FCU | White Plains | NY | C- | D+ | D+ | 1.4 | 0.85 | 0.0 | 44.1 | 0.0 | 0.0 | 10.0 | 21.0 |
| SCFE CU INC | Portsmouth | OH | D | D | D | <1 | -3.31 | 0.0 | 64.0 | 0.0 | 0.0 | 9.1 | 10.4 |
| SCHENECTADY COUNTY EMPL FCU | Schenectady | NY | E+ | E+ | E+ | 4.3 | -5.35 | 0.0 | 68.4 | 0.0 | 12.5 | 6.3 | 8.3 |
| SCHLUMBERGER EMPL CU | Sugar Land | TX | A+ | A+ | A+ | 793.2 | 11.02 | 0.0 | 11.0 | 11.8 | 67.6 | 10.0 | 11.0 |
| SCHNEIDER COMMUNITY CU | Green Bay | WI | C | C- | C+ | 18.8 | 1.70 | 0.0 | 44.2 | 5.4 | 0.0 | 10.0 | 17.5 |
| SCHOFIELD FCU | Wahiawa | HI | B+ | B+ | B+ | 33.5 | -7.51 | 0.5 | 12.1 | 12.0 | 9.8 | 10.0 | 18.0 |
| SCHOOL DISTRICT 218 EMPL FCU | Oak Lawn | IL | D+ | D+ | D+ | 12.2 | -3.67 | 0.0 | 10.0 | 0.0 | 0.0 | 6.9 | 8.9 |

| Asset Quality Index | Non-Performing Loans as a % of Total Loans | Non-Performing Loans as a % of Capital | Net Charge-Offs Avg Loans | Profitability Index | Net Income ($Mil) | Return on Assets | Return on Equity | Net Interest Spread | Overhead Efficiency Ratio | Liquidity Index | Liquidity Ratio | Hot Money Ratio | Stability Index |
|---|---|---|---|---|---|---|---|---|---|---|---|---|---|
| 0.0 | 4.01 | 53.7 | 1.34 | 0.4 | 0.0 | -4.37 | -52.29 | 12.02 | 142.9 | 0.5 | 3.8 | 61.6 | 3.4 |
| 8.5 | 0.20 | 0.4 | 0.38 | 3.3 | 0.0 | 0.38 | 1.39 | 4.18 | 84.4 | 4.5 | 14.1 | 0.0 | 6.9 |
| 3.4 | 4.34 | 31.2 | 6.92 | 1.6 | -0.1 | -1.10 | -15.32 | 3.80 | 107.5 | 5.6 | 29.1 | 0.0 | 1.0 |
| 9.7 | 0.55 | 0.7 | -0.29 | 1.5 | 0.0 | 0.06 | 0.20 | 3.72 | 95.6 | 6.7 | 82.8 | 0.0 | 6.3 |
| 8.1 | 0.11 | 1.5 | 0.30 | 1.7 | 0.0 | 0.07 | 0.80 | 3.67 | 93.3 | 4.4 | 23.7 | 8.4 | 3.2 |
| 9.4 | 0.35 | 2.4 | 0.12 | 3.8 | 0.6 | 0.49 | 5.52 | 2.85 | 82.1 | 4.5 | 18.2 | 7.7 | 6.2 |
| 3.5 | 2.22 | 18.8 | 0.39 | 3.8 | 8.5 | 0.41 | 3.77 | 3.73 | 83.0 | 1.4 | 6.2 | 17.6 | 7.6 |
| 9.8 | 0.29 | 1.4 | 0.03 | 9.4 | 65.4 | 1.26 | 9.29 | 2.47 | 60.7 | 3.5 | 26.0 | 13.2 | 10.0 |
| 10.0 | 0.00 | 0.0 | -0.01 | 2.4 | 0.1 | 0.20 | 2.41 | 2.65 | 92.9 | 3.8 | 25.7 | 12.9 | 4.0 |
| 6.0 | 1.43 | 11.7 | 0.23 | 6.1 | 1.7 | 0.89 | 10.22 | 4.79 | 83.3 | 4.4 | 20.3 | 5.2 | 6.3 |
| 8.5 | 0.00 | 0.0 | 0.00 | 0.1 | 0.0 | -0.41 | -1.62 | 2.32 | 126.7 | 5.4 | 53.2 | 0.0 | 6.2 |
| 10.0 | 0.35 | 1.7 | 0.08 | 3.2 | 2.3 | 0.32 | 3.10 | 2.62 | 87.7 | 3.8 | 24.8 | 9.7 | 7.4 |
| 7.1 | 0.83 | 7.4 | 0.21 | 6.2 | 7.6 | 0.96 | 12.10 | 3.10 | 69.4 | 3.8 | 14.2 | 9.4 | 6.2 |
| 10.0 | 0.00 | 0.0 | 0.00 | 4.1 | 0.1 | 0.64 | 1.65 | 2.05 | 64.3 | 6.6 | 76.1 | 2.4 | 7.6 |
| 10.0 | 0.00 | 0.0 | 0.00 | 0.0 | -0.1 | -1.57 | -14.33 | 1.71 | 174.1 | 5.1 | 26.3 | 10.7 | 4.4 |
| 3.7 | 4.85 | 20.9 | 1.39 | 8.7 | 0.2 | 1.15 | 8.91 | 6.08 | 61.2 | 4.9 | 19.1 | 0.0 | 7.1 |
| 9.2 | 0.36 | 1.3 | -0.06 | 3.4 | 0.4 | 0.37 | 2.25 | 1.33 | 75.7 | 4.0 | 13.3 | 0.0 | 7.9 |
| 1.2 | 4.98 | 30.6 | -0.64 | 6.1 | 0.3 | 2.14 | 28.13 | 7.96 | 83.5 | 5.3 | 35.1 | 3.7 | 4.1 |
| 4.4 | 3.05 | 17.8 | 0.08 | 4.9 | 0.1 | 0.50 | 5.33 | 4.23 | 84.2 | 4.4 | 19.8 | 5.3 | 4.3 |
| 10.0 | 0.58 | 0.9 | 0.38 | 4.3 | 0.1 | 0.55 | 4.37 | 1.37 | 58.5 | 5.0 | 22.5 | 0.0 | 6.1 |
| 9.7 | 0.30 | 1.9 | 0.20 | 5.7 | 4.8 | 0.77 | 8.11 | 3.35 | 81.2 | 3.5 | 12.1 | 6.3 | 7.6 |
| 5.0 | 0.53 | 9.6 | 0.89 | 5.7 | 0.2 | 0.71 | 5.42 | 4.85 | 68.0 | 2.2 | 13.2 | 22.6 | 7.1 |
| 3.5 | 1.63 | 17.5 | 0.16 | 1.9 | 0.0 | 0.30 | 4.29 | 4.31 | 92.2 | 3.8 | 14.5 | 0.0 | 1.0 |
| 8.7 | 0.00 | 0.0 | 0.00 | 0.3 | 0.0 | -1.01 | -6.52 | 5.37 | 127.3 | 4.4 | 54.6 | 31.3 | 5.3 |
| 6.9 | 0.34 | 4.1 | 0.22 | 8.2 | 4.5 | 1.14 | 10.67 | 2.49 | 61.4 | 1.7 | 2.6 | 13.6 | 9.0 |
| 8.7 | 0.74 | 3.7 | 0.09 | 6.8 | 16.3 | 1.01 | 9.70 | 2.43 | 61.1 | 3.3 | 10.6 | 13.1 | 8.3 |
| 4.4 | 5.38 | 13.8 | 0.00 | 2.0 | 0.0 | 0.24 | 1.09 | 3.92 | 88.9 | 6.7 | 56.9 | 0.0 | 7.1 |
| 10.0 | 0.60 | 0.6 | -0.15 | 0.0 | 0.0 | -0.65 | -2.95 | 1.46 | 147.4 | 5.8 | 45.9 | 0.0 | 5.3 |
| 8.6 | 0.01 | 0.1 | 0.25 | 3.9 | 0.3 | 0.64 | 8.31 | 3.28 | 84.0 | 5.0 | 27.3 | 2.1 | 2.8 |
| 10.0 | 0.00 | 0.0 | -0.09 | 2.4 | 0.0 | 0.13 | 1.54 | 2.36 | 96.1 | 6.9 | 43.3 | 0.0 | 3.1 |
| 10.0 | 0.02 | 0.1 | 0.05 | 3.0 | 0.4 | 0.27 | 2.41 | 1.81 | 82.6 | 7.5 | 80.3 | 0.0 | 7.4 |
| 8.8 | 0.60 | 3.2 | 0.46 | 5.1 | 3.8 | 0.81 | 9.29 | 3.38 | 76.1 | 4.3 | 17.5 | 8.8 | 6.4 |
| 2.4 | 3.11 | 33.6 | 0.37 | 2.3 | 0.2 | 0.21 | 3.86 | 4.83 | 90.4 | 3.9 | 14.9 | 0.5 | 4.2 |
| 9.4 | 0.83 | 2.9 | 0.65 | 5.6 | 0.8 | 0.90 | 6.55 | 3.24 | 62.2 | 3.3 | 20.0 | 17.4 | 9.1 |
| 4.4 | 2.35 | 12.7 | -0.24 | 1.5 | 0.0 | -0.08 | -0.88 | 4.47 | 103.3 | 6.5 | 53.7 | 0.0 | 1.0 |
| 7.3 | 1.46 | 6.4 | 0.40 | 3.6 | 0.4 | 0.52 | 4.28 | 2.79 | 87.4 | 4.9 | 28.1 | 5.4 | 7.4 |
| 6.1 | 0.39 | 4.9 | 0.30 | 5.2 | 0.3 | 0.88 | 9.66 | 3.89 | 77.0 | 4.3 | 25.9 | 6.5 | 5.0 |
| 3.7 | 3.47 | 21.7 | 0.20 | 3.7 | 0.0 | 0.51 | 4.84 | 5.23 | 89.7 | 4.5 | 24.3 | 0.0 | 4.6 |
| 9.1 | 0.71 | 4.4 | -0.28 | 4.0 | 0.1 | 0.57 | 5.03 | 3.06 | 86.2 | 3.9 | 10.7 | 7.1 | 5.5 |
| 3.7 | 1.18 | 21.1 | 0.75 | 0.5 | -0.3 | -1.20 | -18.59 | 5.01 | 99.7 | 4.1 | 16.6 | 3.2 | 2.1 |
| 6.0 | 5.30 | 15.6 | 0.03 | 3.9 | 0.0 | 0.59 | 2.84 | 3.12 | 81.4 | 4.1 | 25.2 | 0.0 | 3.7 |
| 0.0 | 16.11 | 80.6 | 2.95 | 4.4 | 0.0 | 0.74 | 10.26 | 8.89 | 76.9 | 6.8 | 55.9 | 0.0 | 3.5 |
| 9.0 | 1.48 | 3.3 | 0.95 | 3.2 | 0.1 | 0.53 | 2.88 | 2.90 | 76.9 | 4.5 | 19.4 | 8.2 | 5.9 |
| 9.8 | 0.54 | 1.3 | 0.57 | 3.9 | 0.1 | 0.54 | 3.59 | 3.75 | 86.8 | 6.3 | 56.7 | 2.0 | 6.6 |
| 8.4 | 1.90 | 5.5 | 0.46 | 3.0 | 0.1 | 0.29 | 2.21 | 4.32 | 89.6 | 6.5 | 58.0 | 1.0 | 6.1 |
| 7.2 | 4.62 | 6.4 | 9.52 | 2.8 | 0.0 | -1.47 | -8.22 | 3.06 | 91.9 | 7.0 | 79.6 | 0.0 | 7.1 |
| 6.4 | 0.62 | 5.2 | 0.24 | 2.8 | 0.0 | 0.23 | 2.74 | 3.80 | 89.8 | 3.1 | 7.4 | 7.9 | 2.3 |
| 7.1 | 0.94 | 7.5 | 0.76 | 4.6 | 3.3 | 0.75 | 6.80 | 3.19 | 71.5 | 3.1 | 12.7 | 15.0 | 6.8 |
| 9.2 | 0.64 | 2.6 | 0.86 | 5.6 | 4.3 | 0.89 | 7.72 | 4.30 | 77.7 | 6.5 | 39.7 | 4.4 | 7.4 |
| 7.6 | 0.68 | 4.3 | 1.05 | 10.0 | 3.2 | 1.49 | 12.49 | 5.42 | 69.3 | 2.1 | 9.6 | 16.2 | 8.1 |
| 8.5 | 0.38 | 2.3 | 0.25 | 4.4 | 2.5 | 0.54 | 5.61 | 4.04 | 88.0 | 4.3 | 16.3 | 6.6 | 6.7 |
| 9.5 | 0.78 | 2.6 | 0.32 | 2.9 | 0.2 | 0.26 | 2.06 | 2.33 | 87.9 | 4.9 | 38.2 | 1.9 | 8.0 |
| 4.0 | 0.77 | 10.9 | 0.52 | 3.8 | 0.2 | 0.46 | 5.89 | 3.96 | 83.9 | 1.7 | 10.0 | 22.1 | 3.1 |
| 7.2 | 0.32 | 0.6 | 17.76 | 2.4 | 0.0 | 0.09 | 0.45 | 5.40 | 72.3 | 5.7 | 26.3 | 0.0 | 6.2 |
| 2.9 | 2.50 | 14.4 | 0.00 | 3.8 | 0.0 | 0.40 | 4.00 | 5.90 | 93.1 | 5.8 | 35.8 | 0.0 | 5.3 |
| 3.9 | 0.82 | 6.4 | 0.09 | 1.3 | 0.0 | -0.27 | -3.35 | 4.58 | 102.0 | 4.3 | 11.1 | 0.0 | 1.0 |
| 10.0 | 0.46 | 1.1 | 0.17 | 9.2 | 8.0 | 1.36 | 12.90 | 2.04 | 50.8 | 5.0 | 9.9 | 2.7 | 10.0 |
| 9.5 | 0.54 | 1.9 | 0.41 | 2.3 | 0.0 | 0.17 | 0.98 | 4.34 | 92.5 | 4.1 | 9.0 | 0.0 | 5.5 |
| 9.4 | 0.00 | 0.0 | 0.00 | 5.0 | 0.2 | 0.73 | 4.86 | 2.37 | 81.1 | 4.0 | 16.4 | 8.7 | 7.8 |
| 10.0 | 0.00 | 0.0 | 0.93 | 2.7 | 0.0 | 0.26 | 3.08 | 1.43 | 78.2 | 5.0 | 14.8 | 0.0 | 3.8 |

www.weissratings.com
183
Data as of September 30, 2015

| Name | City | State | Rating | 2014 Rating | 2013 Rating | Total Assets ($Mil) | One Year Asset Growth | Comm-ercial Loans | Cons-umer Loans | Mort-gage Loans | Secur-ities | Capital-ization Index | Net Worth Ratio |
|---|---|---|---|---|---|---|---|---|---|---|---|---|---|
| | | | | | | | | Asset Mix (As a % of Total Assets) | | | | | |
| SCHOOL DISTRICT 3 FCU | Colorado Springs | CO | B- | B- | B- | 22.4 | 4.73 | 3.8 | 11.6 | 28.3 | 6.3 | 10.0 | 12.1 |
| SCHOOL DISTRICTS 162/163 EMPL FCU | Park Forest | IL | C | C | C | 1.8 | -1.90 | 0.0 | 22.1 | 0.0 | 0.0 | 10.0 | 22.9 |
| SCHOOL EMPL CU | Superior | WI | D+ | D+ | D | 2.2 | -1.93 | 0.0 | 56.3 | 0.0 | 0.0 | 10.0 | 16.0 |
| SCHOOL EMPL LORAIN COUNTY CU INC | Elyria | OH | C- | C | C | 155.7 | 0.33 | 0.0 | 17.2 | 8.9 | 31.9 | 9.1 | 10.5 |
| SCHOOL SYSTEMS FCU | Troy | NY | C | C | C | 76.1 | 2.37 | 0.0 | 12.5 | 10.1 | 21.8 | 5.7 | 7.7 |
| SCHOOLS FCU | Rancho Dominguez | CA | C+ | C+ | C+ | 113.3 | 2.86 | 0.8 | 25.1 | 28.6 | 23.4 | 8.8 | 10.3 |
| SCHOOLS FINANCIAL CU | Sacramento | CA | A- | A- | A- | 1591.0 | 5.66 | 3.3 | 37.6 | 11.2 | 35.6 | 9.0 | 10.4 |
| SCHOOLSFIRST FCU | Santa Ana | CA | A | A | A | 11438.8 | 9.73 | 1.0 | 20.3 | 21.9 | 43.0 | 10.0 | 11.7 |
| SCHUYLKILL FCU | Pottsville | PA | D- | D- | D | 14.1 | -2.27 | 0.0 | 14.7 | 8.2 | 57.8 | 5.7 | 7.7 |
| SCIENCE PARK FCU | New Haven | CT | D | D | C- | 4.8 | -1.93 | 0.0 | 25.7 | 0.0 | 0.0 | 10.0 | 28.1 |
| SCIENT FCU | Groton | CT | C | C+ | C+ | 232.3 | 5.48 | 1.2 | 44.8 | 27.1 | 4.4 | 6.5 | 8.6 |
| SCIENTIFIC RESEARCH PARTNERS CU | Kansas City | MO | E+ | E+ | E+ | 1.1 | -0.09 | 0.0 | 70.8 | 0.0 | 0.0 | 5.7 | 7.8 |
| ▲ SCOTT & WHITE EMPL CU | Temple | TX | D- | E | E- | 41.1 | 5.39 | 0.3 | 22.9 | 6.9 | 11.5 | 4.4 | 6.4 |
| SCOTT ASSOCIATES CU INC | Marysville | OH | C | C | C | 10.7 | -6.44 | 0.0 | 41.9 | 0.0 | 0.9 | 10.0 | 13.3 |
| SCOTT CU | Edwardsville | IL | B- | B+ | A- | 1017.0 | 0.88 | 2.3 | 61.7 | 10.0 | 0.0 | 6.8 | 8.8 |
| SCRANTON TIMES DOWNTOWN FCU | Scranton | PA | D+ | D+ | C- | 11.2 | -3.24 | 5.7 | 11.7 | 49.5 | 0.0 | 8.2 | 9.8 |
| ▲ SCURRY COUNTY SCHOOL FCU | Snyder | TX | B- | C+ | D | 11.2 | 7.03 | 0.0 | 43.0 | 0.0 | 0.0 | 10.0 | 16.4 |
| SEA AIR FCU | Seal Beach | CA | D+ | C- | C | 143.5 | -1.29 | 4.1 | 12.3 | 5.8 | 14.1 | 10.0 | 25.7 |
| SEA COMM FCU | Massena | NY | A | A | A | 494.8 | 2.90 | 2.9 | 15.9 | 18.3 | 47.2 | 10.0 | 13.0 |
| ▲ SEA WEST COAST GUARD FCU | Oakland | CA | B- | C+ | C | 337.8 | 1.14 | 0.3 | 9.1 | 25.8 | 6.6 | 10.0 | 19.5 |
| SEABOARD FCU | Bucksport | ME | C+ | C+ | C+ | 117.4 | 4.90 | 6.6 | 20.5 | 37.9 | 13.4 | 7.1 | 9.1 |
| SEABOARD GATEWAY FCU | Evansville | IN | C | C- | C+ | 1.5 | 2.65 | 0.0 | 50.2 | 0.0 | 0.0 | 10.0 | 22.6 |
| SEAGOVILLE FCU | Seagoville | TX | C+ | C+ | B- | 16.5 | 1.41 | 0.0 | 27.5 | 0.0 | 0.0 | 10.0 | 15.2 |
| SEAPORT FCU | Elizabeth | NJ | B+ | B+ | B | 61.4 | 6.92 | 0.0 | 31.8 | 8.9 | 0.8 | 10.0 | 15.3 |
| ▼ SEARS SPOKANE EMPL FCU | Spokane | WA | E+ | E+ | E+ | 4.9 | 4.86 | 0.0 | 50.2 | 8.5 | 0.0 | 7.0 | 9.0 |
| ▼ SEASONS FCU | Middletown | CT | D+ | C+ | B- | 153.9 | 5.50 | 0.0 | 46.7 | 8.1 | 5.4 | 5.8 | 7.9 |
| SEATTLE METROPOLITAN CU | Seattle | WA | B+ | B | B | 676.1 | 11.59 | 10.8 | 24.4 | 28.9 | 16.0 | 8.4 | 9.9 |
| SEBASTICOOK VALLEY FCU | Pittsfield | ME | B- | B- | C+ | 87.3 | 8.13 | 1.5 | 23.0 | 33.7 | 0.0 | 7.8 | 9.5 |
| SECNY FCU | Syracuse | NY | B | B | B- | 159.8 | 5.20 | 0.0 | 13.6 | 33.0 | 5.0 | 6.0 | 8.0 |
| SECTION 705 FCU | Lafayette | LA | C+ | C | C+ | 32.0 | 0.76 | 0.0 | 40.2 | 20.9 | 17.4 | 8.7 | 10.1 |
| SECURED ADVANTAGE FCU | Simpsonville | SC | C | C | C | 79.5 | 0.73 | 0.0 | 20.0 | 19.1 | 2.3 | 10.0 | 12.2 |
| ▲ SECURITY CU | Flint | MI | B- | C+ | C+ | 391.7 | 2.15 | 2.8 | 31.5 | 9.0 | 32.6 | 6.9 | 8.9 |
| ▼ SECURITY FIRST FCU | Edinburg | TX | D+ | C | C+ | 374.1 | -0.21 | 0.6 | 44.8 | 24.7 | 6.2 | 7.2 | 9.1 |
| SECURITY PLUS FCU | Russellville | KY | D+ | D | D | 1.0 | -2.12 | 0.0 | 46.9 | 0.0 | 0.0 | 10.0 | 33.2 |
| SECURITY SERVICE FCU | San Antonio | TX | B- | B- | B- | 9052.4 | 11.17 | 3.8 | 73.1 | 17.6 | 0.1 | 6.2 | 8.2 |
| SECURITYPLUS FCU | Woodlawn | MD | C- | D+ | D+ | 358.1 | 1.02 | 6.2 | 32.5 | 18.8 | 24.5 | 7.5 | 9.3 |
| SECURTRUST FCU | Southaven | MS | B+ | B | B | 18.4 | 10.36 | 1.6 | 44.4 | 21.2 | 0.0 | 10.0 | 22.2 |
| SEG FCU | Laurel | MT | C+ | C+ | C+ | 14.2 | 5.19 | 0.0 | 46.7 | 4.9 | 0.0 | 10.0 | 12.6 |
| SEI FCU | Pocatello | ID | D+ | C- | C | 18.5 | 11.53 | 0.4 | 45.9 | 0.0 | 0.0 | 8.9 | 10.2 |
| SELCO COMMUNITY CU | Eugene | OR | A- | A- | A- | 1272.6 | 6.16 | 10.7 | 40.9 | 22.0 | 8.5 | 9.4 | 10.6 |
| SELECT EMPL CU | Sterling | IL | C- | C- | C- | 39.5 | 6.71 | 0.0 | 27.1 | 27.8 | 0.0 | 5.2 | 7.2 |
| SELECT FCU | San Antonio | TX | B | B | B | 37.4 | 8.44 | 5.2 | 61.5 | 16.6 | 0.0 | 10.0 | 14.0 |
| SELECT SEVEN FCU | Johnson City | TN | B- | B | B | 48.9 | 5.44 | 0.0 | 56.1 | 17.2 | 0.0 | 10.0 | 11.9 |
| SELF MEMORIAL HOSPITAL FCU | Greenwood | SC | C+ | C | C | 13.8 | 4.83 | 0.0 | 55.0 | 0.0 | 0.0 | 10.0 | 13.0 |
| SELF RELIANCE (NJ) FCU | Clifton | NJ | B | B | B | 98.7 | 2.85 | 5.0 | 0.9 | 51.4 | 11.3 | 10.0 | 15.9 |
| SELF RELIANCE BALTIMORE FCU | Baltimore | MD | E | E- | E- | 18.3 | -4.10 | 0.0 | 2.7 | 45.5 | 6.7 | 6.3 | 8.3 |
| SELF RELIANCE NY FCU | New York | NY | A | A | A | 1147.0 | 7.40 | 28.9 | 0.3 | 60.7 | 27.3 | 10.0 | 16.8 |
| ▲ SELF-HELP CU | Durham | NC | B- | C- | C- | 670.4 | 0.04 | 8.1 | 7.4 | 53.9 | 7.4 | 10.0 | 13.8 |
| ▲ SELF-HELP FCU | Durham | NC | B- | C- | D | 606.0 | 10.93 | 8.7 | 9.3 | 58.4 | 1.8 | 10.0 | 18.0 |
| SELFRELIANCE UKRAINIAN AMERICAN FCU | Chicago | IL | A- | B+ | B | 435.8 | 2.04 | 17.0 | 1.5 | 44.5 | 40.4 | 10.0 | 21.0 |
| SELH FCU | Mandeville | LA | D | D | D | 3.0 | -4.34 | 0.0 | 30.9 | 0.1 | 0.0 | 10.0 | 21.3 |
| SEMICONDUCTOR OF MAINE FCU | South Portland | ME | C | C+ | C+ | 14.4 | 4.10 | 0.0 | 24.5 | 34.6 | 0.0 | 10.0 | 13.2 |
| SEMINOLE PUBLIC SCHOOLS FCU | Seminole | TX | C- | C- | C | 7.8 | -5.32 | 0.0 | 42.7 | 0.8 | 0.0 | 10.0 | 19.6 |
| SENECA NATION OF INDIANS FCU | Irving | NY | D | U | U | <1 | NA | 0.0 | 12.4 | 0.0 | 0.0 | 10.0 | 61.9 |
| SENTINEL FCU | Ellsworth AFB | SD | C+ | C+ | C+ | 105.6 | 77.80 | 12.9 | 28.9 | 16.9 | 0.5 | 6.8 | 8.8 |
| SENTRY CU | Stevens Point | WI | B+ | B+ | B+ | 89.4 | 2.27 | 0.0 | 15.0 | 37.3 | 0.0 | 10.0 | 15.1 |
| SEQUOIA FCU | Redwood City | CA | B- | C+ | C- | 28.6 | 2.30 | 0.0 | 13.8 | 15.1 | 0.0 | 10.0 | 12.7 |
| SERVCO FCU | Bensalem | PA | D+ | D+ | D+ | 2.3 | -10.27 | 0.0 | 12.0 | 0.0 | 0.0 | 10.0 | 21.3 |
| SERVICE 1 FCU | Norton Shores | MI | A | A | A | 102.8 | 4.07 | 0.0 | 39.0 | 9.9 | 3.8 | 10.0 | 16.6 |
| ▲ SERVICE 1ST CU | Tampa | FL | B- | C | C- | 17.1 | -1.39 | 1.3 | 38.2 | 22.6 | 0.0 | 10.0 | 11.5 |

| Asset Quality Index | Non-Performing Loans as a % of Total Loans | as a % of Capital | Net Charge-Offs Avg Loans | Profitability Index | Net Income ($Mil) | Return on Assets | Return on Equity | Net Interest Spread | Overhead Efficiency Ratio | Liquidity Index | Liquidity Ratio | Hot Money Ratio | Stability Index |
|---|---|---|---|---|---|---|---|---|---|---|---|---|---|
| 9.9 | 0.08 | 0.3 | 0.23 | 4.0 | 0.1 | 0.50 | 4.15 | 2.74 | 80.8 | 5.4 | 46.7 | 2.4 | 6.5 |
| 10.0 | 0.77 | 0.7 | 0.00 | 2.7 | 0.0 | 0.15 | 0.67 | 3.95 | 94.6 | 7.7 | 88.8 | 0.0 | 5.7 |
| 4.3 | 3.09 | 11.9 | -0.10 | 2.8 | 0.0 | 0.38 | 2.71 | 3.64 | 88.9 | 4.6 | 23.3 | 0.0 | 6.5 |
| 9.0 | 1.11 | 3.9 | 0.37 | 2.0 | 0.0 | 0.03 | 0.28 | 2.90 | 95.7 | 5.2 | 27.7 | 5.8 | 6.1 |
| 6.6 | 1.76 | 9.1 | 0.09 | 2.8 | 0.1 | 0.23 | 3.12 | 2.50 | 88.5 | 4.7 | 24.5 | 1.8 | 3.3 |
| 7.9 | 0.83 | 6.6 | 0.43 | 3.2 | 0.3 | 0.34 | 3.38 | 4.23 | 82.5 | 4.3 | 18.7 | 3.6 | 6.9 |
| 9.8 | 0.32 | 1.7 | 0.35 | 5.9 | 10.0 | 0.85 | 8.11 | 2.72 | 71.5 | 4.3 | 13.5 | 1.6 | 7.2 |
| 9.6 | 0.52 | 2.2 | 0.37 | 6.7 | 80.4 | 0.96 | 8.30 | 2.40 | 65.9 | 3.3 | 19.4 | 16.6 | 9.2 |
| 9.2 | 0.12 | 2.5 | 0.29 | 1.5 | 0.0 | 0.11 | 1.48 | 3.24 | 100.0 | 4.8 | 13.1 | 0.0 | 2.3 |
| 10.0 | 0.67 | 0.7 | -0.31 | 0.0 | -0.1 | -1.96 | -6.98 | 2.69 | 174.2 | 5.6 | 32.2 | 0.0 | 5.9 |
| 8.1 | 0.45 | 4.9 | 0.78 | 1.4 | -0.3 | -0.16 | -1.96 | 3.72 | 86.3 | 2.5 | 9.4 | 10.5 | 5.2 |
| 3.1 | 2.15 | 18.3 | 0.17 | 1.9 | 0.0 | 0.00 | 0.00 | 4.72 | 100.0 | 4.6 | 26.5 | 0.0 | 1.0 |
| 8.4 | 0.73 | 4.7 | 0.09 | 3.3 | 0.2 | 0.65 | 11.92 | 2.63 | 83.4 | 5.6 | 31.3 | 0.8 | 2.2 |
| 9.7 | 0.63 | 2.2 | 0.35 | 2.5 | 0.0 | 0.23 | 1.80 | 2.98 | 90.0 | 4.4 | 24.6 | 1.1 | 5.7 |
| 4.9 | 1.17 | 10.0 | 1.32 | 4.0 | 5.2 | 0.65 | 7.99 | 3.62 | 65.6 | 3.4 | 16.1 | 10.0 | 5.9 |
| 3.7 | 4.07 | 26.3 | -0.06 | 2.4 | 0.0 | 0.12 | 1.23 | 4.81 | 97.4 | 5.7 | 36.9 | 0.0 | 4.6 |
| 8.0 | 2.21 | 7.0 | 1.38 | 7.0 | 0.1 | 1.09 | 6.75 | 4.84 | 62.7 | 2.6 | 23.3 | 24.8 | 5.7 |
| 10.0 | 1.19 | 0.9 | 1.07 | 0.5 | -0.4 | -0.36 | -1.42 | 1.95 | 104.3 | 3.9 | 32.3 | 17.1 | 7.0 |
| 8.2 | 1.06 | 3.8 | 0.39 | 5.4 | 2.8 | 0.76 | 5.89 | 3.12 | 74.3 | 3.6 | 13.1 | 9.4 | 8.6 |
| 10.0 | 0.38 | 0.7 | 0.08 | 3.5 | 1.5 | 0.58 | 3.01 | 1.98 | 72.9 | 4.3 | 19.9 | 6.8 | 7.3 |
| 5.1 | 2.34 | 19.3 | 0.19 | 3.0 | 0.2 | 0.21 | 2.22 | 3.74 | 91.5 | 3.8 | 16.4 | 6.3 | 6.0 |
| 8.5 | 0.00 | 0.0 | -0.18 | 5.0 | 0.0 | 0.85 | 3.66 | 5.41 | 104.1 | 5.7 | 57.9 | 0.0 | 7.4 |
| 9.7 | 1.05 | 2.2 | 0.22 | 2.6 | 0.0 | 0.28 | 1.87 | 2.21 | 86.4 | 5.5 | 44.3 | 0.0 | 7.2 |
| 9.6 | 0.80 | 2.4 | 0.38 | 5.4 | 0.3 | 0.73 | 4.88 | 3.82 | 78.9 | 4.4 | 24.9 | 6.5 | 7.0 |
| 3.1 | 1.52 | 11.7 | 0.45 | 0.5 | 0.0 | -0.32 | -3.55 | 3.62 | 124.1 | 5.0 | 25.7 | 0.0 | 2.8 |
| 4.1 | 1.22 | 17.4 | 0.88 | 1.2 | -0.5 | -0.46 | -6.30 | 5.17 | 93.0 | 3.3 | 7.6 | 5.2 | 3.4 |
| 7.4 | 0.80 | 6.3 | 0.20 | 5.8 | 2.8 | 0.59 | 5.75 | 3.51 | 84.8 | 3.4 | 9.9 | 4.7 | 7.1 |
| 5.4 | 0.99 | 11.2 | 0.32 | 5.2 | 0.4 | 0.60 | 6.38 | 4.03 | 79.9 | 2.0 | 8.8 | 14.7 | 5.0 |
| 9.5 | 0.40 | 3.2 | 0.08 | 4.1 | 0.7 | 0.54 | 6.97 | 3.19 | 82.6 | 4.2 | 19.7 | 4.6 | 4.8 |
| 7.1 | 0.91 | 5.9 | 0.72 | 2.7 | 0.0 | 0.16 | 1.60 | 4.06 | 83.2 | 3.7 | 10.5 | 3.3 | 4.8 |
| 7.9 | 1.60 | 6.1 | 0.24 | 2.0 | 0.1 | 0.08 | 0.65 | 2.48 | 96.5 | 3.8 | 22.0 | 9.7 | 5.8 |
| 8.1 | 0.66 | 3.9 | 0.63 | 3.9 | 1.5 | 0.51 | 5.84 | 3.52 | 85.9 | 4.5 | 15.7 | 0.9 | 4.4 |
| 5.6 | 1.17 | 11.1 | 2.07 | 1.3 | -0.2 | -0.08 | -0.90 | 4.76 | 81.4 | 3.2 | 15.3 | 13.3 | 4.5 |
| 5.3 | 7.57 | 12.4 | 0.71 | 0.4 | 0.0 | -0.52 | -1.56 | 3.92 | 110.3 | 5.4 | 66.4 | 0.0 | 6.5 |
| 4.6 | 0.96 | 11.1 | 0.80 | 5.1 | 53.9 | 0.84 | 10.06 | 3.21 | 64.1 | 0.7 | 2.1 | 30.3 | 6.6 |
| 6.9 | 1.44 | 9.4 | 0.51 | 2.3 | 0.6 | 0.23 | 2.78 | 3.26 | 85.1 | 4.8 | 27.1 | 1.2 | 4.8 |
| 7.8 | 2.33 | 7.2 | 0.31 | 10.0 | 0.3 | 2.06 | 9.26 | 6.31 | 65.0 | 3.6 | 32.7 | 13.3 | 6.3 |
| 5.4 | 1.47 | 7.6 | 0.55 | 4.8 | 0.1 | 0.74 | 5.83 | 4.32 | 77.4 | 4.7 | 24.8 | 4.2 | 6.7 |
| 1.7 | 2.67 | 29.0 | 1.55 | 4.0 | 0.1 | 0.45 | 4.27 | 5.66 | 81.7 | 3.9 | 9.5 | 0.0 | 4.8 |
| 7.9 | 0.37 | 3.3 | 0.28 | 8.1 | 10.7 | 1.15 | 10.94 | 3.27 | 70.0 | 4.0 | 13.5 | 2.4 | 8.0 |
| 5.5 | 1.69 | 12.7 | 0.39 | 4.1 | 0.2 | 0.53 | 7.60 | 3.96 | 82.7 | 5.6 | 37.0 | 2.1 | 2.7 |
| 4.6 | 1.03 | 9.1 | 0.51 | 9.6 | 0.5 | 1.63 | 12.11 | 6.62 | 67.8 | 1.2 | 8.4 | 24.2 | 7.1 |
| 7.7 | 0.27 | 3.8 | 0.35 | 4.0 | 0.1 | 0.19 | 1.56 | 4.74 | 95.6 | 2.6 | 13.9 | 15.1 | 5.5 |
| 3.7 | 3.91 | 19.3 | 0.12 | 3.8 | 0.0 | 0.28 | 2.30 | 6.59 | 72.5 | 5.5 | 55.7 | 12.9 | 7.1 |
| 9.7 | 0.33 | 2.1 | 0.01 | 3.8 | 0.4 | 0.49 | 3.06 | 2.40 | 78.2 | 4.0 | 32.3 | 12.4 | 7.8 |
| 1.7 | 3.47 | 47.8 | 0.50 | 2.7 | 0.1 | 0.37 | 4.72 | 3.09 | 90.3 | 2.9 | 25.2 | 22.6 | 1.0 |
| 9.0 | 0.42 | 2.0 | 0.06 | 6.2 | 8.0 | 0.95 | 5.71 | 1.89 | 45.2 | 2.6 | 24.3 | 30.9 | 10.0 |
| 3.4 | 4.06 | 29.0 | 0.42 | 6.5 | 4.6 | 0.92 | 11.10 | 4.53 | 65.4 | 4.6 | 29.7 | 12.8 | 7.9 |
| 3.7 | 1.42 | 22.6 | 0.24 | 9.4 | 6.5 | 1.43 | 32.44 | 6.54 | 69.4 | 4.5 | 30.3 | 12.9 | 8.6 |
| 7.4 | 1.78 | 7.2 | 0.09 | 5.7 | 2.9 | 0.90 | 4.35 | 2.81 | 70.1 | 3.3 | 8.5 | 13.1 | 8.1 |
| 6.6 | 4.49 | 7.7 | 6.34 | 0.0 | 0.0 | -1.67 | -7.42 | 7.63 | 102.3 | 7.1 | 65.2 | 0.0 | 5.0 |
| 9.9 | 0.00 | 0.0 | 0.33 | 1.5 | 0.0 | -0.09 | -0.70 | 2.83 | 96.5 | 3.4 | 16.0 | 5.5 | 6.5 |
| 9.6 | 0.52 | 1.3 | 0.03 | 1.6 | 0.0 | 0.03 | 0.17 | 3.20 | 98.9 | 4.9 | 44.6 | 0.0 | 6.7 |
| 10.0 | 0.00 | 0.0 | NA | 0.0 | 0.4 | NA | NA | NA | 25.0 | 6.9 | 356.8 | 48.5 | 0.0 |
| 7.0 | 0.60 | 4.7 | 0.35 | 5.8 | 0.5 | 0.97 | 9.74 | 5.95 | 85.0 | 4.3 | 21.2 | 2.0 | 4.4 |
| 10.0 | 0.09 | 0.4 | 0.03 | 4.4 | 0.4 | 0.63 | 4.16 | 2.63 | 81.9 | 4.7 | 29.3 | 4.3 | 7.6 |
| 9.5 | 1.31 | 3.1 | 0.13 | 3.1 | 0.1 | 0.21 | 1.67 | 3.22 | 92.9 | 5.4 | 20.1 | 0.8 | 5.5 |
| 6.7 | 11.57 | 8.1 | -0.32 | 1.8 | 0.0 | 0.06 | 0.27 | 1.84 | 97.6 | 6.6 | 99.5 | 0.0 | 5.4 |
| 9.3 | 0.43 | 2.1 | 0.25 | 6.2 | 0.7 | 0.96 | 5.87 | 3.47 | 80.8 | 4.2 | 26.2 | 3.0 | 9.0 |
| 9.6 | 0.27 | 1.6 | 0.02 | 7.0 | 0.1 | 1.05 | 9.92 | 3.91 | 89.8 | 3.9 | 12.2 | 0.2 | 5.7 |

| Name | City | State | Rating | 2014 Rating | 2013 Rating | Total Assets ($Mil) | One Year Asset Growth | Commercial Loans | Consumer Loans | Mortgage Loans | Securities | Capitalization Index | Net Worth Ratio |
|------|------|-------|--------|-------------|-------------|---------------------|-----------------------|-------------------|----------------|----------------|------------|----------------------|------------------|
| | | | | | | | | Asset Mix (As a % of Total Assets) | | | | | |
| SERVICE 1ST CU | Greenville | TX | C- | D+ | D+ | 52.6 | 1.67 | 0.0 | 41.8 | 3.7 | 0.0 | 8.6 | 10.0 |
| SERVICE 1ST FCU | Danville | PA | B | B | B+ | 269.7 | 9.27 | 8.8 | 29.7 | 23.3 | 4.9 | 6.3 | 8.3 |
| SERVICE CU | Portsmouth | NH | A- | A | A | 2742.9 | 12.66 | 1.4 | 54.3 | 19.4 | 8.6 | 10.0 | 12.4 |
| SERVICE CU | Green Bay | WI | C- | C- | C- | 15.4 | 0.45 | 0.0 | 24.4 | 8.2 | 0.0 | 10.0 | 15.7 |
| ▲ SERVICE FIRST FCU | Sioux Falls | SD | C- | D+ | D+ | 138.3 | 3.21 | 4.7 | 28.6 | 14.0 | 28.4 | 4.7 | 6.8 |
| ▲ SERVICE ONE CU INC | Bowling Green | KY | B+ | B | B | 134.2 | 5.29 | 1.5 | 21.7 | 33.5 | 10.2 | 9.5 | 10.6 |
| SERVICE PLUS CU | Moline | IL | B- | B- | B- | 20.9 | -0.98 | 0.0 | 20.7 | 42.7 | 0.0 | 10.0 | 13.3 |
| SERVICE STATION DEALERS FCU | Philadelphia | PA | D | C- | C- | <1 | 17.48 | 0.0 | 56.8 | 0.0 | 0.0 | 10.0 | 47.1 |
| SERVICES CENTER FCU | Yankton | SD | C+ | C+ | C+ | 54.9 | 9.18 | 0.6 | 18.2 | 19.9 | 7.7 | 6.7 | 8.7 |
| SERVICES CU | Naperville | IL | B | B | B+ | <1 | -8.14 | 0.0 | 7.0 | 0.0 | 0.0 | 10.0 | 67.5 |
| SERVU FCU | Painted Post | NY | A- | A | A | 261.7 | 6.04 | 0.0 | 41.2 | 3.6 | 0.0 | 10.0 | 12.7 |
| SESLOC FCU | San Luis Obispo | CA | B | B- | B | 685.4 | 8.19 | 5.7 | 17.1 | 31.8 | 29.5 | 7.1 | 9.1 |
| SETTLERS FCU | Bruce Crossing | MI | C+ | C+ | C+ | 20.9 | 10.85 | 1.6 | 42.7 | 18.5 | 0.0 | 9.4 | 10.6 |
| SEVEN SEVENTEEN CU | Warren | OH | A | A- | A- | 844.5 | 2.36 | 9.5 | 23.8 | 37.2 | 16.3 | 10.0 | 12.8 |
| SEVIER COUNTY SCHOOLS FCU | Sevierville | TN | C+ | C+ | C+ | 8.3 | 4.13 | 0.0 | 45.0 | 0.0 | 0.0 | 10.0 | 17.6 |
| SEWERAGE & WATER BOARD EMPL FCU | New Orleans | LA | D | D | C- | 6.7 | -4.01 | 0.0 | 41.7 | 0.0 | 0.0 | 10.0 | 13.4 |
| SF BAY AREA EDUCATORS CU | San Francisco | CA | D- | D- | D- | 19.7 | 0.53 | 0.0 | 24.2 | 17.4 | 0.0 | 5.1 | 7.1 |
| SF POLICE CU | San Francisco | CA | A- | A- | B+ | 797.1 | 3.69 | 8.6 | 13.0 | 38.2 | 26.5 | 10.0 | 14.5 |
| SHACOG FCU | Carnegie | PA | E+ | E+ | E+ | 2.3 | 3.14 | 0.0 | 53.4 | 0.0 | 0.0 | 4.9 | 6.9 |
| SHAKER HEIGHTS FCU | Shaker Heights | OH | D | D | D | 2.1 | 3.08 | 0.0 | 27.9 | 0.0 | 0.0 | 10.0 | 13.0 |
| ▼ SHAMROCK FCU | Dumas | TX | C | B- | B- | 47.3 | 0.80 | 0.0 | 61.4 | 0.0 | 0.0 | 10.0 | 12.7 |
| ▼ SHAMROCK FOODS FCU | Phoenix | AZ | D | D+ | D+ | 5.1 | 14.04 | 0.0 | 75.7 | 0.0 | 0.0 | 7.0 | 9.0 |
| SHARE ADVANTAGE CU | Duluth | MN | C | C | C | 38.6 | 4.56 | 5.4 | 13.2 | 24.8 | 3.2 | 6.6 | 8.6 |
| ▲ SHARED RESOURCES CU | Pasadena | TX | C | C | C | 26.5 | 10.11 | 0.0 | 54.6 | 13.0 | 0.0 | 9.1 | 10.4 |
| SHAREFAX CU INC | Batavia | OH | B | B | B | 332.1 | 3.40 | 2.6 | 31.9 | 20.9 | 15.3 | 8.2 | 9.8 |
| SHAREPOINT CU | Hopkins | MN | B | B- | B- | 185.3 | 1.26 | 5.9 | 23.1 | 21.1 | 23.1 | 10.0 | 12.2 |
| ▲ SHARON CU | Sharon | MA | B | B- | B- | 473.1 | 0.62 | 5.2 | 8.7 | 48.3 | 23.1 | 10.0 | 12.1 |
| SHARONVIEW FCU | Fort Mill | SC | A- | A- | A- | 1186.0 | 9.36 | 0.3 | 30.0 | 44.6 | 5.1 | 10.0 | 11.6 |
| ▲ SHAW UNIV FCU | Raleigh | NC | C- | D+ | D+ | <1 | 10.59 | 0.0 | 45.4 | 0.0 | 0.0 | 10.0 | 23.7 |
| SHAW-ROSS EMPL CU | Miami | FL | C+ | C+ | C+ | 6.6 | 2.86 | 0.0 | 0.0 | 0.0 | 56.1 | 10.0 | 11.5 |
| SHAWNEE TVA EMPL FCU | West Paducah | KY | C- | C- | D+ | 6.5 | -6.22 | 0.0 | 28.0 | 0.0 | 0.0 | 10.0 | 16.7 |
| SHEBOYGAN AREA CU | Sheboygan | WI | B- | C+ | C | 44.3 | 10.68 | 0.4 | 31.3 | 14.1 | 0.0 | 10.0 | 11.8 |
| SHEET METAL WORKERS FCU | Indianapolis | IN | D- | E+ | E+ | 7.5 | -3.20 | 0.0 | 31.6 | 0.0 | 0.0 | 7.3 | 9.2 |
| SHELBY COMMUNITY FCU | Shelby | MT | D | D+ | C- | 6.3 | 1.93 | 0.0 | 18.8 | 0.0 | 0.0 | 10.0 | 16.5 |
| SHELBY COUNTY FCU | Memphis | TN | C+ | C+ | C+ | 55.3 | 2.79 | 0.0 | 39.1 | 1.7 | 14.0 | 10.0 | 15.7 |
| SHELBY/BOLIVAR COUNTY FCU | Boyle | MS | B- | C+ | C+ | 2.0 | 0.10 | 0.0 | 35.7 | 0.0 | 0.0 | 10.0 | 25.0 |
| SHELL COMMUNITY FCU | Wood River | IL | C- | C- | C- | 109.4 | 2.31 | 0.1 | 60.0 | 15.7 | 3.4 | 8.4 | 10.0 |
| SHELL FCU | Deer Park | TX | A- | A- | A- | 738.4 | 10.06 | 0.8 | 55.5 | 22.1 | 2.4 | 9.0 | 10.4 |
| SHELL GEISMAR FCU | Gonzales | LA | C | C- | C+ | 29.0 | 2.35 | 0.0 | 28.7 | 2.0 | 26.7 | 10.0 | 11.6 |
| SHELL WESTERN STATES FCU | Martinez | CA | D+ | C- | B- | 97.7 | -1.96 | 1.1 | 4.8 | 4.5 | 26.7 | 6.2 | 8.4 |
| SHELTER INSURANCE FCU | Columbia | MO | C | C | C | 30.1 | 1.02 | 0.0 | 21.3 | 0.0 | 20.0 | 10.0 | 11.4 |
| SHENANGO CHINA AREA FCU | New Castle | PA | C+ | C+ | C+ | 14.2 | -2.43 | 0.0 | 34.9 | 5.1 | 0.0 | 10.0 | 19.3 |
| ▲ SHERCHEM FCU | Ashtabula | OH | C- | D+ | D+ | 3.0 | -3.66 | 0.0 | 41.6 | 0.0 | 0.0 | 10.0 | 16.1 |
| SHERIDAN COMMUNITY FCU | Sheridan | WY | B | B | B | 39.3 | 7.05 | 0.9 | 73.8 | 5.0 | 0.0 | 10.0 | 11.3 |
| SHERWIN FCU | Portland | TX | C- | C | C+ | 9.8 | -11.40 | 0.0 | 32.1 | 0.0 | 0.0 | 10.0 | 27.0 |
| SHERWIN WILLIAMS EMPL CU | South Holland | IL | D | D+ | D+ | 30.4 | 0.93 | 0.0 | 10.7 | 4.2 | 57.9 | 10.0 | 14.7 |
| SHILOH BAPTIST FCU | Waukegan | IL | C- | D+ | D | <1 | -9.69 | 0.0 | 28.4 | 0.0 | 0.0 | 8.0 | 9.7 |
| SHILOH ENGLEWOOD FCU | Chicago | IL | C+ | C | C- | <1 | -1.56 | 0.0 | 0.0 | 0.0 | 0.0 | 10.0 | 29.0 |
| SHIPBUILDERS CU | Manitowoc | WI | B+ | B+ | B+ | 72.5 | 3.62 | 11.2 | 25.6 | 34.0 | 0.0 | 10.0 | 13.1 |
| SHORE TO SHORE COMMUNITY FCU | Trenton | MI | C- | C | C- | 51.6 | 3.16 | 0.3 | 29.2 | 5.2 | 30.9 | 6.4 | 8.4 |
| SHORELINE CU | Manitowoc | WI | C+ | C- | D | 95.1 | 0.86 | 5.7 | 34.5 | 30.3 | 11.8 | 7.8 | 9.5 |
| ▼ SHORELINE FCU | Muskegon | MI | D- | C | C | 17.3 | -6.30 | 0.0 | 17.3 | 19.3 | 0.0 | 6.7 | 8.7 |
| SHOW-ME CU | Mexico | MO | B- | B- | B- | 27.0 | 1.03 | 0.0 | 27.3 | 30.3 | 0.0 | 10.0 | 12.1 |
| SHPE FCU | Greensburg | LA | D- | E+ | E+ | 2.8 | 10.46 | 0.0 | 58.4 | 0.0 | 0.0 | 7.7 | 9.4 |
| SHREVEPORT FCU | Shreveport | LA | B | B | B | 106.8 | 7.08 | 0.1 | 55.0 | 15.0 | 7.0 | 10.0 | 15.4 |
| SHREVEPORT POLICE FCU | Shreveport | LA | E+ | E+ | E+ | 5.4 | -5.10 | 0.0 | 70.7 | 0.0 | 0.0 | 6.6 | 8.6 |
| SHREWSBURY FCU | Shrewsbury | MA | D | C- | C | 124.9 | 3.11 | 1.3 | 15.7 | 17.1 | 25.7 | 5.8 | 7.8 |
| SHUFORD FCU | Hickory | NC | C- | C | C- | 22.1 | -11.57 | 0.3 | 32.4 | 22.7 | 3.4 | 10.0 | 11.9 |
| ▼ SHYANN FCU | Cheyenne | WY | D+ | C | C | 8.5 | 8.08 | 0.0 | 27.5 | 10.5 | 0.0 | 10.0 | 13.0 |
| SIDNEY FCU | Sidney | NY | B | B+ | B+ | 413.4 | 7.13 | 1.4 | 38.0 | 9.4 | 24.1 | 10.0 | 13.2 |

| Asset Quality Index | Non-Performing Loans as a % of Total Loans | Non-Performing Loans as a % of Capital | Net Charge-Offs Avg Loans | Profitability Index | Net Income ($Mil) | Return on Assets | Return on Equity | Net Interest Spread | Overhead Efficiency Ratio | Liquidity Index | Liquidity Ratio | Hot Money Ratio | Stability Index |
|---|---|---|---|---|---|---|---|---|---|---|---|---|---|
| 7.8 | 0.50 | 2.4 | 0.55 | 2.4 | 0.1 | 0.29 | 2.97 | 2.68 | 87.6 | 4.6 | 13.2 | 0.2 | 4.3 |
| 7.1 | 0.60 | 5.7 | 0.27 | 4.4 | 0.9 | 0.47 | 5.54 | 3.86 | 83.5 | 2.9 | 6.6 | 4.2 | 5.7 |
| 8.5 | 0.20 | 1.6 | 0.32 | 5.0 | 13.6 | 0.68 | 5.58 | 2.59 | 80.4 | 2.2 | 6.7 | 16.5 | 8.7 |
| 10.0 | 0.00 | 0.0 | -0.05 | 1.6 | 0.0 | 0.11 | 0.66 | 2.05 | 95.5 | 5.1 | 35.1 | 0.0 | 7.1 |
| 4.9 | 1.11 | 18.7 | 0.07 | 3.2 | 0.4 | 0.39 | 6.91 | 3.26 | 88.6 | 4.6 | 16.3 | 2.8 | 2.0 |
| 9.7 | 0.43 | 2.4 | 0.24 | 5.6 | 0.9 | 0.85 | 8.00 | 4.09 | 79.6 | 3.7 | 15.7 | 10.2 | 6.7 |
| 9.2 | 0.75 | 3.7 | 0.23 | 4.3 | 0.1 | 0.44 | 3.40 | 3.49 | 82.2 | 4.5 | 19.3 | 1.9 | 6.7 |
| 8.3 | 1.09 | 1.4 | -0.78 | 0.0 | 0.0 | -6.24 | -12.29 | 9.96 | 200.0 | 6.5 | 67.3 | 0.0 | 4.7 |
| 9.3 | 0.12 | 0.8 | 0.09 | 3.7 | 0.2 | 0.45 | 5.19 | 2.85 | 88.4 | 4.7 | 36.3 | 0.7 | 4.6 |
| 10.0 | 0.00 | 0.0 | 0.00 | 7.8 | 0.0 | 0.98 | 1.47 | 14.04 | 33.3 | 9.8 | 285.2 | 0.0 | 6.3 |
| 7.5 | 0.82 | 5.1 | 0.16 | 5.0 | 1.3 | 0.68 | 5.43 | 3.39 | 79.7 | 4.3 | 18.4 | 2.4 | 8.3 |
| 7.6 | 1.21 | 7.0 | 0.11 | 6.2 | 5.0 | 0.99 | 11.25 | 2.65 | 70.9 | 4.7 | 17.2 | 5.8 | 6.0 |
| 6.6 | 0.85 | 6.3 | 0.25 | 7.5 | 0.2 | 1.07 | 10.00 | 5.82 | 80.8 | 3.4 | 21.5 | 10.0 | 5.0 |
| 9.0 | 0.45 | 2.5 | 0.36 | 6.9 | 6.6 | 1.03 | 8.42 | 3.95 | 75.8 | 3.6 | 10.7 | 3.2 | 8.6 |
| 8.8 | 0.65 | 1.7 | 0.04 | 3.2 | 0.0 | 0.35 | 2.31 | 2.55 | 84.0 | 6.2 | 58.4 | 1.5 | 7.4 |
| 9.9 | 0.60 | 1.9 | 0.29 | 0.0 | -0.1 | -1.64 | -11.62 | 5.07 | 118.4 | 6.0 | 39.0 | 0.0 | 5.6 |
| 10.0 | 0.06 | 0.4 | 0.02 | 1.4 | 0.0 | -0.03 | -0.38 | 3.04 | 100.9 | 5.1 | 33.9 | 0.0 | 2.4 |
| 8.4 | 0.13 | 2.8 | 0.46 | 4.7 | 3.7 | 0.63 | 4.46 | 3.46 | 78.1 | 3.7 | 10.0 | 8.7 | 8.9 |
| 4.9 | 0.83 | 6.3 | 0.00 | 1.8 | 0.0 | 0.34 | 5.23 | 3.49 | 87.8 | 5.9 | 48.5 | 0.0 | 1.0 |
| 1.7 | 23.05 | 47.3 | 0.00 | 2.0 | 0.0 | 0.13 | 1.00 | 3.36 | 95.4 | 6.2 | 55.7 | 0.0 | 5.6 |
| 8.2 | 0.14 | 0.8 | 0.05 | 0.6 | -0.4 | -1.20 | -9.35 | 1.96 | 142.5 | 4.3 | 25.8 | 5.7 | 6.5 |
| 7.5 | 0.17 | 1.5 | 0.32 | 4.6 | 0.0 | 0.62 | 6.56 | 6.17 | 90.7 | 4.6 | 20.6 | 0.0 | 2.3 |
| 7.7 | 0.03 | 1.6 | 0.05 | 5.5 | 0.3 | 0.90 | 10.78 | 3.94 | 78.7 | 3.9 | 14.7 | 1.0 | 4.5 |
| 5.9 | 0.78 | 5.4 | 0.22 | 3.3 | 0.1 | 0.37 | 3.57 | 3.75 | 91.3 | 3.0 | 19.0 | 8.5 | 4.5 |
| 6.8 | 1.06 | 7.6 | 0.36 | 4.5 | 1.3 | 0.53 | 5.67 | 2.31 | 75.0 | 3.2 | 24.4 | 19.5 | 5.9 |
| 8.9 | 0.56 | 3.1 | 0.19 | 4.4 | 1.0 | 0.71 | 5.82 | 3.28 | 82.3 | 3.3 | 15.9 | 7.2 | 7.1 |
| 9.8 | 0.35 | 1.9 | -0.08 | 4.2 | 2.2 | 0.63 | 5.35 | 2.46 | 79.3 | 3.5 | 11.5 | 7.7 | 7.7 |
| 7.5 | 0.68 | 5.4 | 0.46 | 5.9 | 7.5 | 0.87 | 7.45 | 3.64 | 71.6 | 1.5 | 11.4 | 22.3 | 8.2 |
| 7.2 | 1.48 | 2.7 | 2.53 | 3.2 | 0.0 | 0.23 | 0.95 | 5.04 | 80.0 | 5.4 | 70.4 | 0.0 | 5.2 |
| 10.0 | 0.36 | 0.3 | 1.94 | 2.5 | 0.0 | 0.24 | 2.12 | 0.92 | 40.6 | 8.0 | 88.6 | 0.0 | 5.1 |
| 8.9 | 0.10 | 2.3 | 0.65 | 1.7 | 0.0 | 0.06 | 0.37 | 2.69 | 85.1 | 4.4 | 22.1 | 0.0 | 6.6 |
| 7.3 | 1.44 | 6.6 | -0.32 | 7.2 | 0.4 | 1.33 | 12.10 | 3.68 | 82.7 | 4.6 | 34.0 | 1.6 | 5.0 |
| 5.7 | 1.97 | 7.8 | 0.61 | 2.5 | 0.0 | 0.16 | 1.74 | 2.48 | 87.0 | 4.8 | 25.8 | 0.0 | 1.7 |
| 8.0 | 4.06 | 6.7 | 1.46 | 0.0 | 0.0 | -0.92 | -5.53 | 3.22 | 107.5 | 6.3 | 35.9 | 0.0 | 6.7 |
| 7.5 | 1.80 | 4.8 | 0.94 | 2.7 | 0.1 | 0.24 | 1.57 | 3.72 | 87.8 | 4.8 | 17.9 | 5.2 | 6.3 |
| 9.1 | 2.41 | 3.8 | 0.00 | 8.9 | 0.0 | 1.38 | 5.71 | 9.93 | 82.4 | 7.5 | 74.8 | 0.0 | 5.7 |
| 8.4 | 0.13 | 1.1 | 0.18 | 2.3 | 0.2 | 0.24 | 2.76 | 3.30 | 94.1 | 3.3 | 10.2 | 3.9 | 4.9 |
| 7.3 | 0.38 | 3.4 | 0.47 | 7.5 | 5.4 | 0.99 | 10.11 | 3.92 | 77.4 | 3.1 | 9.9 | 9.9 | 7.4 |
| 7.5 | 1.15 | 4.8 | 0.35 | 2.3 | 0.1 | 0.26 | 2.28 | 3.47 | 92.6 | 4.9 | 22.7 | 3.1 | 5.7 |
| 10.0 | 0.14 | 0.2 | 0.63 | 1.1 | -0.1 | -0.06 | -0.80 | 1.54 | 98.2 | 5.0 | 11.9 | 0.0 | 3.3 |
| 10.0 | 0.00 | 0.0 | 0.00 | 2.4 | 0.1 | 0.23 | 2.00 | 1.89 | 86.8 | 6.6 | 63.9 | 0.0 | 5.9 |
| 7.0 | 2.20 | 5.7 | 0.34 | 2.7 | 0.0 | 0.29 | 1.57 | 3.29 | 87.9 | 3.9 | 21.6 | 7.7 | 7.0 |
| 9.4 | 0.49 | 1.6 | 0.00 | 1.4 | 0.0 | 0.13 | 0.82 | 2.61 | 93.1 | 4.4 | 22.5 | 0.0 | 6.6 |
| 7.7 | 0.15 | 1.1 | 0.30 | 6.2 | 0.3 | 0.86 | 7.63 | 3.98 | 77.7 | 2.3 | 8.6 | 13.6 | 6.2 |
| 9.6 | 0.37 | 0.5 | 5.11 | 0.0 | -0.4 | -4.99 | -18.41 | 3.99 | 115.5 | 5.8 | 42.0 | 0.0 | 4.9 |
| 7.3 | 5.14 | 6.0 | 5.80 | 0.4 | -0.1 | -0.23 | -1.57 | 2.62 | 100.5 | 5.6 | 21.6 | 0.5 | 5.3 |
| 7.1 | 2.41 | 4.9 | 0.00 | 4.4 | 0.0 | 0.00 | 0.00 | 2.75 | 100.0 | 6.6 | 75.9 | 0.0 | 3.7 |
| 10.0 | 0.00 | 0.0 | 0.00 | 2.5 | 0.0 | -0.53 | -1.80 | 1.05 | 200.0 | 8.2 | 136.5 | 0.0 | 7.8 |
| 6.6 | 1.14 | 6.6 | 0.17 | 7.5 | 0.6 | 1.08 | 8.46 | 4.71 | 75.3 | 3.0 | 6.5 | 4.4 | 7.2 |
| 7.0 | 0.74 | 3.6 | 0.38 | 3.3 | 0.1 | 0.35 | 4.38 | 3.51 | 90.2 | 4.6 | 16.7 | 2.4 | 2.9 |
| 5.3 | 0.63 | 5.8 | 0.18 | 4.5 | 0.3 | 0.44 | 4.61 | 3.82 | 91.7 | 3.4 | 6.3 | 1.3 | 4.0 |
| 7.6 | 1.16 | 5.7 | 0.33 | 0.3 | -0.8 | -5.90 | -122.99 | 2.83 | 139.7 | 5.7 | 40.8 | 0.8 | 4.7 |
| 8.5 | 0.53 | 3.1 | 0.22 | 3.2 | 0.1 | 0.29 | 2.42 | 4.40 | 87.4 | 4.6 | 24.2 | 5.8 | 6.1 |
| 0.7 | 7.24 | 45.7 | 0.35 | 7.4 | 0.0 | 1.24 | 13.39 | 6.11 | 69.3 | 3.9 | 16.7 | 0.0 | 4.8 |
| 4.5 | 2.27 | 16.7 | 0.32 | 6.7 | 0.7 | 0.89 | 7.51 | 7.40 | 87.6 | 2.1 | 17.0 | 42.6 | 7.2 |
| 1.8 | 2.87 | 25.9 | 0.12 | 4.6 | 0.0 | 0.98 | 12.04 | 5.49 | 81.5 | 3.5 | 8.1 | 0.0 | 1.0 |
| 8.8 | 0.90 | 5.9 | 0.12 | 0.8 | -0.1 | -0.06 | -0.83 | 2.43 | 101.1 | 4.2 | 24.7 | 3.3 | 4.2 |
| 3.4 | 3.39 | 25.7 | 0.26 | 2.7 | 0.0 | 0.14 | 1.22 | 5.07 | 92.5 | 3.4 | 17.4 | 5.9 | 5.1 |
| 9.8 | 0.00 | 0.0 | 0.21 | 1.0 | 0.0 | -0.51 | -3.80 | 2.69 | 123.1 | 5.8 | 42.1 | 0.0 | 7.0 |
| 8.8 | 0.62 | 3.3 | 0.41 | 4.3 | 1.5 | 0.50 | 3.84 | 3.57 | 85.9 | 3.7 | 6.8 | 3.0 | 8.0 |

| Name | City | State | Rating | 2014 Rating | 2013 Rating | Total Assets ($Mil) | One Year Asset Growth | Commercial Loans | Consumer Loans | Mortgage Loans | Securities | Capitalization Index | Net Worth Ratio |
|---|---|---|---|---|---|---|---|---|---|---|---|---|---|
| SIERRA CENTRAL CU | Yuba City | CA | B+ | A- | A | 772.1 | 5.65 | 0.6 | 45.2 | 18.2 | 1.6 | 10.0 | 11.6 |
| SIERRA PACIFIC FCU | Reno | NV | B- | B- | C+ | 109.4 | 3.04 | 4.8 | 33.6 | 7.1 | 7.7 | 10.0 | 12.6 |
| SIERRA POINT CU | South San Francisc | CA | D | D- | D- | 27.5 | -0.38 | 17.2 | 10.9 | 36.3 | 28.6 | 6.5 | 8.6 |
| ▲ SIGNAL FINANCIAL FCU | Kensington | MD | C | C- | C+ | 316.0 | 2.03 | 20.8 | 19.0 | 46.5 | 17.4 | 10.0 | 11.2 |
| SIGNATURE FCU | Alexandria | VA | A- | A- | B+ | 292.8 | 4.74 | 6.2 | 28.5 | 25.2 | 2.5 | 10.0 | 12.7 |
| SIGNET FCU | Paducah | KY | A- | B+ | A- | 221.1 | 5.89 | 3.7 | 14.9 | 28.7 | 30.9 | 10.0 | 16.5 |
| SIKESTON PUBLIC SCHOOLS CU | Sikeston | MO | C | C | C | 4.9 | -2.93 | 0.0 | 38.7 | 0.0 | 0.0 | 10.0 | 14.1 |
| SIKORSKY FINANCIAL CU | Stratford | CT | B- | B- | B- | 691.5 | 0.25 | 0.0 | 15.7 | 22.1 | 35.9 | 10.0 | 11.0 |
| SILGAN WHITE CAP CU | Downers Grove | IL | C- | C- | D+ | 2.9 | 6.15 | 0.0 | 42.9 | 0.0 | 0.0 | 10.0 | 30.5 |
| ▲ SILVER STATE SCHOOLS CU | Las Vegas | NV | C- | D | D- | 660.7 | 2.46 | 0.3 | 11.5 | 49.5 | 11.5 | 4.9 | 6.9 |
| SILVERADO CU | Angwin | CA | D+ | C- | D+ | 40.7 | -1.49 | 7.7 | 5.3 | 64.0 | 0.0 | 5.9 | 7.9 |
| ▼ SIMPLOT EMPL CU | Caldwell | ID | C- | C | C+ | 18.7 | -1.90 | 0.0 | 50.0 | 0.0 | 7.0 | 10.0 | 15.4 |
| SIMPLY SERVICE FCU | Belle Fourche | SD | C+ | C+ | C+ | 14.6 | 4.04 | 0.0 | 24.6 | 4.9 | 0.0 | 10.0 | 14.3 |
| ▲ SING SING EMPL FCU | Ossining | NY | C+ | C | C+ | 7.3 | 12.23 | 0.0 | 51.8 | 1.8 | 0.0 | 10.0 | 15.7 |
| SINGING RIVER FCU | Moss Point | MS | C | C | C | 194.1 | -0.92 | 9.3 | 46.7 | 35.1 | 0.5 | 6.3 | 8.3 |
| ▲ SIOUX EMPIRE FCU | Sioux Falls | SD | C | C | C+ | 95.1 | 6.75 | 0.2 | 40.6 | 3.8 | 0.0 | 5.6 | 7.6 |
| SIOUX FALLS FCU | Sioux Falls | SD | B+ | A- | A- | 232.5 | 4.96 | 4.7 | 31.4 | 5.4 | 0.0 | 10.0 | 11.3 |
| ▲ SIOUX VALLEY COMMUNITY CU | Sioux City | IA | C+ | C- | D+ | 26.4 | 9.19 | 3.9 | 39.5 | 6.6 | 0.0 | 10.0 | 15.5 |
| SIOUX VALLEY COOP FCU | Watertown | SD | B- | B- | B- | 15.7 | 2.89 | 0.0 | 53.7 | 0.0 | 0.0 | 10.0 | 20.9 |
| SIOUXLAND FCU | South Sioux City | NE | A | A | A | 160.9 | 4.10 | 4.2 | 34.6 | 36.2 | 0.0 | 10.0 | 15.3 |
| ▲ SISKIYOU CENTRAL CU | Yreka | CA | C | C- | C- | 56.7 | -7.58 | 0.0 | 31.8 | 1.4 | 20.3 | 8.9 | 10.2 |
| ▲ SISSETON-WAHPETON FCU | Agency Village | SD | C | C- | C- | 5.7 | 34.15 | 0.0 | 34.9 | 0.0 | 0.0 | 10.0 | 14.6 |
| SISTERS HOSPITAL EMPL FCU | Buffalo | NY | D | D- | D | 7.8 | 6.05 | 0.0 | 30.6 | 2.4 | 77.5 | 5.8 | 7.8 |
| SIU CU | Carbondale | IL | B- | B- | B | 301.1 | 6.35 | 6.1 | 42.4 | 11.5 | 21.7 | 6.5 | 8.5 |
| SIUE CU | Edwardsville | IL | D | D | D | 17.5 | -5.18 | 0.0 | 24.6 | 13.2 | 32.6 | 6.4 | 8.4 |
| SIXTH AVENUE BAPTIST FCU | Birmingham | AL | E+ | E+ | E+ | 4.2 | -6.21 | 0.0 | 34.8 | 16.8 | 0.0 | 6.0 | 8.0 |
| ▲ SJP FCU | Buffalo | NY | C+ | C- | C | 43.4 | 11.02 | 2.5 | 13.3 | 17.3 | 0.0 | 7.5 | 9.3 |
| SKEL-TEX CU | Skellytown | TX | C+ | C+ | C+ | 6.0 | 5.32 | 0.0 | 53.8 | 0.0 | 0.0 | 10.0 | 18.5 |
| SKY FCU | Livingston | MT | C | C- | D+ | 86.6 | -1.11 | 11.1 | 18.2 | 29.3 | 0.7 | 7.7 | 9.5 |
| SKYLINE CU | Nashville | TN | C+ | C+ | C | 16.2 | 2.17 | 0.0 | 33.0 | 6.9 | 0.0 | 10.0 | 18.0 |
| SKYLINE FINANCIAL FCU | Waterbury | CT | D+ | D | C- | 30.9 | -3.20 | 0.0 | 36.0 | 22.9 | 0.0 | 10.0 | 14.8 |
| SKYONE FCU | Hawthorne | CA | B+ | A- | A- | 437.5 | 2.67 | 6.9 | 28.1 | 22.8 | 26.9 | 9.6 | 10.8 |
| SKYWARD CU | Wichita | KS | A | A | A | 254.2 | 7.47 | 2.0 | 27.6 | 7.0 | 52.8 | 10.0 | 17.2 |
| SLO CU | San Luis Obispo | CA | C+ | B- | B- | 33.7 | -2.69 | 0.0 | 7.5 | 0.7 | 45.3 | 10.0 | 16.2 |
| SLOAN PUBLIC SCHOOLS FCU | Cheektowaga | NY | E+ | D | D | 2.2 | 5.98 | 0.0 | 77.2 | 0.0 | 0.0 | 5.3 | 7.3 |
| SM FCU | Shawnee Mission | KS | B | B | A- | 62.7 | 4.38 | 0.0 | 6.8 | 66.6 | 4.7 | 10.0 | 16.5 |
| ▼ SM FCU | Philadelphia | PA | D | D+ | C+ | <1 | -14.00 | 0.0 | 9.3 | 0.0 | 0.0 | 6.1 | 9.3 |
| SMART FCU | Columbus | OH | C- | C | C | 30.7 | 0.07 | 0.0 | 24.5 | 0.0 | 15.7 | 8.9 | 10.2 |
| ▲ SMART FINANCIAL CU | Houston | TX | B+ | B | B+ | 632.2 | 6.33 | 12.3 | 36.4 | 19.3 | 16.5 | 7.5 | 9.3 |
| SMITH & NEPHEW EMPL CU | Memphis | TN | D+ | C- | C | 7.8 | -5.91 | 0.0 | 29.4 | 0.0 | 0.0 | 10.0 | 17.7 |
| SMMH FCU | Pittsburgh | PA | C | C | C | 5.3 | 1.61 | 0.0 | 28.1 | 0.0 | 0.0 | 10.0 | 16.6 |
| SMSD FCU | Buffalo | NY | C+ | C+ | C+ | 2.1 | 1.24 | 0.0 | 37.6 | 0.0 | 0.0 | 10.0 | 17.9 |
| ▲ SMW 104 FCU | San Leandro | CA | C- | D | D | 85.9 | 1.12 | 0.0 | 19.8 | 0.0 | 0.0 | 5.8 | 7.8 |
| SMW FCU | Lino Lakes | MN | C+ | C+ | B- | 71.1 | 14.10 | 1.6 | 47.8 | 23.3 | 0.0 | 9.7 | 10.8 |
| SNAKE RIVER FCU | Twin Falls | ID | C | C | D+ | 6.4 | 8.00 | 0.0 | 74.7 | 0.0 | 0.0 | 10.0 | 11.8 |
| SNO FALLS CU | Snoqualmie | WA | C+ | C- | D+ | 52.3 | 6.95 | 0.0 | 40.2 | 10.9 | 14.2 | 6.7 | 8.7 |
| SNOCOPE CU | Everett | WA | C- | C- | D+ | 49.1 | 2.87 | 0.0 | 51.6 | 16.8 | 4.3 | 6.3 | 8.4 |
| SO-VAL TEL FCU | Fresno | CA | D+ | C | D+ | 15.9 | 2.65 | 0.0 | 18.5 | 2.8 | 61.3 | 7.1 | 9.1 |
| SOCAL FCU | Canoga Park | CA | D | D | C- | <1 | -14.53 | 0.0 | 0.0 | 0.0 | 0.0 | 10.0 | 22.9 |
| SOCIAL SECURITY CU | Birmingham | AL | C+ | C+ | B- | 29.1 | -0.19 | 0.0 | 38.2 | 19.1 | 0.0 | 10.0 | 20.7 |
| SOFTITE COMMUNITY FCU | Martins Ferry | OH | B- | B- | B | 17.6 | 2.11 | 0.0 | 29.0 | 0.0 | 0.0 | 10.0 | 14.6 |
| ▼ SOLANO FIRST FCU | Fairfield | CA | B- | B+ | B+ | 129.9 | 4.01 | 5.9 | 28.5 | 16.8 | 21.1 | 7.0 | 9.0 |
| SOLARITY CU | Yakima | WA | A | A- | A- | 601.9 | 12.42 | 6.5 | 19.6 | 32.9 | 14.8 | 10.0 | 15.0 |
| SOLIDARITY COMMUNITY FCU | Kokomo | IN | C | C | B- | 208.6 | 2.22 | 1.2 | 48.1 | 9.5 | 13.7 | 9.6 | 10.7 |
| SOLON/CHAGRIN FALLS FCU | Solon | OH | C+ | C+ | C+ | 8.1 | -3.64 | 0.0 | 13.1 | 0.0 | 4.4 | 10.0 | 14.3 |
| SOLUTIONS FCU | Elmira | NY | C+ | C+ | C | 21.7 | 4.10 | 0.0 | 40.8 | 0.0 | 0.0 | 9.7 | 10.8 |
| ▲ SOMERSET FCU | Somerset | MA | C | C- | C- | 138.0 | 0.27 | 2.5 | 5.1 | 49.4 | 32.4 | 10.0 | 15.1 |
| SOMERVILLE MASS FIREFIGHTERS FCU | Somerville | MA | C+ | C+ | C+ | 7.2 | 1.74 | 0.0 | 17.9 | 0.0 | 0.0 | 10.0 | 14.5 |
| ▲ SOMERVILLE MUNICIPAL FCU | Somerville | MA | B- | C+ | C- | 38.0 | 5.77 | 0.0 | 6.9 | 33.2 | 0.0 | 10.0 | 14.9 |
| SOMERVILLE SCHOOL EMPL FCU | Somerville | MA | D+ | D+ | D+ | 27.1 | 9.01 | 0.0 | 5.8 | 0.0 | 4.2 | 10.0 | 15.1 |

| Asset Quality Index | Non-Performing Loans as a % of Total Loans | as a % of Capital | Net Charge-Offs Avg Loans | Profitability Index | Net Income ($Mil) | Return on Assets | Return on Equity | Net Interest Spread | Overhead Efficiency Ratio | Liquidity Index | Liquidity Ratio | Hot Money Ratio | Stability Index |
|---|---|---|---|---|---|---|---|---|---|---|---|---|---|
| 7.5 | 0.46 | 3.2 | 0.56 | 5.5 | 4.6 | 0.81 | 7.07 | 4.36 | 72.2 | 4.5 | 29.7 | 12.5 | 7.5 |
| 8.1 | 0.61 | 2.9 | 0.14 | 3.2 | 0.3 | 0.36 | 2.83 | 2.73 | 86.6 | 5.5 | 43.1 | 1.1 | 7.3 |
| 7.9 | 0.40 | 3.1 | 0.16 | 0.8 | 0.0 | -0.03 | -0.34 | 4.37 | 101.9 | 4.5 | 12.7 | 0.0 | 3.3 |
| 6.8 | 0.91 | 5.8 | 0.40 | 2.2 | 0.2 | 0.07 | 0.61 | 3.61 | 93.1 | 3.0 | 8.0 | 7.3 | 6.4 |
| 9.6 | 0.25 | 1.6 | 0.27 | 5.3 | 1.7 | 0.79 | 6.32 | 3.45 | 75.2 | 2.3 | 20.0 | 25.4 | 7.5 |
| 8.9 | 1.17 | 3.6 | 0.16 | 6.0 | 1.6 | 0.98 | 6.08 | 2.59 | 61.9 | 5.1 | 28.4 | 2.5 | 8.6 |
| 9.8 | 0.49 | 1.4 | 0.33 | 3.1 | 0.0 | 0.38 | 2.73 | 2.09 | 78.6 | 4.6 | 40.7 | 8.9 | 6.5 |
| 9.4 | 0.60 | 2.5 | 0.45 | 3.8 | 2.7 | 0.50 | 4.73 | 2.74 | 78.6 | 4.9 | 17.0 | 3.4 | 6.9 |
| 7.6 | 4.92 | 6.9 | 0.36 | 0.9 | 0.0 | -0.19 | -0.61 | 2.27 | 90.5 | 5.5 | 73.4 | 0.0 | 6.0 |
| 5.5 | 1.00 | 19.6 | 0.31 | 9.8 | 10.5 | 2.12 | 37.62 | 3.85 | 66.9 | 4.7 | 24.3 | 7.8 | 5.0 |
| 9.9 | 0.02 | 0.2 | 0.02 | 1.6 | 0.0 | -0.01 | -0.12 | 3.33 | 103.3 | 3.8 | 19.1 | 3.5 | 3.1 |
| 8.0 | 0.63 | 2.3 | 1.39 | 0.4 | -0.1 | -0.99 | -6.40 | 4.02 | 97.3 | 4.6 | 26.4 | 1.4 | 5.9 |
| 7.7 | 1.15 | 3.5 | 0.75 | 3.8 | 0.0 | 0.27 | 1.93 | 3.15 | 90.8 | 5.7 | 52.5 | 4.9 | 6.3 |
| 5.6 | 1.45 | 5.1 | 0.74 | 10.0 | 0.2 | 3.18 | 20.69 | 7.77 | 62.4 | 4.3 | 18.1 | 0.0 | 5.0 |
| 3.4 | 0.75 | 15.8 | 0.81 | 3.8 | 0.5 | 0.35 | 4.33 | 4.73 | 80.4 | 0.9 | 3.2 | 28.3 | 4.9 |
| 6.3 | 0.87 | 6.7 | 0.26 | 2.9 | 0.2 | 0.29 | 3.85 | 3.28 | 94.6 | 4.9 | 28.4 | 2.7 | 3.5 |
| 7.9 | 0.69 | 3.8 | 0.38 | 6.2 | 1.8 | 1.02 | 10.40 | 3.18 | 75.9 | 4.5 | 29.5 | 2.0 | 7.0 |
| 8.2 | 1.58 | 5.6 | 0.24 | 2.9 | 0.1 | 0.33 | 2.10 | 3.53 | 86.0 | 5.1 | 39.5 | 0.0 | 7.1 |
| 6.2 | 1.42 | 4.6 | 0.15 | 10.0 | 0.3 | 2.54 | 12.54 | 4.55 | 43.7 | 3.7 | 18.0 | 0.0 | 8.7 |
| 8.9 | 0.53 | 2.7 | 0.07 | 7.1 | 1.2 | 1.01 | 6.87 | 3.70 | 79.9 | 3.2 | 20.1 | 6.3 | 9.4 |
| 9.4 | 0.54 | 2.1 | 0.03 | 2.9 | 0.2 | 0.35 | 3.54 | 2.78 | 90.9 | 5.1 | 19.6 | 0.0 | 4.5 |
| 8.1 | 3.48 | 7.5 | -1.10 | 4.1 | 0.0 | 0.70 | 6.07 | 13.36 | 87.9 | 7.8 | 91.1 | 0.0 | 5.6 |
| 9.9 | 0.12 | 0.5 | -0.05 | 2.0 | 0.0 | 0.34 | 4.15 | 2.95 | 84.2 | 5.9 | 40.8 | 0.0 | 1.7 |
| 6.6 | 1.18 | 8.0 | 0.44 | 3.9 | 1.1 | 0.48 | 5.57 | 2.95 | 78.8 | 3.8 | 13.6 | 5.6 | 5.3 |
| 6.4 | 1.65 | 9.2 | 0.18 | 3.0 | 0.1 | 0.35 | 4.44 | 3.35 | 88.6 | 4.2 | 12.2 | 0.9 | 3.0 |
| 3.1 | 4.21 | 28.0 | 0.22 | 2.9 | 0.0 | 0.22 | 2.82 | 4.82 | 95.2 | 4.9 | 19.4 | 0.0 | 1.0 |
| 3.5 | 1.18 | 11.6 | 0.29 | 9.8 | 0.5 | 1.44 | 15.85 | 4.78 | 60.8 | 0.7 | 1.8 | 26.5 | 5.4 |
| 4.7 | 3.29 | 10.0 | 0.00 | 6.9 | 0.0 | 0.81 | 4.35 | 3.89 | 63.3 | 4.8 | 25.6 | 0.0 | 4.3 |
| 3.3 | 0.46 | 20.8 | 0.17 | 4.4 | 0.4 | 0.61 | 6.73 | 4.37 | 87.2 | 3.6 | 22.7 | 8.3 | 3.9 |
| 7.4 | 2.50 | 5.9 | 0.14 | 4.9 | 0.1 | 0.90 | 4.91 | 2.41 | 84.1 | 5.2 | 38.1 | 0.0 | 6.2 |
| 9.6 | 0.62 | 2.6 | 0.06 | 1.1 | 0.0 | 0.14 | 0.96 | 3.36 | 96.6 | 3.7 | 15.7 | 4.0 | 6.1 |
| 8.8 | 0.55 | 3.3 | 0.42 | 4.2 | 0.8 | 0.23 | 2.23 | 3.19 | 84.6 | 2.8 | 10.2 | 13.7 | 6.6 |
| 9.9 | 0.46 | 1.3 | 0.26 | 9.5 | 2.6 | 1.35 | 8.39 | 2.86 | 62.6 | 3.4 | 1.7 | 11.5 | 9.7 |
| 10.0 | 0.00 | 0.0 | 0.08 | 2.7 | 0.1 | 0.28 | 1.72 | 2.41 | 87.5 | 5.0 | 21.4 | 8.3 | 6.9 |
| 8.4 | 0.00 | 0.0 | 0.00 | 0.9 | 0.0 | 0.00 | 0.00 | 3.06 | 97.4 | 4.7 | 20.6 | 0.0 | 2.3 |
| 9.5 | 0.15 | 0.7 | 0.01 | 4.1 | 0.3 | 0.60 | 3.61 | 1.27 | 52.7 | 3.1 | 22.7 | 8.2 | 7.8 |
| 6.4 | 0.00 | 0.0 | 0.00 | 0.1 | 0.0 | -2.75 | -24.24 | 0.00 | 300.0 | 8.8 | 103.8 | 0.0 | 4.8 |
| 7.7 | 0.93 | 3.5 | 0.36 | 1.6 | 0.0 | -0.06 | -0.60 | 2.91 | 99.0 | 4.7 | 18.7 | 1.2 | 4.2 |
| 9.4 | 0.19 | 1.7 | 0.59 | 5.3 | 4.1 | 0.88 | 10.78 | 4.06 | 81.5 | 4.4 | 17.4 | 2.0 | 5.3 |
| 9.5 | 0.52 | 0.9 | 0.89 | 0.6 | 0.0 | -0.33 | -2.03 | 3.17 | 100.4 | 5.7 | 57.2 | 3.1 | 5.7 |
| 9.9 | 0.66 | 1.1 | 0.72 | 2.9 | 0.0 | 0.18 | 1.06 | 2.70 | 92.6 | 5.8 | 32.1 | 0.0 | 6.6 |
| 8.5 | 1.71 | 3.6 | 0.00 | 3.7 | 0.0 | 0.49 | 2.84 | 4.33 | 63.0 | 7.5 | 73.7 | 0.0 | 7.2 |
| 9.8 | 0.06 | 0.3 | 0.22 | 2.0 | 0.2 | 0.29 | 3.74 | 2.16 | 90.1 | 4.1 | 32.6 | 11.3 | 2.5 |
| 6.1 | 0.45 | 3.4 | 0.25 | 4.6 | 0.4 | 0.71 | 6.64 | 4.25 | 84.3 | 1.9 | 4.6 | 14.8 | 5.3 |
| 7.3 | 0.00 | 0.0 | 1.21 | 7.6 | 0.0 | 0.91 | 8.03 | 4.83 | 72.9 | 2.0 | 6.1 | 13.1 | 4.3 |
| 5.2 | 0.78 | 6.5 | 0.11 | 6.3 | 0.3 | 0.89 | 10.34 | 3.94 | 88.2 | 4.1 | 24.3 | 0.3 | 3.3 |
| 6.4 | 0.42 | 3.3 | 0.16 | 4.1 | 0.2 | 0.49 | 6.09 | 4.09 | 89.8 | 3.4 | 13.0 | 5.5 | 3.3 |
| 7.3 | 1.81 | 5.6 | 1.18 | 1.2 | -0.1 | -0.46 | -4.97 | 3.17 | 98.8 | 5.4 | 22.8 | 0.0 | 4.4 |
| 10.0 | NA | 0.0 | 0.00 | 0.2 | 0.0 | -0.22 | -1.11 | 2.44 | 112.5 | 9.0 | 128.7 | 0.0 | 6.2 |
| 9.3 | 1.18 | 3.3 | 0.43 | 3.2 | 0.1 | 0.41 | 1.99 | 3.46 | 82.7 | 4.1 | 24.9 | 1.6 | 6.9 |
| 6.9 | 2.11 | 8.2 | -0.16 | 9.0 | 0.3 | 2.11 | 15.31 | 5.54 | 80.0 | 5.8 | 32.0 | 0.0 | 6.3 |
| 7.8 | 0.46 | 3.7 | 0.03 | 3.5 | 0.3 | 0.29 | 3.16 | 4.04 | 92.1 | 4.6 | 19.4 | 2.9 | 5.6 |
| 8.3 | 0.52 | 2.8 | 0.20 | 9.0 | 6.7 | 1.55 | 10.88 | 3.40 | 63.5 | 3.7 | 26.2 | 6.8 | 10.0 |
| 7.9 | 0.47 | 3.5 | 0.33 | 2.8 | 0.6 | 0.36 | 3.57 | 3.22 | 88.1 | 4.1 | 11.9 | 0.5 | 5.7 |
| 9.9 | 0.00 | 0.0 | -0.04 | 4.7 | 0.1 | 0.74 | 5.26 | 2.35 | 60.3 | 4.5 | 26.2 | 0.0 | 7.2 |
| 7.1 | 0.96 | 5.8 | 0.06 | 4.2 | 0.1 | 0.44 | 4.12 | 3.78 | 89.4 | 4.6 | 31.0 | 0.7 | 5.3 |
| 8.5 | 0.22 | 0.9 | 0.15 | 2.1 | 0.3 | 0.32 | 2.35 | 3.17 | 89.6 | 3.7 | 14.3 | 6.8 | 7.7 |
| 10.0 | 0.00 | 0.0 | 0.00 | 3.0 | 0.0 | 0.29 | 2.04 | 2.11 | 84.3 | 5.6 | 34.2 | 0.0 | 7.7 |
| 10.0 | 0.34 | 1.1 | 0.02 | 3.3 | 0.1 | 0.41 | 2.73 | 2.39 | 85.6 | 4.2 | 24.8 | 2.9 | 6.6 |
| 10.0 | 0.33 | 0.8 | 0.00 | 1.1 | 0.0 | -0.08 | -0.52 | 1.93 | 104.0 | 5.1 | 48.6 | 2.6 | 6.8 |

| Name | City | State | Rating | 2014 Rating | 2013 Rating | Total Assets ($Mil) | One Year Asset Growth | Asset Mix (As a % of Total Assets) | | | | Capital- ization Index | Net Worth Ratio |
|---|---|---|---|---|---|---|---|---|---|---|---|---|---|
| | | | | | | | | Comm- ercial Loans | Cons- umer Loans | Mort- gage Loans | Secur- ities | | |
| ▼ SONOMA COUNTY GRANGE CU | Santa Rosa | CA | C- | C | B- | 40.6 | 10.36 | 8.4 | 14.3 | 50.9 | 0.0 | 10.0 | 13.4 |
| ▲ SONOMA FCU | Santa Rosa | CA | C | C- | D+ | 22.6 | 14.12 | 1.0 | 13.8 | 26.4 | 0.0 | 6.6 | 8.6 |
| ▲ SONY SAN DIEGO EMPL FCU | San Diego | CA | D | D+ | D | 6.9 | 1.45 | 0.0 | 23.4 | 35.5 | 0.0 | 7.6 | 9.4 |
| SOO CO-OP CU | Sault Sainte Marie | MI | C+ | C+ | B- | 154.7 | 2.11 | 0.9 | 35.2 | 19.7 | 3.6 | 9.6 | 10.7 |
| ▲ SOO LINE CU | Savage | MN | D+ | D | D- | 41.3 | 2.16 | 0.2 | 39.7 | 8.8 | 20.2 | 5.5 | 7.5 |
| ▲ SOO SELECT CU | Thief River Falls | MN | B- | C | C- | 14.3 | 0.17 | 0.2 | 41.2 | 0.0 | 0.0 | 10.0 | 11.3 |
| ▼ SOOPER CU | Arvada | CO | C+ | B- | B | 308.2 | 5.65 | 6.9 | 29.8 | 24.5 | 17.3 | 10.0 | 11.8 |
| SORENG EMPL CU | Itasca | IL | D+ | D+ | D | 1.2 | 6.53 | 0.0 | 11.2 | 0.0 | 0.1 | 10.0 | 26.7 |
| SORG BAY WEST FCU | Middletown | OH | D | D | D | 8.3 | 2.57 | 0.0 | 31.7 | 11.3 | 0.0 | 7.9 | 9.6 |
| SOUND CU | Tacoma | WA | A | A- | A- | 1208.2 | 7.84 | 3.9 | 38.6 | 17.7 | 15.3 | 10.0 | 13.5 |
| ▲ SOUNDVIEW FINANCIAL CU | Bethel | CT | C | C | D+ | 33.1 | 1.70 | 0.0 | 25.1 | 0.0 | 1.3 | 10.0 | 12.2 |
| SOURCEONE CU | Chicago | IL | D | D+ | C- | 12.6 | -1.40 | 0.0 | 11.9 | 0.0 | 0.0 | 10.0 | 13.9 |
| SOUTH ATLANTIC FCU | Boca Raton | FL | C- | C- | D | 12.8 | -0.43 | 0.0 | 48.1 | 0.0 | 0.0 | 8.6 | 10.0 |
| ▲ SOUTH BAY CU | Redondo Beach | CA | B+ | B- | C- | 84.9 | 0.72 | 6.4 | 29.1 | 38.6 | 16.3 | 10.0 | 11.1 |
| SOUTH BEND FIREFIGHTERS FCU | South Bend | IN | A- | A- | A- | 36.9 | 7.23 | 0.0 | 39.5 | 16.8 | 0.0 | 10.0 | 24.5 |
| SOUTH BEND POST OFFICE CU | South Bend | IN | D | D+ | D+ | 9.4 | -4.40 | 0.0 | 34.4 | 0.0 | 19.3 | 10.0 | 11.4 |
| SOUTH BEND TRANSIT FCU | South Bend | IN | C | C- | C- | 4.0 | 5.71 | 0.0 | 57.1 | 0.8 | 0.0 | 10.0 | 25.5 |
| SOUTH CAROLINA FCU | North Charleston | SC | A- | B | B- | 1387.7 | 5.08 | 1.9 | 30.5 | 31.8 | 2.8 | 10.0 | 11.3 |
| SOUTH CAROLINA METHODIST CONFERENC | Columbia | SC | D | D | D | 5.7 | 0.86 | 0.4 | 41.9 | 2.5 | 0.0 | 8.9 | 10.2 |
| SOUTH CAROLINA NATIONAL GUARD FCU | Columbia | SC | A- | A- | A- | 62.2 | 6.52 | 0.0 | 43.1 | 0.0 | 21.5 | 10.0 | 18.7 |
| SOUTH CENTRAL CU | Jackson | MI | C | B- | B- | 65.8 | 1.62 | 0.0 | 20.8 | 3.9 | 2.7 | 10.0 | 13.6 |
| SOUTH CENTRAL MISSOURI CU | Willow Springs | MO | C | C | C | 12.0 | -1.45 | 0.0 | 21.7 | 0.0 | 0.0 | 10.0 | 11.8 |
| SOUTH CHARLESTON EMPL FCU | South Charleston | WV | B | B | B | 19.6 | -2.69 | 0.0 | 23.9 | 2.0 | 18.2 | 10.0 | 38.4 |
| SOUTH COAST ILWU FCU | North Bend | OR | C | C | C | 16.5 | 3.60 | 1.6 | 32.9 | 17.9 | 0.0 | 10.0 | 13.2 |
| ▲ SOUTH COMMUNITY CU | Sullivan | MO | C- | D+ | D | 8.5 | -0.06 | 0.0 | 37.0 | 0.0 | 0.0 | 10.0 | 12.2 |
| ▲ SOUTH DIVISION CU | Evergreen Park | IL | B- | C+ | D | 48.2 | -3.34 | 3.5 | 24.7 | 10.6 | 1.0 | 10.0 | 11.3 |
| SOUTH FLORIDA EDUCATIONAL FCU | Miami | FL | B- | B- | B | 927.2 | 4.95 | 0.0 | 16.2 | 4.6 | 42.5 | 10.0 | 20.6 |
| SOUTH FLORIDA FCU | Miami | FL | C+ | C- | C+ | 33.5 | 11.88 | 0.0 | 34.5 | 2.1 | 14.7 | 8.2 | 9.8 |
| SOUTH HILLS HEALTHCARE FCU | Pittsburgh | PA | D- | D | D | 9.2 | 8.37 | 0.0 | 37.9 | 0.0 | 13.1 | 6.9 | 8.9 |
| ▲ SOUTH JENNINGS CATHOLIC FCU | Jennings | LA | D+ | D | D | 1.5 | -1.93 | 0.0 | 31.4 | 0.0 | 0.0 | 10.0 | 14.7 |
| ▼ SOUTH JERSEY FCU | Deptford | NJ | C | C+ | B- | 330.2 | 2.15 | 0.0 | 21.5 | 8.5 | 32.8 | 7.4 | 9.3 |
| SOUTH JERSEY GAS EMPL FCU | Williamstown | NJ | C | C+ | C+ | 10.7 | -3.38 | 0.0 | 15.3 | 0.0 | 0.0 | 10.0 | 21.5 |
| SOUTH LOUISIANA HIGHWAY FCU | Bridge City | LA | C | C | C | 6.1 | 0.60 | 0.0 | 35.9 | 0.0 | 0.0 | 10.0 | 26.2 |
| SOUTH METRO FCU | Prior Lake | MN | B | B | B | 98.4 | 7.24 | 6.2 | 29.9 | 13.6 | 17.6 | 8.8 | 10.2 |
| ▼ SOUTH SAN FRANCISCO CITY EMPL FCU | South Francisc | CA | D | D | D+ | 3.1 | -7.31 | 0.0 | 21.1 | 0.0 | 0.0 | 10.0 | 16.9 |
| ▼ SOUTH SANPETE CU | Manti | UT | D | D+ | C+ | <1 | 14.82 | 0.0 | 58.0 | 0.0 | 0.0 | 10.0 | 11.3 |
| SOUTH SHOP FCU | Alsip | IL | B- | B- | B- | 13.3 | 4.64 | 0.0 | 39.7 | 0.0 | 0.0 | 10.0 | 14.0 |
| SOUTH SHORE RAILROAD EMPL FCU | Michigan City | IN | E+ | E+ | E+ | 3.8 | -4.95 | 0.0 | 49.6 | 0.0 | 0.0 | 5.3 | 7.3 |
| ▼ SOUTH SIDE COMMUNITY FCU | Chicago | IL | D- | D | D- | 4.0 | -4.57 | 0.0 | 5.8 | 8.4 | 0.0 | 7.9 | 9.6 |
| SOUTH TEXAS AREA RESOURCES CU | Corpus Christi | TX | C | C | C- | 44.2 | 2.57 | 0.0 | 35.6 | 3.8 | 0.0 | 10.0 | 13.1 |
| ▼ SOUTH TEXAS FCU | McAllen | TX | D- | D | D- | 46.3 | 5.58 | 0.0 | 55.9 | 2.6 | 14.1 | 4.7 | 6.7 |
| ▼ SOUTH TEXAS REGIONAL FCU | Laredo | TX | E+ | D- | D | 7.4 | 7.38 | 0.0 | 45.0 | 0.0 | 0.0 | 6.3 | 8.3 |
| SOUTH TOWNS COMMUNITY FCU | Lackawanna | NY | D- | D- | D- | 15.0 | 4.86 | 0.0 | 15.2 | 16.7 | 0.0 | 5.7 | 7.7 |
| ▼ SOUTHBRIDGE CU | Southbridge | MA | D | C- | C- | 163.0 | -2.47 | 11.6 | 14.8 | 45.1 | 16.9 | 10.0 | 12.8 |
| SOUTHCOAST HEALTH SYSTEM FCU | New Bedford | MA | B- | B- | B | 50.0 | 3.36 | 0.0 | 10.6 | 13.3 | 16.9 | 10.0 | 12.3 |
| SOUTHEAST FCU | Cornelia | GA | A- | A- | A- | 52.6 | 8.27 | 1.9 | 35.1 | 43.6 | 0.0 | 10.0 | 16.5 |
| SOUTHEAST FINANCIAL CU | Franklin | TN | D | D | D | 431.7 | -2.45 | 8.6 | 33.1 | 22.8 | 1.5 | 5.5 | 7.5 |
| ▲ SOUTHEAST LOUISIANA VETERANS HEALTH | New Orleans | LA | C | D+ | D+ | 1.8 | -4.97 | 0.0 | 45.8 | 0.0 | 0.0 | 10.0 | 13.5 |
| ▲ SOUTHEAST MICHIGAN STATE EMPL FCU | Southfield | MI | C | D+ | C- | 33.3 | 3.99 | 0.0 | 24.2 | 2.6 | 16.9 | 10.0 | 11.1 |
| SOUTHEAST MISSOURI COMMUNITY CU | Park Hills | MO | C- | C- | C- | 6.1 | 8.61 | 0.0 | 48.8 | 0.0 | 0.0 | 10.0 | 12.4 |
| SOUTHEAST TEXAS EMPL FCU | Orange | TX | D- | D- | D | 8.8 | 2.39 | 0.0 | 35.2 | 0.0 | 0.0 | 6.8 | 8.8 |
| SOUTHEASTERN ARIZONA FCU | Douglas | AZ | C | C | C+ | 31.9 | 7.10 | 0.0 | 59.7 | 6.5 | 0.0 | 10.0 | 11.8 |
| SOUTHEASTERN FCU | Valdosta | GA | B | B | B | 222.2 | 12.08 | 12.2 | 38.3 | 19.0 | 11.9 | 7.4 | 9.3 |
| ▲ SOUTHEASTERN OHIO CU | Cambridge | OH | B | C+ | C- | 26.0 | 6.14 | 0.0 | 56.0 | 0.0 | 0.0 | 10.0 | 11.7 |
| SOUTHERN BAPTIST CHURCH OF NEW YOR | New York | NY | D | D | C- | <1 | 0.00 | 0.0 | 17.3 | 0.0 | 0.0 | 10.0 | 14.6 |
| SOUTHERN CHAUTAUQUA FCU | Lakewood | NY | B- | B- | C | 65.9 | 10.83 | 0.0 | 49.7 | 6.6 | 0.0 | 10.0 | 11.1 |
| SOUTHERN CU | Fayetteville | GA | C | C | C | 347.9 | 7.63 | 0.1 | 23.8 | 7.0 | 30.6 | 9.2 | 10.4 |
| SOUTHERN CU | Chattanooga | TN | C | C | C | 21.0 | 4.64 | 0.0 | 48.8 | 10.6 | 0.0 | 10.0 | 13.7 |
| SOUTHERN FCU | Houston | TX | A- | A- | A- | 90.3 | 7.74 | 0.0 | 57.1 | 0.0 | 0.0 | 10.0 | 27.1 |
| ▼ SOUTHERN GAS FCU | Little Rock | AR | D | D+ | C- | 6.5 | 10.93 | 0.0 | 36.1 | 0.5 | 0.0 | 10.0 | 22.8 |

Arrows denote recent upgrades ▲ or downgrades ▼
190
www.weissratings.com

| Asset Quality Index | Non-Performing Loans | | Net Charge-Offs | Profitability Index | Net Income ($Mil) | Return on Assets | Return on Equity | Net Interest Spread | Overhead Efficiency Ratio | Liquidity Index | Liquidity Ratio | Hot Money Ratio | Stability Index |
|---|---|---|---|---|---|---|---|---|---|---|---|---|---|
| | as a % of Total Loans | as a % of Capital | Avg Loans | | | | | | | | | | |
| 9.6 | 0.21 | 1.1 | 0.10 | 1.6 | 0.0 | -0.06 | -0.44 | 3.44 | 100.6 | 3.3 | 15.2 | 6.9 | 6.3 |
| 9.2 | 0.10 | 0.8 | 0.00 | 7.4 | 0.2 | 1.17 | 13.97 | 4.27 | 69.7 | 3.5 | 13.7 | 5.0 | 3.8 |
| 9.4 | 0.04 | 0.3 | 0.31 | 0.8 | 0.0 | -0.34 | -3.77 | 3.74 | 109.0 | 3.9 | 41.6 | 18.4 | 3.9 |
| 7.4 | 0.66 | 4.3 | 0.46 | 3.2 | 0.3 | 0.23 | 2.19 | 3.80 | 87.3 | 4.5 | 23.8 | 4.4 | 6.8 |
| 4.9 | 0.65 | 7.4 | 0.14 | 3.8 | 0.1 | 0.47 | 6.33 | 3.74 | 94.7 | 3.6 | 14.1 | 0.6 | 2.8 |
| 8.5 | 0.82 | 3.4 | -1.00 | 8.4 | 0.2 | 1.35 | 12.66 | 3.74 | 77.6 | 4.6 | 28.5 | 4.2 | 6.3 |
| 9.1 | 0.68 | 3.6 | 0.24 | 2.7 | 0.2 | 0.08 | 0.63 | 3.64 | 87.8 | 4.2 | 21.9 | 5.0 | 7.2 |
| 8.0 | 12.88 | 5.1 | 0.85 | 0.8 | 0.0 | -0.12 | -0.42 | 2.05 | 111.8 | 5.8 | 52.6 | 0.0 | 5.4 |
| 6.0 | 0.69 | 9.0 | 0.28 | 2.1 | 0.0 | 0.03 | 0.34 | 4.63 | 97.7 | 4.1 | 18.1 | 9.1 | 3.7 |
| 9.3 | 0.21 | 1.3 | 0.26 | 9.8 | 12.3 | 1.38 | 12.24 | 3.64 | 67.8 | 4.3 | 14.8 | 4.2 | 8.8 |
| 8.0 | 1.11 | 4.6 | 0.50 | 2.2 | 0.0 | 0.13 | 1.03 | 3.26 | 90.5 | 4.3 | 24.7 | 1.8 | 5.7 |
| 10.0 | 0.83 | 0.8 | 1.02 | 0.2 | -0.1 | -0.51 | -3.68 | 1.79 | 116.8 | 5.0 | 16.8 | 0.0 | 5.1 |
| 5.9 | 1.39 | 7.5 | 1.33 | 4.7 | 0.1 | 0.76 | 8.01 | 4.66 | 72.0 | 4.4 | 15.0 | 0.0 | 3.7 |
| 9.8 | 0.21 | 1.5 | 0.29 | 8.5 | 0.9 | 1.38 | 14.29 | 3.82 | 70.9 | 3.4 | 11.9 | 4.8 | 5.3 |
| 9.4 | 0.75 | 2.1 | 0.29 | 7.9 | 0.3 | 1.12 | 4.54 | 3.17 | 68.2 | 4.0 | 19.8 | 0.0 | 8.2 |
| 8.8 | 0.79 | 2.4 | 1.08 | 0.3 | 0.0 | -0.43 | -3.89 | 2.72 | 101.0 | 5.0 | 19.2 | 0.0 | 4.8 |
| 5.7 | 5.14 | 11.2 | 1.22 | 5.5 | 0.0 | 0.87 | 3.32 | 5.08 | 67.4 | 5.0 | 35.2 | 0.0 | 4.3 |
| 8.3 | 0.36 | 2.8 | 0.21 | 6.0 | 10.1 | 0.98 | 8.83 | 3.60 | 82.3 | 3.9 | 14.7 | 2.8 | 7.0 |
| 5.5 | 2.42 | 11.6 | 0.31 | 2.4 | 0.0 | 0.19 | 1.84 | 5.21 | 94.9 | 5.6 | 72.2 | 3.3 | 5.0 |
| 9.6 | 0.30 | 0.8 | 0.40 | 8.0 | 0.5 | 1.16 | 6.41 | 4.40 | 73.4 | 5.3 | 38.1 | 11.4 | 7.5 |
| 8.6 | 0.93 | 3.0 | 0.66 | 2.7 | 0.2 | 0.30 | 2.31 | 2.66 | 87.7 | 4.3 | 16.0 | 5.0 | 6.1 |
| 9.9 | 0.09 | 0.2 | -0.04 | 1.7 | 0.0 | 0.11 | 0.95 | 1.64 | 93.5 | 4.5 | 2.0 | 0.0 | 5.7 |
| 10.0 | 2.29 | 1.6 | 0.12 | 5.1 | 0.1 | 0.70 | 1.86 | 2.89 | 73.4 | 4.8 | 33.3 | 9.8 | 7.5 |
| 9.8 | 0.01 | 0.1 | 0.30 | 2.1 | 0.0 | 0.06 | 0.43 | 3.33 | 92.6 | 5.1 | 51.0 | 0.0 | 7.1 |
| 9.1 | 0.03 | 0.1 | 0.45 | 5.5 | 0.1 | 1.05 | 8.81 | 4.92 | 84.2 | 6.7 | 54.7 | 0.0 | 4.3 |
| 8.1 | 1.82 | 6.4 | 2.19 | 4.0 | 0.2 | 0.62 | 6.34 | 4.05 | 83.2 | 5.1 | 27.8 | 2.3 | 4.5 |
| 10.0 | 0.48 | 0.5 | 0.52 | 3.6 | 3.3 | 0.48 | 2.31 | 3.03 | 81.9 | 6.8 | 41.9 | 5.2 | 8.2 |
| 7.7 | 0.22 | 1.5 | -1.55 | 6.1 | 0.6 | 2.60 | 26.15 | 5.02 | 91.4 | 3.1 | 6.0 | 7.1 | 3.2 |
| 4.6 | 4.07 | 16.3 | 0.64 | 3.5 | 0.0 | 0.40 | 4.48 | 3.13 | 79.5 | 5.0 | 19.1 | 0.0 | 2.3 |
| 6.5 | 1.49 | 3.5 | 2.82 | 1.3 | 0.0 | -0.09 | -0.59 | 5.04 | 101.8 | 6.1 | 50.7 | 0.0 | 5.0 |
| 6.5 | 1.54 | 8.2 | 2.00 | 1.7 | -0.3 | -0.12 | -1.39 | 3.14 | 89.3 | 4.3 | 15.5 | 6.5 | 4.7 |
| 10.0 | 0.98 | 0.7 | -0.08 | 2.1 | 0.0 | 0.15 | 0.70 | 1.79 | 71.3 | 7.6 | 60.1 | 0.0 | 5.9 |
| 6.4 | 7.99 | 10.7 | 1.13 | 4.2 | 0.0 | 0.46 | 1.77 | 4.68 | 70.2 | 6.6 | 65.2 | 0.0 | 6.6 |
| 8.9 | 0.04 | 0.2 | 0.03 | 4.3 | 0.3 | 0.39 | 3.80 | 3.92 | 92.2 | 2.5 | 14.5 | 18.1 | 5.6 |
| 10.0 | 0.61 | 0.7 | -1.49 | 0.1 | 0.0 | -0.34 | -2.00 | 1.66 | 171.9 | 6.8 | 81.0 | 0.0 | 4.7 |
| 2.5 | 5.56 | 27.7 | 0.00 | 1.6 | 0.0 | 0.00 | 0.00 | 1.82 | 88.9 | 5.8 | 32.1 | 0.0 | 6.3 |
| 6.6 | 3.51 | 9.7 | 0.80 | 6.8 | 0.1 | 1.11 | 7.99 | 3.85 | 57.9 | 4.7 | 18.6 | 0.0 | 5.7 |
| 4.2 | 1.81 | 13.8 | 0.96 | 3.0 | 0.0 | 0.40 | 6.04 | 3.55 | 96.9 | 4.3 | 21.0 | 0.0 | 1.0 |
| 0.3 | 26.18 | 72.4 | 1.04 | 2.1 | 0.0 | -1.36 | -20.10 | 2.68 | 124.1 | 6.9 | 59.6 | 4.3 | 5.1 |
| 9.7 | 0.31 | 1.0 | 0.07 | 2.4 | 0.1 | 0.17 | 1.32 | 2.87 | 96.7 | 5.0 | 27.8 | 3.6 | 5.8 |
| 2.7 | 2.62 | 22.4 | 0.72 | 3.9 | 0.1 | 0.39 | 5.75 | 4.72 | 82.9 | 4.4 | 22.7 | 0.2 | 1.7 |
| 3.5 | 2.23 | 17.4 | 0.66 | 1.3 | 0.0 | -0.48 | -5.20 | 4.65 | 98.7 | 5.3 | 38.4 | 0.0 | 1.0 |
| 8.5 | 0.50 | 2.5 | 1.09 | 1.6 | 0.0 | 0.05 | 0.70 | 3.03 | 97.3 | 5.6 | 26.8 | 0.0 | 2.8 |
| 6.3 | 1.90 | 11.4 | 0.14 | 0.1 | -0.7 | -0.55 | -4.34 | 3.29 | 112.5 | 3.2 | 7.7 | 7.3 | 7.2 |
| 8.9 | 1.33 | 4.6 | 0.01 | 3.0 | 0.1 | 0.26 | 2.07 | 2.91 | 91.0 | 6.1 | 40.8 | 0.0 | 6.3 |
| 9.1 | 0.04 | 1.3 | 0.17 | 10.0 | 0.6 | 1.52 | 9.11 | 4.66 | 74.5 | 2.6 | 11.6 | 12.0 | 8.0 |
| 2.3 | 1.41 | 33.1 | 3.15 | 0.8 | -2.2 | -0.68 | -9.45 | 4.67 | 90.6 | 3.3 | 15.3 | 12.5 | 3.4 |
| 8.3 | 0.48 | 1.5 | -0.85 | 5.8 | 0.0 | 1.27 | 9.86 | 6.60 | 108.8 | 6.4 | 61.8 | 0.0 | 4.3 |
| 7.6 | 2.43 | 5.9 | 0.84 | 2.3 | 0.1 | 0.29 | 2.68 | 3.01 | 87.0 | 4.9 | 24.9 | 2.2 | 4.7 |
| 8.0 | 0.12 | 0.7 | -0.04 | 2.3 | 0.0 | 0.09 | 0.71 | 3.52 | 96.5 | 4.6 | 21.9 | 0.0 | 6.6 |
| 7.8 | 0.75 | 3.5 | 0.68 | 0.6 | 0.0 | -0.18 | -2.08 | 3.09 | 89.2 | 3.5 | 40.3 | 19.8 | 3.0 |
| 6.8 | 0.55 | 5.6 | 0.37 | 2.4 | 0.1 | 0.29 | 2.55 | 3.12 | 87.3 | 4.2 | 26.3 | 1.5 | 6.3 |
| 7.0 | 1.02 | 7.3 | 0.62 | 4.9 | 1.0 | 0.60 | 6.57 | 3.92 | 78.9 | 4.2 | 19.3 | 6.8 | 5.9 |
| 5.8 | 2.14 | 10.2 | 0.31 | 9.5 | 0.4 | 1.82 | 16.68 | 4.62 | 66.2 | 4.2 | 16.3 | 0.0 | 6.0 |
| 10.0 | 0.00 | 0.0 | 12.12 | 0.0 | 0.0 | -1.23 | -7.62 | 2.34 | 166.7 | 7.8 | 98.5 | 0.0 | 6.6 |
| 4.4 | 1.84 | 15.8 | 0.48 | 6.7 | 0.5 | 0.94 | 11.60 | 4.91 | 76.7 | 2.6 | 21.7 | 14.5 | 4.3 |
| 10.0 | 0.17 | 0.7 | 0.37 | 2.8 | 0.9 | 0.35 | 3.38 | 2.62 | 88.6 | 4.8 | 17.3 | 4.2 | 5.9 |
| 6.1 | 1.79 | 8.4 | 0.39 | 3.0 | 0.0 | 0.24 | 1.78 | 3.84 | 88.2 | 4.9 | 35.7 | 1.0 | 6.2 |
| 6.6 | 1.91 | 4.9 | 0.31 | 10.0 | 2.1 | 3.24 | 12.21 | 5.05 | 29.2 | 3.9 | 40.0 | 7.1 | 9.6 |
| 9.7 | 0.31 | 0.6 | -0.05 | 0.2 | 0.0 | -0.40 | -1.70 | 3.34 | 109.2 | 5.3 | 50.5 | 0.0 | 6.2 |

| Name | City | State | Rating | 2014 Rating | 2013 Rating | Total Assets ($Mil) | One Year Asset Growth | Commercial Loans | Consumer Loans | Mortgage Loans | Securities | Capitalization Index | Net Worth Ratio |
|------|------|-------|--------|-------------|-------------|---------------------|----------------------|------------------|----------------|----------------|------------|----------------------|-----------------|
| SOUTHERN LAKES CU | Kenosha | WI | D+ | D+ | D+ | 87.4 | 3.12 | 0.7 | 50.7 | 11.0 | 15.3 | 6.0 | 8.0 |
| SOUTHERN MASS CU | Fairhaven | MA | C | C+ | C- | 200.1 | -2.81 | 0.3 | 10.6 | 33.4 | 18.4 | 9.8 | 10.9 |
| SOUTHERN MIDDLESEX COUNTY TEACHERS | East Brunswick | NJ | C- | C- | C- | 31.8 | 0.19 | 0.0 | 11.5 | 10.9 | 3.4 | 8.4 | 9.9 |
| SOUTHERN MISSISSIPPI FCU | Hattiesburg | MS | D+ | D | D | 29.0 | 2.27 | 0.0 | 44.7 | 0.8 | 0.0 | 7.0 | 9.0 |
| SOUTHERN PINE CU | Valdosta | GA | B- | B- | B- | 44.0 | 1.84 | 0.0 | 14.9 | 32.3 | 0.0 | 10.0 | 17.3 |
| SOUTHERN RESEARCH INSTITUTE EMPL FC | Birmingham | AL | C- | C- | C- | 5.9 | -2.33 | 0.0 | 1.9 | 1.5 | 0.0 | 10.0 | 24.3 |
| SOUTHERN SECURITY FCU | Collierville | TN | B- | B | B- | 139.6 | 4.74 | 0.0 | 24.2 | 24.2 | 13.0 | 8.6 | 10.0 |
| SOUTHERN SELECT COMMUNITY CU | Kannapolis | NC | C- | C- | C | 32.7 | -1.48 | 0.0 | 25.4 | 25.3 | 5.3 | 10.0 | 12.7 |
| SOUTHERN STAR CU | Houston | TX | C+ | C | C | 23.0 | 0.53 | 0.0 | 41.5 | 8.3 | 0.0 | 10.0 | 16.5 |
| SOUTHERN TEACHERS & PARENTS FCU | Baton Rouge | LA | C- | D+ | D | 28.2 | 0.41 | 0.0 | 32.1 | 13.8 | 32.4 | 6.2 | 8.2 |
| SOUTHERNMOST FCU | Key West | FL | C+ | C+ | C+ | 13.3 | 9.96 | 0.0 | 52.6 | 0.0 | 0.0 | 10.0 | 21.3 |
| SOUTHLAND CU | Los Alamitos | CA | B- | B | B+ | 578.6 | 17.99 | 8.9 | 29.2 | 26.4 | 13.0 | 10.0 | 11.1 |
| SOUTHLAND FCU | Lufkin | TX | C | C | C | 37.1 | 11.23 | 0.0 | 61.7 | 0.2 | 0.0 | 10.0 | 11.2 |
| SOUTHPOINT FCU | Sleepy Eye | MN | B+ | A- | A | 291.4 | 3.13 | 19.6 | 9.3 | 49.4 | 15.9 | 10.0 | 14.3 |
| SOUTHSHORE CU | Cudahy | WI | E+ | E+ | D- | 17.8 | 3.74 | 1.1 | 36.5 | 7.1 | 0.0 | 4.6 | 6.6 |
| SOUTHWEST 66 CU | Odessa | TX | B | B | B | 83.8 | -0.36 | 5.3 | 21.3 | 12.9 | 27.3 | 9.6 | 10.7 |
| SOUTHWEST AIRLINES FCU | Dallas | TX | A | A | A | 381.5 | 10.69 | 0.0 | 46.0 | 13.6 | 10.6 | 10.0 | 12.9 |
| SOUTHWEST COLORADO FCU | Durango | CO | B | B | B- | 43.1 | 7.18 | 1.2 | 10.5 | 10.8 | 0.0 | 10.0 | 11.7 |
| SOUTHWEST COMMUNITIES FCU | Carnegie | PA | D+ | D+ | D | 14.4 | 0.41 | 0.5 | 26.4 | 16.8 | 0.0 | 9.4 | 10.6 |
| ▲ SOUTHWEST COUNTIES SCHOOL EMPL CU | Neosho | MO | D | D- | D | 2.2 | 5.20 | 0.0 | 37.9 | 0.0 | 0.0 | 6.7 | 8.9 |
| SOUTHWEST FCU | Albuquerque | NM | C | C | C | 57.5 | 4.12 | 0.0 | 30.7 | 10.6 | 13.4 | 6.4 | 8.6 |
| SOUTHWEST FINANCIAL FCU | Dallas | TX | B+ | B | B | 54.5 | 17.63 | 0.0 | 69.2 | 2.1 | 0.5 | 10.0 | 17.4 |
| SOUTHWEST HEALTH CARE CU | Phoenix | AZ | D+ | D+ | D+ | 15.2 | 2.34 | 0.0 | 48.7 | 0.0 | 31.4 | 9.0 | 10.3 |
| SOUTHWEST HERITAGE CU | Odessa | TX | B+ | B+ | B | 115.7 | 6.65 | 11.3 | 35.6 | 15.5 | 2.6 | 7.2 | 9.1 |
| SOUTHWEST KANSAS COMMUNITY CU | Dodge City | KS | D | D | D | 4.1 | -13.87 | 0.0 | 57.7 | 0.0 | 0.0 | 10.0 | 11.9 |
| SOUTHWEST LOUISIANA CU | Lake Charles | LA | A- | A- | B | 87.6 | 10.29 | 0.0 | 39.6 | 12.0 | 0.0 | 10.0 | 14.2 |
| ▼ SOUTHWEST MONTANA COMMUNITY FCU | Anaconda | MT | C+ | B | B | 102.7 | 1.63 | 1.4 | 16.8 | 24.8 | 18.8 | 10.0 | 13.6 |
| ▲ SOUTHWEST OKLAHOMA FCU | Lawton | OK | B+ | B | C+ | 89.2 | 1.94 | 1.5 | 21.5 | 5.7 | 56.9 | 9.1 | 10.4 |
| ▲ SOUTHWEST RESEARCH CENTER FCU | San Antonio | TX | C | C- | C- | 70.3 | 1.89 | 0.0 | 35.8 | 1.3 | 30.1 | 7.1 | 9.1 |
| SP TRAINMEN FCU | Houston | TX | D | D | D+ | 3.4 | 6.11 | 0.0 | 25.3 | 0.0 | 62.4 | 10.0 | 33.8 |
| SPACE AGE FCU | Aurora | CO | C+ | C+ | C+ | 109.0 | 2.28 | 0.0 | 65.6 | 1.2 | 6.0 | 6.6 | 8.6 |
| ▼ SPACE AGE TULSA FCU | Tulsa | OK | C | C+ | C+ | 16.6 | -0.57 | 0.0 | 37.0 | 0.0 | 0.0 | 10.0 | 16.4 |
| ▲ SPACE CITY CU | Houston | TX | D+ | D | D | 70.4 | 3.31 | 0.6 | 66.7 | 8.1 | 0.0 | 7.6 | 9.4 |
| SPACE COAST CU | Melbourne | FL | B+ | B | B- | 3471.3 | 7.37 | 3.5 | 39.1 | 23.1 | 8.3 | 10.0 | 13.4 |
| SPARTAN FCU | Spartanburg | SC | B- | B- | B- | 13.5 | 3.99 | 0.0 | 33.4 | 5.5 | 0.0 | 10.0 | 12.9 |
| SPARTANBURG CITY EMPL CU | Spartanburg | SC | C- | C- | D+ | 4.6 | 6.56 | 0.0 | 52.2 | 0.0 | 0.0 | 10.0 | 24.8 |
| SPC BROOKLYN FCU | Brooklyn | NY | D | D+ | C- | <1 | -3.37 | 0.0 | 22.8 | 0.0 | 0.0 | 6.8 | 8.8 |
| SPC CU | Hartsville | SC | C+ | B- | B- | 141.1 | 5.08 | 5.4 | 33.3 | 20.5 | 12.5 | 8.4 | 9.9 |
| ▲ SPCO CU | Houston | TX | C- | D+ | D | 38.1 | 3.17 | 1.0 | 29.1 | 47.3 | 0.0 | 9.8 | 10.9 |
| ▲ SPE FCU | State College | PA | D+ | D | D | 77.3 | 0.65 | 17.9 | 17.6 | 26.3 | 33.6 | 6.4 | 8.5 |
| SPECIAL METALS FCU | New Hartford | NY | C+ | C+ | C+ | 10.9 | 3.02 | 0.0 | 33.1 | 0.0 | 0.0 | 10.0 | 13.1 |
| SPELC FCU | Lake Charles | LA | E+ | E+ | E+ | 11.4 | 0.65 | 0.0 | 47.3 | 0.2 | 0.0 | 5.3 | 7.3 |
| SPENCERPORT FCU | Spencerport | NY | C- | C- | D+ | 25.5 | 1.71 | 0.0 | 27.1 | 11.6 | 28.8 | 6.5 | 8.5 |
| ▲ SPERRY ASSOCIATES FCU | Garden City Park | NY | D | E+ | E | 242.9 | -5.21 | 1.8 | 12.7 | 22.4 | 32.8 | 5.5 | 7.6 |
| SPIRE CU | Falcon Heights | MN | B- | B | B | 801.6 | 3.92 | 7.5 | 28.4 | 24.9 | 23.4 | 7.1 | 9.1 |
| SPIRIT OF ALASKA FCU | Fairbanks | AK | B+ | B+ | B+ | 144.1 | 5.30 | 11.4 | 12.9 | 34.3 | 10.0 | 10.0 | 11.0 |
| SPIRIT OF AMERICA FCU | Lincoln | NE | C- | C- | C- | 38.7 | 8.18 | 0.0 | 20.7 | 0.2 | 0.0 | 6.0 | 8.1 |
| SPOJNIA CU | Scranton | PA | D+ | D+ | D+ | 14.1 | -5.18 | 0.0 | 10.0 | 15.8 | 44.1 | 10.0 | 17.5 |
| ▲ SPOKANE CITY CU | Spokane | WA | C | C- | D+ | 33.5 | -0.13 | 0.0 | 40.7 | 11.3 | 0.0 | 9.2 | 10.5 |
| SPOKANE FCU | Spokane | WA | C+ | C+ | B- | 138.0 | 4.33 | 1.0 | 30.5 | 27.0 | 1.4 | 8.0 | 9.7 |
| SPOKANE FIREFIGHTERS CU | Spokane | WA | B | B- | B | 45.0 | 6.38 | 0.0 | 25.7 | 22.0 | 37.6 | 10.0 | 16.6 |
| SPOKANE LAW ENFORCEMENT CU | Spokane | WA | B | B- | B- | 38.2 | -1.76 | 0.0 | 19.1 | 35.1 | 20.6 | 10.0 | 15.7 |
| SPOKANE MEDIA FCU | Spokane | WA | D | D | D | 10.3 | -0.87 | 0.0 | 38.2 | 12.0 | 0.0 | 5.8 | 7.8 |
| SPOKANE TEACHERS CU | Liberty Lake | WA | A- | A- | A- | 2142.1 | 8.66 | 11.0 | 32.9 | 40.7 | 7.2 | 10.0 | 11.2 |
| SPRING MILL EMPL FCU | Roaring Spring | PA | C- | C+ | C | 36.5 | 2.68 | 0.0 | 17.8 | 2.3 | 1.6 | 7.9 | 9.6 |
| SPRINGDALE P P G FCU | Springdale | PA | C- | C- | C | 1.2 | -3.91 | 0.0 | 41.9 | 0.0 | 0.0 | 10.0 | 22.6 |
| SPRINGFIELD CATHOLIC CU | Springfield | MO | D+ | D+ | D+ | 4.0 | -7.42 | 0.0 | 45.8 | 0.0 | 0.0 | 10.0 | 18.0 |
| SPRINGFIELD CITY EMPL CU | Springfield | IL | C | C | C- | 10.7 | 1.42 | 0.0 | 39.8 | 0.0 | 2.0 | 10.0 | 12.3 |
| ▲ SPRINGFIELD FIREFIGHTERS CU | Springfield | IL | C+ | C | C | 3.7 | -0.27 | 0.0 | 31.2 | 0.0 | 0.0 | 10.0 | 14.9 |
| SPRINGFIELD POSTAL EMPL FCU | Springfield | OH | D+ | D+ | C- | 5.0 | -0.89 | 0.0 | 48.2 | 0.0 | 38.7 | 10.0 | 14.1 |

| Asset Quality Index | Non-Performing Loans as a % of Total Loans | as a % of Capital | Net Charge-Offs Avg Loans | Profitability Index | Net Income ($Mil) | Return on Assets | Return on Equity | Net Interest Spread | Overhead Efficiency Ratio | Liquidity Index | Liquidity Ratio | Hot Money Ratio | Stability Index |
|---|---|---|---|---|---|---|---|---|---|---|---|---|---|
| 6.9 | 0.46 | 3.8 | 0.14 | 1.4 | 0.0 | -0.05 | -0.59 | 2.55 | 97.5 | 3.4 | 8.0 | 4.3 | 3.2 |
| 9.1 | 0.65 | 3.2 | 0.03 | 2.9 | 0.4 | 0.24 | 2.11 | 2.59 | 91.2 | 3.6 | 18.1 | 6.0 | 7.4 |
| 8.0 | 0.95 | 3.0 | 0.08 | 2.3 | 0.1 | 0.20 | 2.22 | 1.99 | 87.5 | 4.9 | 24.3 | 2.6 | 4.5 |
| 1.7 | 4.65 | 45.5 | 1.39 | 8.5 | 0.3 | 1.14 | 13.66 | 6.29 | 70.5 | 4.2 | 23.0 | 4.7 | 3.7 |
| 6.7 | 2.59 | 7.8 | 0.16 | 3.3 | 0.1 | 0.39 | 2.28 | 2.33 | 80.2 | 4.7 | 24.1 | 0.0 | 6.9 |
| 10.0 | 0.00 | 0.0 | -0.87 | 1.5 | 0.0 | -0.04 | -0.19 | 1.18 | 106.4 | 5.7 | 32.4 | 0.0 | 6.9 |
| 9.3 | 0.42 | 2.5 | 0.35 | 3.8 | 0.5 | 0.45 | 5.16 | 3.24 | 87.8 | 4.1 | 16.8 | 5.6 | 5.8 |
| 6.3 | 1.79 | 10.0 | 0.54 | 2.0 | 0.0 | 0.08 | 0.65 | 3.75 | 93.1 | 4.1 | 15.7 | 1.5 | 5.1 |
| 6.5 | 2.33 | 9.1 | 1.02 | 3.5 | 0.1 | 0.45 | 2.78 | 4.74 | 81.8 | 4.7 | 35.6 | 3.5 | 6.6 |
| 6.3 | 1.16 | 7.8 | 0.32 | 2.8 | 0.0 | 0.08 | 1.04 | 4.58 | 97.4 | 4.2 | 17.9 | 8.7 | 3.1 |
| 8.4 | 0.27 | 0.7 | 0.74 | 4.1 | 0.1 | 0.57 | 2.52 | 6.00 | 87.9 | 5.5 | 43.9 | 7.3 | 6.3 |
| 6.3 | 1.33 | 8.3 | 0.53 | 3.6 | 1.6 | 0.38 | 3.48 | 3.95 | 87.6 | 3.9 | 16.5 | 9.9 | 6.9 |
| 3.7 | 2.04 | 19.2 | 1.00 | 10.0 | 0.5 | 1.74 | 16.67 | 5.24 | 56.3 | 2.0 | 13.5 | 22.6 | 6.3 |
| 9.0 | 0.45 | 2.5 | 0.03 | 4.0 | 1.0 | 0.46 | 3.21 | 2.89 | 86.5 | 3.2 | 6.9 | 6.9 | 8.9 |
| 5.9 | 1.27 | 10.4 | 0.80 | 0.4 | -0.1 | -0.33 | -4.97 | 3.18 | 97.0 | 4.2 | 21.7 | 0.7 | 0.3 |
| 6.4 | 2.27 | 8.8 | 0.56 | 3.9 | 0.2 | 0.30 | 2.92 | 3.33 | 87.1 | 4.3 | 17.7 | 7.0 | 5.2 |
| 7.7 | 0.33 | 2.0 | 0.53 | 9.1 | 3.5 | 1.26 | 10.36 | 4.15 | 69.8 | 3.8 | 14.4 | 4.3 | 8.1 |
| 10.0 | 0.05 | 0.1 | 0.55 | 5.1 | 0.3 | 0.80 | 6.98 | 2.08 | 69.7 | 5.2 | 34.4 | 2.0 | 6.1 |
| 1.7 | 4.96 | 35.6 | 0.87 | 1.5 | 0.0 | -0.12 | -1.12 | 3.91 | 96.2 | 4.2 | 24.0 | 1.7 | 4.9 |
| 7.4 | 1.08 | 4.6 | 1.63 | 3.1 | 0.0 | 0.37 | 4.21 | 4.26 | 75.0 | 6.6 | 42.8 | 0.0 | 2.3 |
| 6.5 | 0.22 | 6.2 | 0.14 | 2.6 | 0.1 | 0.14 | 1.70 | 4.00 | 96.9 | 3.8 | 8.3 | 5.4 | 3.4 |
| 6.0 | 1.33 | 5.1 | 2.69 | 7.0 | 0.3 | 0.72 | 4.21 | 5.61 | 70.1 | 3.2 | 23.8 | 14.6 | 6.6 |
| 6.2 | 1.17 | 6.4 | 0.66 | 1.6 | 0.0 | -0.04 | -0.34 | 3.99 | 99.0 | 4.0 | 7.8 | 0.0 | 4.1 |
| 8.2 | 0.28 | 3.5 | 0.13 | 7.2 | 0.9 | 1.00 | 11.43 | 3.94 | 76.4 | 3.0 | 18.0 | 12.0 | 7.0 |
| 5.7 | 0.97 | 4.7 | 0.21 | 0.5 | 0.0 | -0.65 | -5.66 | 5.15 | 115.5 | 5.7 | 43.0 | 0.0 | 4.1 |
| 6.8 | 1.13 | 6.5 | 1.16 | 10.0 | 1.4 | 2.23 | 16.33 | 5.77 | 64.6 | 3.9 | 26.7 | 1.8 | 7.3 |
| 10.0 | 0.40 | 1.9 | 0.06 | 2.4 | 0.1 | 0.12 | 0.87 | 2.53 | 94.4 | 4.5 | 24.8 | 5.2 | 8.2 |
| 8.0 | 0.82 | 2.8 | 0.35 | 5.6 | 0.5 | 0.73 | 7.10 | 2.99 | 73.4 | 4.5 | 8.0 | 3.7 | 5.3 |
| 7.0 | 0.80 | 4.1 | 0.19 | 2.8 | 0.2 | 0.29 | 3.25 | 2.75 | 89.0 | 4.3 | 29.1 | 5.8 | 3.5 |
| 10.0 | 0.00 | 0.0 | 0.45 | 0.0 | 0.0 | -1.29 | -3.72 | 4.21 | 135.2 | 5.3 | 26.8 | 0.0 | 5.6 |
| 6.3 | 0.38 | 4.9 | 0.32 | 2.9 | 0.2 | 0.26 | 3.04 | 4.42 | 91.8 | 3.3 | 13.1 | 7.3 | 5.0 |
| 9.5 | 0.50 | 1.3 | 0.29 | 1.9 | 0.0 | 0.04 | 0.25 | 3.42 | 94.2 | 5.1 | 38.1 | 0.8 | 6.8 |
| 4.9 | 0.37 | 5.4 | 0.47 | 4.8 | 0.3 | 0.49 | 5.77 | 4.61 | 84.8 | 2.8 | 9.4 | 7.5 | 3.8 |
| 5.3 | 1.85 | 12.9 | 0.63 | 9.8 | 50.8 | 2.00 | 15.88 | 3.35 | 58.8 | 3.9 | 15.6 | 3.0 | 9.4 |
| 9.9 | 0.07 | 0.8 | 0.61 | 4.1 | 0.0 | 0.29 | 2.33 | 4.58 | 87.6 | 7.0 | 55.7 | 0.0 | 6.7 |
| 8.2 | 0.00 | 0.0 | 0.00 | 2.3 | 0.0 | 0.17 | 0.70 | 4.00 | 93.3 | 4.5 | 40.9 | 0.0 | 6.6 |
| 0.3 | 43.70 | 122.9 | 0.00 | 4.2 | 0.0 | 0.86 | 9.52 | 3.16 | 70.0 | 7.1 | 79.1 | 0.0 | 3.5 |
| 8.4 | 0.45 | 3.5 | 0.52 | 3.1 | 0.3 | 0.28 | 3.45 | 4.49 | 89.6 | 4.5 | 17.4 | 3.8 | 5.7 |
| 7.1 | 0.88 | 6.8 | 0.24 | 2.5 | 0.1 | 0.17 | 1.52 | 4.39 | 92.3 | 2.0 | 11.0 | 25.5 | 3.4 |
| 6.3 | 0.72 | 5.3 | 0.63 | 1.4 | 0.0 | 0.02 | 0.31 | 3.88 | 93.2 | 4.0 | 8.6 | 0.6 | 3.2 |
| 8.3 | 1.74 | 6.5 | -0.37 | 4.3 | 0.0 | 0.54 | 4.17 | 3.92 | 84.8 | 5.3 | 42.5 | 4.7 | 5.6 |
| 5.9 | 0.41 | 3.0 | 0.25 | 2.0 | 0.0 | 0.21 | 2.89 | 2.85 | 89.3 | 4.8 | 35.9 | 0.1 | 1.7 |
| 8.7 | 0.19 | 1.3 | 0.27 | 2.0 | 0.0 | 0.06 | 0.68 | 2.96 | 93.6 | 4.2 | 14.7 | 0.0 | 3.6 |
| 1.7 | 5.03 | 35.3 | 0.14 | 4.0 | 0.3 | 0.15 | 2.03 | 2.61 | 92.2 | 3.3 | 6.0 | 8.5 | 3.8 |
| 8.7 | 0.39 | 3.1 | 0.02 | 4.0 | 2.9 | 0.48 | 5.39 | 2.70 | 89.0 | 3.6 | 4.9 | 2.3 | 5.9 |
| 5.9 | 0.84 | 11.5 | 0.42 | 4.6 | 0.6 | 0.56 | 5.14 | 4.41 | 84.5 | 3.7 | 20.6 | 3.5 | 7.0 |
| 7.6 | 0.86 | 4.7 | 0.28 | 2.3 | 0.0 | 0.11 | 1.50 | 2.60 | 93.6 | 4.9 | 39.3 | 1.7 | 3.2 |
| 10.0 | 0.52 | 0.9 | 0.06 | 0.7 | 0.0 | -0.12 | -0.68 | 2.08 | 105.4 | 5.1 | 29.5 | 8.4 | 5.7 |
| 5.6 | 0.97 | 6.9 | 0.18 | 3.1 | 0.1 | 0.36 | 3.47 | 3.80 | 88.7 | 4.1 | 23.6 | 2.8 | 4.7 |
| 8.9 | 0.40 | 3.3 | 0.41 | 3.1 | 0.3 | 0.27 | 2.76 | 3.25 | 84.1 | 3.4 | 10.2 | 4.4 | 5.9 |
| 8.3 | 0.80 | 2.5 | 0.09 | 5.7 | 0.3 | 0.98 | 5.88 | 2.62 | 71.0 | 4.3 | 16.7 | 4.5 | 6.7 |
| 8.7 | 0.09 | 0.4 | 0.34 | 4.8 | 0.2 | 0.79 | 5.13 | 3.18 | 81.4 | 4.0 | 13.3 | 3.2 | 6.6 |
| 7.1 | 0.42 | 3.3 | 0.04 | 2.4 | 0.0 | 0.16 | 2.19 | 3.63 | 94.2 | 4.4 | 36.2 | 5.3 | 2.3 |
| 8.4 | 0.38 | 2.8 | 0.28 | 7.4 | 17.7 | 1.13 | 10.26 | 3.52 | 69.8 | 2.2 | 6.5 | 12.6 | 8.8 |
| 7.7 | 0.97 | 2.9 | 0.31 | 2.3 | 0.0 | 0.09 | 0.95 | 2.30 | 87.9 | 5.9 | 34.0 | 0.0 | 4.8 |
| 9.5 | 1.45 | 2.7 | 0.00 | 1.4 | 0.0 | -0.12 | -0.51 | 3.51 | 104.0 | 6.7 | 67.3 | 0.0 | 6.9 |
| 5.8 | 3.84 | 11.1 | 0.45 | 0.7 | 0.0 | -0.29 | -1.67 | 4.10 | 105.0 | 4.5 | 24.0 | 0.0 | 6.1 |
| 9.1 | 0.43 | 1.6 | 0.08 | 2.3 | 0.0 | 0.25 | 2.04 | 2.65 | 90.7 | 5.2 | 34.1 | 0.0 | 6.1 |
| 7.2 | 3.05 | 6.3 | 0.00 | 7.1 | 0.1 | 2.49 | 17.97 | 6.03 | 37.8 | 7.4 | 76.9 | 0.0 | 5.0 |
| 5.6 | 3.24 | 10.1 | 3.28 | 0.4 | -0.1 | -2.24 | -15.60 | 4.32 | 95.5 | 4.3 | 12.3 | 0.0 | 5.0 |

| Name | City | State | Rating | 2014 Rating | 2013 Rating | Total Assets ($Mil) | One Year Asset Growth | Asset Mix (As a % of Total Assets) | | | | Capital- ization Index | Net Worth Ratio |
|------|------|-------|--------|-------------|-------------|---------------------|-----------------------|-----------|-----------|-----------|-----------|--------|--------|
| | | | | | | | | Comm- ercial Loans | Cons- umer Loans | Mort- gage Loans | Secur- ities | | |
| SPRINGFIELD STREET RAILWAY EMPL CU | Springfield | MA | C+ | C+ | C+ | 1.6 | 2.61 | 0.0 | 41.2 | 0.0 | 0.0 | 10.0 | 22.2 |
| SPRUANCE CELLOPHANE CU | North Chesterfield | VA | D- | D- | D+ | 6.0 | 5.97 | 0.0 | 38.1 | 11.4 | 0.0 | 6.7 | 8.7 |
| ▲ SRI FCU | Menlo Park | CA | C+ | C | D+ | 78.7 | 2.43 | 0.1 | 10.7 | 19.4 | 28.2 | 6.1 | 8.8 |
| SRP FCU | North Augusta | SC | B | B+ | B+ | 713.9 | 4.97 | 2.0 | 37.1 | 11.3 | 25.8 | 7.8 | 9.5 |
| SRU FCU | Slippery Rock | PA | B | B | B | 41.1 | 7.18 | 0.8 | 11.6 | 8.9 | 35.4 | 10.0 | 11.0 |
| ▼ SS PETER & PAUL FCU | Allentown | PA | D+ | D+ | C- | <1 | 3.47 | 0.0 | 33.0 | 0.0 | 0.0 | 10.0 | 18.4 |
| ▼ SSMOK EMPL FCU | Oklahoma City | OK | D+ | C- | C- | 7.8 | 0.12 | 0.0 | 42.8 | 0.0 | 0.0 | 10.0 | 18.5 |
| ST AGNES EMPL CU | Fond du Lac | WI | D | D | D | 7.2 | -10.00 | 0.0 | 39.0 | 2.8 | 0.0 | 6.8 | 8.8 |
| ST ANDREW KIM FCU | Palisades Park | NJ | C | C- | D- | 2.1 | -7.71 | 0.0 | 42.8 | 0.0 | 0.0 | 10.0 | 12.4 |
| ▲ ST ANNE CU | New Bedford | MA | D | D- | D+ | 16.3 | -3.60 | 0.0 | 15.9 | 38.8 | 10.5 | 9.0 | 10.4 |
| ST ANNES CU OF FALL RIVER | Fall River | MA | C | C | C | 861.2 | 2.84 | 10.5 | 12.6 | 48.4 | 11.4 | 7.9 | 9.6 |
| ST ANNS ARLINGTON FCU | Arlington | VA | C | C | C | 2.6 | -8.76 | 0.0 | 11.4 | 12.2 | 0.0 | 10.0 | 12.6 |
| ST ANTHONY OF NEW BEDFORD FCU | New Bedford | MA | D | D+ | C | 10.3 | 2.60 | 0.5 | 12.5 | 14.1 | 0.0 | 9.0 | 10.4 |
| ST ANTHONY OF PADUA FCU | Fall River | MA | C | C | C+ | 26.0 | 2.93 | 0.0 | 4.0 | 30.4 | 0.0 | 10.0 | 23.3 |
| ST ATHANASIUS CU | Jesup | IA | D+ | D | C- | <1 | 18.23 | 0.0 | 94.4 | 0.0 | 0.0 | 10.0 | 15.4 |
| ST AUGUSTINE CU | Scott City | MO | D- | D- | D- | 1.6 | 15.55 | 0.0 | 42.1 | 0.0 | 0.0 | 5.1 | 7.1 |
| ▲ ST AUGUSTINE PRESBYTERIAN FCU | Bronx | NY | C- | D+ | C- | <1 | 8.51 | 0.0 | 3.9 | 0.0 | 42.2 | 10.0 | 11.8 |
| ST BERNARD PARISH SCHOOL BOARD EMPL | Chalmette | LA | B- | B- | B- | 15.0 | 8.58 | 0.0 | 23.0 | 0.0 | 45.3 | 10.0 | 23.6 |
| ST CLOUD FCU | Saint Cloud | MN | B | B | B- | 120.4 | 9.89 | 1.9 | 42.1 | 25.3 | 0.0 | 6.7 | 8.7 |
| ST COLMAN & AFFILIATES FCU | Cleveland | OH | E+ | E+ | E+ | 6.5 | 1.92 | 0.0 | 54.8 | 0.0 | 0.0 | 6.6 | 8.6 |
| ▲ ST COLUMBKILLE FCU | Parma | OH | C+ | C | C- | 24.9 | -0.87 | 0.0 | 10.6 | 19.3 | 20.8 | 6.6 | 8.6 |
| ST ELIZABETH CU | Northampton | PA | B- | B- | C+ | 10.4 | 1.17 | 0.0 | 4.8 | 10.8 | 0.0 | 10.0 | 18.4 |
| ▲ ST ELIZABETH EMPL CU | Appleton | WI | C- | C- | C- | 4.6 | -0.60 | 0.0 | 45.3 | 0.0 | 0.0 | 10.0 | 14.8 |
| ST FRANCIS FCU | Greenville | SC | C+ | C+ | C+ | 8.4 | 1.79 | 0.0 | 48.7 | 0.0 | 0.0 | 10.0 | 18.0 |
| ST FRANCIS MEDICAL CENTER FCU | Honolulu | HI | D+ | D | D | 9.7 | -2.09 | 0.0 | 67.3 | 0.0 | 0.0 | 10.0 | 12.4 |
| ST FRANCIS X FCU | Petoskey | MI | A | A | A- | 115.9 | 6.50 | 3.8 | 8.0 | 39.2 | 22.0 | 10.0 | 14.7 |
| ST GERTRUDES CU | Mora | NM | E+ | E+ | E+ | 1.6 | -7.39 | 0.0 | 35.6 | 19.1 | 0.0 | 6.7 | 8.7 |
| ▼ ST GREGORY PARISH CU | Chicago | IL | D- | D- | E+ | <1 | 10.84 | 0.0 | 20.7 | 0.0 | 0.0 | 7.0 | 9.0 |
| ▼ ST HELEN FCU | Dayton | OH | D- | D | C- | 2.6 | 1.24 | 0.0 | 43.9 | 0.0 | 0.0 | 9.8 | 10.9 |
| ST HELENA PARISH CU | Chicago | IL | C | C- | C- | <1 | 24.21 | 0.0 | 58.5 | 0.0 | 0.0 | 10.0 | 11.0 |
| ▼ ST HELENS COMMUNITY FCU | Saint Helens | OR | C- | B- | C+ | 182.3 | 2.06 | 25.8 | 26.5 | 35.9 | 8.8 | 5.5 | 7.5 |
| ST JAMES AME CHURCH FCU | Miami | FL | D | D | C- | <1 | -7.60 | 0.0 | 10.0 | 0.0 | 0.0 | 10.0 | 21.0 |
| ST JAMES HOSPITAL EMPL FCU | Chicago Heights | IL | D | D | D+ | 9.9 | 3.96 | 0.0 | 37.9 | 0.0 | 0.0 | 7.3 | 9.2 |
| ST JAMES PARISH CU | Cincinnati | OH | C | C | C | 6.2 | -6.99 | 2.0 | 36.1 | 0.0 | 22.0 | 10.0 | 14.5 |
| ST JAMES PUBLIC SCHOOLS FCU | Saint James | MN | C | C | C- | 2.6 | -11.08 | 2.5 | 28.5 | 0.3 | 5.3 | 10.0 | 12.7 |
| ST JEANS CU | Lynn | MA | C | C+ | C+ | 207.0 | 34.48 | 3.3 | 14.5 | 38.8 | 6.4 | 8.4 | 10.0 |
| ST JOE VALLEY CU | Saint Maries | ID | E+ | E+ | E+ | 6.9 | -4.39 | 0.0 | 15.1 | 13.8 | 0.0 | 4.1 | 6.1 |
| ST JOHN SELF-HELP FCU | Reserve | LA | D | D | D+ | 1.3 | -5.28 | 0.0 | 13.9 | 1.8 | 0.0 | 10.0 | 37.7 |
| ST JOHN UNITED FCU | Buffalo | NY | C- | D | D+ | 1.2 | 8.70 | 0.0 | 16.9 | 0.0 | 0.0 | 10.0 | 13.9 |
| ST JOHNS BUFFALO FCU | Buffalo | NY | D | D | D- | 3.9 | 0.10 | 0.0 | 40.5 | 9.0 | 24.0 | 8.7 | 10.1 |
| ST JOSEPH HOSPITAL EMPLS CU | Nashua | NH | D | D | C- | 6.2 | -7.55 | 0.0 | 35.4 | 0.0 | 0.0 | 8.6 | 10.1 |
| ST JOSEPH MEDICAL CENTER MD FCU | Towson | MD | B- | B- | B- | 14.4 | 2.31 | 0.0 | 33.4 | 0.0 | 44.3 | 10.0 | 13.8 |
| ST JOSEPH TEACHERS CU | Saint Joseph | MO | E+ | E+ | E+ | 7.9 | 7.35 | 0.0 | 27.8 | 0.0 | 0.0 | 5.1 | 7.1 |
| ▼ ST JOSEPHS BROADMOOR FCU | Shreveport | LA | D | D | E+ | 6.2 | -9.25 | 2.2 | 19.6 | 20.1 | 0.0 | 9.1 | 10.4 |
| ST JOSEPHS CANTON PARISH FCU | Canton | OH | D | D | D+ | 44.0 | 0.26 | 1.8 | 30.0 | 5.3 | 9.1 | 5.6 | 7.6 |
| ST JOSEPHS HOSPITAL FCU | Tampa | FL | B+ | B+ | B+ | 37.1 | 3.91 | 0.0 | 43.3 | 0.0 | 20.1 | 10.0 | 13.8 |
| ▲ ST JUDE CU | Chicago | IL | C- | D+ | D+ | <1 | -5.19 | 0.0 | 22.4 | 0.0 | 0.0 | 10.0 | 21.7 |
| ST JULES CU | Lafayette | LA | D | D+ | D+ | 10.7 | 1.83 | 0.0 | 35.6 | 5.9 | 0.0 | 6.0 | 8.0 |
| ST LANDRY PARISH FCU | Opelousas | LA | E+ | E+ | E+ | 6.6 | -0.30 | 0.0 | 27.7 | 16.5 | 0.0 | 4.7 | 6.7 |
| ▲ ST LOUIS COMMUNITY CU | Saint Louis | MO | B | B | B- | 238.1 | 0.92 | 1.0 | 31.6 | 3.5 | 24.9 | 10.0 | 14.3 |
| ▼ ST LOUIS FIREFIGHTERS & COMMUNITY CU | Saint Louis | MO | D+ | C- | D+ | 17.9 | 2.56 | 0.0 | 17.1 | 0.0 | 4.8 | 10.0 | 13.7 |
| ST LOUIS NEWSPAPER CARRIERS CU | Fenton | MO | C | C | C- | 13.0 | 0.27 | 0.0 | 7.7 | 59.9 | 0.0 | 9.4 | 10.6 |
| ST LOUIS POLICEMENS CU | Saint Louis | MO | C+ | C+ | C- | 19.4 | -2.88 | 0.0 | 24.1 | 0.0 | 7.6 | 10.0 | 15.8 |
| ST LUDMILA S CU | Cedar Rapids | IA | D+ | D+ | D+ | <1 | -1.46 | 0.0 | 64.8 | 0.0 | 0.0 | 10.0 | 26.4 |
| ▲ ST MARK CU | Chicago | IL | C | C- | C- | <1 | -1.48 | 0.0 | 6.8 | 0.0 | 0.0 | 10.0 | 13.7 |
| ▼ ST MARKS FCU | New York | NY | D | C- | C+ | <1 | -19.64 | 0.0 | 0.0 | 0.0 | 0.0 | 10.0 | 16.1 |
| ST MARTIN DE PORRES PARISH FCU | Chicago | IL | C | C | D+ | <1 | 8.21 | 0.0 | 0.0 | 0.0 | 0.0 | 9.2 | 10.4 |
| ST MARY CU | Walsenburg | CO | C- | C- | C- | 8.9 | -0.98 | 0.0 | 18.1 | 11.3 | 0.0 | 10.0 | 16.5 |
| ▲ ST MARY PARISH SCHOOL EMPL FCU | Franklin | LA | C- | D+ | C- | <1 | -4.21 | 0.0 | 48.1 | 0.0 | 0.0 | 10.0 | 21.2 |
| ST MARYS & AFFILIATES CU | Madison | WI | C | C | C+ | 33.4 | 0.69 | 1.8 | 29.8 | 15.4 | 0.9 | 8.7 | 10.1 |

| Asset Quality Index | Non-Performing Loans as a % of Total Loans | as a % of Capital | Net Charge-Offs Avg Loans | Profitability Index | Net Income ($Mil) | Return on Assets | Return on Equity | Net Interest Spread | Overhead Efficiency Ratio | Liquidity Index | Liquidity Ratio | Hot Money Ratio | Stability Index |
|---|---|---|---|---|---|---|---|---|---|---|---|---|---|
| 9.8 | 0.75 | 1.3 | 0.00 | 4.5 | 0.0 | 0.42 | 1.88 | 6.70 | 90.0 | 6.1 | 47.9 | 0.0 | 6.9 |
| 9.8 | 0.13 | 0.8 | 0.04 | 0.4 | 0.0 | -0.60 | -6.48 | 4.73 | 117.4 | 4.8 | 18.0 | 0.0 | 3.3 |
| 6.4 | 0.05 | 7.9 | -0.01 | 3.6 | 0.2 | 0.39 | 4.93 | 2.65 | 86.7 | 4.7 | 20.6 | 2.3 | 3.9 |
| 7.1 | 1.12 | 7.4 | 0.71 | 5.3 | 4.5 | 0.83 | 9.06 | 3.39 | 79.7 | 4.4 | 15.8 | 2.3 | 6.1 |
| 8.4 | 0.57 | 1.9 | 0.57 | 5.3 | 0.2 | 0.74 | 6.77 | 2.25 | 64.9 | 5.6 | 27.8 | 0.4 | 5.9 |
| 6.3 | 7.27 | 15.6 | 0.00 | 0.0 | 0.0 | -3.00 | -14.41 | 3.60 | 57.1 | 6.5 | 43.5 | 0.0 | 6.8 |
| 9.8 | 0.13 | 1.7 | 0.00 | 0.8 | 0.0 | -0.22 | -1.20 | 3.67 | 106.3 | 4.2 | 7.7 | 0.0 | 5.8 |
| 9.7 | 0.00 | 0.0 | 0.37 | 0.8 | 0.0 | -0.59 | -6.69 | 2.85 | 119.7 | 6.1 | 49.8 | 0.0 | 4.2 |
| 8.3 | 2.09 | 6.3 | -0.30 | 7.2 | 0.0 | 1.48 | 13.01 | 5.43 | 92.5 | 7.5 | 85.2 | 0.0 | 4.7 |
| 8.7 | 0.08 | 0.4 | 0.12 | 0.7 | 0.0 | -0.08 | -0.79 | 2.86 | 102.7 | 4.9 | 41.1 | 6.4 | 4.2 |
| 7.5 | 0.67 | 6.0 | 0.07 | 3.1 | 2.5 | 0.39 | 4.21 | 2.46 | 85.8 | 2.5 | 16.1 | 15.5 | 6.9 |
| 10.0 | 0.00 | 0.0 | 0.00 | 3.1 | 0.0 | 0.29 | 2.42 | 2.35 | 85.7 | 4.2 | 5.9 | 0.0 | 5.7 |
| 10.0 | 0.03 | 0.1 | 0.62 | 0.5 | 0.0 | -0.49 | -4.56 | 2.76 | 110.8 | 5.2 | 29.3 | 0.0 | 4.3 |
| 9.5 | 1.59 | 2.6 | 0.09 | 2.4 | 0.0 | 0.22 | 0.95 | 2.16 | 86.5 | 4.4 | 21.0 | 6.0 | 7.0 |
| 4.7 | 0.48 | 2.6 | 0.00 | 4.5 | 0.0 | 0.62 | 4.00 | 5.67 | 84.0 | 2.7 | 7.2 | 0.0 | 3.7 |
| 9.3 | 0.00 | 0.0 | 0.00 | 2.1 | 0.0 | 0.19 | 2.40 | 1.62 | 93.8 | 4.5 | 8.8 | 0.0 | 1.7 |
| 8.2 | 0.00 | 0.0 | 0.00 | 1.5 | 0.0 | 0.00 | 0.00 | 0.00 | 0.0 | 7.0 | 57.8 | 0.0 | 6.6 |
| 10.0 | 0.99 | 1.3 | -0.03 | 5.0 | 0.1 | 0.80 | 3.28 | 2.64 | 66.7 | 6.2 | 62.1 | 1.1 | 7.3 |
| 7.4 | 0.50 | 4.6 | 0.25 | 6.4 | 0.9 | 0.99 | 11.45 | 3.54 | 78.4 | 2.8 | 5.9 | 3.8 | 5.7 |
| 2.4 | 3.84 | 25.0 | 1.31 | 3.3 | 0.0 | 0.25 | 2.88 | 4.73 | 79.0 | 4.2 | 27.1 | 0.0 | 1.0 |
| 10.0 | 0.01 | 0.1 | 0.00 | 3.7 | 0.1 | 0.49 | 5.88 | 2.02 | 72.9 | 5.3 | 28.6 | 0.0 | 4.0 |
| 10.0 | 0.00 | 0.0 | 0.00 | 4.3 | 0.1 | 0.67 | 3.70 | 1.95 | 66.0 | 4.9 | 7.5 | 0.0 | 7.8 |
| 8.7 | 0.33 | 1.0 | 0.00 | 1.5 | 0.0 | 0.09 | 0.59 | 3.41 | 92.1 | 5.3 | 23.3 | 0.0 | 6.1 |
| 7.2 | 1.26 | 3.5 | 0.29 | 9.7 | 0.1 | 1.49 | 8.27 | 6.15 | 73.5 | 5.8 | 31.6 | 0.0 | 5.7 |
| 0.7 | 9.55 | 39.5 | 1.71 | 10.0 | 0.1 | 1.51 | 13.01 | 7.32 | 43.5 | 5.9 | 42.4 | 0.0 | 6.2 |
| 7.1 | 1.28 | 7.1 | 0.01 | 9.8 | 1.3 | 1.52 | 10.31 | 3.81 | 64.2 | 2.1 | 3.7 | 17.1 | 9.7 |
| 1.7 | 7.38 | 45.1 | 0.36 | 3.5 | 0.0 | 0.49 | 5.84 | 6.76 | 86.8 | 5.1 | 38.8 | 0.0 | 1.0 |
| 1.7 | 27.27 | 50.0 | 0.00 | 4.1 | 0.0 | 0.39 | 4.17 | 5.23 | 77.8 | 8.1 | 85.6 | 0.0 | 5.5 |
| 8.2 | 1.15 | 4.8 | 1.81 | 0.0 | 0.0 | -1.22 | -10.85 | 2.64 | 120.4 | 5.5 | 49.0 | 0.0 | 6.2 |
| 4.9 | 1.32 | 5.0 | 0.00 | 8.7 | 0.0 | 1.19 | 10.26 | 11.59 | 85.7 | 6.1 | 45.7 | 0.0 | 6.7 |
| 6.1 | 0.50 | 5.3 | 0.35 | 1.9 | 0.1 | 0.08 | 1.09 | 4.08 | 92.5 | 3.6 | 15.0 | 7.1 | 4.5 |
| 10.0 | 0.00 | 0.0 | 1.73 | 0.2 | 0.0 | -0.98 | -4.71 | 9.41 | 142.9 | 8.5 | 102.8 | 0.0 | 6.2 |
| 8.3 | 0.97 | 4.0 | 0.00 | 0.8 | 0.0 | -0.12 | -1.31 | 3.29 | 100.3 | 4.5 | 14.8 | 0.0 | 3.0 |
| 9.1 | 0.91 | 3.0 | -0.55 | 2.9 | 0.0 | 0.30 | 2.11 | 3.23 | 88.2 | 4.6 | 19.9 | 0.0 | 6.2 |
| 9.8 | 0.00 | 0.0 | 0.00 | 1.6 | 0.0 | -0.10 | -0.82 | 2.36 | 104.4 | 5.2 | 42.7 | 0.0 | 5.6 |
| 9.0 | 0.36 | 3.1 | 0.12 | 2.8 | 0.3 | 0.26 | 2.80 | 3.21 | 91.2 | 3.1 | 15.4 | 15.1 | 6.0 |
| 9.9 | 0.00 | 0.0 | 0.00 | 1.5 | 0.0 | -0.06 | -0.95 | 2.97 | 101.8 | 5.2 | 29.6 | 0.0 | 1.0 |
| 10.0 | 0.00 | 0.0 | 0.63 | 0.0 | 0.0 | -1.42 | -3.73 | 1.70 | 181.3 | 6.8 | 126.7 | 0.0 | 5.2 |
| 6.6 | 3.39 | 7.5 | 0.00 | 2.1 | 0.0 | 0.34 | 2.53 | 7.25 | 81.8 | 7.7 | 77.2 | 0.0 | 4.9 |
| 5.4 | 0.47 | 2.8 | 0.95 | 2.3 | 0.0 | 0.10 | 1.01 | 4.79 | 94.7 | 3.9 | 4.4 | 0.0 | 3.8 |
| 8.9 | 0.74 | 2.8 | 0.06 | 1.2 | 0.0 | 0.08 | 0.87 | 2.96 | 102.4 | 5.2 | 20.4 | 0.0 | 4.7 |
| 9.6 | 0.76 | 1.9 | 0.00 | 4.1 | 0.1 | 0.61 | 4.44 | 2.33 | 74.4 | 5.5 | 28.8 | 0.0 | 6.7 |
| 7.2 | 1.10 | 5.2 | -0.35 | 3.8 | 0.0 | 0.47 | 6.58 | 3.57 | 87.0 | 5.7 | 28.3 | 0.0 | 1.7 |
| 5.7 | 1.85 | 9.8 | -0.14 | 1.5 | 0.0 | -0.36 | -3.46 | 3.68 | 121.6 | 5.0 | 41.5 | 11.1 | 4.1 |
| 4.9 | 1.99 | 11.5 | 1.44 | 3.1 | 0.1 | 0.27 | 3.69 | 3.60 | 84.3 | 5.5 | 34.8 | 0.7 | 2.4 |
| 9.8 | 0.29 | 0.9 | 0.15 | 8.4 | 0.3 | 1.14 | 8.45 | 4.30 | 69.3 | 3.0 | 10.6 | 17.4 | 7.9 |
| 9.5 | 0.00 | 0.0 | -3.58 | 2.2 | 0.0 | 0.30 | 1.40 | 3.60 | 87.5 | 7.1 | 65.3 | 0.0 | 4.9 |
| 7.8 | 0.78 | 4.4 | 0.65 | 0.7 | 0.0 | -0.26 | -3.24 | 2.83 | 102.7 | 5.4 | 34.5 | 0.0 | 3.2 |
| 0.3 | 12.87 | 85.5 | 1.39 | 0.0 | -0.1 | -1.14 | -16.31 | 4.38 | 127.1 | 5.1 | 49.2 | 0.0 | 2.5 |
| 8.7 | 1.53 | 4.5 | 1.49 | 4.0 | 1.1 | 0.61 | 4.59 | 3.81 | 86.0 | 5.2 | 26.5 | 2.5 | 7.0 |
| 8.9 | 1.61 | 3.5 | 0.24 | 0.8 | 0.0 | -0.27 | -1.87 | 4.39 | 98.9 | 6.6 | 37.9 | 2.0 | 6.2 |
| 9.4 | 0.18 | 1.2 | 0.00 | 3.3 | 0.0 | 0.24 | 2.25 | 1.25 | 80.3 | 3.5 | 5.6 | 0.0 | 5.4 |
| 9.3 | 2.23 | 4.1 | 0.53 | 3.1 | 0.1 | 0.42 | 2.69 | 2.75 | 79.5 | 5.5 | 15.9 | 0.0 | 6.7 |
| 4.5 | 6.84 | 15.8 | 0.00 | 1.5 | 0.0 | 0.00 | 0.00 | 3.49 | 100.0 | 5.7 | 49.0 | 0.0 | 6.9 |
| 10.0 | 0.00 | 0.0 | 0.00 | 1.9 | 0.0 | 0.20 | 1.47 | 1.69 | 100.0 | 8.1 | 89.2 | 0.0 | 6.3 |
| 9.5 | 50.00 | 3.5 | 57.14 | 0.0 | 0.0 | -3.17 | -20.20 | 0.00 | 400.0 | 7.4 | 111.9 | 0.0 | 6.2 |
| 9.7 | 0.00 | 0.0 | 0.00 | 2.6 | 0.0 | -0.64 | -6.06 | 6.20 | 300.0 | 8.3 | 90.5 | 0.0 | 4.3 |
| 7.2 | 3.72 | 6.2 | -0.29 | 2.5 | 0.0 | 0.18 | 1.09 | 3.01 | 92.4 | 6.9 | 56.7 | 0.0 | 6.4 |
| 4.4 | 2.54 | 5.4 | 1.63 | 6.1 | 0.0 | 1.28 | 6.20 | 8.59 | 83.3 | 5.9 | 64.4 | 0.0 | 3.7 |
| 9.6 | 0.06 | 0.3 | 0.31 | 2.5 | 0.1 | 0.21 | 2.11 | 2.70 | 91.5 | 4.7 | 49.0 | 4.8 | 5.0 |

| Name | City | State | Rating | 2014 Rating | 2013 Rating | Total Assets ($Mil) | One Year Asset Growth | Commercial Loans | Consumer Loans | Mortgage Loans | Securities | Capitalization Index | Net Worth Ratio |
|------|------|-------|--------|-------------|-------------|---------------------|-----------------------|------------------|----------------|----------------|------------|----------------------|-----------------|
| ST MARYS ASSUMPTION PARISH FCU | Swanton | OH | C- | C- | C- | 1.2 | -11.09 | 0.0 | 8.9 | 0.0 | 0.0 | 10.0 | 15.4 |
| ST MARYS BANK CU | Manchester | NH | C | C | C+ | 880.1 | 7.66 | 10.5 | 41.2 | 32.5 | 2.8 | 5.8 | 7.8 |
| ST MARYS CU | Marlborough | MA | C | B- | B- | 732.4 | 8.56 | 4.7 | 31.8 | 38.5 | 13.6 | 9.2 | 10.5 |
| ▼ ST MATTHEWS FCU | Virginia Beach | VA | C- | C | C | 6.0 | 4.60 | 0.0 | 24.9 | 0.0 | 13.7 | 10.0 | 16.5 |
| ST MICHAELS FALL RIVER FCU | Fall River | MA | C+ | C+ | C+ | 38.5 | 0.16 | 14.7 | 9.9 | 66.0 | 0.0 | 9.4 | 10.6 |
| ST MICHAELS FCU | Craig | CO | D | D- | D- | 1.0 | 9.73 | 0.0 | 27.3 | 0.0 | 0.0 | 6.5 | 8.5 |
| ST MONICA FCU | Gary | IN | C- | C- | C+ | <1 | -8.60 | 0.0 | 0.0 | 0.0 | 0.0 | 9.1 | 10.4 |
| ▼ ST NICHOLAS FCU | Wilkes-Barre | PA | D- | D | D+ | 4.9 | -3.70 | 2.0 | 23.2 | 3.1 | 63.1 | 9.6 | 10.7 |
| ▲ ST PASCHAL BAYLONS FCU | Highland Heights | OH | C- | D+ | D | 5.7 | -10.00 | 0.0 | 6.0 | 0.0 | 0.0 | 10.0 | 13.4 |
| ST PATRICKS PARISH CU | Fairfield | VT | D+ | D+ | D+ | <1 | -1.21 | 0.0 | 42.2 | 0.0 | 0.0 | 10.0 | 12.6 |
| ST PATS EMPL FCU | Missoula | MT | D+ | D+ | D | 3.7 | 0.27 | 0.0 | 45.4 | 0.0 | 0.0 | 7.8 | 9.5 |
| ST PAUL AME ZION CHURCH CU | Cleveland | OH | D+ | C- | C- | <1 | 1.79 | 0.0 | 50.2 | 0.0 | 0.0 | 10.0 | 21.6 |
| ST PAUL FCU | Saint Paul | MN | A | A- | B+ | 140.9 | 6.43 | 1.3 | 30.4 | 31.5 | 0.0 | 10.0 | 12.0 |
| ST PAULS FCU | Philadelphia | PA | D+ | C- | C | <1 | -3.15 | 0.0 | 13.8 | 0.0 | 0.0 | 10.0 | 22.8 |
| ST PAULS PARISH FCU | Akron | OH | D | D | D | 4.7 | -1.17 | 0.0 | 16.8 | 13.1 | 32.3 | 10.0 | 19.4 |
| ST PHILIPS CHURCH FCU | New York | NY | C | C | C+ | 1.6 | -6.17 | 0.0 | 4.4 | 0.0 | 0.0 | 10.0 | 24.4 |
| ST PIUS X CHURCH FCU | Rochester | NY | C+ | C | C- | 65.0 | -3.12 | 0.8 | 27.1 | 29.9 | 14.0 | 9.4 | 10.6 |
| ST STEPHENS FCU | Houston | TX | C+ | C | C- | <1 | 1.90 | 0.0 | 45.8 | 0.0 | 0.0 | 10.0 | 52.6 |
| ST TAMMANY FCU | Slidell | LA | C+ | C | C- | 19.8 | 0.91 | 0.0 | 62.9 | 0.0 | 5.1 | 10.0 | 11.3 |
| ST THOMAS CU | Nashville | TN | E+ | E+ | E+ | 24.3 | 0.36 | 0.0 | 31.4 | 25.1 | 0.0 | 6.0 | 8.0 |
| ST THOMAS EMPL FCU | Saint Paul | MN | D+ | D+ | D+ | 3.9 | 8.68 | 0.0 | 42.6 | 0.0 | 29.9 | 8.1 | 9.8 |
| ST THOMAS FCU | Charlotte Amalie | VI | B+ | B+ | B+ | 54.4 | 5.07 | 0.0 | 53.4 | 0.0 | 5.5 | 10.0 | 28.3 |
| ST THOMAS MORE FCU | Arlington | VA | C- | C | D+ | <1 | -0.92 | 0.0 | 16.4 | 0.0 | 33.3 | 10.0 | 37.5 |
| ▲ ST VINCENTS MEDICAL CENTER FCU | Bridgeport | CT | C- | D+ | C- | 19.6 | 1.85 | 0.0 | 15.7 | 0.0 | 66.1 | 10.0 | 11.7 |
| STALEY CU | Decatur | IL | C+ | B- | B- | 124.2 | -0.19 | 0.5 | 33.2 | 35.9 | 10.5 | 8.1 | 9.8 |
| ▲ STAMFORD FCU | Stamford | CT | B- | C+ | C+ | 57.3 | 2.97 | 0.0 | 21.4 | 14.2 | 0.0 | 10.0 | 11.2 |
| STAMFORD HEALTHCARE CU INC | Stamford | CT | C+ | C+ | C+ | 17.8 | 3.44 | 0.0 | 20.3 | 0.0 | 8.4 | 9.6 | 10.8 |
| STAMFORD POSTAL EMPL FCU | Stamford | CT | C- | D+ | C- | 12.6 | -2.44 | 0.0 | 26.7 | 0.0 | 0.0 | 10.0 | 27.0 |
| ▼ STANDARD REGISTER FCU | Dayton | OH | C+ | B- | C | 40.0 | -5.18 | 11.2 | 32.2 | 22.9 | 6.9 | 10.0 | 18.5 |
| STANDARD STEEL EMPL FCU | Burnham | PA | E+ | E+ | E+ | 5.5 | 0.38 | 0.0 | 26.7 | 6.5 | 49.5 | 5.4 | 7.4 |
| STANFORD FCU | Palo Alto | CA | A- | A- | B+ | 1821.2 | 8.98 | 13.0 | 6.0 | 43.3 | 28.0 | 7.8 | 9.5 |
| STANWOOD AREA FCU | New Stanton | PA | D- | D- | D+ | 12.2 | -6.05 | 0.4 | 22.6 | 0.0 | 0.0 | 9.8 | 10.9 |
| STAR CHOICE CU | Bloomington | MN | C- | C- | C | 47.0 | 0.44 | 1.1 | 33.0 | 32.1 | 0.0 | 7.1 | 9.1 |
| STAR CU | Madison | WI | B- | B- | B- | <1 | 5.71 | 0.0 | 0.0 | 0.0 | 0.0 | 10.0 | 56.8 |
| STAR HARBOR FCU | Rancho Dominguez | CA | D | D | C- | 13.6 | -0.85 | 4.0 | 34.0 | 9.8 | 0.0 | 10.0 | 17.4 |
| STAR OF TEXAS CU | Austin | TX | C+ | C+ | B- | 34.9 | 5.01 | 10.9 | 16.0 | 26.3 | 1.4 | 10.0 | 11.5 |
| STAR ONE CU | Sunnyvale | CA | A- | A- | A- | 7760.2 | 13.70 | 1.0 | 3.0 | 33.5 | 49.6 | 9.8 | 10.9 |
| STAR TECH FCU | Greenwood Village | CO | C- | C- | C- | 8.2 | 3.52 | 0.6 | 45.7 | 0.0 | 0.0 | 10.0 | 18.0 |
| STAR USA FCU | Charleston | WV | C- | D+ | C- | 160.6 | -4.18 | 5.6 | 29.5 | 16.8 | 17.9 | 7.0 | 9.0 |
| ▼ STARCOR CU | Becker | MN | C- | C | C+ | 7.9 | -1.88 | 0.0 | 66.9 | 0.0 | 0.0 | 10.0 | 14.3 |
| STARK FCU | Canton | OH | C | C | C- | 111.8 | 2.16 | 6.1 | 25.4 | 11.6 | 2.3 | 9.8 | 10.8 |
| STARK METROPOLITAN HOUSING AUTHORIT | Canton | OH | D | D+ | C | 1.4 | -17.77 | 0.0 | 70.9 | 0.0 | 0.0 | 5.8 | 7.8 |
| STARR COUNTY TEACHERS FCU | Rio Grande City | TX | B- | B- | B- | 27.0 | 7.02 | 0.0 | 37.2 | 0.0 | 0.0 | 10.0 | 17.2 |
| STATE AGENCIES FCU | Shreveport | LA | B- | B- | B- | 9.5 | 4.35 | 0.0 | 30.4 | 11.2 | 0.0 | 10.0 | 22.8 |
| STATE COLLEGE FCU | State College | PA | D | D | D+ | 15.2 | -1.26 | 0.0 | 25.9 | 17.3 | 13.4 | 5.9 | 7.9 |
| STATE CS EMPL FCU | Watertown | NY | C+ | C+ | C+ | 15.9 | 6.69 | 0.0 | 48.5 | 0.0 | 17.4 | 10.0 | 12.7 |
| STATE CU | Charleston | WV | A- | A- | A- | 61.7 | 3.59 | 0.0 | 26.4 | 29.3 | 2.8 | 10.0 | 13.0 |
| STATE DEPT FCU | Alexandria | VA | B+ | B+ | B | 1677.9 | 5.88 | 1.0 | 11.0 | 28.7 | 44.5 | 7.8 | 9.5 |
| STATE EMPL CU | Alton | IL | C | C | C- | 5.5 | -3.09 | 0.0 | 80.2 | 0.0 | 0.0 | 10.0 | 18.9 |
| STATE EMPL CU | Raleigh | NC | B- | B- | C+ | 31162.0 | 7.77 | 1.4 | 10.3 | 44.7 | 0.6 | 5.8 | 7.8 |
| STATE EMPL CU | Santa Fe | NM | A- | A- | A- | 417.2 | 5.48 | 3.5 | 48.9 | 27.9 | 8.0 | 10.0 | 11.7 |
| STATE EMPL CU OF MARYLAND INC | Linthicum | MD | B | B | B+ | 2923.3 | 5.41 | 5.0 | 24.0 | 39.4 | 11.3 | 8.8 | 10.2 |
| STATE EMPL FCU | Albany | NY | B- | B- | B- | 3002.3 | 7.21 | 7.1 | 22.5 | 24.2 | 33.7 | 5.2 | 7.3 |
| STATE FARM FCU | Bloomington | IL | B | B+ | B+ | 3954.2 | 1.24 | 0.0 | 20.7 | 0.0 | 75.9 | 10.0 | 12.4 |
| STATE HIGHWAY CU | Union Gap | WA | C+ | C+ | B | 27.9 | -5.57 | 3.2 | 15.3 | 30.3 | 0.0 | 10.0 | 15.8 |
| STATE HIGHWAY PATROL FCU | Columbus | OH | B | B- | B- | 60.5 | -2.77 | 0.0 | 25.8 | 13.1 | 17.2 | 10.0 | 12.4 |
| STATE POLICE CU INC | Meriden | CT | B- | B- | B- | 60.7 | 0.13 | 0.0 | 4.1 | 26.8 | 6.2 | 10.0 | 15.0 |
| ▼ STATE SERVICE CU | Indianapolis | IN | D | D+ | D+ | 4.7 | -0.61 | 0.0 | 31.5 | 0.2 | 0.0 | 10.0 | 12.0 |
| STATE UNIV OF NY GENESEO FCU | Geneseo | NY | C+ | C+ | B- | 6.2 | 8.66 | 0.0 | 20.1 | 18.3 | 0.0 | 10.0 | 27.5 |
| ▲ STATEWIDE FCU | Flowood | MS | B- | C+ | C+ | 107.4 | 6.42 | 0.0 | 21.5 | 10.2 | 31.1 | 6.0 | 8.0 |

| Asset Quality Index | Non-Performing Loans as a % of Total Loans | Non-Performing Loans as a % of Capital | Net Charge-Offs / Avg Loans | Profitability Index | Net Income ($Mil) | Return on Assets | Return on Equity | Net Interest Spread | Overhead Efficiency Ratio | Liquidity Index | Liquidity Ratio | Hot Money Ratio | Stability Index |
|---|---|---|---|---|---|---|---|---|---|---|---|---|---|
| 9.0 | 0.00 | 0.0 | 0.00 | 1.5 | 0.0 | -0.11 | -0.70 | 1.00 | 122.2 | 6.1 | 61.9 | 0.0 | 7.0 |
| 7.7 | 0.33 | 3.9 | 0.25 | 3.2 | 2.7 | 0.42 | 5.80 | 2.87 | 84.9 | 3.1 | 11.2 | 6.2 | 5.1 |
| 8.2 | 0.44 | 3.3 | 0.12 | 2.7 | 1.3 | 0.23 | 2.19 | 2.39 | 89.3 | 2.2 | 2.1 | 13.4 | 7.4 |
| 7.1 | 5.10 | 11.3 | 0.37 | 2.5 | 0.0 | 0.02 | 0.13 | 6.17 | 95.1 | 7.1 | 57.7 | 0.0 | 6.7 |
| 5.2 | 1.61 | 12.0 | 0.33 | 3.6 | 0.1 | 0.38 | 3.68 | 5.12 | 83.1 | 3.8 | 19.8 | 3.2 | 5.6 |
| 7.3 | 1.23 | 4.0 | 0.00 | 2.7 | 0.0 | 0.40 | 4.71 | 2.79 | 63.6 | 7.7 | 74.7 | 0.0 | 2.3 |
| 10.0 | 0.00 | 0.0 | 0.00 | 1.9 | 0.0 | 0.00 | 0.00 | 3.81 | 100.0 | 8.7 | 98.9 | 0.0 | 5.3 |
| 4.9 | 1.49 | 6.6 | 2.41 | 0.1 | 0.0 | -0.64 | -5.87 | 2.80 | 122.9 | 4.6 | 18.4 | 0.0 | 4.3 |
| 8.9 | 5.08 | 2.8 | 0.00 | 1.6 | 0.0 | 0.07 | 0.52 | 0.96 | 94.9 | 6.3 | 74.0 | 0.0 | 4.7 |
| 1.2 | 7.00 | 35.2 | 0.00 | 7.6 | 0.0 | 1.35 | 11.49 | 5.54 | 66.7 | 5.4 | 31.9 | 0.0 | 7.2 |
| 7.8 | 0.27 | 1.4 | 0.00 | 5.0 | 0.0 | 0.71 | 7.73 | 3.01 | 71.8 | 4.6 | 31.0 | 7.0 | 3.0 |
| 6.5 | 3.48 | 7.3 | 0.00 | 1.0 | 0.0 | -0.60 | -2.72 | 4.27 | 112.5 | 6.6 | 62.7 | 0.0 | 6.8 |
| 8.5 | 0.22 | 2.8 | 0.22 | 9.3 | 1.6 | 1.61 | 13.38 | 3.65 | 62.8 | 4.2 | 24.8 | 5.5 | 7.8 |
| 8.3 | 5.88 | 3.5 | 0.00 | 0.8 | 0.0 | 0.00 | 0.00 | 1.61 | 100.0 | 7.0 | 40.4 | 0.0 | 6.5 |
| 9.0 | 2.80 | 4.9 | -0.75 | 0.0 | 0.0 | -0.90 | -4.68 | 2.01 | 157.1 | 4.9 | 21.4 | 0.0 | 5.9 |
| 8.5 | 12.82 | 4.9 | 0.00 | 2.6 | 0.0 | 0.00 | 0.00 | 1.92 | 91.7 | 8.1 | 86.4 | 0.0 | 5.6 |
| 3.9 | 2.08 | 19.8 | 1.06 | 3.6 | 0.2 | 0.45 | 4.35 | 3.48 | 77.1 | 2.1 | 7.6 | 14.5 | 4.8 |
| 7.5 | 4.03 | 3.4 | 2.82 | 7.0 | 0.0 | 0.94 | 1.79 | 6.31 | 82.4 | 6.4 | 54.2 | 0.0 | 5.0 |
| 5.8 | 0.72 | 4.0 | 0.86 | 8.8 | 0.2 | 1.21 | 11.12 | 6.69 | 71.0 | 5.1 | 26.4 | 0.0 | 5.1 |
| 6.2 | 0.57 | 6.2 | 0.62 | 1.9 | 0.0 | 0.03 | 0.41 | 4.31 | 89.7 | 3.6 | 24.4 | 4.7 | 1.7 |
| 8.1 | 0.54 | 2.3 | 1.28 | 1.9 | 0.0 | 0.04 | 0.36 | 2.32 | 98.2 | 5.1 | 29.1 | 0.0 | 5.1 |
| 8.6 | 0.79 | 1.5 | 0.77 | 5.7 | 0.3 | 0.85 | 2.96 | 6.26 | 78.0 | 5.2 | 37.3 | 0.0 | 7.6 |
| 4.5 | 34.88 | 16.4 | 0.00 | 3.9 | 0.0 | 0.29 | 0.82 | 1.91 | 100.0 | 8.0 | 133.7 | 0.0 | 3.7 |
| 8.5 | 1.11 | 2.8 | 0.00 | 1.7 | 0.0 | 0.08 | 0.72 | 2.63 | 98.2 | 4.6 | 3.7 | 0.0 | 5.5 |
| 8.7 | 0.36 | 3.9 | 0.25 | 3.6 | 0.4 | 0.45 | 5.34 | 3.41 | 86.9 | 3.4 | 7.3 | 3.1 | 5.3 |
| 9.8 | 0.47 | 2.3 | 0.33 | 3.3 | 0.2 | 0.35 | 3.13 | 3.85 | 88.8 | 4.0 | 26.4 | 3.5 | 5.1 |
| 9.9 | 0.53 | 1.2 | 0.00 | 3.6 | 0.1 | 0.47 | 4.49 | 3.16 | 89.2 | 5.0 | 19.0 | 0.0 | 5.3 |
| 9.0 | 3.22 | 3.4 | 0.11 | 1.7 | 0.0 | 0.12 | 0.47 | 3.66 | 98.7 | 6.4 | 41.1 | 0.0 | 5.4 |
| 9.6 | 0.25 | 0.8 | 0.20 | 1.0 | -0.1 | -0.44 | -2.36 | 3.71 | 111.0 | 4.2 | 22.5 | 1.7 | 5.6 |
| 9.8 | 0.25 | 1.2 | 0.00 | 0.3 | 0.0 | -0.39 | -5.10 | 3.21 | 109.9 | 5.2 | 21.6 | 0.0 | 2.7 |
| 9.6 | 0.09 | 0.6 | -0.05 | 7.1 | 14.5 | 1.10 | 11.39 | 2.84 | 64.2 | 4.1 | 26.7 | 12.6 | 7.4 |
| 6.8 | 2.02 | 6.2 | 0.73 | 0.4 | 0.0 | -0.29 | -2.80 | 2.79 | 104.4 | 5.0 | 24.7 | 0.0 | 4.3 |
| 7.1 | 0.11 | 1.6 | 0.40 | 3.5 | 0.1 | 0.30 | 3.35 | 4.22 | 86.6 | 3.0 | 7.1 | 2.6 | 3.1 |
| 10.0 | NA | 0.0 | NA | 7.6 | 0.0 | 3.81 | 6.35 | -8.33 | 100.0 | 9.5 | 206.7 | 0.0 | 3.9 |
| 8.8 | 0.98 | 2.5 | 1.38 | 0.0 | -0.1 | -0.90 | -4.98 | 3.45 | 98.4 | 4.8 | 33.3 | 0.0 | 5.4 |
| 8.8 | 0.98 | 3.9 | 0.06 | 3.0 | 0.1 | 0.30 | 2.58 | 3.35 | 92.7 | 5.1 | 41.8 | 2.1 | 5.5 |
| 10.0 | 0.03 | 0.1 | 0.02 | 5.4 | 44.4 | 0.79 | 7.17 | 1.41 | 43.3 | 4.8 | 17.3 | 2.1 | 9.2 |
| 8.7 | 0.00 | 0.0 | 0.00 | 3.7 | 0.0 | 0.51 | 2.75 | 3.80 | 82.4 | 4.4 | 31.9 | 0.0 | 6.6 |
| 6.3 | 0.48 | 8.2 | 0.17 | 2.0 | 0.1 | 0.06 | 0.74 | 3.09 | 98.1 | 3.4 | 9.1 | 8.1 | 5.2 |
| 4.0 | 2.59 | 15.2 | 0.74 | 5.3 | 0.0 | 0.46 | 3.34 | 7.94 | 85.3 | 2.8 | 10.3 | 8.4 | 3.7 |
| 8.0 | 1.30 | 5.2 | 0.51 | 2.9 | 0.2 | 0.20 | 1.83 | 2.66 | 84.8 | 5.3 | 39.4 | 1.0 | 6.6 |
| 0.0 | 11.45 | 73.2 | 2.82 | 0.0 | 0.0 | -3.67 | -42.67 | 10.12 | 115.6 | 5.4 | 30.4 | 0.0 | 4.7 |
| 9.6 | 0.60 | 1.5 | 0.16 | 3.6 | 0.1 | 0.33 | 1.94 | 6.15 | 92.7 | 6.3 | 34.6 | 0.0 | 6.7 |
| 9.9 | 0.00 | 0.0 | 0.03 | 9.5 | 0.1 | 1.66 | 7.47 | 4.35 | 64.7 | 4.0 | 10.9 | 6.2 | 6.3 |
| 9.7 | 0.06 | 0.4 | 0.02 | 2.0 | 0.0 | 0.28 | 3.66 | 2.68 | 86.8 | 4.3 | 15.5 | 0.0 | 3.7 |
| 8.2 | 0.03 | 0.2 | 0.01 | 2.4 | 0.0 | 0.10 | 0.80 | 3.89 | 96.8 | 4.3 | 20.7 | 4.0 | 5.3 |
| 9.9 | 0.44 | 1.9 | 0.06 | 7.5 | 0.5 | 1.05 | 8.28 | 3.73 | 73.8 | 4.5 | 26.0 | 0.5 | 7.6 |
| 10.0 | 0.27 | 1.5 | 0.14 | 4.4 | 8.9 | 0.71 | 8.07 | 2.36 | 74.2 | 4.6 | 37.1 | 7.5 | 6.9 |
| 5.2 | 1.76 | 7.0 | 1.26 | 9.7 | 0.2 | 3.58 | 20.63 | 6.52 | 52.1 | 3.7 | 29.7 | 8.9 | 5.0 |
| 6.6 | 1.58 | 11.0 | 0.25 | 4.1 | 132.0 | 0.58 | 7.43 | 3.27 | 72.1 | 6.4 | 44.8 | 4.4 | 7.5 |
| 7.1 | 0.35 | 3.0 | 0.36 | 8.8 | 3.6 | 1.16 | 10.75 | 3.60 | 72.2 | 2.8 | 5.5 | 9.4 | 8.7 |
| 6.9 | 1.04 | 8.1 | 0.43 | 4.2 | 12.5 | 0.57 | 5.72 | 3.11 | 77.9 | 3.4 | 10.3 | 7.1 | 7.1 |
| 6.9 | 0.72 | 7.3 | 0.32 | 4.0 | 11.7 | 0.53 | 7.36 | 2.93 | 82.9 | 4.2 | 21.4 | 2.1 | 5.1 |
| 10.0 | 0.30 | 0.5 | 0.66 | 4.1 | 18.0 | 0.61 | 4.94 | 0.80 | 33.5 | 5.5 | 37.1 | 0.0 | 8.1 |
| 10.0 | 0.00 | 0.0 | -0.04 | 2.4 | 0.0 | 0.16 | 1.03 | 2.32 | 93.1 | 4.4 | 31.0 | 6.0 | 6.8 |
| 9.9 | 0.62 | 2.2 | 0.31 | 4.2 | 0.3 | 0.62 | 5.19 | 2.75 | 74.4 | 4.2 | 22.2 | 4.7 | 5.8 |
| 9.1 | 1.75 | 4.3 | 0.05 | 3.0 | 0.2 | 0.38 | 2.58 | 2.22 | 83.2 | 4.5 | 32.7 | 6.7 | 7.3 |
| 7.8 | 2.32 | 7.7 | 3.36 | 0.1 | -0.1 | -3.21 | -24.28 | 3.72 | 110.0 | 5.8 | 51.5 | 2.9 | 5.8 |
| 9.9 | 0.55 | 0.8 | 0.00 | 4.0 | 0.0 | 0.47 | 1.65 | 4.13 | 87.3 | 6.3 | 43.4 | 0.0 | 7.5 |
| 9.5 | 0.47 | 2.4 | 0.23 | 4.2 | 0.6 | 0.69 | 8.78 | 3.35 | 82.3 | 5.3 | 19.3 | 0.0 | 4.9 |

| Name | City | State | Rating | 2014 Rating | 2013 Rating | Total Assets ($Mil) | One Year Asset Growth | Commercial Loans | Consumer Loans | Mortgage Loans | Securities | Capitalization Index | Net Worth Ratio |
|------|------|-------|--------|-------------|-------------|---------------------|-----------------------|------------------|----------------|----------------|------------|---------------------|-----------------|
| STATIONERY CU | Saint Joseph | MO | C+ | C | D+ | 12.2 | 3.99 | 0.0 | 35.5 | 0.0 | 0.0 | 10.0 | 14.1 |
| STEAMFITTERS PHILA FCU | West Chester | PA | C- | C- | D+ | 1.2 | 3.30 | 0.0 | 58.9 | 0.0 | 0.0 | 10.0 | 11.3 |
| STEC FCU | Victoria | TX | D+ | D | D+ | 8.4 | -2.60 | 0.0 | 23.1 | 0.0 | 0.0 | 10.0 | 12.2 |
| STEEL VALLEY FCU | Cleveland | OH | D- | D- | D+ | 31.4 | -8.58 | 0.0 | 31.3 | 21.2 | 6.4 | 5.0 | 7.0 |
| STEPHENS COUNTY COMMUNITY FCU | Toccoa | GA | C- | D+ | C- | <1 | 5.13 | 0.0 | 5.5 | 0.0 | 0.0 | 8.1 | 9.8 |
| STEPHENS-ADAMSON EMPL CU | Clarksdale | MS | C+ | C+ | C+ | <1 | -1.47 | 0.0 | 36.6 | 0.0 | 0.0 | 10.0 | 37.3 |
| STEPHENS-FRANKLIN TEACHERS FCU | Toccoa | GA | C+ | C+ | C+ | 19.6 | -1.19 | 1.1 | 20.7 | 23.0 | 0.0 | 10.0 | 20.1 |
| ▼ STEPPING STONES COMMUNITY FCU | Wilmington | DE | C+ | B- | B- | 1.3 | -16.47 | 0.0 | 3.2 | 0.0 | 0.0 | 10.0 | 23.0 |
| STERLING FCU | Sterling | CO | B+ | A- | A- | 134.1 | 5.04 | 7.0 | 10.5 | 14.8 | 10.1 | 10.0 | 14.5 |
| ▼ STERLING HEIGHTS COMMUNITY FCU | Sterling Heights | MI | D+ | C | C+ | 12.6 | -7.43 | 0.0 | 18.9 | 15.5 | 56.2 | 10.0 | 13.1 |
| STERLING UNITED FCU | Evansville | IN | C+ | B- | B- | 67.9 | 5.02 | 0.6 | 52.4 | 29.0 | 0.0 | 9.0 | 10.3 |
| STEWARTS FCU | Ballston Spa | NY | C+ | C | C | 10.2 | 9.32 | 0.0 | 31.9 | 0.0 | 0.0 | 10.0 | 13.1 |
| STOCKTON COMMUNITY FCU | Stockton | CA | C- | C | C | 5.5 | 5.34 | 0.0 | 21.3 | 0.0 | 0.0 | 9.9 | 10.9 |
| STONEHAM MUNICIPAL EMPL FCU | Stoneham | MA | C | C+ | C+ | 33.9 | 6.44 | 0.0 | 18.1 | 10.5 | 0.0 | 6.8 | 8.8 |
| STOPPENBACH CU | Jefferson | WI | C | C | C- | 1.3 | 6.21 | 0.0 | 62.1 | 0.0 | 0.0 | 10.0 | 30.0 |
| STOUGHTON TOWN EMPL FCU | Stoughton | MA | D | D | C- | 2.7 | 0.52 | 0.0 | 39.5 | 0.0 | 0.0 | 10.0 | 12.1 |
| STOUGHTON US RUBBER EMPL CU | Stoughton | WI | D+ | D+ | D+ | 1.3 | -5.66 | 0.0 | 23.1 | 0.0 | 0.0 | 10.0 | 16.7 |
| STP EMPL FCU | Duncansville | PA | C- | C | C | 1.4 | 5.82 | 0.0 | 74.3 | 0.0 | 0.0 | 10.0 | 12.3 |
| ▲ STRAIT VIEW CU | Port Angeles | WA | B+ | B | B | 53.9 | 10.96 | 0.0 | 27.7 | 11.3 | 0.0 | 9.9 | 10.9 |
| ▲ STRAITS AREA FCU | Cheboygan | MI | B- | C+ | C+ | 77.7 | 9.11 | 0.3 | 23.8 | 16.1 | 10.6 | 7.3 | 9.2 |
| STRATEGIC FCU | Sterling | VA | E+ | E+ | E+ | 17.5 | -1.25 | 0.0 | 25.4 | 10.6 | 0.0 | 5.6 | 7.6 |
| STRATFORD MUNICIPAL EMPL FCU | Stratford | CT | D- | D | D | 4.6 | -4.76 | 0.0 | 32.0 | 0.0 | 0.0 | 9.6 | 10.8 |
| STRATTON AIR NATIONAL GUARD FCU | Scotia | NY | C- | C- | C- | 1.0 | -5.09 | 0.0 | 79.7 | 0.0 | 0.0 | 10.0 | 28.4 |
| ▲ STREATOR COMMUNITY CU | Streator | IL | C | C- | C- | 25.5 | 2.75 | 0.0 | 25.3 | 12.1 | 0.0 | 7.0 | 9.0 |
| STREATOR ONIZED CU | Streator | IL | A | A | A | 200.7 | 4.17 | 0.0 | 56.4 | 13.1 | 4.2 | 10.0 | 13.2 |
| STRIP STEEL COMMUNITY FCU | Weirton | WV | C | C | C- | 44.1 | 1.48 | 0.0 | 17.7 | 13.8 | 25.2 | 10.0 | 20.1 |
| ▲ STRUTHERS FCU | Struthers | OH | D | D- | D- | 16.7 | 5.64 | 0.0 | 38.4 | 1.7 | 24.8 | 5.6 | 7.6 |
| ▼ STSP FCU | Mandeville | LA | D+ | C- | C | <1 | 4.49 | 0.0 | 44.0 | 0.0 | 0.0 | 7.7 | 9.5 |
| SUBIACO FCU | Subiaco | AR | B- | B- | B | 28.9 | 0.38 | 0.3 | 13.6 | 17.8 | 0.0 | 10.0 | 12.8 |
| SUFFOLK FCU | Medford | NY | C+ | B- | B- | 959.3 | 5.24 | 7.4 | 11.4 | 33.1 | 35.1 | 9.0 | 10.3 |
| SUFFOLK VA CITY EMPL FCU | Suffolk | VA | D- | D | D | 4.2 | -1.10 | 0.0 | 60.5 | 0.0 | 0.0 | 5.9 | 7.9 |
| SUGAR GROWERS FCU | Santa Rosa | TX | C | C | C | 2.4 | -5.84 | 0.0 | 23.4 | 0.0 | 0.0 | 10.0 | 35.6 |
| SUGAR VALLEY FCU | Scottsbluff | NE | C | C+ | C+ | 8.7 | -0.25 | 0.0 | 41.1 | 0.0 | 0.0 | 10.0 | 21.5 |
| SUGARDALE EMPL CU | Canton | OH | D+ | D | D- | 4.0 | -2.76 | 0.0 | 35.9 | 13.1 | 0.0 | 6.7 | 8.7 |
| SUMA YONKERS FCU | Yonkers | NY | B | B- | B | 303.6 | 3.53 | 8.6 | 0.8 | 55.6 | 12.7 | 10.0 | 14.8 |
| SUMMIT CU | Greensboro | NC | A- | A- | A- | 181.8 | 16.29 | 1.0 | 39.7 | 23.1 | 7.1 | 10.0 | 12.1 |
| SUMMIT CU | Madison | WI | A | A | A- | 2314.5 | 12.39 | 8.7 | 20.2 | 43.5 | 15.5 | 10.0 | 11.5 |
| SUMMIT FCU | Rochester | NY | C+ | C+ | C+ | 783.8 | 7.32 | 0.0 | 55.3 | 20.2 | 5.3 | 7.9 | 9.6 |
| SUMMIT FCU | Akron | OH | C | C | C | 42.7 | 1.26 | 0.0 | 22.6 | 19.9 | 0.0 | 10.0 | 12.3 |
| SUMMIT HAMPTON ROADS FCU | Norfolk | VA | C- | C- | C- | 13.3 | -4.15 | 0.3 | 35.6 | 6.9 | 0.0 | 10.0 | 16.6 |
| SUMMIT RIDGE CU | Lee's Summit | MO | D | D+ | D | 15.9 | 0.74 | 0.0 | 52.1 | 0.0 | 0.0 | 7.5 | 9.3 |
| SUMTER CITY CU | Sumter | SC | C- | C | C- | 3.2 | 2.92 | 0.0 | 36.8 | 0.0 | 0.0 | 10.0 | 14.4 |
| SUN COMMUNITY FCU | El Centro | CA | B+ | B+ | A- | 341.4 | 13.01 | 18.2 | 25.9 | 39.0 | 12.9 | 10.0 | 11.4 |
| ▲ SUN CU | Hollywood | FL | B | B | B- | 71.4 | 2.94 | 0.0 | 26.3 | 16.3 | 0.5 | 10.0 | 11.1 |
| SUN EAST FCU | Aston | PA | C | C | C+ | 472.9 | -1.75 | 9.0 | 30.2 | 21.7 | 8.2 | 6.5 | 8.5 |
| SUN FCU | Maumee | OH | C+ | C+ | C+ | 469.9 | -5.73 | 6.0 | 14.2 | 34.5 | 26.3 | 6.9 | 9.0 |
| ▼ SUN-PACIFIC FCU | Richmond | CA | D+ | C- | C+ | 21.9 | 1.32 | 0.0 | 32.3 | 0.0 | 8.9 | 10.0 | 16.2 |
| SUNCOAST CU | Tampa | FL | B+ | B+ | B- | 6627.1 | 13.95 | 0.6 | 32.7 | 29.8 | 20.1 | 7.4 | 9.3 |
| SUNCOMP EMPL FCU | Bristol | VA | B | B | B | 5.7 | 7.64 | 0.0 | 70.7 | 0.0 | 0.0 | 10.0 | 49.6 |
| SUNFLOWER FCU | Valley Center | KS | D+ | C- | D+ | <1 | 7.61 | 0.0 | 80.7 | 0.0 | 0.0 | 10.0 | 18.3 |
| SUNFLOWER UP FCU | Marysville | KS | D- | E+ | E+ | 6.7 | 14.89 | 0.0 | 78.9 | 0.0 | 0.0 | 5.8 | 7.8 |
| SUNKIST EMPL FCU | Valencia | CA | D+ | D+ | C- | 5.4 | -2.77 | 0.0 | 15.3 | 0.0 | 0.0 | 10.0 | 19.2 |
| SUNLAND CU | Marianna | FL | D+ | D | D | 2.5 | -7.26 | 0.0 | 65.0 | 0.0 | 0.0 | 10.0 | 26.2 |
| SUNLIGHT FCU | Cody | WY | A | A- | A- | 105.8 | 2.06 | 0.0 | 24.5 | 3.9 | 0.0 | 10.0 | 13.1 |
| SUNMARK FCU | Latham | NY | B- | B- | B- | 473.5 | 9.57 | 11.2 | 25.0 | 35.7 | 0.7 | 6.8 | 8.8 |
| SUNNYSIDE CU | Sunnyside | UT | D+ | D+ | C | 3.1 | -8.10 | 0.0 | 27.8 | 15.6 | 0.0 | 10.0 | 12.2 |
| ▼ SUNRISE FAMILY CU | Bay City | MI | C | C+ | C | 105.3 | 4.01 | 0.2 | 23.4 | 20.8 | 10.1 | 7.4 | 9.2 |
| SUNSET SCIENCE PARK FCU | Portland | OR | B+ | B+ | B | 41.4 | 9.79 | 3.7 | 9.7 | 59.3 | 4.8 | 10.0 | 11.4 |
| SUNSTATE FCU | Gainesville | FL | A- | A- | A- | 330.3 | 6.14 | 14.4 | 33.5 | 38.1 | 7.6 | 10.0 | 11.4 |
| SUNTIDE CU | Corpus Christi | TX | C+ | B- | B+ | 88.4 | -2.69 | 0.0 | 53.0 | 16.8 | 0.0 | 10.0 | 11.1 |

| Asset Quality Index | Non-Performing Loans as a % of Total Loans | as a % of Capital | Net Charge-Offs Avg Loans | Profitability Index | Net Income ($Mil) | Return on Assets | Return on Equity | Net Interest Spread | Overhead Efficiency Ratio | Liquidity Index | Liquidity Ratio | Hot Money Ratio | Stability Index |
|---|---|---|---|---|---|---|---|---|---|---|---|---|---|
| 8.7 | 0.83 | 2.4 | 0.23 | 3.7 | 0.1 | 0.50 | 3.56 | 4.14 | 87.6 | 5.1 | 30.5 | 0.0 | 6.2 |
| 3.6 | 1.92 | 13.1 | -0.13 | 6.9 | 0.0 | 1.65 | 15.15 | 4.76 | 60.5 | 4.1 | 15.6 | 0.0 | 6.2 |
| 9.6 | 0.78 | 1.8 | -0.11 | 1.0 | 0.0 | 0.05 | 0.39 | 1.81 | 90.7 | 4.9 | 28.8 | 0.0 | 4.5 |
| 2.7 | 3.83 | 29.5 | 2.67 | 6.1 | 0.6 | 2.43 | 40.82 | 6.33 | 77.4 | 4.8 | 40.6 | 10.6 | 1.5 |
| 10.0 | 0.00 | 0.0 | 0.00 | 4.2 | 0.0 | 0.82 | 8.33 | 2.13 | 50.0 | 8.7 | 99.3 | 0.0 | 4.9 |
| 9.9 | 0.00 | 0.0 | 0.00 | 2.4 | 0.0 | 0.00 | 0.00 | 8.51 | 100.0 | 6.9 | 53.0 | 0.0 | 7.8 |
| 7.1 | 3.55 | 9.2 | -0.01 | 2.7 | 0.0 | 0.14 | 0.71 | 3.52 | 95.6 | 4.3 | 22.6 | 3.1 | 7.0 |
| 9.4 | 23.91 | 3.6 | 0.00 | 2.7 | 0.0 | -2.23 | -9.49 | 1.10 | 383.3 | 8.2 | 117.5 | 0.0 | 9.7 |
| 10.0 | 0.22 | 0.4 | 0.02 | 5.3 | 0.8 | 0.74 | 5.22 | 2.48 | 71.1 | 6.0 | 33.5 | 2.1 | 9.3 |
| 7.0 | 5.41 | 14.4 | 1.09 | 0.6 | -0.2 | -1.49 | -11.13 | 3.72 | 115.7 | 4.3 | 13.8 | 4.4 | 4.5 |
| 5.1 | 0.81 | 6.6 | 0.42 | 4.1 | 0.3 | 0.57 | 5.68 | 4.03 | 81.3 | 2.0 | 9.4 | 14.2 | 4.8 |
| 9.9 | 0.21 | 0.7 | 0.03 | 3.2 | 0.0 | 0.23 | 1.92 | 3.63 | 92.5 | 6.1 | 36.4 | 0.0 | 6.8 |
| 10.0 | 0.16 | 0.5 | 0.00 | 0.8 | 0.0 | -0.48 | -4.20 | 3.46 | 113.0 | 4.6 | 9.0 | 0.0 | 5.0 |
| 8.4 | 0.01 | 0.0 | 0.06 | 2.8 | 0.1 | 0.29 | 3.26 | 2.31 | 89.3 | 4.8 | 23.7 | 1.8 | 4.1 |
| 8.0 | 0.95 | 2.2 | -0.57 | 4.3 | 0.0 | 0.51 | 1.70 | 7.67 | 91.1 | 5.8 | 48.3 | 0.0 | 7.1 |
| 9.9 | 0.09 | 0.3 | 0.00 | 0.2 | 0.0 | -0.38 | -3.21 | 1.64 | 125.8 | 5.2 | 28.2 | 0.0 | 5.2 |
| 7.1 | 5.00 | 6.5 | -0.78 | 2.1 | 0.0 | 0.31 | 1.85 | 2.14 | 100.0 | 6.2 | 44.3 | 0.0 | 5.3 |
| 7.6 | 0.54 | 3.3 | 0.00 | 2.6 | 0.0 | 0.27 | 2.27 | 2.75 | 87.0 | 4.9 | 24.8 | 0.0 | 6.4 |
| 6.0 | 0.39 | 7.4 | 0.16 | 7.3 | 0.4 | 1.10 | 11.31 | 4.32 | 61.2 | 6.7 | 46.9 | 2.2 | 5.4 |
| 5.9 | 1.02 | 7.8 | 0.56 | 5.1 | 0.4 | 0.73 | 7.85 | 3.67 | 75.0 | 4.2 | 17.5 | 5.4 | 4.9 |
| 6.3 | 1.28 | 10.2 | 0.05 | 2.3 | 0.0 | 0.33 | 4.45 | 3.02 | 91.9 | 4.0 | 5.3 | 0.0 | 1.7 |
| 5.2 | 4.10 | 11.7 | 2.74 | 0.0 | -0.1 | -1.49 | -13.18 | 4.03 | 141.0 | 6.6 | 44.0 | 0.0 | 5.2 |
| 8.2 | 0.00 | 0.0 | 0.00 | 2.9 | 0.0 | 0.36 | 1.38 | 3.65 | 88.0 | 4.4 | 25.0 | 0.0 | 6.9 |
| 10.0 | 0.11 | 0.5 | 0.03 | 2.9 | 0.1 | 0.31 | 3.60 | 2.77 | 91.7 | 4.6 | 11.5 | 5.4 | 4.5 |
| 8.2 | 0.55 | 3.1 | 0.26 | 6.7 | 1.5 | 1.02 | 7.88 | 3.59 | 71.8 | 3.3 | 24.9 | 11.8 | 8.7 |
| 10.0 | 0.79 | 1.3 | -0.01 | 2.3 | 0.1 | 0.22 | 1.16 | 1.81 | 89.7 | 5.0 | 41.8 | 3.7 | 6.5 |
| 7.4 | 0.48 | 2.6 | 0.22 | 3.5 | 0.1 | 0.48 | 6.55 | 3.46 | 86.4 | 4.7 | 17.7 | 0.0 | 2.3 |
| 9.6 | 0.33 | 1.5 | 0.00 | 0.2 | 0.0 | -1.74 | -16.67 | 9.89 | 143.5 | 6.8 | 50.6 | 0.0 | 4.4 |
| 8.1 | 1.47 | 5.0 | 0.57 | 2.9 | 0.1 | 0.23 | 1.76 | 2.57 | 78.4 | 4.8 | 30.5 | 4.4 | 6.1 |
| 8.4 | 0.72 | 4.1 | 0.12 | 3.2 | 2.6 | 0.37 | 3.65 | 2.65 | 85.0 | 3.8 | 8.6 | 5.6 | 7.4 |
| 4.4 | 0.95 | 6.9 | -0.43 | 5.7 | 0.0 | 1.20 | 16.14 | 7.90 | 91.5 | 4.8 | 27.7 | 3.3 | 1.7 |
| 9.8 | 0.00 | 0.0 | 4.71 | 1.9 | 0.0 | -1.08 | -3.14 | 2.69 | 55.3 | 5.0 | 37.9 | 0.0 | 6.4 |
| 7.9 | 2.60 | 5.4 | 0.28 | 7.1 | 0.1 | 1.27 | 6.28 | 2.93 | 66.4 | 5.0 | 44.9 | 0.0 | 5.0 |
| 9.2 | 0.39 | 2.2 | 0.07 | 5.9 | 0.0 | 0.79 | 9.55 | 4.91 | 82.8 | 4.9 | 17.0 | 0.0 | 3.0 |
| 5.2 | 3.58 | 14.9 | 0.00 | 4.3 | 1.5 | 0.67 | 4.54 | 1.98 | 64.9 | 2.0 | 15.5 | 24.9 | 8.5 |
| 7.1 | 1.23 | 7.9 | 0.80 | 7.8 | 1.4 | 1.14 | 10.58 | 5.48 | 76.1 | 2.5 | 12.6 | 17.2 | 7.0 |
| 7.6 | 0.67 | 4.6 | 0.37 | 9.1 | 21.5 | 1.30 | 11.32 | 3.16 | 64.9 | 3.0 | 8.4 | 6.6 | 8.6 |
| 8.1 | 0.28 | 2.7 | 0.23 | 3.5 | 2.6 | 0.45 | 4.82 | 3.05 | 84.0 | 2.0 | 5.8 | 12.9 | 6.7 |
| 9.3 | 0.08 | 1.7 | 0.16 | 1.7 | 0.0 | -0.06 | -0.53 | 2.79 | 99.8 | 5.3 | 51.9 | 0.7 | 6.3 |
| 9.9 | 0.12 | 0.3 | 0.21 | 1.9 | 0.0 | 0.19 | 1.16 | 3.48 | 96.4 | 5.7 | 32.7 | 2.3 | 6.2 |
| 3.5 | 3.16 | 16.1 | 1.14 | 0.6 | -0.1 | -0.46 | -4.84 | 3.85 | 94.7 | 3.6 | 14.8 | 9.9 | 4.5 |
| 8.8 | 1.82 | 4.7 | 0.11 | 1.0 | 0.0 | -0.35 | -2.27 | 4.10 | 113.3 | 7.1 | 68.8 | 0.0 | 7.0 |
| 8.1 | 0.38 | 3.2 | 0.56 | 5.2 | 1.9 | 0.76 | 6.81 | 3.82 | 78.2 | 3.1 | 15.5 | 12.6 | 6.6 |
| 8.9 | 0.42 | 3.1 | 0.84 | 4.0 | 0.3 | 0.54 | 4.96 | 2.96 | 82.9 | 4.5 | 30.3 | 2.9 | 5.9 |
| 6.4 | 0.87 | 8.5 | 0.35 | 2.8 | 1.6 | 0.45 | 5.89 | 3.22 | 87.6 | 2.6 | 8.7 | 11.1 | 4.8 |
| 5.6 | 2.46 | 18.4 | 0.36 | 2.8 | 1.0 | 0.27 | 3.37 | 2.87 | 86.8 | 3.0 | 8.1 | 12.8 | 4.6 |
| 9.8 | 0.83 | 2.2 | 1.49 | 0.0 | -0.2 | -1.17 | -7.10 | 4.53 | 94.4 | 4.4 | 31.3 | 4.1 | 5.4 |
| 6.0 | 1.36 | 11.1 | 0.47 | 8.9 | 59.8 | 1.24 | 14.18 | 2.62 | 68.3 | 3.4 | 16.3 | 6.5 | 7.8 |
| 8.4 | 0.00 | 0.0 | -0.03 | 10.0 | 0.1 | 3.27 | 6.25 | 5.94 | 48.8 | 4.0 | 35.0 | 0.0 | 5.7 |
| 0.7 | 11.08 | 43.0 | 0.00 | 4.2 | 0.0 | 0.57 | 3.03 | 7.82 | 86.4 | 4.7 | 24.2 | 0.0 | 6.8 |
| 4.9 | 0.61 | 7.8 | 0.09 | 9.5 | 0.1 | 1.74 | 23.91 | 5.93 | 71.9 | 2.9 | 4.1 | 0.0 | 2.3 |
| 10.0 | 2.31 | 1.9 | 0.00 | 1.1 | 0.0 | -0.07 | -0.38 | 2.24 | 104.7 | 6.2 | 46.0 | 0.0 | 6.0 |
| 5.5 | 3.40 | 8.3 | 1.78 | 4.6 | 0.0 | 1.05 | 4.20 | 5.65 | 82.9 | 4.6 | 39.0 | 0.0 | 3.7 |
| 9.8 | 0.30 | 0.8 | 0.11 | 6.0 | 0.8 | 1.00 | 8.03 | 2.95 | 69.5 | 5.0 | 22.2 | 4.1 | 8.2 |
| 5.3 | 1.26 | 14.9 | 0.16 | 5.4 | 2.9 | 0.84 | 10.74 | 3.82 | 84.1 | 2.3 | 2.0 | 6.5 | 4.9 |
| 7.6 | 0.00 | 0.0 | -0.31 | 1.0 | -0.1 | -3.22 | -24.21 | 4.07 | 171.0 | 4.8 | 36.5 | 3.8 | 4.7 |
| 8.9 | 0.35 | 2.9 | 0.59 | 2.5 | 0.1 | 0.10 | 1.09 | 3.60 | 87.3 | 4.8 | 30.8 | 7.6 | 5.7 |
| 9.9 | 0.12 | 0.8 | -0.06 | 9.4 | 0.5 | 1.46 | 13.25 | 3.69 | 63.5 | 3.3 | 13.4 | 8.5 | 6.7 |
| 6.9 | 0.69 | 6.1 | 0.37 | 6.6 | 2.4 | 0.98 | 8.60 | 4.66 | 80.6 | 3.3 | 5.8 | 2.5 | 7.5 |
| 2.6 | 3.47 | 22.0 | 3.10 | 2.5 | -0.9 | -1.25 | -10.86 | 7.54 | 71.1 | 2.6 | 20.1 | 24.9 | 6.6 |

| Name | City | State | Rating | 2014 Rating | 2013 Rating | Total Assets ($Mil) | One Year Asset Growth | Asset Mix (As a % of Total Assets) | | | | Capital-ization Index | Net Worth Ratio |
|---|---|---|---|---|---|---|---|---|---|---|---|---|---|
| | | | | | | | | Comm-ercial Loans | Cons-umer Loans | Mort-gage Loans | Secur-ities | | |
| SUNWEST EDUCATIONAL CU | Pueblo | CO | C+ | B- | B- | 114.9 | 4.29 | 3.6 | 30.5 | 21.0 | 1.1 | 7.0 | 9.0 |
| SUNWEST FCU | Phoenix | AZ | B | B | B+ | 292.7 | 5.04 | 0.0 | 65.3 | 0.5 | 10.5 | 10.0 | 14.8 |
| SUNY FREDONIA FCU | Fredonia | NY | C | C | C | 25.1 | 6.60 | 0.0 | 34.9 | 0.0 | 0.0 | 10.0 | 11.0 |
| SUPERIOR CHOICE CU | Superior | WI | A- | A- | A- | 299.9 | 8.67 | 19.1 | 13.5 | 55.4 | 3.4 | 10.0 | 11.6 |
| SUPERIOR CU | Collegeville | PA | E+ | E+ | D- | 48.0 | -0.21 | 0.0 | 33.7 | 27.5 | 1.0 | 6.3 | 8.3 |
| SUPERIOR CU INC | Lima | OH | A+ | A+ | A+ | 519.1 | 8.04 | 12.1 | 16.0 | 39.0 | 20.4 | 10.0 | 15.9 |
| SUPERIOR MUNICIPAL EMPL CU | Superior | WI | C- | D+ | C- | 3.0 | -2.94 | 0.0 | 63.8 | 0.0 | 0.0 | 10.0 | 17.9 |
| SUPERIOR SAVINGS CU | Massillon | OH | D+ | D+ | D | 22.3 | 3.06 | 0.0 | 59.8 | 1.3 | 0.3 | 7.5 | 9.3 |
| SUSQUEHANNA VALLEY FCU | Camp Hill | PA | C- | D+ | D | 65.7 | 1.06 | 0.7 | 19.6 | 12.1 | 1.5 | 5.9 | 7.9 |
| SUSSEX COUNTY FCU | Seaford | DE | A- | A- | A- | 253.6 | 0.54 | 1.6 | 8.4 | 33.5 | 42.8 | 10.0 | 14.0 |
| SUWANNEE RIVER FCU | Live Oak | FL | C+ | C+ | C | 17.1 | 5.85 | 0.0 | 24.8 | 20.9 | 0.0 | 10.0 | 11.6 |
| SWEDISHAMERICAN FCU | Rockford | IL | D- | D- | D- | 4.8 | -2.60 | 0.0 | 26.2 | 0.0 | 0.0 | 6.6 | 8.6 |
| SWEENY TEACHERS FCU | Sweeny | TX | D | D | C- | 2.9 | 1.91 | 0.0 | 52.6 | 0.0 | 0.0 | 10.0 | 11.0 |
| SWEET HOME FCU | Amherst | NY | D | D | C- | 27.5 | 1.24 | 0.0 | 14.4 | 18.4 | 4.9 | 6.4 | 8.4 |
| SWEETEX CU | Longview | TX | C+ | C+ | B- | 11.9 | 0.20 | 0.0 | 16.0 | 13.1 | 0.0 | 10.0 | 28.3 |
| SWEETWATER FCU | Rock Springs | WY | C | C- | C- | 21.1 | 0.40 | 0.0 | 16.8 | 9.4 | 0.0 | 10.0 | 12.7 |
| SWEETWATER REGIONAL FCU | Sweetwater | TX | C | C+ | C+ | 11.1 | -5.81 | 0.4 | 30.0 | 0.4 | 0.0 | 10.0 | 15.5 |
| SWEMP FCU | Texarkana | TX | C- | C- | C- | 9.2 | -1.72 | 0.0 | 63.3 | 0.0 | 0.0 | 10.0 | 16.2 |
| SWINDELL-DRESSLER CU | Pittsburgh | PA | D+ | C- | C | 6.0 | -5.62 | 0.0 | 10.6 | 0.0 | 71.0 | 10.0 | 14.6 |
| SYCAMORE FCU | Talladega | AL | B | B | B | 15.0 | 2.79 | 0.0 | 32.4 | 37.9 | 0.0 | 10.0 | 20.1 |
| ▲ SYLVANIA AREA FCU | Sylvania | OH | C- | D+ | D- | 20.4 | -4.21 | 0.0 | 24.8 | 3.0 | 32.6 | 8.4 | 10.0 |
| SYMPHONY FCU | Boston | MA | E+ | E+ | E+ | 3.5 | -5.89 | 0.0 | 14.1 | 14.3 | 0.0 | 8.3 | 9.9 |
| SYNERGY FCU | San Antonio | TX | A | A | A | 223.0 | 5.72 | 0.0 | 32.0 | 31.7 | 8.5 | 10.0 | 12.0 |
| SYNERGY PARTNERS CU | Chicago | IL | C- | C- | C- | 13.0 | -5.96 | 0.0 | 11.1 | 0.0 | 0.0 | 10.0 | 19.1 |
| SYRACUSE COOPERATIVE FCU | Syracuse | NY | E- | E- | E- | 21.8 | 3.04 | 8.4 | 11.6 | 64.0 | 0.8 | 5.2 | 7.2 |
| SYRACUSE FIRE DEPT EMPL FCU | Syracuse | NY | B+ | B+ | B+ | 78.9 | 0.75 | 0.0 | 17.9 | 35.0 | 1.9 | 10.0 | 12.5 |
| SYRACUSE POSTAL FCU | Syracuse | NY | C | C- | C | 11.5 | -14.75 | 1.3 | 26.2 | 0.0 | 0.0 | 10.0 | 11.7 |
| T & FS EMPL CU | Port Arthur | TX | D+ | C- | C | <1 | 1.71 | 0.0 | 75.7 | 0.0 | 0.0 | 10.0 | 24.4 |
| T & P LONGVIEW FCU | Longview | TX | B- | B- | B | 10.9 | 3.35 | 0.0 | 52.3 | 14.5 | 0.0 | 10.0 | 18.2 |
| T H P FCU | Terre Haute | IN | D | D+ | C- | 4.4 | -0.34 | 0.0 | 64.7 | 0.0 | 0.0 | 10.0 | 21.8 |
| T&I CU | Clawson | MI | C+ | C+ | C+ | 70.8 | 0.53 | 0.0 | 3.3 | 28.3 | 0.0 | 10.0 | 19.1 |
| TABERNACLE FCU | Augusta | GA | D | C- | C- | <1 | -7.06 | 0.0 | 27.9 | 0.0 | 0.0 | 5.0 | 7.6 |
| TACOMA LONGSHOREMEN CU | Fife | WA | A- | A- | B- | 82.1 | 7.60 | 0.0 | 12.9 | 7.9 | 0.0 | 10.0 | 11.7 |
| TACOMA NARROWS FCU | Ruston | WA | D+ | D+ | D+ | 8.4 | -1.07 | 0.0 | 28.1 | 2.8 | 0.0 | 10.0 | 14.8 |
| TACONNET FCU | Winslow | ME | C | C | C | 58.6 | 7.28 | 0.6 | 30.4 | 27.0 | 0.0 | 6.0 | 8.0 |
| TAFT EMPL CU | Hahnville | LA | C- | C | C- | 2.6 | 3.66 | 0.0 | 54.9 | 0.0 | 0.0 | 10.0 | 19.6 |
| TAHQUAMENON AREA CU | Newberry | MI | C | C | C | 60.5 | 0.84 | 1.3 | 11.3 | 20.9 | 47.8 | 9.4 | 10.6 |
| TALERIS CU INC | Cleveland | OH | D | D+ | C | 67.9 | -2.06 | 11.8 | 35.8 | 20.8 | 14.0 | 10.0 | 16.9 |
| TALLAHASSEE FCU | Tallahassee | FL | D | D+ | C- | 5.4 | -5.35 | 0.0 | 26.6 | 4.5 | 7.4 | 10.0 | 18.5 |
| TALLAHASSEE-LEON FCU | Tallahassee | FL | C- | C- | C- | 45.8 | 4.86 | 0.0 | 47.2 | 4.5 | 5.3 | 5.9 | 7.9 |
| TAMPA BAY FCU | Tampa | FL | B+ | B+ | B | 269.9 | 16.03 | 0.3 | 39.6 | 22.8 | 3.1 | 7.9 | 9.6 |
| ▼ TAMPA LONGSHOREMENS FCU | Tampa | FL | C | C+ | B- | <1 | 0.22 | 0.0 | 32.4 | 0.0 | 0.0 | 10.0 | 44.3 |
| TAMPA POSTAL FCU | Lutz | FL | C+ | B- | C+ | 76.1 | 4.46 | 0.0 | 28.1 | 8.8 | 28.8 | 10.0 | 14.4 |
| TANDEM FCU | Warren | MI | D+ | D+ | C | 21.3 | -2.33 | 0.0 | 22.2 | 4.9 | 65.8 | 10.0 | 20.0 |
| ▲ TANGIPAHOA PARISH TEACHERS CU | Amite | LA | C+ | C | C | 31.3 | -0.21 | 0.0 | 14.5 | 9.6 | 63.8 | 10.0 | 29.9 |
| TANNER EMPL CU | Salt Lake City | UT | D+ | D+ | D+ | 5.5 | -2.81 | 0.0 | 60.9 | 0.0 | 0.0 | 10.0 | 11.8 |
| TAPCO CU | Tacoma | WA | B- | C+ | C | 316.0 | 5.81 | 12.1 | 35.7 | 25.3 | 20.9 | 6.3 | 8.3 |
| TAPPAN COMMUNITY CU INC | Mansfield | OH | C+ | C | C | 14.0 | -3.02 | 0.0 | 6.9 | 0.0 | 79.4 | 10.0 | 21.0 |
| TARRANT COUNTYS CU | Fort Worth | TX | C+ | C+ | C | 77.2 | 5.96 | 0.1 | 68.9 | 8.1 | 0.0 | 7.0 | 9.0 |
| TAUNTON FCU | Taunton | MA | A- | A- | B+ | 144.4 | 8.91 | 9.7 | 13.6 | 53.3 | 3.2 | 10.0 | 12.2 |
| TAUPA LITHUANIAN FCU | South Boston | MA | D | D- | D- | 22.1 | 0.98 | 7.9 | 4.3 | 47.6 | 0.0 | 6.7 | 8.7 |
| TAYCO EMPL FCU | South Shore | KY | D | D | C- | 3.2 | -1.55 | 0.0 | 21.0 | 0.0 | 0.0 | 10.0 | 30.7 |
| TAYLOR CU | Medford | WI | C- | C- | B- | 55.5 | 6.58 | 1.7 | 19.6 | 39.1 | 0.0 | 9.6 | 10.7 |
| TAYLORVILLE COMMUNITY CU | Taylorville | IL | B | B- | C+ | 43.9 | 4.19 | 0.2 | 32.1 | 44.5 | 0.0 | 10.0 | 11.4 |
| TAYLORVILLE SCHOOL EMPL CU | Taylorville | IL | C | C- | C- | 1.8 | -6.79 | 0.0 | 34.2 | 0.0 | 0.0 | 10.0 | 17.7 |
| TAZEWELL COUNTY GOVERNMENT EMPL CU | Pekin | IL | D | D | D+ | 1.6 | -15.42 | 0.0 | 60.6 | 0.0 | 0.0 | 10.0 | 11.1 |
| TAZEWELL COUNTY SCHOOL EMPL CU | Pekin | IL | D | D+ | D | 23.9 | -3.16 | 0.0 | 14.5 | 0.8 | 0.0 | 10.0 | 11.5 |
| TBA CU | Traverse City | MI | A | A | A | 167.8 | 3.53 | 6.6 | 43.0 | 24.8 | 9.9 | 10.0 | 14.7 |
| ▲ TBC FCU | Richmond | VA | D+ | D+ | D+ | <1 | 0.00 | 0.0 | 44.9 | 0.0 | 0.0 | 6.1 | 8.8 |
| TC TEACHERS FCU | Texas City | TX | D | D | C- | 7.9 | -4.68 | 0.0 | 23.6 | 0.0 | 0.0 | 10.0 | 17.0 |

| Asset Quality Index | Non-Performing Loans | | Net Charge-Offs Avg Loans | Profitability Index | Net Income ($Mil) | Return on Assets | Return on Equity | Net Interest Spread | Overhead Efficiency Ratio | Liquidity Index | Liquidity Ratio | Hot Money Ratio | Stability Index |
|---|---|---|---|---|---|---|---|---|---|---|---|---|---|
| | as a % of Total Loans | as a % of Capital | | | | | | | | | | | |
| 9.8 | 0.32 | 1.9 | 0.35 | 3.5 | 0.3 | 0.36 | 4.03 | 3.50 | 84.7 | 4.9 | 38.0 | 4.7 | 5.5 |
| 7.9 | 0.61 | 3.6 | 0.43 | 3.9 | 1.1 | 0.49 | 3.65 | 3.87 | 85.4 | 3.1 | 13.1 | 9.3 | 7.3 |
| 6.7 | 3.24 | 10.7 | 0.09 | 5.5 | 0.2 | 0.91 | 8.51 | 2.32 | 69.9 | 4.8 | 21.6 | 0.0 | 5.3 |
| 5.4 | 1.14 | 10.5 | 0.34 | 10.0 | 3.0 | 1.36 | 12.71 | 4.55 | 68.7 | 1.5 | 6.2 | 21.9 | 9.1 |
| 0.3 | 6.73 | 59.2 | 1.27 | 1.5 | 0.0 | 0.08 | 1.20 | 4.49 | 88.6 | 3.9 | 28.1 | 9.4 | 2.6 |
| 9.5 | 0.41 | 1.8 | 0.06 | 9.5 | 5.2 | 1.35 | 8.63 | 2.80 | 67.2 | 3.6 | 16.7 | 7.9 | 10.0 |
| 7.8 | 0.49 | 2.2 | 0.00 | 2.4 | 0.0 | 0.22 | 1.23 | 5.04 | 93.5 | 3.6 | 15.6 | 0.0 | 6.6 |
| 5.7 | 0.73 | 5.0 | 0.51 | 3.3 | 0.1 | 0.28 | 2.99 | 3.95 | 92.9 | 2.4 | 12.7 | 27.3 | 3.0 |
| 7.1 | 0.80 | 5.6 | 0.30 | 3.5 | 0.2 | 0.43 | 5.65 | 3.22 | 87.6 | 4.6 | 22.1 | 1.1 | 2.0 |
| 9.4 | 0.74 | 3.3 | 0.17 | 5.5 | 1.5 | 0.80 | 5.75 | 3.11 | 67.4 | 4.0 | 18.0 | 5.9 | 7.8 |
| 8.3 | 0.81 | 3.4 | 0.28 | 3.8 | 0.1 | 0.40 | 3.48 | 3.71 | 85.9 | 4.9 | 14.3 | 0.8 | 6.8 |
| 7.1 | 1.45 | 4.7 | 0.10 | 1.5 | 0.0 | 0.19 | 2.28 | 2.63 | 91.8 | 6.1 | 50.2 | 0.0 | 1.0 |
| 8.3 | 0.28 | 1.5 | -0.15 | 0.6 | 0.0 | -0.28 | -2.47 | 4.05 | 110.1 | 4.9 | 35.3 | 0.0 | 5.0 |
| 9.9 | 0.07 | 0.4 | 0.31 | 1.3 | 0.0 | -0.02 | -0.29 | 3.87 | 96.9 | 5.0 | 15.1 | 0.8 | 3.6 |
| 10.0 | 0.00 | 0.0 | 0.00 | 2.7 | 0.0 | 0.39 | 1.40 | 2.42 | 83.3 | 5.0 | 35.9 | 0.0 | 7.0 |
| 9.9 | 0.23 | 0.6 | 0.00 | 2.2 | 0.0 | 0.24 | 2.01 | 2.77 | 91.5 | 4.6 | 22.6 | 4.6 | 6.2 |
| 9.0 | 1.88 | 3.8 | 1.02 | 0.4 | 0.0 | -0.45 | -2.99 | 3.24 | 101.0 | 4.4 | 29.9 | 11.0 | 5.7 |
| 8.1 | 0.35 | 1.5 | 0.19 | 4.1 | 0.0 | 0.62 | 3.99 | 2.75 | 76.5 | 3.5 | 22.7 | 4.0 | 7.4 |
| 10.0 | 1.18 | 0.9 | -0.20 | 0.4 | 0.0 | -0.69 | -4.76 | 2.11 | 132.3 | 5.1 | 20.2 | 0.0 | 4.5 |
| 7.3 | 1.06 | 6.8 | 0.27 | 10.0 | 0.3 | 2.69 | 13.90 | 6.94 | 53.9 | 4.4 | 17.4 | 0.0 | 6.3 |
| 6.9 | 1.36 | 4.9 | 0.25 | 2.4 | 0.0 | 0.19 | 1.98 | 2.29 | 93.5 | 4.7 | 17.0 | 0.0 | 4.2 |
| 1.7 | 0.00 | 42.6 | 0.10 | 3.5 | 0.0 | 0.55 | 5.88 | 6.08 | 123.3 | 4.3 | 28.2 | 12.6 | 2.8 |
| 9.7 | 0.22 | 1.3 | 0.07 | 8.0 | 1.9 | 1.15 | 9.90 | 2.78 | 60.2 | 3.5 | 22.7 | 10.6 | 8.9 |
| 10.0 | 0.50 | 0.3 | 1.03 | 1.9 | 0.0 | 0.22 | 1.18 | 2.21 | 91.1 | 5.0 | 26.7 | 4.6 | 5.8 |
| 0.3 | 7.00 | 211.0 | 0.43 | 2.2 | 0.0 | 0.00 | 0.00 | 5.05 | 98.1 | 1.8 | 6.4 | 16.4 | 0.0 |
| 7.1 | 1.24 | 5.9 | 0.06 | 5.9 | 0.6 | 0.96 | 8.02 | 3.51 | 71.9 | 4.7 | 26.8 | 3.7 | 6.5 |
| 8.1 | 2.07 | 4.4 | -0.61 | 4.4 | 0.1 | 0.71 | 7.18 | 2.55 | 74.4 | 4.6 | 6.1 | 0.0 | 5.2 |
| 3.1 | 4.61 | 14.3 | 3.83 | 2.2 | 0.0 | -1.53 | -6.03 | 12.42 | 84.9 | 4.4 | 17.8 | 0.0 | 6.4 |
| 8.2 | 0.06 | 0.3 | 0.03 | 8.4 | 0.1 | 1.55 | 8.54 | 5.58 | 71.4 | 4.0 | 19.0 | 4.4 | 6.3 |
| 8.2 | 0.00 | 0.0 | -0.13 | 0.3 | 0.0 | -0.27 | -1.25 | 3.13 | 116.4 | 3.8 | 20.6 | 0.0 | 6.6 |
| 10.0 | 0.06 | 0.1 | 0.08 | 2.8 | 0.2 | 0.31 | 1.70 | 2.00 | 82.5 | 7.0 | 56.9 | 0.0 | 7.0 |
| 4.2 | 2.22 | 4.2 | 59.26 | 3.2 | 0.0 | -32.38 | -566.67 | 10.13 | 71.4 | 7.8 | 76.0 | 0.0 | 1.7 |
| 10.0 | 0.03 | 0.1 | 0.34 | 5.5 | 0.5 | 0.81 | 7.05 | 2.10 | 58.2 | 4.9 | 16.9 | 0.0 | 5.5 |
| 9.2 | 0.00 | 3.2 | 0.42 | 0.9 | 0.0 | -0.03 | -0.21 | 3.22 | 98.4 | 3.9 | 14.4 | 8.5 | 5.5 |
| 6.4 | 0.53 | 6.1 | 0.23 | 5.5 | 0.3 | 0.68 | 8.59 | 5.25 | 84.4 | 3.6 | 12.3 | 7.1 | 2.9 |
| 5.3 | 2.76 | 7.8 | 0.23 | 6.5 | 0.0 | 0.93 | 4.75 | 5.03 | 79.4 | 5.1 | 43.1 | 0.0 | 4.3 |
| 6.8 | 1.86 | 7.6 | 0.28 | 2.8 | 0.1 | 0.22 | 2.04 | 3.52 | 93.0 | 4.9 | 16.7 | 1.3 | 5.2 |
| 6.5 | 1.41 | 6.3 | 0.78 | 0.5 | -0.4 | -0.69 | -4.36 | 4.27 | 101.2 | 3.9 | 10.4 | 1.3 | 5.0 |
| 7.6 | 4.08 | 7.5 | 0.00 | 0.2 | 0.0 | -0.86 | -4.74 | 4.18 | 117.9 | 4.7 | 16.6 | 0.0 | 4.9 |
| 5.7 | 0.70 | 5.8 | 0.67 | 3.7 | 0.1 | 0.34 | 4.32 | 5.68 | 90.3 | 5.4 | 25.1 | 1.4 | 2.9 |
| 6.9 | 0.83 | 7.1 | 0.50 | 6.2 | 1.5 | 0.76 | 7.93 | 3.93 | 76.2 | 3.9 | 18.6 | 4.4 | 6.0 |
| 4.5 | 24.67 | 16.6 | -0.95 | 5.2 | 0.0 | 0.55 | 1.30 | 17.02 | 76.2 | 8.4 | 125.2 | 0.0 | 4.3 |
| 10.0 | 0.15 | 0.4 | 0.60 | 2.6 | 0.1 | 0.14 | 1.00 | 3.30 | 89.3 | 4.1 | 15.1 | 7.2 | 6.3 |
| 10.0 | 0.34 | 0.5 | 0.37 | 1.1 | 0.0 | -0.06 | -0.31 | 3.23 | 103.2 | 4.4 | 10.7 | 4.7 | 5.4 |
| 10.0 | 2.08 | 1.8 | 0.30 | 2.7 | 0.1 | 0.36 | 1.22 | 2.20 | 75.1 | 5.7 | 32.2 | 0.5 | 6.8 |
| 6.1 | 1.08 | 6.3 | 0.14 | 3.6 | 0.0 | 0.55 | 4.81 | 4.22 | 87.8 | 4.3 | 23.1 | 0.0 | 6.0 |
| 8.9 | 0.30 | 3.3 | 0.13 | 4.6 | 1.6 | 0.70 | 8.50 | 3.50 | 81.0 | 3.9 | 13.9 | 3.2 | 5.1 |
| 10.0 | 4.23 | 1.5 | 2.40 | 2.7 | 0.0 | 0.27 | 1.28 | 2.13 | 89.2 | 5.8 | 18.4 | 0.0 | 5.9 |
| 5.4 | 0.66 | 5.9 | 0.70 | 4.5 | 0.2 | 0.31 | 3.46 | 5.66 | 87.0 | 3.3 | 14.1 | 6.6 | 4.3 |
| 5.7 | 2.23 | 13.9 | 0.47 | 9.4 | 1.5 | 1.41 | 11.64 | 5.38 | 74.0 | 2.9 | 13.9 | 7.0 | 8.7 |
| 3.7 | 3.83 | 28.1 | 0.15 | 2.9 | 0.1 | 0.30 | 3.53 | 2.80 | 85.4 | 3.2 | 28.0 | 29.1 | 2.3 |
| 10.0 | 0.00 | 0.0 | 0.00 | 0.0 | 0.0 | -0.78 | -2.53 | 1.70 | 157.6 | 7.0 | 61.4 | 0.0 | 6.1 |
| 6.1 | 1.36 | 7.9 | 0.08 | 2.2 | 0.1 | 0.13 | 1.15 | 3.40 | 93.1 | 4.0 | 22.2 | 2.4 | 5.4 |
| 9.0 | 0.27 | 3.6 | -0.01 | 5.0 | 0.3 | 0.84 | 7.75 | 3.91 | 79.1 | 3.5 | 12.9 | 0.0 | 6.4 |
| 8.6 | 2.44 | 4.4 | 0.00 | 3.1 | 0.0 | 0.44 | 2.54 | 2.01 | 80.8 | 4.6 | 14.0 | 0.0 | 7.0 |
| 3.6 | 3.01 | 17.0 | 0.00 | 1.2 | 0.0 | -1.10 | -9.77 | 4.80 | 85.5 | 4.6 | 27.6 | 0.0 | 5.7 |
| 9.5 | 2.53 | 3.4 | -0.48 | 0.3 | -0.1 | -0.46 | -4.03 | 1.64 | 124.8 | 5.0 | 24.8 | 0.0 | 4.2 |
| 8.8 | 0.37 | 2.2 | 0.17 | 6.4 | 1.1 | 0.85 | 6.11 | 3.75 | 76.5 | 2.6 | 9.4 | 11.4 | 9.2 |
| 9.9 | 0.00 | 0.0 | 0.00 | 5.7 | 0.0 | 0.97 | 13.33 | 11.30 | 100.0 | 7.0 | 59.7 | 0.0 | 3.0 |
| 8.8 | 3.82 | 5.9 | 0.20 | 0.5 | 0.0 | -0.16 | -0.99 | 2.82 | 105.5 | 5.3 | 20.9 | 0.0 | 6.1 |

201

| Name | City | State | Rating | 2014 Rating | 2013 Rating | Total Assets ($Mil) | One Year Asset Growth | Asset Mix (As a % of Total Assets) | | | | Capital-ization Index | Net Worth Ratio |
|------|------|-------|--------|-------------|-------------|--------|--------|--------------------|--------|--------|--------|--------|--------|
| | | | | | | | | Comm-ercial Loans | Cons-umer Loans | Mort-gage Loans | Secur-ities | | |
| TCP CU | Rural Hall | NC | C | C | D+ | 11.4 | -11.31 | 0.0 | 22.1 | 27.0 | 0.0 | 10.0 | 16.7 |
| TCT FCU | Ballston Spa | NY | B- | B- | C+ | 172.0 | 12.12 | 5.2 | 22.9 | 17.5 | 24.2 | 5.7 | 7.7 |
| ▼ TCWH #585 FCU | Washington | PA | D- | D | D+ | <1 | -7.86 | 0.0 | 79.3 | 0.0 | 0.0 | 7.3 | 9.2 |
| TEA FCU | Houma | LA | E+ | E+ | E+ | 2.2 | 8.66 | 0.0 | 41.8 | 0.0 | 0.0 | 5.8 | 7.8 |
| TEACHERS ALLIANCE FCU | Longview | TX | D+ | D | D | 1.4 | -9.79 | 0.0 | 32.7 | 0.0 | 0.0 | 10.0 | 27.5 |
| TEACHERS CU | South Bend | IN | B- | B- | B- | 2781.0 | 7.08 | 8.1 | 48.8 | 32.9 | 8.3 | 6.2 | 8.2 |
| TEACHERS CU | Oklahoma City | OK | C | C | C | 6.9 | 1.66 | 0.0 | 22.9 | 0.0 | 0.0 | 10.0 | 35.7 |
| TEACHERS CU | Beloit | WI | C- | C- | C | 20.9 | 5.34 | 0.0 | 13.5 | 14.8 | 0.0 | 10.0 | 15.2 |
| TEACHERS FCU | Hauppauge | NY | B | B+ | B+ | 5186.3 | 6.15 | 1.5 | 18.7 | 22.3 | 44.6 | 8.8 | 10.2 |
| TEAM & WHEEL FCU | Winston-Salem | NC | B- | B- | B- | 10.4 | -0.18 | 0.0 | 52.8 | 0.0 | 0.0 | 10.0 | 15.1 |
| ▼ TEAM FINANCIAL FCU | Houston | TX | E+ | D | D | 7.0 | 10.42 | 0.0 | 43.9 | 0.0 | 0.0 | 5.3 | 7.3 |
| TEAM FIRST FCU | Lancaster | PA | C- | C | C+ | 9.6 | -2.64 | 0.0 | 17.3 | 13.3 | 0.0 | 10.0 | 20.3 |
| TEAM ONE CU | Saginaw | MI | B | B+ | B+ | 441.7 | 10.62 | 8.9 | 33.7 | 31.3 | 18.2 | 9.5 | 10.7 |
| TEAMSTERS COUNCIL #37 FCU | Portland | OR | C+ | B- | B- | 55.5 | 2.95 | 0.9 | 22.4 | 15.7 | 0.0 | 10.0 | 12.7 |
| TEAMSTERS CU | Detroit | MI | C | C | D+ | 13.5 | 0.37 | 0.3 | 27.6 | 0.2 | 8.9 | 10.0 | 12.8 |
| TEAMSTERS CU | Blaine | MN | D | D | D+ | 9.8 | 8.19 | 0.0 | 48.5 | 0.0 | 0.0 | 7.7 | 9.5 |
| TEAMSTERS LOCAL #222 FCU | Salt Lake City | UT | D+ | D | D+ | 2.6 | -1.22 | 0.0 | 38.3 | 0.0 | 0.0 | 7.6 | 9.4 |
| ▲ TEAMSTERS LOCAL #238 CU | Cedar Rapids | IA | D+ | D- | D- | 8.2 | -12.97 | 0.0 | 44.2 | 0.0 | 0.0 | 10.0 | 11.3 |
| TEAMSTERS LOCAL 30 FCU | Jeannette | PA | D- | D- | D+ | 3.7 | -1.71 | 0.0 | 53.1 | 0.0 | 2.4 | 2.7 | 4.9 |
| TEAMSTERS LOCAL 697 FCU | Wheeling | WV | C- | D+ | D- | 1.9 | -10.88 | 0.0 | 51.8 | 0.0 | 0.0 | 10.0 | 13.9 |
| TEAMSTERS LOCAL 92 FCU | Canton | OH | D- | D- | D | 2.0 | 3.30 | 0.0 | 70.9 | 0.0 | 6.2 | 7.3 | 9.2 |
| TEAMSTERS LOCAL UNION #270 FCU | New Orleans | LA | C- | D+ | C- | <1 | 3.75 | 0.0 | 42.5 | 0.0 | 0.0 | 10.0 | 17.6 |
| ▲ TEANECK FCU | Teaneck | NJ | C- | D+ | C- | 12.1 | 1.08 | 0.0 | 9.6 | 7.2 | 2.1 | 10.0 | 15.9 |
| TECH CU | Crown Point | IN | C- | D+ | C | 326.1 | 0.58 | 15.1 | 32.1 | 19.7 | 7.2 | 6.3 | 8.3 |
| TECHNICOLOR FCU | Burbank | CA | C | C | D+ | 47.3 | 7.85 | 1.0 | 16.6 | 58.9 | 9.6 | 7.3 | 9.2 |
| TECHNOLOGY CU | San Jose | CA | B+ | B+ | B+ | 1992.6 | 10.68 | 8.4 | 6.5 | 39.5 | 25.6 | 9.2 | 10.5 |
| TECU | Wichita | KS | C+ | C+ | C+ | 73.4 | 4.40 | 0.0 | 65.1 | 3.0 | 3.4 | 8.2 | 9.8 |
| TEE-PAK CU | Danville | IL | B- | B- | B- | 17.9 | 1.87 | 0.0 | 39.6 | 20.3 | 0.0 | 10.0 | 18.9 |
| TEG FCU | Poughkeepsie | NY | B- | B- | C+ | 227.3 | 9.42 | 8.6 | 34.3 | 23.7 | 9.9 | 7.1 | 9.1 |
| TEL-U-WATT FCU | Minot | ND | E+ | E+ | D | 5.0 | 3.70 | 0.0 | 51.3 | 0.0 | 0.0 | 6.8 | 8.9 |
| ▲ TELBEC FCU | Beckley | WV | B | B- | C+ | 13.9 | 4.31 | 0.0 | 51.5 | 26.6 | 0.0 | 10.0 | 12.1 |
| TELCO COMMUNITY CU | Asheville | NC | A- | A- | A- | 141.1 | 16.36 | 0.8 | 36.1 | 27.6 | 0.8 | 8.0 | 9.7 |
| ▼ TELCO CU | Tarboro | NC | D | D+ | C- | 52.8 | -0.60 | 0.0 | 43.3 | 11.6 | 0.0 | 10.0 | 21.7 |
| TELCO PLUS CU | Longview | TX | C- | C | C | 64.6 | -0.40 | 0.0 | 31.9 | 17.9 | 0.0 | 10.0 | 13.6 |
| ▼ TELCO ROSWELL NEW MEXICO FCU | Roswell | NM | C+ | C+ | C+ | 7.0 | -4.92 | 0.0 | 48.2 | 0.0 | 0.0 | 10.0 | 23.2 |
| TELCO-TRIAD COMMUNITY CU | Sioux City | IA | B- | B- | C | 81.1 | 9.76 | 0.2 | 37.8 | 5.6 | 0.0 | 10.0 | 12.2 |
| TELCOE FCU | Little Rock | AR | A | A | A | 327.7 | 3.13 | 0.3 | 11.7 | 14.1 | 63.3 | 10.0 | 21.5 |
| TELCOMM CU | Springfield | MO | A- | A- | A | 133.2 | 5.46 | 0.7 | 17.9 | 11.7 | 4.0 | 10.0 | 13.8 |
| TELHIO CU | Columbus | OH | C+ | C | C+ | 547.7 | 3.30 | 8.5 | 30.1 | 28.6 | 6.8 | 8.4 | 10.0 |
| TEMPLE SANTA FE COMMUNITY CU | Temple | TX | D | D | D+ | 16.4 | -6.04 | 0.0 | 32.6 | 12.2 | 0.0 | 6.0 | 8.0 |
| TEMPLE-INLAND FCU | Diboll | TX | B- | B- | B- | 14.3 | 2.23 | 0.0 | 39.0 | 0.0 | 0.0 | 10.0 | 14.1 |
| ▲ TENN-AM WATER CO FCU | Chattanooga | TN | C+ | C- | C- | 3.2 | -9.36 | 0.0 | 47.8 | 0.0 | 0.0 | 10.0 | 26.1 |
| TENNESSEE CU | Nashville | TN | C- | C- | C | 287.5 | 3.31 | 0.0 | 21.0 | 20.2 | 23.8 | 8.1 | 9.7 |
| TENNESSEE DEPT OF SAFETY CU | Nashville | TN | C | C | C | 9.1 | 1.90 | 0.0 | 51.6 | 0.0 | 0.0 | 10.0 | 20.1 |
| TENNESSEE EMPL CU | Nashville | TN | C+ | C | C | 16.2 | -1.11 | 0.0 | 31.7 | 9.6 | 0.0 | 10.0 | 14.3 |
| TENNESSEE MEMBERS 1ST FCU | Oak Ridge | TN | C- | C | D+ | 81.4 | -2.67 | 0.7 | 11.0 | 19.1 | 37.8 | 10.0 | 11.9 |
| TENNESSEE RIVER FCU | Counce | TN | C+ | C+ | B- | 18.7 | 0.98 | 0.0 | 28.9 | 17.7 | 0.0 | 10.0 | 23.0 |
| TENNESSEE VALLEY FCU | Chattanooga | TN | A | A | A | 1109.4 | 8.19 | 8.5 | 32.4 | 18.4 | 22.5 | 10.0 | 12.7 |
| TERMINAL CU | Metairie | LA | C+ | C+ | C | 18.2 | -1.95 | 0.0 | 10.0 | 21.2 | 42.7 | 10.0 | 13.7 |
| TERMINALS FCU | Carteret | NJ | C- | C | C | 1.0 | -12.15 | 0.0 | 37.2 | 1.6 | 0.0 | 10.0 | 26.1 |
| TES REGIONAL HEALTHCARE FCU | Shreveport | LA | C- | C- | C- | 23.8 | -2.02 | 0.0 | 18.3 | 9.0 | 0.0 | 10.0 | 15.7 |
| ▲ TESORO NORTHWEST FCU | Anacortes | WA | C- | D | C- | 13.5 | 0.70 | 0.0 | 37.9 | 0.2 | 0.0 | 10.0 | 24.7 |
| TEWKSBURY FCU | Tewksbury | MA | B | B | B- | 52.9 | 2.06 | 0.0 | 20.1 | 13.4 | 7.3 | 10.0 | 11.8 |
| TEX-MEX CU | Laredo | TX | B- | B- | B- | 10.8 | -8.60 | 0.0 | 32.4 | 0.0 | 0.1 | 10.0 | 23.8 |
| TEXACO OF HOUMA CU | Houma | LA | D+ | D+ | D+ | 4.9 | -2.47 | 0.0 | 56.3 | 0.0 | 0.0 | 10.0 | 17.3 |
| TEXANS CU | Richardson | TX | F | F | F | 1407.7 | -0.47 | 0.9 | 24.4 | 19.6 | 39.0 | 0.1 | 3.2 |
| TEXAR FCU | Texarkana | TX | A | A | A | 331.4 | 5.78 | 1.4 | 33.0 | 21.2 | 20.5 | 10.0 | 12.5 |
| TEXARKANA TERMINAL EMPL FCU | Texarkana | TX | D | D | D+ | 13.3 | 5.69 | 0.0 | 51.8 | 0.0 | 0.0 | 8.5 | 10.0 |
| ▲ TEXAS ASSNS OF PROFESSIONALS FCU | San Antonio | TX | C- | D+ | D- | 29.7 | 11.57 | 5.5 | 5.1 | 64.3 | 0.0 | 6.2 | 8.2 |
| ▲ TEXAS BAY CU | Houston | TX | B+ | B | B | 357.3 | 16.37 | 0.1 | 45.6 | 29.3 | 1.7 | 8.9 | 10.3 |

| Asset Quality Index | Non-Performing Loans as a % of Total Loans | Non-Performing Loans as a % of Capital | Net Charge-Offs Avg Loans | Profitability Index | Net Income ($Mil) | Return on Assets | Return on Equity | Net Interest Spread | Overhead Efficiency Ratio | Liquidity Index | Liquidity Ratio | Hot Money Ratio | Stability Index |
|---|---|---|---|---|---|---|---|---|---|---|---|---|---|
| 7.4 | 1.18 | 3.3 | 0.12 | 3.2 | 0.0 | 0.31 | 1.97 | 4.48 | 84.1 | 6.2 | 45.4 | 4.7 | 5.7 |
| 9.2 | 0.37 | 3.1 | 0.12 | 4.8 | 0.9 | 0.74 | 9.54 | 3.51 | 77.1 | 3.5 | 4.4 | 2.8 | 4.2 |
| 4.7 | 0.87 | 6.7 | 0.00 | 0.4 | 0.0 | -0.60 | -6.67 | 7.24 | 105.6 | 4.7 | 21.4 | 0.0 | 4.0 |
| 1.7 | 7.64 | 37.8 | 0.78 | 2.0 | 0.0 | -0.06 | -0.76 | 5.33 | 97.7 | 5.7 | 49.2 | 5.1 | 1.0 |
| 4.3 | 17.03 | 19.5 | 2.12 | 1.6 | 0.0 | 0.19 | 0.72 | 9.88 | 92.7 | 7.8 | 92.7 | 0.0 | 4.7 |
| 6.3 | 0.30 | 5.8 | 0.20 | 3.7 | 9.1 | 0.45 | 5.50 | 2.48 | 82.9 | 2.8 | 7.9 | 5.4 | 6.0 |
| 10.0 | 1.69 | 1.1 | 0.00 | 3.2 | 0.0 | 0.27 | 0.77 | 4.26 | 90.4 | 5.0 | 31.1 | 0.0 | 6.2 |
| 8.5 | 1.76 | 3.6 | 0.15 | 1.8 | 0.0 | 0.07 | 0.46 | 2.28 | 96.3 | 4.6 | 23.5 | 1.0 | 7.1 |
| 9.7 | 0.52 | 2.5 | 0.15 | 4.3 | 21.4 | 0.55 | 5.66 | 1.76 | 75.2 | 3.6 | 17.6 | 10.7 | 8.1 |
| 8.5 | 0.00 | 1.4 | 0.40 | 5.5 | 0.1 | 0.71 | 4.72 | 6.39 | 86.3 | 4.3 | 29.4 | 1.2 | 5.8 |
| 4.7 | 2.71 | 18.2 | 0.27 | 1.5 | 0.0 | 0.00 | 0.00 | 5.29 | 100.0 | 6.0 | 49.8 | 3.1 | 1.0 |
| 9.7 | 1.32 | 2.7 | 0.60 | 1.2 | 0.0 | -0.12 | -0.61 | 2.56 | 107.7 | 4.7 | 13.7 | 0.0 | 6.7 |
| 4.8 | 2.29 | 15.9 | 0.77 | 4.2 | 1.4 | 0.44 | 4.14 | 3.90 | 80.4 | 3.2 | 11.9 | 6.4 | 6.5 |
| 10.0 | 0.07 | 0.5 | 0.29 | 2.3 | 0.1 | 0.11 | 0.85 | 2.86 | 93.5 | 5.7 | 57.4 | 6.8 | 6.1 |
| 10.0 | 0.78 | 1.9 | 0.57 | 2.2 | 0.0 | 0.12 | 0.93 | 4.10 | 97.9 | 6.0 | 45.1 | 1.4 | 5.9 |
| 4.7 | 0.90 | 6.7 | 0.13 | 4.0 | 0.0 | 0.49 | 5.13 | 4.61 | 86.2 | 3.2 | 14.4 | 11.5 | 2.3 |
| 6.7 | 1.20 | 6.4 | 0.00 | 3.9 | 0.0 | 0.50 | 5.63 | 4.13 | 94.3 | 4.2 | 14.2 | 0.0 | 3.0 |
| 6.6 | 2.56 | 9.4 | 0.14 | 2.0 | 0.0 | 0.28 | 2.78 | 3.04 | 92.6 | 5.1 | 39.0 | 0.0 | 4.2 |
| 4.7 | 1.42 | 15.4 | 0.13 | 0.1 | -0.1 | -2.40 | -43.80 | 4.93 | 183.3 | 4.7 | 11.0 | 0.0 | 2.2 |
| 5.9 | 1.64 | 5.5 | 0.92 | 3.6 | 0.0 | 0.33 | 2.52 | 7.09 | 93.8 | 6.5 | 52.7 | 0.0 | 6.0 |
| 2.7 | 0.61 | 18.9 | 0.00 | 2.5 | 0.0 | 0.13 | 1.43 | 4.92 | 98.8 | 3.6 | 24.8 | 13.6 | 1.7 |
| 7.2 | 1.63 | 3.7 | 0.00 | 6.4 | 0.0 | 1.73 | 9.76 | 12.09 | 74.3 | 7.2 | 69.1 | 0.0 | 4.3 |
| 9.9 | 1.99 | 2.4 | 0.39 | 1.2 | 0.0 | 0.04 | 0.28 | 2.17 | 98.3 | 4.9 | 15.9 | 0.0 | 6.5 |
| 7.7 | 0.53 | 4.6 | 0.24 | 2.5 | 0.9 | 0.36 | 4.53 | 2.92 | 89.5 | 4.0 | 30.9 | 8.1 | 4.5 |
| 8.7 | 0.27 | 2.1 | 0.09 | 4.1 | 0.2 | 0.63 | 6.90 | 4.12 | 83.3 | 3.0 | 9.5 | 9.9 | 3.8 |
| 9.9 | 0.21 | 1.2 | -0.06 | 5.6 | 12.0 | 0.84 | 7.86 | 2.81 | 74.5 | 4.4 | 22.0 | 4.7 | 7.9 |
| 5.6 | 0.57 | 4.7 | 0.55 | 3.2 | 0.1 | 0.22 | 2.27 | 3.97 | 87.0 | 3.0 | 11.9 | 8.2 | 4.9 |
| 9.4 | 0.85 | 2.8 | 0.72 | 5.6 | 0.1 | 0.75 | 4.13 | 4.26 | 79.1 | 4.5 | 28.2 | 0.7 | 7.4 |
| 6.5 | 1.07 | 8.6 | 0.44 | 5.6 | 1.4 | 0.81 | 9.77 | 4.68 | 80.7 | 3.2 | 10.9 | 9.9 | 5.4 |
| 2.0 | 2.64 | 19.5 | 0.08 | 2.7 | 0.0 | 0.13 | 1.53 | 1.10 | 84.2 | 3.9 | 22.3 | 0.0 | 1.0 |
| 8.2 | 0.36 | 2.3 | 0.79 | 9.5 | 0.2 | 1.47 | 12.76 | 4.17 | 63.5 | 3.3 | 12.5 | 3.5 | 6.3 |
| 6.4 | 1.21 | 9.7 | 0.38 | 7.1 | 0.9 | 0.85 | 8.61 | 4.42 | 80.3 | 3.9 | 19.4 | 4.7 | 7.0 |
| 8.7 | 1.53 | 4.1 | 0.41 | 0.3 | -0.3 | -0.67 | -3.08 | 3.14 | 113.6 | 3.8 | 15.0 | 6.8 | 5.3 |
| 9.1 | 0.66 | 2.7 | 0.49 | 1.6 | 0.0 | 0.01 | 0.11 | 3.22 | 94.7 | 4.9 | 35.5 | 2.7 | 6.1 |
| 4.3 | 4.08 | 12.5 | 0.24 | 10.0 | 0.1 | 2.23 | 10.38 | 6.48 | 54.6 | 2.8 | 54.5 | 38.3 | 8.3 |
| 8.2 | 0.56 | 3.2 | 0.20 | 3.1 | 0.2 | 0.27 | 2.27 | 3.99 | 90.7 | 3.7 | 25.5 | 9.0 | 5.8 |
| 10.0 | 0.15 | 0.2 | 0.01 | 7.1 | 3.2 | 1.29 | 5.81 | 1.85 | 48.4 | 3.5 | 26.0 | 15.8 | 9.9 |
| 9.6 | 1.07 | 3.2 | 0.28 | 5.2 | 0.7 | 0.72 | 5.28 | 2.85 | 78.2 | 4.5 | 31.9 | 4.5 | 8.7 |
| 7.1 | 0.93 | 7.3 | 0.58 | 3.6 | 1.8 | 0.44 | 4.49 | 3.44 | 79.8 | 3.7 | 17.0 | 7.7 | 6.8 |
| 7.8 | 0.73 | 5.9 | -0.03 | 1.1 | 0.0 | 0.04 | 0.72 | 3.63 | 100.8 | 4.7 | 36.5 | 4.4 | 2.5 |
| 8.4 | 0.89 | 3.4 | 0.02 | 4.6 | 0.1 | 0.64 | 5.00 | 2.52 | 79.5 | 4.5 | 24.6 | 0.0 | 7.5 |
| 8.7 | 0.26 | 0.5 | 0.47 | 7.0 | 0.0 | 1.55 | 6.42 | 2.65 | 110.0 | 5.6 | 47.6 | 0.0 | 5.0 |
| 10.0 | 0.31 | 1.5 | 0.43 | 2.0 | 0.1 | 0.07 | 0.75 | 3.07 | 92.5 | 5.3 | 27.6 | 5.7 | 5.3 |
| 8.7 | 0.10 | 0.3 | -0.09 | 4.0 | 0.0 | 0.53 | 2.65 | 3.21 | 86.0 | 4.6 | 17.7 | 0.8 | 7.4 |
| 9.9 | 0.64 | 1.8 | 1.61 | 2.6 | 0.0 | 0.29 | 2.09 | 3.49 | 86.6 | 3.4 | 24.6 | 20.1 | 6.0 |
| 6.9 | 2.00 | 8.4 | 0.62 | 1.0 | -0.1 | -0.18 | -1.54 | 2.52 | 100.9 | 4.3 | 25.9 | 6.9 | 4.6 |
| 9.4 | 0.72 | 2.8 | 0.27 | 4.2 | 0.1 | 0.72 | 3.20 | 3.46 | 67.1 | 4.2 | 28.0 | 3.9 | 7.2 |
| 9.5 | 0.36 | 1.9 | 0.25 | 7.9 | 9.3 | 1.13 | 9.16 | 3.21 | 69.4 | 4.7 | 19.4 | 1.9 | 9.3 |
| 3.7 | 8.62 | 23.0 | 0.52 | 8.1 | 0.2 | 1.09 | 8.14 | 2.89 | 56.1 | 3.8 | 34.8 | 18.8 | 6.4 |
| 3.0 | 8.86 | 23.1 | 0.00 | 8.2 | 0.0 | 1.43 | 6.20 | 6.81 | 69.2 | 5.4 | 36.0 | 0.0 | 6.5 |
| 10.0 | 0.22 | 0.6 | 0.06 | 1.7 | 0.0 | 0.02 | 0.12 | 2.35 | 99.3 | 4.8 | 22.1 | 3.4 | 6.6 |
| 6.8 | 3.95 | 7.9 | 0.91 | 1.9 | 0.0 | 0.29 | 1.17 | 3.63 | 94.4 | 4.9 | 23.9 | 0.0 | 5.1 |
| 6.3 | 1.90 | 10.2 | 0.13 | 4.4 | 0.2 | 0.51 | 4.44 | 3.40 | 86.3 | 3.5 | 22.5 | 8.3 | 5.6 |
| 9.5 | 0.67 | 1.8 | 0.11 | 3.0 | 0.0 | 0.05 | 0.21 | 4.27 | 108.3 | 3.3 | 60.3 | 30.8 | 6.6 |
| 1.8 | 7.13 | 26.1 | 0.39 | 2.7 | 0.0 | 0.38 | 2.24 | 2.42 | 83.5 | 4.2 | 39.2 | 0.0 | 6.9 |
| 3.7 | 0.34 | 29.2 | 0.21 | 9.5 | 21.1 | 1.93 | 85.25 | 2.72 | 54.3 | 4.9 | 18.2 | 0.8 | 2.5 |
| 8.9 | 0.50 | 3.4 | 0.46 | 7.7 | 2.5 | 1.04 | 8.33 | 3.81 | 73.2 | 2.3 | 8.4 | 21.0 | 8.7 |
| 2.0 | 1.77 | 20.3 | 1.53 | 1.4 | 0.0 | -0.04 | -0.40 | 5.03 | 91.6 | 3.0 | 17.6 | 14.7 | 3.5 |
| 5.3 | 0.17 | 8.8 | -0.04 | 5.5 | 0.2 | 0.89 | 11.09 | 4.34 | 85.7 | 1.1 | 7.9 | 25.5 | 3.7 |
| 5.4 | 1.18 | 10.1 | 1.05 | 7.9 | 3.9 | 1.52 | 15.15 | 4.96 | 70.2 | 3.6 | 18.5 | 7.0 | 6.0 |

| Name | City | State | Rating | 2014 Rating | 2013 Rating | Total Assets ($Mil) | One Year Asset Growth | Commercial Loans | Consumer Loans | Mortgage Loans | Securities | Capitalization Index | Net Worth Ratio |
|---|---|---|---|---|---|---|---|---|---|---|---|---|---|
| | | | | | | | | Asset Mix (As a % of Total Assets) | | | | | |
| TEXAS COASTAL COMMUNITY FCU | Beaumont | TX | C+ | C+ | C+ | 24.5 | 2.27 | 0.0 | 34.3 | 0.0 | 0.0 | 10.0 | 15.5 |
| TEXAS DOW EMPL CU | Lake Jackson | TX | B | B | B | 2703.8 | 15.83 | 1.2 | 55.5 | 27.4 | 0.0 | 6.5 | 8.5 |
| TEXAS DPS CU | Austin | TX | D+ | D+ | D+ | 66.2 | 2.18 | 0.0 | 28.7 | 19.2 | 17.0 | 6.5 | 8.5 |
| TEXAS FARM BUREAU FCU | Waco | TX | C | C | D+ | 6.5 | 2.45 | 0.0 | 43.0 | 0.0 | 0.0 | 10.0 | 18.2 |
| ▲ TEXAS FCU | Dallas | TX | D | D- | D- | 61.7 | -2.85 | 0.0 | 30.5 | 14.5 | 14.6 | 5.0 | 7.0 |
| TEXAS GULF CAROLINA EMPL CU | Aurora | NC | C | C | C | 2.5 | 6.83 | 0.0 | 37.4 | 3.0 | 0.0 | 10.0 | 35.4 |
| TEXAS HEALTH CU | Austin | TX | B- | B- | B- | 74.2 | 3.36 | 3.5 | 28.5 | 42.6 | 0.0 | 9.1 | 10.4 |
| ▼ TEXAS HEALTH RESOURCES CU | Dallas | TX | D+ | C- | D | 18.0 | 6.00 | 0.0 | 37.1 | 3.3 | 0.0 | 6.1 | 8.1 |
| TEXAS LEE FCU | Houston | TX | C | C+ | C+ | <1 | 30.05 | 0.0 | 48.6 | 0.0 | 0.0 | 10.0 | 21.1 |
| TEXAS PARTNERS FCU | Killeen | TX | C | C | C | 144.3 | 1.79 | 0.0 | 19.1 | 5.2 | 27.3 | 5.5 | 7.5 |
| ▲ TEXAS PEOPLE FCU | Fort Worth | TX | C- | D+ | C- | 22.0 | -0.56 | 0.0 | 57.2 | 0.9 | 0.0 | 10.0 | 19.6 |
| TEXAS PLAINS FCU | Amarillo | TX | B | B | B+ | 32.8 | 2.94 | 0.0 | 63.0 | 1.5 | 0.0 | 10.0 | 13.9 |
| TEXAS TECH FCU | Lubbock | TX | B+ | B+ | B | 112.1 | 3.04 | 0.0 | 38.7 | 18.2 | 0.2 | 8.9 | 10.3 |
| TEXAS TELCOM CU | Dallas | TX | B+ | B+ | B | 56.7 | 36.03 | 0.7 | 45.7 | 8.1 | 6.9 | 10.0 | 13.1 |
| ▲ TEXAS TRUST CU | Mansfield | TX | B- | C+ | B | 895.9 | 3.81 | 17.1 | 35.1 | 25.1 | 14.1 | 10.0 | 11.5 |
| TEXAS WORKFORCE CU | San Antonio | TX | E+ | D- | D- | 10.4 | 3.27 | 0.0 | 55.4 | 11.5 | 0.0 | 6.7 | 8.7 |
| TEXASGULF FCU | Wharton | TX | A- | A- | B+ | 87.6 | 7.29 | 0.0 | 49.3 | 18.1 | 0.0 | 10.0 | 11.7 |
| TEXELL CU | Temple | TX | A | A | A | 272.2 | 16.23 | 10.5 | 42.0 | 26.7 | 3.5 | 10.0 | 11.4 |
| TEXHILLCO SCHOOL EMPL FCU | Kerrville | TX | E | E | D- | 14.6 | 10.62 | 0.0 | 54.1 | 0.0 | 0.0 | 5.2 | 7.2 |
| TEXOMA COMMUNITY CU | Wichita Falls | TX | B+ | B | B | 114.7 | 3.89 | 1.3 | 45.6 | 15.9 | 0.0 | 8.8 | 10.2 |
| TEXOMA EDUCATORS FCU | Sherman | TX | B- | B- | B- | 74.5 | 10.12 | 0.0 | 29.6 | 0.0 | 7.0 | 10.0 | 14.6 |
| TEXOMA FCU | Fritch | TX | C+ | C | C | 13.2 | -0.91 | 0.0 | 25.0 | 0.0 | 1.6 | 10.0 | 18.1 |
| TEXSTAR FCU | Kenedy | TX | D+ | D+ | C- | 24.5 | 5.63 | 0.0 | 13.3 | 1.2 | 0.0 | 6.3 | 8.4 |
| THD DISTRICT 17 CU | Bryan | TX | C | C | C- | 3.0 | -5.99 | 0.0 | 33.8 | 0.0 | 0.0 | 10.0 | 23.0 |
| THD-6 CU | Odessa | TX | D+ | D+ | C- | 3.8 | 2.28 | 0.0 | 57.4 | 0.0 | 0.0 | 10.0 | 12.3 |
| THINKWISE FCU | San Bernardino | CA | B+ | A- | A- | 75.9 | 12.53 | 13.2 | 22.5 | 24.9 | 6.9 | 10.0 | 14.5 |
| THIOKOL ELKTON FCU | Elkton | MD | C | C- | C- | 21.5 | -0.56 | 0.0 | 15.0 | 3.8 | 0.1 | 10.0 | 14.0 |
| THIRD COAST FCU | Corpus Christi | TX | B- | B- | B+ | 13.9 | 0.05 | 0.0 | 46.5 | 0.0 | 0.0 | 10.0 | 24.6 |
| THIRD DISTRICT HIGHWAY FCU | Lafayette | LA | C | C | C | 16.3 | -0.38 | 0.0 | 13.0 | 0.6 | 0.0 | 10.0 | 11.7 |
| ▲ THORNAPPLE CU | Hastings | MI | C | C | C | 20.4 | 14.38 | 0.0 | 51.6 | 17.1 | 5.1 | 7.6 | 9.4 |
| THREE RIVERS CU | Bainbridge | GA | C+ | C+ | C+ | 15.4 | 8.12 | 0.0 | 31.1 | 6.1 | 0.0 | 10.0 | 12.1 |
| THREE RIVERS FCU | Fort Wayne | IN | A | A | B | 787.7 | 4.42 | 10.5 | 19.4 | 29.1 | 23.8 | 10.0 | 12.9 |
| ▲ THRIVE FCU | Muncie | IN | C | C- | C | 48.8 | 3.30 | 1.4 | 25.2 | 14.7 | 3.4 | 10.0 | 12.6 |
| THRIVENT FCU | Appleton | WI | C+ | C+ | B | 467.4 | -0.25 | 20.2 | 5.0 | 39.1 | 29.8 | 9.8 | 10.9 |
| THUNDER BAY AREA CU | Alpena | MI | D+ | D+ | D+ | 22.3 | 1.12 | 4.5 | 29.5 | 20.5 | 23.3 | 7.9 | 9.6 |
| THUNDERBOLT AREA FCU | Millville | NJ | D | D | D- | 19.9 | 1.16 | 0.0 | 17.6 | 4.0 | 4.9 | 6.7 | 8.7 |
| TICONDEROGA FCU | Ticonderoga | NY | D+ | D | D+ | 93.2 | 0.76 | 0.1 | 13.5 | 6.7 | 53.4 | 8.7 | 10.2 |
| TIDEWATER DOMINION EMPL FCU | Norfolk | VA | D- | D- | D+ | 8.6 | -3.17 | 0.0 | 16.3 | 9.6 | 0.0 | 5.4 | 7.4 |
| TIMBERLAND FCU | Du Bois | PA | C+ | C+ | C+ | 58.5 | -0.83 | 0.0 | 34.2 | 3.1 | 0.0 | 8.5 | 10.0 |
| TIMBERLINE FCU | Crossett | AR | C | C | C | 78.9 | 0.74 | 3.6 | 22.0 | 19.3 | 26.7 | 10.0 | 20.4 |
| TIMES FCU | Honolulu | HI | E+ | E+ | D- | 8.0 | -7.43 | 0.0 | 30.1 | 0.0 | 0.0 | 4.6 | 6.6 |
| TIMES FREE PRESS CU | Chattanooga | TN | C | C | C | 2.1 | -6.08 | 0.0 | 69.2 | 0.0 | 0.0 | 10.0 | 31.4 |
| TIMKEN AEROSPACE FCU | Lebanon | NH | C- | C- | C | 7.0 | 3.53 | 0.0 | 48.5 | 0.1 | 0.0 | 10.0 | 12.8 |
| TIN MILL EMPL FCU | Weirton | WV | D | D | C- | 18.6 | -2.39 | 0.0 | 8.5 | 11.0 | 0.0 | 10.0 | 20.3 |
| TINKER FCU | Oklahoma City | OK | B+ | B+ | B | 3375.3 | 4.49 | 0.0 | 52.6 | 3.5 | 32.3 | 8.9 | 10.3 |
| TIOGA AREA FCU | Wellsboro | PA | E+ | D- | D | 5.8 | 6.50 | 0.0 | 24.1 | 0.0 | 11.2 | 5.7 | 7.7 |
| ▼ TIP OF TEXAS FCU | El Paso | TX | C- | C- | D+ | 22.2 | 0.65 | 0.0 | 46.0 | 7.8 | 0.0 | 10.0 | 17.7 |
| TIPPECANOE FCU | Lafayette | IN | C- | C | C | 12.5 | 1.05 | 0.0 | 34.3 | 0.0 | 0.0 | 10.0 | 12.6 |
| TITAN FCU | Pleasant Gap | PA | C+ | C+ | C+ | 45.5 | 3.40 | 0.0 | 14.7 | 14.0 | 37.6 | 9.7 | 10.8 |
| TLC COMMUNITY CU | Adrian | MI | A | A | A- | 401.0 | 9.11 | 1.9 | 20.1 | 27.0 | 38.8 | 10.0 | 14.2 |
| TLCU FINANCIAL | Mishawaka | IN | B- | C+ | B- | 35.3 | 3.30 | 0.0 | 22.3 | 3.6 | 0.0 | 10.0 | 16.2 |
| ▲ TMH FCU | Tallahassee | FL | B | C | B | 55.9 | 6.66 | 10.4 | 38.4 | 15.8 | 0.0 | 9.6 | 10.8 |
| TNCONNECT CU | Knoxville | TN | D | D | D | 48.8 | 4.88 | 0.0 | 51.3 | 8.0 | 0.2 | 6.1 | 8.1 |
| TOBACCO VALLEY TEACHERS FCU | Enfield | CT | C- | C- | C- | 38.2 | 6.64 | 0.0 | 22.2 | 7.5 | 38.3 | 7.5 | 9.3 |
| ▲ TOLEDO FIRE FIGHTERS FCU | Toledo | OH | C | C- | C- | 31.0 | 0.88 | 0.0 | 28.1 | 7.6 | 16.0 | 10.0 | 13.1 |
| ▲ TOLEDO METRO FCU | Toledo | OH | B- | C+ | C+ | 42.9 | 8.48 | 0.0 | 60.0 | 11.3 | 19.4 | 9.4 | 10.6 |
| ▲ TOLEDO POLICE FCU | Toledo | OH | C+ | C | C- | 33.3 | 2.61 | 0.0 | 25.5 | 12.1 | 3.2 | 9.3 | 10.5 |
| TOLEDO POSTAL EMPL CU INC | Toledo | OH | D+ | C- | C | 4.8 | -3.77 | 1.9 | 24.9 | 1.9 | 0.0 | 10.0 | 19.3 |
| TOLEDO TEAMSTERS FCU | Toledo | OH | E+ | E+ | E+ | 5.2 | 1.24 | 2.3 | 31.3 | 11.9 | 0.0 | 0.0 | 2.3 |
| TOLEDO URBAN FCU | Toledo | OH | E+ | E+ | E+ | 5.8 | 21.51 | 1.0 | 66.2 | 7.7 | 0.0 | 4.1 | 6.2 |

| Asset Quality Index | Non-Performing Loans as a % of Total Loans | Non-Performing Loans as a % of Capital | Net Charge-Offs Avg Loans | Profitability Index | Net Income ($Mil) | Return on Assets | Return on Equity | Net Interest Spread | Overhead Efficiency Ratio | Liquidity Index | Liquidity Ratio | Hot Money Ratio | Stability Index |
|---|---|---|---|---|---|---|---|---|---|---|---|---|---|
| 5.4 | 2.23 | 10.3 | 0.33 | 8.2 | 0.3 | 1.70 | 11.34 | 5.92 | 78.1 | 3.9 | 25.8 | 6.4 | 5.0 |
| 4.9 | 0.95 | 10.3 | 0.76 | 6.3 | 16.8 | 0.87 | 10.15 | 4.37 | 74.8 | 2.0 | 6.5 | 13.6 | 5.8 |
| 7.3 | 0.52 | 3.2 | 0.29 | 1.6 | 0.1 | 0.11 | 1.24 | 2.95 | 94.1 | 4.6 | 22.7 | 1.2 | 3.4 |
| 9.7 | 0.19 | 0.5 | -0.04 | 3.6 | 0.0 | 0.55 | 3.08 | 3.85 | 83.7 | 5.7 | 51.2 | 0.0 | 6.6 |
| 7.4 | 0.53 | 3.6 | 0.24 | 0.6 | 0.0 | -0.08 | -1.17 | 3.18 | 99.0 | 5.4 | 21.7 | 0.0 | 1.7 |
| 9.0 | 3.10 | 3.8 | 0.00 | 5.8 | 0.0 | 1.05 | 2.89 | 5.87 | 81.2 | 4.3 | 11.2 | 0.0 | 4.3 |
| 6.4 | 0.83 | 5.7 | 0.69 | 4.9 | 0.3 | 0.55 | 5.31 | 3.78 | 79.5 | 2.9 | 15.1 | 10.6 | 5.2 |
| 5.8 | 0.91 | 6.4 | 1.11 | 3.7 | 0.0 | -0.10 | -1.18 | 4.93 | 88.7 | 5.0 | 43.4 | 0.0 | 3.0 |
| 8.5 | 0.00 | 0.0 | 0.00 | 4.4 | 0.0 | 0.61 | 2.52 | 3.67 | 66.7 | 6.6 | 56.1 | 0.0 | 4.3 |
| 8.8 | 0.37 | 2.2 | 0.89 | 2.7 | 0.2 | 0.15 | 2.05 | 3.78 | 92.7 | 5.7 | 27.9 | 3.8 | 3.8 |
| 7.8 | 0.73 | 3.6 | -0.07 | 1.6 | 0.0 | 0.13 | 0.65 | 4.03 | 97.2 | 3.8 | 26.9 | 1.8 | 5.6 |
| 6.9 | 0.31 | 4.2 | 0.54 | 7.0 | 0.3 | 1.15 | 8.37 | 5.60 | 82.2 | 3.4 | 25.2 | 8.4 | 6.0 |
| 8.7 | 0.45 | 3.3 | 0.49 | 8.5 | 1.2 | 1.42 | 14.56 | 4.74 | 76.9 | 3.2 | 7.5 | 5.9 | 6.6 |
| 7.4 | 0.66 | 3.5 | 0.48 | 9.2 | 0.5 | 1.33 | 10.52 | 4.10 | 64.6 | 3.3 | 27.2 | 25.6 | 6.3 |
| 7.8 | 0.16 | 4.0 | 0.37 | 4.0 | 4.1 | 0.61 | 5.71 | 2.87 | 81.0 | 2.4 | 2.3 | 13.9 | 7.7 |
| 2.7 | 1.52 | 14.1 | 1.32 | 1.2 | 0.0 | -0.29 | -3.22 | 4.13 | 81.2 | 3.1 | 19.0 | 13.3 | 1.0 |
| 8.1 | 0.24 | 2.4 | 0.15 | 9.5 | 1.0 | 1.53 | 13.46 | 3.57 | 56.4 | 2.9 | 10.3 | 12.5 | 7.6 |
| 8.0 | 0.45 | 3.0 | 0.86 | 9.3 | 2.5 | 1.30 | 11.33 | 4.22 | 69.3 | 3.1 | 17.2 | 14.6 | 8.7 |
| 3.0 | 1.47 | 15.9 | 0.74 | 2.3 | 0.0 | 0.08 | 1.02 | 6.10 | 91.6 | 4.2 | 16.0 | 3.4 | 0.7 |
| 6.0 | 0.36 | 4.9 | 0.52 | 6.8 | 0.9 | 1.04 | 10.46 | 4.53 | 75.6 | 3.2 | 12.5 | 11.7 | 6.5 |
| 9.9 | 0.46 | 1.0 | 0.73 | 3.0 | 0.1 | 0.26 | 1.73 | 2.49 | 85.1 | 4.6 | 15.3 | 0.9 | 6.5 |
| 9.1 | 1.26 | 2.3 | 0.09 | 2.9 | 0.0 | 0.32 | 1.79 | 2.05 | 80.1 | 5.8 | 76.2 | 0.9 | 6.8 |
| 8.6 | 1.43 | 2.8 | 0.29 | 2.3 | 0.1 | 0.25 | 3.10 | 2.28 | 85.4 | 5.5 | 20.7 | 1.0 | 3.6 |
| 9.8 | 1.02 | 1.7 | 0.34 | 2.2 | 0.0 | 0.26 | 1.15 | 2.63 | 86.2 | 4.9 | 30.0 | 0.0 | 6.5 |
| 8.2 | 0.36 | 1.9 | 0.27 | 0.3 | 0.0 | -0.60 | -4.77 | 4.12 | 111.1 | 5.0 | 31.6 | 0.0 | 5.8 |
| 7.6 | 1.71 | 8.1 | 0.61 | 3.3 | 0.0 | -0.03 | -0.18 | 4.31 | 93.7 | 4.5 | 25.8 | 9.7 | 6.7 |
| 6.7 | 3.74 | 8.9 | 0.15 | 2.3 | 0.0 | 0.12 | 1.01 | 2.46 | 94.5 | 4.5 | 22.7 | 3.5 | 6.1 |
| 7.2 | 2.29 | 4.4 | 1.95 | 5.6 | 0.1 | 0.86 | 3.58 | 8.28 | 74.4 | 6.7 | 59.7 | 0.0 | 6.4 |
| 9.4 | 1.46 | 2.2 | 1.04 | 1.6 | 0.0 | 0.01 | 0.07 | 1.77 | 84.9 | 5.0 | 25.7 | 0.0 | 4.6 |
| 7.7 | 0.30 | 2.5 | -0.05 | 8.3 | 0.2 | 1.28 | 14.09 | 4.81 | 79.9 | 3.9 | 14.9 | 0.0 | 4.9 |
| 7.2 | 1.72 | 6.9 | 1.85 | 2.5 | 0.0 | 0.01 | 0.07 | 3.56 | 92.1 | 3.2 | 20.3 | 30.7 | 6.7 |
| 8.3 | 0.79 | 3.9 | 0.30 | 7.2 | 5.7 | 0.99 | 7.60 | 3.70 | 77.9 | 3.6 | 9.2 | 2.0 | 9.0 |
| 7.0 | 1.32 | 8.4 | 0.75 | 2.3 | 0.1 | 0.16 | 1.44 | 3.50 | 89.9 | 3.8 | 18.1 | 4.7 | 5.8 |
| 7.4 | 1.08 | 6.5 | 0.07 | 3.2 | 1.1 | 0.31 | 2.99 | 3.32 | 90.0 | 3.3 | 6.6 | 5.2 | 6.6 |
| 6.3 | 0.16 | 6.8 | 0.11 | 3.1 | 0.1 | 0.28 | 2.99 | 3.14 | 91.2 | 4.2 | 11.8 | 0.0 | 4.5 |
| 4.3 | 4.19 | 16.9 | 1.88 | 2.1 | 0.0 | 0.02 | 0.23 | 2.91 | 80.3 | 4.6 | 20.2 | 1.8 | 4.2 |
| 6.8 | 1.63 | 5.0 | 0.78 | 1.7 | 0.2 | 0.24 | 2.45 | 3.33 | 89.7 | 4.9 | 24.6 | 5.4 | 4.0 |
| 8.9 | 0.41 | 1.5 | -0.05 | 0.0 | -0.1 | -0.69 | -9.54 | 2.61 | 127.2 | 5.4 | 21.8 | 2.6 | 2.8 |
| 5.6 | 1.72 | 9.9 | 0.66 | 3.1 | 0.2 | 0.33 | 3.37 | 3.14 | 82.5 | 4.4 | 19.9 | 1.6 | 4.3 |
| 9.2 | 1.00 | 2.8 | 0.31 | 1.7 | 0.1 | 0.08 | 0.39 | 3.26 | 100.3 | 3.6 | 15.9 | 10.4 | 6.6 |
| 9.9 | 0.08 | 0.3 | 1.92 | 1.0 | 0.0 | -0.08 | -1.25 | 3.35 | 94.9 | 5.8 | 40.3 | 0.0 | 1.0 |
| 8.1 | 1.04 | 2.3 | 0.00 | 5.0 | 0.0 | 0.61 | 2.02 | 4.85 | 86.3 | 4.4 | 23.2 | 0.0 | 4.3 |
| 7.5 | 0.14 | 0.7 | 0.06 | 2.1 | 0.0 | 0.00 | 0.00 | 3.03 | 99.4 | 4.7 | 31.7 | 1.5 | 6.2 |
| 9.7 | 2.11 | 2.2 | 0.41 | 0.3 | 0.0 | -0.20 | -0.99 | 1.87 | 108.4 | 7.1 | 73.6 | 0.0 | 5.9 |
| 6.4 | 0.86 | 5.3 | 0.84 | 5.1 | 18.4 | 0.73 | 7.18 | 2.69 | 67.9 | 3.5 | 14.7 | 7.8 | 7.4 |
| 7.6 | 0.63 | 2.2 | 0.96 | 0.7 | 0.0 | -0.41 | -4.94 | 2.25 | 98.8 | 5.9 | 26.3 | 0.0 | 2.7 |
| 5.2 | 3.35 | 13.4 | 1.53 | 1.2 | 0.0 | -0.21 | -1.18 | 4.95 | 84.9 | 4.3 | 20.8 | 4.7 | 5.7 |
| 7.6 | 1.87 | 5.5 | 1.05 | 1.2 | 0.0 | -0.14 | -1.10 | 2.32 | 86.1 | 5.3 | 35.7 | 0.0 | 6.2 |
| 8.4 | 0.87 | 2.7 | 0.11 | 3.5 | 0.2 | 0.46 | 4.25 | 1.64 | 69.9 | 5.6 | 28.4 | 0.0 | 5.4 |
| 9.5 | 0.24 | 1.4 | 0.17 | 8.4 | 3.9 | 1.32 | 9.35 | 2.86 | 72.0 | 3.5 | 8.9 | 6.9 | 8.8 |
| 9.3 | 1.79 | 3.6 | 0.17 | 3.6 | 0.1 | 0.45 | 2.93 | 2.59 | 85.3 | 5.1 | 15.0 | 0.0 | 6.8 |
| 8.2 | 0.21 | 1.2 | 0.13 | 5.4 | 0.4 | 0.89 | 8.29 | 3.77 | 86.1 | 4.6 | 32.8 | 7.2 | 4.7 |
| 4.7 | 0.93 | 9.0 | 0.17 | 1.5 | 0.1 | 0.17 | 2.04 | 3.40 | 93.5 | 3.4 | 9.6 | 3.3 | 2.8 |
| 8.8 | 0.20 | 1.0 | 0.05 | 2.2 | 0.1 | 0.20 | 2.19 | 2.85 | 94.3 | 5.0 | 37.8 | 0.0 | 4.4 |
| 10.0 | 0.34 | 1.1 | -0.02 | 2.1 | 0.1 | 0.27 | 2.05 | 3.11 | 97.5 | 6.3 | 44.6 | 2.9 | 5.8 |
| 4.8 | 1.58 | 10.0 | 1.01 | 9.7 | 0.6 | 1.99 | 19.40 | 6.16 | 61.5 | 2.0 | 9.7 | 18.4 | 5.2 |
| 9.6 | 0.39 | 1.5 | 0.14 | 3.3 | 0.1 | 0.46 | 4.45 | 3.29 | 85.1 | 5.2 | 26.5 | 1.7 | 5.6 |
| 9.2 | 1.64 | 2.6 | 0.44 | 0.5 | 0.0 | -0.33 | -1.71 | 3.25 | 108.3 | 6.0 | 38.5 | 0.0 | 6.4 |
| 0.3 | 9.07 | 87.7 | 1.62 | 0.2 | -0.2 | -4.58 | -103.24 | 6.13 | 119.2 | 5.5 | 24.1 | 0.0 | 0.1 |
| 0.0 | 2.78 | 76.4 | 0.22 | 4.5 | 0.0 | 0.32 | 13.44 | 6.66 | 97.4 | 3.1 | 18.0 | 4.4 | 2.5 |

| Name | City | State | Rating | 2014 Rating | 2013 Rating | Total Assets ($Mil) | One Year Asset Growth | Asset Mix (As a % of Total Aseets) | | | | Capital-ization Index | Net Worth Ratio |
|---|---|---|---|---|---|---|---|---|---|---|---|---|---|
| | | | | | | | | Comm-ercial Loans | Cons-umer Loans | Mort-gage Loans | Secur-ities | | |
| TOLNA CO-OPERATIVE FCU | Tolna | ND | C- | C- | C | 1.2 | -13.11 | 0.0 | 17.0 | 0.0 | 0.0 | 10.0 | 18.3 |
| TOMAH AREA CU | Tomah | WI | C- | C | B- | 56.7 | 2.03 | 8.8 | 18.0 | 34.4 | 1.8 | 8.0 | 9.7 |
| TOMBIGBEE FCU | Amory | MS | D | D+ | D+ | 5.7 | 1.27 | 0.0 | 14.5 | 0.0 | 0.0 | 10.0 | 14.0 |
| TOMPKINS EMPL FCU | Ithaca | NY | C- | C | C- | 6.2 | 6.63 | 0.0 | 57.2 | 0.0 | 0.0 | 10.0 | 13.3 |
| ▲ TONAWANDA COMMUNITY FCU | Buffalo | NY | D+ | D | D | 26.5 | 2.15 | 0.0 | 18.1 | 15.4 | 47.8 | 5.7 | 7.7 |
| TONAWANDA VALLEY FCU | Batavia | NY | C | C- | C | 88.4 | 8.68 | 0.1 | 18.9 | 15.4 | 1.8 | 6.7 | 8.7 |
| TONGASS FCU | Ketchikan | AK | B- | C+ | C | 68.8 | 2.84 | 12.1 | 16.1 | 28.1 | 16.0 | 8.4 | 10.0 |
| TOPEKA CITY EMPL CU | Topeka | KS | C | C | C- | 10.4 | 4.24 | 1.5 | 39.5 | 30.0 | 0.0 | 10.0 | 12.4 |
| TOPEKA FIREMENS CU | Topeka | KS | C+ | C+ | C+ | 9.1 | 1.42 | 0.0 | 38.5 | 0.0 | 0.0 | 10.0 | 27.3 |
| TOPEKA POLICE CU | Topeka | KS | D | D | D+ | 6.7 | -7.44 | 0.0 | 71.7 | 0.0 | 0.0 | 10.0 | 11.4 |
| TOPEKA POST OFFICE CU | Topeka | KS | C+ | C+ | C+ | 6.9 | 1.52 | 0.0 | 29.4 | 8.1 | 0.0 | 10.0 | 24.9 |
| ▼ TOPLINE FCU | Maple Grove | MN | C+ | B- | B- | 367.4 | 4.12 | 2.5 | 27.1 | 15.9 | 34.2 | 8.3 | 9.9 |
| TOPMARK FCU | Lima | OH | C+ | C+ | C+ | 27.6 | -3.64 | 0.0 | 48.6 | 6.2 | 18.5 | 10.0 | 13.4 |
| TORCH LAKE FCU | Laurium | MI | D | D- | D | 7.1 | 2.25 | 0.0 | 48.7 | 1.4 | 0.0 | 8.3 | 9.9 |
| TORO EMPL FCU | Bloomington | MN | B | B- | C+ | 27.2 | -0.65 | 0.0 | 34.5 | 11.1 | 3.6 | 10.0 | 12.2 |
| TORRANCE COMMUNITY FCU | Torrance | CA | C+ | B- | C+ | 119.6 | 2.88 | 0.4 | 14.2 | 7.7 | 51.4 | 6.2 | 8.2 |
| TORRINGTON MUNICIPAL & TEACHERS FCU | Torrington | CT | C | C | C | 41.2 | 10.08 | 1.1 | 37.3 | 6.4 | 0.0 | 6.5 | 8.5 |
| TOTAL CHOICE FCU | Hahnville | LA | D- | D- | D- | 51.3 | -1.35 | 0.0 | 39.2 | 15.2 | 29.7 | 4.7 | 6.7 |
| ▲ TOTAL COMMUNITY ACTION FCU | New Orleans | LA | C+ | C | C- | 1.3 | -5.00 | 0.0 | 44.3 | 0.0 | 0.0 | 10.0 | 21.2 |
| TOTAL COMMUNITY CU | Taylor | MI | D+ | D+ | D+ | 59.0 | 4.77 | 0.0 | 19.6 | 2.3 | 61.0 | 5.8 | 7.8 |
| TOUCHSTONE FCU | Wilmington | MA | D | D | D | 17.9 | 0.29 | 0.0 | 25.2 | 4.1 | 14.8 | 6.7 | 8.7 |
| TOWANDA SCHOOL EMPL FCU | Towanda | PA | C+ | C- | D+ | <1 | 4.73 | 0.0 | 41.7 | 0.0 | 0.0 | 10.0 | 15.8 |
| TOWER FAMILY CU | Kalamazoo | MI | D- | D- | D+ | 7.8 | -1.11 | 0.0 | 26.5 | 0.0 | 64.4 | 7.9 | 9.6 |
| TOWER FCU | Laurel | MD | B- | B- | B | 2755.3 | 2.23 | 0.0 | 19.6 | 15.4 | 29.2 | 10.0 | 11.1 |
| TOWN & COUNTRY CU | Minot | ND | B+ | A | A | 372.5 | 2.00 | 61.8 | 12.7 | 38.2 | 0.0 | 10.0 | 13.5 |
| TOWN & COUNTRY FCU | Scarborough | ME | B- | B- | B- | 296.1 | 10.84 | 0.1 | 37.4 | 32.1 | 3.3 | 6.1 | 8.1 |
| TOWN AND COUNTRY CU | Harlan | IA | B- | B- | B- | 18.0 | 5.27 | 1.9 | 36.3 | 33.9 | 0.0 | 10.0 | 12.2 |
| TOWN OF CHEEKTOWAGA FCU | Cheektowaga | NY | B+ | B+ | B+ | 19.0 | 7.02 | 0.0 | 13.6 | 25.2 | 6.5 | 10.0 | 13.9 |
| TOWN OF HEMPSTEAD EMPL FCU | North Baldwin | NY | D+ | D+ | C- | 117.0 | 2.05 | 9.2 | 11.1 | 20.4 | 13.9 | 5.4 | 7.4 |
| TOWN OF PALM BEACH FCU | West Palm Beach | FL | D | D+ | D | 2.7 | -0.19 | 0.0 | 42.3 | 0.0 | 0.0 | 9.0 | 10.4 |
| TOWNS-UNION EDUCATORS FCU | Young Harris | GA | E+ | E+ | D- | 2.2 | -19.15 | 0.0 | 44.1 | 0.0 | 0.0 | 5.2 | 7.2 |
| ▲ TOWPATH CU | Fairlawn | OH | B- | C | C | 114.4 | 0.89 | 2.7 | 38.5 | 8.3 | 27.0 | 10.0 | 12.0 |
| TPC EMPL FCU | Tupelo | MS | E+ | E+ | D- | <1 | 5.37 | 0.0 | 40.1 | 0.0 | 0.0 | 3.6 | 5.6 |
| ▲ TRADEMARK FCU | Augusta | ME | D | D- | D | 80.1 | 4.05 | 0.0 | 21.9 | 22.0 | 0.0 | 10.0 | 12.1 |
| ▲ TRADES & LABOR FCU | Albert Lea | MN | D- | E+ | D | 10.5 | 5.96 | 0.0 | 50.2 | 14.0 | 5.7 | 5.4 | 7.4 |
| TRADESMEN COMMUNITY CU | Des Moines | IA | B | B | B | 46.7 | -0.70 | 3.7 | 35.4 | 8.6 | 15.4 | 10.0 | 14.2 |
| TRADEWINDS CU | Comstock Park | MI | D- | D- | D- | 17.8 | 1.82 | 0.0 | 24.0 | 0.0 | 59.9 | 5.6 | 7.7 |
| TRAILHEAD FCU | Portland | OR | C | C | D+ | 98.7 | 5.62 | 3.2 | 23.5 | 20.2 | 17.9 | 6.6 | 8.7 |
| TRANS TEXAS SOUTHWEST CU | San Angelo | TX | C+ | C+ | C+ | 45.6 | 4.53 | 10.2 | 18.5 | 49.1 | 0.0 | 9.4 | 10.6 |
| TRANSFIGURATION MANHATTAN FCU | New York | NY | D | D+ | C- | <1 | -6.31 | 0.0 | 4.8 | 0.0 | 0.0 | 5.7 | 7.7 |
| TRANSFIGURATION PARISH FCU | Brooklyn | NY | D | D | D | 6.9 | -2.03 | 4.9 | 23.4 | 32.5 | 0.0 | 7.5 | 9.3 |
| TRANSIT AUTHORITY DIVISION B FCU | New York | NY | E+ | E+ | E+ | 5.1 | 1.83 | 0.0 | 41.1 | 0.0 | 0.0 | 5.4 | 7.4 |
| TRANSIT EMPL FCU | Washington | DC | B+ | B+ | B+ | 105.6 | 6.57 | 0.4 | 46.1 | 8.4 | 14.5 | 10.0 | 17.9 |
| TRANSIT FCU | Valley Stream | NY | C- | C | B- | 12.9 | -2.95 | 0.0 | 22.6 | 0.0 | 3.6 | 10.0 | 14.4 |
| ▲ TRANSIT OPERATIONS FCU | Minneapolis | MN | C | D | D+ | 4.2 | 2.41 | 0.0 | 30.5 | 0.0 | 0.0 | 10.0 | 14.1 |
| TRANSIT WORKERS FCU | Philadelphia | PA | D | D | D+ | 20.5 | -0.34 | 0.0 | 46.7 | 0.0 | 0.0 | 10.0 | 17.7 |
| TRANSPORTATION FCU | Alexandria | VA | B- | B- | B | 196.3 | 0.65 | 6.4 | 24.1 | 14.6 | 20.4 | 10.0 | 11.9 |
| TRANSTAR FCU | Houston | TX | E- | E- | E | 35.4 | -6.99 | 0.0 | 38.3 | 16.3 | 31.3 | 1.5 | 4.4 |
| TRANSWEST CU | Salt Lake City | UT | B- | C+ | C- | 122.3 | 5.23 | 2.8 | 20.2 | 42.2 | 7.6 | 5.2 | 7.3 |
| ▲ TRAVIS COUNTY CU | Austin | TX | C- | D+ | D+ | 29.1 | 1.09 | 0.0 | 22.5 | 20.6 | 12.3 | 5.7 | 7.7 |
| TRAVIS CU | Vacaville | CA | A | A | A | 2476.0 | 9.18 | 4.4 | 41.9 | 17.3 | 27.0 | 10.0 | 12.0 |
| TREASURY DEPT FCU | Washington | DC | C | C | C- | 167.8 | -2.62 | 0.0 | 20.5 | 23.9 | 1.8 | 5.1 | 7.1 |
| TREASURY EMPL FCU | Jackson | MS | D+ | D+ | C- | 9.4 | -7.62 | 0.0 | 11.3 | 0.0 | 0.0 | 8.4 | 9.9 |
| ▲ TREMONT CU | Braintree | MA | C- | C- | C- | 168.8 | 0.70 | 1.2 | 16.2 | 23.0 | 12.8 | 10.0 | 12.6 |
| TRENTON NEW JERSEY FIREMEN FCU | Trenton | NJ | D | D+ | D+ | 4.6 | -14.49 | 0.0 | 22.0 | 0.0 | 0.0 | 10.0 | 14.0 |
| TRENTON NEW JERSEY POLICE FCU | Hamilton | NJ | B+ | B- | B- | 25.9 | 4.25 | 0.0 | 25.8 | 14.8 | 19.9 | 10.0 | 14.1 |
| TRENTON TEACHERS FCU | Hamilton Square | NJ | D | D | C- | 2.0 | 2.98 | 0.0 | 22.8 | 0.0 | 0.0 | 10.0 | 13.6 |
| TRI AG FCU | Newtown Square | PA | C- | C- | C- | 1.6 | 0.37 | 0.0 | 40.7 | 0.0 | 0.0 | 10.0 | 13.5 |
| TRI AG WEST VIRGINIA FCU | Morgantown | WV | E+ | D | E+ | 11.0 | 6.09 | 0.0 | 46.7 | 10.3 | 0.0 | 5.2 | 7.2 |
| ▼ TRI BORO FCU | Munhall | PA | C- | C- | C- | 99.6 | -2.69 | 0.0 | 14.9 | 30.5 | 6.8 | 10.0 | 11.2 |

| Asset Quality Index | Non-Performing Loans as a % of Total Loans | as a % of Capital | Net Charge- Offs Avg Loans | Profitability Index | Net Income ($Mil) | Return on Assets | Return on Equity | Net Interest Spread | Overhead Efficiency Ratio | Liquidity Index | Liquidity Ratio | Hot Money Ratio | Stability Index |
|---|---|---|---|---|---|---|---|---|---|---|---|---|---|
| 9.6 | 0.00 | 0.0 | 0.00 | 1.3 | 0.0 | -0.12 | -0.63 | 1.90 | 107.1 | 5.8 | 41.8 | 0.0 | 7.1 |
| 6.6 | 0.79 | 5.5 | -0.03 | 2.5 | 0.0 | 0.10 | 1.05 | 2.86 | 95.8 | 3.8 | 16.1 | 2.2 | 5.2 |
| 9.2 | 1.58 | 2.4 | 1.14 | 0.5 | 0.0 | -0.28 | -2.00 | 2.31 | 102.1 | 6.1 | 49.9 | 0.0 | 5.2 |
| 5.4 | 2.13 | 11.0 | 0.00 | 4.9 | 0.0 | 0.61 | 4.58 | 5.54 | 81.6 | 4.6 | 17.9 | 0.0 | 3.7 |
| 6.4 | 1.39 | 7.1 | 0.10 | 3.5 | 0.1 | 0.54 | 7.27 | 3.30 | 85.3 | 5.1 | 19.1 | 0.0 | 2.4 |
| 10.0 | 0.10 | 0.5 | -0.02 | 3.2 | 0.3 | 0.43 | 4.98 | 2.76 | 87.2 | 5.3 | 27.2 | 0.0 | 4.1 |
| 6.7 | 0.22 | 2.7 | 0.11 | 5.0 | 0.4 | 0.75 | 9.92 | 4.18 | 85.0 | 3.9 | 19.3 | 6.8 | 4.2 |
| 6.1 | 0.88 | 8.2 | 2.13 | 1.9 | 0.0 | -0.08 | -0.61 | 4.93 | 72.3 | 4.6 | 26.1 | 1.7 | 6.2 |
| 9.6 | 0.90 | 1.5 | 0.29 | 2.2 | 0.0 | -0.01 | -0.05 | 1.74 | 81.3 | 5.3 | 42.8 | 0.0 | 7.9 |
| 6.1 | 0.04 | 0.3 | 4.36 | 0.0 | -0.1 | -1.96 | -16.34 | 4.25 | 85.2 | 2.8 | 12.0 | 9.4 | 4.9 |
| 9.3 | 0.80 | 1.6 | 0.04 | 3.6 | 0.0 | 0.41 | 1.63 | 3.36 | 89.1 | 4.9 | 34.3 | 0.0 | 7.6 |
| 7.7 | 0.81 | 5.6 | 0.40 | 3.4 | 1.2 | 0.42 | 4.49 | 2.92 | 85.4 | 3.9 | 15.0 | 2.5 | 5.5 |
| 5.3 | 1.90 | 10.7 | 0.79 | 3.8 | 0.1 | 0.41 | 3.15 | 4.58 | 87.1 | 3.5 | 9.7 | 3.6 | 5.6 |
| 6.1 | 0.84 | 5.0 | -1.13 | 4.2 | 0.1 | 0.99 | 10.84 | 4.01 | 100.4 | 5.0 | 23.6 | 0.0 | 3.0 |
| 8.5 | 0.57 | 3.5 | 0.39 | 5.7 | 0.2 | 0.92 | 7.75 | 3.69 | 77.3 | 4.2 | 23.8 | 1.2 | 5.7 |
| 10.0 | 0.33 | 1.3 | 0.26 | 3.0 | 0.3 | 0.29 | 3.49 | 2.19 | 84.9 | 4.3 | 20.4 | 8.7 | 5.2 |
| 8.6 | 0.27 | 1.6 | -0.05 | 4.4 | 0.2 | 0.68 | 8.10 | 3.57 | 84.8 | 4.4 | 21.2 | 3.1 | 3.4 |
| 4.5 | 1.49 | 12.9 | 0.92 | 0.9 | -0.1 | -0.12 | -1.80 | 3.63 | 85.0 | 3.6 | 10.4 | 5.4 | 1.7 |
| 5.6 | 6.74 | 12.9 | -0.21 | 9.2 | 0.0 | 1.53 | 7.58 | 8.15 | 71.2 | 7.1 | 71.1 | 0.0 | 5.0 |
| 7.7 | 1.10 | 4.4 | 0.14 | 1.8 | 0.1 | 0.20 | 2.66 | 2.94 | 93.8 | 4.6 | 18.3 | 2.0 | 2.7 |
| 9.0 | 0.20 | 1.0 | 0.49 | 2.4 | 0.0 | 0.10 | 1.24 | 3.17 | 96.5 | 5.0 | 30.0 | 0.0 | 2.9 |
| 9.8 | 0.00 | 0.0 | 0.00 | 5.0 | 0.0 | 0.86 | 5.19 | 6.82 | 76.9 | 7.0 | 56.5 | 0.0 | 7.1 |
| 7.1 | 1.29 | 3.6 | 0.13 | 0.2 | 0.0 | -0.41 | -4.22 | 2.72 | 112.5 | 5.0 | 22.5 | 0.0 | 3.7 |
| 9.3 | 0.51 | 3.0 | 0.24 | 3.7 | 10.0 | 0.48 | 4.68 | 2.27 | 78.3 | 6.2 | 37.4 | 2.1 | 7.5 |
| 4.3 | 1.28 | 9.5 | 0.03 | 9.8 | 4.0 | 1.39 | 10.97 | 4.22 | 74.3 | 2.7 | 8.6 | 9.1 | 10.0 |
| 6.0 | 1.44 | 14.1 | 0.42 | 4.1 | 1.2 | 0.53 | 6.43 | 4.23 | 82.6 | 2.6 | 3.9 | 6.7 | 5.7 |
| 8.3 | 0.54 | 4.7 | 0.03 | 6.3 | 0.1 | 0.82 | 6.71 | 5.55 | 79.8 | 2.4 | 6.1 | 11.4 | 5.7 |
| 10.0 | 0.05 | 0.2 | 0.00 | 8.4 | 0.2 | 1.18 | 8.64 | 3.38 | 67.1 | 4.4 | 13.2 | 0.8 | 7.0 |
| 3.7 | 1.91 | 20.9 | 0.07 | 1.8 | 0.2 | 0.17 | 3.54 | 2.87 | 91.6 | 4.2 | 19.5 | 5.5 | 2.6 |
| 6.3 | 1.94 | 7.6 | 0.00 | 2.4 | 0.0 | 0.25 | 2.44 | 4.09 | 92.6 | 5.0 | 39.4 | 0.0 | 4.3 |
| 9.4 | 0.20 | 1.3 | 0.40 | 1.1 | 0.0 | -0.16 | -2.25 | 2.67 | 98.1 | 4.8 | 33.9 | 0.0 | 1.0 |
| 9.0 | 0.60 | 2.8 | 0.52 | 3.6 | 0.4 | 0.43 | 3.71 | 3.99 | 82.0 | 4.1 | 14.0 | 1.9 | 6.1 |
| 4.6 | 1.05 | 6.5 | 0.65 | 0.0 | 0.0 | -3.49 | -56.41 | 13.07 | 132.1 | 7.0 | 57.3 | 0.0 | 4.0 |
| 9.6 | 0.35 | 1.6 | 0.40 | 2.3 | 0.2 | 0.30 | 2.47 | 3.06 | 87.5 | 4.6 | 37.7 | 4.9 | 5.9 |
| 6.5 | 0.07 | 1.2 | 0.56 | 2.6 | 0.0 | 0.23 | 3.18 | 3.88 | 87.9 | 3.2 | 9.3 | 6.2 | 1.7 |
| 7.4 | 1.32 | 5.7 | 0.55 | 7.3 | 0.4 | 1.11 | 8.13 | 3.92 | 74.7 | 4.1 | 19.0 | 3.8 | 6.9 |
| 8.9 | 0.07 | 0.3 | 0.41 | 0.2 | -0.1 | -0.57 | -7.17 | 2.73 | 117.0 | 4.5 | 8.3 | 0.0 | 2.9 |
| 4.2 | 1.60 | 15.8 | 0.42 | 3.6 | 0.3 | 0.41 | 4.85 | 4.23 | 83.8 | 3.7 | 16.1 | 0.6 | 3.7 |
| 6.2 | 0.80 | 5.5 | 0.01 | 4.6 | 0.2 | 0.52 | 4.91 | 3.91 | 86.8 | 2.2 | 25.9 | 20.8 | 6.2 |
| 10.0 | 0.00 | 0.0 | 0.00 | 0.6 | 0.0 | 0.00 | 0.00 | 2.34 | 100.0 | 8.4 | 102.1 | 0.0 | 5.2 |
| 6.2 | 1.04 | 6.2 | 0.11 | 2.7 | 0.0 | 0.02 | 0.21 | 8.98 | 99.7 | 6.3 | 43.4 | 0.0 | 2.3 |
| 5.0 | 1.97 | 10.8 | 0.61 | 5.3 | 0.0 | 0.78 | 11.17 | 4.98 | 80.5 | 4.8 | 38.2 | 0.0 | 1.0 |
| 5.2 | 4.03 | 12.2 | 1.65 | 5.1 | 0.3 | 0.43 | 2.33 | 7.24 | 78.4 | 4.9 | 33.5 | 11.5 | 8.0 |
| 4.3 | 13.77 | 17.3 | 11.29 | 0.3 | -0.6 | -6.09 | -38.32 | 3.46 | 120.2 | 5.3 | 21.5 | 0.0 | 5.4 |
| 10.0 | 0.86 | 1.8 | 0.11 | 3.6 | 0.0 | 0.69 | 4.87 | 3.82 | 81.1 | 6.8 | 60.2 | 0.0 | 6.1 |
| 5.6 | 2.91 | 7.4 | 2.41 | 0.2 | -0.2 | -1.00 | -5.65 | 6.76 | 95.8 | 6.7 | 45.3 | 0.0 | 5.0 |
| 9.8 | 0.23 | 1.4 | 0.34 | 3.7 | 0.6 | 0.38 | 3.73 | 3.91 | 87.5 | 4.2 | 15.9 | 4.8 | 5.5 |
| 4.4 | 1.37 | 14.5 | 2.00 | 0.1 | -0.3 | -0.89 | -18.78 | 4.49 | 89.7 | 3.4 | 10.2 | 7.9 | 0.0 |
| 7.3 | 0.19 | 7.5 | 0.23 | 7.4 | 0.9 | 0.96 | 13.60 | 3.53 | 78.6 | 3.1 | 15.8 | 11.9 | 4.3 |
| 9.9 | 0.03 | 0.2 | 0.05 | 2.1 | 0.0 | 0.19 | 2.46 | 2.75 | 94.0 | 4.3 | 19.4 | 2.5 | 3.4 |
| 9.5 | 0.30 | 1.7 | 0.51 | 7.4 | 16.7 | 0.92 | 7.72 | 3.73 | 71.1 | 3.4 | 11.1 | 7.6 | 9.0 |
| 6.8 | 1.26 | 8.5 | 0.73 | 3.1 | 0.3 | 0.24 | 3.44 | 3.14 | 87.3 | 5.2 | 51.9 | 5.8 | 3.1 |
| 6.9 | 3.32 | 3.9 | 1.34 | 2.3 | 0.0 | 0.24 | 2.61 | 1.83 | 86.2 | 4.9 | 10.3 | 0.0 | 4.5 |
| 5.5 | 4.26 | 18.4 | -0.06 | 2.8 | 0.4 | 0.32 | 2.78 | 3.52 | 106.6 | 4.7 | 20.1 | 2.2 | 7.1 |
| 9.8 | 0.94 | 1.5 | 0.51 | 0.5 | 0.0 | -0.31 | -2.24 | 2.08 | 115.3 | 7.2 | 63.3 | 0.0 | 5.6 |
| 9.3 | 0.88 | 2.7 | 0.70 | 7.0 | 0.2 | 1.07 | 7.79 | 2.77 | 60.9 | 4.4 | 11.5 | 0.0 | 7.5 |
| 10.0 | 0.87 | 1.4 | -0.95 | 0.1 | 0.0 | -0.90 | -8.04 | 17.56 | 137.5 | 8.2 | 88.2 | 0.0 | 5.2 |
| 9.3 | 0.94 | 3.4 | 0.00 | 2.7 | 0.0 | 0.33 | 2.47 | 4.53 | 94.1 | 4.7 | 40.0 | 0.0 | 6.6 |
| 4.1 | 1.31 | 11.5 | 1.06 | 3.0 | 0.0 | 0.14 | 1.90 | 3.74 | 92.2 | 3.5 | 13.2 | 5.1 | 1.7 |
| 8.6 | 0.73 | 4.3 | 0.14 | 1.0 | -0.1 | -0.15 | -1.66 | 3.10 | 103.2 | 4.4 | 15.0 | 1.9 | 4.8 |

| Name | City | State | Rating | 2014 Rating | 2013 Rating | Total Assets ($Mil) | One Year Asset Growth | Asset Mix (As a % of Total Assets) Commercial Loans | Consumer Loans | Mortgage Loans | Securities | Capitalization Index | Net Worth Ratio |
|---|---|---|---|---|---|---|---|---|---|---|---|---|---|
| TRI COUNTY AREA FCU | Pottstown | PA | C | C+ | C | 111.5 | 3.33 | 5.4 | 25.3 | 26.8 | 8.5 | 6.5 | 8.5 |
| TRI STATE RAIL FCU | Erie | PA | C- | D+ | C- | 15.3 | -8.94 | 0.0 | 24.9 | 7.6 | 0.0 | 10.0 | 19.9 |
| TRI-CITIES COMMUNITY FCU | Kennewick | WA | B | B | B- | 30.3 | 5.84 | 0.0 | 30.5 | 25.5 | 0.0 | 9.5 | 10.7 |
| TRI-CITIES CU | Grand Haven | MI | C+ | C+ | C+ | 29.3 | 2.96 | 0.0 | 26.8 | 8.0 | 33.7 | 8.1 | 9.7 |
| TRI-COUNTY CU | Grinnell | KS | C | C | C | 3.6 | 5.77 | 6.2 | 19.4 | 0.0 | 0.0 | 10.0 | 16.9 |
| TRI-COUNTY CU | Panguitch | UT | C- | C- | D+ | <1 | -4.91 | 0.0 | 55.5 | 0.0 | 0.0 | 10.0 | 29.0 |
| ▲ TRI-COUNTY CU | Marinette | WI | C- | D+ | C | 27.1 | 4.82 | 1.7 | 15.2 | 18.8 | 0.0 | 10.0 | 14.5 |
| TRI-COUNTY FCU | Delevan | NY | C | C | C | 3.8 | 0.45 | 0.0 | 35.9 | 0.0 | 0.0 | 10.0 | 19.3 |
| TRI-COUNTY FCU | Shawnee | OK | D | D+ | D+ | 3.2 | 5.51 | 0.0 | 26.7 | 0.0 | 0.0 | 7.4 | 9.3 |
| ▲ TRI-LAKES FCU | Saranac Lake | NY | D | D | D | 13.9 | -0.57 | 0.0 | 30.5 | 17.1 | 0.0 | 5.1 | 7.1 |
| TRI-POINT FCU | Pittsburgh | PA | E+ | E+ | E | 9.1 | -9.13 | 0.0 | 16.8 | 0.0 | 0.0 | 5.4 | 7.4 |
| ▲ TRI-RIVERS FCU | Montgomery | AL | E | E | E+ | 16.6 | -3.93 | 0.1 | 58.6 | 0.8 | 7.6 | 5.7 | 7.7 |
| TRI-TOWN TEACHERS FCU | Westport | CT | D+ | D | D | 18.1 | 2.55 | 0.0 | 31.1 | 36.6 | 2.8 | 7.0 | 9.0 |
| TRI-VALLEY SERVICE FCU | Pittsburgh | PA | D- | D+ | D | 15.1 | -0.46 | 0.0 | 52.5 | 0.0 | 0.0 | 6.6 | 8.6 |
| ▲ TRIAD PARTNERS FCU | Greensboro | NC | D | D- | D | 31.9 | -4.66 | 0.0 | 24.9 | 0.0 | 34.8 | 10.0 | 11.6 |
| TRIANGLE CU | Nashua | NH | C+ | C+ | C+ | 557.8 | 10.38 | 10.3 | 24.4 | 44.0 | 5.9 | 5.8 | 7.8 |
| TRIANGLE CU | Kettering | OH | D- | D | D+ | 17.4 | 1.11 | 0.0 | 11.0 | 6.7 | 7.7 | 9.1 | 10.4 |
| TRIANGLE FCU | Columbus AFB | MS | C+ | C+ | C+ | 74.9 | 2.41 | 0.0 | 35.8 | 4.9 | 0.0 | 7.4 | 9.3 |
| TRIANGLE INTERESTS FCU | Bensalem | PA | C- | C- | D+ | <1 | -7.67 | 0.0 | 13.3 | 0.0 | 0.0 | 10.0 | 14.0 |
| TRIBORO POSTAL FCU | Flushing | NY | C- | C+ | C+ | 129.2 | 0.20 | 0.0 | 4.5 | 4.3 | 86.9 | 10.0 | 14.6 |
| TRICO COMMUNITY FCU | Helena | MT | D+ | D+ | D+ | 23.7 | 5.09 | 0.0 | 35.5 | 0.5 | 0.0 | 6.4 | 8.4 |
| TRICOUNTY FCU | Harlowton | MT | C | D+ | E+ | 1.3 | 3.66 | 0.0 | 69.7 | 0.0 | 0.0 | 9.8 | 10.8 |
| TRINITY BAPTIST CHURCH FCU | Florence | SC | C | C- | C- | 2.5 | -2.31 | 0.0 | 6.6 | 2.7 | 0.0 | 10.0 | 12.0 |
| TRINITY UCC FCU | Chicago | IL | C- | C- | C- | 2.9 | -3.34 | 0.0 | 0.0 | 0.0 | 0.0 | 10.0 | 17.9 |
| TRINITY VALLEY TEACHERS CU | Palestine | TX | B- | C+ | B- | 27.1 | 3.17 | 0.0 | 12.9 | 1.2 | 0.0 | 10.0 | 26.7 |
| TRIPLE C 16 FCU | Baltimore | MD | D | D | D | 3.8 | -6.35 | 0.0 | 31.4 | 10.4 | 0.0 | 10.0 | 25.1 |
| TRIUMPH BAPTIST FCU | Philadelphia | PA | E- | E+ | E+ | <1 | -22.05 | 0.0 | 66.6 | 0.0 | 0.0 | 1.9 | 4.6 |
| TRMC EMPL CU | Orangeburg | SC | C+ | C+ | C+ | 5.1 | 3.72 | 0.0 | 63.9 | 0.0 | 0.0 | 10.0 | 17.6 |
| TRONA VALLEY COMMUNITY FCU | Green River | WY | A- | A- | B+ | 170.7 | 3.37 | 0.5 | 45.6 | 19.1 | 0.0 | 10.0 | 11.7 |
| TROPICAL FINANCIAL CU | Miramar | FL | B- | B- | C- | 575.5 | 5.46 | 1.6 | 27.7 | 32.6 | 15.9 | 7.2 | 9.3 |
| ▼ TROUVAILLE FCU | Philadelphia | PA | D- | D | D | 1.5 | 2.01 | 0.0 | 37.8 | 0.0 | 0.0 | 6.4 | 8.4 |
| TROY AREA SCHOOL EMPL FCU | Columbia Cross Ro | PA | D+ | C- | C | 1.9 | -1.24 | 0.0 | 24.0 | 0.0 | 18.4 | 10.0 | 13.5 |
| TROY FCU | Troy | NY | C | C | C | 2.8 | -2.95 | 0.0 | 41.8 | 0.0 | 0.0 | 10.0 | 13.6 |
| ▲ TRUCHOICE FCU | Portland | ME | B+ | B+ | B+ | 104.1 | 9.89 | 0.0 | 43.2 | 20.9 | 0.0 | 10.0 | 11.2 |
| TRUE NORTH FCU | Juneau | AK | C | C+ | C+ | 136.7 | 8.05 | 12.1 | 32.4 | 23.0 | 1.8 | 5.3 | 7.4 |
| TRUECORE FCU | Newark | OH | C | C- | C- | 150.0 | 23.67 | 5.2 | 18.8 | 33.1 | 4.1 | 6.8 | 8.8 |
| TRUGROCER FCU | Boise | ID | C+ | C+ | B- | 236.3 | 4.21 | 0.0 | 12.8 | 16.8 | 8.0 | 10.0 | 20.7 |
| TRUITY FCU | Bartlesville | OK | C+ | C+ | C+ | 719.0 | 2.26 | 6.1 | 45.8 | 26.1 | 10.1 | 6.2 | 8.2 |
| TRULIANT FCU | Winston-Salem | NC | B | B | B | 1849.7 | 5.55 | 7.9 | 41.0 | 25.1 | 9.2 | 7.6 | 9.4 |
| TRUMARK FINANCIAL CU | Trevose | PA | B+ | A- | A- | 1648.7 | 6.94 | 8.5 | 23.9 | 30.6 | 16.0 | 9.9 | 11.0 |
| ▲ TRUMBULL COUNTY POSTAL EMPL CU | Warren | OH | C- | D | D | 1.2 | -14.13 | 0.0 | 9.3 | 0.0 | 0.0 | 10.0 | 11.4 |
| ▲ TRUMBULL CU | Trumbull | CT | D | D- | D- | 3.6 | 2.11 | 0.0 | 6.1 | 0.0 | 5.4 | 7.1 | 9.1 |
| TRUNORTH FCU | Ishpeming | MI | B- | C+ | C- | 131.9 | 6.55 | 0.0 | 17.4 | 30.6 | 25.8 | 6.8 | 8.8 |
| ▲ TRUPARTNER CU INC | Cincinnati | OH | C | C- | C- | 148.0 | 59.36 | 7.9 | 19.0 | 17.5 | 30.9 | 9.6 | 10.7 |
| TRUSERVICE COMMUNITY FCU | Little Rock | AR | D | D+ | C- | 37.3 | 2.63 | 0.0 | 38.9 | 17.8 | 8.5 | 5.7 | 7.7 |
| TRUST FCU | Chattanooga | TN | C | B- | C+ | 65.6 | 3.94 | 0.4 | 54.3 | 20.8 | 1.5 | 9.8 | 10.8 |
| TRUSTAR FCU | International Falls | MN | A | A | A- | 197.0 | 9.09 | 19.6 | 15.6 | 41.2 | 7.2 | 10.0 | 16.4 |
| TRUSTONE FINANCIAL FCU | Plymouth | MN | B+ | B | B- | 1033.8 | 8.36 | 12.4 | 15.0 | 32.1 | 21.8 | 8.1 | 9.7 |
| TRUSTUS FCU | Midlothian | TX | E+ | E+ | E+ | 7.5 | -14.94 | 0.0 | 47.1 | 0.0 | 0.0 | 5.7 | 7.7 |
| TRUWEST CU | Tempe | AZ | B+ | B+ | A- | 903.8 | 5.35 | 8.7 | 51.0 | 27.6 | 4.4 | 9.7 | 10.8 |
| TSU FCU | Nashville | TN | C+ | C | C- | 1.6 | 14.74 | 0.0 | 47.4 | 0.0 | 0.0 | 10.0 | 14.5 |
| TTCU THE CU | Tulsa | OK | A- | B+ | B+ | 1581.2 | 6.09 | 0.1 | 46.5 | 11.3 | 21.3 | 10.0 | 12.7 |
| TUCOEMAS FCU | Visalia | CA | C- | C- | C- | 214.3 | 2.65 | 0.0 | 39.0 | 16.4 | 9.6 | 6.0 | 8.0 |
| TUCSON FCU | Tucson | AZ | B | B | B- | 376.1 | 6.58 | 2.9 | 49.4 | 11.2 | 20.9 | 7.6 | 9.4 |
| TUCSON OLD PUEBLO CU | Tucson | AZ | C- | C- | C- | 138.3 | 2.18 | 0.1 | 21.8 | 20.0 | 19.3 | 4.9 | 6.9 |
| TULANE/LOYOLA FCU | New Orleans | LA | D- | D | D | 19.6 | -0.44 | 0.0 | 23.9 | 10.1 | 0.0 | 8.4 | 9.9 |
| TULARE COUNTY FCU | Tulare | CA | C- | C | D+ | 87.2 | 7.61 | 0.0 | 49.8 | 13.9 | 11.7 | 5.2 | 7.3 |
| TULIP COOPERATIVE CU | Olympia | WA | E+ | E+ | D- | 2.6 | -5.13 | 0.0 | 38.6 | 0.0 | 0.0 | 3.5 | 5.5 |
| TULSA FCU | Tulsa | OK | D+ | C- | C+ | 685.5 | 2.96 | 2.7 | 29.7 | 18.7 | 25.9 | 6.8 | 8.8 |
| TURBINE FCU | Greenville | SC | D | D+ | C- | 25.1 | 6.30 | 0.0 | 37.2 | 0.5 | 0.0 | 10.0 | 14.3 |

| Asset Quality Index | Non-Performing Loans | | Net Charge-Offs Avg Loans | Profitability Index | Net Income ($Mil) | Return on Assets | Return on Equity | Net Interest Spread | Overhead Efficiency Ratio | Liquidity Index | Liquidity Ratio | Hot Money Ratio | Stability Index |
| --- | --- | --- | --- | --- | --- | --- | --- | --- | --- | --- | --- | --- | --- |
| | as a % of Total Loans | as a % of Capital | | | | | | | | | | | |
| 5.6 | 2.23 | 17.3 | 0.43 | 2.8 | 0.2 | 0.20 | 2.42 | 4.13 | 90.4 | 3.7 | 11.5 | 2.6 | 4.9 |
| 9.5 | 1.59 | 3.2 | -0.11 | 1.7 | 0.0 | 0.15 | 0.79 | 3.13 | 92.7 | 5.3 | 21.7 | | 6.3 |
| 6.5 | 0.87 | 6.0 | 0.14 | 10.0 | 0.4 | 1.58 | 15.23 | 4.77 | 74.9 | 3.8 | 16.3 | 1.8 | 5.9 |
| 9.3 | 0.42 | 1.7 | 0.24 | 3.7 | 0.1 | 0.49 | 5.13 | 2.34 | 82.9 | 4.6 | 19.9 | 0.0 | 4.5 |
| 7.8 | 3.45 | 6.3 | 0.00 | 4.7 | 0.0 | 0.73 | 4.42 | 2.33 | 68.9 | 5.1 | 32.4 | 0.0 | 4.3 |
| 6.8 | 0.00 | 0.0 | 0.00 | 2.0 | 0.0 | 0.00 | 0.00 | 7.33 | 80.0 | 6.7 | 62.2 | 0.0 | 6.5 |
| 8.9 | 1.38 | 4.9 | 0.00 | 1.7 | 0.1 | 0.24 | 1.71 | 2.73 | 92.1 | 4.9 | 39.9 | 4.3 | 6.4 |
| 7.6 | 2.48 | 5.8 | 0.17 | 3.6 | 0.0 | 0.37 | 2.00 | 3.70 | 89.7 | 5.8 | 54.9 | 0.0 | 7.6 |
| 8.7 | 0.00 | 0.0 | 0.11 | 1.5 | 0.0 | 0.00 | 0.00 | 3.20 | 100.0 | 6.0 | 70.1 | 0.0 | 4.3 |
| 6.7 | 1.02 | 7.9 | -0.07 | 4.3 | 0.1 | 0.51 | 7.37 | 4.22 | 89.9 | 4.7 | 22.2 | 0.0 | 2.3 |
| 6.1 | 2.67 | 10.1 | 1.30 | 0.0 | -0.1 | -0.85 | -11.90 | 2.39 | 115.7 | 5.6 | 30.8 | 0.0 | 2.0 |
| 0.6 | 4.06 | 46.8 | 1.70 | 5.4 | 0.2 | 1.18 | 16.17 | 7.85 | 88.5 | 3.1 | 7.2 | 10.0 | 1.8 |
| 5.8 | 0.78 | 6.8 | 0.50 | 5.5 | 0.1 | 0.80 | 9.15 | 5.09 | 79.9 | 3.4 | 12.2 | 8.2 | 3.7 |
| 5.1 | 1.00 | 6.3 | 1.65 | 0.2 | -0.1 | -1.08 | -12.22 | 4.38 | 97.2 | 3.9 | 8.7 | 0.2 | 3.5 |
| 7.9 | 1.90 | 5.9 | 0.89 | 0.3 | -0.1 | -0.21 | -2.31 | 2.73 | 99.9 | 4.5 | 24.8 | 9.3 | 3.3 |
| 6.3 | 0.69 | 7.6 | 0.14 | 3.4 | 1.7 | 0.43 | 5.55 | 2.82 | 82.6 | 2.1 | 8.8 | 13.2 | 5.4 |
| 10.0 | 0.18 | 0.4 | -0.10 | 0.0 | -0.1 | -0.64 | -6.06 | 2.30 | 122.3 | 4.8 | 12.5 | 0.0 | 3.3 |
| 6.0 | 1.66 | 7.8 | 1.43 | 3.7 | 0.2 | 0.38 | 4.19 | 4.28 | 85.1 | 5.9 | 49.9 | 2.3 | 4.0 |
| 10.0 | 0.00 | 0.0 | 0.00 | 1.5 | 0.0 | 0.00 | 0.00 | 0.89 | 100.0 | 6.0 | 74.4 | 0.0 | 5.3 |
| 9.6 | 2.56 | 1.6 | 2.52 | 1.5 | 0.0 | -0.02 | -0.15 | 1.14 | 73.0 | 3.9 | 17.6 | 15.0 | 6.7 |
| 5.7 | 1.01 | 9.7 | 0.53 | 4.6 | 0.1 | 0.65 | 7.91 | 4.45 | 83.7 | 4.2 | 22.1 | 1.4 | 3.0 |
| 8.1 | 0.00 | 0.0 | -0.13 | 8.9 | 0.0 | 2.01 | 18.75 | 6.79 | 75.0 | 4.9 | 23.9 | 0.0 | 3.4 |
| 9.5 | 0.00 | 0.0 | 0.00 | 3.5 | 0.0 | 0.54 | 4.57 | 1.44 | 56.5 | 7.3 | 80.5 | 0.0 | 5.8 |
| 10.0 | 0.00 | 0.0 | 0.00 | 1.7 | 0.0 | 0.09 | 0.51 | 1.15 | 91.7 | 6.1 | 59.2 | 0.0 | 7.0 |
| 10.0 | 0.88 | 0.6 | 0.56 | 3.0 | 0.1 | 0.32 | 1.21 | 2.32 | 85.9 | 6.4 | 73.6 | 1.1 | 6.2 |
| 7.9 | 2.44 | 3.9 | 5.58 | 0.0 | -0.2 | -5.14 | -19.47 | 3.28 | 186.7 | 4.9 | 11.5 | 0.0 | 5.0 |
| 0.0 | 5.70 | 107.1 | 10.48 | 0.0 | 0.0 | -4.16 | NA | 5.39 | 61.4 | 5.3 | 29.3 | 0.0 | 3.5 |
| 7.1 | 0.24 | 1.0 | 1.29 | 9.8 | 0.1 | 1.70 | 9.76 | 11.92 | 63.6 | 6.4 | 62.6 | 0.0 | 5.7 |
| 5.4 | 1.15 | 10.8 | 0.69 | 8.0 | 1.5 | 1.16 | 11.73 | 4.87 | 75.3 | 2.9 | 13.7 | 13.6 | 7.0 |
| 7.1 | 0.62 | 6.0 | 0.26 | 4.6 | 2.8 | 0.66 | 7.98 | 3.63 | 86.2 | 3.8 | 10.4 | 4.7 | 5.3 |
| 5.9 | 1.08 | 5.3 | 6.78 | 1.2 | 0.0 | -2.46 | -38.10 | 13.56 | 90.6 | 7.4 | 66.3 | 0.0 | 3.2 |
| 5.8 | 7.64 | 13.4 | 2.09 | 1.9 | 0.0 | 0.14 | 1.05 | 1.84 | 54.2 | 5.7 | 45.1 | 0.0 | 6.1 |
| 9.8 | 0.00 | 0.0 | 0.74 | 3.2 | 0.0 | 0.28 | 2.08 | 4.24 | 88.9 | 6.1 | 41.4 | 0.0 | 7.0 |
| 7.0 | 0.72 | 5.0 | 0.95 | 5.1 | 0.5 | 0.60 | 5.78 | 5.33 | 82.0 | 3.7 | 10.8 | 1.5 | 7.5 |
| 5.8 | 0.66 | 9.5 | 0.29 | 2.8 | 0.2 | 0.15 | 2.08 | 4.23 | 92.7 | 3.4 | 13.3 | 3.8 | 4.4 |
| 6.7 | 0.74 | 7.4 | 0.29 | 3.0 | 0.5 | 0.43 | 5.57 | 3.35 | 88.3 | 3.7 | 19.1 | 4.5 | 3.6 |
| 10.0 | 0.31 | 0.8 | -0.01 | 2.5 | 0.4 | 0.24 | 1.17 | 1.85 | 92.6 | 5.3 | 45.4 | 6.2 | 7.7 |
| 5.0 | 0.86 | 10.2 | 0.80 | 4.7 | 3.8 | 0.69 | 8.78 | 3.92 | 73.0 | 3.6 | 9.8 | 4.6 | 5.5 |
| 7.2 | 0.43 | 4.8 | 0.52 | 4.2 | 6.9 | 0.50 | 5.57 | 3.36 | 82.2 | 3.0 | 10.9 | 11.6 | 6.7 |
| 7.4 | 0.89 | 6.4 | 0.61 | 4.3 | 5.2 | 0.43 | 3.89 | 3.01 | 72.5 | 3.1 | 14.9 | 9.1 | 8.3 |
| 8.4 | 1.31 | 4.0 | -0.18 | 1.4 | 0.0 | 0.00 | 0.00 | 3.01 | 100.0 | 6.0 | 55.7 | 0.0 | 6.4 |
| 10.0 | 0.00 | 0.0 | 0.00 | 1.0 | 0.0 | 0.04 | 0.41 | 2.27 | 98.2 | 6.4 | 81.6 | 0.0 | 3.7 |
| 9.1 | 0.32 | 2.8 | 0.13 | 4.6 | 0.8 | 0.76 | 8.81 | 3.38 | 77.9 | 4.2 | 13.9 | 3.1 | 5.7 |
| 5.0 | 2.20 | 11.7 | 0.36 | 3.9 | 0.7 | 0.73 | 7.24 | 3.98 | 85.4 | 4.5 | 16.8 | 4.4 | 4.8 |
| 5.9 | 0.58 | 5.4 | 0.53 | 0.9 | -0.1 | -0.44 | -5.62 | 3.87 | 98.6 | 3.4 | 12.4 | 11.6 | 2.4 |
| 2.6 | 2.21 | 21.1 | 0.47 | 6.2 | 0.4 | 0.81 | 7.66 | 4.60 | 78.9 | 2.9 | 7.2 | 3.8 | 5.3 |
| 7.7 | 0.52 | 3.2 | 0.13 | 8.4 | 1.8 | 1.26 | 7.62 | 4.68 | 74.3 | 3.7 | 18.3 | 9.3 | 9.0 |
| 8.6 | 0.29 | 3.2 | 0.11 | 7.2 | 9.6 | 1.27 | 13.40 | 3.49 | 72.9 | 3.4 | 7.8 | 3.7 | 7.4 |
| 5.3 | 0.68 | 5.0 | 0.12 | 0.7 | 0.0 | -0.74 | -9.86 | 6.10 | 111.3 | 5.0 | 16.5 | 0.0 | 1.9 |
| 6.9 | 0.48 | 4.1 | 0.44 | 4.5 | 3.6 | 0.53 | 4.89 | 4.09 | 82.3 | 3.1 | 5.6 | 1.5 | 7.5 |
| 4.4 | 4.32 | 17.7 | 0.25 | 8.6 | 0.0 | 2.17 | 14.88 | 6.74 | 63.0 | 4.1 | 37.6 | 0.0 | 4.3 |
| 5.7 | 1.00 | 6.5 | 0.91 | 7.8 | 15.0 | 1.28 | 10.12 | 3.42 | 57.1 | 2.8 | 4.4 | 10.6 | 8.9 |
| 8.5 | 0.22 | 2.6 | 0.37 | 2.3 | 0.4 | 0.25 | 3.61 | 2.93 | 93.0 | 4.4 | 19.9 | 3.6 | 3.4 |
| 6.2 | 0.22 | 6.6 | 0.78 | 5.6 | 2.3 | 0.83 | 9.64 | 4.36 | 77.8 | 4.2 | 23.4 | 2.4 | 5.6 |
| 7.5 | 0.65 | 4.9 | 0.88 | 2.4 | 0.1 | 0.11 | 1.55 | 3.42 | 93.3 | 4.7 | 15.1 | 2.3 | 3.2 |
| 6.1 | 1.48 | 7.4 | 1.39 | 0.5 | -0.1 | -0.75 | -9.64 | 3.40 | 109.4 | 7.1 | 61.6 | 0.0 | 3.1 |
| 4.4 | 1.12 | 11.2 | 0.31 | 2.6 | 0.1 | 0.13 | 1.81 | 3.68 | 91.0 | 3.9 | 14.4 | 1.3 | 3.1 |
| 0.3 | 1.98 | 104.2 | 1.86 | 1.6 | -0.1 | -3.09 | -387.30 | 7.12 | 120.6 | 6.2 | 35.2 | 0.0 | 2.3 |
| 6.7 | 0.98 | 7.0 | 0.98 | 1.8 | -0.2 | -0.04 | -0.48 | 2.96 | 87.3 | 3.8 | 13.5 | 8.9 | 5.1 |
| 9.8 | 0.58 | 1.9 | 0.12 | 0.2 | -0.1 | -0.33 | -2.22 | 3.10 | 108.1 | 4.3 | 24.2 | 4.2 | 5.5 |

www.weissratings.com
209
Data as of September 30, 2015

| Name | City | State | Rating | 2014 Rating | 2013 Rating | Total Assets ($Mil) | One Year Asset Growth | Asset Mix (As a % of Total Assets) Comm-ercial Loans | Cons-umer Loans | Mort-gage Loans | Secur-ities | Capital-ization Index | Net Worth Ratio |
|---|---|---|---|---|---|---|---|---|---|---|---|---|---|
| ▲ TUSCALOOSA COUNTY CU | Tuscaloosa | AL | D | E+ | E+ | 8.6 | 16.60 | 0.0 | 41.9 | 12.0 | 0.0 | 6.7 | 8.7 |
| TUSCALOOSA CU | Tuscaloosa | AL | C+ | C+ | C+ | 64.6 | 6.87 | 1.2 | 36.6 | 18.7 | 5.5 | 8.6 | 10.1 |
| ▲ TUSCALOOSA VETERANS FCU | Tuscaloosa | AL | B- | C- | D | 39.1 | -1.55 | 2.8 | 11.3 | 20.7 | 0.0 | 10.0 | 11.1 |
| TUSCUMBIA FCU | Tuscumbia | AL | C | C | C+ | 1.4 | -0.35 | 0.0 | 38.7 | 0.0 | 0.0 | 10.0 | 34.8 |
| ▲ TUSKEGEE FCU | Tuskegee | AL | D | E+ | E+ | 6.7 | 14.57 | 0.0 | 40.2 | 24.4 | 0.0 | 8.4 | 10.0 |
| TVA ALLEN STEAM PLANT FCU | Memphis | TN | C | C | C | 3.2 | 0.82 | 0.0 | 25.1 | 0.0 | 0.0 | 10.0 | 17.1 |
| TVA COMMUNITY CU | Muscle Shoals | AL | A- | A | A- | 301.3 | 3.33 | 0.0 | 12.0 | 20.3 | 44.6 | 10.0 | 13.7 |
| TVH FCU | Tuskegee | AL | C- | C- | C- | 4.4 | 2.20 | 0.0 | 55.5 | 0.0 | 0.0 | 10.0 | 26.8 |
| TWIN OAKS FCU | Apple Grove | WV | E+ | D | D | 5.0 | -1.59 | 0.0 | 74.3 | 0.7 | 0.0 | 6.3 | 8.3 |
| TWIN RIVERS FCU | Massena | NY | C | C | C | 27.3 | 2.96 | 0.0 | 29.0 | 13.3 | 0.0 | 10.0 | 11.6 |
| TWIN STATES FCU | Columbus | MS | E+ | E+ | E+ | 4.6 | 1.85 | 0.0 | 51.7 | 0.0 | 0.0 | 6.4 | 8.4 |
| TWINSTAR CU | Lacey | WA | B+ | B+ | B | 1007.3 | 11.40 | 4.4 | 40.0 | 13.1 | 5.3 | 9.0 | 10.4 |
| TWO HARBORS FCU | Two Harbors | MN | B+ | B+ | B+ | 65.7 | 3.84 | 0.1 | 14.1 | 43.0 | 0.0 | 10.0 | 16.6 |
| TWO RIVERS COMMUNITY CU | Two Rivers | WI | D | D | D+ | 6.7 | -9.88 | 0.0 | 7.6 | 22.1 | 0.0 | 10.0 | 26.0 |
| TXDOT CU | Abilene | TX | D+ | C- | C- | 12.2 | 0.96 | 0.0 | 62.1 | 0.0 | 0.0 | 9.4 | 10.6 |
| TYLER CITY EMPL CU | Tyler | TX | B- | B- | B- | 18.1 | 3.84 | 0.0 | 50.7 | 0.0 | 0.0 | 10.0 | 16.6 |
| TYNDALL FCU | Panama City | FL | C+ | C+ | B- | 1191.2 | 3.95 | 0.1 | 34.1 | 11.0 | 32.4 | 9.4 | 10.6 |
| U A P EMPL FCU | Forest | OH | C | C+ | C+ | 1.0 | 4.86 | 0.0 | 31.5 | 0.0 | 0.0 | 10.0 | 11.5 |
| U H S EMPL FCU | Johnson City | NY | D+ | D | D+ | 15.7 | 3.50 | 0.0 | 30.5 | 0.0 | 0.0 | 7.3 | 9.2 |
| U OF P FCU | Philadelphia | PA | D+ | C- | C- | 23.4 | 2.51 | 0.0 | 11.0 | 0.0 | 14.2 | 10.0 | 11.5 |
| U S COURT HOUSE SDNY FCU | New York | NY | D | C- | C- | 3.2 | 0.75 | 0.0 | 72.2 | 0.0 | 0.0 | 10.0 | 22.2 |
| U S EMPL CU | Tomball | TX | D+ | D+ | D+ | 77.0 | -4.69 | 0.0 | 33.1 | 2.2 | 3.4 | 5.8 | 7.8 |
| U S I FCU | La Porte | TX | B | B | B | 16.3 | -2.22 | 0.0 | 22.7 | 0.0 | 0.0 | 10.0 | 28.7 |
| U S P L K EMPL FCU | Leavenworth | KS | C+ | C+ | C+ | 34.6 | -1.27 | 0.0 | 14.8 | 16.0 | 39.3 | 10.0 | 11.5 |
| ▼ U S PIPE BESSEMER EMPL FCU | Bessemer | AL | D+ | D | D+ | 2.8 | -2.88 | 0.0 | 23.8 | 0.0 | 0.0 | 10.0 | 28.7 |
| U T FCU | Knoxville | TN | B- | B- | B- | 235.9 | 5.78 | 10.6 | 35.7 | 27.0 | 11.3 | 6.3 | 8.3 |
| U T U FCU | North Olmsted | OH | D+ | D | D | 2.8 | -14.06 | 0.0 | 8.7 | 0.0 | 0.0 | 10.0 | 12.9 |
| ▲ U-1ST COMMUNITY FCU | Carlsbad | NM | C | C+ | C+ | 7.3 | -1.36 | 0.6 | 40.6 | 0.2 | 0.0 | 10.0 | 12.6 |
| U-HAUL FCU | Phoenix | AZ | D+ | D+ | C | 5.7 | 5.08 | 0.0 | 50.7 | 0.0 | 0.0 | 9.6 | 10.8 |
| UALU 354 FCU | Youngwood | PA | D | D | D | 6.3 | 2.61 | 0.0 | 44.6 | 0.0 | 0.0 | 10.0 | 13.2 |
| UARK FCU | Fayetteville | AR | C+ | C+ | C+ | 50.2 | 6.49 | 0.0 | 47.6 | 10.6 | 0.0 | 8.2 | 9.8 |
| UAW MO-KAN FCU | Kansas City | KS | C- | D+ | C- | 5.6 | -2.29 | 0.0 | 44.9 | 0.0 | 0.0 | 10.0 | 13.8 |
| ▲ UBC CU | Saint Louis | MO | D | D | D+ | 2.1 | 9.86 | 0.0 | 48.1 | 0.0 | 0.0 | 10.0 | 11.0 |
| UBC SOUTHERN COUNCIL OF INDUSTRIAL W | Sibley | LA | C | C | C- | <1 | 0.61 | 0.0 | 65.5 | 0.0 | 0.0 | 10.0 | 38.7 |
| UCB CU | Salt Lake City | UT | C- | C- | D+ | 1.2 | -8.66 | 0.0 | 30.0 | 0.0 | 3.9 | 10.0 | 20.5 |
| UFCW COMMUNITY FCU | Wyoming | PA | B- | B- | B- | 116.0 | 6.46 | 1.4 | 27.5 | 18.7 | 0.0 | 10.0 | 11.6 |
| UFCW LOCAL #72 FCU | Wyoming | PA | D | D+ | D+ | 27.6 | -1.00 | 0.0 | 7.3 | 0.0 | 41.9 | 7.8 | 9.5 |
| ▲ UFCW LOCAL 1776 FCU | Plymouth Meeting | PA | D- | E+ | E+ | 6.8 | 0.74 | 0.7 | 24.9 | 0.0 | 0.0 | 7.1 | 9.0 |
| UFCW LOCAL 23 FCU | Canonsburg | PA | D+ | D+ | D+ | 9.0 | 0.12 | 0.0 | 32.4 | 0.0 | 0.0 | 10.0 | 12.6 |
| ▲ UFIRST FCU | Plattsburgh | NY | B- | C+ | C | 59.6 | 2.34 | 0.0 | 28.8 | 14.3 | 36.6 | 10.0 | 18.6 |
| UINTAH CU | Vernal | UT | C- | C- | C | 3.4 | -0.03 | 0.0 | 33.1 | 0.0 | 0.0 | 10.0 | 14.2 |
| UKRAINIAN FCU | Rochester | NY | B- | B | B | 189.6 | 5.34 | 10.6 | 8.8 | 60.9 | 5.5 | 8.0 | 9.7 |
| UKRAINIAN FUTURE CU | Warren | MI | B+ | B+ | B | 83.7 | 1.61 | 6.6 | 3.0 | 33.9 | 0.2 | 10.0 | 12.0 |
| UKRAINIAN NATIONAL FCU | New York | NY | C | C | C | 143.4 | 1.29 | 16.1 | 1.0 | 53.0 | 11.3 | 9.1 | 10.4 |
| UKRAINIAN SELFRELIANCE FCU | Philadelphia | PA | B- | B- | B | 263.2 | 1.05 | 4.8 | 0.7 | 57.6 | 26.1 | 10.0 | 12.3 |
| UKRAINIAN SELFRELIANCE MICHIGAN FCU | Warren | MI | B | B | C | 113.3 | 1.55 | 1.8 | 2.8 | 24.1 | 30.4 | 10.0 | 11.0 |
| UKRAINIAN SELFRELIANCE NEW ENGLAND F | Wethersfield | CT | D- | D- | D- | 32.3 | -0.49 | 8.2 | 23.8 | 40.7 | 0.0 | 6.3 | 8.3 |
| ▼ UKRAINIAN SELFRELIANCE OF WESTERN PA | Pittsburgh | PA | D | C- | D+ | 6.9 | -0.73 | 0.0 | 4.7 | 19.3 | 0.0 | 10.0 | 13.9 |
| ULSTER FCU | Kingston | NY | C- | C- | C | 108.3 | 2.40 | 3.5 | 10.1 | 11.4 | 34.4 | 6.7 | 8.7 |
| UMASSFIVE COLLEGE FCU | Hadley | MA | B- | B- | B- | 406.3 | 5.39 | 0.0 | 21.4 | 28.8 | 18.1 | 6.4 | 8.4 |
| UMATILLA COUNTY FCU | Pendleton | OR | C+ | B- | B | 45.1 | -0.52 | 0.0 | 15.5 | 15.2 | 0.0 | 9.8 | 10.9 |
| UME FCU | Burbank | CA | B- | C+ | C | 172.7 | 6.40 | 4.7 | 10.3 | 25.1 | 17.7 | 7.0 | 9.0 |
| UMICO FCU | New Hartford | NY | D | D+ | C- | 7.1 | 1.78 | 0.0 | 50.9 | 0.0 | 0.0 | 10.0 | 12.4 |
| ▼ UNCLE CU | Livermore | CA | B- | B | A- | 318.7 | 9.12 | 5.4 | 18.0 | 41.0 | 17.3 | 8.7 | 10.1 |
| UNI CU | Cedar Falls | IA | C | C | C- | 19.3 | -1.57 | 0.0 | 24.4 | 0.0 | 44.0 | 10.0 | 15.9 |
| UNIFIED COMMUNITIES FCU | Belleville | MI | E+ | E | E | 12.8 | 5.61 | 0.0 | 37.2 | 19.6 | 19.2 | 5.1 | 7.1 |
| UNIFIED HOMEOWNERS OF ILLINOIS FCU | Chicago | IL | D | D- | D- | <1 | 4.55 | 0.0 | 63.0 | 0.0 | 0.0 | 10.0 | 13.4 |
| UNIFIED PEOPLES FCU | Cheyenne | WY | A- | A- | A- | 43.1 | -0.91 | 0.0 | 26.8 | 0.8 | 6.1 | 10.0 | 20.1 |
| UNILEVER FCU | Englewood Cliffs | NJ | C- | C- | C- | 44.0 | 3.02 | 0.0 | 4.5 | 54.4 | 0.7 | 5.3 | 7.3 |
| UNION BAPTIST CHURCH FCU | Fort Wayne | IN | C+ | C+ | C | <1 | 0.00 | 0.0 | 20.7 | 0.0 | 0.0 | 10.0 | 12.2 |

| Asset Quality Index | Non-Performing Loans as a % of Total Loans | Non-Performing Loans as a % of Capital | Net Charge-Offs Avg Loans | Profitability Index | Net Income ($Mil) | Return on Assets | Return on Equity | Net Interest Spread | Overhead Efficiency Ratio | Liquidity Index | Liquidity Ratio | Hot Money Ratio | Stability Index |
|---|---|---|---|---|---|---|---|---|---|---|---|---|---|
| 3.9 | 2.60 | 16.6 | 0.44 | 7.8 | 0.1 | 1.26 | 14.90 | 4.63 | 79.7 | 2.1 | 11.1 | 31.5 | 2.3 |
| 5.7 | 1.03 | 9.3 | 0.45 | 4.9 | 0.3 | 0.71 | 7.55 | 3.54 | 79.1 | 3.0 | 22.1 | 16.2 | 4.7 |
| 7.0 | 1.82 | 6.9 | -0.17 | 4.9 | 0.3 | 0.86 | 8.07 | 3.15 | 99.8 | 5.5 | 40.1 | 2.5 | 4.4 |
| 8.9 | 0.00 | 0.0 | -0.57 | 7.4 | 0.0 | 1.66 | 4.90 | 6.19 | 62.7 | 5.0 | 32.8 | 0.0 | 5.0 |
| 1.7 | 0.70 | 46.1 | 0.59 | 9.5 | 0.1 | 2.08 | 30.61 | 8.21 | 64.5 | 4.2 | 31.3 | 8.7 | 2.4 |
| 9.6 | 1.99 | 3.2 | 0.00 | 2.2 | 0.0 | 0.17 | 0.98 | 2.11 | 91.7 | 6.4 | 69.8 | 0.0 | 7.1 |
| 10.0 | 0.48 | 1.8 | 0.11 | 5.9 | 1.9 | 0.85 | 6.51 | 2.39 | 69.6 | 4.2 | 13.1 | 9.1 | 8.7 |
| 6.0 | 3.56 | 7.2 | 2.85 | 2.2 | 0.0 | -0.81 | -2.90 | 7.26 | 74.9 | 5.3 | 39.5 | 0.0 | 6.4 |
| 2.9 | 0.69 | 7.0 | 0.19 | 3.4 | 0.0 | 0.60 | 7.19 | 6.33 | 84.9 | 3.0 | 11.7 | 0.0 | 1.0 |
| 9.1 | 0.51 | 2.1 | 0.08 | 2.3 | 0.0 | 0.18 | 1.61 | 3.54 | 96.5 | 5.3 | 28.5 | 0.8 | 5.7 |
| 2.5 | 2.96 | 19.9 | 0.63 | 4.5 | 0.0 | 0.54 | 6.68 | 5.31 | 88.8 | 4.7 | 19.9 | 2.5 | 1.0 |
| 6.7 | 0.77 | 6.2 | 0.75 | 5.9 | 5.7 | 0.78 | 7.63 | 4.29 | 77.7 | 4.3 | 14.7 | 1.1 | 7.4 |
| 9.8 | 0.18 | 1.1 | 0.02 | 5.0 | 0.3 | 0.70 | 4.21 | 3.23 | 83.3 | 3.7 | 22.1 | 6.3 | 7.7 |
| 10.0 | 0.05 | 0.1 | 0.00 | 0.0 | -0.1 | -1.17 | -4.63 | 2.45 | 161.8 | 5.8 | 35.4 | 0.0 | 6.2 |
| 3.9 | 0.88 | 6.7 | 0.72 | 3.7 | 0.0 | 0.34 | 3.27 | 3.00 | 65.8 | 1.1 | 11.3 | 31.3 | 5.3 |
| 7.8 | 0.79 | 2.7 | 0.35 | 5.1 | 0.1 | 0.80 | 4.98 | 3.79 | 81.1 | 4.9 | 36.1 | 0.0 | 7.1 |
| 9.7 | 0.29 | 1.8 | 0.31 | 3.3 | 3.3 | 0.38 | 3.58 | 2.30 | 85.4 | 3.8 | 22.1 | 9.2 | 7.0 |
| 6.9 | 2.67 | 8.2 | 0.00 | 3.6 | 0.0 | -0.27 | -2.22 | 4.87 | 113.3 | 7.5 | 70.3 | 0.0 | 7.2 |
| 6.0 | 1.44 | 7.9 | -0.21 | 2.2 | 0.0 | 0.24 | 2.56 | 3.60 | 93.4 | 4.2 | 24.1 | 2.7 | 4.7 |
| 10.0 | 0.65 | 1.0 | 1.36 | 0.6 | 0.0 | -0.21 | -1.88 | 3.20 | 98.2 | 6.4 | 36.1 | 0.0 | 5.7 |
| 8.1 | 0.00 | 0.0 | 0.29 | 0.3 | 0.0 | -0.71 | -3.13 | 7.88 | 106.0 | 4.2 | 18.8 | 0.0 | 5.3 |
| 8.7 | 0.52 | 2.4 | 0.25 | 1.6 | 0.0 | 0.04 | 0.56 | 2.14 | 96.0 | 4.2 | 28.3 | 7.8 | 2.3 |
| 10.0 | 0.00 | 0.0 | 0.24 | 4.1 | 0.1 | 0.48 | 1.72 | 2.65 | 82.9 | 5.4 | 40.3 | 0.0 | 7.8 |
| 8.4 | 1.18 | 3.4 | 0.30 | 3.2 | 0.1 | 0.34 | 3.06 | 1.93 | 72.8 | 4.8 | 8.4 | 0.0 | 5.7 |
| 7.7 | 6.21 | 5.7 | -0.35 | 0.8 | 0.0 | -0.23 | -0.81 | 3.75 | 103.0 | 6.7 | 50.4 | 0.0 | 5.1 |
| 9.4 | 0.16 | 1.3 | 0.14 | 3.7 | 0.8 | 0.46 | 5.65 | 3.20 | 84.9 | 4.3 | 14.7 | 3.9 | 5.1 |
| 8.5 | 7.53 | 4.7 | 1.55 | 1.2 | 0.0 | 0.05 | 0.37 | 1.28 | 92.0 | 6.4 | 73.9 | 0.0 | 3.5 |
| 7.1 | 1.94 | 7.9 | 0.26 | 5.8 | 0.0 | 0.72 | 6.62 | 4.81 | 82.4 | 5.5 | 41.3 | 0.0 | 4.3 |
| 2.7 | 6.32 | 21.6 | -0.46 | 1.1 | -0.1 | -1.60 | -14.21 | 5.07 | 71.0 | 5.7 | 53.6 | 0.0 | 6.9 |
| 3.4 | 7.06 | 22.8 | 3.07 | 2.7 | 0.0 | 0.25 | 1.93 | 4.43 | 68.3 | 5.7 | 46.2 | 0.0 | 5.7 |
| 5.7 | 0.50 | 3.3 | 0.23 | 3.9 | 0.2 | 0.49 | 5.05 | 3.45 | 86.8 | 5.1 | 33.3 | 2.0 | 4.7 |
| 6.5 | 2.66 | 12.2 | 0.16 | 2.0 | 0.0 | 0.00 | 0.00 | 3.27 | 99.3 | 4.2 | 9.7 | 0.0 | 5.6 |
| 5.6 | 1.64 | 7.5 | 2.15 | 3.3 | 0.0 | 0.61 | 5.77 | 8.52 | 86.1 | 5.9 | 42.1 | 0.0 | 4.5 |
| 8.4 | 0.23 | 0.4 | 0.59 | 7.4 | 0.0 | 1.18 | 3.15 | 9.66 | 84.4 | 5.3 | 50.7 | 0.0 | 5.0 |
| 8.6 | 1.34 | 1.8 | 0.00 | 1.7 | 0.0 | -0.54 | -2.59 | 6.49 | 96.3 | 7.9 | 88.6 | 0.0 | 6.2 |
| 7.7 | 1.35 | 6.0 | 0.45 | 3.4 | 0.3 | 0.35 | 3.10 | 3.60 | 82.5 | 5.2 | 26.1 | 2.7 | 7.1 |
| 8.4 | 1.13 | 2.0 | 1.06 | 1.1 | 0.0 | -0.12 | -1.20 | 1.92 | 96.2 | 7.2 | 39.9 | 0.0 | 4.7 |
| 5.8 | 0.51 | 2.8 | 0.63 | 6.7 | 0.2 | 2.87 | 38.58 | 6.65 | 62.2 | 6.0 | 51.3 | 0.0 | 1.8 |
| 3.7 | 6.68 | 27.8 | 0.43 | 2.9 | 0.0 | 0.34 | 2.64 | 4.06 | 78.3 | 5.1 | 31.3 | 0.0 | 5.4 |
| 9.6 | 0.45 | 2.0 | 0.18 | 3.8 | 0.2 | 0.47 | 4.00 | 3.76 | 86.5 | 4.3 | 12.9 | 0.0 | 6.8 |
| 8.8 | 0.69 | 2.0 | 0.09 | 1.8 | 0.0 | 0.00 | 0.00 | 3.50 | 100.0 | 7.1 | 65.3 | 0.0 | 6.1 |
| 6.0 | 0.92 | 7.8 | 0.62 | 3.6 | 0.5 | 0.39 | 3.97 | 3.65 | 90.6 | 1.5 | 9.3 | 19.2 | 6.0 |
| 5.8 | 4.12 | 12.8 | -0.07 | 4.5 | 0.3 | 0.53 | 4.52 | 2.33 | 81.8 | 3.9 | 16.8 | 10.3 | 6.8 |
| 3.7 | 4.13 | 24.5 | 0.01 | 2.9 | 0.4 | 0.34 | 3.21 | 2.73 | 87.3 | 2.1 | 15.5 | 30.4 | 6.6 |
| 10.0 | 0.06 | 0.3 | 0.00 | 3.0 | 0.5 | 0.23 | 1.97 | 1.95 | 82.9 | 2.3 | 22.6 | 25.8 | 7.8 |
| 7.9 | 1.36 | 3.3 | 1.56 | 4.6 | 0.5 | 0.62 | 6.28 | 2.06 | 71.4 | 4.0 | 23.9 | 11.6 | 6.3 |
| 3.6 | 0.82 | 19.7 | -0.01 | 1.0 | 0.0 | -0.09 | -1.14 | 3.51 | 105.0 | 3.0 | 23.7 | 10.8 | 2.7 |
| 9.0 | 0.90 | 2.3 | 1.15 | 0.2 | -0.1 | -1.11 | -7.70 | 2.75 | 118.6 | 6.7 | 73.4 | 3.3 | 6.7 |
| 7.6 | 1.88 | 8.3 | 0.40 | 2.4 | 0.2 | 0.20 | 2.35 | 2.57 | 87.3 | 5.0 | 21.7 | 4.2 | 4.6 |
| 6.5 | 1.18 | 10.1 | 0.24 | 3.9 | 1.4 | 0.46 | 5.51 | 3.18 | 82.8 | 3.0 | 11.1 | 9.2 | 5.3 |
| 9.4 | 0.08 | 0.7 | 0.05 | 3.2 | 0.1 | 0.33 | 3.08 | 1.55 | 73.1 | 4.2 | 18.1 | 0.0 | 6.1 |
| 10.0 | 0.18 | 0.8 | 0.34 | 4.6 | 1.0 | 0.74 | 8.47 | 2.72 | 74.1 | 4.7 | 18.1 | 3.8 | 4.9 |
| 7.1 | 0.71 | 3.2 | 0.45 | 0.5 | 0.0 | -0.54 | -4.37 | 4.18 | 100.0 | 6.2 | 42.0 | 0.0 | 5.3 |
| 9.9 | 0.08 | 0.5 | 0.06 | 3.9 | 1.4 | 0.59 | 5.74 | 3.22 | 88.1 | 3.8 | 11.8 | 2.3 | 5.6 |
| 8.1 | 1.29 | 3.7 | 0.14 | 2.6 | 0.0 | 0.04 | 0.28 | 3.01 | 95.1 | 5.1 | 32.0 | 0.6 | 6.2 |
| 6.3 | 0.93 | 7.5 | 0.23 | 2.6 | 0.0 | 0.40 | 5.71 | 4.25 | 93.9 | 3.9 | 6.9 | 0.0 | 1.7 |
| 2.8 | 3.45 | 14.6 | 2.03 | 8.9 | 0.0 | 1.19 | 8.89 | 12.86 | 91.3 | 6.0 | 42.5 | 0.0 | 6.5 |
| 9.9 | 1.27 | 2.3 | 0.38 | 8.2 | 0.4 | 1.27 | 6.59 | 3.38 | 70.4 | 4.7 | 26.5 | 2.8 | 8.0 |
| 10.0 | 0.01 | 0.1 | 0.01 | 2.3 | 0.1 | 0.20 | 2.67 | 2.13 | 90.5 | 2.5 | 17.2 | 28.5 | 3.3 |
| 7.8 | 1.82 | 4.0 | 0.00 | 8.7 | 0.0 | 1.20 | 11.59 | 4.10 | 77.8 | 8.1 | 87.8 | 0.0 | 5.7 |

| Name | City | State | Rating | 2014 Rating | 2013 Rating | Total Assets ($Mil) | One Year Asset Growth | Asset Mix (As a % of Total Assets) | | | | Capital-ization Index | Net Worth Ratio |
|------|------|-------|--------|-------------|-------------|---------------------|----------------------|-------------------|---|---|---|------------------|-----------------|
| | | | | | | | | Comm-ercial Loans | Cons-umer Loans | Mort-gage Loans | Secur-ities | | |
| UNION BAPTIST GREENBURGH FCU | White Plains | NY | C- | C- | D+ | <1 | -5.97 | 0.0 | 20.1 | 0.0 | 0.0 | 10.0 | 35.1 |
| UNION BUILDING TRADES FCU | Parsippany | NJ | C | C- | C- | 74.6 | 2.67 | 0.0 | 9.5 | 11.3 | 5.5 | 10.0 | 13.1 |
| UNION CONGREGATIONAL FCU | New York | NY | C+ | B- | B- | <1 | -24.87 | 0.0 | 0.0 | 0.0 | 0.0 | 10.0 | 21.0 |
| ▼ UNION COUNTY EMPL FCU | Elizabeth | NJ | C- | C | C- | 8.4 | -4.19 | 0.0 | 33.7 | 0.0 | 0.0 | 10.0 | 14.0 |
| UNION FCU | Farmerville | LA | C- | C- | D | <1 | -18.04 | 0.0 | 15.2 | 0.0 | 0.0 | 10.0 | 28.6 |
| UNION FIDELITY FCU | Houston | TX | B- | B- | B | 21.0 | 9.13 | 0.0 | 25.2 | 0.0 | 0.0 | 10.0 | 14.2 |
| ▼ UNION MEMORIAL CU | Saint Louis | MO | D+ | C | B- | <1 | -13.40 | 0.0 | 15.5 | 0.0 | 0.0 | 10.0 | 15.5 |
| UNION OF POLES IN AMERICA CU | Garfield Heights | OH | C- | C- | C- | <1 | 1.96 | 0.0 | 49.3 | 0.0 | 0.0 | 10.0 | 14.1 |
| UNION OIL SANTA FE SPRINGS EMPL FCU | Brea | CA | D | D | C- | 4.9 | -9.94 | 0.0 | 3.6 | 0.0 | 0.0 | 10.0 | 14.9 |
| UNION PACIFIC CALIFORNIA EMPL FCU | Los Alamitos | CA | D | D+ | D | 8.7 | -5.87 | 0.0 | 41.8 | 14.9 | 0.0 | 8.2 | 9.8 |
| UNION PACIFIC EMPL CU | Beaumont | TX | C | C | C- | 4.0 | -17.02 | 0.0 | 36.1 | 0.0 | 0.0 | 10.0 | 16.5 |
| UNION PACIFIC OF ARKANSAS FCU | North Little Rock | AR | B | B | B- | 27.2 | 2.88 | 0.0 | 43.9 | 6.1 | 0.0 | 10.0 | 16.4 |
| UNION PACIFIC STREAMLINER FCU | Omaha | NE | E+ | E+ | D- | 24.4 | -2.99 | 2.3 | 43.9 | 3.9 | 0.0 | 0.8 | 4.0 |
| UNION SQUARE CU | Wichita Falls | TX | C | C+ | B- | 332.1 | 1.05 | 5.7 | 27.0 | 30.2 | 9.9 | 10.0 | 11.6 |
| UNION TRADES FCU | Parkersburg | WV | C | C- | C- | 23.5 | 3.27 | 0.0 | 36.3 | 4.9 | 0.0 | 9.9 | 10.9 |
| UNION YES FCU | Orange | CA | E | E+ | E+ | 51.8 | 0.35 | 6.8 | 14.3 | 24.0 | 0.0 | 1.3 | 4.4 |
| ▼ UNION-WALLOWA-BAKER FCU | La Grande | OR | C- | C | C+ | 28.7 | 8.34 | 0.0 | 16.0 | 9.1 | 0.0 | 5.3 | 7.3 |
| UNISON CU | Kaukauna | WI | C | C | C | 188.4 | 5.11 | 0.4 | 22.8 | 40.1 | 9.9 | 9.5 | 10.7 |
| UNITED 1ST FCU | Kingsland | GA | B+ | B+ | B | 127.8 | 2.43 | 0.1 | 35.9 | 11.0 | 23.7 | 10.0 | 11.5 |
| ▲ UNITED ADVANTAGE NORTHWEST FCU | Portland | OR | C | C- | D+ | 34.9 | -1.90 | 4.0 | 30.9 | 24.2 | 10.8 | 7.0 | 9.0 |
| ▼ UNITED AMERICA WEST FCU | Panorama City | CA | D- | D+ | D+ | 4.1 | -3.11 | 0.0 | 25.8 | 0.0 | 0.0 | 7.4 | 9.3 |
| UNITED ARKANSAS FCU | Little Rock | AR | B- | C+ | D+ | 26.9 | 2.32 | 0.0 | 44.5 | 0.0 | 0.0 | 10.0 | 15.1 |
| ▼ UNITED ASSN CU | Concord | CA | C+ | B- | B- | 6.0 | 0.22 | 0.0 | 27.4 | 0.0 | 0.0 | 10.0 | 15.1 |
| UNITED BAY COMMUNITY CU | Bay City | MI | D+ | C- | D | 183.5 | 0.27 | 0.6 | 21.6 | 26.0 | 32.0 | 5.2 | 7.3 |
| UNITED BUSINESS & INDUSTRY FCU | Plainville | CT | C- | C | C+ | 84.3 | 1.49 | 0.0 | 49.9 | 13.1 | 8.2 | 6.0 | 8.0 |
| ▼ UNITED CATHOLICS FCU | West Covina | CA | D- | D | D- | 30.8 | 3.52 | 0.0 | 27.9 | 23.9 | 1.5 | 4.5 | 6.5 |
| UNITED CHURCHES CU | Taylor | MI | D | D | E+ | 16.4 | 0.26 | 0.3 | 13.2 | 3.3 | 65.1 | 5.3 | 7.3 |
| UNITED COMMUNITY CU | Quincy | IL | C | C | D+ | 65.3 | 2.93 | 0.0 | 33.4 | 38.7 | 0.0 | 7.2 | 9.2 |
| UNITED COMMUNITY CU | Galena Park | TX | C | C | C | 91.2 | 7.04 | 0.0 | 79.8 | 6.9 | 0.2 | 6.7 | 8.7 |
| ▲ UNITED COMMUNITY FCU | West Mifflin | PA | D | D | C- | 90.1 | 113.05 | 2.5 | 23.1 | 7.6 | 21.6 | 10.0 | 11.0 |
| UNITED CONSUMERS CU | Independence | MO | B- | B- | C+ | 128.0 | 3.35 | 4.0 | 38.5 | 23.6 | 2.7 | 10.0 | 11.2 |
| UNITED CU | Council Bluffs | IA | C- | C- | C- | 15.8 | 5.81 | 0.0 | 22.1 | 0.0 | 45.0 | 7.6 | 9.4 |
| ▼ UNITED CU | Chicago | IL | D | D+ | D+ | 162.4 | 3.76 | 0.0 | 21.8 | 16.5 | 24.8 | 10.0 | 11.4 |
| UNITED CU | Warsaw | IN | C | C | C+ | 11.2 | 1.38 | 0.0 | 42.5 | 0.0 | 0.0 | 10.0 | 13.1 |
| UNITED CU | Ness City | KS | D | D | D- | 8.9 | 5.44 | 1.4 | 17.8 | 0.0 | 0.0 | 6.5 | 8.5 |
| UNITED CU | Mexico | MO | B+ | B+ | A- | 153.8 | 7.99 | 1.7 | 32.2 | 23.4 | 2.7 | 9.0 | 10.4 |
| UNITED CU | Tyler | TX | C- | C- | C- | 29.0 | 13.18 | 0.0 | 52.9 | 9.9 | 0.0 | 6.5 | 8.5 |
| UNITED EDUCATIONAL CU | Battle Creek | MI | C+ | C+ | C+ | 121.0 | 2.92 | 1.3 | 11.0 | 10.7 | 46.7 | 8.2 | 9.8 |
| UNITED EDUCATORS CU | Apple Valley | MN | C+ | C+ | C- | 157.3 | 4.38 | 0.0 | 19.4 | 7.8 | 13.4 | 7.7 | 9.5 |
| UNITED EMPL CU | Albert Lea | MN | B- | B- | B- | 32.6 | 0.61 | 0.1 | 43.2 | 0.0 | 0.0 | 10.0 | 13.5 |
| UNITED ENERGY CU | Humble | TX | C | C | C | 24.7 | 3.70 | 0.0 | 52.6 | 0.4 | 0.0 | 10.0 | 18.7 |
| UNITED EQUITY CU | Decatur | IL | B- | B | B | 38.7 | 0.15 | 0.0 | 37.6 | 6.5 | 12.4 | 10.0 | 12.1 |
| UNITED FCU | Saint Joseph | MI | A- | A- | A- | 1985.0 | 11.03 | 12.7 | 31.2 | 39.1 | 6.2 | 8.7 | 10.1 |
| UNITED FCU | Morgantown | WV | A- | A- | A- | 79.9 | 8.24 | 6.8 | 11.8 | 38.9 | 3.5 | 10.0 | 18.8 |
| ▲ UNITED FINANCIAL CU | Whittier | CA | B- | C | C+ | 37.0 | 0.37 | 7.3 | 14.4 | 40.1 | 0.0 | 10.0 | 16.2 |
| ▲ UNITED FINANCIAL CU | Saginaw | MI | B- | C+ | C+ | 183.2 | 2.22 | 0.3 | 21.7 | 34.6 | 29.3 | 7.8 | 9.6 |
| UNITED FINANCIAL SERVICES FCU | Scotch Plains | NJ | D | D+ | D+ | 19.6 | -1.75 | 8.6 | 6.6 | 20.8 | 6.3 | 10.0 | 14.2 |
| ▲ UNITED HEALTH CU | Burlingame | CA | C- | D+ | D+ | 65.6 | 2.12 | 2.3 | 18.6 | 19.9 | 2.3 | 7.9 | 9.6 |
| UNITED HERITAGE CU | Austin | TX | B- | B- | B- | 841.0 | 5.72 | 8.8 | 27.7 | 36.2 | 7.2 | 6.5 | 8.5 |
| UNITED HOSPITAL CENTER FCU | Bridgeport | WV | B- | B | B | 11.3 | 2.58 | 0.0 | 30.7 | 0.0 | 0.0 | 10.0 | 13.6 |
| UNITED INVESTORS FCU | Linden | NJ | D- | D- | D- | 3.8 | -6.42 | 0.0 | 20.9 | 0.0 | 0.0 | 6.2 | 8.3 |
| UNITED LABOR CU | Kansas City | MO | D- | D- | D | 12.3 | 4.62 | 0.0 | 56.1 | 0.0 | 0.0 | 5.4 | 7.4 |
| UNITED LOCAL CU | Fresno | CA | B | B | A- | 107.6 | -1.62 | 7.6 | 48.6 | 29.1 | 1.6 | 10.0 | 17.1 |
| UNITED MEMBERS FCU | Tulsa | OK | C | C | C | 12.9 | -0.16 | 0.0 | 10.5 | 3.2 | 18.2 | 10.0 | 14.2 |
| UNITED METHODIST CONNECTIONAL FCU | Marietta | GA | C | C | C | 27.2 | 2.13 | 6.0 | 37.9 | 21.9 | 0.9 | 7.8 | 9.5 |
| UNITED METHODIST FCU | Montclair | CA | C | C | C- | 87.5 | 0.30 | 8.4 | 11.0 | 22.3 | 10.1 | 6.2 | 8.2 |
| UNITED METHODIST FINANCIAL CU | North Canton | OH | C | C | C- | 85.6 | -10.18 | 29.4 | 5.3 | 33.0 | 45.4 | 8.8 | 10.7 |
| UNITED METHODIST FIRST CHOICE FCU | Rapid City | SD | E+ | E+ | D- | 4.4 | -0.05 | 43.7 | 30.8 | 53.3 | 0.9 | 5.1 | 7.1 |
| UNITED METHODIST OF MISSISSIPPI FCU | Booneville | MS | D- | D- | D- | <1 | -3.34 | 0.0 | 35.8 | 0.0 | 0.0 | 5.0 | 7.0 |
| UNITED NATIONS FCU | Long Island City | NY | B | B | B | 4297.0 | 3.64 | 1.9 | 11.6 | 29.2 | 48.3 | 8.5 | 10.0 |

| Asset Quality Index | Non-Performing Loans as a % of Total Loans | as a % of Capital | Net Charge-Offs Avg Loans | Profitability Index | Net Income ($Mil) | Return on Assets | Return on Equity | Net Interest Spread | Overhead Efficiency Ratio | Liquidity Index | Liquidity Ratio | Hot Money Ratio | Stability Index |
|---|---|---|---|---|---|---|---|---|---|---|---|---|---|
| 5.6 | 21.67 | 11.3 | 9.52 | 1.0 | 0.0 | -1.27 | -3.70 | 3.03 | 150.0 | 8.2 | 125.8 | 0.0 | 7.6 |
| 6.1 | 3.24 | 11.6 | -0.12 | 2.0 | 0.1 | 0.12 | 0.92 | 3.22 | 98.2 | 4.5 | 24.8 | 4.5 | 5.6 |
| 10.0 | 0.00 | 0.0 | 0.00 | 2.7 | 0.0 | -0.46 | -2.19 | 1.01 | 100.0 | 5.2 | 8.1 | 0.0 | 7.5 |
| 7.8 | 2.26 | 5.2 | 1.40 | 1.4 | 0.0 | -0.71 | -4.86 | 4.56 | 97.9 | 7.0 | 72.3 | 0.0 | 6.2 |
| 6.8 | 0.00 | 0.0 | 0.00 | 2.6 | 0.0 | -1.98 | -7.02 | 5.34 | 141.7 | 5.4 | 68.1 | 0.0 | 5.0 |
| 10.0 | 0.24 | 0.5 | 0.48 | 4.4 | 0.1 | 0.58 | 3.95 | 3.32 | 81.9 | 5.7 | 47.6 | 6.8 | 6.8 |
| 1.2 | 32.61 | 50.0 | 0.00 | 2.6 | 0.0 | 0.00 | 0.00 | 3.57 | 100.0 | 7.0 | 46.1 | 0.0 | 9.0 |
| 6.6 | 0.92 | 2.9 | 0.00 | 2.7 | 0.0 | 0.15 | 1.07 | 1.89 | 91.7 | 5.2 | 49.7 | 0.0 | 7.0 |
| 9.9 | 0.00 | 0.0 | 1.11 | 0.0 | 0.0 | -0.90 | -5.89 | 1.85 | 149.3 | 5.6 | 27.7 | 0.0 | 6.1 |
| 6.8 | 0.97 | 5.9 | 0.56 | 3.6 | 0.0 | 0.03 | 0.31 | 5.96 | 95.0 | 5.0 | 32.0 | 0.0 | 3.0 |
| 9.3 | 0.00 | 0.0 | 0.13 | 2.8 | 0.0 | -0.30 | -1.81 | 4.39 | 93.7 | 4.5 | 15.2 | 0.0 | 5.5 |
| 6.8 | 2.24 | 7.7 | 0.13 | 4.6 | 0.1 | 0.60 | 3.73 | 3.68 | 84.3 | 4.3 | 29.7 | 7.9 | 7.5 |
| 3.7 | 1.95 | 26.1 | 0.33 | 2.4 | 0.1 | 0.46 | 12.73 | 3.35 | 88.0 | 4.7 | 31.9 | 0.0 | 0.0 |
| 7.0 | 1.27 | 8.3 | 0.10 | 2.0 | 0.3 | 0.11 | 0.94 | 2.91 | 94.0 | 3.3 | 16.2 | 8.0 | 7.0 |
| 5.7 | 1.34 | 8.2 | 0.64 | 6.4 | 0.2 | 1.10 | 10.44 | 4.48 | 78.0 | 4.1 | 12.7 | 2.2 | 5.0 |
| 9.9 | 0.06 | 0.5 | 0.03 | 1.6 | 0.0 | 0.07 | 1.55 | 3.39 | 99.8 | 5.4 | 27.0 | 3.1 | 0.7 |
| 7.2 | 1.22 | 5.7 | 0.47 | 1.2 | -0.1 | -0.35 | -4.68 | 2.67 | 104.0 | 6.2 | 41.7 | 1.4 | 3.3 |
| 9.5 | 0.23 | 1.8 | 0.10 | 2.8 | 0.3 | 0.23 | 2.12 | 3.18 | 91.7 | 4.2 | 16.4 | 4.4 | 6.5 |
| 9.0 | 0.56 | 2.8 | 0.67 | 4.3 | 0.6 | 0.59 | 5.21 | 3.35 | 87.2 | 3.9 | 10.5 | 7.3 | 6.8 |
| 6.8 | 0.25 | 1.8 | -0.25 | 4.5 | 0.2 | 0.57 | 6.45 | 4.92 | 90.4 | 3.5 | 9.5 | 4.4 | 3.6 |
| 6.0 | 1.99 | 5.7 | 3.11 | 0.8 | -0.1 | -2.19 | -21.80 | 4.17 | 104.4 | 5.8 | 46.7 | 0.0 | 3.5 |
| 9.6 | 0.69 | 2.2 | 0.20 | 3.4 | 0.1 | 0.50 | 3.35 | 2.65 | 82.6 | 4.2 | 22.7 | 2.5 | 6.9 |
| 10.0 | 0.42 | 0.8 | 0.18 | 4.8 | 0.0 | 0.62 | 4.15 | 2.12 | 87.2 | 5.0 | 33.0 | 0.0 | 7.1 |
| 6.0 | 1.13 | 9.5 | 0.46 | 1.7 | 0.0 | 0.03 | 0.35 | 3.15 | 92.7 | 4.2 | 19.0 | 0.6 | 4.2 |
| 6.6 | 0.22 | 2.2 | 0.23 | 2.0 | 0.0 | 0.05 | 0.58 | 3.41 | 96.8 | 3.4 | 8.9 | 4.4 | 3.4 |
| 5.7 | 1.29 | 12.7 | -0.16 | 2.6 | 0.0 | 0.17 | 2.57 | 3.18 | 97.6 | 3.8 | 15.9 | 6.7 | 1.7 |
| 10.0 | 0.08 | 0.3 | 0.09 | 2.7 | 0.0 | 0.29 | 3.95 | 2.16 | 97.5 | 5.3 | 38.5 | 0.0 | 2.0 |
| 6.1 | 0.65 | 5.2 | 0.22 | 8.2 | 0.6 | 1.17 | 13.24 | 4.63 | 73.8 | 4.4 | 26.4 | 2.6 | 3.1 |
| 5.4 | 0.51 | 5.1 | 0.33 | 4.1 | 0.4 | 0.56 | 6.43 | 4.27 | 86.2 | 2.2 | 5.7 | 8.9 | 3.9 |
| 7.1 | 1.64 | 6.3 | 0.40 | 1.0 | 0.0 | -0.05 | -0.48 | 3.14 | 95.1 | 4.8 | 23.1 | 1.5 | 4.6 |
| 3.7 | 3.09 | 24.0 | 0.88 | 3.6 | 0.4 | 0.36 | 3.24 | 4.19 | 82.5 | 3.2 | 13.8 | 8.1 | 6.5 |
| 6.1 | 1.65 | 9.4 | 0.19 | 2.6 | 0.0 | 0.18 | 1.91 | 2.87 | 93.9 | 4.7 | 22.5 | 5.0 | 4.5 |
| 9.5 | 0.84 | 2.6 | 0.50 | 0.1 | -1.1 | -0.83 | -7.52 | 2.77 | 115.6 | 4.6 | 26.2 | 4.7 | 6.5 |
| 9.7 | 0.46 | 1.6 | 1.04 | 2.3 | 0.0 | 0.11 | 0.91 | 3.64 | 93.5 | 4.7 | 23.8 | 0.0 | 6.0 |
| 9.6 | 0.46 | 1.4 | 0.00 | 3.0 | 0.0 | 0.38 | 4.65 | 2.00 | 83.0 | 5.4 | 38.4 | 0.0 | 3.0 |
| 7.4 | 0.56 | 4.3 | 0.57 | 5.7 | 1.0 | 0.85 | 8.88 | 4.04 | 77.2 | 3.7 | 25.5 | 3.5 | 6.5 |
| 4.9 | 0.34 | 5.2 | 0.84 | 4.3 | 0.1 | 0.37 | 4.55 | 5.01 | 81.6 | 2.1 | 21.6 | 25.7 | 3.3 |
| 10.0 | 0.25 | 1.0 | 0.12 | 3.4 | 0.3 | 0.33 | 3.53 | 2.63 | 89.3 | 4.5 | 12.1 | 4.0 | 5.6 |
| 8.6 | 0.44 | 3.4 | 0.31 | 3.4 | 0.5 | 0.41 | 4.46 | 3.28 | 84.4 | 3.4 | 6.5 | 3.2 | 5.7 |
| 9.8 | 0.32 | 1.4 | 0.04 | 3.4 | 0.1 | 0.47 | 3.56 | 2.22 | 82.3 | 4.1 | 25.7 | 0.5 | 6.8 |
| 7.8 | 0.55 | 1.6 | 1.17 | 2.6 | 0.0 | 0.11 | 0.61 | 4.90 | 91.3 | 4.8 | 52.5 | 9.3 | 5.6 |
| 7.5 | 0.87 | 5.9 | 0.30 | 3.0 | 0.1 | 0.20 | 1.72 | 3.27 | 90.3 | 4.1 | 12.8 | 3.0 | 6.3 |
| 7.3 | 0.56 | 4.6 | 0.60 | 5.7 | 10.6 | 0.74 | 7.24 | 4.22 | 74.2 | 2.2 | 5.5 | 11.7 | 7.8 |
| 7.1 | 3.10 | 10.6 | 0.51 | 9.8 | 1.1 | 1.81 | 9.78 | 4.12 | 59.7 | 2.9 | 17.0 | 14.1 | 9.3 |
| 6.2 | 2.46 | 13.4 | 0.40 | 4.9 | 0.3 | 0.97 | 6.12 | 3.38 | 75.8 | 4.1 | 24.7 | 8.2 | 5.8 |
| 6.7 | 0.94 | 6.8 | 0.55 | 4.3 | 0.9 | 0.62 | 6.61 | 3.10 | 76.4 | 3.0 | 7.6 | 11.0 | 5.5 |
| 8.2 | 1.10 | 2.7 | 0.34 | 0.2 | -0.1 | -0.45 | -3.17 | 2.62 | 116.3 | 4.7 | 26.7 | 2.7 | 5.6 |
| 7.4 | 0.47 | 2.4 | 0.76 | 2.8 | 0.1 | 0.16 | 1.71 | 3.35 | 93.7 | 4.3 | 17.5 | 1.7 | 3.8 |
| 9.6 | 0.05 | 0.5 | 0.07 | 4.1 | 3.1 | 0.50 | 6.12 | 2.74 | 84.9 | 3.4 | 17.3 | 10.1 | 5.8 |
| 7.6 | 1.78 | 5.1 | 0.15 | 4.1 | 0.0 | 0.45 | 3.26 | 2.56 | 83.6 | 6.5 | 43.4 | 0.0 | 7.2 |
| 5.0 | 2.25 | 11.0 | 6.42 | 0.6 | 0.0 | -0.10 | -1.26 | 4.34 | 103.8 | 6.1 | 33.6 | 0.0 | 3.4 |
| 3.8 | 1.05 | 7.9 | 2.27 | 3.5 | 0.0 | 0.25 | 3.48 | 6.41 | 77.9 | 4.5 | 26.9 | 2.9 | 2.3 |
| 8.1 | 0.08 | 0.7 | 0.31 | 3.5 | 0.4 | 0.43 | 2.55 | 3.47 | 91.2 | 2.6 | 9.9 | 13.8 | 7.4 |
| 9.9 | 1.42 | 1.6 | 0.12 | 2.6 | 0.0 | 0.37 | 2.57 | 2.20 | 84.6 | 5.3 | 23.1 | 0.0 | 5.7 |
| 7.7 | 0.09 | 1.0 | 0.16 | 2.6 | 0.0 | 0.15 | 1.61 | 3.81 | 95.7 | 3.4 | 22.1 | 5.5 | 4.6 |
| 8.4 | 0.91 | 4.5 | 0.22 | 5.3 | 0.6 | 0.86 | 10.97 | 2.82 | 73.4 | 3.9 | 24.2 | 10.7 | 2.9 |
| 9.3 | 0.29 | 1.1 | 0.06 | 2.5 | -0.1 | -0.07 | -0.77 | 2.33 | 103.5 | 4.3 | 23.9 | 12.9 | 4.4 |
| 6.0 | 0.08 | 5.7 | 0.11 | 1.8 | 0.0 | 0.00 | 0.00 | 4.50 | 97.7 | 3.3 | 6.4 | 0.0 | 1.0 |
| 9.4 | 0.00 | 0.0 | 0.00 | 0.0 | 0.0 | -0.98 | -13.33 | 2.94 | 133.3 | 5.9 | 53.1 | 0.0 | 3.0 |
| 8.9 | 0.75 | 3.9 | 0.33 | 4.2 | 18.5 | 0.58 | 5.97 | 2.61 | 75.1 | 4.1 | 21.8 | 8.2 | 7.0 |

| Name | City | State | Rating | 2014 Rating | 2013 Rating | Total Assets ($Mil) | One Year Asset Growth | Asset Mix (As a % of Total Assets) | | | | Capital- ization Index | Net Worth Ratio |
|---|---|---|---|---|---|---|---|---|---|---|---|---|---|
| | | | | | | | | Comm- ercial Loans | Cons- umer Loans | Mort- gage Loans | Secur- ities | | |
| UNITED NEIGHBORHOOD FCU | Augusta | GA | D+ | C- | C | 2.0 | 11.17 | 0.0 | 51.1 | 0.0 | 0.0 | 8.1 | 9.7 |
| ▲ UNITED NEIGHBORS FCU | Watertown | NY | D | D | D | 6.9 | 6.97 | 0.0 | 60.6 | 0.0 | 0.0 | 7.5 | 9.3 |
| UNITED NORTHWEST FCU | Norton | KS | B+ | B+ | B+ | 40.2 | 5.86 | 3.7 | 25.1 | 15.6 | 2.7 | 10.0 | 13.8 |
| ▲ UNITED POLES FCU | Perth Amboy | NJ | E+ | E- | E- | 37.1 | -0.18 | 1.2 | 11.0 | 43.3 | 31.8 | 6.0 | 8.0 |
| UNITED POLICE FCU | Miami | FL | C | B- | B | 48.7 | 7.22 | 0.0 | 19.1 | 2.8 | 47.0 | 10.0 | 16.7 |
| ▲ UNITED SAN ANTONIO COMMUNITY FCU | San Antonio | TX | C | D+ | D | 224.0 | 3.88 | 6.6 | 33.4 | 30.2 | 9.2 | 6.7 | 8.8 |
| UNITED SAVERS TRUST CU | Houston | TX | E+ | E+ | D- | 6.6 | -7.00 | 0.0 | 62.6 | 0.0 | 0.0 | 5.9 | 7.9 |
| UNITED SAVINGS CU | Fargo | ND | B+ | B+ | B+ | 47.7 | 14.87 | 3.4 | 32.1 | 28.8 | 0.0 | 10.0 | 17.9 |
| UNITED SERVICE COMMUNITY CU | West Des Moines | IA | C+ | C+ | C | 40.0 | -0.49 | 2.0 | 21.1 | 5.8 | 6.1 | 7.7 | 9.5 |
| UNITED SERVICES FCU | Toledo | OH | D | D | C- | 6.6 | -4.19 | 0.0 | 23.4 | 1.3 | 3.8 | 10.0 | 16.7 |
| UNITED SOUTHEAST FCU | Bristol | TN | B- | B- | B | 147.9 | -0.62 | 0.0 | 31.9 | 13.1 | 6.3 | 10.0 | 13.1 |
| UNITED STATES SENATE FCU | Alexandria | VA | B | B- | B- | 574.9 | 1.45 | 10.7 | 16.9 | 21.3 | 9.5 | 10.0 | 11.2 |
| ▼ UNITED TELETECH FINANCIAL FCU | Tinton Falls | NJ | C | C+ | C+ | 327.2 | 3.31 | 12.3 | 24.1 | 14.6 | 11.5 | 8.8 | 10.2 |
| UNITED VIP CU | Sterling Heights | MI | D | D | C- | 16.3 | 0.40 | 0.0 | 7.4 | 2.5 | 1.3 | 8.9 | 10.3 |
| UNITEDONE CU | Manitowoc | WI | A- | A- | B | 185.4 | 2.57 | 7.7 | 22.1 | 44.2 | 4.8 | 10.0 | 11.8 |
| ▲ UNITUS COMMUNITY CU | Portland | OR | B+ | C+ | C+ | 971.8 | 4.77 | 5.8 | 36.2 | 24.0 | 23.6 | 8.4 | 9.9 |
| ▲ UNITY CATHOLIC FCU | Parma | OH | C- | D+ | D+ | 68.1 | -3.02 | 0.6 | 25.5 | 17.5 | 23.5 | 7.5 | 9.4 |
| UNITY CU | Warren | MI | C+ | C+ | C+ | 45.3 | -0.02 | 0.5 | 10.6 | 6.2 | 23.0 | 10.0 | 16.6 |
| UNITY FCU | Oaklyn | NJ | C- | C- | C- | 3.4 | -8.42 | 0.0 | 48.0 | 0.0 | 0.0 | 10.0 | 17.0 |
| UNITY ONE CU | Fort Worth | TX | C+ | C | C | 215.7 | 4.05 | 0.0 | 31.4 | 3.8 | 13.2 | 6.0 | 8.2 |
| UNIV & COMMUNITY FCU | Stillwater | OK | B | B | B- | 105.4 | 2.44 | 3.3 | 21.8 | 19.9 | 35.0 | 7.9 | 9.7 |
| UNIV & STATE EMPL CU | San Diego | CA | B+ | A- | B+ | 816.3 | 4.16 | 5.0 | 19.7 | 32.4 | 25.5 | 7.7 | 9.5 |
| UNIV CU | Los Angeles | CA | B- | C+ | C- | 535.4 | 10.54 | 0.8 | 11.9 | 27.9 | 30.8 | 7.0 | 9.0 |
| UNIV CU | Miami | FL | D | D+ | D | 190.6 | 1.17 | 1.2 | 12.3 | 7.6 | 14.9 | 7.8 | 9.6 |
| UNIV CU | Orono | ME | B- | B | B | 265.5 | 2.64 | 2.6 | 24.7 | 44.7 | 9.2 | 6.9 | 8.9 |
| UNIV FCU | Grand Forks | ND | C+ | C+ | C | 29.1 | -0.50 | 0.0 | 26.5 | 0.0 | 1.8 | 7.0 | 9.0 |
| UNIV FCU | Austin | TX | B | B | B- | 1927.0 | 8.30 | 2.5 | 37.0 | 34.7 | 4.4 | 6.2 | 8.2 |
| UNIV FIRST FCU | Salt Lake City | UT | A- | A- | A- | 755.7 | 9.25 | 9.6 | 45.2 | 15.7 | 11.8 | 9.5 | 10.7 |
| UNIV OF HAWAII FCU | Honolulu | HI | A- | A- | B+ | 565.7 | 1.82 | 6.1 | 6.3 | 10.3 | 44.9 | 10.0 | 11.2 |
| UNIV OF ILLINOIS EMPL CU | Champaign | IL | C+ | C | C | 298.3 | 1.19 | 0.1 | 50.9 | 18.1 | 3.1 | 5.9 | 7.9 |
| UNIV OF IOWA COMMUNITY CU | North Liberty | IA | B+ | B+ | B | 3117.0 | 26.07 | 15.2 | 27.1 | 45.3 | 0.0 | 6.2 | 8.2 |
| UNIV OF KENTUCKY FCU | Lexington | KY | A | A | A- | 594.8 | 10.20 | 3.1 | 32.7 | 18.2 | 11.2 | 10.0 | 11.1 |
| ▲ UNIV OF LOUISIANA FCU | Lafayette | LA | C+ | C- | C- | 42.3 | -4.83 | 0.0 | 29.7 | 17.4 | 5.7 | 10.0 | 11.3 |
| UNIV OF MICHIGAN CU | Ann Arbor | MI | B | B- | B- | 638.9 | 13.53 | 0.1 | 30.8 | 21.6 | 27.4 | 7.3 | 9.2 |
| UNIV OF NEBRASKA FCU | Lincoln | NE | C- | C- | C+ | 91.7 | 5.80 | 0.0 | 23.8 | 17.9 | 9.2 | 6.2 | 8.2 |
| UNIV OF PENNSYLVANIA STUDENTS FCU | Philadelphia | PA | C | C | C | 6.7 | 0.18 | 0.0 | 0.7 | 0.0 | 8.2 | 10.0 | 11.1 |
| UNIV OF SOUTH ALABAMA FCU | Mobile | AL | C+ | C+ | C+ | 39.5 | 7.53 | 0.0 | 23.0 | 1.2 | 0.0 | 8.6 | 10.1 |
| UNIV OF TOLEDO FCU | Toledo | OH | C | C | C | 66.4 | 4.10 | 3.9 | 19.4 | 16.6 | 23.9 | 10.0 | 11.3 |
| UNIV OF VIRGINIA COMMUNITY CU | Charlottesville | VA | B+ | A- | A- | 715.0 | 4.83 | 3.5 | 20.4 | 16.1 | 44.0 | 10.0 | 11.3 |
| ▲ UNIV OF WISCONSIN CU | Madison | WI | B | B- | B+ | 2011.4 | 7.52 | 0.1 | 21.2 | 19.1 | 15.7 | 6.4 | 8.4 |
| ▲ UNIV OF WISCONSIN-OSHKOSH CU | Oshkosh | WI | D | E+ | E+ | 24.8 | 2.65 | 0.5 | 10.0 | 43.6 | 6.3 | 5.4 | 7.4 |
| UNIV SETTLEMENT FCU | New York | NY | D+ | C- | C- | <1 | -12.76 | 0.0 | 19.9 | 0.0 | 0.0 | 9.9 | 11.0 |
| ▼ UNIVERSAL 1 CU | Dayton | OH | C- | C+ | C | 391.4 | 4.27 | 2.3 | 60.2 | 10.5 | 6.5 | 6.5 | 8.5 |
| UNIVERSAL CITY STUDIOS CU | Burbank | CA | C | C | C- | 66.7 | -5.64 | 0.0 | 18.9 | 20.7 | 0.0 | 7.0 | 9.0 |
| ▼ UNIVERSAL COOP FCU | Rio Grande | PR | D+ | C- | C | 23.0 | 11.33 | 0.0 | 43.8 | 18.6 | 16.7 | 6.6 | 8.6 |
| ▼ UNIVERSAL CU | Independence | KS | D | D+ | D+ | 1.1 | -1.59 | 0.0 | 33.8 | 0.0 | 0.0 | 10.0 | 35.5 |
| UNIVERSAL FCU | Huntington | WV | C+ | C+ | B- | 78.5 | 3.26 | 0.1 | 20.9 | 20.0 | 1.9 | 10.0 | 13.9 |
| ▼ UNIWYO FCU | Laramie | WY | B- | B | B | 268.8 | 5.25 | 6.3 | 35.2 | 13.8 | 13.5 | 9.7 | 10.9 |
| UNO FCU | New Orleans | LA | B- | C+ | C+ | 25.5 | 3.58 | 0.0 | 38.2 | 2.9 | 0.0 | 10.0 | 11.4 |
| UP CATHOLIC CU | Marquette | MI | A- | A- | A- | 152.4 | 5.70 | 11.4 | 20.3 | 20.1 | 36.6 | 10.0 | 14.5 |
| UP CONNECTION FCU | Omaha | NE | C- | C- | C | 34.3 | 6.30 | 0.0 | 19.1 | 21.9 | 22.8 | 10.0 | 12.8 |
| UP EMPL FCU | North Little Rock | AR | C | C- | C- | 4.2 | -7.70 | 0.0 | 38.1 | 1.0 | 0.0 | 10.0 | 23.2 |
| UP STATE CU | Escanaba | MI | C- | C- | D+ | 64.3 | 28.53 | 1.0 | 31.8 | 22.6 | 0.7 | 6.2 | 8.2 |
| ▲ UPPER CUMBERLAND FCU | Crossville | TN | B- | C+ | C+ | 53.0 | 6.07 | 0.0 | 37.7 | 27.0 | 0.9 | 6.5 | 8.5 |
| UPPER DARBY BELLTELCO FCU | Upper Darby | PA | C- | D+ | C+ | 57.4 | 4.88 | 1.5 | 9.6 | 5.2 | 0.0 | 10.0 | 11.4 |
| UPPER MICHIGAN COMMUNITY CU | Munising | MI | D+ | C- | C | 34.2 | 7.56 | 1.0 | 25.5 | 21.0 | 0.0 | 5.6 | 7.6 |
| ▼ UPS CU | Cincinnati | OH | D+ | C- | D+ | 3.7 | -0.05 | 0.0 | 52.8 | 0.0 | 0.0 | 10.0 | 18.9 |
| UPS EMPL CU | Memphis | TN | B+ | B+ | B+ | 17.7 | 7.83 | 0.0 | 58.9 | 0.9 | 0.0 | 10.0 | 22.5 |
| UPS EMPL FCU | Ontario | CA | C | C+ | C+ | 30.7 | 3.09 | 0.0 | 19.7 | 15.9 | 0.0 | 8.4 | 9.9 |
| UPSTATE FCU | Anderson | SC | C | C | C- | 44.6 | 12.67 | 0.0 | 63.1 | 0.1 | 0.0 | 6.4 | 8.5 |

| Asset Quality Index | Non-Performing Loans as a % of Total Loans | as a % of Capital | Net Charge-Offs Avg Loans | Profitability Index | Net Income ($Mil) | Return on Assets | Return on Equity | Net Interest Spread | Overhead Efficiency Ratio | Liquidity Index | Liquidity Ratio | Hot Money Ratio | Stability Index |
|---|---|---|---|---|---|---|---|---|---|---|---|---|---|
| 1.0 | 7.28 | 35.0 | 6.37 | 1.6 | 0.0 | -2.84 | -25.60 | 10.23 | 79.3 | 4.8 | 44.7 | 14.1 | 6.9 |
| 5.1 | 0.78 | 6.7 | 0.77 | 7.0 | 0.1 | 1.32 | 15.40 | 5.16 | 67.1 | 3.4 | 4.4 | 0.0 | 3.0 |
| 9.2 | 0.72 | 2.4 | 0.21 | 7.2 | 0.3 | 1.09 | 7.73 | 3.23 | 69.1 | 4.8 | 22.5 | 3.7 | 7.0 |
| 3.4 | 3.73 | 33.8 | 0.11 | 3.7 | 0.2 | 0.66 | 8.34 | 3.44 | 86.8 | 3.8 | 13.9 | 3.9 | 3.0 |
| 8.2 | 2.80 | 4.3 | 0.02 | 1.9 | 0.0 | -0.04 | -0.26 | 2.61 | 101.2 | 5.0 | 11.0 | 1.7 | 6.4 |
| 7.2 | 0.72 | 6.7 | 0.24 | 3.4 | 0.8 | 0.47 | 5.71 | 3.73 | 84.6 | 3.4 | 9.7 | 8.1 | 4.1 |
| 3.9 | 0.27 | 10.8 | 0.16 | 1.1 | 0.0 | -0.30 | -4.06 | 5.05 | 104.3 | 3.8 | 23.9 | 6.0 | 1.0 |
| 9.4 | 0.50 | 2.0 | 0.10 | 9.1 | 0.5 | 1.51 | 8.26 | 4.74 | 71.7 | 3.8 | 21.5 | 4.3 | 7.6 |
| 8.7 | 0.37 | 1.2 | 0.16 | 4.2 | 0.2 | 0.55 | 6.04 | 2.71 | 81.0 | 5.5 | 21.2 | 0.0 | 5.1 |
| 10.0 | 0.00 | 0.0 | 0.73 | 0.2 | 0.0 | -0.41 | -2.52 | 2.66 | 112.9 | 5.2 | 31.1 | 0.0 | 6.2 |
| 8.5 | 0.53 | 2.8 | 0.28 | 3.2 | 0.4 | 0.33 | 2.56 | 3.21 | 88.8 | 3.5 | 11.5 | 6.2 | 7.3 |
| 8.9 | 0.59 | 3.5 | 0.22 | 4.8 | 2.9 | 0.65 | 6.01 | 4.32 | 74.9 | 6.4 | 47.6 | 7.1 | 7.5 |
| 2.7 | 3.64 | 30.5 | 0.67 | 2.5 | 0.6 | 0.23 | 2.22 | 4.19 | 86.0 | 3.5 | 10.5 | 2.8 | 6.2 |
| 9.7 | 1.32 | 1.5 | 0.00 | 0.6 | 0.0 | -0.19 | -1.82 | 2.24 | 107.4 | 5.3 | 23.1 | 2.9 | 4.3 |
| 6.7 | 0.89 | 6.0 | 0.53 | 6.0 | 1.2 | 0.85 | 7.39 | 3.85 | 81.2 | 3.7 | 14.8 | 4.0 | 7.8 |
| 9.0 | 0.40 | 2.6 | 0.25 | 5.7 | 6.9 | 0.96 | 9.49 | 3.05 | 74.1 | 3.9 | 14.4 | 5.0 | 6.6 |
| 6.2 | 1.55 | 9.0 | 0.26 | 2.3 | 0.1 | 0.27 | 2.92 | 3.18 | 89.8 | 4.0 | 18.6 | 2.6 | 3.5 |
| 9.7 | 1.14 | 1.7 | 0.21 | 2.5 | 0.1 | 0.19 | 1.21 | 2.32 | 91.7 | 5.3 | 30.6 | 1.6 | 6.7 |
| 8.8 | 0.36 | 1.2 | -0.14 | 3.8 | 0.0 | 0.43 | 2.61 | 5.21 | 92.5 | 4.7 | 35.9 | 0.0 | 5.7 |
| 7.4 | 0.53 | 5.3 | 0.67 | 3.6 | 0.5 | 0.33 | 4.25 | 4.61 | 81.4 | 3.5 | 6.9 | 3.3 | 4.3 |
| 8.9 | 0.54 | 2.6 | 0.29 | 4.6 | 0.5 | 0.67 | 7.40 | 2.56 | 77.3 | 4.5 | 29.6 | 4.7 | 5.7 |
| 9.5 | 0.46 | 2.7 | 0.52 | 4.7 | 3.3 | 0.55 | 5.56 | 3.40 | 84.7 | 3.8 | 13.9 | 2.9 | 7.3 |
| 9.7 | 0.34 | 1.7 | 0.12 | 4.2 | 3.0 | 0.78 | 9.94 | 2.61 | 73.2 | 5.1 | 20.7 | 1.7 | 5.4 |
| 9.4 | 0.64 | 1.9 | 1.79 | 0.3 | -0.6 | -0.44 | -4.55 | 2.86 | 94.9 | 5.5 | 27.2 | 2.6 | 4.8 |
| 5.7 | 1.45 | 13.5 | 0.45 | 3.7 | 0.6 | 0.33 | 3.57 | 4.34 | 86.9 | 3.2 | 3.8 | 2.8 | 6.0 |
| 9.1 | 0.36 | 2.2 | 0.22 | 5.7 | 0.2 | 0.98 | 11.25 | 3.37 | 73.9 | 4.2 | 12.6 | 1.3 | 4.4 |
| 8.7 | 0.21 | 2.3 | 0.54 | 6.2 | 13.6 | 0.96 | 11.97 | 4.24 | 78.7 | 4.0 | 10.7 | 1.6 | 5.9 |
| 6.8 | 0.38 | 3.6 | 0.56 | 7.7 | 6.5 | 1.17 | 11.07 | 3.35 | 66.0 | 3.5 | 9.5 | 3.4 | 7.8 |
| 9.2 | 0.44 | 3.1 | 0.18 | 6.2 | 4.0 | 0.95 | 8.53 | 2.37 | 58.2 | 4.9 | 19.1 | 5.0 | 7.8 |
| 5.2 | 0.78 | 8.1 | 0.93 | 4.1 | 1.3 | 0.58 | 7.58 | 4.72 | 76.0 | 3.2 | 8.6 | 2.8 | 4.2 |
| 6.4 | 0.56 | 6.2 | 0.33 | 9.5 | 34.3 | 1.63 | 19.35 | 3.07 | 48.3 | 0.9 | 10.2 | 37.2 | 7.6 |
| 7.6 | 0.76 | 5.1 | 1.02 | 7.2 | 4.2 | 0.97 | 8.83 | 4.44 | 63.1 | 2.7 | 13.6 | 16.4 | 8.6 |
| 7.0 | 0.48 | 3.3 | 1.62 | 3.8 | 0.2 | 0.58 | 6.72 | 3.93 | 86.3 | 4.4 | 31.4 | 6.7 | 3.6 |
| 6.5 | 1.58 | 10.8 | 0.57 | 5.4 | 4.4 | 0.94 | 10.04 | 3.35 | 72.8 | 3.8 | 12.5 | 4.0 | 5.7 |
| 8.5 | 0.34 | 1.9 | 0.14 | 2.3 | 0.2 | 0.25 | 3.00 | 2.82 | 91.6 | 5.1 | 24.3 | 0.7 | 3.7 |
| 10.0 | 0.75 | 0.1 | -2.72 | 3.1 | 0.0 | 0.60 | 5.72 | 2.24 | 84.1 | 7.5 | 56.1 | 0.0 | 4.1 |
| 8.7 | 0.58 | 1.5 | 0.52 | 3.5 | 0.1 | 0.46 | 4.47 | 2.02 | 83.8 | 5.6 | 37.4 | 0.7 | 5.6 |
| 9.6 | 0.76 | 2.8 | 0.12 | 2.3 | 0.1 | 0.16 | 1.38 | 2.47 | 94.7 | 4.7 | 32.7 | 2.8 | 5.6 |
| 9.6 | 0.35 | 1.5 | 0.72 | 5.1 | 3.9 | 0.73 | 6.53 | 3.37 | 75.0 | 4.5 | 10.8 | 2.6 | 7.5 |
| 7.2 | 0.78 | 5.7 | 0.38 | 6.8 | 19.8 | 1.34 | 16.14 | 3.53 | 70.9 | 4.4 | 19.1 | 3.1 | 5.5 |
| 5.0 | 0.44 | 4.4 | 0.05 | 1.9 | 0.0 | 0.17 | 2.35 | 3.38 | 95.5 | 4.4 | 15.7 | 0.4 | 3.0 |
| 10.0 | 0.00 | 0.0 | 0.00 | 1.1 | 0.0 | -0.36 | -3.33 | 5.37 | 114.3 | 7.5 | 61.2 | 0.0 | 4.9 |
| 4.1 | 1.47 | 12.4 | 1.29 | 2.1 | 0.2 | 0.07 | 0.77 | 3.82 | 76.6 | 3.3 | 16.8 | 10.2 | 5.1 |
| 5.1 | 1.18 | 9.1 | 0.33 | 4.1 | 0.2 | 0.35 | 4.56 | 4.69 | 92.0 | 4.0 | 12.0 | 5.9 | 3.5 |
| 3.4 | 2.57 | 21.5 | 1.59 | 4.2 | 0.0 | 0.17 | 1.93 | 6.01 | 70.6 | 4.3 | 19.2 | 6.4 | 3.0 |
| 7.8 | 7.04 | 7.2 | -1.89 | 0.1 | 0.0 | -1.40 | -3.90 | 5.62 | 131.0 | 6.5 | 67.8 | 0.0 | 5.0 |
| 7.7 | 1.83 | 6.1 | 0.15 | 2.5 | 0.1 | 0.21 | 1.67 | 2.92 | 91.3 | 4.7 | 13.1 | 1.0 | 6.8 |
| 8.6 | 0.45 | 2.7 | 0.53 | 3.7 | 1.1 | 0.56 | 5.27 | 3.31 | 78.1 | 3.5 | 19.7 | 7.5 | 7.0 |
| 8.0 | 1.16 | 4.8 | 0.35 | 3.5 | 0.1 | 0.43 | 3.73 | 3.59 | 85.2 | 5.2 | 43.9 | 1.2 | 6.1 |
| 7.2 | 0.68 | 5.7 | 0.13 | 6.6 | 1.2 | 1.10 | 7.57 | 3.38 | 69.2 | 4.2 | 14.0 | 4.6 | 8.6 |
| 9.4 | 0.01 | 0.0 | 0.56 | 1.9 | 0.0 | 0.17 | 1.35 | 3.32 | 90.9 | 4.0 | 14.1 | 5.1 | 5.9 |
| 8.3 | 1.51 | 2.9 | 0.20 | 2.9 | 0.0 | 0.28 | 1.22 | 7.30 | 96.5 | 7.1 | 68.1 | 0.0 | 5.9 |
| 4.3 | 0.56 | 12.1 | 0.40 | 4.1 | 0.2 | 0.55 | 6.47 | 4.83 | 85.8 | 4.2 | 15.8 | 1.5 | 3.7 |
| 7.7 | 0.47 | 3.7 | 0.16 | 9.3 | 0.5 | 1.39 | 16.46 | 5.14 | 77.4 | 4.0 | 14.6 | 3.0 | 4.5 |
| 5.2 | 4.42 | 13.4 | 2.88 | 3.3 | 0.3 | 0.59 | 5.26 | 3.13 | 88.9 | 5.5 | 31.7 | 6.3 | 4.8 |
| 4.9 | 1.21 | 10.6 | 0.43 | 1.9 | 0.0 | -0.09 | -1.08 | 4.09 | 94.0 | 4.9 | 22.9 | 2.4 | 3.3 |
| 8.6 | 0.10 | 0.3 | -0.07 | 0.9 | 0.0 | -0.28 | -1.52 | 5.12 | 104.6 | 5.4 | 38.3 | 0.0 | 6.4 |
| 8.2 | 0.64 | 1.9 | 0.52 | 10.0 | 0.2 | 1.74 | 7.86 | 6.40 | 70.0 | 4.0 | 20.6 | 3.1 | 7.0 |
| 10.0 | 0.19 | 0.7 | 0.12 | 2.5 | 0.1 | 0.22 | 2.30 | 3.18 | 94.4 | 4.4 | 28.1 | 6.7 | 4.2 |
| 5.2 | 0.45 | 4.2 | 0.30 | 7.9 | 0.4 | 1.10 | 13.37 | 5.38 | 82.7 | 3.5 | 14.1 | 9.4 | 4.0 |

| Name | City | State | Rating | 2014 Rating | 2013 Rating | Total Assets ($Mil) | One Year Asset Growth | Asset Mix (As a % of Total Assets) | | | | Capital-ization Index | Net Worth Ratio |
|------|------|-------|--------|-------------|-------------|---------------------|----------------------|-------------------|---|---|---|----------------------|-----------------|
| | | | | | | | | Comm-ercial Loans | Cons-umer Loans | Mort-gage Loans | Secur-ities | | |
| ▼ UPSTATE MILK EMPL FCU | Cheektowaga | NY | D | D+ | C- | 2.9 | 6.05 | 0.0 | 36.2 | 0.0 | 50.8 | 8.2 | 9.8 |
| UPSTATE TELCO FCU | Gloversville | NY | D+ | C | C- | 5.3 | 6.15 | 0.0 | 28.5 | 0.0 | 0.1 | 10.0 | 15.2 |
| URBAN STREET BISCUIT WKRS FCU | Buffalo | NY | C- | C- | C- | 1.1 | -7.76 | 0.0 | 39.4 | 0.0 | 0.0 | 10.0 | 22.4 |
| ▼ URBAN UPBOUND FCU | Long Island City | NY | D+ | B- | C | <1 | -9.89 | 0.0 | 12.8 | 0.0 | 0.0 | 6.7 | 8.8 |
| URBANA MUNICIPAL EMPL CU | Urbana | IL | D | D | D+ | 3.6 | 3.78 | 0.0 | 60.4 | 0.0 | 0.0 | 6.3 | 8.3 |
| URBANA POSTAL CU | Urbana | IL | C- | C- | C- | <1 | -16.79 | 0.0 | 91.6 | 0.0 | 0.0 | 10.0 | 15.1 |
| URE FCU | East Pittsburgh | PA | C- | C- | C- | 9.4 | 2.08 | 0.0 | 46.2 | 0.0 | 0.0 | 10.0 | 15.7 |
| URW COMMUNITY FCU | Danville | VA | B | B | B- | 142.2 | 19.69 | 1.8 | 69.5 | 14.4 | 0.0 | 7.7 | 9.5 |
| US #1364 FCU | Merrillville | IN | B+ | B+ | B- | 106.5 | 3.91 | 0.0 | 27.0 | 25.7 | 0.0 | 8.0 | 9.7 |
| ▲ US COMMUNITY CU | Nashville | TN | B- | C+ | C+ | 160.1 | 4.15 | 1.6 | 35.0 | 18.3 | 12.4 | 10.0 | 13.1 |
| US EAGLE FCU | Albuquerque | NM | B | B | B | 854.8 | 5.59 | 6.4 | 50.0 | 18.8 | 20.0 | 9.3 | 10.6 |
| US EMPL CU | Chicago | IL | C | C | C+ | 82.5 | 1.04 | 5.4 | 19.2 | 1.4 | 37.2 | 10.0 | 12.4 |
| US EMPL FCU | Fairmont | WV | C- | D+ | C- | <1 | 11.42 | 0.0 | 72.5 | 0.0 | 0.0 | 10.0 | 15.4 |
| US EMPL OC FCU | Oklahoma City | OK | A- | A- | B | 147.1 | 3.35 | 0.0 | 59.6 | 14.4 | 10.8 | 10.0 | 12.2 |
| US FCU | Burnsville | MN | B+ | B+ | B | 1024.1 | 5.57 | 4.6 | 35.2 | 29.7 | 11.6 | 8.5 | 10.0 |
| US POSTAL SERVICE FCU | Clinton | MD | B- | B- | C | 204.3 | 1.69 | 0.0 | 23.1 | 18.2 | 16.8 | 10.0 | 11.6 |
| US WEATHER BUREAU NY FCU | Bohemia | NY | C- | C- | C- | 1.7 | -4.32 | 0.0 | 3.9 | 0.0 | 0.0 | 10.0 | 12.2 |
| USAGENCIES CU | Portland | OR | C+ | B- | B- | 79.0 | 2.50 | 0.0 | 25.9 | 16.8 | 0.0 | 8.6 | 10.1 |
| USALLIANCE FCU | Rye | NY | B- | B- | C+ | 1077.0 | 17.73 | 3.0 | 15.4 | 25.8 | 4.4 | 6.0 | 8.1 |
| USB EMPL FCU | Wilmington | CA | D | D | C- | 2.3 | -2.21 | 0.0 | 17.3 | 0.0 | 17.7 | 10.0 | 27.5 |
| USC CU | Los Angeles | CA | B- | B- | B- | 422.4 | 5.65 | 0.9 | 29.3 | 22.4 | 10.1 | 6.2 | 8.2 |
| USEM MENA FCU | Mena | AR | C+ | C+ | C+ | 2.4 | -0.38 | 0.0 | 45.1 | 0.0 | 0.0 | 10.0 | 17.3 |
| USF FCU | Tampa | FL | B- | B | B | 499.0 | 13.71 | 1.4 | 40.6 | 27.2 | 12.9 | 9.3 | 10.5 |
| USNE PENITENTIARY EMPL FCU | Lewisburg | PA | C- | C- | D | 13.0 | 1.82 | 0.0 | 27.3 | 0.0 | 51.1 | 7.2 | 9.1 |
| USSCO JOHNSTOWN FCU | Johnstown | PA | C+ | C+ | B- | 99.9 | 1.68 | 6.9 | 14.0 | 13.2 | 27.4 | 8.4 | 10.0 |
| USTC EMPL CU | Nashville | TN | B- | C+ | C+ | 2.0 | 6.48 | 0.0 | 76.2 | 0.0 | 0.0 | 10.0 | 16.9 |
| USX FCU | Cranberry Township | PA | B- | B- | B- | 223.0 | 5.50 | 0.0 | 35.4 | 22.7 | 26.0 | 10.0 | 14.4 |
| UTAH COMMUNITY FCU | Provo | UT | A- | A- | A- | 1021.6 | 8.96 | 9.1 | 29.6 | 19.4 | 10.3 | 9.5 | 10.7 |
| UTAH FCU | Salt Lake City | UT | C+ | C+ | C | 18.1 | 4.74 | 1.0 | 28.6 | 20.4 | 30.4 | 10.0 | 12.0 |
| UTAH FIRST FCU | Salt Lake City | UT | A- | A- | B | 267.5 | 4.55 | 13.3 | 28.9 | 29.6 | 0.0 | 9.7 | 10.8 |
| UTAH HERITAGE CU | Moroni | UT | C+ | C | C | 57.0 | 11.46 | 5.6 | 25.0 | 26.8 | 0.0 | 7.4 | 9.3 |
| UTAH POWER CU | Salt Lake City | UT | A+ | A+ | A+ | 552.5 | 4.53 | 0.5 | 17.3 | 19.6 | 48.5 | 10.0 | 13.5 |
| ▼ UTAH PRISON EMPL CU | Draper | UT | D | D+ | D | 4.0 | -3.08 | 0.0 | 48.9 | 0.0 | 0.0 | 9.1 | 10.4 |
| UTICA DISTRICT TELEPHONE EMPL FCU | Utica | NY | B | B- | B- | 35.8 | 2.94 | 0.0 | 15.7 | 12.6 | 0.0 | 10.0 | 27.7 |
| UTICA GAS & ELECTRIC EMPL FCU | New Hartford | NY | B+ | B+ | B+ | 57.7 | 2.42 | 2.2 | 12.7 | 32.0 | 27.6 | 10.0 | 17.7 |
| UTICA POLICE DEPT FCU | Utica | NY | C- | D+ | C- | 7.2 | -0.46 | 0.0 | 47.4 | 0.6 | 44.0 | 10.0 | 15.4 |
| UTILITIES CU | Eau Claire | WI | C- | C- | C- | 8.1 | -4.04 | 0.0 | 29.0 | 0.0 | 0.0 | 10.0 | 11.1 |
| UTILITIES EMPL CU | Wyomissing | PA | B+ | A- | A- | 1110.8 | 1.28 | 0.4 | 7.0 | 11.8 | 71.7 | 10.0 | 14.1 |
| UTILITY DISTRICT CU | Oakland | CA | C | C | C | 30.0 | 1.77 | 0.0 | 16.6 | 11.8 | 6.4 | 6.4 | 8.4 |
| UTILITY EMPL FCU | Hoquiam | WA | C | C | C | 3.7 | -6.07 | 0.0 | 34.0 | 0.0 | 0.0 | 10.0 | 12.3 |
| V SUAREZ EMPL FCU | Bayamon | PR | E+ | D- | D- | <1 | 6.73 | 0.0 | 0.0 | 0.0 | 0.0 | 4.5 | 6.5 |
| VA DESERT PACIFIC FCU | Signal Hill | CA | A- | A- | A- | 65.9 | 5.69 | 3.9 | 33.9 | 22.9 | 30.0 | 10.0 | 15.5 |
| VA HOSPITAL FCU | Little Rock | AR | D | D | D- | 8.6 | 3.01 | 0.0 | 75.9 | 0.0 | 0.0 | 7.8 | 9.6 |
| ▼ VA PITTSBURGH EMPL FCU | Pittsburgh | PA | D+ | C | B- | 19.8 | 1.49 | 0.0 | 22.6 | 0.0 | 5.1 | 10.0 | 11.1 |
| ▼ VAC EMPL FCU | Bath | NY | D+ | D+ | C | 24.1 | 0.30 | 0.0 | 13.0 | 2.7 | 68.0 | 10.0 | 17.1 |
| VACATIONLAND FCU | Sandusky | OH | A- | A- | B+ | 177.1 | 4.70 | 11.2 | 32.7 | 21.2 | 11.1 | 9.5 | 10.7 |
| VAH LYONS EMPL FCU | Lyons | NJ | B- | B- | B- | 43.1 | 1.87 | 0.0 | 21.3 | 0.0 | 0.0 | 9.0 | 10.3 |
| VALDOSTA TEACHERS FCU | Valdosta | GA | C- | C | C | 9.6 | 0.18 | 0.0 | 37.9 | 2.9 | 0.0 | 10.0 | 14.9 |
| ▼ VALEX FCU | Pineville | LA | C- | C | D+ | 18.8 | 3.85 | 0.0 | 43.0 | 11.3 | 0.0 | 8.5 | 10.0 |
| VALLEY 1ST COMMUNITY FCU | Monessen | PA | C+ | C+ | C+ | 84.9 | -1.80 | 0.4 | 7.7 | 24.4 | 0.0 | 10.0 | 22.1 |
| VALLEY BELL FCU | Charleston | WV | C- | D+ | C | <1 | -2.66 | 0.0 | 47.3 | 0.0 | 0.0 | 10.0 | 24.6 |
| VALLEY BOARD FCU | Halltown | WV | D | D | D+ | <1 | 1.60 | 0.0 | 62.2 | 0.0 | 0.0 | 10.0 | 33.1 |
| VALLEY CATHOLIC FCU | Simsbury | CT | E+ | E+ | D | <1 | -9.55 | 2.3 | 54.3 | 0.0 | 0.0 | 6.1 | 8.1 |
| VALLEY COMMUNITIES CU | Mosinee | WI | B- | B- | B | 136.1 | 6.30 | 0.2 | 21.4 | 47.1 | 0.1 | 10.0 | 14.3 |
| VALLEY COMMUNITY CU | Waynesboro | VA | E+ | D- | D- | 8.3 | -15.92 | 3.6 | 25.1 | 36.0 | 20.5 | 6.2 | 8.2 |
| VALLEY CU | Tuscumbia | AL | B+ | B+ | B+ | 67.8 | 4.57 | 0.2 | 21.8 | 16.4 | 17.0 | 10.0 | 16.9 |
| VALLEY CU | Salem | OR | B- | B- | C+ | 67.6 | 4.66 | 2.4 | 29.1 | 6.3 | 0.0 | 8.7 | 10.1 |
| VALLEY EDUCATORS CU | Alamosa | CO | D- | D- | E+ | 4.9 | -1.12 | 0.0 | 56.5 | 0.0 | 0.0 | 8.4 | 9.9 |
| VALLEY FCU | Brownsville | TX | B+ | A- | A- | 61.3 | 8.35 | 0.0 | 56.4 | 2.4 | 0.0 | 10.0 | 14.5 |
| VALLEY FCU OF MONTANA | Billings | MT | A- | A- | A- | 211.9 | 4.51 | 0.0 | 47.1 | 7.7 | 0.0 | 10.0 | 11.0 |

| Asset Quality Index | Non-Performing Loans as a % of Total Loans | Non-Performing Loans as a % of Capital | Net Charge-Offs Avg Loans | Profitability Index | Net Income ($Mil) | Return on Assets | Return on Equity | Net Interest Spread | Overhead Efficiency Ratio | Liquidity Index | Liquidity Ratio | Hot Money Ratio | Stability Index |
|---|---|---|---|---|---|---|---|---|---|---|---|---|---|
| 5.1 | 3.30 | 12.6 | 1.22 | 1.5 | 0.0 | -0.05 | -0.47 | 2.89 | 87.3 | 5.2 | 23.3 | 0.0 | 5.2 |
| 9.5 | 0.69 | 1.3 | 1.60 | 0.4 | 0.0 | -0.98 | -6.05 | 3.94 | 101.8 | 6.9 | 51.2 | 0.0 | 6.0 |
| 8.9 | 1.30 | 2.3 | 1.82 | 2.3 | 0.0 | 0.12 | 0.53 | 3.01 | 113.6 | 7.2 | 164.0 | 0.0 | 5.4 |
| 6.7 | 10.53 | 15.6 | 0.00 | 3.6 | 0.0 | -4.16 | -47.18 | 6.67 | 207.1 | 8.6 | 101.1 | 0.0 | 3.0 |
| 6.2 | 0.58 | 3.8 | -0.06 | 4.1 | 0.0 | 0.60 | 7.26 | 4.71 | 76.4 | 4.2 | 24.9 | 0.0 | 2.3 |
| 5.8 | 1.53 | 8.8 | -0.16 | 4.6 | 0.0 | 0.67 | 4.80 | 4.56 | 86.7 | 3.3 | 9.5 | 0.0 | 3.7 |
| 2.7 | 6.30 | 22.4 | 0.13 | 6.5 | 0.1 | 1.06 | 7.07 | 4.14 | 75.6 | 4.1 | 12.0 | 0.0 | 6.8 |
| 5.0 | 0.88 | 10.1 | 0.92 | 9.5 | 2.5 | 2.43 | 26.69 | 6.28 | 52.8 | 1.1 | 3.3 | 22.8 | 6.7 |
| 9.2 | 0.42 | 2.8 | 0.08 | 6.9 | 0.8 | 1.01 | 11.60 | 2.29 | 71.5 | 3.0 | 21.4 | 13.7 | 6.5 |
| 9.7 | 0.12 | 0.6 | 0.54 | 3.5 | 0.4 | 0.36 | 2.80 | 4.73 | 89.7 | 3.9 | 13.0 | 4.8 | 7.0 |
| 5.2 | 0.67 | 7.9 | 0.68 | 4.7 | 4.2 | 0.66 | 6.34 | 3.46 | 71.0 | 3.1 | 5.3 | 7.1 | 7.2 |
| 9.8 | 0.71 | 1.4 | 0.49 | 2.1 | 0.1 | 0.13 | 1.05 | 2.51 | 94.6 | 5.5 | 23.2 | 1.5 | 5.4 |
| 5.9 | 0.00 | 0.0 | 0.00 | 3.4 | 0.0 | 0.35 | 2.17 | 4.79 | 87.0 | 5.1 | 29.1 | 0.0 | 7.2 |
| 6.2 | 0.69 | 6.3 | 0.38 | 5.8 | 1.0 | 0.86 | 7.87 | 3.60 | 76.0 | 2.8 | 7.0 | 10.3 | 8.0 |
| 7.3 | 0.63 | 5.2 | 0.42 | 5.8 | 6.2 | 0.81 | 8.04 | 3.18 | 66.4 | 3.1 | 11.5 | 7.5 | 7.5 |
| 6.1 | 2.87 | 11.2 | 0.73 | 3.2 | 0.5 | 0.31 | 2.68 | 3.09 | 90.7 | 4.2 | 30.5 | 4.0 | 6.7 |
| 10.0 | 0.00 | 0.0 | 0.00 | 1.7 | 0.0 | 0.08 | 0.64 | 1.46 | 89.5 | 6.1 | 43.2 | 0.0 | 4.9 |
| 9.1 | 0.27 | 1.6 | 0.04 | 3.3 | 0.2 | 0.37 | 3.71 | 2.72 | 89.0 | 4.9 | 36.1 | 1.0 | 5.2 |
| 5.7 | 1.50 | 15.2 | 0.44 | 5.6 | 6.0 | 0.79 | 10.46 | 4.16 | 68.7 | 2.1 | 15.0 | 21.3 | 5.6 |
| 9.3 | 6.39 | 3.9 | 0.00 | 0.3 | 0.0 | -0.29 | -1.07 | 2.07 | 114.7 | 5.6 | 56.0 | 0.0 | 6.4 |
| 7.5 | 0.79 | 6.8 | 0.27 | 3.9 | 1.7 | 0.55 | 6.65 | 2.85 | 80.7 | 4.0 | 14.5 | 3.9 | 5.2 |
| 7.4 | 1.17 | 3.7 | 0.55 | 8.3 | 0.0 | 1.55 | 9.76 | 3.65 | 50.0 | 5.6 | 53.4 | 0.0 | 5.0 |
| 7.9 | 0.59 | 4.6 | 0.66 | 3.7 | 1.8 | 0.49 | 4.53 | 3.48 | 79.5 | 3.6 | 15.1 | 6.6 | 6.7 |
| 9.2 | 0.71 | 2.4 | 0.17 | 2.8 | 0.0 | 0.35 | 3.88 | 1.54 | 75.0 | 5.0 | 13.4 | 0.0 | 4.5 |
| 7.2 | 0.57 | 2.6 | -0.06 | 2.7 | 0.2 | 0.21 | 2.11 | 2.58 | 96.3 | 4.3 | 10.1 | 0.3 | 5.7 |
| 8.0 | 0.33 | 1.4 | 1.00 | 10.0 | 0.0 | 2.98 | 17.97 | 9.15 | 58.1 | 4.8 | 25.0 | 0.0 | 5.7 |
| 7.9 | 1.25 | 5.8 | 0.58 | 3.3 | 0.6 | 0.35 | 2.43 | 3.85 | 85.4 | 3.7 | 10.2 | 3.2 | 7.4 |
| 8.8 | 0.28 | 2.9 | 0.17 | 8.3 | 10.0 | 1.34 | 12.79 | 3.23 | 70.7 | 4.5 | 18.8 | 3.3 | 8.2 |
| 9.7 | 0.26 | 1.2 | 0.54 | 3.3 | 0.1 | 0.44 | 3.62 | 3.16 | 83.6 | 4.1 | 12.8 | 4.9 | 5.5 |
| 8.9 | 0.17 | 2.3 | 0.26 | 8.4 | 2.4 | 1.22 | 11.60 | 4.74 | 77.4 | 3.1 | 10.6 | 7.4 | 7.0 |
| 4.9 | 1.27 | 10.2 | 0.35 | 6.0 | 0.4 | 0.86 | 9.32 | 4.66 | 79.2 | 2.9 | 19.5 | 18.2 | 4.2 |
| 9.9 | 0.33 | 1.1 | 0.10 | 6.8 | 4.1 | 0.98 | 7.48 | 1.92 | 56.1 | 4.3 | 11.1 | 1.0 | 9.9 |
| 3.3 | 2.16 | 12.4 | 0.16 | 2.1 | 0.0 | -0.50 | -4.71 | 4.64 | 110.5 | 6.0 | 40.5 | 0.0 | 4.6 |
| 9.6 | 1.31 | 2.3 | -0.31 | 4.5 | 0.2 | 0.72 | 2.72 | 2.71 | 73.1 | 4.1 | 9.8 | 2.9 | 6.5 |
| 7.6 | 1.66 | 5.6 | 0.03 | 8.8 | 0.6 | 1.36 | 7.99 | 3.51 | 60.8 | 3.1 | 13.7 | 10.8 | 8.0 |
| 5.4 | 2.41 | 6.9 | 2.16 | 4.0 | 0.0 | 0.61 | 4.06 | 2.54 | 50.0 | 4.4 | 12.0 | 0.0 | 3.7 |
| 10.0 | 0.12 | 0.5 | 0.00 | 1.8 | 0.0 | 0.03 | 0.30 | 2.25 | 91.8 | 5.1 | 28.7 | 0.0 | 5.3 |
| 10.0 | 0.46 | 0.9 | 0.19 | 4.3 | 5.0 | 0.60 | 4.32 | 1.56 | 63.8 | 5.3 | 33.1 | 2.2 | 9.2 |
| 9.1 | 0.29 | 1.1 | 0.00 | 3.6 | 0.1 | 0.45 | 5.40 | 2.81 | 85.7 | 4.8 | 15.9 | 0.4 | 3.8 |
| 9.7 | 0.07 | 0.2 | 0.00 | 3.0 | 0.0 | 0.36 | 2.97 | 2.38 | 83.6 | 6.5 | 59.5 | 0.0 | 5.7 |
| 7.7 | 0.42 | 2.6 | 2.55 | 0.6 | 0.0 | -0.95 | -12.90 | 7.98 | 122.2 | 6.4 | 49.9 | 0.0 | 4.1 |
| 8.4 | 0.06 | 0.2 | 0.36 | 9.8 | 0.9 | 1.78 | 11.51 | 4.28 | 68.8 | 3.6 | 6.3 | 2.9 | 8.0 |
| 4.4 | 0.86 | 8.2 | -0.18 | 3.4 | 0.0 | 0.52 | 5.29 | 3.47 | 97.8 | 3.3 | 21.4 | 5.2 | 2.3 |
| 10.0 | 0.50 | 1.2 | 0.82 | 0.9 | 0.0 | -0.06 | -0.57 | 3.13 | 95.0 | 5.9 | 35.4 | 0.0 | 4.9 |
| 10.0 | 0.00 | 0.0 | 0.00 | 0.9 | 0.0 | -0.13 | -0.77 | 2.21 | 100.0 | 4.9 | 18.6 | 0.5 | 6.5 |
| 8.8 | 0.40 | 2.3 | 0.28 | 6.4 | 1.2 | 0.93 | 8.93 | 4.11 | 79.6 | 3.7 | 12.8 | 3.1 | 7.4 |
| 9.6 | 0.86 | 1.7 | 0.00 | 3.5 | 0.1 | 0.45 | 4.38 | 2.15 | 67.1 | 5.1 | 19.8 | 0.0 | 5.1 |
| 9.0 | 0.57 | 1.9 | 0.32 | 2.3 | 0.0 | 0.12 | 0.85 | 4.80 | 94.7 | 5.0 | 32.6 | 0.0 | 6.5 |
| 7.1 | 1.39 | 7.3 | -0.66 | 3.2 | 0.0 | 0.23 | 2.36 | 3.81 | 91.5 | 4.5 | 23.4 | 5.0 | 4.5 |
| 7.0 | 5.32 | 8.5 | 0.50 | 2.9 | 0.2 | 0.32 | 1.48 | 2.52 | 81.0 | 4.6 | 21.2 | 1.9 | 6.5 |
| 2.5 | 11.90 | 23.1 | 0.00 | 7.1 | 0.0 | 2.60 | 11.11 | 8.44 | 40.0 | 7.0 | 65.8 | 0.0 | 5.7 |
| 8.5 | 0.00 | 0.0 | 0.00 | 0.0 | 0.0 | -2.07 | -6.20 | 10.88 | 111.1 | 5.9 | 54.1 | 0.0 | 5.4 |
| 1.9 | 4.70 | 26.7 | 4.49 | 1.3 | 0.0 | -0.13 | -1.71 | 6.61 | 100.0 | 6.2 | 53.3 | 0.0 | 1.0 |
| 9.4 | 0.26 | 1.3 | 0.01 | 3.9 | 0.5 | 0.51 | 3.59 | 3.69 | 86.6 | 3.9 | 23.4 | 2.7 | 8.3 |
| 0.3 | 5.10 | 51.8 | 1.34 | 1.4 | 0.0 | -0.30 | -3.87 | 5.37 | 85.3 | 3.3 | 7.1 | 9.4 | 2.1 |
| 6.6 | 1.22 | 12.8 | 0.17 | 4.5 | 0.3 | 0.54 | 3.22 | 3.54 | 82.9 | 4.6 | 24.0 | 6.6 | 7.2 |
| 5.5 | 1.34 | 12.4 | 0.28 | 5.1 | 0.3 | 0.56 | 5.52 | 5.09 | 78.0 | 4.9 | 27.9 | 8.5 | 5.2 |
| 1.2 | 4.77 | 29.7 | -0.04 | 6.3 | 0.0 | 0.92 | 9.50 | 6.28 | 84.0 | 4.2 | 28.2 | 9.0 | 4.0 |
| 6.7 | 0.83 | 3.5 | 2.08 | 6.4 | 0.4 | 0.77 | 5.38 | 7.11 | 71.5 | 4.4 | 28.8 | 3.3 | 8.2 |
| 6.1 | 0.69 | 4.9 | 0.49 | 5.5 | 1.3 | 0.83 | 7.78 | 4.07 | 75.1 | 3.5 | 14.3 | 2.7 | 6.7 |

Data as of September 30, 2015

| Name | City | State | Rating | 2014 Rating | 2013 Rating | Total Assets ($Mil) | One Year Asset Growth | Asset Mix (As a % of Total Assets) | | | | Capital-ization Index | Net Worth Ratio |
|---|---|---|---|---|---|---|---|---|---|---|---|---|---|
| | | | | | | | | Comm-ercial Loans | Cons-umer Loans | Mort-gage Loans | Secur-ities | | |
| VALLEY FIRST CU | Modesto | CA | B | B | B+ | 547.9 | 5.03 | 1.0 | 41.0 | 7.6 | 23.7 | 9.1 | 10.4 |
| VALLEY GAS EMPL CU | Jackson | MS | C- | C- | C- | 6.3 | -6.11 | 0.0 | 14.7 | 0.0 | 0.0 | 10.0 | 23.5 |
| VALLEY HILLS FCU | San Bernardino | CA | C- | C | C | 3.1 | 4.24 | 0.0 | 49.0 | 0.0 | 0.0 | 10.0 | 12.7 |
| ▲ VALLEY ISLE COMMUNITY FCU | Kahului | HI | D+ | D | D+ | 112.6 | 1.83 | 0.0 | 19.1 | 7.4 | 24.1 | 9.1 | 10.4 |
| VALLEY OAK CU | Three Rivers | CA | C- | D+ | C+ | 49.2 | 4.55 | 0.0 | 62.2 | 2.4 | 0.0 | 8.8 | 10.2 |
| VALLEY ONE COMMUNITY FCU | Steubenville | OH | D | D+ | D | 31.8 | 0.97 | 0.3 | 12.6 | 5.9 | 14.3 | 9.5 | 10.6 |
| VALLEY PRIDE FCU | Kingston | PA | D | D | C- | 6.5 | 2.59 | 0.0 | 12.2 | 0.0 | 18.3 | 10.0 | 17.1 |
| ▼ VALLEY STATE EMPL CU | Saginaw | MI | D | D+ | C- | 25.0 | 8.41 | 0.0 | 49.0 | 15.6 | 13.6 | 9.4 | 10.6 |
| VALLEY WIDE FCU | Vernal | UT | D | D+ | C- | <1 | 8.68 | 0.0 | 53.2 | 0.0 | 0.0 | 10.0 | 19.3 |
| VALLEY WIDE OF PA FCU | Tarentum | PA | D+ | D | D | 1.6 | 1.62 | 0.0 | 41.3 | 0.0 | 0.0 | 10.0 | 18.3 |
| VALLEYSTAR CU | Martinsville | VA | B- | B | B | 273.4 | -0.36 | 2.6 | 22.3 | 28.2 | 9.6 | 10.0 | 15.4 |
| ▼ VALOR FCU | Scranton | PA | C | B- | C+ | 227.8 | 9.26 | 8.1 | 34.5 | 18.2 | 2.5 | 5.4 | 7.4 |
| VALWOOD PARK FCU | Carrollton | TX | C+ | C+ | C+ | 20.7 | 5.00 | 0.0 | 56.5 | 1.1 | 0.0 | 10.0 | 15.4 |
| VAN CORTLANDT COOPERATIVE FCU | Bronx | NY | B+ | A- | A- | 77.5 | -1.71 | 18.0 | 1.5 | 14.3 | 41.3 | 10.0 | 14.1 |
| VANDERBILT UNIV EMPL CU | Nashville | TN | C- | C- | C- | 36.1 | 6.48 | 0.0 | 11.9 | 0.5 | 0.0 | 7.0 | 9.0 |
| ▼ VANTAGE CU | Bridgeton | MO | C- | C+ | C | 766.5 | 4.38 | 0.0 | 49.5 | 7.7 | 5.3 | 6.8 | 8.8 |
| VANTAGE POINT FCU | Hopewell | VA | B+ | B+ | B+ | 31.2 | 0.82 | 0.0 | 26.2 | 7.1 | 29.2 | 10.0 | 13.5 |
| VANTAGE TRUST FCU | Wilkes-Barre | PA | D- | D- | D | 58.2 | -4.88 | 0.0 | 8.8 | 13.5 | 21.5 | 6.7 | 8.7 |
| VANTAGE WEST CU | Tucson | AZ | A- | A- | A- | 1532.9 | 13.61 | 6.8 | 64.7 | 21.6 | 1.8 | 10.0 | 11.8 |
| VAPR FCU | San Juan | PR | C- | C- | C+ | 206.3 | 7.16 | 0.0 | 56.3 | 4.3 | 28.0 | 6.0 | 8.0 |
| VARIAN FCU | Salt Lake City | UT | C | C | C | 13.6 | 0.12 | 0.0 | 28.7 | 3.3 | 52.2 | 10.0 | 18.7 |
| VARICK MEMORIAL FCU | Hempstead | NY | D- | D | C- | <1 | -11.80 | 0.0 | 28.3 | 0.0 | 0.0 | 10.0 | 12.4 |
| VASCO FCU | Latrobe | PA | C- | C | C | 24.0 | 3.38 | 0.0 | 14.6 | 0.0 | 5.0 | 10.0 | 11.5 |
| VATAT CU | Austin | TX | C- | C- | C- | 7.4 | 0.23 | 0.0 | 63.6 | 0.0 | 0.0 | 10.0 | 16.9 |
| ▼ VELMA FCU | Velma | OK | E+ | E+ | D- | 2.6 | 6.94 | 0.0 | 49.1 | 0.0 | 0.0 | 6.9 | 9.0 |
| VELOCITY COMMUNITY FCU | Palm Beach Garden | FL | C | C | C | 300.9 | 4.65 | 0.0 | 23.5 | 17.0 | 46.8 | 10.0 | 12.6 |
| VELOCITY CU | Austin | TX | A | A | A | 784.4 | 14.19 | 0.4 | 61.0 | 1.5 | 10.4 | 10.0 | 12.6 |
| VENTURA COUNTY CU | Ventura | CA | B | B+ | B+ | 719.2 | 5.34 | 3.6 | 46.0 | 24.2 | 8.9 | 7.1 | 9.1 |
| VERIDIAN CU | Waterloo | IA | A- | A- | A- | 2764.2 | 11.43 | 5.7 | 31.8 | 28.9 | 14.1 | 9.3 | 10.5 |
| ▲ VERITAS FCU | Franklin | TN | C | C | C | 39.9 | 5.31 | 0.0 | 43.4 | 14.9 | 2.5 | 7.8 | 9.5 |
| VERITY CU | Seattle | WA | B+ | B+ | B | 461.2 | 6.78 | 3.1 | 23.3 | 29.4 | 18.5 | 8.1 | 9.8 |
| VERMILION SCHOOL EMPL CU | Abbeville | LA | C- | C- | C- | 14.3 | 2.70 | 0.0 | 21.7 | 0.0 | 0.0 | 7.1 | 9.1 |
| VERMILLION FCU | Vermillion | SD | B- | B- | B | 15.8 | -3.90 | 1.5 | 24.5 | 10.4 | 3.2 | 10.0 | 11.9 |
| VERMONT FCU | Burlington | VT | B- | B | B | 450.1 | 8.12 | 9.4 | 16.6 | 28.5 | 32.7 | 6.5 | 8.5 |
| VERMONT STATE EMPL CU | Montpelier | VT | C+ | C+ | C+ | 680.9 | 4.70 | 9.0 | 16.8 | 45.6 | 17.0 | 6.3 | 8.3 |
| ▲ VERMONT VA FCU | White River Junctio | VT | D+ | D+ | D+ | 23.2 | 2.73 | 0.0 | 17.6 | 12.4 | 2.1 | 7.0 | 9.0 |
| ▲ VERVE A CU | Oshkosh | WI | B+ | B | A- | 727.4 | 24.88 | 22.7 | 21.5 | 52.3 | 0.1 | 10.0 | 11.1 |
| VETERANS HEALTH ADMINISTRATION CU | Detroit | MI | D | C- | C | 3.8 | 24.17 | 0.0 | 25.6 | 0.0 | 0.0 | 7.0 | 9.0 |
| VIA CU | Marion | IN | B | B | B+ | 311.4 | 1.03 | 0.6 | 26.7 | 20.2 | 42.5 | 10.0 | 12.2 |
| VIBE CU | Novi | MI | B- | B | B- | 451.8 | 9.13 | 5.5 | 11.0 | 47.0 | 15.1 | 10.0 | 15.0 |
| VIBRANT CU | Moline | IL | B | B | B+ | 492.9 | 2.70 | 7.1 | 38.0 | 31.1 | 0.0 | 9.7 | 10.8 |
| ▲ VICKSBURG RAILROAD CU | Vicksburg | MS | D+ | D | D+ | 12.3 | -0.48 | 0.0 | 30.8 | 13.6 | 0.0 | 10.0 | 31.3 |
| VICKSWOOD CU | Vicksburg | MS | C+ | C+ | C+ | 11.0 | 2.21 | 0.0 | 16.9 | 0.0 | 0.0 | 10.0 | 22.7 |
| VICTOR VALLEY FCU | Victorville | CA | E+ | E+ | E+ | 8.5 | -4.70 | 0.0 | 26.3 | 0.0 | 0.0 | 6.4 | 8.4 |
| VICTORIA CITY-COUNTY EMPL FCU | Victoria | TX | C- | C- | C | 7.3 | -6.02 | 0.0 | 37.2 | 0.0 | 0.0 | 10.0 | 15.7 |
| ▼ VICTORIA FCU | Victoria | TX | D | C | D+ | 11.0 | 3.76 | 0.0 | 40.2 | 4.6 | 0.0 | 8.7 | 10.1 |
| ▲ VICTORIA TEACHERS FCU | Victoria | TX | C | C- | C- | 15.9 | 3.34 | 0.0 | 25.6 | 5.1 | 0.0 | 10.0 | 28.2 |
| VICTORY/PIATERER MUTUAL BENEFIT ASSN | East Hartford | CT | D+ | D+ | D+ | 2.3 | -6.29 | 0.0 | 3.6 | 6.6 | 63.9 | 10.0 | 15.3 |
| VIDOR TEACHERS FCU | Vidor | TX | C | C | C | 3.2 | 8.55 | 0.0 | 61.2 | 0.0 | 0.0 | 10.0 | 14.6 |
| VIGO COUNTY FCU | Terre Haute | IN | D- | E+ | D- | 35.0 | -1.62 | 0.0 | 51.4 | 2.6 | 23.3 | 5.2 | 7.2 |
| VILLAGE COMMUNITY CU | Dearborn | MI | C+ | C+ | C+ | 20.8 | 10.41 | 0.9 | 36.2 | 14.0 | 17.8 | 10.0 | 11.1 |
| VILLAGE CU | Des Moines | IA | B- | C+ | C- | 11.6 | 7.69 | 5.5 | 38.7 | 16.7 | 0.0 | 10.0 | 13.2 |
| VIRGINIA BEACH POSTAL FCU | Virginia Beach | VA | C- | C- | D+ | 6.9 | 0.17 | 0.0 | 54.7 | 0.0 | 0.0 | 10.0 | 11.3 |
| ▼ VIRGINIA BEACH SCHOOLS FCU | Virginia Beach | VA | D+ | C+ | C | 87.1 | 2.12 | 4.9 | 20.8 | 6.4 | 23.1 | 5.7 | 7.8 |
| VIRGINIA BOXER FCU | Richmond | VA | C- | C- | C- | 2.8 | -4.47 | 0.0 | 28.9 | 0.0 | 0.0 | 10.0 | 17.5 |
| VIRGINIA COOPERATIVE CU | Virginia | MN | C- | D+ | D | 21.1 | 5.96 | 0.9 | 23.8 | 20.9 | 17.8 | 6.3 | 8.3 |
| VIRGINIA CU INC | Richmond | VA | B+ | B+ | B | 2809.9 | 7.33 | 1.0 | 38.0 | 21.5 | 29.0 | 8.4 | 9.9 |
| ▼ VIRGINIA EDUCATORS CU | Newport News | VA | D+ | C+ | B- | 60.4 | 1.79 | 0.0 | 26.7 | 3.6 | 2.2 | 8.2 | 11.1 |
| VIRGINIA STATE UNIV FCU | South Chesterfield | VA | E | E | E- | 8.6 | -10.85 | 3.1 | 58.2 | 9.2 | 0.0 | 0.8 | 4.1 |
| VIRGINIA TRAILWAYS FCU | Charlottesville | VA | D+ | D- | D- | 2.4 | 1.20 | 0.0 | 51.6 | 0.4 | 0.0 | 9.7 | 10.9 |

| Asset Quality Index | Non-Performing Loans as a % of Total Loans | Non-Performing Loans as a % of Capital | Net Charge-Offs Avg Loans | Profitability Index | Net Income ($Mil) | Return on Assets | Return on Equity | Net Interest Spread | Overhead Efficiency Ratio | Liquidity Index | Liquidity Ratio | Hot Money Ratio | Stability Index |
|---|---|---|---|---|---|---|---|---|---|---|---|---|---|
| 9.8 | 0.22 | 1.1 | -0.06 | 4.3 | 2.7 | 0.65 | 6.44 | 3.45 | 90.1 | 5.0 | 23.5 | 4.5 | 6.8 |
| 10.0 | 0.11 | 0.1 | 0.29 | 1.6 | 0.0 | 0.02 | 0.09 | 1.98 | 97.8 | 5.8 | 39.4 | 0.0 | 6.5 |
| 8.6 | 0.06 | 0.3 | 0.78 | 3.5 | 0.0 | 0.26 | 2.09 | 4.09 | 83.0 | 4.9 | 27.9 | 0.0 | 5.5 |
| 9.9 | 0.56 | 2.1 | 0.47 | 1.8 | 0.3 | 0.31 | 3.29 | 3.04 | 85.4 | 4.2 | 14.6 | 7.7 | 5.3 |
| 5.6 | 0.58 | 5.2 | 0.62 | 2.1 | 0.0 | 0.04 | 0.43 | 4.86 | 95.3 | 3.4 | 16.6 | 8.1 | 3.5 |
| 7.7 | 1.37 | 3.9 | 0.22 | 1.2 | 0.0 | -0.09 | -0.91 | 2.35 | 100.6 | 5.0 | 17.8 | 0.0 | 3.7 |
| 9.7 | 2.89 | 2.0 | 1.50 | 0.0 | -0.1 | -1.50 | -8.48 | 2.05 | 212.9 | 7.5 | 61.6 | 0.0 | 5.0 |
| 0.7 | 4.95 | 36.5 | 0.36 | 0.9 | 0.0 | -0.11 | -0.99 | 3.25 | 76.0 | 3.3 | 10.9 | 6.4 | 5.4 |
| 8.4 | 0.00 | 0.0 | 2.59 | 0.2 | 0.0 | -1.20 | -5.67 | 4.67 | 130.0 | 6.2 | 47.0 | 0.0 | 6.4 |
| 5.2 | 4.28 | 16.3 | 0.52 | 4.2 | 0.0 | 0.94 | 5.29 | 7.11 | 74.0 | 4.8 | 25.9 | 0.0 | 3.7 |
| 7.3 | 1.54 | 7.0 | 0.66 | 2.8 | 0.4 | 0.20 | 1.35 | 2.76 | 87.4 | 4.0 | 24.0 | 3.5 | 7.9 |
| 2.8 | 3.09 | 30.8 | 1.05 | 1.2 | -1.6 | -0.92 | -11.54 | 3.25 | 102.5 | 2.6 | 22.5 | 20.6 | 5.3 |
| 7.5 | 0.50 | 3.6 | 0.07 | 3.0 | 0.1 | 0.34 | 2.19 | 3.20 | 88.9 | 4.1 | 28.4 | 0.0 | 7.1 |
| 6.3 | 3.62 | 9.5 | 0.10 | 4.5 | 0.3 | 0.58 | 4.25 | 2.29 | 70.8 | 4.5 | 16.3 | 8.5 | 7.5 |
| 9.8 | 0.28 | 1.3 | 0.04 | 2.1 | 0.0 | 0.14 | 1.57 | 3.44 | 94.6 | 6.8 | 48.9 | 0.0 | 4.4 |
| 5.5 | 0.82 | 7.4 | 1.03 | 2.2 | 0.3 | 0.05 | 0.66 | 4.47 | 86.5 | 4.2 | 17.4 | 2.3 | 5.3 |
| 9.3 | 0.87 | 2.3 | 0.52 | 4.3 | 0.1 | 0.52 | 3.95 | 3.02 | 81.0 | 5.0 | 40.6 | 3.4 | 6.0 |
| 5.3 | 4.65 | 17.0 | 0.97 | 0.0 | -0.4 | -0.92 | -11.35 | 2.54 | 114.2 | 5.3 | 25.8 | 1.2 | 2.9 |
| 5.9 | 0.70 | 5.4 | 0.84 | 6.0 | 9.1 | 0.82 | 6.93 | 4.35 | 70.0 | 2.2 | 3.8 | 9.7 | 8.2 |
| 5.6 | 1.14 | 10.2 | 0.87 | 2.1 | 0.3 | 0.16 | 2.07 | 3.28 | 81.7 | 2.5 | 8.9 | 16.6 | 4.5 |
| 9.9 | 0.00 | 0.0 | 0.20 | 2.5 | 0.0 | 0.33 | 1.84 | 2.49 | 87.1 | 4.2 | 3.5 | 1.1 | 7.2 |
| 0.3 | 52.83 | 133.3 | 0.00 | 0.6 | 0.0 | -1.49 | -12.70 | 8.33 | 133.3 | 7.7 | 74.6 | 0.0 | 4.2 |
| 9.6 | 0.97 | 2.2 | 0.51 | 1.5 | 0.0 | -0.03 | -0.29 | 1.82 | 92.2 | 5.3 | 53.8 | 4.4 | 6.1 |
| 8.0 | 0.00 | 0.0 | 0.00 | 2.7 | 0.0 | 0.23 | 1.39 | 3.63 | 93.0 | 2.6 | 21.1 | 11.1 | 7.5 |
| 0.0 | 7.40 | 51.6 | 0.00 | 3.8 | 0.0 | 0.58 | 6.46 | 4.10 | 79.7 | 4.6 | 36.4 | 0.0 | 4.2 |
| 9.8 | 0.41 | 1.5 | 0.38 | 2.2 | 0.5 | 0.23 | 1.83 | 3.11 | 93.1 | 4.5 | 17.1 | 0.8 | 6.8 |
| 7.7 | 0.48 | 4.0 | 0.47 | 10.0 | 12.2 | 2.14 | 19.34 | 4.19 | 51.5 | 2.5 | 8.8 | 14.3 | 9.1 |
| 7.1 | 0.42 | 3.8 | 0.62 | 4.0 | 2.6 | 0.48 | 5.33 | 3.71 | 75.4 | 3.4 | 16.2 | 6.5 | 6.8 |
| 7.1 | 0.75 | 5.5 | 0.48 | 6.7 | 22.1 | 1.08 | 10.43 | 2.90 | 67.2 | 2.2 | 8.7 | 16.2 | 8.3 |
| 4.1 | 0.68 | 14.2 | 1.12 | 5.6 | 0.2 | 0.77 | 8.34 | 5.07 | 84.0 | 4.7 | 29.1 | 3.6 | 4.9 |
| 8.3 | 0.49 | 3.6 | 0.57 | 6.2 | 2.8 | 0.83 | 8.77 | 3.87 | 79.6 | 3.6 | 8.8 | 5.6 | 5.7 |
| 8.6 | 0.85 | 2.5 | -0.07 | 3.2 | 0.1 | 0.46 | 5.12 | 2.03 | 76.8 | 5.8 | 47.3 | 0.0 | 4.8 |
| 9.8 | 0.03 | 0.1 | -0.26 | 4.3 | 0.1 | 0.66 | 5.61 | 3.23 | 86.7 | 5.4 | 34.2 | 0.8 | 6.7 |
| 7.3 | 0.71 | 4.9 | 0.53 | 3.8 | 1.6 | 0.48 | 5.39 | 2.77 | 82.6 | 3.3 | 5.6 | 9.9 | 5.8 |
| 5.9 | 1.41 | 12.2 | 0.20 | 3.3 | 2.1 | 0.41 | 4.90 | 2.95 | 83.1 | 3.2 | 8.2 | 5.0 | 6.2 |
| 6.2 | 3.15 | 11.7 | 0.13 | 3.4 | 0.1 | 0.50 | 5.81 | 2.63 | 79.7 | 5.1 | 35.1 | 0.0 | 3.0 |
| 5.6 | 1.05 | 9.2 | 0.20 | 6.4 | 4.3 | 0.94 | 8.08 | 3.72 | 75.4 | 2.6 | 4.2 | 4.7 | 8.0 |
| 9.5 | 0.19 | 0.6 | 0.64 | 2.2 | 0.0 | -0.10 | -1.17 | 12.46 | 94.8 | 6.4 | 76.8 | 17.1 | 4.0 |
| 9.3 | 0.54 | 2.4 | 0.31 | 4.6 | 1.6 | 0.70 | 5.88 | 2.59 | 77.0 | 4.6 | 40.1 | 4.4 | 7.4 |
| 9.6 | 0.36 | 2.2 | 0.19 | 3.1 | 0.8 | 0.23 | 1.46 | 3.66 | 92.3 | 4.3 | 25.2 | 5.4 | 7.3 |
| 7.5 | 0.45 | 4.5 | 0.35 | 4.3 | 2.3 | 0.61 | 5.84 | 3.49 | 81.9 | 2.4 | 8.5 | 10.0 | 6.8 |
| 8.9 | 2.32 | 3.9 | 0.39 | 1.5 | 0.0 | 0.11 | 0.35 | 3.53 | 97.2 | 5.3 | 40.7 | 1.4 | 6.1 |
| 10.0 | 0.58 | 0.5 | 0.30 | 2.2 | 0.0 | 0.16 | 0.70 | 2.07 | 89.9 | 6.1 | 50.1 | 0.0 | 7.0 |
| 6.5 | 1.94 | 6.3 | 0.57 | 0.5 | 0.0 | -0.24 | -2.96 | 2.86 | 104.7 | 5.2 | 18.3 | 0.0 | 2.8 |
| 8.9 | 0.94 | 3.0 | 0.69 | 1.8 | 0.0 | 0.00 | 0.00 | 3.72 | 93.1 | 2.6 | 15.0 | 25.4 | 6.0 |
| 6.3 | 0.69 | 4.1 | 2.06 | 0.8 | -0.1 | -1.39 | -12.74 | 3.63 | 88.1 | 4.5 | 34.8 | 8.4 | 4.7 |
| 10.0 | 0.06 | 0.1 | 0.11 | 2.0 | 0.0 | 0.13 | 0.45 | 2.03 | 91.0 | 5.9 | 66.1 | 0.0 | 7.0 |
| 5.0 | 25.21 | 16.0 | 0.00 | 0.7 | 0.0 | -2.31 | -14.55 | 1.86 | -121.1 | 7.9 | 105.8 | 0.0 | 7.2 |
| 7.8 | 0.47 | 2.3 | 0.00 | 3.5 | 0.0 | 0.39 | 2.57 | 2.80 | 81.8 | 3.8 | 31.7 | 17.6 | 7.0 |
| 4.3 | 1.01 | 11.6 | 0.21 | 1.9 | 0.1 | 0.28 | 5.69 | 2.97 | 90.5 | 4.3 | 14.3 | 0.8 | 1.7 |
| 6.8 | 0.66 | 3.1 | 0.92 | 5.7 | 0.1 | 0.85 | 7.57 | 4.73 | 80.0 | 3.9 | 6.6 | 1.4 | 4.8 |
| 6.8 | 1.59 | 7.1 | 0.50 | 6.2 | 0.1 | 1.03 | 8.21 | 6.39 | 74.7 | 5.7 | 39.6 | 0.0 | 5.7 |
| 5.4 | 1.61 | 7.9 | 1.22 | 4.4 | 0.0 | 0.23 | 2.07 | 5.18 | 78.6 | 4.5 | 16.2 | 0.0 | 3.7 |
| 8.1 | 0.44 | 2.3 | 0.39 | 1.4 | -0.2 | -0.36 | -4.63 | 3.46 | 100.9 | 4.9 | 15.0 | 0.1 | 3.4 |
| 7.5 | 5.06 | 8.7 | 1.15 | 1.4 | 0.0 | -0.05 | -0.27 | 3.67 | 101.4 | 5.0 | 31.7 | 0.0 | 6.1 |
| 7.7 | 0.68 | 3.8 | 0.12 | 3.9 | 0.1 | 0.49 | 5.87 | 3.57 | 90.4 | 5.1 | 25.1 | 0.0 | 3.4 |
| 7.1 | 1.04 | 7.1 | 0.66 | 6.4 | 19.2 | 0.93 | 10.25 | 3.27 | 71.4 | 3.2 | 10.5 | 7.7 | 6.9 |
| 8.0 | 0.83 | 2.6 | 0.76 | 1.7 | -0.1 | -0.14 | -1.26 | 5.11 | 97.0 | 7.6 | 65.2 | 1.4 | 5.0 |
| 0.7 | 4.07 | 45.4 | 4.16 | 0.0 | -0.2 | -2.30 | -48.09 | 7.32 | 91.6 | 4.3 | 16.6 | 0.0 | 0.0 |
| 2.8 | 3.39 | 16.5 | 0.52 | 3.4 | 0.0 | 0.45 | 4.09 | 6.82 | 91.9 | 6.4 | 49.9 | 0.0 | 5.0 |

| Name | City | State | Rating | 2014 Rating | 2013 Rating | Total Assets ($Mil) | One Year Asset Growth | Commercial Loans | Consumer Loans | Mortgage Loans | Securities | Capitalization Index | Net Worth Ratio |
|---|---|---|---|---|---|---|---|---|---|---|---|---|---|
| VIRGINIA UNITED METHODIST CU INC | Glen Allen | VA | D- | D- | D | 16.6 | -8.08 | 12.2 | 38.6 | 0.0 | 4.5 | 6.7 | 8.7 |
| VIRIVA COMMUNITY CU | Warminster | PA | D | D+ | D+ | 62.2 | -5.80 | 13.9 | 12.1 | 23.6 | 25.4 | 10.0 | 11.9 |
| VISION FINANCIAL FCU | Durham | NC | B- | C+ | C+ | 54.4 | 22.29 | 0.0 | 63.3 | 0.0 | 0.0 | 10.0 | 11.3 |
| VISION ONE CU | Sacramento | CA | B+ | B+ | B+ | 66.2 | 10.12 | 45.0 | 0.0 | 1.2 | 0.0 | 10.0 | 13.6 |
| VISIONARY FCU | Bridgeville | PA | D | D+ | D- | 35.6 | 6.76 | 0.5 | 20.5 | 0.0 | 4.5 | 5.3 | 7.3 |
| VISIONS FCU | Endicott | NY | A- | A- | A- | 3457.5 | 2.52 | 12.6 | 16.7 | 35.8 | 30.0 | 10.0 | 13.2 |
| VITAL FCU | Spartanburg | SC | B- | B- | B- | 41.3 | 1.83 | 3.5 | 56.8 | 3.5 | 0.0 | 9.0 | 10.4 |
| VITELCO EMPL FCU | Charlotte Amalie | VI | C | C | B- | 2.3 | -0.83 | 0.0 | 42.8 | 0.0 | 0.0 | 10.0 | 19.3 |
| VONS EMPL FCU | El Monte | CA | A+ | A+ | A+ | 452.7 | 6.41 | 0.3 | 23.4 | 26.2 | 3.2 | 10.0 | 21.0 |
| ▲ VOYAGE FCU | Sioux Falls | SD | B- | C+ | C+ | 79.8 | 6.57 | 4.4 | 37.1 | 23.8 | 2.5 | 8.7 | 10.2 |
| ▼ VUE COMMUNITY CU | Bismarck | ND | B- | B | B+ | 55.4 | 7.34 | 6.3 | 8.4 | 23.6 | 23.5 | 9.2 | 10.5 |
| VULCRAFT EMPL FCU | Saint Joe | IN | C | C | C | 3.3 | 9.59 | 0.0 | 45.5 | 0.0 | 0.0 | 10.0 | 13.3 |
| VYSTAR CU | Jacksonville | FL | B+ | B+ | B | 5597.8 | 8.66 | 2.9 | 29.1 | 34.5 | 19.5 | 7.4 | 9.3 |
| W N M H CU | Winfield | KS | C+ | C+ | C+ | 1.5 | -4.04 | 0.0 | 83.2 | 0.0 | 0.0 | 10.0 | 13.8 |
| W S P CU | Waupun | WI | D+ | D+ | D+ | 3.2 | -3.57 | 0.0 | 32.0 | 0.0 | 0.0 | 10.0 | 15.1 |
| W T COMMUNITY FCU | Cincinnati | OH | D | D | D+ | 3.3 | 0.62 | 0.0 | 59.0 | 0.0 | 0.0 | 10.0 | 11.3 |
| W T N M ATLANTIC FCU | Denver City | TX | D | D | D+ | 1.8 | 6.31 | 0.0 | 34.4 | 0.0 | 0.0 | 10.0 | 16.8 |
| W-BEE FCU | Wilkes-Barre | PA | C- | C- | C | 38.5 | 0.00 | 0.0 | 4.5 | 0.0 | 33.8 | 5.4 | 7.4 |
| WABELLCO FCU | Washington | PA | D+ | D+ | D | 11.7 | -5.72 | 0.0 | 11.7 | 0.0 | 6.9 | 9.3 | 10.5 |
| WACO FCU | Waco | TX | D | D- | D- | 14.8 | 6.46 | 0.0 | 29.4 | 2.3 | 0.0 | 6.0 | 8.0 |
| WACONIZED FCU | Waco | TX | D | D | C- | 4.6 | -2.64 | 0.0 | 38.0 | 0.0 | 0.0 | 10.0 | 23.5 |
| WADENA FCU | Wadena | MN | B- | B- | B | 13.6 | 2.21 | 0.0 | 16.5 | 2.1 | 0.0 | 10.0 | 22.1 |
| WAIALUA FCU | Waialua | HI | C+ | C+ | C+ | 48.6 | -6.44 | 0.0 | 8.6 | 5.0 | 3.0 | 10.0 | 13.1 |
| WAILUKU FCU | Kahului | HI | A- | B+ | B+ | 46.9 | 6.64 | 7.8 | 13.0 | 16.3 | 6.6 | 10.0 | 15.1 |
| ▼ WAKARUSA VALLEY CU | Lawrence | KS | D | C- | C- | 3.6 | -1.82 | 0.0 | 50.0 | 0.0 | 0.0 | 8.5 | 11.8 |
| WAKEFERN FCU | Elizabeth | NJ | D+ | D+ | C- | 9.1 | 8.72 | 0.0 | 7.5 | 1.1 | 21.4 | 10.0 | 22.6 |
| WAKEFIELD TOWN EMPL FCU | Wakefield | MA | C | C | C | 3.6 | -1.23 | 0.0 | 27.8 | 0.0 | 0.0 | 10.0 | 14.9 |
| WAKOTA FCU | South Saint Paul | MN | C | C- | C | 22.6 | 1.61 | 0.0 | 54.0 | 6.6 | 1.1 | 8.7 | 10.1 |
| WALKER COUNTY EDUCATORS FCU | Chickamauga | GA | B- | B- | B- | 10.2 | 5.72 | 0.0 | 44.9 | 3.3 | 0.0 | 10.0 | 28.3 |
| WALKER COUNTY FCU | Huntsville | TX | B- | C+ | C+ | 28.1 | 2.68 | 0.0 | 44.2 | 0.0 | 3.9 | 9.6 | 10.7 |
| WALLED LAKE SCHOOL EMPL FCU | Walled Lake | MI | C | C+ | C | 96.5 | 0.54 | 0.1 | 9.8 | 19.1 | 43.6 | 10.0 | 11.5 |
| WALLINGFORD MUNICIPAL FCU | Wallingford | CT | E | E | D- | 18.3 | 6.33 | 0.0 | 26.6 | 0.7 | 2.7 | 4.2 | 6.2 |
| WALTHAM MUNICIPAL EMPL CU | Waltham | MA | D+ | D+ | D+ | 8.8 | 6.24 | 0.0 | 19.2 | 0.0 | 0.0 | 10.0 | 18.0 |
| ▼ WALTON COUNTY TEACHERS FCU | Defuniak Springs | FL | D+ | C- | C+ | 18.7 | 12.32 | 0.0 | 34.9 | 2.5 | 0.0 | 6.5 | 8.6 |
| WANIGAS CU | Saginaw | MI | A | A | A- | 299.9 | 1.90 | 0.0 | 23.6 | 37.6 | 23.5 | 10.0 | 13.0 |
| ▲ WARD COUNTY CU | Monahans | TX | D+ | D | D+ | 15.4 | -4.89 | 0.8 | 26.1 | 0.0 | 59.4 | 7.4 | 9.2 |
| ▼ WARD FCU | Philadelphia | PA | D- | D | D+ | <1 | -1.92 | 0.0 | 29.4 | 0.0 | 0.0 | 5.2 | 7.2 |
| WARDEN CAPTREE FCU | Brooklyn | NY | D | D | D | <1 | -5.10 | 0.0 | 10.8 | 0.0 | 0.0 | 10.0 | 33.5 |
| WARE COUNTY SCHOOL EMPL FCU | Waycross | GA | E+ | E+ | E+ | 4.4 | -1.02 | 0.0 | 30.9 | 3.2 | 0.0 | 6.3 | 8.3 |
| WARREN CU | Waterloo | IA | C | C | C | 4.1 | -8.84 | 0.0 | 18.9 | 0.0 | 0.0 | 10.0 | 24.6 |
| WARREN FCU | Cheyenne | WY | B+ | B | B- | 573.2 | 9.10 | 7.5 | 40.0 | 18.3 | 2.0 | 8.2 | 9.8 |
| WARREN MUNICIPAL FCU | Warren | MI | E | E+ | E+ | 16.7 | -0.21 | 0.0 | 15.8 | 9.5 | 59.6 | 5.2 | 7.2 |
| ▲ WASATCH PEAKS FCU | Ogden | UT | B- | C+ | C+ | 276.9 | 5.41 | 10.9 | 26.3 | 28.0 | 5.5 | 8.8 | 10.2 |
| WASHINGTON AREA TEACHERS FCU | Washington | PA | C- | C | B- | 63.1 | 2.69 | 1.0 | 13.7 | 10.5 | 38.1 | 7.9 | 9.8 |
| WASHINGTON COUNTY TEACHERS FCU | Hagerstown | MD | B+ | B+ | B+ | 58.7 | 0.08 | 0.0 | 17.6 | 15.1 | 0.0 | 10.0 | 14.5 |
| WASHINGTON EDUCATIONAL ASSN FCU | Franklinton | LA | D | D | D+ | <1 | 2.90 | 0.0 | 49.6 | 0.0 | 0.0 | 10.0 | 14.2 |
| WASHINGTON GAS LIGHT FCU | Springfield | VA | C | C | C | 94.5 | 3.53 | 0.0 | 22.9 | 2.7 | 45.8 | 10.0 | 17.1 |
| WASHINGTON STATE EMPL CU | Olympia | WA | A- | A- | A- | 2331.5 | 8.81 | 9.2 | 37.7 | 21.2 | 9.1 | 9.5 | 10.7 |
| WASHINGTON TYPOGRAPHIC FCU | Washington | DC | D | D | D | 3.5 | 4.96 | 0.0 | 50.5 | 0.0 | 0.0 | 10.0 | 11.4 |
| WASHTENAW FCU | Ypsilanti | MI | C- | C- | C- | 37.0 | 1.57 | 1.3 | 22.4 | 21.4 | 0.0 | 6.9 | 8.9 |
| WAT FCU | Williamsport | PA | E- | E- | E- | 10.9 | -0.64 | 0.0 | 25.6 | 0.0 | 42.3 | 1.3 | 4.4 |
| WATER AND POWER COMMUNITY CU | Los Angeles | CA | B | B- | B | 552.7 | 5.60 | 1.0 | 13.8 | 25.1 | 43.8 | 6.6 | 8.6 |
| WATER-LIGHT CU | Superior | WI | D+ | D+ | C- | 1.4 | 4.90 | 0.0 | 29.4 | 0.0 | 0.0 | 10.0 | 14.0 |
| WATERBURY CONNECTICUT TEACHER FCU | Middlebury | CT | B+ | B+ | B+ | 227.9 | -1.91 | 0.0 | 28.4 | 2.8 | 0.0 | 10.0 | 13.0 |
| WATERBURY POLICE FCU | Waterbury | CT | D+ | D+ | D | 5.3 | 0.09 | 0.0 | 42.9 | 0.0 | 0.0 | 10.0 | 17.4 |
| WATERBURY POSTAL EMPL FCU | Waterbury | CT | C | C | C | 11.1 | -1.61 | 0.0 | 15.1 | 0.0 | 0.0 | 10.0 | 20.2 |
| WATERFRONT FCU | Seattle | WA | C- | D+ | D | 56.6 | 0.67 | 0.0 | 31.5 | 6.8 | 37.5 | 5.4 | 7.5 |
| WATERLOO FIREMENS CU | Waterloo | IA | C- | C- | C- | 2.0 | -0.05 | 0.0 | 72.4 | 0.0 | 0.0 | 10.0 | 12.3 |
| WATERTOWN MUNICIPAL CU | Watertown | MA | D | D+ | C | 12.0 | -1.27 | 0.0 | 4.3 | 15.0 | 9.5 | 10.0 | 28.0 |
| WATERTOWN POSTAL FCU | Watertown | NY | D | C- | C- | 8.4 | 6.94 | 0.0 | 25.6 | 0.0 | 0.0 | 8.3 | 9.9 |

| Asset Quality Index | Non-Performing Loans as a % of Total Loans | as a % of Capital | Net Charge-Offs Avg Loans | Profitability Index | Net Income ($Mil) | Return on Assets | Return on Equity | Net Interest Spread | Overhead Efficiency Ratio | Liquidity Index | Liquidity Ratio | Hot Money Ratio | Stability Index |
|---|---|---|---|---|---|---|---|---|---|---|---|---|---|
| 5.3 | 1.53 | 9.6 | -0.18 | 0.8 | -0.1 | -0.46 | -5.55 | 3.66 | 109.7 | 4.1 | 17.0 | 6.6 | 2.6 |
| 5.6 | 4.03 | 15.6 | 0.00 | 0.6 | -0.3 | -0.60 | -5.40 | 3.58 | 110.5 | 4.7 | 18.0 | 2.4 | 4.6 |
| 2.7 | 3.47 | 23.8 | 0.84 | 5.4 | 0.3 | 0.87 | 7.49 | 4.37 | 75.6 | 2.8 | 13.4 | 15.1 | 5.3 |
| 5.9 | 0.09 | 0.5 | 0.00 | 9.0 | 0.6 | 1.23 | 9.04 | 4.92 | 75.0 | 1.7 | 19.5 | 39.9 | 8.5 |
| 6.2 | 1.53 | 9.0 | 0.74 | 1.2 | 0.0 | -0.03 | -0.47 | 3.16 | 86.6 | 5.7 | 34.0 | 0.3 | 2.2 |
| 7.0 | 1.66 | 8.3 | 0.20 | 5.4 | 20.4 | 0.79 | 6.31 | 2.37 | 65.4 | 3.2 | 7.2 | 7.9 | 9.4 |
| 7.1 | 0.38 | 2.6 | 0.35 | 8.0 | 0.4 | 1.24 | 12.45 | 4.56 | 79.3 | 3.9 | 14.6 | 6.2 | 5.1 |
| 8.5 | 1.54 | 3.3 | 0.14 | 3.9 | 0.0 | 0.50 | 2.44 | 8.75 | 91.8 | 7.1 | 70.1 | 0.0 | 7.8 |
| 10.0 | 0.40 | 1.0 | 0.47 | 8.8 | 4.3 | 1.28 | 6.17 | 3.42 | 73.6 | 3.5 | 45.4 | 19.4 | 8.3 |
| 5.8 | 0.92 | 6.8 | 0.36 | 4.9 | 0.4 | 0.72 | 7.19 | 3.77 | 79.9 | 3.4 | 8.7 | 1.0 | 4.6 |
| 6.8 | 1.10 | 5.0 | 0.07 | 3.8 | 0.2 | 0.45 | 4.25 | 3.03 | 83.5 | 4.5 | 29.1 | 1.5 | 5.5 |
| 8.4 | 0.00 | 0.0 | 0.00 | 4.3 | 0.0 | 0.65 | 4.71 | 3.85 | 77.6 | 5.8 | 41.0 | 0.0 | 7.3 |
| 9.0 | 0.32 | 2.6 | 0.36 | 5.4 | 30.6 | 0.74 | 7.88 | 2.61 | 77.0 | 3.9 | 25.6 | 8.8 | 7.6 |
| 4.7 | 1.53 | 9.3 | -0.23 | 10.0 | 0.0 | 1.68 | 12.24 | 5.58 | 75.3 | 3.1 | 13.5 | 0.0 | 8.9 |
| 6.4 | 3.68 | 8.6 | 0.82 | 2.2 | 0.0 | 0.08 | 0.55 | 1.85 | 73.2 | 6.3 | 66.1 | 0.0 | 6.0 |
| 5.6 | 1.76 | 11.4 | 0.00 | 1.2 | 0.0 | 0.08 | 0.73 | 3.13 | 97.5 | 4.0 | 11.6 | 0.0 | 4.8 |
| 8.6 | 1.44 | 3.4 | 0.19 | 0.2 | 0.0 | -0.37 | -2.17 | 3.90 | 108.0 | 4.2 | 62.9 | 16.5 | 5.2 |
| 9.5 | 0.99 | 2.0 | 0.00 | 2.0 | 0.0 | 0.08 | 1.02 | 1.85 | 92.3 | 7.6 | 52.1 | 0.0 | 3.2 |
| 6.5 | 1.69 | 5.8 | 0.00 | 1.6 | 0.0 | 0.03 | 0.33 | 2.71 | 101.0 | 4.6 | 14.2 | 0.0 | 4.2 |
| 8.1 | 0.70 | 3.3 | 0.18 | 2.5 | 0.0 | 0.27 | 3.30 | 3.74 | 95.6 | 4.9 | 29.0 | 8.9 | 2.3 |
| 8.3 | 2.21 | 4.7 | 0.36 | 0.3 | 0.0 | -0.64 | -2.69 | 4.90 | 109.6 | 4.1 | 6.3 | 0.0 | 5.7 |
| 9.9 | 2.38 | 2.2 | 0.38 | 4.3 | 0.1 | 0.65 | 2.97 | 2.70 | 71.3 | 6.2 | 41.9 | 0.0 | 6.9 |
| 8.9 | 1.98 | 3.3 | 0.03 | 2.9 | 0.1 | 0.25 | 2.07 | 1.79 | 76.0 | 5.0 | 25.4 | 0.0 | 5.6 |
| 7.5 | 2.05 | 7.7 | 0.05 | 9.8 | 0.6 | 1.71 | 11.36 | 3.88 | 70.7 | 3.4 | 12.3 | 14.5 | 8.3 |
| 4.2 | 3.16 | 14.6 | 0.55 | 0.5 | 0.0 | -0.77 | -6.36 | 2.69 | 129.3 | 3.2 | 34.0 | 17.2 | 6.4 |
| 9.8 | 1.22 | 0.5 | 0.00 | 1.0 | 0.0 | -0.06 | -0.26 | 1.35 | 103.7 | 5.7 | 25.1 | 0.0 | 6.6 |
| 9.7 | 0.90 | 1.6 | 0.93 | 2.2 | 0.0 | 0.18 | 1.25 | 3.06 | 90.9 | 4.9 | 25.5 | 0.0 | 7.4 |
| 5.2 | 0.68 | 4.7 | 0.87 | 6.4 | 0.2 | 1.01 | 10.31 | 4.41 | 75.3 | 3.5 | 16.4 | 2.1 | 4.3 |
| 9.5 | 0.95 | 2.0 | 0.37 | 6.3 | 0.0 | 0.59 | 2.04 | 3.65 | 80.2 | 4.7 | 47.1 | 2.8 | 8.9 |
| 6.7 | 1.17 | 5.1 | 0.59 | 5.7 | 0.2 | 0.91 | 8.65 | 4.28 | 79.2 | 5.4 | 41.7 | 7.6 | 5.1 |
| 10.0 | 0.64 | 1.7 | -0.03 | 2.7 | 0.2 | 0.26 | 2.32 | 2.28 | 89.5 | 4.5 | 16.2 | 4.8 | 6.4 |
| 8.2 | 0.99 | 4.2 | 0.03 | 1.0 | 0.0 | 0.00 | 0.00 | 2.02 | 97.9 | 4.9 | 16.9 | 0.0 | 0.7 |
| 10.0 | 0.00 | 0.0 | 0.00 | 0.8 | 0.0 | -0.08 | -0.42 | 2.23 | 104.8 | 5.8 | 32.7 | 0.0 | 6.8 |
| 4.9 | 3.17 | 15.9 | 0.38 | 1.7 | 0.0 | -0.18 | -2.02 | 5.71 | 103.0 | 6.7 | 49.8 | 0.0 | 3.4 |
| 8.8 | 0.65 | 3.3 | 0.47 | 7.4 | 2.4 | 1.06 | 8.30 | 3.61 | 72.6 | 3.6 | 6.4 | 3.0 | 8.4 |
| 8.3 | 0.09 | 0.3 | 0.05 | 2.3 | 0.0 | 0.18 | 2.08 | 3.42 | 96.1 | 3.8 | 8.9 | 13.8 | 4.2 |
| 10.0 | 0.00 | 0.0 | 0.00 | 0.2 | 0.0 | -0.94 | -11.11 | 8.60 | 133.3 | 7.8 | 73.9 | 0.0 | 2.8 |
| 2.3 | 84.38 | 25.7 | 0.00 | 0.0 | 0.0 | -0.65 | -1.99 | 0.91 | 200.0 | 8.2 | 134.9 | 0.0 | 4.8 |
| 8.5 | 0.21 | 1.3 | 0.38 | 2.0 | 0.0 | 0.03 | 0.37 | 3.12 | 100.0 | 3.4 | 38.9 | 25.4 | 1.7 |
| 9.3 | 0.83 | 1.0 | 1.71 | 4.3 | 0.0 | 0.62 | 2.67 | 3.52 | 81.6 | 5.2 | 30.8 | 0.0 | 5.6 |
| 5.4 | 0.96 | 8.8 | 0.62 | 8.6 | 5.2 | 1.26 | 13.03 | 4.05 | 67.0 | 1.6 | 7.1 | 18.7 | 7.5 |
| 5.0 | 3.18 | 13.1 | 0.33 | 1.1 | 0.0 | -0.05 | -0.77 | 2.93 | 102.4 | 4.7 | 7.7 | 0.0 | 1.0 |
| 8.8 | 0.21 | 1.6 | 0.28 | 4.7 | 1.3 | 0.66 | 6.77 | 3.89 | 81.6 | 3.0 | 11.1 | 11.7 | 5.5 |
| 6.2 | 1.69 | 7.0 | -0.01 | 0.6 | -0.2 | -0.44 | -4.53 | 2.74 | 115.9 | 5.1 | 20.1 | 3.2 | 4.5 |
| 9.7 | 0.77 | 2.0 | 0.35 | 3.6 | 0.2 | 0.41 | 2.89 | 2.54 | 72.3 | 6.9 | 55.5 | 1.4 | 6.9 |
| 4.6 | 2.82 | 9.7 | 2.78 | 1.5 | 0.0 | 0.14 | 0.95 | 6.03 | 92.9 | 5.2 | 21.1 | 0.0 | 5.3 |
| 9.7 | 1.08 | 2.4 | 0.79 | 1.9 | 0.0 | 0.02 | 0.13 | 3.11 | 89.3 | 4.1 | 21.9 | 13.1 | 6.1 |
| 7.0 | 0.57 | 5.0 | 0.98 | 7.9 | 19.3 | 1.13 | 10.80 | 4.56 | 65.0 | 3.7 | 12.4 | 2.7 | 7.9 |
| 4.4 | 3.96 | 16.3 | -0.92 | 1.6 | 0.0 | 0.28 | 2.42 | 3.76 | 123.7 | 5.4 | 30.7 | 0.0 | 5.0 |
| 7.7 | 1.21 | 6.7 | 0.59 | 2.2 | 0.0 | 0.05 | 0.56 | 3.73 | 94.0 | 4.5 | 13.9 | 1.7 | 3.7 |
| 0.3 | 6.41 | 51.4 | 4.60 | 0.0 | -0.3 | -3.29 | -76.43 | 3.27 | 99.3 | 6.1 | 31.7 | 0.0 | 1.5 |
| 8.0 | 1.23 | 5.5 | 0.42 | 4.4 | 3.2 | 0.80 | 9.26 | 3.03 | 76.2 | 4.7 | 11.9 | 3.4 | 6.0 |
| 7.1 | 2.70 | 6.8 | 0.00 | 1.4 | 0.0 | 0.10 | 0.69 | 3.29 | 93.3 | 5.1 | 39.9 | 0.0 | 7.0 |
| 9.4 | 0.66 | 3.3 | 0.18 | 4.7 | 1.3 | 0.74 | 5.98 | 2.90 | 72.0 | 4.0 | 34.3 | 3.3 | 7.8 |
| 5.0 | 6.52 | 18.4 | 0.29 | 1.1 | 0.0 | -0.19 | -1.14 | 5.85 | 105.7 | 5.9 | 49.5 | 0.0 | 5.4 |
| 8.5 | 5.38 | 4.7 | 0.20 | 1.8 | 0.0 | 0.10 | 0.48 | 1.77 | 87.3 | 6.1 | 71.6 | 0.0 | 6.1 |
| 9.2 | 0.02 | 0.5 | 0.67 | 3.6 | 0.1 | 0.30 | 4.20 | 3.77 | 86.2 | 4.7 | 21.9 | 0.9 | 2.1 |
| 8.3 | 0.00 | 0.0 | 0.00 | 1.9 | 0.0 | 0.20 | 1.61 | 2.35 | 93.8 | 4.0 | 18.9 | 0.0 | 6.1 |
| 10.0 | 0.00 | 0.0 | 0.00 | 0.0 | -0.1 | -1.00 | -3.56 | 2.15 | 161.9 | 7.1 | 65.1 | 0.0 | 6.9 |
| 7.2 | 1.71 | 4.8 | 2.28 | 1.4 | 0.0 | -0.10 | -0.96 | 1.62 | 65.7 | 5.0 | 27.0 | 0.0 | 4.4 |

| Name | City | State | Rating | 2014 Rating | 2013 Rating | Total Assets ($Mil) | One Year Asset Growth | Commercial Loans | Consumer Loans | Mortgage Loans | Securities | Capitalization Index | Net Worth Ratio |
|---|---|---|---|---|---|---|---|---|---|---|---|---|---|
| ▲ WATSONVILLE HOSPITAL FCU | Watsonville | CA | C | C | C | 12.2 | 1.51 | 0.0 | 24.1 | 0.0 | 0.0 | 10.0 | 11.8 |
| WAUKEGAN MUNICIPAL EMPL CU | Waukegan | IL | C+ | C | D+ | <1 | -2.86 | 0.0 | 86.8 | 0.0 | 0.0 | 10.0 | 15.7 |
| WAUNA FCU | Clatskanie | OR | B | B | B | 187.8 | 10.59 | 8.5 | 28.2 | 34.2 | 17.4 | 6.5 | 8.5 |
| ▲ WAVE FCU | Warwick | RI | C- | C- | D+ | 106.8 | -1.95 | 1.2 | 10.7 | 27.9 | 0.5 | 10.0 | 11.8 |
| WAWA EMPL CU | Media | PA | D+ | D | C- | 14.9 | 4.45 | 0.0 | 30.1 | 0.0 | 0.0 | 7.3 | 9.2 |
| WAY CU | New Knoxville | OH | D+ | D+ | D+ | 14.3 | 18.86 | 0.0 | 0.0 | 0.0 | 72.4 | 6.3 | 8.4 |
| WAYCOSE FCU | Huntington | WV | C- | C- | C- | 2.7 | -0.04 | 0.0 | 58.3 | 0.0 | 0.0 | 10.0 | 16.0 |
| WAYLAND TEMPLE BAPTIST FCU | Philadelphia | PA | C | C- | C- | <1 | 3.47 | 0.0 | 22.5 | 0.0 | 0.0 | 10.0 | 15.3 |
| WAYNE COUNTY COMMUNITY FCU | Smithville | OH | D+ | C- | C- | 46.2 | -0.20 | 0.6 | 14.8 | 5.5 | 59.6 | 6.1 | 8.2 |
| ▼ WAYNE COUNTY FCU | Richmond | IN | D- | D | D+ | 10.8 | 3.62 | 0.0 | 23.5 | 6.2 | 0.0 | 6.6 | 8.6 |
| WAYNE-WESTLAND FCU | Westland | MI | B- | B- | B- | 84.7 | 6.96 | 0.9 | 21.5 | 10.8 | 43.0 | 8.3 | 10.1 |
| WAYNESBORO EMPL CU INC | Waynesboro | VA | E+ | E+ | E+ | 3.9 | -4.39 | 0.0 | 51.3 | 0.0 | 0.0 | 6.8 | 8.8 |
| WBH EMPL FCU | Paducah | KY | C+ | B- | B- | 13.4 | -2.58 | 0.0 | 31.9 | 1.0 | 0.0 | 10.0 | 15.1 |
| WBRT FCU | Port Allen | LA | C- | C- | D+ | 2.4 | 0.85 | 0.0 | 58.8 | 0.0 | 0.0 | 10.0 | 26.2 |
| WCG EMPL CU | Martin | TN | C | C | C | 1.0 | -3.43 | 0.0 | 53.2 | 0.0 | 0.0 | 10.0 | 17.8 |
| ▲ WCLA CU | Olympia | WA | B- | C | C- | 43.3 | 10.46 | 77.1 | 1.3 | 9.6 | 9.9 | 10.0 | 11.5 |
| WCU CU | Decatur | AL | C- | C | C | 23.1 | 5.07 | 0.0 | 38.9 | 8.8 | 19.5 | 8.0 | 9.6 |
| WE FLORIDA FINANCIAL | Margate | FL | A- | A- | B+ | 458.0 | 11.27 | 2.5 | 40.0 | 12.2 | 0.2 | 9.8 | 10.9 |
| WEA CU | Madison | WI | D+ | C- | C- | 27.1 | -1.52 | 6.7 | 23.2 | 23.8 | 5.8 | 9.6 | 10.7 |
| WEATHERHEAD CC FCU | Columbia City | IN | D+ | C- | C | 12.5 | 8.23 | 0.0 | 40.1 | 0.0 | 0.0 | 9.6 | 10.8 |
| WEBER STATE FCU | Ogden | UT | B- | C+ | C+ | 99.5 | 0.87 | 8.9 | 27.7 | 39.7 | 6.6 | 8.0 | 9.7 |
| WEBSTER CITY MUNICIPAL CU | Webster City | IA | C- | C | C- | <1 | -2.48 | 0.0 | 30.5 | 0.0 | 0.0 | 10.0 | 32.0 |
| WEBSTER FCU | Webster | NY | D- | D- | D- | 14.8 | 4.78 | 0.0 | 35.8 | 8.1 | 0.0 | 6.0 | 8.0 |
| WEBSTER FIRST FCU | Worcester | MA | A | A | A | 821.4 | 28.68 | 9.9 | 6.5 | 59.1 | 15.5 | 10.0 | 18.5 |
| ▼ WEBSTER UNITED FCU | Minden | LA | D | D+ | D+ | 4.0 | -2.12 | 0.0 | 64.9 | 0.0 | 0.0 | 10.0 | 20.3 |
| WEE FCU | Parkersburg | WV | B- | B- | B- | 16.8 | 7.79 | 0.9 | 22.2 | 17.7 | 0.0 | 9.8 | 10.9 |
| WELCOME FCU | Morrisville | NC | C | B- | C+ | 87.2 | 0.19 | 0.0 | 28.3 | 11.3 | 7.5 | 10.0 | 12.4 |
| WELD SCHOOLS CU | Greeley | CO | C | C | C | 63.4 | 5.05 | 0.0 | 23.9 | 9.6 | 0.0 | 6.3 | 8.3 |
| WELLESLEY MUNICIPAL EMPL FCU | Wellesley | MA | C- | C | C | 28.7 | 1.86 | 0.0 | 17.5 | 12.5 | 0.0 | 10.0 | 11.2 |
| WELLSPRING FCU | Bridge City | TX | C | C | C | 40.1 | 6.30 | 0.0 | 52.3 | 10.6 | 0.0 | 7.2 | 9.2 |
| ▼ WENATCHEE VALLEY FCU | East Wenatchee | WA | D | C- | C | 29.4 | -2.09 | 0.0 | 38.9 | 3.6 | 9.2 | 6.3 | 8.3 |
| WEOKIE CU | Oklahoma City | OK | B+ | B+ | A- | 1014.1 | 0.75 | 7.8 | 20.2 | 29.5 | 35.4 | 9.7 | 10.8 |
| WEPAWAUG-FLAGG FCU | Hamden | CT | B- | B- | B- | 108.3 | 36.62 | 2.1 | 10.4 | 13.1 | 45.0 | 9.3 | 10.5 |
| WEPCO FCU | Bloomington | MD | C+ | C+ | C+ | 199.0 | 0.39 | 1.8 | 46.6 | 16.7 | 17.4 | 9.1 | 10.4 |
| WES CU | Willoughby | OH | D | D- | D+ | 10.9 | 2.04 | 0.0 | 28.3 | 0.0 | 51.4 | 9.0 | 10.3 |
| WESCOM CENTRAL CU | Pasadena | CA | B- | B- | B- | 3238.8 | 15.83 | 2.2 | 14.2 | 26.7 | 36.8 | 4.9 | 7.5 |
| WESLA FCU | Shreveport | LA | D | D | D+ | 78.9 | -0.53 | 0.0 | 16.6 | 3.8 | 0.0 | 10.0 | 16.5 |
| WESLEY AME ZION FCU | Philadelphia | PA | D | D | C- | <1 | 3.70 | 0.0 | 0.0 | 0.0 | 0.0 | 10.0 | 28.6 |
| ▼ WESLEY MEDICAL CU | Wichita | KS | D | D+ | C- | 5.7 | -1.32 | 0.0 | 28.9 | 0.0 | 0.0 | 10.0 | 11.5 |
| ▼ WEST BRANCH VALLEY FCU | Williamsport | PA | D | C- | D+ | 36.0 | -0.20 | 0.1 | 19.3 | 22.1 | 11.9 | 5.5 | 7.6 |
| WEST COAST FCU | Clearwater | FL | D+ | D | D+ | 14.7 | -1.52 | 0.0 | 36.7 | 0.4 | 19.7 | 8.3 | 9.8 |
| ▼ WEST COAST FEDERAL EMPL CU | Sarasota | FL | C- | C+ | C | 30.8 | 3.26 | 0.0 | 14.6 | 8.9 | 26.0 | 10.0 | 12.8 |
| WEST COMMUNITY CU | O'Fallon | MO | B- | B- | B- | 169.4 | 6.61 | 10.5 | 28.9 | 25.1 | 2.0 | 6.6 | 8.6 |
| WEST DENVER COMMUNITY CU | Denver | CO | C- | C- | C- | 9.2 | 1.34 | 0.0 | 26.0 | 5.7 | 0.0 | 10.0 | 12.4 |
| WEST FINANCIAL CU | Medina | MN | C | C | D+ | 24.8 | 3.46 | 4.7 | 17.4 | 38.8 | 0.0 | 8.1 | 9.8 |
| ▼ WEST HOLMES SCHOOL EMPL CU INC | Millersburg | OH | C | C+ | C+ | <1 | -2.25 | 0.0 | 35.9 | 0.0 | 0.0 | 10.0 | 15.1 |
| WEST HUDSON TEACHERS FCU | North Arlington | NJ | D | D | D+ | 7.1 | 1.01 | 0.0 | 17.1 | 0.0 | 0.0 | 9.0 | 10.3 |
| WEST JEFFERSON FCU | Marrero | LA | E+ | E+ | E+ | 5.9 | 0.63 | 0.0 | 50.0 | 0.0 | 0.0 | 4.3 | 6.3 |
| WEST MAUI COMMUNITY FCU | Lahaina | HI | C- | C- | C- | 35.7 | 2.34 | 0.0 | 10.9 | 0.0 | 24.3 | 10.0 | 22.7 |
| WEST METRO SCHOOLS CU | Hopkins | MN | B+ | B+ | B+ | 25.8 | -1.86 | 0.0 | 30.6 | 3.7 | 0.0 | 10.0 | 19.3 |
| WEST MICHIGAN CU | Grand Rapids | MI | A | A | A | 142.7 | 4.17 | 0.0 | 28.2 | 9.5 | 25.2 | 10.0 | 16.9 |
| WEST MICHIGAN POSTAL SERVICE FCU | Muskegon | MI | E+ | E+ | E+ | 6.0 | -2.84 | 0.0 | 41.6 | 0.0 | 0.0 | 6.1 | 8.1 |
| WEST MONROE FCU | West Monroe | LA | D+ | C- | C- | 4.8 | 2.30 | 0.0 | 31.7 | 9.3 | 0.0 | 9.7 | 10.8 |
| ▲ WEST OAHU COMMUNITY FCU | Waianae | HI | C+ | D+ | D+ | 34.3 | 2.27 | 0.0 | 15.9 | 4.2 | 16.0 | 10.0 | 13.6 |
| WEST ORANGE MUNICIPAL FCU | West Orange | NJ | E+ | E+ | E+ | 6.9 | -2.02 | 0.9 | 50.3 | 0.9 | 0.0 | 6.9 | 8.9 |
| WEST PENN P&P FCU | Beaver | PA | D+ | C- | C- | 11.4 | -4.95 | 0.0 | 21.0 | 3.6 | 0.0 | 10.0 | 17.3 |
| WEST SIDE BAPTIST CHURCH FCU | Saint Louis | MO | C | C- | C | <1 | 7.67 | 0.0 | 15.8 | 0.0 | 0.0 | 10.0 | 19.8 |
| WEST SPRINGFIELD FCU | West Springfield | MA | D+ | D- | D | 26.9 | 5.03 | 0.0 | 9.6 | 8.7 | 29.9 | 6.5 | 8.5 |
| WEST TENNESSEE CU | Memphis | TN | D | D+ | D+ | 16.1 | 0.36 | 0.5 | 27.9 | 2.3 | 0.0 | 10.0 | 11.1 |
| WEST TEXAS EDUCATORS CU | Odessa | TX | C- | D+ | D+ | 55.4 | 1.61 | 0.5 | 37.4 | 8.5 | 13.7 | 5.8 | 7.8 |

| Asset Quality Index | Non-Performing Loans as a % of Total Loans | as a % of Capital | Net Charge-Offs Avg Loans | Profitability Index | Net Income ($Mil) | Return on Assets | Return on Equity | Net Interest Spread | Overhead Efficiency Ratio | Liquidity Index | Liquidity Ratio | Hot Money Ratio | Stability Index |
|---|---|---|---|---|---|---|---|---|---|---|---|---|---|
| 7.5 | 1.08 | 3.5 | 0.69 | 2.4 | 0.0 | 0.15 | 1.32 | 3.09 | 95.2 | 4.7 | 19.8 | 2.1 | 5.6 |
| 8.0 | 0.00 | 0.0 | 0.00 | 8.9 | 0.0 | 1.41 | 9.84 | 5.33 | 74.4 | 3.0 | 10.6 | 0.0 | 5.0 |
| 7.0 | 0.26 | 5.6 | 0.34 | 5.0 | 1.1 | 0.78 | 9.02 | 4.23 | 82.8 | 3.2 | 4.0 | 4.5 | 5.0 |
| 8.0 | 0.85 | 5.0 | 0.21 | 1.7 | 0.2 | 0.21 | 1.81 | 3.22 | 92.4 | 4.2 | 20.6 | 2.7 | 6.2 |
| 9.1 | 0.70 | 2.8 | 0.35 | 1.4 | 0.0 | 0.01 | 0.10 | 2.73 | 95.9 | 5.8 | 39.5 | 3.5 | 4.1 |
| 10.0 | NA | 0.0 | NA | 1.8 | 0.0 | 0.09 | 1.01 | 1.12 | 90.9 | 6.0 | 36.0 | 0.0 | 0.8 |
| 5.4 | 2.14 | 7.4 | 1.56 | 2.9 | 0.0 | 0.22 | 1.55 | 4.53 | 88.2 | 5.4 | 48.3 | 0.0 | 6.5 |
| 9.7 | 0.00 | 0.0 | 2.30 | 1.8 | 0.0 | 0.00 | 0.00 | 3.57 | 100.0 | 6.4 | 85.9 | 0.0 | 7.2 |
| 6.7 | 1.72 | 5.4 | 1.12 | 1.2 | -0.1 | -0.18 | -2.14 | 2.45 | 93.6 | 5.4 | 31.5 | 2.4 | 3.4 |
| 10.0 | 0.00 | 0.0 | 0.04 | 0.3 | 0.0 | -0.28 | -3.08 | 2.37 | 108.1 | 5.2 | 31.6 | 0.0 | 3.5 |
| 6.8 | 1.87 | 8.9 | 0.31 | 4.5 | 0.4 | 0.64 | 6.79 | 3.13 | 83.6 | 4.6 | 13.1 | 3.2 | 4.5 |
| 2.5 | 4.87 | 24.5 | 0.44 | 2.0 | 0.0 | 0.10 | 1.16 | 5.92 | 98.0 | 6.1 | 62.5 | 0.0 | 1.0 |
| 9.9 | 0.21 | 0.5 | 0.43 | 1.6 | 0.0 | -0.08 | -0.53 | 3.34 | 94.2 | 5.5 | 30.5 | 2.0 | 7.1 |
| 4.7 | 6.39 | 14.6 | 0.91 | 5.8 | 0.0 | 0.73 | 2.81 | 9.90 | 87.3 | 6.0 | 42.5 | 0.0 | 3.7 |
| 8.7 | 0.19 | 0.5 | 0.00 | 2.2 | 0.0 | 0.00 | 0.00 | 2.56 | 100.0 | 5.8 | 57.0 | 0.0 | 7.7 |
| 5.3 | 0.00 | 0.0 | 0.00 | 9.8 | 0.7 | 2.14 | 19.42 | 3.85 | 48.6 | 0.8 | 3.5 | 45.2 | 8.2 |
| 9.1 | 0.00 | 0.0 | 0.22 | 1.9 | 0.0 | -0.09 | -0.96 | 4.32 | 100.4 | 5.3 | 22.7 | 1.0 | 4.4 |
| 6.5 | 1.39 | 7.9 | 0.83 | 5.4 | 2.1 | 0.64 | 5.59 | 4.01 | 78.0 | 4.1 | 33.3 | 12.8 | 6.6 |
| 5.8 | 0.90 | 8.9 | 0.03 | 1.8 | 0.0 | 0.06 | 0.60 | 2.95 | 97.2 | 4.2 | 23.3 | 0.5 | 5.0 |
| 8.4 | 0.15 | 0.7 | 0.39 | 0.2 | -0.1 | -0.51 | -4.45 | 2.70 | 106.0 | 5.0 | 21.4 | 0.0 | 5.2 |
| 8.2 | 0.15 | 1.7 | 0.19 | 4.7 | 0.5 | 0.66 | 6.99 | 3.82 | 82.8 | 3.1 | 7.9 | 5.7 | 4.7 |
| 6.6 | 12.59 | 11.5 | 0.00 | 1.9 | 0.0 | 0.00 | 0.00 | 3.89 | 107.7 | 6.2 | 103.1 | 0.0 | 6.9 |
| 8.0 | 0.15 | 1.3 | 0.30 | 0.3 | -0.1 | -0.44 | -5.52 | 3.14 | 108.8 | 4.0 | 12.8 | 0.0 | 3.4 |
| 7.3 | 1.02 | 5.0 | 0.06 | 7.7 | 6.5 | 1.16 | 6.38 | 3.64 | 68.4 | 3.0 | 8.7 | 9.5 | 9.5 |
| 0.5 | 12.08 | 41.8 | 1.39 | 3.4 | 0.0 | 0.00 | 0.00 | 5.98 | 67.1 | 3.7 | 6.7 | 0.0 | 6.7 |
| 7.6 | 0.65 | 2.4 | -0.16 | 5.4 | 0.1 | 0.83 | 7.59 | 3.87 | 76.1 | 6.3 | 48.4 | 4.1 | 6.4 |
| 7.3 | 1.41 | 6.1 | 0.34 | 2.1 | 0.0 | 0.03 | 0.25 | 4.25 | 97.0 | 6.4 | 41.0 | 0.5 | 5.7 |
| 10.0 | 0.13 | 0.7 | -0.18 | 3.2 | 0.2 | 0.36 | 4.40 | 2.62 | 89.3 | 5.5 | 37.4 | 1.2 | 3.6 |
| 10.0 | 0.33 | 1.2 | 0.18 | 1.6 | 0.0 | -0.01 | -0.08 | 1.89 | 94.8 | 4.6 | 26.5 | 2.3 | 6.0 |
| 4.1 | 1.27 | 11.3 | 0.75 | 4.6 | 0.1 | 0.35 | 3.77 | 5.96 | 87.7 | 3.4 | 18.3 | 13.1 | 4.3 |
| 5.5 | 0.45 | 9.6 | 1.31 | 0.9 | -0.2 | -1.03 | -12.16 | 4.60 | 95.6 | 5.3 | 27.5 | 1.5 | 3.4 |
| 9.8 | 0.26 | 1.5 | 0.21 | 5.1 | 5.9 | 0.76 | 7.13 | 2.22 | 71.2 | 4.6 | 55.6 | 14.9 | 8.0 |
| 7.2 | 2.67 | 14.7 | -0.01 | 3.5 | 0.3 | 0.38 | 3.13 | 3.11 | 88.7 | 4.7 | 14.0 | 4.8 | 5.4 |
| 6.1 | 0.91 | 7.1 | 0.43 | 3.7 | 0.7 | 0.48 | 5.05 | 3.60 | 78.0 | 4.4 | 12.8 | 0.7 | 5.7 |
| 6.9 | 2.52 | 6.7 | 0.00 | 1.0 | 0.0 | 0.04 | 0.35 | 2.42 | 95.6 | 4.7 | 17.6 | 0.0 | 3.8 |
| 8.4 | 0.44 | 3.9 | 0.12 | 3.9 | 16.0 | 0.68 | 10.64 | 2.85 | 86.0 | 4.2 | 23.7 | 9.0 | 4.9 |
| 8.9 | 1.56 | 2.9 | 1.78 | 0.0 | -0.5 | -0.79 | -5.29 | 2.35 | 108.2 | 5.2 | 32.8 | 0.3 | 5.1 |
| 10.0 | 0.00 | 0.0 | 0.00 | 0.0 | 0.0 | -10.53 | -32.43 | 0.00 | 0.0 | 9.4 | 140.5 | 0.0 | 6.5 |
| 9.2 | 1.53 | 4.3 | 0.21 | 0.0 | 0.0 | -1.02 | -8.49 | 2.36 | 139.0 | 6.1 | 74.3 | 4.0 | 6.0 |
| 10.0 | 0.01 | 0.1 | 0.22 | 1.0 | 0.0 | -0.16 | -2.13 | 2.98 | 103.6 | 4.0 | 13.4 | 3.3 | 3.1 |
| 8.6 | 0.31 | 3.2 | 0.41 | 1.5 | 0.0 | 0.11 | 1.10 | 3.83 | 95.7 | 6.0 | 33.7 | 0.0 | 4.2 |
| 8.5 | 1.45 | 3.3 | -0.03 | 1.1 | 0.0 | -0.14 | -1.04 | 3.03 | 114.8 | 5.4 | 28.1 | 0.9 | 5.4 |
| 5.4 | 1.40 | 14.6 | 0.29 | 4.9 | 0.9 | 0.68 | 8.49 | 4.67 | 86.6 | 2.9 | 6.2 | 2.8 | 5.1 |
| 9.6 | 0.81 | 2.3 | -0.04 | 1.9 | 0.0 | 0.00 | 0.00 | 3.38 | 101.9 | 5.3 | 19.5 | 0.0 | 5.8 |
| 4.1 | 1.34 | 18.8 | 0.24 | 6.8 | 0.2 | 0.86 | 9.16 | 5.41 | 83.7 | 3.4 | 11.4 | 1.5 | 4.5 |
| 7.6 | 3.67 | 8.5 | 0.00 | 2.0 | 0.0 | 0.00 | 0.00 | 3.05 | 100.0 | 7.2 | 57.9 | 0.0 | 7.7 |
| 6.0 | 5.44 | 10.6 | 0.00 | 1.0 | 0.0 | -0.15 | -1.45 | 3.00 | 107.5 | 6.4 | 33.9 | 0.0 | 4.5 |
| 3.6 | 1.22 | 9.7 | 0.55 | 0.3 | 0.0 | -0.44 | -7.05 | 3.66 | 102.8 | 6.1 | 48.1 | 0.0 | 2.1 |
| 10.0 | 0.10 | 0.1 | 0.69 | 1.2 | -0.1 | -0.52 | -2.29 | 1.77 | 124.6 | 4.9 | 34.4 | 6.6 | 7.3 |
| 10.0 | 0.04 | 0.1 | 0.08 | 4.9 | 0.2 | 0.79 | 4.26 | 3.20 | 76.3 | 4.7 | 36.7 | 4.0 | 7.2 |
| 9.6 | 0.51 | 1.4 | 0.27 | 6.6 | 1.1 | 1.03 | 6.26 | 3.13 | 70.9 | 4.2 | 20.4 | 3.9 | 8.8 |
| 6.4 | 0.63 | 7.3 | 0.82 | 0.7 | 0.0 | -0.63 | -7.68 | 3.71 | 99.5 | 3.6 | 29.1 | 11.3 | 2.9 |
| 6.9 | 1.96 | 8.5 | 0.18 | 2.9 | 0.0 | 0.22 | 2.06 | 3.56 | 92.5 | 5.7 | 65.3 | 0.0 | 4.7 |
| 9.3 | 2.54 | 4.1 | 0.80 | 3.3 | 0.2 | 0.55 | 4.25 | 2.59 | 78.9 | 4.6 | 22.2 | 5.0 | 5.6 |
| 5.0 | 1.44 | 8.9 | 0.25 | 2.1 | 0.0 | -0.06 | -0.65 | 4.88 | 98.9 | 4.1 | 16.2 | 0.0 | 1.0 |
| 9.5 | 0.78 | 2.2 | 0.57 | 0.5 | 0.0 | -0.41 | -2.42 | 3.01 | 111.2 | 5.2 | 17.0 | 1.1 | 6.6 |
| 6.3 | 9.80 | 7.6 | 4.85 | 2.4 | 0.0 | 0.00 | 0.00 | 5.52 | 71.4 | 8.3 | 103.5 | 0.0 | 7.7 |
| 7.1 | 1.39 | 5.0 | 0.05 | 1.6 | 0.0 | 0.22 | 2.57 | 2.27 | 99.8 | 5.2 | 38.8 | 1.8 | 2.8 |
| 9.8 | 0.54 | 1.6 | 0.06 | 0.0 | -0.2 | -1.43 | -12.30 | 2.84 | 148.3 | 4.9 | 20.8 | 6.8 | 6.1 |
| 5.3 | 2.18 | 12.3 | 1.16 | 3.4 | 0.2 | 0.42 | 5.51 | 4.08 | 75.7 | 4.8 | 22.7 | 3.2 | 3.1 |

| Name | City | State | Rating | 2014 Rating | 2013 Rating | Total Assets ($Mil) | One Year Asset Growth | Asset Mix (As a % of Total Assets) | | | | Capital-ization Index | Net Worth Ratio |
|------|------|-------|--------|-------------|-------------|---------------------|----------------------|------------------------------------|--|--|--|----------------------|-----------------|
| | | | | | | | | Comm-ercial Loans | Cons-umer Loans | Mort-gage Loans | Secur-ities | | |
| WEST VIRGINIA CENTRAL CU | Parkersburg | WV | B+ | B+ | B+ | 145.8 | 10.71 | 6.8 | 31.0 | 27.4 | 12.6 | 7.4 | 9.3 |
| WEST VIRGINIA FCU | South Charleston | WV | C | C | C | 148.2 | -3.62 | 6.3 | 19.2 | 15.7 | 14.5 | 10.0 | 11.6 |
| ▲ WEST VIRGINIA STATE CONVENTION CU | Hilltop | WV | D | D- | D | <1 | -0.87 | 0.0 | 30.6 | 0.0 | 0.0 | 7.9 | 9.6 |
| WEST YORK AREA SCHOOL DISTRICT EMPL | York | PA | E+ | E+ | D- | 4.7 | 0.11 | 0.0 | 34.5 | 0.0 | 0.0 | 6.1 | 8.1 |
| WEST-AIRCOMM FCU | Beaver | PA | C+ | C+ | C+ | 201.8 | 1.62 | 3.7 | 30.2 | 15.8 | 5.4 | 7.0 | 9.0 |
| ▼ WESTACRES CU | West Bloomfield | MI | D | D+ | D+ | 8.2 | -5.49 | 0.0 | 3.8 | 23.8 | 55.0 | 9.6 | 10.7 |
| ▲ WESTAR FCU | Camillus | NY | C | C- | C- | 24.3 | 5.29 | 0.0 | 22.3 | 3.4 | 0.0 | 7.1 | 9.1 |
| WESTBY CO-OP CU | Westby | WI | A- | A- | B+ | 410.1 | 7.18 | 38.1 | 19.1 | 39.8 | 11.0 | 10.0 | 15.1 |
| WESTCONSIN CU | Menomonie | WI | A- | A- | B+ | 978.2 | 8.41 | 15.0 | 23.6 | 37.7 | 9.8 | 10.0 | 11.8 |
| WESTEDGE FCU | Bellingham | WA | B- | B- | B | 54.3 | 2.82 | 0.0 | 21.2 | 12.8 | 7.4 | 10.0 | 14.1 |
| WESTERLY COMMUNITY CU | Westerly | RI | B- | C+ | C+ | 229.0 | 0.29 | 11.1 | 5.6 | 61.9 | 6.1 | 7.3 | 9.3 |
| WESTERN CONNECTICUT FCU | Bethel | CT | E- | E- | E- | 24.2 | 2.55 | 0.3 | 13.2 | 39.2 | 24.5 | 3.6 | 5.6 |
| WESTERN COOPERATIVE CU | Williston | ND | B+ | A- | A- | 334.7 | -0.45 | 27.4 | 18.4 | 14.2 | 22.1 | 9.0 | 10.3 |
| WESTERN DISTRICTS MEMBERS CU | Grand Rapids | MI | B+ | B+ | B | 37.7 | 5.92 | 0.0 | 17.6 | 11.6 | 45.8 | 10.0 | 19.0 |
| WESTERN DIVISION FCU | Williamsville | NY | B | B | B+ | 134.3 | 1.05 | 0.0 | 13.7 | 11.5 | 2.2 | 10.0 | 14.8 |
| WESTERN FCU | Hawthorne | CA | B | B | B- | 2131.8 | 7.72 | 8.6 | 28.3 | 31.8 | 23.5 | 7.9 | 9.6 |
| WESTERN HEALTHCARE FCU | Concord | CA | C | C+ | C- | 36.5 | 2.84 | 10.7 | 30.5 | 27.8 | 0.0 | 7.1 | 9.1 |
| ▼ WESTERN HERITAGE CU | Alliance | NE | C- | C | C | 79.0 | 1.73 | 0.0 | 39.4 | 11.2 | 22.8 | 7.5 | 9.4 |
| WESTERN ILLINOIS CU | Macomb | IL | C- | C- | C | 20.7 | 9.64 | 0.0 | 54.6 | 5.5 | 0.0 | 6.5 | 8.5 |
| WESTERN ILLINOIS SCHOOL EMPL CU | Quincy | IL | D+ | D+ | D+ | 21.6 | 1.88 | 0.0 | 43.7 | 0.0 | 0.0 | 7.1 | 9.0 |
| ▲ WESTERN INDIANA CU | Sullivan | IN | C- | C- | C+ | 24.0 | 0.26 | 50.8 | 3.2 | 40.0 | 0.0 | 10.0 | 14.4 |
| WESTERN NEW YORK FCU | West Seneca | NY | C+ | C+ | C+ | 44.1 | 5.74 | 0.0 | 33.2 | 21.4 | 5.8 | 7.5 | 9.4 |
| WESTERN REGION FCU | Cleveland | OH | B- | B- | B- | 13.0 | -2.86 | 0.0 | 38.4 | 0.1 | 26.9 | 10.0 | 15.0 |
| WESTERN ROCKIES FCU | Grand Junction | CO | D+ | D+ | C- | 112.2 | 2.18 | 0.8 | 22.5 | 12.2 | 44.0 | 7.3 | 9.2 |
| WESTERN SPRINGS FCU | Western Springs | IL | C | C | C | 3.3 | -3.73 | 0.0 | 33.2 | 0.0 | 0.0 | 10.0 | 12.5 |
| WESTERN STATES REGIONAL FCU | Los Angeles | CA | C+ | C | C- | <1 | 4.53 | 0.0 | 32.5 | 0.0 | 0.0 | 10.0 | 33.9 |
| WESTERN SUN FCU | Broken Arrow | OK | B | B | B | 146.5 | 9.65 | 0.2 | 56.3 | 2.7 | 0.0 | 10.0 | 11.9 |
| WESTERN VISTA FCU | Cheyenne | WY | B | B | B+ | 136.7 | 4.70 | 3.2 | 31.7 | 14.6 | 21.8 | 10.0 | 13.2 |
| WESTERRA CU | Denver | CO | B+ | B+ | B+ | 1326.0 | 5.38 | 6.3 | 37.4 | 27.4 | 13.7 | 10.0 | 12.3 |
| WESTEX COMMUNITY CU | Kermit | TX | B+ | B+ | B | 71.8 | 13.91 | 1.1 | 34.8 | 14.8 | 21.2 | 10.0 | 11.1 |
| WESTEX FCU | Lubbock | TX | B | B | B | 61.5 | 3.36 | 0.0 | 24.1 | 6.0 | 17.1 | 10.0 | 12.2 |
| WESTFIELD AREA FCU | Westfield | NY | E+ | E+ | E+ | 3.4 | 2.79 | 0.0 | 48.2 | 0.0 | 20.7 | 5.3 | 7.3 |
| WESTMARK CU | Idaho Falls | ID | B | B+ | B+ | 620.5 | 6.32 | 0.1 | 46.4 | 30.8 | 1.7 | 7.1 | 9.0 |
| WESTMINSTER FCU | Westminster | CO | C | C+ | C+ | 34.8 | 5.67 | 1.4 | 36.5 | 9.4 | 1.1 | 7.6 | 9.4 |
| WESTMORELAND COMMUNITY FCU | Greensburg | PA | D | D | C- | 68.8 | 2.27 | 0.0 | 53.2 | 0.5 | 0.5 | 5.9 | 7.9 |
| ▼ WESTMORELAND FEDERAL EMPL FCU | Greensburg | PA | D+ | D | D | 7.0 | -6.52 | 0.0 | 19.6 | 13.2 | 0.0 | 10.0 | 47.0 |
| WESTMORELAND WATER FCU | Greensburg | PA | C+ | C+ | C+ | 17.2 | 3.63 | 0.1 | 24.3 | 0.0 | 0.0 | 10.0 | 12.2 |
| ▼ WESTPORT FCU | Westport | MA | D | D | D | 56.3 | 2.56 | 0.0 | 3.2 | 24.4 | 20.0 | 6.0 | 8.0 |
| WESTSIDE COMMUNITY FCU | Churchville | NY | D | D+ | D+ | 14.8 | 1.25 | 0.0 | 21.2 | 8.7 | 0.0 | 6.0 | 8.0 |
| WESTSTAR CU | Las Vegas | NV | A- | B+ | B+ | 144.2 | 6.30 | 0.2 | 40.5 | 20.8 | 7.1 | 10.0 | 12.8 |
| WEXFORD COMMUNITY CU | Cadillac | MI | C- | D+ | D+ | 48.7 | 6.65 | 0.0 | 28.2 | 5.6 | 49.3 | 5.9 | 7.9 |
| WEYCO COMMUNITY CU | Plymouth | NC | D | D+ | C+ | 77.8 | -1.98 | 2.6 | 10.8 | 18.6 | 0.0 | 10.0 | 12.8 |
| WH NICHOLS EMPL FCU | Devens | MA | D | D | D+ | 1.1 | -7.06 | 0.0 | 36.9 | 0.0 | 0.0 | 10.0 | 19.9 |
| ▲ WHARTON COUNTY TEACHERS CU | Wharton | TX | C | C- | C- | 11.2 | -0.35 | 0.0 | 3.9 | 0.0 | 0.0 | 10.0 | 16.6 |
| WHATCOM EDUCATIONAL CU | Bellingham | WA | A+ | A+ | A+ | 1173.8 | 11.02 | 17.0 | 14.8 | 46.6 | 0.4 | 10.0 | 16.3 |
| WHEAT STATE CU | Wichita | KS | E | E | D | 19.5 | -0.73 | 1.1 | 57.7 | 12.8 | 0.0 | 6.1 | 8.1 |
| WHEATLAND FCU | Lancaster | PA | C- | C | C- | 53.1 | 0.40 | 0.8 | 24.5 | 32.7 | 3.7 | 7.5 | 9.4 |
| WHETELCO FCU | Wheeling | WV | D+ | D+ | C- | 3.9 | 0.21 | 0.0 | 17.6 | 0.0 | 0.0 | 10.0 | 38.7 |
| ▼ WHITE COUNTY FCU | Searcy | AR | D | D+ | C- | 14.4 | 4.54 | 0.0 | 55.0 | 0.0 | 0.0 | 6.9 | 8.9 |
| WHITE CROWN FCU | Denver | CO | C | C- | C | 59.7 | 0.81 | 9.3 | 15.2 | 28.3 | 23.9 | 7.3 | 9.3 |
| WHITE EAGLE CU | Augusta | KS | A- | B+ | A- | 91.5 | 4.60 | 0.0 | 46.9 | 2.5 | 0.6 | 10.0 | 12.0 |
| ▲ WHITE EARTH RESERVATION FCU | Mahnomen | MN | D | D- | D | 1.6 | -5.78 | 0.0 | 54.3 | 0.0 | 0.0 | 7.0 | 9.0 |
| WHITE GOLD CU | Raceland | LA | C- | C- | C | <1 | 0.21 | 0.0 | 57.1 | 0.0 | 0.0 | 10.0 | 29.7 |
| WHITE HAVEN CENTER EMPL FCU | White Haven | PA | D- | D- | D- | 1.4 | 3.70 | 0.0 | 59.2 | 0.0 | 0.0 | 6.1 | 8.2 |
| WHITE HOUSE FCU | Washington | DC | D | D | D | 53.9 | -6.51 | 0.0 | 24.3 | 7.9 | 40.8 | 5.4 | 7.4 |
| WHITE PINE CU | Pierce | ID | D+ | C- | D+ | 7.5 | -6.79 | 0.0 | 62.8 | 0.0 | 0.0 | 10.0 | 13.6 |
| ▲ WHITE PLAINS P O EMPL FCU | White Plains | NY | D+ | D | D+ | 1.3 | -11.69 | 0.0 | 21.8 | 0.0 | 0.0 | 10.0 | 26.9 |
| ▼ WHITE RIVER CU | Rochester | VT | D | D+ | D+ | 34.4 | 6.41 | 0.0 | 28.4 | 28.6 | 11.0 | 6.3 | 8.4 |
| WHITE RIVER CU | Enumclaw | WA | A- | A- | B+ | 65.1 | 7.15 | 0.3 | 33.8 | 3.4 | 0.0 | 10.0 | 14.2 |
| ▲ WHITE ROCK FCU | Philadelphia | PA | C | C | C+ | <1 | 2.33 | 0.0 | 5.7 | 0.0 | 24.1 | 8.7 | 10.1 |

| Asset Quality Index | Non-Performing Loans as a % of Total Loans | Non-Performing Loans as a % of Capital | Net Charge-Offs Avg Loans | Profitability Index | Net Income ($Mil) | Return on Assets | Return on Equity | Net Interest Spread | Overhead Efficiency Ratio | Liquidity Index | Liquidity Ratio | Hot Money Ratio | Stability Index |
|---|---|---|---|---|---|---|---|---|---|---|---|---|---|
| 8.9 | 0.41 | 3.1 | 0.09 | 7.0 | 1.2 | 1.12 | 12.66 | 2.76 | 69.2 | 3.9 | 13.7 | 0.0 | 6.4 |
| 8.1 | 1.09 | 5.1 | 0.10 | 2.5 | 0.2 | 0.15 | 1.38 | 2.82 | 93.8 | 4.5 | 24.2 | 6.2 | 6.5 |
| 3.4 | 8.57 | 26.1 | 0.00 | 7.1 | 0.0 | 1.22 | 12.70 | 4.69 | 50.0 | 6.7 | 39.6 | 0.0 | 3.0 |
| 8.1 | 0.57 | 3.1 | 0.86 | 0.0 | 0.0 | -0.47 | -5.78 | 2.92 | 96.9 | 5.5 | 50.1 | 0.0 | 2.2 |
| 9.6 | 0.27 | 1.7 | 0.32 | 2.9 | 0.4 | 0.29 | 3.27 | 3.06 | 86.1 | 3.9 | 31.7 | 11.0 | 5.5 |
| 9.8 | 0.49 | 1.4 | 0.00 | 0.2 | 0.0 | -0.52 | -4.86 | 1.64 | 150.7 | 6.5 | 71.0 | 0.0 | 5.0 |
| 9.5 | 0.14 | 0.8 | -0.13 | 3.7 | 0.1 | 0.55 | 6.25 | 3.15 | 85.5 | 4.2 | 9.9 | 0.0 | 4.0 |
| 6.1 | 1.18 | 6.2 | 0.19 | 9.2 | 3.9 | 1.30 | 8.77 | 4.04 | 68.5 | 3.3 | 11.6 | 6.5 | 9.5 |
| 6.1 | 0.97 | 6.6 | 0.19 | 9.0 | 10.9 | 1.49 | 13.38 | 3.66 | 77.6 | 3.1 | 8.5 | 8.1 | 8.7 |
| 9.1 | 0.50 | 1.3 | 0.33 | 2.9 | 0.1 | 0.22 | 1.61 | 2.81 | 88.7 | 4.3 | 19.7 | 7.2 | 6.3 |
| 7.0 | 0.47 | 5.4 | 0.14 | 4.4 | 0.9 | 0.54 | 6.31 | 3.52 | 84.9 | 2.5 | 4.4 | 8.5 | 5.6 |
| 3.2 | 3.27 | 34.7 | 0.90 | 3.8 | 0.1 | 0.50 | 9.23 | 3.71 | 90.5 | 3.5 | 9.8 | 2.9 | 0.0 |
| 8.6 | 0.39 | 2.2 | 0.03 | 4.7 | 1.4 | 0.52 | 5.59 | 3.61 | 83.5 | 4.8 | 14.9 | 0.0 | 7.3 |
| 10.0 | 0.32 | 0.6 | -0.04 | 4.6 | 0.1 | 0.37 | 1.96 | 3.44 | 90.9 | 5.5 | 23.0 | 0.0 | 7.5 |
| 10.0 | 0.07 | 0.2 | -0.14 | 4.9 | 0.7 | 0.72 | 4.97 | 2.30 | 75.2 | 5.0 | 26.2 | 1.7 | 8.1 |
| 6.9 | 0.94 | 7.4 | 0.64 | 4.8 | 11.1 | 0.71 | 8.12 | 4.11 | 76.2 | 3.5 | 20.9 | 8.2 | 6.0 |
| 9.5 | 0.10 | 0.7 | 0.28 | 3.2 | 0.1 | 0.31 | 3.38 | 4.03 | 93.8 | 4.3 | 13.7 | 0.4 | 3.9 |
| 7.1 | 0.63 | 4.8 | 0.14 | 2.2 | 0.1 | 0.16 | 1.72 | 3.43 | 92.4 | 3.3 | 19.1 | 12.7 | 4.5 |
| 7.4 | 0.45 | 3.1 | 0.56 | 5.6 | 0.1 | 0.93 | 11.26 | 3.77 | 73.0 | 4.6 | 20.6 | 0.3 | 3.7 |
| 4.5 | 3.49 | 16.1 | 0.16 | 5.3 | 0.1 | 0.82 | 9.22 | 1.97 | 49.2 | 5.3 | 50.5 | 0.0 | 3.7 |
| 4.0 | 2.00 | 10.2 | 0.02 | 4.1 | 0.1 | 0.52 | 3.57 | 3.71 | 84.5 | 3.4 | 21.5 | 13.1 | 7.1 |
| 8.5 | 0.57 | 3.8 | 0.38 | 6.6 | 0.3 | 1.05 | 11.39 | 4.91 | 75.6 | 4.5 | 17.9 | 3.0 | 4.2 |
| 8.3 | 1.68 | 4.3 | 0.40 | 4.1 | 0.0 | 0.45 | 3.05 | 4.03 | 89.0 | 4.8 | 26.2 | 3.0 | 5.7 |
| 10.0 | 0.42 | 2.1 | -0.01 | 1.5 | 0.0 | 0.01 | 0.17 | 2.97 | 99.5 | 5.1 | 23.3 | 1.2 | 4.5 |
| 10.0 | 0.00 | 0.0 | 0.00 | 2.4 | 0.0 | 0.27 | 2.30 | 1.99 | 83.3 | 5.1 | 35.4 | 0.0 | 6.1 |
| 9.9 | 0.86 | 0.8 | 0.00 | 4.8 | 0.0 | 0.77 | 2.21 | 3.64 | 75.0 | 6.5 | 59.2 | 0.0 | 6.1 |
| 4.0 | 1.78 | 13.0 | 0.75 | 7.8 | 1.2 | 1.16 | 9.65 | 4.53 | 65.0 | 1.9 | 21.8 | 20.0 | 7.7 |
| 8.2 | 0.96 | 4.4 | 0.04 | 4.0 | 0.7 | 0.64 | 4.77 | 3.47 | 86.5 | 3.9 | 12.0 | 6.6 | 8.2 |
| 9.6 | 0.10 | 0.5 | 0.08 | 4.3 | 5.3 | 0.54 | 4.31 | 2.81 | 86.2 | 4.0 | 20.7 | 6.1 | 8.0 |
| 8.2 | 0.90 | 5.3 | 0.30 | 8.0 | 0.5 | 1.02 | 11.13 | 4.88 | 79.0 | 4.3 | 21.0 | 11.7 | 6.1 |
| 8.4 | 1.51 | 5.5 | 0.45 | 4.2 | 0.1 | 0.10 | 0.82 | 4.24 | 90.0 | 5.4 | 39.0 | 11.2 | 6.6 |
| 2.7 | 2.54 | 20.3 | 0.42 | 0.8 | 0.0 | -0.48 | -6.35 | 4.61 | 108.7 | 5.0 | 28.2 | 0.0 | 2.8 |
| 8.3 | 0.08 | 1.0 | 0.28 | 4.4 | 2.4 | 0.53 | 5.90 | 2.90 | 77.9 | 1.9 | 2.9 | 12.3 | 7.0 |
| 7.1 | 0.69 | 4.3 | 0.16 | 2.3 | 0.0 | 0.05 | 0.53 | 3.72 | 97.4 | 4.5 | 16.3 | 2.2 | 3.9 |
| 5.0 | 0.93 | 8.3 | 0.56 | 2.1 | 0.0 | 0.05 | 0.69 | 3.90 | 87.0 | 3.7 | 16.3 | 2.9 | 2.9 |
| 9.2 | 1.84 | 1.6 | 0.96 | 0.5 | 0.0 | -0.06 | -0.12 | 3.10 | 119.9 | 6.3 | 72.3 | 0.0 | 4.7 |
| 10.0 | 0.00 | 0.0 | 0.18 | 3.1 | 0.0 | 0.33 | 2.70 | 2.16 | 81.2 | 5.3 | 38.8 | 0.0 | 6.1 |
| 7.2 | 0.55 | 2.5 | 0.26 | 0.8 | 0.1 | 0.29 | 3.80 | 2.78 | 87.1 | 5.2 | 28.6 | 2.7 | 2.7 |
| 9.6 | 0.31 | 1.8 | 0.09 | 1.2 | 0.0 | -0.05 | -0.68 | 2.75 | 94.8 | 5.0 | 16.3 | 0.0 | 3.5 |
| 8.3 | 0.23 | 1.3 | 0.47 | 5.4 | 0.8 | 0.74 | 5.88 | 3.88 | 88.5 | 4.8 | 25.5 | 1.2 | 7.7 |
| 9.0 | 0.58 | 2.6 | 0.17 | 4.3 | 0.3 | 0.77 | 9.95 | 3.08 | 84.1 | 4.9 | 18.9 | 2.2 | 2.7 |
| 7.2 | 2.58 | 6.4 | 0.92 | 0.3 | -0.2 | -0.27 | -2.10 | 2.42 | 112.8 | 5.0 | 30.5 | 6.3 | 4.7 |
| 9.4 | 1.22 | 2.2 | 0.00 | 0.0 | 0.0 | -1.02 | -4.98 | 3.14 | 138.9 | 7.2 | 74.8 | 0.0 | 4.8 |
| 10.0 | 0.00 | 0.0 | 0.14 | 2.0 | 0.0 | 0.13 | 0.79 | 1.59 | 91.2 | 5.7 | 32.4 | 0.0 | 6.7 |
| 9.3 | 0.35 | 1.3 | 0.17 | 9.0 | 10.8 | 1.28 | 7.66 | 3.73 | 71.2 | 5.4 | 25.9 | 0.2 | 9.5 |
| 3.9 | 1.36 | 13.0 | 1.04 | 2.5 | 0.0 | 0.26 | 3.35 | 5.01 | 86.3 | 2.6 | 8.5 | 9.6 | 1.0 |
| 6.7 | 0.72 | 5.3 | 0.13 | 1.8 | 0.0 | -0.10 | -1.09 | 3.55 | 100.5 | 3.9 | 13.6 | 1.1 | 4.0 |
| 9.9 | 4.80 | 2.2 | 0.00 | 0.5 | 0.0 | -0.34 | -0.88 | 2.07 | 105.4 | 5.2 | 10.6 | 0.0 | 5.2 |
| 1.4 | 1.85 | 27.0 | 0.91 | 4.9 | 0.1 | 0.87 | 10.10 | 5.04 | 70.4 | 4.4 | 24.6 | 0.0 | 2.8 |
| 9.8 | 0.04 | 0.2 | -0.14 | 2.6 | 0.2 | 0.36 | 4.22 | 3.12 | 90.1 | 4.8 | 21.4 | 1.9 | 4.5 |
| 8.2 | 0.15 | 1.4 | 0.98 | 6.1 | 0.6 | 0.89 | 7.57 | 4.81 | 78.6 | 4.4 | 26.0 | 5.1 | 6.4 |
| 7.9 | 0.19 | 1.6 | 0.13 | 9.1 | 0.0 | 1.97 | 32.00 | 7.62 | 93.0 | 5.0 | 30.5 | 6.9 | 1.8 |
| 6.0 | 3.30 | 6.3 | 0.00 | 1.5 | 0.0 | -0.28 | -0.95 | 6.39 | 100.0 | 6.5 | 56.5 | 0.0 | 7.8 |
| 1.9 | 3.32 | 21.1 | 2.24 | 3.9 | 0.0 | 0.50 | 6.06 | 8.10 | 58.5 | 6.2 | 44.1 | 0.0 | 1.0 |
| 6.4 | 1.46 | 8.3 | 0.61 | 1.2 | -0.1 | -0.17 | -2.72 | 3.65 | 99.2 | 6.0 | 38.3 | 2.3 | 1.1 |
| 6.5 | 0.98 | 5.3 | 0.50 | 3.1 | 0.0 | 0.27 | 2.12 | 4.43 | 92.0 | 3.2 | 24.2 | 16.4 | 5.6 |
| 10.0 | 0.00 | 0.0 | 0.00 | 1.4 | 0.0 | 0.20 | 0.78 | 3.13 | 92.6 | 5.9 | 37.6 | 0.0 | 5.8 |
| 4.8 | 1.04 | 9.6 | 0.38 | 0.2 | -0.2 | -0.81 | -9.23 | 4.56 | 112.1 | 4.7 | 17.1 | 0.7 | 3.2 |
| 8.9 | 0.73 | 3.9 | 0.20 | 8.3 | 0.5 | 1.12 | 8.04 | 3.29 | 74.8 | 4.7 | 24.5 | 2.1 | 7.2 |
| 9.9 | 0.00 | 0.0 | 0.00 | 6.2 | 0.0 | 1.21 | 12.28 | 2.10 | 22.2 | 7.2 | 39.6 | 0.0 | 4.3 |

www.weissratings.com
225
Data as of September 30, 2015

| Name | City | State | Rating | 2014 Rating | 2013 Rating | Total Assets ($Mil) | One Year Asset Growth | Asset Mix (As a % of Total Assets) Commercial Loans | Consumer Loans | Mortgage Loans | Securities | Capitalization Index | Net Worth Ratio |
|---|---|---|---|---|---|---|---|---|---|---|---|---|---|
| ▼ WHITE ROSE CU | York | PA | D- | C- | B- | 64.2 | 3.19 | 0.2 | 24.5 | 14.0 | 20.0 | 9.6 | 10.7 |
| WHITE SANDS FCU | Las Cruces | NM | B- | B- | B- | 275.6 | 4.47 | 0.0 | 52.9 | 15.1 | 13.8 | 6.6 | 8.7 |
| WHITEFISH CU ASSN | Whitefish | MT | A- | B | C | 1291.1 | 2.99 | 10.0 | 1.3 | 44.7 | 39.0 | 10.0 | 11.8 |
| WHITEHALL CU | Columbus | OH | D | D | D+ | 17.9 | -0.84 | 0.0 | 29.8 | 0.0 | 0.0 | 10.0 | 11.3 |
| ▼ WHITESVILLE COMMUNITY CU | Whitesville | KY | C | C+ | C+ | 22.0 | 7.22 | 0.0 | 9.0 | 18.1 | 0.0 | 10.0 | 11.4 |
| WHITEWATER COMMUNITY CU | Harrison | OH | D+ | D | D | 6.5 | 3.02 | 0.0 | 74.9 | 0.0 | 0.0 | 8.5 | 10.0 |
| WHITEWATER REGIONAL FCU | Connersville | IN | C- | C- | C- | 7.2 | 4.95 | 0.6 | 62.9 | 0.0 | 0.0 | 10.0 | 13.7 |
| WHITING REFINERY FCU | Whiting | IN | B+ | B+ | B+ | 47.3 | 0.09 | 0.2 | 6.7 | 11.3 | 46.1 | 10.0 | 26.1 |
| WICHITA FALLS FCU | Wichita Falls | TX | C+ | C+ | C+ | 21.1 | 4.17 | 0.0 | 35.5 | 2.7 | 0.0 | 10.0 | 12.5 |
| WICHITA FALLS TEACHERS FCU | Wichita Falls | TX | B | B- | C+ | 73.2 | 4.01 | 0.0 | 37.1 | 0.2 | 37.8 | 10.0 | 11.1 |
| WICHITA FCU | Wichita | KS | B | B | B+ | 97.4 | 11.06 | 0.1 | 60.1 | 10.6 | 2.5 | 10.0 | 14.8 |
| WICKLIFFE PAPER MILL FCU | Wickliffe | KY | C- | C- | C- | 7.8 | -4.57 | 0.0 | 34.8 | 0.0 | 0.0 | 10.0 | 15.9 |
| WIDGET FCU | Erie | PA | C+ | B- | B- | 273.0 | 4.91 | 0.0 | 33.1 | 19.3 | 17.5 | 8.0 | 9.7 |
| WILDFIRE CU | Saginaw | MI | C+ | C+ | B- | 683.5 | 0.93 | 5.1 | 15.4 | 33.5 | 37.1 | 10.0 | 13.1 |
| WILKES-BARRE CITY EMPL FCU | Wilkes-Barre | PA | C | C | B- | 37.3 | -4.44 | 0.2 | 16.2 | 16.4 | 33.3 | 10.0 | 11.8 |
| WILLIAMSON COUNTY CATHOLIC CU | Herrin | IL | E+ | E+ | E+ | 2.3 | 3.96 | 0.0 | 69.1 | 0.0 | 0.0 | 5.5 | 7.5 |
| WILLIAMSPORT TEACHERS CU | South Williamsport | PA | C | C | C+ | 9.9 | 1.33 | 0.0 | 24.2 | 18.1 | 0.0 | 10.0 | 21.2 |
| WILLIAMSVILLE FCU | Amherst | NY | D | D | D+ | 12.3 | 2.48 | 0.0 | 13.9 | 14.6 | 0.0 | 8.7 | 10.1 |
| WILLIS CU | Nashville | TN | B- | B- | C+ | 18.0 | 11.12 | 0.0 | 67.3 | 0.0 | 0.0 | 9.4 | 10.6 |
| WILLIS KNIGHTON FCU | Shreveport | LA | B- | B- | B | 27.5 | 2.87 | 0.0 | 52.9 | 9.0 | 0.0 | 10.0 | 16.2 |
| WILLOW ISLAND FCU | Saint Marys | WV | E+ | E+ | E+ | 8.5 | 9.51 | 0.0 | 66.6 | 0.0 | 0.0 | 5.5 | 7.5 |
| WILMAC EMPL CU | York | PA | C+ | C+ | C+ | 2.7 | -6.85 | 4.6 | 29.8 | 0.0 | 0.0 | 10.0 | 20.3 |
| WILMINGTON POLICE & FIRE FCU | Wilmington | DE | D | D | C- | 13.8 | -8.57 | 0.0 | 12.2 | 0.0 | 68.5 | 10.0 | 19.4 |
| WILMINGTON POSTAL FCU | Wilmington | DE | C+ | C+ | C+ | 16.0 | -0.40 | 0.0 | 27.1 | 0.0 | 0.1 | 10.0 | 19.3 |
| ▲ WIN-HOOD CO-OP CU | Chicago | IL | D+ | D | E+ | 1.4 | -2.60 | 0.0 | 0.3 | 0.0 | 4.6 | 10.0 | 15.0 |
| ▼ WINCHESTER FCU | Winchester | MA | D+ | D+ | C- | 2.4 | 4.33 | 0.0 | 45.3 | 0.0 | 0.0 | 10.0 | 14.7 |
| ▼ WINDSOR COUNTY SOUTH CU | Springfield | VT | D | C- | C | 8.3 | 18.85 | 0.0 | 13.7 | 31.0 | 0.0 | 10.0 | 11.8 |
| ▲ WINDSOR LOCKS FCU | Windsor Locks | CT | C | C+ | C+ | 51.9 | 2.54 | 1.0 | 7.6 | 45.1 | 0.5 | 10.0 | 11.3 |
| WINDTHORST FCU | Windthorst | TX | B | B- | B | 50.5 | 3.15 | 10.6 | 11.9 | 17.6 | 0.0 | 10.0 | 15.5 |
| ▼ WINDWARD COMMUNITY FCU | Kailua | HI | D+ | C | C | 91.4 | 7.07 | 2.5 | 21.1 | 9.3 | 3.2 | 5.6 | 7.6 |
| WINGS FINANCIAL CU | Apple Valley | MN | B+ | B+ | A- | 4192.1 | 4.45 | 1.9 | 12.3 | 21.5 | 49.4 | 10.0 | 11.2 |
| WINNEBAGO COMMUNITY CU | Oshkosh | WI | B | B- | B- | 87.7 | 8.50 | 0.2 | 12.8 | 50.3 | 0.0 | 9.0 | 10.4 |
| ▲ WINSLOW COMMUNITY FCU | Winslow | ME | C | C | C | 35.5 | 11.36 | 0.3 | 44.6 | 11.7 | 0.0 | 6.5 | 8.6 |
| WINSLOW SANTA FE CU | Winslow | AZ | B | B | B | 13.0 | 4.80 | 0.0 | 29.6 | 0.0 | 0.0 | 10.0 | 13.1 |
| WINSLOW SCHOOL EMPL FCU | Winslow | AZ | C- | C- | C | 4.4 | 3.55 | 0.0 | 45.4 | 0.0 | 0.0 | 10.0 | 14.1 |
| WINSOUTH CU | Gadsden | AL | C+ | C+ | C | 238.2 | 0.80 | 6.3 | 27.6 | 35.0 | 16.2 | 6.6 | 8.9 |
| WINSTON-SALEM FCU | Winston-Salem | NC | B | B- | B- | 61.3 | 0.00 | 0.1 | 36.8 | 24.0 | 4.4 | 10.0 | 13.6 |
| WINTHROP AREA FCU | Winthrop | ME | C+ | C | C | 61.7 | 3.77 | 0.0 | 15.2 | 37.6 | 0.0 | 8.3 | 9.9 |
| WINTHROP-UNIV HOSPITAL EMPL FCU | Mineola | NY | B- | B- | C+ | 30.2 | 5.79 | 0.0 | 39.0 | 0.0 | 0.0 | 8.9 | 10.3 |
| ▲ WIREGRASS FCU | Dothan | AL | D+ | D | D | 43.6 | 1.46 | 0.0 | 64.5 | 10.5 | 0.0 | 6.5 | 8.5 |
| WIREMENS CU INC | Parma | OH | C | C+ | C+ | 25.2 | -2.14 | 0.0 | 26.5 | 6.8 | 41.3 | 10.0 | 23.4 |
| WISCONSIN LATVIAN CU INC | Milwaukee | WI | C | C | C | 2.6 | -1.66 | 0.0 | 11.2 | 24.0 | 0.0 | 10.0 | 11.8 |
| ▲ WISCONSIN MEDICAL CU | Green Bay | WI | C- | C- | C- | 10.0 | 6.87 | 0.0 | 23.2 | 24.3 | 0.0 | 8.0 | 9.6 |
| ▼ WIT FCU | Rochester | NY | C- | C | C | 12.0 | 6.49 | 1.8 | 42.0 | 14.9 | 8.0 | 10.0 | 13.4 |
| WITCO HOUSTON EMPL CU | Rosenberg | TX | C- | D+ | D+ | 1.7 | 1.13 | 0.0 | 55.1 | 0.0 | 0.0 | 10.0 | 20.1 |
| WJC FCU | Damascus | VA | E+ | E+ | E+ | 3.7 | -0.08 | 0.0 | 75.0 | 0.0 | 0.0 | 6.6 | 8.6 |
| WNC COMMUNITY CU | Waynesville | NC | B- | B | B | 76.7 | 2.07 | 0.0 | 7.6 | 40.5 | 2.3 | 10.0 | 15.3 |
| WOBURN MUNICIPAL FCU | Woburn | MA | D | D | D | 43.2 | 3.68 | 0.0 | 10.8 | 9.5 | 2.3 | 6.2 | 8.3 |
| WOD FCU | Forty Fort | PA | E+ | E+ | E+ | 2.9 | -13.84 | 0.0 | 21.0 | 0.0 | 54.9 | 6.3 | 8.3 |
| WOLF POINT FCU | Wolf Point | MT | C+ | B- | B | 14.1 | 20.35 | 0.0 | 36.2 | 0.0 | 0.0 | 10.0 | 14.3 |
| WOOD COUNTY COMMUNITY FCU | Parkersburg | WV | E+ | E+ | D- | 18.0 | 1.57 | 0.0 | 31.1 | 6.0 | 0.0 | 4.4 | 6.4 |
| WOOD COUNTY EMPL CU | Wisconsin Rapids | WI | C- | D+ | D+ | 1.2 | -5.15 | 0.0 | 91.5 | 0.0 | 0.0 | 10.0 | 13.9 |
| WOODCO FCU | Perrysburg | OH | D+ | D | D | 9.6 | -1.34 | 0.0 | 38.2 | 13.7 | 0.0 | 7.6 | 9.4 |
| WOODLAWN FCU | Pawtucket | RI | E | E | D- | 13.1 | -1.75 | 4.7 | 27.7 | 18.4 | 0.0 | 5.6 | 7.6 |
| WOODMEN FCU | Omaha | NE | C- | C- | C- | 8.2 | 6.17 | 0.0 | 19.4 | 15.2 | 0.0 | 10.0 | 14.8 |
| WOODSTONE CU | Federal Way | WA | C- | C- | C | 96.5 | 4.61 | 3.2 | 58.3 | 6.1 | 11.5 | 8.9 | 10.3 |
| WOR CO FCU | Pocomoke City | MD | D+ | D+ | C- | 2.4 | 3.57 | 0.0 | 27.6 | 0.0 | 0.0 | 10.0 | 14.0 |
| ▼ WORCESTER CU | Worcester | MA | D | D | D+ | 77.1 | -0.62 | 0.0 | 15.3 | 31.5 | 14.1 | 7.7 | 9.5 |
| WORCESTER FIRE DEPT CU | Worcester | MA | C | C+ | C+ | 38.2 | -2.01 | 0.0 | 13.5 | 10.2 | 5.8 | 10.0 | 14.3 |
| WORCESTER POLICE DEPT CU | Worcester | MA | C+ | C+ | C+ | 15.7 | 9.75 | 0.7 | 42.0 | 19.6 | 0.0 | 10.0 | 12.6 |

| Asset Quality Index | Non-Performing Loans | | Net Charge-Offs Avg Loans | Profitability Index | Net Income ($Mil) | Return on Assets | Return on Equity | Net Interest Spread | Overhead Efficiency Ratio | Liquidity Index | Liquidity Ratio | Hot Money Ratio | Stability Index |
|---|---|---|---|---|---|---|---|---|---|---|---|---|---|
| | as a % of Total Loans | as a % of Capital | | | | | | | | | | | |
| 7.7 | 0.60 | 3.0 | 0.51 | 0.1 | -0.5 | -1.00 | -9.02 | 3.40 | 114.8 | 4.3 | 22.4 | 0.4 | 5.2 |
| 8.1 | 0.34 | 3.2 | 0.26 | 4.2 | 1.2 | 0.60 | 7.01 | 3.52 | 79.7 | 3.9 | 12.0 | 4.7 | 5.2 |
| 5.6 | 1.54 | 16.4 | -0.15 | 6.4 | 9.4 | 0.98 | 8.39 | 2.35 | 70.7 | 4.9 | 19.8 | 0.0 | 8.1 |
| 6.9 | 2.49 | 9.1 | 0.34 | 0.3 | 0.0 | -0.29 | -2.62 | 2.71 | 102.8 | 4.1 | 14.7 | 4.6 | 5.6 |
| 9.8 | 1.01 | 2.6 | -0.02 | 1.9 | 0.0 | 0.03 | 0.26 | 2.39 | 98.3 | 6.2 | 43.4 | 0.0 | 6.6 |
| 8.4 | 0.02 | 0.2 | 0.11 | 4.7 | 0.0 | 0.84 | 8.73 | 3.55 | 86.7 | 4.0 | 23.8 | 4.2 | 3.7 |
| 7.8 | 0.87 | 3.9 | 0.33 | 4.4 | 0.0 | 0.68 | 4.97 | 3.59 | 79.2 | 4.1 | 11.5 | 0.0 | 4.3 |
| 10.0 | 0.08 | 0.7 | 0.39 | 4.0 | 0.2 | 0.53 | 2.05 | 1.60 | 59.0 | 5.4 | 35.9 | 0.0 | 7.4 |
| 9.7 | 0.02 | 0.1 | 0.07 | 3.6 | 0.1 | 0.50 | 4.71 | 3.33 | 88.4 | 4.8 | 35.3 | 4.9 | 5.5 |
| 8.2 | 0.96 | 5.0 | 0.36 | 4.8 | 0.4 | 0.74 | 6.77 | 4.01 | 79.2 | 4.2 | 8.6 | 2.0 | 5.1 |
| 6.2 | 0.74 | 4.8 | 1.37 | 4.8 | 0.4 | 0.62 | 4.09 | 5.48 | 75.8 | 2.3 | 11.9 | 18.4 | 6.1 |
| 9.8 | 0.29 | 0.7 | -0.04 | 2.0 | 0.0 | 0.10 | 0.65 | 2.55 | 96.4 | 4.7 | 32.7 | 3.6 | 6.9 |
| 9.1 | 0.39 | 2.5 | 0.30 | 3.3 | 0.7 | 0.34 | 3.68 | 3.05 | 87.3 | 3.5 | 14.2 | 6.0 | 5.9 |
| 9.4 | 0.67 | 3.0 | 0.24 | 2.3 | 1.2 | 0.23 | 1.87 | 2.90 | 89.7 | 3.0 | 11.2 | 14.1 | 8.0 |
| 7.9 | 0.50 | 3.2 | 1.15 | 1.9 | 0.1 | 0.36 | 3.13 | 2.34 | 94.1 | 5.4 | 40.4 | 0.0 | 4.2 |
| 4.4 | 0.56 | 5.9 | 0.22 | 4.6 | 0.0 | 0.70 | 9.58 | 3.59 | 81.3 | 3.9 | 16.6 | 0.0 | 1.7 |
| 10.0 | 0.02 | 0.1 | 0.00 | 2.3 | 0.0 | 0.22 | 1.02 | 2.57 | 88.7 | 5.6 | 34.0 | 0.0 | 7.2 |
| 9.8 | 0.15 | 0.5 | 0.00 | 0.5 | 0.0 | -0.19 | -1.93 | 2.39 | 109.1 | 5.5 | 32.3 | 0.0 | 4.7 |
| 5.7 | 0.29 | 3.3 | 0.44 | 7.6 | 0.1 | 0.91 | 8.47 | 5.02 | 80.1 | 4.8 | 39.7 | 13.4 | 5.0 |
| 6.8 | 0.43 | 2.2 | 0.23 | 5.1 | 0.2 | 0.78 | 4.89 | 3.86 | 84.8 | 3.6 | 14.8 | 9.1 | 7.1 |
| 2.7 | 1.02 | 11.1 | 0.81 | 3.4 | 0.0 | 0.33 | 4.25 | 4.88 | 85.5 | 3.2 | 15.6 | 7.2 | 1.0 |
| 8.7 | 1.93 | 3.9 | -0.12 | 4.5 | 0.0 | 0.42 | 2.19 | 2.91 | 73.2 | 6.8 | 52.7 | 0.0 | 6.9 |
| 10.0 | 0.00 | 0.0 | -0.61 | 0.0 | -0.1 | -0.77 | -3.99 | 2.30 | 130.5 | 5.4 | 43.1 | 11.3 | 4.7 |
| 9.6 | 1.67 | 3.3 | -0.09 | 4.0 | 0.1 | 0.64 | 3.41 | 3.13 | 77.9 | 4.4 | 21.2 | 1.5 | 6.8 |
| 3.6 | 4.22 | 16.2 | -9.62 | 7.3 | 0.1 | 6.31 | 53.83 | 5.05 | 76.3 | 4.7 | 39.1 | 0.0 | 4.3 |
| 7.1 | 1.68 | 5.1 | 0.00 | 0.8 | 0.0 | -0.66 | -4.58 | 3.64 | 108.1 | 4.5 | 27.4 | 0.0 | 6.4 |
| 10.0 | 0.20 | 0.8 | 0.03 | 0.0 | -0.1 | -0.75 | -6.08 | 2.78 | 117.7 | 5.9 | 58.0 | 0.0 | 6.4 |
| 6.0 | 2.10 | 15.5 | 0.48 | 1.9 | 0.0 | -0.04 | -0.32 | 3.61 | 96.9 | 3.4 | 8.4 | 5.3 | 5.7 |
| 9.5 | 0.13 | 0.3 | 0.05 | 4.8 | 0.3 | 0.84 | 5.48 | 2.32 | 65.9 | 4.6 | 60.0 | 12.7 | 7.6 |
| 5.2 | 2.65 | 15.0 | 1.10 | 1.5 | -0.1 | -0.09 | -1.14 | 3.34 | 89.1 | 5.0 | 28.4 | 1.2 | 3.0 |
| 10.0 | 0.24 | 1.2 | 0.12 | 4.7 | 20.5 | 0.66 | 6.00 | 1.92 | 71.7 | 4.0 | 17.7 | 10.3 | 7.9 |
| 8.9 | 0.25 | 2.3 | 0.11 | 5.2 | 0.5 | 0.84 | 8.10 | 3.12 | 77.9 | 3.5 | 22.7 | 7.1 | 5.6 |
| 7.4 | 0.26 | 2.0 | 0.57 | 4.3 | 0.1 | 0.53 | 6.18 | 3.91 | 79.0 | 3.6 | 14.5 | 5.9 | 3.8 |
| 10.0 | 0.03 | 0.1 | 0.10 | 6.0 | 0.1 | 0.89 | 6.94 | 4.29 | 67.7 | 7.0 | 44.8 | 0.0 | 5.9 |
| 6.7 | 1.05 | 3.4 | -0.06 | 5.3 | 0.0 | 0.78 | 5.66 | 5.00 | 80.0 | 6.5 | 56.6 | 0.0 | 4.3 |
| 6.2 | 0.85 | 10.4 | 0.37 | 3.7 | 0.9 | 0.50 | 6.55 | 3.31 | 85.4 | 3.3 | 12.7 | 7.9 | 4.6 |
| 5.4 | 2.76 | 17.4 | 0.73 | 7.8 | 0.7 | 1.42 | 10.77 | 5.73 | 79.1 | 2.8 | 6.6 | 8.8 | 6.1 |
| 5.5 | 0.28 | 9.5 | 0.14 | 3.4 | 0.2 | 0.44 | 4.45 | 2.79 | 82.2 | 3.8 | 30.1 | 11.4 | 5.1 |
| 6.9 | 1.64 | 8.1 | 0.99 | 7.6 | 0.3 | 1.11 | 11.32 | 6.09 | 72.7 | 4.8 | 38.6 | 10.4 | 5.2 |
| 4.7 | 0.49 | 7.1 | 0.62 | 2.0 | 0.0 | 0.06 | 0.69 | 4.38 | 93.0 | 2.9 | 10.2 | 11.1 | 3.1 |
| 7.7 | 2.24 | 4.0 | 0.27 | 2.4 | 0.0 | 0.21 | 0.95 | 2.67 | 91.9 | 4.4 | 11.2 | 0.0 | 7.4 |
| 10.0 | 0.00 | 0.0 | 0.00 | 3.8 | 0.0 | 0.62 | 5.41 | 3.36 | 78.0 | 5.2 | 41.9 | 0.0 | 6.3 |
| 6.8 | 1.00 | 5.9 | 0.05 | 4.1 | 0.0 | 0.54 | 5.64 | 3.65 | 87.3 | 4.2 | 17.9 | 0.0 | 5.5 |
| 5.8 | 1.90 | 12.9 | 0.71 | 1.4 | 0.0 | -0.26 | -1.89 | 5.47 | 93.0 | 1.8 | 11.3 | 14.9 | 6.7 |
| 7.2 | 1.31 | 4.2 | 0.00 | 3.3 | 0.0 | 0.40 | 1.98 | 5.02 | 87.8 | 5.9 | 40.7 | 0.0 | 6.5 |
| 0.7 | 5.41 | 48.9 | 0.25 | 8.0 | 0.0 | 1.60 | 20.16 | 6.99 | 71.9 | 3.2 | 13.4 | 0.0 | 3.2 |
| 8.1 | 0.64 | 4.2 | 0.33 | 3.5 | 0.2 | 0.40 | 2.59 | 2.91 | 77.7 | 5.1 | 22.5 | 0.3 | 7.2 |
| 10.0 | 0.00 | 0.0 | 0.81 | 0.8 | 0.0 | -0.08 | -0.93 | 2.45 | 99.7 | 5.5 | 28.9 | 1.5 | 3.3 |
| 10.0 | 0.00 | 0.0 | 0.00 | 0.7 | 0.0 | -0.25 | -3.32 | 2.97 | 109.0 | 5.4 | 17.1 | 0.0 | 2.1 |
| 8.8 | 1.28 | 3.8 | -0.07 | 3.9 | 0.0 | 0.43 | 2.69 | 3.94 | 89.3 | 7.0 | 64.2 | 0.0 | 6.5 |
| 6.3 | 0.70 | 6.8 | 1.81 | 0.0 | -0.2 | -1.39 | -19.53 | 3.02 | 122.1 | 5.0 | 11.8 | 2.1 | 1.3 |
| 8.0 | 0.00 | 0.0 | 0.00 | 3.8 | 0.0 | 0.56 | 4.19 | 4.19 | 85.7 | 2.7 | 3.1 | 0.0 | 3.7 |
| 9.6 | 0.10 | 0.8 | -0.04 | 3.7 | 0.0 | 0.53 | 5.74 | 3.88 | 87.8 | 4.4 | 25.0 | 0.0 | 3.0 |
| 3.6 | 2.72 | 23.0 | 0.63 | 2.1 | 0.0 | 0.16 | 2.15 | 6.34 | 96.3 | 5.2 | 43.5 | 10.4 | 1.0 |
| 10.0 | 0.38 | 1.0 | -0.07 | 1.4 | 0.0 | -0.11 | -0.77 | 3.06 | 103.1 | 5.1 | 20.8 | 1.6 | 6.9 |
| 5.6 | 0.56 | 4.6 | 0.78 | 0.7 | -0.3 | -0.45 | -4.37 | 3.70 | 94.0 | 3.0 | 9.1 | 8.7 | 4.1 |
| 6.0 | 5.64 | 10.5 | 1.88 | 0.7 | 0.0 | -0.54 | -3.94 | 4.14 | 117.9 | 6.1 | 26.9 | 0.0 | 5.2 |
| 6.1 | 0.99 | 6.4 | 0.26 | 0.8 | -0.1 | -0.23 | -2.47 | 3.46 | 101.0 | 4.3 | 17.5 | 4.4 | 4.2 |
| 9.3 | 1.21 | 2.6 | 0.58 | 1.7 | 0.0 | -0.04 | -0.29 | 2.09 | 95.0 | 4.6 | 12.5 | 2.1 | 6.6 |
| 8.9 | 0.00 | 0.0 | -0.07 | 3.6 | 0.1 | 0.43 | 3.34 | 4.43 | 98.9 | 4.3 | 22.9 | 7.1 | 6.8 |

| Name | City | State | Rating | 2014 Rating | 2013 Rating | Total Assets ($Mil) | One Year Asset Growth | Asset Mix (As a % of Total Assets) | | | | Capital-ization Index | Net Worth Ratio |
|------|------|-------|--------|-------------|-------------|---------------------|----------------------|-----------|--------|--------|--------|-----------------------|-----------------|
| | | | | | | | | Comm-ercial Loans | Cons-umer Loans | Mort-gage Loans | Secur-ities | | |
| WORKERS CU | Fitchburg | MA | A | A | A | 1270.5 | 13.37 | 5.4 | 12.5 | 41.2 | 22.3 | 10.0 | 12.0 |
| WORKERS FCU | Stafford Springs | CT | E- | E- | E- | 20.6 | -1.82 | 0.0 | 22.6 | 16.5 | 0.0 | 3.6 | 5.6 |
| WORKMENS CIRCLE CU | Savannah | GA | A- | A- | A- | 60.9 | 3.29 | 50.6 | 2.1 | 53.6 | 0.0 | 10.0 | 19.2 |
| WORZALLA PUBLISHING EMPL CU | Stevens Point | WI | C- | C- | C- | 1.2 | -3.19 | 0.0 | 15.5 | 0.0 | 0.0 | 10.0 | 20.5 |
| ▲ WR GRACE MARYLAND EMPL FCU | Curtis Bay | MD | D | D | C- | 3.3 | -3.32 | 0.0 | 12.0 | 0.0 | 82.0 | 10.0 | 11.3 |
| WRIGHT CU | Toccoa | GA | B- | C+ | C+ | 12.2 | 2.85 | 0.0 | 19.1 | 19.5 | 0.0 | 10.0 | 16.1 |
| WRIGHT-DUNBAR AREA CU | Dayton | OH | D+ | D+ | C- | <1 | -5.56 | 0.0 | 18.3 | 0.0 | 0.0 | 10.0 | 16.8 |
| WRIGHT-PATT CU INC | Beavercreek | OH | A | A | A | 3141.1 | 8.20 | 2.9 | 49.3 | 16.2 | 6.2 | 10.0 | 11.7 |
| WSSC FCU | Laurel | MD | C | C | C | 24.2 | 5.40 | 0.0 | 53.7 | 0.0 | 0.0 | 10.0 | 11.1 |
| WUFFACE FCU | Richmond | IN | C- | C- | C | 4.6 | 3.49 | 0.0 | 36.3 | 0.0 | 0.0 | 9.2 | 10.5 |
| WV NATIONAL GUARD FCU | Charleston | WV | B+ | B | B- | 42.0 | 3.72 | 0.5 | 28.7 | 4.5 | 0.0 | 10.0 | 11.6 |
| ▲ WVU EMPL FCU | Morgantown | WV | B | B- | C+ | 33.3 | 8.09 | 0.0 | 30.5 | 0.0 | 0.0 | 9.0 | 10.4 |
| WYHY FCU | Cheyenne | WY | A | A | A- | 203.8 | 6.00 | 1.9 | 41.1 | 25.7 | 2.2 | 10.0 | 11.5 |
| WYMAR FCU | Geismar | LA | A | A- | A- | 90.6 | 3.06 | 0.2 | 17.1 | 30.7 | 24.7 | 10.0 | 14.8 |
| WYO CENTRAL FCU | Casper | WY | C- | C | C | 30.2 | 4.16 | 0.8 | 34.8 | 9.1 | 0.0 | 8.1 | 9.7 |
| ▼ WYOCHEM FCU | Green River | WY | D | D+ | C- | 18.2 | -0.22 | 0.0 | 43.0 | 0.0 | 0.0 | 6.4 | 8.4 |
| WYOMING AREA FCU | Wyoming | PA | D | D | C- | 8.1 | 0.70 | 0.0 | 2.1 | 0.0 | 55.1 | 6.3 | 8.3 |
| WYOMING COUNTY SCHOOL EMPL FCU | Tunkhannock | PA | C- | C | C- | 15.5 | 2.71 | 0.0 | 18.9 | 23.6 | 8.3 | 9.0 | 10.3 |
| WYOMING VALLEY WEST COMMUNITY FCU | Edwardsville | PA | D | D | D | 9.4 | 5.35 | 4.0 | 21.9 | 0.0 | 22.1 | 5.8 | 7.9 |
| WYROPE WILLIAMSPORT FCU | South Williamsport | PA | C | C+ | C+ | 31.3 | -0.60 | 0.0 | 23.5 | 0.1 | 53.1 | 10.0 | 11.3 |
| ▲ XAVIER UNIV FCU | New Orleans | LA | D+ | D+ | C+ | 2.6 | 11.06 | 0.0 | 17.6 | 0.0 | 0.0 | 10.0 | 11.3 |
| XCEED FINANCIAL FCU | El Segundo | CA | C | C | C | 908.0 | -6.84 | 7.5 | 23.0 | 39.4 | 0.7 | 7.0 | 9.0 |
| XCEL FCU | Bloomfield | NJ | C+ | C+ | C+ | 169.1 | 6.75 | 5.5 | 44.7 | 14.1 | 0.4 | 5.8 | 7.8 |
| ▲ XPLORE FCU | New Orleans | LA | B- | C- | C- | 138.7 | 2.21 | 0.0 | 23.2 | 22.4 | 1.5 | 6.7 | 8.7 |
| Y-12 FCU | Oak Ridge | TN | B | B | B | 873.0 | 19.40 | 5.4 | 42.2 | 33.6 | 5.3 | 7.2 | 9.1 |
| YANTIS FCU | Yantis | TX | C | C | C+ | 24.7 | -1.58 | 5.2 | 9.5 | 26.6 | 0.0 | 10.0 | 13.9 |
| YELLOWSTONE FCU | Yellowstone Nation | WY | E+ | E+ | E+ | 4.6 | -6.75 | 0.0 | 51.5 | 2.5 | 0.0 | 4.3 | 6.3 |
| YHA SOUTH UNIT FCU | Youngstown | OH | D | D | C- | 1.6 | -9.32 | 0.0 | 21.4 | 0.0 | 12.4 | 10.0 | 26.1 |
| YOAKUM COUNTY FCU | Plains | TX | C+ | C+ | B- | 8.7 | -0.90 | 0.0 | 31.9 | 0.0 | 0.0 | 10.0 | 18.1 |
| YOGAVILLE FCU | Buckingham | VA | C+ | C+ | C+ | 6.0 | 9.39 | 0.0 | 7.9 | 21.2 | 0.0 | 10.0 | 14.6 |
| YOLO FCU | Woodland | CA | A- | A- | B+ | 237.2 | 8.19 | 6.9 | 12.1 | 33.1 | 0.4 | 8.9 | 10.3 |
| YONKERS POSTAL EMPL CU | Yonkers | NY | C | C+ | C+ | 7.9 | 1.77 | 0.0 | 26.7 | 0.0 | 46.0 | 10.0 | 17.1 |
| ▼ YONKERS TEACHERS FCU | Yonkers | NY | B- | B+ | A- | 55.2 | 3.86 | 0.0 | 7.9 | 0.0 | 24.3 | 10.0 | 12.3 |
| YORK COUNTY FCU | Sanford | ME | B+ | B+ | B- | 222.4 | 7.77 | 2.0 | 23.3 | 38.6 | 3.9 | 9.2 | 10.5 |
| YORK EDUCATIONAL FCU | York | PA | D | D | D | 31.9 | 1.84 | 0.0 | 18.7 | 9.7 | 18.2 | 5.6 | 7.6 |
| YORKVILLE COMMUNITY FCU | Yorkville | OH | C- | C | C- | 10.3 | -4.38 | 0.0 | 30.5 | 0.0 | 0.0 | 10.0 | 15.5 |
| YOUNGSTOWN CITY SCHOOLS CU | Youngstown | OH | C+ | C+ | C+ | 8.9 | -3.58 | 0.0 | 33.3 | 0.0 | 5.6 | 10.0 | 29.8 |
| YOUNGSTOWN FIREFIGHTERS CU | Youngstown | OH | D | D+ | C | 1.3 | -58.68 | 0.0 | 0.0 | 0.0 | 0.0 | 10.0 | 100.0 |
| YOUNGSTOWN OHIO CITY EMPL FCU | Youngstown | OH | D | D+ | C- | 3.2 | -0.86 | 0.0 | 39.5 | 0.0 | 3.0 | 10.0 | 11.3 |
| YOUR CHOICE FCU | Altoona | PA | C- | C- | C- | 10.7 | 2.76 | 0.0 | 21.8 | 8.6 | 27.6 | 10.0 | 13.2 |
| ▲ YOUR HOMETOWN FCU | Mayfield | KY | D+ | D+ | D+ | 18.1 | -2.87 | 0.0 | 14.5 | 32.1 | 0.0 | 8.1 | 9.7 |
| YOUR LEGACY FCU | Tiffin | OH | C | C | C | 54.3 | 5.29 | 4.2 | 22.0 | 20.8 | 16.3 | 7.9 | 9.7 |
| YS FCU | Yellow Springs | OH | C | C | C | 16.0 | -2.05 | 0.0 | 16.5 | 0.1 | 10.5 | 8.8 | 10.2 |
| YUMA COUNTY FCU | Yuma | CO | C+ | C+ | B- | 32.3 | 3.13 | 0.7 | 7.2 | 12.0 | 0.0 | 10.0 | 11.5 |
| ▲ ZACHARY COMMUNITY FCU | Zachary | LA | C | C- | C | <1 | 0.97 | 0.0 | 37.8 | 0.0 | 0.0 | 10.0 | 33.0 |
| ZEAL CU | Livonia | MI | A | A | A | 527.4 | 5.23 | 0.0 | 26.6 | 19.2 | 37.9 | 10.0 | 14.1 |
| ZELLCO FCU | Bogalusa | LA | A- | A- | A- | 56.6 | -0.08 | 1.3 | 26.9 | 24.0 | 0.0 | 10.0 | 34.2 |
| ZIA CU | Los Alamos | NM | C | C | C | 131.2 | 1.58 | 0.0 | 24.2 | 22.0 | 20.9 | 7.1 | 9.1 |
| ZIEGLER FCU | Bloomington | MN | C+ | C+ | C+ | 4.4 | -2.25 | 0.0 | 22.3 | 0.0 | 0.0 | 10.0 | 15.6 |
| ZION HILL BAPTIST CHURCH FCU | Los Angeles | CA | D | D | C- | <1 | 12.14 | 0.0 | 18.6 | 0.0 | 0.0 | 10.0 | 29.9 |

| Asset Quality Index | Non-Performing Loans as a % of Total Loans | Non-Performing Loans as a % of Capital | Net Charge-Offs Avg Loans | Profitability Index | Net Income ($Mil) | Return on Assets | Return on Equity | Net Interest Spread | Overhead Efficiency Ratio | Liquidity Index | Liquidity Ratio | Hot Money Ratio | Stability Index |
|---|---|---|---|---|---|---|---|---|---|---|---|---|---|
| 7.4 | 0.98 | 6.1 | 0.43 | 8.7 | 13.2 | 1.45 | 11.89 | 3.48 | 59.8 | 2.1 | 11.4 | 17.2 | 9.0 |
| 1.7 | 2.31 | 48.4 | -0.06 | 0.6 | 0.0 | -0.20 | -3.46 | 3.87 | 121.0 | 3.3 | 9.6 | 6.6 | 0.0 |
| 7.6 | 0.00 | 0.0 | 0.00 | 9.8 | 1.0 | 2.22 | 11.79 | 3.67 | 29.3 | 4.6 | 27.1 | 6.8 | 9.9 |
| 10.0 | 0.00 | 0.0 | -1.30 | 1.3 | 0.0 | 0.00 | 0.00 | 1.90 | 100.0 | 7.3 | 55.5 | 0.0 | 5.7 |
| 10.0 | 0.24 | 0.3 | -0.28 | 0.2 | 0.0 | -0.55 | -4.90 | 2.43 | 122.8 | 5.0 | 10.9 | 0.0 | 5.7 |
| 9.7 | 0.46 | 1.2 | -0.03 | 4.5 | 0.1 | 0.66 | 4.13 | 3.56 | 81.1 | 5.4 | 45.1 | 6.7 | 7.1 |
| 3.7 | 20.83 | 23.8 | 0.00 | 2.3 | 0.0 | 0.29 | 1.73 | 2.89 | 90.0 | 6.0 | 45.0 | 0.0 | 5.6 |
| 6.8 | 0.69 | 4.6 | 0.67 | 9.2 | 33.8 | 1.46 | 12.81 | 3.48 | 61.9 | 4.0 | 20.3 | 7.7 | 8.9 |
| 6.6 | 1.20 | 6.2 | 0.36 | 4.2 | 0.1 | 0.71 | 6.44 | 4.14 | 81.5 | 4.2 | 29.9 | 4.3 | 5.4 |
| 9.9 | 0.00 | 1.0 | 0.57 | 2.0 | 0.0 | 0.23 | 2.21 | 3.15 | 100.8 | 6.7 | 47.8 | 0.0 | 4.3 |
| 8.5 | 0.68 | 2.3 | 2.37 | 8.8 | 0.5 | 1.52 | 13.58 | 3.09 | 41.8 | 5.0 | 16.4 | 0.0 | 6.3 |
| 9.5 | 0.42 | 1.2 | 0.80 | 6.3 | 0.3 | 1.08 | 10.88 | 3.18 | 60.7 | 5.8 | 30.0 | 0.3 | 5.1 |
| 8.7 | 0.16 | 2.6 | 0.20 | 7.2 | 1.4 | 0.95 | 8.31 | 3.82 | 72.6 | 1.7 | 5.8 | 16.2 | 8.1 |
| 8.8 | 0.84 | 3.3 | -0.02 | 9.2 | 1.1 | 1.68 | 11.70 | 2.95 | 53.0 | 3.8 | 18.3 | 11.1 | 7.9 |
| 3.1 | 2.60 | 22.0 | 0.15 | 3.9 | 0.1 | 0.48 | 5.17 | 4.13 | 85.4 | 3.6 | 9.0 | 3.7 | 4.2 |
| 5.8 | 1.26 | 7.4 | 0.79 | 2.0 | -0.1 | -0.51 | -5.53 | 3.59 | 103.7 | 5.3 | 36.3 | 4.0 | 4.1 |
| 10.0 | 0.00 | 0.0 | 0.00 | 1.2 | 0.0 | -0.02 | -0.20 | 1.30 | 103.9 | 7.1 | 39.8 | 0.0 | 3.9 |
| 3.7 | 5.25 | 26.7 | 0.44 | 5.0 | 0.1 | 0.69 | 6.73 | 2.90 | 68.3 | 5.2 | 29.5 | 0.0 | 4.7 |
| 10.0 | 0.06 | 0.4 | 0.23 | 4.1 | 0.0 | 0.34 | 4.37 | 4.19 | 85.5 | 6.3 | 47.5 | 0.0 | 3.0 |
| 6.3 | 1.68 | 7.5 | 0.58 | 2.4 | 0.0 | 0.14 | 1.29 | 2.25 | 85.2 | 4.5 | 21.7 | 1.4 | 5.6 |
| 6.3 | 8.06 | 12.2 | -0.32 | 1.7 | 0.0 | 0.20 | 1.83 | 1.80 | 83.9 | 6.6 | 91.6 | 0.0 | 4.7 |
| 7.5 | 0.53 | 5.7 | 0.25 | 2.3 | 0.9 | 0.13 | 1.50 | 2.89 | 93.5 | 2.5 | 14.1 | 20.7 | 5.3 |
| 5.5 | 1.31 | 14.6 | 0.59 | 4.8 | 0.7 | 0.57 | 7.86 | 5.15 | 81.2 | 1.1 | 4.0 | 20.5 | 4.5 |
| 9.8 | 0.46 | 2.5 | 0.17 | 4.2 | 0.8 | 0.72 | 8.90 | 3.09 | 82.2 | 4.5 | 22.5 | 1.5 | 5.2 |
| 8.0 | 0.29 | 4.2 | 0.34 | 6.5 | 6.7 | 1.10 | 12.94 | 3.28 | 70.0 | 2.2 | 7.2 | 14.7 | 5.9 |
| 6.9 | 0.65 | 3.5 | 0.33 | 2.0 | 0.0 | 0.19 | 1.41 | 2.79 | 85.8 | 3.1 | 21.3 | 16.2 | 6.0 |
| 8.7 | 0.00 | 0.0 | -0.05 | 0.4 | 0.0 | -0.15 | -2.29 | 3.07 | 103.7 | 5.2 | 36.6 | 0.0 | 1.2 |
| 10.0 | 0.00 | 0.0 | -1.81 | 0.0 | 0.0 | -1.26 | -4.67 | 3.60 | 132.5 | 7.0 | 62.3 | 0.0 | 5.1 |
| 9.2 | 0.16 | 0.4 | 0.00 | 6.3 | 0.1 | 0.84 | 4.73 | 3.56 | 68.7 | 5.4 | 60.3 | 0.0 | 5.0 |
| 8.6 | 1.54 | 5.1 | 0.09 | 7.5 | 0.1 | 1.17 | 8.01 | 3.89 | 57.3 | 4.9 | 41.6 | 14.8 | 5.0 |
| 8.9 | 0.19 | 1.3 | 0.16 | 7.9 | 2.0 | 1.12 | 11.12 | 3.55 | 75.3 | 4.6 | 30.4 | 4.5 | 6.6 |
| 8.3 | 2.82 | 4.3 | 2.75 | 2.2 | 0.0 | -0.14 | -0.79 | 3.60 | 73.2 | 5.2 | 19.3 | 0.0 | 6.8 |
| 10.0 | 2.19 | 1.5 | 0.06 | 3.4 | 0.1 | 0.34 | 2.79 | 1.34 | 73.7 | 5.1 | 20.4 | 0.0 | 5.8 |
| 7.1 | 1.15 | 9.7 | 0.46 | 5.4 | 1.2 | 0.74 | 7.16 | 4.40 | 79.5 | 2.7 | 11.4 | 10.9 | 7.2 |
| 8.1 | 0.25 | 1.8 | -0.01 | 1.6 | 0.0 | 0.09 | 1.29 | 3.09 | 96.0 | 4.1 | 9.9 | 0.7 | 2.5 |
| 6.3 | 5.20 | 10.8 | 1.31 | 0.9 | 0.0 | -0.22 | -1.41 | 2.60 | 93.1 | 5.3 | 35.1 | 0.0 | 6.2 |
| 9.5 | 1.91 | 2.2 | 0.40 | 3.6 | 0.0 | 0.38 | 1.31 | 2.42 | 83.2 | 4.9 | 35.5 | 0.0 | 7.6 |
| 10.0 | NA | 0.0 | 0.00 | 0.0 | -0.1 | -5.01 | -8.17 | 1.79 | 561.1 | 4.0 | NA | 101.0 | 5.7 |
| 8.2 | 0.85 | 3.0 | 1.82 | 0.0 | 0.0 | -0.79 | -6.76 | 3.12 | 121.6 | 5.1 | 53.0 | 0.0 | 5.4 |
| 6.5 | 4.38 | 10.3 | 0.59 | 1.3 | 0.0 | 0.11 | 0.85 | 2.81 | 94.5 | 5.2 | 19.2 | 0.0 | 5.7 |
| 6.1 | 1.21 | 6.4 | 0.01 | 1.4 | 0.0 | 0.01 | 0.15 | 3.06 | 100.9 | 5.3 | 34.1 | 1.4 | 4.4 |
| 9.6 | 0.19 | 1.5 | 0.01 | 3.2 | 0.1 | 0.36 | 3.75 | 2.97 | 92.0 | 4.1 | 13.4 | 1.4 | 4.9 |
| 9.6 | 0.11 | 0.7 | 0.05 | 3.8 | 0.1 | 0.42 | 4.16 | 3.49 | 91.2 | 4.7 | 22.8 | 1.9 | 4.7 |
| 10.0 | 0.05 | 0.2 | 0.01 | 2.5 | 0.1 | 0.19 | 1.71 | 2.28 | 92.6 | 4.7 | 29.6 | 5.0 | 6.4 |
| 6.4 | 2.41 | 2.6 | 1.52 | 7.9 | 0.0 | 1.87 | 5.88 | 5.49 | 71.4 | 7.0 | 92.8 | 0.0 | 5.0 |
| 8.3 | 1.17 | 4.5 | 0.83 | 9.5 | 5.3 | 1.34 | 9.75 | 3.66 | 67.5 | 3.9 | 5.6 | 2.5 | 9.6 |
| 8.6 | 1.50 | 3.1 | 0.44 | 8.6 | 0.6 | 1.28 | 3.93 | 5.98 | 75.4 | 6.5 | 54.9 | 1.4 | 7.3 |
| 6.8 | 1.14 | 6.8 | 0.28 | 3.1 | 0.4 | 0.37 | 4.16 | 4.40 | 92.5 | 3.2 | 15.5 | 16.0 | 5.0 |
| 10.0 | 0.58 | 1.0 | -0.34 | 3.5 | 0.0 | 0.45 | 2.94 | 3.31 | 74.2 | 7.7 | 85.1 | 0.0 | 6.5 |
| 8.1 | 9.30 | 5.4 | -3.03 | 0.0 | 0.0 | -3.60 | -10.96 | 2.96 | 220.0 | 6.0 | 25.9 | 0.0 | 5.1 |

 Data as of September 30, 2015

# Section II

# Weiss
# Recommended Companies

A compilation of those

## Credit Unions

receiving a Weiss Safety Rating
of A+, A, A-, or B+.

Institutions are ranked by Safety Rating
in each state where they have a branch location.

# Section II Contents

This section provides a list of Weiss Recommended companies and contains all financial institutions receiving a Safety Rating of A+, A, A-, or B+. Recommended institutions are listed in each state in which they currently operate one or more branches. If a company is not on this list, it should not be automatically assumed that the firm is weak. Indeed, there are many firms that have not achieved a B+ or better rating but are in good condition with adequate resources to weather an average recession. Not being included in this list should not be construed as a recommendation to immediately withdraw deposits or cancel existing financial arrangements.

Institutions are ranked within each state by their Weiss Safety Rating, and then listed alphabetically by city. Companies with the same rating should be viewed as having the same relative safety regardless of their ranking in this table.

1. **Institution Name**

   The name under which the institution was chartered. A company's name can be very similar to, or the same as, the name of other companies which may not be on our Recommended List, so make sure you note the exact name, city, and state of the main branch listed here before acting on this recommendation.

2. **City**

   The city in which the institution's headquarters or main office is located. With the adoption of intrastate and interstate branching laws, many institutions operating in your area may actually be headquartered elsewhere. So, don't be surprised if the location cited is not in your particular city.

3. **State**

   The state in which the institution's headquarters or main office is located. With the adoption of interstate branching laws, some institutions operating in your area may actually be headquartered in another state. Even so, there are no restrictions on your ability to do business with an out-of-state institution.

4. **Telephone**

   The telephone number for the institution's headquarters, or main office. If the number listed is not in your area, or a local phone call, consult your local phone directory for the number of a location near you.

5. **Safety Rating**

   Weiss rating assigned to the institution at the time of publication. Our ratings are designed to distinguish levels of insolvency risk and are measured on a scale from A to F based upon a wide range of factors. Highly rated companies are, in our opinion, less likely to experience financial difficulties than lower rated firms. See *About Weiss Safety Ratings* for more information and a description of what each rating means.

## Alabama

| City | Name | Telephone | City | Name | Telephone |
|------|------|-----------|------|------|-----------|

### Rating: A

| City | Name | Telephone |
|------|------|-----------|
| DECATUR | FAMILY SECURITY CU | (256) 340-2000 |

### Rating: A-

| City | Name | Telephone |
|------|------|-----------|
| BIRMINGHAM | ACIPCO FCU | (205) 328-4371 |
| TUSCALOOSA | ALABAMA CU | (205) 348-5944 |
| GADSDEN | ALABAMA TEACHERS CU | (256) 543-7040 |
| MONTGOMERY | MAX CU | (334) 260-2600 |
| PENNINGTON | NAHEOLA CU | (205) 654-2370 |
| HUNTSVILLE | REDSTONE FCU | (256) 837-6110 |
| MUSCLE SHOALS | TVA COMMUNITY CU | (256) 383-1019 |

### Rating: B+

| City | Name | Telephone |
|------|------|-----------|
| CHILDERSBURG | COOSA PINES FCU | (256) 378-5559 |
| GADSDEN | FAMILY SAVINGS CU | (256) 543-9530 |
| DOTHAN | FIVE STAR CU | (334) 793-7714 |
| ANNISTON | FORT MCCLELLAN CU | (256) 237-2113 |
| MUSCLE SHOALS | LISTERHILL CU | (256) 383-9204 |
| TUSCALOOSA | RIVERFALL CU | (205) 759-1505 |
| TUSCUMBIA | VALLEY CU | (256) 381-4800 |

## Alaska

| City | Name | Telephone | City | Name | Telephone |
|------|------|-----------|------|------|-----------|

| **Rating:** | | **A** |
|---|---|---|

| ANCHORAGE | CU 1 | (907) 339-9485 |
|---|---|---|

| **Rating:** | | **A-** |
|---|---|---|

| FAIRBANKS | MAC FCU | (907) 474-1291 |
|---|---|---|

| **Rating:** | | **B+** |
|---|---|---|

| PALMER | MATANUSKA VALLEY FCU | (907) 745-4891 |
|---|---|---|
| ANCHORAGE | NORTHERN SKIES FCU | (907) 561-1407 |
| FAIRBANKS | SPIRIT OF ALASKA FCU | (907) 459-5900 |

# Arizona

| City | Name | Telephone | City | Name | Telephone |
|------|------|-----------|------|------|-----------|
| **Rating:** | **A** | | | | |
| PHOENIX | ARIZONA FCU | (602) 683-1000 | | | |
| PHOENIX | DESERT SCHOOLS FCU | (602) 433-7000 | | | |
| **Rating:** | **A-** | | | | |
| GLENDALE | CU WEST | (602) 631-3200 | | | |
| TUCSON | VANTAGE WEST CU | (520) 298-7882 | | | |
| **Rating:** | **B+** | | | | |
| PHOENIX | ARIZONA STATE CU | (602) 467-4081 | | | |
| TUCSON | HUGHES FCU | (520) 794-8341 | | | |
| TUCSON | PIMA FCU | (520) 887-5010 | | | |
| TEMPE | TRUWEST CU | (480) 441-5900 | | | |

## Arkansas

| City | Name | Telephone | City | Name | Telephone |
|------|------|-----------|------|------|-----------|

### Rating: A

| City | Name | Telephone |
|------|------|-----------|
| LITTLE ROCK | TELCOE FCU | (501) 375-5321 |

### Rating: A-

| City | Name | Telephone |
|------|------|-----------|
| WARREN | ARKANSAS SUPERIOR FCU | (870) 226-3534 |

### Rating: B+

| City | Name | Telephone |
|------|------|-----------|
| LITTLE ROCK | BAPTIST HEALTH FCU | (501) 202-2373 |
| PINE BLUFF | PINE FCU | (870) 247-5100 |

## California

| City | Name | Telephone | City | Name | Telephone |
|------|------|-----------|------|------|-----------|
| | | | SIGNAL HILL | VA DESERT PACIFIC FCU | (562) 498-1250 |
| | | | WOODLAND | YOLO FCU | (530) 668-2700 |

### Rating: A+

| City | Name | Telephone |
|------|------|-----------|
| SAN BERNARDINO | ARROWHEAD CENTRAL CU | (909) 383-7300 |
| LONG BEACH | LONG BEACH FIREMENS CU | (562) 597-0351 |
| SAN DIEGO | SAN DIEGO COUNTY CU | (877) 732-2848 |
| EL MONTE | VONS EMPL FCU | (626) 444-1972 |

### Rating: A

| City | Name | Telephone |
|------|------|-----------|
| RIVERSIDE | ALTURA CU | (888) 883-7228 |
| PASADENA | E-CENTRAL CU | (626) 799-6000 |
| FRESNO | EDUCATIONAL EMPL CU | (559) 437-7700 |
| MONTEREY PARK | F&A FCU | (323) 268-1226 |
| STOCKTON | FINANCIAL CENTER CU | (209) 948-6024 |
| ARCADIA | FOOTHILL FCU | (626) 445-0950 |
| FRESNO | FRESNO COUNTY FCU | (559) 252-5000 |
| SACRAMENTO | GOLDEN 1 CU | (916) 732-2900 |
| WILMINGTON | ILWU CU | (310) 834-6411 |
| WESTMINSTER | LBS FINANCIAL CU | (714) 893-5111 |
| BURBANK | LOGIX FCU | (800) 328-5328 |
| SAN DIEGO | MISSION FCU | (858) 524-2850 |
| LIVERMORE | OPERATING ENGINEERS LOCAL UNION #3 | (925) 454-4000 |
| PLEASANTON | PATELCO CU | (415) 442-6200 |
| SANTA ROSA | REDWOOD CU | (707) 545-4000 |
| SACRAMENTO | SACRAMENTO CU | (916) 444-6070 |
| BAKERSFIELD | SAFE 1 CU | (661) 327-3818 |
| SANTA ANA | SCHOOLSFIRST FCU | (714) 258-4000 |
| VACAVILLE | TRAVIS CU | (707) 449-4000 |

### Rating: A-

| City | Name | Telephone |
|------|------|-----------|
| LA HABRA | AMERICAN FIRST CU | (800) 290-1112 |
| SAN PEDRO | BOPTI FCU | (310) 832-0227 |
| RIVERSIDE | BOURNS EMPL FCU | (951) 781-5600 |
| SAN DIEGO | CALIFORNIA COAST CU | (858) 495-1600 |
| SANTA MONICA | CALIFORNIA LITHUANIAN CU | (310) 828-7095 |
| OAKLAND | CHEVRON FCU | (800) 232-8101 |
| SAN DIMAS | CHRISTIAN COMMUNITY CU | (626) 915-7551 |
| ANAHEIM | CU OF SOUTHERN CALIFORNIA | (866) 287-6225 |
| LOS ANGELES | FARMERS INSURANCE GROUP FCU | (800) 877-2345x |
| TORRANCE | HONDA FCU | (310) 217-8600 |
| BAKERSFIELD | KERN SCHOOLS FCU | (661) 833-7900 |
| HANFORD | KINGS FCU | (559) 582-4438 |
| SAN DIEGO | NORTH ISLAND FINANCIAL CU | (858) 769-7600 |
| SANTA ANA | ORANGE COUNTYS CU | (714) 755-5900 |
| BURBANK | PARTNERS FCU | (407) 354-5100 |
| CERRITOS | POPA FCU | (562) 229-9181 |
| CHATSWORTH | PREMIER AMERICA CU | (818) 772-4000 |
| SACRAMENTO | SCHOOLS FINANCIAL CU | (916) 569-5400 |
| SAN FRANCISCO | SF POLICE CU | (415) 564-3800 |
| PALO ALTO | STANFORD FCU | (650) 723-2509 |
| SUNNYVALE | STAR ONE CU | (408) 543-5202 |

### Rating: B+

| City | Name | Telephone |
|------|------|-----------|
| SALINAS | ALLUS CU | (831) 540-4627 |
| SAN DIEGO | CABRILLO CU | (858) 547-7400 |
| SACRAMENTO | CAHP CU | (916) 362-4191 |
| GLENDALE | CALIFORNIA CU | (800) 334-8788 |
| LA CANADA FLINT | CALTECH EMPL FCU | (818) 952-4444 |
| EUREKA | COAST CENTRAL CU | (707) 445-8801 |
| LOMPOC | COASTHILLS CU | (805) 733-7600 |
| SAN JOSE | COMMONWEALTH CENTRAL CU | (408) 531-3100 |
| HANFORD | FAMILIES & SCHOOLS TOGETHER FCU | (559) 584-0922 |
| LOS ANGELES | FIREFIGHTERS FIRST CU | (323) 254-1700 |
| HOLLYWOOD | FIRST ENTERTAINMENT CU | (888) 800-3328 |
| MOUNTAIN VIEW | FIRST TECHNOLOGY FCU | (855) 855-8805 |
| SACRAMENTO | FIRST US COMMUNITY CU | (916) 576-5700 |
| BAKERSFIELD | KERN FCU | (661) 327-9461 |
| GLENDALE | LOS ANGELES FCU | (818) 242-8640x |
| OAKLAND | MATSON EMPL FCU | (510) 628-4358 |
| MERCED | MERCED SCHOOL EMPL FCU | (209) 383-5550 |
| SAN JOSE | MERIWEST CU | (408) 972-5222 |
| MONTEREY | MONTEREY CU | (831) 647-1000 |
| SYLMAR | OLIVE VIEW EMPL FCU | (818) 367-1057 |
| PASADENA | PARSONS FCU | (626) 440-7000 |
| REDWOOD CITY | PROVIDENT CU | (650) 508-0300 |
| REDWOOD CITY | SAN MATEO CU | (650) 363-1725 |
| YUBA CITY | SIERRA CENTRAL CU | (800) 222-7228 |
| HAWTHORNE | SKYONE FCU | (310) 491-7500 |
| REDONDO BEACH | SOUTH BAY CU | (310) 374-3436 |
| EL CENTRO | SUN COMMUNITY FCU | (760) 337-4200 |
| SAN JOSE | TECHNOLOGY CU | (408) 467-2380 |
| SAN BERNARDINO | THINKWISE FCU | (909) 882-2911 |
| SAN DIEGO | UNIV & STATE EMPL CU | (858) 795-6100 |
| SACRAMENTO | VISION ONE CU | (916) 363-4293 |

## Colorado

| City | Name | Telephone | City | Name | Telephone |
|------|------|-----------|------|------|-----------|

### Rating: A+

| City | Name | Telephone |
|------|------|-----------|
| DENVER | ROCKY MOUNTAIN LAW ENFORCEMENT F | (303) 458-6660 |

### Rating: A

| City | Name | Telephone |
|------|------|-----------|
| AURORA | AURORA FCU | (303) 755-2572 |
| GREENWOOD VIL | BELLCO CU | (303) 689-7800 |
| GOLDEN | COORS CU | (303) 279-6414 |
| LAKEWOOD | CU OF DENVER | (303) 234-1700 |
| DENVER | DENVER COMMUNITY CU | (303) 573-1170 |
| COLORADO SPRIN | ENT FCU | (719) 574-1100 |
| LONE TREE | PUBLIC SERVICE CU | (303) 691-2345 |

### Rating: A-

| City | Name | Telephone |
|------|------|-----------|
| BROOMFIELD | COMMUNITY FINANCIAL CU | (303) 469-5366 |
| GRAND JUNCTION | GRAND JUNCTION FCU | (970) 243-1370 |
| CENTENNIAL | METRUM COMMUNITY CU | (303) 770-4468 |

### Rating: B+

| City | Name | Telephone |
|------|------|-----------|
| COLORADO SPRIN | AVENTA CU | (719) 482-7600 |
| LITTLETON | COLORADO CU | (303) 978-2274 |
| GRAND JUNCTION | COLORAMO FCU | (970) 243-7280 |
| BOULDER | ELEVATIONS CU | (303) 443-4672 |
| PUEBLO | MINNEQUA WORKS CU | (719) 544-6928 |
| ARVADA | PARTNER COLORADO CU | (303) 422-6221 |
| STERLING | STERLING FCU | (970) 522-0111 |
| DENVER | WESTERRA CU | (303) 321-4209 |

## Connecticut

| City | Name | Telephone | City | Name | Telephone |
|------|------|-----------|------|------|-----------|

**Rating:**        **B+**

| City | Name | Telephone |
|------|------|-----------|
| ROCKY HILL | NUTMEG STATE FINANCIAL CU | (860) 513-5000 |
| MIDDLEBURY | WATERBURY CONNECTICUT TEACHER FC | (203) 758-9500 |

## Delaware

| City | Name | Telephone | City | Name | Telephone |
|------|------|-----------|------|------|-----------|

### Rating: A-

| City | Name | Telephone |
|------|------|-----------|
| SEAFORD | SUSSEX COUNTY FCU | (302) 629-0100 |

## District of Columbia

| City | Name | Telephone | City | Name | Telephone |
|------|------|-----------|------|------|-----------|
| **Rating:** | **A-** | | | | |
| WASHINGTON | IDB-IIC FCU | (202) 623-3363 | | | |
| **Rating:** | **B+** | | | | |
| WASHINGTON | TRANSIT EMPL FCU | (202) 832-5100 | | | |

# Florida

| City | Name | Telephone | City | Name | Telephone |
|------|------|-----------|------|------|-----------|

## Rating: A

| City | Name | Telephone |
|------|------|-----------|
| JACKSONVILLE | COMMUNITY FIRST CU OF FLORIDA | (904) 354-8537 |
| JACKSONVILLE | JM ASSOCIATES FCU | (904) 378-4588 |
| PANAMA CITY | PANHANDLE EDUCATORS FCU | (850) 769-3306 |
| WEST PALM BEAC | PBC CU | (561) 686-4006 |

## Rating: A-

| City | Name | Telephone |
|------|------|-----------|
| DUNEDIN | ACHIEVA CU | (727) 431-7680 |
| JONESVILLE | CAMPUS USA CU | (352) 335-9090 |
| ROCKLEDGE | COMMUNITY CU OF FLORIDA | (321) 690-2328 |
| TALLAHASSEE | FIRST COMMERCE CU | (850) 488-0035 |
| LAKELAND | MIDFLORIDA CU | (863) 688-3733 |
| PENSACOLA | MY PENSACOLA FCU | (850) 432-9939 |
| PENSACOLA | PEN AIR FCU | (850) 505-3200 |
| LAKELAND | PUBLIX EMPL FCU | (863) 683-6404 |
| TAMPA | RAILROAD & INDUSTRIAL FCU | (813) 621-6661 |
| GAINESVILLE | SUNSTATE FCU | (352) 381-5200 |
| MARGATE | WE FLORIDA FINANCIAL | (954) 745-2400 |

## Rating: B+

| City | Name | Telephone |
|------|------|-----------|
| MIAMI | BAPTIST HEALTH SOUTH FLORIDA FCU | (305) 412-9920 |
| PENSACOLA | CENTRAL CU OF FLORIDA | (850) 474-0970 |
| CHIPLEY | COMMUNITY SOUTH CU | (850) 638-8376 |
| DORAL | DADE COUNTY FCU | (305) 471-5080 |
| JACKSONVILLE | FIRST FLORIDA CU | (904) 359-6800 |
| TALLAHASSEE | FLORIDA STATE UNIV CU | (850) 224-4960 |
| PENSACOLA | GULF WINDS FCU | (850) 479-9601 |
| DELRAY BEACH | IBM SOUTHEAST EMPL CU | (561) 982-4700 |
| MARIANNA | JACKSON COUNTY TEACHERS CU | (850) 526-4470 |
| MIAMI LAKES | JETSTREAM FCU | (305) 821-7060 |
| BRADENTON | MANATEE COMMUNITY FCU | (941) 748-7704 |
| ORLANDO | ORLANDO FCU | (407) 835-3500 |
| LARGO | PINELLAS FCU | (727) 586-4422 |
| MELBOURNE | SPACE COAST CU | (321) 752-2222 |
| TAMPA | ST JOSEPHS HOSPITAL FCU | (813) 870-4362 |
| TAMPA | SUNCOAST CU | (813) 621-7511 |
| TAMPA | TAMPA BAY FCU | (813) 247-4414 |
| JACKSONVILLE | VYSTAR CU | (904) 777-6000 |

## Georgia

| City | Name | Telephone | City | Name | Telephone |
|------|------|-----------|------|------|-----------|

### Rating: A+

| | | |
|---|---|---|
| WARNER ROBINS | ROBINS FCU | (478) 923-3773 |

### Rating: A

| | | |
|---|---|---|
| MACON | CGR CU | (478) 745-0494 |

### Rating: A-

| | | |
|---|---|---|
| ATLANTA | DELTA COMMUNITY CU | (404) 715-4725 |
| JESUP | INTERSTATE UNLIMITED FCU | (912) 427-3904 |
| MARIETTA | LGE COMMUNITY CU | (770) 424-0060 |
| CORNELIA | SOUTHEAST FCU | (706) 776-2145 |
| SAVANNAH | WORKMENS CIRCLE CU | (912) 356-9225 |

### Rating: B+

| | | |
|---|---|---|
| WOODSTOCK | CU OF GEORGIA | (678) 322-2000 |
| DULUTH | GEORGIA UNITED CU | (770) 476-6400 |
| BRUNSWICK | MARSHLAND COMMUNITY FCU | (912) 279-2000 |
| KINGSLAND | UNITED 1ST FCU | (912) 729-2800 |

# Hawaii

| City | Name | Telephone | City | Name | Telephone |
|------|------|-----------|------|------|-----------|

## Rating:         A

| City | Name | Telephone |
|------|------|-----------|
| WAILUKU | MAUI COUNTY FCU | (808) 244-7968 |
| ELEELE | MCBRYDE FCU | (808) 335-3365 |

## Rating:         A-

| City | Name | Telephone |
|------|------|-----------|
| HONOLULU | HAWAIIAN TEL FCU | (808) 832-8700 |
| HONOLULU | UNIV OF HAWAII FCU | (808) 983-5500 |
| KAHULUI | WAILUKU FCU | (808) 244-7981 |

## Rating:         B+

| City | Name | Telephone |
|------|------|-----------|
| HONOLULU | HAWAIIUSA FCU | (808) 534-4300 |
| LIHUE | KAUAI COMMUNITY FCU | (808) 245-6791 |
| WAHIAWA | SCHOFIELD FCU | (808) 624-9884 |

## Idaho

| City | Name | Telephone | City | Name | Telephone |
|---|---|---|---|---|---|

### Rating: A

| City | Name | Telephone |
|---|---|---|
| REXBURG | BEEHIVE FCU | (208) 656-1000 |
| BOISE | ICON CU | (208) 344-7948 |

### Rating: A-

| City | Name | Telephone |
|---|---|---|
| CHUBBUCK | IDAHO CENTRAL CU | (208) 239-3000 |
| KAMIAH | KAMIAH COMMUNITY CU | (208) 935-0277 |
| LEWISTON | POTLATCH NO ONE FCU | (208) 746-8900 |

## Illinois

| City | Name | Telephone | City | Name | Telephone |
|------|------|-----------|------|------|-----------|

### Rating:                    A

| City | Name | Telephone |
|------|------|-----------|
| OSWEGO | EARTHMOVER CU | (630) 844-4950 |
| STREATOR | STREATOR ONIZED CU | (815) 673-1589 |

### Rating:                    A-

| City | Name | Telephone |
|------|------|-----------|
| VERNON HILLS | BAXTER CU | (800) 388-7000 |
| PEORIA | CITIZENS EQUITY FIRST CU | (309) 633-7000 |
| ELGIN | CORPORATE AMERICA FAMILY CU | (847) 214-2000 |
| OTTAWA | FINANCIAL PLUS CU | (815) 433-1496 |
| NAPERVILLE | HEALTHCARE ASSOCIATES CU | (630) 276-5555 |
| QUINCY | MEMBERS FIRST COMMUNITY CU | (217) 223-4377 |
| JOLIET | NUMARK CU | (815) 729-3211 |
| CHICAGO | SELFRELIANCE UKRAINIAN AMERICAN FC | (773) 328-7500 |

### Rating:                    B+

| City | Name | Telephone |
|------|------|-----------|
| BETHALTO | 1ST MIDAMERICA CU | (618) 258-3168 |
| GURNEE | ABBOTT LABORATORIES EMPL CU | (847) 688-8000 |
| CHICAGO | ALLIANT CU | (773) 462-2000 |
| MOLINE | DEERE EMPL CU | (309) 743-1000 |
| ROCK ISLAND | GAS & ELECTRIC CU | (309) 793-3610 |
| SPRINGFIELD | HEARTLAND CU | (217) 726-8877 |
| BLOOMINGTON | IAA CU | (309) 557-2541 |
| SYCAMORE | ILLINOIS COMMUNITY CU | (815) 895-4541 |
| DECATUR | LAND OF LINCOLN CU | (217) 864-3030 |
| MOLINE | MOLINE MUNICIPAL CU | (309) 797-2185 |

## Indiana

| City | Name | Telephone | City | Name | Telephone |
|------|------|-----------|------|------|-----------|

### Rating:      A

| City | Name | Telephone |
|------|------|-----------|
| FORT WAYNE | THREE RIVERS FCU | (260) 490-8328 |

### Rating:      A-

| City | Name | Telephone |
|------|------|-----------|
| COLUMBUS | CENTRA CU | (812) 376-9771 |
| ODON | CRANE FCU | (812) 863-7000 |
| INDIANAPOLIS | ELEMENTS FINANCIAL FCU | (317) 524-5076 |
| TIPTON | ENCOMPASS FCU | (765) 675-8848 |
| KOKOMO | FINANCIAL BUILDERS FCU | (765) 455-0500 |
| BLOOMINGTON | INDIANA UNIV CU | (812) 855-7823 |
| SOUTH BEND | SOUTH BEND FIREFIGHTERS FCU | (574) 287-6161 |

### Rating:      B+

| City | Name | Telephone |
|------|------|-----------|
| EVANSVILLE | EVANSVILLE FCU | (812) 424-2621 |
| EVANSVILLE | EVANSVILLE TEACHERS FCU | (812) 477-9271 |
| FORT WAYNE | MIDWEST AMERICA FCU | (260) 482-3334 |
| WEST LAFAYETTE | PURDUE FCU | (765) 497-3328 |
| MERRILLVILLE | US #1364 FCU | (219) 769-1700 |
| WHITING | WHITING REFINERY FCU | (219) 659-3254 |

## Iowa

| City | Name | Telephone | City | Name | Telephone |
|------|------|-----------|------|------|-----------|

### Rating: A

| City | Name | Telephone |
|------|------|-----------|
| CEDAR FALLS | CEDAR FALLS COMMUNITY CU | (319) 266-7531 |
| FORT DODGE | CITIZENS COMMUNITY CU | (515) 955-5524 |
| DUBUQUE | DUPACO COMMUNITY CU | (563) 557-7600 |

### Rating: A-

| City | Name | Telephone |
|------|------|-----------|
| ESTHERVILLE | EMPL CU | (712) 362-5897 |
| DAVENPORT | FAMILY CU | (563) 388-8328 |
| WATERLOO | VERIDIAN CU | (319) 236-5600 |

### Rating: B+

| City | Name | Telephone |
|------|------|-----------|
| CAMANCHE | 1ST GATEWAY CU | (563) 243-4121 |
| NEWTON | ADVANTAGE CU | (641) 792-5660 |
| BETTENDORF | ASCENTRA CU | (563) 355-0152 |
| DES MOINES | DES MOINES POLICE OFFICERS CU | (515) 243-2677 |
| HIAWATHA | FIRST FCU | (319) 743-7806 |
| FORT DODGE | FORT DODGE FAMILY CU | (515) 573-1160 |
| OTTUMWA | MERIDIAN CU | (641) 684-4207 |
| HUMBOLDT | POWER CO-OP EMPL CU | (515) 332-4096 |
| DES MOINES | PREMIER CU | (515) 282-1611 |
| AMES | RIVER VALLEY CU | (515) 232-1654 |
| NORTH LIBERTY | UNIV OF IOWA COMMUNITY CU | (319) 339-1000 |

## Kansas

| City | Name | Telephone | City | Name | Telephone |
|------|------|-----------|------|------|-----------|

### Rating:                          A

| City | Name | Telephone |
|------|------|-----------|
| WICHITA | SKYWARD CU | (316) 517-6578 |

### Rating:                          A-

| City | Name | Telephone |
|------|------|-----------|
| LENEXA | COMMUNITYAMERICA CU | (913) 905-7000 |
| WICHITA | CU OF AMERICA | (316) 265-3272 |
| AUGUSTA | WHITE EAGLE CU | (316) 775-7591 |

### Rating:                          B+

| City | Name | Telephone |
|------|------|-----------|
| TOPEKA | ENVISTA CU | (785) 228-0149 |
| BELOIT | FARMWAY CU | (785) 738-2224 |
| LEAVENWORTH | FRONTIER COMMUNITY CU | (913) 651-6575 |
| TOPEKA | KANSAS BLUE CROSS-BLUE SHIELD CU | (785) 291-8774 |
| OVERLAND PARK | MAZUMA CU | (816) 361-4194 |
| WICHITA | MERITRUST CU | (316) 683-1199 |
| NORTON | UNITED NORTHWEST FCU | (785) 877-5191 |

## Kentucky

| City | Name | Telephone | City | Name | Telephone |
|------|------|-----------|------|------|-----------|

### Rating: A+

| City | Name | Telephone |
|------|------|-----------|
| RADCLIFF | FORT KNOX FCU | (502) 942-0254 |

### Rating: A

| City | Name | Telephone |
|------|------|-----------|
| FRANKFORT | COMMONWEALTH CU | (502) 564-4775 |
| LOUISVILLE | KENTUCKY TELCO FCU | (502) 459-3000 |
| LEXINGTON | UNIV OF KENTUCKY FCU | (859) 264-4200 |

### Rating: A-

| City | Name | Telephone |
|------|------|-----------|
| ASHLAND | ASHLAND CU | (606) 329-5489 |
| PADUCAH | C-PLANT FCU | (270) 554-0287 |
| LOUISVILLE | L&N FCU | (502) 368-5858 |
| PADUCAH | SIGNET FCU | (270) 443-5261 |

### Rating: B+

| City | Name | Telephone |
|------|------|-----------|
| MIDDLESBORO | ARH FCU | (606) 248-8566 |
| LOUISVILLE | BEACON COMMUNITY CU | (502) 366-6022 |
| EDGEWOOD | COVE FCU | (859) 292-9000 |
| LOUISVILLE | LOUISVILLE GAS & ELECTRIC CO CU | (502) 627-3140 |
| ASHLAND | MEMBERS CHOICE CU | (606) 326-8000 |
| BOWLING GREEN | SERVICE ONE CU INC | (270) 796-8500 |

## Louisiana

| City | Name | Telephone | City | Name | Telephone |
|------|------|-----------|------|------|-----------|

### Rating: A

| City | Name | Telephone |
|------|------|-----------|
| WEST MONROE | OUACHITA VALLEY FCU | (318) 387-4592 |
| GEISMAR | WYMAR FCU | (225) 339-7191 |

### Rating: A-

| City | Name | Telephone |
|------|------|-----------|
| BATON ROUGE | BATON ROUGE FIRE DEPT FCU | (225) 274-8383 |
| BATON ROUGE | DEPT OF CORRECTIONS CU | (225) 342-6618 |
| LAFAYETTE | LAFAYETTE SCHOOLS FCU | (337) 989-2800 |
| LA PLACE | LOUISIANA FCU | (985) 652-4990 |
| LAKE CHARLES | SOUTHWEST LOUISIANA CU | (337) 477-9190 |
| BOGALUSA | ZELLCO FCU | (985) 732-7522 |

### Rating: B+

| City | Name | Telephone |
|------|------|-----------|
| BATON ROUGE | BATON ROUGE TELCO FCU | (225) 924-8900 |
| DERIDDER | BOISE SOUTHERN EMPL FCU | (337) 463-7529 |
| ALEXANDRIA | CENLA FCU | (318) 445-7388 |
| PLAQUEMINE | ESSENTIAL FCU | (225) 353-8238 |
| PINEVILLE | HEART OF LOUISIANA FCU | (318) 619-1900 |
| NEW ORLEANS | JEFFERSON PARISH EMPL FCU | (504) 736-6144 |
| LAFAYETTE | MAPLE FCU | (337) 233-6264 |
| NEW ORLEANS | NEW ORLEANS POLICE DEPT EMPL CU | (504) 658-5570 |
| SHREVEPORT | PROFESSIONAL FIRE FIGHTERS CU | (318) 603-0626 |

## Maine

| City | Name | Telephone | City | Name | Telephone |
|------|------|-----------|------|------|-----------|

### Rating: A-

| City | Name | Telephone |
|------|------|-----------|
| SOUTH PORTLAN | COAST LINE CU | (207) 799-7245 |
| BATH | MIDCOAST FCU | (207) 443-5531 |
| JAY | OTIS FCU | (207) 897-0900 |
| MEXICO | OXFORD FCU | (207) 369-9976 |
| LEWISTON | RAINBOW FCU | (207) 784-5435 |

### Rating: B+

| City | Name | Telephone |
|------|------|-----------|
| FORT KENT | ACADIA FCU | (207) 834-6167 |
| BRUNSWICK | ATLANTIC REGIONAL FCU | (207) 725-8728 |
| AUGUSTA | CAPITAL AREA FCU | (207) 622-3442 |
| CARIBOU | COUNTY FCU | (207) 498-8756 |
| FALMOUTH | CUMBERLAND COUNTY FCU | (207) 878-3441 |
| GARDINER | GARDINER FCU | (207) 582-2676 |
| SACO | SACO VALLEY CU | (207) 282-6169 |
| PORTLAND | TRUCHOICE FCU | (207) 772-0808 |
| SANFORD | YORK COUNTY FCU | (207) 324-7511 |

# Maryland

| City | Name | Telephone | City | Name | Telephone |
|------|------|-----------|------|------|-----------|

## Rating: A

| City | Name | Telephone |
|------|------|-----------|
| LUTHERVILLE | FIRST FINANCIAL OF MARYLAND FCU | (410) 321-6060 |
| UPPER MARLBOR | NASA FCU | (301) 249-1800 |

## Rating: A-

| City | Name | Telephone |
|------|------|-----------|
| CUMBERLAND | FIRST PEOPLES COMMUNITY FCU | (301) 784-3000 |
| BALTIMORE | JOHNS HOPKINS FCU | (410) 534-4500 |
| HYATTSVILLE | LIBRARY OF CONGRESS FCU | (202) 707-5852 |
| FREDERICK | NYMEO FCU | (240) 436-4000 |

## Rating: B+

| City | Name | Telephone |
|------|------|-----------|
| GREENBELT | EDUCATIONAL SYSTEMS FCU | (301) 779-8500 |
| LARGO | MONEY ONE FCU | (301) 925-4600 |
| HAGERSTOWN | WASHINGTON COUNTY TEACHERS FCU | (301) 790-3131 |

## Massachusetts

| City | Name | Telephone | City | Name | Telephone |
|------|------|-----------|------|------|-----------|

### Rating:      A

| City | Name | Telephone |
|------|------|-----------|
| NEEDHAM | DIRECT FCU | (781) 455-6500 |
| SPRINGFIELD | GREATER SPRINGFIELD CU | (413) 782-3161 |
| LYNN | RIVER WORKS CU | (781) 599-0096 |
| WORCESTER | WEBSTER FIRST FCU | (508) 671-5000 |
| FITCHBURG | WORKERS CU | (978) 345-1021 |

### Rating:      A-

| City | Name | Telephone |
|------|------|-----------|
| DORCHESTER | BOSTON FIREFIGHTERS CU | (617) 288-2420 |
| MARLBOROUGH | DIGITAL FCU | (508) 263-6700 |
| ROCKLAND | ROCKLAND FCU | (781) 878-0232 |
| TAUNTON | TAUNTON FCU | (508) 824-6466 |

### Rating:      B+

| City | Name | Telephone |
|------|------|-----------|
| CAMBRIDGE | HARVARD UNIV EMPL CU | (617) 495-4460 |
| SPRINGFIELD | PIONEER VALLEY FCU | (413) 733-2800 |
| QUINCY | QUINCY CU | (617) 479-5558 |

## Michigan

| City | Name | Telephone | City | Name | Telephone |
|------|------|-----------|------|------|-----------|
| | | | OSCODA | NORTHLAND AREA FCU | (989) 739-1401 |
| | | | WATERFORD | OAKLAND COUNTY CU | (248) 886-0144 |

### Rating: A

| City | Name | Telephone | City | Name | Telephone |
|------|------|-----------|------|------|-----------|
| GRAND RAPIDS | AAC CU | (616) 459-4429 | GRAND RAPIDS | OPTION 1 CU | (616) 243-0125 |
| MUSKEGON | BEST FINANCIAL CU | (231) 733-1329 | PORTLAND | PORTLAND FCU | (517) 647-7571 |
| PLYMOUTH | COMMUNITY FINANCIAL CU | (734) 453-1200 | ROMULUS | PUBLIC SERVICE CU | (734) 641-8400 |
| DEARBORN | DFCU FINANCIAL CU | (313) 336-2700 | WARREN | UKRAINIAN FUTURE CU | (586) 757-1980 |
| FLINT | DORT FCU | (810) 767-8390 | GRAND RAPIDS | WESTERN DISTRICTS MEMBERS CU | (616) 241-2516 |
| AUBURN HILLS | GENISYS CU | (248) 322-9800 | | | |
| SAINT JOSEPH | HONOR CU | (269) 983-6357 | | | |
| BATTLE CREEK | KELLOGG COMMUNITY FCU | (269) 968-9251 | | | |
| GRAND RAPIDS | LAKE MICHIGAN CU | (616) 242-9790 | | | |
| MARSHALL | MARSHALL COMMUNITY CU | (269) 781-9885 | | | |
| LATHRUP VILLAG | MICHIGAN FIRST CU | (248) 443-4600 | | | |
| NORTON SHORES | SERVICE 1 FCU | (231) 739-5068 | | | |
| PETOSKEY | ST FRANCIS X FCU | (231) 347-8480 | | | |
| TRAVERSE CITY | TBA CU | (231) 946-7090 | | | |
| ADRIAN | TLC COMMUNITY CU | (517) 263-9120 | | | |
| SAGINAW | WANIGAS CU | (989) 759-5780 | | | |
| GRAND RAPIDS | WEST MICHIGAN CU | (616) 451-4567 | | | |
| LIVONIA | ZEAL CU | (734) 522-3700 | | | |

### Rating: A-

| City | Name | Telephone |
|------|------|-----------|
| JACKSON | AMERICAN 1 CU | (517) 787-6510 |
| ROCHESTER HILL | CHIEF FINANCIAL FCU | (248) 335-9493 |
| KALAMAZOO | CONSUMERS CU | (269) 345-7804 |
| AUBURN HILLS | CORNERSTONE COMMUNITY FINANCIAL C | (248) 340-9310 |
| MONROE | EDUCATION PLUS CU | (734) 242-3765 |
| FLINT | FINANCIAL PLUS CU | (810) 244-2200 |
| CLINTON TOWNS | MICHIGAN SCHOOLS AND GOVERNMENT | (586) 263-8800 |
| EAST LANSING | MICHIGAN STATE UNIV FCU | (517) 333-2424 |
| BATTLE CREEK | OMNI COMMUNITY CU | (269) 441-1400 |
| LIVONIA | PARKSIDE CU | (734) 525-0700 |
| GRAND RAPIDS | PREFERRED CU | (616) 942-9630 |
| SAINT JOSEPH | UNITED FCU | (269) 982-1400 |
| MARQUETTE | UP CATHOLIC CU | (906) 228-7080 |

### Rating: B+

| City | Name | Telephone |
|------|------|-----------|
| PARCHMENT | ADVIA CU | (844) 238-4228 |
| SOUTHFIELD | ALLIANCE CATHOLIC CU | (248) 663-4006 |
| ROGERS CITY | CALCITE CU | (989) 734-4130 |
| CLINTON TOWNS | CENTRAL MACOMB COMMUNITY CU | (586) 466-7800 |
| ROSEVILLE | CHRISTIAN FINANCIAL CU | (586) 772-6330 |
| FARMINGTON HIL | COMMUNITY CHOICE CU | (877) 243-2528 |
| KENTWOOD | COMMUNITY WEST CU | (616) 261-5657 |
| BUCHANAN | COUNTRY HERITAGE CU | (269) 695-2334 |
| JACKSON | CP FCU | (517) 784-7101 |
| BURTON | ELGA CU | (810) 715-3542 |
| MANISTEE | FILER CU | (231) 723-3400 |
| FIFE LAKE | FOREST AREA FCU | (231) 879-4154 |
| FRANKENMUTH | FRANKENMUTH CU | (989) 497-1600 |

## Minnesota

| City | Name | Telephone | City | Name | Telephone |
|------|------|-----------|------|------|-----------|

### Rating:                   A

| City | Name | Telephone |
|------|------|-----------|
| SILVER BAY | NORTH SHORE FCU | (218) 226-4401 |
| SAINT PAUL | ST PAUL FCU | (651) 772-8744 |
| INTERNATIONAL F | TRUSTAR FCU | (218) 283-2000 |

### Rating:                   A-

| City | Name | Telephone |
|------|------|-----------|
| SAINT PAUL | CITY & COUNTY CU | (651) 225-2700 |
| MONTEVIDEO | CO-OP CU OF MONTEVIDEO | (320) 269-2117 |
| FULDA | FULDA AREA CU | (507) 425-2544 |
| SAINT PAUL | HIWAY FCU | (651) 291-1515 |
| ROCHESTER | MAYO EMPL FCU | (507) 535-1460 |
| CLOQUET | MEMBERS COOPERATIVE CU | (218) 879-3304 |
| MANKATO | MINNESOTA VALLEY FCU | (507) 387-3055 |

### Rating:                   B+

| City | Name | Telephone |
|------|------|-----------|
| COON RAPIDS | ANOKA HENNEPIN CU | (763) 422-0290 |
| BAXTER | MID MINNESOTA FCU | (218) 829-0371 |
| CAMBRIDGE | MINNCO CU | (763) 689-1071 |
| CLOQUET | NORTHWOODS CU | (218) 879-4181 |
| SLEEPY EYE | SOUTHPOINT FCU | (507) 794-6712 |
| PLYMOUTH | TRUSTONE FINANCIAL FCU | (763) 544-1517 |
| TWO HARBORS | TWO HARBORS FCU | (218) 834-2266 |
| BURNSVILLE | US FCU | (952) 736-5000 |
| HOPKINS | WEST METRO SCHOOLS CU | (952) 988-4165 |
| APPLE VALLEY | WINGS FINANCIAL CU | (952) 997-8000 |

## Mississippi

| City | Name | Telephone | City | Name | Telephone |
|------|------|-----------|------|------|-----------|
| **Rating:** | **A** | | | | |
| MERIDIAN | 1ST MISSISSIPPI FCU | (601) 693-6873 | | | |
| BILOXI | KEESLER FCU | (228) 385-5500 | | | |
| RIDGELAND | MEMBERS EXCHANGE CU | (601) 922-3350 | | | |
| **Rating:** | **A-** | | | | |
| LAUREL | CENTRAL SUNBELT FCU | (601) 649-7181 | | | |
| GULFPORT | GULF COAST COMMUNITY FCU | (228) 539-7029 | | | |
| JACKSON | MISSISSIPPI FCU | (601) 351-9200 | | | |
| PASCAGOULA | NAVIGATOR CU | (228) 475-7300 | | | |
| **Rating:** | **B+** | | | | |
| MONTICELLO | FERGUSON FCU | (601) 587-4037 | | | |
| SOUTHAVEN | SECURTRUST FCU | (662) 890-8760 | | | |

# Missouri

| City | Name | Telephone | City | Name | Telephone |
|------|------|-----------|------|------|-----------|

## Rating: A

| City | Name | Telephone |
|------|------|-----------|
| SAINT LOUIS | CENTURY CU | (314) 544-1818 |
| SPRINGFIELD | CU COMMUNITY CU | (417) 865-3912 |

## Rating: A-

| City | Name | Telephone |
|------|------|-----------|
| SAINT LOUIS | NEIGHBORS CU | (314) 892-5400 |
| SPRINGFIELD | TELCOMM CU | (417) 886-5355 |

## Rating: B+

| City | Name | Telephone |
|------|------|-----------|
| SAINT LOUIS | FIRST MISSOURI CU | (314) 544-5050 |
| SAINT JOSEPH | GOETZ CU | (816) 232-8754 |
| JEFFERSON CITY | MISSOURI ELECTRIC COOPERATIVES EMP | (573) 634-2595 |
| MEXICO | UNITED CU | (573) 581-8651 |

## Montana

| City | Name | Telephone | City | Name | Telephone |
|------|------|-----------|------|------|-----------|

### Rating: A

| City | Name | Telephone |
|------|------|-----------|
| BILLINGS | BILLINGS FCU | (406) 248-1127 |
| LIBBY | LINCOLN COUNTY CU | (406) 293-7771 |

### Rating: A-

| City | Name | Telephone |
|------|------|-----------|
| SIDNEY | RICHLAND FCU | (406) 482-2704 |
| BILLINGS | VALLEY FCU OF MONTANA | (406) 656-9100 |
| WHITEFISH | WHITEFISH CU ASSN | (406) 862-3525 |

### Rating: B+

| City | Name | Telephone |
|------|------|-----------|
| LEWISTOWN | FERGUS FCU | (406) 535-7478 |
| GLENDIVE | GLENDIVE BN FCU | (406) 377-4250 |
| CIRCLE | MCCONE COUNTY FCU | (406) 485-2288 |
| HELENA | ROCKY MOUNTAIN CU | (406) 449-2680 |

# Nebraska

| City | Name | Telephone | City | Name | Telephone |
|------|------|-----------|------|------|-----------|

## Rating: A

| City | Name | Telephone |
|------|------|-----------|
| OMAHA | METRO HEALTH SERVICES FCU | (402) 551-3052 |
| COLUMBUS | NEBRASKA ENERGY FCU | (402) 563-5900 |
| SOUTH SIOUX CIT | SIOUXLAND FCU | (402) 494-2073 |

## Rating: A-

| City | Name | Telephone |
|------|------|-----------|
| OMAHA | FIRST NEBRASKA EDUCATORS & EMPL GR | (402) 492-9100 |

## Rating: B+

| City | Name | Telephone |
|------|------|-----------|
| COLUMBUS | DALE EMPL CU | (402) 563-6207 |
| OMAHA | FAMILY FOCUS FCU | (402) 933-0233 |
| LINCOLN | LIBERTY FIRST CU | (402) 465-1000 |
| OMAHA | OMAHA FIREFIGHTERS CU | (402) 894-5005 |

## Nevada

| City | Name | Telephone | City | Name | Telephone |
|------|------|-----------|------|------|-----------|

### Rating: A

| City | Name | Telephone |
|------|------|-----------|
| LAS VEGAS | ONE NEVADA CU | (702) 457-1000 |

### Rating: A-

| City | Name | Telephone |
|------|------|-----------|
| BOULDER CITY | BOULDER DAM CU | (702) 293-7777 |
| LAS VEGAS | CLARK COUNTY CU | (702) 228-2228 |
| CARSON CITY | GREATER NEVADA CU | (775) 882-2060 |
| LAS VEGAS | PLUS CU | (702) 871-4746 |
| LAS VEGAS | WESTSTAR CU | (702) 791-4777 |

### Rating: B+

| City | Name | Telephone |
|------|------|-----------|
| FALLON | CHURCHILL COUNTY FCU | (775) 423-7444 |
| HAWTHORNE | FINANCIAL HORIZONS CU | (775) 945-2421 |
| RENO | GREAT BASIN FCU | (775) 333-4228 |

## New Hampshire

| City | Name | Telephone | City | Name | Telephone |
|------|------|-----------|------|------|-----------|

**Rating:**      **A-**

| City | Name | Telephone |
|------|------|-----------|
| PORTSMOUTH | SERVICE CU | (603) 422-8300 |

# New Jersey

| City | Name | Telephone | City | Name | Telephone |
|------|------|-----------|------|------|-----------|

**Rating:**          B+

| City | Name | Telephone |
|------|------|-----------|
| ELIZABETH | SEAPORT FCU | (908) 558-6124 |
| HAMILTON | TRENTON NEW JERSEY POLICE FCU | (609) 570-8155 |

## New Mexico

| City | Name | Telephone | City | Name | Telephone |
|------|------|-----------|------|------|-----------|
| **Rating:** | **A** | | | | |
| ALBUQUERQUE | RIO GRANDE CU | (505) 262-1401 | | | |
| **Rating:** | **A-** | | | | |
| ARTESIA | ARTESIA CU | (575) 748-9779 | | | |
| ALBUQUERQUE | KIRTLAND FCU | (505) 254-4369 | | | |
| ALBUQUERQUE | SANDIA AREA FCU | (505) 292-6343 | | | |
| ALBUQUERQUE | SANDIA LABORATORY FCU | (505) 293-0500 | | | |
| SANTA FE | STATE EMPL CU | (505) 983-7328 | | | |
| **Rating:** | **B+** | | | | |
| SANTA FE | DEL NORTE CU | (505) 455-5228 | | | |
| SANTA FE | GUADALUPE CU | (505) 982-8942 | | | |
| ALAMOGORDO | LOCO CU | (575) 437-3110 | | | |
| ALBUQUERQUE | NUSENDA FCU | (505) 889-7755 | | | |
| ALAMOGORDO | OTERO FCU | (575) 434-8500 | | | |
| ROSWELL | ROSWELL COMMUNITY FCU | (575) 623-7788 | | | |

## New York

| City | Name | Telephone | City | Name | Telephone |
|------|------|-----------|------|------|-----------|

### Rating: A+

| City | Name | Telephone |
|------|------|-----------|
| ROCHESTER | ESL FCU | (585) 336-1000 |

### Rating: A

| City | Name | Telephone |
|------|------|-----------|
| ALBANY | CAPITAL COMMUNICATIONS FCU | (518) 458-2195 |
| ITHACA | CFCU COMMUNITY CU | (607) 257-8500 |
| PLAINVIEW | N C P D FCU | (516) 938-0300 |
| OLEAN | OLEAN AREA FCU | (716) 372-6607 |
| MASSENA | SEA COMM FCU | (315) 764-0566 |
| NEW YORK | SELF RELIANCE NY FCU | (212) 473-7310 |

### Rating: A-

| City | Name | Telephone |
|------|------|-----------|
| OSWEGO | COMPASS FCU | (315) 342-5300 |
| PLATTSBURGH | DANNEMORA FCU | (518) 825-0323 |
| NEW HARTFORD | GPO FCU | (315) 724-1654 |
| CORINTH | HUDSON RIVER COMMUNITY CU | (518) 654-9028 |
| HAMBURG | MERIDIA COMMUNITY FCU | (716) 648-4411 |
| EAST AURORA | MOOG EMPL FCU | (716) 655-2360 |
| PAINTED POST | SERVU FCU | (607) 936-2293 |
| ENDICOTT | VISIONS FCU | (607) 754-7900 |

### Rating: B+

| City | Name | Telephone |
|------|------|-----------|
| NEW YORK | ACTORS FCU | (212) 869-8926 |
| ROCHESTER | ADVANTAGE FCU | (585) 454-5900 |
| LATHAM | COMMUNITY RESOURCE FCU | (518) 783-2211 |
| EAST SYRACUSE | CORE FCU | (315) 656-8220 |
| EAST SYRACUSE | COUNTRYSIDE FCU | (315) 445-2300 |
| SYRACUSE | EMPOWER FCU | (315) 477-2200 |
| ROCHESTER | FAMILY FIRST OF NY FCU | (585) 586-8225 |
| GLOVERSVILLE | FIRST CHOICE FINANCIAL FCU | (518) 725-3191 |
| NEW HARTFORD | FIRST SOURCE FCU | (315) 735-8571 |
| BINGHAMTON | GHS FCU | (607) 723-7962 |
| POUGHKEEPSIE | HUDSON VALLEY FCU | (845) 463-3011 |
| BRIARWOOD | MELROSE CU | (718) 658-9800 |
| BUFFALO | MORTON LANE FCU | (716) 837-2007 |
| WESTBURY | NASSAU EDUCATORS FCU | (516) 561-0030 |
| PORT WASHINGT | PORT WASHINGTON FCU | (516) 883-3537 |
| NEW YORK | PROGRESSIVE CU | (212) 695-8900 |
| OGDENSBURG | SAINT LAWRENCE FCU | (315) 393-3530 |
| SYRACUSE | SYRACUSE FIRE DEPT EMPL FCU | (315) 471-4621 |
| CHEEKTOWAGA | TOWN OF CHEEKTOWAGA FCU | (716) 686-3497 |
| NEW HARTFORD | UTICA GAS & ELECTRIC EMPL FCU | (315) 733-1596 |
| BRONX | VAN CORTLANDT COOPERATIVE FCU | (718) 549-5858 |

## North Carolina

| City | Name | Telephone | City | Name | Telephone |
|------|------|-----------|------|------|-----------|
| **Rating:** | **A** | | | | |
| CHARLOTTE | CHARLOTTE METRO FCU | (704) 375-0183 | | | |
| **Rating:** | **A-** | | | | |
| DURHAM | LATINO COMMUNITY CU | (919) 688-9270 | | | |
| GREENSBORO | SUMMIT CU | (336) 662-6200 | | | |
| ASHEVILLE | TELCO COMMUNITY CU | (828) 252-6458 | | | |
| **Rating:** | **B+** | | | | |
| WINSTON-SALEM | ALLEGACY FCU | (336) 774-3400 | | | |
| CANTON | CHAMPION CU | (828) 648-1515 | | | |
| RALEIGH | COASTAL FCU | (919) 420-8000 | | | |
| RALEIGH | LOCAL GOVERNMENT FCU | (919) 755-0534 | | | |
| WAYNESVILLE | MOUNTAIN CU | (828) 456-8627 | | | |
| GREENSBORO | PREMIER FCU | (336) 370-1286 | | | |

## North Dakota

| City | Name | Telephone | City | Name | Telephone |
|------|------|-----------|------|------|-----------|

### Rating: A

| City | Name | Telephone |
|------|------|-----------|
| JAMESTOWN | FIRST COMMUNITY CU | (701) 252-0360 |
| MINOT | PRAIRIE FCU | (701) 837-5353 |

### Rating: A-

| City | Name | Telephone |
|------|------|-----------|
| BISMARCK | CAPITAL CU | (701) 255-0042 |
| MADDOCK | NORTH STAR COMMUNITY CU | (701) 438-2222 |
| MANDAN | RAILWAY CU | (701) 667-9500 |

### Rating: B+

| City | Name | Telephone |
|------|------|-----------|
| MINOT | AFFINITY FIRST FCU | (701) 857-5541 |
| DEVILS LAKE | CITIZENS COMMUNITY CU | (701) 662-8118 |
| WATFORD CITY | DAKOTA WEST CU | (701) 444-6484 |
| KULM | HOMETOWN CU | (701) 647-2448 |
| MINOT | TOWN & COUNTRY CU | (701) 852-2018 |
| FARGO | UNITED SAVINGS CU | (701) 235-2832 |
| WILLISTON | WESTERN COOPERATIVE CU | (701) 572-4000 |

## Ohio

| City | Name | Telephone | City | Name | Telephone |
|------|------|-----------|------|------|-----------|

### Rating: A+

| City | Name | Telephone |
|------|------|-----------|
| LIMA | SUPERIOR CU INC | (419) 223-9746 |

### Rating: A

| City | Name | Telephone |
|------|------|-----------|
| KETTERING | DAY AIR CU | (937) 643-2160 |
| DOVER | DOVER-PHILA FCU | (330) 364-8874 |
| FREMONT | FREMONT FCU | (419) 334-4434 |
| WEST CHESTER | KEMBA CU | (513) 762-5070 |
| GAHANNA | KEMBA FINANCIAL CU | (614) 235-2395 |
| WARREN | SEVEN SEVENTEEN CU | (330) 372-8100 |
| BEAVERCREEK | WRIGHT-PATT CU INC | (937) 912-7000 |

### Rating: A-

| City | Name | Telephone |
|------|------|-----------|
| CELINA | DYNAMIC FCU | (419) 586-5522 |
| SANDUSKY | VACATIONLAND FCU | (419) 625-9025 |

### Rating: B+

| City | Name | Telephone |
|------|------|-----------|
| CINCINNATI | CHILDRENS MEDICAL CENTER FCU | (513) 636-4470 |
| CINCINNATI | CINFED FCU | (513) 333-3800 |
| YOUNGSTOWN | DOY FCU | (330) 744-5680 |
| CINCINNATI | GENERAL ELECTRIC CU | (513) 243-4328 |
| AKRON | GENFED FINANCIAL CU | (330) 734-0225 |
| CHILLICOTHE | HOMELAND CU | (740) 775-3331 |
| GREENVILLE | MEMBERS CHOICE CU | (937) 548-0360 |
| GARFIELD HEIGHT | OHIO CATHOLIC FCU | (216) 663-8090 |

## Oklahoma

| City | Name | Telephone | City | Name | Telephone |
|------|------|-----------|------|------|-----------|

### Rating: A

| City | Name | Telephone |
|------|------|-----------|
| OKLAHOMA CITY | OKLAHOMA FCU | (405) 524-6467 |

### Rating: A-

| City | Name | Telephone |
|------|------|-----------|
| OKLAHOMA CITY | COMMUNICATION FCU | (405) 879-5600 |
| OKLAHOMA CITY | OKLAHOMA EMPL CU | (405) 606-6328 |
| TULSA | TTCU THE CU | (918) 749-8828 |
| OKLAHOMA CITY | US EMPL OC FCU | (405) 685-6200 |

### Rating: B+

| City | Name | Telephone |
|------|------|-----------|
| DUNCAN | HALLIBURTON EMPL FCU | (580) 255-3550 |
| LAWTON | SOUTHWEST OKLAHOMA FCU | (580) 353-0490 |
| OKLAHOMA CITY | TINKER FCU | (405) 732-0324 |
| OKLAHOMA CITY | WEOKIE CU | (405) 235-3030 |

# Oregon

| City | Name | Telephone | City | Name | Telephone |
|------|------|-----------|------|------|-----------|

## Rating: A

| City | Name | Telephone |
|------|------|-----------|
| PORTLAND | ONPOINT COMMUNITY CU | (503) 228-7077 |

## Rating: A-

| City | Name | Telephone |
|------|------|-----------|
| MILWAUKIE | ADVANTIS CU | (503) 785-2528 |
| CORVALLIS | OREGON STATE CU | (541) 714-4000 |
| MEDFORD | ROGUE CU | (541) 858-7328 |
| EUGENE | SELCO COMMUNITY CU | (800) 445-4483 |

## Rating: B+

| City | Name | Telephone |
|------|------|-----------|
| HOOD RIVER | CASCADE CENTRAL CU | (541) 387-9297 |
| PORTLAND | CASTPARTS EMPL FCU | (503) 771-2464 |
| MILWAUKIE | CLACKAMAS COMMUNITY FCU | (503) 656-0671 |
| PORTLAND | CONSOLIDATED FCU | (503) 232-8070 |
| BEAVERTON | RIVERMARK COMMUNITY CU | (503) 626-6600 |
| PORTLAND | SUNSET SCIENCE PARK FCU | (503) 643-1335 |
| PORTLAND | UNITUS COMMUNITY CU | (503) 227-5571 |

## Pennsylvania

| City | Name | Telephone | City | Name | Telephone |
|------|------|-----------|------|------|-----------|

### Rating: A+

| City | Name | Telephone |
|------|------|-----------|
| PHILADELPHIA | POLICE & FIRE FCU | (215) 931-0300 |

### Rating: A

| City | Name | Telephone |
|------|------|-----------|
| BUTLER | BUTLER ARMCO EMPL CU | (724) 284-2020 |
| WASHINGTON | CHROME FCU | (724) 228-2030 |

### Rating: A-

| City | Name | Telephone |
|------|------|-----------|
| POTTSTOWN | DIAMOND CU | (610) 326-5490 |
| PITTSBURGH | GREATER PITTSBURGH POLICE FCU | (412) 922-4800 |
| ALLENPORT | MON VALLEY COMMUNITY FCU | (724) 326-5632 |
| PHILADELPHIA | PHILADELPHIA FCU | (215) 934-3500 |

### Rating: B+

| City | Name | Telephone |
|------|------|-----------|
| RIDLEY PARK | BHCU | (610) 595-2929 |
| EXTON | CITADEL FCU | (610) 380-6000 |
| CLARION | CLARION FCU | (814) 226-5032 |
| ALLENTOWN | FIRST CLASS FCU | (610) 439-4102 |
| BETHLEHEM | FIRST COMMONWEALTH FCU | (610) 821-2400 |
| NEW CASTLE | GNC COMMUNITY FCU | (724) 652-5783 |
| ALLENTOWN | LEHIGH VALLEY EDUCATORS CU | (610) 820-0145 |
| WORTHINGTON | MOONLIGHT CU | (724) 297-3084 |
| SAINT MARYS | MOUNTAIN LAUREL FCU | (814) 834-9518 |
| HARRISBURG | PENNSYLVANIA STATE EMPL CU | (800) 237-7328 |
| PITTSBURGH | PITTSBURGH FIREFIGHTERS FCU | (412) 928-8500 |
| TREVOSE | TRUMARK FINANCIAL CU | (215) 953-5300 |
| WYOMISSING | UTILITIES EMPL CU | (610) 927-4000 |

## Puerto Rico

| City | Name | Telephone | City | Name | Telephone |
|------|------|-----------|------|------|-----------|
| **Rating:** | **B+** | | | | |
| SAN JUAN | CARIBE FCU | (787) 474-5151 | | | |

## Rhode Island

| City | Name | Telephone | City | Name | Telephone |
|------|------|-----------|------|------|-----------|

**Rating:**        **B+**

| City | Name | Telephone |
|------|------|-----------|
| PAWTUCKET | PAWTUCKET CU | (401) 722-2212 |

## South Carolina

| City | Name | Telephone | City | Name | Telephone |
|------|------|-----------|------|------|-----------|

### Rating: A

| City | Name | Telephone |
|------|------|-----------|
| COLUMBIA | ALLSOUTH FCU | (803) 736-3110 |
| GREENVILLE | GREENVILLE HERITAGE FCU | (864) 467-4160 |
| GREENVILLE | MTC FCU | (864) 908-3469 |
| GREENVILLE | SC TELCO FCU | (864) 232-5553 |

### Rating: A-

| City | Name | Telephone |
|------|------|-----------|
| NORTH CHARLES | CPM FCU | (843) 747-6376 |
| LANCASTER | FOUNDERS FCU | (800) 845-1614 |
| GEORGETOWN | GEORGETOWN KRAFT CU | (843) 546-8494 |
| GREENVILLE | GREENVILLE FCU | (864) 235-6309 |
| COLUMBIA | PALMETTO CITIZENS FCU | (803) 779-1232 |
| COLUMBIA | PALMETTO HEALTH CU | (803) 978-2101 |
| FLORENCE | PEE DEE FCU | (843) 669-0461 |
| COLUMBIA | SC STATE FCU | (803) 343-0300 |
| FORT MILL | SHARONVIEW FCU | (800) 462-4421 |
| NORTH CHARLES | SOUTH CAROLINA FCU | (843) 797-8300 |
| COLUMBIA | SOUTH CAROLINA NATIONAL GUARD FCU | (803) 799-1090 |

### Rating: B+

| City | Name | Telephone |
|------|------|-----------|
| MYRTLE BEACH | CAROLINA TRUST FCU | (843) 448-2133 |
| ROCK HILL | FAMILY TRUST FCU | (803) 367-4100 |

## South Dakota

| City | Name | Telephone | City | Name | Telephone |
|------|------|-----------|------|------|-----------|

### Rating: A-

| City | Name | Telephone |
|------|------|-----------|
| ABERDEEN | ABERDEEN FCU | (605) 225-2488 |
| RAPID CITY | BLACK HILLS FCU | (605) 343-0891 |

### Rating: B+

| City | Name | Telephone |
|------|------|-----------|
| HURON | DAKOTALAND FCU | (605) 352-2845 |
| BRITTON | NORSTAR FCU | (605) 448-2292 |
| SIOUX FALLS | SIOUX FALLS FCU | (605) 334-2471 |

## Tennessee

| City | Name | Telephone | City | Name | Telephone |
|------|------|-----------|------|------|-----------|
| **Rating:** | **A+** | | | | |
| BARTLETT | FIRST SOUTH FINANCIAL CU | (901) 380-7400 | | | |
| **Rating:** | **A** | | | | |
| TULLAHOMA | ASCEND FCU | (931) 455-5441 | | | |
| KINGSPORT | EASTMAN CU | (423) 578-7676 | | | |
| SHELBYVILLE | HERITAGE SOUTH COMMUNITY CU | (931) 680-1400 | | | |
| MEMPHIS | KIMBERLY CLARK CU | (901) 521-4646 | | | |
| JACKSON | LEADERS CU | (731) 664-1784 | | | |
| ELIZABETHTON | NORTHEAST COMMUNITY CU | (423) 547-1200 | | | |
| CHATTANOOGA | TENNESSEE VALLEY FCU | (423) 634-3600 | | | |
| **Rating:** | **A-** | | | | |
| KNOXVILLE | CITY EMPL CU | (865) 824-7200 | | | |
| MEMPHIS | FEDEX EMPL CREDIT ASSN FCU | (901) 344-2500 | | | |
| CLARKSVILLE | FORT CAMPBELL FCU | (931) 431-6800 | | | |
| MEMPHIS | MEMPHIS CITY EMPL CU | (901) 321-1200 | | | |
| CORDOVA | METHODIST HEALTHCARE FCU | (901) 453-3500 | | | |
| **Rating:** | **B+** | | | | |
| ERWIN | CLINCHFIELD FCU | (423) 743-9192 | | | |
| CAMDEN | JOHNSONVILLE TVA EMPL CU | (731) 584-7238 | | | |
| KNOXVILLE | KNOXVILLE TVA EMPL CU | (865) 544-5400 | | | |
| KNOXVILLE | NEW SOUTH CU | (865) 523-0757 | | | |
| OAK RIDGE | ORNL FCU | (865) 688-9555 | | | |
| MEMPHIS | UPS EMPL CU | (901) 396-2132 | | | |

# Texas

| City | Name | Telephone | City | Name | Telephone |
|------|------|-----------|------|------|-----------|
| | | | AUSTIN | AMPLIFY FCU | (512) 836-5901 |
| **Rating:** | **A+** | | DALLAS | BAYLOR HEALTH CARE SYSTEM CU | (214) 820-2342 |
| LONGVIEW | EAST TEXAS PROFESSIONAL CU | (903) 323-0230 | RICHARDSON | BLUE CROSS TEXAS FCU | (972) 766-6732 |
| CORPUS CHRISTI | MEMBERS FIRST CU | (361) 991-6178 | CLUTE | BRAZOSPORT TEACHERS FCU | (979) 265-5333 |
| LIVE OAK | RANDOLPH-BROOKS FCU | (210) 945-3300 | RUSK | CHEROKEE COUNTY FCU | (903) 683-2527 |
| SUGAR LAND | SCHLUMBERGER EMPL CU | (281) 285-4551 | ODESSA | COMPLEX COMMUNITY FCU | (432) 550-9126 |
| | | | DALLAS | CU OF TEXAS | (972) 263-9497 |
| **Rating:** | **A** | | BEAUMONT | DUGOOD FCU | (409) 899-3430 |
| LEAGUE CITY | ASSOCIATED CU OF TEXAS | (409) 945-4474 | FLOYDADA | F C S FCU | (806) 983-5126 |
| AUSTIN | AUSTIN TELCO FCU | (512) 302-5555 | ODESSA | FIRST BASIN CU | (432) 333-5600 |
| DEL RIO | BORDER FCU | (830) 774-2328 | WACO | FIRST CENTRAL CU | (254) 776-9333 |
| DENTON | DATCU CU | (940) 387-8585 | WACO | GENCO FCU | (254) 776-9550 |
| AMARILLO | EDUCATION CU | (806) 358-7777 | HOUSTON | HOUSTON TEXAS FIRE FIGHTERS FCU | (713) 864-0959 |
| WACO | EDUCATORS CU | (254) 776-7900 | TYLER | KELLY COMMUNITY FCU | (903) 597-7291 |
| FORT WORTH | EECU | (817) 882-0000 | LAREDO | LAREDO FCU | (956) 722-3971 |
| FORT WORTH | FORT WORTH CITY CU | (817) 732-2803 | LUFKIN | LUFKIN FCU | (936) 632-4397 |
| PASADENA | GULF COAST EDUCATORS FCU | (281) 487-9333 | PORT NECHES | MCT CU | (409) 727-1446 |
| HOUSTON | HARRIS COUNTY FCU | (713) 755-5160 | MIDLAND | MTCU | (432) 688-7300 |
| HOUSTON | HOUSTON POLICE FCU | (713) 986-0200 | MIDLAND | MY COMMUNITY FCU | (432) 688-8400 |
| BEAUMONT | MOBILOIL FCU | (409) 892-1111 | PHARR | NAFT FCU | (956) 787-2774 |
| PORT NECHES | NECHES FCU | (409) 722-1174 | HOUSTON | NATIONAL OILWELL VARCO EMPL CU | (713) 634-3471 |
| SUGAR LAND | NIZARI PROGRESSIVE FCU | (281) 921-8500 | DALLAS | NEIGHBORHOOD CU | (214) 748-9393 |
| SUGAR LAND | PIONEER MUTUAL FCU | (281) 566-8000 | AMARILLO | SANTA FE FCU | (806) 373-0736 |
| DALLAS | SOUTHWEST AIRLINES FCU | (214) 357-5577 | HOUSTON | SMART FINANCIAL CU | (713) 850-1600 |
| SAN ANTONIO | SYNERGY FCU | (210) 345-2222 | DALLAS | SOUTHWEST FINANCIAL FCU | (214) 630-7111 |
| TEXARKANA | TEXAR FCU | (903) 223-0000 | ODESSA | SOUTHWEST HERITAGE CU | (432) 367-8993 |
| TEMPLE | TEXELL CU | (254) 773-1604 | HOUSTON | TEXAS BAY CU | (713) 852-6700 |
| AUSTIN | VELOCITY CU | (512) 469-7000 | LUBBOCK | TEXAS TECH FCU | (806) 742-3606 |
| | | | DALLAS | TEXAS TELCOM CU | (214) 320-8818 |
| **Rating:** | **A-** | | WICHITA FALLS | TEXOMA COMMUNITY CU | (940) 851-4000 |
| ABILENE | ABILENE TEACHERS FCU | (325) 677-2274 | BROWNSVILLE | VALLEY FCU | (956) 546-3108 |
| BAY CITY | BAYCEL FCU | (979) 244-3995 | KERMIT | WESTEX COMMUNITY CU | (432) 586-6631 |
| SLATON | CAPROCK SANTA FE CU | (806) 828-5825 | | | |
| MEXIA | CENTEX CITIZENS CU | (254) 562-9296 | | | |
| DALLAS | CITY CU | (214) 515-0100 | | | |
| TYLER | COOPERATIVE TEACHERS CU | (903) 561-2603 | | | |
| EDINBURG | EDINBURG TEACHERS CU | (956) 259-3511 | | | |
| BEAUMONT | EDUCATION FIRST FCU | (409) 898-3770 | | | |
| NEDERLAND | FIVEPOINT CU | (409) 962-8793 | | | |
| WACO | MEMBERS CHOICE OF CENTRAL TEXAS F | (254) 776-7070 | | | |
| CORPUS CHRISTI | NAVY ARMY COMMUNITY CU | (361) 986-4500 | | | |
| TEXARKANA | RED RIVER FCU | (903) 793-7681 | | | |
| DALLAS | RESOURCE ONE CU | (214) 319-3100 | | | |
| DEER PARK | SHELL FCU | (713) 844-1100 | | | |
| HOUSTON | SOUTHERN FCU | (713) 232-7774 | | | |
| WHARTON | TEXASGULF FCU | (979) 282-2300 | | | |
| **Rating:** | **B+** | | | | |
| AUSTIN | A+ FCU | (512) 302-6800 | | | |
| AMARILLO | ACCESS COMMUNITY CU | (806) 353-9999 | | | |

## Utah

| City | Name | Telephone | City | Name | Telephone |
|------|------|-----------|------|------|-----------|

### Rating: A+

| City | Name | Telephone |
|------|------|-----------|
| SALT LAKE CITY | UTAH POWER CU | (801) 708-8900 |

### Rating: A

| City | Name | Telephone |
|------|------|-----------|
| BRIGHAM CITY | BOX ELDER COUNTY FCU | (435) 723-3437 |
| OGDEN | GOLDENWEST FCU | (801) 621-4550 |

### Rating: A-

| City | Name | Telephone |
|------|------|-----------|
| RIVERDALE | AMERICA FIRST FCU | (801) 627-0900 |
| WEST JORDAN | CYPRUS FCU | (801) 260-7600 |
| SALT LAKE CITY | HI-LAND CU | (801) 261-8909 |
| WEST JORDAN | MOUNTAIN AMERICA FCU | (801) 325-6228 |
| SPRINGVILLE | NEBO CU | (801) 491-3691 |
| NEPHI | NEPHI WESTERN EMPL FCU | (435) 623-1895 |
| SALT LAKE CITY | UNIV FIRST FCU | (801) 481-8800 |
| PROVO | UTAH COMMUNITY FCU | (801) 223-8188 |
| SALT LAKE CITY | UTAH FIRST FCU | (801) 320-2600 |

### Rating: B+

| City | Name | Telephone |
|------|------|-----------|
| WEST JORDAN | AMERICAN UNITED FAMILY OF CUS FCU | (801) 359-9600 |
| BRIGHAM CITY | MEMBERS FIRST CU | (435) 723-5231 |

# Vermont

| City | Name | Telephone | City | Name | Telephone |
|------|------|-----------|------|------|-----------|

## Rating: A-

| City | Name | Telephone |
|------|------|-----------|
| WILLISTON | NEW ENGLAND FCU | (802) 879-8790 |

## Rating: B+

| City | Name | Telephone |
|------|------|-----------|
| RUTLAND | CU OF VERMONT | (802) 773-0027 |
| RUTLAND | HERITAGE FAMILY FCU | (802) 775-4930 |

# Virgin Islands of the U.S.

| City | Name | Telephone | City | Name | Telephone |
|------|------|-----------|------|------|-----------|

**Rating:**        **B+**

| City | Name | Telephone |
|------|------|-----------|
| CHARLOTTE AMAL | ST THOMAS FCU | (340) 774-1299 |

# Virginia

| City | Name | Telephone | City | Name | Telephone |
|------|------|-----------|------|------|-----------|

## Rating: A

| City | Name | Telephone |
|------|------|-----------|
| VIENNA | NAVY FCU | (703) 255-8000 |

## Rating: A-

| City | Name | Telephone |
|------|------|-----------|
| ROANOKE | BLUE EAGLE CU | (540) 342-3429 |
| FAIRFAX | FAIRFAX COUNTY FCU | (703) 218-9900 |
| CHANTILLY | JUSTICE FCU | (703) 480-5300 |
| ALEXANDRIA | SIGNATURE FCU | (703) 683-7300 |

## Rating: B+

| City | Name | Telephone |
|------|------|-----------|
| CHESAPEAKE | ABNB FCU | (757) 523-5300 |
| FALLS CHURCH | ARLINGTON COMMUNITY FCU | (703) 526-0200 |
| WAYNESBORO | DUPONT COMMUNITY CU | (540) 946-3200 |
| ROANOKE | FREEDOM FIRST FCU | (540) 389-0244 |
| ROANOKE | MEMBER ONE FCU | (540) 982-8811 |
| CHESAPEAKE | N A E FCU | (757) 410-2000 |
| WOODBRIDGE | PWC EMPL CU | (703) 680-1143 |
| ALEXANDRIA | STATE DEPT FCU | (703) 706-5000 |
| CHARLOTTESVILL | UNIV OF VIRGINIA COMMUNITY CU | (434) 964-2001 |
| HOPEWELL | VANTAGE POINT FCU | (804) 541-1473 |
| RICHMOND | VIRGINIA CU INC | (804) 253-6000 |

## Washington

| City | Name | Telephone | City | Name | Telephone |
|------|------|-----------|------|------|-----------|

### Rating: A+

| City | Name | Telephone |
|------|------|-----------|
| BELLINGHAM | WHATCOM EDUCATIONAL CU | (360) 676-1168 |

### Rating: A

| City | Name | Telephone |
|------|------|-----------|
| TUKWILA | BOEING EMPL CU | (206) 439-5700 |
| VANCOUVER | COLUMBIA COMMUNITY CU | (360) 891-4000 |
| SPOKANE VALLEY | NUMERICA CU | (509) 535-7613 |
| SHELTON | OUR COMMUNITY CU | (360) 426-9701 |
| REDMOND | QUALSTAR CU | (425) 643-3400 |
| YAKIMA | SOLARITY CU | (509) 248-1720 |
| TACOMA | SOUND CU | (253) 383-2016 |

### Rating: A-

| City | Name | Telephone |
|------|------|-----------|
| SPOKANE | AVISTA CORP CU | (509) 495-2000 |
| ABERDEEN | GREAT NORTHWEST FCU | (360) 533-9990 |
| LIBERTY LAKE | SPOKANE TEACHERS CU | (509) 326-1954 |
| FIFE | TACOMA LONGSHOREMEN CU | (253) 272-0240 |
| OLYMPIA | WASHINGTON STATE EMPL CU | (360) 943-7911 |
| ENUMCLAW | WHITE RIVER CU | (360) 825-4833 |

### Rating: B+

| City | Name | Telephone |
|------|------|-----------|
| TACOMA | AMERICAS FCU | (253) 964-3113 |
| KENT | CASCADE FCU | (425) 251-8888 |
| RICHLAND | GESA CU | (509) 378-3100 |
| VANCOUVER | IQ CU | (360) 695-3441 |
| BREMERTON | KITSAP CU | (360) 662-2000 |
| EVERETT | NORTHWEST PLUS CU | (425) 297-1000 |
| SPOKANE | PRIMESOURCE CU | (509) 838-6157 |
| SPOKANE | SAFEWAY FCU | (509) 483-9416 |
| SEATTLE | SEATTLE METROPOLITAN CU | (206) 398-5500 |
| PORT ANGELES | STRAIT VIEW CU | (360) 452-3883 |
| LACEY | TWINSTAR CU | (360) 357-9911 |
| SEATTLE | VERITY CU | (206) 440-9000 |

## West Virginia

| City | Name | Telephone | City | Name | Telephone |
|------|------|-----------|------|------|-----------|

### Rating: A-

| City | Name | Telephone |
|------|------|-----------|
| CHARLESTON | CAMC FCU | (304) 388-5700 |
| CHARLESTON | STATE CU | (304) 558-0566 |
| MORGANTOWN | UNITED FCU | (304) 598-5010 |

### Rating: B+

| City | Name | Telephone |
|------|------|-----------|
| CHARLESTON | MEMBERS CHOICE WV FCU | (304) 346-5242 |
| PARKERSBURG | WEST VIRGINIA CENTRAL CU | (304) 485-4523 |
| CHARLESTON | WV NATIONAL GUARD FCU | (304) 342-2422 |

## Wisconsin

| City | Name | Telephone | City | Name | Telephone |
|------|------|-----------|------|------|-----------|

### Rating: A

| City | Name | Telephone |
|------|------|-----------|
| WEST ALLIS | APPLETREE CU | (414) 546-7800 |
| APPLETON | COMMUNITY FIRST CU | (920) 830-7200 |
| ANTIGO | COVANTAGE CU | (715) 627-4336 |
| BELOIT | FIRST COMMUNITY CU OF BELOIT | (608) 362-9077 |
| GREEN BAY | PCM CU | (920) 499-2831 |
| MADISON | SUMMIT CU | (608) 243-5000 |

### Rating: A-

| City | Name | Telephone |
|------|------|-----------|
| ONALASKA | ALTRA FCU | (608) 787-4500 |
| BLACK RIVER FAL | CO-OP CU | (715) 284-5333 |
| RACINE | EDUCATORS CU | (262) 886-5900 |
| FORT ATKINSON | FORT COMMUNITY CU | (920) 563-7305 |
| APPLETON | FOX COMMUNITIES CU | (920) 993-9000 |
| WISCONSIN RAPI | MEMBERS ADVANTAGE CU | (715) 421-1610 |
| EAU CLAIRE | ROYAL CU | (715) 833-8111 |
| SUPERIOR | SUPERIOR CHOICE CU | (715) 392-5616 |
| MANITOWOC | UNITEDONE CU | (920) 684-0361 |
| WESTBY | WESTBY CO-OP CU | (608) 634-3118 |
| MENOMONIE | WESTCONSIN CU | (715) 235-3403 |

### Rating: B+

| City | Name | Telephone |
|------|------|-----------|
| ARCADIA | ARCADIA CU | (608) 323-2126 |
| MILWAUKEE | AURORA CU | (414) 649-7949 |
| GREEN BAY | CAPITAL CU | (920) 494-2828 |
| WAUSAU | CLOVERBELT CU | (715) 842-5693 |
| STEVENS POINT | SENTRY CU | (715) 346-6532 |
| MANITOWOC | SHIPBUILDERS CU | (920) 682-8500 |
| OSHKOSH | VERVE A CU | (920) 236-7040 |

## Wyoming

| City | Name | Telephone | City | Name | Telephone |
|------|------|-----------|------|------|-----------|

### Rating: A

| City | Name | Telephone |
|------|------|-----------|
| CODY | SUNLIGHT FCU | (307) 587-4915 |
| CHEYENNE | WYHY FCU | (307) 638-4200 |

### Rating: A-

| City | Name | Telephone |
|------|------|-----------|
| LANDER | ATLANTIC CITY FCU | (307) 332-5151 |
| GREEN RIVER | TRONA VALLEY COMMUNITY FCU | (307) 875-9800 |
| CHEYENNE | UNIFIED PEOPLES FCU | (307) 632-1476 |

### Rating: B+

| City | Name | Telephone |
|------|------|-----------|
| CHEYENNE | WARREN FCU | (307) 432-5400 |

# Section III

# Rating Upgrades
# and Downgrades

A list of all

## Credit Unions

receiving a rating upgrade or downgrade
during the current quarter.

# Section III Contents

This section identifies those institutions receiving a rating change since the previous edition of this publication, whether it be a rating upgrade, rating downgrade, newly rated company or the withdrawal of a rating.  A rating upgrade or downgrade may entail a change from one letter grade to another, or it may mean the addition or deletion of a plus or minus sign within the same letter grade previously assigned to the company.  Ratings are normally updated once each quarter of the year.  In some instances, however, an institution's rating may be downgraded outside of the normal updates due to overriding circumstances.

1. **Institution Name**    The name under which the institution was chartered. A company's name can be very similar to, or the same as, that of another, so verify the company's exact name, city, and state to make sure you are looking at the correct company.

2. **New Safety Rating**    Weiss rating assigned to the institution at the time of publication.  Our ratings are designed to distinguish levels of insolvency risk and are measured on a scale from A to F based upon a wide range of factors.  Highly rated companies are, in our opinion, less likely to experience financial difficulties than lower rated firms.  See *About Weiss Safety Ratings* for more information and a description of what each rating means.

3. **State**    The state in which the institution's headquarters or main office is located.

4. **Date of Change**    Date that rating was finalized.

## Rating Upgrades

| Name | State | Date of Change |
|------|-------|----------------|

### Rating: B+

| Name | State | Date of Change |
|------|-------|----------------|
| ADVIA CU | MI | 12/16/15 |
| ALLEGACY FCU | NC | 12/16/15 |
| BAYLOR HEALTH CARE SYSTEM CU | TX | 12/16/15 |
| CAPITAL CU | WI | 12/16/15 |
| CHAMPION CU | NC | 12/16/15 |
| COUNTRY HERITAGE CU | MI | 12/16/15 |
| COUNTY FCU | ME | 12/16/15 |
| CP FCU | MI | 12/16/15 |
| DAKOTALAND FCU | SD | 12/16/15 |
| EDUCATIONAL SYSTEMS FCU | MD | 12/16/15 |
| FAMILY TRUST FCU | SC | 12/16/15 |
| FILER CU | MI | 12/16/15 |
| FIRST TECHNOLOGY FCU | CA | 12/16/15 |
| FORT DODGE FAMILY CU | IA | 12/16/15 |
| HARVARD UNIV EMPL CU | MA | 12/16/15 |
| HOMETOWN CU | ND | 12/16/15 |
| IQ CU | WA | 12/16/15 |
| KERN FCU | CA | 12/16/15 |
| MEMBERS FIRST CU | UT | 12/16/15 |
| MOUNTAIN CU | NC | 12/16/15 |
| OAKLAND COUNTY CU | MI | 12/16/15 |
| PORT WASHINGTON FCU | NY | 12/16/15 |
| PORTLAND FCU | MI | 12/16/15 |
| ROSWELL COMMUNITY FCU | NM | 12/16/15 |
| SERVICE ONE CU INC | KY | 12/16/15 |
| SMART FINANCIAL CU | TX | 12/16/15 |
| SOUTH BAY CU | CA | 12/16/15 |
| SOUTHWEST OKLAHOMA FCU | OK | 12/16/15 |
| STRAIT VIEW CU | WA | 12/16/15 |
| TEXAS BAY CU | TX | 12/16/15 |
| TRUCHOICE FCU | ME | 12/16/15 |
| UNITUS COMMUNITY CU | OR | 12/16/15 |
| VERVE A CU | WI | 12/16/15 |

### Rating: B

| Name | State | Date of Change |
|------|-------|----------------|
| 1ST ADVANTAGE FCU | VA | 12/16/15 |
| 4FRONT CU | MI | 12/16/15 |
| ALLIANCE CU | CA | 12/16/15 |
| BAY SHORE CU | WI | 12/16/15 |
| BELEN RAILWAY EMPL CU | NM | 12/16/15 |
| BLACKHAWK COMMUNITY CU | WI | 12/16/15 |
| BLUE CHIP FCU | PA | 12/16/15 |
| BRIGHTSTAR CU | FL | 12/16/15 |
| C C S E FCU | NY | 12/16/15 |
| CENTRIS FCU | NE | 12/16/15 |
| CHAFFEY FCU | CA | 12/16/15 |
| COMMUNITY CHOICE CU | IA | 12/16/15 |
| CRESCENT CU | MA | 12/16/15 |

| Name | State | Date of Change |
|------|-------|----------------|
| DEL-ONE FCU | DE | 12/16/15 |
| DEPT OF LABOR FCU | DC | 12/16/15 |
| DUTRAC COMMUNITY CU | IA | 12/16/15 |
| ELECTRO SAVINGS CU | MO | 12/16/15 |
| FIRELANDS FCU | OH | 12/16/15 |
| FIRST HERITAGE FCU | NY | 12/16/15 |
| FIRST PIONEERS FCU | LA | 12/16/15 |
| FOOTHILLS CU | CO | 12/16/15 |
| FREEDOM CU | PA | 12/16/15 |
| GERBER FCU | MI | 12/16/15 |
| GREENWOOD MUNICIPAL FCU | SC | 12/16/15 |
| HERITAGE CU | WI | 12/16/15 |
| HOLLEY CU | TN | 12/16/15 |
| JEFFERSON FINANCIAL CU | LA | 12/16/15 |
| KEMBA LOUISVILLE CU | KY | 12/16/15 |
| LONG BEACH CITY EMPL FCU | CA | 12/16/15 |
| MARKET USA FCU | MD | 12/16/15 |
| MEMBERS ADVANTAGE COMMUNITY CU | VT | 12/16/15 |
| MIAMI POSTAL SERVICE CU | FL | 12/16/15 |
| NORTH GEORGIA CU | GA | 12/16/15 |
| NORTHSTAR CU | IL | 12/16/15 |
| OKLAHOMA EDUCATORS CU | OK | 12/16/15 |
| PALMETTO FIRST FCU | SC | 12/16/15 |
| PARK COMMUNITY CU INC | KY | 12/16/15 |
| PEOPLES ENERGY CU | IL | 12/16/15 |
| POLISH-AMERICAN FCU | MI | 12/16/15 |
| PUBLIC SERVICE #3 CU | IN | 12/16/15 |
| RALEIGH COUNTY FCU | WV | 12/16/15 |
| RAVALLI COUNTY FCU | MT | 12/16/15 |
| RIVER REGION CU | MO | 12/16/15 |
| RIVERDALE CU | AL | 12/16/15 |
| SHARON CU | MA | 12/16/15 |
| SOUTHEASTERN OHIO CU | OH | 12/16/15 |
| ST LOUIS COMMUNITY CU | MO | 12/16/15 |
| SUN CU | FL | 12/16/15 |
| TELBEC FCU | WV | 12/16/15 |
| TMH FCU | FL | 12/16/15 |
| UNIV OF WISCONSIN CU | WI | 12/16/15 |
| WVU EMPL FCU | WV | 12/16/15 |

### Rating: B-

| Name | State | Date of Change |
|------|-------|----------------|
| ALLCOM CU | MA | 12/16/15 |
| AREA EDUCATIONAL CU | IL | 12/16/15 |
| AUTOTRUCK FINANCIAL CU | KY | 12/16/15 |
| BEACON CU INC | VA | 12/16/15 |
| CALCOM FCU | CA | 12/16/15 |
| CALIFORNIA ADVENTIST FCU | CA | 12/16/15 |
| CANAAN CU | IL | 12/16/15 |
| CATHOLIC & COMMUNITY CU | IL | 12/16/15 |
| CENTRAL CITY CU | WI | 12/16/15 |

## Rating Upgrades

| Name | State | Date of Change | Name | State | Date of Change |
|------|-------|----------------|------|-------|----------------|
| CLEARPATH FCU | CA | 12/16/15 | SELF-HELP FCU | NC | 12/16/15 |
| CONNEXUS CU | WI | 12/16/15 | SERVICE 1ST CU | FL | 12/16/15 |
| CORNERSTONE CU | IL | 12/16/15 | SOMERVILLE MUNICIPAL FCU | MA | 12/16/15 |
| CORRY JAMESTOWN CU | PA | 12/16/15 | SOO SELECT CU | MN | 12/16/15 |
| CU OF EMPORIA | KS | 12/16/15 | SOUTH DIVISION CU | IL | 12/16/15 |
| DALLAS UP EMPL CU | TX | 12/16/15 | STAMFORD FCU | CT | 12/16/15 |
| DISTRICT OF COLUMBIA TEACHERS FCU | DC | 12/16/15 | STATEWIDE FCU | MS | 12/16/15 |
| ELEKTRA FCU | NY | 12/16/15 | STRAITS AREA FCU | MI | 12/16/15 |
| EMBARK FCU | MT | 12/16/15 | TEXAS TRUST CU | TX | 12/16/15 |
| EVOLVE FCU | TX | 12/16/15 | TOLEDO METRO FCU | OH | 12/16/15 |
| FEDSTAR CU | TX | 12/16/15 | TOWPATH CU | OH | 12/16/15 |
| FIRST TRUST CU | IN | 12/16/15 | TUSCALOOSA VETERANS FCU | AL | 12/16/15 |
| FORT FINANCIAL FCU | IN | 12/16/15 | UFIRST FCU | NY | 12/16/15 |
| FRONT ROYAL FCU | VA | 12/16/15 | UNITED FINANCIAL CU | CA | 12/16/15 |
| GABRIELS COMMUNITY CU | MI | 12/16/15 | UNITED FINANCIAL CU | MI | 12/16/15 |
| GLASS CAP FCU | PA | 12/16/15 | UPPER CUMBERLAND FCU | TN | 12/16/15 |
| GREENSBORO MUNICIPAL FCU | NC | 12/16/15 | US COMMUNITY CU | TN | 12/16/15 |
| GROVE CITY AREA FCU | PA | 12/16/15 | VOYAGE FCU | SD | 12/16/15 |
| H M S A EMPL FCU | HI | 12/16/15 | WASATCH PEAKS FCU | UT | 12/16/15 |
| HANIN FCU | CA | 12/16/15 | WCLA CU | WA | 12/16/15 |
| HARBORSTONE CU | WA | 12/16/15 | XPLORE FCU | LA | 12/16/15 |
| HEALTH CARE IDAHO CU | ID | 12/16/15 | | | |
| HOLY TRINITY BAPTIST FCU | PA | 12/16/15 | **Rating:**            **C+** | | |
| HORIZON CU | MO | 12/16/15 | 1ST NORTHERN CALIFORNIA CU | CA | 12/16/15 |
| HOUSATONIC TEACHERS FCU | CT | 12/16/15 | ACCENTRA CU | MN | 12/16/15 |
| INSPIRE FCU | PA | 12/16/15 | ACCLAIM FCU | NC | 12/16/15 |
| JACK DANIEL EMPL CU | TN | 12/16/15 | AEROQUIP CU | MI | 12/16/15 |
| JOPLIN METRO CU | MO | 12/16/15 | ALCO FCU | NY | 12/16/15 |
| KELCO FCU | MD | 12/16/15 | ARROWPOINTE FCU | SC | 12/16/15 |
| KENTUCKY EMPL CU | KY | 12/16/15 | ASSOCIATED HEALTH CARE CU | MN | 12/16/15 |
| LANCASTER-DEPEW FCU | NY | 12/16/15 | BADGER CU | WI | 12/16/15 |
| LAPORTE COMMUNITY FCU | IN | 12/16/15 | BEREA FCU | NY | 12/16/15 |
| LATROBE FCU | PA | 12/16/15 | BIRMINGHAM-BLOOMFIELD CU | MI | 12/16/15 |
| LOUISIANA USA FCU | LA | 12/16/15 | BLACKSTONE RIVER FCU | RI | 12/16/15 |
| MEMBERS CHOICE CU | TX | 12/16/15 | BLAIR COUNTY FCU | PA | 12/16/15 |
| MEMBERS PREFERRED CU | ID | 12/16/15 | BOULEVARD FCU | NY | 12/16/15 |
| NORRISTOWN BELL CU | PA | 12/16/15 | BRAZOS VALLEY SCHOOLS CU | TX | 12/16/15 |
| NORTHERN COLORADO CU | CO | 12/16/15 | BROOKLINE MUNICIPAL CU | MA | 12/16/15 |
| NORTHERN EAGLE FCU | MN | 12/16/15 | CAL-COM FCU | TX | 12/16/15 |
| OAHE FCU | SD | 12/16/15 | CALHOUN-LIBERTY EMPL CU | FL | 12/16/15 |
| OZARK FCU | MO | 12/16/15 | CALIFORNIA COMMUNITY CU | CA | 12/16/15 |
| PACIFIC SERVICE CU | CA | 12/16/15 | CARDINAL CU INC | OH | 12/16/15 |
| PENINSULA FCU | MI | 12/16/15 | CATHOLIC VANTAGE FINANCIAL FCU | MI | 12/16/15 |
| PEOPLES CU | IA | 12/16/15 | CBC FCU | CA | 12/16/15 |
| SAFEAMERICA CU | CA | 12/16/15 | CDC FCU | GA | 12/16/15 |
| SAVANNAH POSTAL CU | GA | 12/16/15 | CDSC LOUISIANA FCU | LA | 12/16/15 |
| SCURRY COUNTY SCHOOL FCU | TX | 12/16/15 | CENTRAL CU OF ILLINOIS | IL | 12/16/15 |
| SEA WEST COAST GUARD FCU | CA | 12/16/15 | COMMUNITY UNITED FCU | GA | 12/16/15 |
| SECURITY CU | MI | 12/16/15 | CONSTRUCTION FCU | MI | 12/16/15 |
| SELF-HELP CU | NC | 12/16/15 | CSD CU | MO | 12/16/15 |

## Rating Upgrades

| Name | State | Date of Change | Name | State | Date of Change |
|------|-------|----------------|------|-------|----------------|
| CU OF ATLANTA | GA | 12/16/15 | ORLEANS PARISH CRIMINAL SHERIFFS CU | LA | 12/16/15 |
| DANVILLE BELL CU | IL | 12/16/15 | P&G MEHOOPANY EMPL FCU | PA | 12/16/15 |
| DOW GREAT WESTERN CU | CA | 12/16/15 | PACIFIC COMMUNITY CU | CA | 12/16/15 |
| EAGLE COMMUNITY CU | CA | 12/16/15 | PACIFIC CREST FCU | OR | 12/16/15 |
| EAST ORANGE VETERANS HOSPITAL FCU | NJ | 12/16/15 | PASADENA SERVICE FCU | CA | 12/16/15 |
| EFCU FINANCIAL FCU | LA | 12/16/15 | PEABODY MUNICIPAL FCU | MA | 12/16/15 |
| EVANSTON FIREMENS CU | IL | 12/16/15 | PEORIA FIRE FIGHTERS CU | IL | 12/16/15 |
| FAMILY COMMUNITY CU | IA | 12/16/15 | PIKES PEAK CU | CO | 12/16/15 |
| FIRST CHOICE CU INC | OH | 12/16/15 | POST OFFICE EMPL CU | LA | 12/16/15 |
| FIRST COAST COMMUNITY CU | FL | 12/16/15 | POSTAL EMPL CU | AL | 12/16/15 |
| FIRST UNITED CU | MI | 12/16/15 | PREMIER MEMBERS CU | CO | 12/16/15 |
| FOCUS CU | FL | 12/16/15 | PVHMC FCU | CA | 12/16/15 |
| GENERAL CU | IN | 12/16/15 | SALINA INTERPAROCHIAL CU | KS | 12/16/15 |
| GP LOUISIANA FCU | LA | 12/16/15 | SANTEE COOPER CU | SC | 12/16/15 |
| GPA CU | GA | 12/16/15 | SING SING EMPL FCU | NY | 12/16/15 |
| GRATIOT COMMUNITY CU | MI | 12/16/15 | SIOUX VALLEY COMMUNITY CU | IA | 12/16/15 |
| GREATER EASTERN CU | TN | 12/16/15 | SJP FCU | NY | 12/16/15 |
| HERITAGE GROVE FCU | OR | 12/16/15 | SPRINGFIELD FIREFIGHTERS CU | IL | 12/16/15 |
| HOLLYFRONTIER EMPL CU | UT | 12/16/15 | SRI FCU | CA | 12/16/15 |
| HTM CU | MA | 12/16/15 | ST COLUMBKILLE FCU | OH | 12/16/15 |
| INOVA FCU | IN | 12/16/15 | TANGIPAHOA PARISH TEACHERS CU | LA | 12/16/15 |
| JAX METRO CU | FL | 12/16/15 | TENN-AM WATER CO FCU | TN | 12/16/15 |
| JERSEY CITY FIREMEN FCU | NJ | 12/16/15 | TOLEDO POLICE FCU | OH | 12/16/15 |
| JERSEY CITY POLICE FCU | NJ | 12/16/15 | TOTAL COMMUNITY ACTION FCU | LA | 12/16/15 |
| KANE COUNTY TEACHERS CU | IL | 12/16/15 | UNIV OF LOUISIANA FCU | LA | 12/16/15 |
| KANSAS CITY CU | MO | 12/16/15 | WEST OAHU COMMUNITY FCU | HI | 12/16/15 |
| KRAFTMAN FCU | LA | 12/16/15 | | | |
| LAKE HURON CU | MI | 12/16/15 | | | |

## Rating:      C

| Name | State | Date of Change | Name | State | Date of Change |
|------|-------|----------------|------|-------|----------------|
| LAKE TRUST CU | MI | 12/16/15 | ALEC FCU | LA | 12/16/15 |
| LANDMARK CU | AL | 12/16/15 | ALEXANDRIA T&P FCU | LA | 12/16/15 |
| LANSING POSTAL COMMUNITY CU | MI | 12/16/15 | ALIQUIPPA TEACHERS FCU | PA | 12/16/15 |
| MARIN COUNTY FCU | CA | 12/16/15 | ANECA FCU | LA | 12/16/15 |
| MCPHERSON COOPERATIVE CU | KS | 12/16/15 | ARK VALLEY CU | KS | 12/16/15 |
| MEADOW GROVE FCU | NE | 12/16/15 | ARMSTRONG COUNTY FEDERAL EMPL FCU | PA | 12/16/15 |
| MEMBERS COMMUNITY CU | IA | 12/16/15 | ATLANTIC CITY POLICE FCU | NJ | 12/16/15 |
| MEMORIAL FCU | MS | 12/16/15 | ATLANTIC HEALTH EMPL FCU | NJ | 12/16/15 |
| MEMPHIS MUNICIPAL EMPL FCU | TN | 12/16/15 | ATTICA-WYOMING CORRECTIONAL EMPL FCU | NY | 12/16/15 |
| MENDO LAKE CU | CA | 12/16/15 | AVH FCU | PA | 12/16/15 |
| MERIDIAN MISSISSIPPI AIR NATIONAL GUARD | MS | 12/16/15 | BADLANDS FCU | MT | 12/16/15 |
| MIL-WAY FCU | AR | 12/16/15 | BEAUMONT COMMUNITY CU | TX | 12/16/15 |
| MISSISSIPPI PUBLIC EMPL CU | MS | 12/16/15 | BELLWETHER COMMUNITY CU | NH | 12/16/15 |
| MUTUAL SECURITY CU | CT | 12/16/15 | BRIDGEWAY FCU | NY | 12/16/15 |
| NESC FCU | MA | 12/16/15 | CALCASIEU TEACHERS & EMPL CU | LA | 12/16/15 |
| NEW COMMUNITY FCU | NJ | 12/16/15 | CAL-ED FCU | PA | 12/16/15 |
| NFG #2 FCU | PA | 12/16/15 | CATHOLIC CU | OH | 12/16/15 |
| NIAGARAS CHOICE FCU | NY | 12/16/15 | CENTRAL COAST FCU | CA | 12/16/15 |
| NONE SUFFER LACK FCU | MD | 12/16/15 | CENTRAL MAINE FCU | ME | 12/16/15 |
| NORTHERN HILLS FCU | SD | 12/16/15 | CHICAGO PATROLMENS FCU | IL | 12/16/15 |
| NRL FCU | VA | 12/16/15 | CITY OF CLARKSBURG FCU | WV | 12/16/15 |
| ONEAL CU | AL | 12/16/15 | CLEVELAND HEIGHTS TEACHERS CU INC | OH | 12/16/15 |

## Rating Upgrades

| Name | State | Date of Change | Name | State | Date of Change |
|------|-------|----------------|------|-------|----------------|
| COMMUNITYWORKS FCU | SC | 12/16/15 | MOUNTAINCREST CU | WA | 12/16/15 |
| CONSUMERS FCU | NY | 12/16/15 | MOWER COUNTY EMPL CU | MN | 12/16/15 |
| CONSUMERS UNION EMPL FCU | NY | 12/16/15 | MUNCIE FCU | IN | 12/16/15 |
| COUNTY CU | MO | 12/16/15 | MUNICIPAL CU | IA | 12/16/15 |
| DE SOTO MO-PAC CU | MO | 12/16/15 | MY HEALTHCARE FCU | FL | 12/16/15 |
| DIXIE LINE CU | TN | 12/16/15 | NAVEO CU | MA | 12/16/15 |
| DU PONT EMPL CU | IA | 12/16/15 | NEW ORLEANS FIREMENS FCU | LA | 12/16/15 |
| EAST CENTRAL MISSISSIPPI CU | MS | 12/16/15 | NIAGARA FALLS TEACHERS FCU | NY | 12/16/15 |
| EDISON FINANCIAL CU INC | OH | 12/16/15 | NOTRE DAME FCU | IN | 12/16/15 |
| EIGHT FCU | OH | 12/16/15 | OHIO TEAMSTERS CU INC | OH | 12/16/15 |
| ELECTRICAL FCU | CO | 12/16/15 | OK MEMBERS FIRST FCU | OK | 12/16/15 |
| ENERGY SERVICES FCU | MN | 12/16/15 | OMAHA DOUGLAS FCU | NE | 12/16/15 |
| ERIE METRO FCU | NY | 12/16/15 | ONE VISION FCU | IN | 12/16/15 |
| EXCEL FCU | GA | 12/16/15 | OSHKOSH TRUCK CU | WI | 12/16/15 |
| FAIRPORT FCU | NY | 12/16/15 | OSNOVA UKRAINIAN FCU | OH | 12/16/15 |
| FAMILY 1ST OF TEXAS FCU | TX | 12/16/15 | PARKS HERITAGE FCU | NY | 12/16/15 |
| FELLOWSHIP BAPTIST CHURCH CU | IL | 12/16/15 | PENINSULA GENERAL HOSPITAL & MEDICAL CTR | MD | 12/16/15 |
| FIRST KINGSPORT CU | TN | 12/16/15 | PEOPLES ADVANTAGE FCU | VA | 12/16/15 |
| FLINT FCU | GA | 12/16/15 | PEORIA HIWAY CU | IL | 12/16/15 |
| FLORENCE FCU | AL | 12/16/15 | PINE BLUFF POSTAL FCU | AR | 12/16/15 |
| FREMONT FIRST CENTRAL FCU | NE | 12/16/15 | PLANITES CU | IL | 12/16/15 |
| GASCO EASTERN DISTRICT FCU | PA | 12/16/15 | POCATELLO SIMPLOT CU | ID | 12/16/15 |
| GEISMAR COMPLEX FCU | LA | 12/16/15 | POLICE CU | WI | 12/16/15 |
| GLAMORGAN EMPL FCU | VA | 12/16/15 | POST OFFICE CU | WI | 12/16/15 |
| HAMLET FCU | NC | 12/16/15 | POSTAL FAMILY FCU | ND | 12/16/15 |
| HARBOR CU | WI | 12/16/15 | PRESSERS UNION LOCAL 12 ILGWU CU | MA | 12/16/15 |
| HARTFORD FIREFIGHTERS FCU | CT | 12/16/15 | PUGET SOUND COOPERATIVE CU | WA | 12/16/15 |
| HERITAGE COMMUNITY CU | CA | 12/16/15 | RIVERSIDE COMMUNITY CU | IL | 12/16/15 |
| HERITAGE VALLEY FCU | PA | 12/16/15 | ROCHESTER & MONROE COUNTY EMPL FCU | NY | 12/16/15 |
| HUB-CO CU | IA | 12/16/15 | S I PHILADELPHIA FCU | PA | 12/16/15 |
| HUTCHINSON GOVERNMENT EMPL CU | KS | 12/16/15 | SAINTS MARGARET & GREGORY FCU | OH | 12/16/15 |
| IBEW 76 FCU | WA | 12/16/15 | SANTA ANA FCU | CA | 12/16/15 |
| ILLINOIS VALLEY CU | IL | 12/16/15 | SHARED RESOURCES CU | TX | 12/16/15 |
| INDUSTRIAL CU OF WHATCOM COUNTY | WA | 12/16/15 | SIGNAL FINANCIAL FCU | MD | 12/16/15 |
| ISSAQUENA COUNTY FCU | MS | 12/16/15 | SIOUX EMPIRE FCU | SD | 12/16/15 |
| JOY EMPL FCU | VA | 12/16/15 | SISKIYOU CENTRAL CU | CA | 12/16/15 |
| KAHULUI FCU | HI | 12/16/15 | SISSETON-WAHPETON FCU | SD | 12/16/15 |
| KEMBA ROANOKE FCU | VA | 12/16/15 | SOMERSET FCU | MA | 12/16/15 |
| KINGSTON TVA EMPL CU | TN | 12/16/15 | SONOMA FCU | CA | 12/16/15 |
| LOC FCU | MI | 12/16/15 | SOUNDVIEW FINANCIAL CU | CT | 12/16/15 |
| MADISON EDUCATION ASSOCIATES CU | FL | 12/16/15 | SOUTHEAST LOUISIANA VETERANS HEALTH CARE | LA | 12/16/15 |
| MANCHESTER MUNICIPAL FCU | CT | 12/16/15 | SOUTHEAST MICHIGAN STATE EMPL FCU | MI | 12/16/15 |
| MARTINSBURG VA CENTER FCU | WV | 12/16/15 | SOUTHWEST RESEARCH CENTER FCU | TX | 12/16/15 |
| MAUMEE VALLEY CU | OH | 12/16/15 | SPOKANE CITY CU | WA | 12/16/15 |
| ME EMPL CU | WI | 12/16/15 | ST MARK CU | IL | 12/16/15 |
| MEMBERS1ST COMMUNITY CU | IA | 12/16/15 | STREATOR COMMUNITY CU | IL | 12/16/15 |
| MERCER COUNTY IMPROVEMENT AUTHORITY FCU | NJ | 12/16/15 | THORNAPPLE CU | MI | 12/16/15 |
| MID DELTA CU | MS | 12/16/15 | THRIVE FCU | IN | 12/16/15 |
| MID PLAINS CU | KS | 12/16/15 | TOLEDO FIRE FIGHTERS FCU | OH | 12/16/15 |
| MONTELL FCU | LA | 12/16/15 | TRANSIT OPERATIONS FCU | MN | 12/16/15 |

## Rating Upgrades

| Name | State | Date of Change | Name | State | Date of Change |
|---|---|---|---|---|---|
| TRUPARTNER CU INC | OH | 12/16/15 | EDUCATIONAL & GOVERNMENTAL EMPL FCU | NY | 12/16/15 |
| U-1ST COMMUNITY FCU | NM | 12/16/15 | EDUCATIONAL COMMUNITY CU | MO | 12/16/15 |
| UNITED ADVANTAGE NORTHWEST FCU | OR | 12/16/15 | EL CAJON FCU | CA | 12/16/15 |
| UNITED SAN ANTONIO COMMUNITY FCU | TX | 12/16/15 | EMPLOYMENT SECURITY EMPL CU | KS | 12/16/15 |
| VERITAS FCU | TN | 12/16/15 | ENERGIZE CU | OK | 12/16/15 |
| VICTORIA TEACHERS FCU | TX | 12/16/15 | EQUITABLE FCU | OH | 12/16/15 |
| WATSONVILLE HOSPITAL FCU | CA | 12/16/15 | FAIRFIELD FCU | AR | 12/16/15 |
| WESTAR FCU | NY | 12/16/15 | FAIRMONT SCHOOL EMPL FCU | MN | 12/16/15 |
| WHARTON COUNTY TEACHERS CU | TX | 12/16/15 | FORREST COUNTY TEACHERS FCU | MS | 12/16/15 |
| WHITE ROCK FCU | PA | 12/16/15 | FORT MORGAN SCHOOLS FCU | CO | 12/16/15 |
| WINDSOR LOCKS FCU | CT | 12/16/15 | FRANKFORT COMMUNITY FCU | MI | 12/16/15 |
| WINSLOW COMMUNITY FCU | ME | 12/16/15 | FRANKLIN REGIONAL SCHOOLS FCU | PA | 12/16/15 |
| ZACHARY COMMUNITY FCU | LA | 12/16/15 | GARLAND COUNTY EDUCATORS FCU | AR | 12/16/15 |
| | | | GEM FCU | ND | 12/16/15 |
| | | | GRAND PRAIRIE CU | TX | 12/16/15 |

## Rating: C-

| Name | State | Date of Change | Name | State | Date of Change |
|---|---|---|---|---|---|
| AGILITY FINANCIAL CU | TN | 12/16/15 | GREATER NILES COMMUNITY FCU | MI | 12/16/15 |
| ALDERSON FCI FCU | WV | 12/16/15 | GREATER PITTSBURGH FCU | PA | 12/16/15 |
| ALIGN CU | MA | 12/16/15 | HARRIS EMPL CU | GA | 12/16/15 |
| BAKERSFIELD CITY EMPL FCU | CA | 12/16/15 | HAWAII LAW ENFORCEMENT FCU | HI | 12/16/15 |
| BAR-CONS FCU | IN | 12/16/15 | HAWAIIAN ELECTRIC EMPL FCU | HI | 12/16/15 |
| BAYONNE HOSPITAL EMPL FCU | NJ | 12/16/15 | HEALTH FACILITIES FCU | SC | 12/16/15 |
| BELLE RIVER COMMUNITY CU | MI | 12/16/15 | HEALTHCARE PLUS FCU | SD | 12/16/15 |
| BERYLCO EMPL CU | PA | 12/16/15 | HEMINGFORD COMMUNITY FCU | NE | 12/16/15 |
| BETHLEHEM 1ST FCU | PA | 12/16/15 | HOLY GHOST PARISH CU | IA | 12/16/15 |
| BOND COMMUNITY FCU | GA | 12/16/15 | HUNTINGTON COUNTY FCU | IN | 12/16/15 |
| BRAZOS COMMUNITY CU | TX | 12/16/15 | IBERVILLE FCU | LA | 12/16/15 |
| BRONCO FCU | VA | 12/16/15 | INNER LAKES FCU | NY | 12/16/15 |
| BUFFALO COMMUNITY FCU | NY | 12/16/15 | JUNIOR COLLEGE FCU | MS | 12/16/15 |
| CALCOE FCU | WA | 12/16/15 | KEKAHA FCU | HI | 12/16/15 |
| CAPITAL AREA REALTORS FCU | MD | 12/16/15 | KONE EMPL CU | IL | 12/16/15 |
| CATHOLICS UNITED CU | KS | 12/16/15 | LENCO CU | MI | 12/16/15 |
| CENTRAL ILLINOIS CU | IL | 12/16/15 | LENNOX EMPL CU | IA | 12/16/15 |
| CHATTANOOGA FIRST FCU | TN | 12/16/15 | LETCHER COUNTY TEACHERS CU | KY | 12/16/15 |
| CHIPHONE FCU | IN | 12/16/15 | LOCAL UNION 392 FCU | OH | 12/16/15 |
| CLAIRTON WORKS FCU | PA | 12/16/15 | LONGVIEW FCU | TX | 12/16/15 |
| COMMUNITY FINANCIAL CU | MO | 12/16/15 | LORMET COMMUNITY FCU | OH | 12/16/15 |
| CONNECTICUT LABOR DEPT FCU | CT | 12/16/15 | LOWLAND CU | TN | 12/16/15 |
| COREPLUS FCU | CT | 12/16/15 | MARYLAND POSTAL FCU | MD | 12/16/15 |
| CORNING CABLE SYSTEMS CU | NC | 12/16/15 | MCKESSON FCU | CT | 12/16/15 |
| COTEAU VALLEY FCU | SD | 12/16/15 | MEADOWS CU | IL | 12/16/15 |
| DECA CU | OH | 12/16/15 | METROWEST COMMUNITY FCU | MA | 12/16/15 |
| DECATUR EARTHMOVER CU | IL | 12/16/15 | MICHIGAN COLUMBUS FCU | MI | 12/16/15 |
| DIEBOLD FCU | OH | 12/16/15 | MIDDLESEX-ESSEX POSTAL EMPL FCU | MA | 12/16/15 |
| DIVISION #6 HIGHWAY CU | MO | 12/16/15 | MONTANA EDUCATORS CU | MT | 12/16/15 |
| DOUGLAS COUNTY CU | WI | 12/16/15 | MPD COMMUNITY CU | TN | 12/16/15 |
| DRESSER ALEXANDRIA FCU | LA | 12/16/15 | MUTUAL FIRST FCU | NE | 12/16/15 |
| EAST ALLEN FCU | IN | 12/16/15 | NEBRASKA STATE EMPL CU | NE | 12/16/15 |
| EAST TRAVERSE CATHOLIC FCU | MI | 12/16/15 | NEW HAVEN POLICE AND MUNICIPAL FCU | CT | 12/16/15 |
| EASTERN KENTUCKY FCU | KY | 12/16/15 | NEW RISING STAR FCU | MI | 12/16/15 |
| ECOLAB CU | MN | 12/16/15 | NEWARK POST OFFICE EMPL CU | NJ | 12/16/15 |

## Rating Upgrades

| Name | State | Date of Change | Name | State | Date of Change |
|------|-------|----------------|------|-------|----------------|
| NIKKEI CU | CA | 12/16/15 | WESTERN INDIANA CU | IN | 12/16/15 |
| NORTH PENN FCU | PA | 12/16/15 | WISCONSIN MEDICAL CU | WI | 12/16/15 |
| NORTHEAST NEBRASKA FCU | NE | 12/16/15 | | | |
| NORTHERN MONTANA HOSPITAL FCU | MT | 12/16/15 | **Rating: D+** | | |
| OHIO VALLEY COMMUNITY CU | OH | 12/16/15 | ALCOA COMMUNITY FCU | AR | 12/16/15 |
| OK FCU | OK | 12/16/15 | AMERICO FCU | PA | 12/16/15 |
| OMAHA FCU | NE | 12/16/15 | ASBESTOS WORKERS LOCAL 14 FCU | PA | 12/16/15 |
| PACIFIC NORTHWEST IRONWORKERS FCU | OR | 12/16/15 | ATL FCU | MI | 12/16/15 |
| PAMPA TEACHERS FCU | TX | 12/16/15 | AVENUE BAPTIST BROTHERHOOD FCU | LA | 12/16/15 |
| PBA FCU | AR | 12/16/15 | BORINQUEN SUR FCU | PR | 12/16/15 |
| PEOPLES COMMUNITY CU | MN | 12/16/15 | BVA FCU | PA | 12/16/15 |
| PEORIA CITY EMPL CU | IL | 12/16/15 | BYKOTA FCU | NY | 12/16/15 |
| POLK COUNTY CU | IA | 12/16/15 | CABOT BOSTON CU | MA | 12/16/15 |
| PORTSMOUTH SCHOOLS FCU | VA | 12/16/15 | CAPITOL CU | TX | 12/16/15 |
| PRESIDENTS FCU | OH | 12/16/15 | CATHOLIC CU | WI | 12/16/15 |
| PROVO POLICE & FIRE DEPT CU | UT | 12/16/15 | CENTRAL FLORIDA POSTAL CU | FL | 12/16/15 |
| QSIDE FCU | NY | 12/16/15 | CHARLESTON FCU | WV | 12/16/15 |
| QUAD CITIES POSTAL CU | IL | 12/16/15 | CHATHAM EBEN COOPERATIVE FCU | MI | 12/16/15 |
| RIVER TOWN FCU | AR | 12/16/15 | CITY CENTER CU | UT | 12/16/15 |
| ROCKFORD BELL CU | IL | 12/16/15 | CITY FCU | TX | 12/16/15 |
| ROCKFORD MUNICIPAL EMPL CU | IL | 12/16/15 | CITY OF MCKEESPORT EMPL FCU | PA | 12/16/15 |
| S T O F F E FCU | OH | 12/16/15 | CLARENCE COMMUNITY & SCHOOLS FCU | NY | 12/16/15 |
| SANTA CRUZ COMMUNITY CU | CA | 12/16/15 | CLARITY CU | ID | 12/16/15 |
| SCENIC FALLS FCU | ID | 12/16/15 | CONSUMERS FCU | SD | 12/16/15 |
| SCF WESTCHESTER NY EMPL FCU | NY | 12/16/15 | CORNER POST FCU | PA | 12/16/15 |
| SERVICE FIRST FCU | SD | 12/16/15 | CORRECTIONAL WORKERS FCU | OK | 12/16/15 |
| SHAW UNIV FCU | NC | 12/16/15 | CROSS VALLEY FCU | PA | 12/16/15 |
| SHERCHEM FCU | OH | 12/16/15 | CSP EMPL FCU | CT | 12/16/15 |
| SILVER STATE SCHOOLS CU | NV | 12/16/15 | DEER LODGE COUNTY SCHOOL EMPL FCU | MT | 12/16/15 |
| SMW 104 FCU | CA | 12/16/15 | DERRY AREA FCU | PA | 12/16/15 |
| SOUTH COMMUNITY CU | MO | 12/16/15 | DESERT MEDICAL FCU | AZ | 12/16/15 |
| SPCO CU | TX | 12/16/15 | EFFINGHAM HIGHWAY CU | IL | 12/16/15 |
| ST AUGUSTINE PRESBYTERIAN FCU | NY | 12/16/15 | ELECTRIC COOPERATIVES FCU | AR | 12/16/15 |
| ST ELIZABETH EMPL CU | WI | 12/16/15 | ELGIN MENTAL HEALTH CENTER CU | IL | 12/16/15 |
| ST JUDE CU | IL | 12/16/15 | ERIE COMMUNITY FCU | OH | 12/16/15 |
| ST MARY PARISH SCHOOL EMPL FCU | LA | 12/16/15 | EVONIK EMPL FCU | AL | 12/16/15 |
| ST PASCHAL BAYLONS FCU | OH | 12/16/15 | FIRST NORTHERN CU | IL | 12/16/15 |
| ST VINCENTS MEDICAL CENTER FCU | CT | 12/16/15 | FIRST SERVICE CU | TX | 12/16/15 |
| SYLVANIA AREA FCU | OH | 12/16/15 | GORMAN-RUPP & ASSOCIATES CU | OH | 12/16/15 |
| TEANECK FCU | NJ | 12/16/15 | GREEN MOUNTAIN CU | VT | 12/16/15 |
| TESORO NORTHWEST FCU | WA | 12/16/15 | HAWAII NATIONAL GUARD FCU | HI | 12/16/15 |
| TEXAS ASSNS OF PROFESSIONALS FCU | TX | 12/16/15 | HEALTH FIRST FCU | ME | 12/16/15 |
| TEXAS PEOPLE FCU | TX | 12/16/15 | HOPES EMPL FCU | NY | 12/16/15 |
| TRAVIS COUNTY CU | TX | 12/16/15 | IBEW LU 66 FCU | TX | 12/16/15 |
| TREMONT CU | MA | 12/16/15 | IBEW/SJ CASCADE FCU | OR | 12/16/15 |
| TRI-COUNTY CU | WI | 12/16/15 | INLAND FCU | CA | 12/16/15 |
| TRUMBULL COUNTY POSTAL EMPL CU | OH | 12/16/15 | KINGS PEAK CU | UT | 12/16/15 |
| UNITED HEALTH CU | CA | 12/16/15 | LAKES FCU | IN | 12/16/15 |
| UNITY CATHOLIC FCU | OH | 12/16/15 | LEXINGTON MA FCU | MA | 12/16/15 |
| WAVE FCU | RI | 12/16/15 | LOUCHEM FCU | KY | 12/16/15 |

## Rating Upgrades

| Name | State | Date of Change | Name | State | Date of Change |
|------|-------|----------------|------|-------|----------------|
| MACON-BIBB EMPL CU | GA | 12/16/15 | CATHOLIC FAMILY CU | MO | 12/16/15 |
| MADISON COUNTY FCU | IN | 12/16/15 | CHRISTOPHER CU | MI | 12/16/15 |
| MESSIAH BAPTIST CHURCH FCU | NJ | 12/16/15 | CONNECTIONS CU | ID | 12/16/15 |
| METRO WIRE FCU | PA | 12/16/15 | CU ONE OF THE OKLAHOMA | OK | 12/16/15 |
| MIDWEST CU | MO | 12/16/15 | DESERT VALLEYS FCU | CA | 12/16/15 |
| MONAD FCU | WA | 12/16/15 | FRATERNAL ORDER OF POLICE CU | OK | 12/16/15 |
| MONROVIA CITY EMPL FCU | CA | 12/16/15 | GEORGIA POWER MACON FCU | GA | 12/16/15 |
| MORTON WEEKS FCU | LA | 12/16/15 | GLAMOUR COMMUNITY FCU | PR | 12/16/15 |
| MUNI EMPL CU | IA | 12/16/15 | HALE COUNTY TEACHERS FCU | TX | 12/16/15 |
| NAVFAC FCU | HI | 12/16/15 | HAMPTON ROADS EDUCATORS CU INC | VA | 12/16/15 |
| NEW CENTURY FCU | IL | 12/16/15 | HARRISON POLICE & FIREMENS FCU | NJ | 12/16/15 |
| NEW YORK STATE EMPL FCU | NY | 12/16/15 | HOOSIER UNITED CU | IN | 12/16/15 |
| NEWSPAPER EMPL CU | NY | 12/16/15 | INTER-AMERICAN FCU | NY | 12/16/15 |
| NORTHEASTERN ENGINEERS FCU | NY | 12/16/15 | IUPAT DC 21 FCU | PA | 12/16/15 |
| OAKDALE CU | WI | 12/16/15 | LANCASTER PENNSYLVANIA FIREMEN FCU | PA | 12/16/15 |
| OREM CITY EMPL FCU | UT | 12/16/15 | MEMBERS CU | CT | 12/16/15 |
| OTERO COUNTY TEACHERS FCU | CO | 12/16/15 | MERCER COUNTY NJ TEACHERS FCU | NJ | 12/16/15 |
| PADUCAH TEACHERS FCU | KY | 12/16/15 | MUTUAL SAVINGS CU | AL | 12/16/15 |
| PASADENA FCU | CA | 12/16/15 | MWPH GRAND LODGE OF ILLINOIS FCU | IL | 12/16/15 |
| PENN SOUTH COOPERATIVE FCU | NY | 12/16/15 | MY CU | CA | 12/16/15 |
| PEPCO FCU | DC | 12/16/15 | NORTHERN CHAUTAUQUA FCU | NY | 12/16/15 |
| PLAIN DEALER FCU | OH | 12/16/15 | PARISH MEMBERS CU | IL | 12/16/15 |
| POWELL SCHOOLS FCU | WY | 12/16/15 | PERSONAL CARE AMERICA FCU | CT | 12/16/15 |
| PROJECTOR FCU | NY | 12/16/15 | PIONEER COMMUNITY FCU | NE | 12/16/15 |
| RESOURCE FCU | TN | 12/16/15 | PORTLAND LOCAL 8 FCU | OR | 12/16/15 |
| RICHMOND COUNTY HEALTH DEPT EMPL CU | GA | 12/16/15 | REGIONAL MEMBERS FCU | GA | 12/16/15 |
| RICHMOND LIGHT EMPL FCU | IN | 12/16/15 | R-G FCU | MO | 12/16/15 |
| RIVER CITIES CU | LA | 12/16/15 | S W E FCU | TX | 12/16/15 |
| RIVERTOWN COMMUNITY FCU | MI | 12/16/15 | SAN JUAN CU | UT | 12/16/15 |
| SOO LINE CU | MN | 12/16/15 | SONY SAN DIEGO EMPL FCU | CA | 12/16/15 |
| SOUTH JENNINGS CATHOLIC FCU | LA | 12/16/15 | SOUTHWEST COUNTIES SCHOOL EMPL CU | MO | 12/16/15 |
| SPACE CITY CU | TX | 12/16/15 | SPERRY ASSOCIATES FCU | NY | 12/16/15 |
| SPE FCU | PA | 12/16/15 | ST ANNE CU | MA | 12/16/15 |
| TBC FCU | VA | 12/16/15 | STRUTHERS FCU | OH | 12/16/15 |
| TEAMSTERS LOCAL #238 CU | IA | 12/16/15 | TEXAS FCU | TX | 12/16/15 |
| TONAWANDA COMMUNITY FCU | NY | 12/16/15 | TRADEMARK FCU | ME | 12/16/15 |
| VALLEY ISLE COMMUNITY FCU | HI | 12/16/15 | TRIAD PARTNERS FCU | NC | 12/16/15 |
| VERMONT VA FCU | VT | 12/16/15 | TRI-LAKES FCU | NY | 12/16/15 |
| VICKSBURG RAILROAD CU | MS | 12/16/15 | TRUMBULL CU | CT | 12/16/15 |
| WARD COUNTY CU | TX | 12/16/15 | TUSCALOOSA COUNTY CU | AL | 12/16/15 |
| WHITE PLAINS P O EMPL FCU | NY | 12/16/15 | TUSKEGEE FCU | AL | 12/16/15 |
| WIN-HOOD CO-OP CU | IL | 12/16/15 | UBC CU | MO | 12/16/15 |
| WIREGRASS FCU | AL | 12/16/15 | UNITED COMMUNITY FCU | PA | 12/16/15 |
| XAVIER UNIV FCU | LA | 12/16/15 | UNITED NEIGHBORS FCU | NY | 12/16/15 |
| YOUR HOMETOWN FCU | KY | 12/16/15 | UNIV OF WISCONSIN-OSHKOSH CU | WI | 12/16/15 |
| | | | WEST VIRGINIA STATE CONVENTION CU | WV | 12/16/15 |

## Rating: D

| Name | State | Date of Change |
|------|-------|----------------|
| BAKER FCU | NJ | 12/16/15 |
| BCM FCU | TX | 12/16/15 |
| BIG BETHEL AME CHURCH FCU | GA | 12/16/15 |

| Name | State | Date of Change |
|------|-------|----------------|
| WHITE EARTH RESERVATION FCU | MN | 12/16/15 |
| WR GRACE MARYLAND EMPL FCU | MD | 12/16/15 |

## Rating: D-

## Rating Upgrades

| Name | State | Date of Change | Name | State | Date of Change |
|------|-------|----------------|------|-------|----------------|
| ALASKA DISTRICT ENGINEERS FCU | AK | 12/16/15 | | | |
| ALLWEALTH FCU | OH | 12/16/15 | | | |
| ANG FCU | AL | 12/16/15 | | | |
| BRENTWOOD BAPTIST CHURCH FCU | TX | 12/16/15 | | | |
| COMMUNITY HEALTHCARE FCU | WA | 12/16/15 | | | |
| ELIZABETH (NJ) FIREMENS FCU | NJ | 12/16/15 | | | |
| HAMPTON ROADS CATHOLIC FCU | VA | 12/16/15 | | | |
| HARRISON TEACHERS FCU | NY | 12/16/15 | | | |
| KALEIDA HEALTH FCU | NY | 12/16/15 | | | |
| LOUISIANA CENTRAL CU | LA | 12/16/15 | | | |
| MESQUITE CU | TX | 12/16/15 | | | |
| MOUNTAIN RIVER CU | CO | 12/16/15 | | | |
| NORTHWEST ARKANSAS FCU | AR | 12/16/15 | | | |
| OUR FAMILY SOCIAL CU | NE | 12/16/15 | | | |
| PATHWAYS FINANCIAL CU INC | OH | 12/16/15 | | | |
| PEOPLES INDEPENDENT CHURCH FCU | CA | 12/16/15 | | | |
| PLAINFIELD POLICE & FIREMENS FCU | NJ | 12/16/15 | | | |
| SAIF FCU | LA | 12/16/15 | | | |
| SCOTT & WHITE EMPL CU | TX | 12/16/15 | | | |
| TRADES & LABOR FCU | MN | 12/16/15 | | | |
| UFCW LOCAL 1776 FCU | PA | 12/16/15 | | | |

## Rating:          E+

| Name | State | Date of Change |
|------|-------|----------------|
| BELLCO FCU | PA | 12/16/15 |
| CATHOLIC UNITED FINANCIAL CU | MN | 12/16/15 |
| CENTRAL JERSEY FCU | NJ | 12/16/15 |
| CLEARCHOICE FCU | PA | 12/16/15 |
| COMMUNITY PLUS FCU | IL | 12/16/15 |
| FIRST PRIORITY CU | TX | 12/16/15 |
| KEYS FCU | FL | 12/16/15 |
| NEIGHBORS 1ST FCU | PA | 12/16/15 |
| NIAGARA-WHEATFIELD FCU | NY | 12/16/15 |
| PRINTING INDUSTRIES CU | CA | 12/16/15 |
| UNITED POLES FCU | NJ | 12/16/15 |

## Rating:          E

| Name | State | Date of Change |
|------|-------|----------------|
| NEW HAVEN COUNTY CU | CT | 12/16/15 |
| TRI-RIVERS FCU | AL | 12/16/15 |

## Rating Downgrades

| Name | State | Date of Change | Name | State | Date of Change |
|------|-------|----------------|------|-------|----------------|
| **Rating:** B- | | | KAUAI GOVERNMENT EMPL FCU | HI | 12/16/15 |
| | | | KBR CU | WA | 12/16/15 |
| CONNECT CU | FL | 12/16/15 | KBR HERITAGE FCU | TX | 12/16/15 |
| EAGLE ONE FCU | DE | 12/16/15 | LOYOLA UNIV EMPL FCU | IL | 12/16/15 |
| FAA CU | OK | 12/16/15 | LYNN MUNICIPAL EMPL CU | MA | 12/16/15 |
| GEMC FCU | GA | 12/16/15 | MBHS FCU | MS | 12/16/15 |
| GROW FINANCIAL FCU | FL | 12/16/15 | MELROSE SCHOOL & MUNICIPAL EMPL FCU | MA | 12/16/15 |
| HAWAII COMMUNITY FCU | HI | 12/16/15 | NATCHEZ-ADAMS EDUCATORS CU | MS | 12/16/15 |
| HUNTINGTONIZED FCU | WV | 12/16/15 | POSTAL GOVERNMENT EMPL FCU | RI | 12/16/15 |
| LETOURNEAU FCU | TX | 12/16/15 | QUAY SCHOOLS FCU | NM | 12/16/15 |
| MAGNOLIA FCU | MS | 12/16/15 | RICHLAND PARISH SCHOOLS FCU | LA | 12/16/15 |
| MERCK EMPL FCU | NJ | 12/16/15 | RUSSELL COUNTRY FCU | MT | 12/16/15 |
| MILL CITY CU | MN | 12/16/15 | SOOPER CU | CO | 12/16/15 |
| MOHAWK VALLEY FCU | NY | 12/16/15 | SOUTHWEST MONTANA COMMUNITY FCU | MT | 12/16/15 |
| OPPORTUNITIES CU | VT | 12/16/15 | STANDARD REGISTER FCU | OH | 12/16/15 |
| PFD FIREFIGHTERS CU INC | VA | 12/16/15 | STEPPING STONES COMMUNITY FCU | DE | 12/16/15 |
| PINE TREE COMMUNITY CU | ID | 12/16/15 | TELCO ROSWELL NEW MEXICO FCU | NM | 12/16/15 |
| PLATINUM FCU | GA | 12/16/15 | TOPLINE FCU | MN | 12/16/15 |
| RED ROCKS CU | CO | 12/16/15 | UNITED ASSN CU | CA | 12/16/15 |
| RIVER REGION FCU | LA | 12/16/15 | | | |
| RIVER VALLEY CU | OH | 12/16/15 | **Rating:** C | | |
| SOLANO FIRST FCU | CA | 12/16/15 | | | |
| UNCLE CU | CA | 12/16/15 | AB&W CU INC | VA | 12/16/15 |
| UNIWYO FCU | WY | 12/16/15 | ALABAMA CENTRAL CU | AL | 12/16/15 |
| VUE COMMUNITY CU | ND | 12/16/15 | ARIZONA CENTRAL CU | AZ | 12/16/15 |
| YONKERS TEACHERS FCU | NY | 12/16/15 | ARRHA CU | MA | 12/16/15 |
| | | | ASCENSION CU | LA | 12/16/15 |
| **Rating:** C+ | | | B P S FCU | TX | 12/16/15 |
| | | | BAY CU | FL | 12/16/15 |
| ALABAMA STATE EMPL CU | AL | 12/16/15 | BAYOU FCU | LA | 12/16/15 |
| ARKANSAS FARM BUREAU FCU | AR | 12/16/15 | BENCHMARK FCU | PA | 12/16/15 |
| BCS COMMUNITY CU | CO | 12/16/15 | BRIDGEWATER CU | MA | 12/16/15 |
| BROWARD HEALTHCARE FCU | FL | 12/16/15 | C T A C AND M FCU | IL | 12/16/15 |
| BUCKS COUNTY EMPL CU | PA | 12/16/15 | CHADRON FCU | NE | 12/16/15 |
| CANYON STATE CU | AZ | 12/16/15 | COLUMBINE FCU | CO | 12/16/15 |
| CENTRAL OKLAHOMA FCU | OK | 12/16/15 | CORAL COMMUNITY FCU | FL | 12/16/15 |
| CLEVELAND SELFRELIANCE FCU | OH | 12/16/15 | DIVISION 10 HIGHWAY EMPL CU | MO | 12/16/15 |
| COMMUNITIES OF ABILENE FCU | TX | 12/16/15 | FOCUS FCU | OK | 12/16/15 |
| CONE CU | WI | 12/16/15 | FONTANA FCU | CA | 12/16/15 |
| CUBA CU | NM | 12/16/15 | GARY POLICE DEPT EMPL FCU | IN | 12/16/15 |
| DELTA COUNTY FCU | CO | 12/16/15 | GENESIS EMPL CU | OH | 12/16/15 |
| DEVILS SLIDE FCU | UT | 12/16/15 | GRANCO FCU | WA | 12/16/15 |
| EDWARDS FCU | CA | 12/16/15 | GREAT LAKES MEMBERS CU | MI | 12/16/15 |
| FLORIDA CENTRAL CU | FL | 12/16/15 | HEALTHCARE FIRST CU | PA | 12/16/15 |
| FREEDOM CU | MA | 12/16/15 | L&N EMPL CU | AL | 12/16/15 |
| GAP FCU | PA | 12/16/15 | LUBBOCK TEACHERS FCU | TX | 12/16/15 |
| GRANITE HILLS CU | VT | 12/16/15 | MACON WATER WORKS CU | GA | 12/16/15 |
| HEALTHSHARE CU | NC | 12/16/15 | MBFT FCU | MD | 12/16/15 |
| JEEP COUNTRY FCU | OH | 12/16/15 | MEMORIAL CU | TX | 12/16/15 |
| JEFFERSON COUNTY FCU | KY | 12/16/15 | MIDWAY FCU | VA | 12/16/15 |
| JORDAN FCU | UT | 12/16/15 | MUHLENBERG COMMUNITY HOSPITAL CU | KY | 12/16/15 |

## Rating Downgrades

| Name | State | Date of Change | Name | State | Date of Change |
|------|-------|--------|------|-------|--------|
| MUNA FCU | MS | 12/16/15 | FORT MCPHERSON CU | GA | 12/16/15 |
| NEW CU | WI | 12/16/15 | FRONTIER COMMUNITY CU | IA | 12/16/15 |
| NEW ORLEANS PUBLIC BELT RR FCU | LA | 12/16/15 | GOLDMARK FCU | MA | 12/16/15 |
| NEWARK BOARD OF EDUCATION EMPL CU | NJ | 12/16/15 | GREATER CENTENNIAL FCU | NY | 12/16/15 |
| ON THE GRID FINANCIAL FCU | GA | 12/16/15 | HARRISON COUNTY POE FCU | MS | 12/16/15 |
| OSWEGO COUNTY FCU | NY | 12/16/15 | HARTFORD MUNICIPAL EMPL FCU | CT | 12/16/15 |
| PACIFIC TRANSPORTATION FCU | CA | 12/16/15 | HARVESTER FINANCIAL CU | IN | 12/16/15 |
| PALISADES FCU | NY | 12/16/15 | HEALTH CARE CU | WI | 12/16/15 |
| PREMIER COMMUNITY CU | CA | 12/16/15 | INLAND VALLEY FCU | CA | 12/16/15 |
| QUALTRUST CU | TX | 12/16/15 | INTERNAL REVENUE FCU | LA | 12/16/15 |
| RACINE MUNICIPAL EMPL CU | WI | 12/16/15 | KILGORE SHELL EMPL FCU | TX | 12/16/15 |
| RAFE FCU | CA | 12/16/15 | LOCAL CU | MI | 12/16/15 |
| S E C U CU | IA | 12/16/15 | LOCKPORT SCHOOLS FCU | NY | 12/16/15 |
| SHAMROCK FCU | TX | 12/16/15 | M A FORD EMPL CU | IA | 12/16/15 |
| SOUTH JERSEY FCU | NJ | 12/16/15 | MALDEN TEACHERS FCU | MA | 12/16/15 |
| SPACE AGE TULSA FCU | OK | 12/16/15 | MEADOWLAND CU | WI | 12/16/15 |
| SUNRISE FAMILY CU | MI | 12/16/15 | MET TRAN FCU | TX | 12/16/15 |
| TAMPA LONGSHOREMENS FCU | FL | 12/16/15 | MINERVA AREA FCU | OH | 12/16/15 |
| UNITED TELETECH FINANCIAL FCU | NJ | 12/16/15 | MOLOKAI COMMUNITY FCU | HI | 12/16/15 |
| VALOR FCU | PA | 12/16/15 | MONROE COUNTY TEACHERS FCU | FL | 12/16/15 |
| WEST HOLMES SCHOOL EMPL CU INC | OH | 12/16/15 | MT JEZREEL FCU | MD | 12/16/15 |
| WHITESVILLE COMMUNITY CU | KY | 12/16/15 | NASHWAUK FCU | MN | 12/16/15 |
|  |  |  | NBA CU | PA | 12/16/15 |

## Rating:     C-

| Name | State | Date of Change | Name | State | Date of Change |
|------|-------|--------|------|-------|--------|
|  |  |  | NEW YORK UNIV FCU | NY | 12/16/15 |
| ACU CU | TX | 12/16/15 | OIL COUNTRY FCU | PA | 12/16/15 |
| APPALACHIAN COMMUNITY FCU | TN | 12/16/15 | PARTNERS 1ST FCU | IN | 12/16/15 |
| ARNOLD BAKERS EMPL FCU | CT | 12/16/15 | PEOPLE FIRST FCU | PA | 12/16/15 |
| ATLANTIC FCU | NJ | 12/16/15 | PINE BLUFF COTTON BELT FCU | AR | 12/16/15 |
| BABBITT STEELWORKERS CU | MN | 12/16/15 | PRESCOTT FCU | AZ | 12/16/15 |
| BATTLE CREEK AREA COMMUNITY FCU | MI | 12/16/15 | QUEENS FCU | HI | 12/16/15 |
| BAYONNE SCHOOL EMPL FCU | NJ | 12/16/15 | RAPIDES FCU | LA | 12/16/15 |
| BOISE FIRE DEPT CU | ID | 12/16/15 | SAKER SHOP RITE FCU | NJ | 12/16/15 |
| BULAB EMPL FCU | TN | 12/16/15 | SIMPLOT EMPL CU | ID | 12/16/15 |
| BUTLER COUNTY TEACHERS FCU | PA | 12/16/15 | SONOMA COUNTY GRANGE CU | CA | 12/16/15 |
| CHEEKTOWAGA COMMUNITY FCU | NY | 12/16/15 | ST HELENS COMMUNITY FCU | OR | 12/16/15 |
| CHICOPEE MUNICIPAL EMPL CU | MA | 12/16/15 | ST MATTHEWS FCU | VA | 12/16/15 |
| CLIFTON NJ POSTAL EMPL FCU | NJ | 12/16/15 | STARCOR CU | MN | 12/16/15 |
| CONNECTION CU | WA | 12/16/15 | TIP OF TEXAS FCU | TX | 12/16/15 |
| COSHOCTON FCU | OH | 12/16/15 | TRI BORO FCU | PA | 12/16/15 |
| CTA SOUTH FCU | IL | 12/16/15 | UNION COUNTY EMPL FCU | NJ | 12/16/15 |
| DEMOCRAT P&L FCU | AR | 12/16/15 | UNION-WALLOWA-BAKER FCU | OR | 12/16/15 |
| DIVISION 726 FCU | NY | 12/16/15 | UNIVERSAL 1 CU | OH | 12/16/15 |
| EATON EMPL FCU | CO | 12/16/15 | VALEX FCU | LA | 12/16/15 |
| ELLISVILLE STATE SCHOOL EMPL CU | MS | 12/16/15 | VANTAGE CU | MO | 12/16/15 |
| ESCU FCU | OH | 12/16/15 | WEST COAST FEDERAL EMPL CU | FL | 12/16/15 |
| EXPRESS CU | WA | 12/16/15 | WESTERN HERITAGE CU | NE | 12/16/15 |
| FAITH BASED FCU | CA | 12/16/15 | WIT FCU | NY | 12/16/15 |
| FANNIE B PECK OF BETHEL AME CHURCH CU | MI | 12/16/15 |  |  |  |

## Rating:     D+

| Name | State | Date of Change |
|------|-------|--------|
| FARMERS BRANCH CITY EMPL FCU | TX | 12/16/15 |
| FINANCIAL PARTNERS FCU | IN | 12/16/15 |

| Name | State | Date of Change |
|------|-------|--------|
| ADVANCE FINANCIAL FCU | IN | 12/16/15 |

## Rating Downgrades

| Name | State | Date of Change | Name | State | Date of Change |
|------|-------|----------------|------|-------|----------------|
| ALLEGHENY CENTRAL EMPL FCU | PA | 12/16/15 | MOHAVE COMMUNITY FCU | AZ | 12/16/15 |
| ALPS FCU | AK | 12/16/15 | MONROEVILLE BORO FCU | PA | 12/16/15 |
| AMBRAW FCU | IL | 12/16/15 | MORRIS SHEPPARD TEXARKANA FCU | TX | 12/16/15 |
| ARKANSAS VALLEY FCU | CO | 12/16/15 | MORRISON EMPL CU | IA | 12/16/15 |
| ARTMET FCU | MA | 12/16/15 | MOTOR CITY COOPERATIVE CU | MI | 12/16/15 |
| BACHARACH EMPL FCU | PA | 12/16/15 | MOTOR COACH EMPL CU | IL | 12/16/15 |
| BASF CHATTANOOGA FCU | TN | 12/16/15 | MOUNT ZION INDIANAPOLIS FCU | IN | 12/16/15 |
| BLOOMFIELD FIRE & POLICE FCU | NJ | 12/16/15 | NATURAL STATE FCU | AR | 12/16/15 |
| BROSNAN YARD FCU | GA | 12/16/15 | NE PA COMMUNITY FCU | PA | 12/16/15 |
| C & R CU | KS | 12/16/15 | NEWARK FIREMEN FCU | NJ | 12/16/15 |
| CARDOZO LODGE FCU | PA | 12/16/15 | NORTH GEORGIA COMMUNITY FCU | GA | 12/16/15 |
| CHEMCO CU | AL | 12/16/15 | NOVAMONT EMPL FCU | WV | 12/16/15 |
| CITY CO FCU | PA | 12/16/15 | ONE SOURCE FCU | TX | 12/16/15 |
| CLARET FCU | PR | 12/16/15 | OUACHITA VALLEY HEALTH SYSTEM FCU | AR | 12/16/15 |
| COMMUNITY POWERED FCU | DE | 12/16/15 | OWENSBORO FCU | KY | 12/16/15 |
| COSDEN FCU | TX | 12/16/15 | PARTHENON FCU | TN | 12/16/15 |
| CROUSE FCU | NY | 12/16/15 | PEOPLES FIRST FCU | AL | 12/16/15 |
| DENNISON FCU | MI | 12/16/15 | PORT OF HAMPTON ROADS ILA FCU | VA | 12/16/15 |
| DESERT SAGE FCU | ID | 12/16/15 | REDIFORM NIAGARA FALLS NY FCU | NY | 12/16/15 |
| DIVISION 694 MOTOR COACH EMPL FCU | TX | 12/16/15 | RIVER VALLEY COMMUNITY FCU | AR | 12/16/15 |
| DOE RUN FCU | KY | 12/16/15 | ROUTE 1 CU | IL | 12/16/15 |
| ELIZABETH POLICE DEPT EMPL FCU | NJ | 12/16/15 | SEASONS FCU | CT | 12/16/15 |
| EM FCU | AZ | 12/16/15 | SECURITY FIRST FCU | TX | 12/16/15 |
| ENERGY FCU | MD | 12/16/15 | SHYANN FCU | WY | 12/16/15 |
| EPB EMPL CU | TN | 12/16/15 | SS PETER & PAUL FCU | PA | 12/16/15 |
| FEDERAL EMPL WEST FCU | CA | 12/16/15 | SSMOK EMPL FCU | OK | 12/16/15 |
| FIDELIS FCU | NY | 12/16/15 | ST LOUIS FIREFIGHTERS & COMMUNITY CU | MO | 12/16/15 |
| FIRST BRISTOL FCU | CT | 12/16/15 | STERLING HEIGHTS COMMUNITY FCU | MI | 12/16/15 |
| FIRST CHEYENNE FCU | WY | 12/16/15 | STSP FCU | LA | 12/16/15 |
| FIRST STATE REFINERY FCU | DE | 12/16/15 | SUN-PACIFIC FCU | CA | 12/16/15 |
| FORT BAYARD FCU | NM | 12/16/15 | TEXAS HEALTH RESOURCES CU | TX | 12/16/15 |
| FORT DIX FCU | NJ | 12/16/15 | U S PIPE BESSEMER EMPL FCU | AL | 12/16/15 |
| GCA FCU | LA | 12/16/15 | UNION MEMORIAL CU | MO | 12/16/15 |
| GENERAL PORTLAND PENINSULAR EMPL FCU | OH | 12/16/15 | UNIVERSAL COOP FCU | PR | 12/16/15 |
| GRAND COUNTY CU | UT | 12/16/15 | UPS CU | OH | 12/16/15 |
| GREATER ALLIANCE FCU | NJ | 12/16/15 | URBAN UPBOUND FCU | NY | 12/16/15 |
| GREATER KC PUBLIC SAFETY CU | MO | 12/16/15 | VA PITTSBURGH EMPL FCU | PA | 12/16/15 |
| HAULPAK FCU | IL | 12/16/15 | VAC EMPL FCU | NY | 12/16/15 |
| HEMA FCU | MD | 12/16/15 | VIRGINIA BEACH SCHOOLS FCU | VA | 12/16/15 |
| HUTCHINSON POSTAL & COMMUNITY CU | KS | 12/16/15 | VIRGINIA EDUCATORS CU | VA | 12/16/15 |
| ILLINOIS STATE POLICE FCU | IL | 12/16/15 | WALTON COUNTY TEACHERS FCU | FL | 12/16/15 |
| KAH CU | IA | 12/16/15 | WESTMORELAND FEDERAL EMPL FCU | PA | 12/16/15 |
| KANSAS CITY P&G EMPL CU | KS | 12/16/15 | WINCHESTER FCU | MA | 12/16/15 |
| KEYSTONE CU | TX | 12/16/15 | WINDWARD COMMUNITY FCU | HI | 12/16/15 |
| KOREAN CATHOLIC FCU | MD | 12/16/15 | | | |
| MANATROL DIVISION EMPL CU | OH | 12/16/15 | **Rating:** D | | |
| MCCOMB FCU | MS | 12/16/15 | ALLOY EMPL CU | WI | 12/16/15 |
| MEMBERSOWN CU | NE | 12/16/15 | ARKANSAS EMPL FCU | AR | 12/16/15 |
| MIDWEST FAMILY FCU | IN | 12/16/15 | BROOKS COMMUNITY FCU | MN | 12/16/15 |
| MODERN EMPL FCU | KY | 12/16/15 | CAANO EMPL FCU | LA | 12/16/15 |

## Rating Downgrades

| Name | State | Date of Change |
|---|---|---|
| CEN TEX MANUFACTURING CU | TX | 12/16/15 |
| COMBINED FCU | AR | 12/16/15 |
| COPOCO COMMUNITY CU | MI | 12/16/15 |
| CORPUS CHRISTI SP CU | TX | 12/16/15 |
| DEEPWATER INDUSTRIES FCU | NJ | 12/16/15 |
| DISTRICT #6 FCU | NY | 12/16/15 |
| EAST BATON ROUGE TEACHERS FCU | LA | 12/16/15 |
| ELECTCHESTER FCU | NY | 12/16/15 |
| ESPEECO FCU | CA | 12/16/15 |
| EW #401 CU | NV | 12/16/15 |
| FAMILY FIRST CU | MI | 12/16/15 |
| GREATER CHRIST BAPTIST CHURCH CU | MI | 12/16/15 |
| GREATER GALILEE BAPTIST CU | WI | 12/16/15 |
| GREATER HARTFORD POLICE FCU | CT | 12/16/15 |
| HARRISON DISTRICT NO TWO FCU | CO | 12/16/15 |
| HEEKIN CAN EMPL CU | OH | 12/16/15 |
| HIGH PEAKS FCU | MT | 12/16/15 |
| HIGH PLAINS FCU | NM | 12/16/15 |
| HOLY REDEEMER COMMUNITY OF SE WISCONSIN | WI | 12/16/15 |
| HOMEPORT FCU | TX | 12/16/15 |
| INTEGRUS CU | IA | 12/16/15 |
| LOCAL 461 FCU | GA | 12/16/15 |
| LOCAL 804 FCU | NY | 12/16/15 |
| MEA CU | IL | 12/16/15 |
| MM EMPL FCU | MT | 12/16/15 |
| MNCPPC FCU | MD | 12/16/15 |
| MOLEX EMPL FCU | IL | 12/16/15 |
| MOUNT ST MARYS HOSPITAL FCU | NY | 12/16/15 |
| NABISCO EMPL CU | VA | 12/16/15 |
| NIAGARA FRONTIER FEDERAL MUNICIPAL CU | NY | 12/16/15 |
| NICE FCU | IL | 12/16/15 |
| PAUL QUINN FCU | NY | 12/16/15 |
| PEAR ORCHARD FCU | TX | 12/16/15 |
| RADIO TELEVISION & COMMUNICATIONS FCU | NY | 12/16/15 |
| ROSLYN CATHOLIC FCU | PA | 12/16/15 |
| SALEM VA MEDICAL CENTER FCU | VA | 12/16/15 |
| SHAMROCK FOODS FCU | AZ | 12/16/15 |
| SM FCU | PA | 12/16/15 |
| SOUTH SAN FRANCISCO CITY EMPL FCU | CA | 12/16/15 |
| SOUTH SANPETE CU | UT | 12/16/15 |
| SOUTHBRIDGE CU | MA | 12/16/15 |
| SOUTHERN GAS FCU | AR | 12/16/15 |
| ST JOSEPHS BROADMOOR FCU | LA | 12/16/15 |
| ST MARKS FCU | NY | 12/16/15 |
| STATE SERVICE CU | IN | 12/16/15 |
| TELCO CU | NC | 12/16/15 |
| UKRAINIAN SELFRELIANCE OF WESTERN PA | PA | 12/16/15 |
| UNITED CU | IL | 12/16/15 |
| UNIVERSAL CU | KS | 12/16/15 |
| UPSTATE MILK EMPL FCU | NY | 12/16/15 |
| UTAH PRISON EMPL CU | UT | 12/16/15 |
| VALLEY STATE EMPL CU | MI | 12/16/15 |
| VICTORIA FCU | TX | 12/16/15 |
| WAKARUSA VALLEY CU | KS | 12/16/15 |
| WEBSTER UNITED FCU | LA | 12/16/15 |
| WENATCHEE VALLEY FCU | WA | 12/16/15 |
| WESLEY MEDICAL CU | KS | 12/16/15 |
| WEST BRANCH VALLEY FCU | PA | 12/16/15 |
| WESTACRES CU | MI | 12/16/15 |
| WESTPORT FCU | MA | 12/16/15 |
| WHITE COUNTY FCU | AR | 12/16/15 |
| WHITE RIVER CU | VT | 12/16/15 |
| WINDSOR COUNTY SOUTH CU | VT | 12/16/15 |
| WORCESTER CU | MA | 12/16/15 |
| WYOCHEM FCU | WY | 12/16/15 |

## Rating: D-

| Name | State | Date of Change |
|---|---|---|
| ANCHOR SEVEN FCU | FL | 12/16/15 |
| ASHLAND COMMUNITY FCU | OH | 12/16/15 |
| BLUEGRASS COMMUNITY FCU | KY | 12/16/15 |
| CANTON POLICE & FIREMENS CU | OH | 12/16/15 |
| COLUMBIA CU | MO | 12/16/15 |
| COMMUNITY FIRST CU | MO | 12/16/15 |
| CTK CU | WI | 12/16/15 |
| EDISON CU | MO | 12/16/15 |
| EMPLOYEES FCU | OK | 12/16/15 |
| FIRST CU | WI | 12/16/15 |
| I F F EMPL FCU | NJ | 12/16/15 |
| IBEW 26 FCU | MD | 12/16/15 |
| ITT ROANOKE EMPL FCU | VA | 12/16/15 |
| JUNCTION BELL FCU | CO | 12/16/15 |
| LONG ISLAND COMMUNITY FCU | NY | 12/16/15 |
| MCKEESPORT BELL FCU | PA | 12/16/15 |
| MEMBERS FINANCIAL FCU | TX | 12/16/15 |
| MEMBERS FIRST OF MARYLAND FCU | MD | 12/16/15 |
| NORTHPARK COMMUNITY CU | IN | 12/16/15 |
| OUR MOTHER OF MERCY PARISH HOUSTON FCU | TX | 12/16/15 |
| POST OFFICE EMPL FCU | LA | 12/16/15 |
| PSE&G NUCLEAR EMPL FCU | NJ | 12/16/15 |
| RECTOR FCU | PA | 12/16/15 |
| ROGERS EMPL FCU | CT | 12/16/15 |
| SHORELINE FCU | MI | 12/16/15 |
| SOUTH SIDE COMMUNITY FCU | IL | 12/16/15 |
| SOUTH TEXAS FCU | TX | 12/16/15 |
| ST GREGORY PARISH CU | IL | 12/16/15 |
| ST HELEN FCU | OH | 12/16/15 |
| ST NICHOLAS FCU | PA | 12/16/15 |
| TCWH #585 FCU | PA | 12/16/15 |
| TROUVAILLE FCU | PA | 12/16/15 |
| UNITED AMERICA WEST FCU | CA | 12/16/15 |

## Rating Downgrades

| Name | State | Date of Change |
|------|-------|----------------|
| UNITED CATHOLICS FCU | CA | 12/16/15 |
| WARD FCU | PA | 12/16/15 |
| WAYNE COUNTY FCU | IN | 12/16/15 |
| WHITE ROSE CU | PA | 12/16/15 |

## Rating: E+

| Name | State | Date of Change |
|------|-------|----------------|
| DESERT COMMUNITIES FCU | CA | 12/16/15 |
| ERRL FCU | PA | 12/16/15 |
| FIRST MIAMI UNIV STUDENT FCU | OH | 12/16/15 |
| FIRST UNITY FCU | MS | 12/16/15 |
| GROTON MUNICIPAL EMPL FCU | CT | 12/16/15 |
| MACHINISTS-BOILERMAKERS FCU | OR | 12/16/15 |
| SEARS SPOKANE EMPL FCU | WA | 12/16/15 |
| SOUTH TEXAS REGIONAL FCU | TX | 12/16/15 |
| TEAM FINANCIAL FCU | TX | 12/16/15 |
| VELMA FCU | OK | 12/16/15 |

## Rating: E

| Name | State | Date of Change |
|------|-------|----------------|
| NIU EMPL FCU | IL | 12/16/15 |

## Rating: E-

| Name | State | Date of Change |
|------|-------|----------------|
| ENTERTAINMENT INDUSTRIES FCU | NJ | 12/16/15 |
| RENAISSANCE COMMUNITY DEVEL CU | NJ | 12/16/15 |

## Rating: F

| Name | State | Date of Change |
|------|-------|----------------|
| BETHEX FCU | NY | 09/18/15 |
| FIRST HAWAIIAN HOMES FCU | HI | 12/30/15 |
| MONTAUK CU | NY | 09/21/15 |

# Appendix

# RECENT CREDIT UNION FAILURES

## 2015

| Institution | Headquarters | Date of Failure | At Date of Failure | |
|---|---|---|---|---|
| | | | Total Assets ($Mil) | Safety Rating |
| First Hawaiian Homes FCU | Hoolehua, HI | 12/9/15 | 3.2 | C+ (Fair) |
| Helping Other People Excel FCU | Jackson, NJ | 11/20/15 | .6 | C (Fair) |
| SWC Credit Union | Tampa, FL | 9/24/15 | 1.9 | D (Weak) |
| Bethex Federal Credit Union | Bronx, NY | 9/18/15 | 12.9 | D (Weak) |
| Montauk Credit Union | New York, NY | 9/18/15 | 178.5 | C (Fair) |
| SCICAP Credit Union | Chariton, IA | 8/28/15 | 2.0 | C (Fair) |
| Alabama One Credit Union | Tuscaloosa, AL | 8/27/15 | 6.0 | D+ (Weak) |
| Lakeside Federal Credit Union | Hammond, IN | 7/16/15 | 8.9 | D (Weak) |
| Trailblazer Federal Credit Union | Washington, PA | 7/10/15 | 4.1 | D (Weak) |
| New Bethel Federal Credit Union | Portsmouth, VA | 4/30/15 | .11 | C- (Fair) |
| TLC Federal Credit Union | Tillamook, OR | 4/30/15 | 109.0 | D (Weak) |
| Montgomery County CU | Dayton, OH | 4/23/15 | 27.3 | D- (Weak) |
| North Dade Comm. Dev FCU | Miami Gardens, FL | 3/31/15 | 3.0 | C (Fair) |
| American Bakery Workers FCU | Philadelphia, PA | 1/30/15 | 4.1 | E+ (Very Weak) |

# 2014

| Institution | Headquarters | Date of Failure | At Date of Failure | |
| --- | --- | --- | --- | --- |
| | | | Total Assets ($Mil) | Safety Rating |
| Metropolitan Church of God CU | Detroit, MI | 12/03/14 | 0.1 | E+ (Very Weak) |
| County & Municipal Empl CU | Edinburg, TX | 10/10/14 | 40.3 | C- (Fair) |
| Republic Hose Employees FCU | Youngstown, OH | 09/30/14 | .6 | E+ (Very Weak) |
| Louden Depot Community CU | Fairfield, IA | 09/05/14 | 5.0 | C+ (Fair) |
| Bensenville Community CU | Bensenville, IL | 07/31/14 | 14.0 | E- (Very Weak) |
| IBEW Local 816 FCU | Paducah, KY | 05/23/14 | 7.9 | D (Weak) |
| Life Line Credit Union Inc | Richmond, VA | 05/23/14 | 7.9 | E+ (Very Weak) |
| Health One Credit Union | Detroit, MI | 05/16/14 | 18.2 | D (Weak) |
| St. Francis Campus Credit Union | Little Falls, MN | 02/14/14 | 51.0 | B (Good) |
| Parsons Pittsburgh CU | Parsons, KS | 01/24/14 | 13.5 | C- (Fair) |

# 2013

| Institution | Headquarters | Date of Failure | At Date of Failure | |
| --- | --- | --- | --- | --- |
| | | | Total Assets ($Mil) | Safety Rating |
| Bagumbayan Credit Union | Chicago, IL | 12/12/13 | 0.1 | C- (Fair) |
| Polish Combatants Credit Union | Bedford, OH | 11/22/13 | 0.1 | B+ (Good) |
| Mayfair Federal Credit Union | Philadelphia, PA | 11/1/13 | 14.3 | C (Fair) |
| Craftsman Credit Union | Detroit, MI | 09/06/13 | 24.1 | D- (Weak) |
| Taupa Lithuanian Credit Union | Clevland, OH | 07/15/13 | 23.6 | C+ (Fair) |
| Ochsner Clinic FCU | New Orleans, LA | 06/28/13 | 9.2 | D- (Weak) |
| PEF Federal Credit Union | Highland Heights, OH | 06/21/13 | 31.3 | E- (Very Weak) |
| First Kingdom Community | Selma, AL | 05/31/13 | 0.1 | E+ (Very Weak) |
| Electrical Workers #527 FCU | Texas City, TX | 05/23/13 | 0.6 | E+ (Very Weak) |
| Lynrocten FCU | Lynchburg, VA | 05/03/13 | 13.8 | B (Good) |
| Shiloh of Alexandria FCU | Alexandria, VA | 04/12/13 | 2.4 | B (Good) |
| I.C.E Federal Credit Union | Inglewood, CA | 03/15/13 | 3.4 | D- (Weak) |
| Pepsi Cola FCU | Buena Park, CA | 03/15/13 | 0.6 | C- (Fair) |
| Amez United Credit Union | Detroit, MI | 02/19/13 | 0.1 | D+ (Weak) |
| NCP Community Development FCU | Norfolk, VA | 02/08/13 | 2.0 | D (Weak) |
| New Covenant Miss Bapt Church CU | Milwaukee, WI | 01/07/13 | 0.5 | E- (Very Weak) |

# 2012

| Institution | Headquarters | Date of Failure | At Date of Failure | |
|---|---|---|---|---|
| | | | Total Assets ($Mil) | Safety Rating |
| Olean Tile Employees FCU | Olean, NY | 12/17/12 | 0.8 | D- (Weak) |
| GIC FCU | Euclid, OH | 12/13/12 | 15.5 | B+ (Very Good) |
| Border Lodge Credit Union | Derby Line, VT | 11/30/12 | 3.1 | D (Weak) |
| Women's Southwest FCU | Dallas, TX | 10/31/12 | 2.1 | E+ (Very Weak) |
| El Paso's Federal Credit Union | El Paso, TX | 9/28/12 | 471.0 | D+ (Weak) |
| United Catholic Credit Union | Temperance, MI | 08/09/12 | 0.2 | C+ (Fair) |
| Trinity Credit Union | Trinidad, CO | 07/27/12 | 4.0 | D- (Weak) |
| USA One National Credit Union | Matteson, IL | 06/05/12 | 37.9 | E- (Very Weak) |
| Wausau Postal Employees CU | Wausau, WI | 05/18/12 | 8.4 | D- (Weak) |
| Shepherd's Federal Credit Union | Charlotte | 03/26/12 | 0.6 | C- (Fair) |
| Telesis Community Credit Union | Chatsworth | 03/23/12 | 318.3 | E+ (Very Weak) |
| AM Community Credit Union | Kenosha, WI | 02/17/12 | 1.2 | E+ (Very Weak) |
| Eastern New York FCU | Napanoch, NY | 01/27/12 | 51.8 | E- (Very Weak) |
| People for People Community Development CU | Philadelphia, PA | 01/06/12 | 1.1 | E+ (Very Weak) |

# 2011

| Institution | Headquarters | Date of Failure | Total Assets ($Mil) | Safety Rating |
|---|---|---|---|---|
| Birmingham Financial FCU | Birmingham, AL | 10/27/11 | 1.3 | E+ (Very Weak) |
| Chetco FCU | Harbor, OR | 09/23/11 | 333.0 | D- (Weak) |
| Sacramento District Postal Employees Credit Union | Sacramento, CA | 08/12/11 | 20.0 | E- (Very Weak) |
| Saguache County Credit Union | Moffat, CO | 07/22/11 | 17.7 | E- (Very Weak) |
| Borinquen FCU | Philadelphia, PA | 06/24/11 | 7.0 | C- (Fair) |
| OUR FCU | Eugene, OR | 06/24/11 | 4.3 | E (Very Weak) |
| St. James AME FCU | Newark, NJ | 06/24/11 | 1.0 | E- (Very Weak) |
| Broome County Teachers FCU | Binghamton, NY | 06/10/11 | 50.4 | N/A |
| Hmong American FCU | St. Paul, MN | 05/04/11 | 2.7 | B- ( Good) |
| Valued Members FCU | Jackson , MS | 05/04/11 | 9.0 | E (Very Weak) |
| Utah Central Credit Union | Salt Lake City, UT | 04/29/11 | 0.1 | E- (Very Weak) |
| Texans Credit Union | Richardson, TX | 04/15/11 | 1,600.0 | E- (Very Weak) |
| Vensure Federal Credit Union | Mesa, AZ | 04/15/11 | 4.7 | B (Good) |
| Mission San Francisco FCU | San Francisco, CA | 04/08/11 | 6.0 | E- (Very Weak) |
| Land of Enchantment Federal CU | Santa Fe, NM | 03/07/11 | 8.6 | E+ (Very Weak) |
| Wisconsin Heights Credit Union | Ogema, WI | 03/04/11 | 0.7 | C- (Fair) |
| NYC OTB Federal Credit Union | New York, NY | 02/23/11 | 1.4 | E+ (Very Weak) |
| Greensburg Community FCU | Greensburg, PA | 02/17/11 | 2.2 | B- (Good) |
| Oakland Municipal CU | Oakland, CA | 02/04/11 | 88.0 | N/A |

# 2010

| Institution | Headquarters | Date of Failure | At Date of Failure | |
|---|---|---|---|---|
| | | | Total Assets ($Mil) | Safety Rating |
| AEA Federal Credit Union | Yuma, Az | 12/17/10 | 309.0 | E- (Very Weak) |
| Beehive Credit Union | Salt Lake City, UT | 12/14/10 | 145.0 | N/A |
| Constitution Corporate FCU | Wallingford, CT | 11/19/10 | N/A | N/A |
| The Union Credit Union | Spokane. WA | 10/29/10 | 11.9 | E- (Very Weak) |
| Phil-Pet Federal Credit Union | Pampa, TX | 10/18/10 | 3.7 | E- (Very Weak) |
| Industries Puerto Rico FCU | Manati, PR | 09/13/10 | 3.6 | E- (Very Weak) |
| Family First FCU | Orem, UT | 07/30/10 | 119.0 | N/A |
| First American Credit Union | Beloit, WI | 08/31/10 | 136.9 | N/A |
| Kappa Alpha Psi | Addison, TX | 08/03/10 | 0.8 | N/A |
| Certified Federal Credit Union | Commerce, CA | 07/31/10 | 37.6 | N/A |
| Norbel Credit Union | Fort Collins, CO | 07/29/10 | 120.0 | N/A |
| Southwest Community FCU | Saint George, UT | 06/30/10 | 139.1 | N/A |
| Arrowhead Central Credit | San Bernardino, CA | 06/25/10 | 876.0 | N/A |
| Orange County Employees CU | Orange, TX | 06/09/10 | 1.7 | N/A |
| Convent Federal Credit Union | New York, NY | 05/17/10 | 0.2 | N/A |
| St. Paul's Croatian FCU | Eastlake, OH | 05/01/10 | 238.8 | N/A |
| Tracy Federal Credit Union | Tracy, CA | 04/27/10 | 25.4 | N/A |
| South End Mutual Benefit Assoc. | Bloomfield, CT | 04/08/10 | 2.4 | N/A |
| Lawrence Cty School Employees | New Castle, PA | 03/05/10 | 2.6 | N/A |
| Mutual Diversified Employees | Santa Ana, CA | 02/26/10 | 6.1 | N/A |
| Friendship Community FCU | Clarksdale, MS | 02/25/10 | 0.9 | N/A |
| Kern Central Credit Union | Bakersfield, CA | 01/08/10 | 34.9 | N/A |

# How Do Banks and Credit Unions Differ?

Since credit unions first appeared in 1946, they have been touted as a low-cost, friendly alternative to banks. But with tightening margins, pressure to compete in technology, branch closures, and the introduction of a host of service fees — some even higher than those charged by banks — the distinction between banks and credit unions has been gradually narrowing. Following are the key differences between today's banks and credit unions.

|  | **Banks** | **Credit Unions** |
|---|---|---|
| **Access** | Practically anyone is free to open an account or request a loan from any bank. There are no membership requirements. | Credit unions are set up to serve the needs of a specific group who share a "common bond." In order to open an account or request a loan, you must demonstrate that you meet the credit union's common bond requirements. |
| **Ownership** | Banks are owned by one or more investors who determine the bank's policies and procedures. A bank's customers do not have direct input into how the bank is operated. | Although they may be sponsored by a corporation or other entity, credit unions are owned by their members through their funds on deposit. Therefore, each depositor has a voice in how the credit union is operated. |
| **Dividends and Fees** | Banks are for-profit organizations where the profits are used to pay dividends to the bank's investors or are reinvested in an effort to increase the bank's value to investors. In an effort to generate more profits, bank services and fees are typically more costly. | Credit unions are not-for-profit organizations. Any profits generated are returned to the credit union's members in the form of higher interest rates on deposits, lower loan rates, and free or low-cost services. |
| **Management and Staffing** | A bank's management and other staff are employees of the bank, hired directly or indirectly by its investors. | Credit unions are frequently run using elected members, volunteer staff, and staff provided by the credit union's sponsor. This helps to hold down costs. |
| **Insurance** | Banks are insured by the Federal Deposit Insurance Corporation, an agency of the federal government. | Credit unions are insured by the National Credit Union Share Insurance Fund, which is managed by the National Credit Union Administration, an agency of the federal government. |

# Glossary

This glossary contains the most important terms used in this publication.

| | |
|---|---|
| **ARM** | Adjustable-Rate Mortgage. This is a loan whose interest rate is tied to an index and is adjusted at a predetermined frequency. An ARM is subject to credit risk if interest rates rise and the borrower is unable to make the mortgage payment. |
| **Average Recession** | A recession involving a decline in real GDP that is approximately equivalent to the average of the postwar recessions of 1957-58, 1960, 1970, 1974-75, 1980 and 1981-82. It is assumed, however, that in today's market, the financial losses suffered from a recession of that magnitude would be greater than those experienced in previous decades. (See also "Severe Recession.") |
| **Board of Directors** | Group of volunteers charged with providing the general direction and control of the credit union. Officers of the credit union (chairman, vice chairman, etc.) are selected from the board membership. |
| **Brokered Deposits** | Deposits that are brought into an institution through a broker. They are relatively costly, volatile funds that are more readily withdrawn from the institution if there is a loss of confidence or intense interest rate competition. Reliance on brokered deposits is usually a sign that the institution is having difficulty attracting deposits from its local geographic markets and could be a warning signal if other institutions in the same areas are not experiencing similar difficulties. |
| **Bylaws** | A codification of the form of organization that the credit union takes and the governance of its day-to-day operations; federal credit unions are required to adopt a basic code approved by the National Credit Union Administration. |
| **Capital** | A measure of a credit union's ability to withstand troubled times. A credit union's base capital represents the total of regular (statutory) reserves, other reserve accounts and undivided earnings. Regulatory capital includes all the above plus allowances for loan and investment losses. (See also "Core Capital") |
| **Cash & Equivalents** | Cash plus highly liquid assets which can be readily converted to cash. |
| **Core (Tier 1) Capital** | A measurement of capital defined by the federal regulatory agencies for evaluating an institution's degree of leverage. Core capital consists of the following: common stockholder's equity, preferred stockholder's equity up to certain limits, and retained earnings net of any intangible assets. |
| **Corporate Credit Union** | A federal or state-chartered credit union that serves other credit unions, providing investment, short-term (liquidity) loans and other services to its member credit unions; they are sometimes refered to as "the credit union's credit union." |
| **Credit Committee** | Optional internal committee of a credit union that considers applications for loans and lines of credit. In the event the credit union has delegated that authority to a loan officer, the credit committee ratifies the applications approved by the loan officer. |

| **Credit Union** | A not-for-profit financial cooperative chartered by the state or federal government and, in most cases, insured by the federal government. It is owned by the members of the credit union. The coopereative is tied to a commonality of interest (such as employer, association or community) that the members or groups of members share. |
|---|---|
| **Credit Union Service Organization** | An organization owned wholly or in part by one or more credit unions to provide service to the credit unions, their members, or both. (CUSO) |
| **Critical Ranges** | Guidelines developed to help you evaluate the levels of each index contributing to a company's Weiss Safety Rating. The sum or average of these grades does not necessarily have a one-to-one correspondence with the final rating for an institution because the rating is derived from a wider range of more complex calculations. |
| **CU** | A common acronym for credit unions. |
| **CUNA** | Credit Union National Association. A national trade association based in Washington, D.C. and Miadison, Wisconson that serves credit unions. |
| **CUSO** | Credit Union Service Organization (see above). |
| **Dividend** | Funds paid to members based on account size and rates declared regularly (monthly, quarterly or annually) by the board of directors for various types of accounts. A dividend represents the payment by the credit union to the member for use of the member's funds. |
| **Equity** | Total assets minus total liabilities. This is the "capital cushion" the institution has to fall back on in times of trouble. (See also "Capital.") |
| **Field of Membership** | Definition of the type of membership generally served by the credit union, e.g.: "defense" credit unions primarily serve members of the armed forces; "education" credit unions primarily serve educators. |
| **Safety Rating** | Weiss Safety Ratings, which grade institutions on a scale from A (Excellent) to F (Failed). Ratings are based on many factors, emphasizing capitalization, asset quality, profitability, liquidity, and stability. |
| **FPR** | Financial Performance Report is a financial anaylysis report derived from Call Report data. |
| **Goodwill** | The value of an institution as a going concern, meaning the value which exceeds book value on a balance sheet. It generally represents the value of a well-respected business name, good customer relations, high employee morale and other intangible factors which would be expected to translate into greater than normal earning power. In a bank or thrift acquisition, goodwill is the value paid by a buyer of the institution in excess of the value of the institution's equity because of these intangible factors. |

**Hot Money**     Individual deposits of $100,000 or more.  These types of deposits are considered "hot money" because they tend to chase whoever is offering the best interest rates at the time and are thus relatively costly and fairly volatile sources of funds.

**Loan Loss Reserves**     The amount of capital an institution sets aside to cover any potential losses due to the nonrepayment of loans.

**National Credit Union Share Insurance Fund**     The federal share insurance fund for credit unions. The fund protects credit union members' shares (up to $250,000) in federal and federally insured, state-chartered credit unions. NCUSIF is backed by the full faith and credit of the United States.

**NCUA**     National Credit Union Association.  An independent federal agency that charters and supervises federal credit unions and insures savings in federal and most state-chartered credit unions.

**Net Charge-offs**     The amount of foreclosed loans written off the institution's books since the beginning of the year, less any previous write-offs that were recovered during the year.

**Net Interest Spread**     The difference between the interest income earned on the institution's loans and investments and the interest expense paid on its interest-bearing deposits and borrowings.  This "spread" is most commonly analyzed as a percentage of average earning assets to show the institution's net return on income-generating assets.

Since the margin between interest earned and interest paid is generally where the company generates the majority of its income, this figure provides insight into the company's ability to effectively manage interest spreads.  A low Net Interest Spread can be the result of poor loan and deposit pricing, high levels of nonaccruing loans, or poor asset/liability management.

**Net Profit or Loss**     The bottom line income or loss the institution has sustained in its most recent reporting period.

**Nonaccruing Loans**     Loans for which payments are past due and full repayment is doubtful.  Interest income on these loans is no longer recorded on the income statement. (See also "Past Due Loans.")

**Nonperform-ing Loans**     The sum of loans past due 90 days or more and nonaccruing loans.  These are loans the institution made where full repayment is now doubtful.  (See also "Past Due Loans" and "Nonaccruing Loans.")

**Past Due Loans**     Loans for which payments are at least 90 days in arears.  The institution continues to record income on these loans, even though none is actually being received, because it is expected that the borrower will eventually repay the loan in full.  It is likely, however, that at least a portion of these loans will move into nonaccruing status. (See also "Nonaccruing Loans.")

| | |
|---|---|
| **Overhead Expense** | Expenses of the institution other than interest expense, such as salaries and benefits of employees, rent and utility expenses, and data processing expenses. A certain amount of "fixed" overhead is required to operate a bank or thrift, so it is important that the institution leverage that overhead to the fullest extent in supporting its revenue-generating activities. |
| **Par Value** | The dollar equivalent of a share required to join a credit union. Par value is determined by the board and typically ranges from $5 to $25. |
| **RBCR** | See "Risk-Based Capital Ratio." |
| **Restructured Loans** | Loans whose terms have been modified in order to enable the borrower to make payments which he otherwise would be unable to make. Modifications could include a reduction in the interest rate or a lengthening of the time to maturity. |
| **Risk-Based Capital Ratio** | A ratio originally developed by the International Committee on Banking as a means of assessing the adequacy of an institution's capital in relation to the amount of credit risk on and off its balance sheet. (See also "Risk-weighted Assets.") |
| **Risk-Weighted Assets** | The sum of assets and certain off-balance sheet items after they have been individually adjusted for the level of credit risk they pose to the institution. Assets with close to no risk are weighted 0%; those with minor risk are weighted 20%; those with low risk, 50%; and those with normal or high risk, 100%. |
| **R.O.A** | Return on Assets calculated as net profit or loss as a percentage of average assets. This is the most commonly used measure of bank profitability. |
| **R.O.E.** | Return on Equity calculated as net profit or loss as a percentage of average equity. This represents the rate of return on the shareholders' investment. |
| **Share Account** | Refers to a regular share savings account or other account that isn't a share certificate account. A regular share account doesn't require a holder to maintain a balance greater than the par value or a notice of intent to withdraw (unless required in the bylaws). Shares are legally defined as equity and represent ownership. |
| **Share Certificate Account** | Account that earns dividends at a specified rate for a specified period of time, if held to maturity; and upon which a penalty may be assessed for premature withdrawal prior to maturity. |
| **Share Draft (checking) Account** | A dividend-earning account from which the holder is authorized to withdraw shares by means of a negotiable or transferable instrument or other order. (similar to a NOW account). |
| **Sponsor** | An organization (such as a corporation, religious congregation or association) that promotes the establishment or continuation of a credit union for its employees or members. |
| **Stockholder's Equity** | See "Equity." |

| | |
|---|---|
| **Supervisory Committee** | Internal committee required for all federal credit unions and most state credit unions. Oversees the credit union's financial operations, conducts internal audits, may arrange for external audits, reports to board of directors and may suspend board members for malfeasance. |
| **Total Assets** | Total resources of an institution, primarily composed of cash, securities (such as municipal and treasury bonds), loans, and fixed assets (such as real estate, buildings, and equipment). |
| **Total Equity** | See "Equity." |
| **Total Liabilities** | All debts owed by an institution. Normally, the largest liability of a bank or thrift is its deposits. |
| **Trust Company** | A financial institution chartered to provide trust services (legal agreements to act for the benefit of another party), which may also be authorized to provide banking services. |
| **Undivided Earnings** | Accumulated net income after distribution to members and provision for reserves required by law, plus or minus increases or decreases in other reserves (such as a special reserve for losses), plus or minus other authorized direct credits or charges for ad justments affecting prior period operations. |